I0801386

Koren Talmud Bavli
THE NOÉ EDITION

YEVAMOT

Steinsaltz Center

KOREN

תלמוד בבלי

KOREN TALMUD BAVLI

THE NOÉ EDITION

יבמות

YEVAMOT

Daf 35b through Daf 53b

COMMENTARY BY

Rabbi Adin Even-Israel Steinsaltz

EDITOR-IN-CHIEF

Rabbi Dr Tzvi Hersh Weinreb

SENIOR CONTENT EDITOR

Rabbi Dr Shalom Z Berger

EXECUTIVE EDITOR

Rabbi Joshua Schreier

STEINSALTZ CENTER
KOREN PUBLISHERS JERUSALEM

Supported by the Matanel Foundation

Koren Talmud Bavli, The Noe Edition
Vol. 14c: Tractate Yevamot, Daf 35b through Daf 53b
Paperback, ISBN, 978-965-7765-66-1

First Hebrew/English paperback edition, 2021

Koren Publishers Jerusalem Ltd.
PO Box 4044, Jerusalem 91040, ISRAEL
PO Box 8531, New Milford, CT 06776, USA
www.korenpub.com

Steinsaltz Center

Steinsaltz Center is the parent organization of institutions established by Rabbi Adin Even-Israel Steinsaltz

PO Box 45187, Jerusalem 91450 ISRAEL
Telephone: +972 2 646 0900, Fax +972 2 624 9454
www.steinsaltz-center.org

הִנֵּה יָמִים בָּאִים, נְאֻם אֲדֹנָי יֱהוִה, וְהִשְׁלַחְתִּי רָעָב בָּאָרֶץ,
לֹא־רָעָב לַלֶּחֶם וְלֹא־צָמָא לַמַּיִם, כִּי אִם־לִשְׁמֹעַ אֵת דִּבְרֵי יהוה.

Behold, days are coming – says the Lord God – I will send a hunger to the land, not a hunger for bread nor a thirst for water, but to hear the words of the Lord. (AMOS 8:11)

The Noé edition of the Koren Talmud Bavli
with the commentary of Rabbi Adin Even-Israel Steinsaltz
is dedicated to all those who open its covers
to quench their thirst for Jewish Knowledge,
in our generation of Torah renaissance.

This beautiful edition is for the young, the aged,
the novice and the savant alike,
as it unites the depth of Torah knowledge
with the best of academic scholarship.

Within its exquisite and vibrant pages,
words become worlds.

It will claim its place in the library of classics,
in the bookcases of the Beit Midrash,
the classrooms of our schools,
and in the offices of professionals and business people
who carve out precious time to grapple with its timeless wisdom.

For the Student and the Scholar

DEDICATED BY LEO AND SUE NOÉ

Introduction by the Publisher

The Talmud has sustained and inspired Jews for thousands of years. Throughout Jewish history, an elite cadre of scholars has absorbed its learning and passed it on to succeeding generations. The Talmud has been the fundamental text of our people.

Beginning in the 1960s, Rabbi Adin Even-Israel Steinsaltz שליט״א created a revolution in the history of Talmud study. His translation of the Talmud, first into modern Hebrew and then into other languages, as well the practical learning aids he added to the text, have enabled millions of people around the world to access and master the complexity and context of the world of Talmud.

It is thus a privilege to present the *Koren Talmud Bavli*, an English translation of the talmudic text with the brilliant elucidation of Rabbi Steinsaltz. The depth and breadth of his knowledge are unique in our time. His rootedness in the tradition and his reach into the world beyond it are inspirational.

Working with Rabbi Steinsaltz on this remarkable project has been not only an honor, but a great pleasure. Never shy to express an opinion, with wisdom and humor, Rabbi Steinsaltz sparkles in conversation, demonstrating his knowledge (both sacred and worldly), sharing his wide-ranging interests, and, above all, radiating his passion. I am grateful for the unique opportunity to work closely with him, and I wish him many more years of writing and teaching.

Our intentions in publishing this new edition of the Talmud are threefold. First, we seek to fully clarify the talmudic page to the reader – textually, intellectually, and graphically. Second, we seek to utilize today's most sophisticated technologies, both in print and electronic formats, to provide the reader with a comprehensive set of study tools. And third, we seek to help readers advance in their process of Talmud study.

To achieve these goals, the *Koren Talmud Bavli* is unique in a number of ways:

- The classic *tzurat hadaf* of Vilna, used by scholars since the 1800s, has been reset for great clarity, and opens from the Hebrew "front" of the book. Full *nikkud* has been added to both the talmudic text and Rashi's commentary, allowing for a more fluent reading with the correct pronunciation; the commentaries of *Tosafot* have been punctuated. Upon the advice of many English-speaking teachers of Talmud, we have separated these core pages from the translation, thereby enabling the advanced student to approach the text without the distraction of the translation. This also reduces the number of volumes in the set. At the bottom of each *daf*, there is a reference to the corresponding English pages. In addition, the Vilna edition was read against other manuscripts and older print editions, so that texts which had been removed by non-Jewish censors have been restored to their rightful place.

- The English translation, which starts on the English "front" of the book, reproduces the *menukad* Talmud text alongside the English translation (in bold) and commentary and explanation (in a lighter font). The Hebrew and Aramaic text is presented in logical paragraphs. This allows for a fluent reading of the text for the non-Hebrew or non-Aramaic reader. It also allows for the Hebrew reader to refer easily to the text alongside. Where the original text features dialogue or poetry, the English text is laid out in a manner appropriate to the genre. Each page refers to the relevant *daf*.

- Critical contextual tools surround the text and translation: personality notes, providing short biographies of the Sages; language notes, explaining foreign terms borrowed from Greek, Latin, Persian, or Arabic; and background notes, giving information essential to the understanding of the text, including history, geography, botany, archaeology, zoology, astronomy, and aspects of daily life in the talmudic era.
- Halakhic summaries provide references to the authoritative legal decisions made over the centuries by the rabbis. They explain the reasons behind each halakhic decision as well as the ruling's close connection to the Talmud and its various interpreters.
- Photographs, drawings, and other illustrations have been added throughout the text – in full color in the Standard and Electronic editions, and in black and white in the Daf Yomi edition – to visually elucidate the text.

This is not an exhaustive list of features of this edition, it merely presents an overview for the English-speaking reader who may not be familiar with the "total approach" to Talmud pioneered by Rabbi Steinsaltz.

Several professionals have helped bring this vast collaborative project to fruition. My many colleagues are noted on the Acknowledgments page, and the leadership of this project has been exceptional.

RABBI MENACHEM EVEN-ISRAEL, DIRECTOR OF THE STEINSALTZ CENTER, was the driving force behind this enterprise. With enthusiasm and energy, he formed the happy alliance with Koren and established close relationships among all involved in the work.

RABBI DR. TZVI HERSH WEINREB שליט"א, EDITOR-IN-CHIEF, brought to this project his profound knowledge of Torah, intellectual literacy of Talmud, and erudition of Western literature. It is to him that the text owes its very high standard, both in form and content, and the logical manner in which the beauty of the Talmud is presented.

RABBI JOSHUA SCHREIER, EXECUTIVE EDITOR, assembled an outstanding group of scholars, translators, editors, and proofreaders, whose standards and discipline enabled this project to proceed in a timely and highly professional manner.

RABBI MEIR HANEGBI, EDITOR OF THE HEBREW EDITION OF THE STEINSALTZ TALMUD, lent his invaluable assistance throughout the work process, supervising the reproduction of the Vilna pages.

RAPHAËL FREEMAN, EXECUTIVE EDITOR OF KOREN, created this Talmud's unique typographic design which, true to the Koren approach, is both elegant and user friendly.

It has been an enriching experience for all of us at Koren Publishers Jerusalem to work with the Steinsaltz Center to develop and produce the *Koren Talmud Bavli*. We pray that this publication will be a source of great learning and, ultimately, greater *avodat Hashem* for all Jews.

Matthew Miller, Publisher
Koren Publishers Jerusalem
Jerusalem 5772

Contents

For the vocalized Vilna Shas layout, please open as a Hebrew book.

Introduction to **Perek IV**

The chapter begins with a consideration of cases in which there was no requirement to perform levirate marriage or *ḥalitza* but nevertheless they were mistakenly performed, e.g., if they were performed with a pregnant woman who later gave birth to a viable offspring. When *ḥalitza* is performed in such cases, the question arises of how to relate to it. Does such an act of *ḥalitza* have any significance? Does it effect any change in the woman's status? Does it render the woman unfit to marry a priest, and will it impact the levirate bond of her rival wife?

If the *yavam* and *yevama* engaged in relations together under the assumption that doing so would achieve the consummation of a levirate marriage, the situation is far more serious. This is because in cases where there is no requirement of levirate marriage, the two are prohibited from engaging in relations with each other by an explicit Torah prohibition. The Gemara discusses their liability for doing so and then further considers the status of a child born from such relations. Is it considered a *mamzer*? Will it be permitted to marry into the priesthood?

In many cases, if a child is born several months after the relations, there could be an uncertainty whether the child is actually the offspring of the original husband or of the *yavam*. If so, the child's status will be subject to uncertainty that will possibly render him a *mamzer*. Moreover, this uncertainty raises issues with regard to the legal status of the child vis-à-vis inheritance. The Gemara considers these issues in depth and discusses what the *halakha* is in various cases that might arise. Following this, the Gemara discusses the steps that should be taken to ensure such uncertainties never arise.

Another central issue discussed in the chapter is the relationship between a *yavam* and his *yevama* before any action has been taken, when there is only a levirate bond between them. In such cases, what rights does the *yavam* have over the property of the *yevama*? Is there a distinction between different categories of property, e.g., property that was bequeathed to her or her previous husband's property? This leads into a discussion of the legal obligations of a *yavam* to a *yevama* following the levirate marriage, especially with regard to the marriage contact.

The chapter concludes with a discussion of the *halakhot* of slaves and of conversion. Upon purchase, a slave must immerse in a ritual bath for the sake of becoming a slave. This is a process similar to conversion, and the Gemara discusses the similarities and the distinctions between the two.

מתני׳ הַחוֹלֵץ לִיבִמְתּוֹ וְנִמְצֵאת מְעוּבֶּרֶת. וְיָלְדָה. בִּזְמַן שֶׁהַוָּלָד שֶׁל קַיָּימָא – הוּא מוּתָּר בִּקְרוֹבוֹתֶיהָ וְהִיא מוּתֶּרֶת בִּקְרוֹבָיו, וְלֹא פְּסָלָהּ מִן הַכְּהוּנָּה.

MISHNA When a man who has a brother dies childless, his widow [*yevama*] and one of his brothers [*yavam*] may perform a ritual through which she is freed of her levirate bonds [*ḥalitza*]. It is then considered, with regard to forbidden relationships, as though they had been married and divorced. Therefore, he is forbidden to her relatives, and she to his. However, with regard to **one who performs *ḥalitza* with his *yevama*** and then **she is found** to have been **pregnant**[H] at the time of the *ḥalitza* **and she gave birth, in the event that the offspring is viable,** the deceased husband has been survived by offspring and so there was never any levirate bond; consequently, the *ḥalitza* that was performed was entirely unnecessary and a meaningless act. As such, **he** remains **permitted to her relatives and she** remains **permitted to his relatives.** Furthermore, since the *ḥalitza* was meaningless, she is not afforded the status of a *ḥalutza*, i.e., a *yevama* who performed *ḥalitza*, a status akin to that of a divorcée. Therefore, the *ḥalitza* **does not disqualify her from** marrying into **the priesthood.**

אֵין הַוָּלָד שֶׁל קַיָּימָא – הוּא אָסוּר בִּקְרוֹבוֹתֶיהָ וְהִיא אֲסוּרָה בִּקְרוֹבָיו, וּפְסָלָהּ מִן הַכְּהוּנָּה.

If **the offspring is not viable,** then it emerges that the *ḥalitza* was indeed necessary. Therefore, **he is forbidden** to engage in relations **with her relatives and she is forbidden** to engage in relations **with his relatives,** as though they had been married and divorced, **and** the *ḥalitza* **disqualifies her from** marrying into **the priesthood,** as she is afforded the status of a *ḥalutza*.

הַכּוֹנֵס אֶת יְבִמְתּוֹ וְנִמְצֵאת מְעוּבֶּרֶת וְיָלְדָה, בִּזְמַן שֶׁהַוָּלָד שֶׁל קַיָּימָא – יוֹצִיא, וְחַיָּיבִין בְּקָרְבָּן.

With regard to **one who consummates** the levirate marriage with **his *yevama*,** i.e., he had intercourse with her under the assumption that there is a levirate bond and so there is a mitzva to do so, **and** then **she is found to** have been **pregnant** at the time of the intercourse **and she gave birth, in the event that the offspring is viable**[H] the deceased brother has been survived by offspring and it is evident that there was never any levirate bond. In that case, the relations they had, rather than being a mitzva, were a violation of the prohibition against engaging in relations with one's brother's wife. Therefore, the *yavam* **must send** her **out,** i.e., they must separate, as she is forbidden to him as his brother's wife, **and** to atone for the forbidden relations that they had, **they are** each **obligated** to bring a sin-**offering,** as is the *halakha* for all who inadvertently transgress a prohibition that, when performed intentionally, is punishable by *karet*.

וְאִם אֵין וָלָד שֶׁל קַיָּימָא – יְקַיֵּים.

And if the offspring is not viable,[H] and therefore there was in fact a levirate bond, **he may maintain** her as his wife since his intercourse with her was a valid consummation of levirate marriage.

HALAKHA

One who performs *ḥalitza* with his *yevama* and then she is found to have been pregnant – הַחוֹלֵץ לִיבִמְתּוֹ וְנִמְצֵאת מְעוּבֶּרֶת: With regard to one who performs *ḥalitza* with his *yevama* and then she is found to have been pregnant at the time, if she later gives birth to viable offspring, the *ḥalitza* is considered of no significance. Therefore, he is permitted to her relatives and she is permitted to his relatives, and the *ḥalitza* does not disqualify her from marrying into the priesthood. If the pregnancy did not result in viable offspring, either because she miscarried or because the child died within thirty days of birth, then the *ḥalitza* is valid. Therefore, he is forbidden to her relatives and she to his, and the *ḥalitza* disqualifies her from the priesthood (Rambam *Sefer Nashim*, *Hilkhot Yibbum VaḤalitza* 1:20; *Shulḥan Arukh*, *Even HaEzer* 164:2).

One who consummates a levirate marriage with his *yevama* and then she is found to have been pregnant with viable offspring – הַכּוֹנֵס יְבִמְתּוֹ וְנִמְצָאָה מְעוּבֶּרֶת בְּבֶן קַיָּימָא: If one had intercourse with his *yevama* and then she was found to have been pregnant at the time, she must separate from him, although there is no need for a bill of divorce, and they are both obligated to bring a sin-offering (Rambam *Sefer Nashim*, *Hilkhot Yibbum VaḤalitza* 1:22 and *Sefer Korbanot*, *Hilkhot Shegagot* 1:1; *Shulḥan Arukh*, *Even HaEzer* 164:5).

One who consummates a levirate marriage with his *yevama* and she miscarries – הַכּוֹנֵס יְבִמְתּוֹ וְהִפִּילָה: In the case of one who consummates a levirate marriage with his *yevama* and then she is found to have been pregnant at the time, if she later miscarries then he is permitted to retain her as his wife. Some say that he is permitted to remain with her only if he married her before her pregnancy was recognizable, but if the pregnancy was already recognizable when he married her, then he is obligated to divorce her (Rema, citing *Tosafot*). In cases where he is permitted to maintain her as his wife, he must repeat the act of intercourse in order to consummate the marriage. This is in accordance with the conclusion of the Gemara that intercourse with a pregnant woman is not considered a valid consummation of levirate marriage (*Nimmukei Yosef*, citing Rabbeinu Yeruḥam). However, if he wishes to separate from her, he must both give her a bill of divorce and perform *ḥalitza* (Rambam *Sefer Nashim*, *Hilkhot Yibbum VaḤalitza* 1:22; *Shulḥan Arukh*, *Even HaEzer* 164:5).

סָפֵק בֶּן תִּשְׁעָה לָרִאשׁוֹן, סָפֵק בֶּן שִׁבְעָה לָאַחֲרוֹן – יוֹצִיא, וְהַוָּלָד כָּשֵׁר, וְחַיָּיבִין בְּאָשָׁם תָּלוּי.

If they consummated the levirate marriage and seven months later she gave birth, there is **uncertainty whether** the child **is nine** months **old**, i.e., counting from conception, and is the offspring **of the first** husband,[H] and as such there was no levirate bond, or **whether** the child is only **seven** months **old** and is the offspring **of the latter** husband, i.e., the *yavam*, and not of the deceased, in which case there was a levirate bond. In that case, due to the possibility that she is forbidden to him as his brother's wife, **he must send** her **out.** However, the lineage of **the child is unflawed,** since regardless of whether it was born of the first or second husband, there was no transgression involved in its conception. Furthermore, to atone for the possibility that they had forbidden relations **they are** both **obligated to bring a guilt**-offering for **uncertainty,**[HB] as is the *halakha* for anyone who is uncertain whether they inadvertently transgressed a prohibition that would require one to bring a sin-offering.

גמ׳ אִיתְּמַר, הַחוֹלֵץ לִמְעוּבֶּרֶת וְהִפִּילָה. רַבִּי יוֹחָנָן אָמַר: אֵינָהּ צְרִיכָה חֲלִיצָה מִן הָאַחִין, רֵישׁ לָקִישׁ אָמַר: צְרִיכָה חֲלִיצָה מִן הָאַחִין.

GEMARA An amoraic dispute **was stated with** regard to **one who performs *ḥalitza* with a pregnant woman**[H] **and she** later **miscarried.** Since she miscarried, she was certainly bound to the *yavam* by a levirate bond and may not marry anyone else; rather, she is obligated to consummate the levirate marriage or perform *ḥalitza*. The question is whether the *ḥalitza* that was performed while she was still pregnant is effective in releasing her from the levirate bond. **Rabbi Yoḥanan**[P] **said: She does not require** another ***ḥalitza* from the brothers. Reish Lakish**[P] **said: She requires** another ***ḥalitza* from the brothers.**[N]

HALAKHA

There is uncertainty whether the child is nine months old and is the offspring of the first husband – סָפֵק בֶּן תִּשְׁעָה לָרִאשׁוֹן: If one consummates a levirate marriage with his *yevama* and seven months later she gives birth, then there is an uncertainty whether the child is nine months old, counting from conception, and is the offspring of the first husband, or whether the child is only seven months old and is the offspring of the *yavam*. Therefore, the *yavam* must separate from her and give her a bill of divorce. The lineage of the child is certainly unflawed; however, any future children that he has with her will have the status of an uncertain *mamzer* (Rambam *Sefer Nashim, Hilkhot Yibbum VaḤalitza* 1:23; *Shulḥan Arukh, Even HaEzer* 164:6).

A guilt-offering for uncertainty – אָשָׁם תָּלוּי: If one consummates a levirate marriage with his *yevama* and she gives birth, and there is an uncertainty whether the child was born after nine months of gestation and is the offspring of the first husband, or after seven months of gestation and is the offspring of the latter husband, the *yavam* is not required to bring a guilt-offering for uncertainty. The *halakha* on this issue is not as ruled in the mishna because the mishna is in accordance with the opinion of Rabbi Eliezer, who holds that a guilt-offering for uncertainty may be brought whenever there exists the possibility that a transgression was performed. However, the Gemara in tractate *Karetot* rejects his opinion and rules that a guilt-offering for uncertainty is brought only in specific cases involving an uncertainty (Rambam *Sefer Korbanot, Hilkhot Shegagot* 8:1–2 and *Leḥem Mishne* and *Mishne LaMelekh* there).

Ḥalitza with a pregnant woman – חֲלִיצַת מְעוּבֶּרֶת: In the case of one who performs *ḥalitza* with his *yevama* and then she is found to have been pregnant at the time, even if the offspring is not viable the *ḥalitza* is considered ineffective and another *ḥalitza* must be performed. Some say it may be performed either with the brother who originally performed *ḥalitza* with her or with any of the brothers. Others argue that this *ḥalitza* may be performed only with one of the other brothers (Rambam *Sefer Nashim, Hilkhot Yibbum VaḤalitza* 1:20; *Shulḥan Arukh, Even HaEzer* 164:2, and in the comment of Rema).

NOTES

She requires *ḥalitza* from the brothers – צְרִיכָה חֲלִיצָה מִן הָאַחִים: The commentaries debate who should perform the additional *ḥalitza* following the miscarriage. Some suggest, in accordance with the plain reading of Reish Lakish's words, that the additional *ḥalitza* cannot be performed by the brother who originally performed it; rather, one of the other brothers should do so. Others suggest the intention is only that she requires an additional *ḥalitza*, but this may be performed by any of the brothers, even the one who originally performed it (see *Tosafot*). The Ramban holds that the original *ḥalitza* is classified as an invalid *ḥalitza* that is partially effective to the extent that the *ḥalitza* of one of the brothers will no longer release her from the levirate bond she has with the other brothers. Consequently, she must now perform a separate *ḥalitza* with each and every one of the brothers.

BACKGROUND

A guilt-offering for uncertainty – אָשָׁם תָּלוּי: The guilt-offering for uncertainty is mentioned in the Torah (Leviticus 5:17–19) and its various *halakhot* are delineated in tractate *Karetot*. The standard case of a guilt-offering for uncertainty is where there is uncertainty whether or not a transgression warranting a sin-offering was committed. For example, if a piece of forbidden fat and a piece of permitted fat were mixed together and one thought that they were both permitted and ate one of them, he must bring a guilt-offering for uncertainty. The offering protects him from punishment until he determines whether or not he actually sinned, and if he did, he must bring a sin-offering.

PERSONALITIES

Rabbi Yoḥanan – רַבִּי יוֹחָנָן: This is Rabbi Yoḥanan bar Nappaḥa, one of the greatest *amora'im*, whose teachings are fundamental components of both the Babylonian Talmud and the Jerusalem Talmud. He resided in Tiberias and lived to an advanced age. Rabbi Yoḥanan was orphaned at a young age, and although his family apparently owned considerable property, he spent virtually all of his resources in his devotion to the study of Torah and eventually became impoverished. In his youth, he had the privilege of studying under Rabbi Yehuda HaNasi, the redactor of the Mishna, but most of his Torah study was accomplished under Rabbi Yehuda HaNasi's students: Ḥizkiya ben Ḥiyya, Rabbi Oshaya, Rabbi Ḥanina, and Rabbi Yannai, who lavished praise upon him. In time, he became the head of the yeshiva in Tiberias, at which point his fame and influence increased greatly.

For many years Rabbi Yoḥanan was the leading rabbinic scholar of the entire Jewish world, not only in Eretz Yisrael but in Babylonia as well, where he was respected by the Babylonian Sages. Many of them immigrated to Eretz Yisrael to become his students. A master of both *halakha* and *aggada*, Rabbi Yoḥanan's teachings in both disciplines are found throughout the Babylonian and Jerusalem Talmuds. As a testament to his intellectual and spiritual stature, the *halakha* is in accordance with his opinion in almost every case, even when Rav or Shmuel, the preeminent *amora'im* of Babylonia, whom he treated deferentially, disagree with him. Only in disputes with his teachers in Eretz Yisrael, such as Rabbi Yannai and Rabbi Yehoshua ben Levi, is the *halakha* not in accordance with his opinion.

Rabbi Yoḥanan was renowned for being handsome, and much was said in praise of his good looks. However, his life was full of suffering; ten of his sons died in his lifetime. There is a geonic tradition that one of his sons was the Babylonian *amora* Rabbi Mattana, who did not predecease him. The death of Rabbi Yoḥanan's disciple-colleague and brother-in-law, Reish Lakish, for which he considered himself responsible, hastened his own death. Rabbi Yoḥanan had many students. In fact, all the *amora'im* of Eretz Yisrael in succeeding generations were his students and benefited from his teachings, to the extent that he is often referred to as the author of the Jerusalem Talmud. His greatest students were his brother-in-law Reish Lakish, Rabbi Elazar, Rabbi Ḥiyya bar Abba, Rabbi Abbahu, Rabbi Yosei bar Ḥanina, Rabbi Ami, and Rabbi Asi.

Reish Lakish – רַבִּי שִׁמְעוֹן בֶּן לָקִישׁ: The name Reish Lakish is actually a contraction of Rabbi Shimon ben Lakish. Reish Lakish was among the greatest *amora'im* in Eretz Yisrael. He was the friend and brother-in-law of Rabbi Yoḥanan.

Reish Lakish lived an extraordinary life. He studied Torah from a young age, but, perhaps due to dire financial straits, he sold himself to a Roman circus as a gladiator. There are many stories in the Talmud that attest to his great strength. Some time later, in the wake of a meeting with Rabbi Yoḥanan, he resumed his Torah study, first as a student of Rabbi Yoḥanan, then as a friend and colleague. He ultimately married Rabbi Yoḥanan's sister.

Many halakhic disagreements between Reish Lakish and Rabbi Yoḥanan concerning central issues of *halakha* are recorded in the Talmud. His objective was not to disagree with Rabbi Yoḥanan but rather to help him hone his opinion through debate. Rabbi Yoḥanan related to him with great respect, often saying: My peer disagrees with me. He was well known for his strict piety, to the extent that one with whom Reish Lakish was seen conversing in public was said to be able to borrow money without guarantors, as Reish Lakish associated only with people beyond reproach. When he died he was survived by his wife and son, who was a child prodigy.

רַבִּי יוֹחָנָן אָמַר: אֵינָהּ צְרִיכָה חֲלִיצָה מִן הָאַחִין – חֲלִיצַת מְעוּבֶּרֶת שְׁמָהּ חֲלִיצָה, וּבִיאַת מְעוּבֶּרֶת שְׁמָהּ בִּיאָה. וְרֵישׁ לָקִישׁ אָמַר: צְרִיכָה חֲלִיצָה מִן הָאַחִין – חֲלִיצַת מְעוּבֶּרֶת לָא שְׁמָהּ חֲלִיצָה, וּבִיאַת מְעוּבֶּרֶת לָא שְׁמָהּ בִּיאָה.

The Gemara elaborates: **Rabbi Yoḥanan said** that **she does not require** another **ḥalitza from the brothers** because he holds: ***Ḥalitza*** performed **with a pregnant woman** who later miscarries **is considered** effective ***ḥalitza*** in order to release her from the levirate bond. **And** similarly, **intercourse with a pregnant woman** who later miscarries **is considered** a valid consummation of levirate marriage through **intercourse,** such that she and the *yavam* are considered to be married. **And Reish Lakish said she requires** another ***ḥalitza* from the brothers** because he holds: ***Ḥalitza*** performed **with a pregnant woman is not considered** effective ***ḥalitza,***[N] **and intercourse with a pregnant woman is not considered** a valid consummation of levirate marriage through **intercourse.** Therefore, after she miscarries, another *ḥalitza* must be performed in order to release her from the levirate bond.

בְּמַאי קָמִפַּלְגִי? אִיבָּעֵית אֵימָא קְרָא, וְאִיבָּעֵית אֵימָא סְבָרָא.

With regard to what principle **do they disagree? If you wish, say** that they disagree over the interpretation of **a verse.**[N] **And if you wish, say** that they disagree on a point of **logical reasoning.**

אִיבָּעֵית אֵימָא סְבָרָא, רַבִּי יוֹחָנָן סָבַר: אִם יָבֹא אֵלִיָּהוּ וְיֹאמַר דְּהָא דְּאִיעַבְּרָא מַפּוֹלֵי מַפְּלָה – מִי לָאו בַּת חֲלִיצָה וְיִבּוּם הִיא? הָשְׁתָּא נַמִי, תִּגְלֵי מִילְּתָא לְמַפְרֵעַ.

If you wish, say that that they disagree over a point of **logical reasoning** in that **Rabbi Yoḥanan holds: If Elijah** the prophet **were to come** at the moment of the *ḥalitza* **and say**[N] **that this** woman **who is pregnant will miscarry, is she not eligible for *ḥalitza* or levirate marriage,** even though she is currently pregnant, since her husband died and will not be survived by offspring? **Now, too,** even though when the *ḥalitza* or levirate marriage is performed it is not known whether or not she will miscarry, **the matter will be revealed retroactively,** i.e., if she ultimately miscarries then it is apparent the *ḥalitza* or levirate marriage was always necessary and is therefore valid.

וְרֵישׁ לָקִישׁ אָמַר: תִּגְלֵי מִילְּתָא לְמַפְרֵעַ לָא אָמְרִינַן.

And Reish Lakish said: We do not say that **the matter will be revealed retroactively**[N] in order to validate the levirate marriage or *ḥalitza*. Since at the time of the levirate marriage or *ḥalitza* it was still unknown whether she would miscarry, the act is considered premature and ineffective.

וְאִיבָּעֵית אֵימָא קְרָא; רַבִּי יוֹחָנָן סָבַר "וּבֵן אֵין לוֹ" אָמַר רַחֲמָנָא, וְהָא לֵית לֵיהּ. וְרֵישׁ לָקִישׁ סָבַר: "וּבֵן אֵין לוֹ" עַיֵּין עָלָיו.

And if you wish, say that they disagree over the interpretation of **a verse** in that **Rabbi Yoḥanan holds: The Merciful One states** in the Torah: "If brothers dwell together, and one of them dies, **and he has no child**" (Deuteronomy 25:5), i.e., the obligation to consummate a levirate marriage or perform *ḥalitza* applies whenever a husband dies and is not survived by offspring. **And this** man, whose wife is currently pregnant, **does not have** any children who will survive him. Therefore, there is an obligation to consummate a levirate marriage or perform *ḥalitza*, and if done, they will be effective. **And Reish Lakish holds:** The phrase **"and he has no [*ein*] child"** is expounded by the Sages to teach that one should **inspect [*ayein*] him** carefully to determine if he is survived by offspring of any form, and currently he is in fact survived by the fetus. Therefore, there is currently no obligation to consummate a levirate marriage or perform *ḥalitza*, and consequently, even if done, they are ineffective.

אֵיתִיבֵיהּ רַבִּי יוֹחָנָן לְרֵישׁ לָקִישׁ: אֵין הַוָּלָד שֶׁל קַיָּימָא – הוּא אָסוּר בִּקְרוֹבוֹתֶיהָ, וְהִיא אֲסוּרָה בִּקְרוֹבָיו. וּפְסָלָהּ מִן הַכְּהוּנָּה. בִּשְׁלָמָא לְדִידִי, דְּאָמֵינָא חֲלִיצַת מְעוּבֶּרֶת שְׁמָהּ חֲלִיצָה – מִשּׁוּם הָכִי פְּסָלָהּ. אֶלָּא לְדִידָךְ, דְּאָמְרַתְּ חֲלִיצַת מְעוּבֶּרֶת לָא שְׁמָהּ חֲלִיצָה – אַמַּאי פְּסָלָהּ מִן הַכְּהוּנָּה?

Rabbi Yoḥanan raised an objection to the opinion of **Reish Lakish** from the mishna: If *ḥalitza* was performed with a pregnant woman, and **the offspring is not viable,** then **he is forbidden to her relatives and she is forbidden to his relatives,** and the *ḥalitza* **disqualifies her from the priesthood.** Rabbi Yoḥanan explains the challenge: **Granted, according to my** opinion, **as I say** that ***ḥalitza*** performed **with a pregnant woman** who later miscarries **is considered** effective ***ḥalitza*, it is due to that** reason that the *ḥalitza* **disqualifies her** from the priesthood. **However, according to your** opinion, **as you say that *ḥalitza*** performed **with a pregnant woman is not considered** effective ***ḥalitza*, why** should the *ḥalitza* **disqualify her from the priesthood?** According to your opinion, shouldn't the *ḥalitza* be entirely disregarded?

NOTES

Ḥalitza performed with a pregnant woman is not considered effective ḥalitza – חֲלִיצַת מְעוּבֶּרֶת לָא שְׁמָהּ חֲלִיצָה: The commentaries debate whether according to Reish Lakish the *ḥalitza* performed with a pregnant woman has any significance. Some suggest that while the *ḥalitza* does not release her from being bound to her *yevamin*, it does preclude her from performing levirate marriage, either specifically with the brother who originally performed *ḥalitza* with her or with any of the brothers. Therefore, her only recourse is to perform another *ḥalitza* following the miscarriage (see Ritva).

If you wish, say a verse, etc. – אִיבָּעֵית אֵימָא קְרָא וכו׳: Normally, in cases where the Gemara suggest that a *halakha* could be based on logical reasoning, if a verse also exists that can teach that same *halakha* the Gemara will ask why the biblical source is necessary at all; does the force of logical reasoning not suffice? Often the justification for the biblical source is based on the fact that if the *halakha* is based on the verse, then some of the details of the *halakha* will be different than if it were solely based on logical reasoning. In this case, as well, there is such a distinction: Were the *halakha* to be purely based on logical reasoning, then Reish Lakish would agree that were Elijah the prophet to actually reveal beforehand that the woman will ultimately miscarry, then the *ḥalitza* would be effective. However, according to his biblical source, the possibility of performing *ḥalitza* with a pregnant woman is entirely precluded, even if it were already known that she will miscarry (*Keren Ora*).

If Elijah were to come and say – אִם יָבֹא אֵלִיָּהוּ וְיֹאמַר: The mishna in tractate *Eduyyot* rules that when Elijah the prophet appears, he will neither inform the people as to what is prohibited or permitted nor introduce new *halakhot*. This is based on the principle that a prophet is neither permitted to legislate *halakha* nor even to resolve halakhic dilemmas. Despite this principle, the Gemara here and elsewhere appears to state that halakhic dilemmas will be resolved by Elijah. Apparently a distinction should be made between deciding halakhic principles, which cannot be done through prophecy, and clarifying questions of fact utilizing his prophetic powers, which is permitted (*Mishne LaMelekh*).

We do not say that the matter will be revealed retroactively – תִּגְלֵי מִילְּתָא לְמַפְרֵעַ לָא אָמְרִינַן: Despite Reish Lakish's claim here, the principle that the facts of a matter can be revealed retroactively is used throughout the Talmud, and it would appear that even Reish Lakish agrees in those instances. What, then, is different about this case? The Ritva suggests that in this case, it is unsound to deduce from the ultimate miscarriage that the pregnancy had always been unviable. It is possible that at the time of the levirate marriage or *ḥalitza* the pregnancy had in fact been viable, and therefore the *yevama* had not been obligated to perform levirate marriage or *ḥalitza* at the time, and it was only afterward that some additional event occurred that caused the miscarriage.

Tosafot suggest that a distinction should be made between cases in which the future is undeterminable based on the current situation and cases where the outcome could be reasonably calculated from the outset. In the former, the facts of the future are considered halakhically meaningless to the extent that even were a prophet to reveal the future, such information would have no relevance to the *halakha* as it is practiced in the present. So too, in the case of *ḥalitza*, since the ultimate miscarriage is not something that could be known in the present, one cannot say the matter is revealed retroactively (see *Gilyonei HaShas*). Rabbi Avraham min HaHar suggests that the principle is applied only in cases of rabbinic law, but not where it would affect a Torah law, as in this case.

Another explanation is cited by the Ritva: According to the verse cited by Reish Lakish, the reason that levirate marriage and *ḥalitza* cannot be performed during pregnancy is because the very existence of the fetus itself is sufficient to exclude this case from the obligation to perform levirate marriage or *ḥalitza*, since it does not fulfill the basic condition that the *yavam* "has no child." If so, the ultimate demise of the fetus is of no relevance.

NOTES

By rabbinic decree and is merely a stringency – מִדְּרַבָּנַן וּלְחוּמְרָא בְּעָלְמָא: The Rashba notes that ostensibly, a similar decree should have been introduced in a case where the offspring was viable. Had an observer only witnessed the *ḥalitza* and been unaware that the offspring ultimately proved to be viable, then if he later saw that the *yavam* and *yevama* were permitted to marry each other's relatives, he might mistakenly conclude that relatives are permitted even in a case where the offspring was not viable and the *ḥalitza* was genuinely required. The Rashba explains that in truth, there is no need to be concerned for such a misunderstanding. The Gemara later explains that in cases where *ḥalitza* was unnecessarily performed, a public announcement is made. This, coupled with the continuing living presence of the offspring, should be sufficient to prevent any misunderstanding.

The Meiri suggests an entirely different approach to this statement of the Gemara and a correspondingly different understanding of the entire talmudic discussion: When the Gemara claims that, according to Reish Lakish, the *halakha* in the mishna is true only by force of a rabbinic decree, it is referring not to the disqualification from the priesthood, but rather to the actual requirement to repeat the *ḥalitza*. According to the Meiri, even Reish Lakish holds that the original *ḥalitza* is valid by Torah law, and consequently he also assumes that it is by Torah law that she is disqualified from the priesthood.

אָמַר לֵיהּ: מִדְּרַבָּנַן, וּלְחוּמְרָא בְּעָלְמָא.

Reish Lakish **said to** Rabbi Yoḥanan: Indeed, by Torah law the *ḥalitza* is to be entirely disregarded. The mishna's ruling that she is disqualified from the priesthood is **by rabbinic decree and is merely a stringency**[N] lest people not realize that she was pregnant and think that a *ḥalutza* is permitted to marry a priest.

אִיכָּא דְּאָמְרִי, אֵיתִיבֵיהּ רֵישׁ לָקִישׁ לְרַבִּי יוֹחָנָן: אֵין הַוָּלָד שֶׁל קַיָּימָא – הוּא אָסוּר בִּקְרוֹבוֹתֶיהָ, וְהִיא אֲסוּרָה בִּקְרוֹבָיו, וּפְסָלָהּ מִן הַכְּהוּנָּה. בִּשְׁלָמָא לְדִידִי, דְּאָמִינָא חֲלִיצַת מְעוּבֶּרֶת לָא שְׁמָהּ חֲלִיצָה – הַיְינוּ דְּקָתָנֵי פְּסָלָהּ מִן הַכְּהוּנָּה לְחוּמְרָא, וְלֹא קָתָנֵי: אֵינָהּ צְרִיכָה חֲלִיצָה מִן הָאַחִין.

There are those **who say** an alternate version of the dispute: **Reish Lakish raised an objection to** the opinion of **Rabbi Yoḥanan** from the mishna: If *ḥalitza* was performed with a pregnant woman and **the offspring is not viable,** then **he is forbidden to her relatives and she is forbidden to his relatives,** and the *ḥalitza* **disqualifies her from the priesthood.** Reish Lakish explains the challenge: **Granted, according to my** opinion, **as I say that** *ḥalitza* performed **with** a **pregnant woman is not considered** effective ***ḥalitza,*** **this is** consistent with **that which is taught** in the mishna: The *ḥalitza* **disqualifies her from the priesthood,** which should be understood **as** a rabbinic **stringency, and** it is understandable that the mishna **does not teach: She does not require** another ***ḥalitza* from the brothers,** because according to my opinion, once she miscarries, she does indeed require another *ḥalitza* from the brothers.

אֶלָּא לְדִידָךְ, אֵינָהּ צְרִיכָה חֲלִיצָה מִן הָאַחִין מִיבָּעֵי לֵיהּ! – אָמַר לֵיהּ: אִין הָכִי נַמִי, וְאַיְּידֵי דְּתָנָא רֵישָׁא לֹא פְּסָלָהּ – תָּנָא סֵיפָא פְּסָלָהּ.

However, according to your opinion that *ḥalitza* performed with a pregnant woman is an effective *ḥalitza*, the mishna **should have** taught the full extent of her permissible status, i.e., that **she does not** even **require** another ***ḥalitza* from the brothers** after she miscarries because the original *ḥalitza* was effective. Rabbi Yoḥanan **said to** Reish Lakish: **Yes, it is indeed so** that she does not require another *ḥalitza* from the brothers, **but since the first clause taught:** The *ḥalitza* **does not disqualify her** from the priesthood, therefore **the latter clause taught:** The *ḥalitza* **disqualifies her** from the priesthood, in order to directly contrast with the first clause rather than teach the greater novelty.

אֵיתִיבֵיהּ רַבִּי יוֹחָנָן לְרֵישׁ לָקִישׁ: אֵין הַוָּלָד שֶׁל קַיָּימָא – יְקַיֵּים. בִּשְׁלָמָא לְדִידִי דְּאָמִינָא חֲלִיצַת מְעוּבֶּרֶת שְׁמָהּ חֲלִיצָה וּבִיאַת מְעוּבֶּרֶת שְׁמָהּ בִּיאָה – מִשּׁוּם הָכִי קָתָנֵי יְקַיֵּים.

Rabbi Yoḥanan raised an objection to the opinion of **Reish Lakish** from the mishna: If a *yavam* had intercourse with his *yevama*, who was pregnant, and **the offspring is not viable,** and therefore she was bound by a levirate bond, **he may maintain** her as his wife. Rabbi Yoḥanan explains the challenge: **Granted, according to my** opinion, **as I say *ḥalitza*** performed **with a pregnant woman is considered** effective ***ḥalitza,*** **and** similarly, **intercourse with a pregnant woman is considered** a valid consummation of levirate marriage through **intercourse,** it is **due to that** reason that the mishna **teaches: He may maintain** her as his wife, because the levirate marriage was indeed valid.

אֶלָּא לְדִידָךְ, דְּאָמְרַתְּ חֲלִיצַת מְעוּבֶּרֶת לָא שְׁמָהּ חֲלִיצָה, וּבִיאַת מְעוּבֶּרֶת לָא שְׁמָהּ בִּיאָה – יַחֲזוֹר וְיִבְעוֹל וִיקַיֵּים מִיבָּעֵי לֵיהּ! – מַאי יְקַיֵּים – יַחֲזוֹר וְיִבְעוֹל וִיקַיֵּים, דְּלָא סַגִּי.

However, according to your opinion, **as you said** that ***ḥalitza*** performed **with a pregnant woman is not considered** effective ***ḥalitza,*** **and intercourse with a pregnant woman is not considered** a valid consummation of levirate marriage through **intercourse,** the mishna **should have** taught that **he should proceed to engage in intercourse** with her again in order to consummate the levirate marriage **and** only then **may he maintain** her as his wife. Reish Lakish responded: **What is** the intention of the mishna when it teaches: **He may maintain** her as his wife? Perforce it means that **he should proceed to engage in intercourse** again with her **and** then **he may maintain** her as his wife, **as** any other way **is insufficient** to release her from the levirate bond. Therefore, it is unnecessary for the mishna to teach this explicitly.

אִיכָּא דְּאָמְרִי, אֵיתִיבֵיהּ רֵישׁ לָקִישׁ לְרַבִּי יוֹחָנָן: אֵין הַוָּלָד שֶׁל קַיָּימָא – יְקַיֵּים. בִּשְׁלָמָא לְדִידִי, דְּאָמִינָא חֲלִיצַת מְעוּבֶּרֶת לָא שְׁמָהּ חֲלִיצָה וּבִיאַת מְעוּבֶּרֶת לָא שְׁמָהּ בִּיאָה, הַיְינוּ דְּקָתָנֵי יְקַיֵּים – יַחֲזוֹר וְיִבְעוֹל וִיקַיֵּים, דְּלָא סַגִּי בְּלָאו הָכִי.

There are those **who say** an alternate version of the dispute: **Reish Lakish raised an objection to** the opinion of **Rabbi Yoḥanan** from the mishna: If a *yavam* had intercourse with his *yevama*, who was pregnant, and **the offspring is not viable,** and therefore she was bound by a levirate bond, **he may maintain** her as his wife. Reish Lakish explains how the mishna poses a challenge to Rabbi Yoḥanan's opinion: **Granted, according to my** opinion, **as I say** that ***ḥalitza*** performed **with a pregnant woman is not considered** effective ***ḥalitza,*** **and intercourse with a pregnant woman is not considered** a valid consummation of levirate marriage through **intercourse, this is** consistent with **that which is taught** in the mishna: **He may maintain** her as a wife, which perforce means **he should proceed to engage in intercourse** with her again **and** then **he may maintain** her as his wife, **as** any other way **is insufficient** to release her from the levirate bond **without this** additional intercourse.

אֶלָּא לְדִידָךְ, רָצָה – יוֹצִיא, רָצָה – יְקַיֵּים, מִיבְּעֵי לֵיהּ! – אִין הָכִי נַמִי, אַיְּידֵי דְּתָנָא רֵישָׁא יוֹצִיא – תָּנָא נַמִי סֵיפָא יְקַיֵּים.

However, according to your opinion that intercourse with a pregnant woman is considered a valid consummation of levirate marriage and therefore she is certainly considered to be his wife, the mishna **should have** taught: **If he wishes he may send her out,** through divorce, or **if he wishes he may maintain** her as a wife. Rabbi Yoḥanan replied: **Yes, it is indeed so, but since the first clause taught: He should send** her **out,** therefore **the latter clause taught: He may maintain** her as a wife, in order to directly contrast the first clause, rather than teach the full *halakha* with all its details.

מֵיתִיבִי: הַכּוֹנֵס אֶת יְבִמְתּוֹ וְנִמְצֵאת מְעוּבֶּרֶת – הֲרֵי זוֹ לֹא תִּנָּשֵׂא צָרָתָהּ, שֶׁמָּא יְהֵא וָלָד בֶּן קַיָּימָא. אַדְּרַבָּה, כִּי הָוֵי הַוָּלָד בֶּן קַיָּימָא מִיפַּטְרָה צָרָתָהּ! אֶלָּא אֵימָא: שֶׁמָּא לֹא יְהֵא הַוָּלָד בֶּן קַיָּימָא.

The Gemara **raises an objection** to the opinion of Rabbi Yoḥanan from a *baraita*: In the case of **one who consummates** the levirate marriage with **his** *yevama*, and he does so under the assumption that there is a levirate bond and he is obligated to consummate a levirate marriage with her, **and** then **she is found to** have been **pregnant** at the time of the intercourse, **a rival wife of this** *yevama* **may not marry, lest the offspring be viable.** Before explaining the challenge, the Gemara notes that the reasoning of the *baraita* appears flawed: **On the contrary, when the offspring is viable,** that is a reason for **her rival wife to be released** from the levirate bond, and she should be able to marry any man. **Rather,** emend the *baraita* and **say: Lest the offspring not be viable.**

וְאִי סָלְקָא דַּעְתָּךְ בִּיאַת מְעוּבֶּרֶת שְׁמָהּ בִּיאָה – אַמַּאי לֹא תִּנָּשֵׂא צָרָתָהּ? תִּיפָּטֵר בְּבִיאָה שֶׁל חֲבֵירְתָהּ!

The Gemara now explains how the *baraita* poses a challenge to Rabbi Yoḥanan's opinion: **And if it enters your mind** to say that **intercourse with a pregnant woman is considered** a valid consummation of levirate marriage through **intercourse, why should her rival wife not** be permitted to **marry?** Indeed, her rival wife **should be released** from the levirate bond **by** virtue **of the intercourse of her fellow** wife. If the deceased had several rival wives, all of them become bound by the levirate bond. However, it is sufficient for one of them to either consummate a levirate marriage or perform *ḥalitza* in order to release the rest of them from their bond and thereby permit them to marry any man.

אָמַר אַבָּיֵי: בְּבִיאָה – כּוּלֵּי עָלְמָא לָא פְּלִיגִי דְּלָא פָּטְרָה, כִּי פְּלִיגִי – בַּחֲלִיצָה.

The Gemara defends Rabbi Yoḥanan's opinion: **Abaye said** that the opinion ascribed to Rabbi Yoḥanan above is not an accurate portrayal of his opinion. Rather, **with regard to intercourse** with a *yevama* who is pregnant at the time, **everyone agrees**[N] **that it does not release** her and her rival wives from the levirate bond; **when they disagree** it is only **with regard to** whether ***ḥalitza***[N] performed with a *yevama* who is pregnant at the time is effective in releasing her and her rival wives from the levirate bond.

רַבִּי יוֹחָנָן סָבַר: חֲלִיצַת מְעוּבֶּרֶת שְׁמָהּ חֲלִיצָה, בִּיאַת מְעוּבֶּרֶת לָא שְׁמָהּ בִּיאָה. רֵישׁ לָקִישׁ סָבַר: בִּיאַת מְעוּבֶּרֶת – לָא שְׁמָהּ בִּיאָה, וַחֲלִיצַת מְעוּבֶּרֶת – לָא שְׁמָהּ חֲלִיצָה.

Abaye continues to explain his opinion: **Rabbi Yoḥanan holds** that ***ḥalitza* with a pregnant woman is considered** effective ***ḥalitza,*** but **intercourse with a pregnant woman is not considered** a valid consummation of levirate marriage through **intercourse** and therefore does not release her and her rival wives from the levirate bond. And **Reish Lakish holds** that **intercourse with a pregnant woman is not considered** a valid consummation of levirate marriage through **intercourse, and *ḥalitza* with a pregnant woman is not considered** effective ***ḥalitza.*** Therefore, the *baraita* cited above does not pose a challenge, since all agree that intercourse with a pregnant woman will not free her or her rival wives from the levirate bond.

אֲמַר לֵיהּ רָבָא: מָה נַפְשָׁךְ: אִי בִּיאַת מְעוּבֶּרֶת שְׁמָהּ בִּיאָה – חֲלִיצַת מְעוּבֶּרֶת שְׁמָהּ חֲלִיצָה, וְאִי בִּיאַת מְעוּבֶּרֶת לָא שְׁמָהּ בִּיאָה – חֲלִיצַת מְעוּבֶּרֶת נַמִי לָא שְׁמָהּ חֲלִיצָה. דְּהָא קַיְימָא לַן

Rava said to him: Whichever way you look at it, one cannot differentiate between the validity of consummating the levirate marriage through intercourse and the validity of *ḥalitza.* **If intercourse with a pregnant woman is considered** a valid consummation of levirate marriage through **intercourse** because if she miscarries it is apparent that there was always an obligation to perform levirate marriage or *ḥalitza,* then perforce ***ḥalitza* with a pregnant woman** should also **be considered** effective ***ḥalitza.* And if intercourse with a pregnant woman is not considered** a valid consummation of levirate marriage through **intercourse** because in her currently pregnant state there is no obligation to perform levirate marriage or *ḥalitza,* then perforce ***ḥalitza* with a pregnant woman** should also **not be considered** effective ***ḥalitza.* As we maintain**

NOTES

With regard to intercourse everyone agrees – בְּבִיאָה כּוּלֵּי עָלְמָא לָא פְּלִיגִי: The commentaries explain that Abaye assumes that the opinion initially ascribed to Rabbi Yoḥanan was never actually said by him. Rather, it was mistakenly assumed to be his opinion by some of his disciples, and it was the disciples of Rabbi Yoḥanan and Reish Lakish, not Rabbi Yoḥanan and Reish Lakish themselves, who then proceeded to debate the viability of that opinion.

When they disagree it is with regard to *ḥalitza* – כִּי פְּלִיגִי בַּחֲלִיצָה: *Tosafot* explain the logic of differentiating between the efficacy of performing a levirate marriage with a pregnant woman and performing *ḥalitza* with a pregnant woman: Rabbi Yoḥanan agrees that the levirate marriage cannot be consummated through intercourse while the *yevama* is still pregnant because there still exists the possibility that the offspring will be viable. Were that to be true, the standard prohibition against engaging in relations with one's brother's wife would remain in force. Consequently, it is certainly forbidden to attempt to consummate the levirate marriage, and therefore doing so is ineffective. In contrast, the act of *ḥalitza* itself is never forbidden, even were it to be unnecessary. Therefore, if it is ultimately revealed that it was necessary, it should certainly be effective. The Rivan suggests that with regard to intercourse, even if it is ultimately revealed that there was an obligation to perform levirate marriage, it is possible for the Sages to retroactively declare the intercourse to have been an illicit act and therefore ineffective in consummating the levirate marriage. However, similar logic could not be applied to invalidate an act of *ḥalitza.*

דְּכָל הָעוֹלָה לְיִבּוּם עוֹלָה לַחֲלִיצָה, וְכָל שֶׁאֵין עוֹלָה לְיִבּוּם – אֵינוֹ עוֹלָה לַחֲלִיצָה!

that anyone who is eligible for levirate marriage[H] **is eligible for *ḥalitza* and anyone who is not eligible for levirate marriage is not eligible for *ḥalitza*.**[N] Therefore, the original understanding of Rabbi Yoḥanan's opinion, that both the intercourse and the *ḥalitza* of a pregnant woman are valid, was accurate.

אֶלָּא אָמַר רָבָא, הָכִי קָאָמַר: הַכּוֹנֵס יְבִמְתּוֹ וְנִמְצֵאת מְעוּבֶּרֶת – הֲרֵי זוֹ לֹא תִּנָּשֵׂא צָרָתָהּ, שֶׁמָּא יְהֵא וָלָד בֶּן קַיָּימָא, וּבִיאַת מְעוּבֶּרֶת לֹא שְׁמָהּ בִּיאָה, וַחֲלִיצַת מְעוּבֶּרֶת לֹא שְׁמָהּ חֲלִיצָה, וְהַוָּלָד אֵינוֹ פּוֹטֵר עַד שֶׁיֵּצֵא לַאֲוִיר הָעוֹלָם.

Rava therefore provides a different defense of Rabbi Yoḥanan's opinion: **Rather, Rava said** that **this is what** the *baraita* **is saying:** In the case of **one who consummates** the levirate marriage **with his *yevama*** under the assumption that there is a mitzva to do so, **and** then **she is found to** have been **pregnant** at the time of the intercourse, **a rival wife**[H] of **this *yevama* may not marry lest the offspring be viable, and intercourse with a woman pregnant** with viable offspring **is not considered** a valid consummation of levirate marriage through **intercourse, and *ḥalitza* of a woman pregnant** with viable offspring **is not considered** effective ***ḥalitza*. And** furthermore, even if **the offspring** is viable, it **does not release** her and her rival wives from the levirate bond **until it comes into the air of the world,** i.e., until it is actually born.

תַּנְיָא כְּוָותֵיהּ דְּרָבָא: הַכּוֹנֵס יְבִמְתּוֹ וְנִמְצֵאת מְעוּבֶּרֶת – הֲרֵי זוֹ לֹא תִּנָּשֵׂא צָרָתָהּ, שֶׁמָּא יְהֵא וָלָד בֶּן קַיָּימָא, וְאֵין בִּיאָה וַחֲלִיצָה פּוֹטֶרֶת, אֶלָּא וָלָד פּוֹטֵר, וְהַוָּלָד אֵין פּוֹטְרָהּ עַד שֶׁיֵּצֵא לַאֲוִיר הָעוֹלָם.

It is taught in a *baraita* **in accordance with** the opinion **of Rava:** In the case of **one who consummates** a levirate marriage with **his *yevama*, and** then **she is found to** have been **pregnant** at the time of the intercourse, **a rival wife of this *yevama* may not marry lest the offspring be viable.** This is because **intercourse or *ḥalitza*** with a woman pregnant with viable offspring **does not release** a *yevama* from the levirate bond; **rather,** the **offspring releases** her. **And** furthermore, even if **the offspring** is viable, it **does not release her** and her rival wives from the levirate marriage bond **until it comes into the air of the world.**

טַעְמָא – דְּשֶׁמָּא יְהֵא וָלָד בֶּן קַיָּימָא הוּא, הָא לָא הָוֵי וָלָד בֶּן קַיָּימָא – מִיפְּטַר צָרָתָהּ. לֵימָא תֶּיהֱוֵי תְּיוּבְתָּא דְּרֵישׁ לָקִישׁ!

The Gemara explains that the *baraita* appears to contradict Reish Lakish's opinion: According to the *baraita*, **the** only **reason** that levirate marriage with the pregnant *yevama* does not permit the rival wife to marry **is as** the *baraita* stated: **Lest the offspring be viable.** By inference, **were the offspring not viable, her rival wife would be released** from the levirate bond. If so, **let us say that** this *baraita* **is a conclusive refutation** of the opinion **of Reish Lakish.**

אָמַר לָךְ רֵישׁ לָקִישׁ, הָכִי קָתָנֵי: הַכּוֹנֵס יְבִמְתּוֹ וְנִמְצֵאת מְעוּבֶּרֶת – הֲרֵי זוֹ לֹא תִּנָּשֵׂא צָרָתָהּ, שֶׁמָּא לֹא יְהֵא הַוָּלָד בֶּן קַיָּימָא, וַחֲלִיצַת מְעוּבֶּרֶת לֹא שְׁמָהּ חֲלִיצָה, וּבִיאַת מְעוּבֶּרֶת לֹא שְׁמָהּ בִּיאָה.

The Gemara defends Reish Lakish's opinion: **Reish Lakish** could have **said to you: This is what** the *baraita* **is teaching:** In the case of **one who consummates** a levirate marriage with **his *yevama*, and** then **she was found to** have been **pregnant** at the time of the intercourse, **a rival wife of this *yevama* may not marry lest the offspring not be viable,** which would mean that all the rival wives are bound by the levirate bond. **And** even if one of those wives has intercourse or preforms *ḥalitza* with the *yavam*, it would be ineffective in releasing them from the levirate bond because ***ḥalitza* with a pregnant woman is not be considered** effective ***ḥalitza*, and intercourse with a pregnant woman is not considered** a valid consummation of levirate marriage through **intercourse.**

וְאִם תֹּאמַר: הַלֵּךְ אַחַר רוֹב נָשִׁים, וְרוֹב נָשִׁים וָלָד מְעַלְּיָא יָלְדָן? – וָלָד אֵין פּוֹטֵר עַד שֶׁיֵּצֵא לַאֲוִיר הָעוֹלָם.

Reish Lakish explains the need for the final clause of the *baraita*: **And** even **if you say:** Let the wives marry without the need for any levirate marriage or *ḥalitza* because one should **follow the majority of women, and the majority of women give birth to a full-fledged,** i.e., viable, **offspring,** and therefore one should presume no levirate bond exists, to counter this claim the *baraita* concludes: Even if the offspring will be viable, an **offspring does not release** a *yevama* and her rival wives from the levirate bond **until it comes into the air of the world.**

HALAKHA

Anyone who is eligible for levirate marriage, etc. – **כָּל הָעוֹלָה לְיִבּוּם וכו׳**: Whenever a woman is ineligible to consummate a levirate marriage, she is also ineligible to perform *ḥalitza* (Rambam *Sefer Nashim, Hilkhot Yibbum VaḤalitza* 1:19).

The rival wife of a pregnant *yevama* – **צָרַת יְבָמָה מְעוּבֶּרֶת**: If a *yevama* who is pregnant with a child from her deceased husband consummates a levirate marriage or performs *ḥalitza*, her rival wife is prohibited from remarrying until the child is born (Rambam *Sefer Nashim, Hilkhot Yibbum VaḤalitza* 1:22; *Shulḥan Arukh, Even HaEzer* 164:3).

NOTES

Anyone who is not eligible for levirate marriage is not eligible for *ḥalitza* – **כָּל שֶׁאֵין עוֹלָה לְיִבּוּם אֵינוֹ עוֹלָה לַחֲלִיצָה**: This principle is generally taken to mean that anyone who is precluded from consummating levirate marriage is not bound by a levirate bond and therefore does not need to perform *ḥalitza*. However, this poses a difficulty, as there are some cases where although it is forbidden to consummate levirate marriage, *ḥalitza* is nevertheless still required in order to release the *yevama* from the levirate bond. This is the case, for example, when the *yavam* is prohibited from engaging in relations with the *yevama* by force of a negative mitzva that does not carry the punishment of *karet*. The Meiri suggests that the principle is indeed sound because, by Torah law, when the levirate marriage is prohibited only by force of a negative mitzva that does not carry the punishment of *karet*, the mitzva to consummate levirate marriage overrides the prohibition. As such, by Torah law, she is in fact eligible to consummate a levirate marriage and therefore is also eligible to perform *ḥalitza*. Therefore, although the Sages decreed that one should not consummate the levirate marriage in such a case, there is still a need to perform *ḥalitza*.

The Ritva suggests a different approach. He explains that even when levirate marriage in such cases is forbidden by Torah law, *ḥalitza* is nevertheless required. He cites the Gemara elsewhere that provides a biblical source that teaches that in cases where the relationship between the *yavam* and the *yevama* is forbidden only by force of a negative mitzva, *ḥalitza* is required. The Gemara's principle here, however, relates exclusively to cases in which the relationship is forbidden by force of a negative mitzva that does carry the punishment of *karet*. In contrast to the above opinions, the Rambam appears to understand the principle in a more limited fashion. According to him, the principle states only that if at any point in time the option to consummate the levirate marriage is proscribed, then at that time, one cannot perform *ḥalitza* either. However, that does not necessarily mean that the *yevama* will be released from the levirate bond. Rather, she will have to wait until, if ever, it is possible to consummate the levirate marriage, at which point she may perform *ḥalitza* if she wishes.

This principle is unanimously accepted. However, in the Gemara, Rava adduces it as support for his understanding of Rabbi Yoḥanan's opinion. How does Abaye justify his understanding in light of the principle? The Ritva explains: Abaye assumes that if it emerges that the offspring is not viable, then it emerges in retrospect that in fact the woman was always eligible for levirate marriage. As such, it is incorrect to automatically consider a pregnant woman as ineligible. Therefore, if she performs *ḥalitza* it will be valid. However, according to Rava, while she is actually pregnant, even should the fetus not survive, she is deemed ineligible to consummate a levirate marriage at that time. Therefore, there is no possibility of performing *ḥalitza* either.

אָמַר רַבִּי אֶלְעָזָר: אֶפְשָׁר, אִיתָא לְהָא דְּרֵישׁ לָקִישׁ וְלֹא תְּנַן לַהּ בְּמַתְנִיתִין?! – נְפַק, דַּק וְאַשְׁכַּח, דִּתְנַן: הָאִשָּׁה שֶׁהָלַךְ בַּעְלָהּ וְצָרָתָהּ לִמְדִינַת הַיָּם, וּבָאוּ וְאָמְרוּ לָהּ: ״מֵת בַּעְלֵךְ״ – הֲרֵי זוֹ לֹא תִּנָּשֵׂא וְלֹא תִּתְיַיבֵּם, עַד שֶׁתֵּדַע שֶׁמָּא מְעוּבֶּרֶת הִיא צָרָתָהּ.

Rabbi Elazar said: Is it **possible** that **there is** halakhic acceptance **of this**[N] opinion **of Reish Lakish and it was not** hinted to by something **taught in the Mishna? He went out** of the study hall, carefully **checked** the *mishnayot*, **and found** one that supported Reish Lakish's opinion, **as we learned** in a mishna: In the case of **a woman whose husband and rival wife went overseas,**[H] **and** then witnesses **came and said to her: Your husband died,** and her husband had a brother, **this** woman **may neither marry** someone other than his brother, **nor may she enter into levirate marriage** with that brother, **until she knows** whether **perhaps her rival wife is pregnant.** If she discovers that her rival wife is not pregnant, she would then be able to perform levirate marriage or *ḥalitza*. If she discovers her rival wife is pregnant, she would have to wait to see if the pregnancy is viable. If it is found to be viable, only at that point would she be permitted to marry someone else.

בִּשְׁלָמָא יַבּוּמֵי לָא – שֶׁמָּא יְהֵא וָלָד בֶּן קַיָּימָא, וְיִפְגַּע בְּאִיסּוּר אֵשֶׁת אָח דְּאוֹרָיְיתָא. אֶלָּא לֹא תַּחֲלוֹץ, אַמַּאי? בִּשְׁלָמָא תַּחֲלוֹץ בְּתוֹךְ תִּשְׁעָה וְתִנָּשֵׂא בְּתוֹךְ תִּשְׁעָה – לָא, הַיְינוּ סָפֵק.

Rabbi Elazar explains how this mishna supports Reish Lakish's opinion: **Granted, she may not enter levirate marriage** as **perhaps** her rival wife is pregnant and the **offspring will be viable, and** therefore by consummating the levirate marriage the *yavam* would **encounter the Torah prohibition against** engaging in relations with one's **brother's wife. But why may she not perform *ḥalitza*? Granted, she may not perform *ḥalitza* during the** first **nine** months following her husband's death **and** then proceed to also **marry during** those **nine** months; **this is** prohibited due to the fact that there is the **uncertainty** whether her rival wife is pregnant with viable offspring, in which case she would be released from the levirate bond.

אֶלָּא תַּחֲלוֹץ בְּתוֹךְ תִּשְׁעָה, וְתִנָּשֵׂא לְאַחַר תִּשְׁעָה!

But let her perform *ḥalitza* during the first **nine** months following her husband's death **and** then wait to **marry** until **after** those **nine** months. By that point in time, even if the rival wife was pregnant she would have already given birth. If the offspring was viable, then it emerges that there was never a levirate bond, and if it is not viable, then she was released from her levirate bond through the *ḥalitza* she performed. Either way, she would now be permitted to remarry. Why, then, does the mishna not consider this possibility? Rabbi Elazar claims that the only explanation for this is if the mishna assumes that *ḥalitza* performed while one of the wives of the deceased is pregnant is not effective. As such, the mishna is a proof for Reish Lakish's opinion.

וּלְטַעְמִיךְ: תַּחֲלוֹץ וְתִנָּשֵׂא לְאַחַר תִּשְׁעָה!

The Gemara rejects Rabbi Elazar's proof: But even **according to your reasoning** that *ḥalitza* with a pregnant woman is not effective, the mishna should have considered an additional possibility: **Let her perform *ḥalitza* and marry,** doing both **after nine** months have passed since the death of her husband.Doing so should be effective according to both Reish Lakish and Rabbi Yoḥanan.

אֶלָּא: בַּר מִינָּהּ דְּהַהִיא, דְּאַבָּיֵי בַּר אַבָּא וְרַב חִינָּנָא בַּר אַבָּיֵי דְּאָמְרִי תַּרְוַויְיהוּ: שֶׁמָּא יְהֵא וָלָד בֶּן קַיָּימָא, וְנִמְצָא אַתָּה מַצְרִיכָהּ כָּרוֹז לִכְהוּנָּה.

Rather, the discussion of this topic should be held **apart from that** mishna, as the true reason for that mishna's ruling is **as** it is **Abaye bar Abba and Rav Ḥinnana bar Abaye who both say** that she is prohibited from performing *ḥalitza* while one of the wives of the deceased is pregnant because **perhaps the offspring will be viable,** in which case any *ḥalitza* performed would be entirely unnecessary and therefore meaningless, and she would remain permitted to marry into the priesthood, as the opening mishna of the chapter rules. However, in this situation people might not realize that the *ḥalitza* she performed was meaningless, and they would think she is a *ḥalutza*, who is prohibited from marrying a priest. **And it would** therefore **emerge** that if she were allowed to perform *ḥalitza* while pregnant, it is possible that **you will** ultimately **require a public announcement** to be made **for her**[N] to attest to the fact that she is in fact still permitted **to** marry into the **priesthood.**

NOTES

Is it possible that there is halakhic acceptance of this – אֶפְשָׁר אִיתָא לְהָא: The Rivan notes that since ultimately the *halakha* is ruled in accordance with Reish Lakish's opinion, it would be peculiar if his opinion was not hinted to somewhere in the Mishna.

It would emerge that you will require a public announcement for her – וְנִמְצָא אַתָּה מַצְרִיכָהּ כָּרוֹז: *Tosafot* and other early commentaries note that a public announcement is made only if the woman is otherwise suitable for the priesthood, in order to indicate that despite the fact that she performed *ḥalitza*, it does not disqualify her, since it was meaningless. Therefore, had she been divorced or had some other disqualification, since no public announcement is made, it should follow that she should not need to wait for nine months before performing *ḥalitza*. The Meiri notes that this is stated explicitly in the Jerusalem Talmud, and the Ramban suggests that this is indicated by the precise formulation of the mishna, which chooses to refer to her simply as: A woman, as opposed to: The *yevama*, which suggests that the mishna relates to a standard woman who had not been previously divorced.

HALAKHA

A woman whose husband and rival wife went overseas – הָאִשָּׁה שֶׁהָלַךְ בַּעְלָהּ וְצָרָתָהּ לִמְדִינַת הַיָּם: In the case of a woman whose husband and rival wife went to a country overseas, and then witnesses came and said to her: Your husband died, the woman may neither perform *ḥalitza* nor consummate levirate marriage until it is established whether the rival wife has given birth (Rambam *Sefer Nashim, Hilkhot Yibbum VaḤalitza* 3:16; *Shulḥan Arukh, Even HaEzer* 156:13).

NOTES

The *halakha* is in accordance with the opinion of Reish Lakish – הִלְכְתָא כְּוָותֵיהּ דְּרֵישׁ לָקִישׁ: According to Reish Lakish, if a woman is pregnant at the time of her husband's death, then at that moment she is ineligible to consummate a levirate marriage. The early commentaries raise the following question: If so, she should be entirely released from any levirate bond based on the principle, developed in the Gemara elsewhere, that the levirate bond is formed at the moment of the husband's death; therefore, if she is not subject to the requirement to consummate a levirate marriage at that point, then no bond is formed at all. Why, then, is she obligated to perform levirate marriage or *ḥalitza* if the offspring proves not to be viable? The early commentaries explain that even according to Reish Lakish, the requirement to consummate a levirate marriage does apply to a pregnant woman from the moment of her husband's death, and therefore a levirate bond is formed. However, since she is pregnant, she must first wait until the viability of the offspring is determined before she is able to act upon it (Rashba).

In these three – בְּהָנֵי תְּלָת: Generally, in disputes between Rabbi Yoḥanan and Reish Lakish the *halakha* is ruled in accordance with the opinion of Rabbi Yoḥanan. Therefore, it was necessary to delineate those cases in which the *halakha* is atypically decided in accordance with the opinion of Reish Lakish.

Many of the early commentaries note that there are many other cases in which the *halakha* is ruled in accordance with the opinion of Reish Lakish. Why, then, did Rava list only three cases? The Meiri suggests that Rava meant only to clarify the *halakha* in those three cases but never to suggest that these are the only cases in which the *halakha* is ruled in accordance with the opinion of Reish Lakish. Others suggest that Rava considered only those disputes about actions whose actual performance is never prohibited, e.g., *ḥalitza* (*Tosefot Ḥad MiKamma'ei*; Rabbi Avraham min HaHar; see *Arukh LaNer*).

וְלַצְרְכָהּ! דִּלְמָא אִיכָּא אִינִישׁ דַּהֲוֵי בַּחֲלִיצָה וְלָא הֲוֵי בְּהַכְרָזָה, וְאָתֵי לְמֵימַר: קָשְׁרֵי חֲלוּצָה לְכֹהֵן.

The Gemara wonders why this poses a problem: **But** why not let her perform *ḥalitza* while still pregnant, and then if it becomes necessary, **require** a public announcement to be made **for her?** The Gemara explains why one should avoid having to rely on a public announcement: **Perhaps there were some people who were** present **at the *ḥalitza* and were not** present **at the public announcement, and** when that the courts permit her to marry a priest **they might come to say** that **they are permitting a *ḥalutza*** to marry **a priest.**

אָמַר לֵיהּ אַבָּיֵי: מִידֵי לֹא תַּחֲלוֹץ וְלֹא תִּתְיַיבֵּם קָתָנֵי? לֹא תִּנָּשֵׂא וְלֹא תִּתְיַיבֵּם קָתָנֵי, בְּלֹא חֲלִיצָה, אֲבָל אִי חָלֵיץ לָהּ – הָכִי נַמִי דִּשְׁרְיָא.

Abaye suggests another rejection of Rabbi Elazar's proof from that mishna: **Abaye said to** Rabbi Elazar: The very formulation of the mishna refutes Reish Lakish's opinion, as **does** the mishna **teach** that **she may neither perform *ḥalitza* nor enter into levirate marriage?** No, the mishna **teaches** only that **she may neither be married nor enter into levirate marriage,** which implies only that she may not marry **without** first performing ***ḥalitza*, but if** the *yavam* **performs *ḥalitza* with her, she would indeed be permitted** to marry after nine months have passed since her husband's death. This understanding of the mishna undermines the basis of Rabbi Elazar's proof from the mishna.

תַּנְיָא כְּוָותֵיהּ דְּרֵישׁ לָקִישׁ: הַחוֹלֵץ לִמְעוּבֶּרֶת וְהִפִּילָה – צְרִיכָה חֲלִיצָה מִן הָאַחִין.

Even if that mishna does not support Reish Lakish's opinion, nevertheless **it is taught** in a *baraita* **in accordance with** the opinion **of Reish Lakish:** In the case of **one who performs *ḥalitza* with a pregnant woman and she miscarries, she requires** another ***ḥalitza* with the brothers** in order to release her from the levirate bond. The *baraita* assumes that the original *ḥalitza* is ineffective because it was done while she was still pregnant, which is accordance with the opinion of Reish Lakish.

אָמַר רָבָא: הִלְכְתָא כְּוָותֵיהּ דְּרֵישׁ לָקִישׁ בְּהָנֵי תְּלָת: חֲדָא – הָא דַּאֲמַרַן. אִידָךְ – דִּתְנַן: הַמְחַלֵּק נְכָסָיו עַל פִּיו, רִיבָּה לְאֶחָד וּמִיעֵט לְאֶחָד, וְהִשְׁוָה לָהֶם אֶת הַבְּכוֹר – דְּבָרָיו קַיָּימִין.

Rava said: The *halakha* is in accordance with the opinion **of Reish Lakish**[N] **in these three**[N] disputes: **One, this** dispute **that we** already **stated** with regard to the *ḥalitza* of a pregnant woman. **The other** dispute concerns that **which we learned** in a mishna: In the case of **one who verbally divides up his possessions**[H] among his descendants, stating how he wishes his estate to be divided after his death, if **he increases** the proportion of his estate that should go **to one** of his children **or decreases** the proportion of his estate that should go **to** another **one** of his children, **or** if **he equally** distributes **between them** the double portion of **the firstborn,** then **his words are binding.**

וְאִם אָמַר מִשּׁוּם יְרוּשָּׁה – לֹא אָמַר כְּלוּם. כָּתַב, בֵּין בַּתְּחִלָּה בֵּין בַּסּוֹף בֵּין בָּאֶמְצַע, מִשּׁוּם מַתָּנָה – דְּבָרָיו קַיָּימִין.

But if he said explicitly that the receipt of those portions should be considered **as an inheritance,** then it as though the verbal division of his property that **he said is nothing,** i.e., it is non-binding, since his words directly contradict the *halakhot* of inheritance as they are written in the Torah.[B] However, if he wrote a will and somewhere therein **he wrote, whether at the beginning, whether at the end, or whether in the middle,** that the receipt of the portions should be considered **as a gift,** as opposed to an inheritance, then **his words are binding.**

HALAKHA

One who verbally divides up his possessions – הַמְחַלֵּק נְכָסָיו עַל פִּיו: In the case of one who is mortally ill who divides up his possessions, if he increases or decreases the proportion of his estate that should go to each child, or if he equally distributes the double portion of the firstborn between them, then his words are binding. However, if he states explicitly that the receipt of those portions should be considered an inheritance, then it as though he did not say anything and the inheritance is allotted according to the standard conventions. If he wrote a will and somewhere therein he wrote, whether at the beginning, middle, or end, that the receipt of the portions should be considered a gift, then even if he also referred to the portions as an inheritance, his words are binding (Rambam *Sefer Mishpatim*, *Hilkhot Naḥalot* 6:5; *Shulḥan Arukh*, *Ḥoshen Mishpat* 281:7).

BACKGROUND

The laws of inheritance – דִּינֵי יְרוּשָּׁה: The basic *halakhot* of inheritance are stated in Numbers 27:8–11 in the following manner: If one dies without sons, the inheritance is given to his daughter. If he has no daughters, the inheritance passes to his father. If the father is no longer alive, then it passes to the father's heirs. In addition, the firstborn son receives a double portion of the inheritance (Deuteronomy 21:17). The *halakhot* of inheritance apply only to property that the deceased had not already given away. During his lifetime he is entitled to divide up his possessions in whatever way he wishes, and he may even write a will just prior to his death dividing them up in whatever way he desires.

Perek **IV**
Daf **35** Amud **b**

ואמר ריש לקיש: לעולם לא קנה עד שיאמר "פלוני ופלוני ירשו שדה פלונית ופלונית שנתתים להם במתנה וירשום".

Reish Lakish and Rabbi Yoḥanan dispute whether one must state that the receipt of the portions should be considered as a gift with regard to each recipient, or whether stating it with regard to one of them is enough to indicate that it is true for all. **And Reish Lakish said:** The inheritors **will only ever acquire** the portions as defined by the owner of the possessions **once he says: So-and-so and so-and-so shall inherit such and such a field and such and such** a field **that I have given to them as a gift, and they shall inherit them,** i.e., he must state explicitly for each recipient that their receipt of the portions should be considered a gift.[H] Rava ruled that in this dispute as well, the *halakha* is in accordance with Reish Lakish.

ואידך – דתנן: הכותב כל נכסיו לבנו לאחר מותו, האב אינו יכול למכור – מפני שנתנן לבן, והבן אינו יכול למכור – מפני שהן ברשות האב – מכר האב מכורין עד שימות הוא. מכר הבן – אין ללוקח כלום עד שימות האב.

And the other dispute concerns that **which we learned** in a mishna: In the case of **one who writes** a bill transferring ownership of **all of his possessions to his son** stating that the transfer should take effect immediately so that the son should gain the rights to use the possessions **after his death,**[H] then although **the father** retained for himself the right to use the possessions until his death, he **is unable to sell** the possessions **due to** the fact **that he gave them to the son, and the son is unable to sell** the possessions **due to** the fact **that they are** still **in the father's possession. If the father sold**[H] the possessions, then **they are sold** to the extent that the purchaser may use them **until** the father **dies. If the son sold**[H] the possessions during his father's lifetime, **the purchaser does not** receive **any** rights to use the possessions **until the father dies.**

ואיתמר, מכר הבן בחיי האב, ומת הבן בחיי האב, רבי יוחנן אמר: לא קנה לוקח, וריש לקיש אמר: קנה לוקח.

And an amoraic dispute **was stated** in the case in which **the son sold** the possessions **during the father's lifetime, and** then **the son died during the father's lifetime,**[H] following which the father died as well. **Rabbi Yoḥanan said: The purchaser does not acquire** anything, **and Reish Lakish said: The purchaser does acquire** the possessions.

רבי יוחנן אמר: לא קנה לוקח, קנין פירות כקנין הגוף דמי.

The Gemara explains their reasoning: **Rabbi Yoḥanan said** that **the purchaser does not acquire** anything, because he holds that the **ownership of** the rights to an item and its **produce is tantamount to the ownership of the item itself,**[B] i.e., the actual title to it. Since the father retained the rights to use the possessions until his death, as long as he lives he is considered to hold the title to them. Therefore, the son's sale can be effective only after the father's death, at which point the son becomes the title owner. However, if the son dies first, then since he never gained the title to the items, his sale can never come to fruition.

וריש לקיש אמר: קנה לוקח, קנין פירות לאו כקנין הגוף דמי.

And Reish Lakish said: The purchaser does acquire the possessions, as Reish Lakish holds that the **ownership of** the rights to an item and its **produce is not tantamount to the ownership of the item itself,** i.e., the actual title to it. Therefore, although the father is still alive, the son immediately gains the full title to the possessions, which he may sell to someone else. Nevertheless, since the father retains the rights to use the possessions, the purchaser may use the possessions he acquired only when the father dies.

HALAKHA

Inheritance and gift – ירושה ומתנה: With regard to one who is mortally ill, who divides up his possessions in a manner that departs from the standard conventions: If he expresses his wishes in a single unbroken statement, then as long as he refers to the receipt of those portions as a gift, even if he also refers to them as an inheritance, his words are binding. This is true even if he mentions that the portions should be considered a gift with respect to only one of the recipients or one of the possessions; provided he mentioned at some point in the statement that it should be considered a gift, it is all considered a gift. However, if he made two or more separate statements, then he must make it explicitly clear that his intention is that each part of the division should be considered a gift. This is in accordance with the opinion of Reish Lakish (Rambam *Sefer Mishpatim, Hilkhot Naḥalot*, 6:6; *Shulḥan Arukh, Ḥoshen Mishpat* 281:7).

One who writes a bill of all of his possessions to his son after his death – הכותב כל נכסיו לבנו לאחר מותו: If a father wrote a bill stating that the son should be able to use his possessions following the father's death, it is prohibited for both the father and the son to sell those possessions (Rambam *Sefer Kinyan, Hilkhot Zekhiya* 12:13; *Shulḥan Arukh, Ḥoshen Mishpat* 257:1).

The father sold – מכר האב: If the father transgressed and sold the possessions that he had promised to his son, then the sale takes effect to the extent that the purchaser has the rights to the use and produce of those possessions until the death of the father. However, upon the father's death, the son becomes the owner of those rights. If at the time of the father's death there was produce that was still attached to the possessions, e.g., produce that grew on the land and was not yet harvested, the son must pay the purchaser its value. Any produce that was already detached belongs to the purchaser. Some (Rema; see *Tur* and *Beit Yosef*, citing Rashbam) argue with this and claim that upon the father's death, the son becomes the owner even of the produce that has already been detached (Rambam *Sefer Kinyan, Hilkhot Zekhiya* 12:13; *Shulḥan Arukh, Ḥoshen Mishpat* 257:3).

The son sold – מכר הבן: If the son transgressed and sold the possessions promised to him by his father, then the purchaser has no rights to them until the death of the father (Rambam *Sefer Kinyan, Hilkhot Zekhiya* 12:13; *Shulḥan Arukh, Ḥoshen Mishpat* 257:4).

The son sold the possessions and then died during the father's lifetime – מכר הבן ומת בחיי אביו: If the son sold the possessions promised to him by his father and then died during the father's lifetime, following which the father died, the purchaser acquires the possessions upon the death of the father. This is because the father retained only the rights to the use and produce of the possessions, and the ownership of the rights to an item and its produce is not tantamount to the ownership of the item itself. This is in accordance with the opinion of Reish Lakish (Rambam *Sefer Kinyan, Hilkhot Zekhiya* 12:13; *Shulḥan Arukh, Ḥoshen Mishpat* 257:5).

BACKGROUND

Ownership of the rights to an item and its produce is tantamount to the ownership of the item itself – קנין פירות כקנין הגוף דמי: If an item was acquired for its produce, one may derive benefit from it, but according to some authorities one cannot perform actions that require actual ownership of the item, e.g., bringing first fruits or selling the item to others. However, other authorities maintain that even if an item is acquired for its produce, this is akin to the purchase of the item itself, and it may be used for these activities.

"אֵין הַוָּלָד שֶׁל קַיָּימָא" כו׳. תָּנָא: מִשּׁוּם רַבִּי אֱלִיעֶזֶר אָמְרוּ: יוֹצִיא בְּגֵט.

§ The mishna states that if a *yavam* consummates a levirate marriage with his *yevama* while she is pregnant, if it emerges that **the offspring is not viable** then he may maintain her as his wife because his intercourse with her was a valid consummation of levirate marriage. An opposing opinion **is taught** in a *baraita*: **In the name of Rabbi Eliezer they said: He must send her out with a bill of divorce.**[N] Although it emerged that the levirate marriage took effect, since at the time he consummated the levirate marriage it was prohibited to do so because the *yevama* was pregnant, he is therefore penalized and required to separate from her.

אָמַר רָבָא: רַבִּי מֵאִיר וְרַבִּי אֱלִיעֶזֶר אָמְרוּ דָּבָר אֶחָד. רַבִּי אֱלִיעֶזֶר – הָא דַּאֲמָרַן,

Rava said: Rabbi Meir and Rabbi Eliezer said the same thing, i.e., they both expressed the same opinion that if one marries a woman whom he is prohibited from marrying, he is penalized and required to divorce her, even if the reason for the prohibition no longer applies. **Rabbi Eliezer's** opinion was expressed in **this** ruling **we have** just **stated.**

רַבִּי מֵאִיר – דְּתַנְיָא: לֹא יִשָּׂא אָדָם מְעוּבֶּרֶת חֲבֵירוֹ וּמֵינֶקֶת חֲבֵירוֹ, וְאִם נָשָׂא – יוֹצִיא, וְלֹא יַחֲזִיר עוֹלָמִית, דִּבְרֵי רַבִּי מֵאִיר. וַחֲכָמִים אוֹמְרִים: יוֹצִיא, וְלִכְשֶׁיַּגִּיעַ זְמַנּוֹ לִכְנוֹס – יִכְנוֹס.

Where was **Rabbi Meir's** opinion expressed? **As it is taught** in a *baraita*: **A man may not marry a woman who is pregnant** with the child **of another man, nor a woman who is nursing** the child **of another** man.[H] **And if he** transgressed and **married** her, he is penalized for violating the prohibition, and **he must divorce** her with a bill of divorce, **and he may never take** her **back;**[H] this is **the statement of Rabbi Meir. And the Rabbis say: He must send** her **out, and when the time comes** in which it is permitted **to marry** her, i.e., after the child is weaned, **he may** then **marry** her again.

אָמַר לֵיהּ אַבָּיֵי: מִמַּאי? דִּלְמָא לָא הִיא, עַד כָּאן לָא קָאָמַר רַבִּי אֱלִיעֶזֶר הָכָא – אֶלָּא מִשּׁוּם דְּקָפָגַע בְּאִיסּוּר אֵשֶׁת אָח דְּאוֹרָיְיתָא, אֲבָל הָתָם דְּרַבָּנַן – כְּרַבָּנַן סְבִירָא לֵיהּ.

Abaye said to him: From where do you deduce that they are of one opinion? **Perhaps that is not so,** as it is possible that **Rabbi Eliezer states** his ruling **only here,** in the case of a *yavam* who consummated a levirate marriage with his *yevama* while she was still pregnant, **due to** the fact that by doing so he risks the possibility that the offspring will be viable, in **which** case **he encounters the Torah prohibition against** engaging in relations with one's **brother's wife. However, there,** in the case where one married a woman who is pregnant with the child of another man, **which is a rabbinic** prohibition, it is possible that **he holds in accordance with** the opinion of the **Rabbis** who argue with Rabbi Meir.

אִי נַמִי: עַד כָּאן לָא קָאָמַר רַבִּי מֵאִיר הָתָם – אֶלָּא מִשּׁוּם דְּרַבָּנַן, וַחֲכָמִים עָשׂוּ חִיזּוּק לְדִבְרֵיהֶם יוֹתֵר מִשֶּׁל תּוֹרָה. אֲבָל הָכָא – מִדְּאוֹרָיְיתָא, מִפְרָשׁ פָּרְשִׁי מִינָּהּ.

Alternatively, it is also possible that **Rabbi Meir states** his ruling **only there,** in the case where one married a woman who is pregnant with the child of another man, **due to** the fact **that** doing so is a violation of a **rabbinic** prohibition, and therefore it is possible that this is one of the cases in which **the Sages reinforced their pronouncements**[N] **with greater** severity **than** prohibitions of **Torah law** so that people would not treat them lightly. **However, here,** in the case of a *yavam* who consummated a levirate marriage with his *yevama* while she was still pregnant, where there was a risk of transgressing a prohibition written **in the Torah,** since people are generally careful to **distance themselves from** a Torah prohibition, there is no need to further penalize someone who nevertheless transgressed.

NOTES

He must send her out with a bill of divorce – **יוֹצִיא בְּגֵט**: Although Rabbi Eliezer's statement is not accepted as the *halakha*, the early commentaries discussed the meaning and rationale of his claim and thereby clarified important principles that lie at the heart of the Gemara's discussion.

Rashi's version of the Gemara text is the same as that which appears in the standard Vilna edition: He must send her out with a bill of divorce. This suggests that nothing more than a bill of divorce is necessary in order to permit her to remarry. The early commentaries note that, ostensibly, this is true only according to the opinion of Rabbi Yoḥanan that the consummation of a levirate marriage with a pregnant woman who later miscarries is valid. Since the marriage is valid, only a divorce is needed to dissolve it. However, according to the opinion of Reish Lakish, the consummation of the levirate marriage performed while the woman was pregnant was invalid, and therefore the couple was never actually married. As such, the levirate bond still exists, and it should be necessary to either repeat the consummation or perform *ḥalitza*. Some commentaries suggest that Rashi's version of the text may be resolved according to the conclusion of the Gemara that the mishna is referring to a case in which, following the miscarriage, the *yavam* indeed repeated the consummation. As such, all would agree that the couple was actually married and that only a bill of divorce is necessary (*Tosafot Yeshanim*; *Tosefot HaRosh*). Other commentaries explain that Rabbi Eliezer's intention was not to suggest that a bill of divorce is sufficient, as certainly according to Reish Lakish it is necessary to perform *ḥalitza*, since the levirate bond remains. Rather, the intention is that in addition to the *ḥalitza*, a bill of divorce is also required (Rambam; Rid; Maharam MiRotenburg).

The Rashba had a different version of the Gemara's text that merely states: He must send her out. According to this version, the Rashba explains, *ḥalitza* alone is sufficient and there is no need for a bill of divorce. The Ritva suggests further that the ambiguity provided by this version of the text means that it can be interpreted as meaning through a bill of divorce, according to the opinion of Rabbi Yoḥanan, or as referring to *ḥalitza*, according to the opinion of Reish Lakish.

The Rivan claims that Rabbi Eliezer's statement was never meant to explain how she should be permitted to remarry; rather, the intention was to teach that a penalty is imposed upon the *yavam* for unlawfully consummating the levirate marriage. He is therefore required to hand her a bill of divorce; by doing so it becomes prohibited for him to repeat the consummation, and therefore his only recourse is to perform *ḥalitza* (see *Baḥ*).

Reinforced their pronouncements – **עָשׂוּ חִיזּוּק לְדִבְרֵיהֶם**: *Tosafot* note that in many cases throughout the Gemara, Rabbi Meir is of the opinion that the Sages reinforced their pronouncements to be equally as severe as Torah law, but not to have greater severity. They raise various distinctions between the case here and those cases. Most commentaries suggest a simple distinction should be drawn between cases involving rabbinic prohibitions and those involving rabbinic enactments in monetary matters. In the former, Rabbi Meir is very strict and holds that in order to prevent laxity it was necessary for the rabbinic prohibitions to be more severe than Torah law. This is also the reason that in many cases, Rabbi Meir rules that when the Sages provided specific formulations to be used in the fulfillment of mitzvot or in creating a bill of divorce, if one deviates from those formulations, the entire matter is null and void even if the change does not affect the essential meaning. However, in monetary matters, the Sages deemed it sufficient if the rabbinic law was applied with equal severity to that of Torah law (Ramban).

HALAKHA

A woman who is pregnant with the child of another man nor a woman who is nursing the child of another man – **מְעוּבֶּרֶת חֲבֵירוֹ וּמֵינֶקֶת חֲבֵירוֹ**: It is prohibited to marry a woman who is pregnant with the child of another man or a woman who is nursing the child of another man, until the child reaches twenty-four months of age. It makes no difference whether the woman is a widow, divorced, or became pregnant out of wedlock. Some are more lenient in the latter case (Rema, citing Maharai Mintz). If the child died within that time, or if the child had already been weaned while the mother was still married to the child's father, or if the mother had never been able to nurse, it is permitted to marry her (Rambam *Sefer Nashim*, *Hilkhot Geirushin* 11:25; *Shulḥan Arukh*, *Even HaEzer* 13:11).

One who married a woman who is pregnant with the child of another man or a woman who is nursing the child of another man – **הַנּוֹשֵׂא מְעוּבֶּרֶת וּמֵינֶקֶת חֲבֵירוֹ**: If one transgressed and married a woman who is pregnant with the child of another man or a woman who is nursing the child of another man, he is ostracized until he divorces her with a bill of divorce, even if he is a priest and would thereby be prohibited from remarrying her. If he is an Israelite, then he is allowed to later remarry her once the child reaches twenty-four months of age. This is in accordance with the opinion of the Rabbis (Rambam *Sefer Nashim*, *Hilkhot Geirushin* 11:28 and in the comment of Ra'avad; *Shulḥan Arukh*, *Even HaEzer* 13:12).

אָמַר רָבָא: וּלְדִבְרֵי חֲכָמִים יוֹצִיאָהּ בְּגֵט. אָמַר מָר זוּטְרָא: דַּיְקָא נַמִי, דְּקָתָנֵי יוֹצִיא, וְלֹא קָתָנֵי יַפְרִישׁ, שְׁמַע מִינַּהּ.

Rava said: According to the statement of the Rabbis who dispute Rabbi Meir and require one who married a pregnant woman to send her out, the intention is that **he must send her out with a bill of divorce** and not merely separate from her. **Mar Zutra said:** The language the Rabbis used **is also precise, as they teach: He must send** her **out, and** they **do not teach: He must separate** himself from her. **Conclude from here** that Rava's claim is correct.

אָמַר לֵיהּ רַב אַשִׁי לְרַב הוֹשַׁעְיָא בְּרֵיהּ דְּרַב אִידִי: הָתָם תְּנַן, רַבָּן שִׁמְעוֹן בֶּן גַּמְלִיאֵל אוֹמֵר: כׇּל שֶׁשָּׁהָא בְּאָדָם שְׁלֹשִׁים יוֹם – אֵינוֹ נֵפֶל. הָא לֹא שָׁהָא – סְפֵיקָא הָוֵי.

Rav Ashi said to Rav Hoshaya, son of Rav Idi: We learned in a *baraita* **there** that **Rabban Shimon ben Gamliel says: Any human** baby **that survives for thirty days**[H] after its birth **is not** to be considered **a stillbirth.** Rather, the baby is considered to be viable, and so the wife of the baby's father is never subject to any obligation of levirate marriage. **But,** by inference, **were it not to survive** for thirty days, **there would be uncertainty** whether the baby was viable or not.

וְאִיתְּמַר, מֵת בְּתוֹךְ שְׁלֹשִׁים יוֹם, וְעָמְדָה וְנִתְקַדְּשָׁה.

And an amoraic dispute **was stated** in the case in which the only offspring of a man **died during** the first **thirty days** of its life, **and** the widow, under the misconception that she was exempt from any obligation of levirate marriage, **arose and was betrothed.**[H]

רָבִינָא מִשְּׁמֵיהּ דְּרָבָא אָמַר: אִם אֵשֶׁת יִשְׂרָאֵל הִיא – חוֹלֶצֶת, וְאִם אֵשֶׁת כֹּהֵן הִיא – אֵינָהּ חוֹלֶצֶת.

Ravina said in the name of Rava: If she became the **wife of an Israelite,** i.e., the man who betrothed her was not a priest, then **she performs *ḥalitza*** with the *yavam* due to the uncertainty whether or not the offspring was viable, and then they may remain married. **But if she** became the **wife of a priest, she does not perform *ḥalitza***[N] with him because if she were to do so, she would become a *ḥalutza* and would therefore be prohibited from remaining married to her husband, who is a priest. Therefore, in this case, in order to allow her to remain married to her husband, the Sages did not require her to be concerned for the possibility that the offspring was not viable.

רַב מְשַׁרְשִׁיָּא מִשְּׁמֵיהּ דְּרָבָא אָמַר: אַחַת זוֹ וְאַחַת זוֹ חוֹלֶצֶת.

The Gemara cites a different version of Rav's opinion: **Rav Mesharshiyya said in the name of Rava: Both this** woman **and that** woman **perform *ḥalitza*,** even though by doing so, if she was betrothed to a priest, she would become forbidden to him.

אֲמַר לֵיהּ רָבִינָא לְרַב מְשַׁרְשִׁיָּא:

Ravina said to Rav Mesharshiyya:

NOTES

If she became the wife of a priest she does not perform *ḥalitza* – אִם אֵשֶׁת כֹּהֵן הִיא אֵינָהּ חוֹלֶצֶת: The Gemara will explain that since her performance of *ḥalitza* would prohibit her from remaining married to her husband, the Sages were willing to rely on the opinion of the Rabbis who disagree with Rabban Shimon ben Gamliel and hold that even if the child does not survive for thirty days it is considered viable. This is especially reasonable because both opinions agree that by Torah law the child is considered viable; the dispute is only whether, by rabbinic law, the case should be treated as one of doubt.

Some question why the *ḥalitza* should not be performed in this case. The *halakha* is that if a *ḥalitza* is performed and it is uncertain whether it was valid, it does not disqualify the *yevama* from marrying a priest. In the case here, too, the *ḥalitza* is performed only to satisfy the possibility that the child was not viable. If so, why does Rava rule that she should not perform *ḥalitza*? To resolve this difficulty, a distinction must be drawn between two cases of uncertainty. The *halakha* that an uncertain *ḥalitza* does not disqualify a woman from marrying a priest applies only to cases where there is clearly a levirate bond, but it is uncertain whether the man who performed the *ḥalitza* was actually the *yavam*. However, in this case, the *ḥalitza* was certainly performed by the *yavam*, and the only question is whether it was necessary. Therefore it is treated like any other case of uncertainty in Torah law, in which one must be stringent, and so if *ḥalitza* was performed, the couple would have to divorce (Rid).

HALAKHA

Any human baby that survives for thirty days – כׇּל שֶׁשָּׁהָא בְּאָדָם שְׁלֹשִׁים יוֹם: Any child of whom it is known that he completed nine months in the womb is considered viable from the moment of birth. If it is not known whether he completed a full nine months, then once he lives for thirty days he is considered viable, and only then will the child's existence free his father's wives from the obligation to perform levirate marriage or *ḥalitza*. Some say that this is true only when his fingernails and hair have grown, as this is proof that the he has reached his ninth month (Rema, citing *Tur*). If the child survived thirty days and then died, and no one checked whether his fingernails and hair had grown, one may rely upon the first opinion (*Beit Shmuel*; *Taz*; Rambam *Sefer Nashim*, *Hilkhot Yibbum* 1:5; *Shulḥan Arukh*, *Even HaEzer* 156:4).

Died during the first thirty days and she arose and was betrothed – מֵת בְּתוֹךְ שְׁלֹשִׁים וְעָמְדָה וְנִתְקַדְּשָׁה: In the case of a *yevama* who gave birth to a child and it was not known whether he reached his ninth month, and then he died within thirty days of his birth, including on the thirtieth day, the *yevama* must perform *ḥalitza* since it is uncertain whether the child was viable. This is in accordance with the opinion of the Rabbis. Even if she was betrothed or married, she must still perform *ḥalitza*, and only then is she permitted to her husband. In the event that the *yavam* was not available to perform the *ḥalitza*, she may remain with her husband until the *yavam* becomes available (Rema, citing Mahari Mintz). However, if she was betrothed to a priest, she is not required to perform *ḥalitza* because if she were to do so she would become prohibited to her husband. In the event that the priest divorced her or died, ideally she should then perform *ḥalitza* in order to become permitted to non-priests. This is in accordance with the opinion of Ravina (Rambam *Sefer Nashim*, *Hilkhot Yibbum* 2:21; *Shulḥan Arukh*, *Even HaEzer* 164:7).

באורתא אמר רבא הכי, ובצפרא הדר ביה. אמר ליה: שריתו? יהא רעוא דתשתרו אף תרבא.

In the evening Rava stated this ruling in accordance with the way you cited him, **but in the morning he retracted** his opinion and ruled as I cited him. Rav Mesharshiyya **said to him: Do you** really **permit** her to marry without *ḥalitza*? He added sarcastically: **May it be** God's **will that you will even permit** forbidden **fats** [*tarba*][N] as well. In Rav Mesharshiyya's opinion, the prohibition against the widow remarrying without *ḥalitza* was as obvious as the prohibition of forbidden fats.

הכא גבי מעוברת חבירו ומינקת חבירו הנשואה לכהן, מאי? מי עבוד רבנן תקנתא לכהן, או לא?

After citing this dispute, Rav Ashi said to Rav Hoshaya, son of Rav Idi: According to Rava's citation of Rav, when a woman is married to a priest, the Sages were more lenient in order to allow the couple to remain married. **Here, with regard to a woman who is pregnant** with the child **of another** man **or a woman who is nursing** the child **of another** man, **who is married to a priest, what** is the *halakha*? **Did the Sages enact an ordinance for** the benefit of **a priest** and say that it is sufficient for him to separate from his wife and he does not need to divorce her, **or not?**

אמר ליה: הכי השתא! בשלמא התם, כיון דאיכא רבנן דפליגי עליה דרבן שמעון בן גמליאל, דאמרי: אף על גב דלא שהא ולד מעליא הוי, גבי אשת כהן, כיון דלא אפשר, עבדינן כרבנן.

He said to him: How can these cases **be compared? Granted, there,** in the case where the offspring died during its first thirty days of life, **since there are the Rabbis who disagree with Rabban Shimon ben Gamliel concerning it, as they say** that **although** the offspring **did not survive** for thirty days **it is** nevertheless considered **a full-fledged,** i.e., viable, **offspring,** therefore, **with regard to the wife of a priest, since it is not possible** for her to perform *ḥalitza* and remain permitted to her husband, **we** will be lenient and **act in accordance with** the opinion **of the Rabbis.**

אבל הכא, כמאן נעביד? אי כרבי מאיר – הא אמר יוציא ולא יחזיר עולמית, ואי כרבנן – האמרי בגט.

However, here, in the case of a woman who is pregnant with or nursing the child of another man, **in accordance with whose** opinion **should we act? If** we act **in accordance with** the opinion of **Rabbi Meir,** it will be of no benefit to the priest because Rabbi Meir **said** even with regard to the wife of an Israelite that **he must divorce** her **and may never take** her **back. And if** we act **in accordance with** the opinion of **the Rabbis,** it will also be of no benefit to the priest because **they say** he must send her out **with a bill of divorce** and only remarry her at a later point. Since there is no opinion that does not require a bill of divorce to be given, there is no possibility to be lenient in this case by not requiring a bill of divorce to be given.

איתמר, קדשה בתוך שלשה וברח פליגי בה רב אחא ורפרם, חד אמר: משמתינן ליה, וחד אמר: עירוקיה מסתייה. הוה עובדא, ואמר להו רפרם: עירוקיה מסתייה.

A pregnancy is generally noticeable only after three months have passed. Therefore, during the first three months after a woman is divorced or widowed, she may not remarry due to the possibility that she is pregnant. The Sages decreed that even betrothing her during that time is prohibited, lest one also marry her (see 41a). Concerning this, an amoraic dispute **was stated:** In a case in which a man **betrothed** a woman **during** the **three months** following her divorce or her husband's death, **and then he fled,**[H] **Rav Aḥa and Rafram disagree over** what should be done. **One said: We excommunicate him** for violating the prohibition. **And the other one said: His flight is sufficient for him,**[N] since it proves that he does not intend to marry her until it is determined that she is not pregnant. Therefore, there is no need to penalize him further. The Gemara relates: **There was an incident** like that, **and Rafram said to those** who asked what to do: **His flight is sufficient for him.**

NOTES

That you will even permit fats [*tarba*] – דתשתרו אף תרבא: Why did Rav Mesharshiyya specifically refer to the prohibition of forbidden fats? The *Arukh LaNer* suggests that Rav Mesharshiyya was hinting at the practice of the priests in the Temple to rely upon the opinions that it is permitted to eat the fats lining the stomach of an animal (see *Ḥullin* 49a). Accordingly, Rav Mesharshiyya was suggesting that since Rava's intention was to issue a ruling that would assist the priesthood, he should continue on that path and also rule that the fats lining the stomach are permitted.

Some early commentaries had a different version of the Gemara's text. In place of the word *tarba*, meaning fats, their text had *tarka*, meaning a divorcée. Accordingly, Rav Mesharshiyya was saying that if one permits a *yevama* to marry without *ḥalitza* then one will eventually also permit other types of forbidden marriages, even a divorcée to a priest (*Tosefot HaRosh*; Ritva on *Shabbat* 136b).

His flight is sufficient for him – עירוקיה מסתייה: The early commentaries discussed why the fact that he fled should save him from being excommunicated. The discussion surrounds the question of why he is excommunicated if he does not flee. Rashi, Ra'avad, and others explain that he is excommunicated in order to compel him to divorce his wife, so that he will not engage in intercourse before the appropriate time. Therefore, if he flees and it is clear that he has no intention of doing so in the immediate future, there is no need to excommunicate him. Accordingly, it is even appropriate to advise the husband in such a situation to flee rather than divorce his wife or suffer excommunication (Rosh). According to other opinions, the reason he is excommunicated is as a punishment for violating the pronouncements of the Sages (Rambam; see Ritva and *Maggid Mishne*). If so, it would seem that when he flees from his wife, he is not excommunicated because the very fact that he is unable to return to her until the appropriate time is itself considered a sufficient punishment.

HALAKHA

He betrothed her during the three months, and then he fled – קידשה בתוך שלשה וברח: One who betroths a woman during the three months following her divorce or her husband's death is excommunicated. Some say that he must divorce her, and then, if he is an Israelite and she is not pregnant, he may remarry her after three months. However, if he is a priest, he will be prohibited from remarrying her (*Tur*). Some say that if he betrothed her and was unaware of the fact that this was prohibited, he need not divorce her, and it is sufficient for the couple to separate (Mahari Weil). Others argue that even such a case requires a divorce (*Terumat HaDeshen*). In a case where the man is a priest, one may rely on the lenient opinion (Rema).

If he betrothed her and then fled, he is not excommunicated. This is in accordance with the opinion of Rafram in the Gemara. Furthermore, he even may be advised to flee *ab initio* (*Tur*). In a case in which not only did he betroth her, but he also married her, the Rambam rules that it is still sufficient for him to flee, whereas others (*Beit Shmuel*) rule that in such a case he must divorce her (Rambam *Sefer Nashim*, *Hilkhot Geirushin* 11:28; *Shulḥan Arukh*, *Even HaEzer* 13:10).

״סָפֵק בֶּן תֵּשַׁע״ וכו׳. אֲמַר לֵיהּ רָבָא לְרַב נַחְמָן: לֵימָא הַלֵּךְ אַחַר רוֹב נָשִׁים, וְרוֹב נָשִׁים לְתִשְׁעָה יָלְדָן!

§ The mishna states that if a *yevama* consummated the levirate marriage and gave birth seven months later, there is **an uncertainty whether** the child **is nine** months **old,** counting from conception, and is the offspring of the first husband, i.e., the deceased brother, or whether the child is only seven months old and is the offspring of the second husband. If it is the child of the first husband, then there was never any obligation of levirate marriage, and the supposed consummation was in fact forbidden by penalty of *karet*. Due to that possibility, both the man and the woman are obligated to bring a guilt-offering for uncertainty. **Rava said to Rav Naḥman:** How can they bring a guilt-offering for uncertainty? **Let us say: Follow** the **majority of women, and** since the **majority of women give birth after nine** months, it should be presumed that the child is the offspring of the deceased brother. Accordingly, the couple would be obligated to bring a certain sin-offering, not a guilt-offering for uncertainty.

אֲמַר לֵיהּ: נָשֵׁי דִּידַן – לְשִׁבְעָה יָלְדָן. אֲמַר לֵיהּ: נָשֵׁי דִּידְכוּ הָווּ רוּבָּא דְּעָלְמָא?

Rav Naḥman **said to him:** The **women of our** family regularly **give birth after seven** months. Therefore, how can you presume that this woman gave birth after nine months? Rava **said to him: Do** the **women of your** family **constitute the majority** of the women of **the world?** Ultimately, the majority of women give birth after nine months, and one should therefore presume accordingly in a case of uncertainty.

אֲמַר לֵיהּ: הָכִי קָאָמִינָא, רוֹב נָשִׁים יָלְדָן לְתִשְׁעָה וּמִיעוּט לְשִׁבְעָה, וְכָל הַיּוֹלֶדֶת לְתִשְׁעָה – עוּבָּרָהּ נִיכָּר לִשְׁלִישׁ יָמֶיהָ. וְזוֹ, הוֹאִיל וְלֹא הוּכַּר עוּבָּרָהּ לִשְׁלִישׁ יָמֶיהָ – אִיתְרַע לֵיהּ רוּבָּא.

Rav Naḥman **said to him: This is what I am saying:** Although it is true that the **majority of women give birth after nine** months **and** only **a minority** give birth **after seven,** still, in the case of **every** woman **who gives birth after nine** months, **her fetus is** already **recognizable after a third of her days,** i.e., in the third month of her pregnancy. Accordingly, in the case of **this** woman, **since her fetus was not recognizable after a third of her days,** as were it already recognizable at that point then it would be obvious that the child was the offspring of the first husband, therefore, the ability to presume she is like the **majority** of women **is compromised,** and the uncertainty as to who the father of the child is remains. Consequently, the *yavam* and *yevama* should each bring a guilt-offering for uncertainty.

אִי כָּל הַיּוֹלֶדֶת לְתִשְׁעָה עוּבָּרָהּ נִיכָּר לִשְׁלִישׁ יָמֶיהָ, הָא מִדְּלָא הוּכַּר לִשְׁלִישׁ יָמֶיהָ – עוּבָּרָהּ וַדַּאי בַּר שִׁבְעָה לְבַתְרָאָה הוּא! אֶלָּא אֵימָא: רוֹב הַיּוֹלֶדֶת לְתִשְׁעָה עוּבָּרָהּ נִיכָּר לִשְׁלִישׁ יָמֶיהָ, וְהַאי מִדְּלָא הוּכַּר לִשְׁלִישׁ יָמֶיהָ – אִיתְרַע לֵיהּ רוּבָּא.

The Gemara asks: **If** it is true that in the case of **every** woman **who gives birth after nine** months, **her fetus is** already **recognizable after a third of her days,** then with regard to **this** woman, **from** the fact that her fetus **was not recognized after a third** of her days, it follows that **her fetus was certainly** only **seven** months **old** and is the offspring **of the latter** husband, i.e., the *yavam*. If so, it is clear the *yavam* is father of the child and there should be no need to bring an offering at all. **Rather,** one must emend Rav Naḥman's words and **say:** In the **majority** of cases, with regard to a woman **who gives birth after nine** months, **her fetus is** already **recognizable after a third of her days, and** with regard to **this** woman, **from** the fact that her fetus **was not recognized after the a third** of her days, the ability to presume she is like the **majority** of women **is compromised.**

תָּנוּ רַבָּנַן: רִאשׁוֹן רָאוּי לִהְיוֹת כֹּהֵן גָּדוֹל, וְשֵׁנִי מַמְזֵר מִסָּפֵק. רַבִּי אֱלִיעֶזֶר בֶּן יַעֲקֹב אוֹמֵר: אֵין מַמְזֵר מִסָּפֵק.

§ The mishna states that the child of the *yevama* has unflawed lineage since regardless of whether it is the offspring of the deceased husband or the *yavam*, there was no transgression involved in its conception. With regard to this case, **the Sages taught** in a *baraita*: The **first** child **is** even **fit to become a High Priest.** However, since it is possible that the child is the offspring of the deceased husband, in which case the widow remains forbidden to the *yavam* as his brother's wife, if she has a **second** child with her *yavam* then that child is a ***mamzer* due to an uncertainty** with regard to his status. **Rabbi Eliezer ben Ya'akov says: One is not** rendered **a *mamzer* due to uncertainty.**

מַאי קָאָמַר? אֲמַר אַבַּיֵי: הָכִי קָאָמַר, רִאשׁוֹן רָאוּי לִהְיוֹת כֹּהֵן גָּדוֹל, וְשֵׁנִי – סְפֵק מַמְזֵר, וְאָסוּר בְּמַמְזֶרֶת. רַבִּי אֱלִיעֶזֶר אוֹמֵר: אֵינוֹ סְפֵק מַמְזֵר אֶלָּא וַדַּאי מַמְזֵר, וּמוּתָּר בְּמַמְזֶרֶת.

The meaning of Rabbi Eliezer ben Ya'akov's statement and how he differs from the first *tanna* is unclear. The Gemara clarifies: **What is the** ***baraita*** **saying? Abaye said: This is what it is saying:** The **first** child is even **fit to become a High Priest. And** if she has a **second** child, his status as a ***mamzer*** **is uncertain and** therefore he is both prohibited from marrying an Israelite woman of unflawed lineage, since he might actually be a *mamzer*, **and he is** also **prohibited from** marrying **a** ***mamzeret***, since he might not be a *mamzer*. **Rabbi Eliezer** ben Ya'akov **says: He is not** treated like one whose status as **a** ***mamzer*** is **uncertain; rather,** due to the uncertainty concerning his status **he is** treated like one who is **definitely a** ***mamzer*****, and he is permitted to** marry **a** ***mamzeret***. In other words, Rabbi Eliezer ben Ya'akov holds that even one whose status as a *mamzer* is uncertain is permitted to marry one who is definitely a *mamzeret*.

רָבָא אֲמַר, הָכִי קָאָמַר: רִאשׁוֹן – רָאוּי לִהְיוֹת כֹּהֵן גָּדוֹל, וְשֵׁנִי – מַמְזֵר וַדַּאי מִסָּפֵק, וּמוּתָּר בְּמַמְזֶרֶת. וְרַבִּי אֱלִיעֶזֶר בֶּן יַעֲקֹב אוֹמֵר: אֵין וַדַּאי מַמְזֵר מִסָּפֵק, אֶלָּא סְפֵק מַמְזֵר, וְאָסוּר בְּמַמְזֶרֶת.

Rava said: This is what the *baraita* **is saying:** The **first** child **is** even **fit to become a High Priest. And** if she has **a second** child, he is treated as though he **is definitely a** ***mamzer*** **due to the uncertainty** concerning his status,[N] **and** therefore **he is permitted to** marry a *mamzeret*, i.e., this *tanna* holds that even one whose status as a *mamzer* is uncertain is permitted to marry one who is definitely a *mamzeret*. **And Rabbi Eliezer ben Ya'akov says: He is not** treated as though he is **definitely a** ***mamzer*** **due to an uncertainty** concerning his status; **rather,** his status as a ***mamzer*** is **uncertain**[H] and he is treated accordingly, **and** therefore he is both prohibited from marrying an Israelite woman of unflawed lineage since he might be a *mamzer*, **and he is** also **prohibited from** marrying **a** ***mamzeret*** since he might not be a *mamzer*.

וְקָמִיפַּלְגִי בִּדְרַבִּי אֶלְעָזָר. דִּתְנַן, רַבִּי אֶלְעָזָר אוֹמֵר: וַדָּאָן בְּוַדָּאָן – מוּתָּר. וַדָּאָן בִּסְפֵקָן, וּסְפֵקָן בְּוַדָּאָן, וּסְפֵקָן בִּסְפֵקָן – אָסוּר.

The Gemara explains: **And** Abaye and Rava **disagree with regard to** whether the *halakha* is decided in accordance with the opinion **of Rabbi Elazar. As we learned** in a mishna (*Kiddushin* 74a): With regard to the prohibition against marrying people with certain types of flawed lineage, **Rabbi Elazar said:** The marriage of **those** people whose flawed lineage status is **certain to those** whose status is **certain is permitted,** but the marriage of **those** whose status is **certain to those** whose status is **uncertain, and** the marriage of **those** whose status is **uncertain to those** whose status is **certain, and** even the marriage of **those** whose status is **uncertain to those** whose status is **uncertain, is prohibited.**[H]

וְאֵלּוּ הֵן סְפֵקָן: שְׁתוּקִי וַאֲסוּפִי וְכוּתִי,

The mishna concludes: **And these are those** who are considered to have an **uncertain** status:[H] **A child of unknown paternity** [*shetuki*], although his mother's identity is known; **and a foundling** who was found abandoned in the streets; **and a Samaritan** [*Kuti*],[B] who is possibly a *mamzer* since the Samaritans do not accept and abide by the *halakhot* of marriage.

וַאֲמַר רַב יְהוּדָה אֲמַר רַב: הֲלָכָה כְּרַבִּי אֶלְעָזָר. כִּי אָמְרִיתָהּ קַמֵּיהּ דִּשְׁמוּאֵל אֲמַר לִי: הִלֵּל שָׁנָה עֲשָׂרָה יוֹחֲסִין עָלוּ מִבָּבֶל: כָּהֲנֵי, לְוָיֵי, וְיִשְׂרְאֵלֵי, חֲלָלֵי, גֵּיורֵי, חֲרוּרֵי, מַמְזֵרֵי, נְתִינֵי, שְׁתוּקֵי, וַאֲסוּפֵי. וְכוּלָּן מוּתָּרִין לָבֹא זֶה בָּזֶה,

And with regard to this mishna **Rav Yehuda said** that **Rav said:** The ***halakha*** **is in accordance with** the opinion of **Rabbi Elazar.** But **when I said this** *halakha* of Rav's **in the presence of Shmuel, he said to me: Hillel taught** in a *baraita* that **ten** categories of **lineage came up from Babylon** to Eretz Yisrael: **Priests; Levites; and Israelites; priests disqualified due to flawed lineage** [***ḥalallim***]; **converts; freed slaves;** ***mamzerim*****; Gibeonites;** ***shetukei*****; and foundlings. And it is permitted** for **all** men and women in these categories **to marry one another,** i.e., the list is arranged such that the marriage between people in any two categories that are adjacent to one another is permitted. This is possible only if one assumes that it is permitted for one whose flawed lineage status is uncertain to marry one whose flawed lineage status is certain.

NOTES

He is definitely a ***mamzer*** **due to the uncertainty concerning his status** – **מַמְזֵר וַדַּאי מִסָּפֵק**: In tractate *Kiddushin*, Rava is cited as saying that one whose status as a *mamzer* is uncertain is permitted to marry an Israelite woman of unflawed lineage. However, this would appear to conform to neither opinion in the *baraita*, according to the way Rava explains it. Some have suggested that a distinction should be drawn between different cases of uncertainty. The *baraita* here concerns a case where there is a specific reason to be concerned that the child is a *mamzer*; if the first child is the son of the previous husband then the second one will be a *mamzer*. Therefore, Rava rules stringently. However, in tractate *Kiddushin*, Rava is considering the cases of a child whose father is entirely unknown and that of a foundling. In those cases, there are no specific indications that the child might be a *mamzer*; rather, there is simply a total lack of knowledge about the child's lineage. Rava therefore rules leniently that there is no need to open a Pandora's box of possibilities, and therefore in such a case there is no prohibition preventing him from marrying an Israelite woman of unflawed lineage (*Mei Naftoaḥ*). Alternatively, one could suggest a resolution based on the opinion of the Rambam that according to Torah law, one whose status as *mamzer* is uncertain is actually permitted to marry an Israelite woman of unflawed lineage. Accordingly, it can be explained that Rava in tractate *Kiddushin* was referring to Torah law, whereas here he is referring to the fact that according to rabbinic law it is prohibited.

HALAKHA

He is not definitely a ***mamzer*** **due to an uncertainty, rather his status as a** ***mamzer*** **is uncertain** – **אֵין וַדַּאי מַמְזֵר מִסָּפֵק אֶלָּא סְפֵק מַמְזֵר**: If a *yevama* and her *yavam* consummate the levirate marriage within three months of her husband's death, and then she gives birth to a viable child and there is an uncertainty whether the child was born after nine months of gestation and is the offspring of the first husband, or whether it was born after only seven months of gestation and is the offspring of the *yavam*, that child has unflawed lineage. If the *yavam* does not divorce her, and they have another child together, the second child's status as a *mamzer* is uncertain. He is therefore prohibited from marrying an Israelite woman of unflawed lineage, since he might be a *mamzer*, and he is also prohibited from marrying a *mamzeret*, as he might not be a *mamzer*. This is in accordance with the opinion of Rabbi Eliezer ben Ya'akov, as explained by Rava (Rambam *Sefer Nashim, Hilkhot Yibbum* 1:23; *Shulḥan Arukh, Even HaEzer* 4:25; 164:6).

Certain and uncertain disqualifications from marriage – **פְּסוּלֵי חִיתּוּן וַדַּאי וְסָפֵק**: By Torah law one whose status as a *mamzer* is uncertain is permitted to marry an Israelite of unflawed lineage. However, by rabbinic law it is prohibited. Only one who is definitely a *mamzer* is permitted to marry a *mamzeret*; if the status of the man, the woman, or both is uncertain, then they are prohibited from marrying one another (Rambam *Sefer Kedusha, Hilkhot Issurei Bia* 15:21; *Shulḥan Arukh, Even HaEzer* 4:24).

Uncertainties with regard to one's status as a ***mamzer*** – **סְפֵקֵי מַמְזֵר**: An uncertainty whether one is a *mamzer* can be created in various ways, e.g., whenever a child is born to a woman from a man who is not her husband in a case where her marital status is uncertain. This can occur either when there is uncertainty concerning the validity of the original betrothal or when there is uncertainty concerning the divorce from, or death of, her husband. A child whose father's identity is not known is also considered to be one whose status as a *mamzer* is uncertain (Rambam *Sefer Kedusha, Hilkhot Issurei Bia* 15:21; *Shulḥan Arukh, Even HaEzer* 4:24, 31, 36).

BACKGROUND

Samaritan [*Kuti*] – **כּוּתִי**: This term is used to describe the non-Jews who settled in Samaria and the surrounding territory after the exile of the ten tribes. Though they converted to Judaism, they had ulterior motives for doing so (see II Kings, chapter 17), and were not scrupulous in their observance of the mitzvot. Accordingly, it was a matter of debate among the Sages whether or not they were to be considered as Jews. In later generations, they abandoned Jewish practices entirely, and the Sages decreed that they should be treated as non-Jews.

וְאַתְּ אָמְרַתְּ הֲלָכָה כְּרַבִּי אֶלְעָזָר?!

After citing the baraita taught by Hillel, which assumes that it is permitted for one whose flawed lineage status is uncertain to marry one whose flawed lineage status is certain, Shmuel concluded: The *halakha* is certainly decided in accordance with the opinion of Hillel, **and yet you,** Rabbi Yehuda, **said the *halakha* is in accordance with** the opinion of **Rabbi Elazar,** which states that a marriage between two people whose flawed lineage status is uncertain is prohibited; your ruling is incorrect.

אַבַּיֵי סָבַר לַהּ כִּשְׁמוּאֵל דְּאָמַר הֲלָכָה כְּהִלֵּל, וּמוֹקֵי לַהּ רַבִּי אֱלִיעֶזֶר בֶּן יַעֲקֹב אַלִּיבָּא דְּהִלְכְתָא כִּי הֵיכִי דְּלָא תִּקְשֵׁי הִלְכְתָא אַהִלְכְתָא.

The Gemara proceeds to explain the dispute between Abaye and Rava: **Abaye holds in accordance with** the opinion of **Shmuel, who said** that **the *halakha* is** decided **in accordance with** the opinion of **Hillel** that it is permitted for one whose flawed lineage status is uncertain to marry one whose flawed lineage status is certain. Therefore, Abaye **establishes that** opinion of **Rabbi Eliezer ben Ya'akov** to be **in accordance with** this ***halakha*, in order that there should not be a contradiction between** one ***halakha***, i.e., that the *halakha* is always decided in accordance with the opinion of Hillel, **and** another ***halakha***, i.e., that the *halakha* is always decided in accordance with the opinion of Rabbi Eliezer ben Ya'akov.

רָבָא סָבַר לַהּ כְּרַב, דְּאָמַר הֲלָכָה כְּרַבִּי אֶלְעָזָר, וּמוֹקֵי לַהּ לְדְרַבִּי אֱלִיעֶזֶר בֶּן יַעֲקֹב אַלִּיבָּא דְּהִלְכְתָא, כִּי הֵיכִי דְּלָא תִּקְשֵׁי

Rava, however, **holds in accordance with** the opinion of **Rav, who said:** The ***halakha*** is decided **in accordance with** the opinion of **Rabbi Elazar** that the marriage of those whose status is certain to those whose status is uncertain is prohibited. Therefore, Rava **establishes that** opinion **of Rabbi Eliezer ben Ya'akov** to be **in accordance with** this ***halakha*, so that there should not be a contradiction** between

Perek IV
Daf 37 Amud b

הִלְכְתָא אַהִלְכְתָא.

one ***halakha***, i.e., that the *halakha* in this case is in accordance with the opinion of Rav, **and** another ***halakha***, i.e., that the *halakha* is always decided in accordance with the opinion of Rabbi Eliezer ben Ya'akov.

אֲמַר אַבַּיֵי: מְנָא אָמִינָא לַהּ דְּכׇל סְפֵיקָא לְרַבִּי אֱלִיעֶזֶר בֶּן יַעֲקֹב כְּוַדַּאי מְשַׁוֵּי לֵיהּ –

Abaye said: From where do I say that concerning **anyone** whose status as a *mamzer* is **uncertain, according to** the opinion of **Rabbi Eliezer ben Ya'akov they are treated equivalently to** one who is **definitely** a *mamzer*?

דְּתַנְיָא, רַבִּי אֱלִיעֶזֶר בֶּן יַעֲקֹב אוֹמֵר: הֲרֵי שֶׁבָּא עַל נָשִׁים הַרְבֵּה וְאֵין יוֹדֵעַ עַל אֵיזוֹ מֵהֶן בָּא. וְכֵן הִיא, שֶׁבָּאוּ עָלֶיהָ אֲנָשִׁים הַרְבֵּה וְאֵינָהּ יוֹדַעַת בְּאֵיזֶה מֵהֶן קִבְּלָה, נִמְצָא אָב נוֹשֵׂא אֶת בִּתּוֹ וְאָח נוֹשֵׂא אֶת אֲחוֹתוֹ, וְנִתְמַלֵּא כׇּל הָעוֹלָם כּוּלּוֹ מַמְזֵרִין, וְעַל זֶה נֶאֱמַר "וּמָלְאָה הָאָרֶץ זִמָּה".

As it is taught in a *baraita* that **Rabbi Eliezer ben Ya'akov says:** With regard to one **who engaged in intercourse with** and impregnated **many women, but he does not know with which** women **he had intercourse, and similarly,** with regard to a woman, if **many men had intercourse with her** and she became pregnant, **but she does not know from which man she received** the seed that caused her to become pregnant, since the identities of the parents of those children are not known, **it could emerge** that **a father marries his daughter, and a brother marries his sister. And** in this way, **the entire world could become filled with *mamzerim*. And concerning this, it is stated: "And lest the land become full of lewdness"** (Leviticus 19:29). Abaye demonstrates his claim from the fact that even though it is not certain that the children in this situation are *mamzerim*, nevertheless, Rabbi Eliezer ben Ya'akov labels them as *mamzerim* and not as those whose status as a *mamzer* is uncertain.[N]

וְרָבָא אָמַר לָךְ: הָכִי קָאָמַר: "זוֹ מַה הִיא".

And Rava could have **said to you: This is what** the verse **is saying:** The word "lewdness [*zima*]" can be understood as an acronym of the words: *Zo ma hi,* meaning: **What is this.**[N] It is plausible to say that Rabbi Eliezer ben Ya'akov's citation of this verse indicates that he regards their status to be uncertain.

NOTES

One whose status as a *mamzer* is uncertain is treated the same way as one who is definitely a *mamzer* – סְפֵיקָא כְּוַדַּאי: Rashi explains that Abaye derives his proof from the fact that Rabbi Eliezer ben Ya'akov relates to the children whose *mamzer* status is uncertain as though they were definitely *mamzerim*. Another possible interpretation is that Abaye's proof is derived from Rabbi Eliezer ben Ya'akov's extended formulation. It would have been sufficient if he had highlighted the possibility that a father might marry his daughter and a brother his sister; why did he continue to emphasize: The entire world will become filled with *mamzerim*? Apparently, Rabbi Eliezer ben Ya'akov was also concerned that the children in these cases, whose status as a *mamzer* would be uncertain, would later marry people who are definitely *mamzerim* and in that way the number of *mamzerim* in the world would be greatly increased. The only reason to be concerned for that possibility is if one holds that one whose status as a *mamzer* is uncertain is permitted to marry one who is definitely a *mamzer*. From here Abaye derives his proof (*Yosef Lekah*).

What is this – זוֹ מַה הִיא: According to Rava, the verse should not be understood as labeling the children in such cases as *mamzerim*; rather, that if one is not careful the world could become filled with people whose lineage status is not known (Rivan).

יָתֵר עַל כֵּן אָמַר רַבִּי אֱלִיעֶזֶר בֶּן יַעֲקֹב: לֹא יִשָּׂא אָדָם אִשָּׁה בִּמְדִינָה זוֹ, וְיֵלֵךְ וְיִשָּׂא אִשָּׁה בִּמְדִינָה אַחֶרֶת, שֶׁמָּא יִזְדַּוְּוגוּ זֶה לָזֶה וְנִמְצָא אָח נוֹשֵׂא אֶת אֲחוֹתוֹ.

The Gemara cites the continuation of the *baraita*: **Furthermore, Rabbi Eliezer ben Ya'akov said** that even in marriage, one should be careful not to create a situation that could lead to the birth of *mamzerim*. Therefore, **a man should not marry a woman in this country and** then **go and marry** another **woman in a different country,**[H] **lest** a son from one marriage and a daughter from the other, unaware that they are both children of the same father, **unite with one another, and it could emerge** that **a brother marries his sister**, the children of whom would be *mamzerim*.

אִינִי? וְהָא רַב, כִּי אִיקְלַע לְדַרְדְּשִׁיר [מַכְרִיז] וְאָמַר: מַאן הָוְיָא לְיוֹמָא. וְרַב נַחְמָן, כִּי אִיקְלַע לְשַׁכַנְצִיב [מַכְרִיז] וְאָמַר: מַאן הָוְיָא לְיוֹמָא!

The Gemara asks: **Is that so; is** there really such a prohibition? **But didn't Rav, when he happened** to come **to Dardeshir, make a public announcement saying: Which** woman **will be** my wife **for the day,** i.e., for the duration of his visit? Since his wife did not accompany him to Dardeshir, he wished to be married to another woman while he was there, in order to avoid a situation that could lead him to having forbidden thoughts. **And** also **Rav Naḥman, when he happened** to come **to Shakhnetziv, made a public announcement saying: Which** woman **will be** my wife **for the day?**[N] It would appear, from the fact that both Sages married wives in two different places, that there is no prohibition in doing so.

שָׁאנֵי רַבָּנַן דִּפְקִיעַ שְׁמַיְיהוּ.

The Gemara rejects the proof: **Sages are different, as their names are renowned,** and therefore their children are always identified by their connection to their father. Therefore, Rabbi Eliezer ben Ya'akov's concern does not apply to them.

וְהָאֲמַר רָבָא: תְּבָעוּהָ לִינָּשֵׂא וְנִתְפַּיְּיסָה – צְרִיכָה לֵישֵׁב שִׁבְעָה נְקִיִּים!

The Gemara examines Rav and Rav Naḥman's actions: **But didn't Rava say:** With regard to a woman **who had an offer of marriage and accepted,** the emotional excitement may have caused her to have a flow of menstrual blood, which would making her ritually impure and prohibit her from engaging in intercourse. Even if she was unaware of any flow, she must consider the possibility that it occurred. To purify herself, **she needs to wait seven** consecutive days that are **clean**[B] from any flow of menstrual blood[H] and then immerse in a ritual bath. Only then may she marry. If so, how could Rav and Rav Naḥman marry women on the day they arrived?

NOTES

Which will be for the day – מַאן הָוְיָא לְיוֹמָא: The commentaries discuss why Rav and Rav Naḥman required a wife for one day, as there are many instances recounted in the Talmud where the same Sages went to different places, and they did not take a wife on those occasions. Moreover, if they intended to divorce these wives, they would be in violation of the dictum that one may not marry a woman with the intention of divorcing her. Indeed, the Rif and the Rosh do not quote this practice, and it appears that they do not consider it to be *halakha*.

Some later authorities suggest that Rav and Rav Naḥman were traveling to meet with the non-Jewish ruler, and it was the custom of the ruler to provide a mistress for those who visited him (see *Avoda Zara* 76b). Therefore, Rav and Rav Naḥman asked to marry a wife so that they would not be offered a mistress by the ruler, since the custom was to offer a mistress only to one who came without his wife (*Imrei David*).

HALAKHA

One should not marry women in different countries – לֹא יִשָּׂא נָשִׁים בְּכַמָּה מְדִינוֹת: A man should not marry a woman in one country and then go and marry another woman in a different country, lest a son from one marriage and a daughter from the other unite with one another and have children, who would be *mamzerim*. This is in accordance with the ruling of Rabbi Eliezer ben Ya'akov. However, if the man is renowned such that any children he has will be identified by their connection to their father, then it is permissible. This is in accordance with the Gemara's initial explanation of the actions of Rav and Rav Naḥman. The *Beit Shmuel* notes that the Rif and Rosh do not refer to this exception, and it would seem that they hold that the Gemara retracted this explanation in its conclusion. This is possible if one assumes that according to the conclusion of the Gemara, Rav and Rav Naḥman never actually married the women in the towns they visited (Rambam *Sefer Kedusha, Hilkhot Issurei Bia* 21:29; *Shulḥan Arukh, Even HaEzer* 2:11).

A woman who has an offer of marriage must wait seven clean days – תְּבָעוּהָ לִינָּשֵׂא יוֹשֶׁבֶת שִׁבְעָה נְקִיִּים: A woman who had an offer of marriage and accepted may not marry immediately; rather, she must count seven clean days since she may have experienced a flow of blood without being aware of it. She must check herself during those seven days to ensure she has not experienced any additional flow. Ideally, this should be done each day (Rema, based on the *Beit Yosef*). The Rambam rules that if the husband is a Torah scholar then she may marry him immediately, since he can be trusted to be careful not to engage in sexual relations with her. This ruling is based on the Gemara here. The Ra'avad disagrees and rules that the prohibition applies to a Torah scholar as well. It would appear that the majority of halakhic authorities concur with the opinion of the Ra'avad (Rambam *Sefer Kedusha, Hilkhot Issurei Bia* 11:9; *Shulḥan Arukh, Yoreh De'a* 192:1).

BACKGROUND

Seven clean days – שִׁבְעָה נְקִיִּים: When a woman accepts an offer of marriage, the emotional excitement can bring on early menstruation. This is especially true for a woman whose cycle is not totally regular. Furthermore, it is possible that out of her desire for her future husband, she may have experienced other vaginal secretions that masked the sensation of the flow of blood; therefore, even if she did not see or feel the release of blood, she must consider the possibility that there was blood. Consequently, she must observe the purification process for a menstruating woman and wait seven clean days before immersing in a ritual bath.

רַבָּנַן שְׁלוּחַיְיהוּ הֲווּ מְשַׁדְּרִי, וּמוֹדְעִי לְהוּ, וְאִיבָּעֵית אֵימָא: לְרַבָּנַן יִחוּדֵי בְּעָלְמָא הוּא דִּמְיַיחֲדִי לְהוּ, דְּאָמַר מָר: אֵינוֹ דּוֹמֶה מִי שֶׁיֵּשׁ לוֹ פַּת בְּסַלּוֹ לְמִי שֶׁאֵין לוֹ פַּת בְּסַלּוֹ.

The Gemara explains: These **Sages would send messengers** seven days ahead of their arrival and **they** would **inform** the women of the Sage's arrival. In this way, the woman who agreed to marry the Sage would have time to count the seven clean days. **And if you wish, say** that **the Sages'** intentions **were merely to be in seclusion** [*meyaḥadi*] **with** the woman[N] but not to engage in intercourse with her. Therefore, it was permitted to marry her even if she became ritually impure. Being in seclusion with a woman was sufficient to help the Sages avoid any forbidden thoughts, **as the Master said: One who has bread in his basket**[N] **is incomparable to one who does not have bread in his basket,** i.e., just as the knowledge that food is readily available is sufficient to psychologically alleviate one's feelings of hunger, so too, the knowledge that one's sexual desires could be met lessens the strength of the desire itself.

תַּנְיָא, רַבִּי אֱלִיעֶזֶר בֶּן יַעֲקֹב אוֹמֵר: לֹא יִשָּׂא אָדָם אִשָּׁה וְדַעְתּוֹ לְגָרְשָׁהּ, מִשּׁוּם שֶׁנֶּאֱמַר ״אַל תַּחֲרֹשׁ עַל רֵעֲךָ רָעָה וְהוּא יוֹשֵׁב לָבֶטַח אִתָּךְ״.

The Gemara cites an additional statement of Rabbi Eliezer ben Ya'akov: It is **taught** in a *baraita* that **Rabbi Eliezer ben Ya'akov says: A man should not marry his wife** when at the same time **his intention is to divorce her,**[NH] **because it is stated: "Do not devise evil against your neighbor, as he dwells securely with you"** (Proverbs 3:29). It is wrong for one to intend to undermine the feelings of security that another has with him.

סָפֵק וְיָבָם שֶׁבָּאוּ לַחֲלֹק בְּנִכְסֵי מִיתְנָא.

§ The mishna raises a case in which a *yavam* consummated the levirate marriage with his *yevama* and seven months later she gave birth. With respect to that child, there is an uncertainty whether he is the child of the deceased brother or whether he is the child of the *yavam*. The Gemara discusses the ramifications of this uncertainty in a dispute concerning inheritance. The case concerns one whose identity as the son of the deceased is **uncertain, and a *yavam*** who consummated the levirate marriage with the *yevama*, **who** both **came to divide up**[N] the **possessions of the deceased** brother[H] and each one claims to be the sole heir.

HALAKHA

A man should not marry his wife when at the same time his intention is to divorce her – לֹא יִשָּׂא אָדָם אִשְׁתּוֹ וְדַעְתּוֹ לְגָרְשָׁהּ: It is prohibited for a man to marry a woman if at the same time his intention is to divorce her, because it is stated: "Do not devise evil against your neighbor, as he dwells securely with you" (Proverbs 3:29). This is in accordance with the ruling of Rabbi Eliezer ben Ya'akov. The Rambam and *Shulḥan Arukh* rule that if he informs her in advance that his intention is only to be married for a short time, then it is permissible. It would appear that this ruling is based on the Gemara here (*Beit Yosef*; see *Derisha*; Rambam *Sefer Kedusha, Hilkhot Issurei Bia* 21:28 and *Sefer Nashim, Hilkhot Geirushin* 10:21; *Shulḥan Arukh, Even HaEzer* 2:10; 119:1).

The son of uncertain descent and the *yavam* who came to divide up the possessions of the deceased brother – סָפֵק וְיָבָם שֶׁבָּאוּ לַחֲלוֹק בְּנִכְסֵי הַמֵּת: If a *yavam* consummated the levirate marriage within three months of his brother's death and seven months later the *yevama* gave birth, then there is an uncertainty whether that child is the offspring of the deceased brother or of the *yavam*. If that child and the *yavam* come to divide up the possessions of the deceased, the possessions are to be divided up equally between them (Rambam *Sefer Mishpatim, Hilkhot Naḥalot* 5:4; *Shulḥan Arukh, Even HaEzer* 163:3).

NOTES

Their intentions were merely to be in seclusion [*meyaḥadi*] with the woman – יִחוּדֵי בְּעָלְמָא הוּא דִּמְיַיחֲדִי לְהוּ: This statement of the Gemara raises numerous difficulties: If a newlywed bride became impure from experiencing a menstrual flow before the couple had managed to consummate their marriage, it is prohibited for them to be in seclusion together, even if they do not engage in relations. Why, then, was it permitted for these Sages? Furthermore, since it was actually prohibited to engage in relations with these women, how was the Sages' seclusion with them considered like the case of one who has bread in his basket? Rabbi Avraham min HaHar raises an additional question: According to the opinion of the Rambam, one may not marry a woman who is ritually impure following her menstruation since there is no immediate possibility of engaging in relations with her. Why, then, was it permitted for these Sages to marry in such a manner?

With regard to the prohibition against being secluded with a bride who experienced a menstrual flow, numerous resolutions have been offered: *Tosafot* on *Yoma* 18b suggest that the prohibition does not actually apply to a newlywed couple but only to an unmarried man and his future bride. However, once they are married, there is no prohibition. The Rambam suggests that the prohibition is only due to the concern that the couple will not be able to withstand their desires and will engage in relations. This concern does not apply to a Torah scholar, and therefore he may be secluded with his newlywed wife in all circumstances.

The Rid interprets the prohibition as being limited to being in the same room; however, it is permitted for the couple to be in the same house. *Tosafot* here explain that from the outset the Sages would inform the women that their intention was only to be secluded with them, but not to engage in relations. Therefore, the excitement of marriage was not so great that it would lead to the women experiencing a flow. Accordingly, it was actually perfectly permissible for them to marry these women, and therefore the Sages could certainly be considered like one who has bread in his basket.

Other commentaries read the Gemara in a way that avoids the questions altogether. The Ra'avad and Meiri claim that these Sages never actually married these women. When the Gemara says *meyaḥadi*, the intention is not that the Sages were in seclusion with them; rather, they would merely designate them to be available to marry. Therefore, there was no question of any prohibition involved. Alternatively, the Ramban explains that the statement that they would merely be in seclusion with the women is not an alternative answer but a continuation of the first answer: They would inform the women of their arrival ahead of time, and even so, due to Rabbi Eliezer ben Ya'akov's concerns, they would not actually engage in relations with them. This answer also resolves a further difficulty raised by some of the early commentaries: If the Gemara's original suggestion that the Sages' names are renowned was rejected, then what would happen if these new wives did become pregnant and give birth to a child? Couldn't this lead to the eventual creation of *mamzerim*? However, according to the Ramban's explanation there was never any possibility of actually having children.

One who has bread in his basket – מִי שֶׁיֵּשׁ לוֹ פַּת בְּסַלּוֹ: The term: Bread in one's basket, is used literally to explain why the manna caused suffering to the Jews in the desert, as they did not have bread in their basket for the next day (*Yoma* 74b). However, bread is also a euphemism for a wife, as the Torah says with regard to Potiphar that he did not deny Yosef anything "save the bread that he did eat" (Genesis 39:6), and the Sages understand this to be a reference to his wife (*Bereshit Rabba* 86:6). Rashi also uses the same euphemism to explain Jethro's words with regard to Moses: "Call him, that he may eat bread" (Exodus 2:20) as a reference to the possibility that Moses will marry one of his daughters (*Menuḥat Aharon*).

A man should not marry his wife when at the same time his intention is to divorce her – לֹא יִשָּׂא אָדָם אִשְׁתּוֹ וְדַעְתּוֹ לְגָרְשָׁהּ: The reason for the prohibition is that doing so undermines the woman's trust, as indicated by the biblical source of the prohibition. Therefore, if the man would first inform the woman of his intentions to divorce her, it would be permitted (see HALAKHA). Therefore, it must be that in the cases of Rav and Rav Naḥman cited in the Gemara, they would make their intentions clear before marrying the women for the duration of their visits, as is already hinted to by the concluding phrase of their requests: Which woman will be my wife for the day (Rid; see Meiri).

One whose identity is uncertain and a *yavam* who came to divide up – סָפֵק וְיָבָם שֶׁבָּאוּ לַחֲלוֹק: The Rashba asks: Since the *yavam* consummated the levirate marriage, the possessions are considered to be under his control. Therefore, even if an uncertainty arises concerning who has a right to those possessions, that uncertainty should not be significant enough to allow the possessions to be removed from his control and divided up between the two sides. In resolution of this difficulty, the Rashba explains that the fact that in the majority of cases a woman gives birth after nine months supports the claim of the son of uncertain descent that he is in fact the son of the deceased, since he was born less than nine months after his mother remarried. The Gemara later explains that the force of this majority is not sufficient to award the inheritance to him; since her pregnancy was not noticeable after three months, the ability to presume that she is like the majority of women is compromised. Nevertheless, the force of the majority is still sufficient to allow the possessions to be removed from the control of the *yavam* and then, due to the uncertainty, to be divided up between them.

NOTES

This is property of uncertain ownership – **הֲוֵי מָמוֹן הַמּוּטָּל בְּסָפֵק**: Normally, in cases of property of uncertain ownership the *halakha* is that the property is left with the one who currently has control of it, based on the principle: The burden of proof rests upon the claimant. However, since in this case neither litigant has stronger control over the possessions, they are divided equally between the two sides (*Tosafot*; see the comments of Rashba cited on the previous page). The Ritva adds that since the case is one of inheritance, each side is considered to be equally in control of the possessions. He explains that this is why it is not appropriate in this case to remove the possessions from the parties and then award them based upon the discretion of the court, or alternatively to allow the parties to settle their differences by themselves and award the possessions according to their resolution. Furthermore, the court only ever resorts to using these methods when there is a possibility that the uncertainty will be resolved; however, in this case, the uncertainty is intractable.

HALAKHA

The son of uncertain descent and the sons of the *yavam* – **סָפֵק וּבְנֵי יָבָם**: If the son of uncertain descent and the sons of the *yavam* come to divide up the possessions of the deceased, then since the sons of the *yavam* concede that at the very least the son of uncertain descent has a right to a portion as one of the brothers, he takes that portion. The rest of the possessions are then divided into two, half going to the son of uncertain descent and the other half being split between the sons of the *yavam* (Rosh; *Tur*, citing Rashi). The Rambam rules that all of the deceased's possessions are to be split equally between the son of uncertain descent and the sons of the *yavam* (Rambam *Sefer Mishpatim*, *Hilkhot Naḥalot* 5:4; *Shulḥan Arukh*, *Even HaEzer* 163:4).

סָפֵק אָמַר: אֲנָא בַּר מִיתְנָא הוּא, וְנִכְסֵי דִּידִי הוּא. וְיָבָם אָמַר: אַתְּ בְּרַאי דִּידִי אַתְּ, וְלֵית לָךְ וְלֹא מִידֵי בְּנִכְסֵי. הֲוֵי מָמוֹן הַמּוּטָּל בְּסָפֵק, וּמָמוֹן הַמּוּטָּל בְּסָפֵק – חוֹלְקִין.

The one of **uncertain** descent **said: I am the son of the deceased,** and therefore, as the only heir, his **possessions are mine. And the *yavam* said** to him: **You are my son, and you have absolutely no** rights **to the possessions;** rather, by virtue of the fact that I consummated the levirate marriage with the widow of the deceased, I should inherit him. The Gemara rules on this case: This **is** a case of **property of uncertain ownership,**[N] as there is no way to determine who is the rightful heir, and the *halakha* is that **property of uncertain ownership** the claimants **divide up** between them.

סָפֵק וּבְנֵי יָבָם שֶׁבָּאוּ לַחֲלוֹק בְּנִכְסֵי מִיתְנָא, סָפֵק אָמַר: הַהוּא גַּבְרָא בַּר מִיתְנָא הוּא, וְנִכְסֵי דִּידִי הוּא. בְּנֵי יָבָם אָמְרִי: אַתְּ אָחִינוּ אַתְּ, וּמְנָתָא הוּא דְּאִית לָךְ בַּהֲדַן.

The Gemara brings another case, that of one concerning whom there is **uncertainty** whether he is the son of the deceased or of the *yavam* **and the sons of the *yavam*,**[H] who consummated the levirate marriage with the *yevama* and has since died, **who came to divide up** the **possessions of the deceased,** and each one makes claim to the inheritance. The one of **uncertain** descent **said: That man,** referring to himself, **is the son of the deceased, and** therefore, as his sole heir, his **possessions are mine.** And the **sons of the *yavam* said** to him: **You are our brother, and** our uncle, the deceased, was not survived by any offspring and so by virtue of our father's levirate marriage he inherited our uncle's possessions, and now that our father has died and we are dividing up his possessions **you have** a right to inherit only **a portion** of the inheritance **together with us.**

סְבוּר רַבָּנַן קַמֵּיהּ דְּרַב מְשַׁרְשִׁיָּא לְמֵימַר: מַתְנִיתִין הִיא, דִּתְנַן: הוּא אֵינוֹ יוֹרֵשׁ אוֹתָם, וְהֵם יוֹרְשִׁין אוֹתוֹ.

The Rabbis who studied **before Rav Mesharshiyya thought to say:** This case **is** analogous to a case in **a mishna, as we learned** a similar case in a mishna (100a) in which a woman gave birth shortly after remarrying and there is uncertainty whether the child's father is the first or second husband. The mishna considers a case in which the husbands died and were each survived by a set of sons: If a son from either set died, the other sons of that set will inherit from him because as brothers they have an uncontested claim to the inheritance. However, **he,** the son of uncertain descent, **does not inherit** from **them** because his claim as a brother is uncertain and is therefore not powerful enough to allow him to take part of the inheritance from the other sons. **However,** if the son of uncertain descent died, **they,** the sons of both husbands, **will** jointly **inherit** from **him.** The claims of each set of sons to be his brothers are equally uncertain; therefore, since there is no one who has a definite claim to his inheritance, his possessions are split between them.

וְהָכָא אִיפְּכָא, הָתָם אָמְרִי לֵיהּ: אַיְיתִי רְאָיָה וּשְׁקוֹל.

The Rabbis qualify their comparison of the cases: **But here,** the positions are **in reverse,** as follows: **There,** in the case of the mishna, when one of the sons dies, **they,** the other sons of that set, can **say to him,** the son of uncertain descent: **Bring proof** that you are actually a son of our father **and** only then can you **take** a portion. Since he cannot prove this, he will not receive any of the inheritance.

הָכָא אָמַר לְהוּ: אַיְיתוּ רְאָיָה וּשְׁקוֹלוּ.

However, **here,** in the case where the son of uncertain descent is in dispute with the sons of the *yavam*, **he,** the son of uncertain descent, can **say to them: Bring proof** that I am not the son of the deceased, **and** only then can you **take** a portion together with me. The Rabbis claim that the principle in both cases is identical: When one party has an uncontested claim to the inheritance, and another party advances a claim to receive part of the inheritance that is based on an uncertainty, the uncertain claim is not accepted. In the mishna's case, it is the son of uncertain descent who has an uncertain claim. The Rabbis suggest that the reverse is true in the Gemara's case: The son of uncertain decent has an uncontested claim to the inheritance because whether he is the son of the first or second husband, he certainly has a right to some inheritance. It is the sons of the *yavam* who have an uncertain claim because they have a right to the inheritance only if the son of uncertain decent is actually their brother.

אמר להו רב משרשיא: מי דמי? התם – אינהו ודאי, ואיהו ספק. הכא – אידי ואידי ספק.

Rav Mesharshiyya said to them: Is the case in the mishna really **comparable? There,** in the mishna's case, when one of the sons dies, **they,** the other sons in that set, have a **definite** claim to the inheritance, since their claim is based on the fact that they are the dead son's brothers, which is certainly true, **and he,** the son of uncertain descent, only has an **uncertain** claim. However, **here, each** party has only an **uncertain** claim.[N] Although the son of uncertain descent claims that ultimately, whatever the nature of his relationship with the deceased is, he should have the right to inherit, nevertheless, since it is not actually known what that relationship is, his claim in reality is merely a composite of uncertain claims.

אלא, אי דמיא למתניתין – [להא] דמיא: לספק ובני יבם שבאו לחלוק בנכסי יבם גופיה, דהתם אמרי ליה: אייתי ראיה דאחונא את ושקול.

Having rejected the analogy offered by the Rabbis, Rav Mesharshiyya offers his own analogy to the case in the mishna that the Rabbis cited: **Rather, if** there is a case that **is analogous to** the case in **the mishna,** then it is **to this** following case that it is **analogous:** It is comparable **to** a case in which following the levirate marriage a son was born, and there is uncertainty whether he is the son of the deceased or of the *yavam*, and that son of **uncertain** descent **and the sons of the *yavam* come to divide up** the **possessions of the *yavam* himself. As there,** those who are unquestionably the sons of the *yavam* have a definite claim; therefore, **they** can **say to him,** the son of uncertain descent: **Bring proof that you are** actually **our brother and** only then can you **take** a portion. Since he cannot prove this, he will not receive any of the inheritance.

ספק ובני יבם שבאו לחלוק בנכסי יבם, לבתר דפלג יבם בנכסי מיתנא.

The Gemara brings yet another case, that of one concerning whom there is an **uncertainty** whether he is the son of the deceased or of the *yavam* **and the sons of the** *yavam*, i.e., the sons of the man who consummated the levirate marriage with the *yevama* and has since died, **who came to divide up** the **possessions of the** *yavam*[H] **after the** *yavam* had already **divided up**[N] the **possessions of the deceased** brother between himself and the son of uncertain descent, as per the Gemara's ruling in the first case above.

בני יבם אמרי: אייתי ראיה דאחונא את ושקול. אמר להו ספק: מה נפשייכו, אי אחוכון אנא – הבו לי מנתא בהדייכו, ואי בר מיתנא אנא – הבו לי פלגא דפלג אבוכו בהדאי.

The *yavam* then died and his sons and the son of uncertain descent each made a claim to the inheritance: **The sons of the *yavam* say** to the son of uncertain descent: **Bring proof that you are our brother, and** only then can you **take** a portion. The son of **uncertain** descent **said to them: Whichever way you** look at it, I should receive a portion of the inheritance. **If** you assume that **I am your brother,** then **give me a portion** of the inheritance **together with** all of **you, and if** you assume that **I am the son of the deceased,** then **give me the half** of the possessions **that your father** took when he **divided up** the possessions **with me** upon the deceased's death, because if you assume I am his son, then I am his sole heir and your father never had any rights to his possessions.

NOTES

Each party has only an uncertain claim – אידי ואידי ספק: Ostensibly, Rav Mesharshiyya's claim that in the Gemara's case each party has only an uncertain claim is difficult, because, as the Rabbis explained, whether the son of uncertain descent is the son of the first or second husband, he has a claim to the possessions. Why then does Rav Mesharshiyya's state that his claim is considered uncertain? Rashi explains that the key issue in defining a claim as certain is whether the potential heir can substantiate the nature of his relationship with the deceased. Since in this case he cannot, his claim is defined as uncertain. The later commentaries explain that this is uniquely true of inheritance rights. In regular monetary disputes, it is indeed sufficient to demonstrate that whatever the situation is, one has a right to the possessions. This is because the basis of one's rights to the possessions is one's acquisition of them, which exists even if unverified. However, in the *halakhot* of inheritance, one's rights to the possessions are merely a function of having the status of an heir, which is based on one's relationship to the deceased. That status can be established only once the relationship is verified. Therefore, as long as one cannot substantiate the precise nature of one's relationship with the deceased, one's claim is always defined as uncertain.

Had already divided up – פלג: The Gemara does not consider what the *halakha* would be had the possessions of the deceased not yet been divided between the son of uncertain descent and the *yavam*. The Rashba, *Tosafot*, and others assume that in such a case, the claim of the son of uncertain descent would certainly be accepted.

The Rashba notes that since the *yavam* consummated the levirate marriage, it would seem that at that time he had an undisputed claim to the possessions. If so, this case should be dependent on the dispute between Admon and the Rabbis cited later in the Gemara, yet the Gemara does not connect the two. Therefore, it would seem that a distinction should be drawn between the two cases. The dispute between Admon and the Rabbis concerns a case where one's rights to the possessions were achieved through an act of acquisition. Only in this case is it possible to say that his act of acquisition strengthens his claim to the extent that it can withstand certain future developments that would have otherwise undermined his rights. However, in a case of inheritance, the fact that someone claimed to have a right to the inheritance and took control of those possessions does not strengthen his claim in any way.

HALAKHA

The son of uncertain descent and the sons of the *yavam*, with regard to the possessions of the *yavam* – ספק ובני יבם בנכסי יבם: If the son of uncertain descent and the sons of the *yavam* come to divide up the possessions of the *yavam* after the *yavam* had previously divided up the possessions of his deceased brother between himself and the son of uncertain descent: If the son of uncertain descent claims that he is either willing to return the portion of the possessions of the deceased that he originally received and instead receive an portion equal to the sons of the *yavam*, or he will insist on receiving all of the possessions of the deceased, his claim is not heeded. This is in accordance with the opinion of Rav, who holds that the original verdict stands. However, the *Taz* and others rule that the original verdict is reconsidered (based on the *Tur*, citing Rosh). According to the *Beit Shmuel*, if the possessions of the deceased had not yet been divided up between the *yavam* and the son of uncertain descent, then the claim would be successful. Furthermore, if the son of uncertain descent had already obtained control of the possessions, they would not be removed from him (Rambam *Sefer Mishpatim*, *Hilkhot Naḥalot* 5:4; *Shulḥan Arukh*, *Even HaEzer* 163:5).

רבי אבא אמר רב: קם דינא. רבי ירמיה אמר: הדר דינא.

The son of uncertain descent's claim assumes that the original verdict to divide up the possessions of the deceased between the two sides may be reexamined in light of later developments. This assumption, however, is subject to a dispute: **Rabbi Abba said** that **Rav said: The** original **verdict stands,**[N] i.e., the original division of the deceased's possessions is considered a closed matter, and the new dispute concerning the possessions of the *yavam* is considered independently of it. Accordingly, the son of uncertain descent's claim cannot succeed, and so he receives no portion of the inheritance of the *yavam*. **Rabbi Yirmeya said: The** original **verdict is reconsidered** in light of the new circumstances, and therefore in this case the son of uncertain descent can put forward his undeniable claim to some of the possessions of the *yavam* based on the original uncertainties that existed with regard to the division of the deceased's possessions.

לימא בפלוגתא דאדמון ורבנן קמיפלגי, דתנן: מי שהלך למדינת הים ואבדה לו דרך שדהו, אדמון אמר: ילך בקצרה. וחכמים אומרים: יקח לו דרך במאה מנה, או יפרח באויר.

Let us say that Rabbi Abba and Rabbi Yirmeya **disagree over the dispute between Admon**[P] **and the Rabbis. As we learned** in a mishna (*Ketubot* 109b): With regard to **one** who owns a field and has the rights to a path that passes through land belonging to another, and **he traveled to a country overseas, and** when he returned the **path to his field was lost,**[H] i.e., he forgot where the path was located, **Admon says: He may go** only **on the shortest** path to his field, as although it is not known where the path is, he definitely did have a path, and therefore at the very least he has a right to the shortest path. **The Rabbis say: He must** either **purchase for himself** a new **path for** whatever price is asked, even if it is **one hundred dinars, or he will** have to **fly through the air** to reach his field, i.e., as long as he cannot prove where the original path was, he has no rights to any other path.

והוינן בה: לרבנן; שפיר קאמר אדמון! ואמר רב יהודה אמר רב: הכא במאי עסקינן – כגון שהקיפוה ארבעה בני אדם מארבע רוחות.

And we discussed the mishna and thereby established the parameters of the dispute as follows: It is difficult **for the Rabbis** because **Admon is saying well,** i.e., the logic of his opinion would seem to be compelling. **And** in defense of the Rabbis' opinion, **Rav Yehuda said** that **Rav said: With what are we dealing here?** It is with a case **where** his field was **surrounded by four individuals** who owned the land **on** each of its **four sides.** Therefore, he cannot demand a path from any one of the surrounding owners, since each one can deflect his claim by suggesting that the path might have passed through one of the other owners' land.

אי הכי, מאי טעמא דאדמון? ואמר רבא: בארבעה דאתו מכח ארבעה, וארבעה דאתו מכח חד – כולי עלמא לא פליגי, דמצו מדחי ליה.

However, this creates a further difficulty: **If so,** that the surrounding land is owned by different people, **what is Admon's rationale** for ruling that the owner of the field has a claim to the shortest path? **And** in order to justify Admon's opinion, **Rava said: With regard to** a case in which there are **four** current owners **who came** to own their land **on the basis of** purchase from **four** previous owners, i.e., each of the current owners acquired their land from a different previous owner, **and** also in a case in which there are **four** current owners **who came** to own their land **on the basis of** purchase from **one** previous owner who originally owned all four pieces of land, **everyone agrees that** the current owners **are able to deflect him** and his claim to a path.

כי פליגי – בחד דאתי מכח ארבעה. אדמון סבר: מצי אמר ליה: מכל מקום דרכי גבך הוא. ורבנן סברי, דאמר ליה: אי שתקת – שתקת, ואי לא – מהדרנא שטרא למרייהו, ולא מצית לאשתעויי דינא בהדייהו.

When they disagree, it is **in** a case in **which** there is only **one** current owner of all four pieces of land, **who came** to own his land **on the basis of** purchase from **four** previous owners. **Admon holds** that the owner of the field **can say to** the current owner of the surrounding land: **Whichever** way you construe the case, **my path** to my field is somewhere **with you** in the surrounding land. **And the Rabbis hold** that the owner of the surrounding land can deflect this claim because **he can say to him: If you** do not press your claim and **are silent,** then **be silent,** and I will sell you a path at a reasonable price. **But if not,** and you insist on pressing your claim, then **I will return the bills** of purchase of the land **to their** previous **owners,**[N] **and** then **you will not be able to** successfully **engage in a legal dispute with them,** as each one could claim that the path went through one of the other pieces of land not owned by them.

NOTES

The verdict stands – קם דינא: The *Terumat HaDeshen* suggests a rationale for this opinion: At the time of the original verdict to split up the possessions, it is assumed that the parties accepted the verdict and gave up any rights to those possessions awarded to the other party. This is true even though they believe the verdict to have been in error. Therefore, it is obvious that they cannot come later and try to regain those rights. See the Jerusalem Talmud for further discussion of this topic. From the discussion there it would appear that in the case of the sons of *yavam*, they would be able to offer a claim based on a reconsideration of the original verdict.

I will return the bills of purchase of the land to their previous owners – מהדרנא שטרא למרייהו: *Tosafot* ask: Why doesn't the field owner respond: True, if you actually return the surrounding land to the previous owners then I would not able to make a claim to my path; however, until you actually do so, my claim is valid and you should provide me with a path? The early commentaries answer that the statement of the owner of the surrounding land is not to be taken as a threat. Indeed, it is possible that the previous owners will not be interested in repurchasing the land. Rather, his statement is simply his way of highlighting the fact that the land was originally in the possession of four previous owners who could have easily deflected the field owner's claim to a path. He therefore claims that since they could have done so, and he purchased the land from them, he also has the right to do so (Ritva; *Nimmukei Yosef*).

PERSONALITIES

Admon – אדמון: The Admon cited here is Admon ben Gaddai, one of the Sages of Jerusalem in the generation before the destruction of the Temple. Admon was one of two edict judges in Jerusalem who stood at the head of the city judges. It was their responsibility, and part of their authority, to establish amendments and pass permanent public edicts in matters of robbery or damages. Several halakhic rulings are presented in Admon's name in tractate *Ketubot* (108b–110a).

HALAKHA

One whose path to his field was lost – מי שאבדה דרך שדהו: With regard to one who owns a field and has the rights to a path leading to his field that passes through land belonging to another, and he traveled to a country overseas and when he returned the path to his field was lost, if the surrounding land currently belongs to a single owner and had always belonged to a single owner, then the field owner may demand that the owner of the surrounding land provide him with at least the shortest path to his field. This is in accordance with the conclusion of the Gemara that in such a case everyone agrees with the ruling of Admon. However, if the surrounding land is currently owned by numerous individuals, even if they purchased their pieces of land from a single previous owner, then the owner of the field has no right to claim a path, and if he wants one, he much purchase it. This is also the ruling if the land is currently owned by a single individual who purchased it from numerous previous owners. This is in accordance with the opinion of the Rabbis (Rambam *Sefer Mishpatim, Hilkhot To'en VeNitan* 15:11; *Shulḥan Arukh, Hoshen Mishpat* 178:1–2).

לֵימָא רַבִּי אַבָּא דְּאָמַר כְּרַבָּנַן.

Having established the parameters of the dispute, the Gemara suggests: **Let us say** that the statement of **Rabbi Abba, who said** that the original verdict stands, **is in accordance with** the opinion of **the Rabbis.** When the owner of the field forgot where his path was located, the surrounding land was owned by four different owners, and therefore at that time the verdict was that he had no ability to successfully claim his path. The Rabbis apparently assume that that verdict stands, and therefore the field owner is considered to have lost any rights to the path. Consequently, even if the surrounding pieces of land are later purchased by a single person, the owner of the field cannot make a claim for his path.

וְרַבִּי יִרְמְיָה דְּאָמַר כְּאַדְמוֹן?

The Gemara continues: **And** the statement of **Rabbi Yirmeya, who said** that the original verdict is repealed, **is in accordance with** the opinion of **Admon.** Admon apparently assumes that although the original verdict was that the field owner has no ability to successfully claim his path, nevertheless, that does not mean he loses his rights to the path. Rather, once the situation changes and the surrounding pieces of land are purchased by a single person, the original uncertainty is revived to allow him to make a claim for at least the shortest path to his field.

אָמַר לָךְ רַבִּי אַבָּא: אֲנָא דַּאֲמַרִי אֲפִילּוּ כְּאַדְמוֹן. עַד כָּאן לָא קָאָמַר אַדְמוֹן הָתָם – אֶלָּא מִשּׁוּם דְּאָמַר לֵיהּ: מִמָּה נַפְשָׁךְ

The Gemara rejects the comparison: **Rabbi Abba** could have **said to you: When I stated** my ruling, it was **even in accordance with** the opinion of **Admon. Admon states** his ruling **only there,** in the case of the lost path, **because** the field owner **said to** the owner of the surrounding land: **Whichever way you** look at it,

Perek **IV**
Daf **38** Amud **a**

דַּרְכִּי חַד גַּבָּךְ הוּא, אֲבָל הָכָא – מִי אִיכָּא לְמֵימַר הָכִי?

my one path is with you[N] in one of your pieces of land. Since his claim is based on facts that are clear and certain, his claim is successful. **However, here,** in the dispute over the inheritance, **is** the son of uncertain descent **able to state** a claim like **this?** Although the son of uncertain descent claims that ultimately, whatever the nature of his relationship with the deceased is, he should have the right to inherit, nevertheless, since it is not actually known what that relationship is, his claim in reality is merely a composite of uncertain claims.

וְרַבִּי יִרְמְיָה אָמַר לָךְ: אֲנָא דַּאֲמַרִי אֲפִילּוּ לְרַבָּנַן, עַד כָּאן לָא קָאָמְרִי רַבָּנַן הָתָם אֶלָּא מִשּׁוּם דְּאָמַר לֵיהּ: אִי שָׁתְקַתְּ – שָׁתְקַתְּ, וְאִי לָא – מַהֲדַרְנָא שְׁטָרָא לְמָרַיְיהוּ, וְלָא מָצֵית לְאִשְׁתַּעוּיֵי דִּינָא בַּהֲדַיְיהוּ. אֲבָל הָכָא – מִי אִיכָּא לְמֵימַר הָכִי?

And Rabbi Yirmeya could have **said to you: I stated** my ruling **even in accordance with** the opinion of **the Rabbis,** since perhaps **the Rabbis state** their ruling **only there,** in the case of the lost path, **because** the owner of the surrounding land **said to** the field owner: **If you** do not press your claim and **are silent,** then **be silent** and I will sell you the path at a reasonable price; **but if not,** then **I will return the bills** of purchase of the pieces of land **to their** previous **owners** and then **you will not be able to** successfully **engage in a legal dispute with them.** He is successful with this claim because it is within his power to return the fields and thereby recreate the original circumstances in which the owner of the field would forfeit the path. **However, here, are** the sons of the *yavam* **able to state** a claim like **this?** The original circumstance, in which the inheritance of the deceased had still not been divided, cannot be recreated. Therefore, a claim based on that circumstance will be unsuccessful.

NOTES

My one path is with you – דַּרְכִּי גַּבָּךְ הִיא: The commentary here is in accordance with the explanation of Rashi that the distinction between the two cases is whether or not the claim is definite or uncertain. Other commentaries suggest a different interpretation: The distinction lies in whether it is possible to offer a claim based on the current situation. In the case of the path, the field owner's claim is tendered irrespective of any dealings he had with the previous owners of the surrounding pieces of land; it is made against the current owner of the surrounding land based on his ownership of it. However, in the dispute over the inheritance, the claim relates to the original situation, before the inheritance was divided; a situation that no longer exists (Rid; Rabbi Avraham min HaHar).

HALAKHA

One of uncertain descent and the *yavam* with regard to the possessions of the grandfather – סָפֵק וְיָבָם בְּנִכְסֵי סָבָא: In a case where the *yavam* and one of uncertain descent, who is either the son of the deceased or the son of the *yavam*, came to divide up the possessions of the grandfather, i.e., the father of the *yavam*, and the son of uncertain descent claims that he is the son of the deceased and therefore a portion of the possessions should be awarded to him, his claim is not accepted and all of the property is awarded to the *yavam* (Rambam *Sefer Mishpatim, Hilkhot Naḥalot* 5:5; *Shulḥan Arukh, Even HaEzer* 163:6).

One of uncertain descent and the sons of the *yavam* with regard to the possessions of the grandfather – סָפֵק וּבְנֵי יָבָם בְּנִכְסֵי סָבָא: In a case in which the sons of the *yavam* and one of uncertain descent, who is either the son of the deceased or the son of the *yavam*, came to divide up the possessions of the grandfather, i.e., the father of the *yavam*, the portion that each party concedes to the other side is awarded to that side, and then the remaining possessions are divided up between them, half given to the son of uncertain descent and the other half divided between those who are definitely sons of the *yavam* (Rambam *Sefer Mishpatim, Hilkhot Naḥalot* 5:5; *Shulḥan Arukh, Even HaEzer* 163:7).

LANGUAGE

One-sixth [*danka*] – דַּנְקָא: *Danka* is a Persian monetary unit that appears in Middle Persian sources as dāng. This unit was equal to one-sixth of a dinar. The term was then borrowed to refer to one-sixth of anything, as in this passage.

סָפֵק וְיָבָם שֶׁבָּאוּ לַחֲלוֹק בְּנִכְסֵי סָבָא, סָפֵק אָמַר: הַאי גַּבְרָא בַּר מִיתְנָא הוּא, וּפַלְגָא דִּידִי הוּא. יָבָם אָמַר: אַתְּ בְּרַאי דִּידִי אַתְּ, וְלֵית לָךְ וְלָא מִידֵי,

The Gemara brings another case, that of one of **uncertain** descent, who is either the son of the deceased or the son of the *yavam*, **and the *yavam* who came to divide up** the **possessions of the grandfather,**[H] i.e., the father of the *yavam* and the deceased, and each one made a claim to the inheritance. The son of **uncertain** descent **said: That man,** referring to himself, **is the son of the deceased, and** therefore **half** of the possessions **are mine** because the inheritance should be split between the two sons, i.e., the deceased and the *yavam*, and since I am the sole heir of the deceased, I should receive his portion. **The *yavam* said** to him: **You are my son, and** therefore **you have absolutely no** rights to the possessions; rather, I should receive all the inheritance. One half is mine because I am the grandfather's son, and the other half, which would have gone to my deceased brother, I should receive by virtue of the fact that I consummated the levirate marriage with his widow.

הֲוֵי יָבָם וַדַּאי, וְסָפֵק סָפֵק – וְאֵין סָפֵק מוֹצִיא מִידֵי וַדַּאי.

The Gemara rules on this case: This is a case in which **the *yavam* has a definite** claim[N] because he is the grandfather's son, **and the** son of **uncertain** descent has only **an uncertain** claim, and the *halakha* is that one with **an uncertain claim cannot extract** property **from** one who has **a definite** claim to it. Therefore, the *yavam* receives all the inheritance.

סָפֵק וּבְנֵי יָבָם שֶׁבָּאוּ לַחֲלוֹק בְּנִכְסֵי סָבָא, סָפֵק אָמַר: הַהוּא גַּבְרָא בַּר מִיתְנָא הוּא, וּפַלְגָא דִּידִי הוּא. וּבְנֵי יָבָם אָמְרִי: אֲחוּנָא אַתְּ, וּמְנָתָא אִית לָךְ בַּהֲדַן.

The Gemara raises yet another case, that of one of **uncertain** descent, who is either the son of the deceased or the son of the *yavam*, **and the sons of the *yavam* who came to divide up** the **possessions of the grandfather,**[H] and each one made a claim to the inheritance. The son of **uncertain** descent **said: That man,** referring to himself, **is the son of the deceased, and** therefore **half** of the possessions **are mine** because the inheritance should be split between the two sons, i.e., the deceased and the *yavam*, and since I am the lone heir of the deceased I should receive his portion. **And the sons of the *yavam* said: You are our brother, and** therefore **you** should **receive** only **a portion together with us.**

פַּלְגָא דְּקָמוֹדֵי לְהוּ – שָׁקְלִי, תִּילְתָּא דְּקָא מוֹדוּ לֵיהּ – שָׁקֵיל. פָּשׁ לְהוּ דַּנְקָא, הָוֵי מָמוֹן הַמּוּטָּל בְּסָפֵק – וְחוֹלְקִין.

The Gemara rules on this case: **The half** of the grandfather's possessions **that** the son of uncertain descent **concedes** belongs **to them,** the sons of the *yavam*, **they take** for themselves. By claiming to be the son of the brother who died first, he forfeits any rights to the other brother's portion. **The third** of the grandfather's possessions **that** the sons of the *yavam* **concede** belong **to him,** the son of uncertain descent, **he takes** for himself. By claiming he is their brother, they admit that he should at least receive an equal portion to them, which would mean one-third if they are three. This **leaves them** with **one-sixth** [*danka*][L] of the possessions that **is property of uncertain ownership, and** so **they** should **divide it up** between them.

NOTES

The *yavam* has a definite claim – הֲוֵי יָבָם וַדַּאי: Rashi and Rivan explain that his claim is deemed to be definite because he will definitely receive at least some portion of the inheritance. Therefore, he is considered to have control over the property, and the son of uncertain descent, whose claim is uncertain, is not able to extract any of that property from him. *Tosafot* question Rashi's opinion: Why should the fact that he definitely has a right to a portion of the inheritance grant him control over all of it? *Tosafot* therefore reject Rashi's explanation and suggest that the *yavam* is considered to have a definite claim because he indisputably has the status of an heir of the deceased; the only question is how much of the inheritance he should receive. However, the son of uncertain descent may not be an heir at all. Therefore, since the very basis of his right to inherit is uncertain, it is inappropriate that he should receive anything in the presence of one who is certainly an heir. The *Arukh LaNer* defends Rashi's explanation. He suggests that with regard to inheritance, the fact that one has a definite right to part of an inheritance proves that ultimately he has the basis for a claim to all the inheritance. Therefore, his claim is considered to be definite.

סָבָא וְיָבָם בְּנִכְסֵי סָפֵק, אוֹ סָבָא וְסָפֵק בְּנִכְסֵי יָבָם –

The Gemara presents two additional cases. One is a case where a son of uncertain descent, who is either the son of the deceased or the son of the *yavam*, died, and **the grandfather and the *yavam*** come to divide up the **possessions of the** son of **uncertain** descent. In the absence of any children, a father inherits from his son. The grandfather claims that the son of uncertain descent was actually the son of the deceased, and since the deceased has already died, the grandfather should be next in line to inherit from him. The *yavam* claims that the son of uncertain descent was his own son, and therefore he should inherit from him. **Or,** the second case is one in which the *yavam* died and **the grandfather and the** son of **uncertain** descent[N] come to divide up the **possessions of the *yavam*.** The son of uncertain descent claims to be the lone son of the *yavam* and therefore he should inherit, whereas the grandfather claims that the son of uncertain descent was the son of the deceased and that the *yavam* died childless, and therefore the grandfather, who is the father of the *yavam*, should inherit from him.

הָוֵי מָמוֹן הַמּוּטָּל בְּסָפֵק, וְחוֹלְקִין.

The Gemara rules in these cases: This **is** a case of **property of uncertain ownership, and** so **they** should **divide up** the possessions between them.[H]

מתני׳ שׁוֹמֶרֶת יָבָם שֶׁנָּפְלוּ לָהּ נְכָסִים, מוֹדִים בֵּית שַׁמַּאי וּבֵית הִלֵּל שֶׁמּוֹכֶרֶת וְנוֹתֶנֶת וְקַיָּים.

MISHNA With regard to **a widow waiting for her *yavam***[N] to either consummate a levirate marriage or perform *ḥalitza* with her, i.e., a *yevama*, **to whom property was bequeathed:**[H] **Beit Shammai and Beit Hillel** both **agree that she may sell or give** away that property *ab initio*, **and** that if she did, the transfer **is valid.** Since she has only a levirate bond with the *yavam*, she retains total control of the property. This is in contrast to a betrothed woman, concerning whom Beit Hillel rule that she may not sell such property because her betrothed also has rights to it (*Ketubot* 78a).

מֵתָה – מַה יֵּעָשֶׂה בִּכְתוּבָּתָהּ וּבִנְכָסִים הַנִּכְנָסִים וְיוֹצְאִין עִמָּהּ? בֵּית שַׁמַּאי אוֹמְרִים: יַחֲלוֹקוּ יוֹרְשֵׁי הַבַּעַל עִם יוֹרְשֵׁי הָאָב, וּבֵית הִלֵּל אוֹמְרִים: נְכָסִים בְּחֶזְקָתָן: כְּתוּבָּה בְּחֶזְקַת יוֹרְשֵׁי הַבַּעַל, נְכָסִים הַנִּכְנָסִים וְיוֹצְאִין עִמָּהּ בְּחֶזְקַת יוֹרְשֵׁי הָאָב.

If she **died, what should be done with** the money assured to her in **her marriage contract** by her deceased husband **and with** her **property that enters and leaves** the marriage **with her,** in which a husband only ever has a usufructuary interest?[H] **Beit Shammai say: The husband's heirs,** i.e., the *yavam*, who stands to inherit from the husband when he consummates the levirate marriage, **should divide up** the property **together with** her **father's heirs,** i.e., the woman's family. **And Beit Hillel say:** The **property** retains **its** previous ownership **status.**[N] Therefore, money assured to her in her **marriage contract** remains **in the possession of the husband's heirs.** Since it was to be paid from the husband's own property, the money is retained by his estate and passes to his heirs. And her **property that enters and leaves** the marriage **with her** remains **in the possession of the father's heirs.** Since those properties belonged to her, upon her death they are inherited by her father or his heirs.

NOTES

The grandfather and the son of uncertain descent – סָבָא וְסָפֵק: The grandfather in this case is unquestionably the father of the *yavam*; it is only the son whose identity is uncertain. If so, ostensibly, this is an additional case in which one party, in this case the grandfather, has a definite claim to the inheritance, whereas the other party, in this case the son of uncertain descent, has only an uncertain claim. Why, then, does the Gemara not adduce the *halakha* it cited above that in such cases the inheritance is awarded to the party with the definite claim? The early commentaries explain that whenever one is survived by a son, the other relatives are not considered to have the status of heirs at all. Therefore, although the grandfather's identity is unquestioned, his status as an heir is uncertain. Since both parties have equally uncertain claims, the possessions are divided between them (see Rid and Ramban).

A widow waiting for her *yavam* – שׁוֹמֶרֶת יָבָם: The Hebrew term for this woman is a *shomeret yavam*. The root *sh-m-r* usually denotes the concept of guarding. However, Rashi here and elsewhere notes that in this context the word denotes waiting, in this case for her *yavam*. Rashi cites proof for this from other instances in the Gemara (*Ketubot* 62b) and the Bible (Genesis 37:11; see *Tosefot Yom Tov*).

The property retains its previous ownership status – נְכָסִים בְּחֶזְקָתָן: According to this version of the mishna's text, which is the version cited by the *ge'onim*, it would appear that Beit Hillel first present a principle: The property retains its previous ownership status, and then proceed to demonstrate its application to the marriage contract and to the property that enters and leaves the marriage with her. This version does not mention explicitly what should be done with guaranteed property, i.e., property that the wife brings with her into the marriage that is explicitly recorded in the marriage contract and whose value the husband guarantees will be returned to her in the event of payment of the marriage contract. However, since such property is written as part of the marriage contract, it is assumed that it is treated in the same way as the marriage contract itself. This is how Rabbeinu Tam, the Rashba, and many other early commentaries rule.

Other early commentaries have a different version of the mishna's text that states: The property retains its previous ownership status and the marriage contract remains in the possession of the husband's heirs. The addition of the conjunctive: And, before: The marriage contract, indicates that the *halakha* cited concerning the marriage contract is not an elaboration of a previous principle but a new case. Accordingly, the opening clause: The property retains its previous ownership status, should not be taken as a principle but as an independent case. Therefore, according to this version the mishna actually presents three different cases: First it states what should be done with: The property, which is a reference to her guaranteed property; then it states what should be done with her marriage contract, which refers to both its principal value and any additional sums the husband may have promised; and finally it states what should be done with her property that enters and leaves the marriage with her. Although this version does explicitly make reference to her guaranteed property, it does not state what precisely should be done with it. However, the Gemara elsewhere (see *Bava Batra* 158a) elaborates on this point and rules that the property should be split between the parties. This is how Rashi on *Ketubot* 80a explains the mishna, and the Rambam rules accordingly.

HALAKHA

The grandfather and the *yavam*, the grandfather and the son of uncertain descent – סָבָא וְיָבָם, סָבָא וְסָפֵק: If a son of uncertain descent, who is either the son of the deceased or the son of the *yavam*, died, and the grandfather claims that the son of uncertain descent was actually the son of the deceased, and so the grandfather should inherit from him, and the *yavam* claims that the son of uncertain descent was his own son, and so he should inherit from him, then they should divide up the possessions equally between them. The same *halakha* would apply if the *yavam* died and the grandfather and the son of uncertain descent both claimed the possessions of the *yavam* (Rambam *Sefer Mishpatim*, *Hilkhot Naḥalot* 5:5; *Shulḥan Arukh*, *Even HaEzer* 163:8).

A widow waiting for her *yavam* to whom property was bequeathed – שׁוֹמֶרֶת יָבָם שֶׁנָּפְלוּ לָהּ נְכָסִים: If a widow waiting for her *yavam* is bequeathed property after she already happened before the *yavam* for levirate marriage, she is in full possession of that property; she may sell or give away the property *ab initio*. The Ran rules that this is the *halakha* even if the *yavam* had performed levirate betrothal with her (Rambam *Sefer Mishpatim*, *Hilkhot Naḥalot* 3:10 and *Sefer Nashim*, *Hilkhot Ishut* 22:10; *Shulḥan Arukh*, *Even HaEzer* 160:5).

Inheritance of a widow waiting for her *yavam* – יְרוּשַּׁת שׁוֹמֶרֶת יָבָם: If a widow waiting for her *yavam* dies, her heirs inherit the property that enters and leaves the marriage with her, and the husband's heirs inherit the money assured to her in the marriage contract. With regard to her guaranteed property, some say it is divided up equally between her heirs and her husband's heirs (Rashi; Rambam). Others say that the guaranteed property is awarded to the husband's heirs (Rabbeinu Tam; Rosh). Even according to the first opinion, if the husband's heirs had already taken control of the property, it is not to be removed from their possession (Ran). Some rule that in places where the custom is always to perform *ḥalitza* and never to allow levirate marriage, the husband's heirs gain no entitlement to the property (Rema, citing Maharik; Rambam *Sefer Nashim*, *Hilkhot Ishut* 22:10; *Shulḥan Arukh*, *Even HaEzer* 160:7).

HALAKHA

If the *yavam* consummated the levirate marriage with her then her legal status is that of his wife – כְּנָסָהּ הֲרֵי הִיא כְּאִשְׁתּוֹ: If a *yavam* consummated a levirate marriage with his *yevama*, then her legal status is that of his wife in every sense and he is able to separate from her only by means of a bill of divorce; afterward, if he wishes, he may remarry her (Rambam *Sefer Nashim*, *Hilkhot Ishut* 22:10; *Shulḥan Arukh*, *Even HaEzer* 168:1).

Her marriage contract is payable from the property of her first husband – כְּתוּבָּה עַל נִכְסֵי בַּעְלָהּ הָרִאשׁוֹן: The marriage contract that a *yavam* gives to his *yevama* has to be paid only from the possessions he inherits from her first husband (Rambam *Sefer Nashim*, *Hilkhot Ishut* 22:10 and *Hilkhot Yibbum* 1:1; *Shulḥan Arukh*, *Even HaEzer* 166:4, 168:3).

כְּנָסָהּ – הֲרֵי הִיא כְּאִשְׁתּוֹ לְכָל דָּבָר, וּבִלְבַד שֶׁתְּהֵא כְּתוּבָּה עַל נִכְסֵי בַּעְלָהּ הָרִאשׁוֹן.

If the *yavam* **consummated the levirate marriage with her, then** her legal status is **that of his wife**[H] **in every sense,** and therefore the *yavam* has the same rights to her property as in a regular marriage. **And** the **only** exception to this is **that** her **marriage contract will** still **be** payable **from the property of her first husband**[H] and not from the property of the *yavam*.

גמ׳ מַאי שְׁנָא רֵישָׁא דְּלָא פְּלִיגִי, וּמַאי שְׁנָא סֵיפָא דִּפְלִיגִי?

GEMARA The Gemara asks: **What is different** about **the first clause,** concerning a *yevama* who is still alive, **that** Beit Shammai **do not disagree** with Beit Hillel that the woman has full possession of the property since there is only a levirate bond but no marriage, **and what is different** about **the latter clause that** Beit Shammai **disagree** with Beit Hillel and rule that the *yavam* does take a share of the property, which would imply that the levirate bond alone is sufficient to afford the *yavam* rights over her property?[N]

אָמַר עוּלָּא: רֵישָׁא – דְּנָפְלָה כְּשֶׁהִיא אֲרוּסָה, וְסֵיפָא – דְּנָפְלָה כְּשֶׁהִיא נְשׂוּאָה.

Ulla said: The two clauses concern different cases: **The first clause** concerns a case **where she happened** before her *yavam* for levirate marriage at a time **when she was a betrothed woman**[N] and only then did she come into the possession of property. Since when she was betrothed her husband did not have any rights to the property, neither does the *yavam*. **And the latter clause** concerns a case **where she happened** before her *yavam* at a time **when she was a married woman.** In such a case, were her husband still alive, he would have full rights to the property; therefore, so does the *yavam*.

וְקָסָבַר עוּלָּא: זִיקַת אֲרוּסָה – עוֹשָׂה סְפֵק אֲרוּסָה,

The Gemara explains: **And Ulla holds** that a levirate **bond** formed **with a betrothed woman affords** her a status equivalent to **a woman** about whom there is an **uncertainty** whether she is **betrothed,**[N]

NOTES

Interpretations of the mishna – פֵּירוּשֵׁי הַמִּשְׁנָה: The Gemara presents four different interpretations of the mishna in the name of Ulla, Rabba, Abaye, and Rava. The commentaries discuss the principal differences between the various opinions, as well as the question of which opinion was accepted as the *halakha*. In a responsum, Rav Hai Gaon claims that all of the opinions here are only explications of Beit Shammai's opinion. Accordingly, the entire talmudic discussion is irrelevant to the *halakha* since the *halakha* is in accordance with the opinion of Beit Hillel recorded in the mishna (see Ramban).

Where she happened before her *yavam* when she was a betrothed woman – דְּנָפְלָה כְּשֶׁהִיא אֲרוּסָה: This version of the Gemara text, which is also the version cited by Rashi, states: Where she happened. Accordingly, the mishna concerns a case where the property fell to her only after her husband had already died and she was awaiting levirate marriage. The distinction between the clauses lies in the strength of the levirate bond, which is dependent upon her status when her husband died. The *ge'onim*, however, had an alternate version that states: Where they fell to her, with the word they being a reference to the property. According to this version, the property fell to her when she was still married to her previous husband, and the distinction between the cases is due to whether her husband gained ownership of that property. If she was already married at the time, then when the property fell to her, her husband instantly gained rights to it, and those rights will pass over to the *yavam*. However, if she was still only betrothed to her husband at the time, the property would remain fully in her possession (see Rashba and Ritva).

Affords her a status equivalent to a woman about whom there is an uncertainty whether she is betrothed – עוֹשָׂה סְפֵק אֲרוּסָה: Rashi questions why it is necessary to afford her such a status; in truth, the *yavam* has no rights to property that is bequeathed to his *yevama* while she is still awaiting levirate marriage. Accordingly, the Gemara could have simply stated: A levirate bond formed with a betrothed woman is nothing. Rashi explains that the Gemara avoided describing her levirate bond in this way because doing so could have given the incorrect impression that there is no levirate bond at all and that she does not even require *ḥalitza*. By describing the bond in the way it did, the Gemara clarifies that although the bond indeed exists, nevertheless it does not afford the *yavam* with any rights.

The Rashba takes issue with Rashi's assertion that the *yavam* has no rights to her property. See his commentary for a resolution of Rashi's opinion He notes that in the mishna in *Ketubot* 78a, Beit Hillel rule that a betrothed woman may not sell property that was bequeathed to her *ab initio* because her husband also has rights to it. As such, it is clear why the Gemara could not have stated: The levirate bond is nothing, because were she to have already come into the possession of the property while betrothed to her previous husband, the levirate bond formed with the *yavam* would also prevent her from selling that property *ab initio*.

זִיקַת נְשׂוּאָה עוֹשָׂה סָפֵק נְשׂוּאָה.

and a levirate **bond** formed **with a married woman affords** her a status equivalent to that of **a woman** for whom there is an **uncertainty** whether she is **married,** i.e., when her husband dies, the same level of relationship that existed with the first husband is created with the *yavam*. However, since the new relationship exists only by virtue of a levirate bond, it exists to a lower degree, and so the rights afforded to the *yavam* are more limited than those the first husband would have enjoyed; the rights granted to the *yavam* are equivalent to the rights of husband in a case where there is uncertainty whether that level of relationship exists at all.

זִיקַת אֲרוּסָה עוֹשָׂה סָפֵק אֲרוּסָה, דְּאִי סָלְקָא דַּעְתָּךְ וַדַּאי אֲרוּסָה – מוֹדִים בֵּית הִלֵּל שֶׁמּוֹכֶרֶת וְנוֹתֶנֶת וְקַיָּים?!

The Gemara proceeds to demonstrate this: It must be that a levirate **bond** formed **with a betrothed woman affords** her a status equivalent to that of **a woman** for whom there is an **uncertainty** whether she is **betrothed, because if it enters your mind** to suggest that her status is equivalent to that of **a definitely betrothed woman, would Beit Hillel concede that she may sell or give** away her property *ab initio*, **and that** if she does the transfer **is valid?**

וְהָתְנַן: נָפְלוּ לָהּ נְכָסִים מִשֶּׁנִּתְאָרְסָה, בֵּית שַׁמַּאי אוֹמְרִים: תִּמְכּוֹר, וּבֵית הִלֵּל אוֹמְרִים: לֹא תִּמְכּוֹר. אֵלּוּ וְאֵלּוּ מוֹדִים שֶׁאִם מָכְרָה וְנָתְנָה – קַיָּים. אֶלָּא שְׁמַע מִינָּהּ: זִיקַת אֲרוּסָה – עוֹשָׂה סָפֵק אֲרוּסָה.

But didn't we learn in a mishna (*Ketubot* 78a): If **property was bequeathed to** a woman **after she was betrothed,**[H] **Beit Shammai say: She may sell** that property, **and Beit Hillel say: She may not sell** that property. However, **both agree that if she sold** it **or gave** it **away,** the transfer **is valid.** The mishna clearly states that according to Beit Hillel, a woman who is definitely betrothed may not sell the property *ab initio*. **Rather, conclude from here,** from the fact that here Beit Hillel permit the *yevama* to sell her property *ab initio*, that a levirate **bond** formed **with a betrothed woman affords** her a status equivalent to that of **a woman** for whom there is an **uncertainty** whether she is **betrothed.**

זִיקַת נְשׂוּאָה עוֹשָׂה סָפֵק נְשׂוּאָה, דְּאִי סָלְקָא דַּעְתָּךְ וַדַּאי נְשׂוּאָה בֵּית שַׁמַּאי אוֹמְרִים יַחֲלוֹקוּ יוֹרְשֵׁי הַבַּעַל עִם יוֹרְשֵׁי הָאָב?!

Similarly, it must be that a levirate **bond** formed **with a married woman affords** her a status equivalent to that of **a woman** for whom there is an **uncertainty** whether she is **married, because if it enters your mind** to suggest that her status is equivalent to that of **a definitely married woman,** would **Beit Shammai say** that **the husband's heirs should divide up** the property **together with the father's heirs?**

וְהָתְנַן: נָפְלוּ לָהּ נְכָסִים מִשֶּׁנִּישֵּׂאת – אֵלּוּ וְאֵלּוּ מוֹדִים שֶׁאִם מָכְרָה וְנָתְנָה שֶׁהַבַּעַל מוֹצִיא מִיַּד הַלָּקוֹחוֹת. אֶלָּא שְׁמַע מִינָּהּ: זִיקַת נְשׂוּאָה עוֹשָׂה סָפֵק נְשׂוּאָה.

But didn't we learn in a mishna (*Ketubot* 78a): If **property was bequeathed to** a woman **after she was married,**[H] **both** Beit Hillel and Beit Shammai **agree that if she sold** the property **or gave** it away, then **the husband repossesses** it **from the purchasers. Rather, conclude from here,** from the fact that here Beit Shammai assume the rights of the *yavam* are limited, that a levirate **bond** formed **with a married woman affords** her a status equivalent to **a woman** for whom there is an **uncertainty** whether she is **married.**

אֲמַר לֵיהּ רַבָּה: אַדְּמִפַּלְגִי בְּגוּפָהּ וּלְאַחַר מִיתָה, לִפְלְגוּ בְּחַיֶּיהָ וּלְפֵירוֹת!

Rabba challenges Ulla's understanding of the mishna: **Rabba said to him:** If your explanation is correct, then in the latter clause, **instead of disagreeing** with regard to who has the rights to the property **itself,** which necessitates considering the case **after** her **death, let** Beit Hillel and Beit Shammai **disagree with regard to** the more immediate case **when she is** still **alive and** dispute who has the rights **to** the use and **produce**[N] of the property.

NOTES

Let them disagree with regard to the case when she is alive and dispute the rights to the produce – לִפְלְגוּ בְּחַיֶּיהָ וּלְפֵירוֹת: The early commentaries already note that this is certainly not the halakhic conclusion, as it is undisputed that the *halakha* is that before he consummates the levirate marriage the *yavam* has no rights to the use and produce of the property of the *yevama* (see Rashba). Rather, this statement of Rabba is only in accordance with the opinion of Ulla (see *Yosef Lekah*).

HALAKHA

A betrothed woman's property – נִכְסֵי אֲרוּסָה: A betrothed woman may not sell property belonging to her *ab initio*, but if she does so, the sale is valid (Rambam *Sefer Nashim, Hilkhot Ishut* 22:8; *Shulḥan Arukh, Even HaEzer* 90:11, 160:5).

A married woman's property – נִכְסֵי נְשׂוּאָה: If a married woman sold her property of which the husband has a usufructuary interest, even if that property fell to her as an inheritance prior to her betrothal, then her husband continues to have rights to the use of that property as long as they are married. If she dies, he may also repossess the property from the buyer and need not compensate the buyer monetarily. Some (*Tur*; Rosh) say that he may repossess the property even while she is still alive (Rambam *Sefer Nashim, Hilkhot Ishut* 22:7; *Shulḥan Arukh, Even HaEzer* 90:9).

NOTES

One who has an uncertain claim cannot extract property from one who has a definite claim to it – אֵין סָפֵק מוֹצִיא מִידֵי וַדַּאי: The Gemara discusses this principle in tractate *Pesaḥim* (9a) and suggests based on various sources that an uncertainty can override even a certainty. One example given is that of one who leaned over a pit, and it is known that at some point a corpse lay at the bottom of the pit. If the corpse was still there when he leaned over the pit, then he would be rendered ritually impure. However, there is uncertainty whether the corpse is in fact still there, since an animal may have dragged it away. The existence of that uncertainty is sufficient to undermine the certainty that there was a corpse there, and accordingly the person who leaned over the pit may be deemed ritually pure (see the Gemara there).

Why, then, does the Gemara here state unequivocally that an uncertainty cannot override a certainty? It would seem that with regard to monetary claims the *halakha* is different, due to the principle that the burden of proof rests upon the claimant. The later authorities explain that in the case in the Gemara here, although the woman presents a definite claim, since her status is uncertain that impacts her claim and prevents her from being able to lay claim to the property.

אֶלָּא אֲמַר רַבָּה: אִידִי וְאִידִי דִּנְפַלָה כְּשֶׁהִיא נְשׂוּאָה, וְזִיקַת נְשׂוּאָה – עוֹשָׂה סָפֵק נְשׂוּאָה. רֵישָׁא דְּאִיהִי קַיְימָא – הֲוָה לָהּ אִיהִי וַדַּאי וְאִינְהוּ סָפֵק וְאֵין סָפֵק מוֹצִיא מִידֵי וַדַּאי.

Rather, Rabba said a different resolution to the apparent inconsistency in Beit Shammai's rulings: Both **this** first clause **and that** latter clause of the mishna concern a case in **which she happened** before her *yavam* for levirate marriage **once she was** already **a married woman, and** a levirate **bond** formed **with a married woman affords** her a status equivalent to that of **a woman** about whom there is an **uncertainty** whether she is **married.** The distinction between the two clauses is as follows: In the **first clause, where she is alive, she has a certain** claim to the property, **while they,** i.e., the *yavam*, are considered to have only **an uncertain claim** to the property, as she has the status of a woman for whom there is an uncertainty whether she is married. **And** since one who has **an uncertain claim cannot extract** property **from** one who has **a definite** claim to it,[N] she therefore retains full possession of the property.

סֵיפָא דְּמֵתָה – הַלָּלוּ בָּאִין לִירַשׁ וְהַלָּלוּ בָּאִין לִירַשׁ, וְיַחֲלוֹקוּ.

In **the latter clause,** however, **where she died,** neither party has a definite claim; rather, **these** heirs of the father **come to inherit, and those** heirs of the husband **come to inherit, and** therefore **they should divide up** the property.

אֵיתִיבֵיהּ אַבַּיֵי: וּלְבֵית שַׁמַּאי אֵין סָפֵק מוֹצִיא מִידֵי וַדַּאי?! וְהָתְנַן: נָפַל הַבַּיִת עָלָיו וְעַל אָבִיו, עָלָיו וְעַל מוֹרִישָׁיו, וְהָיוּ עָלָיו כְּתוּבַּת אִשָּׁה וּבַעַל חוֹב,

Abaye raised an objection to Rabba's opinion: **But** is it true that **according to Beit Shammai,** one with **an uncertain claim cannot extract** property **from** one who has **a definite** claim to it? **Didn't we learn** in a mishna (*Bava Batra* 157a): In a case where **a house collapsed upon** a person **and upon his father,**[H] or **upon him and upon those** from **whom he** stood to **inherit, and there were** outstanding debts **against** that person from his **wife's marriage contract and** to **a creditor,** but he had no money with which to pay those debts, and it is not known who died first, the following situation arises: If the father died first, then before the son died he had already inherited the father's property and therefore the son's creditors gained a lien over that property and have the rights to collect their debts from that property even after the son's death.

יוֹרְשֵׁי הָאָב אוֹמְרִים: הַבֵּן מֵת רִאשׁוֹן וְאַחַר כָּךְ מֵת הָאָב. וּבַעַל חוֹב אוֹמֵר: הָאָב מֵת רִאשׁוֹן וְאַחַר כָּךְ מֵת הַבֵּן,

Accordingly, the father's heirs and the creditor offer opposing claims: **The father's heirs say: The son died first and** only **afterward the father died.** Therefore, the creditor never gained any rights to collect from the property. **And the creditor says: The father died first and** only **afterward the son died.** Therefore, the father's property was liened to the son's debts, and the creditor has a right to collect.

בֵּית שַׁמַּאי אוֹמְרִים: יַחֲלוֹקוּ, וּבֵית הִלֵּל אוֹמְרִים: נְכָסִים בְּחֶזְקָתָן.

The mishna continues: **Beit Shammai say: They should divide up** the property between them. **And Beit Hillel say:** The **property** retains **its** previous ownership **status,** which in this case means that since the last known possessor was the father, so the father's heirs gain full rights to it.

וְהָא הָכָא, יוֹרְשֵׁי הָאָב – וַדַּאי, וּבַעַל חוֹב – סָפֵק, וְקָאָתֵי סָפֵק וּמוֹצִיא מִידֵי וַדַּאי!

Abaye explains his proof: **Isn't** it the case **here** that **the father's heirs** have a **definite** claim **and the creditor** has only **an uncertain** claim? Therefore, since Beit Shammai rule that the property should be divided up, it is apparent that they hold that one with **an uncertain claim can extract** property **from** one who has **a definite** claim to it.

HALAKHA

A house collapsed upon a person and upon his father – נָפַל הַבַּיִת עָלָיו וְעַל אָבִיו: If a house collapsed upon a person and his father or anyone else from whom he stood to inherit, and it was unknown whether that person or his father died first, and there were outstanding debts against that person from his wife's marriage contract and to a creditor, this gives rise to the following situation: The father's heirs can claim that the son died first and since he had no properties of his own any debts against him became void, and the wife and the creditors can claim that the father died first, and so the son inherited from him before dying, and they therefore have a right to collect their debts from that money. The *halakha* in this case is that the property remains in the possession of the father's heirs, and the burden of proof rests upon the wife and the creditors. This ruling is in accordance with the opinion of Beit Hillel (Rambam *Sefer Mishpatim, Hilkhot Naḥalot* 5:8; *Shulḥan Arukh, Ḥoshen Mishpat* 280:12).

קָסָבְרִי בֵּית שַׁמַּאי: שְׁטָר הָעוֹמֵד לִגְבּוֹת כִּגְבוּי דָּמֵי.

Rabba rejects the proof: Beit Shammai's ruling in this case cannot be adduced as a proof because **Beit Shammai hold:** A debt recorded in **a bill of debt that is awaiting collection**[N] **is as though it was already collected** to the extent that the creditor is considered to be in possession of the debt. Therefore, the creditor is considered to be in possession of the property to the same extent as the father's heirs; consequently, the property is divided between them.

וּמְנָא תֵּימְרָא – דִּתְנַן: מֵתוּ בַּעֲלֵיהֶן עַד שֶׁלֹּא שָׁתוּ, בֵּית שַׁמַּאי אוֹמְרִים: נוֹטְלוֹת כְּתוּבָּתָן וְאֵינָן שׁוֹתוֹת, וּבֵית הִלֵּל אוֹמְרִים: אוֹ שׁוֹתוֹת אוֹ לֹא נוֹטְלוֹת כְּתוּבָּתָן.

And from where do you say that Beit Shammai hold this opinion? **As we learned** in a mishna (*Sota* 24a): A married woman who secluded herself with another man after her husband had warned her not to do so is suspected of having committed adultery. To establish her guilt or innocence she is brought to the Temple, where she drinks the bitter waters. With regard to such women, if **their husbands died before they drank**[H] the bitter waters, **Beit Shammai say: They collect** the money assured to them in **their marriage contracts and do not drink** the waters. **And Beit Hillel say: Either they drink,** and if they survive they collect their marriage contracts, **or** they do not drink and **they cannot collect their marriage contracts,** and all the husband's property passes to his heirs.

אוֹ שׁוֹתוֹת?! ״וְהֵבִיא הָאִישׁ אֶת אִשְׁתּוֹ״ אָמַר רַחֲמָנָא, וְלֵיכָּא! אֶלָּא: מִתּוֹךְ שֶׁלֹּא שׁוֹתוֹת לֹא נוֹטְלוֹת כְּתוּבָּתָן.

The Gemara clarifies the statement of Beit Hillel: Did Beit Hillel really mean: **Either they drink,** which implies they may actually choose to drink? But doesn't **the Merciful One state: "And the man shall bring his wife"** (Numbers 5:15), which indicates that the ritual of drinking the bitter waters applies only when the husband is still alive, **and** in this case **there is no** husband to do so; consequently, she should not be able to drink. **Rather,** Beit Hillel's intent is as follows: The only means by which a suspected adulteress is able to collect her marriage contract is by drinking the bitter waters and proving her innocence. Therefore, where this is not possible due to the death of the husband, **since** the wives **do not drink, they cannot collect their marriage contracts.**

וְהָא הָכָא, דְּסָפֵק הוּא, סָפֵק זִנַּאי סָפֵק לֹא זִנַּאי, וְקָאָתֵי סָפֵק וּמוֹצִיא מִידֵי וַדַּאי! אֶלָּא שְׁמַע מִינָּהּ: שְׁטָר הָעוֹמֵד לִגְבּוֹת כִּגְבוּי דָּמֵי.

Rabba explains his proof from this mishna: **Isn't** it the case **here that** the wife's claim to her marriage contract **is uncertain** because there is **uncertainty whether she was unfaithful or whether she was not unfaithful, and** so it would appear that one with **an uncertain** claim **is coming and undermining** the **definite** claim of the husband's heirs? This is untenable, as even were one to hold that someone with an uncertain claim can extract property from someone who has a definite claim to it, that would only allow for the money to be divided between the two sides, whereas in this case Beit Shammai rule that the creditor collects the entire debt. **Rather, conclude from** that mishna that Beit Shammai hold that a debt recorded in **a bill of debt that is awaiting collection is** considered **as though it were already collected** to the extent that the one who is owed the money is considered to be in possession of the debt. It is due to this reason that she is empowered to be able to collect her marriage contract.

וְאַבַּיֵי, לוֹתְבֵיהּ מֵהָא! דִּלְמָא כְּתוּבַּת אִשָּׁה שָׁאנֵי, מִשּׁוּם חִינָּא.

The Gemara asks: **And** why did **Abaye** object to Rabba's opinion based on the mishna in tractate *Bava Batra*? **Let him object to** Rabba's opinion **based on this**[N] mishna in tractate *Sota* since based on Abaye's assumption that a bill of debt is not considered as though it were already collected, this mishna perforce demonstrates that Beit Shammai hold that one with an uncertain claim can extract property from one who has a definite claim to it. The Gemara answers: Abaye did not object based on this mishna because he reasoned that **perhaps a woman's marriage contract is different** from a regular bill of debt in that the Sages uniquely reinforced a woman's hold over the debt in her marriage contract **due to** the increased **desirability**[N] that this would bring her when trying to remarry. This would ensure that she would bring some money with her into a new marriage.

NOTES

A bill of debt that is awaiting collection, etc. – שְׁטָר הָעוֹמֵד לִגְבּוֹת וכו׳: Rav Hai Gaon raises a difficulty with Rabba's claim. Even if one concedes that in general a bill of debt that is awaiting collection is considered as though it was already collected, it is unreasonable to apply that principle in a case such as this, where the son did not have any property. Therefore, he claims that the Gemara's question was not resolved by the Gemara.

And Abaye, let him object to Rabba's opinion based on this – וְאַבַּיֵי לוֹתְבֵיהּ מֵהָא: Rashi explains that the Gemara's difficulty is with the fact that Abaye raised his objection from a mishna in tractate *Bava Batra*, a tractate in the order of *Nezikin*, when he could have raised his objection from a mishna in tractate *Sota*, which, like tractate *Yevamot*, is in the order of *Nashim*. *Tosafot Yeshanim* explain differently: Since the Gemara had not yet demonstrated that according to Beit Shammai a document awaiting collection is considered as though it is already collected, the mishna in tractate *Sota* presents a more immediate difficulty: Why indeed should those women receive their marriage contracts, since isn't it the *halakha* that one with an uncertain claim cannot extract property from one who has a definite claim to it?

Tosafot note further that in any case the mishna proves difficult for Abaye's opinion because it states that she receives the entire marriage contract, whereas according to Abaye, Beit Shammai should hold that she should receive only half (see *Tosefot HaRosh*). *Tosafot* suggest that since the woman is able to present a definite claim that she was not unfaithful, whereas her relatives' claims are only uncertain, she is therefore in a stronger position and so she is awarded her entire marriage contract. Ramban offers an additional answer: Since Beit Shammai hold that one with an uncertain claim can extract property from one who has a definite claim to it, it would appear that they regard an uncertain claim to be like a definite claim. Therefore, it is possible that one follows the principle that unless proven otherwise, one presumes the original status remains unchanged and therefore one should presume the woman was not unfaithful. Consequently, she should receive the entire value of her marriage contract. It is also possible that Abaye holds that the mishna in tractate *Sota* does not actually mean that she collects the entire marriage contract but only that she collects from it; she would never actually receive more than half.

Due to desirability – מִשּׁוּם חִינָּא: *Tosafot* on *Ketubot* 84a cite the explanation of Rabbeinu Ḥananel that reinforcing the marriage contract makes women more attractive to men since it ensures that a woman will bring some money with her into a new marriage. Rashi on *Ketubot* 84a and *Arakhin* 22a suggests a different explanation: Reinforcing the marriage contract is not designed to make women more desirable to men but to make the institution of marriage more desirable to women. The existence of a strong marriage contract reduces the likelihood that the husband will divorce the wife without careful consideration, as the divorce would create a financial burden upon him.

This explanation would appear to assume that a woman is reluctant to marry and the Sages therefore needed to take steps to encourage her. However, this would seem to contradict another statement of the Sages that a woman wishes to marry as she cannot bear to be alone (*Kiddushin* 41a), and based on this concept the Sages ruled that a marriage contract is collected from the husband's lowest-quality possessions in order to make the institution of marriage more appealing to men. *Tosafot* raise this difficulty to Rashi's opinion but claim that it does not pose a full refutation because one cannot draw comparisons between different rabbinic decrees. The reason for this is that often, in one instance the Sages will favor one party while in another instance they may favor the other party.

HALAKHA

Their husbands died before they drank – מֵתוּ בַּעֲלֵיהֶן עַד שֶׁלֹּא שָׁתוּ: If a woman secluded herself with another man after her husband had warned her not to do so and her husband then died, she may not drink the bitter waters and does not receive her marriage contract. This is in accordance with the opinion of Beit Hillel, according to the conclusion of the Gemara (Rambam *Sefer Nashim*, *Hilkhot Sota* 2:7).

וְלוֹתְבֵיהּ כְּתוּבָּה דְּמַתְנִיתִין!

The Gemara asks again concerning Abaye's decision to object to Rabba's opinion based on the mishna in *Bava Batra*: **Let him object to** Rabba's opinion **based on** the case of the **marriage contract in the mishna** here (38a). In its latter clause, the mishna states that if a widow waiting for her *yavam* dies, Beit Shammai rule that her marriage contract and other property are divided between her father's heirs and the *yavam*. In that case, the *yavam* has certain possession of that property, and the father's heirs come with an uncertain claim to collect the value of the marriage contract. The fact that Beit Shammai rule that they should divide up the value of the marriage contract between them demonstrates that they hold that one with an uncertain claim can extract property from one who has a definite claim to it.

לָא פְּלִיגִי. וְלָא? וְהָא קָתָנֵי: מֵתָה, מַה יֵּעָשֶׂה בִּכְתוּבָּתָהּ וּבִנְכָסִים הַנִּכְנָסִים וְיוֹצְאִין עִמָּהּ? בֵּית שַׁמַּאי אוֹמְרִים: יַחֲלוֹקוּ יוֹרְשֵׁי הַבַּעַל עִם יוֹרְשֵׁי הָאָב, וּבֵית הִלֵּל אוֹמְרִים: נְכָסִים בְּחֶזְקָתָן!

The Gemara responds: In truth, Beit Shammai **do not disagree** on that point. The Gemara challenges this claim: Do they **not** disagree? **But it is** explicitly **taught** in the mishna that they disagree in that case: If the widow waiting for her *yavam* **died, what should be done with** the money assured to her in **her marriage contract, and with** her **property that enters and leaves** the marriage **with her? Beit Shammai say: The husband's heirs should divide up** the property **together with the father's heirs. And Beit Hillel say:** The **property** retains **its** previous ownership **status.**

הָכִי קָאָמַר: מֵתָה, מַה יֵּעָשֶׂה בִּכְתוּבָּתָהּ, וּשְׁבָקָהּ. נְכָסִים הַנִּכְנָסִים וְהַיּוֹצְאִים עִמָּהּ, בֵּית שַׁמַּאי אוֹמְרִים: יַחֲלוֹקוּ יוֹרְשֵׁי הַבַּעַל עִם יוֹרְשֵׁי הָאָב וּבֵית הִלֵּל אוֹמְרִים נְכָסִים בְּחֶזְקָתָן.

The Gemara answers: **This is what** that mishna **is saying:** If she **died, what should be done with** the money assured to her in **her marriage contract? And** the *tanna* then **left** this question unanswered, and addressed an additional case: What should be done with her **property that enters and leaves** the marriage **with her? Beit Shammai say: The husband's heirs should divide up** the property **together with the father's heirs. And Beit Hillel say:** The **property** retains **its** previous ownership **status.**

אֲמַר רַב אַשִׁי: מַתְנִיתִין נַמִּי דַּיְקָא, דְּקָתָנֵי: יַחֲלוֹקוּ יוֹרְשֵׁי הַבַּעַל עִם יוֹרְשֵׁי הָאָב, וְלֹא קָתָנֵי יוֹרְשֵׁי הָאָב עִם יוֹרְשֵׁי הַבַּעַל – שְׁמַע מִינָּהּ.

Rav Ashi said: The language of **the mishna is also precise** according to this interpretation, **as it teaches:** Beit Shammai say that **the husband's heirs should divide up** the property **together with the father's heirs,** which implies that the father's heirs had de facto possession of the property and the husband's heirs then came and divided that property with them. This is true with regard to her property that enters and leaves the marriage with her. **And** the mishna **does not teach** using the reverse formulation: Beit Shammai say that **the father's heirs should divide up** the property **together with the husband's heirs,** which would imply that the husband's heirs had *de facto* possession of the property; this is true with regard to the payment of the marriage contract. **Conclude from here** that Beit Shammai did not rule what should be done with the payment of the marriage contract, as the Gemara claimed.

אַבַּיֵי אֲמַר: רֵישָׁא דְּנָפְלוּ לָהּ כְּשֶׁהִיא שׁוֹמֶרֶת יָבָם, סֵיפָא דְּנָפְלוּ לָהּ כְּשֶׁהִיא תַּחְתָּיו דְּבַעַל.

The Gemara presents a third resolution to the apparent inconsistency in Beit Shammai's rulings in the mishna: **Abaye said: The first clause** concerns a case in **which property was bequeathed to her when she was** still **a widow waiting for her** *yavam* to perform levirate marriage or *ḥalitza*, and **the latter clause** concerns a case in **which property was bequeathed to her when she was still under,** i.e., married to, **her** first **husband,**[N] before he died.

NOTES

The latter clause concerns a case in which property was bequeathed to her when she was under her husband – סֵיפָא דְּנָפְלוּ לָהּ כְּשֶׁהִיא תַּחְתָּיו דְּבַעַל: Most commentaries claim that the present version of the Gemara's text is the correct version: When she was under her husband. Rav Hai Gaon had another version that states: When she was under him. This allows for Rav Hai Gaon's unique explanation that the reference is not to being married to her husband, but to being under the *yavam*, i.e., being bound to him through a levirate bond. Accordingly, the dispute between Beit Hillel and Beit Shammai is, in Abaye's opinion, whether the *yavam* is entitled to at least a portion of the property that enters and leaves the marriage with the woman, of which the husband has a usufructuary interest. Do the rights of the *yavam* fully parallel those of her husband, in which case he would have rights, or does he have weaker rights, in which case he should not be entitled to them at all?

וקסבר אביי ידו כידה.

And Abaye holds that according to Beit Hillel, with regard to the husband's rights to his wife's property, **his hand is like her hand,** but not any stronger. Accordingly, the *yavam* has a weaker hand in her property than she does, because the rights of a *yavam* are always weaker than those of the husband himself. Therefore, she is considered to be in possession of the property, and when she dies, her heirs, i.e., her father and his heirs, inherit it. However, Beit Shammai assume that the husband's hand is stronger than his wife's hand. Therefore, the hand of the *yavam*, which is weaker than the husband's hand, is nevertheless equally as strong as the hand of the *yevama*, and therefore they rule that if she dies, the *yavam* and her heirs divide up the property.

אמר ליה רבא. אי דנפלי לה כשהיא תחתיו דבעל – דכולי עלמא לא פליגי דידו עדיפא מידה.

Rava[N] **said to him:** I hold that **if** the property **was bequeathed to her when she was** still **under the** first **husband, everyone,** i.e., both Beit Hillel and Beit Shammai, **agrees that his hand is stronger than her hand,** and therefore the hand of the *yavam* will be equally as strong as that of the *yevama*, and if she dies the property will be divided between the two sides.

אלא: אידי ואידי דנפלו לה כשהיא שומרת יבם, רישא – דלא עבד בה מאמר, סיפא – דעבד בה מאמר.

Therefore, Rava presents his own resolution to the apparent inconsistency in Beit Shammai's rulings in the mishna: **Rather, both this** first clause **and that** latter clause concern cases in **which** property **was bequeathed to her when she was a widow waiting for her** ***yavam*****. The first clause** concerns a case in **which the** *yavam* **had not performed a levirate betrothal with her,**[N] and **the latter clause** concerns a case in **which he had performed a levirate betrothal with her.**

וקסבר רבא: מאמר לבית שמאי עושה ודאי ארוסה וספק נשואה, ודאי ארוסה – לדחות בצרה, וספק נשואה – לחלוק בנכסים.

The Gemara explains the rationale behind Rava's explanation: **And Rava holds** that **according to Beit Shammai a levirate betrothal** with a *yevama* **affords** her a status equivalent in some aspects to a woman who is **definitely betrothed and** in other aspects to a woman about whom there is **uncertainty** whether she is **married.** The Gemara elucidates: She is similar to a woman who is **definitely betrothed** with regard **to nullifying** the levirate bond of **her rival wife,** so that the rival wife need not perform levirate marriage or *ḥalitza*. **And** she is similar to a woman about whom there is **uncertainty** whether she is **married** with regard to empowering the *yavam* **to divide up the property** that she attained while she was waiting for her *yavam*.

NOTES

The opinions of Abaye and Rava – שיטות אביי ורבא: The commentaries offer various interpretations of the dispute between Abaye and Rava (see Ramban and Rashba, who elucidate them). According to Rashi, Abaye assumes that Beit Hillel hold that a husband's hand over the possessions is equally as strong as his wife's, while in a case where a *yevama* is still awaiting levirate marriage the hand of the *yavam* is weaker than that of the *yevama*. Therefore, in the latter case, if she dies, any property that fell to her will remain in her and her heirs' possession. Beit Shammai, however, hold that a husband's hand is stronger than the hand of his wife, and therefore the hand of a *yavam* is equally as strong as that of the *yevama*. Accordingly, in the latter case, if she dies, any property that fell to her should be divided up between the heirs of the *yevama* and the *yavam*. According to Rava, all agree that the husband's hand is stronger than that of his wife, and that if property fell to a woman awaiting levirate marriage then the hand of the *yavam* and that of the *yevama* are equally strong, and therefore they divide up the property between them. The dispute between Beit Hillel and Beit Shammai lies in the case where the *yavam* performed levirate betrothal. In that case, Beit Shammai hold that the betrothal affords her a status of a fully betrothed woman.

The Rif holds that according to Abaye, all agree that a husband's hand and his wife's are equally strong. Beit Shammai hold that when a woman happens before her *yavam* for levirate marriage, all of the husband's rights are transferred to the *yavam*, and so upon her death her heirs and the *yavam* or his heirs divide up the property equally between them. Beit Hillel hold that the husband's rights are not transferred to the *yavam*, and therefore the woman's property is awarded to her heirs. Rava claims that all agree that the hand of the *yavam* is actually stronger than that of the woman, and therefore upon her death her property that was bequeathed to her while she was married to her husband will go to his heirs. However, the Gemara here is discussing only property that she received once she was already awaiting levirate marriage.

The Rambam, Razah, and Ramban assume that the dispute between Abaye and Rava relates only to the opinion of Beit Shammai, but according to Beit Hillel the levirate bond does not render her equivalent even to a betrothed woman, and therefore the property is certainly fully in her possession and will pass to her heirs.

The first clause concerns a case in which he had not performed a levirate betrothal with her – רישא דלא עבד בה מאמר: The Ritva explains that the distinction between the cases applies in cases in which property was bequeathed to her before the levirate betrothal was performed. Other commentaries differ, suggesting that in that case, even Beit Shammai would hold that the husband's heirs would have rights to the property. Instead, they explain that the dispute lies only in cases where she died, as then there would indeed be a difference if the levirate betrothal had taken place (*Keren Ora*).

NOTES

And it was stated in the name of Rabbi Yosei, son of Rabbi Ḥanina – וְאִיתְּמַר מִשְּׁמֵיהּ דְּרַבִּי יוֹסֵי בְּרַבִּי חֲנִינָא: The Jerusalem Talmud also records an analysis of the distinction between the first and latter clauses of the mishna. There, Rabbi Yosei explains that the first clause concerns a case where the woman inherited property prior to her happening before her *yavam* for levirate marriage, and the latter clause concerns a case where the property was bequeathed to her after she was already awaiting levirate marriage. However, the *Penei Moshe* suggests modifying the text in a way that renders Rabbi Yosei bar Ḥanina's explanation consistent with Abaye's explanation in the Gemara here. Rabbi Zeira explains there that according to Beit Shammai, the *yavam* is afforded a status similar to that of a man concerning whom it is uncertain whether he is the husband. The *halakha* in such a case is that the property is divided equally between the parties. According to Beit Hillel, the status of the *yavam* vis-à-vis the inheritance is the same as that of any husband. Even so, since even a regular husband does not have full ownership of his wife's property but only a usufructuary interest in it, the *yavam* cannot lay claim to her property either. According to this opinion, Beit Shammai and Beit Hillel dispute what should be done with the value of the marriage contract as well, as is implied by the straightforward reading of the mishna, as opposed to Abaye's interpretation on 38b.

And there is nothing more – וְתוּ לָא מִידֵּי: Other commentaries explain that the Gemara's intention is to say that the inference from the formulation of the mishna is very convincing and no objection can be raised against it (Rabbi Avraham min HaHar).

HALAKHA

If he consummated the levirate marriage with her then her legal status is that of his wife in every sense – כְּנָסָהּ הֲרֵי הִיא כְּאִשְׁתּוֹ לְכָל דָּבָר: Once the *yavam* consummates the levirate marriage with his *yevama*, she is considered to be his wife in every sense. Therefore, the only way to divorce her is to by means of a bill of divorce, and following the divorce he is permitted to remarry her (Rambam *Sefer Nashim, Hilkhot Yibbum* 1:15; *Shulḥan Arukh, Even HaEzer* 168:1).

אִיתְּמַר מִשְּׁמֵיהּ דְּרַבִּי אֶלְעָזָר כְּוָותֵיהּ דְּרָבָא וְאִיתְּמַר מִשְּׁמֵיהּ דְּרַבִּי יוֹסֵי בְּרַבִּי חֲנִינָא כְּוָותֵיהּ דְּאַבָּיֵי.

The Gemara notes: An interpretation of the mishna **was stated in the name of Rabbi Elazar** that is **in accordance with** the opinion **of Rava. And** an interpretation of the mishna **was stated in the name of Rabbi Yosei, son of Rabbi Ḥanina**[N] that is **in accordance with** the opinion **of Abaye.**

וּמִי אָמַר רַבִּי אֶלְעָזָר הָכִי? וְהָא אָמַר רַבִּי אֶלְעָזָר: מַאֲמָר לְבֵית שַׁמַּאי אֵינָהּ קוֹנָה אֶלָּא לִדְחוֹת צָרָה בִּלְבָד!

The Gemara objects: **And did Rabbi Elazar** actually **state this** interpretation that is in accordance with the opinion of Rava? **But didn't Rabbi Elazar say: According to Beit Shammai a levirate betrothal acquires** the *yevama* **only** with regard **to nullifying** the levirate bond of **a rival wife** so that she need not perform levirate marriage or *ḥalitza*? This implies that it does not acquire her with regard to enabling the *yavam* to inherit from her. This, then, stands in contrast to Rava's interpretation.

אֵיפוֹךְ. וְאִי בָּעֵית אֵימָא: לְעוֹלָם לָא תֵּיפוֹךְ, אָמַר לָךְ רַבִּי אֶלְעָזָר: כִּי אָמְרִי אֲנָא – דְּלָא סַגִּי לַהּ בְּגֵט, אֶלָּא דְּבָעֵי נָמֵי חֲלִיצָה, לַחֲלוֹק בִּנְכָסִים דְּלָא קָנֵי – מִי אֲמַרִי?

The Gemara offers two possible solutions: **Reverse** the opinions, so that Rabbi Elazar is in accordance with Abaye, and Rabbi Yosei, son of Rabbi Ḥanina, is in accordance with Rava. **And if you wish, say** instead: **Actually, do not reverse** the opinions, since Rabbi Elazar can be understood to be in accordance with the opinion of Rava, as **Rabbi Elazar** could have **said to you: When I said** the statement that implies that a levirate betrothal acquires in a very limited sense, the intention was only that its acquisition is limited in **that** giving her **a bill of divorce** is still **insufficient for her** in order to release her from the levirate bond; **rather, she also needs** to perform *ḥalitza.* But to suggest **that he does not acquire** her with regard **to dividing up** the **property** she attained, **did I say that?** Certainly not, as in fact a levirate betrothal acquires her to that extent as well, as Rava assumes.

אָמַר רַב פַּפָּא: דַּיְיקָא דְּמַתְנִיתִין כְּוָותֵיהּ דְּאַבָּיֵי. וְאַף עַל גַּב דְּקַשְׁיָא ״מֵתָה״,

Rav Pappa said: The precise formulation of the mishna is in accordance with the opinion of **Abaye, even though** according to his opinion **it is difficult** that the mishna discusses the case in which **she died.**

דְּקָתָנֵי: ״נְכָסִים הַנִּכְנָסִים וְיוֹצְאִים עִמָּהּ״, מַאי נִכְנָסִין וּמַאי יוֹצְאִין? לָאו נִכְנָסִין: לִרְשׁוּת הַבַּעַל, וְיוֹצְאִים: מֵרְשׁוּת הַבַּעַל לִרְשׁוּת הָאָב,

The Gemara explains Rav Pappa's statement: The precise formulation of the mishna is in accordance with the opinion of Abaye, **as it teaches:** Her **property that enters and leaves** the marriage **with her. What** is the meaning of: **That enters, and what** is the meaning of: **That leaves? Is it not: That enters into the domain of the husband and leaves the domain of the husband** when she dies, and then enters **into the domain of the father?** Interpreted in this way, the mishna explicitly considers the period in which she was still married to her first husband, and likewise, the case in which she came into the possession of property should be understood as referring to a case in which she did so while still married. This is consonant with Abaye's interpretation, but not with Rava's.

וְאַף עַל גַּב דְּקַשְׁיָא מֵתָה, אַדְּמִפַּלְגִי בְּגוּפָהּ וּלְאַחַר מִיתָה לִפְלְגוּ בְּחַיֶּיהָ וּלְפֵירוֹת.

And when Rav Pappa said: **Even though** according to his opinion **it is difficult** that the mishna discusses the case in which **she died,** he meant as follows: **Instead of disputing** who has the rights to the property **itself,** which necessitates considering the case **after** her **death, let** Beit Hillel and Beit Shammai **dispute** the more immediate case **when she is** still **alive and** dispute who has the rights to the use and **produce** of the property.

וְתוּ לָא מִידֵּי.

The Gemara concludes: **And there is nothing more**[N] to say concerning this matter, i.e., as Rav Pappa noted, while it is undeniable that the mishna's formulation supports Abaye's interpretation, it is equally true that the case discussed by the mishna would appear to challenge his interpretation.

״כְּנָסָהּ הֲרֵי הִיא״ כו׳. לְמַאי הִלְכְתָא? אָמַר רַבִּי יוֹסֵי בַּר חֲנִינָא: לוֹמַר שֶׁמְּגָרְשָׁהּ בְּגֵט וּמַחֲזִירָהּ.

§ The mishna states: If the *yavam* **consummated the levirate marriage with her, then** her legal status is that of his wife in every sense.[H] The Gemara asks: **With regard to what *halakha*** is this said? **Rabbi Yosei bar Ḥanina said:** It is **to say that** once they have consummated the levirate marriage, the only way to legally dissolve the marriage is if **he divorces her with a bill of divorce,** but *ḥalitza* is of no avail, **and** after divorcing her, he is permitted to **take her back** to be his wife, as the prohibition against engaging in relations with one's brother's wife does not apply to her.

מגרשה בגט פשיטא! סלקא דעתך אמינא: הואיל וכתיב "ולקחה לו לאשה ויבמה" אמר רחמנא, ועדיין יבומי הראשון עליה. בחליצה – אין, בגט – לא, קא משמע לן.

The Gemara examines the first clause of Rabbi Yosei bar Ḥanina's statement: **Isn't it obvious** that to sever his relationship with her, **he divorces her with a bill of divorce?** The Gemara explains: It is necessary to teach this because **it could enter your mind to say** that **since it is written: "And take her to him to be his wife and consummate the levirate marriage with her"** (Deuteronomy 25:5), continuing to refer to the marriage as a levirate marriage even after the verse has stated that he took her as a wife, one might claim **the Merciful One is saying** that the **original levirate** bond **continues to be upon her,** and therefore, **with *ḥalitza*, yes,** they can sever the relationship, but **with a bill of divorce, no,** the relationship would not be severed. Therefore, the mishna **teaches us** that she is considered to be his wife to the extent that the relationship can be severed with a bill of divorce alone.

"מחזירה". פשיטא! סלקא דעתך אמינא: מצוה דרמיא רחמנא עליה עבדה. השתא תיקום עליה באיסור אשת אח – קא משמע לן

The Gemara examines the second clause: **Isn't it obvious** that after divorcing her, he is permitted to **take her back** to be his wife? The Gemara explains: It is necessary to teach this because **it could enter your mind to say** that the **mitzva that the Merciful One imposes upon him, he has performed,** and therefore **now** that there is no longer any mitzva to marry her, **she should** once again **be established** as forbidden **to him by the prohibition** against engaging in relations with one's **brother's wife.** To dispel this notion, the mishna **teaches us** that she is considered to be his wife to the extent that there is no longer any prohibition against remarrying her.

ואימא הכי נמי! אמר קרא: "ולקחה לו לאשה", כיון שלקחה – הרי היא כאשתו לכל דבר.

The Gemara challenges this ruling: **But** why not **say** that this **is indeed so,** that she should be forbidden to him? The Gemara explains: **The verse states: "And take her to him to be his wife"** (Deuteronomy 25:5), indicating that **once he has taken her,** her legal status is **that of his wife in every sense.**

"ובלבד שתהא כתובתה" כו'. מאי טעמא? אשה הקנו לו מן השמים.

§ The mishna states: The **only** exception to this is **that** her **marriage contract will** still **be** payable from the property of her first husband and not from the property of the *yavam*. The Gemara asks: **What is the reason** for this? The Gemara explains: **A wife was acquired to him by Heaven,** and since he did not choose her as a wife, he did not obligate himself to pay her marriage contract.

ואי לית לה מן הראשון – התקינו לה משני, כדי שלא תהא קלה בעיניו להוציאה.

The Gemara qualifies the mishna's ruling: **And if she has no** ability to collect her marriage contract **from the first** husband,[H] since he died without leaving any property with which to pay it, the Sages **instituted an ordinance for her** benefit that she must receive a new marriage contract **from** her **second** husband, i.e., the *yavam*. This was instituted **so that she will not be demeaned in his eyes such that** he will easily **divorce her,** since doing so would incur a financial burden on his part.

מתני׳ מצוה בגדול לייבם, לא רצה – מהלכין על כל האחין, לא רצו – חוזרין אצל גדול, ואומרים לו: עליך מצוה, או חלוץ או ייבם.

MISHNA The **mitzva** of levirate marriage **is for the eldest** of the brothers **to consummate the levirate marriage.**[H] If the eldest **does not want** to do so,[H] the court **goes to each of the** other **brothers** and requires them to do so. **If they do not want** to do so, the court **returns to** the **eldest** brother **and says to him:** The **mitzva is** incumbent **upon you; either perform *ḥalitza* or consummate the levirate marriage.**

תלה בקטן עד שיגדיל. או בגדול עד שיבא ממדינת הים, או חרש או שוטה – אין שומעין לו, אלא אומרים לו: עליך מצוה, או חלוץ או ייבם.

If a brother **made** his decision **dependent** upon the possibility that one of his other brothers will eventually consummate the levirate marriage, saying that he will do so only if they do not, then whether he makes it dependent **upon** a brother who is currently **a minor,**[H] meaning that the *yevama* should wait **until he matures, or upon** his **eldest brother,** who is not currently present, meaning the *yevama* should wait **until he comes from overseas, or** upon a brother who is **a deaf-mute or an imbecile,**[N] as perhaps they will recover from their disability, the court **does not listen to him; rather,** the judges of the court **say to him:** The **mitzva is** incumbent **upon you; either perform *ḥalitza* or consummate the levirate marriage.**

HALAKHA

And if she has no ability to collect her marriage contract from the first husband – ואי לית לה מן הראשון: If the deceased brother had no property, the *yavam* must give the *yevama* a marriage contract for one hundred dinars payable from his property, so that she will not be demeaned in his eyes such that he will easily divorce her (Rambam *Sefer Nashim, Hilkhot Ishut* 22:14; *Shulḥan Arukh, Even HaEzer* 168:9, and in the comment of Rema).

The mitzva is for the eldest to consummate the levirate marriage – מצוה בגדול לייבם: The mitzva of levirate marriage is for the eldest of the brothers to consummate the levirate marriage or perform *ḥalitza*. If he does not wish to do so or is incapable of doing so (Rivash), then the other brothers, starting with the next oldest and proceeding in descending order of age, are required to do so. If they refuse, the eldest brother is again required to either consummate the levirate marriage or perform *ḥalitza* (Rambam *Sefer Nashim, Hilkhot Yibbum* 2:6, 7; *Shulḥan Arukh, Even HaEzer* 161:4).

The eldest does not want to consummate the levirate marriage – לא רצה לייבם: If the eldest brother refuses to either consummate the levirate marriage or perform *ḥalitza*, he is forced to perform *ḥalitza*. This is true even though there is a younger brother who could do so, and even if the eldest brother had taken an oath not to do so, because since there is a mitzva incumbent upon him, the oath does not take effect (Rema). Nevertheless, to avoid a situation where it would appear as though he is violating his oath, he is first to be released from his oath (Rivash; Rambam *Sefer Nashim, Hilkhot Yibbum* 2:7; *Shulḥan Arukh, Even HaEzer* 161:4).

He made it dependent upon a minor – תלה בקטן: If a brother does not wish to consummate the levirate marriage or perform *ḥalitza* immediately, but instead says that he wishes to wait for a brother who is a minor to mature, or for a brother who is a deaf-mute to heal, or for an older brother to return from overseas, this is not accepted, and he must consummate the levirate marriage with her or perform *ḥalitza* immediately (Rambam *Sefer Nashim, Hilkhot Yibbum* 2:8–9; *Shulḥan Arukh, Even HaEzer* 161:5).

NOTES

A deaf-mute or an imbecile – או חרש או שוטה: Rambam, in his Commentary on the Mishna, along with most of the other commentaries, explains that the intention here is that the eldest brother wished to wait for the possibility that a brother who is a deaf-mute or imbecile will be healed. It would appear, however, that *Tosafot* understand that his request is that the deaf-mute or imbecile should consummate the levirate marriage in their current disabled state. Accordingly, *Tosafot* assume that a levirate marriage with such an individual is valid. Nevertheless, a *yevama* is never compelled to enter into levirate marriage in such a case.

גמ׳ אִיתְּמַר, בִּיאַת קָטָן וַחֲלִיצַת גָּדוֹל, פְּלִיגִי בָּהּ רַבִּי יוֹחָנָן וְרַבִּי יְהוֹשֻׁעַ בֶּן לֵוִי, חַד אֲמַר: בִּיאַת קָטָן עֲדִיפָא, וְחַד אֲמַר: חֲלִיצַת גָּדוֹל עֲדִיפָא.

GEMARA An amoraic dispute **was stated: Rabbi Yoḥanan and Rabbi Yehoshua ben Levi disagree with regard to** a case in which there is the choice between **consummation of** the levirate marriage by **a younger** brother [*katan*][N] **or** *ḥalitza* performed **by the eldest** brother. **One said:** The **consummation of** the levirate marriage by **a younger** brother **is preferable, and the other one said:** *Ḥalitza* performed by the **eldest** brother **is preferable.**[H]

מַאן דְּאָמַר בִּיאַת קָטָן עֲדִיפָא – דְּהָא מִצְוָה בְּיִיבּוּם, וּמַאן דְּאָמַר חֲלִיצַת גָּדוֹל עֲדִיפָא – בִּמְקוֹם גָּדוֹל – בִּיאַת קָטָן לָאו כְּלוּם הִיא.

The Gemara explains: With regard to **the one who said** that **consummation of** the levirate marriage by **a younger** brother **is preferable,** this is due to the fact **that the mitzva** of levirate marriage **is through** the actual **consummation of the levirate marriage,** and therefore preference is always given to consummation over the performance of *ḥalitza*. **And the one who said *ḥalitza*** performed **by** the **eldest** brother **is preferable,** this is because **in the presence of** the **eldest** brother, the **consummation of** the levirate marriage by **a younger** brother **is** considered **nothing.**

תְּנַן: לֹא רָצָה – מַחֲזִירִין עַל כָּל הָאַחִין. מַאי לָאו: לֹא רָצָה לְיַיבֵּם אֶלָּא לַחֲלוֹץ, וְקָתָנֵי: מְהַלְּכִין אֵצֶל הָאַחִין, שְׁמַע מִינָּהּ בִּיאַת קָטָן עֲדִיפָא –

The Gemara suggests proof for the first opinion: **We learned** in the mishna: If the eldest **does not want** to consummate the levirate marriage, the court **goes to each of the** other **brothers** and requires them to do so. The Gemara suggests: **What, is it not that he does not want to consummate the levirate marriage but** is willing **to perform *ḥalitza*? And** yet the mishna **teaches:** The court **goes to each of the** other **brothers** and requires them to consummate the levirate marriage. If so, **conclude from here** that the **consummation** of the levirate marriage by **a younger** brother **is preferable.**

לָא, לֹא רָצָה לַחֲלוֹץ וְלֹא לְיַיבֵּם, דִּכְוָותָהּ גַּבֵּי הָאַחִין לֹא רָצוּ – לֹא לַחֲלוֹץ וְלֹא לְיַיבֵּם, אַמַּאי חוֹזְרִים אֵצֶל הַגָּדוֹל, לְמִיכְפְּיֵיהּ – לִכְפְּיֵיהּ לְדִידְהוּ! כֵּיוָן דְּמִצְוָה עֲלֵיהּ דִּידֵיהּ רַמְיָא – לְדִידֵיהּ כָּיְיפִינַן.

The Gemara rejects the proof: **No,** the mishna might concern a case where the eldest **does not want** either **to perform *ḥalitza* or to consummate the levirate marriage,** and it is only because he is unwilling to do either that the other brothers are considered. The Gemara asks: If this is so, then **in the corresponding situation** in the mishna in which **the brothers do not want** to do so, the case must be that they do not want either **to perform *ḥalitza* or to consummate the levirate marriage.** But if so, **why should** the court invest the extra effort to **return to the eldest** brother[N] **to force him** to fulfill his duty? **Let** the court **force** the other brothers to fulfill their duty. The Gemara responds: **Since the mitzva is incumbent upon** the eldest brother *ab initio*, **it is he who is forced.**

תְּנַן: תָּלָה בְּקָטָן עַד שֶׁיַּגְדִּיל – אֵין שׁוֹמְעִין לוֹ. וְאִי בִּיאַת קָטָן עֲדִיפָא, אַמַּאי אֵין שׁוֹמְעִין לוֹ? נִינְטַר דִּלְמָא גָּדֵיל וּמְיַיבֵּם!

The Gemara suggests another proof: **We learned** in the mishna: If a brother makes his decision **dependent upon** a brother who is currently **a minor,** the court **does not listen to him.** The Gemara suggests: **And if** the **consummation of** the levirate marriage by **a minor is preferable, why shouldn't** the court **listen to him? Let** the court **wait,** as **perhaps he will mature and consummate the levirate marriage.** Rather, it would appear that the mishna assumes that consummation by a younger brother is not preferable.

וְלִיטַעֲמִיךְ, וּבְגָדוֹל עַד שֶׁיָּבֹא מִמְּדִינַת הַיָּם אֵין שׁוֹמְעִין לוֹ, אַמַּאי? נִינְטַר, דִּלְמָא אָתֵי וְחָלֵיץ! אֶלָּא: כָּל שֶׁהוּיֵי מִצְוָה לָא מַשְׁהִינַן.

The Gemara responds: **But** even **according to your reasoning** that *ḥalitza* performed by an elder brother is preferable, what about the next case in the mishna, where a brother asks to wait **until the eldest brother comes from overseas?** In that case, as well, the mishna rules: **They do not listen to him;** but **why shouldn't** they listen to him? **Let** the court **wait,** as **perhaps he will come and** at the very least **perform *ḥalitza*.**[N] **Rather,** it is clear that the reason for the mishna's ruling is that **we do not delay the performance of any mitzva;**[N] therefore, if one of the brothers is currently unable to perform the mitzva, he is not considered at all. Consequently, no proof can be derived from the mishna.

NOTES

The consummation of a younger brother [*katan*] – בִּיאַת קָטָן: The Gemara here uses the term *katan*, which normally refers to a minor. However, Rashi explains that in this case the reference is not to a minor but to a younger brother who is already an adult and therefore fully capable of consummating the marriage according to all opinions. Others explain that the reference here is to an actual minor, but one who is above nine years of age, from which point his act of sexual intercourse has legal significance (Rivan; Meiri; see Rashba and Ritva).

Why should they return to the eldest brother – אַמַּאי חוֹזְרִין אֵצֶל הַגָּדוֹל: Ostensibly, it would seem that the very fact that the younger brothers are considered demonstrates that the consummation of a younger brother is preferable to the *ḥalitza* of the eldest, as if that were not the case, why wouldn't the eldest brother immediately be forced to perform *ḥalitza*? The reason that a proof cannot be drawn from here is because compulsion is always considered a last resort. Therefore, even if the *ḥalitza* of the eldest brother is preferable to the consummation of a younger brother, the consummation of a younger brother is nevertheless preferable to the forced *ḥalitza* of the eldest brother (*Yosef Lekaḥ*).

Perhaps he will come and perform *ḥalitza* – דִּלְמָא אָתֵי וְחָלֵיץ: The Gemara mentions the possibility that the eldest brother might perform *ḥalitza* to emphasize that the eldest brother is preferred even if he does not intend to consummate the marriage (Rashba; Meiri; see *Haggahot Rav Yeshaya Pick-Berlin*).

We do not delay the performance of any mitzva – כָּל שֶׁהוּיֵי מִצְוָה לָא מַשְׁהִינַן: The *Ḥayyei Adam* cites the *Terumat HaDeshen*, who infers from the mishna here that one may delay the performance of a mitzva if doing so will enable one to perform it in its optimal manner later. This is derived from the fact that the mishna states only that one does not wait for the older brother to return from overseas in order to perform levirate marriage. By implication, if he were in the same country but merely not available immediately, then one should wait. Apparently, this is because the short delay is acceptable in order to perform a mitzva in its optimal manner. However, the *Sefer Ḥasidim* cites the verse: "I made haste and did not delay to observe Your commandments" (Psalms 119:60), and interprets it to mean that one should not delay performing a mitzva even if it could be performed in a more complete manner later. The *Ḥayyei Adam* notes that this is also implied by the straightforward reading of the Gemara, which states without qualifications that one should not delay the performance of a mitzva.

HALAKHA

The consummation of a younger brother and the *ḥalitza* of the eldest brother – בִּיאַת קָטָן וַחֲלִיצַת גָּדוֹל: If the eldest brother does not wish to consummate the levirate marriage but only to perform *ḥalitza*, and a younger brother is willing to consummate the levirate marriage, then the consummation of the younger brother is preferable. Whenever *ḥalitza* is performed, preference is given to the eldest brother. This is the case today, as according to many opinions levirate marriage is never performed nowadays. Even those authorities who hold that levirate marriage is still performed agree that if the *yevama* does not wish to enter into levirate marriage then *ḥalitza* is performed, giving preference to the eldest brother (Rema, citing *Terumat HaDeshen*; *Shulḥan Arukh*, *Even HaEzer* 161:6).

אִית דְּאָמְרִי: בְּבִיאָה – כּוּלֵּי עָלְמָא לָא פְּלִיגִי דְּבִיאַת קָטָן עֲדִיפָא. כִּי פְּלִיגִי – בַּחֲלִיצַת קָטָן,

There are those **who say** that the dispute is more limited: **When** there is the possibility of **consummating** the levirate marriage, **everyone agrees that** the **consummation of** the levirate marriage by **a younger** brother **is preferable** to the *ḥalitza* of the eldest brother. **When they disagree** it is **with regard to the** significance of the ***ḥalitza* of a younger** brother.

וְהָכִי אִיתְּמַר: חֲלִיצַת קָטָן וַחֲלִיצַת גָּדוֹל – פְּלִיגִי בָּהּ רַבִּי יוֹחָנָן וְרַבִּי יְהוֹשֻׁעַ בֶּן לֵוִי. חַד אֲמַר: חֲלִיצַת גָּדוֹל עֲדִיפָא, וְחַד אֲמַר: כִּי הֲדָדֵי נִינְהוּ.

And this is how the dispute **was stated: Rabbi Yoḥanan and Rabbi Yehoshua ben Levi disagree with regard to** a case in which there is choice between the ***ḥalitza* of a younger** brother **or** the ***ḥalitza*** of the **eldest** brother. **One said:** The ***ḥalitza*** **of the eldest** brother **is preferable.**[H] **And the other one said:** The two options **are equivalent.**

מַאן דְּאָמַר חֲלִיצַת גָּדוֹל עֲדִיפָא – דְּהָא מִצְוָה בְּגָדוֹל. וְאִידַּךְ: כִּי אָמְרִינַן מִצְוָה בְּגָדוֹל – לְעִנְיַן יִבּוּם, אֲבָל לְעִנְיַן חֲלִיצָה – כַּהֲדָדֵי נִינְהוּ.

The Gemara explains: With regard to **the one who said** that the ***ḥalitza*** **of the eldest** brother **is preferable,** this is due to the fact **that** the **mitzva** of levirate marriage and *ḥalitza* **is** incumbent **upon** the **eldest** brother. **And the other** Sage would respond to this claim by saying that **when we say** that the **mitzva is** incumbent **upon** the **eldest** brother, that is only **with regard to** the consummation of the **levirate marriage; however, with regard to** performing ***ḥalitza,*** all the brothers **are equivalent.**

תְּנַן: לֹא רָצוּ – חוֹזְרִין אֵצֶל גָּדוֹל, מַאי לָאו: לֹא רָצוּ לְיַיבֵּם אֶלָּא לַחֲלוֹץ, וְקָתָנֵי חוֹזְרִין אֵצֶל גָּדוֹל, וּשְׁמַע מִינַּהּ: חֲלִיצַת גָּדוֹל עֲדִיפָא!

The Gemara suggests a proof for the first opinion: **We learned** in the mishna: If the younger brothers **do not want** to consummate the levirate marriage, the court **returns to** the **eldest** brother and demands that he at least perform *ḥalitza*. The Gemara suggests: **What, is it not** that the other brothers **did not want to consummate the levirate marriage but** are willing **to perform *ḥalitza*? And** yet the mishna **teaches:** The court **returns to** the **eldest** brother so that he can perform *ḥalitza*. If so, **conclude from here** that the ***ḥalitza*** of the **eldest** brother **is preferable.**

לָא, לֹא רָצוּ – לֹא לַחֲלוֹץ וְלֹא לְיַיבֵּם. דִּכְוָותֵיהּ גַּבֵּי גָּדוֹל – לֹא רָצָה לֹא לַחֲלוֹץ וְלֹא לְיַיבֵּם, אֶלָּא אַמַּאי חוֹזְרִין אֵצֶל גָּדוֹל, לְמִכְפְּיֵיהּ? לִכְפַּיְיהוּ לְדִידְהוּ! כֵּיוָן דְּמִצְוָה עֲלֵיהּ דִּידֵיהּ רַמְיָא – לְדִידֵיהּ כָּיְיפִינַן.

The Gemara rejects the proof: **No,** the mishna might concern a case where the other brothers **did not want** either **to perform *ḥalitza* or to consummate the levirate marriage,** and it is only because they are unwilling to do either that the court returns to the eldest brother. The Gemara asks: If this is so, then **in the corresponding** situation in which the mishna states: The **eldest** brother **does not want** to do so, the case must be that he does not want either **to perform *ḥalitza* or to consummate the levirate marriage. But** if so, when the younger brothers also refuse, **why should** the court invest the extra effort to **return to the eldest** brother **to force him** to fulfill his duty? **Let** the court **force them,** i.e., the younger brothers, to fulfill their duty. The Gemara responds: **Since the mitzva is incumbent upon** the eldest brother *ab initio*, **it is he who is forced.**

תָּא שְׁמַע: תָּלָה בְּגָדוֹל עַד שֶׁיָּבֹא מִמְּדִינַת הַיָּם – אֵין שׁוֹמְעִין לוֹ. וְאִי סָלְקָא דַּעְתָּךְ: חֲלִיצַת גָּדוֹל עֲדִיפָא, אַמַּאי אֵין שׁוֹמְעִין לוֹ? נִינְטַר דִּלְמָא אָתֵי וְחָלֵיץ!

Come and hear another proof from the mishna: If a younger brother makes his decision **dependent upon** the **eldest brother,** who is currently unavailable, suggesting that the *yevama* wait **until he comes from overseas,** the court **does not listen to him. And if it enters your mind** to suggest that the ***ḥalitza*** of the **eldest** brother **is preferable, why doesn't** the court **listen to him? Let** the court **wait,** as **perhaps he will come and perform *ḥalitza*.** Rather, it would appear that the mishna assumes that the with regard to performing *ḥalitza*, all the brothers are equivalent.

HALAKHA

***Ḥalitza* of a younger brother and the eldest brother – חֲלִיצַת קָטָן וְגָדוֹל:** If the brothers are willing only to perform *ḥalitza* but not to consummate the levirate marriage, then it is preferable for the *ḥalitza* to be performed by the eldest brother. This is especially true nowadays, when *ḥalitza* takes precedence over consummating the levirate marriage. Even according to the opinions that the consummation of the levirate marriage takes precedence, if the *yevama* wishes to perform *ḥalitza* then *ḥalitza* is preferred (Rema, citing *Terumat HaDeshen*; *Shulḥan Arukh, Even HaEzer* 161:6).

ולטעמיך, בקטן עד שיגדיל אין שומעין לו, אמאי? נינטר דלמא גדיל ומייבם, (אי נמי אתי איהו ומייבמה). אלא כל שהויי מצוה לא שהינן.

The Gemara challenges this: **But** even **according to your reasoning,** you certainly agree that the possibility of consummating the levirate marriage is always preferable. If so, what about the previous case in the mishna, where the eldest brother asks to wait **until** his brother who is **a minor will mature?** In that case as well the mishna rules: The court **does not listen to him;** but **why shouldn't** the court **listen to him? Let** the court **wait,** as **perhaps he will come and consummate the levirate marriage. Alternatively,** in the case where the eldest brother is overseas, let the court wait, as perhaps **he will come and consummate the levirate marriage with her. Rather,** it is clear that the reason for the mishna's ruling is that **we do not delay the performance of a mitzva.** Therefore, if one of the brothers is currently unable to perform the mitzva, he is not considered at all. Consequently, no proof can be derived from the mishna.

תנן התם: מצות יבום קודמת למצות חליצה – בראשונה שהיו מתכוונין לשם מצוה, עכשיו שאין מתכוונין לשם מצוה – אמרו: מצות חליצה קודמת למצות יבום.

§ **We learned** in a mishna **there** (*Bekhorot* 13a): The **mitzva of** consummating the **levirate marriage takes precedence over** the **mitzva of** performing *ḥalitza*;[H] this applied **initially, when** *yevamin* **would have intent for the sake of** fulfilling **the mitzva. Now, that they do not have intent for the sake of** fulfilling **the mitzva,** the Sages **say:** The **mitzva of** performing *ḥalitza* **takes precedence over** the **mitzva of** consummating the **levirate marriage.**

אמר רב: אין כופין: כי אתו לקמיה דרב אמר להו: אי בעית – חלוץ, אי בעית – ייבם, בדידך תלא רחמנא, "ואם לא יחפוץ האיש", הא אם חפץ – אי בעי חליץ, אי בעי ייבם.

Rav said: Nevertheless, the court **does not force**[N] a *yavam* to perform *ḥalitza*, and if he wishes it is still permitted to consummate the levirate marriage. The Gemara relates: **When a** *yavam* and a *yevama* **would come before Rav, he would say to them: If you want, perform** ***ḥalitza*****,** and **if you want, consummate the levirate marriage, as the Merciful One makes** the matter **dependent upon your** will, as it is stated: **"And if the man does not wish** to take his *yevama*" (Deuteronomy 25:7) then he should perform *ḥalitza*. This implies that the Torah requires him to perform *ḥalitza* only if he does not wish to consummate the levirate marriage, **but if he wishes** to do so, then the matter is dependent upon him, and **if he wants, he performs** ***ḥalitza*****,** or **if he wants, he consummates the levirate marriage.**

ואף רב יהודה סבר אין כופין. מדאתקין רב יהודה בגיטא דחליצה: איך פלונית בת פלוני אקריבת ית פלוני יבמה קדמנא לבי דינא, ואשתמודעינהו דאחוה דמיתנא מאבא ניהו, ואמרי ליה: אי צבית ליבם – יבם, ואי לא – איטלע לה רגליך דימינא.

The Gemara notes: **And even Rav Yehuda holds** that the court **does not force** a *yavam* to perform *ḥalitza* if he wishes to consummate the levirate marriage. This is apparent **from** the fact **that Rav Yehuda enacted** in his court that the following formulation should be used **in the bill of** ***ḥalitza*****:**[H] **That so-and-so, daughter of so-and-so, brought so-and-so, her** ***yavam*****, before the court; and we identified him, that he was** indeed **the paternal brother of the deceased, and we said to him: If you desire to consummate the levirate marriage,** then **consummate the levirate marriage, and if not, extend your right foot toward** your *yevama* so that she may perform *ḥalitza* by removing your shoe.[B]

HALAKHA

Levirate marriage and ***ḥalitza*** **– יבום וחליצה:** The mitzva to consummate levirate marriage takes precedence over the mitzva of performing *ḥalitza* (Rif; Rambam). This is in accordance with the opinion of the Rabbis and the statement of Rami bar Ḥama. Others say that the mitzva of performing *ḥalitza* takes precedence (Rashi). This is in accordance with the opinion of Abba Shaul and the assumption of Rav Naḥman bar Yitzḥak. According to the first opinion, in a case where the *yavam* wishes to consummate the levirate marriage and the *yevama* does not, if she does not have a sufficiently valid reason to refuse, then she is categorized as rebellious and does not receive the money allotted to her in her marriage contract. According to the second opinion, she is not categorized as rebellious for refusing to consummate the levirate marriage, and so when she performs *ḥalitza* she receives the payment of her marriage contract. According to this opinion, although the *yavam* is not forced to perform *ḥalitza*, he can be tricked into doing so (*Tur*, citing Rabbeinu Tam and Rosh). If the *yavam* falls into the category of one who, were he to be married, would be forced to divorce his wife, then he is also forced to perform *ḥalitza* (*Tur*, citing *Smag*).

Some say that even if both the *yavam* and the *yevama* wish to consummate the levirate marriage, they are not permitted to do so unless it is clear that they are doing so for the sake of the fulfilling the mitzva (*Tur*, citing Rabbeinu Tam; see *Yam shel Shlomo*). The custom is not to force *ḥalitza* unless the *yavam* refuses both to consummate the levirate marriage and to perform *ḥalitza* (Maharam Padua). In recent generations, especially in Ashkenazic communities, the custom is not to allow levirate marriage under any circumstances, although there have been some questionable exceptions to this principle. This has also become the accepted practice in Eretz Yisrael (Rambam *Sefer Nashim, Hilkhot Yibbum VaḤalitza* 1:2, 3:7; *Shulḥan Arukh, Even HaEzer* 165:1).

Bill of ***ḥalitza*** **– גט חליצה:** Although there is no requirement for the *ḥalitza* to be documented in writing, it was nevertheless customary for the court to grant the *yevama* a document as proof that she performed *ḥalitza* and that she is now permitted to marry a man from the general public. There was a standard formulation for this document, as is clear from the statements of Rav Yehuda and Rabbi Ḥiyya bar Avya. In some places it is not customary to write a bill of *ḥalitza*; however the better custom is to write one (*Be'er Heitev*; Rambam *Sefer Nashim, Hilkhot Yibbum* 4:30; *Tur, Even HaEzer* 169; *Shulḥan Arukh, Even HaEzer* 169:56).

BACKGROUND

The order of ***ḥalitza*** **– סדר חליצה:** A mishna in Chapter Twelve describes the order of the *ḥalitza* ceremony and stresses that the ceremony was performed in Hebrew. The bill of *ḥalitza* mentioned here is a later addition, written in Aramaic and designed to enable the woman to later prove that she has performed the mitzva of *ḥalitza* and is therefore allowed to remarry. The Rif formulated a complete version of the bill of *ḥalitza*, including the details mentioned, e.g., the requirement that the witnesses see the woman's saliva and that they recognize both the woman as the wife of the deceased and the man as his brother. The Rif also adds which phrases from the Torah must be said by the man and which by the woman and by the court, as well as describing the type of shoe required for the performance of *ḥalitza*.

NOTES

The court does not force – אין כופין: This statement of Rav can be understood in different ways. Rashi and most of the other commentaries understand it to mean that a *yavam* is not to be forced to perform *ḥalitza* if he wishes to consummate the levirate marriage, and that this is true even if one asserts that the mitzva of *ḥalitza* takes precedence. Rabbeinu Ḥananel and Rabbeinu Tam explain Rav's statement in the opposite manner: The *yavam* will not be forced to consummate the levirate marriage, even in cases where one assumes his motives will be pure.

It is similarly unclear to whom Rav's statement applies; who is not to be forced? Rashi explains that where both the *yavam* and the *yevama* are willing to consummate the levirate marriage, they cannot be forced to perform *ḥalitza* even if *ḥalitza* is considered preferable. Others explain that Rav was referring only to the *yavam*, meaning that he cannot be forced to consummate the levirate marriage; alternatively he was referring only to the *yevama*, meaning that she is never forced to consummate the levirate marriage.

The *Gilyonei HaShas* cites a geonic responsum that explains that the dispute with regard to compulsion is dependent upon the broader issue as to whether or not *ḥalitza* is valid if not agreed to by both parties. If the *ḥalitza* requires mutual consent, then there can be no forced *ḥalitza*. According to that opinion, the opinions that do allow for a forced *ḥalitza* must be explained as one of the cases in which the Sages retroactively annulled the original marriage, consequently obviating any need for a valid *ḥalitza*. Nevertheless, an act of *ḥalitza* is still required because otherwise it would be appear as though the *yevama* had been released from her levirate bonds without performing an act that would release her.

וְאִיטְלַע לָהּ רַגְלָא דִּימִינָא, וּשְׁרַת סֵינֵיהּ מֵעַל רַגְלוֹהִי, וְיָרְקַת בְּאַנְפּוֹהִי רוּקָא דְּמִתְחַזְיָא לְבֵי דִינָא עַל אַרְעָא.

The bill of *ḥalitza* would continue with the account of what transpired: **And he extended** [*itla*] **his right foot**[N] **toward her and she removed his shoe from upon his foot and she spat toward his face spittle, which was visible to the court,** and which landed **upon the ground.**

וְרַבִּי חִיָּיא בַּר אָוְיָא מְסַיֵּים בָּהּ מִשְּׁמֵיהּ דְּרַב יְהוּדָה: וְאַקְרֵינְהוּ מַה דִּכְתִיב בִּסְפַר אוֹרַיְיתָא דְּמֹשֶׁה.

And Rabbi Ḥiyya bar Avya in the name of Rav Yehuda would conclude the formulation of the bill of *ḥalitza* with an additional sentence: **And we dictated to the** *yavam* **that which is written in the book of the Torah of Moses,** i.e., those declarations that the *yavam* and the *yevama* are required to make.

אִשְׁתְּמוֹדְעִינְהוּ, פְּלִיגִי בָּהּ רַב אַחָא וְרָבִינָא. חַד אָמַר: בְּעֵדִים, וְחַד אָמַר: אֲפִילּוּ קָרוֹב, אֲפִילּוּ אִשָּׁה. וְהִלְכְתָא: גִּלּוּיֵי מִילְּתָא בְּעָלְמָא הוּא, וַאֲפִילּוּ קָרוֹב וַאֲפִילּוּ אִשָּׁה.

The Gemara clarifies the intention of the phrase: **And we identified him**[H] as the brother of the deceased. **Rav Aḥa and Ravina disagree concerning** this phrase: **One said** that this identification must be made **through** legally valid **witnesses, and the other one said** that **even** the testimony of **a relative**[N] and **even** the testimony **a woman** is accepted in this case. The Gemara concludes: **And the *halakha* is** that the identification of the brother is considered to be **merely revealing** the facts of **the matter,** and therefore, **even a relative and even a woman** may tender this information.

בָּרִאשׁוֹנָה שֶׁהָיוּ מִתְכַּוְּונִין לְשֵׁם מִצְוָה – מִצְוַת יִבּוּם קוֹדֶמֶת לְמִצְוַת חֲלִיצָה, וְעַכְשָׁיו שֶׁאֵין מִתְכַּוְּונִין לְשֵׁם מִצְוָה – אָמְרוּ: מִצְוַת חֲלִיצָה קוֹדֶמֶת לְמִצְוַת יִבּוּם.

The Gemara paraphrases the mishna from tractate *Bekhorot*: **Initially, when** *yevamin* **would have intent for the sake of** fulfilling **the mitzva** of consummating the levirate marriage, **the mitzva** of consummating the **levirate marriage took precedence over the mitzva** of performing ***ḥalitza*. And now that they do not have intent for the sake of** fulfilling **the mitzva,** the Sages **say: The mitzva** of performing ***ḥalitza* takes precedence over the mitzva** of consummating the **levirate marriage.**

אָמַר רָמִי בַּר חָמָא אָמַר רַבִּי יִצְחָק: חָזְרוּ לוֹמַר מִצְוַת יִבּוּם קוֹדֶמֶת לְמִצְוַת חֲלִיצָה. אָמַר לֵיהּ רַב נַחְמָן בַּר יִצְחָק: אַכְשׁוּר דָּרֵי?!

Rami bar Ḥama said that **Rabbi Yitzḥak said:** In later generations **they went back to** once again **saying** that **the mitzva of** consummating the **levirate marriage takes precedence over the mitzva of** performing ***ḥalitza*. Rav Naḥman bar Yitzḥak said to him** in wonderment: Could it be that **the** later **generations improved** their spiritual level and now intend to consummate the levirate marriage solely for sake of fulfilling the mitzva?

מֵעִיקָּרָא סָבְרִי לַהּ כְּאַבָּא שָׁאוּל, וּלְבַסּוֹף סָבְרִי לַהּ כְּרַבָּנַן.

The Gemara explains that this does not mean that the later generations improved themselves; rather, **initially they held in accordance with** the opinion of **Abba Shaul,** and so the mitzva of performing *ḥalitza* took precedence, **and in the end they held in accordance with** the opinion of **the Rabbis,**[N] and so the mitzva of consummating the levirate marriage took precedence.

HALAKHA

Identification of the *yavam* and the *yevama* – הַכָּרַת הַיָּבָם וְהַיְּבָמָה: The court must substantiate that the man coming to perform *ḥalitza* is the paternal brother of the deceased, that the two brothers coexisted, and that this woman was the wife of the deceased. There is no need for two qualified witnesses to testify in this matter; rather, any testimony suffices, even that of a close relative, a woman, or anyone else generally disqualified from giving testimony. Even written testimony is acceptable if the parties can be recognized thereby (*Be'er Heitev*, citing Maharshdam). Some (*Be'er Heitev*, citing Rivash) say that a disqualified witness may not testify at the time of the *ḥalitza* itself; rather, the court must first confirm the identities of the *yavam* and the *yevama* and only then may the *ḥalitza* be performed (Rambam *Sefer Nashim, Hilkhot Yibbum VaḤalitza* 4:31; *Shulḥan Arukh, Even HaEzer* 169:8; 157:2; *Seder Ḥalitza* 38).

NOTES

He extended [*itla*] his right foot – אִיטְלַע...רַגְלָא דִּימִינָא: Rashi interprets the word *itla* as meaning incline. Accordingly, the phrase means that the *yavam* presented his foot to his *yevama* by extending it toward her. The commentaries explain that Rashi understood that the Aramaic word is related to the Hebrew word *tzela*, which can mean a side; Rashi similarly translates the phrase: "*Tzela hamishkan*" (Exodus 26:26) as being the side of the Tabernacle (Rabbi Yehuda al-Madari; *Noda Bihuda*). Rabbi Avraham min HaHar cites Rashi as explaining *itla* to mean prepare. The *Arukh* writes that the word means remove. Clearly the intention is not that he should remove his shoe; rather, it must mean that he should allow his shoe to be removed by her. Later commentaries note that it appears that the *Arukh* had a variant text of the Gemara that could support such a meaning. Other commentaries explain that the word means limp, and the intention is that the *yavam* should forcefully plant his foot on the ground to the point that he appears like one with a limp, who distributes his weight unequally by supporting himself on one leg (Meiri; Rabbi Avraham min HaHar; *Noda Bihuda*).

Even the testimony of a relative, etc. – אֲפִילּוּ קָרוֹב וכו׳: The early commentaries, based on the comments of the Rif, explain that this is certainly not to say that the court actually relied entirely on the testimony of a close relative or woman. Rather, in all cases the court would allow for the performance of *ḥalitza* only if they were certain of the identities of the parties involved. The novelty of the ruling is that it allows the court not to follow the standard protocol by which facts are established only through formal testimony supplied by independent valid witnesses (Meiri; *Tosafot*; see HALAKHA).

The dispute between Abba Shaul and the Rabbis – מַחְלוֹקֶת אַבָּא שָׁאוּל וַחֲכָמִים: The Gemara never explicitly rules on the dispute between the Rabbis and Abba Shaul as to whether nowadays one may consummate a levirate marriage even though there are reservations concerning one's purity of motives. The Gemara here appears to be inclined toward the opinion of the Rabbis; however, in other places the Gemara appears to accept the opinion of Abba Shaul. Already during the period of the *ge'onim* different communities followed different opinions. In Neharde'a the practice was to act in accordance with Abba Shaul, and in Sura the opinion of the Rabbis was followed. In later generations, the Sephardic commentaries generally permitted the consummation of the levirate marriage, while Ashkenazic commentaries permitted only *ḥalitza*.

HALAKHA

The mitzva of levirate marriage – מִצְוַת יִבּוּם: If one's paternal brother died childless, one is commanded to take his brother's widow in levirate marriage, whether she was married or only betrothed to his brother (Rambam *Sefer Nashim, Hilkhot Yibbum* 1:1; *Shulḥan Arukh, Even HaEzer* 156:1).

דְּתַנְיָא, אַבָּא שָׁאוּל אוֹמֵר: הַכּוֹנֵס אֶת יְבִמְתּוֹ לְשֵׁם נוֹי, וּלְשׁוּם אִישׁוּת, וּלְשׁוּם דָּבָר אַחֵר – כְּאִילּוּ פּוֹגֵעַ בְּעֶרְוָה, וְקָרוֹב אֲנִי בְּעֵינַי לִהְיוֹת הַוָּלָד מַמְזֵר. וַחֲכָמִים אוֹמְרִים: ״יְבָמָהּ יָבֹא עָלֶיהָ״ – מִכׇּל מָקוֹם.

As it is taught in a *baraita*: **Abba Shaul says** that **one who consummates** a levirate marriage **with his** ***yevama*** **for the sake of** her **beauty, or for the sake of marital relations,**[N] **or for the sake of another matter,**[N] e.g., he wishes to inherit her husband's estate, **it is** considered **as though he encountered a forbidden relation, and I am inclined to view the offspring** born from such a union **as a** ***mamzer***. Since the prohibition against engaging in relations with one's brother's wife is overridden only for the sake of fulfilling the mitzva of consummating the levirate marriage, when one does not have the intention to fulfill that mitzva, the baseline prohibition applies, and so any offspring from the union will be *mamzerim*. **The Rabbis say:** The Torah states: **"Her brother-in-law will have intercourse with her"** (Deuteronomy 25:5), which indicates that he should do so **in any case,** even if his intentions are not solely for the sake of fulfilling the mitzva.[N]

מַאן תַּנָּא לְהָא דְּתָנוּ רַבָּנַן: ״יְבָמָהּ יָבֹא עָלֶיהָ״ מִצְוָה. שֶׁבַּתְּחִלָּה הָיְתָה עָלָיו בִּכְלַל הֶיתֵּר, נֶאֶסְרָה, וְחָזְרָה וְהוּתְּרָה, יָכוֹל תַּחְזוֹר לְהֶיתֵּירָהּ הָרִאשׁוֹן – תַּלְמוּד לוֹמַר ״יְבָמָהּ יָבֹא עָלֶיהָ״ מִצְוָה.

The Gemara asks: **Who is the** ***tanna*** who **taught** the following *baraita* **that the Sages taught:** The Torah states: **"Her brother-in-law will have intercourse with her"** (Deuteronomy 25:5); this is to be considered **a mitzva, as initially,** before she was married to his brother, **she was among** all other women who are **permitted to him,** and then when she married his brother **she became forbidden** to him, **and** when his brother died without offspring **she reverted** from her forbidden status **and became permitted to him.** One **might** have thought that **she would revert to her original permitted status;** therefore, **the verse states: "Her brother-in-law will have intercourse with her"** to teach that it is in fact **a mitzva** to do so.[H]

NOTES

For the sake of marital relations – לְשׁוּם אִישׁוּת: *Tosafot* explain that the use of the term: For the sake of marital relations, as it is used here differs from its use later in the Gemara. In the present context, such motivation is presented as being contemptible. Accordingly, the phrase means either that he desires to gain the status of a married man (*Tosafot*), that he desires the woman (Rivan), or that he wishes for her to serve him (*Otzar HaShitot*). However, later in the Gemara the phrase is used in contrast to the phrase: For the sake of her beauty. This implies that the phrase: For the sake of marital relations, indicates a more noble intention, i.e., that he wishes to have children with her. Nevertheless, even such motivation is still deficient in a case of a levirate marriage, where one must have intention for the specific goals of the levirate marriage (see *Otzar HaShitot*).

For the sake of another matter – לְשׁוּם דָּבָר אַחֵר: Rivan and others offer that the reference is to a case where the *yavam* is motivated by financial gain, either that he had his eye on her possessions or that he wants to inherit from his brother. Others interpret this to mean illicit sexual relations (*Ḥokhmat Manoaḥ*). Both positions find support in earlier sources.

The opinions of Abba Shaul and the Rabbis – שִׁיטוֹת אַבָּא שָׁאוּל וַחֲכָמִים: The early commentaries are divided as to what extent Abba Shaul intended to say that lack of appropriate motives would actually result in the violation of a prohibition, the offspring of which would be *mamzerim*. The Ramban understands Abba Shaul's opinion in the most extreme sense, i.e., when the *yavam* lacks the appropriate motives he does not acquire the *yevama* at all, and the children of such a union would actually be *mamzerim*. Others suggest that under all circumstances the *yavam* certainly acquires the *yevama*; Abba Shaul's point is that if the *yavam* lacks pure motives, then he transgresses a Torah prohibition by engaging in intercourse with her (*Keren Ora*). Still others hold that even Abba Shaul agrees that since the *yavam* is obligated to consummate the levirate marriage, there can be no Torah prohibition involved in doing so, even if he has impure motives. Nevertheless, the Sages prohibited the consummation of the levirate marriage unless his motives were pure. This interpretation explains why Abba Shaul specifically stated: As though he encountered a forbidden relation, and: I am inclined to view the offspring as a *mamzer*, instead of simply stating that the *yavam* encountered a forbidden relation and the offspring is a *mamzer* (*Nimmukei Yosef*).

Some commentaries explain that the dispute between Abba Shaul and the Rabbis hinges on the question of why it is permitted to consummate a levirate marriage in the first place, given that generally one is prohibited from engaging in relations with his brother's wife. They explain that Abba Shaul understood that in every case of levirate marriage there is a clash between two factors: The mitzva to consummate the levirate marriage and the prohibition against engaging in relations with one's brother's wife. The principle in such a case is that by performing the mitzva, one is permitted to disregard the prohibition. Accordingly, if one does not intend to fulfill the mitzva, one necessarily encounters the prohibition without permission to do so. This is readily understandable based on the comments of the Ramban that a mitzva overrides a prohibition because the former is an expression of one's love for God and the latter of one's awe, and when there is a choice between them, one should express one's love. As such, when one performs the mitzva not out of love but for some ulterior motive, the basis for permitting the prohibition is undermined. The Rabbis disagreed with the entire basis of this argument. They understood that it is not that the mitzva of levirate marriage overrides the prohibition against engaging in relations with one's brother's wife; rather, the scope of the prohibition itself is limited and does not apply to any case in which there is the possibility of consummating a levirate marriage. As such, the permission to consummate the levirate marriage is entirely unrelated to the intentions of the *yavam*, since there is simply no prohibition to speak of (*Kovetz He'arot*).

מַאן תָּנָא? אָמַר רַבִּי יִצְחָק בַּר אַבְדִּימִי: אַבָּא שָׁאוּל הִיא, וְהָכִי קָאָמַר: ״יְבָמָהּ יָבֹא עָלֶיהָ״ מִצְוָה, שֶׁבִּתְחִלָּה הָיְתָה עָלָיו בִּכְלַל הֶיתֵּר, רָצָה לְשֵׁם נוֹי – כּוֹנְסָהּ, רָצָה לְשׁוּם אִישׁוּת – כּוֹנְסָהּ.

Who is the *tanna* who taught this *baraita*? Rav Yitzḥak bar Avdimi said: It is Abba Shaul, and this is what the *baraita* is saying: "Her brother-in-law will have intercourse with her" teaches that it is permitted to engage in intercourse with her only when his intention is to fulfill a mitzva, as initially, before she was married to his brother, she was among all other women who are permitted to him, and so, if he wished, then even for the sake of her beauty he was permitted to marry her, or similarly, if he wished, then even for the sake of marital relations he was permitted to marry her.

נֶאֶסְרָה, חָזְרָה וְהוּתְּרָה, יָכוֹל תַּחֲזוֹר לְהֶיתֵּירָהּ הָרִאשׁוֹן – תַּלְמוּד לוֹמַר ״יְבָמָהּ יָבֹא עָלֶיהָ״, לְמִצְוָה.

When she married his brother she became forbidden to him, and when his brother died without offspring she reverted from her forbidden status and became permitted to him. One might have thought that she would fully revert to her original permitted status; therefore, the verse states: "Her brother-in-law will have intercourse with her" to teach that he is permitted to marry her only when his intention is for the mitzva.

רָבָא אָמַר: אֲפִילּוּ תֵּימָא רַבָּנַן, וְהָכִי קָאָמַר: ״יְבָמָהּ יָבֹא עָלֶיהָ״ – מִצְוָה. שֶׁבִּתְחִלָּה הָיְתָה בִּכְלַל הֶיתֵּר. רָצָה – כּוֹנְסָהּ, רָצָה – אֵינוֹ כּוֹנְסָהּ.

Rava said: You can even say that the *baraita* is in accordance with the Rabbis, and this is what the *baraita* is saying: "Her brother-in-law will have intercourse with her" indicates that it is a mitzva to consummate the levirate marriage, as initially, before she was married to his brother, she was among all other women who are permitted to him, and so if he wished, he was permitted to marry her, or if he wished, he was permitted to choose not to marry her.

נֶאֶסְרָה, חָזְרָה וְהוּתְּרָה, יָכוֹל תַּחֲזוֹר לְהֶיתֵּירָהּ הָרִאשׁוֹן; רָצָה – כּוֹנְסָהּ, רָצָה – אֵינוֹ כּוֹנְסָהּ. רָצָה אֵינוֹ כּוֹנְסָהּ?

When she married his brother she became forbidden to him, and when his brother died without offspring she reverted from her forbidden status and became permitted to him. One might have thought that she would fully revert to her original permitted status, so that if he wishes, he may marry her, or if he wishes, he may choose not to marry her.

הָא אֲגִידָה בֵּיהּ, בִּכְדֵי תֵּיפּוֹק?! אֶלָּא אֵימָא: רָצָה – כּוֹנְסָהּ, רָצָה – חוֹלֵץ לָהּ. תַּלְמוּד לוֹמַר: ״יְבָמָהּ יָבֹא עָלֶיהָ״ – מִצְוָה.

The Gemara interjects that the logic of this last statement seems implausible: Does he really have the option to do as he wishes? Isn't she bound to him with a levirate bond? Could it be that she will be released from that bond without doing anything? Rather, emend the previous argument and instead say: One might think that if he wishes, he may marry her, or if he wishes not to do so, he performs *ḥalitza* with her. Therefore, the verse states: "Her brother-in-law will have intercourse with her," to teach that it is now a mitzva to consummate the marriage, and doing so is preferable to performing *ḥalitza*.

אֵימָא רֵישָׁא: ״מַצּוֹת תֵּאָכֵל בְּמָקוֹם קָדוֹשׁ״ – מִצְוָה,

The *baraita* under discussion also presents another case that follows a similar model of initially being permitted, then prohibited, and then once again permitted. The Gemara analyzes the explanations of Rav Yitzḥak and Rava based on that clause of the *baraita*: Say the first clause and try to explain it in a way consistent with the various explanations of the latter clause: The Torah states concerning the meal-offerings eaten by the priests: "It shall be eaten unleavened in a sacred place" (Leviticus 6:9); this indicates that doing so is a mitzva,

Perek **IV**
Daf **40** Amud **a**

שֶׁבִּתְחִלָּה הָיְתָה עָלָיו בִּכְלַל הֶיתֵּר, נֶאֶסְרָה, וְחָזְרָה וְהוּתְּרָה, יָכוֹל תַּחֲזוֹר לְהֶיתֵּירָהּ הָרִאשׁוֹן – תַּלְמוּד לוֹמַר ״מַצּוֹת תֵּאָכֵל בְּמָקוֹם קָדוֹשׁ״ מִצְוָה.

as initially, before the flour was consecrated, it was among all other foods that are permitted to him, and then when the flour was consecrated as a meal-offering, it became forbidden to him, and then once a handful of the offering was brought on the altar, it reverted from its forbidden status and became permitted to him. One might have thought that it would revert to its original permitted status; therefore, the verse states: "It shall be eaten unleavened in a sacred place" (Leviticus 6:9), which indicates that it is a mitzva[H] to eat it.

HALAKHA

It shall be eaten unleavened…indicates that it is a mitzva – מַצּוֹת תֵּאָכֵל...מִצְוָה: After the handful has been taken from the meal-offering and burned on the altar, it is a positive mitzva for the priests to eat the remainder of the offering (Rambam *Sefer Avoda*, *Hilkhot Ma'aseh HaKorbanot* 10:2).

NOTES

What two manners are there – מַאי תְּרֵי גַּוְונֵי אִיכָּא: One could suggest that according to the opinion that in general the fulfillment of mitzvot is achieved only when one has intention to fulfill them, there is a very simple way of explaining the clause concerning the meal-offering: If it is eaten with intention to fulfill the mitzva, then it is permitted; otherwise it would be prohibited due to the general prohibition against benefiting from consecrated items. The *Keren Ora* suggests that the Gemara did not raise this option because even if in general one requires intention for the fulfillment of mitzvot, this might not apply to the consumption of sacred foods. The reason for this would be that their consumption by the priesthood is referred to as being given "for anointment" (Numbers 18:8), which the Gemara in *Zevaḥim* interprets elsewhere as meaning that it is to be eaten in grandeur, as kings eat. As such, it is possible that when eating it the priests are not required to focus on the fact that doing so is a mitzva but instead may eat it for their own purposes; provided they eat it with appetite, they fulfill what is required of them. Another resolution can be offered based on the opinion of *Tosafot* and Ran in tractate *Pesaḥim*. They explain that mitzvot that require one to eat never require specific intent to fulfill the mitzva, since the benefit of eating perforce defines the act as one of intention.

One who eats through an act of excessive eating on Yom Kippur – הָאוֹכֵל אֲכִילָה גַּסָּה בְּיוֹם הַכִּפּוּרִים: From the statement of Reish Lakish alone it would appear that the reason for the exemption is because the prohibition against eating on Yom Kippur is expressed by the Torah as one of affliction, which suggests that only acts that alleviate one's affliction are prohibited. Therefore, excessive eating, which causes one discomfort, should not be prohibited. This is the interpretation of Rabbi Avraham min HaHar. Accordingly, although excessive eating might be considered an unusual act of eating, it certainly has the legal status of an act of eating, and therefore one who eats forbidden foods in such a manner would be liable for doing so. The Meiri disagrees and claims that Reish Lakish's teaching is not unique to Yom Kippur; rather, it is a principle that an excessive act of eating does not have the legal status of an act of eating. Therefore, it applies to all cases in which an act of eating is necessary. This is also the opinion of the *Maggid Mishne* and the Ran. Accordingly, even if one were to eat forbidden foods through an act of excessive eating, one would be exempt.

Tosafot note that the Gemara states elsewhere that one who eats the Paschal lamb through an act of excessive eating does fulfill one's obligation, even though doing so is not the proper way to fulfill the mitzva. This would appear to imply, contrary to the Gemara here, that an act of excessive eating does have the legal status of an act of eating. To resolve this difficulty, *Tosafot* differentiate between two levels of excessiveness. The Gemara here discusses the case of one who has eaten to the point at which eating anything else would be repulsive to him. At that point, any further eating does not have the legal status of an act of eating; one in that state would not fulfill his obligation to eat the Paschal lamb. The Gemara that states that one does fulfill one's obligation of eating the Paschal lamb concerns an earlier stage, where one has already eaten to satiation, but further eating is still not repulsive. Eating in this manner, while inappropriate for the Paschal lamb, is certainly considered an act of eating.

The Ramban suggests a different distinction. The Gemara concerning the Paschal lamb does not actually discuss a case of excessive eating at all; rather, it concerns the motivation for eating the offering and discusses the case of one who, although he has still not achieved satiation, eats the Paschal lamb as part of an attempt to gorge himself. This is apparent from the precise formulation of the Gemara there, which states that he ate the Paschal lamb: For the stage of gorging. The Ramban offers an additional resolution that since the mitzva of the Paschal lamb is primarily fulfilled through its sacrifice and not through its consumption, the requirement to eat does not demand the same strict standards for an act of eating that apply elsewhere, and therefore even an act of excessive eating is sufficient. A similar approach is also suggested by *Tosafot Yeshanim*.

בִּשְׁלָמָא לְרָבָא, דְּאָמַר הָא מַנִּי רַבָּנַן הִיא – הָכָא הָכִי קָאָמַר: ״מַצּוֹת תֵּאָכֵל בְּמָקוֹם קָדוֹשׁ״ מִצְוָה. שֶׁבַּתְּחִלָּה הָיְתָה עָלָיו בִּכְלַל הֶיתֵּר, רָצָה – אוֹכְלָהּ, רָצָה – אֵינוֹ אוֹכְלָהּ. (נֶאֶסְרָה, חָזְרָה וְהוּתְּרָה, יָכוֹל תַּחֲזוֹר לְהֶיתֵּירָהּ הָרִאשׁוֹן) – רָצָה אוֹכְלָהּ, רָצָה אֵינוֹ אוֹכְלָהּ.

The Gemara asks: **Granted, according to Rava, who said:** In accordance with **whose** opinion **is this** *baraita*? **It is** in accordance with the opinion of **the Rabbis;** according to him, **here,** in the first clause, **this is what** the *baraita* **is saying: "It shall be eaten unleavened in a sacred place"** indicates that it is a **mitzva** for the priest who prepares the offering to eat it himself. **As, initially,** before the flour was consecrated, **it was among** all other foods that are **permitted to him:** If **he wishes, he may eat it, and if he wishes, he may** choose **not to eat it.** When the flour was consecrated, **it became forbidden** to him, **and** then once a handful was brought on the altar, **it reverted** from its forbidden status **and became permitted to him.** One **might** have thought that **it would revert to its original permitted status,** so that if **he wishes, he may eat it, and** if **he wishes, he may** choose **not to eat it.**

רָצָה אֵינוֹ אוֹכְלָהּ?! וְהָכְתִיב ״וְאָכְלוּ אֹתָם אֲשֶׁר כֻּפַּר בָּהֶם״ מְלַמֵּד שֶׁהַכֹּהֲנִים אוֹכְלִים וּבְעָלִים מִתְכַּפְּרִין!

The Gemara interjects that the logic of this last statement seems implausible: Could it be that if **he wishes, he may** choose **not** to **eat it? But isn't it written: "And they shall eat those things through which atonement is attained"** (Exodus 29:33), which **teaches that the priests eat** portions of the offering **and** by their doing so **the owners** who brought the offering **attain atonement?**[H] Clearly, then, the eating of the offerings is not volitional.

אֶלָּא: רָצָה – הוּא אוֹכְלָהּ, רָצָה – כֹּהֵן אַחֵר אוֹכְלָהּ, תַּלְמוּד לוֹמַר ״מַצּוֹת תֵּאָכֵל בְּמָקוֹם קָדוֹשׁ״ – מִצְוָה.

Rather, the *baraita* should be understood as saying: One might have thought that if **he wishes, he may eat it, and if he wishes, another priest may eat it;** therefore, **the verse states: "It shall be eaten unleavened in a sacred place"** (Leviticus 6:9), to teach that it is a **mitzva** for the priest who prepares the offering to eat it himself. This explanation of the first clause of the *baraita* is entirely consistent with Rava's explanation of the latter clause concerning the mitzvot of levirate marriage. In his opinion, both clauses demonstrate that there is a mitzva to perform an action in a case where one might have thought there was none.

אֶלָּא לְרַב יִצְחָק בַּר אַבְדִּימִי, דְּאָמַר אַבָּא שָׁאוּל הִיא – הָכָא מַאי תְּרֵי גַּוְונֵי אִיכָּא?

However, according to Rav Yitzḥak bar Avdimi, who said that the *baraita* **is** in accordance with the opinion of **Abba Shaul** and explained the *baraita* accordingly as teaching the correct manner in which the mitzva is to be performed, **here,** in the first clause concerning the meal-offering, **what two manners** of eating **are there**[N] of which one would be prohibited?

וְכִי תֵּימָא: רָצָה – לְתֵאָבוֹן אוֹכְלָהּ, רָצָה – אֲכִילָה גַּסָּה אוֹכְלָהּ, אֲכִילָה גַּסָּה מִי שְׁמָהּ אֲכִילָה? וְהָאָמַר רֵישׁ לָקִישׁ: הָאוֹכֵל אֲכִילָה גַּסָּה בְּיוֹם הַכִּפּוּרִים – פָּטוּר מִ״לֹּא תְעֻנֶּה״!

And if you would say that the *baraita* might refer to two types of eating and is saying: One might have thought that if **he wishes he may eat it with an appetite, and if he wishes he may eat it** though an act of **excessive eating,** forcing himself to eat despite already being fully satiated; perforce this is not correct, as does **excessive eating have the** legal **status of** an act of **eating? Didn't Reish Lakish say: One who eats** through an act of **excessive eating on Yom Kippur**[NH] **is exempt from** the punishment of *karet* indicated in the verse: "For whatever soul it be that **shall not be afflicted** in that same day shall be cut off from his people" (Leviticus 23:29)? From this it is apparent that excessive eating does not have the legal status of an act of eating.

HALAKHA

The priests eat and the owners attain atonement – הַכֹּהֲנִים אוֹכְלִים וּבְעָלִים מִתְכַּפְּרִין: There is a positive mitzva for the priests to eat the meat of sin-offerings and guilt-offerings, and through their doing so the owners of those offerings attain atonement. Similarly, the consumption of other offerings by the priests is also a positive mitzva (Rambam *Sefer Avoda, Hilkhot Ma'aseh HaKorbanot* 10:1).

Excessive eating on Yom Kippur – אֲכִילָה גַּסָּה בְּיוֹם הַכִּפּוּרִים: If one eats excessively on Yom Kippur, e.g., if one continues to eat in addition to that which he ate prior to the onset of Yom Kippur to the point that he is repulsed by his food, he is exempt. Some rule that he would still be liable for eating sweet foods, since one continues to have an appetite for such foods even after one is fully satiated (Rema, citing *Kol Bo*). However, even for such foods, if one reached a point where he found even them to be repulsive, he would be exempt (*Baḥ*; Rambam *Sefer Zemanim, Hilkhot Shevitat Asor* 2:7; *Shulḥan Arukh, Oraḥ Ḥayyim* 612:6).

אֶלָּא: רָצָה – מַצָּה אוֹכְלָהּ, רָצָה – חָמֵץ אוֹכְלָהּ,

The Gemara therefore suggests a different interpretation of the *baraita* that is consistent with Rav Yitzhak's opinion: **Rather,** say the *baraita* is referring to two different manners in which the meal-offering was prepared: If **he wishes he may eat it unleavened,** and if **he wishes he may eat it leavened.**

וְהָכְתִיב ״לֹא תֵאָפֶה חָמֵץ חֶלְקָם״, וְאָמַר רֵישׁ לָקִישׁ: וַאֲפִילּוּ חֶלְקָם לֹא תֵאָפֶה חָמֵץ! אֶלָּא: רָצָה – מַצָּה אוֹכְלָהּ, רָצָה – חָלוּט אוֹכְלָהּ.

The Gemara interjects that the logic of this last statement seems implausible: Could it be that if he wishes, the offering could be leavened? **But isn't it written: "Their portion shall not be baked leavened"** (Leviticus 6:10),[H] **and Reish Lakish said** that both the handful brought on the altar **and even the** priest's **portion shall not be baked leavened? Rather,** the *baraita* should be understood as saying: One might have thought that if **he wishes he may eat it unleavened,** and if **he wishes he may eat it** even if it was prepared by being **boiled.**[H] Therefore, the verse taught that one must eat it unleavened. Understood in this way, this clause of the *baraita* is also consistent with Rav Yitzhak's opinion.

הַאי חָלוּט הֵיכִי דָּמֵי? אִי מַצָּה הִיא – הָא מַצָּה הִיא, וְאִי לָא מַצָּה הִיא – ״מַצּוֹת״ אָמַר רַחֲמָנָא!

The Gemara asks: With regard to **this** possibility of eating the meal-offering **boiled, what are the circumstances,** i.e., how is it classified? **If it is** considered to be **unleavened** because it is presumed that the flour never managed to rise before it was cooked, **then it is unleavened** and there is no reason to prohibit its use; **and if it is not** considered to be **unleavened** because it is presumed that the flour managed to rise before it was cooked, then it is certainly disqualified from use because **the Merciful One states** that the offering must be **"unleavened"** (Leviticus 10:12).[N] How, then, could one ever have questioned whether it is permitted to eat the meal-offering if it was boiled?

לָא, לְעוֹלָם אֵימָא לָךְ מַצָּה הִיא, וּלְהָכִי תְּנָא בֵּיהּ קְרָא – לְעַכֵּב.

The Gemara explains: **No; actually, I** could **say to you** that the boiled meal-offering **is** considered to be **unleavened, and** nevertheless it is disqualified because it is **for this** very reason that **the verse repeated** the requirement that it be unleavened, in order **to invalidate** a meal-offering that was boiled.

אֶלָּא חָלוּט מַצָּה הִיא דְּקָאָמְרִינַן, לְמַאי הִלְכְתָא? לוֹמַר שֶׁאָדָם יוֹצֵא בָּהּ יְדֵי חוֹבָתוֹ בְּפֶסַח, אַף עַל פִּי דְּחַלְטֵיהּ מֵעִיקָּרָא, כֵּיוָן דַּהֲדַר אֲפָיֵיהּ בְּתַנּוּר – ״לֶחֶם עוֹנִי״ קָרֵינָא בֵּיהּ, וְאָדָם יוֹצֵא בָּהּ יְדֵי חוֹבָתוֹ בְּפֶסַח.

The Gemara asks: **But** if boiled flour is invalid as a meal offering, then with regard to this statement **that we said** that **boiled** flour **is unleavened, for what *halakha*** is it relevant? The Gemara answers: It is **to say that a person fulfills his obligation with it on Passover.** This is because **even though he initially boiled it, since he subsequently baked it in an oven, it is called "bread of affliction"** (Deuteronomy 16:3),[N] **and** therefore **a person fulfills his obligation with it on Passover.**

מתני׳ הַחוֹלֵץ לִיבִמְתּוֹ – הֲרֵי הוּא כְּאֶחָד מִן הָאַחִין לְנַחֲלָה, וְאִם יֵשׁ שָׁם אָב – נְכָסִים שֶׁל אָב. הַכּוֹנֵס אֶת יְבִמְתּוֹ זָכָה בִּנְכָסִים שֶׁל אָחִיו. רַבִּי יְהוּדָה אוֹמֵר: בֵּין כָּךְ וּבֵין כָּךְ, אִם יֵשׁ שָׁם אָב – נְכָסִים שֶׁל אָב.

MISHNA **One who performs *halitza* with his *yevama* is like** any **one of the** other **brothers with respect to the inheritance**[H] of the deceased brother's estate, i.e., each of the brothers takes an equal share of the inheritance. **And if there is a father** of the deceased, who is still alive, **the property** of the deceased **belongs to the father. One who consummates** levirate marriage with **his *yevama***[H] thereby **acquires** his deceased **brother's property** solely for himself. **Rabbi Yehuda says: In either** case, whether he consummated the levirate marriage or performed *halitza*, **if there is a father** who is still alive, **the property belongs to the father.**

גמ׳ פְּשִׁיטָא! סָלְקָא דַּעְתָּךְ אָמֵינָא: חֲלִיצָה בִּמְקוֹם יִבּוּם קַיְימָא, וְנִשְׁקוֹל כּוּלְּהוּ נִכְסֵי, קָא מַשְׁמַע לָן.

GEMARA The Gemara asks with regard to the opening clause of the mishna: The fact that one who performs *halitza* does not gain any special rights to the inheritance of the deceased brother **is obvious;** why did the mishna teach it? The Gemara answers: **It could enter your mind to say** that the ***halitza* takes the place of the levirate marriage and** therefore the brother who performs *halitza* **should take all the property** in the same way as one who consummates the levirate marriage. Therefore, the mishna **teaches us** that this is not the case.

HALAKHA

Their portion shall not be baked leavened – לֹא תֵאָפֶה חָמֵץ חֶלְקָם: Although the priests are permitted to eat the remainders of the meal-offerings together with other foods prepared in any manner, it is nevertheless prohibited to eat them leavened. If the remainders of the meal-offerings became leavened, the priests responsible for doing so would transgress a negative mitzva and receive lashes. This is in accordance with the opinion of Reish Lakish (Rambam *Sefer Avoda, Hilkhot Ma'aseh HaKorbanot* 12:14).

Boiled unleavened bread – מַצָּה חֲלוּטָה: Flour scalded in boiling water and then baked is regarded as unleavened, and consequently one could fulfill one's obligation to eat *matza* on Passover by eating it. However, nowadays, no one knows how to scald the flour with enough speed and care to ensure it does not rise and become leavened. Therefore, flour boiled in water is considered to be leavened and is forbidden (*Tur*, citing the *ge'onim*; Rambam *Sefer Zemanim, Hilkhot Hametz UMatza* 6:6; *Shulhan Arukh, Orah Hayyim* 454:3).

The status of one who performs *halitza* is like any one of the brothers with respect to the inheritance – הַחוֹלֵץ דִּינוֹ כְּאֶחָד הָאַחִים לְנַחֲלָה: One who performs *halitza* with his *yevama* is like any one of the other brothers with respect to the inheritance of the deceased brother's estate. Each of the brothers takes an equal share of the inheritance. If the father is still alive, then he alone inherits from his son. The Rema notes that even if the *yavam* wishes to consummate the levirate marriage but the *yevama* refuses him, he still does not attain any rights to the deceased brother's estate. In some communities the custom has developed that the one who performs *halitza* receives half of the brother's estate (*Shulhan Arukh, Even HaEzer* 163:2).

One who consummates levirate marriage with his *yevama* – הַכּוֹנֵס אֶת יְבִמְתּוֹ: One who consummates levirate marriage with his *yevama* thereby acquires his deceased brother's property and any property that the brother was already due to inherit at the time of his death. However, he does not gain the rights to inherit the property that his brother would have inherited, were he still alive, if it only becomes available after his brother's death. This is in accordance with the opinion of the Rabbis (Rambam *Sefer Mishpatim, Hilkhot Nahalot* 3:7; *Shulhan Arukh, Even HaEzer* 163:1).

NOTES

The Merciful One states "unleavened" – מַצּוֹת אָמַר רַחֲמָנָא: Rashi claims the Gemara is citing the verse: "And eat it unleavened beside the altar" (Leviticus 10:12), which, although it concerns only one specific type of meal-offering, is understood to be true for all meal-offerings (see *Tosafot*). Other commentaries suggest that the Gemara is not citing a verse but is referring to the *halakha* that is established from the verse previously cited by the Gemara: "Their portion shall not be baked with leaven" (Leviticus 6:10), which teaches the requirement that all meal-offerings must be unleavened (*Tosafot Yeshanim*). The Rashba questions why, according to Rashi's understanding, there is a need for a verse to teach the requirement that the meal-offering be unleavened, given that there is already another verse prohibiting one from baking a leavened meal-offering. He explains that the additional verse is required to emphasize that it is not sufficient if the meal-offering is not leavened; rather, it must be baked such that it is clearly unleavened.

Bread of affliction – לֶחֶם עוֹנִי: Some commentaries explain that by describing the *matza* that one is required to eat on Passover as bread of affliction, the Torah indicates that it should be of an inferior quality, similar to the bread eaten by the poor. When *matza* is boiled its texture is enhanced, and it is no longer similar to the bread eaten by the poor (Razah and Ra'avad; see Rashi on *Pesahim* 36b). Others explain that dough boiled in water cannot be classified as bread (Rabbeinu Yehonatan of Lunel on *Pesahim* 36b). However, if it is baked again in an oven its original texture is restored, and in that case it may be used for the mitzva.

NOTES

Since he caused her to forfeit the possibility of levirate marriage – הוֹאִיל וְאַפְסְדָהּ מִיבּוּם: Some commentaries question why one who performs *ḥalitza* should be penalized. They note that *ḥalitza* is performed only after it is clarified that none of the brothers are willing to consummate the levirate marriage. If so, the one who ultimately performs *ḥalitza* is not preventing her from consummating the levirate marriage, as that possibility had already been ruled out. They explain that the case here must be one in which a younger brother performed *ḥalitza* before his older brothers had been given the opportunity to consummate the levirate marriage. As such, his *ḥalitza* actually precluded the possibility of her consummating the levirate marriage with the brothers he preempted, and therefore there is reason to assume that he should be penalized (see *Arukh LaNer* and *Yosef Lekaḥ*).

It is written: He shall succeed in the name of his dead brother, but not in the name of his father – יָקוּם עַל שֵׁם אָחִיו כְּתִיב וְלֹא עַל שֵׁם אָבִיו: The underlying principle indicated by this inference is that despite the fact that he consummated the levirate marriage, the *yavam* does not become entitled to the portion of his father's estate that would have been awarded to his deceased brother were he still alive. Therefore, according to Rabbi Yehuda, if the father is still alive at the time of the brother's death then the father takes full ownership of his estate, and when the father subsequently dies, the *yavam* who consummated the levirate marriage has no more claim to the estate than any of the other brothers. Many commentaries assume that this principle is similarly true according to the Rabbis. They explain that the Rabbis dispute Rabbi Yehuda's opinion only in their claim that even if the father is still alive when the brother dies, the *yavam* inherits the brother's estate at that time. However, even the Rabbis agree that when the father subsequently dies, the *yavam* does not become entitled to the portion of his father's estate that would have been awarded to his deceased brother (Rambam; Ramban). Other commentaries claim that the Rabbis do in fact dispute this principle and that according to them, when a *yavam* consummates the levirate marriage he becomes entitled not only to the estate of his deceased brother as it exists at that time, but also to his brother's inheritance rights, which will became germane only at a later date. Therefore, when the father subsequently dies, the *yavam* does receive both the portion that is due to him as a son, and the portion that would have been awarded to his brother (see *Yam shel Shlomo*).

HALAKHA

The father of the deceased take precedence over all the father's descendants – הָאָב קוֹדֵם לְכָל יוֹצְאֵי חֲלָצָיו: If one dies without descendants, then his father is entitled to his inheritance. If the father is not alive, the inheritance passes on to the father's descendants, e.g., the deceased's brothers; if they are not alive, the inheritance passes on to their descendants (Rambam *Sefer Mishpatim*, *Hilkhot Naḥalot* 1:2; *Shulḥan Arukh*, *Ḥoshen Mishpat* 276:1).

אִי הָכִי ״הֲרֵי הוּא כְּאֶחָד מִן הָאַחִים״? אֵינוֹ אֶלָּא כְּאֶחָד מִן הָאַחִים מִיבְּעֵי לֵיהּ!

The Gemara asks: **If so,** that the mishna's point is to teach that by performing *ḥalitza* one is not afforded any additional rights to the inheritance, why is the mishna formulated as: **He is like** any **one of the** other **brothers,** placing the emphasis on what he gains? **It should have** instead taught: **He is** still **only like one of the** other **brothers,** which would emphasize the mishna's point that by performing *ḥalitza* he does not gain any additional rights.

אֶלָּא, סָלְקָא דַּעְתָּךְ אָמִינָא: הוֹאִיל וְאַפְסְדָהּ מִיבּוּם לִקְנְסֵיהּ, קָא מַשְׁמַע לָן.

Rather, the mishna needs to teach the opening clause in this manner because **it could enter your mind to say** that **since** by performing *ḥalitza* with his *yevama* **he caused her to forfeit** the possibility of consummating the **levirate marriage,**[N] **he should be penalized** and should forfeit any entitlement to his brother's property. Therefore the mishna **teaches us** that this is not so.

״אִם יֵשׁ שָׁם אָב״. דַּאֲמַר מָר: אָב קוֹדֵם לְכָל יוֹצְאֵי יְרֵכוֹ.

§ The mishna states: **If there is a father** of the deceased, who is still alive, the property of the deceased belongs to the father. The Gemara explains: **As the Master said** with regard to the laws of inheritance (*Bava Batra* 115a): **A father** of the deceased **takes precedence over all** the father's **descendants.**[H] Therefore, since the father is still alive, the brothers do not inherit at all.

״הַכּוֹנֵס אֶת יְבִמְתּוֹ״ וכו׳. מַאי טַעְמָא? ״יָקוּם עַל שֵׁם אָחִיו״ אָמַר רַחֲמָנָא, וַהֲרֵי קָם.

The mishna states: **One who consummates** levirate marriage with his *yevama* thereby acquires his deceased brother's property. The Gemara asks: **What is the reason** for this? **The Merciful One states** in the Torah: **"He shall succeed in the name of his** dead **brother"** (Deuteronomy 25:6), **and he has succeeded** him by marrying his wife; consequently, he succeeds him by acquiring his property as well.

״רַבִּי יְהוּדָה אוֹמֵר״ וכו׳. אָמַר עוּלָּא: הֲלָכָה כְּרַבִּי יְהוּדָה. וְכֵן אָמַר רַבִּי יִצְחָק נַפָּחָא: הֲלָכָה כְּרַבִּי יְהוּדָה.

§ The mishna continues by citing an opposing opinion. **Rabbi Yehuda says:** In either case, whether he consummated levirate marriage or performed *ḥalitza*, if there is a father who is still alive, the property belongs to the father. The Gemara cites a ruling on this dispute: **Ulla said:** The ***halakha*** **is in accordance with** the opinion of **Rabbi Yehuda. And similarly, Rabbi Yitzḥak Nappaḥa said: The** ***halakha*** **is in accordance with** the opinion of **Rabbi Yehuda.**

וַאֲמַר עוּלָּא וְאִיתֵימָא רַבִּי יִצְחָק נַפָּחָא: מַאי טַעֲמָא דְּרַבִּי יְהוּדָה – דִּכְתִיב ״וְהָיָה הַבְּכוֹר אֲשֶׁר תֵּלֵד״, כִּבְכוֹר: מַה בְּכוֹר אֵין לוֹ בְּחַיֵּי הָאָב – אַף הַאי נַמִי אֵין לוֹ בְּחַיֵּי הָאָב.

And Ulla said, and some say that it was **Rabbi Yitzḥak Nappaḥa** who said: **What is the reason** for the opinion **of Rabbi Yehuda? As it is written: "And it shall be that the firstborn that she bears** shall succeed in the name of his dead brother" (Deuteronomy 25:6). The term "firstborn" is understood to be a reference to the *yavam*. By referring to him in this way the Torah indicates that his rights to his brother's estate are **like** those of **a firstborn** child's rights to his father's estate: **Just as a firstborn has no** rights to any of his father's estate **during the lifetime of the father,** and he may take his double portion only upon the father's death, **so too, this** ***yavam*** **as well has no** rights to any of his brother's estate **during the lifetime of the father.**

אִי מַה בְּכוֹר נוֹטֵל פִּי שְׁנַיִם לְאַחַר מִיתַת הָאָב – אַף הַאי נוֹטֵל פִּי שְׁנַיִם לְאַחַר מִיתַת הָאָב!

The Gemara asks: **If** there is truly a comparison between the *yavam* who consummated the levirate marriage and a firstborn, then one should also say that **just as the firstborn takes a double portion** of his father's estate **after the death of the father, so too, this** ***yavam*** **should** become entitled to **take a double portion** of the father's estate **after the father's death,** i.e., the portion due to him as a son, and that portion that would have been awarded to his brother. However, this is not the case; if the *yavam* is not actually the father's firstborn then he receives only an equal portion of the inheritance together with the other brothers.

מִידֵי ״יָקוּם עַל שֵׁם אָבִיו״ כְּתִיב? ״יָקוּם עַל שֵׁם אָחִיו״ כְּתִיב, וְלֹא ״עַל שֵׁם אָבִיו״!

The Gemara explains: **Is it written** in the Torah: **He shall succeed in the name of his father?** No, **it is written: "He shall succeed in the name of his dead brother,"** which indicates that he succeeds his brother **but not in the name of his father,**[N] i.e., the Torah never granted him any special entitlement to his father's estate, and so he should not receive a double portion of it.

אֵימָא: הֵיכָא דְּלֵיכָּא אָב דְּלִשְׁקוֹל נַחֲלָה – תִּתְקַיֵּים מִצְוַת יִבּוּם, הֵיכָא דְּאִיכָּא אָב, [דְּלָא] שָׁקֵיל נַחֲלָה – לֹא תִּתְקַיֵּים מִצְוַת יִבּוּם!

The Gemara asks: Since Rabbi Yehuda holds that the *halakha* that the *yavam* inherits from his brother, which is stated in the verses describing levirate marriage, applies only when the father is no longer alive, perhaps the other *halakhot* in those verses also apply only when the father is no longer alive, and accordingly one should **say: When there is no father** who is still alive, which means **that the** *yavam* **takes the inheritance,** only then **should the mitzva of levirate marriage apply,** but **when there is a father** who is still alive, which means **that the** *yavam* **does not take the inheritance,** in that case **the mitzva of levirate marriage should not apply.**

מִידֵי יִבּוּם בְּנַחֲלָה תָּלָה רַחֲמָנָא? יַבּוּמֵי מְיַבְּמֵי, וְאִי אִיכָּא נַחֲלָה – שָׁקְלֵי, וְאִי לָא – לָא שָׁקֵיל.

The Gemara rejects the possibility of saying this: **Does the Merciful One make** the mitzva of **levirate marriage dependent upon inheritance?**[N] Certainly not; rather, in all cases the *yavam* **should consummate the levirate marriage, and** then **if there is an inheritance** to which he is entitled, **he takes** it, **and if not, he does not take** it.

יְתֵיב רַבִּי חֲנִינָא קָרָא קַמֵּיהּ דְּרַבִּי יַנַּאי, וִיתֵיב וְקָאָמַר: הֲלָכָה כְּרַבִּי יְהוּדָה. אֲמַר לֵיהּ: פּוּק קְרִי קְרָיָיךְ לְבָרָא, אֵין הֲלָכָה כְּרַבִּי יְהוּדָה.

Rabbi Ḥanina Kara, the Bible expert,[P] **was sitting before Rabbi Yannai, and he was sitting and saying:** The *halakha* **is in accordance with** the opinion of **Rabbi Yehuda.** Rabbi Yannai **said to him: Leave** the study hall **and recite your verses outside,** as you are incorrect in your ruling; in fact, the *halakha* **is not in accordance with** the opinion of **Rabbi Yehuda.**

תָּנֵי תַּנָּא קַמֵּיהּ דְּרַב נַחְמָן: אֵין הֲלָכָה כְּרַבִּי יְהוּדָה. אָמַר לֵיהּ: אֶלָּא כְּמַאן, כְּרַבָּנַן? פְּשִׁיטָא, יָחִיד וְרַבִּים הֲלָכָה כְּרַבִּים!

In another incident, **a** *tanna*[N] who would recite *baraitot* in the study hall **taught** a *baraita* **before Rav Naḥman:** The *halakha* **is not in accordance with** the opinion of **Rabbi Yehuda. Rav Naḥman said to him: But** then it follows that **in accordance with whose** opinion is the *halakha*? It is the opinion of **the Rabbis.** The Gemara asks: But this fact **is obvious,** as in a dispute between **one** individual Sage **and many**[N] other Sages, the *halakha* is always decided in accordance with the opinion of **the many.**

אָמַר לֵיהּ: אִסְמְיֵיהּ?! אָמַר לֵיהּ: לָא, אַתְּ "הֲלָכָה" אַתְנְיָיךְ, וּמוּקְשָׁה הוּא דְּאַקְשֵׁי לָךְ, וְאַפַּכְתְּ, וּלְמַאי דְּאַפַּכְתְּ – שַׁפִּיר אַפַּכְתְּ.

The *tanna* **said to him:** Are you saying that this statement in the *baraita* is unnecessary and so **I should remove that** ruling from the *baraita* when I recite it in the future? Rav Naḥman **said to him: No,** do not remove it, as although the statement is unnecessary, it is correct. Rav Naḥman explained further: It must be that originally the *baraita* that **you were taught** stated: The *halakha* is in accordance with the opinion of Rabbi Yehuda, and **that** ruling **was difficult for you** because you knew that the *halakha* is always decided in accordance with many, **and so you reversed** the statement of the *baraita* to say, as you presently recited it, that the *halakha* is not in accordance with the opinion of Rabbi Yehuda. **And** with regard to the manner in **which you reversed it, you reversed it well,** and therefore you should leave it in its current form.

מתני׳ הַחוֹלֵץ לִיבִמְתּוֹ – הוּא אָסוּר בִּקְרוֹבוֹתֶיהָ, וְהִיא אֲסוּרָה בִּקְרוֹבָיו.

MISHNA In the case of **one who performs *ḥalitza* with his *yevama*,** by rabbinic decree it is as though she had been married to him and then he divorced her. Consequently, **he is forbidden** to engage in relations **with her relatives**[H] **and she is forbidden** to engage in relations **with his relatives.**

NOTES

Does the Merciful One make levirate marriage dependent upon inheritance – מִידֵי יִבּוּם בְּנַחֲלָה תָּלָה רַחֲמָנָא: The Gemara elsewhere (see 17b) does appear to link the mitzva of levirate marriage with the ability to inherit the deceased brother's property. However, in truth, there is a clear distinction between the two discussions. The Gemara that links the two concerns the question of which fraternal relationships qualify for the mitzva to apply and establishes that only brothers who can inherit from one another are obligated in the mitzva of levirate marriage toward each other's wives. The Gemara here that states that the mitzva is not dependent on whether the *yavam* can inherit the deceased brother's property is discussing a case where the *yavam* has the appropriate fraternal relationship, but in the present circumstances he will not actually inherit from the deceased brother because the father is still alive. In summary, the relationship which creates the possibility of inheritance must exist in order for the mitzva to apply, but there is no need for the *yavam* to actually inherit from his brother (*Tosefot HaRosh*; *Tosafot Yeshanim*).

***Tanna* – תַּנָּא:** The *tanna* referred to here is not a Sage from the tannaitic period. Rather, the term refers to those who memorized large numbers of *mishnayot* and *baraitot* to be able to quote them for the Sages who were engaged in analysis. Occasionally, the Sage had to emend the versions of these sources that had become corrupted or that represented minority opinions that had been rejected.

It is obvious, as in a dispute between one and many, etc. – פְּשִׁיטָא, יָחִיד וְרַבִּים וכו׳: The early commentaries point out that apparently it is not so obvious that the *halakha* should be decided in accordance with the opinion of the Rabbis because the Gemara itself cites many Sages who in fact ruled in accordance with the opinion of Rabbi Yehuda, and many more rulings to this effect are cited in the Jerusalem Talmud. They explain that what truly troubled Rav Naḥman was not the actual ruling in accordance with the opinion of the Rabbis but the roundabout formulation of the *baraita*: If the *halakha* is indeed in accordance with the opinion of the Rabbis, why didn't it simply say so explicitly, since the reason to rule in accordance with their opinion is not because of some issue with Rabbi Yehuda's opinion but simply because they represent the majority (Rashba; Ritva).

PERSONALITIES

Rabbi Ḥanina Kara, the Bible expert – רַבִּי חֲנִינָא קָרָא: A second-generation *amora* in Eretz Yisrael, Rabbi Ḥanina was a disciple of Rabbi Ḥanina bar Ḥama, Rabbi Ḥanina the Great, and Rabbi Yannai. Apparently, Rabbi Ḥanina not only taught young children but was also a Bible expert, which is why he was called *Kara*, meaning: The reader. He is mentioned in the Talmud and the midrash in discussions with his two teachers, both on matters relating to his work and on other halakhic matters.

HALAKHA

One who performs *ḥalitza* with his *yevama* is forbidden to engage in relations with her relatives – הַחוֹלֵץ לִיבִמְתּוֹ אָסוּר בִּקְרוֹבוֹתֶיהָ: One who performs *ḥalitza* with his *yevama* is forbidden to her relatives, i.e., her mother, her mother's mother, etc., since by rabbinic decree it is considered as though she was actually married to him and then he divorced her. Similarly, she is forbidden to his relatives (Rambam *Sefer Nashim*, *Hilkhot Yibbum VaḤalitza* 1:13; *Shulḥan Arukh*, *Even HaEzer* 162:3).

HALAKHA

He is permitted to a relative of a rival wife of his *ḥalutza* – מוּתָּר בִּקְרוֹבַת צָרַת חֲלוּצָתוֹ: It is permitted to marry a sister or any other relatives of a rival wife of one's *ḥalutza* (Rambam *Sefer Nashim, Hilkhot Yibbum VaḤalitza* 1:13; *Shulḥan Arukh, Even HaEzer* 162:4).

He is forbidden to engage in relations with a rival wife of a relative of his *ḥalutza* – אָסוּר בְּצָרַת קְרוֹבַת חֲלוּצָתוֹ: If one performed *ḥalitza* with his *yevama*, and her sister or other relative was married to another brother, who also died, such that the relative and her rival wife happened before him for levirate marriage, then just as the relative of the *ḥalutza* is forbidden to him, so too, her rival wife is forbidden to him, and they must perform *ḥalitza* but may not consummate the levirate marriage. This is in accordance with the ruling of the Rambam and most of the commentaries (Rambam *Sefer Nashim, Hilkhot Yibbum VaḤalitza* 6:20; *Shulḥan Arukh, Even HaEzer* 162:5, 174:3).

הוּא אָסוּר בְּאִמָּהּ, וּבְאֵם אִמָּהּ, וּבְאֵם אָבִיהָ, וּבְבִתָּהּ, וּבְבַת בִּתָּהּ, וּבְבַת בְּנָהּ, וּבַאֲחוֹתָהּ בִּזְמַן שֶׁהִיא קַיֶּימֶת, וְהָאַחִין מוּתָּרִין.

Accordingly, **he is forbidden** to engage in relations **with her mother,**[N] **and with her mother's mother, and with her father's mother, and with her daughter, and with her daughter's daughter, and with her son's daughter, and with her sister while** his *yevama* **is still alive.** However, **the** other **brothers** who did not perform *ḥalitza* **are permitted** to her relatives.

וְהִיא אֲסוּרָה בְּאָבִיו, וּבַאֲבִי אָבִיו, וּבִבְנוֹ, וּבְבֶן בְּנוֹ, בְּאָחִיו, וּבְבֶן אָחִיו.

And she is forbidden to engage in relations **with his father,**[N] **and with his father's father, and with his son, and with his son's son, and with his brother, and with his brother's son.**

מוּתָּר אָדָם בִּקְרוֹבַת צָרַת חֲלוּצָתוֹ, וְאָסוּר בְּצָרַת קְרוֹבַת חֲלוּצָתוֹ.

The mishna states an additional principle: **A man is permitted** to engage in relations **with a relative of a rival wife of his *ḥalutza*,**[H] i.e., his *yevama* with whom he performed *ḥalitza*. Since he did not perform *ḥalitza* with her, she is not regarded as though she had actually been married to him. However, **he is forbidden** to engage in relations **with a rival wife of a relative of his *ḥalutza*,**[HN] i.e., in addition to being forbidden to the relatives of his *ḥalutza*, he is also forbidden to their rival wives.

גמ׳ אִיבַּעְיָא לְהוּ: גָּזְרוּ שְׁנִיּוֹת בַּחֲלוּצָה אוֹ לָא?

GEMARA **A dilemma was raised before** the Sages: In addition to the Torah prohibition against engaging in relations with one's wife's close relatives, the Sages decreed that it is also prohibited to engage in relations with one's wife's secondary relatives, i.e., those who are less closely related and so are permitted by Torah law. Since the Sages decreed that a *ḥalutza* is to be regarded as though she had actually been married to the one who performed *ḥalitza*, such that her close relatives are forbidden to him, did **they** also **decree** that the prohibition of **secondary** forbidden **relationships** should also apply **in the case of a *ḥalutza*, or not?**

NOTES

He is forbidden to engage in relations with her mother, etc. – הוּא אָסוּר בְּאִמָּהּ וכו׳: The prohibition against engaging in relations with the relatives of one's wife continues to remain in force even should the couple divorce. By Torah law this prohibition applies only in a case of a true marriage. However, by rabbinic law the prohibition is also applied to a *yavam* and *yevama* by virtue of the levirate bond between them, which, in certain respects, is akin to a marriage. It is explained in the Jerusalem Talmud that although the levirate bond is sufficient to generate a prohibition while the bond exists, nevertheless, unlike a true marriage, that prohibition does not continue once the bond is dissolved. Therefore, if the *yevama* dies, the prohibition ends immediately and the relatives of the *yevama* are again permitted to all of the brothers; this is also true in a case in which one of the brothers performs *ḥalitza*, since *ḥalitza* dissolves the levirate bond. However, in that case, the Sages decreed that with respect to the brother who actually performed *ḥalitza*, the prohibition continues. This is due to the fact that *ḥalitza* is viewed as equivalent to a divorce, and therefore the Sages decreed that with respect to the brother who actually performed *ḥalitza* the prohibition continues as though he had actually been married to the *yevama* and then divorced her.

And she is forbidden to engage in relations with his father, etc. – וְהִיא אֲסוּרָה בְּאָבִיו וכו׳: The commentaries note that some of the relatives listed in the mishna are forbidden irrespective of the fact that the *yavam* performed *ḥalitza*. For example, the *yevama* is forbidden to the father of the one who performed *ḥalitza* by virtue of the fact that he is also the father of her deceased husband, and therefore she is forbidden to him as his daughter-in-law. Therefore, while conceding that in fact it was not necessary to list all of the relatives in the mishna, the commentaries explain that for the sake of completeness the mishna chose to list them all (*Gilyon Maharsha*, citing Responsa of Rabbi Shmuel Abuhav).

He is forbidden to engage in relations with a rival wife of a relative of his *ḥalutza* – אָסוּר בְּצָרַת קְרוֹבַת חֲלוּצָתוֹ: Rashi describes the case very simply: If the *ḥalutza* had a relative, e.g., a sister, and that relative was married to a man who had another wife, then that wife would also be forbidden. However, the Ramban, the Rashba, and many others question Rashi's explanation (see *Tosafot* on 41a): If Rashi is correct, it emerges that the *halakha* is stricter with regard to the relatives of a *ḥalutza*, who are forbidden by rabbinic decree, than with the relatives who are forbidden by Torah law, since the *halakha* permits one to engage in relations with the rival wives of relatives forbidden by Torah law. Therefore, many of the early commentaries (see the *Halakhot Gedolot*, Rambam, and Rid) explain that the mishna's prohibition applies only in a case in which both the relative and her rival wife are also bound by a levirate bond to the same brother. This could occur if a brother performed *ḥalitza* with his *yavama* and then his brother married a female relative of the first brother's *ḥalutza* and an additional wife, and then he died. The relative and her rival wife would then be bound by a levirate bond to the first brother. Since it is prohibited for the first brother to consummate the levirate marriage with the relative, since she is the relative of his *ḥalutza*, it is also prohibited for him to consummate the levirate marriage with her rival wife.

The *Yam shel Shlomo* defends Rashi's opinion and notes that it would appear that both the Rif and Rabbeinu Ḥananel also understood this in the same manner. He explains that it is true that according to this opinion a unique stringency exists in the case of a *ḥalutza* but suggests that this is the meaning of the Gemara's question at the end of this *amud*: What is different about this woman, the relative of the rival wife, who is permitted, and what is different about that woman, the rival wife of a relative, who is forbidden? The Gemara explains there that this stringency is necessary because since the case is very complex, people might not appreciate all of the nuances of the case and draw incorrect conclusions from it. To prevent any misunderstanding, the Sages decreed that the rival wife should be forbidden as well, similar to the standard case of a levirate bond with a forbidden relative and a rival wife (see *Arukh LaNer*).

בְּעֶרְוָה דְּאוֹרַיְיתָא גְּזוּר בְּהוּ רַבָּנַן שְׁנִיּוֹת, בַּחֲלוּצָה לָא גְּזוּר רַבָּנַן שְׁנִיּוֹת, אוֹ דִּלְמָא לָא שְׁנָא?

The Gemara presents the sides of the dilemma: Did **the Sages decree** that the prohibition of **secondary** forbidden **relationships** applies only **in** a case where there is a relative with whom **relations** are **forbidden by Torah** law, but **in** the case of a ***ḥalutza***, whose relatives are forbidden only by rabbinic decree, **they did not decree** that there should be a prohibition of **secondary** forbidden **relationships? Or perhaps** the case of a ***ḥalutza*** **is no different,**[H] and since the basis of the rabbinic prohibition applying to her relatives is that it is considered as though she had actually been married to her *yavam*, the prohibition should extend to her secondary relatives as well?

תָּא שְׁמַע: "הוּא אָסוּר בְּאִמָּהּ וּבְאֵם אִמָּהּ", וְאִילּוּ "אֵם אֵם אִמָּהּ" – לָא קָתָנֵי.

The Gemara suggests: **Come** and **hear** a proof from the mishna: A *yavam* **is prohibited** from engaging in relations **with** the **mother of** his *ḥalutza* **and with her mother's mother. However,** the mishna **does not teach** that it is prohibited to engage in relations with **her mother's mother's mother,** which is one of the secondary relationships. This would suggest that the prohibition of secondary relationships does not apply in this case.

דִּלְמָא הַיְינוּ טַעְמָא דְּלָא תָּנֵי – מִשּׁוּם דְּקָבָעֵי לְמִיתְנֵי סֵיפָא "וְהָאַחִין מוּתָּרִין", וְאִי תָּנָא "אֵם אֵם אִמָּהּ" הֲוָה אָמֵינָא: הָאַחִין מוּתָּרִין דַּוְקָא בְּאֵם אֵם אִמָּהּ, אֲבָל בְּאֵם אִמָּהּ וּבְאִמָּהּ לָא.

The Gemara rejects the proof: **Perhaps this is the reason that** the mishna **does not teach** that case, **because it needs to teach in the latter clause:** However, **the** other **brothers** who did not perform *ḥalitza* **are permitted** to her relatives. **And if it** had **taught** the prohibition of **her mother's mother's mother** in the first clause, **I would** mistakenly **say** that **the brothers are permitted specifically to her mother's mother's mother, but not to her mother's mother.** Therefore, no proof can be adduced from that case of the mishna.

וְלִיתְנֵי "אֵם אֵם אִמָּהּ" וְלִיתְנֵי "הָאַחִין מוּתָּרִין בְּכוּלָּן"! קַשְׁיָא.

The Gemara objects: **But** if he is forbidden to the great-grandmother, then **let it teach: Her mother's mother's mother** in the first clause, **and** then **let it teach: The brothers are permitted to all of them,** in the latter clause. This would avoid the concern stated above. The fact that the mishna did not do so would suggest that he is not forbidden to the great-grandmother, or any other secondary relatives. The Gemara concludes: Indeed, this is **difficult**, but still inconclusive.

תָּא שְׁמַע: הִיא אֲסוּרָה בְּאָבִיו וּבַאֲבִי אָבִיו. קָתָנֵי מִיהָא אֲבִי אָבִיו, מַאי לָאו – מִשּׁוּם חוֹלֵץ, דְּהָוְיָא לֵיהּ כַּלַּת בְּנוֹ!

The Gemara suggests: **Come** and **hear** another proof from the mishna: **She is prohibited** from engaging in relations **with his father, and with his father's father.** The Gemara explains the proof: **In any case,** the mishna **teaches** that she is forbidden to **his father's father. What, is it not** that she is forbidden to him **due to** the rabbinic decree that it is considered as though she had actually been married to **the one who performed *ḥalitza*** with her, and therefore she is forbidden to the grandfather because **she is considered to be** the grandfather's **son's daughter-in-law,** i.e., the wife of one of the grandfather's grandsons, which is a secondary relationship? If so, the mishna explicitly demonstrates that the prohibition of secondary relationships also applies in the case of a *ḥalutza*.

לָא, מִשּׁוּם מִיתְנָא, דְּהָוְיָא לֵיהּ כַּלַּת בְּנוֹ.

The Gemara rejects the proof: **No,** she is forbidden to his grandfather **due to** her previous marriage with **the deceased,** whose relatives are forbidden to her by Torah law, and it is due to that relationship **that she is considered** the grandfather's **son's daughter-in-law.** Therefore, no proof can be adduced from that case of the mishna.

תָּא שְׁמַע: וּבְבֶן בְּנוֹ. מַאי לָאו – מִשּׁוּם חוֹלֵץ, דְּהָוְיָא לֵיהּ (מִשּׁוּם) אֵשֶׁת אֲבִי אָבִיו!

The Gemara suggests: **Come** and **hear** another proof from the mishna: **And** she is prohibited from engaging in relations **with his son's son.** The Gemara explains the proof: **What, is it not** that she is forbidden to him **due to** the rabbinic decree that it is considered as though she had actually been married to **the one who performed *ḥalitza*** with her, and **she is** therefore forbidden to his grandson because **she is considered to be the wife** of that grandson's **father's father,** which is a secondary relationship? If so, the mishna explicitly demonstrates that the prohibition of secondary relationships also applies in the case of a *ḥalutza*.

HALAKHA

Secondary forbidden relationships of a *ḥalutza* – שְׁנִיּוֹת בַּחֲלוּצָה: Just as the Sages prohibited relations with secondary relatives in the case of relatives who are forbidden by Torah law, they also prohibited relations with secondary relatives in the case of a *ḥalutza*. This is in accordance with the conclusion of the Gemara (Rambam *Sefer Nashim, Hilkhot Yibbum VaḤalitza* 1:12; *Shulḥan Arukh, Even HaEzer* 162:3).

BACKGROUND

She is forbidden to his son's son – אֲסוּרָה בְּבֶן בְּנוֹ: For example, Reuven and Shimon are the sons of Ya'akov and Leah. Shimon married Miriam and died childless, so that Miriam happened before Reuven for levirate marriage. Reuven performed *ḥalitza* with Miriam. Accordingly, Miriam is forbidden to Reuven's relatives as follows: She is forbidden to Reuven's paternal grandfather, Yitzḥak, since she is the daughter-in-law of his son, and she is forbidden to Reuven's maternal grandfather, Lavan, since she is the daughter-in-law of his daughter. She is also forbidden to Yoel and Mikha, the sons of Reuven's son and daughter, respectively. The reason she is forbidden to Yoel is both because it is considered as though she had actually been married to Reuven and therefore she is considered to be the wife of Yoel's paternal grandfather, and also because she was married to Shimon and therefore she was the wife of Yoel's paternal grandfather's brother. She is forbidden to Mikha due to the fact that it is considered as though she had actually been married to Reuven and therefore she is considered to be the wife of Mikha's maternal grandfather, which is a secondary forbidden relationship. However she would not be forbidden due to the fact that she was married to Shimon, because that renders her the wife of the brother of Mikha's maternal grandfather, which is a permitted relationship.

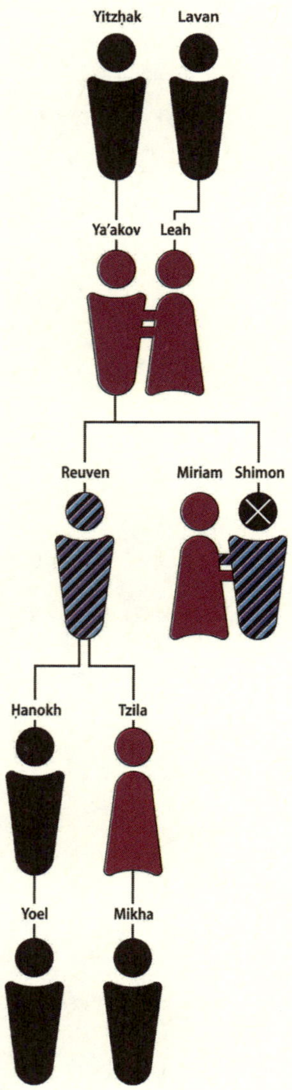

לָא, מִשּׁוּם מִיתְנָא, וְהָוְיָא לָהּ אֵשֶׁת אֲחִי אֲבִי אָבִיו.

The Gemara rejects the proof: **No,** she is forbidden to his grandson **due to** her previous marriage with **the deceased,** whose relatives are forbidden to her by Torah law, and it is due to that relationship that **she is considered to be the wife of a brother of** that grandson's **father's father,** which is also a forbidden secondary relationship. Therefore, no proof can be adduced from that case of the mishna.

הָא אֲמֵימַר מַכְשַׁר בְּאֵשֶׁת אֲחִי אֲבִי אָבִיו!

The Gemara asks: **But Ameimar rules permissible** the marriage of a man **to the wife of a brother of** that man's **father's father.** Accordingly, the prohibition in the mishna cannot be due to that relationship.

אֲמֵימַר מוֹקֵי לָהּ בְּבַר בְּרָא דְּסָבָא.

The Gemara explains: **Ameimar** would **establish** the mishna's case of: His son's son, as referring to engaging in relations **with a son of a son of the grandfather.** The mishna states that she is forbidden to his father, to his father's father, to his son, and to his son's son. The Gemara assumed that antecedent of the pronoun: His, in the phrase: To his son and to his son's son, is the one who performed *ḥalitza*. As such, the mishna teaches that she is forbidden to the son and grandson of the one who performed *ḥalitza* with her, which are secondary relationships. Ameimar, however, would claim the antecedent of this pronoun is the father's father, which immediately precedes it in the mishna. As such, the mishna is teaching that she is forbidden to the grandfather of the one who performed *ḥalitza* with her, to that grandfather's sons, i.e., the brothers of the deceased, and to the grandfather's sons' sons, i.e., the nephews of the deceased. The *yevama* is forbidden to these relatives by Torah law. Therefore, no proof can be derived from that case of the mishna.

אִי הָכִי, הַיְינוּ אָחִיו וּבֶן אָחִיו! תָּנָא אָחִיו מִן הָאָב, וְקָתָנֵי אָחִיו מִן הָאֵם

The Gemara challenges this understanding of: His son and his son's son: But **if so, these** relatives **are** none other than **his brother and the son of his brother,** who are already explicitly mentioned in the mishna. The Gemara explains: This is not a case of unnecessary repetition because the mishna first **teaches** that she is forbidden to **his paternal** half **brother and** then **teaches** that she is forbidden to **his maternal** half **brother** as well.

תָּא שְׁמַע, דְּתָנֵי רַבִּי חִיָּיא: אַרְבַּע מִדִּבְרֵי תוֹרָה, וְאַרְבַּע מִדִּבְרֵי סוֹפְרִים. אָב וּבְנוֹ, אָחִיו וּבֶן אָחִיו – מִדִּבְרֵי תוֹרָה, אֲבִי אָבִיו וַאֲבִי אִמּוֹ, בֶּן בְּנוֹ, וּבֶן בִּתּוֹ – מִדִּבְרֵי סוֹפְרִים.

The Gemara suggests: **Come** and **hear** a proof from a *baraita* **that Rabbi Ḥiyya taught:** Of the relatives who are forbidden to a *ḥalutza*, **four** are forbidden **by Torah law and four by rabbinic law,** as follows: **The father** of the deceased husband, **and his son,**[N] **his brother, and his brother's son** are forbidden **by Torah law; his father's father, and his mother's father, his son's son,**[B] **and his daughter's son** are forbidden **by rabbinic law.**

קָתָנֵי מִיהָא אֲבִי אָבִיו, מַאי לָאו מִשּׁוּם חוֹלֵץ, וְהָוְיָא לָהּ כַּלַּת בְּנוֹ!

In any case, the *baraita* **teaches** that she is forbidden to **his father's father. What, is it not** that she is forbidden to him **due to** the rabbinic decree that it is considered as though she had actually been married to **the one who performed** ***ḥalitza*** with her, and therefore she is forbidden to the grandfather because **she is considered to be** the grandfather's **son's daughter-in-law,** which is a secondary forbidden relationship? This would prove that the prohibition of secondary relationships applies in the case of a *ḥalutza*.

NOTES

The father and his son, etc. – אָב וּבְנוֹ וכו׳: Most commentaries explain that the phrase: The father and his son, in the *baraita* is referring to the father and son of the one who performed *ḥalitza*. The difficulty with this understanding is that the *baraita* continues to mention the prohibition of the brother of the one who performed *ḥalitza* and the brother's son, even though both the son of the one who performed *ḥalitza* and the son of his brother are forbidden to the *ḥalutza* for the identical reason that they are the sons of her deceased husband's brother. The commentaries concede this point and explain that the mishna wished to organize those forbidden to the *ḥalutza* by their relationship to the one who performed *ḥalitza*. The Maharam MiRotenburg suggests an explanation that avoids this difficulty. He interprets the reference: His son, not as a reference to the son of the one who performed *ḥalitza* but to the son of the father of the one who performed *ḥalitza*, who is mentioned immediately before. As such, it refers to the paternal half brother of the one who performed *ḥalitza*. He then proceeds to explain that when the *baraita* continues to refer to the brother of the one who performed *ḥalitza*, the reference is to his maternal half brother (*Tosefot HaRosh*).

לָא, מִשּׁוּם מִיתְנָא, דְּהָוְיָא לָהּ כַּלַּת בְּנוֹ.	The Gemara rejects the proof: **No,** she is forbidden **due to** her previous marriage with **the deceased,** whose relatives are forbidden to her by Torah law, and it is due to that relationship that **she is considered** the grandfather's **son's daughter-in-law.** Therefore, no proof can be adduced from that case of the *baraita.*
תָּא שְׁמַע: אֲבִי אִמּוֹ – מַאי לָאו מִשּׁוּם חוֹלֵץ, דְּהָוְיָא לָהּ כַּלַּת בִּתּוֹ!	The Gemara proceeds to consider whether proof may be adduced from each of the other secondary relationships listed in the *baraita:* **Come** and **hear** a proof from that which the *baraita* teaches: She is forbidden to **his mother's father.** The Gemara explains the proof: **What, is it not** that she is forbidden to him **due to** the rabbinic decree that it is considered as though she had actually been married to **the one who performed *ḥalitza*** with her, and therefore she is forbidden to the grandfather because **she is considered to be** the grandfather's **daughter's daughter-in-law,** which is a secondary relationship? This would prove that the prohibition of secondary relationships applies in the case of a *ḥalutza.*
לָא, מִשּׁוּם מִיתְנָא, דְּהָוְיָא לָהּ כַּלַּת בִּתּוֹ.	The Gemara rejects the proof: **No,** she is forbidden **due to** her previous marriage with **the deceased,** whose relatives are forbidden to her by Torah law, and it is due to that relationship that **she is considered** the grandfather's **daughter's daughter-in-law.** Therefore, no proof can be adduced from that case of the *baraita.*
תָּא שְׁמַע: וּבֶן בְּנוֹ, מַאי לָאו מִשּׁוּם חוֹלֵץ, דְּהָוְיָא לָהּ אֵשֶׁת אֲבִי אָבִיו!	**Come** and **hear** a proof from that which the *baraita* teaches: **And** she is forbidden to **his son's son.** The Gemara explains the proof: **What, is it not** that she is forbidden to him **due to** the rabbinic decree that it is considered as though she had actually been married to **the one who performed *ḥalitza*** with her, and so she is forbidden to his grandson because **she is considered to be the wife** of that grandson's **father's father,** which is a secondary relationship? If so, the *baraita* explicitly demonstrates that the prohibition of secondary relationships applies in the case of a *ḥalutza.*
לָא, מִשּׁוּם מִיתְנָא, וְהָוְיָא לָהּ אֵשֶׁת אֲחִי אֲבִי אָבִיו.	The Gemara rejects the proof: **No,** she is forbidden to his grandson **due to** her previous marriage with **the deceased,** whose relatives are forbidden to her by Torah law, and due to that relationship **she is considered to be the wife of a brother of** that grandson's **father's father,** which is also a forbidden secondary relationship. Therefore, no proof can be adduced from that case of the *baraita.*
וְהָא אֲמֵימַר מַכְשִׁיר בְּאֵשֶׁת אֲחִי אֲבִי אָבִיו! אֲמֵימַר מוֹקִים לָהּ מִשּׁוּם חוֹלֵץ, וְקָסָבַר גָּזְרוּ שְׁנִיּוֹת בַּחֲלוּצָה.	The Gemara asks: **But didn't Ameimar rule permissible** the marriage of a man **with the wife of a brother of his father's father?** Accordingly, the prohibition in the mishna cannot be due to that relationship. The Gemara concedes: **Ameimar** would **establish** the mishna's case of: His son's son, **as** being **due to** the rabbinic decree that it is considered as though she had actually been married to **the one who performed *ḥalitza*** with her, **and** as such it is evident that **he holds** that the Sages **decreed** that the prohibition of **secondary** forbidden **relationships** should apply **in** the case of **a *ḥalutza.***
תָּא שְׁמַע: וּבֶן בִּתּוֹ, מַאי לָאו מִשּׁוּם חוֹלֵץ, דְּהָוְיָא לָהּ אֵשֶׁת אֲבִי אִמּוֹ!	The Gemara continues to seek proof for those who disagree with Ameimar: **Come** and **hear** a proof from that which the *baraita* teaches: **And** she is forbidden to **his daughter's son.** The Gemara explains the proof: **What, is it not** that she is forbidden to him **due to** the rabbinic decree that it is considered as though she had actually been married to the **one who performed *ḥalitza*** with her, and so **she is** forbidden to his grandson because **she is considered to be the wife** of that grandson's **mother's father,** which is a secondary relationship? If so, the *baraita* explicitly demonstrates that the prohibition of secondary relationships applies in the case of a *ḥalutza.*
לָא, מִשּׁוּם מִיתְנָא דְּהָוְיָא לָהּ אֵשֶׁת אֲחִי אֲבִי אִמּוֹ. וְהָא גַּבֵּי שְׁנִיּוֹת עֶרְוָה לָא גָּזְרוּ!	The Gemara rejects the proof: **No,** she is forbidden to his grandson **due to** her previous marriage with **the deceased,** whose relatives are forbidden to her by Torah law, and due to that relationship **she is considered to be the wife of a brother of** the grandson's **mother's father.** The Gemara challenges this: **But** the Sages did **not decree** that such a person is included **among** those relatives who are forbidden as **secondary** forbidden **relationships.**

PERSONALITIES

Rav Tovi bar Kisna – רַב טוֹבִי בַּר קִיסְנָא: A second-generation *amora* who lived in Babylonia, Rav Tovi was a disciple of Shmuel, and most of his statements cite his teacher as their source. He is also known as Rav Tavi bar Kisna (*Eiruvin* 104b) and Rav Tavyomi bar Kisna (*Menaḥot* 70a).

אֶלָּא לָאו מִשּׁוּם חוֹלֵץ, וּשְׁמַע מִינַּהּ: גָּזְרוּ שְׁנִיּוֹת בַּחֲלוּצָה, שְׁמַע מִינַּהּ.

Rather, is it not, as the Gemara initially assumed, that she is forbidden to him **due to** the rabbinic decree that it is considered as though she had actually been married to **the one who performed *ḥalitza*** with her, **and** therefore must one not **conclude from** this case that the Sages **decreed** that the prohibition of **secondary** forbidden **relationships** should apply **in** the case of **a *ḥalutza*?** The Gemara confirms: One should indeed **conclude from it** that this is so.

״מוּתָּר אָדָם״ וכו׳. אָמַר רַב טוֹבִי בַּר קִיסְנָא אָמַר שְׁמוּאֵל: הַבָּא עַל צָרַת חֲלוּצָה – הַוָּלָד מַמְזֵר. מַאי טַעְמָא – בְּאִיסּוּרָהּ קַיְימָא.

§ The mishna states: **A man is permitted** to engage in relations with a relative of a rival wife of his *ḥalutza*; however, he is prohibited from engaging in relations with a rival wife of a relative of his *ḥalutza*. The Gemara cites a ruling: **Rav Tovi bar Kisna**[P] **said** that **Shmuel said:** With regard to **one who engages in intercourse with a rival wife** of his ***ḥalutza*, the offspring** of that union **is a *mamzer*. What is the reason** for this ruling? It is that **she remains in her** original **prohibition.**

Normally, it is prohibited to engage in relations with one's brother's wife. However, when there is a mitzva to consummate levirate marriage, that prohibition does not apply, due to the levirate bond between the *yavam* and *yevama*. Although following *ḥalitza* the levirate bond is dissolved, the woman's status as a *ḥalutza* means that only the lesser prohibition against marrying a *ḥalutza* applies to her, and she does not return to her original forbidden status. Shmuel claims that the rival wives of the *ḥalutza* are not considered to be represented in her act of *ḥalitza*; consequently, they are not afforded a status similar to that of the *ḥalutza* herself. Therefore, he assumes that following *ḥalitza* the rival wives once again become subject to the original prohibition against marrying a brother's wife. Since that prohibition entails *karet*, any offspring born from such a union is a *mamzer*.

אֲמַר רַב יוֹסֵף: אַף אֲנַן נַמִי תָּנֵינָא: מוּתָּר אָדָם בִּקְרוֹבַת צָרַת חֲלוּצָתוֹ. אִי אָמְרַתְּ בִּשְׁלָמָא צָרָה אַבָּרַאי – מִשּׁוּם הָכִי מוּתָּר בַּאֲחוֹתָהּ.

Rav Yosef said: We, too, learned this though an inference from the mishna: **A man is permitted** to engage in relations **with a relative of a rival wife of his *ḥalutza*.** Rav Yosef explains the inference: **Granted, if you say** that **a rival wife is outside,** i.e., she is not represented in the *ḥalitza* of the *ḥalutza* and so she is not afforded a status similar to that of the *ḥalutza* herself, then it is **due to that** reason that **he is permitted** to engage in relations **with her sister** and other relatives, because since they are not the relatives of his *ḥalutza*, there is no reason for them to be forbidden.

אֶלָּא אִי אָמְרַתְּ צָרָה כַּחֲלוּצָה דָּמְיָא – אַמַּאי מוּתָּר?

However, if you say that **a rival wife is** afforded a status **similar to** that of **the *ḥalutza*** herself, **why is he permitted** to her relatives? Rather, from the fact that the relatives of the rival wives are permitted, it is apparent that the rival wives are not represented in the *ḥalitza*. As such, it follows that they should return to their original forbidden status of a brother's wives, as Shmuel claims.

לֵימָא תֶּיהֱוֵי תְּיוּבְתָּא דְּרַבִּי יוֹחָנָן, דְּאָמַר: בֵּין הוּא בֵּין אַחִין אֵין חַיָּיבִין לֹא עַל הַחֲלוּצָה כָּרֵת, וְלֹא עַל צָרָתָהּ כָּרֵת!

The Gemara suggests: **Shall we say,** then, that this mishna **is a conclusive refutation of** the opinion of **Rabbi Yoḥanan?**[N] As Rabbi Yoḥanan **said: Neither he** who performed the *ḥalitza* **nor his brothers are liable to** receive ***karet***; they are **neither** liable to receive ***karet*** **on account of** engaging in relations with **the *ḥalutza*, nor** are they liable to receive ***karet*** **on account of** engaging in relations with **her rival wife.**

NOTES

Shall we say that this is a conclusive refutation of the opinion of Rabbi Yoḥanan – לֵימָא תֶּיהֱוֵי תְּיוּבְתָּא דְּרַבִּי יוֹחָנָן: An objection to Rabbi Yoḥanan's opinion could be raised on different grounds: According to his opinion a rival wife is considered as though she herself had performed *ḥalitza*, since the *ḥalutza* is considered to have represented her in the act of *ḥalitza*, and furthermore, all of the brothers are considered as though they had themselves performed the *ḥalitza* since they were all represented by the brother who actually performed the act of *ḥalitza*. In that case, why aren't all of the brothers forbidden to the relatives of all of the rival wives? The commentaries explain that clearly the suggested explanation for the prohibition with regard to the rival wives of the relatives of the *ḥalutza*, i.e., that the relatives accompany her to court, does not exist when it comes to the brothers, who do not accompany each other to court (see Ritva). Moreover, since the prohibition is only rabbinic in nature, the Sages were not so stringent as to render the relative of a rival wife like the *ḥalutza* herself (*Tosafot*; Meiri).

אָמַר לָךְ רַבִּי יוֹחָנָן: וְתִסְבְּרָא אֲחוֹת חֲלוּצָה דְּאוֹרַיְיתָא? וְהָאָמַר רֵישׁ לָקִישׁ: כָּאן שָׁנָה רַבִּי: אֲחוֹת גְּרוּשָׁה – מִדִּבְרֵי תוֹרָה, אֲחוֹת חֲלוּצָה – מִדִּבְרֵי סוֹפְרִים.

The Gemara responds: **Rabbi Yoḥanan** could have **said to you: But** how can **you understand** it that way? Why do you assume that if the rival wives are considered to be represented in the *ḥalitza* that perforce means that their relatives should be forbidden to the *yavam*? Is **a sister of** one's ***ḥalutza*** forbidden **by Torah** law? **Didn't Reish Lakish say** with regard to another mishna (41a): **Here, Rabbi** Yehuda HaNasi **taught:** Engaging in relations with **a sister of** one's **divorcée** is forbidden **by Torah law,** whereas engaging in relations with **a sister of** one's ***ḥalutza*** **is** forbidden **by rabbinic law.** Since the prohibition with regard to the relatives of one's *ḥalutza* is rabbinic, it is reasonable to assume that it was applied to only the wife who actually performed *ḥalitza* and not extended to her rival wives, even if they are considered to be represented in her *ḥalitza* to the extent that they do not return to their original forbidden status.

מַאי שְׁנָא הַאי, וּמַאי שְׁנָא הַאי?

§ The Gemara questions the distinction indicated by the mishna: **What is different** about **this** woman, the relative of a rival wife of one's *ḥalutza,* that she is permitted, **and what is different** about **that** woman, the rival wife of a relative of one's *ḥalutza,* that she is forbidden?

Perek **IV**
Daf **41** Amud **a**

הָךְ דְּאָזְלָא בַּהֲדָהּ לְבֵי דִּינָא – גְּזַרוּ בְּהוּ רַבָּנַן, הַאי דְּלָא אָזְלָא בַּהֲדָהּ לְבֵי דִּינָא – לָא גְּזַרוּ בְּהוּ רַבָּנַן.

The Gemara explains: With regard to **that** woman, the relative of the *ḥalutza,* **who** often **goes together with** the *ḥalutza*[N] **to court,** since she is present in the court during the *ḥalitza,* people might mistakenly assume that it was she who actually performed *ḥalitza.* Were the *yavam* permitted to marry her rival wife, people might incorrectly conclude that it is permitted to marry the rival wife of one's *ḥalutza.* To preclude this possibility, **the Sages decreed with regard to her** that her rival wife should be forbidden. However, with regard to **this** woman, the rival wife of the *ḥalutza,* **who does not go together with** the *ḥalutza* **to court,** since she is never present in the court during the *ḥalitza,* there is no concern that people will mistake her for the *ḥalutza* herself. Consequently, **the Sages did not** see any reason to **decree with regard to her** that her relatives should be forbidden.

מתני׳ הַחוֹלֵץ לִיבִמְתּוֹ, וְנָשָׂא אָחִיו אֶת אֲחוֹתָהּ, וָמֵת – חוֹלֶצֶת וְלֹא מִתְיַבֶּמֶת. וְכֵן הַמְגָרֵשׁ אֶת אִשְׁתּוֹ, וְנָשָׂא אָחִיו אֶת אֲחוֹתָהּ וָמֵת – הֲרֵי זוֹ פְּטוּרָה.

MISHNA In the case of a *yavam* **who performed *ḥalitza* with his *yevama* and then his brother married her sister**[H] **and died,** the sister **performs *ḥalitza*** with the *yavam*, **but she may not enter into levirate marriage** with him, since as a sister of his *ḥalutza* she is forbidden to him. **And similarly,** in the case of **one who divorced his wife and his brother married her sister and died,**[H] **then that** woman **is exempt** both from *ḥalitza* and from consummating levirate marriage, since as the sister of his former wife she is forbidden to him.

HALAKHA

One who performed *ḥalitza* with his *yevama* and then his brother married her sister – הַחוֹלֵץ לִיבִמְתּוֹ וְנָשָׂא אָחִיו אֶת אֲחוֹתָהּ: If a *yavam* performed *ḥalitza* with his *yevama* and then his brother married her sister or one of her other relatives, and then the brother died, the sister or other relative happens for levirate marriage before the *yavam* who originally performed the *ḥalitza*. However, as a relative of his *ḥalutza*, she is forbidden to him. Therefore, she performs *ḥalitza* but may not consummate the levirate marriage. Similarly, her rival wife performs *ḥalitza* but may not enter into levirate marriage (Rambam *Sefer Nashim, Hilkhot Yibbum VaḤalitza* 6:20; *Shulḥan Arukh, Even HaEzer* 174:3).

The sister of his divorcée – אֲחוֹת גְּרוּשָׁתוֹ: If one divorces his wife and then her sister falls before him for levirate marriage, she is exempt from both *ḥalitza* and from levirate marriage because, as long as his former wife is alive, her sister is prohibited by Torah law from engaging in relations with him (Rambam *Sefer Nashim, Hilkhot Yibbum VaḤalitza* 6:9; *Shulḥan Arukh, Even HaEzer* 173:1).

NOTES

That woman who goes together with the *ḥalutza* – הָךְ דְּאָזְלָא בַּהֲדָהּ: The version of the Gemara cited here has: That woman who goes together with her. Based on this version, Rashi, Rabbeinu Ḥananel, and the Rif explain that: Goes with her, is referring to people that accompany the *ḥalutza* to court. Based on this, they explain that since the relative of the *ḥalutza* accompanies her to court, some people might mistakenly think that it was the relative who performed *ḥalitza*. Therefore, it is necessary to render the rival wife of the relative of the *ḥalutza* forbidden, just as the rival wife of the *ḥalutza* herself is forbidden. However, since the rival wife never accompanies the *ḥalutza*, there is no concern that people might mistakenly think she performed the *ḥalitza*, and so there is no need to render her relatives forbidden.

Tosafot and other early commentaries challenge this explanation; *Yam shel Shlomo* suggests a defense of Rashi's opinion. *Tosafot* themselves suggest that a different version of the Gemara is preferable, which states: That woman who goes with him, where him refers to the *yavam* who performed the *ḥalitza*. Accordingly, the Gemara's distinction is simply between the *ḥalutza*, who actually underwent the *ḥalitza*, and her rival wives, who did not. The Sages expanded the prohibition only to the relatives of the former. The Ramban writes that this version is to be preferred but he questions the authenticity of this version of the text.

Based on the present version of the Gemara, the Maharam MiRotenburg suggests a third interpretation. He understands that the Gemara is referring to a point in time after the *ḥalitza* has already been performed, when the relatives of the *ḥalutza* go to court to inquire as to their status. At that point, the relatives of the *ḥalutza* are instructed that they may not marry the *yavam*. The Gemara states that since the relatives are accompanied by their rival wives, and there is a possibility that people will confuse them, the Sages also rendered the rivals wives of the relatives forbidden (*Tosefot HaRosh*).

שׁוֹמֶרֶת יָבָם שֶׁקִּידֵּשׁ אָחִיו אֶת אֲחוֹתָהּ, מִשּׁוּם רַבִּי יְהוּדָה בֶּן בְּתֵירָא אָמְרוּ: אוֹמְרִים לוֹ: הַמְתֵּן עַד שֶׁיַּעֲשֶׂה אָחִיךָ מַעֲשֶׂה.

In the case of **a widow waiting for her** ***yavam*** to consummate levirate marriage or perform *ḥalitza* with her, and the **brother of** the *yavam* **betrothed her sister,**[H] **they said in the name of Rabbi Yehuda ben Beteira: They say to** the brother: **Wait** and do not marry[N] the woman you betrothed **until your brother performs an act,**[N] either of *ḥalitza* or of consummating the levirate marriage, as until he does there remains a levirate bond between the *yevama* and each of the brothers, and it is prohibited to marry the sister of a woman to whom one is bound by a levirate bond.

חָלַץ לָהּ אָחִיו אוֹ כְּנָסָהּ – יִכְנוֹס אֶת אִשְׁתּוֹ. מֵתָה הַיְבָמָה – יִכְנוֹס אֶת אִשְׁתּוֹ. מֵת יָבָם – יוֹצִיא אֶת אִשְׁתּוֹ בְּגֵט, וְאֵשֶׁת אָחִיו בַּחֲלִיצָה.

If a **brother of** the one who betrothed the sister of the *yevama* **performed** ***ḥalitza*** **with** the *yevama* **or consummated a levirate marriage with her,** since by doing so the levirate bond between the *yevama* and the one who betrothed her sister is dissolved, **he may** then **enter into marriage** with **his wife,** who until that point was only betrothed to him, as she is no longer the sister of a woman to whom he is bound by a levirate bond. Similarly, if **the** ***yevama*** **died,** since his levirate bond to her is dissolved upon her death, **he may** proceed to **enter into marriage** with **his** betrothed **wife.** However, if the ***yavam*** **died**[H] without performing an act that would have dissolved the levirate bond, **he must divorce his wife with a bill of divorce,**[N] as she is forbidden to him as the sister of a woman to whom he is bound by a levirate bond, **and his brother's wife** he must send out **with** ***ḥalitza,***[N] as she is forbidden to him as the sister of his divorcée.

גמ׳ מַאי ״וְכֵן״? אֵימָא: אֲבָל הַמְגָרֵשׁ.

GEMARA The mishna considers two cases in which there is no possibility of consummating levirate marriage with a *yevama*. In the first case the reason is that she is the sister of one's *ḥalutza*, and in the second it is that she is the sister of one's divorcée. The mishna appears to compare the two cases by introducing the second case with: And similarly. The Gemara questions this: **What is the meaning of: And similarly?** The two cases are not similar; in the first case the *yevama* must perform *ḥalitza*, and in the second she is entirely exempt from the need to do anything. The Gemara answers: Emend the mishna and **say: However, one who divorces.**[N]

HALAKHA

A widow waiting for her *yavam* and the brother of the *yavam* betrothed her sister – שׁוֹמֶרֶת יָבָם שֶׁקִּידֵּשׁ אָחִיו אֶת אֲחוֹתָהּ: It is prohibited for one to marry a relative of a woman to whom one is bound by a levirate bond. Therefore, if a woman happens for levirate marriage before a number of brothers, and one of them betroths her sister, it is prohibited for him to proceed to marry the relative he betrothed until after one of the other brothers either consummates the levirate marriage with the *yevama* or performs *ḥalitza* with her, thereby dissolving the levirate bond between her and the other brothers. Some say that if the brother who betrothed the sister transgressed and proceeded to marry her, then the levirate bond to him is thereby dissolved, and so he is allowed to engage in relations with his wife even before his brother performs levirate marriage or *ḥalitza* (*Tosafot*; Rosh). Rabbeinu Gershom Meor HaGola issued a ban prohibiting a man from being married to two women. Some say that included in the ban is the case of a *yavam* who is bound by a levirate bond to a *yevama*, such that it is prohibited for the *yavam* to marry any other woman until he has first performed *ḥalitza* with the *yevama* (Mahari Mintz). However, if the woman he wishes to marry had committed herself to marry him before the *yevama* happened before him for levirate marriage, then he is permitted to marry her even before he performs *ḥalitza* (*Haggahot Mordekhai*; Rambam *Sefer Nashim, Hilkhot Yibbum VaḤalitza* 1:14; *Shulḥan Arukh, Even HaEzer* 159:5).

The *yavam* died, etc. – מֵת יָבָם וכו׳: With regard to a *yavam* who is bound to his *yevama* through a levirate bond, who transgressed and betrothed the sister of his *yevama*, if his other brothers die, since the woman is then bound to him alone, he must divorce the betrothed sister with a bill of divorce and release his *yevama* by performing *ḥalitza* (Rambam *Sefer Nashim, Hilkhot Yibbum VaḤalitza* 1:14; *Shulḥan Arukh, Even HaEzer* 159:7).

NOTES

Wait and do not marry – הַמְתֵּן: The marriage process consists of two distinct stages. In the first stage, termed *kiddushin* or *eirusin*, a legal bond is formed between the couple that defines the woman as a wife to the extent that the dissolution of that bond requires a divorce, and sexual relations with other men are considered adulterous and are punishable by death. However, the couple may still not yet live together as man and wife, and most of the couple's mutual obligations do no yet apply. This stage is usually translated as "betrothal," even though that term fails to convey the fact that this stage is not a precursor to a marriage, but actually the first stage of the marriage.

The second stage of marriage, termed *nissuin*, and translated simply as "marriage," is usually effected by having the couple stand under a marriage canopy together or being secluded together. At this stage, the couple may live together as man and wife and all of the various mutual obligations apply.

The mishna discusses various situations in which one of a number of brothers, who were all bound through a levirate bond to a *yevama*, proceeded to betroth her sister. Due to the bond he has with the *yevama* he is forbidden to engage in relations with the sister. As such, he may not continue to complete the second stage of his marriage with her since the purpose of that stage is for them to live together as man and wife. Nevertheless, should another one of his brothers either consummate levirate marriage with the *yevama*, or perform *ḥalitza* with her, since that will dissolve the levirate bond between her and the other brothers, there will no longer be any impediment to completing the marriage with her sister.

Wait until your brother performs an act – הַמְתֵּן עַד שֶׁיַּעֲשֶׂה אָחִיךָ מַעֲשֶׂה: The commentaries explain that Rabbi Yehuda ben Beteira holds that the levirate bond is substantial, meaning that to a certain extent it is as though he is already married to her. Accordingly, the woman he betrothed is regarded as though she is his wife's sister, and therefore it is forbidden for him to now proceed to marry her. However, the commentaries explain that despite this, Rabbi Yehuda ben Beteira does not demand that he divorce the woman he betrothed; there is no need to take such drastic action because there is a possibility that she will be rendered entirely permissible through an action of his brother (*Tosefot HaRosh*).

Some commentaries raise the following question: Even if one holds that the levirate bond is substantial, shouldn't the brother's levirate bond to the *yevama* be entirely dissolved by virtue of his betrothal of her sister, since by doing so he renders the *yevama* forbidden to him by Torah law? They explain that since the levirate bond was in place before the betrothal, the strength of betrothal itself is deficient, and so it is not sufficiently efficacious to negate the bond (Rid; see Rashba).

He must divorce his wife with a bill of divorce, etc. – יוֹצִיא אֶת אִשְׁתּוֹ בְּגֵט וכו׳: The mishna on 29a discusses a similar case in which ultimately, he is prohibited from living with either his wife or his *yevama*, and expresses the lament: Woe is him on account of his wife, and woe is him on account of his brother's wife. *Tosafot* question why that expression of lament does not appear in this case as well. They suggest that the expression is used only where no prohibition was involved in the man's marriage to his wife, as in the case on 29a. However, in this case the situation was created due to the *yavam* marrying a woman whom he was forbidden to marry. Therefore, it is inappropriate to lament the situation. The Rivan explains that the lament is appropriate only in a case in which he had already lived together with his wife. However, in this case, the woman was only betrothed to him; therefore, since the couple is not as closely bound as was the couple in the first case, the pain of the ruling is less pronounced.

And his brother's wife with *ḥalitza* – וְאֵשֶׁת אָחִיו בַּחֲלִיצָה: This act of *ḥalitza* is required only by rabbinic decree, since as his wife's sister, the *yevama* is forbidden to her *yavam* by Torah law, and therefore by Torah law the *ḥalitza* is unnecessary. Alternatively, since he betrothed the sister of the *yevama* after the levirate bond to the *yevama* was already in place, the strength of betrothal itself is deficient, and so the bond is compromised, but only partially. As such, it is no longer possible to consummate the levirate marriage, but *ḥalitza* is necessary to fully dissolve the bond (Rashba; Ritva).

Say: However, one who divorces – אֵימָא אֲבָל הַמְגָרֵשׁ: One later commentary explains that the use of the phrase: And similarly, suggests only that there is some connection between the prohibitions with regard to the sister of one's divorcée and the sister of one's *ḥalutza*. When the Gemara suggests the emendation to: However, it is not rejecting that assumption and suggesting that the mishna should be emended; rather, it is simply explaining the correct interpretation of the phrase: And similarly, used in the mishna. The phrase should not be understood as implying that the *halakha* in both cases is the same; rather, it indicates only that the reason for the rabbinic prohibition with regard to the sister of one's *ḥalutza* is on account of the Torah prohibition with regard to the sister of one's divorcée (*Mei Naftoaḥ*).

אָמַר רֵישׁ לָקִישׁ: כָּאן שָׁנָה רַבִּי: אֲחוֹת גְּרוּשָׁה – מִדִּבְרֵי תוֹרָה, אֲחוֹת חֲלוּצָה – מִדִּבְרֵי סוֹפְרִים.

The Gemara explains the reason for the difference between the two cases: **Reish Lakish said: Here,** through this mishna, **Rabbi** Yehuda HaNasi **taught** that **a sister of** one's **divorcée**[H] is forbidden to him **by Torah law,** and that is why she is entirely exempt, whereas **a sister of a *ḥalutza***[H] is forbidden to him only **by rabbinic law,** and therefore, since there is still a levirate bond between her and the *yavam*, she requires *ḥalitza* to release her from it.

״שׁוֹמֶרֶת יָבָם שֶׁקִּידֵּשׁ״ וכו׳. אָמַר שְׁמוּאֵל: הֲלָכָה כְּדִבְרֵי רַבִּי יְהוּדָה בֶּן בְּתֵירָא.

§ The mishna states that in the case of **a widow waiting for her *yavam*** where the brother of the *yavam* **betrothed** her sister, Rabbi Yehuda ben Beteira said that the brother may not proceed to marry his betrothed. The Gemara cites a ruling on this matter: **Shmuel said:** The ***halakha* is in accordance with the statement of Rabbi Yehuda ben Beteira.**

אִיבַּעְיָא לְהוּ: מֵתָה אִשְׁתּוֹ, מַהוּ בִּיבִמְתּוֹ? רַב וְרַבִּי חֲנִינָא דְּאָמְרִי תַּרְוַיְיהוּ: מֵתָה אִשְׁתּוֹ מוּתָּר בִּיבִמְתּוֹ, שְׁמוּאֵל וְרַב אַסִּי דְּאָמְרִי תַּרְוַיְיהוּ: מֵתָה אִשְׁתּוֹ אָסוּר בִּיבִמְתּוֹ.

A dilemma was raised before the Sages: If a *yavam* is betrothed to the sister of his *yevama*, then since the *yevama* is his betrothed wife's sister, it is forbidden for him to consummate a levirate marriage with her. However, if **his** betrothed **wife died, what is the *halakha* with regard to his *yevama*;** is he then permitted to consummate a levirate marriage with her? It is **Rav and Rabbi Ḥanina who both say: If his wife died, he is permitted to** consummate a levirate marriage with **his *yevama***.[H] Their opinion is disputed by **Shmuel and Rav Asi, who both say: If his wife died, he is forbidden to his *yevama*.**

אָמַר רָבָא: מַאי טַעְמָא דְּרַב? מִשּׁוּם דְּהָוֵאי יְבָמָה שֶׁהוּתְּרָה, וְנֶאֶסְרָה, וְחָזְרָה וְהוּתְּרָה – תַּחֲזוֹר לְהֶיתֵּירָהּ הָרִאשׁוֹן.

Rava said: What is Rav's reasoning?[N] She is permitted **due to the fact that she is a *yevama* who,** when her husband died, **was permitted** to the *yavam*, **and** then when the *yavam* betrothed her sister **she became forbidden** to him as his wife's sister, **and then** when his wife died the *yevama* **reverted** to her original status **and was permitted** to him. As such, **she should** also **revert to her original permitted status** with regard to levirate marriage and be permitted to consummate a levirate marriage with the *yavam*.

מְתִיב רַב הַמְנוּנָא: שְׁלֹשָׁה אַחִין, שְׁנַיִם נְשׂוּאִין שְׁתֵּי אֲחָיוֹת וְאֶחָד מוּפְנֶה, מֵת אֶחָד מִבַּעֲלֵי אֲחָיוֹת וְעָשָׂה בָּהּ מוּפְנֶה מַאֲמָר, וְאַחַר כָּךְ מֵת אָחִיו הַשֵּׁנִי,

Rav Hamnuna raised an objection from that which was taught in a *baraita*: With regard to a case of **three brothers, two** of whom **are married to two sisters and one** of whom **is a bachelor,** if **one of the sisters' husbands died and the bachelor performed levirate betrothal** with that sister, **and afterward the second brother** who was married to the other sister **died,** and so his wife also happened before the bachelor for levirate marriage, the bachelor is then bound to each of the sisters through a levirate bond. In such a case it is prohibited for the bachelor to consummate a levirate marriage with either one, as it is prohibited to marry the sister of a woman to whom one is bound through a levirate bond.

וְאַחַר כָּךְ מֵתָה אִשְׁתּוֹ אַחֲרָיו – אוֹתָהּ יְבָמָה חוֹלֶצֶת וְלֹא מִתְיַבֶּמֶת.

And if afterward the wife of the second brother **died after him,** i.e., after her husband had already died, which restored the original situation in which the bachelor was bound by a levirate bond only to the widow of the first brother, then in such a case **that *yevama***, the widow of the first brother, **performs *ḥalitza* but may not enter into levirate marriage.**

HALAKHA

A sister of one's divorcée – אֲחוֹת גְּרוּשָׁה: If one divorces his wife, then her sister is forbidden to him by Torah law as long as the divorcée remains alive, irrespective of whether the sister is only a paternal or maternal half sister and irrespective of whether she was born in or out of wedlock (Rambam *Sefer Nashim, Hilkhot Issurei Bia* 2:7; *Shulḥan Arukh, Even HaEzer* 15:26).

A sister of a *ḥalutza* – אֲחוֹת חֲלוּצָה: The sister of one's *ḥalutza* is forbidden to him by rabbinic law (Rambam *Sefer Nashim, Hilkhot Yibbum VaḤalitza* 1:13; *Shulḥan Arukh, Even HaEzer* 162:3).

If His wife died he is permitted to his *yevama* – מֵתָה אִשְׁתּוֹ, מוּתָּר בִּיבִמְתּוֹ: With regard to one who betrothed the sister of his *yevama*, if the woman betrothed to him died, then he is permitted to consummate a levirate marriage with his *yevama*, or if he wishes he may perform *ḥalitza*. This is in accordance with the opinion of Rabbi Ḥanina (Rambam *Sefer Nashim, Hilkhot Yibbum VaḤalitza* 7:8; *Shulḥan Arukh, Even HaEzer* 159:7).

NOTES

What is Rav's reasoning – מַאי טַעְמָא דְּרַב: The later commentaries explains that the dispute between Rav and Shmuel here is not limited to the specific principle of whether a woman who is permitted, then forbidden, and then permitted again may consummate a levirate marriage. Rather, it is a fundamental dispute concerning the very nature of the allowance to marry one's brother's wife in a case of levirate marriage. Normally, one is prohibited from engaging in relations with the wife of one's brother. However, in the case of a levirate marriage it is permitted and a mitzva to do so. Rav assumes that in the case of a *yevama* who is permitted, then forbidden, and then permitted again, one may proceed to consummate the levirate marriage; he understands that the prohibition against engaging in relations with one's brother's wife is itself limited in that it does not apply in a situation where there is a mitzva of levirate marriage. Therefore, once any additional reason to prevent the levirate marriage is removed, the *yavam* may proceed to consummate the levirate marriage with the *yevama* without any concern about that prohibition. Shmuel, however, assumes that the prohibition against engaging in relations with one's brother's wife does fundamentally apply even in a situation where there is a mitzva of levirate marriage, but that in order to enable the fulfillment of the mitzva, the prohibition is waived. Therefore, should an additional prohibition be applied to his brother's wife that will inhibit the fulfillment of the mitzva, then since there is no longer a mitzva of levirate marriage, the original prohibition against engaging in relations with one's brother's wife is reinstated. Consequently, even should the additional prohibition be removed, the prohibition with regard to one's brother's wife will remain in force and the couple may not consummate the levirate marriage (*Mei Naftoaḥ*; *Yosef Lekaḥ*).

וְאַמַּאי? תֶּיהֱוֵי כִּיבָמָה שֶׁהוּתְּרָה, וְנֶאֶסְרָה, וְחָזְרָה וְהוּתְּרָה – תַּחְזוֹר לְהֶיתֵּירָה הָרִאשׁוֹן!

Rav Hamnuna explains the challenge from the *baraita*: **But why** may she not consummate the levirate marriage? **She should be like a** ***yevama*** **who was** initially **permitted** to her *yavam*, **and** then **became forbidden** to him, **and then reverted** to her original status **and was permitted, and so** in this case **she should** also **revert to her original permitted status** with regard to levirate marriage and be permitted to consummate a levirate marriage with him. The fact that the *baraita* rules that she is prohibited from consummating the marriage demonstrates that she does not revert to her original permitted status.

אִישְׁתִּיק. לְבָתַר דִּנְפַק אֲמַר: אַמַּאי לָא אָמְרַתְּ לֵיהּ רַבִּי אֱלִיעֶזֶר הִיא, דְּאָמַר: כֵּיוָן שֶׁעָמְדָה עָלָיו שָׁעָה אַחַת בְּאִיסּוּר נֶאֶסְרָה עָלָיו עוֹלָמִית?

Rava **was silent,** as he had no immediate answer. **After** Rav Hamnuna **left** the study hall, Rava **said** to himself: **Why did you not say to him** that the *baraita* does not pose a challenge because **it is** in accordance with the opinion of **Rabbi Elazar,**[N] **who said** in a mishna (108b) with regard to the case of a man who divorced his wife, remarried her, and then died childless, that the *yevama* may not consummate levirate marriage with her *yavam* because **once** a *yevama* **has stood** before her *yavam* **in a forbidden state,** even **for a single moment, she** remains **forbidden to him forever,** and in that case, during the period she was divorced from her husband she was forbidden to her *yavam*? The Rabbis, however, disagree with his opinion, and the *halakha* is ruled in accordance with their opinion.

הֲדַר אֲמַר: אֵימוּר דְּאָמַר רַבִּי אֱלִיעֶזֶר – הֵיכָא דְּלָא חֲזְיָא בִּשְׁעַת נְפִילָה, אֲבָל הֵיכָא דַּחֲזְיָא בִּשְׁעַת נְפִילָה – מִי אָמַר?

He then said to himself: It is not certain that the *baraita* is in accordance with the opinion of Rabbi Elazar because one could **say**[N] **that Rabbi Elazar said** his opinion only **where she was not suitable** for the *yavam*, i.e., she was forbidden to him, already from **the time** of her **happening** before her *yavam* for levirate marriage at the moment of her husband's death. **However, where she was suitable** for her *yavam* **at the time of** her **happening** before him and became forbidden to him only at some later point, as in the case of a *yavam* who betrothed the sister of his *yevama*, **did he** actually **say** that if the reason for the prohibition is removed then she does not return to her permissible state? If the *baraita* does not represent the opinion of Rabbi Elazar, then it must be unanimously agreed upon, and therefore it indeed poses a challenge.

הֲדַר אֲמַר: אִין, וְהָתַנְיָא: רַבִּי אֱלִיעֶזֶר אוֹמֵר: מֵתָה יְבִמְתּוֹ – מוּתָּר בְּאִשְׁתּוֹ, מֵתָה אִשְׁתּוֹ אוֹתָהּ יְבָמָה חוֹלֶצֶת וְלֹא מִתְיַבֶּמֶת.

He then said: Yes, actually, Rabbi Elazar did state his opinion even in such a case, **and so it is taught** in a *baraita*: With regard to a *yavam* who betrothed the sister of his *yevama*, **Rabbi Elazar says:** If **his** ***yevama*** **dies, he is permitted to his wife.** If **his wife dies, that** ***yevama*** **performs** ***ḥalitza*** **but may not enter into levirate marriage** with him. Therefore, the challenge from the *baraita* can be dismissed since it represents only Rabbi Elazar's opinion.

לֵימָא שְׁמוּאֵל וְרַב אַסִּי דְּאָמְרִי כְּרַבִּי אֱלִיעֶזֶר!

The Gemara suggests: **Shall we say** that **Shmuel and Rav Asi, who say** that she may not consummate the levirate marriage, hold **in accordance with** the opinion of **Rabbi Elazar?**

NOTES

It is in accordance with the opinion of Rabbi Elazar, etc. – **רַבִּי אֱלִיעֶזֶר הִיא וכו׳**: In the Jerusalem Talmud, this suggestion of Rav to link the *baraita* cited by Rav Hamnuna to the opinion of Rabbi Elazar is cited as an explicit statement of Rabbi Yoḥanan.

He then said, say, etc. – **הֲדַר אֲמַר אֵימוּר וכו׳**: The advantage of this suggestion is that if the *baraita* is not in accordance with the opinion of Rabbi Elazar, as taught in the mishna on 108b, then it is not subject to his dispute with the Rabbis and perforce it must be based upon an additional, unanimously agreed-upon principle. If so, it can provide a halakhic basis for the opinion of Shmuel and Rav Asi, since otherwise this *baraita*, which is the only support for their opinion, is in accordance only with an opinion that is not accepted as the *halakha*. In fact, Shmuel and Rav Asi themselves would have to explain the *baraita* in this way. However, Rava concludes that the *baraita* is in accordance only with the opinion of Rabbi Elazar, and therefore the *baraita* is not to be accepted as the *halakha* (*Tosefot HaRosh*; Rashba).

אפילו תימא כרבנן, עד כאן לא קמיפלגי רבנן עליה דרבי אלעזר – אלא משום דמנפילה ואילך לא מיתסר עלייהו, אבל הכא דאיתסר – אפילו רבנן מודו.

The Gemara rejects this: **You** can **even say** that they hold **in accordance with** the opinion of **the Rabbis,** as perhaps **the Rabbis disagree with Rabbi Elazar** in the case of a man who divorced and remarried his wife and then died childless **only due to** the fact **that** in that case, **from** the time of her **happening** for levirate marriage **and onward she was not forbidden to them,** i.e., her *yevamin*. The fact that the prohibition between her and her *yevamin* ended before she ever happened before them for levirate marriage means it has no bearing on her current eligibility for levirate marriage. **However, here,** in the case where the *yavam* betrothed the sister of his *yevama*, since **she became forbidden** after she had already happened before him for levirate marriage, **even the Rabbis** would **agree** that she remains permanently ineligible to consummate levirate marriage with him.

מתני׳ היבמה לא תחלוץ ולא תתייבם עד שיש לה שלשה חדשים. וכן כל שאר הנשים לא יתארסו ולא ינשאו עד שיהו להן שלשה חדשים אחד בתולות ואחד בעולות, אחד גרושות ואחד אלמנות, אחד נשואות ואחד ארוסות.

MISHNA **A** *yevama* **may neither perform** *ḥalitza* **nor enter into levirate marriage until she has** waited **three months**[H] from the time of her husband's death. **And similarly, all other women may not be betrothed**[H] **and may not marry until they have** waited **three months** since their previous marriage ended. This waiting period is necessary so that, should a woman give birth shortly after remarrying, it will be obvious who the father of the child is. This applies **both to virgins and non-virgins, both to divorcées and widows,** and **both to women** who were **married** to their previous husbands **and women** who were only **betrothed.** All of these women must wait three months before remarrying even though for some of them the reason for doing so does not apply.

רבי יהודה אומר: הנשואות יתארסו, והארוסות ינשאו, חוץ מן הארוסות שביהודה, מפני שלבו גס בה.

Rabbi Yehuda says: The women who were **married** to their previous husbands **may be betrothed, and the women** who were only **betrothed** to their previous husbands **may marry** without waiting three months. This is true **except for the betrothed women that are in** the area of **Judea,**[B] **due to** the fact **that** the groom **is familiar with her.** The custom in Judea was for the couple to be secluded together before the marriage so that they would become familiar with each other. This led to the possibility that they might cohabit even during their betrothal period. Rabbi Yehuda holds that one does not need to wait three months whenever the reason for doing so does not apply.

רבי יוסי אומר: כל הנשים יתארסו, חוץ מן האלמנה,

Rabbi Yosei says: All of the women[N] **may be betrothed** within three months even if they were previously married, **except for a widow,**

HALAKHA

A ***yevama*** **may not perform** ***ḥalitza*** **until she has waited three months – היבמה לא תחלוץ עד שלשה חדשים:** A woman who happened before her *yavam* for levirate marriage may neither perform *ḥalitza* nor enter into levirate marriage before first waiting ninety days, excluding the day of her husband's death and the day of her levirate marriage or *ḥalitza* (Rambam *Sefer Nashim, Hilkhot Yibbum VaḤalitza* 1:19; *Shulḥan Arukh, Even HaEzer* 164:1).

All other women may not be betrothed, etc. – כל שאר הנשים לא יתארסו וכו׳: Any woman who was divorced or widowed is forbidden to be betrothed or enter into levirate marriage with her *yavam* until she first waits ninety days, excluding the day of her husband's death or her divorce and the day of the betrothal. This is in accordance with the opinion of the first *tanna*, who is Rabbi Meir, and Rabbi Meir's opinion concerning decrees is also accepted as the *halakha*. However, it is permitted during this ninety-day period for the woman to commit herself to marry another man without actual betrothal (*Beit Yosef*, citing Rosh and *Terumat HaDeshen*; Rambam *Sefer Nashim, Hilkhot Geirushin* 11:18; *Shulḥan Arukh, Even HaEzer* 13:1).

BACKGROUND

The betrothed women that are in Judea – הארוסות שביהודה: Tractate *Ketubot* (12a) recounts that it was the custom in Judea for a couple to be secluded together before the marriage so that they would become familiar with each other. This was done despite the fact that this involved a certain compromise on the standards of modesty, as doing so could result in the couple engaging in sexual relations. The reason for the custom was that, at the time, the local gentile ruler would often force brides-to-be to first engage in sexual relations with him before entering their marriage. Although the communities would do everything in their power to prevent this, it was not always possible to avoid it. When it did occur, it could often lead to disharmony between the couple. Therefore, it was decided that before a couple would married, they should first be secluded together and thereby develop a close relationship between them that could help them withstand an assault from the local ruler.

NOTES

Rabbi Yosei says: All of the women, etc. – רבי יוסי אומר: כל הנשים וכו׳: Rashi explains that Rabbi Yosei fundamentally accepts the opinion of Rabbi Yehuda that the need for a waiting period applies only when there is both the possibility that the woman might already be pregnant from the previous husband and the possibility that she could become pregnant from the new husband. He disagrees only in the case of a widow. He would agree that a woman who was only betrothed to her previous husband is permitted to marry a new husband without waiting. However, other early commentaries argue that from the Gemara there is no indication that Rabbi Yosei agrees with Rabbi Yehuda on this point. Furthermore, the simple import of his words: All of the women may be betrothed, implies that he permits women to be betrothed without waiting, but never to marry during that three-month period. Therefore, they suggest that Rabbi Yosei actually represents a third opinion, and that his ruling concerning a widow is an additional, but independent, stringency (Rashba; Ritva; *Nimmukei Yosef*).

מִפְּנֵי הָאִיבּוּל.

due to the mourning period she must observe for her deceased husband.

גמ׳ בִּשְׁלָמָא לֹא תִתְיַיבֵּם – שֶׁמָּא יִהְיֶה הַוָּלָד בֶּן קַיָּימָא, וְקָא פָּגַע בְּאִיסּוּר אֵשֶׁת אָח דְּאוֹרַיְיתָא. אֶלָּא לֹא תַחְלוֹץ – אַמַּאי?

GEMARA The Gemara questions the mishna's opening clause: **Granted, she should not enter into levirate marriage,**[N] as she might already be pregnant, which would still not be noticeable during the first three months, and **perhaps the baby will be viable.** In that case it would emerge that she was never subject to the mitzva of levirate marriage, and therefore, if the *yavam* consummates a levirate marriage **he will have encountered the Torah prohibition against** engaging in relations with one's **brother's wife. However, why should she not perform *ḥalitza*?**

לֵימָא תֶּיהֱוֵי תְּיוּבְתָּא דְּרַבִּי יוֹחָנָן דְּאָמַר: חֲלִיצַת מְעוּבֶּרֶת שְׁמָהּ חֲלִיצָה! וְלָאו מִי אוֹתְבִינֵיהּ לְרַבִּי יוֹחָנָן חֲדָא זִימְנָא? לֵימָא מֵהָא נַמִי תֶּיהֱוֵי תְּיוּבְתָּא!

The Gemara suggests: **Let us say** that this mishna, which states that a pregnant woman should not perform *ḥalitza*, **is a conclusive refutation of** the opinion of **Rabbi Yoḥanan, who said** that **a *ḥalitza*** performed **with a pregnant woman** who later miscarries **is considered** a valid ***ḥalitza*.** The Gemara asks: **But didn't they** already **conclusively refute** the opinion of **Rabbi Yoḥanan one time** previously from other sources? The Gemara rephrases the suggestion: **Let us say** that **from this** mishna **as well there is a conclusive refutation** of the opinion of Rabbi Yoḥanan.

לָא, הָכָא הַיְינוּ טַעְמָא שֶׁמָּא יְהֵא וָלָד בֶּן קַיָּימָא, וְנִמְצֵאת אַתָּה מַצְרִיכָהּ כָּרוֹז לִכְהוּנָּה.

The Gemara deflects this suggestion: **No,** it is possible that in the mishna **here, this is the reason** that she may not perform *ḥalitza*: **Perhaps** the **offspring will be viable,** in which case although she performed the act of *ḥalitza*, it is entirely meaningless since it was completely unnecessary, and she would remain permitted to marry into the priesthood. However, this could lead to a problem: People might not realize that the *ḥalitza* she performed was meaningless, and they would think she is a *ḥalutza* who is prohibited from marrying a priest. **It would** therefore **emerge** that if you permit her to perform *ḥalitza* even though it is possible that she is pregnant, it could be that **you will** ultimately **require a public announcement** to be made **for her** to attest to the fact that the *ḥalitza* she performed was meaningless and she is in fact still permitted to marry **into the priesthood.**

וְנִצְרְכָהּ! דִּלְמָא אִיכָּא דַּהֲוָאי בַּחֲלִיצָה וְלֹא הֲוֵי בַּהַכְרָזָה, וּמַפְסְלוּהָ מִן הַכְּהוּנָּה.

The Gemara wonders why this poses a problem: **But** why not let her perform *ḥalitza* even though it is possible she is pregnant, and then, if it becomes necessary, **require** a public announcement to be made **for her?** The Gemara explains why one should avoid having to rely on a public announcement: **Perhaps there will be some** people **who are** present **at the *ḥalitza* but were not** present **at the public announcement, and** those people **will** incorrectly **disqualify her from** marrying into **the priesthood.** To avoid this situation, the mishna rules that she should wait three months before performing *ḥalitza*.

NOTES

Granted, she should not enter into levirate marriage – בִּשְׁלָמָא לֹא תִתְיַיבֵּם: The waiting period is required only due to the possibility that the *yevama* might be pregnant from her previous husband. Therefore there should be no requirement to wait for a *yevama* who was only betrothed to her previous husband, as it can be assumed she is not pregnant since it is forbidden to engage in relations during the betrothal period. Nevertheless, the Sages required the waiting period in all cases. Were they not to have required it a case in which the *yevama* had only been betrothed, people could have made a mistaken comparison and incorrectly concluded that even where the *yevama* was in fact pregnant from her deceased husband, it is permitted for her to consummate a levirate marriage immediately, which would be violation of a prohibition that entails *karet*. Therefore, to avoid any confusion, the Sages required the waiting period in all cases (Ritva).

תֵּינַח אַלְמָנָה, גְּרוּשָׁה מַאי אִיכָּא לְמֵימַר? מִשּׁוּם דְּמַפְסִיד לָהּ מְזוֹנוֹת.

The Gemara asks: This answer **works out well** with regard to a **widow** because as a widow she is currently still permitted to marry into the priesthood, but with regard to **a divorcée**, who is already prohibited from marrying into the priesthood, **what is there to say**; why shouldn't she perform *ḥalitza* immediately? The Gemara provides an alternative reason to delay the *ḥalitza*: The reason is **because** by performing *ḥalitza* immediately **she will forfeit the sustenance payments** from her deceased husband's estate, which she otherwise would have been entitled to for the first three months. Since she is not permitted to remarry during those three months, she will have no means of support. Therefore, she should wait until after three months have passed before performing *ḥalitza*.

תֵּינַח נְשׂוּאָה, אֲרוּסָה גְּרוּשָׁה מַאי אִיכָּא לְמֵימַר?

The Gemara asks: This answer **works out well** with regard to a **woman** who was **married** to her previous husband and who is therefore entitled to sustenance payments, but with regard to a **divorcée who** was only **betrothed** to her previous husband, **what is there to say?** She is neither entitled to receive sustenance payments nor is she permitted to marry into the priesthood. Why, then, shouldn't she perform *ḥalitza* immediately?

אֶלָּא מִשּׁוּם דְּרַבִּי יוֹסֵי. דְּתַנְיָא: מַעֲשֶׂה בְּאָדָם אֶחָד שֶׁבָּא לִפְנֵי רַבִּי יוֹסֵי, אָמַר לוֹ: מַהוּ לַחֲלוֹץ בְּתוֹךְ שְׁלֹשָׁה? אָמַר לוֹ: לֹא תַּחֲלוֹץ. וְתַחֲלוֹץ וּמַה בְּכָךְ?

The Gemara therefore provides an alternative reason to delay the *ḥalitza*: **Rather,** it is **due to that** which **Rabbi Yosei** stated, **as it is taught** in a *baraita*: There was **an incident involving a certain man who came before Rabbi Yosei.** The man **said to him: What is** the *halakha* with regard **to performing *ḥalitza* within three** months of the husband's death? **He said to him: She may not perform *ḥalitza*.** He asked him: **Let her perform *ḥalitza*; what** would be the problem **with that?** Even if she is pregnant, no prohibition will have been transgressed.

קָרָא עָלָיו מִקְרָא זֶה: ״וְאִם לֹא יַחְפֹּץ״ הָא אִם חָפֵץ – יַבֵּם, כָּל הָעוֹלֶה לְיִבּוּם – עוֹלֶה לַחֲלִיצָה כו׳.

To explain his ruling, Rabbi Yosei **recited this verse about him: "And if the man does not wish** to take his *yevama*" (Deuteronomy 25:7) in levirate marriage, then he must perform *ḥalitza*. By inference, the possibility of performing *ḥalitza* exists only in a case in which **if he wishes he may consummate the levirate marriage.** This teaches the principle that **one who is eligible for levirate marriage**[H] **is eligible for *ḥalitza*,** and one who is ineligible for levirate marriage is ineligible for *ḥalitza*. This includes even a woman who is temporarily prohibited from marrying, e.g., a woman in the first three months following a previous marriage.

מְתִיב רַב חִינָּנָא: הַסְּפֵקוֹת חוֹלְצוֹת וְלֹא מִתְיַבְּמוֹת.

Rav Ḥinnana raised an objection from the following *baraita*: **Those women** whose status as a *yevama* **is uncertain perform *ḥalitza* but may not enter into levirate marriage.** According to this *baraita*, there are in fact cases in which a woman is eligible for *ḥalitza* but may not enter into levirate marriage.

מַאי סְפֵקוֹת? אִילֵימָא סָפֵק קִדּוּשִׁין אַמַּאי לֹא מִתְיַבְּמוֹת? תִּתְיַיבֵּם וְאֵין בְּכָךְ כְּלוּם!

The Gemara clarifies the case: **What is** the case of **women** whose status as a *yevama* **is uncertain? If we say** it is referring to a woman whose **betrothal** to her previous husband **is uncertain,** then **why does she not enter into levirate marriage? Let her enter into levirate marriage,** and there is **no** problem **with that,** because if the betrothal was never valid, then she is permitted to the *yavam* as she is not his brother's wife; and if it was valid, then she is now obligated to enter into levirate marriage with him.[H]

אֶלָּא לָאו – סָפֵק שֶׁקִּידֵּשׁ אַחַת מִשְּׁתֵּי אֲחָיוֹת וְאֵינוֹ יוֹדֵעַ אֵיזוֹ מֵהֶן קִידֵּשׁ, וְקָתָנֵי: חוֹלֶצֶת!

Rather, is it not referring to a case of **uncertainty** in **which** a man **betrothed one of two sisters and he does not know which** one **of them he betrothed?** If that man then died childless, the *yavam* may not consummate the levirate marriage with either sister because it is possible that he will do so with the sister who was not betrothed to his brother, who is therefore forbidden to him as the sister of a woman who is bound to him by a levirate bond. This is in fact the case of the *baraita*, **and the** *baraita* **teaches** that **she performs *ḥalitza*,** even though she is not permitted to enter into levirate marriage.

HALAKHA

One who is eligible for levirate marriage, etc. – כָּל הָעוֹלָה לְיִבּוּם וכו׳: A *yevama* may not consummate levirate marriage until she has waited ninety days from the day of her husband's death. Since she is ineligible for levirate marriage, she is also ineligible for *ḥalitza* (Rambam *Sefer Nashim, Hilkhot Yibbum VaḤalitza* 1:19).

A woman whose betrothal is uncertain with regard to levirate marriage – סָפֵק מְקוּדֶּשֶׁת לְעִנְיַן יִבּוּם: If a woman's betrothal to her husband was uncertain and her husband died, and the woman happened before her *yavam* for levirate marriage, he may consummate the levirate marriage with her since there is no reason to prohibit it (Rambam *Sefer Nashim, Hilkhot Yibbum VaḤalitza* 6:7; *Shulḥan Arukh, Even HaEzer* 173:15).

הָכִי הָשְׁתָּא?! הָתָם, אִם יָבֹא אֵלִיָּהוּ וְיֹאמַר דְּהָא קִידֵּשׁ – בַּת חֲלִיצָה וְיִיבּוּם הִיא,

The Gemara rejects the proof: **How can** these cases **be compared? There,** in the case of uncertainty, **if Elijah were to come and say that** the man **betrothed this one** of the sisters, then **she would be eligible for *ḥalitza* and levirate marriage.** It is clear, then, that fundamentally the sister who was betrothed is actually eligible for levirate marriage, and it is merely a lack of knowledge that prevents her from entering into it.

הָכָא אִם יָבֹא אֵלִיָּהוּ וְיֹאמַר דְּהָא לָא אִיעַבְּרָה – מִי מַשְׁגַּח בֵּיהּ וְיַבְּמִינַן לָהּ? הָא קְטַנָּה דְּלָאו בַּת אִיעַבּוּרֵי הִיא, וַאֲפִילּוּ הָכִי צְרִיכָה לְהַמְתִּין שְׁלֹשָׁה חֳדָשִׁים,

However, **here,** with regard to a woman during the first three months following her previous marriage, **if Elijah were to come and say that this** woman **is not pregnant, would one pay heed to him and would we allow the** *yavam* **to consummate levirate marriage?** Certainly not, **as** is evident from the fact that **a minor girl, who cannot become pregnant, must** also **wait three months.**[H] Evidently, the requirement to wait three months applies in all situations, even those in which the reason for the requirement is irrelevant. Therefore, by virtue of that decree the *yevama* is considered to be fundamentally ineligible for levirate marriage and similarly is ineligible for *ḥalitza*.

תָּנוּ רַבָּנַן: יְבָמָה, שְׁלֹשָׁה חֳדָשִׁים הָרִאשׁוֹנִים – נִזּוֹנֶת מִשֶּׁל בַּעַל, מִכָּאן וְאֵילָךְ – אֵינָהּ נִזּוֹנֶת לֹא מִשֶּׁל בַּעַל וְלֹא מִשֶּׁל יָבָם.

§ The Gemara mentioned that a *yevama* is supported from her deceased husband's estate. It now proceeds to cite a *baraita* that teaches this *halakha*: **The Sages taught: A** *yevama* during **the first three months** following her husband's death **receives sustenance** payments[H] **from the husband's** estate.[N] This is because her previous marriage to him is the cause of her current unmarried state, since is it due to that marriage that she must first wait three months before remarrying. **From this point forward, she does not receive sustenance** payments, **neither from the husband's** estate **nor from the** ***yavam,*** as he has not yet consummated a levirate marriage with her.

עָמַד בַּדִּין וּבָרַח – נִזּוֹנֶת מִשֶּׁל יָבָם.

The *baraita* continues: If the *yavam* **was brought to judgment** and it was decided that he was obligated to either consummate the levirate marriage with her or perform *ḥalitza,* **and he ran away**[N] to avoid doing so, **she receives sustenance** payments **from** the estate **of the** ***yavam,*** which is his penalty for neglecting his duty.

נָפְלָה לִפְנֵי יָבָם קָטָן (מַאי)? מִיָּבָם – לֵית לָהּ, מִבַּעַל – מַאי?

The Gemara asks: If **she happened before** her *yavam* who is **a minor**[H] for levirate marriage, **what is** the *halakha*? **From the** ***yavam*** **she does not have** any right to sustenance payments because, as a minor, he is unable to consummate a levirate marriage, but as to payments **from** her **husband's** estate, **what** is the *halakha*? Since his death placed her in a situation that forces her to remain in an unmarried state, does his estate have to take the responsibility of supporting her?

פְּלִיגִי בָּהּ רַב אַחָא וְרָבִינָא; חַד אָמַר: אִית לָהּ, וְחַד אָמַר: לֵית לָהּ, וְהִלְכְתָא: לֵית לָהּ, מִשְּׁמַיָּא קְנָסוּהָ.

Rav Aḥa and Ravina disagree with regard to this matter: **One said she does have** rights to sustenance payments, **and the other one said she does not have** any rights. **And the** ***halakha*** is that **she does not have** any rights to sustenance payments. This is because the husband is not considered to be responsible for her situation; rather, it is thought that **she was penalized by Heaven.**[N]

תָּנוּ רַבָּנַן: יְבָמָה שֶׁחָלְצוּ לָהּ אַחִים בְּתוֹךְ שְׁלֹשָׁה – צְרִיכָה לְהַמְתִּין שְׁלֹשָׁה חֳדָשִׁים,

§ **The Sages taught:** In the case of a ***yevama*** **with whom the brothers** of her deceased husband **performed** ***ḥalitza*** **within three** months of her husband's death, she still **needs to wait three months** before remarrying.

NOTES

For three months she receives sustenance payments from the husband's estate – שְׁלֹשָׁה חֳדָשִׁים נִזּוֹנֶת מִשֶּׁל בַּעַל: One of the conditions of the marriage contract is that in the event of the husband's death, the widow may remain in her husband's home and be sustained from his estate. This right continues to exist as long as the woman maintains her connection to her deceased husband and refrains from attempts to remarry. However, this is not true of a *yevama*. Since there is a mitzva to either consummate the levirate marriage or perform *ḥalitza*, she is automatically considered as though she is in the process of remarrying and therefore loses the right to be sustained from her husband's estate. However, during the first three months following her husband's death she is not permitted to proceed due to the rabbinic decree. Therefore, during that period she is not considered to be in the process of remarrying, and consequently she retains the rights to be sustained from her husband's estate.

He was brought to judgment and he ran away – עָמַד בַּדִּין וּבָרַח: Rashi explains that the *yavam* ran away to avoid complying with the court's ruling, and his obligation to provide subsistence for her is a penalty for neglecting his duty. However, most of the other early commentaries explain that the *baraita* is referring to a man who was forced to run away due to circumstances beyond his control. Nevertheless, since when he was brought to court, the court fixed a date by which he was expected to consummate the levirate marriage, when that date arrives he automatically takes on the financial responsibilities of a husband to support his wife. The *halakha* is the same in any case of a man who betrothed a woman and a date is set for them to be married; when the date arrives he takes on financial responsibility for her irrespective of whether he actually marries her (Ramban).

She was penalized by Heaven – מִשְּׁמַיָּא קְנָסוּהָ: Despite the Gemara's conclusion, several *ge'onim* ruled that in cases such as this, especially where the woman is unable to sustain herself through her own efforts, she should receive sustenance payments from the dowry that she brought with her to her previous marriage. Later, when the *yavam* matures, if he consummates the levirate marriage with her, he will take whatever is left of the dowry, and if he performs *ḥalitza* then she receives the remainder of the marriage contract.

HALAKHA

A minor girl must wait – קְטַנָּה צְרִיכָה לְהַמְתִּין: When the Sages decreed that no woman may marry until she has first waited three months since the end of her previous marriage, they did not distinguish between cases, and therefore even a woman who is unfit for childbirth, e.g., a minor, is included in the decree (Rambam *Sefer Nashim, Hilkhot Geirushin* 11:20; *Shulḥan Arukh, Even HaEzer* 13:1).

Sustenance payments for a *yevama* – מְזוֹנוֹת יְבָמָה: A *yevama* receives sustenance payments from her husband's estate, like any other widow, for the first three months following his death. From this point onward, she does not receive sustenance payments either from the husband or from the *yavam*. If, after three months, she demanded that the *yavam* consummate levirate marriage and he agreed to do so, or even if he did not agree (Rambam), then even if he was ultimately prevented from doing so due to circumstances beyond his control he becomes obligated to provide her with sustenance payments. If he ran away to avoid doing so, it would seem that he is obligated to provide for her according to all opinions (*Beit Shmuel*; Rambam *Sefer Nashim, Hilkhot Ishut* 18:15; *Shulḥan Arukh, Even HaEzer* 160:1).

She happened before her *yavam* who is a minor – נָפְלָה לִפְנֵי יָבָם קָטָן: In the case of a *yevama* who happened before a *yavam* who is a minor, after three months she no longer receives sustenance payments from the estate of the husband or that of the *yavam* until the *yavam* reaches maturity (*Beit Shmuel*; Rambam *Sefer Nashim, Hilkhot Ishut* 18:17; *Shulḥan Arukh, Even HaEzer* 160:3).

לְאַחַר שְׁלֹשָׁה – אֵין צְרִיכָה לְהַמְתִּין שְׁלֹשָׁה חֳדָשִׁים.

If they performed the *ḥalitza* **after three** months, **she does not need to wait three months** and may marry immediately.

הֱוֵי הַשְּׁלֹשָׁה חֳדָשִׁים שֶׁאָמְרוּ – מִשְּׁעַת מִיתַת הַבַּעַל, וְלֹא מִשְּׁעַת חֲלִיצַת הַיָּבָם.

The Gemara infers from the latter clause of the *baraita*: It **must be** that **the three months that are stated** throughout the *baraita* are counted **from the time of the husband's death and not from the time of the *ḥalitza* of the *yavam*.**[H]

מַאי שְׁנָא מִגֵּט, דְּרַב אָמַר מִשְּׁעַת נְתִינָה וּשְׁמוּאֵל אָמַר מִשְּׁעַת כְּתִיבָה?

The Gemara asks: In **what** way is this case **different from** the case of **a bill of divorce,**[H] **where Rav said** that the three months are counted **from the time of the giving** of the bill of divorce, **and Shmuel said** that the count is **from the time of the writing** of the bill. If a couple is secluded together after the bill of divorce is written, the bill of divorce is invalid. Therefore, there is no concern that they were secluded from that time. This is why Shmuel holds that the three months are counted from the writing. Rav apparently assumes that even so, the count always begins from the formal end of the marriage and not from the point from which there was no possibility of her becoming pregnant. Why, then, does the *baraita* not rule also in the case when a woman happens for levirate marriage, that the count should begin from the point of *ḥalitza*, since the marriage is only fully severed at that point?

אָמַר רָבָא: קַל וָחוֹמֶר: אִיסּוּר כָּרֵת הִתַּרְתָּ, אִיסּוּר לָאו לֹא כׇּל שֶׁכֵּן?

Rava said: With regard to a *yevama*, all agree that the count begins from the time of her husband's death. This can be derived through an ***a fortiori*** inference, as follows: **If a prohibition** that entails ***karet***, i.e., the prohibition against engaging in relations with one's brother's wife in the event she is pregnant and not subject to levirate marriage, **you have permitted** after three months from the husband's death, then in the case of a standard **negative prohibition,** such as the prohibition against engaging in relations with a woman within three months of the death of her previous husband, is it **not all the more so**[N] clear that she should be permitted to remarry after three months from her husband's death? Therefore, even Rav agrees that in this case, the count begins from the husband's death.

״וְכֵן שְׁאָר כׇּל הַנָּשִׁים״. בִּשְׁלָמָא יְבָמָה – כְּדַאֲמַרַן. אֶלָּא שְׁאָר כׇּל הַנָּשִׁים אַמַּאי?

§ The mishna states: **And similarly, all other women may** not be betrothed or marry until they have waited three months. The Gemara asks: **Granted, a *yevama*** has to wait, **in accordance with** the reason **that we said,** that if she is pregnant with viable offspring, consummating the levirate marriage would violate the prohibition against engaging in relations with one's brother's wife. **But** with regard to **all other women, why** shouldn't they remarry immediately even if they are pregnant?

אָמַר רַב נַחְמָן אָמַר שְׁמוּאֵל: מִשּׁוּם דְּאָמַר קְרָא ״לִהְיוֹת לְךָ לֵאלֹהִים וּלְזַרְעֲךָ אַחֲרֶיךָ״ לְהַבְחִין בֵּין זַרְעוֹ שֶׁל רִאשׁוֹן לְזַרְעוֹ שֶׁל שֵׁנִי.

Rav Naḥman said that **Shmuel said:** It is **due to** the fact **that the verse states** with regard to Abraham: **"To be a God to you and your seed after you"** (Genesis 17:7), which indicates that the Divine Presence rests with someone only when his seed can be identified as being descended from him, i.e., there are no uncertainties with regard to their lineage. Therefore, to prevent any uncertainties concerning the lineage of her child, the woman must wait so that it will be possible **to distinguish**[N] **between the seed of the first** husband **and the seed of the second** husband. After three months, if she has conceived from her previous husband, the pregnancy will already be noticeable.

מְתִיב רָבָא: לְפִיכָךְ גֵּר וְגִיּוֹרֶת צְרִיכִין לְהַמְתִּין שְׁלֹשָׁה חֳדָשִׁים, הָכָא מַאי לְהַבְחִין אִיכָּא?

Rava raised an objection from a *baraita*: **Therefore,** on account of the requirement to wait three months, **a male convert and a female convert** who were originally married to each other and converted **need to wait three months**[H] before they may remarry following their conversion. Rava asks: **Here,** in this case, **what** reason **is there to distinguish?** Even if they do not wait and she is found to be pregnant, it is clear who the child's parents are.

HALAKHA

From when does a *yevama* wait – **מִמָּתַי מַמְתִּינָה הַיְבָמָה**: A *yevama* who performed *ḥalitza* within three months of her husband's death must still complete the three-month wait after her husband's death before remarrying. If she performed *ḥalitza* after three months had already passed, she need not wait any longer (Rambam *Sefer Nashim, Hilkhot Yibbum VaḤalitza* 1:19; *Shulḥan Arukh, Even HaEzer* 164:1).

From when does a divorcée wait – **מִמָּתַי מַמְתִּינָה גְּרוּשָׁה**: A divorcée must wait three months from the writing of her bill of divorce before remarrying. This applies even if the bill was made conditional or was given only some time later. This is in accordance with the opinion of Shmuel. Most halakhic authorities rule in accordance with his opinion because in tractate *Ketubot* Rav Ashi, one of the latest of the *amora'im*, rules in accordance with his opinion (*Kesef Mishne*). This is also the final ruling in the Jerusalem Talmud. However, the Rema (citing *Tur* and Rosh) rules that it is correct to be stringent and count from the time that the bill of divorce was given (Rambam *Sefer Nashim, Hilkhot Geirushin* 11:19; *Shulḥan Arukh, Even HaEzer* 13:1).

Separation of male and female converts – **הַפְרָשַׁת גֵּר וְגִיּוֹרֶת**: A maidservant or female convert who was married prior to conversion must wait ninety days before remarrying. This applies even to a husband and wife who converted together; they must separate from each other for that period. This is required so that it will be possible to distinguish between seed that was sown in sanctity and seed that was not sown in sanctity (Rambam *Sefer Nashim, Hilkhot Geirushin* 11:21; *Shulḥan Arukh, Even HaEzer* 13:5).

NOTES

A standard negative prohibition, all the more so – **אִיסּוּר לָאו לֹא כׇּל שֶׁכֵּן**: This reasoning cannot be applied in the case of a divorcée since she is still considered fully married until she has actually received a bill of divorce (Rivan).

To distinguish – **לְהַבְחִין**: The later commentaries deliberate whether the fact that a biblical source is cited renders this a true exegetical inference, which would mean that the need to distinguish is by Torah law, or whether the requirement is a rabbinic decree and the verse is cited merely as support for it. The *Keren Ora* states that the need to distinguish is a rabbinic decree, while *Arukh LaNer* cites the *Targum Yerushalmi* and certain formulations of the Rambam that suggest that the requirement is by Torah law.

Yosef Lekaḥ writes that although the concern of being unable to distinguish between the seed of the first and second husbands might seem unlikely, nevertheless, since remarriage for women is so common it is reasonable to assume that even this unusual situation will eventually arise.

NOTES

Between seed that was sown in sanctity – בֵּין זֶרַע שֶׁנִּזְרַע בִּקְדוּשָּׁה: If the child was conceived before his parents' conversions, the child would also have the status of a convert. As such, if the child was a female she would be prohibited from marrying into the priesthood (Rivan). Furthermore, as a convert, the child would not inherit from his convert father. Some assume that halakhically, the child would be considered as though he were not descended from his father for all other matters as well.

Rava stated, it is a rabbinic decree, etc. – רָבָא אָמַר גְּזֵירָה וכו׳: An additional reason for the decree is cited in the *She'iltot deRav Aḥai Gaon*, and it is possible that this reason actually appeared in the author's version of the Gemara: Lest he set slaves free. The *Gilyonei HaShas* explains the concern: When one owns slaves and dies, his mastery over his slaves is inherited by his children. If the child in this case incorrectly identified who his father was, and then upon that father's death the son frees the father's slaves, his release of the slaves would be entirely ineffectual since he is not truly that father's son and does not actually inherit from him. This would create a situation where those slaves, assuming that they had been lawfully freed, might proceed to marry Jewish women, when in fact they would be prohibited from doing so because they remained slaves. A similar explanation can be offered for the requirement to distinguish between seed in the case of a maidservant, which requires her to wait three months after her release. Since her offspring conceived before her release would have the status of slaves, whereas those conceived after her release would be fully Jewish, there is a concern that her offspring might actually be slaves but will act as though they are free.

The Rivash notes that based on all the reasons that the Gemara provides, it would appear that when a man remarries his divorcée without her having since remarried in the interim, there is no reason to require her to wait three months.

In all of those cases I identify – בְּכוּלָּן אֲנִי קוֹרֵא בָּהֶן: According to *Tosafot*, the phrase: All of those cases, refers to all *yevamot* who are prohibited from marrying. However, Rashi and the Meiri explain that it refers to all cases of women who are prohibited from remarrying. This includes even cases such as those in which the evidence of a husband's death is not sufficient to allow a woman to remarry; even in such cases, the ultimate reason for the prohibitions is to prevent people from engaging in forbidden relations.

BACKGROUND

Born after eight months of pregnancy – אִי נַמִּי לְתַמְנְיָא יָלְדָה: During talmudic times conventional wisdom held that a child born during the eighth month of pregnancy had no chance of survival, while a child born during the seventh month, and even one born during the sixth month, was more likely to survive. Nowadays, a baby born in the eighth month is considered to have greater chances of survival than one born earlier. Accordingly, despite the fact that the Gemara says that one may not desecrate the Shabbat to save a child born during the eighth month (*Shabbat* 135a), nowadays, since the child is likely to survive, the later authorities maintain that one may desecrate Shabbat to save him or her (*Minḥat Yitzḥak* 4:123; *Ḥazon Ish*, *Yoreh De'a* 155:3).

הָכָא נַמִּי: אִיכָּא לְהַבְחִין בֵּין זֶרַע שֶׁנִּזְרַע בִּקְדוּשָּׁה לְזֶרַע שֶׁלֹּא נִזְרַע בִּקְדוּשָּׁה.

The Gemara explains: **Here, too, there is** a need **to distinguish between seed that was sown in sanctity,**[N] i.e., a child conceived by a Jewish parents, **and seed that was not sown in sanctity,** i.e., a child conceived by gentile parents.

רָבָא אָמַר: גְּזֵירָה שֶׁמָּא יִשָּׂא אֶת אֲחוֹתוֹ מֵאָבִיו, וִייַבֵּם אֵשֶׁת אָחִיו מֵאִמּוֹ,

Rava stated a different reason for the need to wait: It is a rabbinic **decree**[N] **lest** a child be born and be incorrectly identified as the son of his mother's second husband when he is fact the son of her first husband. This could result in him **marrying his paternal sister,** unaware of the true relationship between them, **or consummating a levirate marriage with the wife of his maternal brother** under the misconception that his maternal brother was also his paternal brother. This would be prohibited because the prohibition to engage in relations with one's brother's wife is waived only in the case where there is a mitzva of levirate marriage, which applies only to paternal brothers.

וְיוֹצִיא אֶת אִמּוֹ לַשּׁוּק, וְיִפְטוֹר אֶת יְבִמְתּוֹ לַשּׁוּק.

Or in the event that his mother's second husband died and he was assumed to be his only offspring, **he would cause his mother to go out** and be permitted **to the** general **public** because, under the misconception that he was the offspring of the deceased, he assumed that there was no mitzva of levirate marriage. **Or,** in the event that his maternal brother died childless and the brother's widow became subject to levirate marriage, under the misconception that he was the paternal brother of the deceased he might perform *ḥalitza* and **permit** his supposed ***yevama*** **to** marry a man from **the** general **public.** To avoid these problems, the Sages decreed that a woman must wait before remarrying.

מְתִיב רַב חֲנַנְיָה: בְּכוּלָּן אֲנִי קוֹרֵא בָּהֶן מִשּׁוּם תַּקָּנַת עֶרְוָה, וְכָאן מִשּׁוּם תַּקָּנַת וָלָד. וְאִם אִיתָא – כּוּלְּהוּ מִשּׁוּם תַּקָּנַת עֶרְוָה!

Rav Ḥananya raised an objection from a *baraita*: **In all of those** cases where the Sages prohibit a woman from marrying or consummating a levirate marriage, **I identify**[N] that the prohibition is **due to an ordinance** instituted to prevent a violation of **forbidden relations, and here,** with regard to the prohibition against marrying within three months, it is **due to an ordinance for** the benefit of **the offspring.** Rav Ḥananya explains the challenge: **And if it is so** that Rava's understanding of the prohibition against marrying within three months is correct, then **all of the** cases of forbidden marriages are **due to an ordinance** to prevent violation of **forbidden relations.** However, the *baraita* indicates otherwise.

הַאי מִשּׁוּם תַּקָּנַת וָלָד דְּלָא לִפְגַּע בְּהוּ עֶרְוָה.

The Gemara defends Rava's opinion and explains that the *baraita* can be interpreted in a way that is consistent with his understanding: When the *baraita* says that **this** prohibition is **due to an ordinance for** the benefit of **the offspring,** it means **that** due to the prohibition the offspring **will not encounter** a prohibition of **forbidden relations.**

בִּשְׁלָמָא תַּמְתִּין שְׁנֵי חֳדָשִׁים וְתִנָּשֵׂא, לָא – דְּהַיְינוּ סְפֵיקָא, אִי בַּר תִּשְׁעָה לְקַמָּא אִי בַּר שִׁבְעָה לְבַתְרָא.

§ The Gemara analyzes the prohibition against marrying before three months have passed: **Granted, she should not wait** for only **two months and** then **marry, as this is** still a case that could give rise to **an uncertainty whether** the child born to her seven months after remarrying **is nine** months **old,** i.e., counting from conception, and it is the offspring **of the first** husband, or **whether** the child is only **seven** months **old** and is the offspring **of the latter** husband.

אֶלָּא, תַּמְתִּין חוֹדֶשׁ אֶחָד וְתִנָּשֵׂא: וְאִי לְשִׁבְעָה יָלְדָה – הַאי בַּר שִׁבְעָה לְבַתְרָא הוּא, וְאִי לְתַמְנְיָא יָלְדָה – הַאי בַּר תִּשְׁעָה לְקַמָּא הוּא.

However, let her wait only **one month and** then **marry, and** then, since it is presumed that a baby born during its eighth month since conception is not viable[B] but a baby born during its seventh or nine month is viable, **if after seven** months since remarrying **she gives birth,** then the child **is** clearly **seven** months old and **is** the offspring **of the latter** husband, **and if after eight** months since remarrying **she gives birth,** then **this** child **is** clearly **nine** months **old and is** the offspring **of the first** husband. Why, then, is there a need to wait three months?

אִי נַמִי לִתְמַנְיָא יָלְדָה – אִיכָּא לְמֵימַר דְּבַתְרָא הוּא, דִּלְמָא אִישְׁתַּהוּיֵי אִישְׁתְּהָא חוֹדֶשׁ אֶחָד וְאִיעַבַּר.

The Gemara explains: **Even if she gave birth after eight** months since remarrying **one could say that** the child is the offspring **of the latter** husband,[N] as **perhaps she waited one month** after remarrying **and conceived** only then. As such, the baby would be only seven months old, and that would explain its viability.

וְתַמְתִּין שְׁנֵי חֳדָשִׁים וּמֶחֱצָה וְתִנָּשֵׂא, דְּאִי לְשִׁבְעָה יָלְדָה – הַאי בַּר שִׁבְעָה לְבַתְרָא הוּא. וְאִי לְשִׁיתָּא וּפַלְגָּא יָלְדָה – הַאי בַּר תִּשְׁעָה לְקַמָּא הוּא, דְּאִי בַּר בַּתְרָא הוּא – בַּר שִׁיתָּא וּפַלְגָּא לָא חַיֵּי!

The Gemara asks further: **But let her wait for two and a half months and** then **marry, as, if after seven** months since remarrying **she gives birth,** then **this** child **is** clearly **seven** months **old and** is the offspring **of the latter** husband. **And if after six and a half** months since remarrying **she gives birth,** then **this** child **is** clearly **nine** months **old** and **is** the offspring **of the first** husband, because **if** one would suggest **it is** the offspring **of the latter** husband, in that case it would be **six and a half** months **old,** at **which** age it **cannot survive.**

אִי נַמִי לְשִׁיתָּא וּפַלְגָּא יָלְדָה – אִיכָּא לְמֵימַר דְּבַתְרָא הוּא, דְּאָמַר מָר זוּטְרָא: אֲפִילּוּ לְמַאן דְּאָמַר יוֹלֶדֶת לְתִשְׁעָה אֵינָהּ יוֹלֶדֶת לְמִקּוּטָּעִין – יָלְדָה לְשִׁבְעָה יוֹלֶדֶת לְמִקּוּטָּעִין,

The Gemara objects: **Even if after six and a half** months since remarrying **she gave birth, one could say that** the child is the offspring **of the latter** husband, **as Mar Zutra said: Even according to the one who says** that **a woman who gives birth after nine** months **does not give birth after an incomplete** number of months, i.e., she carries for a full nine months, nevertheless, **a woman who gives birth after seven months can give birth after an incomplete** number of months, and therefore it is possible that the baby was actually born after six and a half months.

שֶׁנֶּאֱמַר ״וַיְהִי לִתְקֻפוֹת הַיָּמִים״ מִיעוּט ״תְּקוּפוֹת״ – שְׁתַּיִם, מִיעוּט ״יָמִים״ – שְׁנַיִם.

This fact is derived from the verse concerning the birth of Samuel the prophet, **as it is stated: "And it came to pass, when the seasons of the days had come,** that Hannah conceived, and bore a son" (I Samuel 1:20). How much time is indicated by the phrase "the seasons of the days"? **The minimal sense of** the word **"seasons" is two,** and since each season of the year is three months, that indicates six months. **The minimal sense of** the word **"days" is two.** Accordingly, one may conclude that Samuel the prophet was born after six months and two days.

וְתַמְתִּין מַשֶּׁהוּ וְתִנָּשֵׂא, וְכִי מָלוּ שְׁלֹשָׁה חֳדָשִׁים לִבְדְּקָהּ!

The Gemara suggests further: **But let her wait any** minimal **amount** of time, less than a month, **and** then **marry,** and then **when three months** after the end of her first marriage **are complete, examine her** body to see if she is noticeably pregnant. If she is, then perforce the baby is the offspring of her previous husband because a pregnancy is not noticeable until three months.

אָמַר רַב סָפְרָא: אֵין בּוֹדְקִין אֶת הַנְּשׂוּאוֹת, שֶׁלֹּא יִתְגַּנּוּ עַל בַּעֲלֵיהֶן. וְנִבְדְּקָהּ בְּהִלּוּכָהּ?

Rav Safra said: This solution is not possible because **one does not examine** the bodies of **married women so as not to shame them before their husbands.** The Gemara suggests: **But let her be examined through the way she walks,**[NB] since after three months a pregnant woman walks differently than a woman who is not pregnant.

אָמַר רָמִי בַּר חָמָא: אִשָּׁה מְחַפָּה עַצְמָהּ, כְּדֵי שֶׁיִּירַשׁ בְּנָהּ בְּנִכְסֵי בַּעְלָהּ.

Rami bar Ḥama said: A woman who conceived from her previous husband would **mask herself** by purposefully walking in a manner in which her pregnancy will not be discerned, so that her child will be identified as the son of her new husband **in order that her child will** ultimately **inherit her** new **husband's property.** Therefore, it is impossible to rely upon a test of this kind. In summary, the Gemara has demonstrated that it would be ineffective to wait any less than three months.

הֵיכָא דְּקִים לַן דִּמְעוּבֶּרֶת הִיא תִּנָּשֵׂא, אַלְמָה תַּנְיָא: לֹא יִשָּׂא אָדָם מְעוּבֶּרֶת חֲבֵירוֹ וּמֵינֶקֶת חֲבֵירוֹ, וְאִם נָשָׂא יוֹצִיא וְלֹא יַחֲזִיר עוֹלָמִית.

§ The Gemara asks: In cases **where we are convinced that she is pregnant, let her marry** immediately, as the reason to wait three months does not apply. **Why,** then, **is it taught** in a *baraita*: **A man may not marry a woman who is pregnant** with the child of **another** man, **nor a woman who is nursing** the child **of another** man;[H] **and if he** transgressed and **married** her, he is penalized for violating the prohibition, and **he must divorce** her **and may never take** her **back?**

NOTES

One could say that the child is the offspring of the latter husband, etc. – **אִיכָּא לְמֵימַר דְּבַתְרָא הוּא וכו׳:** Why didn't the Gemara reject the possibility of waiting one month also due to the possibility that she had become pregnant from her previous husband one month before the end of the marriage? In that case, if a baby boy was born after eight months that child would actually be nine months old and the offspring of the first husband. Rashi suggests that Gemara could have considered this possibility; however, since in any case the Gemara rejects the possibility of waiting one month for the reasons it mentions, it was not necessary to state another reason. Others suggest that the Gemara considered it preferable to provide reasons that pertain to all cases, even to a case where she had been married to her previous husband for only a single day (Ramban; *Tosefot HaRosh*).

But let her be examined through the way she walks – **וְנִבְדְּקָהּ בְּהִלּוּכָהּ:** Rashi and Rivan cite the *ge'onim*, who explain that the fetus of a pregnant woman rests on one side of the womb and causes her steps to be uneven.

BACKGROUND

Let her be examined through the way she walks – **וְנִבְדְּקָהּ בְּהִלּוּכָהּ:** Rashi cites the explanation of the *ge'onim* that the woman's footprints are examined. There is also an additional change in pregnant women: Their posture becomes less stable in that the upper body begins to arch back more and more as the pregnancy progresses. This small change is discernible already in the first months of pregnancy. A woman who wishes to hide her state can do so by purposefully altering her posture. If she does so, her pregnancy will not be evident for some time.

HALAKHA

Pregnant and nursing women – **מְעוּבֶּרֶת וּמֵינֶקֶת:** A man may not marry a woman who is pregnant with the child of another man. He may also not marry a woman who is nursing the child of another man within twenty-four months of its birth. If he transgressed and married such a woman, he must divorce her with a bill of divorce. This applies even if he is a priest. If he is a non-priest he is permitted to remarry her after the nursing period has ended (Rambam *Sefer Nashim*, *Hilkhot Geirushin* 11:25; *Shulḥan Arukh*, *Even HaEzer* 13:11).

גְּזֵירָה שֶׁמָּא תַּעֲשֶׂה עוּבָּרָהּ סַנְדָּל, אִי הָכִי – דִּידֵיהּ נַמִּי,

The Gemara explains: This prohibition is a rabbinic **decree lest** she become pregnant a second time and **her** original **fetus will be deformed** into the shape of **a sandal fish.** The Gemara asks: **If so, even** if his wife is pregnant with **his own** child, the same concern applies.

אִי לְמַאן דַּאֲמַר בְּמוֹךְ – בְּמוֹךְ, וְאִי לְמַאן דַּאֲמַר מִן הַשָּׁמַיִם יְרַחֲמוּ – מִן הַשָּׁמַיִם יְרַחֲמוּ,

The Gemara responds: She is permitted to engage in relations, both **if** one holds **in accordance with the one who said** that a young girl, for whom it is dangerous to become pregnant, is permitted to engage in relations **using a** contraceptive **resorbent** placed at the entrance to her womb, then also a woman pregnant with her husband's child may engage in relations **using a resorbent, and** similarly **if** one holds **in accordance with the one who said** a young girl is permitted to engage in relations in her usual manner and **Heaven will have mercy** upon her[N] and prevent any mishap, then in this case as well a pregnant woman should continue to engage in relations and **Heaven will have mercy** upon her.

הָכָא נַמִּי: אִי לְמַאן דְּאָמַר בְּמוֹךְ – בְּמוֹךְ, אִי לְמַאן דְּאָמַר מִן הַשָּׁמַיִם יְרַחֲמוּ – מִן הַשָּׁמַיִם יְרַחֲמוּ!

The Gemara objects: But **here, too,** in the case of a woman who is pregnant with the child of another man, these solutions could be employed: Both **if** one holds **in accordance with the one who says** that a young girl may engage in relations **using a resorbent,** in this case as well she may do so **using a resorbent, and** similarly **if** one holds **in accordance with the one who says** that **Heaven will have mercy** upon her, in this case as well **Heaven will have mercy** upon her.

אֶלָּא מִשּׁוּם דְּחָסָה. אִי הָכִי דִּידֵיהּ נַמִּי! דִּידֵיהּ חָיֵיס עִילָּוֵיהּ. הָכָא נַמִּי חָיֵיס עִילָּוֵיהּ!

The Gemara suggests a different reason for the prohibition against marrying a woman who is pregnant with the child of another man: **Rather,** it is **due to the** damage that could be caused to the fetus by the **pressure**[N] applied to it at the time of intercourse. The Gemara asks: **If so, even** if his wife his pregnant with **his own** child, the same concern applies. The Gemara explains: When it is **his own** child, **he has mercy upon it** and tries not to apply too much pressure. The Gemara asks: But **here, too,** when it is the child of another man, **he will have mercy upon it,** as certainly one is careful not to cause harm to any human life and will be careful not to press down too hard.

אֶלָּא: סְתָם מְעוּבֶּרֶת לְמֵינִקָה קַיְימָא,

The Gemara suggests a different reason: **Rather,** the reason for the prohibition is that **a typical pregnant woman is poised to nurse** her child once it is born;

NOTES

Heaven will have mercy upon her – מִן הַשָּׁמַיִם יְרַחֲמוּ: This concept, based on the verse: "The Lord preserves the simple" (Psalms 116:6), applies only when one acts normally and does not take unusual risks. When there is definite danger involved, one is not permitted to take the risk and rely on God's protection. In the case here, there is only a very slight risk involved, and therefore this concept can be applied (Meiri; Ridvaz 3:596; *Aḥiezer* 1:23).

Due to the pressure – מִשּׁוּם דְּחָסָה: Usually when the Gemara challenges the logic of a given answer and proceeds by saying: Rather, it indicates that the given answer is rejected. Accordingly, it would appear that the Gemara here rejects the suggestion that the concern that the man might damage the fetus by applying too much pressure could be the reason for the prohibition. However, the Rambam does cite this reason when he codifies the *halakha*. Some suggest that the Rambam understood that the Gemara never meant to reject the reasons it raised; it merely held that they were insufficient. It is also possible that the Rambam had a different version of the Gemara text and that in his version the Gemara never stated: Rather. Alternatively, it is possible that the Rambam drew a distinction between the case of a pregnant woman and that of a nursing woman, and different reasons apply to each case (see *Kesef Mishne* and *Ha'amek She'ala*).

Perek **IV**
Daf **42** Amud **b**

דִּלְמָא אִיעַבְּרָה, וּמִיעַכַּר חֲלָבָהּ, וְקָטְלָה לֵיהּ. אִי הָכִי דִּידֵיהּ נַמִּי! דִּידֵיהּ מְמַסְמְסָא לֵיהּ בְּבֵיצִים וְחָלָב. דִּידָהּ נַמִּי מְמַסְמְסָא לֵיהּ בְּבֵיצִים וְחָלָב! לָא יָהֵב לָהּ בַּעַל. וְלִיתְבָּעִינֵיהּ לַיּוֹרְשִׁים! אָמַר אַבַּיֵי: אִשָּׁה בּוֹשָׁה לָבֹא לְבֵית דִּין, וְהוֹרֶגֶת אֶת בְּנָהּ.

therefore, one should be concerned that **perhaps she will become pregnant and her milk will dry up**[B] during pregnancy, **and** the lack of milk will **kill** her newborn child. The Gemara asks: **If so, even** if his wife is pregnant with **his own** child, the same concern applies. The Gemara explains: For **his own** child, **she will feed** [*memasmesa*][L] **him**[N] **with eggs and milk** as a substitute for the mother's milk. The Gemara asks: Even if the child is not his, it is still the mother's child, and for **her** child **she will also feed him with eggs and milk.** The Gemara answers: **The husband will not give her** money to procure food for a child that is not his. The Gemara asks: **But she could sue** her first husband's **heirs** to provide subsistence for the child. **Abaye said: A woman is embarrassed to come to court, and** therefore she will not obtain enough sustenance for him. Consequently, **she** effectively **kills her son** as a result.

BACKGROUND

She will become pregnant and her milk will dry up – אִיעַבְּרָה וּמִיעַכַּר חֲלָבָהּ: The hormone responsible for producing milk in the mother's body also substantially hinders ovulation. As such, women generally do not become pregnant while nursing. However, if a nursing woman does become pregnant, the hormones that are then released into her body can affect the mother's milk and produce a change in the quality of the milk.

LANGUAGE

She will feed [*memasmesa*] – מְמַסְמְסָא: This verb apparently has two meanings: It can mean to soften or mash, which fits well with the current version of the Gemara, as the verb is applied to eggs. It can also mean to calm or give encouragement. Accordingly, in the Gemara here it would mean to calm the hungry infant by providing him with these foods. Indeed, Rashi translates the word here to mean that she feeds her child.

NOTES

She will feed him – מְמַסְמְסָא לֵיהּ: Rashi explains the word as a reference to feeding. The Rivan explains it refers to preparing the food. Both of them assume that the food is for the baby. However, the *Ha'amek She'ala* cites the Rambam's version of the text, which implies that the eggs were not for the child but for the mother. He explains that sexual relations can affect a woman's milk, causing it to dry up, but consuming eggs can help restore the flow.

״אַחַת בְּתוּלוֹת וְאַחַת בְּעוּלוֹת״. הֵי נִיהוּ בְּתוּלוֹת וְהֵי נִיהוּ אֲרוּסוֹת, הֵי נִיהוּ בְּעוּלוֹת וְהֵי נִיהוּ נְשׂוּאוֹת?

§ The mishna states: The requirement to wait three months before remarrying applies **both to virgins and non-virgins,** both to divorcées and to widows, and both to women who were married to their previous husbands and to women who were only betrothed. The Gemara asks: **Which** women **are** referred to as **virgins**[N] **and which are** referred to as those who were **betrothed?** Although the two terms appear to be synonymous, since a virgin will be subject to levirate marriage only if she was betrothed, they must certainly refer to two different categories of women. Similarly, **which** women **are** referred to as **non-virgins and which are** referred to as **married,** as a married woman is always considered to be a non-virgin?

אָמַר רַבִּי יְהוּדָה הָכִי קָאָמַר: אַחַת בְּתוּלוֹת וְאַחַת בְּעוּלוֹת שֶׁנִּתְאַרְמְלוּ אוֹ שֶׁנִּתְגָּרְשׁוּ, בֵּין מִן הָאֵרוּסִין בֵּין מִן הַנִּשּׂוּאִין.

Rabbi Yehuda said this is what the mishna **is saying:** The requirement to wait applies **to both virgins and non-virgins who were widowed or divorced, whether from betrothal or from marriage,** i.e., the mishna does not list different categories of women but instead establishes a general principle.

רַבִּי אֶלְעָזָר לָא עָל לְבֵי מִדְרְשָׁא, אַשְׁכְּחֵיהּ לְרַבִּי אַסִי, אֲמַר לֵיהּ: מַאי אֲמוּר רַבָּנַן בְּבֵי מִדְרְשָׁא? אֲמַר לֵיהּ, הָכִי אָמַר רַבִּי יוֹחָנָן: הֲלָכָה כְּרַבִּי יוֹסֵי.

The Gemara relates: **Rabbi Elazar did not enter the study hall** one day. **He found Rabbi Asi** and **said to him: What was said by the Sages in the study hall** today? **He said to him: This** is what **Rabbi Yoḥanan said:** The ***halakha* is in accordance with** the opinion of **Rabbi Yosei** that a woman is permitted to be betrothed even before three months have passed, since the reason for waiting does not apply in that case.

מִכְּלָל דִּיחִידָאָה פָּלֵיג עֲלֵיהּ? אִין, וְהָתַנְיָא: הֲרֵי שֶׁהָיְתָה רְדוּפָה לֵילֵךְ לְבֵית אָבִיהָ, אוֹ שֶׁהָיָה לָהּ כַּעַס בְּבֵית בַּעְלָהּ, אוֹ שֶׁהָיָה בַּעְלָהּ חָבוּשׁ בְּבֵית הָאֲסוּרִין, אוֹ שֶׁהָיָה בַּעְלָהּ זָקֵן אוֹ חוֹלֶה, אוֹ שֶׁהָיְתָה הִיא חוֹלָה,

Rabbi Elazar said: **From the fact** that Rabbi Yoḥanan needed to state this, it would seem **that** there is **an individual** opinion that **disagrees with him,**[N] even though no such opinion is mentioned in the mishna. Rabbi Asi answered: **Yes,** that is correct, **and so it is taught** in a *baraita* in the *Tosefta* (*Yevamot* 6:6): With regard to a woman who is certainly not pregnant, for example, a woman who, at the time of her husband's death, had not lived with her husband for some time because she always eagerly hurried, like **one pursued, to go to her father's house, or because she had** been subject to **anger in her husband's house, or because her husband had been incarcerated in prison, or because her husband was elderly or infirm, or because she was infirm.**

אוֹ שֶׁהִפִּילָה אַחַר מִיתַת בַּעְלָהּ, אוֹ שֶׁהָיְתָה עֲקָרָה, אוֹ זְקֵנָה, אוֹ קְטַנָּה, אוֹ אַיְלוֹנִית, אוֹ שֶׁאֵינָהּ רְאוּיָה לֵילֵד – צְרִיכָה לְהַמְתִּין שְׁלֹשָׁה חֳדָשִׁים, דִּבְרֵי רַבִּי מֵאִיר. רַבִּי יְהוּדָה מַתִּיר לֵיאָרֵס וְלִינָּשֵׂא מִיָּד.

Or a woman who could not be pregnant **because she miscarried after her husband's death, or because she was barren,**[N] **or elderly, or a minor, or a sexually underdeveloped woman** [***aylonit***], **or** if for some other reason **she was unsuited to give birth;**[N] even though the reason for the decree to wait three months does not apply to such a woman, nevertheless, **she must wait three months.** This is **the statement of Rabbi Meir. Rabbi Yehuda permits** such women **to be betrothed or to marry immediately.** It is apparent from the *baraita* that the question of whether a woman is required to wait the three months when the reason to do so does not apply is subject to a dispute.

אָמַר רַבִּי חִיָּיא בַּר אַבָּא: חָזַר בּוֹ רַבִּי יוֹחָנָן. אֲמַר רַב יוֹסֵף: אִי הֲדַר בֵּיהּ – מִמַּתְנִיתִין דְּכַרְמָא הֲדַר בֵּיהּ. דְּתַנְיָא, אָמַר רַבִּי יִשְׁמָעֵאל בְּנוֹ שֶׁל רַבִּי יוֹחָנָן בֶּן בְּרוֹקָה: שָׁמַעְתִּי מִפִּי חֲכָמִים בְּכֶרֶם בְּיַבְנֶה: כּוּלָּן צְרִיכוֹת לְהַמְתִּין שְׁלֹשָׁה חֳדָשִׁים.

Rabbi Ḥiyya bar Abba said: Rabbi Yoḥanan retracted his statement that the *halakha* is in accordance with the opinion of Rabbi Yosei. **Rav Yosef said:** Even **if he** wanted to **retract** his statement, would **he retract from the *baraita*** that records the opinions of the Sages **of the vineyard** of Yavne? **As it is taught** in a *baraita*: **Rabbi Yishmael, son of Rabbi Yoḥanan ben Beroka, said: I heard from the mouth of the Sages in the vineyard of Yavne**[B] that **all** those women enumerated in the *baraita* above **need to wait three months.**[H] If the great Sages of Yavne held in accordance with the opinion Rabbi Yosei, then the *halakha* is certainly in accordance with his opinion.

NOTES

Which are virgins – הֵי נִיהוּ בְּתוּלוֹת: Rashi assumes that the case of a virgin *yevama* is one in which she was widowed from betrothal. Accordingly the Gemara's question is that the cases of virgins and women who were betrothed are synonymous; why then are they listed as though they are two distinct cases? However, other early commentaries highlight that it is also possible that a married woman might be a virgin if she had not yet had the opportunity to consummate her marriage. Therefore, the *Arukh LaNer* explains the Gemara's question differently: A betrothed woman is certainly a virgin, and as such the additional reference to a virgin is superfluous.

That an individual opinion disagrees with him – דִּיחִידָאָה פָּלֵיג עֲלֵיהּ: In his Commentary on the Mishna, the Rambam explains that even in those places where the Mishna mentions the opinion of a single Sage, it does not necessarily mean that it was only that Sage who held that opinion. Rather, many other Sages held that opinion; the Sage mentioned was merely the leading exponent of it. However, when the Mishna cites an unattributed opinion or states: The Rabbis said, this is an indication that Rabbi Yehuda HaNasi maintained that the majority of the Sages held in accordance with that opinion.

Barren – עֲקָרָה: The Rivan and other commentaries explain that this refers to a woman whose womb had been removed. They explain that although the term barren is typically used in a more general sense, since the list here concludes with reference to a woman who is unsuited to give birth, which is a general statement, the earlier reference to a barren woman must be understood as referring to a specific case.

She was unsuited to give birth – שֶׁאֵינָהּ רְאוּיָה לֵילֵד: Rashi explains that this is referring to a woman who took a drug that rendered her barren. The Rif writes that this is referring to a woman above the age of forty, or to a woman who had been married for ten years without children, since in such cases the Gemara states elsewhere that such women are no longer suitable for childbirth.

BACKGROUND

The vineyard of Yavne – כֶּרֶם בְּיַבְנֶה: According to an ancient tradition, the Sanhedrin in Yavne was called a vineyard because when it was in session, the Sages themselves, along with their students, would sit in rows, like the rows of a vineyard (Jerusalem Talmud). It is also possible that the Sanhedrin may have been situated near vineyards, lending the name a double meaning.

HALAKHA

Which women require a waiting period for the purposes of distinguishing – אֵיזוֹ נָשִׁים צְרִיכוֹת הַבְחָנָה: The rabbinic decree that any woman who had been married must wait three months until she remarries is applied irrespective of whether the reason to wait is relevant. Therefore, a woman must wait even if it is clear that she is not pregnant, e.g., if she did not have the opportunity to engage in sexual relations with her husband, or if she is elderly, or a minor, or an *aylonit*, or if for some other reason she is unsuited to give birth. This is in accordance with the opinion of Rabbi Meir, as the *halakha* is ruled in accordance with his opinion in all cases of rabbinic decrees (Rambam *Sefer Nashim, Hilkhot Geirushin* 11:20; *Shulḥan Arukh, Even HaEzer* 13:1).

אֲמַר לֵיהּ רַבִּי יִרְמְיָה לְרַבִּי זְרִיקָא: כִּי עָיְילַתְּ לְקַמֵּיהּ דְּרַבִּי אַבָּהוּ רְמִי לֵיהּ: מִי אֲמַר רַבִּי יוֹחָנָן הֲלָכָה כְּרַבִּי יוֹסֵי? וְהָאָמַר רַבִּי יוֹחָנָן: הֲלָכָה כִּסְתָם מִשְׁנָה, וּתְנַן: כׇּל הַנָּשִׁים לֹא יִנָּשְׂאוּ וְלֹא יִתְאָרְסוּ עַד שֶׁיְּהוּ לָהֶם שְׁלֹשָׁה חֳדָשִׁים, אַחַת בְּתוּלוֹת וְאַחַת בְּעוּלוֹת!

Rabbi Yirmeya said to Rabbi Zerika: When you come before Rabbi Abbahu, raise the following **contradiction: Did Rabbi Yoḥanan** actually **say** that **the *halakha* is in accordance with** the opinion of **Rabbi Yosei? Didn't Rabbi Yoḥanan say** that the ***halakha*** is always established **in accordance with** the ruling of **an unattributed mishna? And we learned** in the mishna an unattributed ruling: **All women may not marry and may not be betrothed until they** have waited **three months** since their previous marriage ended; this applies to **both virgins and non-virgins.**

אֲמַר לֵיהּ: דִּרְמָא לָךְ הָא – לָא חָשׁ לְקִמְחֵיהּ; סְתָם וְאַחַר כָּךְ מַחֲלוֹקֶת הִיא, וְאֵין הֲלָכָה כִּסְתָם. דְּאָמַר רַב פָּפָּא וְאִיתֵּימָא רַבִּי יוֹחָנָן: מַחֲלוֹקֶת וְאַחַר כָּךְ סְתָם – הֲלָכָה כִּסְתָם, סְתָם וְאַחַר כָּךְ מַחֲלוֹקֶת – אֵין הֲלָכָה כִּסְתָם

When Rabbi Zerika went and asked, Rabbi Abbahu **said to him:** The one **who raised this contradiction to you** is clearly **not concerned for his flour;**[N] this is a case of **an unattributed** ruling **followed by a dispute**[N] on that ruling, and in such cases the ***halakha* is not** necessarily **in accordance with the unattributed opinion. As Rav Pappa said, and some say** it was **Rabbi Yoḥanan** who said the following principle: When the Mishna first records **a dispute, and afterward** it records only one side of that dispute as **an unattributed opinion,** then **the *halakha* is in accordance with the unattributed opinion.** However, when the Mishna first records **an unattributed opinion and afterward** records that the ruling is subject to **a dispute, the *halakha* is not** necessarily **in accordance with the unattributed opinion.** In each case, the later reference is considered to be a summary of the matter.

מִסְתַּמֵּיךְ וְאָזֵיל רַבִּי אַבָּהוּ אַכַּתְפֵּיהּ דְּרַבִּי נַחוּם שַׁמָּעֵיהּ, מְנַקֵּיט וְאָזֵיל הִלְכְתָא מִינֵּיהּ. בְּעָא מִינֵּיהּ: מַחֲלוֹקֶת וְאַחַר כָּךְ סְתָם מַאי? אֲמַר לֵיהּ: הֲלָכָה כִּסְתָם. סְתָם וְאַחַר כָּךְ מַחֲלוֹקֶת מַאי? אֲמַר לֵיהּ: אֵין הֲלָכָה כִּסְתָם.

§ The Gemara relates: **Rabbi Abbahu would walk while leaning upon the shoulder of Rabbi Naḥum, his attendant,** and along the way Rabbi Naḥum would **walk and gather halakhic rulings from him.** Once, Rabbi Naḥum **asked him:** When the Mishna first records **a dispute, and afterward** it records only one side of that dispute as **an unattributed opinion, what** is the *halakha*? Rabbi Abbahu **said to him:** The ***halakha* is in accordance with the unattributed opinion.** Rabbi Naḥum then asked: When the Mishna first records **an unattributed opinion and afterward** records that the ruling is subject to **a dispute, what** is the *halakha*? Rabbi Abbahu **said to him:** The ***halakha* is not** necessarily **in accordance with the unattributed opinion.**[N]

סְתָמָא דְּמַתְנִיתִין וּמַחֲלוֹקֶת בְּבָרַיְיתָא מַאי? אֲמַר לֵיהּ: הֲלָכָה כִּסְתָם. מַחֲלוֹקֶת בְּמַתְנִיתִין וּסְתָמָא בְּבָרַיְיתָא מַאי? אֲמַר לֵיהּ:

Rabbi Naḥum asked: When a ruling is recorded in **the Mishna** as **unattributed and** it is subject to **a dispute in a *baraita*, what** is the *halakha*?[N] Rabbi Abbahu **said to him:** The ***halakha* is in accordance with** the **unattributed opinion** in the Mishna. Rabbi Naḥum then asked: When **the Mishna** records that a matter is subject to **a dispute, and** only one side is recorded as **an unattributed opinion in a *baraita*, what** is the *halakha*? Rabbi Abbahu **said to him:**

NOTES

He is not concerned for his flour – לָא חָשׁ לְקִמְחֵיהּ: Rashi explains the analogy as referring to one who does not show care and concern for the items that he himself produces. *Arukh* interprets it as a reference to one who is not wary of wasting his flour; here, he wasted the energy he gained from the bread he had eaten because he did not study thoroughly enough. Rabbi Avraham min HaHar explains the reference is to one who is not sufficiently aware of his own flour, i.e., one who does not taste his own food, which in this case is referring to one not paying attention to the words he says. The *ge'onim* had a different version of the text, which states: He does not fear that which is before him, meaning that he does not perceive that which is found directly before him.

An unattributed ruling followed by a dispute – סְתָם וְאַחַר כָּךְ מַחֲלוֹקֶת: The early commentaries engaged in a detailed clarification of this principle. For example, does it apply only to cases where named Sages are in dispute, or also to cases where an individual Sage disagrees with an unattributed opinion? The Meiri cites an opinion, also mentioned in *Sefer HaKeritut*, that whenever the Mishna cites a dispute between a named Sage and an unattributed opinion, the *halakha* is not necessarily in accordance with the unattributed opinion, irrespective of whether the unattributed opinion is cited first or last in the mishna. The commentaries also discuss whether this principle applies only when the opinions appear together within a single mishna or even when they appear in different *mishnayot* within the same tractate. The Gemara states in one place that the tractates of the Mishna are not ordered sequentially, so that if in one tractate a dispute is cited and in another tractate one of the opinions is cited as unattributed, one cannot claim that the opinions in one tractate were recorded before the other in order to determine what the *halakha* should be. However, some claim that there is a specific sequencing of the orders of the Mishna, and therefore if the two *mishnayot* appear in different orders, the principle can be applied (see *Tosefot Yom Tov* on *Sota*, chapter 9, *Sha'ar HaMelekh*, and *Arukh LaNer*).

The *halakha* is not in accordance with the unattributed opinion – אֵין הֲלָכָה כִּסְתָם: Ramban, Rashba, Ritva, and *Nimmukei Yosef* all note that the only intent of this statement is that in such a case Rabbi Yoḥanan's principle that the *halakha* is always established in accordance with the ruling of an unattributed mishna does not apply. It does not mean to state positively that the *halakha* is never in accordance with the unattributed opinion, but only that it is not necessarily so. Therefore, in such cases, the dispute must be analyzed based on the standard principles of halakhic decision-making.

A ruling recorded in the Mishna as unattributed and subject to a dispute in a *baraita* – סְתָם בְּמִשְׁנָה וּמַחֲלוֹקֶת בְּבָרַיְיתָא: The essence of this question lies in the fact that it was the disciples of Rabbi Yehuda HaNasi, the redactor of the Mishna, who taught the *baraitot*. It is therefore possible that they received Rabbi Yehuda HaNasi's final opinion on a matter and that he may have retracted his ruling recorded in the Mishna. The Rashba writes (*Bava Kama* 102a) that although the Gemara here states that one disregards the *baraita* in such a case, there are other *amora'im* who hold that the *baraita* does indeed carry greater authority than an unattributed mishna.

וכי רבי לא שנאה רבי חייא מכן לו?

If Rabbi Yehuda HaNasi **had not taught** that ruling in the Mishna,[N] **from where would Rabbi Ḥiyya,** his disciple and redactor of the *baraitot,* **have known it?** Since the source of the unattributed ruling in the *baraita* is certainly the dispute recorded in the mishna, its lack of attribution in the *baraita* only reflects the fact that Rabbi Ḥiyya ruled in accordance with that opinion, but that cannot be used to indicate that it is the accepted *halakha.*

אמר ליה: והא תנן: מסרק של פשתן שניטלו שיניו, ונשתיירו בו שתים – טמאות, ואחת – טהורה. וכולן שניטלו אחת אחת בפני עצמן – טמאות.

Rabbi Naḥum questioned the principle that the *halakha* is always in accordance with an unattributed ruling in a mishna and **said to** Rabbi Ḥiyya: **Didn't we learn** in a mishna (*Kelim* 13:8): **A comb** made for combing beaten **flax**[H] in preparation for spinning, from **which its teeth were removed**[N] and only **two** of its teeth **remained in it,** is still suitable for combing. It is therefore considered a utensil and will become **ritually impure** if it comes in contact with ritual impurity. However, if only **one** tooth remained, so that the comb was no longer suitable for combing, it is no longer considered a utensil and so will remain **ritually pure** even if it comes in contact with ritual impurity. **And** with regard to **any** of the teeth **that were individually removed on their own,** since they do serve a purpose, e.g., they may be embedded and used as hooks, they are considered utensils and can become **ritually impure.**

של צמר שניטלו שיניו אחת מבינתים – טהור, נשתיירו בו שלש במקום אחד – טמא, היתה החיצונה אחת מהן – טהור. ניטלו שנים ועשאן למלקט – טמאות, אחת והתקינה לנר או למתוח – טמאה.

A comb made for combing **wool**[BHN] **from which every other one of its teeth were removed,** so that no two consecutive teeth remained in place, is no longer suitable for combing and so will remain **ritually pure.** If **three** teeth **remained in it in a single place** so that it could still be used for combing, then it could become **ritually impure.** However, if **one of those** teeth **was the external** frame of the comb itself, then it could not function as a comb, and so it will remain **ritually pure.** If **two** of the teeth **were removed and made into** small **pincers,** then they could become **ritually impure.** Alternatively, if **one** of the teeth was removed, **and it was prepared** in a manner that made it suitable **for** use in cleaning **an oil lamp**[N] **or for stretching**[N] ropes, then it would be considered a utensil and could become **ritually impure.**[H]

BACKGROUND

Combs for wool and flax – מסרקי צמר ופשתן: From the various descriptions in the Mishna and Talmud, it would appear that the comb made for flax was a large instrument with which the stalks of flax were combed in order to prepare them for spinning. The body of the comb and its external teeth were constructed from wood, while the internal teeth were metal nails. It is for this reason that no combs of this kind remain from that period, because wood generally decomposes, at which point any nails fall out.

There are differing opinions concerning the structure of the comb made for wool. Some explain that it was made in a similar fashion to the one for flax, the only difference being its thickness and the proximity of the teeth. Others, however, explain that the comb made for wool was an entirely different tool. It was constructed from a wooden board, or a pair of wooden boards, also known as cards, upon which several rows of metal nails were fastened. The combing was achieved by dragging the wool over the boards. According to this description, the Gemara's distinction between internal teeth and external teeth refers to the different rows of teeth.

Dried flax with threshing comb

Pair of wool cards

HALAKHA

A comb made for flax – מסרק של פשתן: With regard to a comb made for combing flax, from which the teeth were removed: If two teeth remain, the comb remains susceptible to ritual impurity, but if only a single tooth remains it is no longer susceptible to ritual impurity (Rambam *Sefer Tahara, Hilkhot Kelim* 11:4).

A comb made for wool – מסרק של צמר: With regard to a comb made for combing wool, from which the teeth were removed, if three teeth remain in a single place, the comb remains susceptible to ritual impurity. However, if one of the three was the external frame, it would not be susceptible to ritual impurity. The *Kesef Mishne* questions why the Rambam rules in accordance with this mishna even though the Gemara states that it is not ruled as *halakha* (see NOTES; Rambam *Sefer Tahara, Hilkhot Kelim* 11:3).

The teeth of the comb – שיני המסרק: If two teeth of a comb were removed and made into pincers, or if a single tooth was removed and prepared for an oil lamp or for stretching, then they are susceptible to ritually impurity. If that tooth was large and thick, then even if it was not specially prepared, it is susceptible to ritual impurity. This is in accordance with the resolution suggested by Rav Pappa (Rambam *Sefer Tahara, Hilkhot Kelim* 11:3).

NOTES

If Rabbi Yehuda HaNasi had not taught it, etc. – וכי רבי לא שנאה וכו׳: The Gemara assumes that since Rabbi Ḥiyya was Rabbi Yehuda HaNasi's disciple, it does not stand to reason that he would formulate an opinion as though it were the conclusive *halakha* when Rabbi Yehuda HaNasi clearly decided not to teach that opinion in such a way (Rav Sherira Gaon). The Maharik adds that Rabbi Yehuda HaNasi had a far greater breadth of knowledge than Rabbi Ḥiyya, and so it is improbable that Rabbi Ḥiyya would be aware that a certain opinion had been accepted as the *halakha* if Rabbi Yehuda HaNasi was not.

A comb whose teeth were removed, etc. – מסרק שניטלו שיניו וכו׳: Utensils are susceptible to ritual impurity only when they serve a useful purpose. Even if they break and no longer serve their original purpose, if they serve some other useful purpose they can still become impure. The import of this mishna is to define at which point a comb is considered broken to the extent that it no longer serves any useful purpose and therefore is no longer susceptible to ritual impurity.

Combs made for wool and flax – מסרקי צמר ופשתן: The early commentaries describe the differences between the two types of combs: The Rivan explains that the teeth of a flax comb are narrower than those of a wool comb. However, the Meiri claims the opposite to be true and adds that they are also distinct in their form and structure.

It was prepared for an oil lamp – התקינה לנר: Rashi suggests that this means that the tooth of the comb can be used to clean out the lamp. The Rivan suggests that a wax candle could be attached to it.

For stretching – למיתוח: The Rambam, in his commentary on the Mishna on *Kelim* 13:6, explains that this term refers to wrapping a thread around a stick to make the thread easier to use.

וְקַיְימָא לָן דְּאֵין הֲלָכָה כְּאוֹתָהּ מִשְׁנָה! אֲמַר לֵיהּ: בַּר מִינָּהּ דְּהַהִיא, דְּרַבִּי יוֹחָנָן וְרֵישׁ לָקִישׁ דְּאָמְרִי תַּרְוַיְיהוּ: זוֹ אֵינָהּ מִשְׁנָה.

Rabbi Naḥum posed his question: **But we maintain that the *halakha* is not in accordance with that mishna.**[N] This would seem to contradict the principle that the *halakha* is always in accordance with an unattributed opinion. Rabbi Ḥiyya **said to** Rabbi Naḥum that the principle applies to all cases **apart from this** mishna, **as** with regard to this particular mishna there are **Rabbi Yoḥanan and Reish Lakish who both say: This is not** an authoritative **mishna,** and so it cannot be relied upon for a halakhic ruling.

מַאי טַעֲמָא? אֲמַר רַב הוּנָא בַּר מָנוֹחַ מִשְּׁמֵיהּ דְּרַב אִידִי בְּרֵיהּ דְּרַב אִיקָא: מִשּׁוּם דְּקַשְׁיָא רֵישָׁא לְסֵיפָא. דְּקָתָנֵי: שֶׁל צֶמֶר שֶׁנִּיטְּלוּ שִׁינָּיו אַחַת מִבֵּינְתַיִם – טָהוֹר, הָא נִשְׁתַּיְּירוּ בּוֹ שְׁתַּיִם בְּמָקוֹם אֶחָד – טָמֵא, וַהֲדַר תָּנֵי: נִשְׁתַּיְּירוּ בּוֹ שָׁלֹשׁ – טָמֵא, שָׁלֹשׁ – אִין, שְׁתַּיִם – לָא!

The Gemara asks: **What is the reason** to say that the mishna is not authoritative? **Rav Huna bar Manoaḥ said in the name of Rav Idi, son of Rav Ika:** It is **because the first clause** of that mishna **contradicts the latter clause, as it teaches:** A comb used **for wool from which every other one of its teeth were removed** is no longer considered a utensil, and so it will remain **ritually pure. This** implies that **were two** teeth **to remain in it in one place,** it could become **ritually impure. And then** the mishna **continues and teaches:** If **three** teeth **remained in it in a single place** it is still considered a utensil and so it could become **ritually impure.** This indicates that if there are **three, yes,** it could become ritually impure, but if there are **two, no,** it would not become ritually impure.

וּמַאי קוּשְׁיָא? דִּלְמָא הָא בְּגַוָּויָתָא הָא בְּבָרַיָּיתָא!

The Gemara asks: **But what** is the **difficulty? Perhaps this** ruling that if two teeth remain it is considered a utensil is referring to **the internal** teeth, found in the middle of the frame, while **that** ruling that it is not considered a utensil is referring to **the outer** teeth, which are adjacent to the frame of the comb, which makes them unsuitable for use.

אֶלָּא מֵהָכָא, דְּקָתָנֵי: וְכוּלָּן שֶׁנִּיטְּלוּ אַחַת אַחַת בִּפְנֵי עַצְמָן טְמֵאוֹת, וְאַף עַל גַּב דְּלָא הִתְקִינָהּ. אֵימָא סֵיפָא: אַחַת וְהִתְקִינָהּ לְנֵר אוֹ לְמִיתּוּחַ – טְמֵאָה. הִתְקִינָהּ – אִין, לֹא הִתְקִינָהּ – לָא!

Rather, the difficulty with the mishna is **from here, as it teaches: And any** of the teeth **that were individually removed on their own,** since they can serve a useful purpose they are considered utensils and can become **ritually impure. And** the implication is that this is true **even though** the tooth **was not prepared** for that purpose. But **say the latter clause** as follows: If **one** of the teeth was removed, **and it was prepared** in a manner that rendered it suitable **for** use in cleaning **an oil lamp or for stretching** ropes, then it would be considered a utensil and could become **ritually impure.** The implication is that if **it was prepared** for use, then **yes,** it would be considered a utensil, but if **it was not prepared** for use, then **no,** it would not be considered a utensil.

אֲמַר אַבַּיֵי: וּמַאי קוּשְׁיָא? דִּלְמָא הָא בְּקַתַּיְיהוּ, הָא בְּלָא קַתַּיְיהוּ.

Abaye said: But what is the **difficulty? Perhaps this** ruling, that further preparation is not required before it is considered a utensil, is referring to a case where the teeth were removed **with their base,** which allows them to be used immediately for various functions, whereas **that** ruling, that it is considered a utensil only once it is prepared for use, is referring to a case where the teeth were removed **without their base** and therefore require further preparation before they can be used.

אָמַר רַב פַּפָּא: וּמַאי קוּשְׁיָא? וְדִלְמָא הָא – בְּקַטִּינָתָא, הָא – בְּאַלִּימָתָא.

Rav Pappa stated an alternative resolution: **But what** is the **difficulty? Perhaps this** ruling that further preparation is not required is referring to a case where the teeth **were narrow,** whereas **that** ruling that it is considered a utensil only once it is prepared for use is referring to a case where the teeth **were thick.**

אֶלָּא: מִשּׁוּם דִּמְסַיְּימֵי בָּהּ דַּוְוקָנֵי: זוֹ רַבִּי שִׁמְעוֹן.

Rather, the reason that the mishna is not accepted as authoritative is not due to some difficulty in the formulation of the mishna, but **because those who are exact**[B] in their rendition of the tradition **conclude** this mishna with: **This is** the statement of **Rabbi Shimon.** In other words, this mishna is not unattributed but presents the minority opinion of a single Sage, and it is for this reason that it is not accepted as authoritative.

שָׁלַח רַבִּי חִיָּיא בַּר אָבִין: מְאָרְסִין תּוֹךְ שְׁלֹשָׁה, וְכֵן עוֹשִׂים מַעֲשֶׂה.

§ **Rabbi Ḥiyya bar Avin sent** a message from Eretz Yisrael with regard to the *halakha* cited in the mishna: **One may betroth** a woman, but not marry her, **within three** months of her previous marriage; **and so one acts in practice.**

NOTES

But we maintain that the *halakha* is not in accordance with that mishna – וְקַיְימָא לָן דְּאֵין הֲלָכָה כְּאוֹתָהּ מִשְׁנָה: Despite the Gemara's claim, the Rambam rules in accordance with this mishna. In addition, it appears that Rabbeinu Shimshon also rules in this manner. The *Yam shel Shlomo* explains that although the Gemara identifies the various difficulties inherent in the mishna, the mishna is nevertheless ruled as *halakha*, and ultimately the Rabbis disagree with Rabbi Shimon only on a single point, i.e., the question of ritual impurity for the teeth removed from the comb. Rabbi Shimon holds that these do not require preparation in order to be susceptible to ritual impurity, while the Rabbis hold that they do require preparation (see *Keren Ora* and *Arukh LaNer*).

BACKGROUND

Those who are exact – דַּוְוקָנֵי: Apparently, there were a number of Sages who were relied upon to establish the precise formulation of the mishna. Rav Sherira Gaon explains in his famous letter concerning the composition of the Mishna that this is why the Gemara is often willing to delete parts of a mishna or even an entire mishna on occasion, as sometimes the current version is erroneous or was not transmitted reliably.

וְכֵן הָיָה רַבִּי אֶלְעָזָר מְלַמְּדֵנוּ מִשּׁוּם רַבִּי חֲנִינָא הַגָּדוֹל: רוּבּוֹ שֶׁל רִאשׁוֹן, וְרוּבּוֹ שֶׁל שְׁלִישִׁי, וְאֶמְצָעִי שָׁלֵם.

And so Rabbi Elazar would teach us in the name of Rabbi Ḥanina the Great[P] that the three months are counted as follows: One counts **the majority of** the days **of the first** month,[N] **and the majority of the third** month, **and the entire middle** month.

אֲמֵימַר שְׁרָא לְיָאֲרֵס בְּיוֹם תִּשְׁעִים. אֲמַר לֵיהּ רַב אַשִׁי לַאֲמֵימַר: וְהָא רַב וּשְׁמוּאֵל דְּאָמְרִי תַּרְוַיְיהוּ: צְרִיכָה לְהַמְתִּין שְׁלֹשָׁה חֳדָשִׁים, חוּץ מִיּוֹם שֶׁמֵּת בּוֹ וְחוּץ מִיּוֹם שֶׁנִּתְאָרְסָה בּוֹ! הַהוּא לְעִנְיַן מֵינֶקֶת. אִיתְּמַר, דְּרַב וּשְׁמוּאֵל דְּאָמְרִי תַּרְוַיְיהוּ: צְרִיכָה לְהַמְתִּין עֶשְׂרִים וְאַרְבָּעָה חֹדֶשׁ, חוּץ מִיּוֹם שֶׁנּוֹלַד בּוֹ וְחוּץ מִיּוֹם שֶׁנִּתְאָרְסָה בּוֹ.

Ameimar permitted one to betroth a woman **on the ninetieth day**[N] itself. **Rav Ashi said to Ameimar: Didn't Rav and Shmuel both say** that **she needs to wait three** full **months, excluding the day on which** the husband **died and excluding the day on which she is betrothed?** It is apparent that it is still prohibited to betroth a woman on the ninetieth day itself. Ameimar said to him: **That** which you heard, that the days of the husband's death and of the betrothal are not included, **was stated** only **with regard to a nursing woman,** as it was **Rav and Shmuel** who **both said:** A nursing woman **needs to wait twenty-four months** before being betrothed, **excluding the day on which** the baby **was born and excluding the day on which she is betrothed.**

וְהָא הַהוּא דַּעֲבַד סְעוּדַת אֵירוּסִין בְּיוֹם תִּשְׁעִים, וְאַפְסְדֵיהּ רָבָא לִסְעוּדָתֵיהּ! הַהִיא סְעוּדַת נִשּׂוּאִין הֲוַאי.

The Gemara asks: **Wasn't** there an incident concerning **a certain** person **who prepared a betrothal feast on the ninetieth day** following the death of the woman's first husband, **and Rava caused him to forfeit his feast** by prohibiting the betrothal on that day? The Gemara answers: **That** feast **was** actually **a marriage feast,** but had it been a betrothal feast it would have been permitted.

וְהִלְכְתָא: צְרִיכָה לְהַמְתִּין עֶשְׂרִים וְאַרְבָּעָה חוֹדֶשׁ, חוּץ מִיּוֹם שֶׁנּוֹלַד בּוֹ וְחוּץ מִיּוֹם שֶׁנִּתְאָרְסָה בּוֹ. וּצְרִיכָה לְהַמְתִּין שְׁלֹשָׁה חֳדָשִׁים, חוּץ מִיּוֹם שֶׁמֵּת בּוֹ וְחוּץ מִיּוֹם שֶׁנִּתְאָרְסָה בּוֹ.

The Gemara summarizes: **The *halakha* is** that a nursing mother **needs to wait twenty-four months,**[N] **excluding the day on which** the baby **was born and excluding the day on which she is betrothed. And** if she was widowed but was not nursing, then **she needs to wait** only **three months, excluding the day on which** her previous husband **died and excluding the day on which she is betrothed.**[H]

"חוּץ מִן הָאַלְמָנָה" וכו׳. אָמַר רַב חִסְדָּא: קַל וָחוֹמֶר, וּמַה בְּמָקוֹם שֶׁאָסוּר לְכַבֵּס – מוּתָּר לְיָאֲרֵס, מָקוֹם שֶׁמּוּתָּר לְכַבֵּס – אֵינוֹ דִּין שֶׁמּוּתָּר לְיָאֲרֵס!

§ The mishna states that Rabbi Yosei says: All women may be betrothed within three months **except for a widow,** due to the mourning period she must observe for her deceased husband. **Rav Ḥisda** questioned the mishna's ruling and **said:** Based on an ***a fortiori*** inference, it should be permitted for a woman to be betrothed during the thirty-day mourning period for her husband: If during another period of mourning, which the Gemara will specify, **when it is prohibited to launder** clothes, **it is permitted to be betrothed,** then during the thirty-day morning period for a husband, **when it is permitted to launder** clothes, **isn't it logical that it** should also be **permitted to be betrothed?**

PERSONALITIES

Rabbi Ḥanina the Great – רַבִּי חֲנִינָא הַגָּדוֹל: This is Rabbi Ḥanina bar Ḥama, who is labeled this way because he was one of the outstanding Sages of his generation. In the Jerusalem Talmud he is known as Rabbi Ḥanina Rabba, which bears the same meaning. This epithet is generally used when Rabbi Ḥanina is mentioned alongside another Sage of that name, in this case Rabbi Ḥanina Kara, to differentiate between them.

NOTES

The majority of the first month – רוּבּוֹ שֶׁל רִאשׁוֹן: The Rivan claims that this novel ruling is limited and applies only to a woman who was merely betrothed to her previous husband. However, even Rabbi Ḥanina would concede that a woman who was married would have to wait three complete months.

Some commentaries suggest the basis for Rabbi Ḥanina's ruling is to be found in the narrative of Tamar, where it states that her pregnancy was discernible "about three months after" (Genesis 38:24), which they interpret to mean that there was not three full months but some part of them.

On the ninetieth day – בְּיוֹם תִּשְׁעִים: In the *She'iltot deRav Aḥai Gaon* it is written that the reason that the woman is permitted to marry on the ninetieth day itself is based on the principle that in many cases, once a portion of the day has passed it is considered as though the entire day had passed.

Twenty-four months, etc. – עֶשְׂרִים וְאַרְבָּעָה חוֹדֶשׁ וכו׳: The geonic responsa and several *midrashim* see an allusion to this *halakha* in the verse: "You shall not cook [*tevashel*] a kid in its mother's milk" (Exodus 23:19). The numerical value of the Hebrew word *tevashel* is 732, which is exactly the number of days in two solar years plus two additional days. However, the later commentaries discuss whether the twenty-four months referred to here are based on the solar or the lunar calendar, as well as what the *halakha* would be if one of the years were a leap year.

HALAKHA

The time of betrothal following the waiting period – זְמַן הָאֵירוּסִין אַחַר הַמְתָּנָה: Pregnant women and nursing mothers may not be betrothed, and certainly not married, until the period of nursing has ended. The time established by the Sages for this period is twenty-four months, excluding the day of the child's birth and the day of the betrothal. A woman who is widowed or divorced and is not pregnant or nursing must wait ninety days, excluding the day of the husband's death or the divorce and the day of the betrothal (Rambam *Sefer Nashim, Hilkhot Geirushin* 11:26; *Shulḥan Arukh, Even HaEzer* 13:1, 11).

מאי היא? דתנן: שבת שחל תשעה באב בתוכה – אסור לספר ולכבס, ובחמישי מותר מפני כבוד השבת. ותניא: קודם הזמן הזה העם ממעטין בעסקיהם מלישא ומליתן, מלבנות ולנטוע, ומארסין אבל לא כונסין, ואין עושין סעודת אירוסין.

The Gemara explains the cases involved: **What is** the period of mourning to which Rav Ḥisda is referring? **As we learned** in a mishna (*Ta'anit* 26b): During **the week in which the Ninth of Av occurs,**[H] **it is prohibited to cut** hair **and to launder** clothes, **but on Thursday it is permitted**[N] **in deference to Shabbat. And it is taught** in a *baraita*: **Prior to this time**[H] **the public reduce their activities,** refraining **from business transactions,**[N] **from building and planting, and they may betroth** women **but may not marry** them,[H] **and they may not make a betrothal feast.** The Gemara assumes that the *baraita* is referring to the days immediately preceding the Ninth of Av. Accordingly, during the days prior to the Ninth of Av it is prohibited to launder clothes, but it is permitted to be betrothed. It was upon this period of time that Rav Ḥisda based his *a fortiori* inference.

כי תניא ההיא – קודם דקודם (תניא).

To defend Rav Yosei's ruling in the mishna, the Gemara explains: **When that** *baraita* **is taught, it is taught** with regard to the period **prior to** the period that is **prior** to the Ninth of Av, i.e., the days prior to the week in which the Ninth of Av occurs. It is only then that it is permitted to be betrothed, but during the week in which the Ninth of Av occurs it is prohibited. Therefore, the basis of Rav Ḥisda's *a fortiori* inference is undermined.

אמר רבא: וקודם דקודם נמי, קל וחומר: ומה במקום שאסור לישא וליתן – מותר ליארס, מקום שמותר לישא וליתן – אינו דין שמותר ליארס?!

Rava said: From the period **prior to** the period that is **prior** to the Ninth of Av, a challenge to Rabbi Yosei's ruling can **also** be advanced based on an ***a fortiori*** inference, as follows: If in a period of mourning **when it is prohibited to conduct business transactions, it is permitted to be betrothed,** then during the thirty-day morning period for a husband, **when it is permitted to conduct business transactions, isn't it logical that it** should also be **permitted to be betrothed?**

לא תימא דרבי יוסי אומר כל הנשים יתארסו, אלא אימא: כל הנשים ינשאו.

The Gemara accepts the conclusion of this *a fortiori* inference and therefore concludes: **Do not say** that **Rabbi Yosei says: All women may be betrothed** within three months; **rather,** emend his statement to **say: All women may be married** within three months except for a widow. However, even Rabbi Yosei agrees that it is permitted for a widow to be betrothed during this period.

HALAKHA

The week in which the Ninth of Av occurs – שבת שחל תשעה באב בתוכה: It is prohibited to cut hair and to launder clothing during the week in which the Ninth of Av occurs. Laundered clothes may be worn only on Shabbat. There are several opinions with regard to which activities are classified as laundering and are therefore prohibited. This is the Sephardic custom. The Rema explains that it was customary to be more stringent and to adopt all of these restrictions from the first day of the month of Av. This is the Ashkenazic custom (Rambam *Sefer Zemanim, Hilkhot Ta'anit* 5:6; *Shulḥan Arukh, Oraḥ Ḥayyim* 551:3).

Prior to this time – קודם הזמן הזה: Business transactions are reduced from the first day of the month of Av, and joyful building or planting is not performed unless it is done for the sake of a mitzva (Ran). This is in accordance with the Gemara in tractate *Ta'anit* (Rambam *Sefer Zemanim, Hilkhot Ta'anit* 5:6; *Shulḥan Arukh, Oraḥ Ḥayyim* 551:2).

Betrothal and marriage in the month of Av – אירוסין ונשואין בחודש אב: It is prohibited to marry from the first day of Av until after the fast of the Ninth of Av, and betrothal feasts are also not permitted. However, it is permitted to perform a betrothal without a feast even on the Ninth of Av itself. This is in accordance with the Gemara in tractate *Ta'anit* (Rambam *Sefer Nashim, Hilkhot Ishut* 10:14; *Shulḥan Arukh, Oraḥ Ḥayyim* 551:2).

NOTES

On Thursday it is permitted – ובחמישי מותר: This ruling is not cited in the various codifications of *halakha*. The commentaries explain that this is because this *halakha* applies only when the Ninth of Av occurs on a Friday, in which case it is necessary to prepare for Shabbat on Thursday. However, once the calendar was fixed so that the Ninth of Av never occurs on a Friday, this *halakha* became obsolete (*Maggid Mishne*).

From business transactions – מלישא וליתן: This *halakha* is not cited by many of the early halakhic authorities. The commentaries explain that those authorities hold that refraining from business transactions was only a custom of the especially pious, or a regional custom limited to some places. The *Yam shel Shlomo* explains that there is an established ruling that since it was often very difficult for Jews in exile to earn a livelihood in any way other than business, it is improper to prohibit it (see *Tosafot* and *Tosafot Yeshanim*).

Perek **IV**
Daf **43** Amud **b**

ולית ליה לרבי יוסי להבחין?

The Gemara asks: **But does Rabbi Yosei not accept** that there is a decree to wait three months in order **to distinguish** between the seed of the first and second husbands? According to the Gemara's emendation of his statement, it would appear there is no case in which Rabbi Yosei applies the decree.

לית ליה. ואיבעית אימא: לעולם אית ליה, ואימא, רבי יוסי אומר: כל ארוסות גרושות ינשאו.

The Gemara answers: Indeed, **he does not accept** the decree. **And if you wish, say** that **actually, he does accept** the decree and applies it in the case of a married woman who was divorced. And with regard to the challenge to his opinion from the *a fortiori* inference, emend the mishna and **say: Rabbi Yosei says** that **all** women who **were** only **betrothed** to their previous husbands and then **divorced may be married** within three months, since the reason to wait does not apply in this case.

אי הכי היינו רבי יהודה! איכא בינייהו נשואה ליארס; רבי יהודה סבר: נשואה מותרת ליארס, ורבי יוסי סבר: נשואה אסורה ליארס.

The Gemara asks: **If so,** then **this** opinion of Rabbi Yosei is identical to the opinion of **Rabbi Yehuda.** What difference is there between them? The Gemara answers: **There is** a practical difference **between them** in the case of a woman who was **married** to her previous husband and seeks **to be betrothed. Rabbi Yehuda holds** that **it is permitted to betroth** a woman who was **married** to her previous husband without first waiting three months. **And Rabbi Yosei holds** that **it is prohibited to betroth** a woman who was **married** to her previous husband without first waiting three months.

וסבר רבי יוסי נשואה אסורה ליארס? והתניא, רבי יוסי אומר: כל הנשים יתארסו, חוץ מן האלמנה מפני האיבול, וכמה איבול שלה – שלשים יום. וכולן לא ינשאו עד שיהו להן שלשה חדשים!

The Gemara asks: **But does Rabbi Yosei** really **hold** that **it is prohibited to betroth** a woman who was **married** to her previous husband without first waiting three months? **Isn't it taught** in a *baraita*: **Rabbi Yosei says** that **all women may be betrothed** without waiting **except for a widow, due to the mourning period** she must observe for her deceased husband; **and how long is her mourning period?** It is **thirty days. And none of them may be married until they have** waited **three months.**

האי מאי קושיא? אילימא דקתני, רבי יוסי אומר: כל הנשים יתארסו – מי אלימא ממתניתין דאוקימנא בארוסות גרושות ינשאו – הכא נמי כל ארוסות גרושות ינשאו.

The Gemara clarifies the question: **What difficulty does this** *baraita* pose? **If we say that** the *baraita* **teaches: Rabbi Yosei says** that **all women may be betrothed** without waiting, **is** the *baraita* **stronger than the mishna**[N] **that was established** as teaching that women who were only **betrothed** to their previous husbands and then **divorced may be married** within three months? **Here, too,** the *baraita* could be established as teaching that **all** women who were only **betrothed** to their previous husbands and then **divorced may be married** within three months.

אלא מסיפא, דקתני: וכולן לא ינשאו עד שיהו להן שלשה חדשים. אינסובי הוא – דלא, הא איתרוסי – שפיר דמי.

Rather, the difficulty arises **from the latter clause that teaches: And none of them may marry until they have** waited **three months.** This implies that Rabbi Yosei holds that it is specifically **marrying that** is **not** permitted, **but betrothing seems well** and is permitted. This challenges the Gemara's original claim that Rabbi Yosei disagrees with Rabbi Yehuda on this point.

אמר רבא, תריץ ואימא הכי: רבי יוסי אומר כל ארוסות גרושות ינשאו, חוץ מן האלמנה מפני האיבול, וכמה איבול שלה – שלשים יום. ונשואות לא יתארסו עד שיהא להן שלשה חדשים.

Rava said: Resolve the difficulty **and** emend Rabbi Yosei's statement to **say this: Rabbi Yosei says** that **all** women who were only **betrothed** to their previous husbands and then **divorced may marry** within three months **except for a widow, due to the mourning period** she must observe for her deceased husband. **And how long is her mourning period?** It is **thirty days. And** women who were **married** to their previous husbands **may not be betrothed until they have** waited **three months.**

ואלמנה מן האירוסין מי אית לה איבול? והתני רבי חייא בר אמי: אשתו ארוסה – לא אונן ולא מיטמא לה, וכן היא לא אוננת ולא מיטמאה לו. מתה – אינו יורשה, מת הוא – גובה כתובתה.

The Gemara asks: **But does** a woman who became **a widow from betrothal have** to observe **a mourning period** for her husband? **Didn't Rabbi Ḥiyya bar Ami teach** in a *baraita*: If one's **wife** to whom he was **betrothed** died, **he does not observe** a period of **acute mourning** for her, **and** if he is a priest **he is not** permitted **to become ritually impure for her. And similarly,** if he dies, **she does not observe** a period of **acute mourning** for him **and she does not become ritually impure for him.**[N] **If she dies, he does not inherit from her. If he dies, she collects** payment of **her marriage contract.** The *baraita* demonstrates that a widow is required to mourn her husband only if she was married to him and not merely betrothed. If so, clearly Rabbi Yosei's ruling in the mishna is referring to married women. Accordingly, all of the Gemara's emendations of Rabbi Yosei's statement, in order to defend his statement from Rav Ḥisda's *a fortiori* inference, are refuted.

NOTES

Is the *baraita* stronger than the mishna – מי אלימא ממתניתין: Since the language of the Mishna is assumed to be more exact than that of the *baraitot*, being that the latter were not proofread and examined to the same extent, it often happens that the Gemara revises the language found in a *baraita* or assumes that its formulation is not exact. Consequently, if the same expression is found in both a mishna and in a *baraita*, and it is revised or understood to be imprecise in the mishna, then it stands to reason that the same expression must be revised in the *baraita* as well.

She does not become ritually impure for him – לא מיטמאה לו: The early commentaries note that this clause of the *baraita* is strange because a woman is never prohibited from becoming ritually impure, even if she is the daughter or wife of a priest. Rashi apparently avoided this difficulty by explaining that the intention of the *baraita* is just that a betrothed woman is not obliged to involve herself with his burial, which will usually result in her becoming ritually impure.

אֶלָּא תַּנָּאֵי הִיא. דְּתַנְיָא: מֵרֹאשׁ חֹדֶשׁ וְעַד הַתַּעֲנִית הָעָם מְמַעֲטִין מֵעִסְקֵיהֶן, מִלִּישָּׂא וּמִלִּיתֵּן, מִלִּבְנוֹת וְלִנְטוֹעַ, וּמִלֵּיאָרֵס וּמִלִּישָּׂא. שַׁבָּת שֶׁחָל תִּשְׁעָה בְּאָב בְּתוֹכָהּ – אָסוּר לְסַפֵּר וּלְכַבֵּס (וְאָסוּר לֵיאָרֵס). וְיֵשׁ אוֹמְרִים: כָּל הַחֹדֶשׁ אָסוּר.

Rather, it must be that the question of whether it is permitted to betroth a woman during the period prior to the week of the Ninth of Av is subject to a dispute between *tanna'im*. **As it is taught** in a *baraita*: **From the New Moon** of Av **and until the fast** on the ninth, **the public reduces its activities,** refraining **from business transactions, from building and planting, and from betrothing and marrying.** During **the week in which the Ninth of Av occurs, it is prohibited to cut** hair **and to launder** clothes, **and it is prohibited to be betrothed. And some say: It is prohibited for the entire month.** The Gemara's challenge to Rabbi Yosei's opinion that it is prohibited for a widow to be betrothed during her mourning period was based on an *a fortiori* inference that assumes that it is permitted to be betrothed during the mourning period preceding the week of the Ninth of Av. However, since this ruling is subject to a dispute, Rabbi Yosei could reject the *a fortiori* inference by stating that he holds in accordance with the opinion that it is in fact prohibited to be betrothed during that period.

מַתְקִיף לָהּ רַב אַשִׁי: מִמַּאי דְּלֵיאָרֵס – לֵיאָרֵס מַמָּשׁ? דִּלְמָא לְמִיעֲבַד סְעוּדַת אֵירוּסִין הוּא דְּאָסוּר, הָא לֵיאָרֵס – שַׁפִּיר דָּמֵי.

Rav Ashi strongly objects to this: From where is it known **that** when the *baraita* prohibits one **to be betrothed,** it is referring to **actually betrothing? Perhaps it is** only **to make a betrothal feast that is prohibited, but** merely **to be betrothed seems well** and is permitted.

אִי הָכִי, מִלִּישָּׂא? לִינְסֵיב נַמִי לְמִיעֲבַד סְעוּדַת נִשּׂוּאִין הוּא דְּאָסוּר, הָא לִישָּׂא – שַׁפִּיר דָּמֵי! הָכִי הַשְׁתָּא! בִּשְׁלָמָא נִשּׂוּאִין בְּלֹא סְעוּדָה – אִיכָּא שִׂמְחָה, אֶלָּא אֵירוּסִין בְּלֹא סְעוּדָה – מִי אִיכָּא שִׂמְחָה?

The Gemara questions Rav Ashi's objection: **If so,** then with regard to the prohibition **against marrying** as well one could make the same claim: With regard to the prohibition **to marry, too, it is only to make a marriage feast that is prohibited, but** merely **to marry seems well** and is permitted. The Gemara rejects its question: **How can these cases be compared? Granted,** from **a marriage,** even **without a feast, there is joy, but** from **a betrothal without a feast,**[N] **is there** any **joy?** It is merely a legal ceremony.

אֶלָּא אֲמַר רַב אַשִׁי: שָׁאנֵי אֲבֵילוּת חֲדָשָׁה מֵאֲבֵילוּת יְשָׁנָה, וְשָׁאנֵי אֲבֵילוּת דְּרַבִּים מֵאֲבֵילוּת דְּיָחִיד.

Rather, Rav Ashi stated a different resolution of Rav Yosei's opinion: **New mourning,** i.e., the mourning for a relative who has just passed away, **is different**[N] **from old mourning,** i.e., the mourning over historic events such as the destruction of the Temple, and it is appropriate to be more lenient in the latter. **And the mourning of the public**[N] **is different from the** private **mourning of the individual,** and it is appropriate to be more stringent in the latter. As such, it is not possible to form an *a fortiori* inference from the *halakhot* of mourning for the Temple to those of a wife mourning for her husband.

מתני׳ אַרְבָּעָה אַחִין נְשׂוּאִין אַרְבַּע נָשִׁים, וָמֵתוּ. אִם רָצָה הַגָּדוֹל שֶׁבָּהֶם לְיַיבֵּם אֶת כּוּלָּן – הָרְשׁוּת בְּיָדוֹ.

MISHNA In a case of **four brothers**[H] **married to four women and** some of the brothers **died** childless, their wives thereby become *yevamot*. **If the eldest of** the brothers who survived **wished to consummate the levirate marriage with all of** his *yevamot*, **he has permission** to do so.

מִי שֶׁהָיָה נָשׂוּי לִשְׁתֵּי נָשִׁים וָמֵת – בִּיאָתָהּ אוֹ חֲלִיצָתָהּ שֶׁל אַחַת מֵהֶן פּוֹטֶרֶת צָרָתָהּ.

In the case of **one who was married to two women**[H] **and died** childless, the **intercourse or** ***ḥalitza*** **of** either **one of** the wives with the *yavam* **releases her rival wife** from the levirate bond, and the rival wife need not enter into levirate marriage or perform *ḥalitza*.

NOTES

Betrothal without a feast – אֵירוּסִין בְּלֹא סְעוּדָה: In the time of the Talmud formal betrothal would take place long in advance of marriage, often a year beforehand. Following the betrothal, the bride and groom are still not permitted to live together. Consequently, betrothal alone does not lead to a sense of joy unless a celebratory feast to mark the event is prepared, in which fine foods, meat, and wine are available. In contrast, the marriage represents the beginning of the couple's life together, and therefore it is a joyous occasion even if it is not celebrated with a feast.

New mourning is different, etc. – שָׁאנֵי אֲבֵילוּת חֲדָשָׁה וכו׳: Rashi explains that the mourning for the Ninth of Av is less severe than the mourning of a private individual on two counts, both because it is public and because it is old. Rabbeinu Tam raises a challenge to this in *Tosafot*: If this is so, then the *a fortiori* objection raised earlier by Rav Ḥisda is indeed valid. Ramban suggests a further objection, pointing out the repetitive language utilized in the Gemara, which states: New mourning is different from old mourning and the mourning of the public is different from the private mourning of the individual. This seems to imply that there is not a single difference, but rather two differences. The commentaries suggest that the aspects of some rulings on the Ninth of Av may be more lenient, while others must be more stringent, and therefore it is not possible to draw inferences from these *halakhot* to matters concerning private individuals.

Rabbeinu Tam holds that the *halakha* must be ruled stringently with regard to actions performed in the public sphere in matters of public mourning, as were it not so, it would appear that there is no need to be concerned over displays of mourning at all. However, in private matters such as betrothals, there is no reason to be stringent. The Ramban explains differently: Since the mourning on the Ninth of Av is old, people might tend to treat it lightly. Therefore, a stringent ruling was put in place with regard to laundering clothes, a restriction that does not exist in cases of new mourning. On the other hand, were the Sages to permit betrothal in cases of private mourning, people might end up preparing feasts to celebrate the event, and no one would stop them, whereas in cases of public mourning others would certainly prevent the one performing the betrothal from performing any prohibited actions.

The Meiri explains that public mourning is less intense, and so to emphasize the period, the Sages were more stringent in the matter of laundering clothes. However, they were concerned that if they were to impose a rabbinic decree against betrothals during periods of public mourning, people might not obey, and so they did not do so.

Mourning of the public – אֲבֵילוּת דְּרַבִּים: Rivan explains that public mourning is less intense because in such cases people comfort one another. Similarly, the Meiri explains that this type of mourning is in itself a partial consolation.

HALAKHA

Four brothers, etc. – אַרְבָּעָה אַחִין וכו׳: In a case where one had a number of brothers who died childless, so that their wives happened before him for levirate marriage, then if he has the means to do so, he must consummate levirate marriage with all of them, or he may perform *ḥalitza* with all of them, or he may consummate levirate marriage with some and perform *ḥalitza* with the others. However, he may do so with only one wife from each brother (Rambam *Sefer Nashim*, *Hilkhot Yibbum VaḤalitza* 1:11; *Shulḥan Arukh*, *Even HaEzer* 161:8).

One who was married to several women – מִי שֶׁהָיָה נָשׂוּי לְכַמָּה נָשִׁים: If a man married to several women died childless and was survived by his brother, then once that brother either consummates levirate marriage or performs *ḥalitza* with one of the wives, all of her rival wives are thereby released from their levirate bond (Rambam *Sefer Nashim*, *Hilkhot Yibbum VaḤalitza* 1:9; *Shulḥan Arukh*, *Even HaEzer* 161:1).

הָיְתָה אַחַת כְּשֵׁרָה וְאַחַת פְּסוּלָה, אִם הָיָה חוֹלֵץ – חוֹלֵץ לַפְּסוּלָה, וְאִם הָיָה מְיַיבֵּם – מְיַיבֵּם לַכְּשֵׁרָה.

If **one** of these women **was fit** to marry into the priesthood **and one was unfit,**[H] then **if he performs *ḥalitza*, he should perform *ḥalitza* with the unfit** woman rather than with the one who is fit for the priesthood, since doing so with the woman who is fit would needlessly disqualify her from marrying into the priesthood. **But if he consummates the levirate marriage, he may consummate the levirate marriage with** the one who is **fit**.

גמ׳ אַרְבָּעָה אַחִין סָלְקָא דַּעְתָּךְ? אֶלָּא אֵימָא: אַרְבָּעָה מֵאַחִין.

GEMARA The simple reading of the mishna's first clause implies that all four brothers died. The Gemara questions this: Can it **enter your mind** to say that all **four brothers** died? If they all died, then who remains to consummate the levirate marriage? **Rather,** emend the mishna and **say** instead: **Four** married men **of** a set of more than four **brothers** died.

״הָרְשׁוּת בְּיָדוֹ״. וְשָׁבְקִי לֵיהּ? וְהָתַנְיָא: ״וְקָרְאוּ לוֹ זִקְנֵי עִירוֹ״ – הֵן וְלֹא שְׁלוּחָן, ״וְדִבְּרוּ אֵלָיו״ – מְלַמֵּד שֶׁמַּשִּׂיאִין לוֹ עֵצָה הַהוֹגֶנֶת לוֹ,

The mishna continues: If the eldest of them wished to consummate the levirate marriage with all of his *yevamot*, **he has permission** to do so. The Gemara asks: **Do they** actually **leave him**[N] to do so? **Isn't it taught** in a *baraita*: The verse states: **"And the Elders of his city shall call him"** (Deuteronomy 25:8), which indicates that **they,** the Elders, **and not their agent,** should call him. The verse continues: **"And they speak to him";**[H] this phrase **teaches that they offer him advice that is appropriate for him.**

שֶׁאִם הָיָה הוּא יֶלֶד וְהִיא זְקֵנָה, הוּא זָקֵן וְהִיא יַלְדָּה – אוֹמְרִין לוֹ: מַה לְּךָ אֵצֶל יַלְדָּה, מַה לְּךָ אֵצֶל זְקֵנָה? כְּלַךְ אֵצֶל שֶׁכְּמוֹתְךָ, וְאַל תָּשִׂים קְטָטָה בְּבֵיתְךָ.

The *baraita* explains: Appropriate advice means **that if he was a young man and she an elderly woman** or if **he was an elderly man and she a young woman, they say to him: What do you want with a young woman** when you are elderly? Or: **What do you want with an elderly woman** when you are young? **Go after your own kind,** i.e., a woman of a similar age, **and do not place discord in your household** that could be caused by marrying a woman of a significantly different age. From the *baraita* it is apparent that if consummating the levirate marriage will ultimately lead to contention between the couple, it is preferable to perform *ḥalitza*. Similarly, in the case of the mishna, marrying four women will likely lead to contention since it is difficult to support so many people, and poverty will lead to strife. Therefore, the *yavam* should not be allowed to consummate levirate marriages with all of them.

לָא צְרִיכָא, דְּאֶפְשָׁר לֵיהּ. אִי הָכִי, אֲפִילּוּ טוּבָא נַמִי! עֵצָה טוֹבָה קָא מַשְׁמַע לַן: אַרְבַּע – אִין, טְפֵי – לָא, כִּי הֵיכִי דְּנִמְטְיֵיהּ עוֹנָה בְּחֹדֶשׁ.

The Gemara qualifies the mishna's case: **No,** it is **necessary** to teach that he has permission to consummate the levirate marriage with all of his *yevamot* in the case **where it is possible for him** to provide for all four women. The Gemara asks: **If so,** then the same should be true **even** if there are **many** more women **as well;** why does the mishna specifically discuss a case of four women? The Gemara explains: The mishna **teaches us good advice;** in a case of up to **four** women, **yes,** if he can provide for them then it is acceptable to marry all of them. But if there are any **more** than that, **no,**[H] he should not, **in order that he will** be able to **meet the conjugal rights** of each woman at least once **in** each **month.**[N] A Torah scholar is expected to provide conjugal relations once a week. If he marries no more than four women, then that will ensure that each of his wives will receive their conjugal rights at least once a month.

HALAKHA

One was fit and one was unfit – הָיְתָה אַחַת כְּשֵׁרָה וְאַחַת פְּסוּלָה: In a case of several widows of the same man who happen before their *yavam* for levirate marriage, and some of them are fit to marry into the priesthood and some are not, if the *yavam* wishes to consummate the levirate marriage, he may do so with whichever one he chooses. However, if he wishes to perform *ḥalitza*, he should do so with one of the ones who are unfit. Some (*Beit Shmuel*, citing *Beit Yosef*) say that if he willingly violated this *halakha* after having been warned not to do so, then he is excommunicated or receives lashes (Rambam *Sefer Nashim, Hilkhot Yibbum VaḤalitza* 1:10; *Shulḥan Arukh, Even HaEzer* 161:2).

And they shall call him…and they speak to him – וְקָרְאוּ לוֹ...וְדִבְּרוּ אֵלָיו: When *ḥalitza* is to be performed, the norm is for the *yavam* and *yevama* to go to the court in the town of the *yavam*, at which point that court advises them whether it is more appropriate for them to consummate the levirate marriage or to perform *ḥalitza* (Rambam *Sefer Nashim, Hilkhot Yibbum VaḤalitza* 4:1; *Shulḥan Arukh, Even HaEzer* 166:1).

Four wives – אַרְבַּע נָשִׁים: By Torah law a man is permitted to marry as many women as he is able to provide for, i.e., to fulfill his legal obligation to provide them with food, clothing, and conjugal relations. However, the Sages said that one should not marry more than four women, so that he will be able to provide each of them with their conjugal rights at least once in each month. Some (*Beit Shmuel* and *Ḥelkat Meḥokek*) rule that if one belongs to a category of people who are obligated to provide conjugal relations more than once a week, then it would be permitted to marry even more than four women (Rambam *Sefer Nashim, Hilkhot Ishut* 14:1; *Shulḥan Arukh, Even HaEzer* 76:7).

NOTES

Do they leave him – וְשָׁבְקִי לֵיהּ: The early commentaries explain that the mishna's formulation: He has permission to do so, suggests that not only is he not forced to perform *ḥalitza*, but in fact it is entirely acceptable for him to consummate the levirate marriage with all of the *yevamot* and he would not be advised otherwise. The Gemara therefore challenges this understanding because the Gemara considers such a course of action to be inappropriate (Ritva).

Conjugal rights in each month – עוֹנָה בְּחוֹדֶשׁ: The obligation of a husband to provide his wife with conjugal relations varies based on the husband's occupation. Torah scholars are obligated to provide relations once a week, while men in other professions have a more or less frequent obligation dependent on their availability. The commentaries question why the number of women one marries should be based upon the expectations placed on a Torah scholar, when the mishna is certainly not referring only to Torah scholars. Some explain that the limitation of four women is true only in a case of levirate marriage; since the situation was brought about by Heaven and not by the free choice of the *yavam*, he is not expected to provide any more than the more minimal frequency of conjugal relations expected of a Torah scholar (Ritva; *Nimmukei Yosef*). This opinion was not accepted as the *halakha*. One commentary suggests that this number in fact applies only to a Torah scholar and is merely an example of the principle (*Tosefot Yom Tov*). Others suggest that the *halakha* is not based upon the Torah scholars' requirement to provide relations once a week but upon the fact that a Torah scholar is permitted to be absent from the house for up to thirty days without his wife's permission. From that *halakha* it is apparent that it is not considered overly distressing for a woman if she is provided with relations once a month (Rivan). Another commentary explains that the *halakha* is based on the fact that the average woman completes a cycle of menstruation and subsequent ritual purification once a month. At that point she has rights to conjugal relations (*Beit Shmuel*; see *Tosefot Yom Tov*).

״מִי שֶׁהָיָה נָשׂוּי״ וכו׳. וְנַיַיבֵּם לְתַרְוַיְיהוּ! אָמַר רַבִּי חִיָּיא בַּר אַבָּא אָמַר רַבִּי יוֹחָנָן: אָמַר קְרָא ״אֲשֶׁר לֹא יִבְנֶה אֶת בֵּית אָחִיו״ – בַּיִת אֶחָד הוּא בּוֹנֶה, וְאֵין בּוֹנֶה שְׁנֵי בָתִּים.

§ The mishna states: In the case of **one who was married** to two women[H] and died childless, the intercourse or *ḥalitza* of either one of them with the *yavam* releases her rival wife from the levirate bond. The Gemara questions why the mishna considers only the possibility that he would do so with only one of the women: **But let him** instead **consummate levirate marriages with both of them. Rabbi Ḥiyya bar Abba said** that **Rabbi Yoḥanan said: The verse states** that a *yavam* who performs *ḥalitza* is referred to as: "The man **who does not build his brother's house**" (Deuteronomy 25:9). The fact that the word "house" appears in the singular indicates that even had he instead chosen to consummate a levirate marriage, only **one house may he build,** by consummating a levirate marriage with one of his brother's wives, **but he may not build two houses.**

וְנַחֲלוֹץ לְתַרְוַיְיהוּ! אֲמַר מָר זוּטְרָא בַּר טוֹבִיָּה: אָמַר קְרָא ״בֵּית חֲלוּץ הַנָּעַל״ – בַּיִת אֶחָד הוּא חוֹלֵץ, וְאֵין חוֹלֵץ שְׁנֵי בָתִּים.

The Gemara suggests: **But let him perform *ḥalitza* with both of them;** why does the mishna state that he does so with only one woman? **Mar Zutra bar Toviya said: The verse states** that following the *ḥalitza* the man is called: **"The house of him who had his shoe removed"** (Deuteronomy 25:10). The fact that the word "house" appears in the singular indicates that **he performs *ḥalitza* with** only **one house,** i.e., only one of his brother's wives, **and he does not perform *ḥalitza* with two houses.**

וְנַיַיבֵּם לַחֲדָא וְנַחֲלוֹץ לַחֲדָא! – אֲמַר קְרָא ״אִם לֹא יַחְפּוֹץ״ הָא חָפֵץ – יַיבֵּם, כָּל הָעוֹלָה לְיִבּוּם – עוֹלָה לַחֲלִיצָה, כָּל שֶׁאֵין עוֹלָה לְיִיבּוּם – אֵין עוֹלָה לַחֲלִיצָה.

The Gemara suggests: **But let him consummate the levirate marriage with one and perform *ḥalitza* with the other.** The Gemara explains that **the verse states: "If** the man **does not wish** to take his *yevama*" (Deuteronomy 25:7), which implies that with regard to anyone who performs *ḥalitza*, **were he to wish** to, **he could consummate the levirate marriage.** This teaches the principle that only **one who is eligible for levirate marriage is eligible for *ḥalitza*,** but **one who is ineligible for levirate marriage is ineligible for *ḥalitza*.** And since, in the case of the mishna, if the *yavam* consummated the levirate marriage with one of his brother's wives he may not do so with the second, consequently he may not perform *ḥalitza* with her either.

וְעוֹד: שֶׁלֹּא יֹאמְרוּ בַּיִת מִקְצָתוֹ בָּנוּי וּמִקְצָתוֹ חָלוּץ. וְיֹאמְרוּ! אִי דִּמְיַיבֵּם וַהֲדַר חָלֵיץ – הָכִי נַמִי, אֶלָּא [דִּלְמָא] חָלֵיץ וַהֲדַר מְיַיבֵּם, וְקָם לֵיהּ בְּ״לֹא יִבְנֶה״.

And furthermore, an additional reason that one may not do so is so **that** people **should not say**[N] that the brother's **house was partially built** through levirate marriage **and partially released through *ḥalitza*.** The Gemara asks: **And** even if **they will say** that, what of it? The Gemara explains: **If he** first **consummated the levirate marriage** with one wife **and subsequently performed *ḥalitza*** with the other, **indeed,** there is no reason not to do this. **However, perhaps he** might first **perform *ḥalitza*** with one wife **and subsequently consummate levirate marriage** with the other, **and** by doing so **he is liable for** a violation of the prohibition **of: "He does not build** his brother's house" (Deuteronomy 25:9). The verse indicates that one who performs *ḥalitza* has not built his brother's house and is therefore subsequently prohibited from attempting to do so by consummating a levirate marriage with either the *ḥalutza* or any of her rival wives.

וְאֵימָא: כִּי אִיכָּא חֲדָא – תִּתְקַיֵּים מִצְוַת יִבּוּם, כִּי אִיכָּא תַּרְתֵּי – לֹא תִּתְקַיֵּים מִצְוַת יִבּוּם!

The Gemara asks. **But** since the Torah's description of levirate marriage mentions only a case in which the deceased brother had only one wife, **say: When there is only one** wife, **the mitzva of levirate marriage exists,** but **when there are two** wives, **the mitzva of levirate marriage does not exist.**[N]

אִם כֵּן, צָרַת עֶרְוָה דְּאַסַּר רַחֲמָנָא לָמָּה לִי? הַשְׁתָּא, תַּרְתֵּי בְּעָלְמָא אָמְרַתְּ לָאו בְּנֵי חֲלִיצָה וְיִבּוּם נִינְהוּ, צָרַת עֶרְוָה מִיבַּעְיָא?

The Gemara suggests a proof: **If** that were **so, why do I need the** *halakha* concerning **a rival wife of a forbidden relation, which is forbidden by the Merciful One** in the Torah? **Now** that even in the case of **two women in general,** where neither woman is a forbidden relation, **you say** that **they are not eligible for *ḥalitza* and levirate marriage, is it necessary** to say **a rival wife of a forbidden relation** is also forbidden? The fact that the Torah does prohibit a rival wife of a forbidden relation indicates that the mitzva of levirate marriage does exist in a general case of two wives in which neither are a forbidden relation.

HALAKHA

Two wives from a single house – **שְׁתֵּי נָשִׁים מִבַּיִת אֶחָד**: A man is not permitted to consummate levirate marriage with two women who were both married to his brother, as the verse states: "His brother's house," which indicates he may build one house for his brother, but not two (Rambam *Sefer Nashim, Hilkhot Yibbum VaḤalitza* 1:9).

NOTES

And furthermore that people should not say – **וְעוֹד שֶׁלֹּא יֹאמְרוּ**: *Tosafot* challenge the validity of this section of the Gemara. They assert that if it were indeed permitted by Torah law to consummate levirate marriage with one *yevama* and perform *ḥalitza* with the other, then the Sages would not have issued a decree prohibiting it. The Rivan adds further that since the Torah explicitly prohibits such a practice, it is superfluous for the Gemara to suggest additional reasons that it is prohibited. Therefore, they advocate removing this section entirely from the text of the Gemara.

The Ramban, however, presents a defense of this section. He explains that although by Torah law a *yevama* is released through the levirate marriage of her rival wife, one might have thought that it would be appropriate for the Sages to require that *yevama* to perform *ḥalitza* to avoid the appearance of a *yevama* being permitted without taking any action. The reason suggested here by the Gemara explains why the Sages did not do so. A different defense is offered by Rabbi Avraham min HaHar, who suggests that one might have assumed that the principle derived from the verse refers only to women who are forbidden by prohibitions entailing *karet*; however, if the *yevama* was forbidden by a prohibition punishable by lashes, one might have thought she would require *ḥalitza*. Therefore, the Gemara provides an additional reason to cover this case as well.

When there are two wives the mitzva of levirate marriage does not exist – **כִּי אִיכָּא תַּרְתֵּי לֹא תִּתְקַיֵּים מִצְוַת יִבּוּם**: The Gemara above derived from the verse "The man who does not build his brother's house" (Deuteronomy 25:9) that a *yavam* may build only one house by consummating a levirate marriage with one of his brother's wives, but he may not build two houses. Some commentaries note that the underlying assumption of this derivation is that the mitzva of consummating levirate marriage does exist even in a case where there are two wives. Why, then, does the Gemara question that fact here? They explain that were it not for the derivation mentioned later, which proves that the mitzva applies even in a case where the deceased had two wives, the verse "The man who does not build his brother's house" would have been expounded in a different manner, possibly to teach that the mitzva applies only where there is one "house," i.e., wife, but not where there are two (*Tosefot HaRosh*; *Tosafot Yeshanim*).

אַלְמָה לָא? אִיצְטְרִיךְ, סָלְקָא דַּעְתָּךְ אָמִינָא עֶרְוָה אַבְּרַאי קַיְימָא, וְתִתְיַיבֵּם צָרָתָהּ – קָא מַשְׁמַע לַן דַּאֲסִירָא.

The Gemara objects: **Why not?** Even if one assumes that there is no mitzva of levirate marriage when the deceased brother had two wives, **it is** still **necessary** to teach the *halakha* concerning a rival wife of a forbidden relation because it could **enter your mind to say** that since there is no possibility of consummating the levirate marriage with her, **the forbidden relation stands outside** the calculation such that her presence is disregarded, **and her rival wife should enter into levirate marriage** as though she were the only wife. Therefore, the verse needs to **teach us that** the rival wife **is forbidden.**

אֶלָּא: "יְבִמְתּוֹ... יְבִמְתּוֹ" – רִיבָּה.

Rather, the repeated use of the phrase **"his *yevama,*" "his *yevama"*** in the verses concerning levirate marriage **amplifies** the mitzva of levirate marriage so that it applies even when the deceased brother had more than one wife.

"הָיְתָה אַחַת כְּשֵׁרָה". אָמַר רַב יוֹסֵף: כָּאן שָׁנָה רַבִּי: לֹא יִשְׁפּוֹךְ אָדָם מֵי בּוֹרוֹ וַאֲחֵרִים צְרִיכִים לָהֶם.

§ The mishna states: If **one** of these wives of the deceased brother **was fit** for the priesthood and one was unfit, *ḥalitza* should not be performed with the fit woman since doing so would needlessly disqualify her from the priesthood. **Rav Yosef said** that **here,** through this mishna, **Rabbi** Yehuda HaNasi **taught** the principle that one should not perform an action that will needlessly disadvantage others, and so **a person should not spill out water** collected in **his pit**[N] that he does not need **when others are in need of it.**

מתני׳ הַמַּחֲזִיר גְּרוּשָׁתוֹ, וְהַנּוֹשֵׂא חֲלוּצָתוֹ, וְהַנּוֹשֵׂא קְרוֹבַת חֲלוּצָתוֹ – יוֹצִיא, וְהַוָּלָד מַמְזֵר, דִּבְרֵי רַבִּי עֲקִיבָא.

MISHNA With regard to **one who remarries his divorcée** after she had been married to another man from whom she was then widowed or divorced, **or one who marries the woman with whom he performed *ḥalitza* [*ḥalutza*], or one who marries a relative of his *ḥalutza*,** since all such marriages are forbidden he **must divorce** her, **and the offspring** born from such unions **is a *mamzer*;** this is **the statement of Rabbi Akiva.** He holds that even the offspring from relations forbidden by a prohibition punishable by lashes is a *mamzer*.

וַחֲכָמִים אוֹמְרִים: אֵין הַוָּלָד מַמְזֵר. וּמוֹדִים בְּנוֹשֵׂא קְרוֹבַת גְּרוּשָׁתוֹ, שֶׁהַוָּלָד מַמְזֵר.

The Rabbis say: The offspring in those cases **is not a *mamzer*, but they concede with regard to one who marries a relative of his divorcée,** a union forbidden by a prohibition entailing *karet*, **that the offspring is a *mamzer*.** They hold that only the offspring from relations forbidden by a prohibition entailing *karet* is a *mamzer*.

גמ׳ וְסָבַר רַבִּי עֲקִיבָא הַנּוֹשֵׂא קְרוֹבַת חֲלוּצָתוֹ הַוָּלָד מַמְזֵר? וְהָאָמַר רֵישׁ לָקִישׁ, כָּאן שָׁנָה רַבִּי: אֲחוֹת גְּרוּשָׁה – מִדִּבְרֵי תוֹרָה, אֲחוֹת חֲלוּצָה – מִדִּבְרֵי סוֹפְרִים! תְּנִי: קְרוֹבַת גְּרוּשָׁתוֹ.

GEMARA The Gemara asks: **But does Rabbi Akiva** actually **hold** that with regard to **one who marries a relative of his *ḥalutza*, the offspring is a *mamzer*? Didn't Reish Lakish say** that through the mishna **here, Rabbi** Yehuda HaNasi **taught** that **a sister of** one's **divorcée** is forbidden **by Torah law** whereas **a sister of** one's ***ḥalutza*** is forbidden **by rabbinic law?** If a relative of one's *ḥalutza* is forbidden by rabbinic law, how can the offspring of that union be a *mamzer*? The Gemara concedes: Emend the mishna and **teach** instead: **A relative of his divorcée.**[N]

NOTES

A person should not spill out water collected in his pit – לֹא יִשְׁפּוֹךְ אָדָם מֵי בּוֹרוֹ: The Rid writes that this imperative should not be confused with the principle that one compels another to refrain from behavior characteristic of Sodom. That principle teaches that if one denies another the use of his possessions even though doing so would incur no loss or damage to himself, then he should be forced to waive his rights to those possessions. The Rid explains that that principle is limited to cases where there is a specific individual who wishes to use the possessions. The imperative here goes much further in demanding that one not perform an action that could theoretically disadvantage an unidentified person in the future. Accordingly, it would appear that one would not be forcibly compelled to act in this manner. This is also how the *Keneset HaGedola* rules; he explains the Gemara to be indicating the proper course of behavior for ethical living but not a strict requirement. In contrast, Rabbeinu Yeruḥam (cited in *Beit Yosef*) understands the Gemara to actually require such behavior, and he therefore rules that one who refuses to act in a way that will avoid needlessly causing disadvantage to others should be excommunicated and flogged.

Teach: A relative of his divorcée – תְּנִי קְרוֹבַת גְּרוּשָׁתוֹ: According to this emended version of the mishna, Rabbi Akiva states that the offspring resulting from one's union with a relative of his divorcée is a *mamzer*. While Rabbi Akiva certainly holds that this is true, one could question why he would choose to mention such a case. The novelty of Rabbi Akiva's opinion is that he holds that even the offspring from relations forbidden by a prohibition punishable by lashes is a *mamzer*, even though that prohibition is not punishable by *karet*. The prohibition against engaging in relations with a relative of one's divorcée, however, is punishable by *karet*. Therefore, even the Rabbis would agree that the offspring would be a *mamzer*. As such, what advantage is there for Rabbi Akiva to mention this case? One could suggest that Rabbi Akiva's entire statement is directed toward the Rabbis. He mentions the case of a relative of one's divorcée because he knows that the Rabbis agree with him in that case, and then he says that just as they agree in that case, they should agree in the other cases he goes on to enumerate.

הָכִי נַמִּי מִסְתַּבְּרָא, דְּקָתָנֵי סֵיפָא: וּמוֹדִים בְּנוֹשֵׂא קְרוֹבַת גְּרוּשָׁתוֹ שֶׁהַוָּלָד מַמְזֵר. אִי אָמְרַתְּ בִּשְׁלָמָא אַיְירִי בָּהּ – הַיְינוּ דְּקָתָנֵי "וּמוֹדִים", אֶלָּא אִי אָמְרַתְּ לָא אַיְירִי בָּהּ – מַאי "וּמוֹדִים"?

The Gemara notes: **So, too, it is reasonable** that this is the correct version of the mishna, as **the latter clause teaches: But they concede** in the case of **one who marries a relative of his divorcée that the offspring is a *mamzer*. Granted, if you say** that Rabbi Akiva **was talking about that** case, **this is** consistent with **that which** the mishna **teaches: They concede,** which implies that they agree to a case already mentioned. **However, if you say** that he **was not talking about that** case, **what** could the phrase: **They concede,** possibly be referring to?

וְדִלְמָא הָא קָא מַשְׁמַע לַן: דְּיֵשׁ מַמְזֵר מֵחַיָּיבֵי כְּרֵיתוֹת. הָא קָתָנֵי לַהּ לְקַמַּן: אֵיזֶהוּ מַמְזֵר – כׇּל שְׁאֵר בָּשָׂר שֶׁהוּא בְּ"לֹא יָבֹא" דִּבְרֵי רַבִּי עֲקִיבָא, רַבִּי שִׁמְעוֹן הַתִּימְנִי אוֹמֵר: כׇּל שֶׁחַיָּיבִין עָלָיו כָּרֵת בִּידֵי שָׁמַיִם, וַהֲלָכָה כִּדְבָרָיו.

The Gemara objects: **But perhaps this** phrase **teaches us that** the Rabbis concede **that** the offspring **from** forbidden relations for which one **is liable** to receive ***karet* is a *mamzer*.** The Gemara rejects this option: **This is already taught later on** in a mishna (49a): **Which** offspring of forbidden relations has the status of **a *mamzer*?** It is the offspring of a union with **any next of kin that is subject to** a Torah prohibition that one **should not engage in sexual relations** with them; this is **the statement of Rabbi Akiva. Rabbi Shimon HaTimni says:** It is the offspring of a union with **any** forbidden relative **for which one is liable to** receive *karet* **at the hand of Heaven. And the *halakha* is in accordance with his statement.** Since the mishna explicitly rules in accordance with Rabbi Shimon HaTimni, it would be unnecessary for the mishna here to teach that fact.

וְדִלְמָא קָסָתֵים לַן תַּנָּא כְּרַבִּי שִׁמְעוֹן הַתִּימְנִי. אִם כֵּן לִיתְנֵי שְׁאָר חַיָּיבֵי כְּרֵיתוֹת, קְרוֹבַת גְּרוּשָׁתוֹ לָמָּה לִי? אֶלָּא שְׁמַע מִינַּהּ אַיְירִי בָּהּ.

The Gemara persists: **But perhaps the *tanna* taught us as unattributed** a mishna that is **in accordance with** the opinion of **Rabbi Shimon HaTimni**[N] to indicate that this is indeed the accepted *halakha*. The Gemara rejects this: **If so,** then **let him teach other** cases of forbidden relations **for which one is liable to** receive ***karet*; why do I need** the mishna to specifically consider the case of **a relative of one's divorcée? Rather, conclude from this** that Rabbi Akiva indeed **was talking about that** case.

[וְדִלְמָא] לְעוֹלָם לָא אַיְירִי בָּהּ, וְאַיְּידֵי דִּתְנָא מַחֲזִיר גְּרוּשָׁתוֹ וְנוֹשֵׂא חֲלוּצָתוֹ וּקְרוֹבַת חֲלוּצָתוֹ – תָּנֵי נַמִּי קְרוֹבַת גְּרוּשָׁתוֹ.

The Gemara persists: **But perhaps he was not actually talking about that** case, **but since** Rabbi Akiva **taught** the cases of **one who remarries his divorcée,** or **one who marries his *ḥalutza*** or **a relative of his *ḥalutza*,** the mishna **also taught** in the name of the Rabbis the case of one who marries **a relative of his divorcée** because it is a similar case. The Gemara concedes that this would be an acceptable reading of the mishna.

אֶלָּא קְרוֹבַת חֲלוּצָתוֹ לְרַבִּי עֲקִיבָא הָוֵי מַמְזֵר. אֲמַר רַבִּי חִיָּיא בַּר אַבָּא אָמַר רַבִּי יוֹחָנָן: הַיְינוּ טַעֲמָא דְּרַבִּי עֲקִיבָא, דְּאָמַר קְרָא "בֵּית חֲלוּץ הַנָּעַל" – הַכָּתוּב קְרָאוֹ בֵּיתוֹ.

Rather, the mishna should not be emended, and with regard to the Gemara's original question as to how Rabbi Akiva could claim that the offspring from one's union with a relative of his *ḥalutza* is a *mamzer* if that union is forbidden only by rabbinic law, one must conclude that **a relative of one's *ḥalutza*** is forbidden by Torah law **according to Rabbi Akiva** and therefore the offspring **is a *mamzer*. Rabbi Ḥiyya bar Abba said** that **Rabbi Yoḥanan said** that **this is Rabbi Akiva's reasoning: As the verse states: "The house of he who had his shoe removed"** (Deuteronomy 25:10). **The verse called** his relationship with the *ḥalutza* **his house,** indicating that the *ḥalutza* is considered as though she had been married to the *yavam*, and therefore her relative is forbidden to him by Torah law.

אָמַר רַב יוֹסֵף אָמַר רַבִּי שִׁמְעוֹן בַּר רַבִּי: הַכֹּל מוֹדִים בְּמַחֲזִיר גְּרוּשָׁתוֹ

Rav Yosef said that **Rabbi Shimon bar Rabbi** Yehuda HaNasi **said: All agree** in the case of **one who remarries his divorcée**

NOTES

The *tanna* taught us as unattributed a mishna in accordance with the opinion of Rabbi Shimon HaTimni, etc. – **קָסָתֵים לַן תַּנָּא כְּרַבִּי שִׁמְעוֹן הַתִּימְנִי וכו׳**: What advantage is there in having an unattributed mishna in accordance with the opinion of Rabbi Shimon HaTimni when the mishna on 49a already explicitly states: The *halakha* is in accordance with his statement? The advantage is in that there is an accepted principle that the *halakha* may not be derived from the Mishna. Therefore, even when a mishna explicitly states what the *halakha* should be, that statement is not necessarily relied upon as the final *halakha*. This is because that statement might well have been only the opinion of an individual Sage that Rabbi Yehuda HaNasi preserved in his redaction of the Mishna. However, when there is an unattributed mishna in accordance with one opinion, that clearly indicates that the opinion was held by the majority of Sages, and therefore the *halakha* is to be fixed in accordance with that opinion (Ritva).

שֶׁהַוָּלָד פָּגוּם לִכְהוּנָּה. מַאן "הַכֹּל מוֹדִים" – שִׁמְעוֹן הַתִּימְנִי. דְּאַף עַל גַּב דְּאָמַר שִׁמְעוֹן הַתִּימְנִי: אֵין מַמְזֵר מֵחַיָּיבֵי לָאוִין – נְהִי דְּמַמְזֵר לָא הָוֵי, פָּגוּם – מִיהָא הָוֵי,

that the offspring, even if not a *mamzer*, **has flawed** lineage and, if the offspring is a girl, is unfit **to** marry into the **priesthood.** The Gemara clarifies: **Who is included by saying: All agree?**[N] It is **Shimon HaTimni, as although Shimon HaTimni said** that the offspring of relations **for which one is liable for** violating a **prohibition is not a** *mamzer*, nevertheless, **granted** that Shimon HaTimni holds that **he is not a** *mamzer*; he would agree, **however,** that **he is of flawed** lineage.

מִקַּל וָחוֹמֶר מֵאַלְמָנָה. וּמָה אַלְמָנָה לְכֹהֵן גָּדוֹל, שֶׁאֵין אִיסּוּרָהּ שָׁוֶה בַּכֹּל – בְּנָהּ פָּגוּם, זוֹ שֶׁאִיסּוּרָהּ שָׁוֶה בַּכֹּל – אֵינוֹ דִּין שֶׁבְּנָהּ פָּגוּם?

This is derived **through an** ***a fortiori*** **inference from** the *halakha* pertaining to **a widow,** as follows: **Just as** in the case of **a widow** who is married **to a High Priest, where the prohibition** that pertains **to her is not equally applicable to all,** i.e., only a High Priest is prohibited from marrying a widow, and nevertheless **her child** from that union will **have flawed** lineage, then so too with regard to **this** divorcée, who married another man and is therefore prohibited from marrying her original husband, **where the prohibition** that pertains **to her is equally applicable to all** Jews, as the prohibition to remarry one's divorcée after she was married to another man applies to all Jews, **isn't it logical that her child** from that union will have **flawed** lineage?

אִיכָּא לְמִיפְרַךְ: מָה לְאַלְמָנָה – שֶׁכֵּן הִיא עַצְמָהּ מִתְחַלֶּלֶת,

The Gemara raises a number of objections: The logic of this *a fortiori* inference **can be refuted: What** is true with regard **to a widow, where** her union with a High Priest is what makes **her herself disqualified** from subsequently marrying any priest and, if she is the daughter of a priest, from eating *teruma*, is not true with regard to a remarried divorcée, where her remarriage to another man is permitted and is not the cause of any further disqualification. Therefore, one case cannot be deduced from the other.

וְעוֹד: "הִיא תּוֹעֵבָה" כְּתִיב, וְאֵין בָּנֶיהָ תּוֹעֵבִין.

And furthermore,[N] **"She is an abomination"** (Deuteronomy 24:4) **is written** with regard to remarrying with one's divorcée, and the emphasis on the word "she" teaches that only she is considered so, **but her children are not abominations** and they have unflawed lineage.

וְעוֹד, תַּנְיָא: הַמַּחֲזִיר גְּרוּשָׁתוֹ, וְהַנּוֹשֵׂא חֲלוּצָתוֹ, וְהַנּוֹשֵׂא קְרוֹבַת חֲלוּצָתוֹ. רַבִּי עֲקִיבָא אוֹמֵר: אֵין לוֹ בָּהּ קִדּוּשִׁין, וְאֵינָהּ צְרִיכָה הֵימֶנּוּ גֵּט, וְהִיא פְּסוּלָה וּוְלָדָהּ פָּסוּל, וְכוֹפִין אוֹתוֹ לְהוֹצִיא. וַחֲכָמִים אוֹמְרִים: יֵשׁ לוֹ בָּהּ קִדּוּשִׁין, וּצְרִיכָה הֵימֶנּוּ גֵּט, וְהִיא כְּשֵׁרָה וּוְלָדָהּ כָּשֵׁר.

And furthermore, it is taught in a *baraita*: With regard to **one who remarries his divorcée,**[H] **and one who marries his** ***ḥalutza*****, and one who marries a relative of his** ***ḥalutza*****, Rabbi Akiva says** that **one's betrothal of** such women **is not** effective. **And** therefore, even if he attempts to do so, it is meaningless and **she does not require a bill of divorce from him** in order to separate from him. **And** if she has relations with him **she is** rendered **unfit and her child is unfit, and we force him to send** her **away. The Rabbis say** that **one's betrothal of** such women **is** effective, **and** therefore if he betrothed her **she requires a bill of divorce from him, and** if she has relations with him **she** remains **fit and her child is fit.**[N]

לְמַאן – לָאו לִכְהוּנָּה? לָא, לְקָהָל. אִי הָכִי, הִיא כְּשֵׁרָה – לְמַאן? אִילֵימָא לְקָהָל – פְּשִׁיטָא, מִשּׁוּם דְּזִנְּתָה אִפַּסְלָה לְקָהָל? אֶלָּא לָאו – לִכְהוּנָּה,

The Gemara clarifies: When the *baraita* states she and her child are rendered unfit, **to whom** are they unfit to be married? **Is it not to the priesthood? No,** it is **to the congregation** of Israel. **If so,** when the *baraita* states **she is fit, to whom** is she fit to be married? **If we say** it is **to the congregation** of Israel, **this is obvious;** could it be that **because she engaged in forbidden sexual relations that she is rendered unfit from** marrying into **the congregation** of Israel? Although by doing so she is rendered a *zona*, that can disqualify her only from marrying a priest. **Rather, is it not** that the intention is that she is fit **to** marry into **the priesthood?**

NOTES

Who is included by saying: All agree – מַאן הַכֹּל מוֹדִים: The Gemara does not need to mention that Rabbi Yehoshua agrees with this, because that was already made explicit on 15b. There, Rabbi Yehoshua testifies to the fact that such children are fit even to marry into the priesthood (Ritva).

This can be refuted…and furthermore – אִיכָּא לְמִיפְרַךְ...וְעוֹד: The Maharsha notes that it would appear that these two objections stand in direct contradiction to one another. If the objection derived from the *halakha* of a widow were truly compelling, then it would be unnecessary to have a scriptural derivation from the phrase "she is an abomination" to teach that her children have unflawed lineage; that derivation is necessary only to counter the import of the *a fortiori* inference. The Maharsha suggests that it is possible that the one who raised these objections did in fact believe that the objection derived from the *halakha* of a widow is conclusive. He understood that the objection is not contradicted by the subsequent derivation from the phrase: "She is an abomination" because, as the Gemara later suggests, there are other ways to expound the verse. Nevertheless, he cites the derivation from the verse because he reasoned that even if the derivation from the *halakha* of a widow were flawed, then it is still possible to raise the objection from the verse. The *Keren Ora* suggests that the *a fortiori* inference teaches in general about all cases for which one is liable for violating a prohibition, not only the case of one who remarries his divorcée. With regard to one who remarries his divorcée there is an independent reason to assume that the offspring would have flawed lineage because the verse describes the union as "impure" (Deuteronomy 24:4). Therefore, it was necessary to refute both reasons in order to prove that the offspring's lineage would be unflawed.

She remains fit and her child is fit – הִיא כְּשֵׁרָה וּוְלָדָהּ כָּשֵׁר: Some of the early commentaries claim that in all these cases, the woman and her daughter from the forbidden union would even be fit to eat *teruma* if they were to marry a priest or are the daughters of a priest. This is because the verse describing the qualification to eat *teruma* excludes only a woman who had relations with a "common man" (Leviticus 22:12), meaning one who was always forbidden to her, whereas in these cases the man was not initially forbidden to her (*Tosafot*; Rid). However, Rabbeinu Ḥananel claims that in the case of one who remarries his divorcée, the woman and her daughter are rendered unfit to eat *teruma*. This opinion is also found explicitly in the Jerusalem Talmud. The Maharam MiRotenburg explains that this is because the verse describes that union as "impure" (Deuteronomy 24:4).

HALAKHA

One who remarries his divorcée – הַמַּחֲזִיר גְּרוּשָׁתוֹ: It is prohibited to remarry one's divorcée after she had been married or betrothed to another man. This applies even if she had not engaged in intercourse with the other man. If one violates the prohibition, he is flogged and forced to divorce his wife. Nevertheless, she remains fit and her children are fit. This is in accordance with the opinion of the Rabbis (Rambam *Sefer Nashim, Hilkhot Geirushin* 11:12).

NOTES

She is an abomination but her rival wife is not an abomination – הִיא תּוֹעֵבָה וְאֵין צָרָתָהּ תּוֹעֵבָה: The commentaries ask: How would Rabbi Akiva interpret the restrictive implication of the word "she" in the verse: "She is an abomination" (Deuteronomy 24:4)? He is unable to interpret it in either manner suggested by the Gemara: It cannot be teaching about a rival wife because according to Rabbi Akiva, betrothal of a woman forbidden by a standard prohibition does not take effect. Therefore, she cannot have the status of a wife herself, and consequently she cannot have a rival wife. Furthermore, it cannot come to teach that the lineage of the offspring is unflawed, because according to Rabbi Akiva they are *mamzerim*. Some suggest that since the Gemara uses this verse to derive the *halakhot* of a *sota* as well, Rabbi Akiva could claim that the verse comes to exclude the case of a rival wife of a *sota* (*Tosafot Yeshanim*) or to exclude the offspring of a *sota* from having flawed lineage (*Tosefot HaRosh*).

וּמִדְּהִיא לִכְהוּנָּה – וְלָדָהּ נַמִי לִכְהוּנָּה. מִידֵי אִירְיָא? הָא כִּדְאִיתָא וְהָא כִּדְאִיתָא.

The Gemara suggests: **And since** in reference **to her** the word fit in the *baraita* means fit **for the priesthood,** it follows that for **the child as well,** the word fit means fit **for the priesthood.** The Gemara objects: **Are these cases comparable? This** case is **as it is, and that** case is **as it is,** and although the two cases are juxtaposed in the *baraita* they need not be relating to the same issue. Rather, when referring to the mother the *baraita* mentions fitness for the priesthood, and when referring to the child it mentions fitness for the congregation of Israel.

הָכִי נַמִי מִסְתַּבְּרָא, דְּקָתָנֵי רֵישָׁא: הִיא פְּסוּלָה וּוְלָדָהּ פָּסוּל. הִיא פְּסוּלָה לְמַאן? אִילֵּימָא לַקָּהָל – מִשּׁוּם דִּזְנָיָא אִפַּסְלָה לֵיהּ לַקָּהָל? אֶלָּא לָאו – לִכְהוּנָּה,

The Gemara notes: **So, too, it is reasonable** to assume that the two clauses concern different issues, **as the first clause teaches** in the name of Rabbi Akiva: **She is unfit and her child is unfit.** When that first clause states: **She is unfit, to whom** is she unfit to be married? **If we say** it is **to the congregation** of Israel, could it be that **because she engaged in forbidden sexual relations she is rendered unfit to** marry into **the congregation** of Israel? **Rather, is it not** that the intention that she is rendered unfit **to** marry into **the priesthood?**

וּוְלָדָהּ פָּסוּל, לְמַאן? אִילֵּימָא לִכְהוּנָּה – הָא לַקָּהָל כָּשֵׁר? הָאָמַר רַבִּי עֲקִיבָא הַוָּלָד מַמְזֵר! אֶלָּא פְּשִׁיטָא – לַקָּהָל,

And then when the first clause continues and states: **And her child is unfit, to whom** is she unfit to be married? **If we say** that it is **to** the **priesthood, that** would imply that the child **is fit to** marry into **the congregation** of Israel. However, this is untenable because **didn't Rabbi Akiva** himself **say** in the mishna here that **the offspring is a** ***mamzer*** and is unfit from entering the congregation of Israel? **Rather, it is obvious** that the intention of the *baraita* is that the child is unfit even **to** marry into **the congregation** of Israel.

וּמִדְּרֵישָׁא הָא כִּדְאִיתָא וְהָא כִּדְאִיתָא – סֵיפָא נַמִי הָא כִּדְאִיתָא וְהָא כִּדְאִיתָא.

And since in **the first clause** of the *baraita* it is apparent that, although two cases are juxtaposed, **this** case is **as it is and that** case is **as it is,** in **the latter clause as well** one should assume that **this** case is **as it is and that** case is **as it is.**

וְ״הִיא תּוֹעֵבָה״ נַמִי, הִיא תּוֹעֵבָה – וְאֵין צָרָתָהּ תּוֹעֵבָה, אֲבָל בָּנֶיהָ – תּוֹעֲבִין.

Having resolved the objection raised from the *baraita*, the Gemara returns to its preceding objection: **And** the objection raised from the verse: **"She is an abomination,"** in which the Gemara suggested that the emphasis on "she" teaches that only she is an abomination but her children are not, can **also** be resolved, as the emphasis on "she" could be interpreted differently to teach: **"She is an abomination" but her rival wife is not an abomination,**[N] and if they both fell together for levirate marriage, the *yavam* may consummate the levirate marriage with her rival wife. **However,** it is possible that **her children are** in fact **abominations** and are unfit to marry into the priesthood.

אֶלָּא אַלְמָנָה קַשְׁיָא: מָה לְאַלְמָנָה שֶׁכֵּן הִיא עַצְמָהּ מִתְחַלֶּלֶת!

The Gemara concludes: **However,** although two of the objections were resolved, the objection to the logic of the *a fortiori* inference from the case of **a widow** remains **difficult,** as the Gemara noted earlier: **What** is true with regard **to a widow, where** her union with a High Priest is what makes **her herself disqualified** from subsequently marrying any priest and, if she is the daughter of a priest, from eating *teruma*, is not true with regard to a remarried divorcée, where her remarriage to another man is permitted and is not the cause of any further disqualification. Therefore, there is no basis for assuming that the child of one who remarries his divorcée after she had been married to another man will have flawed lineage.

אֶלָּא אִי אִתְּמַר הָכִי אִתְּמַר: אָמַר רַב יוֹסֵף אָמַר רַבִּי שִׁמְעוֹן בְּרַבִּי: הַכֹּל מוֹדִים בְּבָא עַל חַיָּיבֵי כְּרֵיתוֹת שֶׁהַוָּלָד פָּגוּם. מַאן ״הַכֹּל מוֹדִים״ – רַבִּי יְהוֹשֻׁעַ, דְּאַף עַל גַּב דְּאָמַר רַבִּי יְהוֹשֻׁעַ אֵין מַמְזֵר מֵחַיָּיבֵי כְּרֵיתוֹת, נְהִי דְּמַמְזֵר לָא הָוֵי – פָּגוּם מִיהָא הָוֵי,

Rather, if this was stated, it **was stated as follows: Rav Yosef said** that **Rabbi Shimon, son of Rabbi** Yehuda HaNasi, **said: All agree with regard to one who engages in intercourse with** a forbidden relation **for which one is liable to** receive ***karet*** **that the offspring has flawed** lineage. The Gemara clarifies: **Who** is included by saying: **All agree?** It is **Rabbi Yehoshua, as although Rabbi Yehoshua said** in the mishna (49b) **that** the offspring born **from** a union **for which one is liable to** receive ***karet*** **is not a** ***mamzer***, nevertheless, **granted** that Rabbi Yehoshua holds that **he is not a** ***mamzer***; he would agree, **however,** that **he is of flawed** lineage.

מִקַּל וָחוֹמֶר מֵאַלְמָנָה. וּמָה אַלְמָנָה לְכֹהֵן גָּדוֹל, שֶׁאֵין אִיסּוּרָהּ שָׁוֶה בַּכֹּל – בְּנָהּ פָּגוּם, זוֹ שֶׁאִיסּוּרָהּ שָׁוֶה בַּכֹּל – אֵינוֹ דִּין שֶׁבְּנָהּ פָּגוּם?

This is derived **through an *a fortiori* inference from the *halakha* of a widow,** as follows: **Just as** in the case of **a widow** who is married **to High Priest, where the prohibition** that pertains **to her is not equally applicable to all,** i.e., only a High Priest is prohibited from marrying a widow, and nevertheless **her child** from that union will **have flawed** lineage, then so too with regard to **this woman, where the prohibition** that pertains **to her is equally applicable to all** Jews, **isn't it logical that her child** from that union should **have flawed** lineage?

וְכִי תֵּימָא: מָה לְאַלְמָנָה שֶׁכֵּן הִיא עַצְמָהּ מִתְחַלֶּלֶת – הָכָא נַמִי, כֵּיוָן שֶׁבְּעָלָהּ – עֲשָׂאָהּ זוֹנָה.

And if you would say that the logic of this *a fortiori* inference could be refuted in a manner similar to the suggestion above that **what is** true with regard **to a widow, who is herself disqualified** from marrying a priest, is not true with regard to a woman who is forbidden by a prohibition for which one is liable to *karet*, that is not correct because **here, too, once he has engaged in intercourse with her he renders her a *zona*,** and as such she is disqualified from marrying into the priesthood.

אָמַר רַבָּה בַּר בַּר חָנָה אָמַר רַבִּי יוֹחָנָן: הַכֹּל מוֹדִים בְּעֶבֶד וְגוֹי הַבָּא עַל בַּת יִשְׂרָאֵל שֶׁהַוָּלָד מַמְזֵר.

§ The Gemara considers the status of other children born from forbidden unions: **Rabba bar bar Ḥana said** that **Rabbi Yoḥanan said: All agree with regard to a slave**[N] **or a gentile who engaged in intercourse with a Jewish woman that the offspring** born from such a union **is a *mamzer*.**

מַאן "הַכֹּל מוֹדִים" שִׁמְעוֹן הַתִּימְנִי. דְּאַף עַל גַּב דְּאָמַר שִׁמְעוֹן הַתִּימְנִי אֵין מַמְזֵר מֵחַיָּיבֵי לָאוִין – הָנֵי מִילֵּי

The Gemara clarifies: **Who is included by saying: All agree?** It is **Shimon HaTimni, as although Shimon HaTimni said** that the offspring of relations **for which one is liable for** violating **a prohibition is not a *mamzer*, this applies** only

NOTES

All agree with regard to a slave, etc. – **הַכֹּל מוֹדִים בְּעֶבֶד וכו׳**: The early commentaries point out that the inclusive phrase: All agree, should not be understood as including Rabbi Yehoshua. This is because even if it could be proven that Rabbi Yehoshua holds that betrothal is ineffective when performed with relatives who are forbidden by a prohibition for which one is liable to *karet*, nevertheless, he would still hold that the offspring of such unions are not *mamzerim*. Accordingly, in the case of a union with a gentile or a slave, who are entirely excluded from the possibility of betrothal, he would certainly hold that the offspring would not be *mamzerim* (see *Tosafot*, *Tosafot Yeshanim*, and Ramban).

Perek **IV**
Daf **45** Amud **a**

מֵחַיָּיבֵי לָאוִין דְּתָפְסִי בְּהוּ קִדּוּשִׁין, אֲבָל הָכָא – גּוֹי וְעֶבֶד, כֵּיוָן דְּלָא תָּפְסִי בְּהוּ קִדּוּשִׁין – כְּחַיָּיבֵי כָּרֵיתוֹת דָּמֵי.

to forbidden relations **for which one is liable for** violation of **a prohibition** concerning **which a betrothal** between the couple **would take effect. However, here,** with regard **to a gentile and a slave, since their betrothal** of a Jewish woman **would not take effect,**[NH] a union with them **is comparable to** forbidden relations **for which one is liable to** receive ***karet***, and therefore the offspring of such a union will be a *mamzer*.

מֵיתִיבֵי: גּוֹי וְעֶבֶד הַבָּא עַל בַּת יִשְׂרָאֵל – הַוָּלָד מַמְזֵר, רַבִּי שִׁמְעוֹן בֶּן יְהוּדָה אוֹמֵר: אֵין מַמְזֵר אֶלָּא מִמִּי שֶׁאִיסּוּרוֹ אִיסּוּר עֶרְוָה, וְעָנוּשׁ כָּרֵת.

The Gemara **raises an objection** from a *baraita*: In the case of **a gentile or a slave who engaged in intercourse with a Jewish woman, the offspring** born from such a union **is a *mamzer*. Rabbi Shimon ben Yehuda says:** The offspring is **a *mamzer* only** if born **from** relations with **one who is forbidden by a prohibition of forbidden relations** that are **punishable by *karet*.** It is apparent from the *baraita* that one who holds, as does Shimon HaTimni, that only the offspring from forbidden relations for which one is liable to receive *karet* is a *mamzer*, nevertheless holds that the offspring of a slave or gentile and a Jewish woman is not a *mamzer*.

אֶלָּא אָמַר רַב יוֹסֵף: מַאן "הַכֹּל מוֹדִים" – רַבִּי. אַף עַל גַּב דְּרַבִּי אוֹמֵר: אֵין הַדְּבָרִים הַלָּלוּ אֲמוּרִים אֶלָּא לְדִבְרֵי רַבִּי עֲקִיבָא, שֶׁהָיָה עוֹשֶׂה חֲלוּצָה כְּעֶרְוָה, וְלֵיהּ לָא סְבִירָא לֵיהּ – בְּגוֹי וְעֶבֶד מוֹדֶה. דְּכִי אֲתָא רַב דִּימִי אָמַר רַב יִצְחָק בַּר אֲבוּדִימִי מִשּׁוּם רַבֵּינוּ: גּוֹי וְעֶבֶד הַבָּא עַל בַּת יִשְׂרָאֵל – הַוָּלָד מַמְזֵר.

Rather, Rav Yosef said: Who is included by saying: All agree? It is **Rabbi** Yehuda HaNasi, as **although Rabbi** Yehuda HaNasi **says** in a *baraita* (52b) concerning the mishna (50a–51b) that states that a levirate betrothal between a *yavam* and a *yevama* with whom he had already performed *ḥalitza* is ineffective: **This statement was said only according to the statement of Rabbi Akiva, as he would consider a *ḥalutza* like a forbidden relative** such that if the *yavam* betrothed her it would not take effect. **And although** Rabbi Yehuda HaNasi **himself does not hold accordingly** with regard to that issue, **with regard to** the offspring of a union with **a gentile or a slave he concedes** that the offspring is a *mamzer*. **As, when Rav Dimi came** from Eretz Yisrael, he said that **Rav Yitzḥak bar Avudimi said in the name of our Master,** i.e., Rabbi Yehuda HaNasi: With regard to **a gentile or a slave who engaged in intercourse with a Jewish woman, the offspring is a *mamzer*.**

NOTES

The betrothal of a gentile or a slave with a Jewish woman does not take effect – **נָכְרִי וְעֶבֶד לָא תָּפְסִי בְּהוּ קִדּוּשִׁין**: The early commentaries offer various proofs that the betrothal of a gentile or a slave with a Jewish woman is ineffective. With regard to a slave, Rashi cites the homiletic derivation of the verse in which Abraham instructs his slave attendants to "remain here with [*im*] the ass" (Genesis 22:5), to indicate that slaves are considered to be a people [*am*] that is comparable to an ass in that their betrothal is entirely ineffective. With regard to a gentile, he cites the case of the gentile female prisoner of war (see Deuteronomy 21:10–14), from which it is clear that there is no possibility of betrothing her prior to her conversion. See Rashi for additional proofs that he cites in the name of the *She'iltot deRav Aḥai Gaon*. The Ramban also cites an additional proof from the *Mekhilta*: A gentile maidservant may be given to a Hebrew slave in order for them to bear children for their master. When eventually the Hebrew slave goes free, he does not take the gentile maidservant with him; rather, she remains as a slave. The *Mekhilta* demonstrates from here that no marital bond could have existed between them. Through a verbal analogy, the *Mekhilta* derives that the same is true of a gentile.

HALAKHA

Betrothal does not apply to a gentile or a slave – **אֵין קִדּוּשִׁין בְּנָכְרִי וְעֶבֶד**: If a gentile or a slave betroths a Jewish woman, the betrothal does not take effect at all. Similarly, if a Jew betroths a gentile woman or a maidservant, the betrothal does not take effect (Rambam *Sefer Nashim*, *Hilkhot Ishut* 4:15; *Shulḥan Arukh*, *Even HaEzer* 44:8).

PERSONALITIES

Rabbi Aḥa, lord of the capital – רַבִּי אַחָא שַׂר הַבִּירָה: This Rabbi Aḥa was a third-generation *amora* of Eretz Yisrael, and very little is known about his teachers. Apparently there was also a fifth-generation *tanna* in Eretz Yisrael of the same name; they may have been related.

Some explain that the title: Lord of the capital, was based on a family legacy, and that one of his ancestors had been the minister appointed over the capital, i.e., the Temple Mount in Jerusalem.

BACKGROUND

Armon – אַרְמוֹן: Some say that Armon is the name of a place in Eretz Yisrael, possibly Kadesh Naftali. Others suggest that Armon is the Hebraic rendition of the country Armenia. It is reasonable to assume that these captives came from a distant place because it is known that captors would bring Jewish captives from remote locations to Tiberias, at that point the main city of Eretz Yisrael, since the Jewish community there would take great efforts to redeem them.

NOTES

The offspring has flawed lineage and is prohibited from marrying into the priesthood – הַוָּלָד פָּגוּם לִכְהוּנָּה: The early commentaries debate whether this ruling is accepted as *halakha*. Most commentaries hold, based on the Gemara's *a fortiori* inference from the *halakha* of a widow, that a daughter of a gentile or slave with a Jewish woman would certainly be unfit to marry into the priesthood. This also appears to be the conclusion in the Jerusalem Talmud. However, a son from such a union would not be rendered unfit in any way, such that even if he were to father a daughter with a Jewish woman, that daughter would be fit to marry into the priesthood.

Other commentaries disagree and claim that even the daughter of the gentile or slave would be considered fit to marry into the priesthood. They bring support for their opinion from the conclusion of the Gemara's discussion, which states simply that the offspring of a gentile or slave and a Jewish woman is considered fit, without making any further distinctions. They reject the implication of the *a fortiori* inference because according to it, the woman should be rendered a *ḥalala*, who is unfit to marry a priest, and they hold that ultimately the *halakha* is that a woman can be rendered a *ḥalala* only in cases where there is a violation of one of the prohibitions that are unique to the priesthood (see *Yam shel Shlomo*). Some explain that even if the woman who engaged in intercourse with the gentile or slave is disqualified by doing so, the offspring will not be, because the offspring of a gentile with a Jewish woman is never halakhically recognized as relating to him. Since the offspring is not considered to be descended from him it cannot be disqualified on his account (Ritva).

Isn't it logical that her child [*benah*] from that union will have flawed lineage – אֵינוֹ דִּין שֶׁבְּנָהּ פָּגוּם: Rashi and Rivan both note that although the Gemara says *benah*, which literally means: Her son, it should be taken as meaning her child, and the intention is actually a daughter who will be rendered unfit to marry into the priesthood. However, others suggest that the Gemara can be understood as referring to a son. Although normally the status of *ḥalal*, one whose flawed lineage disqualifies him from the priesthood, is applied only to a descendant of a priest, in this case the son would be rendered unfit to the same extent as a *ḥalal* such that if he were to father a daughter with another Jewish woman, that daughter would be unfit to marry into the priesthood.

רַבִּי אַחָא שַׂר הַבִּירָה וְרַבִּי תַּנְחוּם בְּרֵיהּ דְּרַבִּי חִיָּיא אִישׁ כְּפַר עַכּוֹ פְּרוּק הָנְהוּ שְׁבוּיָיתָא דְּאָתוּ מֵאַרְמוֹן לְטִבֶרְיָא. הֲוָה חֲדָא דְּאִיעַבְּרָא מִגּוֹי, וַאֲתוּ לְקַמֵּיהּ דְּרַבִּי אַמִּי. אֲמַר לְהוּ: רַבִּי יוֹחָנָן וְרַבִּי אֶלְעָזָר וְרַבִּי חֲנִינָא דְּאָמְרִי, גּוֹי וְעֶבֶד הַבָּא עַל בַּת יִשְׂרָאֵל הַוָּלָד מַמְזֵר.

The Gemara cites a related incident: **Rabbi Aḥa, lord of the capital,**[P] **and Rabbi Tanḥum, son of Rabbi Ḥiyya, the man of Akko village, redeemed those captives who came from Armon**[B] **to Tiberias. One of them had been impregnated by a gentile, and they came before Rabbi Ami** to ask what the offspring's status would be when born. **He said to them** that **Rabbi Yoḥanan and Rabbi Elazar and Rabbi Ḥanina** all **say:** With regard to **a gentile or a slave who engaged in intercourse with a Jewish woman, the offspring is a** ***mamzer*****.**

אֲמַר רַב יוֹסֵף: רְבוּתָא לְמִחֲשַׁב גַּבְרֵי?! הָא רַב וּשְׁמוּאֵל בְּבָבֶל, וְרַבִּי יְהוֹשֻׁעַ בֶּן לֵוִי וּבַר קַפָּרָא בְּאֶרֶץ יִשְׂרָאֵל, וְאָמְרִי לַהּ: חִלּוּפֵי בַּר קַפָּרָא וְעַיְילֵי זִקְנֵי דָּרוֹם, דְּאָמְרִי: גּוֹי וְעֶבֶד הַבָּא עַל בַּת יִשְׂרָאֵל – הַוָּלָד כָּשֵׁר.

Upon hearing this, **Rav Yosef said: Is it so great to enumerate men?** The fact that several great Sages held this opinion does not prove that their opinion is the accepted *halakha*. **But** there are **Rav and Shmuel in Babylonia, and Rabbi Yehoshua ben Levi and bar Kappara in Eretz Yisrael, and some say to remove bar Kappara** from this list **and insert** instead **the Elders of the South, who** all **say:** With regard to **a gentile or a slave who engaged in intercourse with a Jewish woman,** the lineage of **the offspring is unflawed,** and he or she may marry into the congregation of Israel.

אֶלָּא אֲמַר רַב יוֹסֵף: רַבִּי הִיא. דְּכִי אֲתָא רַב דִּימִי אֲמַר רַבִּי יִצְחָק בַּר אֲבוּדִימִי מִשּׁוּם רַבֵּינוּ אָמְרוּ: גּוֹי וְעֶבֶד הַבָּא עַל בַּת יִשְׂרָאֵל – הַוָּלָד מַמְזֵר.

Rather, Rav Yosef said the *halakha* is in fact that the offspring is a *mamzer* because this **is Rabbi** Yehuda HaNasi's opinion, **as when Rav Dimi came** from Eretz Yisrael he said that **Rav Yitzḥak bar Avudimi said in the name of our Master,** i.e., Rabbi Yehuda HaNasi, that **they say:** With regard to **a gentile or a slave who engaged in intercourse with a Jewish woman, the offspring is a** ***mamzer*****.**

רַבִּי יְהוֹשֻׁעַ בֶּן לֵוִי אוֹמֵר: הַוָּלָד מְקוּלְקָל. לְמַאן? אִילֵימָא לַקָּהָל – הָא אֲמַר רַבִּי יְהוֹשֻׁעַ הַוָּלָד כָּשֵׁר, אֶלָּא לִכְהוּנָּה – דְּכוּלְּהוּ אֲמוֹרָאֵי דְּמַכְשְׁרִי מוֹדוּ שֶׁהַוָּלָד פָּגוּם לִכְהוּנָּה.

Rabbi Yehoshua ben Levi says: The lineage of **the offspring is sullied,** and if the child is a girl she is restricted in whom she may marry. The Gemara asks: **To whom** is she prohibited from marrying? **If we say** it is **to the congregation** of Israel, **but didn't Rabbi Yehoshua** himself **say** that the lineage of **the offspring is unflawed** and he or she may marry into the congregation of Israel? **Rather,** the offspring is prohibited **to** marry into **the priesthood,** as **all of the** ***amora'im*** **who render** the offspring **fit** to enter the congregation of Israel **agree that the offspring has flawed** lineage and is forbidden **to** marry into **the priesthood.**[NH]

מִקַּל וָחוֹמֶר מֵאַלְמָנָה: מָה אַלְמָנָה לְכֹהֵן גָּדוֹל, שֶׁאֵין אִיסּוּרָהּ שָׁוֶה בַּכֹּל – בְּנָהּ פָּגוּם, זוֹ שֶׁאִיסּוּרָהּ שָׁוֶה בַּכֹּל – אֵינוֹ דִּין שֶׁבְּנָהּ פָּגוּם.

This is derived **from an** ***a fortiori*** **inference from the** *halakha* **of a widow,** as follows: **Just as** in the case of **a widow** who is married **to a High Priest, where the prohibition** that pertains **to her is not equally applicable to all** Jews, i.e., only a High Priest is prohibited from marrying a widow, and nevertheless **her child** from that union will **have flawed** lineage, then so too with regard to **this** woman who engaged in relations with a gentile or slave, **where the prohibition** that pertains **to her is equally applicable to all** Jews, **isn't it logical that her child** from that union will **have flawed** lineage?[N]

מָה לְאַלְמָנָה לְכֹהֵן גָּדוֹל שֶׁכֵּן הִיא עַצְמָהּ מִתְחַלֶּלֶת! הָכָא נַמִי, כֵּיוָן שֶׁנִּבְעֲלָה פְּסָלָהּ.

And if one would say that the logic of this *a fortiori* inference could be refuted by claiming that **what** is true **with** regard **to a widow** who is married **to a High Priest, where** her union with him is what makes **her herself disqualified** from subsequently marrying any priest and, if she is the daughter of a priest, from eating *teruma*, is not true with regard to the prohibition against a Jewish woman engaging in relations with a gentile or a slave. This is not correct, because **here, too, once he has engaged in intercourse with her,**[H] he thereby **renders her unfit** to marry into the priesthood.

HALAKHA

The offspring has flawed lineage and is prohibited from marrying into the priesthood – הַוָּלָד פָּגוּם לִכְהוּנָּה: Although the offspring of a gentile or slave who engaged in intercourse with a Jewish woman is fit to marry into the congregation of Israel, if the offspring is a daughter then she is prohibited from marrying a priest. This is in accordance with the Gemara here and several other places where it is stated that this fact is unanimously accepted. Some (Rif; Ramban; Rambam, as explained by *Maggid Mishne*) rule that she is not unfit to marry into the priesthood. Therefore, later commentaries (*Beit Shmuel*; *Ḥelkat Meḥokek*) rule that if the daughter went and married a priest then this lenient opinion may be relied upon, and they need not divorce (Rambam *Sefer Kedusha, Hilkhot Issurei Bia* 15:4; *Shulḥan Arukh, Even HaEzer* 4:4–5, 19; 7:17).

A gentile who engaged in intercourse with a Jewish woman – נָכְרִי הַבָּא עַל בַּת יִשְׂרָאֵל: If a gentile or slave engaged in intercourse with a Jewish woman, she becomes a *zona* and is therefore prohibited from marrying into the priesthood (Rambam *Sefer Kedusha, Hilkhot Issurei Bia* 18:2; *Shulḥan Arukh, Even HaEzer* 6:8).

דאמר רבי יוחנן משום רבי שמעון: מנין לגוי ועבד הבא על הכהנת ועל הלויה ועל הישראלית שפסלוה – שנאמר "ובת כהן כי תהיה אלמנה וגרושה", מי שיש לו אלמנות וגירושין בה, יצאו גוי ועבד שאין להם אלמנות וגירושין בה.

As Rabbi Yoḥanan said in the name of Rabbi Shimon: From where is it derived with regard **to a gentile or a slave who engaged in intercourse with a daughter of a priest or with a female Levite or with a female Israelite that they** thereby **render her unfit** to marry into the priesthood? **As it is stated: "But a priest's daughter when she will become a widow, or a divorcée,** and have no child, she returns to her father's house as in her youth" (Leviticus 22:13). The verse indicates that she returns to her father's house and enjoys the rights of the priesthood only in a case where she engaged in intercourse with **one to whom widowhood and divorce can apply,** i.e., one with whom her marriage would be valid and would be broken only through death or divorce. **Excluded** from this is a union with **a gentile or a slave, to whom neither widowhood nor divorce can apply,** as no marriage bond can be formed with them.

אמר ליה אביי: מאי חזית דסמכת אדרב דימי? סמוך אדרבין! דכי אתא רבין אמר: רבי נתן ורבי יהודה הנשיא מורים בה להיתירא, ומאן רבי יהודה הנשיא – רבי.

Abaye said to Rav Yosef: **What did you see that you rely upon Rav Dimi** and his tradition that Rabbi Yehuda HaNasi holds that the offspring of a gentile or a slave and a Jewish woman is a *mamzer*? **Rely** instead **upon Ravin, as when Ravin came** from Eretz Yisrael **he said that Rabbi Natan and Rabbi Yehuda HaNasi** both **rule** that the offspring is **permitted** to marry into the congregation of Israel. **And who is the Rabbi Yehuda HaNasi** referred to in Ravin's report? It is the one who is simply referred to as **Rabbi,** the redactor of the Mishna, whose opinion is accepted as the *halakha*.

ואף רב מורה בה היתירא, דההוא דאתא לקמיה דרב, אמר ליה: גוי ועבד הבא על בת ישראל מהו?

The Gemara notes: **And even Rav rules** that the offspring is **permitted, as** is evident from an incident involving **a certain** individual **who came before Rav and said to him:** With regard to the offspring of **a gentile or a slave who engaged in intercourse with a Jewish woman,**[H] **what is** its halakhic status?

אמר לו: הולד כשר. אמר ליה: הב לי ברתך! לא יהיבנא לך.

Rav **said to him:** The lineage of **the offspring is unflawed.** The individual who asked the question was himself such a child, and **he said to** Rav: If so, **give me your daughter** in marriage. He said to him: **I will not give** her **to you.**

אמר שימי בר חייא לרב: אמרי אינשי: גמלא במדי אקבא רקדא, הא קבא והא גמלא והא מדי – ולא רקדא!

Shimi bar Ḥiyya,[P] Rav's grandson, **said to Rav: People** often **say** that **a camel in Medes**[NB] can **dance upon** a small space that holds only a single ***kav*** of produce. However, clearly that is an exaggeration, since if one would go to Medes one could demonstrate that **this is** a space that holds a ***kav*, and this is a camel, and this is Medes,** and yet the camel **is not dancing,**[N] i.e., the truth of a statement becomes apparent when it is put to the test. So too, it would appear that you do not truly believe in your ruling because when put to the test, you are unwilling to rely on it.

אמר ליה: אי ניהוי כיהושע בן נון לא יהיבנא ליה ברתי. אמר ליה: אי הוה כיהושע בן נון, אי מר לא יהיב ליה – אחריני יהבי ליה. האי, אי מר לא יהיב ליה – אחריני לא יהבי ליה.

He said to him: Even **if he were** as great **as Joshua, son of Nun, I would not give him**[N] **my daughter** in marriage. My refusal to give her to him in marriage is not that I do not stand by my ruling; it is for other reasons. **He said to him: If he were** as great as **Joshua, son of Nun,** then even **if the Master would not give him** his daughter, **others would** still **give him** their daughters. However, with regard to **this** man, **if the Master does not give him** his daughter, **others will not give him** their daughters either out of fear of damaging the family lineage. Nevertheless, Rav remained unwilling to give his daughter to that individual.

HALAKHA

A gentile or slave who engaged in intercourse with a Jewish woman – גוי ועבד הבא על בת ישראל: With regard to a gentile or slave who engaged in intercourse with a Jewish woman, the offspring of such a union is fit to enter into the congregation of Israel, irrespective of whether the woman was married or unmarried and whether the intercourse was consensual or forced (Rambam *Sefer Kedusha, Hilkhot Issurei Bia* 15:3; *Shulḥan Arukh, Even HaEzer* 4:5, 19).

NOTES

A camel in Medes, etc. – גמלא במדי וכו׳: The Rivan interprets this to mean that the camels there are so well trained that they can stand with all four legs on a space that holds one *kav*. The Meiri explains that it means that the camels there are so small that they can stand inside of a space that holds one *kav*. See the *Arukh LaNer*, who explains how this imagery alludes to a deeper meaning.

This is a *kav*…and it is not dancing – הא קבא...ולא רקדא: One commentary explains that the man who asked the question was himself a Torah scholar and that is why Rav Shimi bar Ḥiyya wanted to intervene on his behalf. He brings support for his claim from the fact that Rav compared the man to the biblical Joshua, which, at the very least, suggests that he was an important figure in his own right (Ya'avetz).

I would not give him – לא יהיבנא ליה: Some explain that Rav's hesitance was because he did not want to introduce anyone with flawed lineage into his family. Possibly he believed that the son of a gentile is unfit for the priesthood; alternatively, Rav considered the very fact that one is descended from a gentile to be a flaw, even if there are no associated prohibitions with that flaw (see Rivan). Others explain that his concerns had nothing to do with the man's lineage but were due to an entirely unrelated issue.

BACKGROUND

A camel in Medes – גמלא במדי: In talmudic literature, Medes is often used as an example of a distant, unknown land. This example was first used in the period of the Mishna, when Medes was far from the Jewish center of life in Eretz Yisrael. Later, when the Jewish community was centered in Babylonia, the example continued to be used despite the fact that Medes is actually near Babylonia.

PERSONALITIES

Shimi bar Hiyya – שימי בר חייא: Rav Shimi bar Ḥiyya was among the second-generation *amora'im* of Babylonia. He was a grandson of Rav and apparently his preeminent disciple and much beloved by him. Even during his grandfather's lifetime, Rav Shimi was recognized as a significant Torah scholar. The Talmud records numerous halakhic teachings of his, both those he transmitted in the name of his grandfather and those of his own. In certain cases he even disagreed with the rulings of his grandfather. Given their close familial relationship, it is clear why here he allowed himself to address Rav in such an informal manner.

BACKGROUND

He placed his eyes upon him and he died – יָהֵיב בֵּיהּ עֵינֵיהּ וּשְׁכֵיב: This concept is mentioned in the Talmud on a number of occasions. The *Or HaḤayyim* on Exodus 11:5 and 23:23 explains that when a righteous person looks at others he can draw out the sparks of holiness that each individual has, and if that individual does not have any other merits to stay alive, he might die as a result. This explanation might be challenged from the fact that the Talmud cites a similar event with Rav Sheshet (*Berakhot* 58b), despite the fact that he was blind. In the *Iggeret HaKodesh* (attributed to the Ramban) it is explained that the word eyes does not literally refer to eyes but rather to the thought process of a righteous person, which can affect other people for good or bad.

לָא הֲוָה קָאָזֵיל מִקַּמֵּיהּ, יָהֵיב בֵּיהּ עֵינֵיהּ וּשְׁכֵיב.

That individual **would not go from** standing **before** Rav and continued to plead with him. Rav **placed his eyes upon him and he died.**[B]

וְאַף רַב מַתָּנָה מוֹרֶה בָּהּ לְהֶיתֵּירָא, וְאַף רַב יְהוּדָה מוֹרֶה בָּהּ לְהֶיתֵּירָא. דְּכִי אֲתָא לְקַמֵּיהּ דְּרַב יְהוּדָה אֲמַר לֵיהּ: זִיל אִיטְמַר, אוֹ נְסֵיב בַּת מִינָךְ. וְכִי אֲתָא לְקַמֵּיהּ דְּרָבָא אֲמַר לֵיהּ: אוֹ גְּלִי, אוֹ נְסֵיב בַּת מִינָךְ.

The Gemara adds: **And even Rav Mattana rules** that the offspring is **permitted, and even Rav Yehuda rules** that the offspring is **permitted, as** is evident from the fact that **when** a child of a gentile or slave and a Jewish woman **came before Rav Yehuda, he said to him: Go** and **conceal** your paternal lineage[N] so that people will not refrain from giving you their daughters in marriage, as it is permitted for you to marry into the congregation of Israel, **or** otherwise, **marry** a woman **of your own kind,** i.e., a woman of similar lineage. **And** similarly, **when** such a person **came before Rava, he said to him: Either go into exile**[N] to a place where your lineage is unknown, so that others will give you their daughters in marriage, **or marry a woman of your own kind.**

שָׁלְחוּ לֵיהּ בְּנֵי בֵּי מִיכְסֵי לְרַבָּה: מִי שֶׁחֶצְיוֹ עֶבֶד וְחֶצְיוֹ בֶּן חוֹרִין הַבָּא עַל בַּת יִשְׂרָאֵל מַהוּ? אֲמַר לְהוּ: הַשְׁתָּא עֶבֶד כּוּלּוֹ אָמְרִינַן כָּשֵׁר – חֶצְיוֹ מִיבַּעְיָא?

The residents of Bei Mikhsei sent the following question **to Rabba:** With regard to the offspring of **one who is a half-slave half-freeman, who engaged in intercourse with a Jewish woman, what is** its halakhic status? **He said to them: Now** that with regard to the offspring of **a full slave we say** that his lineage is **unflawed, is it necessary** to ask about **a half**-slave?

אֲמַר רַב יוֹסֵף: מָרָא דִּשְׁמַעְתְּתָא

Rav Yosef said: The Master who is responsible for dissemination **of this *halakha*** that the offspring of a slave and a Jewish woman is not a *mamzer,*

NOTES

Go and conceal your paternal lineage – זִיל אִיטְמַר: Evidently, Rav Yehuda maintains that the child of a gentile and a Jewish woman is fit to marry even a priest, as if this were not the case his advice might lead to a prohibited marriage, since the daughter of this man might mistakenly think that she is eligible to marry a priest as her father did not disclose his lineage (Rashba). However since the *halakha* is that such a child is considered to be of flawed lineage and may not marry a priest (see *Even HaEzer* 4:5 and 4:19), a father would not be allowed to conceal his lineage.

Another issue that arises from Rav Yehuda's advice is the propriety and ramifications of deceptive behavior between potential marriage partners, which Rav Yehuda appears to be encouraging. Apart from the ethical issues involved, doing so might render the betrothal as mistaken, thereby undermining its validity. The *Tzitz Eliezer* (17:48) suggests that Rav Yehuda's suggestion was permitted only at that time, as it was not universally accepted that the offspring of a gentile and a Jewish woman was of unflawed lineage, and there was a need to establish this *halakha* so that such people would be able to marry and would not be rejected even though they are permitted. However, the *Kehillot Ya'akov* (*Yevamot* 44) maintains that not revealing one's flawed lineage is not considered deceptive whenever the marriage itself is permitted. He rationalizes that even if one would respond unfavorably to certain information concerning lineage before the couple is married, it is obvious that once they are happily married they would not divorce over such an issue. Therefore, it cannot be considered a mistaken betrothal, and so the deception should be permitted for the sake of the mitzva to marry. Alternatively, it is possible that Rav Yehuda was merely advising him to go to a place where people do not examine lineage so closely, where he would have a better chance of marrying (see *Tosafot* on 47a).

Go and conceal your lineage…go into exile – ...זִיל אִיטְמַר גְּלִי: The later commentaries attempted to explain why these Sages differed in their choice of language. One explains that the man who asked this question of Rava was famous in his locale and therefore could not conceal his lineage (*Melo HaRo'im*).

מַנּוּ – רַב יְהוּדָה, וְהָא אָמַר רַב יְהוּדָה: מִי שֶׁחֶצְיוֹ עֶבֶד וְחֶצְיוֹ בֶּן חוֹרִין הַבָּא עַל בַּת יִשְׂרָאֵל – אוֹתוֹ וָלָד אֵין לוֹ תַּקָּנָה.

who is he? He is **Rav Yehuda,** as the Gemara cited above. **But didn't Rav Yehuda** himself **say:** With regard to **one who is a half-slave half-freeman**[H] **who engaged in intercourse with a Jewish woman, that offspring** of that union **has no recourse**[N] to be able to marry? It is apparent, then, that even one who permits the offspring of a slave to marry into the congregation of Israel does not permit the offspring of a half-slave to do so, contrary to Rava's assertion.

כִּי אִיתְּמַר דְּרַב יְהוּדָה כְּגוֹן דְּקַדֵּישׁ בַּת יִשְׂרָאֵל, דְּנִמְצָא צַד עַבְדוּת שֶׁבּוֹ מִשְׁתַּמֵּשׁ בְּאֵשֶׁת אִישׁ.

The Gemara resolves the difficulty: **When** this ruling **of Rav Yehuda was stated,** it was referring to a case **where** the half-slave **betrothed a Jewish woman.**[N] Since a slave's betrothal does not take effect, the result of that betrothal is that the woman is married to only the free half of the half-slave half-freeman, such **that it emerges** that when he has relations with her, the **slave side of him is engaging in relations with a married woman** to whom that side of him is not married, and so the offspring of that union is a *mamzer*.

וְהָאָמְרִי נְהַרְדְּעֵי מִשְּׁמֵיהּ דְּרַבִּי יַעֲקֹב: לְדִבְרֵי הַפּוֹסֵל – פּוֹסֵל אֲפִילּוּ בִּפְנוּיָה, לְדִבְרֵי הַמַּכְשִׁיר – מַכְשִׁיר אֲפִילּוּ בְּאֵשֶׁת אִישׁ.

The Gemara raises an objection: **But didn't** the Sages **of Neharde'a say in the name of Rabbi Ya'akov: According to the statement of the one who renders** the child of a gentile or slave and a Jewish woman **unfit** to marry into the congregation of Israel, **he renders** the child **unfit even when** the mother is **an unmarried woman.** And **according to the statement of the one who renders** the child **fit, he renders** the child **fit even when** the mother **is a married woman.**

וּשְׁנֵיהֶם לֹא לְמֵדוּהָ אֶלָּא מֵאֵשֶׁת אָב – מַאן דְּפָסֵיל סָבַר: מָה אֵשֶׁת אָב דְּלָא תָּפְסִי בָּהּ קִדּוּשִׁין [הַוָּלָד מַמְזֵר] – אַף כָּל דְּלָא תָּפְסִי בָּהּ קִדּוּשִׁין הַוָּלָד מַמְזֵר.

And both of them derived their opinions **only from the** *halakha* of one's **father's wife,**[N] as follows: **The one who renders** the child **unfit holds** that **just as** with regard to one's **father's wife,** one's **betrothal of her does not take effect** even after she is widowed or divorced, and so **the offspring** of such a union **is a** ***mamzer*****, so too,** with regard to **any** one for whom **betrothal of her does not take effect,** including a gentile or a slave, **the offspring is a** ***mamzer*****.**

HALAKHA

A half-slave half-freeman – חֲצִיוֹ עֶבֶד וַחֲצִיוֹ בֶּן חוֹרִין: If a half-slave half-freeman engaged in intercourse with a married woman, then the offspring is forbidden both to a Jewish woman and to a maidservant. If the offspring marries a convert, his children will share his status (Rambam *Sefer Kedusha, Hilkhot Issurei Bia* 15:5; *Shulḥan Arukh, Even HaEzer* 4:17).

NOTES

He has no recourse – אֵין לוֹ תַּקָּנָה: Most of the early commentaries explain that there is no one whom this offspring is permitted to marry because his status is half-*mamzer* and half-fit. He is therefore prohibited from marrying a Jewish woman on account of his *mamzer* status but he may also not marry a *mamzeret* due to his fit status. Furthermore, since he is not a gentile or a slave he is forbidden to a maidservant. However, Rashi appears to explain that the offspring will have full *mamzer* status, and therefore he would be permitted to marry a *mamzeret* or a maidservant. Some explain that Rashi's opinion is based on the *halakha* that the status of a *mamzer* status is transferred to his son, even when there is no transgression involved in his conception, e.g., where a *mamzer* married a female convert. It is apparent from that *halakha* that the *mamzer* status is considered dominant and therefore always defines the offspring. So too, in the case here, if the factors necessary to define the offspring as a *mamzer* exist, even if they exist only with regard to one side of his father, that is sufficient to render the offspring a full *mamzer* (*Mei Naftoaḥ*).

A case where he betrothed a Jewish woman – כְּגוֹן דְּקַדֵּישׁ בַּת יִשְׂרָאֵל: The Gemara in *Gittin* (43a) considers the status of a betrothal performed by a half-slave and remains in doubt as to whether it is at all effective (see *Tosafot* here). From the fact that the Gemara here establishes the case as one where the half-slave betrothed a Jewish woman, apparently the Gemara here assumes that such a betrothal is effective. Nevertheless, it would appear that even if it is effective, the bond between the couple is still incomparable to the bond formed by a standard betrothal. Rather, the betrothal will be effective only to render the woman partially betrothed, a state that is similar to the marital status of a designated maidservant, i.e., a half-free half-slave maidservant who was betrothed to a Hebrew slave (see Leviticus 19:20–22; *Keren Ora*).

They derived their opinions…from a father's wife – לְמֵדוּהָ...מֵאֵשֶׁת אָב: In the Torah, the prohibition against engaging in relations with one's father's wife is juxtaposed to the prohibition against allowing a *mamzer* to enter the congregation of God (Deuteronomy 23:1–3). Based on that juxtaposition, the Gemara derives that only unions that are similar to that of a man with his father's wife will result in the offspring having the status of a *mamzer*. The various opinions concerning who is a *mamzer* are all based on the issue of how to define whether a case is considered to be similar or dissimilar to the case of one's father's wife.

ומאן דמכשר סבר: מה אשת אב, דלדידיה לא תפסי בה קדושין לאחריני תפסי בה קדושין – לאפוקי גוי ועבד דלא תפסי בהו קדושין כלל.

And the one who renders the child **fit holds** that the derivation from the *halakha* of one's father's wife is more limited, and it is derived that the offspring is a *mamzer* only in a case **just like** one's **father's wife,** in **that** although his **betrothal of her does not take effect, with someone else** his **betrothal** of her **does take effect.** This is **to the exclusion of a gentile and a slave, for whom betrothal** of any Jewish woman **does not take effect**[N] **at all,** and so the offspring of such a union will not be a *mamzer*. It is apparent from this statement of the Sages of Neharde'a that according to the lenient opinion, the offspring of a slave is never a *mamzer*, irrespective of the marital status of the Jewish woman. Therefore, the Gemara's resolution is undermined.

אלא, כי איתמר דרב יהודה – כגון שבא על אשת איש ונמצא צד חירות שבו משתמש באשת איש.

The Gemara offers a different resolution: **Rather, when** this statement **of Rav Yehuda was stated,** it was referring to a case **where** the half-slave half-freeman **engaged in intercourse with a married woman** who was married to someone else, **and it** therefore **emerges** that although the woman's union with the slave side of him will not render the offspring a *mamzer*, the **free side of him is engaging in relations with a married woman** to whom he is not married, and due to that side of him the offspring is a *mamzer*.

אמר רבינא אמר לי רב גזא: איקלע רבי יוסי בר אבין לאתרין, והוה עובדא בפנויה – ואכשר, באשת איש – ופסיל. אמר רב ששת: לדידי אמר לי רב גזא: לא רבי יוסי בר אבין הוה, אלא רבי יוסי ברבי זבידא הוה, ואכשר בין בפנויה בין באשת איש. אמר ליה רב אחא בריה דרבה לרבינא: איקלע אמימר לאתרין. ואכשר בין בפנויה בין באשת איש.

Ravina said: Rav Gazza said to me that **Rabbi Yosei bar Avin**[P] once **happened** to come **to our place, and there was an incident involving an unmarried woman** who had engaged in intercourse with a slave, **and** Rabbi Yosei bar Avin **rendered** her offspring **fit** to marry into the congregation of Israel. And there was another incident **involving a married woman** who had engaged in intercourse with a slave, **and he rendered** her offspring **unfit** to marry into the congregation of Israel by ruling the offspring was a *mamzeret*. **Rav Sheshet said: Rav Gazza told me** that it was **not Rabbi Yosei bar Avin; rather, it was Rabbi Yosei, son of Rabbi Zevida, and he rendered** the offspring **fit both in** the case of **an unmarried woman and in** the case of **a married woman. Rav Aḥa, son of Rabba, said to Ravina: Ameimar** once **happened** to come **to our place and rendered** the offspring **fit both in** the case of **an unmarried woman and in** the case of **a married woman.**

והלכתא: גוי ועבד הבא על בת ישראל – הולד כשר, בין בפנויה בין באשת איש.

The Gemara concludes: **And the *halakha* is** that with regard to **a gentile or slave who engaged in intercourse with a Jewish woman,** the lineage of **the offspring is unflawed, whether** she was **an unmarried or a married woman.**

רבא אכשריה לרב מרי בר רחל ומנייה בפורסי דבבל. ואף על גב דאמר מר "שום תשים עליך מלך", כל משימות שאתה משים אל יהו אלא מקרב אחיך, האי כיון דאמו מישראל – "מקרב אחיך" קרינן ביה.

The Gemara cites a related *halakha*: **Rava ruled** that **Rav Mari bar Raḥel,**[P] who was the son of a gentile father and a Jewish mother, was **fit** to marry into the congregation of Israel, **and** furthermore **he appointed him as one of the officials** [*pursei*][L] **of Babylonia. And although the Master said** that from the verse, **"You shall place a king over you** whom the Lord your God shall chose; from among your brethren shall you place a king over you" (Deuteronomy 17:15) it is derived that not only with regard to the kingship but also with regard to **all positions** of authority **that you appoint,** the incumbents **may be selected only from among your brethren**[N] who share your Jewish lineage. Nevertheless, with regard to **this one,** i.e., Rav Mari bar Raḥel, **since his mother is of Jewish** lineage, **we call him "from among your brethren,"**[H] and so he is eligible.

NOTES

To the exclusion of a gentile and a slave, for whom betrothal does not take effect – לאפוקי גוי ועבד דלא תפסי בהו קדושין: The commentaries question the logic of this opinion that when the father of the offspring is a gentile or slave, the marital status of the woman is irrelevant. Ultimately the relations were adulterous and forbidden both for the Jewish woman herself and for the gentile, since adultery is included as one of the Noahide laws; why doesn't that automatically render the offspring a *mamzer*? Because of this difficulty, the Ramban and others prefer an alternative version of the text held by Rav Hai Gaon and the other *ge'onim*. According to that version, the reason that the offspring is not a *mamzer* is not solely dependent on the forbidden status of the union. Rather, it is based on the offspring being descended from a father and mother between whom betrothal is ineffective. The uniqueness of this case, then, is due to the fact that the offspring of a gentile father is never halakhically recognized as relating to him. Consequently, with regard to issues of lineage, the offspring is halakhically considered as having no father, and therefore it cannot be rendered a *mamzer*.

All positions…from among your brethren – כל משימות...מקרב אחיך: The Gemara states that for this *halakha* it is sufficient even if only one's mother is of Jewish lineage. However, *Tosafot* and the other early commentaries note that the Gemara in tractate *Sota* appears to contradict this when it states that although Agrippas's mother was Jewish, since his father was not, he was not halakhically qualified to be king. See *Tosafot* for one resolution of this question. The Ramban suggests that a distinction be made between appointing one to be the king and appointing him to other positions of authority. To be a king one must indeed have both a Jewish mother and father; however, for other positions of authority it is sufficient if only the mother is Jewish. Some suggest that this distinction can be identified in the verse that provides the source of this *halakha*, by splitting it up into two clauses, as follows: "From among your brethren shall you place a king over you" (Deuteronomy 17:15) refers specifically to a king, and the phrase "among your brethren" implies that both parents must be Jewish. However, the continuation of the verse: "You may not put a foreigner over you, who is not your brother," refers to any position of authority where one individual is placed in charge of others, and for that position only someone who is "not your brother" is excluded. One is defined as "not your brother" only if he does not have a Jewish mother (see *Yam shel Shlomo*).

LANGUAGE

Officials [*pursei*] – פורסי: From the Greek ἔφορος, *eforos*, meaning a governor or appointee. In certain locations this became the title of city governors or officials appointed over large populations.

HALAKHA

From among your brethren – מקרב אחיך: It is prohibited to appoint a king over the Jewish people if he descends from a line of converts. It is likewise prohibited to appoint such a man to any position of authority over the Jewish people. If, however, either his father or mother are not from a line of converts, he is eligible (Rambam *Sefer Shofetim*, *Hilkhot Melakhim* 1:4).

PERSONALITIES

Rabbi Yosei bar Avin – רבי יוסי בר אבין: An *amora* from Eretz Yisrael, Rabbi Yosei appears frequently in the Jerusalem Talmud as Rabbi Yosei bar Bun. In the Jerusalem Talmud he is usually the final *amora* mentioned on each topic, and some see his role as similar to that of Rav Ashi in the Babylonian Talmud, who edited and organized the subject matter. In a number of places his name appears with that of Rabbi Yosei bar Zevida, who was apparently his colleague but who does not appear in the Jerusalem Talmud, even though he, too, lived in Eretz Yisrael.

Rav Mari bar Raḥel – רב מרי בר רחל: It would seem that Rav Mari bar Raḥel is the same person referred to various times in the Gemara as Rav Mari, son of Issur the convert. During the wars that took place in Neharde'a, the daughters of the great *amora* Shmuel, the leading Sage of that city, were captured. One of them, Raḥel, was taken by a gentile named Issur, who later became a righteous convert. Nevertheless, since Mari was conceived while his father was not yet Jewish, he was referred to by his matrilineal descent.

Rav Mari grew to become a Torah scholar and was considered one of the leading scholars in his generation. He even debated the great Sages Abaye and Rava, who also lived in his generation. The Gemara often refers to his virtues and to the fact that he was careful to act beyond the requirements of the *halakha*. He was also very wealthy and influential. Two of his sons, Mar Zutra and Rav Ada Saba, were also considered to be among the great scholars of their generation and were contemporaries of Rav Ashi.

§ A gentile slave purchased by a Jew must be circumcised and then immersed in a ritual bath. By being immersed for the sake of slavery, he takes on the status of a full slave, which, among other things, obligates him to keep certain mitzvot. However, if the slave, or any gentile, is immersed for the sake of conversion, he then becomes a full Jew and fully obligated in mitzvot like any other Jew.

עבדיה דרבי חייא בר אמי אטבלה להההיא גויה לשם אנתתא. אמר רב יוסף: יכילנא לאכשורי בה ובברתה.

The Gemara considers the result of different intentions accompanying an immersion: **Rabbi Ḥiyya bar Ami's slave immersed a certain gentile woman for the sake of** having **intimate relations,**[N] i.e., to purify her from her menstrual impurity. **Rav Yosef said: I am able to render** both **her and her daughter fit** to marry into the congregation of Israel.

בה – כדרב אסי, דאמר רב אסי: מי לא טבלה לנדותה?

With regard to her, I can render her fit **in accordance with** the opinion **of Rav Asi, as Rav Asi said** concerning a woman whose status as a convert was unclear but who lived as a part of the Jewish people and acted like all other Jewish women: **Didn't she immerse**[H] **for the sake of** purifying herself from **her menstruation?**[N] Therefore, even if the original immersion was invalid, her intention in subsequent immersions was sufficient to be considered for the sake of conversion, since ultimately she immersed as an expression of her commitment to Judaism. She is therefore fully Jewish.

בברתה – גוי ועבד הבא על בת ישראל הולד כשר.

And **with regard to her daughter,** she is the daughter of **a gentile or slave who engaged in intercourse with a Jewish woman,** and the *halakha* is that the lineage of **the offspring is unflawed.**

ההוא דהוו קרו ליה בר ארמייתא. אמר רב אסי: מי לא טבלה לנדותה? ההוא דהוו קרו ליה בר ארמאה, אמר רבי יהושע בן לוי: מי לא טבל לקריו?

The Gemara details the circumstances of Rav Asi's ruling: There was **a certain** man **whom** people **would call: Son of the Aramean woman,** as they cast aspersions on the validity of his mother's conversion. With regard to that case, **Rav Asi said: Didn't she immerse for the sake of** purifying herself from **her menstruation?** A similar incident is recounted: There was **a certain** man **whom** people **would call: Son of an Aramean man,**[N] as they cast aspersions on the validity of his father's conversion. **Rabbi Yehoshua ben Levi said: Didn't he immerse for the sake of** purifying himself from **his seminal emission?** That intention is sufficient to consider the immersion an immersion for the sake of conversion.

אמר רב חמא בר גוריא אמר רב: הלוקח עבד מן הגוי, וקדם וטבל לשם בן חורין – קנה עצמו בן חורין. מאי טעמא?

Rav Ḥama bar Gurya said that **Rav said:** In the case of a Jew **who purchased a slave from a gentile, and** before he managed to immerse him for the sake of slavery the slave **preempted** him[N] **and immersed for the sake of** conversion to render himself a **freeman,**[H] he thereby **acquired himself** and becomes **a freeman,** i.e., his immersion effects a full conversion and he is no longer a slave. **What is the reason** for this *halakha*?

NOTES

He immersed her for the sake of intimate relations – אטבלה לשם אנתתא: *Tosefot Ḥad MiKamma'ei* and many other early commentaries explain that the woman had already completed all of the various stages of conversion; however, her original immersion was invalid because it had not been done under the direction of a court, and therefore it was not clear that it had been done with the necessary intention. When she later immersed for the sake of purifying herself, in accordance with the *halakha*, that intention itself was sufficient to deem the later immersion as one for the sake of conversion. This is because she performed the immersion as an expression of her commitment to Judaism, and therefore that immersion completed her conversion process (see *Nimmukei Yosef*). However, many other commentaries explain that it was not the actual immersion for the sake of purifying herself that completed her conversion; rather, it merely served as proof that when she had originally immersed as part of her conversion, she had the necessary intentions.

Didn't she immerse for the sake of her menstruation – מי לא טבלה לנדותה: *Tosafot* and the other early commentaries question how this immersion, which was presumably done in private, could possibly be valid, since the Gemara states later (46b) that the conversion process must be done in the presence of a court of three. Some suggest that in fact, a court of three is necessary only when the potential convert formally accepts upon himself to observe the mitzvot, since that is the primary act of conversion. However, the immersion itself may be performed in private. Others suggest that provided it is known to the court that she immersed, that is sufficient, even if they do not actually see the immersion. The Rif rules that a court of three is only ever necessary *ab initio*. Accordingly, the difficulty does not arise, since the Gemara's case here is clearly after the fact.

Whom people would call: Son of an Aramean man – קרו ליה בר ארמאה: Some commentaries ask: If his mother was Jewish, then he would be a full Jew. Furthermore, according to the Gemara's conclusion, with which Rabbi Yehoshua himself concurs, the offspring of a gentile and a Jewish woman is not a *mamzer*. If so, of what significance is it whether his father was a gentile? Some suggest that it is still significant according to the opinions that although he would not be a *mamzer*, he would be unfit for the priesthood (Maharsha). Others suggest that the case was not of the son of a questionable convert, but of a Jew who took a gentile woman in marriage, and it was the conversion of the son himself that was questionable. In support of this suggestion they cite an alternative version of the text that has: Son of an Aramean woman (*Arukh LaNer*; see Meiri).

One who purchased a slave…and the slave preempted him, etc. – הלוקח עבד...וקדם וכו׳: The commentaries explain the connection between this section of the Gemara and the previous one: From the previous Gemara it is apparent that even if a convert immersed in private, not in the presence of the court, the immersion can still be valid because his intention was clear. The main issue in the following section of the Gemara is the very issue of the significance of one's intentions at the time of immersion (*Yosef Lekaḥ*).

HALAKHA

Didn't she immerse, etc. – מי לא טבלה וכו׳: In order to become Jewish, a convert is required to declare that he accepts upon himself to observe the mitzvot, and he must then be circumcised and immersed, all in the presence of a court of three. If a convert did not declare his acceptance of the mitzvot or was not immersed in the presence of a court of three, then the conversion can still be valid if it is apparent that he had continued to observe the mitzvot and Jewish customs and had immersed for the sake of purifying himself from a discharge of semen, or, in the case of a female convert, that she had immersed to purify herself from menstruation. In any case, if the convert marries a Jewish woman, a child born from that union is not rendered unfit (Rambam *Sefer Kedusha, Hilkhot Issurei Bia* 13:9; *Shulḥan Arukh, Yoreh De'a* 268:3).

One who purchased a slave…and he immersed for the sake of rendering him a freeman – הלוקח עבד...וטבל לשם בן חורין: If a Jew purchased a slave from a gentile, and the slave immersed for the sake of conversion, then that immersion effects a full conversion and he becomes a freeman. He must then compensate his previous master with the monetary value of himself when he was a slave (Rema, citing *Nimmukei Yosef*; Rambam *Sefer Kedusha, Hilkhot Issurei Bia* 13:11 and *Sefer Kinyan, Hilkhot Avadim* 8:19; *Shulḥan Arukh, Yoreh De'a* 267:9).

גּוֹי גּוּפָא לָא קָנֵי לֵיהּ, מַאי דְּקָנֵי לֵיהּ – הוּא דְּמַקְנֵי לֵיהּ לְיִשְׂרָאֵל, וְכֵיוָן דְּקָדַם וְטָבַל לְשֵׁם בֶּן חוֹרִין – אַפְקְעֵיהּ לְשִׁעְבּוּדֵיהּ,

His previous **gentile** owner **did not have ownership of the** slave's **body,** since a gentile is unable to have ownership of another's body; rather, he had rights to only the slave's labor. And only **that which he owned in him was he** able to **sell to the Jew.** Therefore, before immersion, the Jew had rights to only the slave's labor, but not ownership of his body, **and** therefore, **once** the slave **preempted** his owner **and immersed for the sake of** conversion to make him **a freeman, he abrogates** his master's **lien** upon him.

כִּדְרָבָא. דְּאָמַר רָבָא: הֶקְדֵּשׁ, חָמֵץ, וְשִׁחְרוּר – מַפְקִיעִין מִידֵי שִׁעְבּוּד.

The Gemara notes: This explanation is **in accordance with** the opinion **of Rava, as Rava said: Consecration** of an item to the Temple, the prohibition of **leavened bread**[H] taking effect upon a leavened food, **and** the **emancipation**[N] of a slave **abrogate** any **lien**[H] that exists upon them.

מְתִיב רַב חִסְדָּא: מַעֲשֶׂה בְּבֵלוֹרְיָא הַגִּיּוֹרֶת שֶׁקָּדְמוּ עֲבָדֶיהָ וְטָבְלוּ לְפָנֶיהָ. וּבָא מַעֲשֶׂה לִפְנֵי חֲכָמִים וְאָמְרוּ: קָנוּ עַצְמָן בְּנֵי חוֹרִין. לְפָנֶיהָ – אִין, לְאַחֲרֶיהָ – לָא!

Rav Ḥisda raised an objection from a *baraita*: There was **an incident involving Beloreya the female convert**[P] **in which her slaves preempted** her **and immersed before her**[N] own immersion for her own conversion. **And** the details of the **incident came before the Sages, and they said:** The slaves **acquired themselves** and became **freemen.** Rav Ḥisda explains how the *baraita* poses a challenge: The *baraita* implies that only because the slaves immersed **before her,** while she was still a gentile, that **yes,** they became freemen; however, had they immersed **after her,**[H] i.e., after she had already converted, then **no,** they would not have become freemen. The reason for this is presumably that upon her conversion she attains the rights to her slaves' bodies, and therefore their immersion for the sake of becoming freemen would be ineffective. However, this contradicts the Gemara's explanation above that when a Jew gains ownership of a slave from a gentile, he has a right to only the slave's labor.

אֲמַר רָבָא: לְפָנֶיהָ – בֵּין בִּסְתָם בֵּין בִּמְפוֹרָשׁ. לְאַחֲרֶיהָ, בִּמְפוֹרָשׁ – אִין, בִּסְתָם – לָא.

To resolve the challenge **Rava said:** When the *baraita* says that because they immersed **before her** they acquired themselves, that is **whether** they immersed **without a specified** intention **or whether** they immersed **with explicit** intention to convert and become freemen. However, had they immersed **after her,** if they did so **with explicit** intention to convert, then **yes,** the immersion would achieve that end, but if they did so **without a specified** intention, then **no,** their immersion would, by default, be considered for the sake of slavery and they would not become free.

אֲמַר רַב אַוְיָא: לֹא שָׁנוּ אֶלָּא בְּלוֹקֵחַ מִן הַגּוֹי, אֲבָל גּוֹי גּוּפֵיהּ – קָנֵי,

Rav Avya[P] **said: They taught** that one acquires only the rights to the slave's labor **only with regard to** a Jew **who purchased** a slave **from a gentile** slave owner, **but if a gentile** sold **his own body** as a slave directly to a Jew, then the Jew **acquires**[H] his body.

HALAKHA

Consecration, leavened bread abrogate a lien – הֶקְדֵּשׁ, חָמֵץ מַפְקִיעִים מִידֵי שִׁעְבּוּד: With regard to consecration, Rabbeinu Tam and the Rambam hold that even consecrating an item with sanctity that inheres only in its value is effective to abrogate a lien upon it, whereas Rashi and the Ra'avad hold this applies only when one consecrates an item to the extent that the item is endowed with inherent sanctity. The abrogation caused by the onset of the prohibition of leavened bread is also true of the onset of any prohibition that prohibits one from gaining any benefit from the item. Even in a case where the lien is abrogated, the debt supported by the lien still exists, and the creditor may still attempt to collect it (Rambam *Sefer Hafla'a, Hilkhot Arakhin* 7:14, and *Sefer Mishpatim, Hilkhot Malve VeLoveh* 18:6–7; *Shulḥan Arukh, Ḥoshen Mishpat* 117:7).

Emancipation abrogates a lien – שִׁחְרוּר מַפְקִיעִין מִידֵי שִׁעְבּוּד: If one designated his slaves to be the sole property from which repayment of his debt may be collected and he then emancipated the slave, then the emancipation is effective and the lien is thereby abrogated. The debtor must still repay the creditor. Although the slave is no longer bound to the debt, the creditor is forced to write a bill of emancipation for him so that he will not later try to claim that the slave should be considered his own due to the lien that once existed upon him (Rambam *Sefer Kinyan, Hilkhot Avadim* 8:16; *Shulḥan Arukh, Yoreh De'a* 267:68).

Before her and after her – לְפָנֶיהָ וְאַחֲרֶיהָ: In a case where a Jew purchases a slave from a gentile and the slave preempts the owner and immerses on his own accord, if he immersed in the presence of his owner then he becomes a freeman, and if the immersion was not in the presence of his owner then he becomes free only if it was explicitly stated that the immersion was for the sake of becoming a freeman. This is according to the opinion of Rambam, based on the version of the text by which the Rif held. The *Shulḥan Arukh*, following the version of the text by which Rashi held, rules: In a case where a convert has owned a slave since before his conversion, if the slave immersed prior to the owner's conversion, the slave would thereby become a freeman, but if he immersed only after the owner's conversion, then he becomes free only if it was explicitly stated that the immersion was for the sake of becoming a freeman (*Tur*, citing Rosh; Rambam *Sefer Kinyan, Hilkhot Avadim* 8:19; *Shulḥan Arukh, Yoreh De'a* 267:9).

A gentile's body is acquired – נָכְרִי גּוּפוֹ קוֹנֶה: If a gentile sells himself as a slave, of his own volition, to a Jew, then the Jew acquires his body, and if the slave immerses, he cannot unilaterally define that immersion as one for the sake of becoming a freeman (*Shulḥan Arukh, Yoreh De'a* 267:9).

PERSONALITIES

Beloreya the female convert – בְּלוֹרְיָא הַגִּיּוֹרֶת: The name Beloreya is probably a variant of the name Valeria, a name used in Rome for women of the gens Valeria, which was one of the most celebrated and wealthy families in Rome. Beloreya converted during the Second Temple period, and the Talmud relates several questions that she posed to Rabban Gamliel concerning the meanings of various verses in the Bible.

Rav Avya – רַב אַוְיָא: A fourth-generation Babylonian *amora*, Rav Avya was a prominent disciple of Rav Huna but also studied in Eretz Yisrael with Rabbi Ami and Rabbi Yoḥanan. Rav Huna respected him greatly and valued his comments and questions. He married the sister of Rami bar Pappa, and some of his children became *amora'im* themselves. The most famous of these children, Rav Aḥa, son of Rav Avya, is quoted many times in the Talmud as a disciple of Rav Ashi.

NOTES

Consecration, leavened bread, and emancipation, etc. – הֶקְדֵּשׁ, חָמֵץ, וְשִׁחְרוּר וכו׳: In the present case, the slave's owner never actually emancipated him. Nevertheless, the slave's immersion rendered him a freeman, and in that way he effectively emancipated himself (*Tosafot Yeshanim*).

And immersed before her – וְטָבְלוּ לְפָנֶיהָ: The early commentaries record two different versions of the Gemara's text here that lead to two fundamentally different conclusions.

The text of the *Halakhot Gedolot*, Rif, and Rambam reads: Immersed in her presence. According to this version, when slaves immerse in the presence of their owner, unless the owner explicitly states otherwise, it is assumed that the owner consents to the fact that their immersion should be for the sake of conversion, and so they become freemen. However, if slaves immerse not in the presence of their owner, they cannot unilaterally define their immersion to be for conversion, and therefore they remain slaves. Essentially, only the owner has the ability to define the nature of her slaves' immersion.

The present text, which is the version by which Rashi and the Razah held, reads: Immersed before her, meaning their immersion preceded her own. According to this version, the ability for the slaves' immersion to effect their conversion is dependent on whether it took place while their owner was a Jew or a gentile. As a gentile, she would have rights to only their labor, and so their immersion could abrogate her lien upon them. However, if she immersed first and was already Jewish, then she would have already attained ownership of their bodies, and therefore they would not be able to immerse for the sake of conversion without her consent.

An underlying assumption of both explanations is that in some cases an immersion whose purpose was unspecified is considered, by default, to be for the sake of conversion. The *Yosef Lekaḥ* explains the rationale for this. In truth, the very act of immersion demonstrates an acceptance of the system of mitzvot; why else would the slaves be immersing? Therefore, unless it is made explicit that the immersion is for the sake of slavery, it is considered for the sake of conversion.

דִּכְתִיב ״וְגַם מִבְּנֵי הַתּוֹשָׁבִים הַגָּרִים עִמָּכֶם מֵהֶם תִּקְנוּ״ – אַתֶּם קוֹנִים מֵהֶם, וְלֹא הֵם קוֹנִים מִכֶּם, וְלֹא הֵם קוֹנִים זֶה מִזֶּה.

As it is written: **"Moreover, of the children of the strangers that sojourn among you, of them you may acquire"** (Leviticus 25:45). The verse states only that **you,** i.e., Jews, **can acquire** a slave **from them,** i.e., a gentile slave, **but they cannot acquire** a slave **from you,** i.e., a Jewish slave, **and they cannot acquire** a slave **from one another.**

וְלֹא הֵם קוֹנִים מִכֶּם, לְמַאי? אִילֵימָא לְמַעֲשֵׂה יָדָיו – אַטּוּ גּוֹי לָא קָנֵי לֵיהּ לְיִשְׂרָאֵל לְמַעֲשֵׂה יָדָיו? וְהָכְתִיב ״אוֹ לְעֵקֶר מִשְׁפַּחַת גֵּר״ וְאָמַר מָר: ״מִשְׁפַּחַת גֵּר״ – זֶה הַגּוֹי! אֶלָּא לָאו – לְגוּפֵיהּ, וְקָאָמַר רַחֲמָנָא ״אַתֶּם קוֹנִין מֵהֶם״ – אֲפִילּוּ גּוּפֵיהּ.

When it is derived that: **But they cannot acquire** slaves **from you, to what** type of acquisition is it referring? **If we say it is for his labor, is that to say** that **a gentile cannot acquire a Jew for his labor?**[H] **Isn't it written:** "And if a stranger who is a settler with you becomes rich, and your brother becomes poor beside him, and he sells himself to the stranger who is a settler with you, **or to the offshoot of a stranger's family"** (Leviticus 25:47), **and the Master said** in explanation of the phrase **"a stranger's family"** that **this** is referring to **a gentile.** If so, the verse explicitly states that a Jew can sell himself as a slave to a gentile. **Rather, is it not** that the reference is **to** selling **his body, and the Merciful One states** that **you,** i.e., Jews, **can acquire** a slave **from them,** which means **even his body.** Accordingly the verse indicates that a Jew can acquire a gentile slave's body, but a gentile is unable to acquire ownership of another's body, even that of another gentile.

פָּרֵיךְ רַב אַחָא: אֵימָא בְּכַסְפָּא וּבִטְבִילָה! קַשְׁיָא.

Rav Aḥa refutes Rav Avya's explanation: **Say** that the verse is referring to acquiring a gentile slave by both purchasing him **with money and** then **by immersing** him for the purpose of slavery, and only in that case does it teach that a Jew acquires the gentile slave's body. However, until he has been immersed the acquisition is not fully complete, and therefore if the slave immerses himself with the intention to become free, then his immersion would achieve that end. The Gemara concedes: This is **difficult.**

אָמַר שְׁמוּאֵל: וְצָרִיךְ לְתָקְפוֹ בַּמַּיִם.

Shmuel said: And if one wishes to ensure that one's slave does not declare the immersion to be for the sake of conversion, then **one needs to hold him tightly**[NH] **in the water** in a way that demonstrates the owner's dominance over the slave at that time, thereby defining the immersion as one for the sake of slavery.

כִּי הַאי דְּמִנְיָמִין, עַבְדֵּיהּ דְּרַב אַשִׁי, בְּעָא לְאַטְבּוּלֵי, מְסָרֵיהּ נִיהֲלַיְיהוּ לְרָבִינָא וּלְרַב אַחָא בְּרֵיהּ דְּרָבָא, אֲמַר לְהוּ: חֲזוּ דְּמִינַּיְיכוּ קָבָעֵית לֵיהּ. רָמוּ לֵיהּ אַרְוִיסָא בְּצַוָּארֵיהּ, אַרְפּוּ לֵיהּ. וְצִמְצְמוּ לֵיהּ.

That is as demonstrated **in this** incident **involving Minyamin, Rav Ashi's slave:** When **he wished to immerse** him, **he passed him to**[N] **Ravina and Rav Aḥa, son of Rava,** to perform the immersion on his behalf, and **he said to them: Be aware that I will claim** compensation **for him from you** if you do not prevent my slave from immersing for the sake of conversion. **They placed a bridle** [***arvisa***][L] **upon his neck,** and at the moment of immersion **they loosened it and** then immediately **tightened it** again while he was still immersed.

אַרְפּוּ לֵיהּ – כִּי הֵיכִי דְּלָא לֶהֱוֵי חֲצִיצָה, צִמְצְמוּ לֵיהּ – כִּי הֵיכִי דְּלָא לִקְדִּים וְלֵימָא לְהוּ: לְשֵׁם בֶּן חוֹרִין אֲנִי טוֹבֵל. בַּהֲדֵי דְּדָלֵי רֵישֵׁיהּ מִמַּיָּא, אַנְחוּ לֵיהּ זוּלְטָא דְּטִינָא אַרֵישֵׁיהּ. וְאָמְרוּ לֵיהּ: זִיל אַמְטֵי לְבֵי מָרָךְ.

The Gemara explains their actions: **They** initially **loosened it in order that there should not be any interposition** between the slave and the water during the immersion, which would invalidate it. **They** immediately **tightened it** again **in order that** the slave **should not preempt** them **and say to them: I am immersing for the sake of** becoming **a freeman. When he lifted his head from the water they placed a bucket of clay**[N] **upon his head and said to him: Go and bring** this **to the house of your master.** They did this in order to demonstrate that the immersion had been successful and that he was still a slave.

NOTES

Then one needs to hold him tightly – וְצָרִיךְ לְתוֹקְפוֹ: Rashi explains that this is necessary to demonstrate the owner's dominance over the slave. However, Rabbeinu Ḥananel and the Rif simply write that the slave must be held tightly in order to ensure the validity of the immersion. Simply read, it would appear that they mean only that the owner should ensure the slave is fully immersed in the water. Based on this understanding of their statements, the Razah rejects their explanation, seemingly because he assumes that it is such an obvious point that is should be unnecessary to state it. However, the Ramban in *Milḥamot HaShem* claims that the Rif's intention is similar to that of Rashi; if the owner is in physical control of the slave's immersion, it is clear that it is the owner who is in charge of the immersion, and therefore the nature of the immersion is defined by his intentions.

He passed him to them – מְסָרֵיהּ נִיהֲלַיְיהוּ: Some commentaries suggest that from the fact that the Gemara mentions the involvement of only two Sages in this incident, it would appear that it is sufficient to have two judges preside over the immersion. The Ramban rejects this possibility outright, insisting that three judges are always required. He explains that even in this incident, there was certainly an additional judge present at the time. Presumably, the third judge was not of equal stature as Ravina and Rav Aḥa, and so he was not mentioned out of deference to them.

They placed a bucket of clay – אַנְחוּ לֵיהּ זוּלְטָא דְּטִינָא: This act was not halakhically significant. It was done only in order to demonstrate and publicize the fact that the man was still a slave so that no one could later suggest that the immersion might have been for the sake of making him a freeman (Rashba; *Nimmukei Yosef*).

LANGUAGE

Bridle [*arvisa*] – אַרְוִיסָא: From the Middle Persian arwēs, meaning a rope or bridle.

HALAKHA

A Hebrew slave sold to a gentile – עֶבֶד עִבְרִי הַנִּמְכָּר לְנׇכְרִי: A Jew may be sold as a slave only to either a born Jew or to a convert, but it is not permitted to sell him to a gentile. This applies both in the case where the court sold the Jew or where the Jew sold himself. Nevertheless, if a Jew sold himself to a gentile, the transaction is valid, even if he sold himself directly into the service of idolatry (Rambam *Sefer Kinyan, Hilkhot Avadim* 1:3).

One needs to hold him tightly – צָרִיךְ לְתָקְפוֹ: One who immerses his slave needs to perform some act of enslavement at the same time. For example, he could hold him tightly in the water. By doing so he prevents the slave from immersing for the sake of becoming a freeman and thereby acquiring himself (Rambam *Sefer Kinyan, Hilkhot Avadim* 8:19 and *Sefer Kedusha, Hilkhot Issurei Bia* 13:11; *Shulḥan Arukh, Yoreh De'a* 267:9).

אָמַר לֵיהּ רַב פָּפָּא לְרָבָא: חָזֵי מָר הָנֵי דְּבֵי פַּפָּא בַּר אַבָּא דְּיָהֲבִי זוּזֵי לְאֶינָשֵׁי לְכַרְגַּיְיהוּ, וּמְשַׁעְבְּדִי בְּהוּ. כִּי נָפְקִי, צְרִיכִי גִּיטָּא דְּחֵירוּתָא אוֹ לָא?

Rav Pappa said to Rava: Has the Master seen those of the house of Pappa bar Abba[P] **who give money** to the tax-collectors **on behalf of** poor **people**[N] **to pay for their poll tax** [*karga*],[L] **and** as a result **they would enslave them.** Anyone who did not pay the tax would be taken as a slave for the king. By paying for such people's taxes, the members of the house of Pappa bar Abba essentially purchased those people, who had become the king's slaves, for themselves. Rav Pappa asked: **When** those slaves **go free, do they require a bill of emancipation,**[N] because the members of the house of Pappa bar Abba actually attained ownership of the slaves' bodies, **or not,** as they were owned only for the sake of their labor?

אָמַר לֵיהּ: אִיכּוּ שְׁכִיבִי לָא אָמְרִי לְכוּ הָא מִילְּתָא, הָכִי אָמַר רַב שֵׁשֶׁת: מוֹהַרְקַיְיהוּ דְּהָנֵי בְּטַפְסָא דְּמַלְכָּא מָנַח, וּמַלְכָּא אֲמַר: מַאן דְּלָא יָהֵיב כַּרְגָּא – מִשְׁתַּעְבַּד לְמַאן דְּיָהֵיב כַּרְגָּא.

He said to him: Were I dead[N] **I could not say this matter to you,** so it is good that you have asked me while I am still alive, as I know that **this** is what **Rav Sheshet said** with regard to the matter: **The writ of slavery** [*moharkayehu*][L] **of these**[H] residents of the kingdom **rests in the treasury** [*tafsa*][L] **of the king,** and in fact all the residents of the kingdom are considered to be full slaves of the king, i.e., he owns their bodies, irrespective of whether they pay their taxes. **And** so when **the king says: One who does not give the poll tax is to be enslaved to the one who does give the poll tax** on his behalf, the king's decree is fully effective in making those residents full slaves of those who paid for them. As such, they will require a bill of emancipation when they are freed.

PERSONALITIES

Pappa bar Abba – פַּפָּא בַּר אַבָּא: Also known as Rav Pappa bar Abba, he was a well-respected and wealthy man who lived during the same time as Rav Pappa (see 21b). It seems that there were close relations between Rav Pappa and the house of Rav Pappa bar Abba; apparently the members of that household related to Rav Pappa as their rabbi and master, asking him various questions in *halakha*. The sons of Rav Pappa bar Abba were Torah scholars and are found participating in talmudic discussions concerning matters of *halakha* together with Rav Pappa and Ravina.

LANGUAGE

Poll tax [*karga*] – כַּרְגָּא: Related to the Middle Persian word harg, meaning tribute.

Writ of slavery [*moharka*] – מוֹהַרְקָא: From the Middle Persian muhrak, which means a document.

Treasury [*tafsa*] – טַפְסָא: The correct reading of this word, preserved in some manuscripts and commentaries, is *sefata*. It apparently is related to the New Persian term safad, meaning basket.

HALAKHA

The writ of slavery of these, etc. – מוֹהַרְקַיְיהוּ דְּהָנֵי וכו׳: If a gentile king declares that all of those who do not pay their taxes shall be sold to those who do, that law is halakhically binding, and a slave acquired in this matter is considered a Canaanite slave in every respect (Rambam *Sefer Kinyan*, *Hilkhot Avadim* 1:8; *Shulḥan Arukh*, *Yoreh De'a* 267:18).

NOTES

Give money on behalf of people, etc. – יָהֲבִי זוּזֵי לְאֶינָשֵׁי וכו׳: The Gemara does not state who these people were. Most commentaries assume that they were gentiles. Accordingly, Rav Pappa's question is whether they were enslaved only for the sake of their labor or even to the extent that their bodies were owned. However, Rabbeinu Ḥananel explains that these people were *gerei toshav*, i.e., gentiles who reside in Eretz Yisrael and observe certain mitzvot. In many regards, the status of a *ger toshav* is not similar to that of other gentiles. Rav Pappa therefore inquired whether or not their bodies can be fully owned as slaves in the same way as a gentile slave. Others explain that these people were Jews. According to this opinion, the question is whether it is possible to become a Hebrew slave in this manner; normally the status of a Hebrew slave is attained only if the Jew either sells himself or is sold as a slave by the court. Although Rav Pappa lived in a generation in which the status of a Hebrew slave could no longer be attained in the standard manner, it is possible that they might still be considered Hebrew slaves since the law of the land defined them as such (Ritva).

Do they require a bill of emancipation – צְרִיכִי גִּיטָּא דְּחֵירוּתָא: According to the opinions that these people were gentiles, various questions are raised: Why did Rav Pappa ask only about the need for a bill of emancipation? Would such slaves also require immersion for the sake of slavery? Why didn't Rav Pappa ask about that as well? The Ramban explains that the issue of immersion is directly dependent on whether there is a need for a bill of emancipation; therefore, there was no need to ask about it. If a bill of emancipation is required, that is because even the slaves' bodies were owned. Therefore, it would also be necessary to immerse them. If there is no need for a bill of emancipation, then it is apparent that they were acquired only for the sake of their labor, and so no immersion would be necessary.

The Gemara above explains that one gentile cannot acquire the body of another. If so, since these slaves were acquired from the gentile king, how is it possible for their new owners to have gained ownership of their bodies, a state which consequently requires a bill of emancipation? The commentaries explain that although it is true that under normal circumstances one gentile cannot acquire the body of another, in the present case the law of the land afforded the king such rights, and such rights are recognized as halakhically binding. This is because the king's ownership is not based on a mutual agreement but on the power of the king over his subjects.

Based on this discussion, some suggest that there may be a further example where one gentile can own the body of another in a case where one gentile takes another as a prisoner of war. In such a case it is possible that since the ownership of the captive is similarly not based on mutual agreement but due to the power of the captor over his captive, in that case as well the captor would acquire ownership of his captive's body (see *Tosefot HaRosh* and Rashba).

Were I dead – אִיכּוּ שְׁכִיבִי: This strange expression was also used once by Rava's teacher Rav Naḥman with regard to his own teacher Shmuel (*Shabbat* 152b), as well as by Rav Yehuda with regard to his teacher Rav (*Avoda Zara* 55a). *Ben Yehoyada* on *Shabbat* 152b suggests that the teachers of these *amoraim* had whispered various teachings to them, and they therefore assumed that no one else had heard them and that if they died, the statements would have been lost forever.

רבי חייא בר אבא איקלע לגבלא. חזא בנות ישראל דמעברן מגרים שמלו ולא טבלו, וחזא חמרא דישראל דמזגי גוים ושתו ישראל, וחזא תורמוסין דשלקי גוים ואכלי ישראל, ולא אמר להו ולא מידי.

§ The Gemara relates: **Rabbi Ḥiyya bar Abba** once **happened** to come **to Gavla.**[B] **He saw Jewish women** there **who had become pregnant from converts who were circumcised but** had still **not immersed** to complete their conversion process; **and he saw wine of Jews that gentiles were pouring,**[N] **and Jews were drinking** it; **and he saw lupines** [*turmusin*][LB] **that gentiles were cooking, and Jews were eating** them; **but he did not say anything to them.**

אתא לקמיה דרבי יוחנן. אמר ליה: צא והכרז על בניהם שהם ממזרים, ועל יינם משום יין נסך, ועל התורמוסן משום בישולי גוים, לפי שאינן בני תורה.

Later, **he came before Rabbi Yoḥanan** and told him what he had witnessed. **Rabbi Yoḥanan said to him: Go and make** a public **declaration concerning their children that they are** *mamzerim*, **and concerning their wine** that it is forbidden **because** it is like **wine poured as an** idolatrous **libation, and concerning their lupines** that they are forbidden **because** they are **food cooked by gentiles.** One should be stringent and make such a declaration **because they are not** well-versed **in Torah,** and if they are left to be lax in this regard they will eventually transgress Torah prohibitions.

על בניהן שהם ממזרים – רבי יוחנן לטעמיה, דאמר רבי חייא בר אבא אמר רבי יוחנן: לעולם אין גר עד שימול ויטבול, וכיון דלא טביל – גוי הוא. ואמר רבה בר בר חנה אמר רבי יוחנן: גוי ועבד הבא על בת ישראל – הולד ממזר.

The Gemara explains: With regard to the declaration **concerning their children that they are** *mamzerim*, **Rabbi Yoḥanan** conforms **to his** standard line of **reasoning** in two *halakhot*: The first is **as Rabbi Ḥiyya bar Abba said** that **Rabbi Yoḥanan said:** One **is never** considered to be **a convert until he has been circumcised and has immersed.**[H] **And since** the convert in the case in Gavla **had not immersed, he is** still considered **a gentile. And** the second *halakha* is as **Rabba bar bar Ḥana said** that **Rabbi Yoḥanan said:** With regard to **a gentile or a slave who engaged in intercourse with a Jewish woman, the offspring** of that union **is a** *mamzer*.

ועל יינם משום יין נסך – משום "לך לך", אמרין נזירא, "סחור סחור, לכרמא לא תקרב".

And the reason to declare **concerning their wine** that it is forbidden **because** it is like **wine poured as an** idolatrous **libation**[H] is that although their wine was not actually poured as an idolatrous libation, it was prohibited by rabbinic decree **due to** the maxim that: **Go, go, we say to a nazirite, go around and go around,** but **do not come near to the vineyard.** Although a nazirite is prohibited only from eating produce of the vine, he is warned not even to come into close proximity of a vineyard as a protective measure to ensure that he will not transgress this prohibition. So too, in many cases, the Sages decreed certain items and actions to be prohibited because they understood that if people would partake of them, they would eventually transgress Torah prohibitions.

NOTES

That gentiles were pouring – דמזגי גוים: Rashi explains that the gentiles did not actually touch the wine itself but merely poured it; nevertheless, that was sufficient to render it forbidden. Apparently, according to Rashi it was this point that provided the novelty of the case, which Rabbi Ḥiyya bar Abba was initially unaware of. Rabbi Avraham min HaHar argues that it was unanimously understood that if a gentile actually pours wine, the wine is thereby rendered forbidden. The novelty in this case was that although the gentiles in fact merely diluted the wine by pouring water into it, the wine was nevertheless forbidden because by pouring the water, they caused the wine to be moved. This is sufficient to render the wine forbidden because the rabbinic prohibition is on account of the fact that idolaters sometimes worship their deity by simply swirling the wine around, and so it applies in any case where a gentile causes the wine to move.

HALAKHA

When is one considered a convert – מתי נחשב גר: One is considered to be a convert only once he has both been circumcised and immersed in a ritual bath. This is in accordance with the opinion of Rabbi Yoḥanan (Rambam *Sefer Kedusha, Hilkhot Issurei Bia* 13:6).

Their wine because of wine poured as a libation – יינם משום יין נסך: It is forbidden to derive benefit from wine touched by gentiles. This is due to a rabbinic decree that was issued on account of wine poured as a libation offering to idols. The Rema cites opinions that nowadays, since idolaters do not pour libation offerings of wine to their idols, it is permitted to derive benefit from their wine, and so it is permissible to take wine from them in exchange for repayment of a debt or in other cases of possible loss (*Tur*, citing Rashbam and Rosh). Nevertheless, one may not trade in it *ab initio* (*Haggahot Maimoniyyot*). There are those who are lenient even in this regard, but it is proper to be stringent (*Smag*; Rambam *Sefer Kedusha, Hilkhot Ma'akhalot Assurot* 11:3; *Shulḥan Arukh, Yoreh De'a* 123:1).

BACKGROUND

Gavla – גבלא: Gavla is apparently a reference to the area of the Golan in the northern part of Eretz Yisrael. Despite the fact that it was relatively close to the centers of the Jewish settlement in Tiberias and its environs, it was nevertheless not considered a place of Torah scholars, and it was populated by both Jews and gentiles.

Lupines – תורמוסין: Lupine is the name of several plants from the legume family, of the *Faboideae* subfamily. White lupine, *Lupinus albus*, and yellow lupine, *Lupinus luteus*, are the most commonly grown kinds. The seeds of lupines, which can grow to a diameter of up to fifteen centimeters, are edible. However, due the presence of alkaloids, the natural taste of the seeds is extremely bitter. In order to prepare them for consumption one must cook them repeatedly in water. To this day the cooked seeds of lupines are sold as a delicacy.

White lupine

European yellow lupine

Lupine seeds

LANGUAGE

Lupine [*turmus*] – תורמוס: From the Greek θέρμος, *thermos*, meaning lupine, the lupine plant from the legume family.

וְעַל תּוּרְמוּסָן מִשּׁוּם בִּשּׁוּלֵי גּוֹיִם – לְפִי שֶׁאֵינָן בְּנֵי תּוֹרָה, הָא בְּנֵי תּוֹרָה שָׁרֵי? וְהָאֲמַר רַב שְׁמוּאֵל בַּר רַב יִצְחָק מִשְּׁמֵיהּ דְּרַב: כָּל הַנֶּאֱכָל כְּמוֹת שֶׁהוּא חַי – אֵין בּוֹ מִשּׁוּם בִּשּׁוּלֵי גּוֹיִם, וְהָא תּוּרְמוּס אֵינוֹ נֶאֱכָל כְּמוֹת שֶׁהוּא חַי, וְיֵשׁ בּוֹ מִשּׁוּם בִּשּׁוּלֵי גּוֹיִם!

And the final declaration **concerning their lupines** that they are forbidden **because** they are **food cooked by gentiles**[NH] is issued **because they are not** well versed **in Torah.**[N] The Gemara expresses astonishment: Does this imply that **were they students of the Torah** their lupines would **be permitted? Didn't Rav Shmuel bar Rav Yitzḥak say in the name of Rav:** Any food item **that is eaten as it is, raw, is not** subject to the prohibition of **food cooked by gentiles,** even when cooked by them? **But a lupine is not eaten as it is, raw, and** therefore **it is subject to** the prohibition of **food cooked by gentiles.**

רַבִּי יוֹחָנָן כְּאִידָךְ לִישָּׁנָא סְבִירָא לֵיהּ דְּאָמַר רַב שְׁמוּאֵל בַּר רַב יִצְחָק מִשְּׁמֵיהּ דְּרַב: כָּל שֶׁאֵין עוֹלֶה עַל שׁוּלְחַן מְלָכִים לֶאֱכוֹל בּוֹ אֶת הַפַּת – אֵין בּוֹ מִשּׁוּם בִּשּׁוּלֵי גּוֹיִם. וְטַעְמָא דְּאֵינָן בְּנֵי תּוֹרָה, הָא בְּנֵי תּוֹרָה – שָׁרֵי.

The Gemara explains that **Rabbi Yoḥanan holds** in this matter **in accordance with** the opinion of **the other version** of what **Rav Shmuel bar Rav Yitzḥak said in the name of Rav: Any** food item that lacks sufficient importance such that it **does not appear on the table of kings** in order **to eat bread with it is not** subject **to** the prohibition of **food cooked by gentiles.** Lupines lack importance and are therefore permitted even if cooked by gentiles. **And** consequently, **the** only **reason** to make a declaration prohibiting the residents of Gavla from eating them is **because they are not** well versed **in Torah,** and if they are left to be lax in this regard they will eventually become lax in actual Torah prohibitions; by inference, to those well versed **in Torah, it is permitted.**

§ During their sojourn in Egypt, the children of Israel had the halakhic status of gentiles. At the revelation at Sinai they entered into a national covenant with God in which they attained their status of the Jewish people. This transformation was essentially the mass conversion of the people, and so their preparation for the revelation provides a paradigm of the process required for conversion for all generations. The *tanna'im* disagree as to which aspects of that original conversion are to be derived for all generations.

תָּנוּ רַבָּנַן: גֵּר שֶׁמָּל וְלֹא טָבַל, רַבִּי אֱלִיעֶזֶר אוֹמֵר הֲרֵי זֶה גֵּר, שֶׁכֵּן מָצִינוּ בַּאֲבוֹתֵינוּ שֶׁמָּלוּ וְלֹא טָבְלוּ. טָבַל וְלֹא מָל, רַבִּי יְהוֹשֻׁעַ אוֹמֵר: הֲרֵי זֶה גֵּר, שֶׁכֵּן מָצִינוּ בָּאִמָּהוֹת שֶׁטָּבְלוּ וְלֹא מָלוּ. וַחֲכָמִים אוֹמְרִים: טָבַל וְלֹא מָל, מָל וְלֹא טָבַל – אֵין גֵּר עַד שֶׁיָּמוֹל וְיִטְבּוֹל.

The Sages taught in a *baraita*: With regard to **a convert who was circumcised but did not immerse, Rabbi Eliezer says** that **this is a convert, as so we found with our forefathers** following the exodus from Egypt **that they were circumcised**[N] **but were not immersed.** With regard to one who **immersed but was not circumcised, Rabbi Yehoshua says** that **this is a convert, as so we found with our foremothers that they immersed but were not circumcised. And the Rabbis say:** Whether **he immersed but was not circumcised** or whether **he was circumcised but did not immerse, he is not a convert until he is circumcised and he immerses.**

וְרַבִּי יְהוֹשֻׁעַ נַמִי – נֵילַף מֵאָבוֹת, וְרַבִּי אֱלִיעֶזֶר נַמִי – נֵילַף מֵאִמָּהוֹת! וְכִי תֵּימָא: אֵין דָּנִין אֶפְשָׁר מִשֶּׁאִי אֶפְשָׁר –

The Gemara questions the opinions in the *baraita*: **But let Rabbi Yehoshua also derive** what is required for conversion **from** our **forefathers;** why didn't he do so? **And let Rabbi Eliezer also derive** the *halakha* **from** our **foremothers;** why didn't he do so? **And if you would say** that Rabbi Eliezer did not derive the *halakha* from our foremothers because he holds **one cannot derive** the **possible from** the **impossible,** i.e., one cannot derive that men do not require circumcision from the *halakha* that women do not require it, because for women it is a physical impossibility, that claim may be refuted.

וְהָתַנְיָא, רַבִּי אֱלִיעֶזֶר אוֹמֵר: מִנַּיִן לְפֶסַח דּוֹרוֹת שֶׁאֵין בָּא אֶלָּא מִן הַחוּלִּין – נֶאֱמַר פֶּסַח בְּמִצְרַיִם וְנֶאֱמַר פֶּסַח בְּדוֹרוֹת, מַה פֶּסַח הָאָמוּר בְּמִצְרַיִם – אֵין בָּא אֶלָּא מִן הַחוּלִּין, אַף פֶּסַח הָאָמוּר לְדוֹרוֹת – אֵין בָּא אֶלָּא מִן הַחוּלִּין.

It would appear that Rabbi Eliezer does not accept that principle, as **isn't it taught** in a *baraita* that **Rabbi Eliezer says: From where** is it derived with regard **to the Paschal lamb** brought throughout the **generations that it may be brought only from non-sacred** animals?[H] **A Paschal lamb is stated** in the Torah **in** reference to the lamb that the Jewish people brought prior to the exodus from **Egypt, and a Paschal lamb is stated in** reference to the yearly obligation throughout the **generations.** The association between them teaches that **just as the Paschal lamb stated in** reference to **Egypt was only brought from non-sacred** animals, since prior to the giving of the Torah there was no possibility to consecrate property, **so too,** with regard to **the Paschal lamb stated** in reference **to** the obligation throughout the **generations, it may be brought only from non-sacred** animals.

NOTES

Food cooked by gentiles – בִּישׁוּלֵי גּוֹיִם: The prohibition against eating foods cooked by gentiles does not stem from concern that some forbidden foods might have been mixed in. Rather, it is an independent rabbinic decree, issued by the Sages, to prevent Jews from intermingling with gentiles. It is for this reason that the prohibition is limited to items of significance, i.e., those that would appear on a king's table, and for which the act of cooking was significant, i.e., the food would not be eaten raw. In such cases, the fact that the gentile provided such foods to the Jews demonstrates a level of devotion and honor that could lead to an undesirable closeness between them.

Because they were not well versed in Torah – שֶׁאֵינָן בְּנֵי תּוֹרָה: This justification for a stringent ruling is offered in several places in the Talmud. It is used in places in which the correct practice requires a nuanced understanding of the *halakha* and the ability to distinguish between permitted practices and similar prohibited ones. In places in which Torah scholars lived, the Sages were lenient based on the assumption that they would know how to maintain the appropriate halakhic distinctions.

Circumcision of our forefathers – מִילָה בַּאֲבוֹתֵינוּ: Although the Torah does not explicitly record the fact that the children of Israel were circumcised prior to the revelation at Sinai, this may be inferred in several ways. The simplest way, suggested by the Rambam, is that they must have circumcised themselves before leaving Egypt in preparation for the Paschal lamb that they brought there, since there is an explicit Torah prohibition prohibiting an uncircumcised male from partaking of the Paschal lamb. Since that circumcision was performed for the sake of observing a mitzva, it was also valid as a preparation for the national conversion that was effected by the revelation at Sinai (see also Ramban).

HALAKHA

Food cooked by gentiles – בִּישׁוּלֵי גּוֹיִם: Any food item that is not eaten raw and appears on the table of kings in order to eat bread with it is subject to the rabbinic prohibition of food cooked by gentiles. This prohibition applies even to food cooked by a gentile in a Jew's house with his utensils. Most commentaries rule that a food is subject to the prohibition only if both the above stated conditions are fulfilled (Rambam *Sefer Kedusha, Hilkhot Ma'akhalot Assurot* 17:14; *Shulḥan Arukh, Yoreh De'a* 113:1).

The Paschal lamb…is brought…from non-sacred animals – פֶּסַח...בָּא...מִן הַחוּלִּין: All offerings brought by an individual, including the Paschal lamb, may be brought only from non-sacred animals (Rambam *Sefer Kedusha, Hilkhot Ma'aseh HaKorbanot* 16:15).

אמר ליה רבי עקיבא: וכי דנין אפשר משאי אפשר? אמר ליה: אף על פי שאי אפשר – ראיה גדולה היא, ונלמד הימנה.

Rabbi Akiva said to him: But can one derive the **possible,** i.e., the *halakha* for the Paschal lamb throughout the generations, where a possibility exists to bring it from consecrated animals, **from** the **impossible,**[N] i.e., from the Paschal lamb in Egypt, where it was not a possibility? Rabbi Eliezer **said to him: Although it was impossible** to bring the Paschal lamb in Egypt from consecrated animals, nevertheless, **it is** still **a great proof, and we may learn from it.** It is apparent, then, that Rabbi Eliezer holds that one can derive the possible from the impossible. Therefore the original question stands: Why didn't Rabbi Eliezer derive from the foremothers that circumcision is not essential for conversion?

אלא

The Gemara concedes: **Rather,** the *baraita* must be reinterpreted as follows:

Perek **IV**
Daf **46** Amud **b**

בטבל ולא מל – כולי עלמא לא פליגי דמהני. כי פליגי – במל ולא טבל. רבי אליעזר יליף מאבות, ורבי יהושע: באבות נמי טבילה הוה.

With regard to one who immersed but was not circumcised, everyone, i.e., both Rabbi Yehoshua and Rabbi Eliezer, **agrees that** the *halakha* is derived from the foremothers that immersion alone **is effective. Where they disagree** is **with regard to one who was circumcised but had not immersed; Rabbi Eliezer derives** that it is effective **from the forefathers, and Rabbi Yehoshua** disagrees because he maintains that **in** the conversion of the **forefathers there was also an immersion.**

מנא ליה? אילימא מדכתיב "לך אל העם וקדשתם היום ומחר וכבסו שמלתם", ומה במקום שאין טעון כבוס – טעון טבילה, מקום שטעון כבוס – אינו דין שטעון טבילה?

The Gemara asks: **From where did he** derive this? **If we say** that he derived it **from** the fact **that it is written** that in preparation for the revelation at Sinai, God commanded Moses: **"Go unto the people and sanctify them today and tomorrow, and let them wash their garments"** (Exodus 19:10), as Rabbi Yehoshua understands that the washing mentioned in this verse is the ritual immersion of clothes, this leads to the following *a fortiori* inference: **Just as in a case where** one became impure through contact with some source of impurity, **washing,** i.e., immersion, of clothes **is not required** but **immersion** of one's body **is required,** then **in a case where washing** of clothes **is required,** as in the preparation for the revelation at Sinai, **isn't it logical that immersion** of one's body **should** also **be required?**

ודלמא נקיות בעלמא?

The Gemara rejects the proof: **But perhaps** when the verse states that they had to wash their clothes, it was **merely for cleanliness** and not for the sake of ritual purity. If so, no *a fortiori* inference can be drawn from it to the case of immersion for ritual purity.

אלא מהכא: "ויקח משה את הדם ויזרק על העם" וגמירי דאין הזאה בלא טבילה.

Rather, Rabbi Yehoshua derived it **from here,** where the verse states with regard to the formation of the covenant at Sinai: **"And Moses took the blood**[N] **and sprinkled it upon the people"** (Exodus 24:8), **and it is learned** as a tradition **that there is no** ritual **sprinkling without immersion.** Therefore, our forefathers also must have immersed at Sinai, and consequently that is also an essential requirement for all conversions.

NOTES

The possible from the impossible – אפשר משאי אפשר: This issue is present in every system of logical thought with regard to logical constructs that are based on inductive reasoning. In fact, in certain areas of mathematics there are proofs based on inducing the possible from the impossible.

NOTES

And Moses took the blood, etc. – ויקח משה את הדם וגו׳: The commentaries note that Onkelos translates this verse as: Moses took the blood and sprinkled it upon the altar to atone for the people, which explicitly assumes that the sprinkling of the blood was not upon the people but upon the altar. Rabbi Eliezer of Metz explains that the Gemara here differs with Onkelos on this matter. However, *Tosafot Yeshanim* suggests that Onkelos's translation might be in accordance with the opinion of Rabbi Eliezer, who does not accept the opinion of Rabbi Yehoshua and could therefore interpret the verse differently. Indeed, Maharatz Ḥayyut notes that elsewhere the Gemara explicitly states that Onkelos's translation is always in accordance with the opinions of Rabbi Eliezer and Rabbi Yehoshua, and if so, it makes sense that it renders the verse here according to one of them. If Rabbi Eliezer does not interpret the verse as Onkelos does, he could explain that it is referring to an act of sprinkling that took place after the giving of the Ten Commandments, as is suggested by the sequence of the verses in the Torah.

וְרַבִּי יְהוֹשֻׁעַ, טְבִילָה בָּאִמָּהוֹת מְנָלַן? סְבָרָא הוּא, דְּאִם כֵּן – בַּמֶּה נִכְנְסוּ תַּחַת כַּנְפֵי הַשְּׁכִינָה?

The Gemara asks: **And** with regard to the opinion of **Rabbi Yehoshua, from where do we** derive that also **in** the case of our **foremothers** there was **immersion?**[N] The Gemara answers: **It is** based on **logical reasoning, as, if so,** that they did not immerse, then **with what were they brought**[N] **under the wings of the Divine Presence?** Therefore, they also must have immersed.

אָמַר רַבִּי חִיָּיא בַּר אַבָּא אָמַר רַבִּי יוֹחָנָן: לְעוֹלָם אֵינוֹ גֵּר עַד שֶׁיָּמוֹל וְיִטְבּוֹל. פְּשִׁיטָא, יָחִיד וְרַבִּים הֲלָכָה כְּרַבִּים!

Rabbi Ḥiyya bar Abba said that **Rabbi Yoḥanan said:** A man is **never** considered a **convert until he is** both **circumcised and has immersed.** The Gemara asks: **Isn't this obvious?** In all disputes between **an individual** Sage **and many** Sages the *halakha* **is in accordance with** the opinion of **the many** Sages; it is therefore obvious that the *halakha* is in accordance with the Rabbis.

מַאן חֲכָמִים – רַבִּי יוֹסֵי.

The Gemara explains: **Who are the Rabbis** referred to in the *baraita*? It is **Rabbi Yosei.** Since Rabbi Yosei is merely an individual Sage, it was necessarily for Rabbi Yoḥanan to state explicitly that the *halakha* is ruled in accordance with his opinion.

דְּתַנְיָא: הֲרֵי שֶׁבָּא וְאָמַר מַלְתִּי וְלֹא טָבַלְתִּי – מַטְבִּילִין אוֹתוֹ, וּמַה בְּכָךְ, דִּבְרֵי רַבִּי יְהוּדָה. רַבִּי יוֹסֵי אוֹמֵר: אֵין מַטְבִּילִין.

Rabbi Yosei's opinion is **as it is taught** in a *baraita*: With regard to a convert **who came and said: I was circumcised** for the sake of conversion **but I did not immerse,** the court **should immerse him,** as **what** would be the problem **with that;** this is **the statement of Rabbi Yehuda.** Since in any case the court immerses him, Rabbi Yehuda does not require proof of the convert's claim that he was circumcised for the sake of conversion because he holds that it is sufficient to be either circumcised or immersed for the sake of conversion. **Rabbi Yosei says:** The court **does not immerse** him. He holds that both circumcision and immersion must be performed specifically for the sake of conversion and are indispensable parts of the conversion process. Therefore, since it is impossible to verify the convert's claim with regard to his circumcision, there is no benefit to having him immerse.

לְפִיכָךְ מַטְבִּילִין גֵּר בְּשַׁבָּת, דִּבְרֵי רַבִּי יְהוּדָה. וְרַבִּי יוֹסֵי אוֹמֵר: אֵין מַטְבִּילִין.

The *baraita* states a ramification of their dispute: **Therefore,** the court **may immerse a convert** who was already circumcised **on Shabbat;** this is **the statement of Rabbi Yehuda.** Since he holds that circumcision alone effected conversion, the immersion will not effect any further change in his status, and so it is permitted on Shabbat. **And Rabbi Yosei says:** The court **may not immerse** him.[NH] Since he holds that both circumcision and immersion are necessary to effect a conversion, the immersion will effect a change in his status by making him Jewish. Therefore it is prohibited to do so on Shabbat by rabbinic decree, because it appears similar to preparing a vessel for use.

אָמַר מָר: לְפִיכָךְ מַטְבִּילִין גֵּר בְּשַׁבָּת, פְּשִׁיטָא, כֵּיוָן דְּאָמַר רַבִּי יְהוּדָה בַּחֲדָא סַגְיָא, הֵיכָא דְּמָל לְפָנֵינוּ – מַטְבִּילִין, מַאי לְפִיכָךְ?

The Gemara analyzes the latter clause: **The Master said** in the *baraita*: **Therefore,** the court **may immerse a convert** who was already circumcised **on Shabbat.** The Gemara asks: **Isn't** this an **obvious** extension of his opinion; **since Rabbi Yehuda said that** either **one** of circumcision or immersion **is sufficient, where** a convert **was circumcised in our presence** the court may certainly **immerse** him, even on Shabbat. **What,** then, is the need for the *baraita* to include the clause that begins with: **Therefore?**

מַהוּ דְּתֵימָא: לְרַבִּי יְהוּדָה טְבִילָה עִיקָּר, וּטְבִילָה בְּשַׁבָּת – לָא, דְּקָא מְתַקֵּן גַּבְרָא, קָא מַשְׁמַע לָן דְּרַבִּי יְהוּדָה אוֹ הָא אוֹ הָא בָּעֵי.

The Gemara explains: It is necessary to explicitly teach this ramification **lest you say** that **according to Rabbi Yehuda the immersion is** in fact **the principal** act that effects conversion, and when he said in the first clause that a convert who claims to have been circumcised should be immersed since there is no problem with that, his reasoning was that he holds it is only immersion that effects the conversion. **And** therefore performing the **immersion on Shabbat** would **not** be permitted, **as it establishes the person** with a new status and so would be prohibited by a rabbinic decree because it appears similar to preparing a vessel for use. The latter clause is therefore necessary to **teach us that Rabbi Yehuda requires either this or that,** i.e., either immersion or circumcision alone is sufficient to effect a conversion.

NOTES

Immersion of the foremothers – טְבִילָה בָּאִמָּהוֹת: The Gemara here is clearly referring to the women who were present at the revelation at Sinai as our foremothers. The Ritva questions the propriety of referring to them as such when the Gemara elsewhere states decisively that only four women are privileged with this title: Sarah, Rebecca, Rachel, and Leah. To resolve this difficulty, the Ritva suggests that the restrictions on the title foremother are limited to its use in prayer. Another resolution is suggested by the *Ahavat Eitan*, who suggests that since the Gemara here is referring to the entire generation and not to any specific individuals, it is acceptable to refer to them as foremothers. The Meiri cites a novel interpretation that the Gemara here is actually referring to the original four Matriarchs. This interpretation assumes that the three Patriarchs and four Matriarchs all required some act of conversion to become the forebearers of the Jewish people. The Patriarchs underwent circumcision, whereas the Matriarchs immersed.

As, if so, with what were they brought – דְּאִם כֵּן בַּמֶּה נִכְנְסוּ: The Rashba asks why the Gemara does not consider the possibility that the sprinkling of blood upon them is what effected their conversion. He answers that even if one were to claim that the sprinkling of the blood was part of the process, one cannot escape the conclusion that there was an immersion, since there is no ritual sprinkling without immersion, and therefore it is reasonable to assume that the immersion itself is part of the process of conversion. Furthermore, it is not certain that the blood was actually sprinkled upon the women; perhaps it was only sprinkled upon the men (see *Tosafot*). In fact, *Tosafot Yeshanim* explain the phrase "upon the people" as excluding the women.

Ultimately, the *halakha* is ruled in accordance with the understanding that the sprinkling was upon both men and women. There is therefore general agreement that full conversion actually involves four requirements: Acceptance of the mitzvot, circumcision, immersion, and sacrifice of a bird as a burnt-offering. The requirement to sacrifice an offering parallels the sprinkling of the blood at Sinai. Nowadays, when it is no longer possible to bring offerings, the conversion is considered valid even without it, as is explained in *Karetot* (9a) and elsewhere.

The court may not immerse a convert on Shabbat – אֵין מַטְבִּילִין גֵּר בְּשַׁבָּת: This ruling stands in contradistinction to the *halakha* that one may immerse on Shabbat in order to purify himself from a state of ritual impurity. Various distinctions have been offered between the two cases: *Tosafot* explain that immersing in order to purify oneself from a state of ritual impurity is a private matter. However, a conversion is performed in the presence of three judges and is therefore considered a public event. Since it is performed in public, the Sages prohibited it since it might appear in the eyes of the public to be similar to preparing a vessel for use. *Tosafot Yeshanim* suggest that immersing in order to purify oneself from a state of ritual impurity is permitted because the change in status is considered minor and is therefore not considered similar to preparing a vessel for use. However, the change effected by conversion is significant and is therefore prohibited. According to the Rambam, the question does not even arise. The Rambam explains that the reason to prohibit the immersion is not because it might resemble preparing a vessel for use but because presiding over conversion is considered to be an act of judgment and it is prohibited for a court to issue judgments on Shabbat.

HALAKHA

Immersion of a convert on Shabbat – טְבִילַת גֵּר בְּשַׁבָּת: Since the immersion of a convert is an act of judgment performed by the court, a convert may not be immersed on Shabbat or on a Festival. Nevertheless, if he does immerse, he is thereby rendered a convert (Rambam *Sefer Kedusha, Hilkhot Issurei Bia* 13:6; *Shulḥan Arukh, Yoreh De'a* 268:4).

רַבִּי יוֹסֵי אוֹמֵר אֵין מַטְבִּילִין. פְּשִׁיטָא, דְּכֵיוָן דְּאָמַר רַבִּי יוֹסֵי תַּרְתֵּי בָּעֵינַן – הַקּוֹנֵי גַּבְרָא בְּשַׁבָּת לָא מְתַקְּנִינַן!

The Gemara analyzes the next statement in the *baraita*: **Rabbi Yosei says:** The court **may not immerse** him. The Gemara asks: **Isn't** this an **obvious** extension of his opinion? **As, since Rabbi Yosei requires two** acts, both circumcision and immersion, to effect conversion, **we may** certainly **not establish** that **person** with a new status **on Shabbat** by completing his conversion by immersing him.

מַהוּ דְּתֵימָא: לְרַבִּי יוֹסֵי מִילָה עִיקָּר, וְהָתָם הוּא דְּלָא הֲוַאי מִילָה בְּפָנֵינוּ, אֲבָל הֵיכָא דַּהֲוָיָא מִילָה בְּפָנֵינוּ – אֵימָא לִיטְבּוֹל זֶה בְּשַׁבְּתָא, קָא מַשְׁמַע לָן דְּרַבִּי יוֹסֵי תַּרְתֵּי בָּעֵי.

The Gemara explains: It is necessary to explicitly teach this ramification **lest you say** that **according to Rabbi Yosei circumcision is** in fact **the principal** act that effects conversion, **and** it is only **there,** in the first clause of the *baraita,* **where the circumcision was not performed in our presence** and so there is no way to verify whether it was done for the sake of conversion, that Rabbi Yosei states that the court should not proceed to immerse him; **however, where the circumcision was performed in our presence,** one might **say** that the conversion was already effected by the circumcision, and therefore **let us immerse this** convert **on Shabbat.** The latter clause is therefore necessary to **teach us that Rabbi Yosei requires two** acts, both circumcision and immersion, to effect conversion.

אֲמַר רַבָּה: עוּבְדָּא הֲוָה בֵּי רַבִּי חִיָּיא בַּר רַבִּי, וְרַב יוֹסֵף מַתְנֵי רַבִּי אוֹשַׁעְיָא בַּר רַבִּי, וְרַב סָפְרָא מַתְנֵי רַבִּי אוֹשַׁעְיָא בְּרַבִּי חִיָּיא, דַּאֲתָא לְקַמֵּיהּ גֵּר שֶׁמָּל וְלֹא טָבַל. אָמַר לֵיהּ שְׁהֵי כָּאן עַד לְמָחָר וְנַטְבִּילְךָ.

Rabba said: There was an incident in the house of Rabbi Ḥiyya bar Rabbi, and as **Rav Yosef teaches** it, **Rabbi Oshaya bar Rabbi** was also present, **and** as **Rav Safra teaches** it, a third Sage, **Rabbi Oshaya, son of Rabbi Ḥiyya,** was also present, **in which a convert came before him who was circumcised but had not immersed. He said to** the convert: **Remain here** with us **until tomorrow,** and then **we will immerse you.**

שְׁמַע מִינָּהּ תְּלָת: שְׁמַע מִינָּהּ גֵּר צָרִיךְ שְׁלֹשָׁה, וּשְׁמַע מִינָּהּ: אֵינוֹ גֵּר עַד שֶׁיִּמּוֹל וְיִטְבּוֹל, וּשְׁמַע מִינָּהּ: אֵין מַטְבִּילִין גֵּר בַּלַּיְלָה. וְנֵימָא: שְׁמַע מִינָּהּ נַמִּי בָּעֵינַן מוּמְחִין! דִּלְמָא דְּאִיקְּלְעוּ.

Rabba said: **Learn from** this incident **three** principles: **Learn from it** that **a convert requires** a court of **three**[N] people to preside over the conversion, as Rav Safra taught that the case involved three Sages. **And learn from it** that **one is not** considered to be a **convert until he has been** both **circumcised and immersed. And learn from it** that the court **may not immerse a convert at night,** as they instructed him to remain there until the following day. The Gemara suggests: **And let us say** that one should **also learn from it** that **we require** a court of **experts** to preside over the conversion, as Rav Safra identified that three expert Sages were present. The Gemara rejects this: **Perhaps they** simply **happened to be** there, but in fact three laymen would suffice.

אָמַר רַבִּי חִיָּיא בַּר אַבָּא אָמַר רַבִּי יוֹחָנָן: גֵּר צָרִיךְ שְׁלֹשָׁה "מִשְׁפָּט" כְּתִיב בֵּיהּ.

Rabbi Ḥiyya bar Abba said that **Rabbi Yoḥanan said: A convert requires** a court of **three** to preside over conversion, because **"judgment," is written with regard to him,** as the verse states: "And one judgment shall be both for you and for the convert that sojourns with you" (Numbers 15:16), and legal judgments require a court of three judges.[H]

תָּנוּ רַבָּנַן: מִי שֶׁבָּא וְאָמַר: "גֵּר אֲנִי", יָכוֹל נְקַבְּלֶנּוּ – תַּלְמוּד לוֹמַר "אִתְּךָ" – בְּמוּחְזָק לָךְ. בָּא וְעֵדָיו עִמּוֹ מִנַּיִן – תַּלְמוּד לוֹמַר "וְכִי יָגוּר אִתְּךָ גֵּר בְּאַרְצְכֶם".

The Sages taught in a *baraita*: With regard to **someone who came and said: I am a convert,**[N] one **might** have thought that **we should accept him;** therefore, **the verse states:** "And if a convert sojourns **with you** in your land, you shall not oppress him" (Leviticus 19:33). The emphasis on "with you" suggests that only someone who was already **presumed by you** to be a valid convert should be accepted as a convert. If **he came and** brought **witnesses** to his conversion **with him, from where** is it derived that he is to be accepted? It is from **the** beginning of that **verse,** which **states: "And if a convert sojourns with you in your land."**

NOTES

A convert requires three – גֵּר צָרִיךְ שְׁלֹשָׁה: The commentaries explain that this is derived from the fact that Rav Safra taught that the case involved three Sages. *Tosafot* explain that this must certainly have been Rav Safra's intention because the third scholar mentioned was not of the same caliber as the first two, and therefore it does not stand to reason that he would name him together with them unless his intention was to teach the need for a court of three. Furthermore, some note that Rav Yosef and Rav Safra would not have been particular to mention the names of the additional Sages who were present just so that the record of events would be more accurate. Rather, they clearly sought to teach a ruling by doing so. This is also suggested by the Gemara's formulation: And Rav Yosef taught, which indicates that he was adding to the statement of Rabba and was not in dispute with him (*Ramat Shmuel*).

Someone who came and said: I am a convert – מִי שֶׁבָּא וְאָמַר: גֵּר אֲנִי: This discussion applies only to one who is known to have been a gentile. If he had not been known originally as a gentile he would be accepted even without proof that he had converted, because he could just as easily have passed himself off as a Jew (Rabbeinu Tam; Ramban; Rashba), or because it is a fact that could easily be verified later and therefore it can be assumed he would not lie about it (Ritva). However, the Rambam writes that this applies only in Eretz Yisrael, whereas elsewhere a convert should never be accepted based on his own testimony without witnesses (Rambam *Sefer Kedusha, Hilkhot Issurei Bia* 13:10).

HALAKHA

Conversion in a court – גִּיּוּר בְּבֵית דִּין: One is considered to be a convert only after he accepts upon himself the yoke of mitzvot, undergoes circumcision, and immerses in a ritual bath. These acts must be performed before three individuals suitable for sitting in judgment and must be done during the day. After the fact, if one immersed at night, the conversion is still valid (Rambam *Sefer Kedusha, Hilkhot Issurei Bia* 13:6; *Shulḥan Arukh, Yoreh De'a* 268:3).

NOTES

I have derived only that a convert is accepted in Eretz Yisrael – אֵין לִי אֶלָּא בָּאָרֶץ: *Tosafot* explain that the Gemara here considers the possibility that conversion would be possible only in Eretz Yisrael. *Tosefot HaRosh* suggests a rationale for such an opinion. In Eretz Yisrael a convert stands to gain from the bounty of the land and the other benefits of living there. Therefore, it is less likely that a convert would revert back to his previous ways if he lives in Eretz Yisrael than if he lives elsewhere. Due to the concern that exists with a convert outside Eretz Yisrael, it is conceivable that the possibility of converting there is entirely precluded.

HALAKHA

One who comes and says: I converted – מִי שֶׁבָּא וְאָמַר נִתְגַּיַּירְתִּי: If one presumed to be a gentile comes and claims to have converted in accordance with the *halakhot* of conversion, whether in Eretz Yisrael or outside Eretz Yisrael, he is not accepted as a convert and may not marry in the congregation of Israel until he brings witnesses to his conversion. This ruling is in accordance with the opinion of the Rabbis (Rambam *Sefer Kedusha*, *Hilkhot Issurei Bia* 13:7; *Shulḥan Arukh*, *Yoreh De'a* 268:10).

אֵין לִי אֶלָּא בָּאָרֶץ, בְּחוּץ לָאָרֶץ מִנַּיִן? תַּלְמוּד לוֹמַר ״אִתְּךָ״ – בְּכָל מָקוֹם שֶׁאִתְּךָ. אִם כֵּן מַה תַּלְמוּד לוֹמַר ״בָּאָרֶץ״ – בָּאָרֶץ צָרִיךְ לְהָבִיא רְאָיָה, בְּחוּץ לָאָרֶץ – אֵין צָרִיךְ לְהָבִיא רְאָיָה. דִּבְרֵי רַבִּי יְהוּדָה. וַחֲכָמִים אוֹמְרִים: בֵּין בָּאָרֶץ בֵּין בְּחוּצָה לָאָרֶץ – צָרִיךְ לְהָבִיא רְאָיָה.

I have derived **only** that a convert is accepted **in Eretz** Yisrael;[N] **from where** do I derive that also **outside** of Eretz Yisrael he is to be accepted? **The verse states "with you,"** which indicates that **in any place that he is with you**, you should accept him. **If so, what** is the meaning when **the verse states: In the land?** This indicates that **in** Eretz Yisrael **he needs to bring evidence** that he is a convert, **but outside** of Eretz Yisrael **he does not need to bring evidence** that he is a convert; rather, his claim is accepted. This is **the statement of Rabbi Yehuda. And the Rabbis say: Whether** he is **in Eretz** Yisrael **or whether** he is **outside** of **Eretz** Yisrael, **he needs to bring evidence.**

בָּא הוּא וְעֵדָיו עִמּוֹ – קְרָא לָמָּה לִי? אָמַר רַב שֵׁשֶׁת, דְּאָמְרִי: שָׁמַעְנוּ שֶׁנִּתְגַּיֵּיר בְּבֵית דִּין שֶׁל פְּלוֹנִי. סָלְקָא דַּעְתָּךְ אָמִינָא: לָא לֵיהֵמְנַיְיהוּ, קָא מַשְׁמַע לָן.

The Gemara analyzes the *baraita*: In the case when **he came** and brought **witnesses** to his conversion **with him, why do I need a verse** to teach that he is accepted? In all cases, the testimony of witnesses is fully relied upon. **Rav Sheshet said:** The case is **where they say: We heard that he converted in** the **court of so-and-so,** but they did not witness the actual conversion. And it is necessary to teach this because it could **enter your mind to say** that **they should not be relied upon;** therefore, the verse **teaches us** that they are relied upon.

״בָּאָרֶץ״, אֵין לִי אֶלָּא בָּאָרֶץ, בְּחוּצָה לָאָרֶץ מִנַּיִן? תַּלְמוּד לוֹמַר ״אִתְּךָ״ – בְּכָל מָקוֹם שֶׁאִתְּךָ. וְהָא אַפִּיקְתֵּיהּ! חֲדָא מֵ״אִתְּךָ״ וַחֲדָא מֵ״עִמָּךְ״.

As cited above, the latter clause of the *baraita* states: "With you **in** your **land**" (Leviticus 19:33). **I have** derived **only** that a convert is accepted **in Eretz** Yisrael; **from where** do I derive that also **outside** of Eretz Yisrael he is to be accepted? **The verse states: "With you,"** which indicates that **in any place that he is with you**, you should accept him. The Gemara asks: **But didn't you** already **expound that** phrase in the first clause of the *baraita* to teach that one doesn't accept the claims of an individual that he is a valid convert? The Gemara explains: **One** of these *halakhot* is derived **from** the phrase **"with you"** in the verse cited, **and the other one** is derived **from** the phrase **"with you"** in a subsequent verse (Leviticus 25:35).

וַחֲכָמִים אוֹמְרִים: בֵּין בָּאָרֶץ בֵּין בְּחוּצָה לָאָרֶץ צָרִיךְ לְהָבִיא רְאָיָה. וְאֶלָּא, הָא כְּתִיב ״בָּאָרֶץ״!

The *baraita* states: **And the Rabbis say: Whether** he is **in Eretz** Yisrael **or whether** he is **outside** of **Eretz Yisrael, he needs to bring evidence.** The Gemara asks: **But isn't "in your land" written** in the verse? How can the Rabbis deny any distinction between the *halakha* inside and outside of Eretz Yisrael?

הַהוּא מִיבָּעֵי לֵיהּ דַּאֲפִילּוּ בָּאָרֶץ מְקַבְּלִים גֵּרִים. דְּסָלְקָא דַּעְתָּךְ אָמִינָא: מִשּׁוּם טִיבוּתָא דְּאֶרֶץ יִשְׂרָאֵל קָמִגַּיְּירִי, וְהָשְׁתָּא נַמִי דְּלֵיכָּא טִיבוּתָא – אִיכָּא לֶקֶט שִׁכְחָה וּפֵאָה וּמַעְשַׂר עָנִי, קָא מַשְׁמַע לָן.

The Gemara explains: **That** phrase **is necessary** to teach **that even in Eretz** Yisrael, the Jewish people should **accept converts, as it could enter your mind to say** that it is only **for the sake of** benefiting from **the goodness of Eretz Yisrael**, and not for the sake of Heaven, that **they are converting,** and therefore they should not be accepted. **And** it could also enter your mind to say that even **nowadays, when** God's blessing has ceased and **there is no** longer **the** original **goodness** from which to benefit, one should still suspect their purity of motives because **there are** the **gleanings,** the **forgotten sheaves, and** the **corners** of fields, **and the poor man's tithe** from which they would benefit by converting. Therefore, the verse **teaches us** that they are accepted even in Eretz Yisrael.

אָמַר רַבִּי חִיָּיא בַּר אַבָּא אָמַר רַבִּי יוֹחָנָן: הֲלָכָה, בֵּין בָּאָרֶץ בֵּין בְּחוּץ לָאָרֶץ – צָרִיךְ לְהָבִיא רְאָיָה. פְּשִׁיטָא, יָחִיד וְרַבִּים הֲלָכָה כְּרַבִּים! מַהוּ דְּתֵימָא: מִסְתַּבֵּר טַעֲמָא דְּרַבִּי יְהוּדָה, דְּקָמְסַיְּיעֵי לֵיהּ קְרָאֵי, קָא מַשְׁמַע לָן.

Rabbi Ḥiyya bar Abba said that **Rabbi Yoḥanan said:** The *halakha* is that **whether** a convert is **in Eretz** Yisrael **or whether** he is **outside of Eretz** Yisrael, **he needs to bring evidence.**[H] The Gemara asks: **Isn't this obvious;** in all disputes between **an individual** Sage **and many** Sages the *halakha* **is in accordance with** the opinion of the **many** Sages. The Gemara explains: It is necessary to state this **lest you say** that **Rabbi Yehuda's reason** is more **logical, being that the verse supports him** when it states: "In your land." Therefore, it is necessary for Rabbi Yoḥanan to **teach us** that the *halakha* is not in accordance with his opinion.

תָּנוּ רַבָּנַן: ״וּשְׁפַטְתֶּם צֶדֶק בֵּין אִישׁ וּבֵין אָחִיו וּבֵין גֵּרוֹ״ מִכָּאן אָמַר רַבִּי יְהוּדָה: גֵּר שֶׁנִּתְגַּיֵּיר בְּבֵית דִּין – הֲרֵי זֶה גֵּר, בֵּינוֹ לְבֵין עַצְמוֹ – אֵינוֹ גֵּר.

The Sages taught: The verse states that Moses charged the judges of a court: **"And judge righteously between a man and his brother, and the convert with him"** (Deuteronomy 1:16). **From here,** based on the mention of a convert in the context of judgment in a court, **Rabbi Yehuda said:** A potential **convert who converts in a court is a valid convert.** However, if he converts **in private, he is not a convert.**

מַעֲשֶׂה בְּאֶחָד שֶׁבָּא לִפְנֵי רַבִּי יְהוּדָה, וְאָמַר לוֹ: נִתְגַּיַּירְתִּי בֵּינִי לְבֵין עַצְמִי. אָמַר לוֹ רַבִּי יְהוּדָה: יֵשׁ לְךָ עֵדִים? אֲמַר לֵיהּ: לָאו. יֵשׁ לְךָ בָּנִים? אֲמַר לֵיהּ: הֵין. אָמַר לוֹ: נֶאֱמָן אַתָּה לִפְסוֹל אֶת עַצְמְךָ, וְאִי אַתָּה נֶאֱמָן לִפְסוֹל אֶת בָּנֶיךָ.

The Gemara relates: There was **an incident involving one** who was presumed to be Jewish **who came before Rabbi Yehuda and said to him: I converted in private,** and therefore I am not actually Jewish. **Rabbi Yehuda said to him: Do you have witnesses**[N] to support your claim? **He said to him: No.** Rabbi Yehuda asked: Do **you have children? He said to him: Yes.** Rabbi Yehuda **said to him: You are deemed credible** in order **to render yourself unfit**[NH] to marry a Jewish woman by claiming that you are a gentile, **but you are not deemed credible** in order **to render your children unfit.**[N]

[וּמִי] אָמַר רַבִּי יְהוּדָה אַבָּנִים לָא מְהֵימַן? וְהָתַנְיָא: ״יַכִּיר״ – יַכִּירֶנּוּ לַאֲחֵרִים. מִכָּאן אָמַר רַבִּי יְהוּדָה: נֶאֱמָן אָדָם לוֹמַר: זֶה בְּנִי בְּכוֹר. וּכְשֵׁם שֶׁנֶּאֱמָן לוֹמַר זֶה בְּנִי בְּכוֹר כָּךְ נֶאֱמָן לוֹמַר: בְּנִי זֶה בֶּן גְּרוּשָׁה הוּא, אוֹ בֶּן חֲלוּצָה הוּא. וַחֲכָמִים אוֹמְרִים: אֵינוֹ נֶאֱמָן.

The Gemara asks: **But did Rabbi Yehuda** actually **say** that **with regard to** his **children he is not deemed credible? But isn't it taught** in a *baraita*: The verse states: **"He shall acknowledge** [*yakir*] the firstborn, the son of the hated, by giving him a double portion of all that he has" (Deuteronomy 21:17). The phrase "he shall acknowledge" is apparently superfluous. It is therefore expounded to teach that the father is deemed credible so that **he can identify him** [*yakirenu*] **to others. From here Rabbi Yehuda said: A man is deemed credible to say: This is my firstborn son,**[H] **and just as he is deemed credible to say: This is my firstborn son, so too,** a priest **is deemed credible to say: This son of mine is a son of a divorced woman** and myself, **or** to say: He is **a son of a *ḥalutza*** and myself, and therefore he is disqualified due to flawed lineage [*ḥalal*]. **And the Rabbis say: He is not deemed credible.**[H] If Rabbi Yehuda holds that a father is deemed credible to render his children unfit, why did he rule otherwise in the case of the convert?

אָמַר רַב נַחְמָן בַּר יִצְחָק, הָכִי קָאָמַר לֵיהּ: לְדִבְרֶיךָ גּוֹי אַתָּה, וְאֵין עֵדוּת לְגוֹי. רָבִינָא אָמַר: הָכִי קָאָמַר לֵיהּ: יֵשׁ לְךָ בָּנִים? הֵין, יֵשׁ לְךָ בְּנֵי בָּנִים? הֵין. אָמַר לֵיהּ: נֶאֱמָן אַתָּה לִפְסוֹל בָּנֶיךָ, וְאִי אַתָּה נֶאֱמָן לִפְסוֹל בְּנֵי בָּנֶיךָ.

Rav Naḥman bar Yitzḥak said that **this is what** Rabbi Yehuda **said to him: According to your statement you are a gentile, and there is no testimony for a gentile,** as a gentile is a disqualified witness. Consequently, you cannot testify about the status of your children and render them unfit. **Ravina said** that **this is what** Rabbi Yehuda **said to him:**[N] **Do you have children? He said: Yes. He said to him: Do you have grandchildren?** He said: **Yes. He said to him: You are deemed credible** in order **to render your children unfit,** based on the phrase "he shall acknowledge," **but you are not deemed credible** in order **to render your grandchildren unfit,**[N] as the verse affords a father credibility only with respect to his children.

HALAKHA

Deemed credible in order to render himself unfit, etc. – נֶאֱמָן לִפְסוֹל עַצְמוֹ וכו׳: With regard to one who was presumed to be Jewish who comes and says that he converted in private, he is deemed credible in order to render himself unfit and is therefore prohibited from marrying a Jewish woman until he converts in the presence of a court. If he has children, he is not deemed credible in order to render his children unfit. This is in accordance with the opinion of Rabbi Yehuda as explained by Rav Naḥman bar Yitzḥak (Rambam *Sefer Kedusha, Hilkhot Issurei Bia* 13:8; *Shulḥan Arukh, Yoreh De'a* 268:11).

He is deemed credible to say: This is my firstborn son – נֶאֱמָן אָדָם לוֹמַר: זֶה בְּנִי בְּכוֹר: A father is deemed credible to say concerning one of his sons, or even concerning someone who was presumed not to be his son at all, that he is in fact his firstborn son. He is likewise deemed credible to say that someone who was presumed to be his firstborn son is not actually his firstborn. The Rema writes that once a father has claimed that a certain person is his firstborn, he can no longer claim that someone else is (*Tur*, citing Ramban; *Beit Yosef*, citing Ran; Rambam *Sefer Mishpatim, Hilkhot Naḥalot* 2:14; *Shulḥan Arukh, Ḥoshen Mishpat* 277:12).

Credibility to render a son unfit – נֶאֱמָנוּת לִפְסוֹל בֵּן: A father is deemed credible to render his son unfit, e.g., if he were to say that the son of his wife is not actually his own son and is therefore a *mamzer*. This is true only if that son does not have any children. If the son does have children, then the father is not believed even with regard to his own son. This is in accordance with the opinion of Ravina. The Rema, citing the Ramah, writes that if the son was presumed to be legitimate based on the testimony of his father, then the father is no longer able to render him unfit. In addition, a man is deemed credible to render unfit only someone who was always presumed to be his son, e.g., the child born to his wife. Therefore, if a single woman announces that her son is actually the child of so-and-so, that man is not deemed credible to claim that the child is a *mamzer* (*Terumat HaDeshen*; Rambam *Sefer Kedusha, Hilkhot Issurei Bia* 15:16; *Shulḥan Arukh, Even HaEzer* 4:29).

NOTES

Do you have witnesses – יֵשׁ לְךָ עֵדִים: *Tosafot* ask how the convert could possibly have had witnesses if he had converted in private. *Tosefot HaRosh* explains that from here it is apparent that the need for a court of three to be present at the conversion is essential, and if three are not present, the conversion is invalid even after the fact. Accordingly, even if two witnesses were present, the conversion would still be defined as being in private. Other commentaries assume that a conversion can be valid even if performed in the presence of a single judge. If so, the question raised by *Tosafot* remains. One commentary suggests that Rav Yehuda's question was whether the individual had witnesses that he converted before he had children (*Yam shel Shlomo*). Alternatively, the Ra'avad suggests that it had previously been assumed that the individual here had always been a Jew. Rav Yehuda therefore asked him to provide witnesses that he was once a gentile (see Ramban and Rabbi Avraham min HaHar).

You are deemed credible in order to render yourself unfit – נֶאֱמָן אַתָּה לִפְסוֹל אֶת עַצְמְךָ: The commentaries explain that since the testimony about his children was inadmissible, none of it could be accepted. Rav Yehuda's ruling that the convert was able to render himself unfit is based on the principle that if one claims that an item or action is prohibited to him, he is thereafter obligated to relate to that item or action as though it were indeed prohibited, irrespective of whether that claim could have been accepted as testimony in court (see *Tosafot* and *Nimmukei Yosef*).

You are not deemed credible in order to render your children unfit – אִין אַתָּה נֶאֱמָן לִפְסוֹל אֶת בָּנֶיךָ: The early commentaries ask: Even if that man was deemed credible with regard to his children, why would that render them unfit, since the *halakha* is that the offspring of a gentile and a Jewish woman is a Jew of unflawed lineage? The commentaries note that it is insufficient to resolve this question by assuming that this statement in accordance with the opinions that the offspring of a gentile and a Jewish woman is unfit for the priesthood, because according to Rabbi Yehuda, even the daughter of a valid convert is unfit to marry into the priesthood (see *Tosafot*, Ra'avad as cited by Ramban, and Rashba). Some explain that Rabbi Yehuda holds in accordance with the opinion of Rabbi Akiva, which is not accepted as *halakha*, that the offspring of a gentile father is actually a *mamzer* (see *Tosafot* and Ramban). Others explain that the case here was that both parents were converts who testified that they had not converted properly, and therefore according to their claim the children were not actually Jewish (Ramban; see *Yam shel Shlomo*). One commentary suggests that the disqualification referred to here is not a halakhic one; rather, it refers to the harm caused to the children's name by virtue of the fact they would be considered to be the children of gentiles (Rabbi Avraham min HaHar).

Ravina said that this is what he said to him, etc. – רָבִינָא אָמַר: הָכִי קָאָמַר לֵיהּ וכו׳: Rav Naḥman bar Yitzhak and Ravina appear to disagree over whether or not a gentile is deemed credible to testify about his son. One commentary explains that their dispute concerns the essential nature of the unique credibility that is afforded to a father with respect to his son. Rav Naḥman bar Yitzhak holds that this credibility is an extension of the standard *halakhot* of testimony. Therefore, just as a gentile is disqualified from providing testimony in a standard case, he is also not deemed credible with respect to his son. Ravina holds that the credibility that is afforded to a father is a unique *halakha* that is not based on the standard *halakhot* of testimony. Accordingly, there is no reason that a gentile should be excluded (*Ḥiddushei Batra*).

You are not deemed credible in order to render your grandchildren unfit – וְאִי אַתָּה נֶאֱמָן לִפְסוֹל בְּנֵי בָנֶיךָ: Most commentaries follow the understanding of this statement suggested by *Tosafot*: Since he is not deemed credible with regard to his grandchildren, then if he has any grandchildren from the children he is testifying about he is not deemed credible with regard to those children either, because rendering his children unfit will perforce have an effect on the status of his grandchildren. In contrast, the *She'iltot deRav Aḥai Gaon* does differentiate between children and grandchildren. He explains that a father is given the unique ability to render his children unfit; however, his power is limited so that no ramifications of his claims will be passed down to affect his grandchildren.

תַּנְיָא נַמִּי הָכִי, רַבִּי יְהוּדָה אוֹמֵר: נֶאֱמָן אָדָם לוֹמַר עַל בְּנוֹ קָטָן, וְאֵין נֶאֱמָן עַל בְּנוֹ גָּדוֹל. וְאָמַר רַבִּי חִיָּיא בַּר אַבָּא אָמַר רַבִּי יוֹחָנָן: לֹא קָטָן קָטָן מַמָּשׁ, וְלֹא גָּדוֹל גָּדוֹל מַמָּשׁ, אֶלָּא, קָטָן וְיֵשׁ לוֹ בָּנִים – זֶהוּ גָּדוֹל, גָּדוֹל וְאֵין לוֹ בָּנִים – זֶהוּ קָטָן.

This opinion of Ravina **is also taught** in a *baraita*: **Rabbi Yehuda says: A man is deemed credible to say about his minor son** that he is unfit, **but he is not deemed credible to say about his adult son** that he is unfit. **And** in explanation of the *baraita*, **Rabbi Ḥiyya bar Abba said** that **Rabbi Yoḥanan said:** The reference to **a minor** son does **not** mean one who is **literally a minor,** who has not yet reached majority, **and** the reference to **an adult** son does **not** mean one who is **literally an adult,** who has reached majority; **rather, a minor who has children, this is** what the *baraita* is referring to as **an adult,** and **an adult who does not have children, this is** what the *baraita* is referring to as **a minor.**

וְהִלְכְתָא כְּוָותֵיהּ דְּרַב נַחְמָן בַּר יִצְחָק. וְהָתַנְיָא כְּוָותֵיהּ דְּרָבִינָא! הַהוּא לְעִנְיַן "יַכִּיר" אִיתְּמַר.

The Gemara concludes: **And the *halakha* is in accordance with** the opinion of **Rav Naḥman bar Yitzḥak.** The Gemara asks: **But isn't it taught** in the *baraita* **in accordance with** the opinion **of Ravina?** If there is a *baraita* that supports his opinion, the *halakha* should be in accordance with his opinion. The Gemara explains: **That** *baraita* **was stated concerning the matter of "he shall acknowledge,"** that a father is deemed credible to render his son unfit; however, if one claims he is a gentile, he is not deemed credible to say the same about his son.

תָּנוּ רַבָּנַן: גֵּר שֶׁבָּא לְהִתְגַּיֵּיר בַּזְּמַן הַזֶּה אוֹמְרִים לוֹ: מָה רָאִיתָ שֶׁבָּאתָ לְהִתְגַּיֵּיר? אִי אַתָּה יוֹדֵעַ שֶׁיִּשְׂרָאֵל בַּזְּמַן הַזֶּה דְּוּוּיִם, דְּחוּפִים, סְחוּפִים וּמְטוֹרָפִין, וְיִסּוּרִין בָּאִין עֲלֵיהֶם? אִם אוֹמֵר: יוֹדֵעַ אֲנִי וְאֵינִי כְּדַאי – מְקַבְּלִין אוֹתוֹ מִיָּד.

§ **The Sages taught** in a *baraita*: With regard to a potential **convert who comes to** a court in order to **convert, at the present time,** when the Jews are in exile, the judges of the court **say to him:**[H] **What did you see that** motivated **you to come to convert? Don't you know that the Jewish people at the present time are anguished, suppressed, despised, and harassed, and hardships are** frequently **visited upon them? If he says: I know, and** although **I am unworthy** of joining the Jewish people and sharing in their sorrow, I nevertheless desire to do so, then the court **accepts him immediately** to begin the conversion process.

וּמוֹדִיעִין אוֹתוֹ מִקְצָת מִצְוֹת קַלּוֹת, וּמִקְצָת מִצְוֹת חֲמוּרוֹת, וּמוֹדִיעִין אוֹתוֹ עֲוֹן לֶקֶט שִׁכְחָה וּפֵאָה וּמַעְשַׂר עָנִי, וּמוֹדִיעִין אוֹתוֹ עָנְשָׁן שֶׁל מִצְוֹת, אוֹמְרִים לוֹ: הֱוֵי יוֹדֵעַ שֶׁעַד שֶׁלֹּא בָּאתָ לְמִדָּה זוֹ, אָכַלְתָּ חֵלֶב – אִי אַתָּה עָנוּשׁ כָּרֵת, חִלַּלְתָּ שַׁבָּת – אִי אַתָּה עָנוּשׁ סְקִילָה. וְעַכְשָׁיו, אָכַלְתָּ חֵלֶב – עָנוּשׁ כָּרֵת, חִלַּלְתָּ שַׁבָּת – עָנוּשׁ סְקִילָה.

And the judges of the court **inform him of some of the lenient mitzvot**[N] **and some of the stringent mitzvot, and they inform him of the sin** of neglecting the mitzva to allow the poor to take **gleanings, forgotten sheaves, and** produce in the **corner** of one's field, **and** about the **poor man's tithe. And they inform him** of **the punishment** for transgressing **the mitzvot,** as follows: **They say to him: Be aware that before you came to this status** and converted, **had you eaten forbidden fat, you would not be punished by *karet*,** and **had you profaned Shabbat, you would not be punished by stoning,** since these prohibitions do not apply to gentiles. **But now,** once converted, **if you have eaten forbidden fat you are punished by *karet*,** and **if you have profaned Shabbat, you are punished by stoning.**

וּכְשֵׁם שֶׁמּוֹדִיעִין אוֹתוֹ עָנְשָׁן שֶׁל מִצְוֹת, כָּךְ מוֹדִיעִין אוֹתוֹ מַתַּן שְׂכָרָן. אוֹמְרִים לוֹ: הֱוֵי יוֹדֵעַ שֶׁהָעוֹלָם הַבָּא אֵינוֹ עָשׂוּי אֶלָּא לַצַּדִּיקִים, וְיִשְׂרָאֵל בַּזְּמַן הַזֶּה אֵינָם יְכוֹלִים לְקַבֵּל

And just as they inform him about the **punishment for** transgressing the **mitzvot, so too, they inform him** about the **reward granted for** fulfilling **them. They say to him: Be aware that the World-to-Come is made only for the righteous,** and if you observe the mitzvot you will merit it, **and** be aware that **the Jewish people, at the present time, are unable to receive** their full reward in this world;

HALAKHA

What is said to one who comes to convert – מָה אוֹמְרִים לַבָּא לְהִתְגַּיֵּיר: When a gentile comes to convert, the judges of the court say to him: For what reason do you seek to convert? Don't you know that the Jewish people are oppressed and suffer nowadays? If he accepts this upon himself, the court informs him of some of the lenient mitzvot and some of the stringent mitzvot, and informs him of the punishment for not observing the mitzvot. The judges should not overwhelm him, nor are they exacting with him, and they inform him of the reward given for performance of the mitzvot in the World-to-Come (Rambam *Sefer Kedusha, Hilkhot Issurei Bia* 13:14; *Shulḥan Arukh, Yoreh De'a* 268:2).

NOTES

Some of the lenient mitzvot – מִקְצָת מִצְוֹת קַלּוֹת: The Meiri explains that since the gentile system of law does not relate to less serious issues and does not demand a commitment to minutiae, it is necessary to teach him some of the more lenient mitzvot and thereby demonstrate that the halakhic system is all-encompassing and relates to every detail of life. If he is unable to commit to this, he is given the opportunity to withdraw.

לֹא רוֹב טוֹבָה וְלֹא רוֹב פּוּרְעָנוּת. וְאֵין מַרְבִּין עָלָיו, וְאֵין מְדַקְדְּקִין עָלָיו.

they are not able to receive either **an abundance of good nor an abundance of calamities,**[N] since the primary place for reward and punishment is in the World-to-Come. **And they do not overwhelm him** with threats, **and they are not exacting with him** about the details of the mitzvot.

קִיבֵּל – מָלִין אוֹתוֹ מִיָּד. נִשְׁתַּיְּירוּ בּוֹ צִיצִין הַמְעַכְּבִין אֶת הַמִּילָה – חוֹזְרִים וּמָלִין אוֹתוֹ שְׁנִיָּה. נִתְרַפֵּא – מַטְבִּילִין אוֹתוֹ מִיָּד. וּשְׁנֵי תַלְמִידֵי חֲכָמִים עוֹמְדִים עַל גַּבָּיו, וּמוֹדִיעִין אוֹתוֹ מִקְצָת מִצְוֹת קַלּוֹת וּמִקְצָת מִצְוֹת חֲמוּרוֹת. טָבַל וְעָלָה – הֲרֵי הוּא כְּיִשְׂרָאֵל לְכָל דְּבָרָיו.

If **he accepts** upon himself all of these ramifications, then **they circumcise him immediately.** If **there** still **remain on him shreds** of flesh from the foreskin **that invalidate the circumcision, they circumcise him again a second** time to remove them. When **he is healed** from the circumcision, **they immerse him**[N] **immediately,**[H] **and two Torah scholars stand over him** at the time of his immersion **and inform him of some of the lenient mitzvot and some of the stringent mitzvot.** Once **he has immersed and emerged, he is like** a born **Jew in every sense.**

אִשָּׁה – נָשִׁים מוֹשִׁיבוֹת אוֹתָהּ בַּמַּיִם עַד צַוָּארָהּ, וּשְׁנֵי תַלְמִידֵי חֲכָמִים עוֹמְדִים לָהּ מִבַּחוּץ, וּמוֹדִיעִין אוֹתָהּ מִקְצָת מִצְוֹת קַלּוֹת וּמִקְצָת מִצְוֹת חֲמוּרוֹת.

For the immersion of **a woman: Women** appointed by the court **seat her in the water** of the ritual bath **up to her neck, and two Torah scholars stand outside** the bath house so as not to compromise her modesty, **and** from there **they inform her of some of the lenient mitzvot and some of the stringent mitzvot.**

אֶחָד גֵּר וְאֶחָד עֶבֶד מְשׁוּחְרָר. וּבִמְקוֹם שֶׁנִּדָּה טוֹבֶלֶת – שָׁם גֵּר וְעֶבֶד מְשׁוּחְרָר טוֹבְלִין. וְכָל דָּבָר שֶׁחוֹצֵץ בִּטְבִילָה – חוֹצֵץ בְּגֵר וּבְעֶבֶד מְשׁוּחְרָר וּבְנִדָּה.

The procedure applies for **both a convert and an emancipated slave**[HN] who, upon immersion at the time of his emancipation, becomes a Jew in every sense. **And in the same place that a menstruating woman immerses,** i.e., in a ritual bath of forty *se'a* of water, **there a convert and an emancipated slave also immerse. And anything that interposes** between one's body and the water of the ritual bath **with regard to immersion**[N] of a ritually impure person, in a manner that would invalidate the immersion, also **interposes** and invalidates the immersion **for a convert, and for an emancipated slave, and for a menstruating woman.**

HALAKHA

Circumcision and immersion – מִילָה וּטְבִילָה: Once a convert has been made aware of the ramifications of conversion and he nevertheless commits to undergo the process, he is circumcised immediately. As soon as his wound heals, he is immersed to complete the process (Rambam *Sefer Kedusha, Hilkhot Issurei Bia* 14:5; *Shulḥan Arukh, Yoreh De'a* 268:2).

Immersion of a convert and an emancipated slave – טְבִילַת גֵּר וְעֶבֶד מְשׁוּחְרָר: A convert or an emancipated slave requires immersion in a ritual bath that is valid for the immersion of a menstruating woman. Any substance that is considered an interposition and would invalidate the immersion of a menstruating woman also invalidates the immersion of a convert or slave (Rambam *Sefer Kedusha, Hilkhot Issurei Bia* 13:13 and *Sefer Tahara, Hilkhot Mikvaot* 2:22; *Shulḥan Arukh, Yoreh De'a* 268:2).

NOTES

Nor an abundance of calamities – וְלֹא רוֹב פּוּרְעָנוּת: This is a continuation of the explanation with regard to the reception of reward for the performance of the mitzvot. Although the Jewish people suffer in exile, the calamities will never dominate to such an extent that the nation might cease to exist completely, as has occurred with other nations (Rabbi Avraham min HaHar).

When he is healed, they immerse him – נִתְרַפֵּא מַטְבִּילִין אוֹתוֹ: The Ramban asks why the convert does not first immerse and only then undergo circumcision; doing so would avoid the delay in the conversion process while the convert waits for his wound to heal. The Ramban suggests that since the circumcision is difficult and painful, the insistence that he perform it first provides another opportunity for him to withdraw from the process.

The basic assumption of the Ramban is that even if the immersion would precede the circumcision, the conversion would be valid. The Ramban adduces proof for this assumption that the order of the two rituals is not essential from the case of a pregnant convert. The Gemara elsewhere states that the immersion of a pregnant woman counts for her fetus as well. However, if the fetus is a male, it will require circumcision once it is born. It would appear, then, that even if the immersion precedes the circumcision the conversion is still valid.

The Rashba and the Ritva reject the Ramban's claim and dismiss his proof. They claim that the immersion must always be the final stage of the process. They bring an analogy to support their claim from the *halakha* of immersing vessels purchased from gentiles, which requires that the vessels first be purged of any non-kosher substances and only then may they be immersed.

With regard to the Ramban's proof, the commentaries suggest various alternative ways to interpret that Gemara. Some claim that the immersion can count for the fetus despite the fact it has not yet been circumcised only because at the time of the immersion the fetus was still unfit for circumcision (*Tosafot*). Others explain that the immersion is effective only according to the opinions that a fetus is halakhically considered to be an extension of the mother's body. Consequently, the immersion alone effects the fetus's conversion (Rid). Other commentaries claim that the immersion is valid for the fetus only if it emerges that the fetus was female, but if the fetus turns out to be male, once it is born it will require first circumcision and then immersion in the correct order (see Rashba).

Immersion of an emancipated slave – טְבִילַת עֶבֶד מְשׁוּחְרָר: The early commentaries debate whether the immersion of a slave upon his emancipation is required by Torah law and effects the full conversion of the slave, rendering him a Jew, or whether it is only a rabbinic requirement and in actual fact the conversion process was completed when he was initially immersed upon becoming a slave, and the emancipation is only to remove his slave status (see *Tosafot*, *Tosefot HaRosh*, and Meiri).

And anything that interposes with regard to immersion – וְכָל דָּבָר שֶׁחוֹצֵץ בִּטְבִילָה: Rashi explains that the Gemara compares the case of a ritually impure person immersing to purify himself to the case of conversion. The present version of the Gemara text supports this. However, other commentaries had a variant text in which the comparison is to the immersion of a woman who is ritually impure due to menstruation, who immerses in order to be permitted to her husband (see Ramban and Ritva).

אָמַר מָר: גֵּר שֶׁבָּא לְהִתְגַּיֵּיר אוֹמְרִים לוֹ: מָה רָאִיתָ שֶׁבָּאתָ לְהִתְגַּיֵּיר? וּמוֹדִיעִים אוֹתוֹ מִקְצָת מִצְוֹת קַלּוֹת וּמִקְצָת מִצְוֹת חֲמוּרוֹת. מַאי טַעְמָא? דְּאִי פָּרֵישׁ – נִפְרוֹשׁ. דְּאָמַר רַבִּי חֶלְבּוֹ: קָשִׁים גֵּרִים לְיִשְׂרָאֵל כְּסַפַּחַת, דִּכְתִיב ״וְנִלְוָה הַגֵּר עֲלֵיהֶם וְנִסְפְּחוּ עַל בֵּית יַעֲקֹב״.

The Gemara analyzes the *baraita*. **The Master said** in the *baraita*: With regard to a potential **convert who comes to** a court in order to **convert,** the judges of the court **say to him: What did you see that** motivated **you to come to convert? And they inform him of some of the lenient mitzvot and some of the stringent mitzvot.** The Gemara asks: **What is the reason** to say this to him? It is so **that if he** is going to **withdraw** from the conversion process, **let him withdraw** already at this stage. He should not be convinced to continue, **as Rabbi Ḥelbo said: Converts are as harmful to the Jewish people as a** leprous **scab** [*sappaḥat*][N] on the skin, **as it is written: "And the convert shall join himself with them, and they shall cleave** [*venispeḥu*] **to the house of Jacob"** (Isaiah 14:1). This alludes to the fact that the cleaving of the convert to the Jewish people is like a scab.

״וּמוֹדִיעִים אוֹתוֹ עֲוֹן לֶקֶט שִׁכְחָה וּפֵאָה וּמַעְשַׂר עָנִי״. מַאי טַעְמָא? אָמַר רַבִּי חִיָּיא בַּר אַבָּא אָמַר רַבִּי יוֹחָנָן: בֶּן נֹחַ נֶהֱרָג עַל פָּחוֹת מִשְׁוֵה פְּרוּטָה, וְלֹא נִיתָּן לְהִשָּׁבוֹן.

The *baraita* continues: **And they inform him of the sin** of neglecting the mitzva to allow the poor to take **gleanings, forgotten sheaves,**[N] **and** produce in the **corner** of one's field, **and** about the **poor man's tithe.** The Gemara asks: **What is the reason** to specifically mention these mitzvot? **Rabbi Ḥiyya bar Abba said** that **Rabbi Yoḥanan said:** Because **a gentile is executed** even **on account of** stealing **less than the value of a** ***peruta,***[H] since gentiles are particular about even such a small loss, **and** an item that a gentile steals **is not subject to being returned,** i.e., he is not obligated to return it to its owner. Since gentiles are unwilling to separate even from items of little value, a potential convert must be made aware that he if converts, he will be required to relinquish some of his property to others.

(וּמוֹדִיעִים אוֹתוֹ עֲוֹן שִׁכְחָה וּפֵאָה). ״וְאֵין מַרְבִּים עָלָיו וְאֵין מְדַקְדְּקִים עָלָיו״. אָמַר רַבִּי אֶלְעָזָר: מַאי קְרָאָה – דִּכְתִיב ״וַתֵּרֶא כִּי מִתְאַמֶּצֶת הִיא לָלֶכֶת אִתָּהּ וַתֶּחְדַּל לְדַבֵּר אֵלֶיהָ״,

The *baraita* continues: **And they inform him of the sin** of neglecting the mitzva to allow the poor to take **gleanings, forgotten sheaves, and** produce in the **corner** of one's field. **And they do not overwhelm him** with threats, **and they are not exacting with him** about the details of the mitzvot, i.e., the court should not overly dissuade the convert from converting. **Rabbi Elazar said: What is the verse** from which this ruling is derived? **As it is written: "And when she saw that she was steadfastly minded to go with her, she left off speaking with her"** (Ruth 1:18). When Naomi set out to return to Eretz Yisrael, Ruth insisted on joining her. The Gemara understands this to mean that Ruth wished to convert. Naomi attempted to dissuade her, but Ruth persisted. The verse states that once Naomi saw Ruth's resolve to convert, she desisted from her attempts to dissuade her. The Gemara infers from here that the same approach should be taken by a court in all cases of conversion.

אָמְרָה לָהּ: אֲסִיר לָן תְּחוּם שַׁבָּת – ״בַּאֲשֶׁר תֵּלְכִי אֵלֵךְ״, אֲסִיר לָן יִחוּד – ״בַּאֲשֶׁר תָּלִינִי אָלִין״,

The Gemara reconstructs the original dialogue in which Naomi attempted to dissuade Ruth from converting: Naomi **said to her:** On Shabbat, **it is prohibited for us** to go beyond **the Shabbat limit.**[NB] Ruth responded: **"Where you go, I shall go"** (Ruth 1:16), and no further. Naomi said to her: **It is forbidden for us to be alone together**[B] with a man with whom it is forbidden to engage in relations. Ruth responded: **"Where you lodge, I shall lodge"** (Ruth 1:16), and in the same manner.

NOTES

Converts are as harmful to the Jewish people as a leprous scab – קָשִׁים גֵּרִים לְיִשְׂרָאֵל כְּסַפַּחַת: Many different interpretations have been suggested in explanation of this statement. *Tosafot* suggest four different explanations. One explanation, also suggested by the Rambam, is that it is common for converts to revert to their old ways and beliefs, and when they do they exert a corrupting influence on other Jews. This is similar to the mixed multitude of peoples who accompanied the Jewish people in the exodus from Egypt and caused the sin of the Golden Calf. *Tosafot* on *Kiddushin* 70b cite the Gemara elsewhere that the continuing exile and dispersion of the Jewish people occurs in order to provide an opportunity for converts to join them. Consequently, it emerges that converts are actually part of the cause of the exile. *Tosafot* there also cite the opinion of Rabbi Avraham the convert. He claims that converts are generally punctilious and strict with regard to the mitzvot, and therefore their behavior casts aspersions on the practice of those born Jews who are not as vigilant.

And they inform him of the sin of gleanings, forgotten sheaves, etc. – וּמוֹדִיעִין אוֹתוֹ עֲוֹן לֶקֶט: Some commentaries connect this statement to the Gemara above (47a), where it is stated that a gentile might seek to convert in order to benefit from gleanings and forgotten sheaves. Consequently, he must be informed that there is a sin involved in denying these items to poor people, and it is not merely a right that the poor have (*Arukh LaNer*).

It is prohibited for us to go beyond the Shabbat limit – אֲסִיר לָן תְּחוּם שַׁבָּת: The Maharsha explains that Naomi informed Ruth of this *halakha* in fulfillment of the requirement to inform a potential convert of some of the lenient mitzvot, of which the Shabbat limit is one.

HALAKHA

A gentile is executed on account of stealing less than the value of a ***peruta*** **– בֶּן נֹחַ נֶהֱרָג עַל פָּחוֹת מִשְׁוֵה פְּרוּטָה:** A gentile is liable for theft and is punished with execution, even for stealing an item whose value is less than a *peruta* (Rambam *Sefer Shofetim*, *Hilkhot Melakhim* 9:9).

BACKGROUND

Shabbat limit – תְּחוּם שַׁבָּת: By rabbinic decree, and some say by Torah law, on Shabbat one is not permitted to travel more than a certain distance away from the place where he established his residence at the onset of Shabbat. That distance is known as the Shabbat limit. Even animals and inanimate objects have a limit, determined by the limit of the person to whose care they are entrusted, beyond which they may not be taken. Generally, the Shabbat limit is defined as two thousand cubits outside of one's city in every direction.

Being alone together – יִחוּד: A man and a woman between whom sexual relations are forbidden are forbidden to be alone together in a manner in which it would be possible for them to engage in intercourse. Typically this means that they may not be secluded in a closed room together. According to tradition, in the era of King David this prohibition was extended to prohibit a man from being alone with an unmarried woman. Exceptions to these rules include a father and daughter and a mother and son. A man is also forbidden to be alone with two women.

מפקדינן שש מאות ושלש עשרה מצות – "עמך עמי", אסיר לן עבודה זרה – "ואלהיך אלהי", ארבע מיתות נמסרו לבית דין – "באשר תמותי אמות", שני קברים נמסרו לבית דין – "ושם אקבר".

Naomi said to her: **We are commanded** to observe **six hundred and thirteen mitzvot.**[N] Ruth responded: **"Your people are my people"** (Ruth 1:16). Naomi said to her: **Idolatrous worship is forbidden to us.**[N] Ruth responded: **"Your God is my God"** (Ruth 1:16). Naomi said to her: **Four types of capital punishment**[B] **were handed over to a court** with which to punish those who transgress the mitzvot. Ruth responded: **"Where you die, I shall die"** (Ruth 1:17). Naomi said to her: **Two burial grounds**[B] **were handed over to the court,** one for those executed for more severe crimes and another for those executed for less severe crimes. Ruth responded: **"And there I shall be buried"** (Ruth 1:17).

מיד – "ותרא כי מתאמצת היא וגו'".

Immediately following this dialogue, the verse states: **"And when she saw that she was steadfastly minded** she left off speaking with her" (Ruth 1:18). Once Naomi saw Ruth's resolve to convert, she desisted from her attempts to dissuade her.

"קיבל – מלין אותו מיד". מאי טעמא? שהויי מצוה לא משהינן.

The *baraita* continues: If **he accepts** upon himself all of these ramifications, then **they circumcise him immediately.** The Gemara asks: **What is the reason** to act immediately? It is that **we do not delay** the performance of **a mitzva.**[N]

"נשתיירו בו ציצין המעכבין המילה" וכו'. כדתנן: אלו הן ציצין המעכבין המילה: בשר החופה את רוב העטרה, ואינו אוכל בתרומה. ואמר רב ירמיה בר אבא אמר רב: בשר החופה רוב גובהה של עטרה.

The *baraita* continues: If **there** still **remain on him shreds**[B] of flesh from the foreskin **that invalidate the circumcision,**[H] he is circumcised a second time to remove them. The Gemara explains: This is **as we learned** in a mishna (*Shabbat* 137a): **These are the shreds** of flesh **that invalidate the circumcision** if they are not cut: Any fragments of **the flesh that cover the greater part of the corona.** If such shreds remain, the child is considered uncircumcised, **and he may not partake of *teruma*. And** in explanation of this mishna, **Rav Yirmeya bar Abba said** that **Rav said:** This also includes **the flesh that covers the greater part of the height of the corona.**

"נתרפא מטבילין אותו מיד", נתרפא – אין, לא נתרפא – לא. מאי טעמא? משום דמיא מרזו מכה.

The *baraita* continues: When **he is healed** from the circumcision, **they immerse him immediately.** The Gemara infers from the precise formulation of the *baraita* that when **he has healed,** then **yes,** he is immersed, but as long as **he has not healed,** then **no,** he is not. **What is the reason** for this? It is **because water agitates a wound.**[B]

"ושני תלמידי חכמים עומדים על גביו". והא אמר רבי חייא אמר רבי יוחנן: גר צריך שלשה! הא אמר רבי יוחנן לתנא: תני שלשה.

The *baraita* continues: **And two Torah scholars stand over him** at the time of his immersion. The Gemara asks: **But didn't Rabbi Ḥiyya say** that **Rabbi Yoḥanan said** that **a convert requires** a court **of three** to be present at his conversion? The Gemara answers: In fact, **Rabbi Yoḥanan said to the *tanna*** reciting the mishna: Do not teach that there are two Torah scholars; rather, **teach** that there are **three.**

"טבל ועלה הרי הוא כישראל לכל דבריו". למאי הלכתא? דאי הדר ביה, ומקדש בת ישראל – ישראל מומר קרינא ביה, וקידושיו קידושין.

The *baraita* continues: Once **he has immersed and emerged he is a Jew**[H] **in every sense.** The Gemara asks: **With regard to what *halakha*** is this said? It is **that if he reverts back** to behaving as a gentile, he nevertheless remains Jewish, **and** so if **he betroths a Jewish woman,** although **he is considered to be an apostate Jew, his betrothal is a valid betrothal.**

BACKGROUND

Four types of capital punishment – ארבע מיתות...בית דין: These capital punishments are prescribed by the Torah and administered by a court of twenty-three members. They are, in diminishing order of severity: Stoning, burning, decapitation, and strangulation.

Two burial grounds – שני קברים: According to *halakha* one may not bury a wicked person adjacent to a righteous person (*Sanhedrin* 47a). Even one who transgressed a severe prohibition must be buried separately from one who transgressed a less severe prohibition. For this reason, the court maintained two separate burial grounds, one for those executed for more serious crimes and one for those executed for less serious crimes.

Shreds – ציצין: Circumcision involves two stages: First, the foreskin covering the corona is removed, and then the underlying membrane is ripped and folded back. Occasionally, and especially if this second stage is not performed in the proper manner, part of the membrane remains in its place, covering the corona. These are the shreds the Gemara refers to here.

Water agitates a wound – מיא מרזו מכה: Submerging a wound in water for an extended period can occasionally result in a light renewal of bleeding. In the Gemara here, however, the reference seems to be to a different phenomenon related specifically to ritual baths. In the Talmudic period, ritual baths were formed from collections of rain water that had been gathered, often in caves and the like. Such water can be presumed to contain different micro-organisms such as bacteria and algae. These could certainly cause the wound to become infected, even severely so.

NOTES

We are commanded to observe six hundred and thirteen mitzvot, etc. – מפקדינן שש מאות ושלש עשרה מצות וכו': Some commentaries explain Naomi's statement and Ruth's response in the following manner: There are many mitzvot that apply only to certain segments of the community, e.g., only to men, priests, etc. Therefore, it is not possible for a single individual to fulfill all six hundred and thirteen mitzvot on his own; rather, their fulfillment is only fully achieved by the collective efforts of the entire people. This is the meaning of Ruth's response: "Your people are my people" (*Iyyun Ya'akov*; *Arukh LaNer*).

Idolatrous worship is forbidden to us – אסיר לן עבודה זרה: The commentaries question why Naomi had to inform Ruth of the prohibition against idolatrous worship when it was already prohibited to Ruth as one of the seven Noahide laws. One commentary suggests that it was necessary because the punishment for a Jew is more severe than the punishment for a gentile (*Shevut Ya'akov*). Others suggest that it was necessary because the prohibition for a Jew is more encompassing: It includes any expression of veneration toward a deity, such as embracing or kissing (Maharsha); it prohibits a Jew from even possessing an object of idolatrous worship in his home (Riaf); a Jew is punished for having idolatrous beliefs even if he never expresses them in action (*Iyyun Ya'akov*); and a Jew is prohibited from associating a deity together with God (*Arukh LaNer*).

We do not delay the performance of a mitzva – שהויי מצוה לא משהינן: Although the Gemara states immediately that converts are as harmful as a leprous scab, and on 109b it is stated: Evil after evil will befall those who accept converts, *Tosafot* explain that this refers only to converts who were not initiated according to the process described in the Gemara or were encouraged to convert even though they were unwilling. However, if a gentile sincerely wishes to convert then there is a mitzva to accept him immediately, and one must not delay the performance of this mitzva. This may be seen from the midrash's comment that Abraham was punished for not accepting Timna when she wished to convert and join his family, and she eventually married Esau's son and gave birth to Amalek. Some early authorities write that the mitzva of converting gentiles is derived from the verse: "And you shall love the convert" (Deuteronomy 10:19), implying that one who desires to convert should be loved and encouraged (Rabbi Yehuda of Barcelona). Others derive the mitzva from the general mitzva to love God, which the *Sifrei* interprets to include Abraham's actions in encouraging people to worship God. In the same way, accepting converts enables them to enter a deeper relationship with God (Rabbi Yeruḥam Fishel Perla).

HALAKHA

Shreds that invalidate the circumcision – ציצין המעכבין המילה: If following circumcision, some of the flesh of the foreskin remains upon the greater part of the height of the corona, even in a single spot, and certainly if it surrounds the entire circumference (*Shakh*), then the circumcision is invalid and the extra flesh must be removed (Rambam *Sefer Ahava, Hilkhot Mila* 2:3; *Shulḥan Arukh, Yoreh De'a* 264:5).

He has immersed and emerged, he is a Jew – טבל ועלה הרי הוא כישראל: Once the conversion process has been completed as required the convert is considered to be a Jew in every sense. Therefore, even if he reverts back to his old ways and engages in idolatrous worship, he is still considered to be a Jew, albeit an apostate Jew, and so if he betroths a Jewish woman, the betrothal takes effect (Rambam *Sefer Kedusha, Hilkhot Issurei Bia* 13:17; *Shulḥan Arukh, Yoreh De'a* 268:2).

HALAKHA

An emancipated slave does not need to accept upon himself – עֶבֶד מְשׁוּחְרָר אֵין צָרִיךְ לְקַבֵּל: At the time of his emancipation, a slave must immerse in the presence of three judges. However, he need not be informed of the basic beliefs and mitzvot and he need not accept these upon himself, since he was already informed of them and accepted them at the time that he was immersed for the sake of becoming a slave (Rambam *Sefer Kedusha, Hilkhot Issurei Bia* 13:12; *Shulḥan Arukh, Yoreh De'a* 267:7).

A beautiful female prisoner of war who accepted the mitzvot upon herself – יְפַת תּוֹאַר שֶׁקִּבְּלָה עָלֶיהָ מִצְוֹת: A beautiful female prisoner of war who accepts the mitzvot upon herself may be immersed for the sake of conversion, upon which she becomes a Jew. In such a case, the procedures described by the Torah do not apply. If she does not initially accept the mitzvot upon herself, then the procedures described by the Torah must be fulfilled. Her captor then resides with her until she agrees to accept the mitzvot upon herself, at which point she may be immersed for the sake of conversion (Rambam *Sefer Shofetim, Hilkhot Melakhim* 8:5).

״אֶחָד גֵּר וְאֶחָד עֶבֶד מְשׁוּחְרָר״. קָסָלְקָא דַּעְתָּךְ לְקַבֵּל עָלָיו עוֹל מִצְוֹת, וּרְמִינְהוּ: בַּמֶּה דְּבָרִים אֲמוּרִים – בְּגֵר, אֲבָל בְּעֶבֶד מְשׁוּחְרָר – אֵין צָרִיךְ לְקַבֵּל!

The *baraita* continues: This applies **both for a convert and for an emancipated slave.** The Gemara considers the meaning of this clause: **If it enters your mind** to interpret the *baraita* to mean that a convert and an emancipated slave are the same **with regard to accepting upon oneself the yoke of mitzvot,** then one could **raise a contradiction** from that which is taught in another *baraita*: **In what** case **is this statement** that there is a need to accept the yoke of mitzvot **said?** It is **with respect to a convert; however, an emancipated slave does not need to accept** upon himself[H] the yoke of mitzvot when he immerses for the sake of emancipation. Rather, the immersion alone is sufficient to emancipate him and thereby render him a Jew.

אָמַר רַב שֵׁשֶׁת: לָא קַשְׁיָא, הָא – רַבִּי שִׁמְעוֹן בֶּן אֶלְעָזָר, הָא – רַבָּנַן.

Rav Sheshet said: This is **not difficult,** as **this** *baraita* that states that an emancipated slave is not required to accept the yoke of mitzvot **is** in accordance with the opinion of **Rabbi Shimon ben Elazar,** whereas **that** *baraita* that implies he is required to do so **is** in accordance with the opinion of **the Rabbis,** the first *tanna* of the following *baraita.*

דְּתַנְיָא, ״וּבָכְתָה אֶת אָבִיהָ וְאֶת אִמָּהּ״ וגו׳ בַּמֶּה דְּבָרִים אֲמוּרִים – שֶׁלֹּא קִבְּלָה עָלֶיהָ, אֲבָל קִבְּלָה עָלֶיהָ – מַטְבִּילָהּ, וּמוּתָּר בָּהּ מִיָּד.

As it is taught in a *baraita*: The Torah permits a Jewish soldier to take a beautiful female prisoner of war out of her captivity in order to marry her. Before he may do so, she must first undergo the process that the Torah describes: "And she shall shave her head, and do her nails; and she shall remove the raiment of her captivity from upon her, and she shall remain in your house **and bewail her father and her mother** a month of days" (Deuteronomy 21:12–13). She may then be immersed for the sake of conversion, even though she does not accept upon herself the yoke of mitzvot. At that point it is permitted to marry her. The *baraita* asks: **Under what** circumstance **are these matters stated?** It is **when she did not accept upon herself** the yoke of mitzvot; **however,** if **she** willingly **accepted upon herself**[H] the yoke of mitzvot, **he may immerse her** for the sake of conversion, **and he is permitted to** marry **her immediately** without the need for her to undergo the process described in the Torah.

רַבִּי שִׁמְעוֹן בֶּן אֶלְעָזָר אוֹמֵר: אַף עַל פִּי שֶׁלֹּא קִבְּלָה עָלֶיהָ – כּוֹפֶה, וּמַטְבִּילָהּ לְשֵׁם שִׁפְחוּת, וְחוֹזֵר וּמַטְבִּילָהּ לְשֵׁם שִׁחְרוּר, וּמְשַׁחְרְרָהּ,

Rabbi Shimon ben Elazar says: Even if she did not accept upon herself the yoke of mitzvot, the need for the process can still be circumvented if **he forces** her **and immerses her for the sake of slavery, and then he again immerses her for the sake of emancipation and** thereby **emancipates her,** rendering her a Jewess. Rabbi Shimon ben Elazar holds that the immersion of a slave for the sake of emancipation is effective even if the slave does not accept upon himself the yoke of mitzvot.

Perek **IV**
Daf **48** Amud **a**

וּמוּתָּר בָּהּ מִיָּד.

And he is permitted to marry **her immediately** afterward, without the need for her to undergo the process described in the Torah. The fact that the Rabbis do not suggest this course of action is evidently because they hold that even if she were to be rendered a slave and then immersed for the sake of emancipation, she would become Jewish only if she also accepted upon herself the yoke of mitzvot. Rav Sheshet assumes that the Rabbis would similarly rule that a regular slave who was immersed for the sake of emancipation becomes Jewish only if he also accepts upon himself the yoke of mitzvot.[N]

NOTES

The dispute between Rabbi Shimon ben Elazar and the Rabbis – מַחְלוֹקֶת רַבִּי שִׁמְעוֹן בֶּן אֶלְעָזָר וַחֲכָמִים: Rabbi Shimon ben Elazar and the Rabbis dispute whether or not a slave who immersed upon his emancipation must accept the yoke of mitzvot in order to become Jewish. The Ramban discusses this dispute at length and suggests three possible interpretations of its parameters (see Rashba).

According to Rashi, all agree that the initial immersion of the slave for the sake of entering into slavery, after he is first purchased from a gentile, may be performed against his will. The dispute here concerns the immersion upon a slave's emancipation: Must that immersion be accompanied by the slave's acceptance of the yoke of mitzvot? The Ramban cites passages in the Jerusalem Talmud and *Pirkei deRabbi Eliezer* that support this interpretation.

A different interpretation, which appears consistent with the rulings of the Rif and Rambam, also assumes that the dispute concerns only the immersion upon a slave's emancipation. However, this interpretation assumes with regard to the initial immersion for the sake of slavery that everyone agrees that it requires the slave's consent.

A third interpretation, suggested by *Tosafot,* is that the dispute concerns both the original immersion for the sake of slavery and the immersion upon emancipation. The Rabbis assume that in both cases the immersion must be performed with the consent of the slave.

אֲמַר רָבָא: מַאי טַעֲמָא דְּרַבִּי שִׁמְעוֹן בֶּן אֶלְעָזָר – דִּכְתִיב "כָּל עֶבֶד אִישׁ מִקְנַת כָּסֶף", עֶבֶד אִישׁ וְלֹא עֶבֶד אִשָּׁה?! אֶלָּא: עֶבֶד אִישׁ אַתָּה מָל בְּעַל כָּרְחוֹ, וְאִי אַתָּה מָל בֶּן אִישׁ בְּעַל כָּרְחוֹ.

Rava said: What is the rationale for Rabbi Shimon ben Elazar's opinion? **As it is written** with regard to the Paschal lamb: **"Every slave of a man that is bought for money,** when you have circumcised him, then he may eat of it" (Exodus 12:44). Could the use of the phrase "slave of a man," rather than just: Slave, possibly indicate that the verse applies only to **a man's slave but not a woman's slave?** Certainly not; **rather,** the phrase "slave of a man" means that the slave himself is a man, i.e., an adult, and teaches that **a slave who is a man you may circumcise against his will,** and there is no need for him to accept upon himself the yoke of mitzvot, **but you may not circumcise** a gentile's **son who is a man,** i.e., an adult who is not a slave, **against his will.**

וְרַבָּנַן? אֲמַר עוּלָּא: כְּשֵׁם שֶׁאִי אַתָּה מָל בֶּן אִישׁ בְּעַל כָּרְחוֹ כָּךְ אִי אַתָּה מָל עֶבֶד אִישׁ בְּעַל כָּרְחוֹ. וְאֶלָּא, הָכְתִיב "כָּל עֶבֶד אִישׁ"! הַהוּא מִיבָּעֵי לֵיהּ לִכְדִשְׁמוּאֵל.

The Gemara asks: **And** how would **the Rabbis** counter this argument? **Ulla said** that the Rabbis reason that **just as you may not circumcise a son who is a man against his will, so too, you may not circumcise a slave who is a man against his will.** The Gemara asks: **But isn't it written: "Every slave of a man"?** The Gemara explains: The Rabbis **require that** verse **for that which Shmuel** said.

דְּאָמַר שְׁמוּאֵל: הַמַּפְקִיר עַבְדּוֹ יָצָא לְחֵירוּת, וְאֵין צָרִיךְ גֵּט שִׁחְרוּר, שֶׁנֶּאֱמַר "כָּל עֶבֶד אִישׁ מִקְנַת כָּסֶף", עֶבֶד אִישׁ וְלֹא עֶבֶד אִשָּׁה? אֶלָּא: עֶבֶד שֶׁיֵּשׁ לוֹ רְשׁוּת לְרַבּוֹ עָלָיו – קָרוּי עֶבֶד, וְשֶׁאֵין רְשׁוּת לְרַבּוֹ עָלָיו – אֵין קָרוּי עֶבֶד.

As Shmuel said: With regard to one **who renounces ownership of his slave,**[H] the slave **is emancipated, and he does not** even **require a bill of emancipation,**[N] **as it is stated: "But every slave of a man that is bought for money."** Could the use of the phrase "slave of a man," rather than just: Slave, possibly indicate that the verse applies only to **a man's slave but not a woman's slave?** Certainly not; **rather,** the use of the phrase indicates that only a **slave whose master has possession of him,** and can rightfully be described as: a slave of a man, **is called a slave, but** a slave **whose master does not have possession of him** is not **called a slave,** and therefore he is considered a freeman and does not require a bill of emancipation.

מַתְקִיף לַהּ רַב פָּפָּא: אֵימוּר דִּשְׁמַעַתְּ לְהוּ לְרַבָּנַן בִּיפַת תּוֹאַר, דְּלָא שַׁיְיכָא בְּמִצְוֹת. אֲבָל עֶבֶד דְּשַׁיֵּיךְ בְּמִצְוֹת – הָכִי נַמִי דַּאֲפִילּוּ רַבָּנַן מוֹדוּ.

Rav Pappa strongly objects to Rav Sheshet's claim that the Rabbis of the *baraita* would hold that a regular slave who was immersed for the sake of emancipation becomes Jewish only if he also accepts upon himself the yoke of mitzvot: **Say that you heard** that **the Rabbis** insist on the acceptance of the yoke of mitzvot **with regard to** the case of **a beautiful female** prisoner of war, **who was not involved in** any **mitzvot** before being emancipated; **however,** with regard to **a slave, who was** initially **involved in mitzvot** before his emancipation, since as a slave he was obligated to observe certain mitzvot, perhaps **even the Rabbis would agree** that there is no need for the slave to accept upon himself the yoke of mitzvot.

דְּתַנְיָא: אֶחָד גֵּר וְאֶחָד לוֹקֵחַ עֶבֶד מִן הַגּוֹי צָרִיךְ לְקַבֵּל. הָא לוֹקֵחַ מִיִּשְׂרָאֵל – אֵין צָרִיךְ לְקַבֵּל,

As it is taught in a *baraita*: **Both** in the case of **a convert and** in the case of **one who purchases a slave from a gentile** whom he is now emancipating, the convert and the slave **need to accept** upon themselves the yoke of mitzvot in order to become Jewish. The Gemara infers: The *baraita* states the need to accept the yoke of mitzvot only in the case where one purchases a slave from a gentile, **but** if **one purchases** a slave **from a Jew,** then the slave **does not need to accept** upon himself the yoke of mitzvot, since he was involved in mitzvot before his emancipation.

מַנִּי? אִי רַבִּי שִׁמְעוֹן בֶּן אֶלְעָזָר – הָאָמַר לוֹקֵחַ מִן הַגּוֹי נַמִי אֵין צָרִיךְ לְקַבֵּל. אֶלָּא לָאו – רַבָּנַן, וּשְׁמַע מִינָּהּ: דְּלוֹקֵחַ מִן הַגּוֹי צָרִיךְ לְקַבֵּל, אֲבָל לוֹקֵחַ מִיִּשְׂרָאֵל – אֵין צָרִיךְ לְקַבֵּל.

In accordance with **whose** opinion is this taught? **If** one suggests that it is in accordance with the opinion of **Rabbi Shimon ben Elazar,** that is incorrect because **didn't he say** that **also** in the case of **one who purchases a slave from a gentile,** the slave **does not need to accept** upon himself the yoke of mitzvot? **Rather, must it not** be in accordance with the opinion of **the Rabbis? And** so, **conclude from** this *baraita* **that** in the case of **one** who **purchases a slave from a gentile,** the slave **needs to accept** upon himself the yoke of mitzvot, **but** in the case of **one who purchases** a slave **from a Jew,**[H] the slave **does not need to accept** upon himself the yoke of mitzvot.

HALAKHA

One who renounces ownership of his slave – הַמַּפְקִיר עַבְדּוֹ: If one renounces ownership of his slave, the slave is set free but still requires a bill of emancipation. This is in accordance with the conclusion of the Gemara in tractate *Gittin* (Rambam *Sefer Kinyan, Hilkhot Avadim* 8:13; *Shulḥan Arukh, Yoreh De'a* 267:64).

One who purchases a slave from a gentile or a Jew – הַלּוֹקֵחַ מִנָּכְרִי וּמִיִּשְׂרָאֵל: If a slave is purchased from a gentile, before the slave is immersed for the sake of slavery, he must willingly accept the yoke of mitzvot upon himself. However, if he was purchased from a Jew, he need not do so (Rambam *Sefer Kedusha, Hilkhot Issurei Bia* 14:9; *Shulḥan Arukh, Yoreh De'a* 267:3).

NOTES

And he does not require a bill of emancipation – וְאֵין צָרִיךְ גֵּט שִׁחְרוּר: This opinion of Shmuel is subject to a debate on *Gittin* 38b. The Gemara there cites the opinion of Rav that although when one renounces ownership of his slave, the slave is no longer subjugated to his master, he still requires a bill of emancipation in order to fully modify his status from a slave to a freeman in order to permit him to marry a Jewish woman.

וְאֶלָּא קַשְׁיָא אֶחָד גֵּר וְאֶחָד עֶבֶד מְשׁוּחְרָר! כִּי תַּנְיָא הַהִיא – לְעִנְיַן טְבִילָה תַּנְיָא.

The Gemara asks: **But** if so, it is **difficult** to understand the meaning of the *baraita* cited above: This applies **both for a convert and for an emancipated slave.** That phrase appears to refer to the need for both a convert and an emancipated slave to accept the yoke of mitzvot, which is mentioned in the *baraita* beforehand. The Gemara explains: **When that** clause **is taught, it is taught** only **with regard to the matter of immersion,**[H] which is mentioned immediately beforehand, but not with regard to the need to accept the yoke of mitzvot that is mentioned prior to that.

תָּנוּ רַבָּנַן: ״וְגִלְּחָה אֶת רֹאשָׁהּ וְעָשְׂתָה אֶת צִפָּרְנֶיהָ״ רַבִּי אֱלִיעֶזֶר אוֹמֵר: תָּקוֹץ, רַבִּי עֲקִיבָא אוֹמֵר: תַּגְדִּיל.

§ Having cited it above, the Gemara focuses on the case of the beautiful female prisoner of war: **The Sages taught:** The verse states: **"And she shall shave her head and do her nails"** (Deuteronomy 21:12).[HN] The phrase "do her nails" is ambiguous. **Rabbi Eliezer says:** It means **she cuts** her nails. **Rabbi Akiva says:** It means **she grows** them.

אָמַר רַבִּי אֱלִיעֶזֶר: נֶאֶמְרָה עֲשִׂיָּה בָּרֹאשׁ וְנֶאֶמְרָה עֲשִׂיָּה בַּצִּפָּרְנַיִם, מַה לְּהַלָּן הַעֲבָרָה – אַף כָּאן הַעֲבָרָה. רַבִּי עֲקִיבָא אוֹמֵר: נֶאֱמַר עֲשִׂיָּה בָּרֹאשׁ, וְנֶאֱמַר עֲשִׂיָּה בַּצִּפָּרְנַיִם. מַה לְּהַלָּן נִיוּוּל – אַף כָּאן נִיוּוּל.

Each *tanna* explains the basis of his opinion: **Rabbi Eliezer said:** An act of **doing is stated with regard to the head,** that she should shave it, **and** an act of **doing is stated with regard to the nails; just as there,** with regard to the hair on her head, the Torah requires its **removal, so too, here,** with regard to her nails, the Torah requires their **removal. Rabbi Akiva says:** An act of **doing is stated with regard to the head,** that she should shave it, **and** an act of **doing is stated with regard to the nails; just as there,** with regard to the hair on her head, the Torah requires that she do something that makes her **repulsive, so too, here,** with regard to her nails, the Torah requires she do something that makes her **repulsive,** i.e., allowing them to grow.

וּרְאָיָה לְדִבְרֵי רַבִּי אֱלִיעֶזֶר ״וּמְפִבֹשֶׁת בֶּן שָׁאוּל יָרַד לִקְרַאת הַמֶּלֶךְ לֹא עָשָׂה רַגְלָיו וְלֹא עָשָׂה שְׂפָמוֹ״. מַאי עֲשִׂיָּה – הַעֲבָרָה.

And a proof for the statement of Rabbi Eliezer may be adduced from the verse that states: **"And Mephibosheth, the son of Saul, came down to meet the king; and he had neither done his feet nor done his mustache"** (II Samuel 19:25). **What** is the meaning of **doing** in that context? Clearly it means the **removal** of his toenails and his mustache.

תָּנוּ רַבָּנַן: ״וּבָכְתָה אֶת אָבִיהָ וְאֶת אִמָּהּ״,

The Sages taught in a *baraita*: The verse states: **"And she shall bewail her father and her mother** a month of days and after that you may come to her" (Deuteronomy 21:13).

Perek **IV**
Daf **48** Amud **b**

רַבִּי אֱלִיעֶזֶר אוֹמֵר: ״אָבִיהָ״ – אָבִיהָ מַמָּשׁ, ״אִמָּהּ״ – אִמָּהּ מַמָּשׁ. רַבִּי עֲקִיבָא אוֹמֵר: ״אָבִיהָ וְאִמָּהּ״ – זוֹ עֲבוֹדָה זָרָה, וְכֵן הוּא אוֹמֵר ״אוֹמְרִים לָעֵץ אָבִי אַתָּה״ וגו׳.

Rabbi Eliezer says: "Her father" means **her actual father** and "her **mother**" means **her actual mother. Rabbi Akiva says: Her father and her mother; this** is referring to the **idolatrous deity** that she had worshiped but will no longer be able to worship, **and so it says: "They say to a tree: You are my father,** and to a stone: You have given birth to us" (Jeremiah 2:27).[H]

״יֶרַח יָמִים״ – יֶרַח שְׁלֹשִׁים יוֹם. רַבִּי שִׁמְעוֹן בֶּן אֶלְעָזָר אוֹמֵר: תִּשְׁעִים יוֹם, ״יֶרַח״ – שְׁלֹשִׁים, ״יָמִים״ – שְׁלֹשִׁים, ״וְאַחַר כֵּן״ – שְׁלֹשִׁים.

The verses states: **"A month of days**[H] and after that you may come to her" (Deuteronomy 21:13). This means **a thirty-day month. Rabbi Shimon ben Elazar says:** She must wait **ninety days.** This is derived as follows: The phrase **"a month"** connotes **thirty** days; the word **"days"** adds another **thirty** days; **and** the words **"after that"** indicate another period equal to one previously mentioned, i.e., a further **thirty** days.

מַתְקִיף לַהּ רָבִינָא: אֵימָא ״יֶרַח״ – שְׁלֹשִׁים, ״יָמִים״ – שְׁלֹשִׁים, ״וְאַחַר כֵּן״ – כִּי הָנֵי! – קַשְׁיָא.

Ravina strongly objects to this: If the words "after that" indicate another period equal to one previously mentioned, then one should **say:** The phrase **"a month"** connotes **thirty** days; the word **"days"** adds another **thirty** days; **and** then the words **"after that"** add another period which is **equal to** the total sum of all **those** days she has already waited, i.e., an additional sixty days. The Gemara concedes: Indeed, this is **difficult.**

HALAKHA

Immersion of an emancipated slave – **טְבִילַת עֶבֶד מְשׁוּחְרָר**: An emancipated slave must be immersed in the presence of three people in order to become Jewish and be allowed to marry a Jewish woman (Rambam *Sefer Kedusha, Hilkhot Issurei Bia* 13:13; *Shulḥan Arukh, Yoreh De'a* 267:3).

And do her nails – **וְעָשְׂתָה אֶת צִפָּרְנֶיהָ**: A beautiful female prisoner of war must grow her fingernails during the month she remains in her captor's home. This is in accordance with the opinion of Rabbi Akiva (Rambam *Sefer Shofetim, Hilkhot Melakhim* 8:5).

NOTES

And do her nails – **וְעָשְׂתָה אֶת צִפָּרְנֶיהָ**: One commentary explains that the dispute between Rabbi Eliezer and Rabbi Akiva is based upon two different understandings of the purpose of the procedures delineated by the Torah: Rabbi Eliezer views the procedures as a process of purification in anticipation of her conversion, which is performed at the conclusion of the process. The shaving of her head is also part of this process and is similar to the preparations of the Levites, who shaved their heads as part of their consecration, and the leper, who shaved as part of his purification process. Apparently, the idea is that in preparation for becoming pure, one should remove extraneous parts of the body. Therefore, he interprets the phrase "do her nails" as referring to removing them. This is paralleled in the custom that an apostate Jew, as part of his process of repentance, would shave his head and cut his nails. According to some opinions, a convert must do so as well.

Rabbi Akiva, however, views the procedures as part of the Torah's attempt to make the woman less appealing in the eyes of her captor in the hope that ultimately he will refrain from taking her as a wife. Accordingly, the purpose of shaving her head is to negatively affect her appearance, and likewise, the phrase "do her nails" refers to letting them grow (Malbim).

It should be noted that Rabbi Akiva certainly was aware of the verse relating to Mephibosheth that supports Rabbi Eliezer's opinion; nevertheless, he understood that the context of the phrase here indicates a meaning other than its standard meaning (*Gilyonei HaShas*).

HALAKHA

She shall bewail her father and her mother – **וּבָכְתָה אֶת אָבִיהָ וְאֶת אִמָּהּ**: A beautiful female prisoner of war, during her month-long stay in her captor's home, cries over her separation from her previous religion and her captor may not prevent her from doing so. This is in accordance with the opinion of Rabbi Akiva (Rambam *Sefer Shofetim, Hilkhot Melakhim* 8:5).

A month of days – **יֶרַח יָמִים**: The time designated for a female prisoner of war to perform the procedures delineated by the Torah is thirty days. This is in accordance with the opinion of the first *tanna*. Nevertheless, her captor must wait an additional two months before taking her in marriage, so that if it later emerges that she is pregnant, it will be clear whether the captor is the father (Rambam *Sefer Shofetim, Hilkhot Melakhim* 8:5 and *Leḥem Mishne* there).

תָּנוּ רַבָּנַן: מְקַיְּימִין עֲבָדִים שֶׁאֵינָם מָלִין, דִּבְרֵי רַבִּי יִשְׁמָעֵאל. רַבִּי עֲקִיבָא אוֹמֵר: אֵין מְקַיְּימִין. אָמַר לֵיהּ רַבִּי יִשְׁמָעֵאל: הֲרֵי הוּא אוֹמֵר "וְיִנָּפֵשׁ בֶּן אֲמָתְךָ"! אָמַר לֵיהּ: בְּלוֹקֵחַ עֶבֶד בֵּין הַשְּׁמָשׁוֹת וְלֹא הִסְפִּיק לְמוֹלוֹ הַכָּתוּב מְדַבֵּר.

§ **The Sages taught** in a *baraita*: **One may maintain**[N] **slaves that are not circumcised** under one's control; this is **the statement of Rabbi Yishmael. Rabbi Akiva says: One may not maintain** such slaves, even for a moment. **Rabbi Yishmael said to him: But it says** with regard to Shabbat: **"And the son of your maidservant will be refreshed"** (Exodus 23:12). The verse prohibits a Jewish master from allowing his slave to perform labor on Shabbat. The Gemara will explain that this is referring to an uncircumcised slave. It is therefore apparent that it is permitted to keep such a slave. Rabbi Akiva **said to him: The verse speaks of one who purchases a slave at twilight**[N] on the eve of Shabbat **and** therefore **does not have the opportunity to circumcise him** before the onset of Shabbat.

דְּכוּלֵּי עָלְמָא מִיהַת "וְיִנָּפֵשׁ בֶּן אֲמָתְךָ" בְּעֶבֶד עָרֵל כְּתִיב, מַאי מַשְׁמַע? דְּתַנְיָא: "וְיִנָּפֵשׁ בֶּן אֲמָתְךָ" – בְּעֶבֶד עָרֵל הַכָּתוּב מְדַבֵּר. אַתָּה אוֹמֵר בְּעֶבֶד עָרֵל, אוֹ אֵינוֹ אֶלָּא בְּעֶבֶד מָהוּל? כְּשֶׁהוּא אוֹמֵר: "לְמַעַן יָנוּחַ עַבְדְּךָ וַאֲמָתְךָ כָּמוֹךָ" – הֲרֵי עֶבֶד מָהוּל אָמוּר, הָא מָה אֲנִי מְקַיֵּים "וְיִנָּפֵשׁ בֶּן אֲמָתְךָ"! – בְּעֶבֶד עָרֵל.

The Gemara notes: **In any event,** in the opinion **of everyone** the verse: **"And the son of your maidservant will be refreshed," is written with regard to an uncircumcised slave. From where is this inferred? As it is taught in a** *baraita*: **"And the son of your maidservant will be refreshed"; the verse speaks of an uncircumcised slave.** Do **you say** it speaks **of an uncircumcised slave, or** perhaps **it is speaking only of a circumcised slave? When it says** elsewhere: "And the seventh day is a Shabbat to the Lord your God, you shall not do any labor, you, and your son, and your daughter, and your slave, and your maidservant… **so that your slave and your maidservant may rest like you"** (Deuteronomy 5:13), **a circumcised slave is** already **mentioned; how,** then, **do I uphold** the verse **"And the son of your maidservant will be refreshed"?** It must refer **to an uncircumcised slave.**

"וְהַגֵּר" – זֶה גֵּר תּוֹשָׁב, אַתָּה אוֹמֵר זֶה גֵּר תּוֹשָׁב. אוֹ אֵינוֹ אֶלָּא גֵּר צֶדֶק? כְּשֶׁהוּא אוֹמֵר "וְגֵרְךָ אֲשֶׁר בִּשְׁעָרֶיךָ" – הֲרֵי גֵּר צֶדֶק אָמוּר, הָא מָה אֲנִי מְקַיֵּים "וְהַגֵּר" – זֶה גֵּר תּוֹשָׁב.

The verse continues: **"And the stranger** [*ger*]" (Exodus 23:12). **This is** referring to a **gentile who observes certain mitzvot** [*ger toshav*].[N] **Do you say** that **this is a** *ger toshav*, **or** perhaps **it is only a righteous convert** [*ger tzedek*], who is a Jew in every sense? **When it says** elsewhere: **"And your stranger** [*ger*] **that is within your gates"** (Deuteronomy 5:13), **a righteous convert is** already **mentioned. How,** then, **do I uphold** the verse **"And the stranger** [*ger*]**"?** It must be that **this is a** *ger toshav*.

אָמַר רַבִּי יְהוֹשֻׁעַ בֶּן לֵוִי: הַלּוֹקֵחַ עֶבֶד מִן הַגּוֹי וְלֹא רָצָה לָמוּל, מְגַלְגֵּל עִמּוֹ עַד שְׁנֵים עָשָׂר חֹדֶשׁ. לֹא מָל – חוֹזֵר וּמוֹכְרוֹ לְגוֹיִם.

Rabbi Yehoshua ben Levi said: In the case of **one who purchases a slave from a gentile** and the slave **does not wish to be circumcised,**[H] **he abides with him up to twelve months.** If, after this period, **he will** still **not be circumcised, he then sells him** on **to gentiles.**

אֲמָרוּהָ רַבָּנַן קַמֵּיהּ דְּרַב פַּפָּא: כְּמַאן – דְּלָא כְּרַבִּי עֲקִיבָא, דְּאִי רַבִּי עֲקִיבָא – הָאָמַר אֵין מְקַיְּימִין! אָמַר לְהוּ רַב פַּפָּא: אֲפִילּוּ תֵּימָא רַבִּי עֲקִיבָא, הָנֵי מִילֵּי – הֵיכָא דְּלָא פַּסְקָא לְמִילְּתֵיהּ, אֲבָל הֵיכָא דְּפַסְקָא לְמִילְּתֵיהּ – פַּסְקָא.

The Sages said this *halakha* **before Rav Pappa** and asked: **In accordance with whose** opinion is it? It seems **that it is not in accordance with** the opinion of **Rabbi Akiva, as, if** it were in accordance with the opinion of **Rabbi Akiva, didn't he say: One may not maintain** an uncircumcised slave even for a moment? Rav Pappa **said to them: You can even say** that it is in accordance with the opinion of **Rabbi Akiva,** since perhaps **that** *halakha* of Rabbi Yehoshua ben Levi **applies** only **where** the slave **did not make his** refusal to be circumcised **explicit;**[N] **however, where he did make his** refusal to be circumcised **explicit,** since **he has made it explicit,** it is prohibited to maintain him, as Rabbi Akiva rules.

אָמַר רַב כָּהֲנָא: אֲמָרִיתָא לִשְׁמַעְתָּא קַמֵּיהּ דְּרַב זְבִיד מִנְּהַרְדְּעָא. אָמַר לִי: אִי הָכִי, כִּי אָמַר לֵיהּ רַבִּי עֲקִיבָא בְּלוֹקֵחַ עֶבֶד בֵּין הַשְּׁמָשׁוֹת – לִישַׁנֵּי לֵיהּ הָא! חֲדָא מִתְּרֵי טַעְמֵי קָאָמַר.

Rav Kahana said: I said this *halakha* **before Rav Zevid from Neharde'a. He said to me: If so,** that Rabbi Akiva agrees that one may temporarily maintain a slave who has not explicitly refused to be circumcised, then **when Rabbi Akiva said to** Rabbi Yishmael that the verse with regard to an uncircumcised slave **is referring to one who purchases a slave at twilight**[N] on the eve of Shabbat, **let him** instead **answer him** that the verse is referring to **this** case of a slave who has not explicitly refused to be circumcised. The Gemara explains: Rabbi Akiva **said** only **one out of two** possible **reasons** why it would be permitted to be in possession of such a slave.

NOTES

One may maintain, etc. – מְקַיְּימִין עֲבָדִים וכו׳: *Tosafot* explain that Rabbi Akiva's opinion is based on the fact that Abraham was commanded to circumcise everyone in his household including his slaves; if so, clearly one is not allowed to leave them uncircumcised. *Tosafot* conclude, therefore, that it is apparent that Rabbi Akiva's prohibition to maintain a slave without circumcision is by Torah law. This also explains why Rabbi Yishmael had to adduce biblical support for his claim that it is permitted to do so (see *Tosefot HaRosh* and *Mekhilta*).

One who purchases a slave at twilight – בְּלוֹקֵחַ עֶבֶד בֵּין הַשְּׁמָשׁוֹת: The Ritva explains that one should not conclude that the verse is referring only to this specific case. Rather, it refers to all cases where, due to some unavoidable circumstances, the master was unable to circumcise his slave before the onset of Shabbat, e.g., if no one who could perform the circumcision was available.

This is a ***ger toshav*** – זֶה גֵּר תּוֹשָׁב: The status of a *ger toshav*, and which mitzvot he is required to observe, is subject to significant debate both in the Gemara and the early commentaries. In order to explain the Gemara here, Rashi cites the opinion that a *ger toshav* must observe the prohibitions of Shabbat in the same manner as a Jew. *Tosafot* and the Ramban object to this explanation and explain that even if he is not obligated to observe Shabbat, it is prohibited by Torah law for him to perform any labor on behalf of a Jew. This is in contrast to the general prohibition against benefiting from labor that a gentile performed for a Jew, which is a rabbinic prohibition. The Ramban also cites an opinion that a *ger toshav* is prohibited from performing labor on Shabbat to the same extent that a Jew is prohibited from performing labor on a Festival. Accordingly, certain labors that are necessary for the preparation of food are permitted.

He did not make his refusal explicit – לָא פַּסְקָה לְמִילְּתֵיהּ: Rashi suggests two interpretations. According to the first, the phrase refers to the slave: As long as the slave does not explicitly state that he will not consent to be circumcised, the master is permitted to maintain him. According to the second interpretation, the phrase refers to the slave owner and should be translated as: He did not fix a time for the matter. Accordingly, it means that it is permitted for an owner to maintain his uncircumcised slave only if he set a time by which he will circumcise him. This time would have to be set at the moment of purchase. *Tosafot* cite the interpretation of Rabbeinu Yitzhak, which is also the explanation of Rav Hai Gaon, that, on the contrary, once the slave has agreed to be circumcised it is then prohibited to maintain him in an uncircumcised state; rather, he must be circumcised and immersed immediately. However, if the slave refuses to be circumcised, then one is allowed to maintain him as such.

HALAKHA

One who purchases a slave from a gentile and he does not wish to be circumcised – הַלּוֹקֵחַ עֶבֶד מִן הַגּוֹי וְלֹא רָצָה לָמוּל: If one purchases a slave from a gentile and the slave does not wish to be circumcised, then he abides with him up to twelve months. If, after this period, the slave still refuses to be circumcised, the master then sells him on to gentiles. This is in accordance with the opinion of Rabbi Yehoshua ben Levi (Rambam *Sefer Ahava*, *Hilkhot Mila* 1:6 and *Sefer Kedusha*, *Hilkhot Issurei Bia* 14:9; *Shulḥan Arukh*, *Yoreh De'a* 267:4).

שָׁלַח רָבִין מִשְּׁמֵיהּ דְּרַבִּי אֶילְעַאי, וְכָל רַבּוֹתַי אָמְרוּ לִי מִשְּׁמוֹ: אֵיזֶהוּ עֶבֶד עָרֵל שֶׁמּוּתָּר לְקַיְּימוֹ – זֶה שֶׁלְּקָחוֹ רַבּוֹ עַל מְנָת שֶׁלֹּא לְמוֹלוֹ. אֲמַרוּהָ רַבָּנַן קַמֵּיהּ דְּרַב פַּפָּא: כְּמַאן – דְּלָא כְּרַבִּי עֲקִיבָא, דְּאִי רַבִּי עֲקִיבָא – הָאֲמַר: אֵין מְקַיְּימִין! אֲמַר לְהוּ רַב פַּפָּא: אֲפִילּוּ תֵּימָא רַבִּי עֲקִיבָא, הָנֵי מִילֵּי – הֵיכָא דְּלָא אַתְנֵי בַּהֲדֵיהּ, אֲבָל הֵיכָא דְּאַתְנֵי – אַתְנֵי.

Ravin[P] sent a message citing a *halakha* **in the name of Rabbi Ilai: And all of my teachers said to me in his name: What is the** case **of an uncircumcised slave whom it is permitted to maintain? This is one whose master purchased him on condition not to circumcise him.**[H] **The Sages said this** *halakha* **before Rav Pappa** and asked: **In accordance with whose** opinion is it? It seems **that it is not in accordance with** the opinion of **Rabbi Akiva, as, if** it were in accordance with the opinion of **Rabbi Akiva, didn't he say: One may not maintain** an uncircumcised slave even for a moment? Rav Pappa **said to them: You** can **even say** it is in accordance with the opinion of **Rabbi Akiva,** since perhaps **that** ruling of Rabbi Akiva **applies** only **where** the master **did not make a condition with regard to** the slave that he would not be circumcised; **however, where he did make** such a **condition,** since **he made a condition,** even Rabbi Akiva would concede it is permitted to maintain him.

אֲמַר רַב כָּהֲנָא: אֲמַרִיתָא לִשְׁמַעְתָּא קַמֵּיהּ דְּרַב זְבִיד מִנְּהַרְדְּעָא, וַאֲמַר לִי: אִי הָכִי, כִּי קָאָמַר לֵיהּ רַבִּי עֲקִיבָא בְּלוֹקֵחַ עֶבֶד בֵּין הַשְּׁמָשׁוֹת וְלֹא הִסְפִּיק לְמוֹלוֹ – לִישְׁנֵי לֵיהּ הָא!

Rav Kahana said: I said this *halakha* **before Rav Zevid from Neharde'a and he said to me: If so,** that Rabbi Akiva agrees that one may maintain a slave who was purchased on condition that he would not be circumcised, then **when Rabbi Akiva said to** Rabbi Yishmael that the verse with regard to an uncircumcised slave **is referring to one who purchases** a **slave at twilight** on the eve of Shabbat **and** therefore **does not** have **the opportunity to circumcise him** before the onset of Shabbat, **let him** instead **answer him** that the verse is referring to **this** case of a slave who was purchased on condition that he would not be circumcised.

וְלִיטַעֲמִיךְ – לִישְׁנֵי לֵיהּ הָךְ! אֶלָּא: חַד מִתְּרֵי וּתְלָת טַעֲמֵי קָאָמַר.

The Gemara responds: **But** even **according to your reasoning** that Rabbi Akiva disagrees, since you do agree with Rav Pappa's resolution of Rabbi Akiva's opinion with the *halakha* of Rabbi Yehoshua ben Levi, **let** Rabbi Akiva **answer him** that the verse is referring to **that** case of a slave who has not explicitly refused to be circumcised. The Gemara answers: Rabbi Akiva **said** only **one out of two or three** possible **reasons** that it would be permitted to be in possession of such a slave.

יָתֵיב רַבִּי חֲנִינָא בַּר פַּפִּי וְרַבִּי אַמִּי וְרַבִּי יִצְחָק נַפָּחָא אַקִּילְעָא דְּרַבִּי יִצְחָק נַפָּחָא, וְיָתְבִי וְקָאָמְרִי: עִיר אַחַת הָיְתָה בְּאֶרֶץ יִשְׂרָאֵל וְלֹא רָצוּ עֲבָדֶיהָ לָמוּל, וְגִלְגְּלוּ עִמָּהֶם עַד שְׁנֵים עָשָׂר חֹדֶשׁ, וְחָזְרוּ וּמְכָרוּם לְגוֹיִם. כְּמַאן –

Rabbi Ḥanina bar Pappi, and Rabbi Ami, and Rabbi Yitzḥak Nappaḥa were sitting in the courtyard of Rabbi Yitzḥak Nappaḥa. They were sitting and saying: There was one city in Eretz Yisrael whose slaves did not wish to be circumcised. Their masters **abided with them until twelve months** had passed **and then sold them to gentiles. In accordance with whose** opinion did they act?

PERSONALITIES

Ravin – רָבִין: Ravin was a fourth-generation *amora* who studied in Eretz Yisrael under Rabbi Abbahu, Rabbi Zeira, and Rabbi Ilai. He is known in the Jerusalem Talmud as Rabbi Avin or Rabbi Bun. He is best known for all of the traditions that he brought with him from Eretz Yisrael to Babylonia, which are frequently quoted in the Talmud with the introductory phrase: When Ravin came. The source of many of the traditions that Ravin brought with him was Rabbi Yoḥanan, and they were considered to be very precise. Apparently, Ravin also returned to visit his teachers in Eretz Yisrael and sent messages, possibly by letter, back to Babylonia, containing the traditions he learned from them (see *Ketubot* 49b and *Bava Metzia* 114a).

HALAKHA

He stipulated not to be circumcised – הִתְנָה שֶׁלֹּא לָמוּל: If a slave stipulated from the outset that he does not wish to be circumcised, and similarly, in times and places when the government prohibited conversion (*Mordekhai*), it is permitted to maintain the slave in one's house for as he long as he wishes. This is in accordance with the opinion of Rabbi Yehoshua ben Levi and Rav Pappa (Rambam *Sefer Ahava, Hilkhot Mila* 1:6; *Shulḥan Arukh, Yoreh De'a* 267:4 and in the comment of Rema).

כי האי תנא. דתניא: הלוקח עבד מן הגוי ולא רצה למול – מגלגל עמו עד שנים עשר חודש, לא מל – חוזר ומוכרו לגוים. רבי שמעון בן אלעזר אומר: אין משהין אותו בארץ ישראל, מפני הפסד טהרות. ובעיר הסמוכה לספר – אין משהין אותו כל עיקר, שמא ישמע דבר, וילך ויאמר לחברו גוי.

It is in accordance with the opinion of **this *tanna*, as it is taught** in a *baraita*: In the case of **one who purchases a slave from a gentile and** the slave **does not wish to be circumcised,** the master **abides with him** for **up to twelve months.** If, after this period, the slave **will** still **not be circumcised,** the master **then sells him to gentiles. Rabbi Shimon ben Elazar says: One may not allow him to remain in Eretz Yisrael due to the loss of ritually pure items** he could cause. As long as the slave remains uncircumcised, he is considered to be a gentile; therefore, by rabbinic decree, ritually pure items that he touches are considered to be impure. **And in a city that is near to the border**[N] **he may not be allowed to remain at all, lest he hear some** secret **matter** concerning security **and go and say** it over **to his fellow gentile** in an enemy country. However, once he has been circumcised and accepted the yoke of mitzvot, this concern no longer exists.

תניא, רבי חנניא בנו של רבן גמליאל אומר: מפני מה גרים בזמן הזה מעונין, ויסורין באין עליהן – מפני שלא קיימו שבע מצות בני נח. רבי יוסי אומר: גר – שנתגייר כקטן שנולד דמי. אלא מפני מה מעונין – לפי שאין בקיאין בדקדוקי מצות כישראל, אבא חנן אומר משום רבי אלעזר: לפי שאין עושין מאהבה אלא מיראה.

§ **It is taught** in a *baraita*: **Rabbi Ḥananya, son of Rabban Gamliel, says: For what reason are converts at the present time**[N] **tormented and hardships come upon them?**[N] It is **because** when they were gentiles **they did not observe the seven Noahide mitzvot. Rabbi Yosei says:** They would not be punished for their deeds prior to their conversion because **a convert who** just **converted is like a child** just **born**[N] in that he retains no connection to his past life. **Rather, for what reason are they tormented?** It is **because they are not** as **well-versed in the intricacies of the mitzvot as** a born **Jew,** and consequently they often inadvertently transgress mitzvot. **Abba Ḥanan says in the name of Rabbi Elazar:** It is **because they observe** mitzvot **not out of love** of God, **but only out of fear** of the punishments for failing to observe them.

אחרים אומרים: מפני ששהו עצמם להכנס תחת כנפי השכינה. אמר רבי אבהו ואיתימא רבי חנינא: מאי קראה – "ישלם ה׳ פעלך ותהי משכרתך שלמה מעם ה׳ אלהי ישראל אשר באת לחסות" וגומר.

Others say: It is **because they waited**[N] **before entering under the wings of the Divine Presence,** i.e., they are punished for not converting sooner than they did. **Rabbi Abbahu said, and some say** it was **Rabbi Ḥanina** who said: **What is the verse**[N] from which it is derived that one should convert at the earliest opportunity? Boaz said to Ruth: **"The Lord shall recompense your work, and your reward shall be complete from the Lord, the God of Israel,** under whose wings **you have come to take refuge"** (Ruth 2:12).

NOTES

A city that is near to the border – **עיר הסמוכה לספר:** The Gemara in tractate *Eruvin* maintains that if marauders attack a border city, one may desecrate the Sabbath to confront them even if their sole intention is to steal produce. The early commentaries explain that that reason for this is because if they would succeed in entering into a border city, that would pose a significant security risk as it would allow them to penetrate further into the country. Similarly, the requirement to decimate an idolatrous city in Eretz Yisrael does not apply if that city is on the border, as doing so might encourage the enemy to attack other cities nearby. In the Gemara here, the concern is that the slave might know the language of the enemies, and since he lives adjacent to the border he would be able to direct them as to how to conquer the border cities (*Meshekh Ḥokhma*).

It remains unclear why, when discussing the fact the slave could disqualify ritually pure items, the *baraita* states: One may not allow him to remain, but when discussing the danger of leaving him near a border city, it states more emphatically: He may not be allowed to remain at all.

Rabbi Moshe Feinstein suggests that it is easier to protect ritually pure items in the short term until one finds a buyer for the slave, and therefore one may delay before selling the slave. However, in a border city, where there is imminent danger that the slave will undermine the security of the city, he must be sold to gentiles immediately.

Converts at the present time – **גרים בזמן הזה:** The commentaries note that the Gemara emphasizes that this question applies specifically to the present time because those who convert at times when the Jews are of superior status are suspected of having chosen to convert not for the sake of Heaven. At the present time, however, when the Jews are downtrodden, it is certain that the conversion is for the sake of Heaven and so the question of why they suffer so much arises (*Iyyun Ya'akov*).

Tormented and hardships come upon them – **מעונין, ויסורין באין עליהן:** The Ritva explains that the question is asked specifically about converts. Born Jews might naturally conclude that they suffer due to the sins of their fathers. Converts, on the other hand, have no apparent reason to be suffering.

Like a child just born – **כקטן שנולד דמי:** A convert is absolved of sins he committed while he was still a gentile only in cases where the punishment is in the hands of Heaven. However, if he was liable to be punished by the courts, converting will not exempt him from his liability (*Tosafot Yeshanim*).

Because they waited – **מפני ששהו עצמן:** One commentary explains that this cannot refer to the fact that they did not decide to convert earlier, as gentiles are not commanded to convert. Rather, it refers to the time between the decision to convert and the actual act of conversion itself; once a convert has decided to convert he should act quickly to complete the process (Ya'avetz).

What is the verse, etc. – **מאי קראה וכו׳:** Rashi and *Tosafot* explain that this verse is cited in support of the opinion attributed to: Others. The Maharsha explains that the proof is derived from the fact that Boaz gave Ruth a double blessing. The blessing: "God shall recompense your work," is for the act of conversion itself, and "Your reward shall be complete" is for the promptness involved. Re'em Horowitz, however, suggests that this verse is cited only to provide a source for the phrase: To enter under the wings of the Divine Presence. The Ritva holds that the verse is adduced to prove the statement of Rabbi Yosei that a convert is like a child just born. See *Arukh LaNer*, who explains how the verse provides proof for all of these positions.

מתני׳ אֵיזֶהוּ מַמְזֵר? כׇּל שְׁאֵר בָּשָׂר שֶׁהוּא בְּ״לֹא יָבֹא״, דִּבְרֵי רַבִּי עֲקִיבָא. שִׁמְעוֹן הַתִּימְנִי אוֹמֵר: כׇּל שֶׁחַיָּיבִים עָלָיו כָּרֵת בִּידֵי שָׁמַיִם. וַהֲלָכָה כִּדְבָרָיו. וְרַבִּי יְהוֹשֻׁעַ אוֹמֵר: כׇּל שֶׁחַיָּיבִין עָלָיו מִיתַת בֵּית דִּין.

MISHNA Which offspring of forbidden relations have the status of a ***mamzer***?[NH] It is the offspring of a union with **any next of kin**[N] **that is subject** to a Torah **prohibition** that **he should not engage in sexual relations** with them; **this is the statement of Rabbi Akiva. Shimon HaTimni**[P] **says:** It is the offspring of a union with any forbidden relation **for which one is liable to** receive ***karet*** **at the hand of Heaven. And the *halakha* is in accordance with his statement.**[N] **Rabbi Yehoshua says:** It is the offspring of a union with **any** forbidden relation **for which one is liable to** receive **court-**imposed **capital punishment.**

אָמַר רַבִּי שִׁמְעוֹן בֶּן עַזַּאי: מָצָאתִי מְגִלַּת יוּחֲסִין בִּירוּשָׁלַיִם וְכָתוּב בָּהּ: אִישׁ פְּלוֹנִי מַמְזֵר מֵאֵשֶׁת אִישׁ, לְקַיֵּים דִּבְרֵי רַבִּי יְהוֹשֻׁעַ.

Rabbi Shimon ben Azzai said: I found a scroll recording people's **lineages in Jerusalem, and it was written in it that so-and-so is a *mamzer***[N] **from** an adulterous union with **a married woman,** a sin punishable by court-imposed capital punishment. The only reason for the scroll to state the reason that this individual is a *mamzer* is in order **to support the statement of Rabbi Yehoshua.**

אִשְׁתּוֹ שֶׁמֵּתָה – מוּתָּר בַּאֲחוֹתָהּ, גֵּירְשָׁהּ וּמֵתָה – מוּתָּר בַּאֲחוֹתָהּ. נִשֵּׂאת לְאַחֵר וּמֵתָה – מוּתָּר בַּאֲחוֹתָהּ. יְבִמְתּוֹ שֶׁמֵּתָה – מוּתָּר בַּאֲחוֹתָהּ, חָלַץ לָהּ וּמֵתָה – מוּתָּר בַּאֲחוֹתָהּ, נִשֵּׂאת לְאַחֵר וּמֵתָה – מוּתָּר בַּאֲחוֹתָהּ.

The mishna delineates the circumstances in which it is prohibited to engage in relations with the sister of one's wife and the sister of one's *yevama*: If a man's **wife died, he is permitted to her sister.**[H] **If he divorced her and** then **she died, he is permitted to her sister.** If he divorced his wife and then **she was married to another** and then **died, he is permitted to her sister.** If **his *yevama* died, he is permitted to her sister. If he performed *ḥalitza* with her and** then **she died, he is permitted to her sister.** If after *ḥalitza* **she was married to another** and then **died, he is permitted to her sister.** The principle underlying all these cases is that the prohibition against engaging in relations with her sister only applies while the wife or *yevama* remain alive, irrespective of their current relationship to the man.

גמ׳ מַאי טַעֲמָא דְּרַבִּי עֲקִיבָא? דִּכְתִיב ״לֹא יִקַּח אִישׁ אֶת אֵשֶׁת אָבִיו וְלֹא יְגַלֶּה כְּנַף אָבִיו״ – כָּנָף שֶׁרָאָה אָבִיו לֹא יְגַלֶּה,

GEMARA What is Rabbi Akiva's reasoning? As it is written: "A man shall not take his father's wife, and he shall not uncover his father's cloak"** (Deuteronomy 23:1). This teaches that a **cloak that his father saw,**[N] i.e., a woman with whom his father engaged in sexual relations, the son **may not uncover.**

HALAKHA

Which offspring have the status of a *mamzer* – אֵיזֶהוּ מַמְזֵר: The offspring born of a forbidden union for which one is liable to *karet* or a court-imposed death penalty is a *mamzer*, irrespective of whether the sexual relations were engaged in willfully or otherwise. This is true with the exception of the offspring of a union with a menstruating woman, which is not a *mamzer*. This is in accordance with the opinion of Shimon HaTimni, since the Gemara rules in accordance with his opinion (Rambam *Sefer Kedusha, Hilkhot Issurei Bia* 15:1; *Shulḥan Arukh, Even HaEzer* 4:13).

If a man's wife died he is permitted to her sister – אִשְׁתּוֹ שֶׁמֵּתָה מוּתָּר בַּאֲחוֹתָהּ: A man's wife's sister is forbidden to him throughout his wife's lifetime, even if they are divorced. After his wife's death, however, he is permitted to marry her sister. It is all the more true that the sister of a *yevama* is permitted to the *yavam* after the death of the *yevama* (Rambam *Sefer Kedusha, Hilkhot Issurei Bia* 2:9; *Shulḥan Arukh, Even HaEzer* 15:26).

PERSONALITIES

Shimon HaTimni – שִׁמְעוֹן הַתִּימְנִי: Shimon HaTimni was a *tanna* during the generation of Rabbi Akiva whose title was derived from his home city of Timna in Judea. He was one of the important Sages of the Sanhedrin in Yavne. He numbers among those few Sages who understood seventy languages. However, due to his young age, he was never ordained, and so he is instead referred to as one who deliberated before the Sages. Despite his young age, and even though he was connected to the disciples of Rabbi Akiva, he was nevertheless not his preeminent disciple. In fact, he occasionally disputed Rabbi Akiva's opinions.

Most statements cited in his name in the Mishna and *baraitot* involve matters of *halakha*, and he seldom comments on issues of *aggada*.

NOTES

Which offspring have the status of a *mamzer* – אֵיזֶהוּ מַמְזֵר: This mishna is not directly related to the general subject matter of this chapter. However, since the previous mishna cites the dispute between Rabbi Akiva and the Rabbis as to whether or not the offspring from various forbidden unions are *mamzerim*, this mishna cites the basic principles behind that dispute (Meiri).

Any next of kin – כׇּל שְׁאֵר בָּשָׂר: The mishna here appears to state that Rabbi Akiva regards only the offspring of forbidden unions between next of kin as *mamzerim*; however, the offspring of other forbidden unions would not be *mamzerim*. This would seem to contradict the mishna on 44a that states that Rabbi Akiva holds that with regard to one who remarries his divorcée after she had been married to another man, the offspring from that union is also a *mamzer*. Rashi suggests that the two *mishnayot* reflect the two different opinions with regard to Rabbi Akiva's position, and the mishna on 44a is in accordance with the understanding of Rabbi Simai. Others reject this suggestion because it would be highly unseemly for the Mishna to cite two statements in the name of a single Sage based on two opposing opinions of what his position is, especially when the two statements are cited in close proximity to each other. The Rashba therefore explains that one must conclude that one's divorcée who remarried is also considered next of kin because the prohibition is based on his close relationship to her.

From the Rambam's Commentary on the Mishna it would appear that he read Rabbi Akiva's statement in this mishna as comprising two clauses: The offspring of a union with any next of kin, or of a union that is subject to a Torah prohibition, is a *mamzer*. His interpretation is supported by the discussion of this mishna in the Jerusalem Talmud. According to this reading, there is no contradiction at all to the previous mishna.

And the *halakha* is in accordance with his statement – וַהֲלָכָה כִּדְבָרָיו: Some early commentaries, including the Rif and Rabbeinu Ḥananel, note that there is a principle, cited in the Jerusalem Talmud on tractate *Pe'a*, that the *halakha* is not decided based on rulings in a mishna. Therefore, despite the fact that this mishna explicitly states that the *halakha* is in accordance with the opinion of Shimon HaTimni, that itself has no force in deciding the ultimate ruling. Some explain that the reason for this is that when Rabbi Yehuda HaNasi redacted the Mishna, he collected and arranged many tannaitic statements that already existed. He would sometimes cite those statements without modification, even if they included claims about what the *halakha* should be. Accordingly, when a mishna includes a statement about the ruling of a *halakha*, it cannot be assumed that it reflects Rabbi Yehuda HaNasi's own opinion, and therefore it does not carry any halakhic weight.

And it was written in it that so-and-so is a *mamzer*, etc. – וְכָתוּב בָּהּ: אִישׁ פְּלוֹנִי מַמְזֵר וכו׳: The purpose of keeping a record of lineages is so that people are aware of whom they may marry and whom they may not. Therefore, it is unnecessary for the scroll to detail the circumstances that led to one gaining a certain status. Accordingly, the fact that this scroll explicitly stated why a certain individual was a *mamzer* suggests that it meant to teach something about who is to be regarded as a *mamzer* (*Yosef Lekaḥ*; see *Tosafot*).

A cloak that his father saw, etc. – כָּנָף שֶׁרָאָה אָבִיו וכו׳: The Gemara explains that this refers to a woman raped by his father. However, it is difficult to understand why the offspring from a union with her would be a *mamzer*, since Rabbi Akiva states in the mishna that only the offspring of a union with a next of kin is a *mamzer*. Some resolve this question by saying that the essence of the condition that the union be with a next of kin is that the prohibition is a function of one's relationship to her. If so, even though a woman his father rapes is not actually a next of kin, since ultimately the prohibition against engaging in relations with her is due to the father's relationship to her, Rabbi Akiva will agree that the offspring of a union with her will be a *mamzer* (Rashash).

וסבר לה כרבי יהודה, דאמר: באנוסת אביו הכתוב מדבר, דהויא לה חייבי לאוין.

And in this interpretation of the verse, Rabbi Akiva **holds in accordance with** the opinion of **Rabbi Yehuda, who said:** The verse states only that such relations are forbidden, but they would not render him liable to receive *karet*; perforce **the verse speaks of a woman raped by one's father,** since **she is** one of the women with whom relations render one **liable for** violating **a prohibition.** The verse could not refer to one's father's wife since relations with her render one liable to receive *karet*.

וסמיך ליה "לא יבא ממזר בקהל ה'". אלמא: מהני הוי ממזר.

The Gemara completes its explanation of Rabbi Akiva's opinion: **And in close proximity to that** verse is the verse: **"A** ***mamzer*** **shall not enter**[N] **into the congregation of the Lord"** (Deuteronomy 23:3). **Apparently,** even **from these** forbidden relations, which render one liable for the violation of a prohibition, the offspring **is a** ***mamzer***.

ולרבי סימאי דמרבה שאר חייבי לאוין דלאו ד"שאר", ולרבי ישבב דמרבה אפילו חייבי עשה –

The Gemara asks: **But according to Rabbi Simai, who** holds that Rabbi Akiva **includes** as a *mamzer* the offspring of all **other** forbidden relations **for which one is liable** for violation of a **prohibition,** even those **that are not** with his **next of kin; and** also **according to Rabbi Yeshevav,**[P] who holds that Rabbi Akiva **includes even** the offspring of relations **for which one is liable for** the violation of a **positive mitzva;** since according to them, Rabbi Akiva includes cases that are not similar to the case a woman raped by his father, what is his source?

נפקא להו מ"ולא".

The Gemara answers: **They derive** it **from** the verse that states: **"And he shall not** uncover his father's cloak" (Deuteronomy 23:1). The word "and" is superfluous and serves to include additional cases.

ושמעון התימני סבר לה כרבנן, דאמרי: בשומרת יבם של אביו הכתוב מדבר, דהויא לה חייבי כריתות, וסמיך ליה "לא יבא ממזר", אלמא: מחייבי כריתות הוי ממזר.

And Shimon HaTimni[N] **holds in accordance with** the opinion of **the Rabbis, who say:** It **is with regard to the widow waiting for his father** to perform **levirate marriage that the verse is speaking,** and it indicates **that she is** one of the women with whom relations **render one liable** to receive *karet*. **And in close proximity to that** verse is the verse: **"A** ***mamzer*** **shall not enter** into the congregation of the Lord" (Deuteronomy 23:3). **Apparently,** only the offspring of a union **for which one is liable** to receive ***karet*** **is a** ***mamzer***.

ורבי יהושע: לכתוב רחמנא "לא יגלה", "לא יקח" ("ולא יגלה") למה לי? אלא לאו הכי קאמר: מ"לא יקח" עד "לא יגלה" – הוי ממזר, טפי – לא הוי ממזר.

And how does **Rabbi Yehoshua**[N] derive his opinion? If the verses should be derived as Rabbi Akiva and Shimon HaTimni suggest, **let the Merciful One write** only: **"He shall not uncover** his father's cloak." It is unnecessary for the verse to mention the prohibition with regard to one's father's wife, as the fact that the offspring of that union is a *mamzer* would be known through an *a fortiori* inference, since that prohibition is more stringent than the one derived from the verse: "And shall not uncover his father's cloak." **Why do I** need both the clause **"a man shall not take** his father's wife" and the clause **"and shall not uncover** his father's cloak"? **Rather, is it not** that **this is what** the Torah **is saying:** Only the offspring of relations with the woman mentioned in the verse **after** the words **"a man shall not take" until** the words **"he shall not uncover,"** i.e., his father's wife, **is a** ***mamzer***, **but** the offspring of relations with the woman mentioned **beyond** that point, i.e., the woman referred to as "his father's cloak," **is not a** ***mamzer***.

אמר אביי: הכל מודים בבא על הנדה

§ **Abaye said: All** *tanna'im* in the mishna **agree with regard to one who engages in sexual relations with a menstruating woman,**[N]

NOTES

And in close proximity to that verse is: "A ***mamzer*** **shall not enter" – וסמיך ליה לא יבא ממזר:** Generally, when a derivation is based on the fact that two verses are in close proximity to each other, the two verses are actually juxtaposed with nothing between them. However, in this case, the two verses are separated by a verse that states that a man whose sexual organs have been damaged is prohibited from marrying into the congregation. *Tosafot* note this difficulty and explain that since a man whose sexual organs have been damaged is unable to father any children, that verse can certainly not be utilized to identify which kinds of forbidden unions result in the offspring being a *mamzer*. Therefore, in this case it is acceptable to base the derivation on the proximity of the verse about a *mamzer* to the verse about a woman with whom one's father engaged in relations (see Ritva and *Nimmukei Yosef*).

The opinion of Shimon HaTimni – שיטת שמעון התימני: From an opinion in the Jerusalem Talmud, as well as from many early commentaries (see Ramban and Rashba), it would appear that Shimon HaTimni arrived at his opinion based on the hermeneutical principle that if a case was included as part of a general category but was singled out to teach something, what it teaches is to be applied not only to that case but to all of the cases in that general category. As applied to this case, it indicates that since the prohibition with regard to one's father's wife appears in Leviticus as part of the general category of incestuous relationships for which one is liable to receive *karet*, and then it is mentioned alone in Deuteronomy in order to teach that the offspring of a union with one's father's wife is a *mamzer*, it therefore teaches that this is true of all the cases in Leviticus, i.e., that the offspring from any one of those relationships is a *mamzer*.

Rabbi Yehoshua's proof – הוכחת רבי יהושע: The commentaries suggest different interpretations of Rabbi Yehoshua's proof here. Rashi explains that since it is unnecessary to state both: "he shall not take" and "he shall not uncover," it is apparent that only the offspring of relations with the woman mentioned in between those phrases, i.e., one's father's wife, is a *mamzer*, as well as all similar cases where one would be liable for a court-imposed death penalty. The *ge'onim*, based on a different version of the text also cited by *Tosafot*, explain that since it is repetitious to state both "he shall not take" and "he shall not uncover," it must be that one should derive the *halakha* of a *mamzer* from the more stringent of the two.

Rabbeinu Ḥananel appears to have had a version of the Gemara in which the continuation: Rather is it not, etc., does not appear at all. Based on that version, he explains that since the expressions "he shall not take" and "he shall not uncover" are repetitious, their use must come to teach that only those prohibitions that are formulated in these ways are included.

All agree with regard to one who engages in sexual relations with a menstruating woman, etc. – הכל מודים בבא על הנדה וכו׳: In the Jerusalem Talmud it is explained that the offspring from relations with a menstruating woman is not a *mamzer* because the woman is not forbidden on account of being a next of kin, which the mishna here states is one of the conditions for the offspring to be a *mamzer*. This fits well with the explanation found in the Jerusalem Talmud that the specific case of one's father's wife teaches about the entire category of forbidden relations recorded in Leviticus. The prohibition against engaging in relations with a menstruating woman is not included in that category. Furthermore, that category of cases is introduced by the statement: "None of you shall approach to any that is next of kin to him, to uncover their nakedness" (Leviticus 18:6), which serves to emphasize that only the offspring from relations with those who are next of kin is a *mamzer*.

Rabbi Yehuda al-Madari notes that in addition to the Gemara's reasoning that betrothal with a menstruating woman takes effect, further proof can be derived from the fact that when a woman menstruates, the betrothal bond is not dissolved. This point, already mentioned by *Tosafot*, serves to prove that a menstruating woman is not to be fully classified in the same manner as other forbidden relations.

PERSONALITIES

Rabbi Yeshevav – רבי ישבב: Rabbi Yeshevav was a third-generation *tanna* and scribe who was a disciple of Rabbi Yehoshua and a contemporary of Rabbi Akiva. He was exceedingly generous, and Rabbi Akiva criticized him for giving too much of his money to charity. Rabbi Yeshevav was one of the ten martyrs who were killed by the Romans during the bar Kokheva rebellion, and according to tradition (*Midrash Eleh Ezkera*), the ninety-year-old Sage told his disciples to support each other and uphold justice and peace. He was then thrown to the dogs and did not merit to be buried.

וְעַל הַסּוֹטָה שֶׁאֵין הַוָּלָד מַמְזֵר.

or with a *sota*,[N] that the offspring is not a *mamzer*.[H]

נִדָּה – דְּהָא תָּפְסִי בָּהּ קִידּוּשִׁין, שֶׁנֶּאֱמַר "וּתְהִי נִדָּתָהּ עָלָיו" – אֲפִילּוּ בִּשְׁעַת נִדָּתָהּ – תָּפְסֵי בָּהּ קִידּוּשִׁין.

With regard to a **menstruating woman** the offspring is not a *mamzer* because one's **betrothal of her takes effect**,[H] **as it is stated: "And her impurity shall be upon him"** (Leviticus 15:24). The phrase "shall be" alludes to the fact that a betrothal with her takes effect. The verse teaches that **even at the time of her** menstrual **impurity, betrothal with her takes effect.**

סוֹטָה נַמִי – דְּהָא תָּפְסֵי בָּהּ קִידּוּשִׁין.

With regard to a ***sota*, too,** the offspring is not a *mamzer* **because** one's **betrothal of her takes effect.**

תַּנְיָא נַמִי הָכִי: הַכֹּל מוֹדִים בְּבָא עַל הַנִּדָּה, וְעַל הַסּוֹטָה, וְעַל שׁוֹמֶרֶת יָבָם – שֶׁאֵין הַוָּלָד מַמְזֵר.

The Gemara notes: **This** teaching of Abaye **is also taught** in a *baraita*: **All agree with regard to one who engages in sexual relations with a menstruating woman, or with a *sota*, or with a widow waiting for her *yavam*** to perform levirate marriage, **that the offspring is not a *mamzer*.**

וְאַבַּיֵי: שׁוֹמֶרֶת יָבָם מְסַפְּקָא לֵיהּ, אִי כְּרַב אִי כִּשְׁמוּאֵל.

The Gemara explains: **And Abaye** did not mention the case of a **widow waiting for her *yavam*** because **he is uncertain**[N] **whether,** if someone other than the *yavam* betrothed her, the *halakha* is **in accordance with** the opinion of **Rav** that it does not take effect or **in accordance with** the opinion of **Shmuel** that it might take effect.

"אָמַר רַבִּי שִׁמְעוֹן בֶּן עַזַּאי" כו׳. תָּנֵי, שִׁמְעוֹן בֶּן עַזַּאי אוֹמֵר: מָצָאתִי מְגִלַּת יוֹחֲסִין בִּירוּשָׁלַיִם, וְכָתוּב בָּהּ: אִישׁ פְּלוֹנִי מַמְזֵר מֵאֵשֶׁת אִישׁ. וְכָתוּב בָּהּ: מִשְׁנַת רַבִּי אֱלִיעֶזֶר בֶּן יַעֲקֹב קַב וְנָקִי. וְכָתוּב בָּהּ: מְנַשֶּׁה הָרַג אֶת יְשַׁעְיָה.

§ The mishna states: **Rabbi Shimon ben Azzai said:** I found a scroll recording people's lineages. The Gemara cites an expanded version of the contents of the scroll. **It is taught** in a *baraita* that **Rabbi Shimon ben Azzai said: I found a scroll** recording people's **lineages, in Jerusalem, and it was written in it**[N] that so-and-so **is a *mamzer*** from an adulterous union with a **married woman. And it was** also **written in it: The teachings of Rabbi Eliezer ben Ya'akov** measure only **a *kav* but are clean** and accurate, and so the *halakha* is decided in accordance with his opinions. **And it was written in it: Manasseh,** king of Israel, **killed Isaiah** the prophet.

HALAKHA

The offspring of a menstruating woman – וְלַד הַנִּדָּה: All agree that a child born from a menstruating woman is not a *mamzer* and is even permitted to marry into the priesthood (*Beit Shmuel*). However, he is considered to be of a sullied status and his family is not held to be of distinguished lineage (Rambam *Sefer Kedusha, Hilkhot Issurei Bia* 15:1; *Shulḥan Arukh, Even HaEzer* 4:3).

Betrothal of a menstruating woman – קִדּוּשֵׁי נִדָּה: If one betroths one of the forbidden relations whom, were he to engage in relations with them, he would be liable to receive *karet* or a court-imposed death penalty, then the betrothal does not take effect. The exception to this principle is a menstruating woman, in whose case the betrothal does take effect. Nevertheless, it is not appropriate to betroth a menstruating woman. The *Taz* writes that nowadays, due to the significant monetary loss involved in rescheduling a wedding if the bride is menstruating, people are not particular about avoiding this situation, but nevertheless one should try to prevent the situation *ab initio* (Rambam *Sefer Nashim, Hilkhot Ishut* 4:12; *Shulḥan Arukh, Even HaEzer* 44:6).

NOTES

Sota – סוֹטָה: The term *sota* is used to describe both a wife who was suspected by her husband of having been unfaithful and a wife who is known to have been unfaithful. In both cases, she is prohibited from engaging in relations with her husband.

Rashi explains that the Gemara here is referring to a case where it is known that she was unfaithful and nevertheless she remained married to her husband. Rashi explains that in this case the reason that everyone agrees that the offspring is not a *mamzer* is because the marriage bond is not abrogated despite the fact that the marriage is prohibited. *Tosafot* argue that the fact that the marriage bond is not abrogated is itself insufficient to explain why the offspring is not a *mamzer*. Therefore, they explain that the case here is where the husband divorced his adulterous wife and then remarried her. It is therefore apparent that his betrothal of her takes effect, and it is this fact that explains why the offspring is not a *mamzer*. Apparently, *Tosafot* assume that the key factor in defining whether the offspring will be a *mamzer* is whether or not the prohibition is a function of the familial relationship between them, i.e., only the offspring of forbidden relations between next of kin is a *mamzer*, and it is this factor that expresses itself in the fact that one cannot effect a betrothal between these relatives.

Rabbeinu Ḥananel writes that although the Gemara here states clearly that the offspring is not a *mamzer*, that is true only according to Torah law. However, by rabbinic law, the offspring is rendered a *mamzer*. He draws proof for his claim from the case of a woman who remarries after a single witness testified that her husband had died. In such a case, if it later emerges that in fact her original husband is still alive, she is prohibited by rabbinic decree from returning to him. If she does return to him and has a child by him, the Sages decreed that it is considered a *mamzer*. Rabbeinu Ḥananel understands that this provides a paradigm for other cases where the marriage is forbidden by rabbinic decree, and that in those cases as well the offspring is rendered a *mamzer* by the Sages. *Tosafot* cite the opinion of Rabbeinu Ḥananel and explain that this decree is a penalty on the couple for ignoring the rabbinic prohibition against their marrying.

Other authorities disagree with Rabbeinu Ḥananel's opinion and claim that the case of a woman who remarried based on the testimony of a single witness is unique because in that case she married her new husband under the assumption that it was a valid course of action. Since the new marriage has the appearance of a valid one, the Sages prohibited her from returning to her original husband. However, in the case of adultery, no such concern exists, and therefore there is no need to render the offspring a *mamzer* (*Tosefot Ḥad MiKamma'ei*; Meiri; see Rashi, *Tosafot*, and Ramban).

He is uncertain, etc. – מְסַפְּקָא לֵיהּ וכו׳: The connection made by the Gemara between whether to rule in accordance with Rav or Shmuel and the status of the offspring as a *mamzer* is far from simple because the prohibition against a *yevama* engaging in relations with someone other than her *yavam* is of an entirely different nature than other forbidden relations (see *Tosafot*). Some explain that even according to the opinion of Rav the betrothal does not take effect; there is no actual negative mitzva against the *yevama* engaging in relations with someone other than her *yavam*. Rather, the reason that betrothal does not take effect is because she is already bound to the *yavam* through a levirate bond, and that bond prevents any other marital bond from taking effect upon her. The offspring of such a union is a *mamzer* for the same reason that some opinions hold that the offspring of a gentile and a Jewish woman is a *mamzer*: Whenever it is not possible to effect a betrothal between two people, the offspring from a union between them is a *mamzer* irrespective of the nature of the prohibition that applies to them.

One commentary suggests that neither Rav nor Shmuel themselves would hold that the offspring is a *mamzer*, since they hold that only the offspring of forbidden relations for which one is liable to receive *karet* is a *mamzer*. Abaye's uncertainty was in accordance with the opinion of Rabbi Akiva that even the offspring of less stringent forbidden relations is a *mamzer* (see Ramban and Rabbi Avraham min HaHar).

A scroll recording people's lineages…and it was written in it, etc. – מְגִלַּת יוֹחֲסִין...וְכָתוּב בָּהּ וכו׳: Ostensibly, the other matters that were written in the scroll were of no relevance to the scroll's main purpose of recording people's lineages. However, some suggest that a connection may be drawn: The statement that the *halakha* is in accordance with Rabbi Eliezer ben Ya'akov could be understood to refer specifically to the fact that the *halakha* is decided in accordance with his opinion with regard to the *halakhot* of lineages. In fact, the Gemara in *Kiddushin* 77a cites a case of lineages where his opinion was followed. With regard to the statement about Manasseh, the relevance may have been related to the fact that Manasseh was the grandson of Isaiah. The scroll wished to proclaim that although lineage may be of some importance, good lineage it is not necessarily a guarantee for success (*Arukh LaNer*).

אֲמַר רָבָא: מֵידַן דַּיְינֵיהּ וּקְטַלֵיהּ. אֲמַר לֵיהּ: מֹשֶׁה רַבָּךְ אֲמַר "כִּי לֹא יִרְאַנִי הָאָדָם וָחָי" וְאַתְּ אָמַרְתְּ "וָאֶרְאֶה אֶת ה׳ יוֹשֵׁב עַל כִּסֵּא רָם וְנִשָּׂא", מֹשֶׁה רַבָּךְ אֲמַר "מִי כַּה׳ אֱלֹהֵינוּ בְּכָל קָרְאֵנוּ אֵלָיו" וְאַתְּ אָמַרְתְּ "דִּרְשׁוּ ה׳ בְּהִמָּצְאוֹ". מֹשֶׁה רַבָּךְ אֲמַר "אֶת מִסְפַּר יָמֶיךָ אֲמַלֵּא" וְאַתְּ אָמַרְתְּ "וְהוֹסַפְתִּי עַל יָמֶיךָ חֲמֵשׁ עֶשְׂרֵה שָׁנָה"!

The Gemara expands on the events surrounding Isaiah's death: **Rava said:** Manasseh **judged him** as a false witness for issuing statements contradicting the Torah **and** only then **killed him.** Manasseh **said to** Isaiah: **Moses your master said** in the Torah: "And He said: You cannot see My face, **for man cannot see Me and live**" (Exodus 33:20), **and** yet **you said: "I saw the Lord sitting upon a high and lofty throne"** (Isaiah 6:1). **Moses your master said:** "For which great nation is there, that has God so near to it, **as the Lord our God is, whenever we call upon Him?"** (Deuteronomy 4:7), **and** yet **you said: "Seek the Lord while He may be found, call upon Him while He is near"** (Isaiah 55:6), which implies that God is not always near. **Moses your master said: "I will fulfill the number of your days"** (Exodus 23:26), which implies that each individual has a preordained allotted lifespan that he cannot outlive, **and** yet **you said** in a prophecy to King Hezekiah: **"And I will add to your days, fifteen years"** (II Kings 20:6).

אֲמַר יְשַׁעְיָה: יָדַעְנָא בֵּיהּ דְּלָא מְקַבֵּל מַה דְּאֵימָא לֵיהּ, וְאִי אֵימָא לֵיהּ – אֲשַׁוְּיֵיהּ מֵזִיד. אֲמַר שֵׁם, אִיבְלַע בְּאַרְזָא. אַתְיוּהָ לְאַרְזָא וְנַסְרוּהָ. כִּי מְטָא לְהָדֵי פּוּמָא – נָח נַפְשֵׁיהּ, מִשּׁוּם דְּאָמַר "וּבְתוֹךְ עַם טְמֵא שְׂפָתַיִם אָנֹכִי יוֹשֵׁב".

Isaiah said to himself: **I know him,** i.e., Manasseh, **that he will not accept whatever** explanation **that I will say to him** to resolve my prophecies with the words of the Torah. **And** even **if I say it to him,**[N] **I will make him into an intentional transgressor** since he will kill me anyway. Therefore, in order to escape, **he uttered a** divine **name and was swallowed within a cedar** tree. Manasseh's servants **brought the cedar** tree **and sawed through it** in order to kill him. **When** the saw **reached to where his mouth was,** Isaiah **died.** He died specifically as this point **due to that which he said: "In the midst of a people of unclean lips,**[N] **I dwell"** (Isaiah 6:5). He was punished for referring to the Jewish people in a derogatory manner.

מִכָּל מָקוֹם קָשׁוּ קְרָאֵי אַהֲדָדֵי!

The Gemara asks: **In any case,** as Manasseh pointed out, these **verses contradict each other;** how are these contradictions to be resolved?

"וָאֶרְאֶה אֶת ה׳" – כִּדְתַנְיָא: כָּל הַנְּבִיאִים נִסְתַּכְּלוּ בְּאַסְפַּקְלַרְיָא שֶׁאֵינָהּ מְאִירָה, מֹשֶׁה רַבֵּינוּ נִסְתַּכֵּל בְּאַסְפַּקְלַרְיָא הַמְּאִירָה.

The Gemara resolves the first contradiction: **"I saw the Lord"** is to be understood **as it is taught** in a *baraita*: **All of the prophets observed** their prophecies **through an obscure looking glass** [*aspaklaria*],[LN] i.e., their prophecies were given as metaphoric visions but were not a direct perception of the matter. However, **Moses our master observed** his prophecies **through a clear looking glass,** i.e., he gained a direct and accurate perception of the matter.

NOTES

If I say it to him, etc. – **אִי אֵימָא לֵיהּ וכו׳**: *Tosafot* cite the interpretation of Rabbeinu Ḥananel that Isaiah could have easily responded that the Torah itself states with regard to the Elders at the revelation at Sinai: "And they saw the God of Israel" (Exodus 24:10), which justifies the use of the verb: See, with regard to God. The *Otzar HaShitot* explains that the Gemara chose not to raise this issue because ultimately the root of the issue is, as the Gemara explains, due to the difference in the level of prophecy between Moses and others. This, then, also explains the verse: "And they saw the God of Israel," which also describes the prophetic vision of the Elders, whose prophecy was not at the level of Moses'. Isaiah could not explain this matter to Manasseh because it would have been damaging to his mission to state that his level of prophecy was comparable to looking through an obscure looking glass, which Manasseh would have taken to mean that his prophecy was unreliable and inaccurate.

Due to that which he said: In the midst of a people of unclean lips – **מִשּׁוּם דְּאָמַר וּבְתוֹךְ עַם טְמֵא שְׂפָתַיִם**: Although Isaiah issued prophetic warnings to the Jewish people that contained much harsher statements, the commentaries explain that there was no claim against him for that because those statements were simply relaying what God had told him to say. He was punished only for expressing his own opinion about the nature of the Jewish people. See the Meiri and *Yam shel Shlomo* who discuss the halakhic conclusions that can be drawn from this Gemara.

The Ritva points out that in that same chapter in Isaiah, God's angels said to Isaiah: "Your iniquity is taken away and your sin shall be expiated" (Isaiah 7:6). This would seem to imply he was forgiven for his sin; why, then, was he later punished? The Ritva explains that Isaiah was forgiven only for expressing his sentiments before God, but he still had no right to later publicly recount what he had said, and he was punished for that. He also suggests another explanation: The phrase "and your sin shall be expiated" is stated in the future tense; it is not saying that he was already forgiven but that ultimately his sin would be expiated though his unseemly death.

Obscure looking glass – **בְּאַסְפַּקְלַרְיָא שֶׁאֵינָהּ מְאִירָה**: The commentaries (*ge'onim*; Rabbeinu Ḥananel; Rambam) wrote at length to explain this matter. Primarily they cite passages from *Vayikra Rabba* that include different tannaitic explanations of the subject. The essential idea is that one who does not see with sufficient clarity mistakenly sees things that do not exist or sees distorted forms. The Rambam, in *Sefer HaMadda* and in his Commentary on the Mishna, explains that only Moses could see God "face to face" (Deuteronomy 34:10) without any intervening imagery. The Ramban hints at a different understanding, according to which the other prophets experienced their prophecies as a mental image, whereas the prophecy of Moses was at such a high level that he gained an intimate understanding of the prophecy without the need for it to be diluted and encapsulated in a prophetic vision.

LANGUAGE

Looking glass [*aspaklaria*] – **אַסְפַּקְלַרְיָא**: Either from the Latin speculum, which is a mirror made of metal, or from the Latin specularis, meaning transparent, i.e., a transparent window. The word apparently entered Hebrew through the Greek **σπεκλάριον**, *speclarion*, meaning a small mirror.

In the Gemara, the word has two connotations: It can mean either a mirror made of metal, or a glass window or looking glass. In the context here, the reference is to the latter.

Ancient optical lens possibly used as a magnifying glass

Ancient Greek mirror

NOTES

This is with regard to the individual and this is with regard to a community – **הָא בְּיָחִיד הָא בְּצִבּוּר**: This distinction is evident in the verses themselves as well. The verse: "Whenever we call upon Him" clearly refers to a group of people, i.e., the community of the Jewish people, and the verse: "Seek the Lord while He may be found" continues "and let the wicked one forsake His way" (Isaiah 55:7), which clearly refers to an individual (Maharsha).

HALAKHA

Ten days of repentance – **עֲשֶׂרֶת יְמֵי תְּשׁוּבָה**: While repentance is always effective, repentance of the individual is especially well received during the ten days between Rosh HaShana and Yom Kippur (Rambam *Sefer HaMadda*, *Hilkhot Teshuva* 2:6).

"דִּרְשׁוּ ה׳ בְּהִמָּצְאוֹ" – הָא בְּיָחִיד הָא בְּצִבּוּר. וְיָחִיד אֵימַת? אָמַר רַב נַחְמָן אָמַר רַבָּה בַּר אֲבוּה: אֵלּוּ עֲשָׂרָה יָמִים שֶׁבֵּין רֹאשׁ הַשָּׁנָה לְיוֹם הַכִּפּוּרִים,

The Gemara resolves the second contradiction: Isaiah's prophecy: **"Seek the Lord while He may be found,"** does not contradict the verse in the Torah that God is near to His nation "whenever we call upon Him," because **this** prophecy of Isaiah was made **with regard to the individual** and **this** verse in the Torah is stated **with regard to a community,**[N] as the prayer of the community is always accepted. The Gemara asks: **And when** is the time that God is to be found near **the individual? Rav Naḥman said Rabba bar Avuh said: These are the ten days between Rosh HaShana and Yom Kippur.**[H]

"אֶת מִסְפַּר יָמֶיךָ אֲמַלֵּא" – תַּנָּאֵי הִיא. דְּתַנְיָא "אֶת מִסְפַּר יָמֶיךָ אֲמַלֵּא"

The resolution of the third contradiction from the verse: **"I will fulfill the number of your days,"** is subject to a dispute between *tanna'im*, **as it is taught** in a *baraita*: The verse states: **"I will fulfill the number of your days";**

Perek **IV**
Daf **50** Amud **a**

אֵלּוּ שְׁנֵי דּוֹרוֹת, זָכָה – מַשְׁלִימִין לוֹ, לֹא זָכָה – פּוֹחֲתִין לוֹ. דִּבְרֵי רַבִּי עֲקִיבָא. וַחֲכָמִים אוֹמְרִים: זָכָה – מוֹסִיפִים לוֹ, לֹא זָכָה – פּוֹחֲתִין לוֹ.

these are the **years of** the **generations,**[N] i.e., the allotted lifespan that is preordained for each individual before birth. If **he is deserving,** God **completes his** allotted lifespan. If **he is not deserving,** God **reduces his** lifespan; this is **the statement of Rabbi Akiva.** Rabbi Akiva assumes one cannot outlive one's preordained allotted lifespan. **The Rabbis say:** If **he is deserving,** God **adds** years **to his** lifespan.[N] If **he is not deserving,** God **reduces his** lifespan. According to the Rabbis, Isaiah's prophecy is referring to one who deserved to have extra years added to his allotted lifespan, and the verse in the Torah is referring to one who deserved to merely complete his lifespan.

אָמְרוּ לוֹ לְרַבִּי עֲקִיבָא: הֲרֵי הוּא אוֹמֵר "וְהוֹסַפְתִּי עַל יָמֶיךָ חֲמֵשׁ עֶשְׂרֵה שָׁנָה"! אָמַר לָהֶם: מִשֶּׁלּוֹ הוֹסִיפוּ לוֹ. תֵּדַע, שֶׁהֲרֵי נָבִיא עוֹמֵד וּמִתְנַבֵּא "הִנֵּה בֵן נוֹלָד לְבֵית דָּוִד יֹאשִׁיָּהוּ שְׁמוֹ" וַעֲדַיִין לֹא נוֹלַד מְנַשֶּׁה.

The Rabbis **said to Rabbi Akiva:** How can you claim that one cannot outlive one's allotted lifespan when **there is** a verse that **states** that Isaiah prophesied to Hezekiah as Hezekiah lay on his deathbed: **"And I will add unto your days fifteen years"?** Rabbi Akiva **said to them:** Those additional years that God **added to his** lifespan are **from his own** allotted lifespan. When Hezekiah sinned God decreed that his lifespan be shortened, but when he repented God allowed him to live out those years. **Know** that this is so, **as a prophet** during the reign of King Jeroboam **stood and prophesied:**[N] **"Behold, a son shall be born unto the House of David, Josiah is his name"** (I Kings 13:2). Josiah was the grandson of Manasseh, Hezekiah's son, and at the time Hezekiah lay on his deathbed, **Manasseh had not yet been born.** Evidently, Hezekiah's preordained allotted lifespan had still not been completed.

NOTES

The years of the generations – **שְׁנֵי דּוֹרוֹת**: Rashi and others interpret this as a reference to the years of life allotted to each generation, which are then divided and are allotted to each individual in that generation. *Tosefot HaRosh* explains that when God makes an accounting of people's lifespans He does so as part of a general decree relating to the lifespans of the entire generation. This is alluded to by the verse: "He that calls the generations from the beginning" (Isaiah 41:4). The *ge'onim* explain that the reference is to the number of years one should live based on his physical structure and health (see Meiri and Rabbi Avraham min HaHar). The Rambam wrote an important treatise in Arabic in which he summarized the various opinions on this subject, from both the philosophical and the medical perspectives.

If he is deserving, God adds years to his lifespan – **זָכָה מוֹסִיפִים לוֹ**: What is the significance of being given a preordained lifespan if one can merit additional years or lose years based on one's actions? The *Tzlaḥ* on *Yoma* 86b suggests that each day has its own unique goals to be fulfilled, and if one did not utilize each day correctly he will be called to account in the World-to-Come. However, if he merits it, he will receive additional days and consequently he will be able to complete the goals that he did not achieve during the amount of time that had been allotted to him.

As a prophet stood and prophesied, etc. – **שֶׁהֲרֵי נָבִיא עוֹמֵד וּמִתְנַבֵּא וכו׳**: In a responsum written by Rav Hai Gaon on this matter he proves from here, as well as from Isaiah's prophecy concerning King Hezekiah's impending demise, that such prophecies are always conditional on one's actions and so one can change his fate by amending his ways and through prayer. See the Rambam, who discusses this subject at length when dealing with prophecy in *Mishne Torah* and elsewhere (see also in *Tosafot*).

וְרַבָּנַן: מִי כְּתִיב מֵחִזְקִיָּה? ״לְבֵית דָּוִד״ כְּתִיב, אִי מֵחִזְקִיָּה נוֹלַד, אִי מֵאֱינָשׁ אַחֲרִינָא.

And what would **the Rabbis** respond to Rabbi Akiva's proof? They could counter: **Is it written** that Josiah was to be born specifically **from** the descendants of **Hezekiah? It is written** only that he would be born **"unto the House of David,"** so **he could be born either from** the descendants of **Hezekiah or from a different person** of the House of David. Accordingly, no proof concerning Hezekiah's allotted lifespan can be deduced from that verse.

״אִשְׁתּוֹ שֶׁמֵּתָה וכו׳ יְבִמְתּוֹ שֶׁמֵּתָה״ וכו׳. אָמַר רַב יוֹסֵף: כָּאן שָׁנָה רַבִּי מִשְׁנָה שֶׁאֵינָהּ צְרִיכָה.

§ The mishna details the prohibition with regard to one's wife's sister in various cases: If a man's **wife died,** he is permitted to her sister; if **his *yevama* died,** he is permitted to her sister. **Rav Yosef said: Here Rabbi** Yehuda HaNasi **taught an unnecessary mishna,**[N] since the prohibition with regard to one's wife's sister and the fact that the prohibition exists only in the lifetime of one's wife is stated explicitly in the Torah, and there is no additional novelty in this mishna's ruling.

הדרן עלך החולץ

NOTES

An unnecessary mishna – מִשְׁנָה שֶׁאֵינָהּ צְרִיכָה: From Rashi's commentary it is clear that he holds that at the very least, the clause referring to the permissibility of one's wife's sister after the wife's death is superfluous, since the matter is stated explicitly in the Torah. However, *Tosafot Yeshanim* suggest that even that clause of the mishna hints at a novelty that is not explicit in the Torah. They explain the novelty is in the case where one's previous wife married another man: Unless she dies, the prohibition with regard to her sister still remains in effect. One might have claimed that since, by marrying another man, the woman was rendered forbidden to her first husband, therefore her sister would become permitted to him. To dispel this notion the mishna teaches that the prohibition remains in force until the wife actually dies. Therefore, *Tosafot Yeshanim* suggest that it is the latter clause, which states that if one's *yevama* died one is permitted to her sister, which is entirely superfluous. Once the mishna has stated the *halakha* in the case of one's wife's sister, it is obviously true in the case of one's *yevama* through an *a fortiori* inference.

However, from an opinion in the Jerusalem Talmud it would appear that the primary novelty in the mishna is to be found specifically in the clause concerning the sister of one's *yevama*. The novelty does not lie in the case itself but in the fact that it implies that even after one's *yevama* dies, the levirate bond continues to exist to the extent that relatives of one's *yevama* will remain forbidden to him. The mishna states that the sister of one's *yevama* is an exception to this principle, but by inference the prohibition to other relatives, e.g., her mother or daughter, continue to apply. *Tosafot Yeshanim* and *Tosefot HaRosh* reject this suggestion.

The Ramban claims that only the clause that relates to the basic case of the sister of one's wife or *yevama* being permitted upon the death of one's wife or *yevama* are considered unnecessary because those cases are explicit in the Torah. However, although the principle is the same in the other cases, since they are not stated explicitly there is value in mentioning them here.

In contrast, the Ritva claims that the entire mishna is unnecessary and rejects the suggestion that the cases were taught to indicate some subtle novelty that may be inferred from them. Rather, the mishna was written to reëmphasize matters that are already known; doing so is considered "making the Torah great and glorious" (Isaiah 42:21).

Summary of **Perek IV**

The chapter began with a discussion of a case in which a woman performed *ḥalitza* or entered into levirate marriage under the assumption that she was required to do so, but it eventually emerged that she was pregnant at the time. The Gemara concludes that the validity of the *ḥalitza* or levirate marriage depends on whether she ultimately required them or not. Therefore, if she ultimately miscarries, in which case it is apparent that she did require them, they are valid. However, if she ultimately gave birth to viable offspring, then the levirate marriage or *ḥalitza* is of no significance.

As part of that discussion, the Gemara considered cases in which a child is born to the *yevama* following levirate marriage and it is unclear whether the child is the offspring of her first husband or the *yavam*. The Gemara then considered the steps that must be taken in all marriages to prevent such uncertainties from arising and to ensure that the lineage of the Jewish people is clear and apparent. The Gemara explained that for this purpose the Sages decreed that no woman should remarry until three months have passed since the end of her previous marriage and it is clear whether or not she is pregnant. With regard to a pregnant or nursing woman the Sages likewise decreed that she should wait a certain period before remarrying.

The Gemara proceeded to examine which cases of forbidden relations produce offspring with *mamzer* status. Although many views on the issue were presented, the accepted opinion is that only offspring from forbidden relations for which one is liable to receive *karet* are *mamzerim*, with the exception of a child born from a union with a menstruating woman, for which the punishment is not *karet*.

The chapter also considered the issues relating to the property of the *yevama* and of her deceased husband. As long as the *yevama* is still awaiting levirate marriage, her property remains her own and under her control. If she dies during that period then that property is bequeathed to her heirs, while the money promised to her in her marriage contract is inherited by her husband's heirs. However, after the levirate marriage the *yevama* is considered to be the wife of the *yavam* in every sense, and therefore the *yavam* has the same level of control over her property as any other husband has over his wife's property. The only exception to this principle is that her marriage contract remains payable from her first husband's estate.

The Gemara also discussed the *halakhot* of conversion and concluded that in order to convert it is necessary to be both circumcised and immersed for the sake of conversion before a court of three judges. A similar process is required for a slave; however, the Gemara examined whether there might be a distinction between the case of a convert and that of a slave with regard to whether it is necessary to willingly accept upon oneself the yoke of the mitzvot.

Introduction to **Perek V**

This chapter deals exclusively with one issue: The relationship between the various acts that a *yavam* might perform with a *yevama*. In total, there are four options: Intercourse or *ḥalitza*, which are effective by Torah law, and levirate betrothal [*ma'amar*] or a bill of divorce [*get*] by rabbinic law. This chapter clarifies the nature of the relationship between these options by discussing the relative efficacy of the modes of acquisition, i.e., intercourse or levirate betrothal, on the one hand, and the modes of release, i.e., *ḥalitza* or a bill of divorce, on the other. These issues come to the fore when two or more of these acts are performed successively, whether they are performed by a single *yavam* with a single *yevama*, a single *yavam* with two *yevamot* who are co-wives, several *yevamin* with one *yevama*, or several *yevamin* with several *yevamot*.

Examination of these various combinations helps clarify the relative legal validity of each of these acts. Does a given act conclusively determine the relationship between the *yavam* and the *yevama*, or does it leave room for a further act that might, if performed, alter matters?

This clarification proves especially important with regard to the two acts that are of rabbinic ordinance: The levirate betrothal and the bill of divorce for a *yevama*. Indeed, the Sages were in dispute with regard to the exact nature of levirate betrothal and its power of acquisition: Does it constitute a fully valid act of acquisition like regular betrothal, does it grant only partial acquisition, or is it merely symbolic and bereft of any legal validity whatsoever? Similarly, with regard to a bill of divorce given to a woman requiring levirate marriage, in what way is this bill similar to an ordinary bill of divorce? To what extent does it serve only as a symbol and merely resemble standard bills of divorce?

The clarification of these relationships and the various rabbinic ordinances involved constitute the subject matter for this chapter.

מתני׳ רַבָּן גַּמְלִיאֵל אוֹמֵר: אֵין גֵּט אַחַר גֵּט, וְלֹא מַאֲמָר אַחַר מַאֲמָר, וְלֹא בְּעִילָה אַחַר בְּעִילָה, וְלֹא חֲלִיצָה אַחַר חֲלִיצָה. וַחֲכָמִים אוֹמְרִים: יֵשׁ גֵּט אַחַר גֵּט, וְיֵשׁ מַאֲמָר אַחַר מַאֲמָר, אֲבָל לֹא אַחַר בְּעִילָה וְלֹא אַחַר חֲלִיצָה כְּלוּם.

MISHNA **Rabban Gamliel says:**[N] **A bill of divorce** [*get*][B] **is not** effective when given **after a bill of divorce** was previously given to a *yevama*. Once a *yevama* receives a bill of divorce from a *yavam*, no bill of divorce given by that *yavam* to her rival wife or a bill of divorce given to her by a different *yavam* is of any effect. **And levirate betrothal**[B] **is not** effective **after** a previous **levirate betrothal** was performed, **and intercourse** with a second *yevama* **is not** effective **after intercourse** with the first one, **and *ḥalitza***[B] **is not** effective **after *ḥalitza*** was previously performed. **But the Rabbis say: A bill of divorce is** effective when given **after a bill of divorce,**[N] **and levirate betrothal is** effective **after levirate betrothal,**[H] **but nothing is** effective **after intercourse**[N] **or after *ḥalitza*.**[H] If a *yavam* has relations with the *yevama* or performs *ḥalitza* with her, no other action performed afterward is effective, whether performed by that *yavam* toward a different *yevama* or by any *yavam* with the original *yevama*.

כֵּיצַד? עָשָׂה מַאֲמָר בִּיבִמְתּוֹ, וְנָתַן לָהּ גֵּט – צְרִיכָה הֵימֶנּוּ חֲלִיצָה. עָשָׂה מַאֲמָר וַחֲלִיצָה – צְרִיכָה הֵימֶנּוּ גֵּט. עָשָׂה מַאֲמָר וּבָעַל – הֲרֵי זוֹ כְּמִצְוָתָהּ.

The mishna elaborates: **How**[N] do these laws work in practice? If a *yavam* **performed levirate betrothal**[N] **with his *yevama*, and he** later **gave her a bill of divorce,**[H] **she** nevertheless **requires *ḥalitza* from him.** The bill of divorce does not fully exempt her from levirate marriage, as the levirate bond remains intact. If **he performed levirate betrothal and** then ***ḥalitza*, she requires a bill of divorce from him** in order to cancel the levirate betrothal. If the *yavam* **performed levirate betrothal and** then engaged in **intercourse** with the *yevama*, **this is** the way to perform levirate marriage **in accordance with its mitzva,** as the Sages instituted this as the proper procedure for a *yavam* to perform levirate marriage.

BACKGROUND

Bill of divorce [*get*] – גֵּט: Although the term *get* is sometimes applied to all legal documents, it is commonly used to refer specifically to a bill of divorce. The basic text of a bill of divorce includes the declaration of the husband that he divorces his wife and that she is permitted to marry any other man. He is identified by his name and his father's name, and his wife is identified by her name and her father's name. The document must contain the date it was written and the signatures of two witnesses. In talmudic times a bill of divorce could be written privately by a scribe at the request of the husband. In later generations it became customary for a bill of divorce to be written in a rabbinical court that had expertise in this field, so that no halakhic difficulties would arise that might lead to the invalidation of the document.

Levirate betrothal – מַאֲמָר: In the context of the *halakhot* of levirate marriage, levirate betrothal refers to an ordinary act of betrothal that is performed prior to the actual levirate marriage. According to the mishna (*Kiddushin* 1:1), betrothal can be performed with money or its equivalent, e.g., a ring, a legal document, or sexual intercourse. According to Torah law levirate marriage can be consummated only by means of sexual intercourse. The Sages ruled that when the *yavam* gives the *yevama* money and states that he is betrothing her and fulfilling the mitzva of levirate marriage by means of this money, they are betrothed by rabbinic law.

Ḥalitza – חֲלִיצָה: When a man dies without children, the Torah obligates his brother to perform levirate marriage with the deceased man's wife. The woman is not permitted to marry out of the family until this obligation is performed. If the brother does not wish to marry the woman he may perform the *ḥalitza* ceremony and thereby release the widow from her bond and allow her to remarry (see Deuteronomy 25:7–10). The term *ḥalitza* is derived from the central element of this ceremony, which involves the widow removing a special sandal from the foot of one of her deceased husband's brothers. *Ḥalitza* must be performed before a rabbinical court.

HALAKHA

A bill of divorce after a bill of divorce, etc. – גֵּט אַחַר גֵּט וכו׳: Levirate betrothal does not serve to completely acquire the *yevama*, nor does a bill of divorce serve to nullify the levirate bond entirely. Therefore any action performed with the *yevama* after levirate betrothal or a bill of divorce is effective, whether it is a bill of divorce, levirate betrothal, intercourse, or *ḥalitza*. This *halakha* applies both to situations of one *yavam* and two *yevamot*, one *yevama* and two *yevamin*, as well as two *yevamot* and two *yevamin*, in accordance with the opinion of the Rabbis (Rambam *Sefer Nashim*, *Hilkhot Yibbum* 5:14; *Shulḥan Arukh*, *Even HaEzer* 170:3).

Nothing is effective after intercourse and *ḥalitza* – לֹא אַחַר בְּעִילָה וַחֲלִיצָה: A *yavam* who has intercourse with a *yevama* has acquired her fully, and similarly *ḥalitza* serves to completely nullify the levirate bond. Consequently, any act performed after intercourse or *ḥalitza* is of no halakhic consequence (Rambam *Sefer Nashim*, *Hilkhot Yibbum* 5:14; *Shulḥan Arukh*, *Even HaEzer* 170:12).

If he performed levirate betrothal and gave a bill of divorce – עָשָׂה מַאֲמָר וְנָתַן גֵּט: If a *yavam* performed levirate betrothal with his *yevama* and gave her a bill of divorce, she still requires *ḥalitza*. If he performed levirate betrothal and *ḥalitza*, she requires a bill of divorce to cancel his levirate betrothal (Rambam *Sefer Nashim*, *Hilkhot Yibbum* 5:4; *Shulḥan Arukh*, *Even HaEzer* 170:2).

NOTES

Rabban Gamliel's opinion – שִׁיטַת רַבָּן גַּמְלִיאֵל: Some early commentaries maintain that Rabban Gamliel's statement with regard to levirate betrothal follows Rabbi Akiva's opinion that betrothal does not take effect on a woman who is forbidden due to a regular prohibition. Accordingly, after the *yavam* performs levirate betrothal with the first *yevama*, the second *yevama* would be forbidden due to the prohibition indicated by the verse: "So shall it be done to the man who does not build his brother's house" (Deuteronomy 25:9); he may build one house, in the singular, but he may not build two houses. Therefore, a second levirate betrothal would not be effective. The Ramban explains that if this is true in cases where the *yavam* consummated the levirate marriage with the first *yevama*, it is true in cases where he merely performed levirate betrothal. *Tosafot*, however, explain that Rabban Gamliel's statement accords with the opinion of the Rabbis, who disagree with Rabbi Akiva and state that betrothal does take effect on a woman forbidden due to a regular prohibition. If the *yavam* had consummated the levirate marriage with the first *yevama*, then betrothal would indeed be effective with the second *yevama*. However, in this case only levirate betrothal was performed, and the Sages did not institute a ruling allowing levirate betrothal to be effective in cases where it was already performed with one *yevama*.

A bill of divorce is effective after a bill of divorce, etc. – יֵשׁ גֵּט אַחַר גֵּט וכו׳: The latter act of giving a bill of divorce or performing levirate betrothal is of legal consequence. Admittedly, such actions do not acquire the *yevama* or nullify the levirate bond completely, but they do serve to connect the *yavam* to the *yevama* and render him forbidden to her relatives (see the *Melekhet Shlomo*).

But nothing is effective after intercourse, etc. – אֲבָל לֹא אַחַר בְּעִילָה וכו׳: As the Gemara will explain, this broad statement is imprecise, for most Sages agree that in certain situations his actions are effective even after intercourse or *ḥalitza*. It is possible that this principle is only according to the opinion of Rabbi Akiva, or that it is stated in a comprehensive manner because it will later be qualified and elucidated.

How – כֵּיצַד: Rashi and *Tosafot* state that this question does not refer particularly to the dispute at the beginning of the mishna. Rather, the mishna details all the various combinations of a bill of divorce, *ḥalitza*, levirate betrothal, and intercourse. This explains why several cases mentioned by the mishna teach us nothing new, or something we easily could have deduced from the other cases, as the *tanna* lists all possibilities.

How…performed levirate betrothal, etc. – כֵּיצַד עָשָׂה מַאֲמָר וכו׳: The mishna first mentions a *yavam* who performed levirate betrothal or gave a bill of divorce because the levirate betrothal and bill of divorce of a *yevama* are rabbinical decrees. Afterward it turns to actions prescribed by the Torah – intercourse and *ḥalitza* (*Nimmukei Yosef*).

HALAKHA

If he gave a bill of divorce and performed levirate betrothal – נָתַן גֵּט וְעָשָׂה מַאֲמָר: If a *yavam* gave a bill of divorce to his *yevama*, and he or his brother subsequently performed levirate betrothal with her, she requires a bill of divorce to cancel the levirate betrothal, and *ḥalitza* to nullify the levirate bond. Similarly, if he gave her a bill of divorce and afterward engaged in intercourse with her, she needs a bill of divorce to cancel the betrothal accomplished by intercourse, and *ḥalitza* to nullify the levirate bond (Rambam *Sefer Nashim, Hilkhot Yibbum* 5:7; *Shulḥan Arukh, Even HaEzer* 170:9).

נָתַן גֵּט וְעָשָׂה מַאֲמָר – צְרִיכָה גֵּט וַחֲלִיצָה. נָתַן גֵּט וּבָעַל – צְרִיכָה גֵּט וַחֲלִיצָה. נָתַן גֵּט וְחָלַץ – אֵין אַחַר חֲלִיצָה כְּלוּם.

If the *yavam* **gave** the *yevama* **a bill of divorce and** afterward **performed levirate betrothal**[H] with her, **she requires** another **bill of divorce** to cancel the levirate betrothal, as well as ***ḥalitza*** to nullify the levirate bond. **If he gave her a bill of divorce and then engaged in intercourse** with her, **she requires a bill of divorce** to cancel the betrothal that took place via intercourse, **and *ḥalitza*** to nullify the levirate bond; the intercourse did not affect the levirate bond because once he gave her a bill of divorce she was forbidden to him. **If he gave** her **a bill of divorce and performed *ḥalitza*, nothing is** effective **after *ḥalitza*,** as the levirate bond was completely nullified.

חָלַץ וְעָשָׂה מַאֲמָר, נָתַן גֵּט וּבָעַל, אוֹ בָּעַל וְעָשָׂה מַאֲמָר, נָתַן גֵּט וְחָלַץ – אֵין אַחַר חֲלִיצָה כְּלוּם.

Similarly, if he **performed *ḥalitza*** with her **and** then either **performed levirate betrothal,** or **gave a bill of divorce, or engaged in intercourse** with her; **alternatively,** if he **engaged in intercourse** with her **and** then either **performed levirate betrothal,** or **gave a bill of divorce, or performed *ḥalitza*** after they engaged in relations, **nothing is** effective **after *ḥalitza*** or intercourse. Any action performed afterward is unrelated to the levirate bond.

Perek **V**
Daf **50** Amud **b**

NOTES

Levirate betrothal with this one and levirate betrothal with that one – מַאֲמָר בָּזוֹ וּמַאֲמָר בָּזוֹ: *Tosafot* ask: Why can't the *yavam* give a bill of divorce for his levirate betrothal and thereby permit the second woman to perform levirate marriage, as this is an effective way of revoking the levirate betrothal according to the Gemara in the third chapter (32a). The Rivan answers that the ruling in the third chapter only applies after the fact; it is forbidden to do so *ab initio*. The *Tosefot HaRosh* holds that there the Gemara is referring only to a case where the brother who performed the levirate betrothal and gave the bill of divorce subsequently died, and therefore that ruling cannot be applied to the case in this mishna. The Ramban cites an explanation of this mishna that maintains that it is speaking only of a man who does not want to perform levirate marriage, but the Ramban rejects this answer. He himself explains that the *tanna* here is stating the basic *halakha*, without mentioning the option instituted by the Sages. Alternatively, this mishna follows the more stringent opinion found in the Gemara there, whereby a bill of divorce given by one of the brothers to the *yevama* disqualifies the levirate betrothal of the other women involved.

She requires a bill of divorce and *ḥalitza* – צְרִיכָה גֵּט וַחֲלִיצָה: *Tosafot* point out that this is correct only according to the opinion that invalid *ḥalitza* serves to exempt the rival wife. According to the opinion that invalid *ḥalitza* must be repeated for both rival wives, one must say that the mishna used the more common singular form, but it actually means that he must perform *ḥalitza* twice. This principle of the singular form of *ḥalitza* used in place of the plural applies here and in similar cases.

אַחַת יְבָמָה אַחַת לְיָבָם אֶחָד, וְאַחַת שְׁתֵּי יְבָמוֹת לְיָבָם אֶחָד. כֵּיצַד? עָשָׂה מַאֲמָר בָּזוֹ וּמַאֲמָר בָּזוֹ – צְרִיכוֹת שְׁנֵי גִּיטִּין וַחֲלִיצָה. מַאֲמָר בָּזוֹ וְגֵט לָזוֹ – צְרִיכָה גֵּט וַחֲלִיצָה. מַאֲמָר בָּזוֹ וּבָעַל אֶת זוֹ – צְרִיכוֹת שְׁנֵי גִּיטִּין וַחֲלִיצָה. מַאֲמָר בָּזוֹ וְחָלַץ לָזוֹ – הָרִאשׁוֹנָה צְרִיכָה גֵּט.

The above principles apply **both** in cases of **one *yevama* to one *yavam*, as well as** in cases of **two *yevamot* to one *yavam*. How so? If he performed levirate betrothal with this** *yevama* **and levirate betrothal with that** one,[NH] i.e., her rival wife, **they require two bills of divorce,** each for her own levirate betrothal, **and *ḥalitza*** with one of them, to release them both from the levirate bond. If he performed **levirate betrothal with this one and** gave **a bill of divorce to that** one,[H] the first woman **requires a bill of divorce** to cancel the levirate betrothal, **and** one of them must receive ***ḥalitza*.**[N] If he performed **levirate betrothal with this one and engaged in intercourse with that one,**[H] **they require two bills of divorce and** he must perform ***ḥalitza*** with one of them. If the *yavam* performed **levirate betrothal with this one and performed *ḥalitza* with that one,**[H] **the first** woman **requires a bill of divorce.**

HALAKHA

Levirate betrothal with this one and levirate betrothal with that one – מַאֲמָר בָּזוֹ וּמַאֲמָר בָּזוֹ: If a *yavam* performed levirate betrothal with one *yevama* and then he, or one of his brothers, performed levirate betrothal with her rival wife, each of the women requires a bill of divorce for the levirate betrothal, and the *yavam* must also perform *ḥalitza* with one of them in order to exempt them both from levirate marriage (Rambam *Sefer Nashim, Hilkhot Yibbum* 5:14; *Shulḥan Arukh, Even HaEzer* 170:6).

Levirate betrothal with this one and a bill of divorce to that one – מַאֲמָר בָּזוֹ וְגֵט לָזוֹ: If a *yavam* performed levirate betrothal with one *yevama*, and subsequently he, or one of his brothers, gave a bill of divorce to her rival wife, he must give a bill of divorce for his levirate betrothal, and he or one of his brothers must perform *ḥalitza* with one of them. Some authorities (*Tur*, citing *Tosafot*) rule that both require *ḥalitza* (Rambam *Sefer Nashim, Hilkhot Yibbum* 5:6; *Shulḥan Arukh, Even HaEzer* 170:7).

Levirate betrothal with this one and engaged in intercourse with that one – מַאֲמָר בָּזוֹ וּבָעַל אֶת זוֹ: If a *yavam* performed levirate betrothal with one *yevama* and he, or one of his brothers, engaged in intercourse with her rival wife, they both require a bill of divorce, and the *yavam* must perform *ḥalitza* with one of them (Rambam *Sefer Nashim, Hilkhot Yibbum* 5:6; *Shulḥan Arukh, Even HaEzer* 170:8).

Levirate betrothal with this one and performed *ḥalitza* with that one – מַאֲמָר בָּזוֹ וְחָלַץ לָזוֹ: If a *yavam* performed levirate betrothal with one *yevama* and he, or one of his brothers, performed *ḥalitza* with the other one, the first woman requires a bill of divorce (Rambam *Sefer Nashim, Hilkhot Yibbum* 5:6; *Shulḥan Arukh, Even HaEzer* 170:7).

גט לזו וגט לזו – צריכות הימנו חליצה. גט לזו ובעל את זו – צריכה גט וחליצה. גט לזו ומאמר בזו – צריכה גט וחליצה. גט לזו וחלץ לזו – אין אחר חליצה כלום.

If the *yavam* gave **a bill of divorce to this** *yevama* **and a bill of divorce to that one,**[H] **they require** ***ḥalitza*** **from him.** If he gave a **bill of divorce to this one and engaged in intercourse with that one,**[H] the latter **requires a bill of divorce and** ***ḥalitza.*** If he gave a **bill of divorce to this** one **and** performed **levirate betrothal with that one,**[H] the latter **requires a bill of divorce and** he must perform ***ḥalitza*** with one of them. If the *yavam* gave **a bill of divorce to this woman and performed** ***ḥalitza*** **with that** one,[H] **nothing is** effective **after** ***ḥalitza,*** and he cannot betroth the rival wife.

חלץ וחלץ, או חלץ ועשה מאמר, נתן גט ובעל, או בעל ובעל, או בעל ועשה מאמר, נתן גט וחלץ – אין אחר חליצה כלום, בין יבם אחד לשתי יבמות. בין שני יבמין ליבמה אחת.

If **he performed** ***ḥalitza*** with one *yevama* **and** then **performed** ***ḥalitza*** with a second *yevama*, **or he performed** ***ḥalitza*** with one *yevama* **and** then proceeded to either **perform levirate betrothal,**[N] **give a bill of divorce, or engage in intercourse** with a second; **alternatively, he engaged in intercourse** with one *yevama* and **engaged in intercourse** with the second *yevama*, **or he engaged in intercourse** with one *yevama* **and** proceeded to either **perform levirate betrothal, give a bill of divorce, or perform** ***ḥalitza*** with the second, **nothing is** effective **after** ***ḥalitza*** or intercourse. These *halakhot* apply **both** in cases of **one** ***yavam*** **to two** ***yevamot,*** **as well as two** ***yevamin*** **to one** ***yevama.***

חלץ ועשה מאמר, נתן גט ובעל, או בעל ועשה מאמר, ונתן גט וחלץ – אין אחר חליצה כלום, בין בתחלה בין באמצע בין בסוף.

If **he performed** ***ḥalitza*** with one *yevama* **and** then proceeded to either **perform levirate betrothal, give a bill of divorce, or engage in intercourse** with a second *yevama*; **alternatively, he engaged in intercourse** with one *yevama* **and** then proceeded to **perform levirate betrothal, or give a bill of divorce, or perform** ***ḥalitza*** with a second *yevama*, **nothing is** effective **after** ***ḥalitza,*** **whether** the *ḥalitza* took place **at the beginning, in the middle,**[N] **or at the end.** All of these *halakhot* accord with the opinion of Rabbi Akiva, who maintains betrothal does not take effect on a woman who is forbidden due to the prohibition against betrothing a *yevama* after *ḥalitza.*[H]

והבעילה, בזמן שהיא בתחלה – אין אחריה כלום. באמצע ובסוף – יש אחריה כלום. רבי נחמיה אומר: אחת בעילה ואחת חליצה, בין בתחלה בין באמצע בין בסוף – אין אחריה כלום.

But with regard to **intercourse, when it is at the beginning,** i.e., the first act the *yavam* performed with his *yevama*, **nothing is** effective **after it** and any subsequent action is void. However, if it was performed **in the middle, and** similarly if it was performed **at the end,** i.e., after some other action that impairs the validity of his intercourse, **something is effective after it.**[H] **Rabbi Neḥemya says: Both** with regard to **intercourse and** ***ḥalitza,*** **whether** performed **at the beginning, in the middle, or at the end, nothing is** effective **after it.**[N] If the *yavam* performed a valid action according to Torah law, any subsequent action is of no consequence according to *halakha.*

NOTES

Performed *ḥalitza* and then proceeded to perform levirate betrothal – חלץ ועשה מאמר: According to Rashi, the mishna here returns to discuss the case of a single *yavam* and *yevama*, and it repeats this case in order to introduce the dispute between Rabbi Neḥemya and the Rabbis. The Rashba and other commentaries claim that it is not necessary to define the case in this way, as this statement can apply to the cases of multiple *yevamin* and *yevamot* as well.

***Ḥalitza* in the middle – חליצה באמצע:** Rashi explains that this refers to a *yavam* who gave a bill of divorce to one *yevama* and performed *ḥalitza* with another *yevama*. If he afterward performs levirate betrothal to either of the women, it is not effective. *Tosefot HaRosh* takes issue with this example, as this *ḥalitza* should not be considered in the middle, for there is nothing that must take place afterward. Instead, this is referring to a case where a *yavam* performed levirate betrothal followed by *ḥalitza*. In that case he must afterward give a bill of divorce to cancel his levirate betrothal. Despite the fact that the *ḥalitza* is considered to be in the middle as further action is demanded on his part, no other actions are effective after the *ḥalitza*.

Nothing is effective after it – אין אחריה כלום: According to Rashi's comments on the mishna, in cases where the *yavam* engaged in intercourse at some stage, nothing is required after it, and she can be released with a bill of divorce without the need for *ḥalitza* (see Maharsha). Other commentaries disagree and maintain that even according to Rabbi Neḥemya, she needs *ḥalitza* to release her from the levirate bond after invalid intercourse. The statement: There is nothing after it, only means that subsequent actions do not create a bond that would forbid him to marry her relatives. Rashi, in his commentary on the Gemara, concurs with this alternate explanation (Ramban).

HALAKHA

A bill of divorce to this one and a bill of divorce to that one – גט לזו וגט לזו: If a *yavam* gave a bill of divorce to one *yevama* and he, or one of his brothers, gave a bill of divorce to her rival wife, he must perform *ḥalitza* with one of them, and each *yavam* is forbidden to the relatives of the women to whom he gave a bill of divorce (Rambam *Sefer Nashim, Hilkhot Yibbum* 5:15; *Shulḥan Arukh, Even HaEzer* 170:1, 5).

A bill of divorce to this one and engaged in intercourse with that one – גט לזו ובעל את זו: If a *yavam* gave a bill of divorce to one *yevama* and he, or one of his brothers, engaged in intercourse with her rival wife, the latter requires a bill of divorce, and he must perform *ḥalitza* with one of them (Rambam *Sefer Nashim, Hilkhot Yibbum* 5:7; *Shulḥan Arukh, Even HaEzer* 170:14).

A bill of divorce to this one and levirate betrothal with that one – גט לזו ומאמר בזו: If a *yavam* gave a bill of divorce to one *yevama* and he, or one of his brothers, performed levirate betrothal with her rival wife, the latter requires a bill of divorce, and he must perform *ḥalitza* with one of them (Rambam *Sefer Nashim, Hilkhot Yibbum* 5:9; *Shulḥan Arukh, Even HaEzer* 170:11).

A bill of divorce to this one and performed *ḥalitza* with that one – גט לזו וחלץ לזו: If a *yavam* gave a bill of divorce to one *yevama* and he, or one of his brothers, performed *ḥalitza* with her rival wife, nothing is necessary after *ḥalitza* (Rambam *Sefer Nashim, Hilkhot Yibbum* 5:14; *Shulḥan Arukh, Even HaEzer* 170:14).

Actions after *ḥalitza* – מעשה לאחר חליצה: If a *yavam* performed *ḥalitza* with his *yevama* and afterward he, or one of his brothers, performed *ḥalitza* with her rival wife or gave her a bill of divorce, this last action is of no consequence; the second *ḥalitza* or bill of divorce does not render her relatives forbidden to him. However, if he or one of his brothers performed levirate betrothal with her rival wife or engaged in intercourse with her, she requires a bill of divorce. The *halakha* does not follow the mishna, which is in accordance with the opinion of Rabbi Akiva (*Shulḥan Arukh, Even HaEzer* 170:13).

Actions after intercourse with a *yevama* – מעשה לאחר ביאה ביבמה: If one of the brothers has relations with the *yevama*, any further nullifying action he or one of his brothers performs with her rival wife is of no effect; it does not render her relatives forbidden to him. However, if any disqualifying action preceded the intercourse, for example if he performed levirate betrothal with the rival wife or gave her a bill of divorce, the act of intercourse does not fully acquire the *yevama*, and she requires a bill of divorce. If at this stage a *yavam* performs levirate betrothal with another rival wife, it serves to forbid him to her relatives. The *halakha* is not in accordance with Rabbi Neḥemya (Rambam *Sefer Nashim, Hilkhot Yibbum* 5:9; *Shulḥan Arukh, Even HaEzer* 170:12, 14).

גמ׳ עַד כָּאן לָא פְּלִיגִי אֶלָּא בְּגֵט אַחַר גֵּט וּמַאֲמָר אַחַר מַאֲמָר, אֲבָל גֵּט אֶחָד בִּיבָמָה [וּמַאֲמָר אֶחָד בִּיבָמָה] – מְהַנֵּי,

GEMARA Rabban Gamliel and the Rabbis **disagree only with regard to** the efficacy of **a bill of divorce** performed **after a bill of divorce and levirate betrothal** performed **after levirate betrothal, but one bill of divorce** given **to a single *yevama*, or one levirate betrothal** performed **with a single *yevama*,**[H] **is effective.** The bill of divorce prevents him from performing levirate marriage, and the levirate betrothal requires a bill of divorce to cancel it, in addition to *ḥalitza*.

מַאי טַעֲמָא אֲמוּר רַבָּנַן גֵּט בִּיבָמָה מְהַנֵּי – מִשּׁוּם דִּמְהַנֵּי בְּעָלְמָא. דְּאִי אָמְרַתְּ לָא מְהַנֵּי, אָמְרִי: גֵּט לְהוֹצִיאָהּ וַחֲלִיצָה לְהוֹצִיאָהּ וּמִדְּגֵט לָא מְהַנֵּי – חֲלִיצָה נַמִּי לָא מְהַנֵּי, וְאָתֵי לְמִיבְעַל אַחַר חֲלִיצָה.

The Gemara elaborates: **What is the reason that the Sages said** that **a bill of divorce is effective for a *yevama*,** despite the fact that she is not his wife? This is **because it is effective in general** in cases of married women. **For if you say** that **it is not effective** in the case of a *yevama*, there are some who might mistakenly **say** the following: **A bill of divorce** is given to a woman in order **to remove her** from her husband, **and *ḥalitza*** likewise serves **to remove her** from the *yavam*; **since a bill of divorce is ineffective** for this *yevama*, ***ḥalitza* is also ineffective**[N] and does not sever their relationship completely. **And** perhaps the *yavam* **will come to engage in intercourse after *ḥalitza*,** which is forbidden by the Torah prohibition derived from the verse: "So shall it be done to the man who does not build his brother's house" (Deuteronomy 25:9).

וּמַאי טַעֲמָא אֲמוּר רַבָּנַן מַאֲמָר בִּיבָמָה מְהַנֵּי – מִשּׁוּם דִּמְהַנֵּי בְּעָלְמָא. דְּאִי אָמְרַתְּ לָא מְהַנֵּי, אָמְרִי: מַאֲמָר לִקְנוֹת וּבִיאָה לִקְנוֹת, וּמִדְּמַאֲמָר לָא מְהַנֵּי – בִּיאָה נַמִּי לָא מְהַנְיָא וְאָתֵי לְמִיבְעַל אַחַר בִּיאָה.

And what is the reason the Sages said that **levirate betrothal is effective for a *yevama*? Because it is effective in general,**[N] as levirate betrothal is essentially an act of betrothal. **For if you say** that **it is not effective,** there are some who might mistakenly **say: Levirate betrothal serves to acquire** a woman **and intercourse** serves **to acquire** a woman in general, as women can be betrothed by intercourse; **since levirate betrothal is ineffective** in the case of a *yevama*, **intercourse is also ineffective,** i.e., it does not acquire a *yevama* completely. **And** he will therefore **come to engage in intercourse** with a rival wife **after intercourse** with the first *yevama*.

וּמַאי טַעֲמָא אֲמוּר רַבָּנַן בִּיאָה פְּסוּלָה יֵשׁ אַחֲרֶיהָ כְּלוּם?

And what is the reason the Sages who disagree with Rabbi Neḥemya **said** that **invalid intercourse,** i.e., intercourse that follows any disqualifying action with the rival wife of a *yevama*, does not fully acquire the *yevama*, such that **something is** effective **after it?** In this case the invalid intercourse does not cancel the levirate bond, and therefore further action with the *yevama* is effective.

אָמְרִי: אִי בִּיאָה אַחַר הַגֵּט הִיא – גְּזֵירָה בִּיאָה אַחַר הַגֵּט מִשּׁוּם בִּיאָה אַחַר חֲלִיצָה, וְאִי בִּיאָה אַחַר מַאֲמָר הִיא – גְּזֵירָה בִּיאָה אַחַר מַאֲמָר מִשּׁוּם בִּיאָה אַחַר בִּיאָה.

The Sages **say: If this is intercourse** performed **after a bill of divorce,** then it is considered invalid due to a rabbinic **decree** with regard to **intercourse after a bill of divorce**[N] **because** of its potential confusion with a case of **intercourse after *ḥalitza*.** The Sages established that invalid intercourse of this kind should not cancel the levirate bond completely, for if it did, then people might come to engage in intercourse after *ḥalitza*, which would violate a Torah prohibition. **And if this is intercourse** performed **after levirate betrothal,** then it is considered invalid due to a rabbinic **decree** with regard to **intercourse after levirate betrothal because** of its potential confusion with a case of **intercourse** with the second *yevama* **after intercourse** with the first. If intercourse after levirate betrothal is effective, people might come to engage in intercourse with a second *yevama* after intercourse with a first, and this is forbidden as the woman is considered his brother's wife who is not eligible for levirate marriage.

וּמַאי טַעֲמָא אֲמוּר רַבָּנַן הַאי חֲלִיצָה פְּסוּלָה אֵין אַחֲרֶיהָ כְּלוּם – אָמְרִי: מַאי לִגְזוֹר? נִגְזוֹר חֲלִיצָה אַחַר הַגֵּט מִשּׁוּם חֲלִיצָה אַחַר חֲלִיצָה – כָּל כִּי הָנֵי תַּחֲלוֹץ וְתֵיזִיל!

And what is the reason the Sages said with regard to **this invalid *ḥalitza*** that **nothing is** effective **after it?** For they **say: What** is the reason that **we should we issue a decree** in that case? **Should we issue a decree** with regard to ***ḥalitza*** performed **after a bill of divorce due to** a concern for ***ḥalitza*** performed **after *ḥalitza*?** In this case there is no concern, as there is no prohibition involved in repeating *ḥalitza*. In **any situation like these, let her continue performing *ḥalitza*,**[N] for no harm is done if *ḥalitza* is performed unnecessarily.

HALAKHA

One bill of divorce or one levirate betrothal – גֵּט אֶחָד וּמַאֲמָר אֶחָד: Everyone agrees that a bill of divorce given to one *yevama* or levirate betrothal performed with one *yevama* serves to forbid the *yavam* to her rival wife and to render the relatives of the *yevama* prohibited to the one who gave the bill of divorce (Rambam *Sefer Nashim, Hilkhot Yibbum* 5:7; *Shulḥan Arukh, Even HaEzer* 170:1).

NOTES

***Ḥalitza* is also ineffective – חֲלִיצָה נַמִּי לָא מְהַנֵּי:** *Tosafot* point out that the Sages did not decree that women in general should require *ḥalitza* when being divorced from their husbands out of a concern that people will confuse the cases, as everyone knows that *ḥalitza* is not relevant for most women. In the Jerusalem Talmud the *halakha* that only a bill of divorce is effective for a married woman, and not *ḥalitza*, is derived from specific verses.

Because it is effective in general – מִשּׁוּם דִּמְהַנֵּי בְּעָלְמָא: The Gemara does not suggest that people will mistakenly conclude that if levirate betrothal is not effective, regular betrothal is also not effective. Even according to the opinion that betrothal by money is not from the Torah, people betroth in this manner all the time and will not doubt its efficacy (Ritva).

A decree with regard to intercourse after a bill of divorce, etc. – גְּזֵירָה בִּיאָה אַחַר הַגֵּט וכו׳: Even though the Sages already prohibited intercourse after a bill of divorce and required the *yavam* to perform *ḥalitza*, they also saw fit to decree that invalid intercourse should not be completely effective, for otherwise the initial prohibition would not be upheld (Rashba; see Ritva).

In any situation like these let her continue performing *ḥalitza* – כָּל כִּי הָנֵי תַּחֲלוֹץ וְתֵיזִיל: Rashi explains this as a straightforward statement: It is of no concern to us if she performs *ḥalitza* several times. The Rashba and the Ritva explain this as a question: Would a woman really perform *ḥalitza* multiple times? With regard to intercourse it makes sense to institute a decree, lest he engage in intercourse after performing *ḥalitza* with her rival wife, but with regard to *ḥalitza* there is no reason to suppose one will want to perform *ḥalitza* again; the *Nimmukei Yosef* offers a slightly different version of the same approach. These different interpretations have halakhic ramifications with regard to the issue of whether it is permitted to perform *ḥalitza* with two *yevamot* (see *Beit Shmuel* and *Arukh LaNer*).

לִיגְזוֹר חֲלִיצָה אַחַר מַאֲמָר מִשּׁוּם חֲלִיצָה אַחַר בִּיאָה – אַטּוּ חֲלִיצָה אַחַר מַאֲמָר מִי לָא בָּעֲיָא גֵּט לְמַאֲמָרוֹ? חֲלִיצָה אַחַר בִּיאָה נַמִּי – בָּעֲיָא גֵּט לְבִיאָתוֹ

Alternatively, **should we issue a decree** stating that other actions are effective after *ḥalitza* is performed **after levirate betrothal due to** the concern for confusion with the case of *ḥalitza* performed **after intercourse?** In this case there is a concern that people will assume that no bill of divorce is required after intercourse so long as the *yavam* performed *ḥalitza*. The Gemara challenges this concern: **Is that to say** that in the case of ***ḥalitza* after levirate betrothal she does not require a bill of divorce for his levirate betrothal,** such that one would conclude the same for *ḥalitza* after intercourse? In the case of *ḥalitza* after levirate betrothal, the woman requires a bill of divorce, and similarly in the case of ***ḥalitza* after intercourse she likewise requires a bill of divorce for his intercourse.** Thus, the same action performed following *ḥalitza* after levirate betrothal is also performed following *ḥalitza* after intercourse, and therefore there is no need to issue a further decree.

אֲמַר רָבָא:

§ **Rava said:**

Perek **V**
Daf נא Amud **a**

מַאי טַעֲמָא דְּרַבָּן גַּמְלִיאֵל – דִּמְסַפְּקָא לֵיהּ: גֵּט, אִי דָּחֵי אִי לָא דָּחֵי, מַאֲמָר, אִי קָנֵי אִי לָא קָנֵי. גֵּט אִי דָּחֵי אִי לָא דָּחֵי, אִי קַמָּא דָּחֵי – בַּתְרָא מַאי קָעָבֵיד? אִי קַמָּא לָא דָּחֵי – בַּתְרָא נַמִּי לָא דָּחֵי.

What is the reason for the ruling of **Rabban Gamliel** that a bill of divorce is not effective after a bill of divorce? It is **because he is uncertain** with regard to **a bill of divorce whether** it effectively **precludes** levirate marriage or **whether it does not preclude** levirate marriage. Similarly, he is uncertain with regard to **levirate betrothal, whether it** effectively **acquires** the *yevama* **or does not acquire** her at all. The Gemara clarifies: With regard to **a bill of divorce,** he is uncertain as to **whether it precludes** levirate marriage **or does not preclude** it. **If the first** bill of divorce **precludes** levirate marriage, **what did he do** by giving **the latter** bill of divorce, **as** it has no substance? Alternatively, **if the first** bill of divorce **does not preclude** levirate marriage, **neither does the latter preclude** levirate marriage.

מַאֲמָר אִי קָנֵי אִי לָא קָנֵי, אִי קַמָּא קָנֵי – בַּתְרָא מַאי קָעָבֵיד? וְאִי קַמָּא לָא קָנֵי – בַּתְרָא נַמִּי לָא קָנֵי.

Likewise, with regard to **levirate betrothal,** he is uncertain as to **whether it acquires** the *yevama* **or does not acquire** her. **If the first** levirate betrothal effectively **acquires** the *yevama*, **what does the last one accomplish? And if the first one does not acquire** her, **the last one also does not acquire** her. For this reason Rabban Gamliel maintains that a bill of divorce is not effective after a bill of divorce was given, and similarly levirate betrothal is not effective after levirate betrothal was performed.[N]

NOTES

The opinions of Rabban Gamliel and the Rabbis – שִׁיטוֹת רַבָּן גַּמְלִיאֵל וַחֲכָמִים: The Jerusalem Talmud provides an analysis of Rabban Gamliel's opinion that is similar to the one found here. There it compares Rabban Gamliel's opinion to that of Rabbi Shimon, who maintains that levirate betrothal either acquires the *yevama* completely or it does not acquire her at all. The Jerusalem Talmud goes on to demonstrate, as Abaye argues here, that Rabban Gamliel must be of the opinion that levirate betrothal and a bill of divorce acquire her to a certain extent. The Rashba and others note that the Gemara here does not inquire into the reason behind the opinion of the Rabbis. Despite the fact that the Gemara briefly states subsequently that the effects of levirate betrothal and a bill of divorce were instituted by the Sages, this sentence does not appear in all versions of the text and is mentioned only incidentally rather than as a full explanation. These commentaries explain that this is because the reasoning of the Rabbis is clear; it is Rabban Gamliel's opinion that requires elucidation. The Rabbis' opinion is that since levirate betrothal is a rabbinic institution, its effect is not complete, and thus both levirate betrothal and a bill of divorce can be effective even after levirate betrothal.

אִיתִיבֵיהּ אַבָּיֵי: וּמוֹדֶה רַבָּן גַּמְלִיאֵל שֶׁיֵּשׁ גֵּט אַחַר מַאֲמָר, וּמַאֲמָר אַחַר הַגֵּט, וְגֵט אַחַר בִּיאָה וּמַאֲמָר, וּמַאֲמָר אַחַר בִּיאָה וָגֵט.

Abaye raised an objection to his opinion from a *baraita*: **And Rabban Gamliel concedes that a bill of divorce is effective after levirate betrothal and levirate betrothal is** effective **after a bill of divorce.** If a *yavam* gave a bill of divorce to one *yevama* and then performed levirate betrothal with the other, or the reverse, both actions would be effective. **And** he also concedes that **a bill of divorce** is effective **after intercourse and levirate betrothal** such that if the *yavam* engaged in levirate betrothal with one *yevama*, engaged in intercourse with a second, and gave a bill of divorce to a third, the bill of divorce is effective and he is prohibited from marrying the relatives of the third *yevama*. **And** he concedes **that levirate betrothal is** effective **after intercourse and a bill of divorce,** such that if he gave a bill of divorce to one woman, engaged in intercourse with a second, and performed levirate betrothal with a third, the levirate betrothal is effective and the third woman requires a bill of divorce.

וְאִי מְסַפְּקָא לֵיהּ לְרַבָּן גַּמְלִיאֵל – תֶּהֱוֵי כְּבִיאָה דִּלְכַתְּחִלָּה, וְתִקְנֵי! דְּהָא תְּנַן: הַבְּעִילָה, בִּזְמַן שֶׁהִיא בַּתְּחִלָּה – אֵין אַחֲרֶיהָ כְּלוּם.

And if Rabban Gamliel is uncertain[N] with regard to the efficacy of levirate betrothal or a bill of divorce, then the third action should never be effective. Either the initial levirate betrothal or bill of divorce was completely effective, in which case any subsequent action is not effective, or these actions are not effective at all and the intercourse that followed them **should be like intercourse** performed **at the beginning, and** it should serve to **acquire** the *yevama* completely, and any actions performed afterward with the rival wife should be of no account. **For we learned** in the mishna: With regard to **intercourse, when it is at the beginning, nothing is** effective **after it.** Consequently, Rabban Gamliel's ruling is difficult.

אֶלָּא אָמַר אַבָּיֵי: לְעוֹלָם פְּשִׁיטָא לֵיהּ לְרַבָּן גַּמְלִיאֵל בְּגֵט דְּדָחֵי, וּמַאֲמָר דְּקָנֵי. מִיהוּ, אָמוּר רַבָּנַן: הָא יְבָמָה, בְּחַד צַד מְהַנֵּי בָּהּ גֵּט, וּבְחַד צַד מְהַנֵּי בָּהּ מַאֲמָר. גֵּט אַחַר גֵּט – לָא דָּחֵי, דְּהָא דָּחָה לֵיהּ קַמָּא, וּמַאֲמָר אַחַר מַאֲמָר – לָא קָנֵי, דְּהָא קָנֵי לֵיהּ קַמָּא. גֵּט אַחַר מַאֲמָר, וּמַאֲמָר אַחַר הַגֵּט – הַאי מִילְּתָא קָא דָּחֵי, וְהַאי מִילְּתָא קָא קָנֵי.

Rather, Abaye said: Actually, it is obvious to Rabban Gamliel that a bill of divorce precludes levirate marriage, **and that levirate betrothal acquires** the *yevama*. **Nevertheless, the Sages said** that with regard to **this *yevama*, in one respect a bill of divorce is effective for her, and in another respect levirate betrothal is effective for her,** but they are not effective in the same manner. Therefore, **a bill of divorce** given **after a bill of divorce does not preclude** levirate marriage, **as the first** bill of divorce **has** already **precluded** it **for him** as much as he can preclude it by means of a bill of divorce. **And levirate betrothal** performed **after levirate betrothal does not acquire** her, **as the first** levirate betrothal **has acquired** her **for him** as much as possible. However, with regard to **a bill of divorce after levirate betrothal, and levirate betrothal after a bill of divorce, this action precludes** levirate marriage **and that action acquires** the *yevama*. Since the acquisition of levirate betrothal and the nullification of a bill of divorce work in different ways, there can be both an acquisition and a nullification, and therefore one can be effective after the other.

וְרַבָּנַן: כָּל חַד וְחַד תִּקִּינוּ לֵיהּ רַבָּנַן גֵּט וּמַאֲמָר בִּיבָמָה.

However, the Rabbis maintain that **the Sages instituted for each and every one** of the brothers-in-law both the nullification of **a bill of divorce and** the acquisition of **levirate betrothal for a *yevama*,** and they decreed that these should be effective for each of the *yevamot*. Therefore the strength of the first bill of divorce or levirate betrothal is equal to that of the second one, and both are effective.

NOTES

And if Rabban Gamliel is uncertain, etc. – וְאִי מְסַפְּקָא לֵיהּ לְרַבָּן גַּמְלִיאֵל וכו׳: Rashi explains this proof in the following manner: If Rabban Gamliel maintains that levirate betrothal either acquires the *yevama* fully or not at all, either way he should not concede in the case of a bill of divorce after intercourse and levirate betrothal. If levirate betrothal acquires her completely the subsequent intercourse and bill of divorce are of no consequence, and if levirate betrothal does not acquire her at all then the intercourse should acquire her fully, and any further action should be ineffective. The early commentaries note that according to Rashi's explanation, Abaye's statement is truncated, as he only mentions one side of the issue (Rashba; Ritva). They therefore prefer the following interpretation of Rabbeinu Ḥananel: If Rabban Gamliel is uncertain as to whether levirate betrothal acquires the *yevama*, how can something that only uncertainly acquires her nullify an act, i.e., intercourse, that definitely acquires her according to Torah law? Therefore, when the intercourse takes place after the levirate betrothal it should acquire her completely and the subsequent bill of divorce should not be effective. However, it has been pointed out that this argument is explained in the Jerusalem Talmud in precisely the manner suggested by Rashi.

וְהַאי בִּיאָה פְּסוּלָה עֲדִיפָא מִמַּאֲמָר, וּגְרִיעָא מִמַּאֲמָר. עֲדִיפָא מִמַּאֲמָר, דְּאִילּוּ מַאֲמָר אַחַר מַאֲמָר לָא מְהַנֵּי, וְאִילּוּ בִּיאָה אַחַר מַאֲמָר – מְהַנֵּי. וּגְרִיעָא מִמַּאֲמָר, דְּאִילּוּ מַאֲמָר אַחַר הַגֵּט קָנֵי לְכוּלֵּיהּ שִׁיּוּרָא דְּגֵט, וְאִילּוּ בִּיאָה אַחַר הַגֵּט – לָא קָנְיָא לֵיהּ לְכוּלֵּיהּ שִׁיּוּרָא דְּגֵט.

Abaye proceeds to explain the rest of Rabban Gamliel's teaching in the *baraita*: **And this invalid intercourse,** i.e., intercourse that was performed after a disqualifying action, such as levirate betrothal or a bill of divorce, **is superior to levirate betrothal**[N] **and** also **inferior to levirate betrothal: It is preferable to levirate betrothal** in the following respect: **whereas levirate betrothal after levirate betrothal is not effective** at all, **intercourse after levirate betrothal is effective,** because intercourse acquires a *yevama* according to Torah law. **And** it is **inferior to levirate betrothal, for whereas levirate betrothal after a bill of divorce** according to Rabban Gamliel **acquires the entire remainder** of the woman left **by the bill of divorce,**[N] such that any further levirate betrothal would be ineffective, **intercourse after a bill of divorce does not acquire the entire remainder** of the woman left **by the bill of divorce,** as it is not considered valid intercourse, and a subsequent levirate betrothal is effective.

תָּנוּ רַבָּנַן: כֵּיצַד אָמַר רַבָּן גַּמְלִיאֵל אֵין גֵּט אַחַר גֵּט? שְׁתֵּי יְבָמוֹת שֶׁנָּפְלוּ לִפְנֵי יָבָם אֶחָד, וְנָתַן גֵּט לָזוֹ וְגֵט לָזוֹ – רַבָּן גַּמְלִיאֵל אוֹמֵר: חוֹלֵץ לָרִאשׁוֹנָה וְאָסוּר בִּקְרוֹבוֹתֶיהָ, וּמוּתָּר בִּקְרוֹבוֹת שְׁנִיָּה.

§ **The Sages taught: How,** i.e., in what case, **did Rabban Gamliel say** that **a bill of divorce is not effective after a bill of divorce?** In the case of **two *yevamot* who happened before one *yavam* and he gave a bill of divorce to this one and a bill of divorce to that one. Rabban Gamliel says: He performs *ḥalitza* with the first one and is forbidden to** marry **her relatives,** as she is his *ḥalutza*, **and he is permitted to marry the relatives of the second one.** Because the bill of divorce he gave the second woman is of no consequence at all, she is merely the rival wife of his *ḥalutza*, and he is therefore permitted to marry her relatives.

וַחֲכָמִים אוֹמְרִים: נָתַן גֵּט לָזוֹ וְגֵט לָזוֹ – אָסוּר בִּקְרוֹבוֹת שְׁתֵּיהֶן, וַחֲלִיצָה לְאַחַת מֵהֶן. וְכֵן אַתָּה אוֹמֵר בִּשְׁנֵי יְבָמִים וִיבָמָה אַחַת.

But the Rabbis say: If he gave a bill of divorce to this one and a bill of divorce to that one,[H] **he is forbidden** to marry **the relatives of both of them, and** he must perform ***ḥalitza* with one of them. And you** would **say the same with regard to two *yevamim* and one *yevama*.** If the two *yevamin* gave one *yevama* a bill of divorce, one after the other, Rabban Gamliel maintains that the bill of divorce of the second *yavam* is of no account, and he is therefore permitted to marry her relatives, whereas the Rabbis hold that it is effective in that it renders him forbidden to her relatives.

כֵּיצַד אָמַר רַבָּן גַּמְלִיאֵל אֵין מַאֲמָר אַחַר מַאֲמָר? שְׁתֵּי יְבָמוֹת שֶׁנָּפְלוּ לִפְנֵי יָבָם אֶחָד וְעָשָׂה מַאֲמָר בְּזוֹ וּמַאֲמָר בְּזוֹ, רַבָּן גַּמְלִיאֵל אוֹמֵר: נוֹתֵן גֵּט לָרִאשׁוֹנָה, וְחוֹלֵץ לָהּ, וְאָסוּר בִּקְרוֹבוֹתֶיהָ, וּמוּתָּר בִּקְרוֹבוֹת שְׁנִיָּה. וַחֲכָמִים אוֹמְרִים: נוֹתֵן גֵּט לִשְׁתֵּיהֶן, וְאָסוּר בִּקְרוֹבוֹת שְׁתֵּיהֶן, וַחֲלִיצָה לְאַחַת מֵהֶן. וְכֵן אַתָּה אוֹמֵר בִּשְׁנֵי יְבָמִים וִיבָמָה אַחַת.

How, with regard to what circumstance, **did Rabban Gamliel say** that **there is no levirate betrothal after levirate betrothal?** In a case of **two *yevamot* who happened before one *yavam*, and he performed levirate betrothal with this one and levirate betrothal with that one,**[H] **Rabban Gamliel says: He gives a bill of divorce to the first one and performs *ḥalitza* with her, and is forbidden to her relatives, but** he **is permitted to the relatives of the second one,** as the levirate betrothal performed with the rival wife is ineffective. **But the Rabbis say: He gives a bill of divorce to both of them,** as the levirate betrothal is effective for both women, **and he is forbidden to the relatives of both of them; and** as for ***ḥalitza*,** he must perform it **with one of them. And you would say the same with regard to two *yevamim* and one *yevama*.** If the first *yavam* performed levirate betrothal with the *yevama*, and the second *yavam* consequently performed levirate betrothal with her, they are both required to give her a bill of divorce and both are forbidden to marry her relatives.

אָמַר מָר: נוֹתֵן גֵּט לָזוֹ וְגֵט לָזוֹ, רַבָּן גַּמְלִיאֵל אוֹמֵר: חוֹלֵץ לָרִאשׁוֹנָה וְאָסוּר בִּקְרוֹבוֹתֶיהָ, וּמוּתָּר בִּקְרוֹבוֹת שְׁנִיָּה. לֵימָא תֶּיהֱוֵי תְּיוּבְתָּא דִּשְׁמוּאֵל, דְּאָמַר שְׁמוּאֵל: חָלַץ לְבַעֲלַת הַגֵּט – לֹא נִפְטְרָה צָרָה!

The Master said above in the *baraita*: **He gives a bill of divorce to this one and a bill of divorce to that one. Rabban Gamliel says: He performs *ḥalitza* with the first one and is forbidden to** marry **her relatives, and he is permitted to** marry **the relatives of the second one.** The Gemara asks: **Shall we say that** this is a **conclusive refutation of** the statement of **Shmuel?**[N] **For Shmuel said: If he performed *ḥalitza* with the woman who received a bill of divorce, the rival wife is not exempted** by this invalid *ḥalitza*. The *yavam* must therefore repeat the *ḥalitza* with the rival wife as well. This appears to contradict the *baraita*, where Rabban Gamliel rules that he has to perform *ḥalitza* with only one of the *yevamot*.

NOTES

This invalid intercourse is superior to levirate betrothal – הַאי בִּיאָה פְּסוּלָה עֲדִיפָא מִמַּאֲמָר: It would appear that one could similarly argue that a bill of divorce is also preferable to levirate betrothal, as it too is effective after levirate betrothal. However, the only reason a bill of divorce takes effect after levirate betrothal is that a bill of divorce works on a different plane than levirate betrothal, i.e., its effectiveness is not related to that of the levirate betrothal. In contrast, the power of acquisition of intercourse is certainly of the same type as levirate betrothal (*Tosafot Yeshanim*).

Acquires the entire remainder left by the bill of divorce – קָנֵי לְכוּלֵּיהּ שִׁיּוּרָא דְּגֵט: No further levirate betrothal is possible after levirate betrothal and a bill of divorce, as even Rabban Gamliel agrees that in the case of levirate betrothal after levirate betrothal and a bill of divorce, the second levirate betrothal is not effective (Ritva).

Shall we say that this is a conclusive refutation of Shmuel – לֵימָא תֶּיהֱוֵי תְּיוּבְתָּא דִּשְׁמוּאֵל: Most early commentaries follow Rashi's explanation that the difficulty only stems from Rabban Gamliel's opinion, as Rabban Gamliel maintains that even though the *yavam* can perform a superior *ḥalitza* with the rival wife, he can nevertheless exempt the rival wife by means of this invalid *ḥalitza*. The opinion of the Rabbis, however, presents no difficulty, for they maintain that the *ḥalitza* of the two rival wives is equally invalid. *Tosafot Yeshanim*, however, claim that the Gemara could have raised the difficulty according to the opinion of the Rabbis, but it preferred to cite Rabban Gamliel, who states this *halakha* explicitly.

HALAKHA

A bill of divorce to this one and a bill of divorce to that one – גֵּט לָזוֹ וְגֵט לָזוֹ: If two rival wives required levirate marriage, and the *yavam* gave a bill of divorce to each of them, he is forbidden to the relatives of both. Similarly, if two *yevamin* gave a bill of divorce to one *yevama*, they are both forbidden to her relatives, and likewise two *yevamin* who gave bills of divorce to two different rival wives, each is prohibited to the relatives of the woman to whom he gave the bill of divorce, in accordance with the opinion of the Rabbis (Rambam *Sefer Nashim, Hilkhot Yibbum* 5:15; *Shulḥan Arukh, Even HaEzer* 170:4).

Levirate betrothal with this one and levirate betrothal with that one – מַאֲמָר בְּזוֹ וּמַאֲמָר בְּזוֹ: If two rival wives happened before one *yavam*, and he performed levirate betrothal with both of them, he is forbidden to marry the relatives of both. Likewise, if two *yevamin* performed levirate betrothal with one *yevama*, they are both forbidden to marry her relatives, and if the two *yevamin* performed levirate betrothal with two different rival wives, each is forbidden to the relatives of the woman with whom he performed the levirate betrothal, as stated by the Rabbis (Rambam *Sefer Nashim, Hilkhot Yibbum* 5:15; *Shulḥan Arukh, Even HaEzer* 170:6).

NOTES

The levirate bond is substantial…the levirate bond is not substantial – יש זיקה...אין זיקה: Although the Torah (Deuteronomy 25:5) forbids a widow requiring levirate marriage from remarrying until *ḥalitza* has been performed, the nature of the connection between her and her *yavam* is not clear. Is this connection seen as a form of betrothal, i.e., the levirate bond is substantial, or is it seen as a unilateral obligation upon the widow to wait for her brother-in-law's action, i.e., the levirate bond is not substantial.

אמר לך שמואל: כי אמרי אנא – אליבא דמאן דאמר יש זיקה, ורבן גמליאל סבר אין זיקה.

The Gemara answers: **Shmuel** could have **said to you: When I said** my above teaching, it was **in accordance with** the opinion **of the one who said that the levirate bond is substantial,** and he must therefore perform a valid *ḥalitza* in order to cancel this bond. A *ḥalitza* performed with a woman who received a bill of divorce is not powerful enough to completely cancel the bond of the rival wife who did not performed *ḥalitza*. **But Rabban Gamliel holds** that **the levirate bond is not substantial,**[N] and therefore any *ḥalitza* that releases one of the women also serves to release the other.

ומדרבן גמליאל סבר אין זיקה

The Gemara asks: **But** if so, **from** the fact that **Rabban Gamliel holds** that **the levirate bond is not substantial,**

NOTES

The Rabbis hold that the levirate bond is substantial – רבנן סברי יש זיקה: Rashi explains that this inference cannot be proven from the mishna, but rather it is logical to assume that just as Rabban Gamliel and the Rabbis disagree with regard to the strength of levirate betrothal, they similarly disagree about the nature of the levirate bond itself. The Ramban and the Rashba, on the other hand, maintain that there is an inherent connection between the nature of the levirate bond and the strength of levirate betrothal. Rabban Gamliel maintains that the levirate bond is not substantial, and therefore levirate betrothal or a bill of divorce performed by one *yavam* is sufficient to nullify the levirate bond between this yevama and the other *yevamin* and between him and the other *yevamot* entirely. The Rabbis, however, maintain that the levirate bond is substantial, and therefore no one act of levirate betrothal or bill of divorce can completely cancel this bond. Therefore, all of the actions performed by all the *yevamin* and *yevamot* are effective.

And the latter clause teaches: And you would say the same, etc. – וקתני סיפא וכן אתה אומר וכו׳: The early commentaries ask: Why does the Gemara cite the latter clause in the *baraita* when it could have equally questioned the statement of Rabba bar Rav Huna by citing a proof from the first part of the *baraita*? With regard to one *yavam* and two *yevamot* the Rabbis rule that a single *ḥalitza* is enough. One could deduce that if a woman requires *ḥalitza* from all the brothers when her *ḥalitza* was invalid, then similarly in a case of one *yavam* and two *yevamot*, he should have to perform *ḥalitza* with all the *yevamot*. They answer that the Gemara could indeed have asked in this manner, but it preferred to raise a difficulty from a source that explicitly states that she does not require *ḥalitza* from all the brothers (*Tosefot HaRosh*; *Tosafot Yeshanim*). However, some authorities learn from the fact that the Gemara specifically cites the latter clause that in the case of invalid *ḥalitza*, it is not necessary to perform *ḥalitza* with all the *yevamot* (*Tosefot Ḥad MiKamma'ei*; Meiri).

Levirate betrothal acquires her as a full-fledged acquisition – מאמר קונה קנין גמור: *Tosafot* point out that these *tanna'im* are not in complete agreement, as they disagree over the particulars of the acquisition. The common denominator is that they consider levirate betrothal to be very powerful. Rashi also notes that this does not mean that all these Sages maintain that levirate betrothal is a full-fledged acquisition, but rather it is at least a significant acquisition. The *Keren Ora* suggests that the shared feature of all these opinions might be that they all view levirate betrothal as having a certain validity from the Torah, not merely as a rabbinical institution.

רבנן סברי יש זיקה. וקתני סיפא: וכן אתה אומר בשני יבמין ויבמה אחת. לימא תיהוי תיובתא דרבה בר רב הונא אמר רב. דאמר רבה בר רב הונא אמר רב: חליצה פסולה – צריכה לחזור על כל האחין!

it can be inferred that **the Rabbis hold that the levirate bond is substantial,**[N] as it is assumed that they disagree with Rabban Gamliel in this regard as well. **And the latter clause** of that *baraita* **teaches: And you would say the same**[N] **with regard to two** *yevamin* **and one** *yevama* such that if the two *yevamin* gave one *yevama* a bill of divorce, she is exempted by the *ḥalitza* of one of them. If so, **let us say that it is a conclusive refutation of** the statement that **Rabba bar Rav Huna** said that **Rav said. For Rabba bar Rav Huna said** that **Rav said:** In cases of **invalid** ***ḥalitza,*** the *yevama* **is required to repeat** the *ḥalitza* **with all the brothers.** If the *ḥalitza* was invalid for some reason, all the brothers must perform *ḥalitza* with the *yevama*, as her bond with them is not canceled by an invalid *ḥalitza*.

אמר לך רבה בר רב הונא: בין לרבן גמליאל בין לרבנן סברי אין זיקה, והכא בגט אחר גט ומאמר אחר מאמר קמיפלגי.

The Gemara responds: **Rabba bar Rav Huna** could have **said to you: Both Rabban Gamliel and the Rabbis hold** that **the levirate bond is not substantial,** whereas my statement is in accordance with the opinion that the levirate bond is substantial. **And here** the dispute does not concern the topic of the levirate bond at all, but rather it only involves the explicitly mentioned issue: They **disagree with regard to** the efficacy of **a bill of divorce after a bill of divorce and levirate betrothal after levirate betrothal.**

אמר מר: עשה מאמר בזו ומאמר בזו, רבן גמליאל אומר: נותן גט לראשונה וחולץ לה, ואסור בקרובותיה, ומותר בקרובות שניה. מכדי קסבר רבן גמליאל אין מאמר אחר מאמר – ראשונה נמי תתייבם! גזירה דלמא אתי לייבומי לשניה.

The Master said above in the *baraita*: If **he performed levirate betrothal with this one and levirate betrothal with that one, Rabban Gamliel says: He gives a bill of divorce to the first one and performs** ***ḥalitza*** **with her and is forbidden to her relatives, but he is permitted to the relatives of the second one.** The Gemara poses a question: **Since Rabban Gamliel holds** that **levirate betrothal is not** effective **after levirate betrothal,** and the second levirate betrothal is of no consequence, the **first** woman **should also be permitted to enter into levirate marriage.** Why must he perform *ḥalitza* with her? The Gemara answers: It is prohibited due to a rabbinic **decree lest he perform levirate marriage with the second** woman. The Sages were concerned that in cases where the *yavam* performed levirate betrothal with both women, if he were permitted to consummate the levirate marriage with the first woman, he might do so with the second woman as well.

אמר רבי יוחנן: רבן גמליאל, ובית שמאי, ורבי שמעון, ובן עזאי ורבי נחמיה – כולהו סבירא להו: מאמר קונה קנין גמור. רבן גמליאל – הא דאמרן.

§ **Rabbi Yoḥanan said: Rabban Gamliel, and Beit Shammai, and Rabbi Shimon, and ben Azzai, and Rabbi Neḥemya, they all hold** that **levirate betrothal acquires** the *yevama* **as a full-fledged acquisition,**[N] like a regular betrothal. The source for **Rabban Gamliel's** opinion is **that which we said** above, that levirate betrothal is not effective after levirate betrothal. Rabbi Yoḥanan maintains that the second levirate betrothal is not effective because she was already fully acquired by the first one.

בית שמאי – דתנן: שלשה אחין, שנים מהם נשואין לשתי אחיות ואחד מופנה, מת אחד מבעלי אחיות ועשה בה מופנה מאמר, ואחר כך מת אחיו השני, בית שמאי אומרים: אשתו עמו, והלזו תצא משום אחות אשה.

The source for the opinion of **Beit Shammai is as we learned** in a mishna: In the case of **three brothers, two** of whom **were married to two sisters, and one who was single,** the following occurred: **The husband of one of the sisters died** childless, leaving behind his wife, **and the single** brother **performed levirate betrothal** with this wife. **Afterward, the second brother died,** whereby the second brother's wife, the sister of the betrothed, happened before him for levirate marriage as well. In this case, **Beit Shammai say: His wife remains with him,** i.e., the woman he betrothed is considered like his wife, and he is not required to divorce her. **And this other leaves** the *yavam* and is exempt from levirate marriage **due to** the fact that she is **the sister of a wife.** This indicates that Beit Shammai hold that the levirate betrothal performed with the first woman makes her fully betrothed, thereby nullifying the levirate bond with her sister.

רבי שמעון – דתניא, אמר להו רבי שמעון לחכמים: אם ביאת ראשון ביאה – ביאת שני אינה ביאה, אם ביאת ראשון אינה ביאה – ביאת שני נמי אינה ביאה. והא ביאת בן תשע, דכמאמר שויוה רבנן, וקאמר רבי שמעון אינה ביאה.

The source for the opinion of **Rabbi Shimon** is based on the following case cited in a mishna (96b): In the case of a boy aged nine years and one day old who had relations with his *yevama*, and afterward his brother, who is also nine years and one day old, had relations with her, the second brother disqualifies her from performing levirate marriage with the first one. Rabbi Shimon says he does not disqualify her. **As it is taught** in a *baraita* that **Rabbi Shimon said to the Rabbis: If the intercourse**[N] **of the first** brother is considered effective **intercourse, the intercourse of** the **second** brother **is not** considered effective **intercourse** such that it would disqualify her from performing levirate marriage with the first brother, as the first brother has already acquired her through his intercourse. **If the intercourse of** the **first** brother **is not** considered effective **intercourse, the intercourse of** the **second** brother **is also not** effective **intercourse. And the Sages considered the intercourse of a nine-year-old** boy[B] **to be like levirate betrothal,**[N] **and Rabbi Shimon says** that the intercourse of the second boy **is not** considered **intercourse.** This proves that in his opinion the intercourse of a nine-year-old fully acquires the *yevama*, and similarly, so does levirate betrothal.

בן עזאי – דתניא, בן עזאי אומר: יש מאמר אחר מאמר בשני יבמין ויבמה אחת, ואין מאמר אחר מאמר בשתי יבמות ויבם אחד. רבי נחמיה – דתנן, רבי נחמיה אומר: אחת בעולה ואחת חליצה, בין בתחלה בין באמצע בין בסוף – אין אחריה כלום. והא ביאה פסולה, דכמאמר שויוה רבנן וקתני: אין אחריה כלום.

This source for **ben Azzai's** opinion is **as it is taught** in a *baraita* that **ben Azzai says: Levirate betrothal is** effective **after levirate betrothal** in the case of **two *yevamin* and one *yevama*, but levirate betrothal is not** effective **after levirate betrothal** in the case of **two *yevamot* and one *yavam*.** Because the latter case involves only one *yavam*, his levirate betrothal fully acquires the *yevama*, and therefore the levirate betrothal he performs with the second woman is of no account, as he is already betrothed to the first *yevama*. The source for **Rabbi Neḥemya's** opinion is **as we learned** in a mishna that **Rabbi Neḥemya says:** With regard to **both intercourse and *ḥalitza*, whether at the beginning, in the middle, or at the end, nothing is** effective **after it. And the Sages considered invalid intercourse** to be **like levirate betrothal,**[N] **and** Rabbi Neḥemya **teaches** that **nothing is** effective **after it.** This indicates that he maintains that no form of acquisition is effective after levirate betrothal, as levirate betrothal completely acquires the *yevama*.

"כיצד עשה מאמר" כו׳.

§ The mishna states: **How so?** If he **performed levirate betrothal** with his *yevama* and gave her a bill of divorce, **etc.**

NOTES

Rabbi Shimon, as it is taught…if the intercourse, etc. – רבי שמעון דתניא...אם ביאת וכו׳: The Ramban asks: Why is it necessary for the Gemara to derive a proof from invalid intercourse, by comparing it to levirate betrothal, when Rabbi Shimon explicitly makes the same claim with regard to levirate betrothal itself (see 19a). He answers, and the Rashba explains similarly, that it is possible that when Rabbi Shimon stated his argument there, he was speaking in accordance with the opinion of the Rabbis only in order to argue against their opinion, whereas he himself does not maintain that opinion (see *Arukh LaNer* and *Yosef Lekaḥ* for a different resolution).

The intercourse of a nine-year-old boy is like levirate betrothal – ביאת בן תשע כמאמר: Some commentaries are puzzled by this *halakha*: Since any type of intercourse acquires a *yevama*, whether it is performed intentionally or unwittingly, why should the intercourse of a nine-year-old not acquire her as well, being that the Sages considered this intercourse to be full-fledged intercourse with regard to forbidden relations? They answer that it is an established *halakha* that the wife of a minor is not fully acquired by him. Although his cohabitation has the status of intercourse, it is not considered an act of acquisition (*Tosefot HaRosh*; see Ramban, who attributes this response to Rabbi Avraham *Av Beit Din* and questions it).

The Sages considered invalid intercourse to be like levirate betrothal – ביאה פסולה דכמאמר שויוה רבנן: The early commentaries raise a serious difficulty: Surely Rabbi Neḥemya distinguishes between invalid intercourse, after which no action is effective, and levirate betrothal, where subsequent action is effective. But if so, how can he prove that invalid intercourse is like levirate betrothal? Rabbeinu Ḥananel cites a proof from a *Tosefta* that states the following: When did they say that nothing is effective after intercourse? When it is at the beginning; but if it is not at the beginning it is like levirate betrothal. He adds that the principle is that an unattributed *Tosefta* follows the opinion of Rabbi Neḥemya, but the Ramban retorts that it is clear from the context that this particular *Tosefta* is not in accordance with Rabbi Neḥemya.

Rabbi Avraham *Av Beit Din* writes that invalid intercourse is like levirate betrothal in that neither of them enables the wife of a priest to eat *teruma*. However, the Ramban and the Rashba question this answer as well. They are similarly dissatisfied with the resolutions offered by *Tosafot*, as they do not fit the wording of the Gemara. The Ramban himself answers that Rabbi Neḥemya maintains that invalid intercourse is like levirate betrothal in that this type of intercourse does not exempt a *yevama* with whom an action had previously been performed. However, Rabbi Neḥemya disagrees with the Rabbis with regard to a different issue, as he maintains that no action is effective after invalid intercourse. His reasoning is that the decrees of the Sages are unnecessary in the case of intercourse, as intercourse is an effective method of acquisition from the Torah, and people will therefore not be confused with regard to its efficacy. The Rashba and the Ritva accept the basic premise of this opinion.

BACKGROUND

The intercourse of a nine-year-old boy – ביאת בן תשע: According to the Sages, sexual intercourse cannot be performed by a boy who is less than nine years old, and therefore it has no halakhic significance. From that age and onward such an act of intercourse is recognized as significant, even prior to the advent of physical maturity.

הַאי גֵּט אַחַר גֵּט הוּא! אֲמַר רַב יְהוּדָה, הָכִי קָאָמַר: גֵּט אַחַר הַגֵּט וּמַאֲמָר אַחַר מַאֲמָר כְּדַאֲמָרַן, יָבָם אֶחָד וִיבָמָה אַחַת כֵּיצַד הַתָּרָתָן? עָשָׂה מַאֲמָר בִּיבִמְתּוֹ וְנָתַן לָהּ גֵּט – צְרִיכָה הֵימֶנּוּ חֲלִיצָה.

The Gemara is puzzled: Is **this case** upon which the mishna elaborates the case of **a bill of divorce after a bill of divorce** that is mentioned first in the mishna? The mishna first is referring to a bill of divorce after a bill of divorce, but when it comes to the specifics, it mentions a bill of divorce after levirate betrothal. **Rav Yehuda said: This is what** the *tanna* **is saying**: With regard to a **bill of divorce after a bill of divorce, and levirate betrothal after levirate betrothal,** it is **as we said** and these cases were explained in the *baraita*, but with regard to **one** *yavam* **and one** *yevama***, how is their** complex bond **released?** He then proceeds to delineate: **If he performed levirate betrothal with his** *yevama* **and gave her a bill of divorce, she requires** *ḥalitza* **from him.**

״עָשָׂה מַאֲמָר וּבָעַל הֲרֵי זוֹ כְּמִצְוָתָהּ״. לֵימָא מְסַיַּיע לֵיהּ לְרַב הוּנָא, דְּאָמַר רַב הוּנָא: מִצְוַת יְבָמָה – מְקַדֵּשׁ וְאַחַר כָּךְ בּוֹעֵל. אֵימָא: אַף זֶה כְּמִצְוָתָהּ.

§ The mishna teaches: If the *yavam* **performed levirate betrothal and engaged in intercourse, this is** done **in accordance with its mitzva.**[H] The Gemara suggests: **Let us say that** this mishna **supports** the statement of **Rav Huna. As Rav Huna said: The mitzva of a** *yevama* **is** properly performed when the *yavam* **betroths** the *yevama* **and** only **afterward engages in intercourse.** This statement indicates that the levirate betrothal is a necessary component of the mitzva, and the mishna seems to imply the same. The Gemara refutes this claim: This is not necessarily the case, as you can read the mishna as stating that **this also is in accordance with its mitzva.** If he performed levirate betrothal and then engaged in intercourse, this too is a proper manner to proceed, but we do not have to interpret the mishna as indicating that this is the only way to fulfill the mitzva.

פְּשִׁיטָא! סָלְקָא דַּעְתָּךְ אָמִינָא: כֵּיוָן דְּאָמַר מָר: הָעוֹשֶׂה מַאֲמָר בִּיבִמְתּוֹ – פָּרְחָה הֵימֶנּוּ זִיקַת יְבָמִין, וְחָלָה עָלָיו זִיקַת אֵרוּסִין וְנִשּׂוּאִין, אֵימָא לָאו מִצְוָה קָעָבֵיד – קָא מַשְׁמַע לָן.

The Gemara asks: **Isn't** this **obvious?** If one can fulfill the mitzva without performing levirate betrothal, why would one think that levirate betrothal is detrimental? The Gemara answers: It was indeed necessary for the mishna to teach us this, for it might **enter your mind to say** that **since the Master said** above (29b): **One who performs levirate betrothal with his** *yevama* **causes the levirate bond to dissipate from himself, and a** standard **bond of betrothal and marriage takes effect on him,** you might **say** that he **no** longer **performs a mitzva** when he carries out levirate marriage, as the levirate bond is no longer in place. The *tanna* therefore **teaches us** that we consider the levirate betrothal and the subsequent intercourse as part of the same process, which constitutes a mitzva.

גּוּפָא אָמַר רַב הוּנָא: מִצְוַת יְבָמִין מְקַדֵּשׁ וְאַחַר כָּךְ בּוֹעֵל, וְאִם בָּעַל וְעָשָׂה מַאֲמָר – קָנָה. אִם בָּעַל וְעָשָׂה מַאֲמָר – פְּשִׁיטָא, דְּהָא קַנְיָהּ בְּבִיאָה! אֶלָּא אֵימָא: אִם בָּעַל בְּלֹא מַאֲמָר – קָנָה.

The Gemara continues: With regard to **the** matter **itself, Rav Huna said: The mitzva of levirate marriage** is properly performed when the *yavam* **betroths** the *yevama* **and afterward engages in intercourse, and if he engaged in intercourse and** later **performed levirate betrothal, he has acquired** the *yevama*. The Gemara is puzzled: **If he engaged in intercourse and** then **performed levirate betrothal it is obvious** that he has acquired her, **as he has** already **acquired her by intercourse.** The levirate betrothal does not affect the issue one way or another. **Rather, say** as follows: **If he engaged in intercourse without** prior **levirate betrothal,** even in that case **he has acquired** her.

HALAKHA

The levirate betrothal of a ***yevama*** **– מַאֲמַר יְבָמָה:** With regard to regular women, the process of marriage involved two stages. The first was betrothal, in which a man would give a woman money or a document or engage in consensual relations with her. This last method was abolished by the *amora* Rav. Through this act of betrothal the man acquired the woman and she was forbidden to all other men. At a later stage, usually a year later, the man would bring the woman into his home as his full-fledged wife. This was done through conjugal relations and was symbolized by the marriage canopy. With regard to a *yevama*, however, the Torah states that a *yavam* can acquire his *yevama* by intercourse alone. Nevertheless, the Sages instituted that he should betroth her with money or a document and that she requires a marriage canopy like all other women (Rema, citing the Rivash). Only afterward should they engage in intercourse (Rambam *Sefer Nashim*, *Hilkhot Yibbum* 2:1–2; *Shulḥan Arukh*, *Even HaEzer* 166:2).

וְהָתַנְיָא: לוֹקֶה! מַכַּת מַרְדּוּת מִדְּרַבָּנַן.

The Gemara challenges this: **But isn't it taught** in a *baraita* that a *yavam* who has intercourse without levirate betrothal **is flogged?**[NH] The Gemara answers: The lashes are not because he transgressed by not performing levirate betrothal, but rather they are **lashes for rebelliousness** given for transgressing a **rabbinic** law, namely for acting in an immodest manner.

דְּרַב מְנַגֵּיד מַאן דִּמְקַדֵּשׁ בְּבִיאָה, וּמַאן דִּמְקַדֵּשׁ בְּשׁוּקָא, וּמַאן דִּמְקַדֵּשׁ בְּלֹא שִׁדּוּכֵי,

The Gemara cites other instances where the Sages administered lashes for immodest behavior. **As Rav** would **flog one who betroths** a woman **by intercourse,**[H] despite the fact that betrothal is effective by this method, because he acted in a promiscuous manner. **And** he would likewise **flog one who betroths** a woman **in the marketplace,**[N] rather than at home, as this too is loose behavior, **and** he would also administer lashes **to one who betroths** a woman **without** a prior **marriage agreement** [*shiddukhei*],[N] as this too is an act of permissiveness.

וּמַאן דִּמְבַטֵּל גִּיטָּא, וּמַאן דִּמְסַר מוֹדָעָא אַגִּיטָּא,

And he would further lash **one who nullifies a bill of divorce**[H] he had earlier sent by declaring in the presence of witnesses that the bill of divorce is nullified. This action is effective, but by doing so he transgresses the rabbinic ordinance of the Sages that bans such an action as it might lead his wife to unlawfully wed another. **And** he would also flog **one who delivers a declaration** preemptively invalidating **a bill of divorce,** by informing three people before giving a bill of divorce that he is not doing so of his own free will and he wants to cancel it ahead of time. Here too he will mislead his wife, who will assume it is a valid bill of divorce.

וּמַאן דְּפָקֵיר שְׁלִיחָא דְּרַבָּנַן, וּמַאן דְּשָׁהֵי שַׁמְתָּא דְּרַבָּנַן עֲלֵיהּ תְּלָתִין יוֹמִין וְלָא אָתֵי לְבֵי דִּינָא וְתָבַע לְשַׁמְתֵּיהּ,

And he would lash **one who behaves irreverently** toward a **messenger of the Sages,**[H] even if the messenger is not a scholar, as he thereby shows disrespect to the Sages themselves. **And** he would administer lashes to **one who remained under an excommunication**[H] **of the Sages** for **thirty days and did not go to the court and petition for** the removal of **his excommunication after** correcting the sin that led to the excommunication in the first place. This behavior demonstrates that he does not care about the excommunication, and is therefore deserving of lashes.

NOTES

But isn't it taught that he is flogged – וְהָתַנְיָא לוֹקֶה: According to Rashi, the assumption of the Gemara at this stage is that he is lashed for transgressing a Torah law. The Rashba and other commentaries support this idea by citing the following homiletic interpretation of the verse that is cited in the Jerusalem Talmud. The Gemara there expounds the verse: "And he shall take her to him to be his wife and consummate the levirate marriage" (Deuteronomy 25:5), in the following manner: "And he shall take her to him to be his wife" by means of betrothal, and afterward he shall "consummate the levirate marriage" through intercourse. It is further explained in the Jerusalem Talmud that this line of reasoning follows the opinion that the action of one who transgresses a Torah law is not effective (see *Arukh LaNer*).

However, the Ritva points out that even according to this opinion the *yavam* should not be liable to lashes, as he has only transgressed a positive mitzva. Furthermore, it is Beit Shammai, not Beit Hillel, who maintain that levirate betrothal acquires the *yevama* by Torah law, and therefore, as the halakha does not accord with Beit Shammai's opinion, it is an established *halakha* that levirate betrothal is only effective by rabbinic decree. *Tosafot* suggest that the Gemara never considered that levirate betrothal is effective by Torah law, but merely that he should be lashed for transgressing a rabbinic ordinance. By not performing levirate betrothal, it is considered as though he had relations with his brother's wife without performing a mitzva. The Ramban explains that the question of the Gemara is not how he can acquire the *yevama* in this way if he receives lashes for his actions, but rather the Gemara is suggesting that he perhaps should be obligated to perform levirate betrothal before he has intercourse with the *yevama* again.

One who betroths a woman in the marketplace, etc. – מַאן דִּמְקַדֵּשׁ בְּשׁוּקָא וכו׳: The objection to this behavior is because the man acted in a disrespectful manner by betrothing in a marketplace or without prior preparation or appeasement of the woman and her family. Betrothing in the market gives the impression of an impromptu decision and is therefore considered licentious, as it is not dissimilar to soliciting a prostitute.

Marriage agreement [*shiddukhei*] – שִׁדּוּכֵי: The Aramaic root *sh-d-kh*, which is apparently the source of the Hebrew word, bears a variety of meanings. It seems that its chief meaning is to silence, from which several other meanings developed, such as to appease or to persuade. This is the likely etymology of the word as an appeasement and agreement between a woman and a man, or two families, as a preparation for marriage.

HALAKHA

If he engaged in intercourse without levirate betrothal he has acquired her and is flogged – בָּעַל בְּלֹא מַאֲמָר קָנָה וְלוֹקֶה: One who has relations with his *yevama* without performing levirate betrothal acquires her, but he receives lashes for rebelliousness from the Sages for acting in an immodest manner (Rambam *Sefer Nashim, Hilkhot Yibbum* 2:2; *Shulḥan Arukh, Even HaEzer* 166:2).

One who betroths a woman by intercourse – מַאן דִּמְקַדֵּשׁ בְּבִיאָה: One who betroths a woman by intercourse, or betroths her in the marketplace, or without a prior marriage agreement, receives lashes for rebelliousness but she is nevertheless betrothed. The Rema (based on *Tur* citing Rosh) writes that the custom is not to lash one who betrothed in the marketplace or without a marriage agreement (Rambam *Sefer Nashim, Hilkhot Ishut* 3:21–22 and *Sefer Kedusha, Hilkhot Issurei Bia* 21:14; *Shulḥan Arukh, Even HaEzer* 26:4).

One who nullifies a bill of divorce, etc. – מַאן דִּמְבַטֵּל גִּיטָּא וכו׳: One who sends a bill of divorce to his wife and subsequently retracts and nullifies it in the presence of witnesses, and similarly one who delivers a declaration preemptively invalidating a bill of divorce, receives lashes for rebelliousness, as stated by Rav (Rambam *Sefer Nashim, Hilkhot Geirushin* 6:26; *Shulḥan Arukh, Even HaEzer* 141:67).

One who behaves irreverently toward a messenger of the Sages – מַאן דְּפָקֵיר שְׁלִיחָא דְּרַבָּנַן: With regard to one who harasses or derides a messenger of the court who is carrying out his duty, if the messenger reports that he was belittled, the messenger is believed like two witnesses, and we place the offender under an excommunication. If there were witnesses to the event, the offender receives lashes for rebelliousness (Rambam *Sefer Shofetim, Hilkhot Sanhedrin* 25:5; *Shulḥan Arukh, Ḥoshen Mishpat* 8:5).

One who remained under an excommunication of the Sages – מַאן דְּשָׁהֵי שַׁמְתָּא דְּרַבָּנַן עֲלֵיהּ: If one was obligated to take an oath by the Sages but he refused to swear, the court places him under an excommunication for thirty days. If he does not come to the court to have the excommunication annulled, the court administers lashes for rebelliousness (Rambam *Sefer Mishpatim, Hilkhot To'en VeNitan* 1:5; *Shulḥan Arukh, Ḥoshen Mishpat* 87:9).

וְעַל חַתְנָא דְּדָאֵיר בְּבֵי חֲמוּהִי. דְּדָאֵיר – אִין, דְּחָלֵיף – לָא. וְהָא הַהוּא דְּחָלֵיף אַבָּבָא דְּבֵי חֲמוּהִי, וְנַגְדֵּיהּ רַב שֵׁשֶׁת! הַהוּא – מֵידָם הֲוָה דָּיֵים מֵחֲמָתֵיהּ.

And he would also lash **a son-in-law who lives in his father-in-law's house,**[NH] as this is likely to lead to temptation between the younger couple and older couple who share the same house. The Gemara asks: With regard to **one who lives** in his father-in-law's house, **yes,** he would lash him, but with regard to **one who** only **passed** through his father-in-law's house at regular intervals, **no,** he would not lash him? **But** an incident occurred involving **a certain** man **who passed by the entrance to his father-in-law's house and Rav Sheshet lashed him.** The Gemara explains: There was a special set of circumstances in that case, as **that** man **was suspected**[H] **with regard to his mother-in-law,** and therefore he was lashed merely for passing near her house, as he thereby gave credence to the rumors.

נְהַרְדְּעֵי אָמְרִי: בְּכוּלְּהוּ לָא מְנַגֵּיד רַב אֶלָּא לִמְקַדֵּשׁ בְּבִיאָה וּבְלֹא שִׁדּוּכֵי. וְאִיכָּא דְּאָמְרִי: אֲפִילּוּ בְּשִׁדּוּכֵי נַמִי, מִשּׁוּם פְּרִיצוּתָא.

The Sages **of Neharde'a**[P] would **say: In all** these cases **Rav would not flog, apart from** the case of one who **betrothed by intercourse and without** a prior **marriage agreement. And there are** those **who say** he would flog a man who betrothed by intercourse **even** if he did so **with** a prior **marriage agreement, due to the immorality** involved, as he must invite witnesses to observe the act.

תָּנוּ רַבָּנַן: כֵּיצַד מַאֲמָר – נָתַן לָהּ כֶּסֶף אוֹ שְׁוֵה כֶּסֶף, וּבִשְׁטָר כֵּיצַד? בִּשְׁטָר כֵּיצַד?! כְּדַאֲמַרַן: כָּתַב לָהּ עַל הַנְּיָיר אוֹ עַל הַחֶרֶס, אַף עַל פִּי שֶׁאֵין בּוֹ שְׁוֵה פְּרוּטָה: "הֲרֵי אַתְּ מְקוּדֶּשֶׁת לִי"! אֲמַר אַבַּיֵי, הָכִי קָאָמַר: שְׁטַר כְּתוּבַּת יְבָמִין כֵּיצַד –

§ **The Sages taught: How is levirate betrothal** performed? **He gives her money or the equivalent** value of **money** and declares: You are hereby betrothed to me. The Gemara asks: **And with a document,**[N] **how** does he betroth her? The Gemara is puzzled by this question: **With a document, how** does he betroth her? It is **as we have said** by the *halakhot* of a regular document of betrothal: **If he wrote to her on paper or on earthenware, even though it is not worth a** *peruta*, the words: **You are hereby betrothed to me,**[H] it is effective. As a document is not effective as a means of betrothal due to its monetary value but rather due to the words it contains, there is no requirement that it be of a minimum value. However, because the *halakhot* of betrothal by a document were already taught, the Gemara is puzzled as to the nature of this question. **Abaye said** that **this is what** the *baraita* **is saying:** With regard to **the document of a marriage contract for levirate marriage, how** is it written? Abaye understands that the question did not refer to the document of betrothal but rather to the marriage contract of a levirate marriage.

כָּתַב לָהּ: אֲנָא פְּלוֹנִי בַּר פְּלוֹנִי קַבֵּילִית יַת פְּלוֹנִית יְבִמְתִּי עֲלַי לְזוּן וּלְפַרְנְסָהּ כָּרָאוּי, וּבִלְבַד שֶׁתְּהֵא כְּתוּבָּתָהּ עַל נִכְסֵי בַּעֲלָהּ הָרִאשׁוֹן. וְאִי לֵית לָהּ מֵרִאשׁוֹן – תַּקִּינוּ לָהּ רַבָּנַן מִשֵּׁנִי, כְּדֵי שֶׁלֹּא תְּהֵא קַלָּה בְּעֵינָיו לְהוֹצִיאָהּ.

The Gemara explains that **he writes to her: I, so-and-so, son of so-and-so, have accepted so-and-so, my** *yevama* **upon me, to feed and maintain her in a fitting manner, provided that her marriage contract will** still **be** payable **from the property of her first husband** and not from the property of the *yavam*.[H] The Gemara adds: **But if the first** husband **does not have** property, **the Sages instituted for her** that she should receive her marriage contract **from the second** husband, i.e., the *yavam*, for the same reason that they instituted the marriage contract in the first place: **So that she will not be demeaned in his eyes such that** he will easily **divorce her.** If he will suffer no financial penalty, he is likely to divorce over the smallest argument.

בְּעָא מִינֵּיהּ אַבַּיֵי מֵרַבָּה: נָתַן לָהּ גֵּט, וְאָמַר: הֲרֵי אַתְּ מְגוֹרֶשֶׁת הֵימֶנִּי, וְאִי אַתְּ מוּתֶּרֶת לְכָל אָדָם, מַהוּ? גֵּט יְבָמָה דְּרַבָּנַן הוּא, גֵּט דִּמְהַנֵּי בְּאֵשֶׁת אִישׁ מְהַנֵּי בִּיבָמָה. גֵּט דְּלָא מְהַנֵּי בְּאֵשֶׁת אִישׁ – לָא מְהַנֵּי בִּיבָמָה. אוֹ דִּלְמָא אָתֵי לְאַחְלוּפֵי בְּגִיטָּא?

§ **Abaye inquired of Rabba:** If a *yavam* **gave** his *yevama* **a bill of divorce, and said** the following formula: **You are hereby divorced from me but you are not permitted to any** other **man, what is** the status of such a bill of divorce? **Is the bill of divorce of a** ***yevama***[H] a bill of divorce **based on rabbinic** law and therefore subject to the *halakhot* of a regular bill of divorce; and consequently, **a bill of divorce that is effective for a married woman is also effective for a** ***yevama***, and **a bill of divorce that is not effective for a married woman is not effective for a** ***yevama***? Since this type of a divorce is invalid in the case of a married woman, it is similarly ineffective in the case of a *yevama*. **Or perhaps** the Sages were concerned that **perhaps** people **will come to confuse** this bill of divorce **with** an unqualified **bill of divorce** given by a *yavam* and they therefore decreed that it should affect the levirate bond, preventing the *yavam* from marrying the *yevama*.

NOTES

A son-in-law who lives in his father-in-law's house – חַתְנָא דְּדָאֵיר בְּבֵי חֲמוּהִי: The *ge'onim* state that there is a concern that the mother-in-law might develop an attraction to her first son-in-law. In addition to the concern with regard to forbidden relations, there is also a concern with regard to the monetary aspects of the arrangement (Rabbi Avraham min HaHar). In this context the Rif cites a saying from *Sefer Ben Sira* quoted in tractate *Bava Batra* (89b): I have found no substance lighter than bran; yet, lighter than bran is a son-in-law who lives in the house of his father-in-law.

A document of betrothal – שְׁטָר קִידּוּשִׁין: The early commentaries explain that an act of using a document to perform levirate betrothal is also called a *ma'amar*, a saying. Admittedly, one who gives a woman a document of betrothal does not have to say anything, but since most betrothals were performed with money, when the man is required to speak, it was called *ma'amar*.

HALAKHA

A son-in-law who lives in his father-in-law's house – חַתְנָא דְּדָאֵיר בְּבֵי חֲמוּהִי: The Sages forbade a son-in-law to live in his father-in-law's house. The Ra'avad writes that if a special area is set aside for him and his wife, it is permitted. It appears that we rely on this opinion in order to be lenient in this area (*Maggid Mishne*; see *Tosafot*). In addition, the early commentaries state in tractate *Kiddushin* that nowadays we are less concerned with regard to this issue (Rambam *Sefer Kedusha, Hilkhot Issurei Bia* 21:15).

He was suspected, etc. – מֵידָם הֲוָה דָּיֵים וכו׳: If one is suspected of involvement with a forbidden relation, or if there are rumors circulating with regard to them, he may not live in the same alleyway as her, nor may he be seen in the same neighborhood, in accordance with Rav Sheshet. The Ra'avad claims that this *halakha* only applies to one's mother-in-law, as she is particularly close to him due to her daughter (Rambam *Sefer Kedusha, Hilkhot Issurei Bia* 2:12).

A document of betrothal – שְׁטָר קִידּוּשִׁין: If one writes a document on paper or any other material, even on something worth less than a *peruta*, that states: You are hereby betrothed to me, and gives it to a woman in the presence of witnesses, she is betrothed. The document must, however, be written in the name of that particular woman (Rambam *Sefer Nashim, Hilkhot Ishut* 3:3; *Shulḥan Arukh, Even HaEzer* 32:1).

The marriage contract of levirate marriage – כְּתוּבַּת יְבָמִין: A *yavam* is also required to write a marriage contract for his *yevama*, but the wording of his contract differs from that of a regular marriage contract. The main difference is that the fiscal responsibility for the marriage contract is upon the property of the deceased brother (Rambam *Sefer Nashim, Hilkhot Yibbum* 4:32).

The bill of divorce of a ***yevama*** **– גֵּט יְבָמָה:** If the *yavam* gives a bill of divorce to the *yevama* he disqualifies her and her rival wives from levirate marriage, both to himself and his brothers. Any bill of divorce that disqualifies a woman for marrying into the priesthood also disqualifies her from levirate marriage (Rambam *Sefer Nashim, Hilkhot Yibbum* 5:1; *Shulḥan Arukh, Even HaEzer* 170:1).

PERSONALITIES

The Sages of Neharde'a – נְהַרְדְּעֵי: The Gemara states elsewhere that anonymous statements attributed to the Sages of Neharde'a refer to Rav Ḥama from Neharde'a, who served as the head of the yeshiva of Neharde'a for several years following the passing of Rav Naḥman bar Yitzḥak. Apparently, Rav Ḥama was related to the house of the Exilarch, and for a time was its official scholar. It is also possible that he was the same Rav Ḥama who met with the king of Persia and discussed Torah matters with him.

[אָמַר לֵיהּ: חָיְישִׁינַן דִּלְמָא אָתֵי לְאַחְלוּפֵי בְּגִיטָּא]. מַתְקִיף לָהּ רַבָּה בַּר חָנָן: אֶלָּא מֵעַתָּה, יְהִיב לָהּ נְיָירָא בְּעָלְמָא הָכִי נָמֵי דְּפָסְלָה? אָמַר לֵיהּ: הָתָם לָא פְּסִיל בִּכְהוּנָּה, הָכָא – קָפָסֵיל בִּכְהוּנָּה.

Rabba **said to him: We are concerned** that **perhaps** they will come to **confuse** this bill of divorce **with a** regular **bill of divorce,** and it therefore disqualifies a *yevama*. **Rabba bar Ḥanan strongly objects to this: However, if that is so,** that we are stringent with the bill of divorce of a *yevama* out of concern that people might confuse the two types of bills of divorce, if **he gives her a mere** piece of **paper,** which does not mention divorce, **so too will it disqualify her? He said to him: There** it is different, as a mere piece of paper has no effect on any other woman, for **it does not disqualify** her **for** marrying into **the priesthood.** If a husband gives his wife a piece of paper that contains nothing about divorce, even if he says: This is a bill of divorce, his action is of no consequence, not even to forbid her to a priest. **Here,** however, a bill of divorce of this kind at least **disqualifies** a woman from marrying **into the priesthood.**[H]

דְּתַנְיָא: ״וְאִשָּׁה גְּרוּשָׁה מֵאִישָׁהּ לֹא יִקָּחוּ״ אֲפִילּוּ לֹא נִתְגָּרְשָׁה אֶלָּא מֵאִישָׁהּ – לֹא יִקָּחוּ, וְהַיְינוּ רֵיחַ הַגֵּט שֶׁפּוֹסֵל בִּכְהוּנָּה.

As it is taught in a *baraita*: "They shall not take a woman that is a harlot, or profaned; **and a woman divorced from her husband they shall not take,** as he is holy to his God" (Leviticus 21:7). This verse lists the women whom a priest is prohibited from marrying. From this verse it can be inferred: **Even if she was only divorced from her husband** who said when giving her a bill of divorce: You are divorced from me, but did not permit her to other men, even such a woman **they may not take** in marriage. Although a bill of divorce of this kind does not permit the woman to others, it does suffice to prohibit her from marrying a priest. **And this is** what is referred to as **the trace of a bill of divorce, which disqualifies** a woman from marrying **into the priesthood.**[N] Since this bill of divorce is valid to a certain extent, it also disqualifies a *yevama*.

אָמַר רָמִי בַּר חָמָא: הֲרֵי אָמְרוּ, אָמַר אֶחָד לַלַּבְלָר ״כְּתוֹב גֵּט לַאֲרוּסָתִי, לִכְשֶׁאֶכְנָסֶנָּה אֲגָרְשֶׁנָּה״ הֲרֵי זֶה גֵּט, מִפְּנֵי שֶׁבְּיָדוֹ לְגָרְשָׁהּ.

Rami bar Ḥama said: They said that **if one said to a scribe** [*lavlar*]:[L] **Write a bill of divorce for my betrothed** now, **such that when I marry her I will divorce her** with the bill of divorce, if he indeed gave her this bill of divorce after their marriage **it is** a valid **bill of divorce.**[H] Why? **Because it is already in his power to divorce her** while she is betrothed to him, and therefore the bill of divorce written during their betrothal is valid.

LANGUAGE

Scribe [*lavlar*] – לַבְלָר: The root of the word is from the Latin librarius, a writer, especially of contracts. *Lavlar* was another name for a scribe or an expert in writing. His field of expertise was not only the writing itself but also the wording of various kinds of contracts.

HALAKHA

A bill of divorce that disqualifies her from marrying into the priesthood – גֵּט הַפּוֹסֵל בִּכְהוּנָּה: A woman who receives a bill of divorce is disqualified from marrying into the priesthood, even if the bill of divorce is invalid because it is an uncertain bill of divorce or if the bill of divorce stated: You are hereby divorced from me, but you are not permitted to any man (Rambam *Sefer Nashim, Hilkhot Geirushin* 10:1; *Shulḥan Arukh*, *Even HaEzer* 6:1).

If he wrote a bill of divorce to his betrothed, etc. – כָּתַב גֵּט לַאֲרוּסָתוֹ וכו׳: If one wrote a bill of divorce to his betrothed in order to divorce her with it after he marries her, it is a valid bill of divorce. This applies only if the bill of divorce includes the date on which it was given, but if he wrote the date on which it was written, it is invalid (Ra'avad; Rabbeinu Tam; Rambam *Sefer Nashim, Hilkhot Geirushin* 3:6; *Shulḥan Arukh, Even HaEzer* 132:1).

NOTES

The trace of a bill of divorce, which disqualifies for the priesthood – רֵיחַ הַגֵּט שֶׁפּוֹסֵל בִּכְהוּנָּה: The trace of a bill of divorce refers to a divorce which is lacking in some way and therefore does not effect a full divorce. Despite the fact that the woman is not divorced, in some cases the trace of a bill of divorce is enough to consider her a divorcée for the purposes of disqualifying her from marrying into the priesthood. In these cases, should her husband subsequently die, she would be considered a divorcée and not a widow who would be permitted to the priesthood. The question of which bills of divorce disqualify a woman for marrying into the priesthood is a matter of dispute among the authorities. The Rambam maintains that any bill of divorce about which the Sages said: It is not a bill of divorce, does not even disqualify a woman for marrying into the priesthood. Only this particular bill of divorce, expressed with the formula: You are divorced from me but you are not permitted to any man, disqualifies her due to its status as the trace of a bill of divorce. The Ra'avad disagrees and claims there are other invalid bills of divorce that prevent her from marrying a priest, depending on their similarity to a proper bill of divorce. The *Migdal Oz* writes that this dispute dates back to Rashi and *Tosafot* as well.

וְלְאִשָּׁה בְּעָלְמָא – אֵין גֵּט, מִפְּנֵי שֶׁאֵין בְּיָדוֹ לְגָרְשָׁהּ. בָּעֵי רָמִי בַּר חָמָא: לִיבִמְתּוֹ מַהוּ? כֵּיוָן דַּאֲגִידָא בֵּיהּ – כַּאֲרוּסָתוֹ דָּמְיָא, אוֹ דִּלְמָא: כֵּיוָן דְּלָא עֲבַד בָּהּ מַאֲמָר – לָא? תֵּיקוּ.

But if he wrote a bill of divorce **for a regular woman** who has no connection to him, even if he later married her, it is **not a** valid **bill of divorce.**[HN] This is **because** at the time of the writing of the bill of divorce, **it is not in his power to divorce her,** and therefore the bill of divorce is of no consequence. All this is evident, but in light of the above *halakhot* **Rami bar Ḥama inquires:** If he wrote a bill of divorce **for his *yevama*** and did not give it to her immediately, but only after they were married, **what is** the *halakha*?[N] Is it a valid bill of divorce or not? The Gemara clarifies the options: On the one hand, **since she is tied to him** she **is considered like his betrothed; or perhaps, since he has not** yet **performed levirate betrothal with her,** she is **not** even considered the equivalent of his betrothed, and the bill of divorce is not effective? The Gemara does not have a resolution for this and states that the question **shall stand** unresolved.

בָּעֵי רַב חֲנַנְיָה: כָּתַב גֵּט לְזִיקָתוֹ וְלֹא לְמַאֲמָרוֹ, לְמַאֲמָרוֹ וְלֹא לְזִיקָתוֹ, מַהוּ? מַאֲמָר עִילָּוֵי זִיקָה קָא רָמֵי, וַהֲוָה לֵיהּ כִּמְגָרֵשׁ חֲצִי אִשָּׁה, וְהַמְגָרֵשׁ חֲצִי אִשָּׁה לֹא עָשָׂה וְלֹא כְּלוּם, אוֹ דִּלְמָא: הַאי לְחוּדֵיהּ קָאֵי וְהַאי לְחוּדֵיהּ קָאֵי?

Rav Ḥananya inquires: If **he wrote a bill of divorce for his levirate bond,** by specifying in the bill of divorce that he is thereby severing the levirate bond between them, **but not for his levirate betrothal,** or if he wrote a bill of divorce **for his levirate betrothal and** stated that it is **not for his levirate bond, what is** the *halakha*?[H] Is the **levirate betrothal superimposed upon the levirate bond,** so that they are considered a single, continuous link, **and he is like one who divorces half a woman, and one who divorces half a woman has done nothing; or perhaps this stands on its own and that stands on its own,** and he can therefore cancel either the levirate bond or the levirate betrothal separately.

וְתִפְשׁוֹט לֵיהּ מִדְּרָבָא, דְּאָמַר רָבָא: נָתַן גֵּט לְמַאֲמָרוֹ – הוּתְּרָה צָרָתָהּ! לְרָבָא – פְּשִׁיטָא לֵיהּ, לְרַב חֲנַנְיָה – מִיבַּעְיָא לֵיהּ, מַאי? תֵּיקוּ.

The Gemara asks: **And why** do you not **resolve** the dilemma **from** a teaching of **Rava? For Rava said:** If a *yavam* **gave a bill of divorce for his levirate betrothal, her rival wife is permitted.** The levirate betrothal he had previously performed is thereby canceled, which leaves the bond intact, and the rival wife of this *yevama* remains available for levirate marriage. This indicates that levirate betrothal and the levirate bond are not connected. The Gemara answers: **To Rava it is obvious, but to Rav Ḥananya it is a dilemma. What,** then, is the *halakha*? Since no other proof is forthcoming, and Rav Ḥananya does not accept the teaching of Rava, the question remains undecided. The Gemara states that the dilemma **shall stand** unresolved.

HALAKHA

If he wrote a bill of divorce to one who is not his wife – כָּתַב גֵּט לְמִי שֶׁאֵינָהּ אִשְׁתּוֹ: If a man wrote a bill of divorce to a woman who is not his wife, with the intention of divorcing her with it after their marriage, the bill of divorce is ineffective. However, if he wrote it to his *yevama* before he married her, it is an uncertain bill of divorce (Rambam *Sefer Nashim, Hilkhot Geirushin* 3:6; *Shulḥan Arukh, Even HaEzer* 132:2).

A bill of divorce for levirate betrothal and a bill of divorce for a levirate bond – גֵּט לְמַאֲמָר וְגֵט לְזִיקָה: If a *yavam* performed levirate betrothal with his *yevama* and afterward gave her a bill of divorce for her levirate bond, he has thereby disqualified her for levirate marriage, both with himself and with the other brothers. If he does not specify the nature of the bill of divorce it is considered to have been written for her levirate bond. In order to permit her to marry any other man she requires another bill of divorce for her levirate betrothal, and *ḥalitza* to release the levirate bond. If he gave her a bill of divorce for her levirate betrothal and not for her levirate bond, she is permitted to the brothers, but not to him. Some say (*Tosafot*; Ra'avad; Rosh) that she is even permitted to him (Rambam *Sefer Nashim, Hilkhot Yibbum* 5:4; *Shulḥan Arukh, Even HaEzer* 170:15).

NOTES

But for a regular woman it is not a bill of divorce – וּלְאִשָּׁה בְּעָלְמָא אֵין גֵּט: Most early commentaries (see *Tosafot*) explain that since he appointed an agent to write the bill of divorce on his behalf, the agent cannot perform something the husband does not have the power to do, and at the time of the appointment he could not have written the bill of divorce himself. Rabbi Avraham min HaHar raises several difficulties with this explanation. He explains that the Rambam has a different opinion: As the woman could not be divorced at that time, the bill of divorce is considered like one that was not written for the sake of a particular woman, and such a bill of divorce is invalid.

For his *yevama* what is the *halakha* – לִיבִמְתּוֹ מַהוּ: Rashi understands this question in a straightforward manner: Is this bill of divorce that she receives when still a *yevama* effective for their divorce after they are married? The Rambam understands the question in a similar vein. *Tosafot*, however, claim that it is obvious that such a bill of divorce cannot be used for divorce after their marriage. Consequently, they explain that the question is whether a bill of divorce written before levirate betrothal can cancel that levirate betrothal. Alternatively, the reference is to the trace of a bill of divorce, i.e., does a bill of divorce of this kind disqualify her for marrying into the priesthood? *Tosafot Yeshanim* note that one might have thought it is evident that this bill of divorce disqualifies her for marrying into the priesthood, as a bill of divorce is effective for a *yevama* even before he has performed levirate betrothal. Nevertheless, there is a difference between the cases, as he does not give her the bill of divorce immediately, but only after their marriage. It is therefore possible that the decree of the Sages with regard to the bill of divorce of a *yevama* no longer applies to a married woman.

Tosefot HaRosh explains that the dilemma is whether his *yevama* is considered like his betrothed, since he can have intercourse with her, even against her will, and then divorce her; or perhaps there is no relationship between them as of yet, since they have yet to engage in relations. A different point is raised by the Ramban: If the question concerns the validity of the bill of divorce according to Torah law, including its ability to effect a regular divorce, why is the rabbinical levirate betrothal mentioned in this connection at all? He concludes that the question concerns the efficacy of this bill of divorce on a rabbinic level, such that if he divorced her with it after their marriage, would she be considered divorced by rabbinic law. Do we say that the fact that he can give her a bill of divorce when she is a *yevama* and thereby disqualify her indicates that there is a connection between them, or perhaps this bill of divorce is completely ineffective after their marriage, as stated by *Tosafot Yeshanim*? All this refers to the stage before levirate betrothal, for once he has performed levirate betrothal with her she is certainly considered his betrothed according to rabbinic law.

The Rashba continues the line of reasoning suggested by the Ramban, but he explains somewhat differently. In his opinion the Gemara is asking a pair of questions that involve two distinct possibilities. First, does the fact that he can perform *ḥalitza* with his *yevama* mean that it is as though he can give her a bill of divorce, and she is considered his betrothed with regard to the validity of this bill of divorce? Second, if we say that *ḥalitza* is dissimilar to a bill of divorce, perhaps this bill of divorce is strong enough to disqualify her from marrying into the priesthood before he performs levirate betrothal.

״חָלַץ וְעָשָׂה מַאֲמָר״. אָמַר רַב יְהוּדָה אָמַר רַב: זוֹ דִּבְרֵי רַבִּי עֲקִיבָא, דְּאָמַר: אֵין קִדּוּשִׁין תּוֹפְסִין בְּחַיָּיבֵי לָאוִין. אֲבָל חֲכָמִים אוֹמְרִים: יֵשׁ אַחַר חֲלִיצָה כְּלוּם.

§ It was taught in the mishna: If the *yavam* **performed *ḥalitza*** **and then performed levirate betrothal,** nothing is effective after *ḥalitza* and this levirate betrothal is not valid. **Rav Yehuda said** that **Rav said: This is the statement of Rabbi Akiva,**[N] **who says** that **betrothal does not take effect on** those who are forbidden as they are **liable for** violating **a prohibition.** Once he has performed *ḥalitza,* the woman is forbidden to him due to the prohibition derived from the verse "So shall it be done to the man who does not build his brother's house" (Deuteronomy 25:9), and betrothal is ineffective. **But the Rabbis say something is** effective **after *ḥalitza*.** Although the woman who performed *ḥalitza* is forbidden to him, if he does betroth her, his betrothal is effective, as with any regular prohibition.

וּמִי מָצֵית מוֹקְמַתְּ לַהּ כְּרַבִּי עֲקִיבָא? וְהָא קָתָנֵי רֵישָׁא: נָתַן גֵּט וְעָשָׂה מַאֲמָר – צְרִיכָה גֵּט וַחֲלִיצָה, וְאִי רַבִּי עֲקִיבָא – כֵּיוָן דִּיהַב לַהּ גֵּט מִי מְהַנֵּי בָּהּ מַאֲמָר?

The Gemara asks: **And can you establish** that the mishna is **in accordance with** the opinion of **Rabbi Akiva? But doesn't the first clause** of the mishna **teach: If he gave a bill of divorce and performed levirate betrothal, she requires a bill of divorce and *ḥalitza*. Now if** this is in accordance with **Rabbi Akiva's** opinion**, once he gave her a bill of divorce, is levirate betrothal effective for her?**

וְהָתַנְיָא, רַבִּי עֲקִיבָא אוֹמֵר: מִנַּיִן לְנוֹתֵן גֵּט לִיבִמְתּוֹ שֶׁנֶּאֶסְרָה עָלָיו עוֹלָמִית – שֶׁנֶּאֱמַר ״לֹא יוּכַל בַּעְלָהּ הָרִאשׁוֹן אֲשֶׁר שִׁלְּחָהּ״ אַחַר שִׁילּוּחַ.

But isn't it taught in a *baraita* that **Rabbi Akiva says: From where** is it derived **that if one gives a bill of divorce to his *yevama*, she is forbidden to him forever** and he no longer has the option of marrying her? As it **is stated** with regard to a woman who was divorced and married another man who subsequently died or divorced her: **"Her former husband, who sent her away, may not** take her again to be his wife" (Deuteronomy 24:4). Rabbi Akiva emphasizes the words "who sent her away," implying that he may not remarry her **after sending** her **away.**[N] This indicates that there is an instance where a husband may not remarry his wife even if she has not married another, merely because he has given her a bill of divorce. This applies to the case of a *yevama* where the bill of divorce she receives renders her permanently prohibited to him. According to Rabbi Akiva, once she is rendered prohibited to him, no further action performed by the *yavam* is effective, so why does the levirate betrothal performed require a bill of divorce?

אָמַר רַב אַשִׁי: גֵּט יְבָמִין מִדְּרַבָּנַן. וּקְרָא – אַסְמַכְתָּא בְּעָלְמָא.

Rav Ashi said: This is not difficult because **the bill of divorce for levirate marriage** was established by the Sages and only has the force of **rabbinic law,**[H] **and the** aforementioned **verse** is not a Torah prohibition, but rather **a mere support.** Therefore there is no Torah prohibition against marrying a *yevama* who received a bill of divorce, and the levirate betrothal performed afterward is effective according to Rabbi Akiva as well.

תַּנְיָא נַמִי הָכִי, אָמַר רַבִּי: אֵין הַדְּבָרִים הַלָּלוּ אֲמוּרִים אֶלָּא לְדִבְרֵי רַבִּי עֲקִיבָא, שֶׁהָיָה עוֹשֶׂה חֲלוּצָה כְּעֶרְוָה. אֲבָל חֲכָמִים אוֹמְרִים: יֵשׁ אַחַר חֲלִיצָה כְּלוּם. וַאֲנִי אוֹמֵר: אֵימָתַי – בִּזְמַן שֶׁקִּדְּשָׁהּ לְשׁוּם אִישׁוּת, אֲבָל קִדְּשָׁהּ לְשׁוּם יִבּוּמוֹת – אֵין אַחַר חֲלִיצָה כְּלוּם.

With regard to the *halakha* of betrothal after *ḥalitza,* the Gemara notes: **This** *halakha* **is also taught** in a *baraita* as **Rabbi** Yehuda HaNasi **said: These matters were only stated in accordance with the statement of Rabbi Akiva, who considers a *yevama* who underwent *ḥalitza* to be** prohibited **like a forbidden relation.** Therefore, any further betrothal is not effective with her, as is the case with forbidden relations. **But the Rabbis say something is** effective **after *ḥalitza*. And I say: When** is betrothal effective after *ḥalitza*? It is effective **when he betrothed for the purpose of marriage,** like the regular betrothal of any ordinary woman. **But** if **he betrothed her** after *ḥalitza* and specified that he is doing so **for the purpose of levirate marriage,** in that case **nothing is** effective **after *ḥalitza*.**

תַּנְיָא אִידַּךְ: הַחוֹלֵץ לִיבִמְתּוֹ, וְחָזַר וְקִדְּשָׁהּ. רַבִּי אוֹמֵר: אִם קִדְּשָׁהּ לְשׁוּם אִישׁוּת – צְרִיכָה הֵימֶנּוּ גֵּט, לְשׁוּם יִבּוּמוֹת – אֵין צְרִיכָה הֵימֶנּוּ גֵּט וַחֲכָמִים אוֹמְרִים: בֵּין שֶׁקִּדְּשָׁהּ לְשׁוּם אִישׁוּת, בֵּין שֶׁקִּדְּשָׁהּ לְשׁוּם יִבּוּמוֹת – צְרִיכָה הֵימֶנּוּ גֵּט.

It is taught in another *baraita*: With regard to **one who performs *ḥalitza* with his *yevama* and then betroths her,**[H] **Rabbi** Yehuda HaNasi **says: If he betrothed her for the purpose** of regular **marriage she requires a bill of divorce from him;** if he betrothed her **for the purpose of levirate marriage she does not require a bill of divorce from him. And the Rabbis say: Whether he betrothed her for the purpose** of regular **marriage, or whether he betrothed her for the purpose of levirate marriage, she requires a bill of divorce from him,** as this betrothal is effective.

NOTES

This is the statement of Rabbi Akiva – זוֹ דִּבְרֵי רַבִּי עֲקִיבָא: In the Jerusalem Talmud, this conclusion is not accepted by all, as there are alternate ways to explain the mishna. For example, Reish Lakish maintains that a woman who performed *ḥalitza* is forbidden to the brothers due to a prohibition for which they are liable to *karet*, as are her rival wives, and therefore betrothal is not effective even according to the Rabbis. Another possibility is that the mishna is in accordance with Rabbi Yehuda HaNasi, and it is discussing a situation where the *yavam* betrothed the *yevama* for the purpose of levirate marriage.

After sending her away – אַחַר שִׁילּוּחַ: Rabbi Akiva maintains that the words "who sent her away" are superfluous, and therefore he reads the verse as speaking of two separate mitzvot. One would therefore read the verse as having two subjects, as follows: "Her former husband" and similarly he "who sent her away," i.e., the *yavam*, "may not return to take her as a wife."

HALAKHA

The validity of a bill of divorce for levirate marriage – תּוֹקֶף גֵּט יְבָמִין: The Sages decreed that the bill of divorce of a *yavam* to his *yevama* is effective, and it disqualifies her and her rival wives from levirate marriage, both with him and his brothers (Rambam *Sefer Nashim, Hilkhot Yibbum* 5:1; *Shulḥan Arukh, Even HaEzer* 170:1).

One who performs *ḥalitza* with his *yevama* and then betroths her – הַחוֹלֵץ לִיבִמְתּוֹ וְחָזַר וְקִדְּשָׁהּ: If one performed *ḥalitza* with his *yevama* and then betrothed her, whether he did so for the purpose of regular marriage or levirate marriage, he is forbidden to marry her; but the betrothal is effective to the extent that she requires a bill of divorce from him (Rambam *Sefer Nashim, Hilkhot Yibbum* 5:15; *Shulḥan Arukh, Even HaEzer* 170:13).

HALAKHA

One who hoes in the property of a convert – הָעוֹדֵר בְּנִכְסֵי הַגֵּר: If one hoes the property of a convert who died without leaving heirs, under the mistaken impression that the land belonged to him, he has not acquired it. However, if he thought it belonged to a particular convert and it actually belonged to a different one, and he intended to acquire the ownerless property, the acquisition is effective (Rambam *Sefer Kinyan, Hilkhot Zekhiya UMattana* 2:13; *Shulḥan Arukh, Ḥoshen Mishpat* 275:25–26).

Levirate betrothal and a levirate bond – מַאֲמַר יְבָמִין וְזִיקַת יְבָמִין: If a *yavam* performed *ḥalitza* with his *yevama* and then betrothed her, whether he said he was doing so with levirate betrothal or with the levirate bond, his betrothal is effective. The *Beit Shmuel* claims that it is only valid by rabbinic law. She then requires a bill of divorce, in accordance with the opinion of the Rabbis (*Shulḥan Arukh, Even HaEzer* 170:14).

אֲמַר רַב יוֹסֵף: מַאי טַעֲמָא דְּרַבִּי – עֲשָׂאוּהָ כְּעוֹדֵר בְּנִכְסֵי הַגֵּר וּכְסָבוּר שֶׁלּוֹ הֵן דְּלָא קָנֵי.

Rav Yosef said: What is the reason for Rabbi Yehuda HaNasi's distinction between one who betroths his *ḥalutza* for the purpose of levirate marriage and one who does so for the purpose of regular marriage? It is because the Sages **considered him like** one who **hoes the property of a convert**[H] who died without leaving heirs. The property of such a convert is ownerless, and whoever takes possession of it acquires its title. As one of the methods of taking possession of land is hoeing, if one hoed the property of this convert with the intention of acquiring it, it belongs to him. However, if he hoed the convert's property **while** mistakenly **thinking** that the land **was his own,** even though he performed an act of acquisition, since he lacked the requisite intention **he has not acquired** the land. Here too, since the *yavam* intended to betroth her for the purpose of levirate marriage, and the levirate bond no longer exists, his action is not effective.

אָמַר לֵיהּ אַבַּיֵי: מִי דָּמֵי? הָתָם – לָא קָא מְכַוֵּין לְמִיקְנֵי, הָכָא – קָא מְכַוֵּין לְמִיקְנֵי. הָא לָא דָּמְיָא אֶלָּא לְעוֹדֵר בְּנִכְסֵי גֵּר זֶה, וּכְסָבוּר שֶׁל גֵּר אַחֵר הוּא, דְּקָנֵי.

Abaye said to him: Are the two situations **comparable?**[N] **There,** in the case of hoeing, **he does not intend to acquire** the land as he works, as he thinks that it is already his, whereas **here he does intend to acquire** the woman. **This case is similar only to the one who hoes the property of this** deceased **convert while thinking it is that of a different convert.** The *halakha* in that case is **that he acquires** the land, despite his imprecise knowledge of what he is acquiring. Here too the betrothal should take effect regardless of his error.

אֶלָּא אֲמַר אַבַּיֵי: הָכָא בְּמַאי עָסְקִינַן – כְּגוֹן דְּאָמַר לָהּ ״הִתְקַדְּשִׁי לִי בְּמַאֲמַר יְבָמִין״. רַבִּי סָבַר: מַאֲמָר עִילָּוֵי זִיקָה קָא רָמֵי, וַאֲתַאי חֲלִיצָה אַפְקַעְתָּהּ לְזִיקָה. וְרַבָּנַן סָבְרִי: הַאי לְחוּדֵיהּ קָאֵי וְהַאי לְחוּדֵיהּ קָאֵי. מֵעִיקָּרָא, אִילּוּ אֲמַר לָהּ ״הִתְקַדְּשִׁי לִי בְּמַאֲמַר יְבָמִין״ מִי לָא מְהַנֵּי? הַשְׁתָּא נַמִי מְהַנֵּי.

Rather, Abaye said that the dispute between Rabbi Yehuda HaNasi and the Rabbis cannot be explained in the above manner. Instead, he suggests: **With what are we dealing here?** It is a case **where he said to** his *ḥalutza*: **Be betrothed to me with levirate betrothal. Rabbi** Yehuda HaNasi **holds** that **levirate betrothal is superimposed upon** the **levirate bond,** and is therefore only possible when the bond exists, **and** since ***ḥalitza* comes** and **releases the levirate bond,** levirate betrothal is not effective for her. **And the Rabbis hold: This,** the levirate bond, **stands on its own, and that,** levirate betrothal, **stands on its own.** Although the bond has been canceled, the formula of: Be betrothed to me with levirate betrothal, is effective. **At the outset,** before *ḥalitza*, **if he had said to her: Be betrothed to me with levirate betrothal,**[N] **would** this **not be** an **effective** betrothal despite the lack of connection between the levirate betrothal and the levirate bond? **Now too** it should be **effective,** even though she performed *ḥalitza*.

רָבָא אֲמַר: אִי דְּאָמַר לָהּ ״בְּמַאֲמַר יְבָמִין״ כּוּלֵּי עָלְמָא לָא פְּלִיגִי דִּמְהַנְּיָא, וְהָכָא בְּמַאי עָסְקִינַן – כְּגוֹן דְּאָמַר לָהּ ״הִתְקַדְּשִׁי לִי בְּזִיקַת יְבָמִין״. רַבִּי סָבַר:

Rava said: If he said to her: Be betrothed to me **with levirate betrothal, everyone agrees that it is effective,** and she is acquired. **And with what are we dealing here?** It is a case **where he said to her: Be betrothed to me with the levirate bond,**[H] and the dispute is as follows: **Rabbi** Yehuda HaNasi **holds**

NOTES

Abaye said to him, Are they comparable – אָמַר לֵיהּ אַבַּיֵי מִי דָּמֵי: The early commentaries are puzzled by Abaye's opinion: After questioning Rav Yosef's comparison to one who hoes a field by asserting that a *yavam* acquires his *yevama* when he betroths her for the purpose of levirate marriage, he himself proceeds to claim that he cannot acquire her by levirate betrothal.

Tosafot offer two explanations, also cited, with slight variations, by *Tosafot Yeshanim*. The Ra'avad explains that Rav Yosef explains Rabbi Yehuda HaNasi's case as one where the *yavam* says he is betrothing so-and-so, his *yevama*. Abaye responds that there is no proof from the wording that he is acquiring her with levirate marriage in mind, as he might merely be mentioning that she was previously his *yevama*. Abaye therefore explains that Rabbi Yehuda HaNasi was referring specifically to one who said that he is acquiring her with levirate betrothal.

If he had said to her, Be betrothed to me with levirate betrothal – אִילּוּ אֲמַר לָהּ הִתְקַדְּשִׁי לִי בְּמַאֲמַר יְבָמִין: The Ritva indicates that a statement of this kind would be effective even with regard to a regular woman, despite the fact that it is not a precise expression of betrothal. Levirate betrothal is in essence an act of betrothal, and there is no reason to distinguish between them. For example, the Gemara in tractate *Kiddushin* 6a states that if one says to a woman: You are hereby tied to me by a bond, she is betrothed.

יֵשׁ זִיקָה, וַאֲתַאי חֲלִיצָה אַפְקְעַתֵּיהּ לְזִיקָה. וְרַבָּנַן סָבְרִי, אֵין זִיקָה. מֵעִיקָּרָא אִילּוּ אֲמַר לַהּ ״הִתְקַדְּשִׁי לִי בְּזִיקַת יְבָמִין״ מִי לָא מְהַנֵּי? הָשְׁתָּא נַמִּי מְהַנֵּי.

that **the levirate bond is substantial,** and this betrothal is based on the levirate bond. **And** in this case, the ***ḥalitza*** **comes** and **releases the levirate bond.** Therefore this type of betrothal does not acquire the *ḥalutza*. **But the Rabbis hold** that **the levirate bond is not substantial,**[N] that is, the bond itself does not create a connection between the *yavam* and *yevama*, and that in general, levirate betrothal acquires a *yevama* as a form of betrothal unrelated to the levirate bond.[N] **And** consequently, **at the outset, if he had said to her: Be betrothed to me by the levirate bond, would** this **not be effective? Now too,** after *ḥalitza*, even without the bond, it should likewise be **effective.**

רַב שֵׁרֵבְיָא אֲמַר: בַּחֲלִיצָה כְּשֵׁרָה, אִי דַּאֲמַר לַהּ ״הִתְקַדְּשִׁי לִי בְּזִיקַת יְבָמִין״ כּוּלֵּי עָלְמָא לָא פְּלִיגִי דְּלָא מְהַנֵּי. וְהָכָא בַּחֲלִיצָה פְּסוּלָה קָמִיפַּלְגִי. מָר סָבַר: חֲלִיצָה פְּסוּלָה פּוֹטֶרֶת, וּמָר סָבַר: חֲלִיצָה פְּסוּלָה אֵינָהּ פּוֹטֶרֶת.

Rav Sherevya suggested a different point of dispute and **said:** In a case when the woman performed **valid *ḥalitza*, if he** later **said to her: Be betrothed to me by the levirate bond, everyone agrees**[N] **that it is not effective,** as there is no longer any bond. **And here,** they **disagree** with regard to one who performed **invalid *ḥalitza*.** One **Sage,** Rabbi Yehuda HaNasi, **holds** that **invalid *ḥalitza* exempts** her from the levirate bond and disqualifies her from betrothal as a *yevama*. **And one Sage,** i.e., the Rabbis, **holds** that **invalid *ḥalitza* does not** fully **exempt** her,[N] and some element of the levirate bond remains intact and she can therefore be betrothed with the levirate bond.

רַב אַשִׁי אֲמַר: דְּכוּלֵּי עָלְמָא חֲלִיצָה פְּסוּלָה אֵינָהּ פּוֹטֶרֶת. וְהָכָא בְּיֵשׁ תְּנַאי בַּחֲלִיצָה קָמִיפַּלְגִי. מָר סָבַר: יֵשׁ תְּנַאי בַּחֲלִיצָה, וּמָר סָבַר: אֵין תְּנַאי בַּחֲלִיצָה.

Rav Ashi said: Everyone agrees that **invalid *ḥalitza* does not exempt** her and does not entirely nullify the bond. **And here** they **disagree** as to whether **a condition is** effective **with regard to *ḥalitza*.** When the *yavam* states he is performing *ḥalitza* on the condition that the *yevama* give him one hundred dinars, for example, is this condition effective and therefore the *ḥalitza* is nullified if the condition is not fulfilled? One **Sage,** i.e., the Rabbis, **holds** that **a condition is** effective **with regard to *ḥalitza*.** If the *yevama* fails to comply with the condition, the *ḥalitza* is ineffective and she can still be betrothed with the levirate bond. **And** one **Sage,** Rabbi Yehuda HaNasi, **holds** that **a condition is not** effective **with regard to *ḥalitza*,**[H] and therefore the *ḥalitza* is always effective as is the subsequent levirate betrothal.

רָבִינָא אֲמַר: דְּכוּלֵּי עָלְמָא יֵשׁ תְּנַאי בַּחֲלִיצָה. וְהָכָא בִּתְנַאי כָּפוּל קָמִיפַּלְגִי; מָר סָבַר: בָּעֵינַן תְּנַאי כָּפוּל, וּמָר סָבַר: לָא בָּעֵינַן תְּנַאי כָּפוּל.

Ravina said: Everyone agrees that **a condition is** effective **with regard to *ḥalitza*, and here** they **disagree with regard to a compound condition.**[HB] One **Sage,** Rabbi Yehuda HaNasi, **holds** that **we require a compound condition.** The man must explicitly stipulate that the *ḥalitza* should be effective if the condition is upheld, and that it should not be effective if she does not fulfill the condition. If he did not state both the positive and negative sides of the condition it does not take effect, and the *ḥalitza* is effective and the levirate bond is canceled. Consequently, betrothal by the levirate bond is ineffective. **And one Sage,** i.e., the Rabbis, **holds that we do not require a compound condition.** Therefore, the condition applies and cancels the *ḥalitza*, which leaves the levirate bond intact.

NOTES

But the Rabbis hold that the levirate bond is not substantial – וְרַבָּנַן סָבְרִי אֵין זִיקָה: It is not that the Rabbis maintain that the levirate bond is not significant at all, as the *yevama* certainly requires levirate marriage. Rather, it means the bond does not have the halakhic force with regard to creating prohibitions, as it is does not create a family connection that would forbid the *yavam* from marrying the relatives of the *yevama* (*Tosefot HaRosh*). Rabbi Avraham min HaHar explains that this opinion holds the levirate bond is not substantial by Torah law but rather by rabbinic law.

The explanations of the dispute between Rabbi Yehuda HaNasi and the Rabbis – פֵּירוּשֵׁי מַחֲלוֹקֶת רַבִּי וְרַבָּנַן: The early commentaries were puzzled by the variety of interpretations of this dispute, as they are based on assumptions that are not accepted as *halakha*. The Rif states, and the Rid writes similarly, that all these explanations of the Gemara are merely hypothetical exercises to sharpen the mind, and it is a mistake to analyze them too closely, as they are not meant as rulings for *halakha*.

Be betrothed to me by the levirate bond, everyone agrees, etc. – הִתְקַדְּשִׁי לִי בְּזִיקַת יְבָמִין כּוּלֵּי עָלְמָא לָא פְּלִיגֵי וכו׳: The *Milḥamot HaShem* had an alternate version of the text that reads: If he said: Be betrothed to me by the levirate bond, everyone agrees that it is effective, as they did not disagree with regard to the levirate bond at all. According to this opinion, which is implied somewhat by Rashi as well, all the suggested interpretations of the dispute are in logical order, in the manner usually signaled by the words: And if you say, etc.

Invalid *ḥalitza* does not exempt her – חֲלִיצָה פְּסוּלָה אֵינָהּ פּוֹטֶרֶת: This suggestion is problematic, as the accepted principle throughout our chapter is that invalid *ḥalitza* exempts the woman and that anything afterward is ineffective. How, then, can the Gemara propose that such a *ḥalitza* does not exempt her? For this reason the Rif claims that this statement refers to the requirement to repeat the *ḥalitza* with the other brothers; and therefore, according to the opinion that invalid *ḥalitza* does not exempt her, she must perform *ḥalitza* with all the brothers. A different interpretation is cited by Rabbi Avraham min HaHar. He contends that invalid *ḥalitza* does not refer to *ḥalitza* performed after another action. Instead, it means *ḥalitza* performed with a pregnant woman, which is ineffective according to Reish Lakish.

HALAKHA

A condition with regard to *ḥalitza* – תְּנַאי בַּחֲלִיצָה: No conditions are effective with regard to *ḥalitza*, and therefore a mistaken *ḥalitza* is valid. For example, if the *yavam* was told to perform *ḥalitza* on condition that the *yevama* should give him a large sum of money, even if it was stated as a compound condition, the *ḥalitza* is valid whether or not she paid him the stipulated amount (Rambam *Sefer Nashim*, *Hilkhot Yibbum* 4:24; *Shulḥan Arukh*, *Even HaEzer* 169:50).

A compound condition – תְּנַאי כָּפוּל: Every condition must include the following four features: It must be double in the sense that he must specify what will happen both if the condition is fulfilled and if it is not fulfilled; the formulation of its positive aspect, i.e., its fulfillment, must precede the negative formulation of the condition; the condition must be stated before the action itself; and the fulfillment of the condition must be feasible. Any condition that lacks one of these elements is discounted (Rambam *Sefer Nashim*, *Hilkhot Ishut* 6:2; *Shulḥan Arukh*, *Even HaEzer* 38:2).

BACKGROUND

A compound condition – תְּנַאי כָּפוּל: This refers to conditions set out when creating contractual obligations. A simple condition merely states the positive side of a commitment: If X, then Y. A compound condition states its negative side, as well: If X, then Y, and if not X, then not Y. Some authorities, basing themselves on the agreement made between Moses and the tribes of Gad and Reuben (see Numbers 32:20–24), maintain that compound conditions are required so that violation of a simple condition, where the negative side of the case is not stated, does not nullify the agreement.

HALAKHA

Nothing is effective after intercourse – אֵין אַחַר בִּיאָה כְּלוּם: If a *yavam* engaged in valid intercourse with the *yevama*, i.e., the intercourse was not preceded by any action that would invalidate it, no action performed afterward is of any effect, whether performed by any other *yavam* with her, or by the *yavam* or one of his brothers with her rival wife, as stated by Abaye and Rava (Rambam *Sefer Nashim*, *Hilkhot Yibbum* 5:14; *Shulḥan Arukh*, *Even HaEzer* 170:12).

"חָלַץ וְעָשָׂה מַאֲמָר וְנָתַן גֵּט וּבָעַל" וכו׳. וְנִיתְנֵי נַמִּי אֵין אַחַר בִּיאָה כְּלוּם! אַבָּיֵי וְרָבָא דְּאָמְרִי תַּרְוַיְיהוּ, תְּנֵי: אֵין אַחַר בִּיאָה כְּלוּם. וְתַנָּא דִּידַן – הַתָּרַת יְבָמָה לַשּׁוּק עֲדִיפָא לֵיהּ.

§ The mishna teaches: If the *yavam* **performed** ***ḥalitza*** **and** then either **performed levirate betrothal, or gave a bill of divorce, or engaged in intercourse,** nothing is effective after *ḥalitza*. The Gemara asks: **And let** the *tanna* **likewise teach** that **nothing is** effective **after intercourse,**[H] for he also mentioned the case of one who engaged in intercourse and then proceeded to perform other actions such as levirate betrothal, divorce and *ḥalitza*. Indeed, **Abaye and Rava both** say that the mishna should **teach: Nothing is** effective **after intercourse,** as this clause is fit to be inserted into the mishna. The Gemara asks: **And the** ***tanna*** **of our** mishna;[N] why did he not state this? The Gemara explains: **The permission for a** ***yevama*** **to** marry a member of the **public is preferable to him.** He preferred to teach cases in which the *yevama* is permitted to marry any man from the general public as opposed to a situation where she is married to the *yavam*.

"אֶחָד יְבָמָה אַחַת אֶחָד שְׁתֵּי יְבָמוֹת". מַתְנִיתִין דְּלָא כְּבֶן עַזַּאי. דְּתַנְיָא, בֶּן עַזַּאי אוֹמֵר: יֵשׁ מַאֲמָר אַחַר מַאֲמָר בִּשְׁנֵי יְבָמִין וִיבָמָה אַחַת, וְאֵין מַאֲמָר אַחַר מַאֲמָר בִּשְׁתֵּי יְבָמוֹת וְיָבָם אֶחָד.

The mishna teaches that all the *halakhot* with regard to levirate betrothal after levirate betrothal and the like apply **both** in cases of **one** ***yevama*** to one *yavam*, **as well as** in cases of **two** ***yevamot*** to one *yavam*. The Gemara comments: **The mishna is not in accordance with** the opinion of **ben Azzai. As it is taught** in a *baraita*: **Ben Azzai says: Levirate betrothal is** effective **after levirate betrothal in** the case of **two** ***yevamin*** **and one** ***yevama*****, but levirate betrothal is not** effective **after levirate betrothal in** the case of **two** ***yevamot*** **and one** ***yavam*****.** The *tanna* of the mishna, in contrast, does not differentiate between the cases.

"כֵּיצַד מַאֲמָר לָזוֹ" וכו׳. לֵימָא מְסַיַּיע לֵיהּ לִשְׁמוּאֵל, דְּאָמַר שְׁמוּאֵל: חָלַץ לְבַעֲלַת מַאֲמָר לֹא נִפְטְרָה צָרָתָהּ,

The mishna further teaches: **How so?** If he performed **levirate betrothal with this** one and performed *ḥalitza* with that one, the first woman requires a bill of divorce to cancel the levirate betrothal. The Gemara suggests: **Let us say** that this teaching **supports** the opinion of **Shmuel.**[N] **As Shmuel said:** If a *yavam* **performed** ***ḥalitza*** **with** the woman **who received levirate betrothal,** then **the rival wife is not exempt** as this *ḥalitza* is invalid. The fact that the Gemara does not state that the *ḥalitza* be performed with the woman who received levirate betrothal indicates that this *ḥalitza* is not a valid *ḥalitza* and would not be sufficient to exempt the rival wife.

NOTES

And the ***tanna*** **of our mishna, etc. – וְתַנָּא דִּידַן וכו׳:** The wording here is confusing, for Abaye and Rava just stated that mishna should be adjusted, which means that in their opinion our *tanna* did in fact include this teaching in the mishna. *Tosafot Yeshanim* suggest that Abaye and Rava were pointing out a *baraita* that explicitly says that nothing is effective after intercourse, as indeed, such a *baraita* is found in the *Tosefta*. After noting that source, the Gemara inquires about the *tanna* of our mishna.

Let us say that this supports Shmuel, etc. – לֵימָא מְסַיַּיע לֵיהּ לִשְׁמוּאֵל וכו׳: *Tosafot* are puzzled by the assertion that this statement is both a support for the opinion of Shmuel and a refutation of the statement of Rav Yosef, for the opposite would appear to be the case; accepting Shmuel's opinion should remove any difficulty with the statement of Rav Yosef. Once it is established that *ḥalitza* with the woman who received levirate betrothal does not exempt the rival wife, it is clear that Rav Yosef's insistence on not performing *ḥalitza* when unnecessary is not relevant to this case, as here it is necessary. They answer that this line should be read as support for Shmuel or a refutation of Rav Yosef. However, the early commentaries point out that the letter *vav* usually means "and" and only rarely means "or" in the Gemara. Some commentaries therefore explain that the Gemara is saying that even according to Shmuel's opinion, if Rav Yosef's opinion is accepted the *yavam* should be obliged to perform *ḥalitza* with the first woman, such that when he later performs *ḥalitza* with the second one he should at least not disqualify her by Torah law (*Tosefot HaRosh*).

Rabbeinu Ḥananel has a very different opinion. He claims that the Gemara is not referring to Rav Yosef's opinion with regard to: He should not pour out the water of his pit, when others require them (12a), indicating that one should not needlessly disqualify a woman, but rather his opinion that: One who hoes the property of a convert…has not acquired it (52b). According to this interpretation, if the *yavam* performed levirate betrothal under the mistaken impression that it fully acquires her as a wife, the acquisition is considered an error, and it should therefore be entirely discounted.

The Ramban objects to this interpretation, as it would mean that the difficulty does not refer to this particular section of the mishna, but to multiple clauses of the mishna, and there was no reason to raise it at this juncture. The Ramban himself suggests that the Sages of the Gemara had a tradition that Rav Yosef disagrees with Shmuel. The *Tosefot HaRosh* similarly explains that the reference here is to Rav Yosef's assertion in tractate *Megilla* (18b) that Shmuel's opinion with regard to the levirate bond is a minority opinion. Therefore, if this mishna supports Shmuel it automatically presents a difficulty to that statement of Rav Yosef.

וּתְיוּבְתָּא דְּרַב יוֹסֵף! מִי קָתָנֵי "חוֹלֵץ"? "חָלַץ" קָתָנֵי, דִּיעֲבַד.

And this would constitute **a conclusive refutation of** Rav Yosef's opinion, for he holds that it is preferable to perform *ḥalitza* with the woman who received levirate betrothal and thereby exempt the second woman. As the first woman requires a bill of divorce and therefore is necessarily disqualified from marrying into the priesthood, it is preferable to perform *ḥalitza* with her as well and consequently leave the second woman eligible to marry a priest. The Gemara refutes this claim: **Does the mishna teach: He should perform *ḥalitza*,** which would imply that the *yavam* should do so *ab initio*? It **teaches** that **he performed *ḥalitza*,** implying that the ruling in the mishna is **after the fact.** Therefore, there is no indication in the mishna that the *yavam* should perform *ḥalitza* with the second woman, and it is possible that if he were to perform *ḥalitza* with the first woman he would thereby exempt the second one. It is simply that the particular case discussed by the mishna here concerns a man who performed levirate betrothal with this woman and *ḥalitza* with that one.

"גֵּט לָזוֹ וְגֵט לָזוֹ" כו׳. לֵימָא מְסַיַּיע לֵיהּ לְרַבָּה בַּר רַב הוּנָא, דְּאָמַר רַבָּה בַּר רַב הוּנָא: חֲלִיצָה פְּסוּלָה – צְרִיכָה לַחֲזוֹר עַל כׇּל הָאַחִין. מַאי "צְרִיכוֹת" צְרִיכוֹת דְּעָלְמָא.

It is further taught in the mishna: If he gave **a bill of divorce to this one and a bill of divorce to that one,** they require *ḥalitza* from him. The Gemara suggests: **Let us say that it supports** the statement of **Rabba bar Rav Huna.**[N] **As Rabba bar Rav Huna said:** In cases of **invalid *ḥalitza*,** the ***yevama* is required to repeat** the *ḥalitza*[H] **with all of the brothers,** as that single invalid *ḥalitza* is insufficient. Similarly, in this case of invalid *ḥalitza*, it would be necessary to perform *ḥalitza* with all of the *yevamot*. The Gemara rejects this suggestion: **What is** the meaning of **require** in this context? It means that such women **require in general.** The plural form does not refer to all the *yevamot* mentioned in the mishna, but rather it means that all *yevamot* in similar situations require *ḥalitza*.

"גֵּט לָזוֹ וְחָלַץ לָזוֹ". לֵימָא מְסַיַּיע לֵיהּ לִשְׁמוּאֵל וְתֶיהְוֵי תְּיוּבְתָּא דְּרַב יוֹסֵף. מִי קָתָנֵי "חוֹלֵץ"? "חָלַץ" קָתָנֵי, דִּיעֲבַד.

It was taught in the mishna: If he gave **a bill of divorce to this one and performed *ḥalitza* with that one,** nothing is effective after *ḥalitza*. The Gemara suggests: **Let us say that this supports** the opinion of **Shmuel,** as it indicates that the *yavam* should perform *ḥalitza* with the rival wife rather than the woman who received a bill of divorce. **And it would likewise be a conclusive refutation of** the opinion of **Rav Yosef,** who prefers performing *ḥalitza* with the disqualified woman. The Gemara again rejects this proof: **Does it teach: He should perform *ḥalitza*,** a ruling *ab initio*? **It teaches: He performed *ḥalitza*,** which is only **after the fact,** meaning he acted in that manner in this particular case.

"חָלַץ וְחָלַץ אוֹ חָלַץ" וכו׳. וְלִיתְנֵי נַמִּי אֵין אַחַר בִּיאָה כְּלוּם! אַבַּיֵּי וְרָבָא דְּאָמְרִי תַּרְוַיְיהוּ, תְּנֵי: אֵין אַחַר בִּיאָה כְּלוּם. וְתַנָּא דִּידַן – הֶתֵּרַת יְבָמָה לַשּׁוּק עֲדִיפָא לֵיהּ.

The mishna taught that if **he performed *ḥalitza*** with one woman **and** then **performed *ḥalitza*** with another one, **or he performed *ḥalitza*** and then proceeded to perform levirate betrothal, nothing is effective after *ḥalitza*. The Gemara suggests: **And let** the *tanna* **also teach: Nothing is** effective **after intercourse,** as this is indicated in the mishna as well. The Gemara answers: Indeed, **Abaye and Rava both say** that it should **teach: Nothing is** effective **after intercourse.** The Gemara comments: **And the *tanna* of our** mishna did not state this because **the permission for a *yevama* to** marry a member of the **public is preferable to him,** and he therefore specified a case that involves *ḥalitza*.

"בֵּין יָבָם אֶחָד לִשְׁתֵּי יְבָמוֹת" כו׳. בִּשְׁלָמָא לְרַבִּי יוֹחָנָן, דְּאָמַר: כּוּלַּהּ בֵּיתָא בְּלָאו קָאֵי, אִיצְטְרִיךְ לְאַשְׁמוֹעִינַן דְּאֵין קִידּוּשִׁין תּוֹפְסִין בְּחַיָּיבֵי לָאוִין.

§ It was taught in the mishna: Nothing is effective after *ḥalitza*, **both** in cases of **one *yavam* to two *yevamot*,** as well as cases of two *yevamin* to one *yevama*. The Gemara comments: **Granted, according to** the opinion of **Rabbi Yoḥanan, who said** that once a *yavam* has performed *ḥalitza* with his *yevama*, **the entire household,** the woman who performed *ḥalitza* as well as her rival wives, **is liable due to a prohibition**[N] derived from the verse "So shall it be done to the man who does not build his brother's house" (Deuteronomy 25:9), but the women are not liable to *karet* due to the prohibition with regard to a brother's wife. In light of Rabbi Yoḥanan's ruling, **it was necessary to teach us that betrothal does not take effect on** the rival wife of the woman who performed *ḥalitza*, despite the fact that she is only **liable for** violating **a prohibition,** in accordance with the opinion of Rabbi Akiva.

NOTES

Let us say that it supports Rabba bar Rav Huna, etc. – לֵימָא מְסַיַּיע לֵיהּ לְרַבָּה בַּר רַב הוּנָא וכו׳: Rashi and other commentaries maintain that the proof is not from this precise section of the mishna that states that both *yevamot* must perform *ḥalitza*, but rather from the continuation: And similarly two *yevamin*, etc., from which we learn that another *ḥalitza* is required even when there are two *yevamin*. The Ritva claims that it is not necessary to explain in this manner, for if invalid *ḥalitza* must be repeated with all the women, it must certainly be repeated with multiple brothers.

The entire household is liable due to a prohibition – כּוּלַּהּ בֵּיתָא בְּלָאו: The Ramban notes that according to Rabbeinu Ḥananel's version of the text (11a), which states that Rabbi Yoḥanan maintains that if one of the brothers has relations with one of the rival wives after *yibbum* has been performed, he violates a prohibition, the Gemara can be read in a straightforward manner. But according to our reading of the text there, which states that in that situation the entire house is liable due to a positive mitzva, the Gemara here is difficult. It must be interpreted as saying that Rabbi Yoḥanan holds that this prohibition is certainly no more than a regular prohibition, and there is a novel ruling being taught if there is a prohibition and all the more so if there is merely a positive mitzva. The novelty in that case would be that betrothal is ineffective for those liable for violating a positive mitzva, as claimed by Rabbi Yesheivav (49a).

HALAKHA

Invalid *ḥalitza*, she is required to repeat it – חֲלִיצָה פְּסוּלָה צְרִיכָה לַחֲזוֹר: The dispute as to whether a woman who performed invalid *ḥalitza* must repeat the ḥalitza with all the brothers is left unresolved by the Gemara here. Indeed, some commentaries claim that according to the opinion that one who performed invalid *ḥalitza* is required to repeat it with all the brothers, the same *halakha* applies to all her rival wives, as they all require *ḥalitza* as well. According to the opinion that she does not require *ḥalitza* from all the brothers, however, a single *ḥalitza* is sufficient, whether we are dealing with two *yevamot* or two *yevamin* (Rambam *Sefer Nashim*, *Hilkhot Yibbum* 5:11; *Shulḥan Arukh*, *Even HaEzer* 170:5).

אֶלָּא לְרֵישׁ לָקִישׁ, דְּאָמַר: כּוּלָּהּ בֵּיתָא בְּכָרֵת קָאֵי – אִיצְטְרִיךְ לְאַשְׁמוֹעִינַן דְּאֵין קִדּוּשִׁין תּוֹפְסִין בְּחַיָּיבֵי כְּרֵיתוֹת?!

However, according to Reish Lakish, who said that the entire household, apart from the woman who received *ḥalitza*, **is liable** to receive *karet*, **was it necessary to teach us that betrothal does not take effect on** forbidden relations for which one is **liable** to receive *karet*? According to Reish Lakish, after the *yavam* performs *ḥalitza*, the mitzva of levirate marriage is canceled and the *karet* prohibition against marrying a brother's wife is once again in force. As all agree that betrothal does not take effect on those liable to receive *karet*, it is unnecessary for the mishna to teach this ruling.

אָמַר לָךְ רֵישׁ לָקִישׁ: וְלִיטַעְמִיךְ, סֵיפָא דְּקָתָנֵי: בָּעַל וְעָשָׂה מַאֲמָר, אִיצְטְרִיךְ לְאַשְׁמוֹעִינַן דְּאֵין קִדּוּשִׁין תּוֹפְסִין בְּאֵשֶׁת אִישׁ?

The Gemara answers: **Reish Lakish** could have **said to you: And according to your reasoning,** that the mishna would not be teaching us an apparently obvious *halakha*, consider the **latter clause** of the mishna, **which teaches** that if a *yavam* **engaged in intercourse and** another *yavam* **performed levirate betrothal** with the same woman, the levirate betrothal is not effective. Now **was it necessary to teach us that betrothal is not effective for a married woman?** Once a *yavam* has engaged in relations with a *yevama* she is his full-fledged wife, and certainly no other betrothal is effective.

אֶלָּא: אַיְּידֵי דְּתָנָא הַתָּרַת יָבָם אֶחָד וִיבָמָה אַחַת – תָּנָא נַמִי שְׁתֵּי יְבָמוֹת וְיָבָם אֶחָד, וְאַיְּידֵי דְּתָנָא שְׁתֵּי יְבָמוֹת וְיָבָם אֶחָד – תָּנָא נַמִי שְׁתֵּי יְבָמִין וִיבָמָה אַחַת.

Rather, it must be that not every clause in the mishna teaches a novel *halakha*, and the reasoning of the *tanna* is as follows: **Since he teaches the release of** the bond between **one *yavam* and one *yevama*, he also teaches** the case of **two *yevamot* and one *yavam*, and since he teaches** the case of **two *yevamot* and one *yavam*, he also teaches** the case of **two *yevamin* and one *yevama*.** The *tanna* therefore listed all possible cases even though we do not learn a novel *halakha* from each and every one.

Perek **V**
Daf **53** Amud **b**

"חָלַץ וְעָשָׂה מַאֲמָר וְנָתַן" וכו׳. בִּשְׁלָמָא חָלַץ וְעָשָׂה מַאֲמָר אִיצְטְרִיךְ, סָלְקָא דַּעְתָּךְ אָמֵינָא: נִגְזוֹר מַאֲמָר דְּבָתַר חֲלִיצָה אַטּוּ מַאֲמָר דְּקַמֵּי חֲלִיצָה – קָא מַשְׁמַע לַן דְּלָא גָּזְרִינַן. אֶלָּא חָלַץ וְנָתַן גֵּט לָמָּה לִי?

§ It was taught in the mishna: If **he performed *ḥalitza* and** then proceeded to either **perform levirate betrothal, or give** a bill of divorce, or engage in intercourse with a second woman, nothing is effective after *ḥalitza*. The Gemara asks: **Granted, it was necessary** to teach that in the case of one who **performed *ḥalitza* and then performed levirate betrothal**[N] the levirate betrothal is not effective. For **it might enter your mind to say** that **we should issue a decree** with regard to **levirate betrothal that** takes place **after *ḥalitza* due to levirate betrothal that** takes place **before *ḥalitza*,** and rule that all levirate betrothal is effective. The mishna therefore **teaches us that we do not issue a decree** in this case. **However,** the case of one who **performed *ḥalitza* and gave a bill of divorce, why do I need** this case? What novelty is there in the teaching that a bill of divorce after *ḥalitza* is not effective?

וּלְטַעְמִיךְ אֵימָא סֵיפָא: בָּעַל וְעָשָׂה מַאֲמָר, בָּעַל וְנָתַן גֵּט – בִּשְׁלָמָא בָּעַל וְנָתַן גֵּט אִיצְטְרִיךְ, סָלְקָא דַּעְתָּךְ אָמֵינָא: נִגְזוֹר גֵּט דְּבָתַר בְּעִילָה אַטּוּ גֵּט דְּקַמֵּי בְּעִילָה, קָא מַשְׁמַע לַן דְּלָא גָּזְרִינַן. אֲבָל בָּעַל וְעָשָׂה מַאֲמָר לָמָּה לִי?

The Gemara answers: **And according to your reasoning,** that each new case must teach something new, **say the latter clause** of the mishna: If **he engaged in intercourse and** then proceeded to **perform levirate betrothal, or give a bill of divorce, or perform *ḥalitza*** with a second woman, nothing is effective. In this case the same question can be asked: **Granted, it was necessary** to teach the case of one who **engaged in intercourse and gave a bill of divorce.** This is because **it might enter your mind to say** that **we should issue a decree** with regard to **a bill of divorce that** is given **after intercourse,**[N] **due to a bill of divorce that** is given **before intercourse,** and decree that this bill of divorce alone is insufficient and she requires *ḥalitza* as well. The mishna therefore **teaches us that we do not issue** such **a decree. But** the case of a *yavam* who **engaged in intercourse and performed levirate betrothal, why do I** need to state it? Once he has engaged in intercourse with her she is his wife in all regards; what difference does levirate betrothal make?

NOTES

It was necessary to teach the case of one who performed *ḥalitza* and then performed levirate betrothal, etc. – חָלַץ וְעָשָׂה מַאֲמָר אִיצְטְרִיךְ וכו׳: The Rosh asks why this justification is necessary as the Gemara could simply have explained as it did on the previous *amud*, that the mishna is emphasizing Rabbi Akiva's opinion that betrothal is ineffective for those liable due to regular prohibitions. He answers that the Gemara preferred to state an alternative explanation than to say that several sections of the mishna teach us the same thing.

We should issue a decree with regard to a bill of divorce that is given after intercourse, etc. – נִגְזוֹר גֵּט דְּבָתַר בְּעִילָה וכו׳: The Rashba and the Ritva explain this statement differently from Rashi. Rashi explains that the decree would require the woman who received a bill of divorce after *ḥalitza* to perform *ḥalitza* again so that it not be confused with a bill of divorce given initially. The others explain that one might have thought that since a bill of divorce given to a *yevama* before intercourse permanently disqualifies her from levirate marriage, we should therefore decree that the bill of divorce she receives after intercourse likewise disqualifies her, and she should once again be considered forbidden to the *yavam* as his brother's wife. The *tanna* therefore teaches that in this case they left the Torah law as it is and did not decree further. The *ge'onim* read: Since a bill of divorce before intercourse is effective, a bill of divorce after intercourse is also effective, a version of the text that supports the Rashba's interpretation.

אֶלָּא: אַיְּידֵי דִּתְנָא חָלַץ וְעָשָׂה מַאֲמָר – תְּנָא נַמִּי בָּעַל וְעָשָׂה מַאֲמָר, וְאַיְּידֵי דְּבָעֵי לְמִיתְנֵי בָּעַל וְנָתַן גֵּט – תְּנָא נַמִּי חָלַץ וְנָתַן גֵּט.

Rather, one must say that **since** the *tanna* **taught** the case of one who **performed *ḥalitza*** **and** then **performed levirate betrothal, he also taught** the case of one who **engaged in intercourse and** then **performed levirate betrothal,** due to the similarity between them. **And since he wished to teach** the case of one who **engaged in intercourse and** then **gave a bill of divorce, he also taught** the case of one who **performed *ḥalitza*** **and** then **gave a bill of divorce.** We should therefore not infer anything from these superfluous cases, as they are merely stated for stylistic reasons.

״בִּזְמַן שֶׁהִיא״ וכו׳. מַתְנִיתִין דְּלָא כִּי הַאי תַּנָּא. דְּתַנְיָא, אַבָּא יוֹסֵי בֶּן יוֹחָנָן אִישׁ יְרוּשָׁלַיִם אוֹמֵר מִשּׁוּם רַבִּי מֵאִיר: אַחַת בְּעִילָה וְאַחַת חֲלִיצָה, בַּתְּחִלָּה – אֵין אַחֲרֶיהָ כְּלוּם, בָּאֶמְצַע וּבַסּוֹף – יֵשׁ אַחֲרֶיהָ כְּלוּם.

§ The mishna taught: With regard to intercourse, **when it is** at the beginning nothing is effective after it, but if it was in the middle or at the end, something is effective after it. The Gemara comments: **The mishna is not in accordance with** the opinion of **this *tanna*. As it is taught** in a *baraita*: **Abba Yosei ben Yoḥanan, a man of Jerusalem, says in the name of Rabbi Meir:** With regard to **both intercourse and *ḥalitza*,** if one of them were performed **at the beginning, nothing is effective after it,** but if they were done **in the middle or at the end,** i.e., they were preceded by some other action, **something is** effective **after it.** According to the mishna, however, nothing is effective after *ḥalitza* regardless of when it was performed.

וְשָׁלֹשׁ מַחֲלוֹקוֹת בַּדָּבָר, תַּנָּא קַמָּא סָבַר: בִּיאָה דְּאִיכָּא לְמִיגְזַר – גָּזְרִינַן, חֲלִיצָה דְּלֵיכָּא לְמִיגְזַר – לָא גָּזְרִינַן.

And therefore it can be concluded that there are **three disputes with regard to this matter,** i.e., three opinions on this issue. **The first *tanna* holds:** In the case of **intercourse** that is preceded by a disqualifying action, **where there is** a reason **to issue a decree,** lest one violate a prohibition by engaging in intercourse after *ḥalitza* or intercourse was performed, **we issue a decree** establishing that invalid intercourse should not be as effective as valid intercourse. With regard to ***ḥalitza*,** however, **where there is no** reason **to issue a decree** as there is no concern of a prohibition even if an action is performed after *ḥalitza*, **we do not issue a decree.**

וְרַבִּי נְחֶמְיָה סָבַר: בִּיאָה נַמִּי לֵיכָּא לְמִיגְזַר. וּדְקָאָמְרַתְּ: לִיגְזוֹר בִּיאָה אַחַר הַגֵּט מִשּׁוּם בִּיאָה אַחַר חֲלִיצָה – כֵּיוָן דַּחֲלִיצָה דְּאוֹרָיְיתָא, מֵידַע יָדְעִי. וּדְקָאָמְרַתְּ לִיגְזוֹר בִּיאָה אַחַר מַאֲמָר מִשּׁוּם בִּיאָה אַחַר בִּיאָה – כֵּיוָן דְּבִיאָה דְּאוֹרָיְיתָא, הָא מֵידַע יָדְעִי. וְאַבָּא יוֹסֵי בֶּן חָנָן סָבַר לַהּ כְּרַבָּנַן דְּגָזְרִי בְּבִיאָה, וְגָזַר חֲלִיצָה מִשּׁוּם בִּיאָה.

And Rabbi Neḥemya holds that with regard to **intercourse there is also no** reason **to issue a decree. And as** for what **you said** in justification of your ruling, **that we should issue a decree** in a case of **intercourse after a bill of divorce due to intercourse after *ḥalitza*,** there is no cause for such a concern. **Since *ḥalitza*** is effective **by Torah law,** people **know** that it is fully effective and cannot be followed by anything, and they will not confuse it with laws instituted by the Sages. **And as** for what **you said that we should issue a decree** with regard to **intercourse after levirate betrothal due to intercourse after intercourse, since** the acquisition of **intercourse** is **by Torah law, this** matter **is known** by people, and they will not err in this regard. **And Abba Yosei ben Ḥanan holds in accordance with** the opinion of **the Rabbis, who issue a decree with regard to intercourse,** but he adds **and issues a decree** with regard to ***ḥalitza*** **due to intercourse.** He therefore does not differentiate between *ḥalitza* and intercourse at all.

הדרן עלך רבן גמליאל

Summary of **Perek V**

From the discussion in this chapter it became clear that neither performing levirate betrothal nor giving a bill of divorce is a completely efficacious act for a woman requiring levirate marriage. While levirate betrothal effects some degree of acquisition and a bill of divorce effects some degree of release, there is room for subsequent acts to be applied, and if performed they are legally binding. This is true regardless of whether the act was performed by the original *yavam* with a different *yevama* or by a different *yavam* with the original *yevama*.

Insofar as intercourse and *ḥalitza* are concerned, we find that their *halakhot* are not identical. On the one hand, intercourse with a *yevama* is completely efficacious, and so long as the intercourse occurred first, i.e., before any other act that might invalidate it, any subsequent act is halakhically insignificant. However, if the act of intercourse followed a different previous act, the intercourse is considered invalid and other subsequent acts have legal implications. On the other hand, with regard to *ḥalitza*, it makes no difference whether it was performed first or after another act; after *ḥalitza* no other act of nullification, neither *ḥalitza* nor a bill of divorce, holds any legal validity. However, acts of acquisition, i.e., intercourse or levirate betrothal, are still efficacious.

In practice, it makes no difference whether any one of these combinations was performed by a single *yavam* with a single *yevama* or two *yevamot*, or by two *yevamin* with a single *yevama* or two *yevamot*. However, if a single *yavam* performed levirate betrothal and engaged in sexual relations with a single *yevama*, this is the proper way to perform the mitzva of levirate marriage. If he engaged in intercourse and then gave her a bill of divorce, then he performed the mitzva of levirate marriage and subsequently divorced the woman.

Halakhic conclusions of this chapter:

First act	Second act	Validity of subsequent acts	What must be done next
Levirate betrothal	Levirate betrothal	All acts are valid	Two bills of divorce and *ḥalitza*
	Bill of divorce	All acts are valid	Bill of divorce for the levirate betrothal and *ḥalitza*
	Intercourse	All acts are valid	Two bills of divorce and *ḥalitza*
	Ḥalitza	Intercourse and levirate betrothal are valid	Bill of divorce
Bill of divorce	Levirate betrothal	All acts are valid	Bill of divorce and *ḥalitza*
	Bill of divorce	All acts are valid	*Ḥalitza*
	Intercourse	All acts are valid	Bill of divorce and *ḥalitza*
	Ḥalitza	Intercourse and levirate betrothal are valid	
Intercourse	Levirate betrothal	All acts are invalid	
	Bill of divorce	All acts are invalid	
	Intercourse	All acts are invalid	
	Ḥalitza	All acts are invalid	
Ḥalitza	Levirate betrothal	Levirate betrothal and intercourse are valid	Bill of divorce
	Bill of divorce	All acts are invalid	
	Intercourse	Levirate betrothal and intercourse are valid	Bill of divorce
	Ḥalitza	All acts are invalid	

Image **Credits**

All images are copyright © Koren Publishers Jerusalem Ltd., except:

p291 1st image © Anneli Salo; **p291** 2nd image © kavring, www.shutterstock.com; **p313** 1st image © Darren Fehrmann; **p313** 2nd image © Alves Gaspar; **p313** 3rd image © Calapito; **p333** 1st image © Geni, GFDL, CC-BY-SA; **p333** 2nd image © Daderot.

My Notes

My Notes

My Notes

My Notes

My Notes

My Notes

תלמוד בבלי

— מהדורת נאה —

יבמות חלק ג

Steinsaltz Center

KOREN

Please note that the number ranges that appear at the bottom of each daf of the Vilna pages indicate the corresponding pages of the Koren Talmud Bavli translation and commentary.

תלמוד בבלי

הוצאת קורן ירושלים

— מהדורת נאה —

מסכת יבמות
דף לה: עד דף נג:

COMMENTARY BY

Rabbi Adin Even-Israel Steinsaltz

EDITOR-IN-CHIEF

Rabbi Dr Tzvi Hersh Weinreb

EXECUTIVE EDITOR

Rabbi Joshua Schreier

•

STEINSALTZ CENTER
KOREN PUBLISHERS JERUSALEM

א א מיי' פ"א מהלכות יבום הלכה כ סמג עשין נא טוש"ע אה"ע סימן קסד סעיף ב:
ב ב מיי' שם הלכה כא טור ש"ע שם סעי"ה:
ג ג מיי' פ"א מהלכות שגגות הלכה א:
ד ד מיי' פ"א מהלכות יבום הלכה כג סמג עשין נא טוש"ע אה"ע סימן קסד סעיף ו:
ה ה מיי' פ"א מהלכות שגגות הלכה א:
ו ו מיי' פ"א מהלכות יבום הלכה כ סמג שם טוש"ע אה"ע סימן קסד סעיף ב:
ז ז מיי' שם טור ש"ע שם סעיף ג:

מתני'

החולץ [א]ליבמתו ונמצאת מעוברת. וילדה. בזמן שהולד של קיימא – הוא מותר בקרובותיה והיא מותרת בקרוביו, ולא פסלה מן הכהונה. אין הולד של קיימא – הוא אסור בקרובותיה והיא אסורה בקרוביו, ופסלה מן הכהונה. [ב]הכונס את יבמתו ונמצאת מעוברת וילדה, בזמן שהולד של קיימא – יוציא, [ג]וחייבין בקרבן. ואם אין ולד של קיימא – יקיים. *[ד]ספק בן תשעה לראשון, ספק בן שבעה לאחרון – יוציא, והולד כשר, [ה]וחייבין באשם תלוי.§

גמ' איתמר, החולץ למעוברת והפילה. רבי יוחנן אמר: אינה צריכה חליצה מן האחין, ר"ל אמר: [ו]צריכה חליצה מן האחין. *ר' יוחנן אמר: א"צ חליצה מן האחין – חליצת מעוברת שמה חליצה, וביאת מעוברת שמה ביאה. ור"ל אמר: צריכה חליצה מן האחין – חליצת מעוברת לא שמה חליצה, [ז]וביאת מעוברת לא שמה ביאה. במאי קמפלגי? *איבעית אימא קרא, ואיבעית אימא סברא. (א) איבעית אימא סברא, רבי יוחנן סבר: אם יבא אליהו ויאמר דהא דאיעברא מפולי מפלה – מי לאו בת חליצה ויבום היא? השתא נמי, תגלי מילתא למפרע. ור"ל אמר: תגלי מילתא למפרע לא אמרינן. ואיבעית אימא קרא; רבי יוחנן סבר °"ובן אין לו" אמר רחמנא, והא לית ליה. ור"ל סבר: "ובן אין לו" *עיין עליו. דברים כה איתיביה ר' יוחנן לר"ל: אין הולד של קיימא – הוא אסור בקרובותיה, והיא אסורה בקרוביו. ופסלה מן הכהונה. בשלמא לדידי, דאמינא חליצת מעוברת שמה חליצה – משום הכי פסלה. אלא לדידך, דאמרת חליצת מעוברת לא שמה חליצה – אמאי פסלה מן הכהונה? א"ל: מדרבנן, ולחומרא בעלמא. א"ד, איתיביה ריש לקיש לר' יוחנן: אין הולד של קיימא – הוא אסור בקרובותיה, והיא אסורה בקרוביו, ופסלה מן הכהונה. בשלמא לדידי, דאמינא חליצת מעוברת לא שמה חליצה – היינו דקתני פסלה מן הכהונה לחומרא, ולא קתני: אינה צריכה חליצה מן האחין. אלא לדידך, אינה צריכה חליצה מן האחין מיבעי ליה! – א"ל: אין הכי נמי, ואיידי דתנא רישא לא פסלה – תנא *סיפא פסלה. איתיביה רבי יוחנן לר"ל: אין הולד של קיימא – יקיים. בשלמא לדידי דאמינא חליצת מעוברת שמה חליצה וביאת מעוברת שמה ביאה – משום הכי קתני יקיים. אלא לדידך, דאמרת חליצת מעוברת לא שמה חליצה, וביאת מעוברת לא שמה ביאה – יחזור ויבעול ויקיים מיבעי ליה! – מאי יקיים – יחזור ויבעול ויקיים, דלא *סגי. איכא דאמרי, איתיביה ר"ל לרבי יוחנן: אין הולד של קיימא – יקיים. בשלמא לדידי, דאמינא חליצת מעוברת לא שמה חליצה וביאת מעוברת לא שמה ביאה, היינו דקתני יקיים – יחזור ויבעול ויקיים, דלא סגי בלאו הכי. אלא לדידך, רצה – יוציא, רצה – יקיים, מיבעי ליה! – אה"נ, איידי דתנא רישא יוציא – תנא נמי סיפא יקיים. מיתיבי: הכונס את יבמתו ונמצאת מעוברת – הרי זו לא תנשא צרתה, שמא יהא ולד בן קיימא. אדרבה, כי הוי הולד בן קיימא מיפטרה צרתה! אלא אימא: שמא לא יהא הולד בן קיימא. ואי ס"ד ביאת מעוברת שמה ביאה – אמאי לא תנשא צרתה? תיפטר בביאה של חבירתה! אמר אביי: בביאה – כולי עלמא לא פליגי דלא פטרה, כי פליגי – בחליצה. רבי יוחנן סבר: חליצת מעוברת שמה חליצה, ביאת מעוברת לא שמה ביאה. ר"ל סבר: ביאת מעוברת – לא שמה ביאה, וחליצת מעוברת – לא שמה חליצה. אמר ליה רבא: מה נפשך: אי ביאת מעוברת שמה ביאה – חליצת מעוברת שמה חליצה, ואי ביאת מעוברת לא שמה ביאה – חליצת מעוברת נמי לא שמה חליצה. דהא קי"ל דכל

בשלמא

רש"י

החולץ הוא מותר בקרובותיה. דלאו חליצה היא, דהא לא בעיא. קרובותיה וקרוביו. מפרש לקמן במתני' הנך דנאסרות על האיש מחמת אשתו, וקרוביו שנאסרים על האשה מחמת בעלה. **אם אין** הולד של קיימא. שהיה נפל. וחייבין בקרבן. שבעל אשת אח שלא במקום מצוה. הולד כשר. ממה נפשך. **גמ'** אינה צריכה חליצה מן האחין. דהך חליצה מעלייתא היא. שמה חליצה. היכא דהפילה, דאיגלאי מילתא דבת חליצה הואי. מדרבנן ולחומרא. דלמא אתי למישרי חלוצה לכהונה, דלא ידעי דהואי מעוברת. היינו דקתני פסולה ולחומרא. ולא קתני בהדיא אין צריכה חליצה מן האחין. אלא לדידך. דאמרת חליצה מעלייתא היא, לישמעינן הא דאינה צריכה חליצה, ואנא ידענא דאסורה בקרוביו ופסלה מן הכהונה. ואיידי דתנא רישא לא פסלה. ולא תנא חליצה, דהתם לא מצי למימר: וצריכה חליצה, תנא נמי סיפא פסלה, ולא איירי בחליצה. **אין הולד** של קיימא יקיים. הכונס יבמתו ונמצאת מעוברת. היינו דקתני יקיים. דלא מצריך ביאה לאחר שהפילה. ואם בא לגרשה בגט – מגרשה, דאיפטרה לה בביאה קמייתא. וביאת מעוברת שמה ביאה, דקס"ד יקיים דקתני מתני' לאו חובה היא, אלא התירא, משום דתנא רישא: אם הולד של קיימא יוציא. דלא סגי בלא"ה. דלא מיפטרה בלא ביאה לאחר שהפילה. דאם לא יחזור ויבעול לא מצי למפטרה בגט, דאין אדם יכול להוציא את יבמתו בגט אא"כ כנסה תחלה, וביאת מעוברת לאו שמה ביאה. ובחליצה נמי לא אפשר למפטרה, הואיל ומ"מ בא עליה. רצה יוציא. בגט, רצה יקיים מיבעי ליה. אלא שמא לא יהא ולד של קיימא. ונמצאת זקוקה ליבם, וביאת מעוברת לא שמה ביאה.

תורה אור

תוספות

החולץ ליבמתו ונמצאת מעוברת. הא דלא נקט החולץ למעוברת כדנקט בגמ' – משום דרבותא היא, דאע"ג דלא היה עוברה ניכר בשעת חליצה, ונראית חליצה מעולה – אפילו הכי לא פסלה בזמן שהולד של קיימא. ובגמ' נקט נמי למעוברת לרבותא, דאע"פ שהוכר עוברה, כיון שהפילה – חליצה מעלייתא הויא. א"נ, נקט נמצאת משום סיפא, דהתם לא מצי למיתני הכונס ליבמתו מעוברת – דא"כ מזיד הוא, ולא מיחייב קרבן, דלא שב מידיעתו הוא.

ונמצאת מעוברת. בחולץ תוך ג' חדשים איירי, דומיא דסיפא דהכונס יבמתו דאיירי תוך ג', דאי לאחר ג' – אמאי חייב קרבן? כיון דרוב נשים עוברן ניכר לשליש, וזו, הואיל ולא הוכר עוברה – מאי הוה ליה למיעבד? וכה"ג אמרינן בשבועות (דף יח. ושם): פרט לאנוס, גבי שלא בשעת וסתה. וא"ת: אם כן, אם אין הולד של קיימא, אמאי אסור בקרובותיה? דתוך שלשה חדשים לאו חליצה היא, דהא תנן לקמן: היבמה לא תחלוץ ולא תתייבם עד שיהיו לה ג' חדשים. ומפרש בגמ' טעמא, דכיון דאינה עולה ליבום – אינה עולה לחליצה! ואר"י: דנהי דלאו חליצה היא מ"מ אסור בקרובותיה, כיון דמדאורייי' הויא חליצה. [א] ועוד: דדיעבד, אם חלצה – אפילו מדרבנן אינה צריכה חליצה אחרת. דאמר לקמן: יבמה שחלצו לה אחין בתוך ג' – צריכה להמתין ג' חדשים, משמע דלא בעיא חליצה.

צריכה חליצה מן האחין. לאו דוקא מן האחין, דה"ה דלא פקעה זיקת החולץ[ב]. אי נמי: מן האחין של מת קאמר. **והא** לית ליה. כיון דהפילה לבסוף. אבל בר קיימא לא. א"נ, כשהוא בר קיימא נפקא לן מ"להקים שם" ומ"לא ימחה" – פרט לזה שאין שמו מחוי. **וריש** לקיש סבר בין אין לו עיין עליו. הואיל ובאותה שעה היה ראוי להתקיים. וא"ת: א"כ, תפטר לשוק בלא חליצה כמו בזרע פסול, דנפקא לן (לעיל דף כב:) נמי מ"אין לו", ואמאי נמי אמרינן לקמן דולד אינו פוטר עד שיצא לאויר העולם! ויש לומר, דאמרינן נמי: עיין עליו שלא תחלוץ ולא תנשא כל זמן שעומדת בספק. **תגלי** מילתא למפרע לא אמרינן. אע"ג דלקמן (דף מא:), גבי ספקות שקידש אחת משתי אחיות חשבינן לה בת חליצה ויבום, כיון דאם יבוא אליהו ויאמר דהא קדיש – לא דמי, דהכא אין זה ספק ראוי להתברר עכשיו, שא"א לידע העתידות. אבל התם א"צ לידע אלא מה שבאותה שעה. וא"ת: לריש לקיש הכונס יבמתו מעוברת והפילה, אמאי פטור מן הקרבן? כיון דביאת מעוברת לא שמה ביאה, א"כ אשת אח שלא במקום מצוה היא! ואר"י: דאפ"ה לא מחייב, מידי דהוה אקטן שבא על יבמתו גדולה, דאמר לקמן° (דף לט) דתגדלנו. **רצה** יוציא רצה יקיים מיבעיא ליה. והא דקתני לעיל גבי ד' אחין: ב"ש אומרים יקיימו, ולא קתני רצו – משום דהתם ליכא למיטעי. **הרי** זו לא תנשא צרתה. כ"ש היא שלא תנשא ושלא תבעל, אלא צרתה איצטריך, שלא תאמר תנשא ממה נפשך. **כולי** עלמא לא פליגי. הא דקאמר לעיל איתיביה הכונס יבמתו – להד"מ, וכה"ג איכא בפרק "המפלת" (נדה דף כז.) גבי פניו ממומסמסין, וכמה דוכתין*. **כי** פליגי בחליצה. וביאה מודה, שלא יבא לידי איסור.

תוספות ישנים

החולץ ליבמתו ונמצאת מעוברת. ומיירי שחלץ לה תוך שלשה חדשים דאי לאחר ג' חדשים לא מצי למימר לקמן בזמן שהולד של קיימא חייבין בקרבן שהרי אנוס הוא אחרי שעשה כתקנת חכמים אלא מיירי תוך שלשה חדשים ומזיד לא הוי דסבור הוא שאינה מעוברת ואע"ג דאמרינן היבמה לא תחלוץ ולא תתייבם עד שיעברו ג' חדשים מ"מ דיעבד שפיר דמי ולהכי נקט [בגמ'] החולץ למעוברת משום דאשמעינן רבותא דאע"ג דידע שפיר שהיא מעוברת קאמר ר' יוחנן דאינה צריכה חליצה מעולה.

תוספות חד מקמאי

היו כהניות נשואות לישראל פסולין לתרומה דבי נשייהו:
פ"ד איתמר החולץ למעוברת והפילה ר"י אומר אינה צריכה חליצה מן האחין ר"ל אמר צריכה חליצה מן האחים חליצת מעוברת לאו שמה חליצת והלכתא כר"ל ומודה ר"ל דפסולה לכהונה לחומרא ופסלה מן האחים וצרתה פסולה לו ולאחין ולחומרא כללא דמילתא חליצת מעוברת שהפילה לאו שמה חליצה לחומרא אבל החולץ למעוברת והולד בן קיימא תרוייהו מודו דלאו שמה חליצה כלל ולא פסלה מן הכהונה תניא הכונס את יבמתו ונמצאת מעוברת הרי זו לא תנשא צרתה [שמא] לא יהיה הולד בן קיימא וביאת מעוברת לאו שמה ביאה וא"ת הלך אחר רוב נשים ורוב נשים וולד של קיימא ילדן ולד אינו פוטר עד שיצא לאויר העולם והא דקתני רישא שמא לא יהא ולד של קיימא לאו דוקא שמא דבין יהא ולד של קיימא ובין לא יהא ולד של קיימא לא תנשא צרתה:

מסורת הש"ס

[כריתות יז:]
[לקמן מא:]
[ברכות ־: קדושין לה: כ"ב ח: ע. ע"ז לז: סנהדרין ל. שבועות כב: וע"ש בתוס' ד"ה אב"א זבחים ב. ז: מנחות ב. יג: עג: חולין קיח: תמורה ל:]
[לעיל כב: וש"נ ועי' מ"ש שם בשם ערוך והסמ"ע והתי"ט]
כדפו"י תנא נמי
[עי' תוס' ב"ב קב: ד"ה כרם ותוס' בכורות ז: ד"ה אלא]

הגהות הב"ח

(א) גמרא איבעית אימא קרא ואיבעית אימא סברא איבעית אימא קרא ר' יוחנן סבר ובן אין וכו' עיין עליו ואיבעית אימא סברא ר' יוחנן סבר אם יבא וכו' לא אמרי' אותיביה רבי יוחנן כצ"ל:

הגהות הגר"א

[א] תוס' ד"ה ונמצאת. ועוד לדיעבד כו'. נ"ב וג"ח הכל לכתחלה לדיעבד אף יבום מהני (עמ"ש רבינו באה"ע סי' קסד ס"ק ב') אלא דבירושלמי אמר בהדיא דצריך חליצה אחרת אבל בגמרא דידן פליגא כמ"ש תוס' ועמש"ש בדברי הירושלמי (ע"ש בס"ק ה): [ב] שם ד"ה צריכה. א"נ מן האחין כו'. נ"ב וע"ל עט ב' במתני' (איילונית שחלצו לה אחין. כ"כ רבינו להדיא באה"ע שם ס"ק ח' בכי"ק ונשמט בדפוס):

גליון הש"ס

תוס' ד"ה תגלי מילתא וכו' דאמר לקמן דף לט וכו'. נ"ל דף קיב ע"ב:

בשלמא בתוך ג' חדשים כו'. אין גירסא זו נכונה, כדפירש בקונטרס. ועוד: דאי אפשר כלל לדקדק מדאינה חולצת תוך ג' לינשא אחר ג', דחליצת מעוברת לא שמה חליצה. דהא ודאי תוך ג' מודה ר' יוחנן דאין חולצת, כדתנן: היבמה לא תחלוץ עד שיהיו לה ג' חדשים. וטעמא, משום דאינה עולה לייבום, דאפי' יבא אליהו ויאמר דלא מיעברא – לאו בת ייבום היא, ולכך אינה עולה לחליצה. אבל בתוך ט' – בת ייבום היא אם יבא אליהו ויאמר דלא מיעברא, או אפילו הפילה. לכך דייק שפיר, אלא ה"ג: תחלוץ בתוך ט' ותנשא לאחר ט'. **ותנשא** לאחר ט'. תימה: דלא מסיק אדעתיה האי ולטעמיך דפריך! **ונמצא** אתה מצריכה כרוז לכהונה. ודוקא בשאר נשים דלאו גרושות איירי. וכן מוקי לה בהדיא בפרק בתרא (לקמן קיט: ושם). והא דפריך לקמן (דף מא:) גבי והיבמה לא תחלוץ עד שיהא לה ג' חדשים, ומפרש בגמרא מעיקרא טעמא שמא יהא ולד של קיימא ונמצא מצריכה כרוז לכהונה, תינח אלמנה, גרושה מאי איכא למימר? אר"י: משום דהתם בא להשמיענו דין כל הנשים שנופלות לייבום, ואם היה דין אחר לגרושה – ה"ל לפרושי. אבל הכא, דאיירי אם אירע בו מעשה באשה שהלך בעלה וצרתה למדינת הים, איירי שפיר דוקא בשאר נשים דלאו גרושות. ועדיפא מינה בפרק בתרא, דמוקי ההיא ד"האשה שלום" דוקא בגרושה, דפריך מינה אההיא דמייתי הכא. **הלכתא** כר"ל בהני תלת. הא דפליגי בפרק ב' דחולין (דף כט: ושם) גבי ישנה שחיטה מתחלה ועד סוף – לא חשיב הכא, אע"ג דסבירא ליה כוותיה בפ' ב' דזבחים (דף ל. ושם) – היינו משום דר"ל משמיה דלוי סבא אמרה. ותימה, דלא חשיב הא דפ"ק דמסכת ע"ז (דף ו: ושם). דתניא כותיה דר"ל דנשא ונתן מותר, כיון דחשיב הכא מידי דתניא כוותיה! ואור"י: דמ"מ, התם הלכתא כר' יוחנן, דהתם, גבי הא דתנן וחכ"א לפניהם אסור לאחריהם מותר, פריך: חכמים היינו ת"ק! ומשני: נשא ונתן איכא בינייהו. ובפרק קמא דסנהדרין (דף טו: ושם) גבי זאב וארי, דתניא כוותיה דר"ל – התם פליגי אליבא דר"א ולא סבירא להו כוותיה*. **משום** ירושה לא אמר כלום. טעמא (ג) מפרש התם במתניתין: לפי שהתנה על מה שכתוב בתורה. ורבי יוחנן בן ברוקא פליג בפרק "יש נוחלין" (ב"ב קל.) ואמר: דאם אמר על מי שראוי ליורשו – דבריו קיימים. וטעמא מפרש התם, משום דכתיב "והיה ביום הנחילו את בניו" – התורה נתנה רשות לאב להנחיל לכל מי שירצה. והא דכתיב "לא יוכל לבכר" – היינו דוקא חלק בכורה, אבל חלק פשיטות – יכול. ורבנן – "ביום הנחילו את בניו" מוקמי לדרשא אחריתי, "ולא יוכל לבכר" איצטריך, משום דהורע כחו, שאין נוטל בראוי כבמוחזק, וס"ד דהורע כחו נמי בהא. א"נ איצטריך, דס"ד כיון דשנואה שנואה בנישואיה – דיכול לבכר. ואמר

---

*[א] דכל העולה ליבום עולה לחליצה, וכל שאין עולה ליבום – אינו עולה לחליצה! אלא אמר רבא, הכי קאמר: [ב] הכונס יבמתו ונמצאת מעוברת – הרי זו לא תנשא צרתה, שמא יהא ולד בן קיימא, וביאת מעוברת לא שמה ביאה, וחליצת מעוברת לא שמה חליצה, והולד אינו פוטר עד שיצא לאויר העולם. תניא כוותיה דרבא: הכונס יבמתו ונמצאת מעוברת – הרי זו לא תנשא צרתה, שמא יהא ולד בן קיימא, ואין ביאה וחליצה פוטרת, אלא ולד פוטר, והולד אין פוטרה עד שיצא לאויר העולם. טעמא – דשמא יהא ולד בן קיימא הוא, הא לא הוי ולד בן קיימא – מיפטר צרתה. לימא תיהוי תיובתא דר"ל! – אמר לך ר"ל, הכי קתני: הכונס יבמתו ונמצאת מעוברת – הרי זו לא תנשא צרתה, שמא לא יהא הולד בן קיימא, וחליצת מעוברת לא שמה חליצה, וביאת מעוברת לא שמה ביאה. וא"ת: הלך אחר רוב נשים, ורוב נשים ולד מעליא ילדן? – ולד אין פוטר עד שיצא לאויר העולם. א"ר אלעזר: אפשר, איתא להא דריש לקיש ולא תנן לה במתניתין?! – נפק, דק ואשכח, דתנן: *האשה שהלך בעלה וצרתה למדינת הים, ובאו ואמרו לה: "מת בעלך" – הרי זו לא תנשא ולא תתייבם, עד שתדע שמא מעוברת היא צרתה. בשלמא יבומי לא – שמא יהא ולד בן קיימא, ויפגע באיסור אשת אח דאורייתא. אלא לא תחלוץ, אמאי? בשלמא תחלוץ בתוך ט' ותנשא בתוך ט' – לא, היינו ספק. אלא תחלוץ בתוך תשעה, ותנשא לאחר תשעה! – ולטעמיך: תחלוץ ותנשא לאחר ט'! אלא: בר מינה דההיא, *דאביי בר *אבא ורב חיננא בר *אביי דאמרי תרוייהו: *שמא יהא ולד בן קיימא, ונמצא אתה מצריכה כרוז לכהונה. – ולצרכה! – דלמא איכא איניש דהוי בחליצה ולא הוי בהכרזה, ואתי למימר: קשרי חלוצה לכהן. א"ל אביי: מידי לא תחלוץ ולא תתייבם קתני? לא תנשא ולא תתייבם קתני, בלא חליצה, אבל אי חליץ לה – הכי נמי דשריא. תניא כוותיה דריש לקיש: [ג] החולץ למעוברת והפילה – צריכה חליצה מן האחין. *אמר רבא: *הלכתא כוותיה דר"ל בהני תלת: חדא – הא דאמרן. אידך – דתנן: *[ד] המחלק נכסיו על פיו, ריבה לאחד ומיעט לאחד, והשוה להם את הבכור – דבריו קיימין. ואם אמר משום ירושה – לא אמר כלום. כתב, בין בתחלה בין בסוף בין באמצע, משום מתנה – דבריו קיימין. ואמר

דכל העולה לייבום כו'. דביאתה פוטרתה. עולה לחליצה. דכתיב (דברים כה) "אם לא יחפוץ האיש לקחת יבמתו (א) וחלצה" וכו'. שמא יהא הולד של קיימא וביאת מעוברת. בולד של קיימא לדברי הכל לא שמה ביאה, דטעמא דרבי יוחנן משום שמא יבא אליהו ויאמר נפל הואי, והכא ליכא למימר הכי. והולד אין פוטר עד שיצא לאויר העולם. הא לא יהא ולד של קיימא. דלמפרע בת יבום היא, הוה מיפטרא צרתה, ואין צריך לחזור ולבעול לאחר הפילה. אמר לך ר"ל הכי קתני. כלומר, לא קתני שמא יהא, אלא שמא לא יהא. והאי דקתני סיפא ולד אינו פוטר כו', דמשמע דבשל קיימא מיירי – הכי קאמר: וא"ת, הלך אחר רוב נשים, ורוב נשים ולד מעליא ילדן, ונהי דביאתה לא פטרה, מיהו פטורה משום הולד – הולד אין פוטר עד שיצא לאויר העולם. שהלך בעלה. ואין לו בנים. לא תנשא. קס"ד אפילו ע"י חליצה קאמר, דלא תנשא לשוק לעולם. היא צרתה. אותה צרתה שהלכה עמו. אבל אי שמעה עליה שאינה מעוברת – תתייבם, ולא חיישינן שמא נשא בעלה אחרת במדינת הים. ולהכי תנן היא צרתה, והכי מפרש בפ' "האשה". אלא לא תחלוץ. ותנשא לשוק. אמאי. אי חליצת מעוברת שמה חליצה תחלוץ ממה נפשך, דבין צרתה מעוברת ובין אינה מעוברת – הרי חליצה פוטרתה. בשלמא תחלוץ בתוך ג' ותנשא בתוך ג'. שמת לא אפשר דהיינו ספק – דבן ט' לראשון או בן ז' לאחרון, דאפילו נשאת כ' ימים (ב) בתוך ג' חדשים וילדה בסוף ט' לבעל הראשון – אכתי איכא למימר שמא בן ז' לאחרון הוא. ואע"פ שאין אלא ו' חדשים וב' ימים, דקי"ל (ר"ה דף יא.): יולדת לז' יולדת למקוטעין. ואע"ג דהיא לאו ודאי מעוברת, דהא מדקדקי שמא מעוברת צרתה, מכלל דאחר זמן מרובה שהלך בעלה למדינת הים קמיירי – לא פלוג רבנן בנשים, אלא כולן צריכות להמתין: א) אלא תחלוץ בתוך ג' ותנשא לאחר כו'. וקשה לי: היכי מצי לאותובי הכי? נהי נמי דחליצת מעוברת שמה חליצה, הני מילי – בנפל, אבל הכא – הא איכא למיחש שמא צרתה מעוברת בולד בן קיימא, ואין ביאה וחליצה פוטרת בה לדברי הכל, אלא ולד. והולד אין פוטר עד שיצא לאויר העולם! ונראה בעיני דה"ג: בשלמא תחלוץ בתוך ט' ותנשא בתוך ט' לא דהיינו ספק שמא יהא ולד צרתה בן קיימא, ואין ביאה וחליצה פוטרת אלא ולד, והולד אין פוטר עד שיצא לאויר העולם. ול"ג "אי בן ט' לראשון", ופירושו היה בספרים משובשים. אלא תחלוץ בתוך ט' ותנשא לאחר ט' ממה נפשך: אי מיעברא צרתה והפילה, או לא מעוברת הואי – הרי חלצה זו. ואי ולד של קיימא הוה – הרי יצא לאויר העולם. אלא לאו, משום שמא מעוברת צרתה היתה בשעת חליצה, ואין הולד של קיימא, וההיא חליצה לא פטרה כר"ל, הואיל ואחת מהן מעוברת לא שייכא חליצה ההיא שעתא, דאמרינן עיין עליו. ולטעמיך. אי טעמא דלא תחלוץ משום ספק מעוברת צרתה בשעת חליצה היא – תחלוץ לאחר ט', דהשתא ודאי לאו מעוברת היא, ותנשא. ומ"ט קתני עד שתדע, ואפי' לסוף כמה שנים? אלא בר מינה דההיא. כלומר, מההיא לא תידוק סייעתא לר"ל. דהא דקתני לא תחלוץ בתוך ט' ותנשא לאחר ט', התם טעמא לאו משום ספק יבמה לשוק הוא, אלא כדאביי בר אבין כו'. שמא יהא ולד. צרתה. בן קיימא. ונמצא חליצתה שלא לצורך, וכשרה לכהונה. ומי שראה בחליצה מחזיקה כפסולה לכהונה, ואתה צריך להכריז: דעו שזו לא פסלתה חליצתה. [א"ל] אביי מידי לא תחלוץ ולא תתייבם קתני. דתידוק מינה סייעתא לר"ל? לא תנשא קתני. דלא תנשא לשוק בלא חליצה לסמוך ולומר צרתי ילדה לבעלי, אע"פ שרוב נשים יולדות. אבל אי חלצה, אפי' בתוך ט' – ה"נ דמשתריא לאחר ט'. דביאת מעוברת וחליצתה – שמה ביאה וחליצה. על פיו. אחרי דברי פיו, ולא בסתם ירושה בשתיקה. ריבה לאחד ומיעט לאחד או שהשוה לו את הבכור דבריו קיימים. דלכולן נתן בחייו, ואין כאן ירושה ליטול בכורה, ולא הפשוטים ליטול בשוה, אלא מה שריבה – ריבה, ומה שמיעט – מיעט. ואם אמר משום ירושה. פלוני יירש שדה פלונית, ופלוני שדה פלונית. לא אמר כלום. שהתנה על מה שכתוב בתורה, ותנאו בטל, הואיל ולא חילק לפשוטים בשוה, ולבכור פי שנים. בתחלה. תנתן שדה פלונית לפלוני ויירשנה. באמצע. יירשה ותנתן לו ויירשה. בסוף. יירשה ותנתן לו. לעולם

עין משפט נר מצוה

ח א מיי' פ"א מהלכות יבום הלכה יט:

ט ב מיי' פ"א שם הלכה כב סמג עשין נ טוש"ע אה"ע סימן קסד סעיף ג:

י ג מיי' שם הלכה כ טוש"ע שם סעיף ב:

יא ד מיי' פ"ו מהלכות נחלות הלכה ה סמג עשין נ טוש"ע ח"מ סימן רפא סעיף ז:

ל"ל אבין [לקמן מח:]

[וע"ע תוס' ב"מ מח. ד"ה נתנה וכו' ותוס' ע"ז עח. ובכורות יג: ד"ה רב אשי]

[עי' תוס' שבת ע: סוף ד"ה נודע לו]

תוספות ישנים

א) ועוד דהו"ל לאתויי בהדיא הא דתנן לקמן לא תחלוץ עד שיעברו עליה ג' חדשים ולפרוך לר' יוחנן תחלוץ בתוך שלשה ותנשא לאחר שלשה. ונהי נמי דלקמן פריך לה הכי הכא הו"ל לאתויי ועוד מאי קאמר ולטעמיך תחלוץ לאחר ג' ותנשא וכו' היכי מצי להנשא לאחר ג' הא שמא צרתה מעוברת מולד בן קיימא ואין החליצה כלום ומשום ולד לא מפטר דולד אינו פוטר עד שיצא לאויר העולם:

תוספות חד מקמאי

תנן האשה שהלך בעלה למ"ה ובאו ואמרו לה מת בעלך ה"ז לא תנשא ולא תתיבם עד שתדע שמא מעוברת היא צרתה. בשלמא מייבם לא דלמא מעברא וקא פגע באיסור אשת אח דאורייתא אלא לא תנשא אמאי בשלמא חליצה בתוך ט' חדשים ונשואין בתוך ט' חדשים לא דהיינו ספיקא שמא יהיה הולד של קיימא ולד אינו פוטר עד שיצא לאויר העולם ותחלוץ בתוך ט' ותנשא לאחר ט' ואסיקנן שמא יהיה ולד של קיימא ונמצאת מצריכה כרוז לכהונה. ולפום האי טעמא אם היתה גרושה שפסולה לכהונה תחלץ ותנשא לאחר ט' חדשים ודוקא לכתחלה הוא דחיישנן לכרוז אבל דיעבד לא דהא תנן החולץ ליבמתו ונמצאת מעוברת וילדה בזמן שהולד של קיימא הוא מותר בקרובותיה והיא מותרת בקרוביו ולא פסלה מן הכהונה אמר רבא הלכתא כותיה דר"ל בהני תלת ואיכא נמי אחריני בפ"ק דע"ז בנשא ונתן לפני אידיהם ר"י אמר אסור ר"ל אמר מותר ותניא כותיה דר"ל אלא באסור [לא] קמיירי אבל החולץ למעוברת מאי איסורא איכא בחליצה. איתמר

[לעיל ג. וש"נ]

הגהות הב"ח

(א) רש"י ד"ה עולה לחליצה וכו' לקחת יבמתו ועלתה וגו' הא חפץ מייבם הס"ד: (ב) ד"ה לא אפשר וכו' כ' ימים בסוף ג' חדשים: (ג) תוס' ד"ה משום וכו' טעמא דמתני' מפרש התם לפי:

לקמן קיט.

[לקמן קיט:]

נ"ל אבין

ב"ב קכט: חולין עז.

ב"ב קכו:

*[א]וְאָמַר ר"ל: לְעוֹלָם לֹא קָנָה עַד שֶׁיֹּאמַר "פְּלוֹנִי וּפְלוֹנִי יִרְשׁוּ שָׂדֶה פְּלוֹנִית וּפְלוֹנִית שֶׁנְּתַתִּים לָהֶם בְּמַתָּנָה וְיִרָשׁוּם". וְאִידָךְ – דִּתְנַן: *[ב]הַכּוֹתֵב כָּל נְכָסָיו לִבְנוֹ לְאַחַר מוֹתוֹ, הָאָב אֵינוֹ יָכוֹל לִמְכּוֹר – מִפְּנֵי שֶׁנְּתָנָן לַבֵּן, וְהַבֵּן אֵינוֹ יָכוֹל לִמְכּוֹר – מִפְּנֵי שֶׁהֵן בִּרְשׁוּת הָאָב – [ג]מָכַר הָאָב מְכוּרִין עַד שֶׁיָּמוּת הוּא. מָכַר הַבֵּן – אֵין לַלּוֹקֵחַ כְּלוּם עַד שֶׁיָּמוּת הָאָב. *וְאִיתְּמַר, מָכַר הַבֵּן בְּחַיֵּי הָאָב, וּמֵת הַבֵּן בְּחַיֵּי הָאָב, רַ' יוֹחָנָן אָמַר: לֹא קָנָה לוֹקֵחַ, וְרֵישׁ לָקִישׁ אָמַר: [ד]קָנָה לוֹקֵחַ. רַ' יוֹחָנָן אָמַר: לֹא קָנָה לוֹקֵחַ, *קִנְיַן פֵּירוֹת כְּקִנְיַן הַגּוּף דָּמֵי. וְר"ל אָמַר: קָנָה לוֹקֵחַ, [ה]קִנְיַן פֵּירוֹת לָאו כְּקִנְיַן הַגּוּף דָּמֵי.§ "אֵין הַוָּלָד שֶׁל קַיָּימָא כו'".§ תָּנָא: מִשּׁוּם רַבִּי אֱלִיעֶזֶר אָמְרוּ: יוֹצִיא בְּגֵט. אָמַר רָבָא: רַ' מֵאִיר וְרַ' אֱלִיעֶזֶר אָמְרוּ דָּבָר אֶחָד. רַבִּי אֱלִיעֶזֶר – הָא דַּאֲמַרַן, ר"מ – דְּתַנְיָא: *[ו]לֹא יִשָּׂא אָדָם מְעוּבֶּרֶת חֲבֵירוֹ וּמֵינֶקֶת חֲבֵירוֹ, וְאִם נָשָׂא – יוֹצִיא, וְלֹא יַחֲזִיר עוֹלָמִית, דִּבְרֵי רַ' מֵאִיר. וַחֲכָמִים אוֹמְרִים: [ז]יוֹצִיא, וְלִכְשֶׁיַּגִּיעַ זְמַנּוֹ לִכְנוֹס – יִכְנוֹס. א"ל אַבַּיֵי: מִמַּאי? דִּלְמָא לָא הִיא, עַד כָּאן לָא קָאָמַר רַ' אֱלִיעֶזֶר הָכָא – אֶלָּא מִשּׁוּם דְּקָפָגַע בְּאִיסּוּר אֵשֶׁת אָח דְּאוֹרַיְיתָא, אֲבָל הָתָם דְּרַבָּנַן – כְּרַבָּנַן סְבִירָא לֵיהּ. אִי נַמִי: עַד כָּאן לָא קָאָמַר רַבִּי מֵאִיר הָתָם – אֶלָּא מִשּׁוּם דְּרַבָּנַן, *וַחֲכָמִים עָשׂוּ חִיזּוּק לְדִבְרֵיהֶם יוֹתֵר מִשֶּׁל תּוֹרָה. אֲבָל הָכָא – מִדְּאוֹרַיְיתָא, מִפְרָשׁ פָּרְשִׁי מִינַּהּ. אָמַר רָבָא: וּלְדִבְרֵי חֲכָמִים [ח]יוֹצִיאָהּ בְּגֵט. אָמַר מָר זוּטְרָא: דַּיְקָא נַמִי, דְּקָתָנֵי יוֹצִיא, וְלֹא קָתָנֵי יַפְרִישׁ, ש"מ. א"ל רַב אַשִׁי לְרַב הוֹשַׁעְיָא בְּרֵיהּ דְּרַב אִידִי: הָתָם *תְּנַן, *) רשב"ג אוֹמֵר: [ט]כָּל שֶׁשָּׁהָא בְּאָדָם ל' יוֹם – אֵינוֹ נֵפֶל. הָא לֹא שָׁהָא – סְפֵיקָא הָוֵי. וְאִיתְּמַר, *מֵת בְּתוֹךְ ל' יוֹם, וְעָמְדָה וְנִתְקַדְּשָׁה. רָבִינָא מִשְּׁמֵיהּ דְּרָבָא אָמַר: [י]אִם אֵשֶׁת יִשְׂרָאֵל הִיא – חוֹלֶצֶת, וְאִם אֵשֶׁת כֹּהֵן הִיא – אֵינָהּ חוֹלֶצֶת. רַב *מְשַׁרְשְׁיָא מִשְּׁמֵיהּ דְּרָבָא אָמַר: אַחַת זוֹ וְאַחַת זוֹ חוֹלֶצֶת. אֲמַר לֵיהּ רָבִינָא לְרַב מְשַׁרְשְׁיָא: בְּאוֹרְתָא

*) שבת קלה: לקמן פ: נדה מד: [תוספתא דשבת פט"ו]

רש"י

לְעוֹלָם לֹא קָנָה כו'. לָאו אַמַּתְנִיתִין פָּלֵיג, אֶלָּא הָתָם בְּ"יֵשׁ נוֹחֲלִין" פְּלִיגִי אַמּוֹרָאֵי בְּדִיּוּקָא דְּמַתְנִי'. דְּכִי אָתָא רָבִין אָמַר: יִרַשׁ פְּלוֹנִי שָׂדֶה פְּלוֹנִי, וְתִנָּתֵן שָׂדֶה פְּלוֹנִי לִפְלוֹנִי, רַבִּי יוֹחָנָן אָמַר: קָנָה אֲפִילּוּ הַאי דִּירוּשָּׁה, דְּמִדְּאַדְכַּר לְשׁוֹן מַתָּנָה בְּהַאי שְׁטַר גַּוָּוהּ לְחַד מִינַּיְיהוּ – כּוּלְּהוּ נַמִי מַתָּנָה נִינְהוּ. וְר"ל אָמַר: לְעוֹלָם לֹא קָנָה הַהוּא דִּירוּשָּׁה, דְּאָמְרִינַן: לְהַאי הָוֵה מַתָּנָה וּלְהַאי יְרוּשָּׁה, עַד שֶׁיֹּאמַר כו', דְּתֵיקוּ לְשׁוֹן מַתָּנָה אַתַּרְוַיְיהוּ. לְאַחַר מוֹתוֹ. שֶׁכָּתַב: מֵהַיּוֹם וּלְאַחַר מִיתָה, וְאֵין לָאָב בָּהֶן אֶלָּא אֲכִילַת פֵּירוֹת בְּחַיָּיו. מָכַר הָאָב מְכוּרִין. לֶאֱכוֹל הַלּוֹקֵחַ פֵּירוֹת כָּל יְמֵי חַיֵּי הָאָב, שֶׁזָּכָה בַּזְּכוּת שֶׁהָיָה לוֹ לָזֶה בָּהֶן. וּמֵת הַבֵּן בְּחַיֵּי הָאָב רַבִּי יוֹחָנָן אָמַר לֹא קָנָה לוֹקֵחַ. אֲפִילּוּ לִכְשֶׁיָּמוּת הָאָב. דְּקִנְיַן פֵּירוֹת שֶׁהָיָה לוֹ לָאָב בַּנְּכָסִים הַלָּלוּ כְּקִנְיַן הַגּוּף דָּמֵי, וְאֵין מְכִירַת הַבֵּן מְכִירָה. וּמַתְנִיתִין דְּקָתָנֵי אֵין לַלּוֹקֵחַ בָּהֶן כְּלוּם עַד שֶׁיָּמוּת הָאָב, הָא כְּשֶׁיָּמוּת הָאָב יֵשׁ לוֹ – הָתָם דְּמִית הָאָב בְּחַיֵּי הַבֵּן, וְנִתְקַיְּימָה הַמַּתָּנָה. וּמַה מָּכַר רִאשׁוֹן לַשֵּׁנִי – כָּל זְכוּת שֶׁתָּבֹא לְיָדוֹ. אֲבָל מֵת הַבֵּן – לֹא בָּא זְכוּת לְיָדוֹ. תָּנָא מִשּׁוּם ר"א כו'. ר' אֱלִיעֶזֶר פָּלֵיג אַסֵּיפָא דְּמַתְנִי', וְקָאֵי אַאֵין הַוָּלָד שֶׁל קַיָּימָא יְקַיֵּים, וְקָאָמַר אִיהוּ: אע"פ שֶׁאֵין הַוָּלָד שֶׁל קַיָּימָא קָנְסִינַן לֵיהּ דְּיוֹצִיא (א) בְּגֵט, מִשּׁוּם דְּנִכְנַס לִסְפֵק אִיסּוּר אֵשֶׁת אָח. וְאע"ג דְּהַשְׁתָּא אִיגַּלַּאי מִילְּתָא דְּיִיבּוּם מְעַלְּיָא הֲוַאי. וּמִיהוּ, בְּגֵט בְּלֹא חֲלִיצָה סַגִּי. דָּבָר אֶחָד. דְּר"מ נַמִי קָנֵיס אֶת הַנּוֹשֵׂא מְעוּבֶּרֶת חֲבֵירוֹ וּמֵינֶקֶת חֲבֵירוֹ (ב) – לְגָרְשָׁהּ. אִשָּׁה שֶׁמֵּת בַּעְלָהּ, וְהִיא מְעוּבֶּרֶת אוֹ מֵנִיקָה, אֲסוּרָה לְהִנָּשֵׂא עַד עֶשְׂרִים וְאַרְבָּעָה חֹדֶשׁ, שֶׁכֵּן תִּינוֹק יוֹנֵק. וְלִכְשֶׁיַּגִּיעַ זְמַנּוֹ לִכְנוֹם. לְסוֹף כ"ד חֹדֶשׁ, יִכְנוֹס. בְּאִיסּוּר אֵשֶׁת אָח. כְּלוֹמַר, שֶׁהֵיקֵל לְהִכָּנֵס לִסְפֵק אֵשֶׁת אָח שֶׁיֵּשׁ לוֹ בָּנִים, דִּדְלְמָא הָוֵי וָלָד שֶׁל קַיָּימָא, הִלְכָּךְ קָנְסִינַן לֵיהּ. אֶלָּא [מִשּׁוּם] דְּרַבָּנַן. דִּמְעוּבֶּרֶת חֲבֵירוֹ מִדְּרַבָּנַן הִיא, וְקָא מְזַלְזְלֵי בָּהּ. וּמִשּׁוּם הָכִי קָנְסוּהוּ דְּלָא לֵיתֵי אַחֲרִינָא לְמֶיעֱבַד הָכִי. אֲבָל הָכָא. יְבָמָה מְעוּבֶּרֶת דְּאוֹרַיְיתָא הִיא, וּבְדִילֵי מִינָּהּ, וְלָא בָּעֵי לְמִיקְנְסֵיהּ לְהַאי אַטּוּ אַחֲרִינֵי. וּלְדִבְרֵי חֲכָמִים. דְּאָמְרִי לִכְשֶׁיַּגִּיעַ זְמַנּוֹ לִכְנוֹס יִכְנוֹס. מִיהוּ, עַד שֶׁיַּגִּיעַ הַזְּמַן יוֹצִיא בְּגֵט, וְלָא סַגִּי לֵיהּ בְּהַפְרָשָׁה בְּעָלְמָא. דְּקָתָנֵי יוֹצִיא. וַחֲכָמִים אוֹמְרִים יוֹצִיא. הָתָם תְּנַן וכו'. מִשּׁוּם דְּקָבָעֵי לְמִבְּעֵי הָכָא מַאי. כָּל שֶׁשָּׁהָה שְׁלֹשִׁים יוֹם. מִשֶּׁנּוֹלַד חַי שְׁלֹשִׁים יוֹם. בְּאָדָם אֵין נֵפֶל. לְהָכִי נָקַט בְּאָדָם, דְּתָנֵי סֵיפָא: וּבִבְהֵמָה ח' יָמִים. אֵינוֹ נֵפֶל. וּפוֹטֵר אֶת אִמּוֹ מִן הַחֲלִיצָה. סְפֵיקָא הוּא. וְחוֹלֶצֶת וְלֹא מִתְיַיבֶּמֶת. וְדַוְקָא אִי מְסַפְּקָא לָן אִי כָּלוּ לוֹ חֳדָשָׁיו אִי לָא, אֲבָל אִי קִים לָן דְּכָלוּ לוֹ חֳדָשָׁיו – תְּנַן בְּמַסֶּכֶת נִדָּה (דף מג:): תִּינוֹק בֶּן יוֹמוֹ פּוֹטֵר מִן הַיִּיבּוּם. מֵת בְּתוֹךְ שְׁלֹשִׁים. בֶּן הַיְבָמָה, וְנִתְקַדְּשָׁה לַשּׁוּק בְּחֶזְקַת שֶׁפְּטוּרָה מִשּׁוּם בְּנָהּ. אִם אֵשֶׁת יִשְׂרָאֵל הִיא. אִם זֶה שֶׁקִּדְּשָׁהּ יִשְׂרָאֵל הוּא, שֶׁאִם תַּחֲלוֹץ מִן הַיָּבָם לְאַחַר קִדּוּשִׁין לֹא תֵּיאָסֵר עַל בַּעְלָהּ – חוֹלֶצֶת. וְאִם זֶה שֶׁקִּדְּשָׁהּ כֹּהֵן הוּא. שֶׁאִם תַּחֲלוֹץ תֵּיאָסֵר עָלָיו – אֵינָהּ חוֹלֶצֶת, וְסָמְכִינַן אַוָּלָד. בְּאוֹרְתָא

תוספות

ואמר ריש לקיש לעולם לא קנה כו'. אע"ג דרבא גופיה קאמר ב"יש נוחלין" (ב"ב דף קל.) דהלכה כרבי יוחנן בן ברוקה – מ"מ נפקא מינה דהלכה כר"ל לענין (ג) [אחר] שאין ראוי ליורשו. **ורבי** יוחנן אמר לא קנה לוקח. וא"ת: לרבי יוחנן, אפי' לא מת הבן בחיי האב נמי לא ליקני, דהוי כמו (ב"מ טז.): מה שאירש מאבא מכור לך, כיון דאיס קנין פירות כקנין הגוף! וי"ל: דלגבי הכי לא אלים קנין פירות לבטל לגמרי קנין הגוף דבן, וכיון דלבסוף אתיא שדה לידי דבן – חשיב מכר. **קנין** פירות בקנין הגוף דמי. מה שהתקינו באושא דאשה שמכרה בנכסי מלוג בחיי בעלה, ומתה, דהבעל מוציא מיד הלקוחות – לרבי יוחנן לא איצטריך). וכן משמע ב"החובל" (ב"ק דף פח: ושם) דמסיק: תקנת אושא לר"ל. א"נ, קנין הגוף דאשה עדיף, שאין לבעל פירות אלא מכחה. ועוד: דאין לבעל פירות אלא בתקנתא דרבנן. וה"ר יעקב דאורליינ"ש תירץ: דאיצטריך תקנתא דאושא להיכא דכתב לה "דין ודברים אין לי בפירות נכסייך"*. **חיזוק** לדבריהם יותר משל תורה. והיא ד"הזהב" (ב"מ נה:) גבי חמשה חומשין דלא עשו אלא כשל תורה – משום דלא איצטריך [לחיזוק]. והכא גבי איסורא הוא דקניס ר"מ, אבל גבי ממונא כגון כתובה – לא עשו חיזוק אפי' כשל תורה, דקאמר ר"מ בפ' "אע"פ" (כתובות נו: ושם): כל המתנה על מה שכתוב בתורה – תנאו בטל, הא בדרבנן – תנאו קיים. וקצת תימה: אי רבנן דהכא היינו ר' יהודה – הא סבירא ליה גבי כתובה דעשו חיזוק לדבריהם יותר משל תורה! וי"ל: דבמילתא דשכיחא עבדו חיזוק, אבל הכא – מילתא דלא שכיחא היא שישא אדם מעוברת חברו ומינקת חברו. **ולא** קתני יפריש. והא דתני בסוטה בפ' "ארוסה" (דף כד. ושם) גבי מעוברת חברו ומינקת חברו יכול הוא להפרישה ולהחזירה לאחר זמן – לשון הפרשה משמע הכי ומשמע הכי, אבל יוציא לא משמע אלא בגט. א"נ: התם, שקינא לה ונסתרה – לא חיישינן שיבא עליה, כיון דאסירא ליה מדאורייתא ולא בעיא גט. והר"ר יוסף מאורליינ"ש הורה מטעם זה באחד שקידש מינקת חברו שלא להצריך גט אלא הפרשה בעלמא (אפילו לרבי מאיר), כיון דבלאו הכי אסורה ליה, דכלה בלא ברכה אסורה לבעלה כנדה. ודוקא בנשא הוא דאמר הכא דבעיא גיטא. אע"ג דנקדש תוך ג' ובהרת, אי לאו דערוקיה מסתייה היה צריך ליתן גט – במעוברת ומינקת חבירו לא החמירו. ואין נראה: דמאי חומרא דכלה בלא ברכה ממינקת חבירו, דתרווייהו מדרבנן. (ד) וקצת היה מדקדק ר"י מהא דתניא התם (כתובות דף ס.): מינקת שמת בעלה – הרי זו לא תארס ולא תנשא, ואם כשאירס צריך ליתן גט – לא איצטריך תו למימר לא תנשא! ומיהו, י"ס דגרסי לא תנשא ולא תארס, ואיכא למימר דזו אף זו קתני. ואפילו גרסינן לא תארס ולא תנשא – מצי למימר דנקט ולא תנשא משום רבי יהודה, דאפילו לינשא שרי בתר י"ח חדש. ובשאלתות דרבי אחאי בפרשה וירא (סימן יג) כתוב גבי מעוברת ומינקת חברו, דהיכא דעבר וקדיש – מפקיע לה בגט מיניה, ואפילו אי הוה כהן – מפסדינן לה מיניה. **הא** לא שהא ספיקא הויא. ב) לא כמו שפי' הקונטרס דפיחק ומת ולד [דהא] אפילו רבנן מודו בפיחק ומת דנפל הוא. אלא כשנפל מן הגג או אכלו ארי איירי, כדאמר בס"פ "ר' אליעזר דמילה" (שבת דף קלו. ושם), והתם פסקינן כרשב"ג. וא"ת: ואמאי לא אזלינן בתר רוב נשים דולד מעליא ילדן? וא"י: דחיישינן למיעוט מצוי כזה, כמו שאין להם סוף (לקמן קכא.) דאשתו אסורה, וגוסס *שאין מעידים עליו להשיא אשתו, אע"ג דשמא התם משום ערוה החמירו, מ"מ כיון דמיעוט של נפלים מצוי – מחמירים ביה. ומחמירים נמי שלא לאכול בהמה תוך ח' ימים, כדאמרינן בס"פ "ר' אליעזר דמילה" (ג"ז שם). ומיהו, לענין אבילות לא החמירו, שיש להקל באבלות כדאמר בפ' "יש בכור" (בכורות מט.): הכל מודים לענין אבלות שאין מתאבלים, דאמר שמואל: הלכה כדברי המיקל באבל. והא דתנן במסכת שמחות: *הספקות אוננים ומתאבלים עליהם – נראה דבספק בן ט' לראשון או ז' לאחרון איירי, דנגאי הדבר שלא יתאבלו לא זה ולא זה, מאחר שודאי קרוב לאחד. **מת** בתוך שלשים יום כו'. נראה דהכי גרסי'. ולא כרש"י *דגרים בפ' "ר"א דמילה" (שבת קלו. ושם): "מת בסוף שלשים יום", כיון דבפרק "יש בכור" (בכורות מט. ושם) אמרינן דיום ל' כשלפניו – מה לי ביום שלשים מה לי תוך שלשים, ולמה ליה למינקט ביום שלשים טפי? ומיהו בה"ג כתב דביום שלשים אפי' פיחק ומת לרבנן לא הוי נפל, דדוקא תוך שלשים הוא דאמר בשבת (ג"ז שם): פיחק ומת לד"ה מת הוא. משמע דגרסינן הכא "מת ביום שלשים", דאי לאו הכי – מנין היה להם חילוק זה? ועוד יש מקיים גירסא זאת אפילו בנפל מן הגג או אכלו ארי, וביום שלשים דוקא סמכי ארבנן. ושמא לענין אבילות נמי חשיב בר קיימא. מי

עין משפט נר מצוה

יב א מיי' פ"ו מהלכות נחלות הלכה ו סמג עשין צו טוש"ע ח"מ סי' רמח סעיף ז:

הגהות הב"ח

גליון הש"ס

תוספות ישנים

תוספות חד מקמאי

איתמר מת בתוך שלשים יום או ביום ל' ועמדה ונתקדשה אמר רבינא משמיה דרבא אם אשת ישראל דהוי] ולד מעלי' אע"ג דלא שהא גבי אשת כהן עבדינן (לחומרא) [לקולא] כרבנן. ודוקא בנפל מן חולצת אם אשת כהן אינה חולצת ושריא לבעלה דכיון דאיכא רבנן דפליגי עליה דרשב"ג (קאי) [דאמרי הגג או אכלו ארי אבל פיחק ומת אף אשת כהן חולצת ואסרינן לה אגברא דקי"ל בפר"א דמילה דפיחק

*באורתא אמר רבא הכי, ובצפרא הדר ביה. א"ל: *שריתוה? יהא רעוא דתשתרו אף תרבא. הכא גבי מעוברת חבירו ומינקת חבירו הנשואה לכהן, מאי? מי עבוד רבנן תקנתא לכהן, או לא? אמר ליה: [א]הכי השתא! בשלמא התם, כיון דאיכא רבנן דפליגי עליה דרשב"ג, דאמרי: אע"ג דלא שהא ולד מעליא הוי, — גבי אשת כהן, כיון דלא אפשר, עבדינן כרבנן. אבל הכא, כמאן נעביד? אי כר' מאיר — הא אמר יוציא ולא יחזיר עולמית, ואי כרבנן — האמרי בגט. איתמר, קדשה בתוך שלשה וברח פליגי בה רב אחא ורפרם, חד אמר: משמתינן ליה, וחד אמר: עירוקיה מסתייה. הוה עובדא, ואמר להו רפרם: [ב]עירוקיה מסתייה.§ "ספק בן תשע וכו'".§ אמר ליה רבא לרב נחמן: לימא הלך אחר רוב נשים, ורוב נשים לתשעה ילדן! אמר ליה: נשי דידן — לשבעה ילדן. א"ל: נשי דידכו הוו רובא דעלמא? א"ל: הכי קאמינא, רוב נשים ילדן לתשעה ומיעוט לשבעה, וכל היולדת לתשעה — *עוברה ניכר לשליש ימיה. וזו, הואיל ולא הוכר עוברה לשליש ימיה — איתרע ליה רובא. אי כל היולדת לתשעה עוברה ניכר לשליש ימיה, הא" מדלא הוכר לשליש ימיה — עוברה ודאי בר שבעה לבתראה הוא! — אלא אימא: רוב היולדת לתשעה עוברה ניכר לשליש ימיה, והאי מדלא הוכר לשליש ימיה — איתרע ליה רובא. ת"ר: *ראשון ראוי להיות כהן גדול, ושני ממזר מספק. רבי אליעזר בן יעקב אומר: *אין ממזר מספק. מאי קאמר? אמר אביי: הכי קאמר, ראשון ראוי להיות כהן גדול, ושני — ספק ממזר, ואסור בממזרת. ר' אליעזר (א) אומר: אינו ספק ממזר אלא ודאי ממזר, ומותר בממזרת. רבא אמר, [ג]הכי קאמר: ראשון — ראוי להיות כהן גדול, ושני — ממזר ודאי מספק, ומותר בממזרת. ורבי אליעזר בן יעקב אומר: אין ודאי ממזר מספק, אלא ספק ממזר, ואסור בממזרת. וקמיפלגי בדרבי אלעזר. דתנן, *רבי אלעזר אומר: [ד]ודאן בודאן — מותר. ודאן בספקן, וספקן בודאן, וספקן בספקן — אסור. [ה]ואלו הן ספקן: שתוקי ואסופי וכותי, *ואמר רב יהודה אמר רב: הלכה כר' אלעזר. כי אמריתה קמיה דשמואל אמר לי: הלל שנה עשרה יוחסין עלו מבבל: כהני, לויי, וישראלי, חללי, גירי, חרורי, ממזרי, נתיני, שתוקי, ואסופי. וכולן מותרין לבא זה בזה — ואת אמרת הלכה כרבי אלעזר?! אביי סבר לה כשמואל דאמר הלכה כהלל, ומוקי לה רבי אליעזר בן יעקב אליבא דהלכתא כי היכי דלא תקשי הלכתא אהלכתא. רבא סבר לה כרב, דאמר הלכה כר' אלעזר, ומוקי לה לדרבי אליעזר בן יעקב אליבא דהלכתא, כי היכי דלא תקשי הלכתא

רש"י

באורתא אמר רבא הכי. כדקאמרת. לצפרא הדר ביה. ושמעתי מפיו שאיה חולצת. הכא מאי. לר' יהושע בריה דרב אידי קבעי לה. מי עביד רבנן תקנתא לכהן. דאע"ג דלישראל בעינן יוציא בגט עד שיגיע זמנו, התם הוא דלכשיגיע זמנו מצי לאהדורה, אבל הכא, דאי מגרש לה לא מצי מהדר לה — תסגי בהפרשה בעלמא. עבדינן כרבנן. וסמכינן אוולד. קדשה בתוך שלשה. שום אלמנה או גרושה. עירוקיה מסתייה. לא בעי למיכפייה דליכתוב גט, דגלי דעתיה דלא בעי לכנוס עד זמנו. ורוב נשים לט' ילדן. ולייתי כוותא, דודאי בר קמא הוא, ואשת אח בת בנים בעל. וזו הואיל ולא הוכר עוברה לשליש ימיה. דאי הוכר לא הוה מספקא לן. לשליש ימיה. דכתיב "ויהי כמשלש חדשים" (בראשית לח). איתרע לה רובא. דלא תשדייה בתר רוב נשים, אלא ספק בתר מיעוט, ספק בתר רוב. ראשון. דספק הוה ראוי להיות כהן גדול ממה נפשך. והשני. אם קיימה עד שילדה לו בן ודאי ממזר מספק שמא ראשון בן המת הוה, וקאי עליה בכרת, ואישתכח האי שני ולד חייבי כריתות, וממזר. מאי קאמר. ר"א בן יעקב, היכי מצי לאפוקי מספק ממזר? אמר אביי כו' ספק ממזר הוי. ואסור בממזרת ובכשרה. ר"א (ב) אומר אין ממזר מספק. אלא כודאי ממזר הוי, ומותר בממזרת. דקסבר: ספיקן בודאן מותר. ושני ממזר ודאי הוי מספק. כלומר, מתוך ספק זה נעשה כודאי ממזר, ומותר בממזרת. וקמיפלגי. אביי ורבא, דמר מוקי רבי אליעזר בן יעקב להיתרא, ומר מוקי ליה לאיסורא, פליגי בדרבי *אליעזר. ודאן בספיקן אסור. שמא הספק כשר הוא, ונמצא בא ממזר בקהל. וכן ספק מבזר בספק ממזרת, דשמא זה פסול וזה כשר. שתוקי. שקורא אביו, ואמו משתקתו. אסופי. שנאסף מן השוק. ובכולהו איכא למיחש שמא מפסול נתעברה. כותי. אין מקפיד על קדושי כסף ושטר, דלית ליה גזירה שוה דקיחה קיחה, וכי מקדש חד — מנסבא לאידך. לפיכך כולן ספק ממזרים הם, שמא נתקדשה אמו לאחר. כי אמריתה. רב יהודה מסיים למילתיה ואזיל: כי אמריתה להא שמעתא דרב אמר הלכה כר"א, קמיה דשמואל, אמר לי כו'. וכולן מותרין לבא זה בזה. אי אמרת (ג) ספיקן בודאן מותר, וכ"ש ספיקן בספיקן — היינו דמשכחת ליה כולן מותרין זה בזה. כהנים לוים וישראלים — מותרין זה בזה, לויי, וישראלי, חללי, גירי, וחרורי, עבדים משוחררים — מותרים זה בזה, גירי, חרורי, ממזרי, ונתיני, שתוקי, ואסופי — מותרים זה בזה, דקהל גרים לא איקרי קהל, לפיכך ממזרים מותרים בהן, וכסדר הזה שנויים בקדושין (דף סט.). ואת אמרת הלכה כר"א. שאין ממזר מותר בשתוקי, ולא שתוקי בשתוקי, ולא שתוקי באסופי (א"כ לא משכחת לה כולהו מעורבים). נתיני. גבעונים שנתגיירו בימי יהושע בערמה, ויש בהן לא עבדות, דכתיב (יהושע ט) "ויתנם יהושע חוטבי עצים ושואבי מים לעדה". הלכתא

תוספות

מי עביד רבנן תקנתא או לא. בעיא זו אליבא דרבנן ולא אליבא דר' מאיר. ומכאן מדקדק בה"ג ובשאלתות דהא דאמר בפ' "אע"פ" (כתובות דף ס: ושם) דהלכה כר"מ בגזרותיו — היינו דוקא בגזרותיו ולא בקנסותיו*. אי כל היולדת כו'. כה"ג דייק בר"פ דכתובות (דף טז:) גבי כל הנישאת בתולה יש לה קול כו', ובפ' "המפלת" (נדה דף כט.) גבי כל היולדות מטנפות. אבל בפרק "ואלו טריפות" (חולין דף נג.), גבי כל הדורס אין לפרעו נשמטת, לא דייק (אע"ג) ד"כל" לאו דוקא. רוב היולדת לט' כו'. וא"ת: מה מועיל המתנת ג' חדשים משום הבחנה? אכתי יכול לבא לידי ספק אם תנשא מיד ותלד לו' חדשים ויום אחד, או אפילו ג' ימים, דיש להסתפק אם הוא בנו של ראשון ולא נקלט הזרע עד יום ג', או הוא בנו של שני, דיולדת לשבעה יולדת למקוטעים! וזהו תימה לומר שתהא האשה צריכה להמתין ג' חדשים וג' ימים, דלקמן משמע דג' חדשים דוקא, דאמר: חוץ מיום שמת בו ויום שנתארסה בו! ואין לומר כיון דהמתינה ג' חדשים שריא לינשא, ולא חיישינן שמא תלד מעֵני לסוף ששה חדשים וב' ימים או ג', דסמכינן ארובא דלט' ילדן, וא"כ דסמכינן ארובא דלט' ילדן — א"כ אפילו תוך ג' חדשים תנשא, דסמכינן ארובא, ואין צריך להמתין אלא חדש אחד, ושוב אין ספק, דאם תלד לסוף ט' ממיתת ראשון — אין להסתפק שמא הוא מז' לאחרון, דאזלינן בתר רוב נשים דלט' ילדן, אלא ע"כ, כל מקום שיכול לבא לידי ספק — החמירו חכמים! וי"ל: דכ"כ לא היה משתהא הכרת העובר של ראשון עד שליש ימיה מן השני. וזו הואיל ולא הוכר. תימה: דאמאי לא מוקמינן לה בחזקת היתר ליבם, ולא יתחייב באשם תלוי, ויהא נמי ולד שני כשר, דסמוך מיעוט יולדת לשבעה אחזקה, ואיתרע ליה רובא, ונסמוך ארובא דעוברה ניכר לשליש ימיה, דלעיל בפ' "ד' אחין" (דף ל:) חשבינן לה חזקה גבי ספק קידושין, ולקמן בפ' בתרא (דף קיט. ושם) אפילו היתה צרתה מעוברת חשבינן לה בחזקת זקוקה? וכ"ת דאיכא רובא אחרינא, דרוב נשים מתעברות ויולדות, לפיכך יש להחזיקה כמעוברת מן הראשון — דאין סברא כלל לומר בנשים ששהו עם בעליהן כמה שנים ולא עיברו ומתו בעליהם דרוב מעוברות, ולקמן (דף קיט.) הוא דאמר לה גבי האשה שהלך בעלה וצרתה למדינת הים! ראשון ראוי להיות כה"ג. והא דאמר בפ"ק דכתובות (דף יג: ושם) גבי עשר כהנים שפירש אחד מהן ובעל הולד שתוקי, שמשתקין אותו מדין כהונה, דבעינן זרעו מיוחס אחריו – לקמן בפ' "נושאין" (דף ק:) פריך לה, ומשני: זרעו מיוחס אחריו דרבנן, וכי גזור רבנן – בזנות, בנישואין – לא גזור. סבר לה כרב דאמר הלכה כר' אלעזר. והא דפריך בגמרא "עשרה יוחסין" (קידושין דף עג. ושם) גבי הא דאמר רבא דבר תורה כו' שתוקי כשר: אלא מעתה שתוקי – שתוקית לא ישא! לאו משום דלרבא שרי שתוקי בשתוקית, אלא משום דגם אליבא דרבנן אמר רבא מילתיה דהתם, להכי פריך דלרבנן נמי שתוקי שתוקית לא ישא.

יהודי

עין משפט נר מצוה

כ א ב מיי' פי"ד מהל' גירושין הלכה כח סמג עשין נ טוש"ע אה"ע סימן יג סעיף יב:

[וע"ע תוס' ב"ק ל: סד"ה וחכמים ותוס' ב"מ עב. ד"ה קונסין ותוס' ב"ב לד: ד"ה וחכ"א ותוס' בכורות כח. ד"ה ר"מ ותוס' זבחים קד. ד"ה אמר ר"ע]

כא ג מיי' פ"א מהלכות יבום הלכה כג סמג לאוין קיז טוש"ע שם סימן ד סעיף כה וסימן קסד סעיף ו:

כב ד מיי' פט"ו מהל' איסורי ביאה הלכה כא סמג שם טוש"ע שם סימן ד סעיף כד:

כג ה מיי' שם וטוש"ע שם סעיף לו וסעיף לח:

תוספות חד מקמאי

דפיהק ומת ד"ה (מותר) [נפל] הוא. עמד וקדשה בתוך ג' חדשים וברח פליגי רב אחא ורפרם חד אמר משמתין ליה עד שיוציאה בגט (ושמואל) [וחד אמר] ערקויי מסתייה דגלי דעתיה שאין דעתו לכנסה עד אחר שלשה חדשים והלכתא ערקויי מסתייה אבל לא ברח יוציא בגט אפי' קדשה ביום השלמת שלשה חדשים דקי"ל צריכה להמתין ג' חדשים חוץ מיום שמת בו וחוץ מיום שנתארסה בו. הרב אלפס כתב לאלמנת חבירו ולגרושת חבירו בתוך ג' חדשים משמע דהא אם קדש אלמנת אחיו א) לא איבעיא ג' חדשים אלא אמר ערקויי מסתייה והראב"ד כתב דה"ה אם קדש אשת אחיו דהא לא פסקא דמתני' אתמהא הא שמעתא:

א) נראה דצ"ל בתוך ג' חדשים לא אמרינן דערוקיה מסתייה דהא אפסקא דמתניתין אתמר הא שמעתתא.

הגהות הב"ח

(א) גמ' ר' אליעזר בן יעקב אומר אינו ספק ממזר אלא ודאי: (ב) רש"י ד"ה ר' אליעזר בן יעקב אומר אין ממזר: (ג) ד"ה וכולן וכו' אי אמרת בשלמא ספקן:

מסורת הש"ס: שבת קלו: | [ס"א שריתוה] | [סנהדרין סט.] | נ"ל אלעזר | קדושין עד. | [שם עה.] | כתובות יג: | ס"א אינו ספק

הלכתא אהלכתא. אמר אביי: מנא אמינא לה דכל ספיקא לר' אליעזר בן יעקב כודאי משוי ליה – דתניא, *ר' אליעזר בן יעקב אומר: [א]הרי שבא על נשים הרבה ואין יודע על איזהו מהן בא. וכן היא, שבאו עליה אנשים הרבה ואינה יודעת מאיזה מהן קבלה, נמצא אב נושא את בתו ואח נושא את אחותו, ונתמלא כל העולם כולו ממזרין, ועל זה נאמר °"ומלאה הארץ זמה". (ויקרא יט) ורבא אמר לך: הכי קאמר: *"זו מה היא". יתר על כן אמר ר' אליעזר בן יעקב: *[ב]לא ישא אדם אשה במדינה זו, וילך וישא אשה במדינה אחרת, שמא יזדווגו זה לזה ונמצא אח נושא את אחותו. איני? והא *רב, כי איקלע לדרדשיר [מכריז] ואמר: מאן הויא ליומא. ורב נחמן, כי איקלע לשכנציב [מכריז] ואמר: מאן הויא ליומא! – [ג]שאני רבנן דפקיע שמייהו. והאמר רבא: *[ד]תבעוה לינשא ונתפייסה – צריכה לישב שבעה נקיים! רבנן שלוחייהו הוו משדרי, ומודעי להו, ואיבעית אימא: לרבנן יחודי בעלמא הוא דמייחדי להו, דאמר מר: *אינו דומה מי שיש לו פת בסלו למי שאין לו פת בסלו. תנא, רבי אליעזר בן יעקב אומר: [ה]לא ישא אדם *אשתו *ודעתו לגרשה, משום שנאמר °"אל תחרש על רעך רעה והוא יושב לבטח אתך". (משלי ג) § ספק ויבם שבאו לחלוק בנכסי מיתנא. ספק אמר: אנא בר מיתנא הוא, ונכסי דידי הוא. ויבם אמר: את בראי דידי את, ולית לך ולא מידי בנכסי. [ו]הוי ממון המוטל בספק, וממון המוטל בספק – חולקין. [ז]ספק ובני יבם שבאו לחלוק בנכסי מיתנא, ספק אמר: ההוא גברא בר מיתנא הוא, ונכסי דידי הוא. בני יבם אמרי: את אחינו את, ומנתא הוא דאית לך בהדן. סבור רבנן קמיה דרב משרשיא למימר: מתניתין היא, דתנן: *הוא אינו יורש אותם, והם יורשין אותו. והכא איפכא, התם אמרי ליה: אייתי ראיה ושקול. הכא אמר להו: אייתו ראיה ושקולו. אמר להו רב משרשיא: מי דמי? התם – אינהו ודאי, ואיהו ספק. הכא – אידי ואידי ספק. אלא, אי דמיא למתני' – [להא] דמיא: לספק ובני יבם שבאו לחלוק בנכסי יבם גופיה, דהתם אמרי ליה: אייתי ראיה דאחונא את ושקול. ספק ובני יבם שבאו לחלוק בנכסי יבם, לבתר דפלג יבם בנכסי מיתנא. בני יבם אמרי: אייתי ראיה דאחונא את ושקול. אמר להו ספק: מה נפשייכו, אי אחוכון אנא – הבו לי מנתא בהדייכו, ואי בר מיתנא אנא – הבו לי פלגא דפלג אבוכון בהדאי. ר' אבא אמר רב: [ח]קם דינא. ר' ירמיה אמר: הדר דינא. לימא בפלוגתא דאדמון ורבנן קמיפלגי, דתנן: *מי שהלך למדינת הים ואבדה לו דרך שדהו, אדמון אמר: ילך בקצרה. וחכ"א: יקח לו דרך במאה מנה, או יפרח באויר. והוינן בה לרבנן; [ט]שפיר קאמר אדמון! ואמר רב יהודה אמר רב: הכא במאי עסקינן – [י]כגון שהקיפוה ארבעה בני אדם מארבע רוחות. א"ה, מ"ט דאדמון? ואמר רבא: [כ]בארבעה דאתו מכח ארבעה, וארבעה דאתו מכח חד – כולי עלמא לא פליגי, דמצו מדחי ליה. כי פליגי – בחד דאתי מכח ארבעה. אדמון סבר: מצי א"ל: מכל מקום דרכי גבך הוא. ורבנן סברי, דא"ל: [ל]אי שתקת – שתקת, ואי לא – מהדרנא שטרא למרייהו, ולא מצית לאשתעויי דינא בהדייהו. לימא ר' אבא דאמר כרבנן, ור' ירמיה דאמר כאדמון. אמר לך ר' אבא: אנא דאמרי אפילו כאדמון. עד כאן לא קאמר אדמון התם – אלא משום דא"ל: ממה נפשך דרכי

דרכי

הלכתא אהלכתא. דקיימא לן: משנת ר"א ב"י קב ונקי, במסכת גיטין (דף סז.). קבלה. נתעברה. ונתמלא כל העולם כולו ממזרים. מספק קרו להו ממזרים. זו מה היא. לשון ספק. יתר על כן. דאפי' הכא, דע"י נשואין הוה והדבר מפורסם, גזר ר"א בן יעקב. מאן הויא ליומי. מי אפלה לינשא לימים שאתעכב כאן. דפקיעי. כ"ע בשמייהו, וקוראין לבתו על שמו. ואם יבא בנו ממקום אחר – ישמע שהיא בת אביו, ויפרוש. שבעה נקיים. שמא מחמת חימוד פרסה נדה, בשעה שנתפייסה. שלוחייהו הוו משדרי. שבעה יומי קודם דאתן. ממון המוטל בספק. שאין זה מוחזק (א) בזה יותר מזה. דאם זה בן המת – אין ליבם בהן כלום, ואם בן היבם הוא – אין לו בהן כלום. הלכך אין כאן מוציא מחברו להטיל עליו הראיה. ספק ובני יבם. הספק מוחזק בהן ביותר, דממה נפשך אית ליה זכיה בגווייהו. אבל בני יבם – שמא אין להם חלק בהם, שזה בן ראשון הוא וכולה שלו. ומשום הכי סבור רבנן למימר היינו מתניתין בפ' "נושאין על האנוסה", דקתני ספק בן תשעה לראשון ספק בן שבעה לאחרון, הוא לא יורש אותן לא זה ולא זה, דבני ראשון מדחו ליה אצל בני אחרון, ובני אחרון – אצל בני ראשון, והם יורשים אותו בין שניהם. והכא אמרינן איפכא. דהוא מוחזק יותר. דהתם להכי מדחו ליה, דאמרי ליה: אייתי ראיה דאחונא את ושקול. והכא נמי אמר להו האי: אייתו ראיה דאחוכון אנא ושקולו. מי דמי התם אינהו ודאי. שהן יודעין מכח מי הן באין לירש. אידי ואידי ספיקא נינהו. שאפילו הספק אין טוען טענת ודאי, ואינו יודע מכח מי הוא בא לירש. בנכסי יבם גופיה. התם מיתוקמא מתניתין, דהוא לא יורש אותן, דאמרי ליה: אייתי ראיה ושקול. אבל בההיא דלעיל – שניהם ספק. ונראה בעיני דההיא מנתא דקמודו ליה – שקיל, ואידך הוי ממון המוטל בספק וחולקין, הוא נוטל החצי ובין כולן החצי. לבתר דפלג יבם. עם ספק בנכסי מיתנא, כדאמרן לעיל דחולקין. אי אחוכון אנא הבו לי מנתא גבייכו. ואי משום דשקלי אנא פלגא בנכסי מיתנא – מהדרנא לכו ההוא פלגא, ונחלוק הכל בשוה, בין נכסי הראשון בין נכסי האחרון. וכגון שהיו נכסי היבם מרובין, ואביו מועטין. קם דינא. אחר שנעשה דין בנכסי המת אין זה יכול לחזור ולערער עליהם, ומה שהוא שואל בנכסי היבם – אמרי ליה: אייתי ראיה. הדר דינא. ומהדרי ליה פלגא דנכסי מיתנא, או פלג כולהו נכסי בשוה. ואבדה דרך שדהו. שהיתה שדהו מוקפת משדות אחרים, והיה לו דרך על אחת מן הרוחות ואבדה, ששכחו על איזה מן הרוחות היתה. ילך בקצרה. יתנו ביניהם דרך קצרה, ולקמן מפרש לה. שפיר קאמר אדמון. קסלקא דעתא שהקיפו אדם אחד מכל רוחותיו, דאמר: אורחיה גביה הוא. ארבעה בני אדם. דכל חד וחד מדחי ליה. דאתו מכח ארבעה. שארבעה אנשים מכרום לאלו. אי שתקת שתקת. ולא אעלה עליך בדמים יקרים.

דרכי

יחודי בעלמא הוו מיחדי. ויש כאן פת בסלו, כיון שאם היה רוצה (ב)היה בא עליה. וכיון שפעמים לא היה בא עליה – לא מיתמדא ולא חזיא. דאי לא תימא הכי – גם להתיחד הוה אסור, כדאמר בפ"ק דכתובות (דף ד. ושם) גבי חתן, אם פרסה אשתו נדה – הוא ישן בין האנשים ואשתו ישנה בין הנשים. ומשום נושא אשה במדינה אחרת נמי ליכא למיחש, שאם היה אירע שבא עליה ונתעברה ממנו היה מוליכה עמו לעירו*.

וממון המוטל בספק חולקים. אפילו רבנן דסומכוס (ב"ק לה:) מודו הכא, דלא שייך כאן המוציא מחבירו עליו הראיה, שאין זה מוחזק יותר מזה, והוי כמו הללו באין לירש והללו באין לירש, דאמר ב"מי שמת" (ב"ב דף קנח:) דיחלוקו. אמר רבי אבא קם דינא. דוקא בתר דפלג, אבל מקמי דפלג – לא. דאמר ליה אי שתקת שתקת. פי': ולא תטול כלום. ולא כמו שפירש בקונט' אי שתקת ומוזילנא לך, דהא קתני יקח לו דרך במאה מנה. ובפ"ק דב"ק (דף ח.) גבי מכרן לאחד כולן נכנסו תחת הבעלים, והויא אשה בזיבורית אע"פ שלקח עידית באחרונה, משום אי שתקת כו' ולא מצי אמרה ליה: לכי תהדר. כיון שאין בא להפקיע מדינא. ובחד דאתי מכח חד לא מצי למימר ואי לא מזבנינא לארבעה – דהא פשיטא, כיון דלא אתי מכח ארבעה – לא שבקינן ליה. ואם תאמר: וארבעה דאתו מכח חד, ליהדר ההוא חד דמי קצרה! וי"ל: דמצי אמר ליה: לא מכרתי אלא מה שיש לי בה.

הוי

כד א מיי' פט"ו מהל' איסורי ביאה הלכה כט:
כה ב ג מיי' פכ"א שם הלכה כט סמג לאוין קכו טוש"ע אה"ע סימן ב סעיף יא:
[ועי' תוס' יומא יח: ד"ה יחודי]
כו ד מיי' פי"א שם הלכה ט סמג לאוין קיא ועשין רמג טוש"ע יד סימן קצב סעיף א:
כז ה מיי' פ"י מהל' גרושין הלכה כא סמג עשין נ טוש"ע אה"ע סימן ב סעיף י וסימן קיט סעיף א:
כח ו מיי' פ"ה מהל' נחלות הלכה ד סמג עשין צ טוש"ע שם סימן קסג סעי' ג:
כט ז מיי' שם טוש"ע שם סעיף ד:
ל ח מיי' שם הלכה ה טוש"ע שם סעי' ה:
לא ט מיי' פט"ו מהל' טוען ונטען הלכה יא טוש"ע ח"מ סימן קמח סעיף ב:
לב י כ ל מיי' שם טוש"ע שם וסעיף א:

נ"ל אשה

[תוספתא דקידושין פ"ה]
[נדרים נא.]
[יומא יח: ע"ש]
שם
ג"ז שם יוד סו.
יומא יח: סז. עד: כתובות סב: סג.
[גיטין ל. כ"ש הטיוב]
לקמן ק:
כתובות קטו: כה"ע

תוספות ישנים

כי פליגי בחד דאתי מכח ארבעה ולא קאמר א) משום דמצי למוכרם לארבעה דאין לנו להעמיד הדבר אלא במה שהוא או במה שהיה: אי לייתת פ"ה ותקח דרך במאה מנה. ותימה דא"ל לכשתהדר שהרי מה יכול להפסידו יותר וא"ל דמוזיל גביה דהא קאמר לעיל יקח לו דרך במאה מנה ואין זה זול. וי"ל דכיון שלקח מהארבעה חשבינן כאילו מוחזר השמקח כבר ולא שייך לכשתהדר וא"כ קאמר ליה אי שתקת שתקת ותקנה ממני ביוקר:

א) חסר כאן וצ"ל ולא קאמר בחד דאתי מכח חד משום דמצי למוכרם וכו' וכ"ה בתוס' כאן בד"ה דאמר ובחד דאתי מכח חד לא מצי למימר וכו'.

תוספות חד מקמאי

ספק ובני יבם שבאו לחלוק בנכסי מיתנא ספק אמר בר מיתנא אנא ונכסי דידי הוו. ובני יבם אמרי ליה את אחינו את ומנתא הוא דאית לך. כתב ר"ש ז"ל דמאי דמודו ליה שקיל והשאר הוי ממון המוטל בספק ויחלוקו והכי משמע במסקנא דשמעתתא. ספק ובני יבם שבאו לחלוק בנכסי יבם בתר דפלג יבם בנכסי (אלמנה) מיתנא. אמר להו ספק אי אחוכון אנא הבו לי א) נכסי דפליג אבוכון בנכסי. ר' אבא אמר קם דינא. ר' ירמיה אמר הדר דינא. משמע לכאורה מדקאמר לבתר דפלג יבם בנכסי מיתנא הא מקמי דפליג בנכסי מיתנא דכ"ע אמר להו מ"נ דלא שייך למימר קם דינא כיון דלא פלג בנכסי ומיהו בפלוגתא דאדמון ורבנן איכא לעיוני בהא מילתא דהא לא קם דינא בהדיה ואפ"ה אמרו רבנן קם דינא. ופסק הרב אלפס כר' אבא דאמר קם דינא כיון דקאי כרבנן. ואע"ג דאמרי' אמר לך ר' ירמיה אנא דאמרי אפילו לרבנן שנויא דחיקא היא. ואע"ג דאיתא בפ' בית כור שני אחים שחלקו ובא להן אח ממדינת הים רב אמר בטלה מחלוקת וקי"ל כוותיה אלמא הדר דינא שאני התם דחלוקה בטעות הוא והרב ר' אפרים (מה') פסק כר' ירמיה: ספק ויבם שבאו לחלוק בנכסי סבא בספק א' אנא בר מיתנא ופלגא דידי ויבם אמר את ברי ולית ליך ולא מידי הוה יבם ודאי וספק ספק ואין ספק מוציא מידי ודאי. סבא ויבם שבאו לחלוק בנכסי

ספק

הגהות הב"ח

(א) רש"י ד"ה ממון וכו' מוחזק בנכסי יותר מזה: (ב) תוס' ד"ה יחודי וכו' היה בא עליה וכו' ועיין ביאור ליבור זה בתשובות ב"ח סימן פ"ב.

דִּרְכִּי חַד גַּבָּךְ הוּא, אֲבָל הָכָא — מִי אִיכָּא לְמֵימַר? הָכִי וְרַבִּי יִרְמְיָה אָמַר לָךְ: אֲנָא דַּאֲמָרִי אֲפִי' לְרַבָּנַן, עַד כָּאן לָא קָאָמְרִי רַבָּנַן הָתָם אֶלָּא מִשּׁוּם דְּא"ל: אִי שָׁתְקַתְּ — שָׁתְקַתְּ, וְאִי לָא — מַהֲדַרְנָא שְׁטָרָא לְמָרֵייהוּ, וְלָא מָצֵית לְאִשְׁתַּעוּיֵי דִּינָא בַּהֲדַיְיהוּ. אֲבָל הָכָא — מִי אִיכָּא לְמֵימַר הָכִי? [א]סָפֵק וְיָבָם שֶׁבָּאוּ לַחֲלוֹק בְּנִכְסֵי סָבָא, סָפֵק אָמַר: הַאי גַּבְרָא בַּר מִיתְנָא הוּא, וּפַלְגָּא דִּידִי הוּא. יָבָם אָמַר: אַתְּ בְּרַאי דִּידִי אַתְּ, וְלֵית לָךְ וְלָא מִידֵי, הָוֵי יָבָם וַדַּאי, וְסָפֵק סָפֵק — *וְאֵין סָפֵק מוֹצִיא מִידֵי וַדַּאי. [ב]סָפֵק וּבְנֵי יָבָם שֶׁבָּאוּ לַחֲלוֹק בְּנִכְסֵי סָבָא, סָפֵק אָמַר: הַהוּא גַּבְרָא בַּר מִיתְנָא הוּא, וּפַלְגָּא דִּידִי הוּא. וּבְנֵי יָבָם אָמְרִי: אָחוּנָא אַתְּ, וּמְנָתָא אִית לָךְ בַּהֲדַן. פַּלְגָּא דְּקָמוֹדֵי לְהוּ — שָׁקְלִי, תִּילְתָּא דְּקָא מוֹדוּ לֵיהּ — שָׁקַל. פָּשׁ לְהוּ דַּנְקָא, הָוֵי מָמוֹן הַמּוּטָּל בְּסָפֵק — וְחוֹלְקִין. [ג]סָבָא וְיָבָם בְּנִכְסֵי סָפֵק, אוֹ סָבָא וְסָפֵק בְּנִכְסֵי יָבָם — הָוֵי מָמוֹן הַמּוּטָּל בְּסָפֵק, וְחוֹלְקִין.§ **מתני'** *[ד]שׁוֹמֶרֶת יָבָם שֶׁנָּפְלוּ לָהּ נְכָסִים, מוֹדִים ב"ש וב"ה שֶׁמּוֹכֶרֶת וְנוֹתֶנֶת וְקַיָּים. מֵתָה — מַה יַּעֲשׂוּ בִּכְתוּבָּתָהּ וּבִנְכָסִים הַנִּכְנָסִים וְיוֹצְאִין עִמָּהּ? ב"ש אוֹמְרִים: יַחֲלוֹקוּ יוֹרְשֵׁי הַבַּעַל עִם יוֹרְשֵׁי הָאָב, וב"ה אוֹמְרִים: [ה]נְכָסִים בְּחֶזְקָתָן: כְּתוּבָּה בְּחֶזְקַת יוֹרְשֵׁי הַבַּעַל, נְכָסִים הַנִּכְנָסִים וְיוֹצְאִין עִמָּהּ בְּחֶזְקַת יוֹרְשֵׁי הָאָב. *[ו]כְּנָסָהּ — הֲרֵי הִיא כְּאִשְׁתּוֹ לְכָל דָּבָר, *[ז]וּבִלְבַד שֶׁתְּהֵא כְּתוּבָּה עַל נִכְסֵי בַּעְלָהּ הָרִאשׁוֹן.§ **גמ'** מ"ש רֵישָׁא דְּלָא פְּלִיגִי, וּמ"ש סֵיפָא דִּפְלִיגִי? אָמַר עוּלָּא: רֵישָׁא — דְּנָפְלָה כְּשֶׁהִיא אֲרוּסָה, וְסֵיפָא — דְּנָפְלָה כְּשֶׁהִיא נְשׂוּאָה. וְקָסָבַר עוּלָּא: זִיקַת אֲרוּסָה — עוֹשָׂה סָפֵק אֲרוּסָה, זִיקַת

רש"י

דִּרְכִּי חַד אִית לִי גַּבָּךְ. וְטַעֲנַת בָּרִי הוּא, דְּיָדַע מַאי קָתָבַע מִינֵּיהּ. מִי אִיכָּא לְמֵימַר הָכִי. הָא לָא יָדַע מַאי קָא תָּבַע מִינֵּיהּ, אִי פַּלְגָּא בְּנִכְסֵי מִיתְנָא (א) אִי פַּלְגָּא מְנָתָא בְּנִכְסֵי יָבָם. וּמִכֹּחַ שְׁתֵּי טְעָנוֹת הוּא בָּא עֲלֵיהֶם, בְּכָל אַחַת וְאַחַת אוֹמְרִים לוֹ: הָבֵא רְאָיָה. סָבָא. אֲבִי הַמֵּת וְהַיָּבָם. הָוֵי יָבָם וַדַּאי. יוֹרֵשׁ, וְיוֹדֵעַ מִכֹּחַ מִי הוּא בָּא וּמוּחְזָק בַּנְּכָסִים, וְלָא דָּמֵי לְהַהִיא דְּרַב מְשַׁרְשְׁיָא דִּלְעֵיל, דְּהָתָם, אַע"ג דְּסָפֵק אִית לֵיהּ זְכִיָּה בַּנְּכָסִים מִמַּה נַּפְשָׁךְ, אֲפִילּוּ הָכִי לָא חֲשִׁיב וַדַּאי, דְּלָא יָדַע מִכֹּחַ מִי הוּא בָּא לִירַשׁ, מִכֹּחַ מַה הוּא בָּא עֲלֵיהֶן. פַּלְגָּא דְּקָא מוֹדֶה לְהוּ שָׁקְלִי. מִשִּׁשָּׁה זְהוּבִים נוֹטְלִין שְׁלֹשָׁה. תִּילְתָּא דְּקָא מוֹדוּ לֵיהּ. שְׁנֵי זְהוּבִים תִּילְתָּא דְּכוּלְּהוּ נִכְסֵי. שָׁקֵיל. דְּהָא אָמְרוּ לֵיהּ אָחוּנָא אַתְּ, וְאִינְהוּ הָווּ תְּרֵי וְאִיהוּ שְׁלִישִׁי. פָּשׁ דַּנְקָא. דְּקָמִינְּצוּ עֲלֵיהּ. הַאי אָמַר: כּוּלֵּיהּ דִּידִי, וְהָנֵי אָמְרִי: כּוּלֵּיהּ דִּידַן. הוּא נוֹטֵל חֶצְיוֹ, וּבֵין שְׁנֵיהֶם חֶצְיוֹ. סָבָא וְיָבָם בְּנִכְסֵי סָפֵק. סָבָא אָמַר: הַאי בַּר מִיתְנָא הוּא, וְכֵיוָן דְּאֵין לוֹ יוֹרֵשׁ אֲנִי קוֹדֵם, דִּתְנַן (ב"ב דף קטו.): הָאָב קוֹדֵם לְכָל יוֹצְאֵי יְרֵכוֹ, וְיָבָם אָמַר בְּנִי הוּא וַאֲנִי יוֹרְשׁוֹ דְּהָאָב קוֹדֵם. אוֹ סָבָא וְסָפֵק בְּנִכְסֵי יָבָם. שֶׁאֵין לַיָּבָם בֵּן אַחֵר. סָבָא אָמַר: אַתְּ בַּר מִיתְנָא, וַאֲנִי יוֹרֵשׁ אֶת בְּנִי מָקוֹם שֶׁאֵין לוֹ בֵּן, וְסָפֵק אָמַר: בְּנוֹ אֲנִי, וַאֲנִי יוֹרְשׁוֹ. חוֹלְקִין. דְּדִלְמָא כּוּלְּהוּ דְּהַאי וְדִלְמָא כּוּלְּהוּ דְּהַאי. וְאֵין לוֹמַר הָאָב וַדַּאי מוּחְזָק, דְּאִם זֶה בְּנוֹ — אֵין כָּאן לָאָב כְּלוּם. **מתני'** שׁוֹמֶרֶת יָבָם. מַמְתֶּנֶת וּמְצַפָּה לַיָּבָם, כְּמוֹ: עֲנִיָּה זוֹ לַשָּׁוְא שָׁמְרָה, בְּ"אַף עַל פִּי" בִּכְתוּבּוֹת (דף סג:). שֶׁנָּפְלוּ לָהּ נְכָסִים. מֵאָבִיהָ. וְסָלְקָא דַּעְתָּן שֶׁנָּפְלוּ לָהּ כְּשֶׁהִיא שׁוֹמֶרֶת יָבָם. וּבִנְכָסִים הַנִּכְנָסִים וְיוֹצְאִים עִמָּהּ. הַיְינוּ נִכְסֵי מְלוֹג, שֶׁהַקֶּרֶן שֶׁלָּהּ קַיָּים, וּכְשֶׁהִיא נִכְנֶסֶת נִכְנָסִין עִמָּהּ, וּכְשֶׁהִיא יוֹצֵאת יוֹצְאִין עִמָּהּ: ה"ג. ב"ש אוֹמְרִים יַחֲלוֹקוּ יוֹרְשֵׁי הַבַּעַל עִם יוֹרְשֵׁי הָאָב. דְּסָפֵק נְשׂוּאָה הִיא, וְזָכָה הַיָּבָם בַּחֲצִי יְרוּשָּׁתוֹ מִסָּפֵק. שֶׁהַבַּעַל יוֹרֵשׁ אֶת אִשְׁתּוֹ, וְזוֹ שֶׁסָּפֵק נְשׂוּאָה הִיא אֶצְלוֹ זָכֵי בְּפַלְגָּא. אֲבָל בִּכְתוּבָּתָהּ מוֹדִים ב"ש דִּבְחֶזְקַת הַבַּעַל הִיא, וְלָא פָּלְגִי בָּהּ יוֹרְשֵׁי הָאָב. וְטַעְמָא דְּכוּלָּהּ מַתְנִיתִין מְפָרֵשׁ בַּגְּמָ'. **גמ'** מַאי שְׁנָא רֵישָׁא דְּל"פ וּמ"ש סֵיפָא דִּפְלִיגִי ב"ש. מַאי שְׁנָא רֵישָׁא כְּשֶׁהִיא קַיֶּימֶת דְּלָא פְּלִיגִי ב"ש, אֶלָּא בְּכֹחַ דִּילָהּ מַחְזְקִינַן לְנִכְסֵי, דְּקָאָמְרִי: מוֹכֶרֶת וְנוֹתֶנֶת לְכַתְּחִלָּה, וּמַאי שְׁנָא סֵיפָא, דִּפְלִיגִי כְּשֶׁמֵּתָה לָא מוֹקְמִי נִכְסֵי מְלוֹג בְּחֶזְקַת יוֹרְשֶׁיהָ? ה"ג. אָמַר עוּלָּא רֵישָׁא דְּנָפְלָה כְּשֶׁהִיא אֲרוּסָה. שֶׁנָּפְלָה לְיִיבּוּם מֵאֵירוּסִין, וְנָפְלוּ הַנְּכָסִים לָהּ כְּשֶׁהִיא שׁוֹמֶרֶת יָבָם. סֵיפָא דְּנָפְלָה. לְפָנָיו לְיִיבּוּם. כְּשֶׁהִיא נְשׂוּאָה. הִלְכָּךְ רֵישָׁא דִּלְגַבֵּי אֲרוּסָה מַמָּשׁ קי"ל לְב"ש תִּמְכּוֹר, כְּדִתְנַן לְקַמָּן, כ"ש זוֹ שֶׁאֵינָהּ אֶלָּא זְקוּקָה בְּעָלְמָא. וּב"ה דְּאָמְרִי בַּאֲרוּסָה וַדַּאי לֹא תִּמְכּוֹר לְכַתְּחִלָּה, אֲבָל אִם מָכְרָה וְנָתְנָה קַיָּים, הָכָא מִשּׁוּם דְּסָפֵק אֲרוּסָה הִיא דַּאֲגִידָא בֵּיהּ, וְלָאו אִשְׁתּוֹ מַמָּשׁ הִיא — מוֹדוּ ב"ה דְּמוֹכֶרֶת וְנוֹתֶנֶת לְכַתְּחִלָּה. סֵיפָא

תוספות

הוי יבם ודאי וספק ספק. פי' בקונטרס: ודאי – שיודע מאיזה כח הוא בא, ומוחזק בנכסים, ולא דמי להוא דרב משרשיא דלעיל, דהתם אע"ג דספק אית ליה בנכסים זכיה ממה נפשך – אפ"ה לא חשיב ודאי, דלא ידע מכח מי הוא בא עליהם. משמע מתוך פירושו דקרי ודאי מה שודאי נוטל חלק בנכסים, ובפרק "מי שמת" (ב"ב דף קנח: ושם), גבי הא דתנן נפל הבית עליו ועל אמו (ב) אלו ואלו מודים שיחלוקו, פירש רבינו שמואל שיחלוקו יורשי האם, דהיינו: אחי האם מאביה, עם יורשי הבן, היינו: אחי הבן מן האב ראובן. ולא רצה לפרש יורשי האם – בני האם דהיינו אחי הבן מן האם דהיינו בנימין – דא"כ ה"ל בנימין ודאי וראובן ספק ואין ספק מוציא מידי ודאי. ואין נראה כלל, דאטו מפני שהוא ודאי במקצת הנכסים יהא ודאי בכולן?! ועוד: דאמר התם, ומייתי ליה לקמן גבי נפל הבית עליו ועל אביו [עליו] ועל מורישיו, והיתה עליו כתובת אשה וב"ח כו', ומסיק דיורשי האב – אחי הבן. אלמא, אע"ג דיש לאב בנים אחרים לא חשבינן להו ודאי. וכן בפ"ק דב"ק (דף ט. ושם) גבי אחים שחלקו ובא ב"ח ונטל חלקו של אחד מהן, דאמר רב אסי: נוטל רביע בקרקע או רביע במעות, משום דמספקא ליה אי כיורשים דמו אי כלקוחות, ולא אמרי' שלא יטול כלום – שהרי זה המוחזק הוא ודאי במקצת נכסים. וכן זה אומר כולה שלי וזה אומר חציה שלי גבי "שנים אוחזים בטלית" (ב"מ דף ב.). אלא הא דקרי הכא יבם ודאי, היינו: משום שהיבם הוא ודאי יורשו של סבא, אבל ספק – הוא ספק אם הוא יורשו כלל. אבל התם, בנפל עליו ועל אמו – לא הוי בנימין ודאי יורש בכל חצי האחר. דאם מתה רחל קודם יוסף – הוי ראובן נמי יורשו. וכן בנפל הבית עליו ועל אביו, אם מת האב קודם – הוי בעל חוב יורש, ולא בן האחר. **ובית** הלל אומרים הנכסים בחזקתן. בפרק "מי שמת" (ב"ב קנח. ושם) פליגי בכהאי גוונא ב"ש וב"ה, גבי נפל הבית עליו ועל אשתו, וקאמר בגמ' בחזקת מי? פירוש: בית הלל דקאמרי נכסים בחזקתן, דהיינו נכסי צאן ברזל – בחזקת מי? ר' אלעזר אומר: בחזקת יורשי האשה, רבי יוחנן אמר: בחזקת יורשי הבעל. וריש לקיש אמר: יחלוקו. ופי' בקונטרס בפרק "האשה שנפלו" (כתובות דף פ: ושם): דכי היכי דפליגי התם – הכי נמי פליגי אמתניתין דהכא! ורבינו תם אומר דלא דמיא הך להתם. דהכא לא פליגי ב"ש בכתובה אלא בנכסי מלוג, כדאמר בגמ' דכתובה שיירה, מדקתני יחלוקו יורשי הבעל עם יורשי אב כו', אבל התם קתני סתמא יחלוקו, משמע דבכתובה נמי פליגי. והיינו טעמא: דהתם, אם הבעל מת תחלה – הויא האשה כמו שגבתה כתובתה, אבל הכא שהיא זקוקה ליבם – אין לאשה כלום בנכסי הבעל עד אחר החליצה, דלא ניתנה כתובה לגבות מחיים, ואפשר דכולהו אמוראי מודו הכא דנכסי צאן ברזל הוי בחזקת יורשי הבעל. והא דלא ערבינהו עם כתובה – כדי ליתן טעם לדבר. כלומר: בחזקת מי שהיו עד עתה, דהיינו בחזקת הבעל. אבל בכתובה – דבר פשוט הוא יותר שהיא בחזקת הבעל מנכסי צאן ברזל שהיא הביאה מבית אביה ושמה אותם לבעל. וכן צ"ל למאן דאמר התם בחזקת יורשי הבעל. ואם תאמר: ולמאן דאמר בחזקת יורשי האשה – מ"ש מנפל הבית עליו ועל אמו, דמודים בית הלל שיחלוקו ולא מוקמינן להו בחזקת יורשי האם? ויש לומר: דשמא קסבר ההוא תנא דירושת יורשי הבעל דרבנן. א"נ: אפילו קסבר דהוי דאורייתא, כיון דלאו מכח קורבה קאתין – מוקמינן להו בחזקת האשה טפי. א"נ: משום הכי לא מוקמינן להו התם בחזקת יורשי האם, משום דרגילות הוא שהאם היא מתה קודם, דקא חשיב בריש "יש נוחלין" (ב"ב דף קח.) פורענות כשהבן מת תחלה, לפיכך לא החזיקום בחזקת האם. ואם תאמר: ויורשי האשה היכי גבו כתובה? (ג) הא קי"ל כרב ושמואל דאמרי בפרק "כל הנשבעין" (שבועות דף מז.) דאין אדם מוריש שבועה לבניו! ומיהו, לב"ש ניחא, דאית להו: שטר העומד לגבות – כגבוי דמי, והוו כמוחזקין בממון. דכמה ברייתות דפריך מינייהו לרב ושמואל בשבועות (ד) משני התם דאתא כב"ש. ולר"א דאמר בחזקת יורשי האשה – ניחא, דאיהו פליג בהדיא בשבועות (דף מח.), אדרב ושמואל, אבל ר' יוחנן, דאמר בחזקת יורשי הבעל, ופי' דנכסים בחזקתם הוא טעם לדבר – למה לי? תיפוק ליה דאין אדם מוריש שבועה לבניו! ויש לומר, דהיא הנותנת: דלפי שהנכסים בחזקת הבעל (ה) אינה מורשת. שאם היו בחזקת האשה היתה מורשת, כמו לבית שמאי דאמרי כגבוי דמי. אי נמי, אר"י: דאיכא לאוקמי במטלטלי, ואיתנהו בעינייהו, שנוטל בלא שבועה. והא דלא משני הכי בשבועות, אלא דוחק להעמידה כב"ש, משום דהתם בכתובה איירי, אבל הכא דאיירי בנכסי צאן ברזל שהביא' מבית אביה, דרגילין להיות בעינייהו, דאין דרך לבעלה למכרן. ואיכא למ"ד לקמן (דף סו:) המכנסת שום לבעלה, אם רצה הבעל למכור – לא ימכור. זיקת

עין משפט נר מצוה

לג א מיי' פ"ה מהלכות נחלות הלכה ד ה סמג עשין צו טוש"ע אה"ע סימן קסג סעיף ו:
לד ב מיי' שם טוש"ע שם סעיף ז:
לה ג מיי' שם טוש"ע שם סעיף ח:
לו ד מיי' פכ"ב מהל' אישות הלכה י ופ"ג מהלכות נחלות הלכה י סמג עשין נא טוש"ע אה"ע סימן קס סעיף ה:
לז ה טוש"ע שם ס"ו:
לח ו מיי' שם טוש"ע אה"ע סי' קסח ס"א:
לט ז מיי' שם ופ"א מהלכות יבום הל' א טוש"ע אה"ע שם סעיף ג וסימן קסו סעיף ד:

תוספות חד מקמאי

ספק או סבא וספק בנכסי יבם חולקין: **מתניתין** שומרת יבם שנפלו לה נכסים מודים ב"ש וב"ה שמוכרת ונותנת וקיים מתה מה יעשו בכתובתה ובנכסים הנכנסין והיוצאין עמהם ב"ש אומרים יחלוקו וב"ה אומרים נכסים בחזקתן וכתובתה בחזקת יורשי הבעל נכסים הנכנסים והיוצאים עמהן בחזקת יורשי האב וה"ה לנצ"ב שהן בחזקת יורשי הבעל כדין כתובתה ואע"ג דגבי נפל הבית עליו ועל אשתו נצ"ב יחלוקו יורשי הבעל עם יורשי האב שאני הכא כיון דשומרת יבם היא יבם במקום בעל קאי וכשם שהוא מוחזק בכתובה כך הוא מוחזק בנצ"ב והרמב"ם כתב גבי שומרת יבם נמי יחלוקו מסקנא דשמעתתא אליבא דהלכתא שומרת יבם מן הארוסין כל הנכסים בחזקתן ל"ש נפלו לה בחיי ארוס ל"ש נפלו לה כשהיא שומרת יבם ל"ש עבד בה מאמר ול"ש לא עבד בה מאמר ל"ש בחייה ולפירות ול"ש מתה ולגוף הנכסים ואם היתה שומרת יבם מן הנשואין ונפלו לה נכסים כשהיא שומרת יבם מוכרת ונותנת נכסים הנכנסין והיוצאים עמה וקיים ואפלו עשה בה מאמר ואם מתה נכסים בחזקתן כתובה ונצ"ב בחזקת יורשי הבעל. נ"מ בחזקת יורשי האב ואפי' עשה בה מאמר ואם היתה שומרת יבם מן הנשואין ונפלו לה נכסים כשהיא תחת בעלה קי"ל כרבא דאמר ידו עדיפא מידה ל"ש עבד בה מאמר ל"ש לא עביד בה מאמר והשתא כשמת הבעל קלישא ליה וידו כידה ויחלוקו הנכנסים הנכנסים והיוצאין עמה. אבל לאביי דאמר אליבא דב"ה דידו כידה השתא כשמת הבעל קלישא ליה ידו ונכסים בחזקת יורשי האב. מיהו קי"ל כרבא ויחלוקו ואע"ג דאמר רב פפא דייקא מתני' כותיה דאביי הלכתא כותיה דרבא דקי"ל כל היכא דפליגי אביי ורבא הלכה כרבא בר מיע"ל קג"ם הלכך הלכתא כרבא ויחלוקו. וי"מ אליבא דרבא דאמר ידו עדיפא מידה נכסים בחזקת יבם. ורש"י כתב ויחלוקו והא דאמר ואע"ג דקשיא מתה לאביי ה"ה לרבא נמי קשיא אדמפלגי לאחר מיתה לפלגו בחייה ולפירות דאליבא דב"ש יחלוקו. וי"מ דלרבא לא קשיא מתה א) דבמתה ה"ה יחלוקו לכ"ע הואיל והללו באים לירש אבל בחייה נכסים בחזקתן אפי' לב"ש אפי' עבד לה מאמר ב) ולפי הפירוש הזה לא הוה צריך לאוקמי רישא בדלא עבד לה מאמר. וה"ל לאוקמי רישא וסיפא בחד טעמא בדעבד לה מאמר:

א) ר"ל כנפלו לה נכסים מתחתי דבעל ול"ש נפלו לה כשהיא שומרת יבם לב"ש יחלוקו. ב) עי' תוס' לקמן לט ד"ה אע"ג.

כתב

מסורת הש"ס

לעיל יט: פסחים ע. וש"נ
כתובות פ:
[לעיל יט: כתובות פ:]
לקמן נב. [פס. כתובות נג: פ:]

הגהות הב"ח

(א) רש"י ד"ה מי איכא וכו' פלגא בנכסי מיתנא אי מנתא כצ"ל ותיבת פלגא נמחק: (ב) תוס' ד"ה הוי יבם וכו' עליו ועל אמו כגון יוסף ורחל אלו ואלו מודים שיחלוקו פי' רבינו שמואל שיחלוקו יורשי האם והיינו אחי האם מן האב לבן עם יורשי הבן: (ג) ד"ה ובית הלל וכו' היכי גבו כתובה. נ"ב כלומר הלא מחוייבת שבועה היתה וכיון שמתה ולא נשבעה הוי מוריש שבועה לבניו [והשאר חסר]: (ד) בא"ד לרב ושמואל בשבועות וקא משני התם. נ"ב כלומר על חדא ברייתא מהנך ברייתות קא משני הא מני ב"ש היא דאמר שטר העומד לגבות כגבוי דמי אלמא דלב"ש ניחא דיכולה להוריש שבועה כיון דהוי כמו שמוחזקין בממון: (ה) בא"ד בחזקת הבעל לכך אינה מורשת שאם היו בחזקת וכו' דאין דרך בעלה למכרן:

מ א ב מיי' פכ"ב מהל' אישות הל' ז סמג לאוין סא טור ש"ע אה"ע סי' צ סעיף יא וסימן קס סעיף ה:

מא ג מיי' שם טוש"ע שם סימן צ סעיף ט:

מב ד מיי' פ"ה מהל' נחלות הלכה ח סמג עשין צו טוש"ע ח"מ סי' רפ סעיף יב:

מג ה מיי' פ"ב מהל' סוטה הל' א סמג עשין מח טור אה"ע סימן קטו וסימן קעח:

תורה אור

זִיקַת נְשׂוּאָה עוֹשָׂה סָפֵק נְשׂוּאָה. זִיקַת אֲרוּסָה עוֹשָׂה סָפֵק אֲרוּסָה, דְּאִי ס"ד וַדַּאי אֲרוּסָה – מוֹדִים ב"ה שֶׁמּוֹכֶרֶת וְנוֹתֶנֶת וְקַיָּים?! וְהָתְנַן: *נָפְלוּ לָהּ נְכָסִים מִשֶּׁנִּתְאָרְסָה, ב"ש אוֹמְרִים: תִּמְכּוֹר, וּב"ה אוֹמְרִים: אלֹא תִּמְכּוֹר. אֵלּוּ וָאֵלּוּ מוֹדִים בשֶׁאִם מָכְרָה וְנָתְנָה – קַיָּים. אֶלָּא ש"מ: זִיקַת אֲרוּסָה – עוֹשָׂה סָפֵק אֲרוּסָה. זִיקַת נְשׂוּאָה עוֹשָׂה סָפֵק נְשׂוּאָה, דְּאִי ס"ד וַדַּאי נְשׂוּאָה ב"ש אוֹמְרִים יַחֲלוֹקוּ יוֹרְשֵׁי הַבַּעַל עִם יוֹרְשֵׁי הָאָב?! וְהָתְנַן: *נָפְלוּ לָהּ נְכָסִים מִשֶּׁנִּישֵּׂאת – אֵלּוּ וָאֵלּוּ מוֹדִים גשֶׁאִם מָכְרָה וְנָתְנָה שֶׁהַבַּעַל מוֹצִיא מִיַּד הַלָּקוּחוֹת. אֶלָּא שְׁמַע מִינָּהּ: זִיקַת נְשׂוּאָה עוֹשָׂה סָפֵק נְשׂוּאָה. אֲמַר לֵיהּ רַבָּה: אַדְּמִפַּלְגִי בְּגוּפָהּ וּלְאַחַר מִיתָה, לִפְלְגוּ בְּחַיֶּיהָ וּלְפֵירוֹת! אֶלָּא אֲמַר רַבָּה: אִידִי וְאִידִי דְּנָפְלָה כְּשֶׁהִיא נְשׂוּאָה, וְזִיקַת נְשׂוּאָה – עוֹשָׂה סָפֵק נְשׂוּאָה. רֵישָׁא דְּאִיהִי קַיְימָא – הֲוָה לָהּ אִיהִי וַדַּאי וְאִינְהוּ סָפֵק *וְאֵין סָפֵק מוֹצִיא מִידֵי וַדַּאי. סֵיפָא דְּמֵתָה – הַלָּלוּ בָּאִין לִירַשׁ וְהַלָּלוּ בָּאִין לִירַשׁ, וְיַחֲלוֹקוּ. אֵיתִיבֵיהּ אַבַּיֵי: וּלְב"ש אֵין סָפֵק מוֹצִיא מִידֵי וַדַּאי?! וְהָתְנַן: *נָפַל הַבַּיִת עָלָיו וְעַל אָבִיו, עָלָיו וְעַל מוֹרִישָׁיו, וְהָיוּ עָלָיו כְּתוּבַּת אִשָּׁה וּבַ"ח, יוֹרְשֵׁי הָאָב אוֹמְרִים: הַבֵּן מֵת רִאשׁוֹן וְאַחַר כָּךְ מֵת הָאָב. וּבַ"ח אוֹמֵר: הָאָב מֵת רִאשׁוֹן וְאח"כ מֵת הַבֵּן, ב"ש אוֹמְרִים: יַחֲלוֹקוּ, וּב"ה אוֹמְרִים: דנְכָסִים בְּחֶזְקָתָן. וְהָא הָכָא, יוֹרְשֵׁי הָאָב – וַדַּאי, וּבַ"ח – סָפֵק, וְקָאָתֵי סָפֵק וּמוֹצִיא מִידֵי וַדַּאי! קָסָבְרִי ב"ש: *שְׁטָר הָעוֹמֵד לִגְבּוֹת כִּגְבוּי דָּמֵי. וּמְנָא תֵּימְרָא – דִּתְנַן: *מֵתוּ בַּעֲלֵיהֶן עַד שֶׁלֹּא שָׁתוּ, ב"ש אוֹמְרִים: נוֹטְלוֹת כְּתוּבָּתָן וְאֵינָן שׁוֹתוֹת, וּב"ה אוֹמְרִים: אוֹ שׁוֹתוֹת אוֹ לֹא נוֹטְלוֹת כְּתוּבָּתָן. אוֹ שׁוֹתוֹת?! °"וְהֵבִיא הָאִישׁ אֶת אִשְׁתּוֹ" אָמַר רַחֲמָנָא, וְלֵיכָּא! אֶלָּא: המִתּוֹךְ שֶׁלֹּא שׁוֹתוֹת לֹא נוֹטְלוֹת כְּתוּבָּתָן. וְהָא הָכָא, דְּסָפֵק הוּא, סָפֵק זַנַּאי סָפֵק לֹא זַנַּאי, וְקָאָתֵי סָפֵק וּמוֹצִיא מִידֵי וַדַּאי! אֶלָּא ש"מ: *שְׁטָר הָעוֹמֵד לִגְבּוֹת כִּגְבוּי דָּמֵי. וְאַבַּיֵי, לוֹתְבֵיהּ מֵהָא! דִּלְמָא כְּתוּבַּת אִשָּׁה שָׁאנֵי, מִשּׁוּם *חִינָּא. וְלוֹתְבֵיהּ כְּתוּבָּה דְּמַתְנִיתִין! לָא פְּלִיגִי. וְלָא? וְהָא *)קָתָנֵי: מֵתָה, מַה יֵּעָשֶׂה בִּכְתוּבָּתָהּ וּבִנְכָסִים הַנִּכְנָסִים וְיוֹצְאִין עִמָּהּ? ב"ש אוֹמְרִים: יַחֲלוֹקוּ יוֹרְשֵׁי הַבַּעַל עִם יוֹרְשֵׁי הָאָב, וּב"ה אוֹמְרִים: נְכָסִים בְּחֶזְקָתָן! הָכִי קָאָמַר: מֵתָה, מַה יֵּעָשֶׂה בִּכְתוּבָּתָהּ, וּשְׁבָקָהּ. נְכָסִים הַנִּכְנָסִים וְהַיּוֹצְאִים עִמָּהּ, ב"ש אוֹמְרִים: יַחֲלוֹקוּ יוֹרְשֵׁי הַבַּעַל עִם יוֹרְשֵׁי הָאָב, וּב"ה אוֹמְרִים: נְכָסִים בְּחֶזְקָתָן. א] אֲמַר רַב אַשִׁי: מַתְנִי' נַמִי דַּיְקָא, דְּקָתָנֵי: יַחֲלוֹקוּ יוֹרְשֵׁי הַבַּעַל עִם יוֹרְשֵׁי הָאָב, •*וְלָא קָתָנֵי יוֹרְשֵׁי הָאָב עִם יוֹרְשֵׁי הַבַּעַל – ש"מ. אַבַּיֵי אֲמַר: רֵישָׁא דְּנָפְלוּ לָהּ כְּשֶׁהִיא שׁוֹמֶרֶת יָבָם, סֵיפָא דְּנָפְלוּ לָהּ כְּשֶׁהִיא תַּחְתָּיו דְּבַעַל. וְקָסָבַר

°במדבר ה

*) כתובות פ:

סֵיפָא. דְּגַבֵּי נְשׂוּאָה בְּעָלְמָא אָמְרִי' לְקַמָּן דִּבְרֵי הַכֹּל מָכְרָה וְנָתְנָה, אֲפִי' בְּדִיעֲבַד – הַבַּעַל מוֹצִיא מִיַּד הַלָּקוֹחוֹת, הָכָא, לְגַבֵּי זִיקַת נְשׂוּאָה, דְּסָפֵק הִיא וְלָא כִּנְשׂוּאָה מַמָּשׁ – קָיְימִי נִכְסֵי בְּסָפֵק. הִלְכָּךְ, לְב"ש חֲלוּקָה עֲדִיפָא, [וּלְב"ה חֲזָקָה עֲדִיפָא]. זִיקַת אֲרוּסָה. זִיקַת יְבָמָה שֶׁנָּפְלָה מִן הָאֵירוּסִין. סָפֵק אֲרוּסָה וְלָא וַדַּאי אֲרוּסָה. וְאַע"ג דִּלְגַבֵּי נְכָסִים אֵין לוֹ שׁוּם כֹּחַ בָּהֶן, וְנִמְצָא שֶׁזִּיקַת אֲרוּסָה אֵינָהּ כְּלוּם – קָרֵי לָהּ סָפֵק אֲרוּסָה, דְּלָא מָצֵי לְמֵימַר קָסָבַר עוּלָּא זִיקַת אֲרוּסָה אֵינָהּ כְּלוּם, דְּהָא בָּעֲיָא חֲלִיצָה. מוֹדִים ב"ה כו'. בִּתְמִיָּה. אֶלָּא ש"מ: כְּסָפֵק אֲרוּסָה הִיא, הִלְכָּךְ תִּמְכּוֹר לְכַתְּחִלָּה. עוֹשָׂה סָפֵק נְשׂוּאָה. כִּדְפָרֵישִׁית לְעֵיל, דְּכֵיוָן דְּוַדַּאי נְשׂוּאָה – הַבַּעַל מוֹצִיא מִיַּד הַלָּקוֹחוֹת, הָכָא דְּסָפֵק נְשׂוּאָה הִיא – הָווּ נְכָסִים בְּסָפֵק, וּלְב"ש חֲלוּקָה עֲדִיפָא, דְּאֵין לָהּ בָּהֶם חֲזָקָה יוֹתֵר מִמֶּנּוּ, דְּיָדוֹ כְּיָדָהּ. וּלְב"ה חֲזָקָה עֲדִיפָא, דְּאֵין יָדוֹ כְּיָדָהּ, הוֹאִיל וְלֹא נָפְלוּ לָהּ כְּשֶׁהָיְתָה תַּחַת הַבַּעַל. אֲמַר לֵיהּ רַבָּה. לְעוּלָּא: אִי טַעְמָא מִשּׁוּם חֲלוּקָה עֲדִיפָא הוּא, אַדְּמִיפַּלְגֵי בְּגוּפָהּ שֶׁל קַרְקַע וּלְאַחַר מִיתָה – לִיפְלְגוּ בְּחַיֶּיהָ וּלְפֵירוֹת, דִּלְב"ש פָּלֵיג יָבָם פֵּירֵי בַּהֲדָהּ, דְּסָפֵק נְשׂוּאָה הִיא. דְּאִילּוּ וַדַּאי נְשׂוּאָה הֲוַאי – הֲוָה שָׁקֵיל לְהוּ בַּעַל כָּרְחָהּ (א), וּלְב"ה נְכָסִים בְּחֶזְקָתָהּ, וְלָא שָׁקֵיל מִידֵּי! וּמִדְּנָקַט מַתְנִי' מִיתָה בְּסֵיפָא – ש"מ טַעֲמַיְיהוּ דְּב"ש בְּרֵישָׁא דְּאַלְמוּהָ לַחֲזָקָה דִּילָהּ, מִשּׁוּם דְּהִיא קַיְימָא. אֶלָּא אֲמַר רַבָּה אִידִי וְאִידִי דְּנָפְלָה. לְיִבּוּם כְּשֶׁהִיא נְשׂוּאָה כו'. אִיהִי וַדַּאי. שֶׁהַקֶּרֶן שֶׁלָּהּ מָה נַפְשָׁךְ, הִלְכָּךְ אַלִּימָא חֲזָקָה דִּילָהּ. סֵיפָא. הוֹאִיל וּמֵתָה, הַלָּלוּ בָּאִים וְטוֹעֲנִים מִכֹּחַ יְרוּשָּׁה, וְהַיָּבָם טוֹעֵן מִכֹּחַ יְרוּשָּׁה. הִלְכָּךְ שְׁנֵיהֶם סָפֵק לְב"ש, דְּאִי זִיקָה כִּכְנוּסָה – אֵין כָּאן לְיוֹרְשֵׁי הָאָב כְּלוּם, שֶׁהַבַּעַל יוֹרֵשׁ שֶׁלָּהּ. וְאִי לָאו כִּכְנוּסָה – אֵין כָּאן לַיָּבָם כְּלוּם, לְפִיכָךְ סָפֵק וְסָפֵק הוּא וְיַחֲלוֹקוּ. וּלְב"ה, הוֹאִיל וְאֵלּוּ קְרוֹבִין וַדָּאִין הֵם, וְהוּחְזְקָה נַחֲלָה זוֹ כְּבָר בְּחֶזְקַת מִשְׁפַּחְתָּן, אָמְרִינַן: אוֹקֵי אַחֶזְקָתָהּ. אֲבָל בְּחַיֶּיהָ וּלְפֵירוֹת – אֲפִי' ב"ש מוֹדוּ דִּנְכָסִים בְּחֶזְקָתַיְיהוּ, וְלָא שָׁקֵיל בַּעַל מִידֵּי: עָלָיו וְעַל יוֹרְשָׁיו ל"ג. נָפַל הַבַּיִת כו'. לוֹ אֵין נְכָסִים, וּלְמוֹרִישָׁיו יֵשׁ נְכָסִים. הַבֵּן מֵת רִאשׁוֹן. וְלֹא זָכָה בְּנִכְסֵי הָאָב, וְאֵין לְב"ח מַה לִּגְבּוֹת. יוֹרְשֵׁי הָאָב וַדַּאי. מוּחְזָקִים, שֶׁבָּאִין מִכֹּחַ יְרוּשָּׁה וַדָּאִית, שֶׁאֲפִי' (ב) הָאָב מֵת רִאשׁוֹן – נִכְסֵי הַבֵּן מִסְתָּמָא נוֹפְלִים לִפְנֵי יוֹרְשִׁין. דְּאִילּוּ ב"ח מִיחֲסַר גּוּבַיְינָא, עַד שֶׁיַּחֲזִיקוּהוּ ב"ד בָּהֶם. וּבַעַל חוֹב סָפֵק. דְּלֹא הוּחְזַק שְׁטָרוֹ עֲלֵיהֶן, וְקָאָתֵי סָפֵק וּמוֹצִיא אֶת הַנְּכָסִים מִידֵי וַדַּאי. כִּגְבוּי דָּמֵי. כְּלוֹמַר, גָּדוֹל כֹּחַ הַשְּׁטָר, וּכְמוֹ שֶׁמּוּחְזָק בַּנְּכָסִים (ג), וַהֲרֵי הֵן קָמוּ בִּמְקוֹם הַבֵּן וּמוּחְזָקִים בַּנְּכָסִים דָּמֵי. הִלְכָּךְ, סָפֵק וְסָפֵק הוּא, וְאֵין כָּאן חֲזָקָה לָזֶה יוֹתֵר מִזֶּה. אִם הָאָב מֵת רִאשׁוֹן – הוּחְזַק ב"ח מִיַּד, וְלָא אָמְרִינַן הָא מְחוּסַּר גּוּבַיְינָא. וְאִם בֵּן מֵת רִאשׁוֹן – הוּחְזְקוּ יוֹרְשִׁים. מֵתוּ בַּעֲלֵיהֶן. כָּל אִשָּׁה שֶׁקִּנֵּא לָהּ בַּעְלָהּ וְנִסְתְּרָה, וּמֵת עַד שֶׁלֹּא שָׁתְתָה – נוֹטֶלֶת כְּתוּבָּתָהּ. וְאַע"פ שֶׁשֶּׁמָּא זִינְּתָה וְאֵין לָהּ כְּתוּבָּה – לֹא שׁוֹתוֹת, דְּבָעֵינַן וְהֵבִיא הָאִישׁ אֶת אִשְׁתּוֹ, וְלֵיכָּא. מִידֵי יוֹרְשֵׁי הַבַּעַל, שֶׁהֵן מוּחְזָקִין וַדַּאי, מוֹצִיאָה זוֹ כְּתוּבָּה מִסָּפֵק. אֶלָּא. לָאו ש"מ קָסָבְרֵי ב"ש: שְׁטָר הָעוֹמֵד לִגְבּוֹת – כִּגְבוּי דָּמֵי, וְכֵיוָן שֶׁמֵּת – עָמְדוּ הַנְּכָסִים מִיַּד בְּחֶזְקַת הָאִשָּׁה, וְיוֹרְשִׁים קָאָתוּ לְאַפּוּקֵי מִינָּהּ מִשּׁוּם סָפֵק זַנַּאי, וְלָא אָתֵי סָפֵק וּמוֹצִיא מִידֵי וַדַּאי. דְּאִי לָא כִּגְבוּי דָּמֵי, וְטַעְמָא מִשּׁוּם דְּאָתֵי סָפֵק וּמוֹצִיא מִידֵי וַדַּאי הוּא – הֲוָה לְהוּ לְמֵימַר יַחֲלוֹקוּ, וְנַשְׁוְויֵי סָפֵק כְּוַדַּאי. אֲבָל לְעַלּוּיֵי מִינֵּיהּ – לֵיכָּא לְמ"ד. וְגַבֵּי נָפַל הַבַּיִת קָאָמַר יַחֲלוֹקוּ, דְּכִי נַמִי אָמְרִי' כִּגְבוּי דָּמֵי – לֹא מָלֵינוּ לְב"ח לְשַׁוְּויֵי וַדַּאי טְפֵי מִיּוֹרְשִׁין, שֶׁהֲרֵי לֹא הוּחְזַק בּוֹ זֶה בַּנְּכָסִים, וְהַשְּׁטָר זֶה יוֹצֵא עָלָיו וְלֹא עַל הָאָב, הִלְכָּךְ סָפֵק וְסָפֵק הוּא: אִם הָאָב מֵת רִאשׁוֹן – נִמְצָא ב"ח וַדַּאי, דְּהַאי שְׁטָר כִּגְבוּי דָּמֵי, וְיוֹרְשִׁים אֵינָם כְּלוּם, וְאִם הַבֵּן מֵת רִאשׁוֹן – נִמְצְאוּ יוֹרְשִׁין וַדָּאִין, וּב"ח אֵין כְּלוּם. וְאַבַּיֵי. דְּלָא אַסֵּיק אַדַּעְתֵּיהּ מֵעִיקָּרָא מִשּׁוּם טַעְמָא דִּשְׁטָר הָעוֹמֵד לִגְבּוֹת, כִּי אוֹתְבֵיהּ לְרַבָּה מִנָּפַל הַבַּיִת, דִּתְנַן בְּ"מִי שֶׁמֵּת" בְּבָבָא בַּתְרָא בְּסֵדֶר יְשׁוּעוֹת. לוֹתְבֵיהּ מֵהָא. דְּמַתְנִי' הִיא בְּסֵדֶר נָשִׁים, דְּהָכָא נַמִי סָפֵק מוֹצִיא מִידֵי וַדַּאי. וְאַבַּיֵי. לְהָכִי לָא אוֹתְבֵיהּ מִכְּתוּבָּה, דְּקָסָבַר: שָׁאנֵי כְּתוּבָּה מִשּׁוּם חִינָּא, שֶׁיִּהְיוּ נוֹשְׂאִין חֵן בְּעֵינֵי הָאֲנָשִׁים וְיִתְרַצּוּ לְהִנָּשֵׂא, לְפִיכָךְ הֶחֱזִיקוּהָ מִסָּפֵק. וְלוֹתְבֵיהּ מִכְּתוּבָּה דְּמַתְנִי'. דְּאָמְרֵי ב"ש יַחֲלוֹקוּ. דְּקס"ד הַשְׁתָּא דְּב"ש נַמִי אַכְּתוּבָּה אָמְרֵי יַחֲלוֹקוּ, וְקָאָתוּ יוֹרְשִׁין דִּידָהּ (ד) מִסָּפֵק וְגָבוּ פַּלְגָּא דִּכְתוּבָּה מִיָּבָם דַּהֲוֵי וַדַּאי. וְהָתָם לֵיכָּא לְמֵימַר מִשּׁוּם חִינָּא, דְּהָתָם מֵתָה, וְגַבֵּי יוֹרְשִׁין לָא חָיְישִׁינַן לְחִינָּא, כִּדְאָמַר בְּ"אַלְמָנָה נִיזּוֹנֶת" (כתובות נג:), אא"כ הָיוּ יוֹרְשֶׁיהָ נְקֵבוֹת. לֹא פְּלִיגִי. דְּמוֹדוּ ב"ש שֶׁהִיא בְּחֶזְקַת יוֹרְשֵׁי הַבַּעַל, דְּלָא נִיתְּנָה כְּתוּבָּה לִגְבּוֹת מֵחַיִּים. וְכָל שֶׁהִיא מֵתָה בְּחַיָּיו שֶׁל יָבָם – לֹא גָּבוּ יוֹרְשִׁים דִּילָהּ כְּתוּבָּה, דְּיָבָם בִּמְקוֹם בַּעַל קָאֵי. וְאַע"ג דִּשְׁמַעִינַן לֵיהּ לְאַבַּיֵי בִּכְתוּבּוֹת פֶּרֶק "הָאִשָּׁה" (דף פא.) נִיתְּנָה כְּתוּבָּה לִגְבּוֹת מֵחַיִּים לְב"ש – הָנֵי מִילֵּי לְהִתְחַיֵּיב יָבָם בִּקְבוּרָתָהּ, דְּקָאָמַר: מִינָּהּ קָא יָרֵית כְּתוּבָּה וְלֹא מֵאָחִיו. אֲבָל דְּלִיפְקוּ יוֹרְשִׁין דִּילָהּ כְּתוּבָּתָהּ – לֹא שְׁמַעִינַן לֵיהּ. דַּיְקָא נַמִי כו'. וְטַעְמָא לָאו מִשּׁוּם דִּשְׁטָר הָעוֹמֵד לִגְבּוֹת הוּא, דְּלֹא נִיתְּנָה כְּתוּבָּה לִגְבּוֹת מֵחַיִּים. יוֹרְשֵׁי הַבַּעַל עִם יוֹרְשֵׁי הָאָב. נִכְסֵי מְלוֹג. אַבַּיֵי. מַהֲדַר אַרֵישָׁא דִּשְׁמַעְתִּין לְתָרוּצֵי, מַאי שְׁנָא רֵישָׁא דְּלָא פְּלִיגֵי וּמַאי שְׁנָא סֵיפָא דִּפְלִיגֵי. וְתָרְצֵיהּ: לָאו מִשּׁוּם דִּבְרֵישָׁא הִיא קַיֶּימֶת וְסֵיפָא מִשּׁוּם דְּלֵיתָא, דְּוַדַּאי סֵיפָא נַמִי אִי כְּשֶׁהִיא שׁוֹמֶרֶת יָבָם נָפְלוּ לָהּ מוֹדוּ ב"ש דְּיוֹרְשֵׁי הָאָב וַדָּאִין וּנְכָסִים בְּחֶזְקָתָן. אֶלָּא: רֵישָׁא דְּנָפְלוּ לָהּ כְּשֶׁהִיא שׁוֹמֶרֶת יָבָם לְפִיכָךְ מוֹכֶרֶת לְכַתְּחִלָּה. וְה"ה אִם מֵתָה – יוֹרְשֶׁיהָ יוֹרְשִׁין אוֹתָהּ, דְּלָא מְהַנְיָא זִיקָה לְמִיקְנֵי נִכְסֵי דְּהַשְׁתָּא. סֵיפָא. דְּנָפְלוּ לָהּ כְּשֶׁהִיא תַּחַת בַּעְלָהּ הָרִאשׁוֹן. וְקָסָבַר

זיקת נשואה עושה ספק נשואה. ואפ"ה, לב"ה הוו בחזקת יורשי האב. דחזקה עדיפא, שיש לנו להחזיק נחלה בחזקת אותו השבט. **דאי** ס"ד ודאי נשואה והתנן נפלו לה כו'. מכמה משניות דתנן פרק "יש נוחלין" (ב"ב דף קח.) שהבעל יורש את אשתו הוה מצי למיפרך! אלא מסיפא דההוא דאייתי לעיל *נ"ל לאיתויי. **הויא** לה איהי ודאי. שהגוף (ה) שלה. **קסברי** ב"ש שטר העומד לגבות כגבוי דמי. אביי גופיה אית ליה הכי בפרק "האשה שנפלו" (כתובות דף פא. ושם), דלבתר דשמע מרבה סברה. **בש"א** נוטלות כתובה ולא שותות. והא דתנן בריש פ' "ארוסה" (סוטה דף כג:): ארוסה ושומרת יבם לא שותות ולא נוטלות כתובתן, ולא פליגי ב"ש! אור"י: דהתם היא נתנה אצבע בין שיניה, שנסתרה ואסרה עצמה על בעלה. אבל הכא, בשעה שנסתרה היתה יכולה ליבדק בשתיה. ועוד: *דבארוסה ושומרת יבם אין לחושבה כעוברת על דת, כיון שאינה יכולה ליבדק, כדקאמר התם בגמ'. **בה"א** או שותות או לא נוטלות כו'. הא דגרס במסכת סוטה (דף כד.) לא שותות ולא נוטלות כתובה*) – כתבו שם כמו שמגיה הש"ס כאן. **ואביי** לותביה מהא. וא"ת: אדרבה, תקשי ליה למה נוטלת כל הכתובה מספק?! וי"ל: לפי שהיא באה בטענת ברי, והיורשין בטענת ספק. וספק

*) לפנינו ליתא האי גירסא

[ניחא ליה]

דבארוסה ושומרת יבם יש לחושבה כצ"ל מהר"ם

תוספות ישנים

ליפלגו מחיים ולפירות. פי' וכשנפלו לה כשהיא נשואה: **סיפא** דמתה הללו באין לירש והללו באין לירש ויחלוקו. ומכל מקום אמרי ב"ה דחזקה עדיפא כיון שהוחזקה נחלה באותו השבט: **אלא** ש"מ קסברי ב"ש שטר העומד לגבות כגבוי דמי. וא"ת ומנלן דלמא טעמא משום דספק מוציא מידי ודאי. וי"ל דא"כ לא הוה לן למימר רק יחלוקו דאין לספק להועיל יותר מן הודאי. וא"ת וכי נמי אמרינן שטר העומד לגבות כגבוי דמי אמאי אמרי' נוטלות כל כתובתן הוה לן למימר יחלוקו עם יורשי הבעל כדאמרינן לעיל נפל הבית עליו ועל מורישיו דבש"א יחלוקו משום דשטר העומד לגבות כגבוי דמי. וי"ל דלא דמי לדלעיל דהא אי הוי כגבוי אין זה אלא כשמת הבן אחריו אבל אם מת האב אחריו אין לזה בעל חוב כלום ואינו כגבוי שהרי אינו עומד לגבות מן האב כי האב לא נתחייב לו שום דבר והבן לא נשאר לו שום דבר ולהכי אמרינן יחלוקו אבל הכא שהאשה ודאי מוחזקת בנכסים מכבר אי אמרינן דשטר העומד לגבות כגבוי דמי כי הכל יודעין כי האשה יש לה דין בכתובה מקודם לכך ואי אמרינן שטר העומד לגבות כגבוי דמי היא מוחזקת מכבר ולכך אמרינן דנוטלת כל כתובתה כי היא ודאית בנכסים שהיא מוחזקת מקודם לכן ואין ספק מוציא מידי ודאי וכפ"ה וזה לשונו דלא דמי לדלעיל הללו באין לירש והללו באין לירש והוי כולם ספק. אבל הכא שהאשה ודאי שהיא מוחזקת בנכסים מכבר משום דשטר העומד לגבות כגבוי דמי א"כ נוטלות כל כתובתן. ואביי לותביה מהא פ"ה למה ליה לעיל למפרך מההיא דנפל הבית דמתנייא בבבא בתרא בסדר ישועות לותביה מהא דמתנייא בסדר נשים דספק מוציא מידי ודאי מן ההיא דמתו בעליהן לא שותות וכו' ונוטלות כתובה. ואינו נראה דהא לא מצי לאותביה מהא טומר דספק מוציא מידי ודאי דא"כ הל"ל יחלוקו כדפ"ה לעיל. אלא נראה דה"פ לותביה מהא מאי טעמא נוטלות כתובה כיון דלא ידע דשטר העומד לגבות כגבוי דמי: ואביי לותביה מכתובה דמתני' דהא ליכא למימר משום חינא אי לאו אם היו היורשים נקבות: **בכתובה** דמתני' לא פליגי. דלא נתנה כתובה לגבות מחיים מחיי הבעל וה"ה מחיי היבם דיבם במקום בעל קאי ואף למ"ד נתנה כתובה לגבות מחיים ה"מ להתחייב בקבורה דחשבינן ליה כאילו ירית כתובה מינה וצריך לקוברה אבל במידי אחרינא

כתובות עח. | ג"ז שם | [לעיל יט: פסחים ע. וש"נ] | ב"ב קנז. | [סוטה כה. וש"נ] | סוטה כד. כתובות פא. | גיטין לו. כתובות פו. שבועות מח. | [ב"מ סב.]

הגהות הב"ח

(א) רש"י ד"ה אמר ליה וכו' בעל כרחה הלכך ולב"ה: (ב) ד"ה יורשי האב וכו' שאפי' אם האב: (ג) ד"ה כגבוי וכו' בנכסים דמי: (ד) ד"ה ולותביה מכתובה וכו' יורשין דידה דספק וגבו: (ה) תוס' ד"ה הויא לה איהי ודאי וכו' שהגוף שלה. נ"ב ולריך לומר דספק איהו נשואה היא ודאי ארוסה:

גליון הש"ס

גמ' ולא קתני יורשי האב עם יורשי הבעל. ע' יומא דף פה ע"ב בתוס' ד"ה ישנים ד"ה תשובה ובר"ש פ"ז מ"ב דטהרות:

הגהות מהר"ב רנשבורג א] אמר רב אשי מתני' נמי דיקא דקתני יחלוקו יורשי הבעל. נ"ב ע' יומא פה ע"ב תוס' ד"ה תשובה

וְקָסָבַר *אַבַּיֵי יָדוֹ כְּיָדָהּ. [א] א"ל רָבָא. אִי דְּנָפְלִי לָהּ כְּשֶׁהִיא תַּחְתָּיו דְּבַעַל — דְּכ"ע לָא פְּלִיגִי דְּיָדוֹ עֲדִיפָא מִיָּדָהּ. אֶלָּא: אִידִי וְאִידִי דְּנָפְלוּ לָהּ כְּשֶׁהִיא שׁוֹמֶרֶת יָבָם, רֵישָׁא — דְּלָא עֲבַד בָּהּ מַאֲמָר, *סֵיפָא — דַּעֲבַד בָּהּ מַאֲמָר. וְקָסָבַר רָבָא: מַאֲמָר לְב"ש עוֹשֶׂה וַדַּאי אֲרוּסָה וּסְפֵק נְשׂוּאָה, וַדַּאי אֲרוּסָה — לִדְחוֹת בְּצָרָה, וּסְפֵק נְשׂוּאָה — לַחֲלוֹק בַּנְּכָסִים. אִיתְּמַר מִשְּׁמֵיהּ דְּרַ' אֶלְעָזָר כְּוָותֵיהּ דְּרָבָא וְאִיתְּמַר מִשְּׁמֵיהּ דְּרַבִּי יוֹסֵי בְּרַבִּי חֲנִינָא כְּוָותֵיהּ דְּאַבַּיֵי. וּמִי אָמַר רַבִּי אֶלְעָזָר הָכִי? וְהָא אָמַר רַבִּי אֶלְעָזָר: *מַאֲמָר לְב"ש אֵינָהּ קוֹנָה אֶלָּא לִדְחוֹת בְּצָרָה בִּלְבָד! אֵיפוֹךְ. וְאִי בָּעֵית אֵימָא: לְעוֹלָם לָא תֵּיפוֹךְ, אֲמַר לָךְ רַבִּי אֶלְעָזָר: כִּי אֲמַרִי אֲנָא — דְּלָא סַגִּי לָהּ בְּגֵט, אֶלָּא דְּבָעֵי נַמִי חֲלִיצָה, לַחֲלוֹק בִּנְכָסִים דְּלָא קָנֵי — מִי אֲמַרִי? אֲמַר רַב פָּפָּא: דַּיְקָא דְּמַתְנִיתִין כְּוָותֵיהּ דְּאַבַּיֵי. וְאע"ג דְּקַשְׁיָא "מֵתָה", דְּקָתָנֵי: "נְכָסִים הַנִּכְנָסִים וְיוֹצְאִים עִמָּהּ", מַאי נִכְנָסִין וּמַאי יוֹצְאִין? לָאו נִכְנָסִין: לִרְשׁוּת הַבַּעַל, וְיוֹצְאִים: מֵרְשׁוּת הַבַּעַל לִרְשׁוּת הָאָב, וְאע"ג דְּקַשְׁיָא מֵתָה, אַדְּמִפַּלְגִי בְּגוּפָהּ וּלְאַחַר מִיתָהּ לִפְלְגוּ בְּחַיֶּיהָ וּלְפֵירוֹת. *וְתוּ לָא מִידֵי.§ "כְּנָסָהּ הֲרֵי הִיא כו'".§ לְמַאי הִלְכְתָא? א"ר יוֹסֵי בַּר חֲנִינָא: *לוֹמַר שֶׁמְּגָרְשָׁהּ בְּגֵט וּמַחֲזִירָהּ. מְגָרְשָׁהּ בְּגֵט פְּשִׁיטָא! סד"א: הוֹאִיל וּכְתִיב °"וּלְקָחָהּ לוֹ לְאִשָּׁה וְיִבְּמָהּ" אָמַר רַחֲמָנָא, וַעֲדַיִין יִבּוּמֵי הָרִאשׁוֹן עָלֶיהָ. בַּחֲלִיצָה — אִין, בְּגֵט — לָא, קמ"ל. "מַחֲזִירָהּ". פְּשִׁיטָא! סד"א: מִצְוָה דְּרָמְיָא רַחֲמָנָא עֲלֵיהּ *עֲבַדָהּ. הָשְׁתָּא תֵּיקוּם עֲלֵיהּ בְּאִיסּוּר אֵשֶׁת אָח — קמ"ל. וְאֵימָא הָכִי נַמִי! אָמַר קְרָא: "וּלְקָחָהּ לוֹ לְאִשָּׁה", כֵּיוָן שֶׁלְּקָחָהּ — הֲרֵי הִיא כְּאִשְׁתּוֹ לְכָל דָּבָר.§ "וּבִלְבַד שֶׁתְּהֵא כְּתוּבָּתָהּ כו'".§ מ"ט? *אִשָּׁה הִקְנוּ לוֹ מִן הַשָּׁמַיִם, ג וְאִי לֵית לָהּ מִן הָרִאשׁוֹן — תַּקִּינוּ לָהּ מִשֵּׁנִי, כְּדֵי שֶׁלֹּא תְּהֵא קַלָּה בְּעֵינָיו לְהוֹצִיאָהּ.§

מתני' *ד מִצְוָה בְּגָדוֹל לְיַיבֵּם, לֹא רָצָה — מְהַלְּכִין עַל כָּל הָאַחִין, לֹא רָצוּ — חוֹזְרִין אֵצֶל גָּדוֹל, וְאוֹמְרִים לוֹ: עָלֶיךָ מִצְוָה, אוֹ חֲלוֹץ אוֹ יַיבֵּם. ה תָּלָה בְּקָטָן עַד שֶׁיַּגְדִּיל. (א) אוֹ בְּגָדוֹל עַד שֶׁיָּבֹא מִמְּדִינַת הַיָּם, אוֹ חֵרֵשׁ אוֹ שׁוֹטֶה — אֵין שׁוֹמְעִין לוֹ, אֶלָּא אוֹמְרִים לוֹ: עָלֶיךָ מִצְוָה, אוֹ חֲלוֹץ אוֹ יַיבֵּם.§

גמ' אִיתְּמַר, בִּיאַת קָטָן וַחֲלִיצַת גָּדוֹל, פְּלִיגִי בָּהּ רַ' יוֹחָנָן וְרַ' יְהוֹשֻׁעַ בֶּן לֵוִי, חַד אָמַר: ו בִּיאַת קָטָן עֲדִיפָא, וְחַד אָמַר: חֲלִיצַת גָּדוֹל עֲדִיפָא. מַאן דְּאָמַר בִּיאַת קָטָן עֲדִיפָא — דְּהָא מִצְוָה בְּיִיבּוּם, וּמַאן דְּאָמַר חֲלִיצַת גָּדוֹל עֲדִיפָא — בִּמְקוֹם גָּדוֹל — בִּיאַת קָטָן לָאו כְּלוּם הִיא. תְּנַן: לֹא רָצָה — מַחֲזִירִין עַל כָּל הָאַחִין. מַאי לָאו: לֹא רָצָה לְיַיבֵּם אֶלָּא לַחֲלוֹץ, וְקָתָנֵי: מְהַלְּכִין אֵצֶל הָאַחִין, שְׁמַע מִינַּהּ בִּיאַת קָטָן עֲדִיפָא — לָא, לֹא רָצָה לַחֲלוֹץ וְלֹא לְיַיבֵּם, דִּכְוָותָהּ גַּבֵּי הָאַחִין לֹא רָצוּ — לֹא לַחֲלוֹץ וְלֹא לְיַיבֵּם, אַמַּאי חוֹזְרִים אֵצֶל הַגָּדוֹל, ז לְמִיכְפְּיֵיהּ — לִכְפְּיֵיהּ לְדִידְהוּ! כֵּיוָן דְּמִצְוָה עֲלֶיהָ דִּידֵיהּ רַמְיָא — לְדִידֵיהּ כָּיְיפִינַן. תְּנַן: תָּלָה בְּקָטָן עַד שֶׁיַּגְדִּיל — אֵין שׁוֹמְעִין לוֹ. וְאִי בִּיאַת קָטָן עֲדִיפָא, אַמַּאי אֵין שׁוֹמְעִין לוֹ? נִינְטַר דִּלְמָא גָּדֵיל וּמְיַיבֵּם! וְלִיטַעְמִיךְ, וּבְגָדוֹל עַד שֶׁיָּבֹא מִמְּדִינַת הַיָּם אֵין שׁוֹמְעִין לוֹ, אַמַּאי? נִינְטַר, דִּלְמָא אָתֵי *וְחָלֵיץ! אֶלָּא: כָּל *) שְׁהוּיֵי מִצְוָה לָא מַשְׁהִינַן. אִית

*) [לקמן מז:]

וְקָסָבַר אַבַּיֵי יָדוֹ כְּיָדָהּ. מִדְּאוֹקִי פְּלוּגְתַּיְיהוּ בְּנָפְלוּ לָהּ (ב) תַּחְתָּיו, וַאֲפִי' הָכִי לְבֵית הִלֵּל נְכָסִים בְּחֶזְקָתָן — קָסָבַר אַבַּיֵי: נְשׂוּאָה יָדוֹ כְּיָדָהּ, וְלֹא יוֹתֵר. הִלְכָּךְ, כְּשֶׁמֵּת וְאֵין לַיָּבָם בָּהּ אֶלָּא זִיקָה — יָדוֹ גְּרִיעָא מִיָּדָהּ, וּנְכָסִים בְּחֶזְקָתָהּ. וּבֵית שַׁמַּאי פְּלִיגֵי וְאָמְרֵי: נְשׂוּאָה, יָדוֹ עֲדִיפָא מִיָּדָהּ, וּכְשֶׁמֵּת — יַד הַיָּבָם כְּיָדָהּ, וְיַחֲלוֹקוּ. וּבִכְתוּבּוֹת בְּ"הַכּוֹתֵב" (דף פג.) נַמִי פְּלִיגֵי אַבַּיֵי וְרָבָא, דְּקָאָמַר אַבַּיֵי: יָדוֹ כְּיָדָהּ, וְרָבָא אָמַר: יָדוֹ עֲדִיפָא מִיָּדָהּ. וְאָמְרִינַן הָתָם: נָפְקָא מִינָּהּ לְשׁוֹמֶרֶת יָבָם. דְּיָדוֹ עֲדִיפָא מִיָּדָהּ. וַאֲפִילוּ בֵּית הִלֵּל מוֹדוּ דְּשָׁקְלֵי יוֹרְשֵׁי הַבַּעַל בַּנְּכָסִים: הָכִי גָּרְסִינַן. אֶלָּא אִידִי וְאִידִי דְּנָפְלוּ לָהּ כְּשֶׁהִיא שׁוֹמֶרֶת יָבָם רֵישָׁא דְּלָא עֲבַד בָּהּ מַאֲמָר. קוֹדֶם שֶׁנָּפְלוּ לָהּ הַנְּכָסִים, הִלְכָּךְ זִיקָה לָא מְהַנְּיָא וְלָא מִידֵי בַּנְּכָסִים. וְסֵיפָא דַּעֲבַד בָּהּ מַאֲמָר. וּבֵית שַׁמַּאי לְטַעְמַיְיהוּ, דְּאָמְרֵי: מַאֲמָר קָנֵי, בְּפֶרֶק "אַרְבָּעָה אַחִין" (לעיל כט.) בֵּית שַׁמַּאי אוֹמְרִים: אִשְׁתּוֹ עִמּוֹ כו', וּב"ה לְטַעְמַיְהוּ, דְּאָמְרֵי: לָא קָנֵי. וְקָסָבַר רָבָא. קָנֵין מַאֲמָר לְב"ש קָנֵי כְּוַדַּאי אֲרוּסָה וּכְסָפֵק נְשׂוּאָה. כְּלוֹמַר, אע"ג דְּב"ש (ג) וַדַּאי אֲרוּסָה מְשַׁוֵּי לָהּ לִדְחוֹת בְּצָרָ' אֲחוֹתָהּ מִשּׁוּם אֲחוֹת אִשָּׁה, כִּדְקָתָנֵי: אִשְׁתּוֹ עִמּוֹ, מִיהוּ לָא כְּוַדַּאי נְשׂוּאָה מְשַׁוֵּי לָהּ, לְמִיקְנֵי יָבָם כּוּלָּהּ יְרוּשָׁה דִּילָהּ, אֶלָּא כִּסְפֵק נְשׂוּאָה, וְיַחֲלוֹקוּ. כְּוָותֵיהּ דְּאַבַּיֵי. דְּסֵיפָא בִּדְנָפְלוּ לָהּ כְּשֶׁהִיא תַּחַת הַבַּעַל. דְּקַשְׁיָא מֵתָה. לְקַמָּן מְפָרֵשׁ. וְיוֹצְאִין מֵרְשׁוּת הַבַּעַל כְּשֶׁמֵּתָה. אַלְמָא דְּנָפְלוּ לָהּ תַּחַת בַּעְלָהּ. אַדְּמִיפַּלְגֵי בְּגוּפָהּ. שֶׁל קַרְקַע, וּלְאַחַר מִיתָהּ. לִיפַלְגוּ בְּחַיֶּיהָ וּלְפֵירוֹת. הוֹאִיל וְטַעְמָא מִשּׁוּם דְּיָדוֹ כְּיָדָהּ. וְתוּ לָא מִידֵי. אֵין לְהָשִׁיב עַל כָּךְ, דְּוַדַּאי דַּיְקָא כְּוָותֵיהּ, וְקַשְׁיָא לֵיהּ מֵתָה. שֶׁמְּגָרְשָׁהּ בְּגֵט. וְלָא בָּעֵי חֲלִיצָה. וּמַחֲזִירָהּ. אִם רָצָה, וְלָא מִיתַּסְרָא עֲלֵיהּ. וְיִבְּמָהּ. אע"פ שֶׁלְּקָחָהּ קָרֵי לֵיהּ "וְיִבְּמָהּ". וְאֵימָא הָכִי נַמִי. אַכּוּלָּהּ מִילְּתָא קָאֵי. וּלְקָחָהּ לוֹ. דְּבִיאָה מָצֵי לְמִכְתַּב, לָמָּה לִי דִּכְתִיב "לְאִשָּׁה"? שְׁמַע מִינַּהּ: הֲרֵי הִיא כְּאִשְׁתּוֹ. "וְיִבְּמָהּ", אִי לִכְדְרַבִּי בְּפ"ק (לעיל דף ח.) לֶאֱסוֹר צָרוֹת וַעֲרָיוֹת, אִי לִכְדְרַבָּנַן — יְיַבְּמָהּ בְּעַל כָּרְחָהּ. אִשָּׁה הִקְנוּ לוֹ. לַיָּבָם. מִן הַשָּׁמַיִם. וְלֹא שֶׁיִּשְׁתַּעְבֵּד נְכָסָיו לִכְתוּבָּתָהּ, וְיָכוֹל לְמוֹכְרָן בְּכָל עֵת שֶׁיִּרְצֶה. וְאִי לֵית לָהּ מֵרִאשׁוֹן. דְּלֵית לֵיהּ נְכָסִים. **מתני'** מִצְוָה בְּגָדוֹל. מִ"וְהָיָה הַבְּכוֹר" (דברים כה). לֹא רָצָה כו'. מְפָרֵשׁ בַּגְּמָ'. תָּלָה בְּקָטָן. קָטָן מַמָּשׁ. וּבְגָדוֹל. (ד) שֶׁהָיָה גָּדוֹל הָאַחִים בִּמְדִינַת הַיָּם, וְיֵשׁ לוֹ אָח כָּאן הַגָּדוֹל מִן הָאַחִין שֶׁלְּפָנֵינוּ. וְתָלָה גָּדוֹל הָאַחִין שֶׁלְּפָנֵינוּ בּוֹ, לוֹמַר: הַמְתִּינוּ לוֹ, שֶׁהוּא גָּדוֹל מִמֶּנִּי, שֶׁמָּא יְיַבֵּם אוֹתָךְ. וְהָכִי מוּכַח בַּגְּמָ', דְּאָמְרִי', ת"ש: וּבְגָדוֹל עַד שֶׁיָּבֹא מִמְּדִינַת הַיָּם — אֵין שׁוֹמְעִין לוֹ. וְאִי ס"ד חֲלִיצַת גָּדוֹל עֲדִיפָא — אַמַּאי אֵין שׁוֹמְעִין לוֹ? נִינְטַר דִּלְמָא אָתֵי וְחָלֵיץ. אַלְמָא אוֹתוֹ שֶׁבִּמְדִינַת הַיָּם גָּדוֹל שֶׁבְּכָל הָאַחִין הוּא. עָלֶיךָ מִצְוָה. שֶׁאע"פ שֶׁאָחִיךָ שֶׁבִּמְדִינַת הַיָּם גָּדוֹל מִמְּךָ, כֵּיוָן דְּאַתָּה גָּדוֹל הָאַחִין שֶׁלְּפָנֵינוּ — עָלֶיךָ מִצְוָה, דְּשָׁהוּיֵי מִצְוָה לָא מַשְׁהִינַן, וְהָכִי מְפָרֵשׁ בַּגְּמָרָא. **גמ'** בִּיאַת קָטָן וַחֲלִיצַת גָּדוֹל. גָּדוֹל רוֹצֶה לַחֲלוֹץ וְקָטָן [מִמֶּנּוּ] רוֹצֶה לְיַיבֵּם. וְהַאי קָטָן — לָאו קָטָן מַמָּשׁ הוּא, דְּקָטָן לָאו בַּר חֲלִיצָה וְיִיבּוּם הוּא, שֶׁמָּא יִמָּצֵא סָרִיס. וַאֲפִי' מַאן דְּלָא חָיֵישׁ לְמִיעוּט, וְקָטָן מוּתָּר לְיַיבֵּם — הָכָא וַדַּאי סוּגְיָא דִּשְׁמַעְתִּין מוֹכְחָא דְּלָאו קָטָן מַמָּשׁ הוּא, מִדְּקָפָרֵיךְ לְקַמָּן: תָּלָה בְּקָטָן עַד שֶׁיַּגְדִּיל, וְשַׁנֵּי לֵיהּ: שְׁהוּיֵי מִצְוָה לָא מַשְׁהִינַן. אַלְמָא: בְּקָטָן מַמָּשׁ כּוּלְּהוּ מוֹדוּ. בִּמְקוֹם גָּדוֹל בִּיאַת קָטָן לָאו כְּלוּם הוּא. דְּהָא מִצְוָה אַגָּדוֹל רָמְיָא. אוּלַי יְיַבְּמֶנָּה. וְאַמַּאי חוֹזְרִין אֵצֶל גָּדוֹל. אִי אָמְרַתְּ בִּשְׁלָמָא דְּכָל לֹא רָצָה וְרָצוּ דְּמַתְנִיתִין אַיִּיבּוּם קָאֵי — לְהָכִי חוֹזְרִין אֵצֶל גָּדוֹל; דְּכֵיוָן דְּכוּלְּהוּ בָּעוּ לְמֵיחַלַּץ, וְאִיהוּ נַמִי בָּעֵי לְמֵיחַלַּץ — אִיהוּ קָדֵים. אֶלָּא אִי אָמְרַתְּ אֲפִילּוּ מֵיחַלַּץ לָא בָּעֵי, אַמַּאי חוֹזְרִין אֵצֶל גָּדוֹל? פְּשִׁיטָא דִּלְמִיכְפְּיֵיהּ לְמֵיחַלַּץ, וְנִכְפִּינַן לְדִידְהוּ, וְלָא נַטְרַח ב"ד כּוּלֵּי הַאי. הָתָם

ושפק נשואה לחלוק בנכסים. לעיל פ' "ד' אחין" (דף כט: ושם) גרס רבה, גבי מאמר לב"ש נישואין עושה או אירוסין עושה, דמתוך תשובתו משמע דמודה דאין יורשה. **אע"ג** דקשיא מתה. לרבא ניחא, דדוקא לאחר מיתה מהני מאמר לחלוק בנכסים, אבל מחיים — לא, דהויא לה איהי ודאי ואינהו ספק. ומ"מ לא בעי רישא לאוקמי בעבד בה מאמר, דמשום דהויא איהי ודאי אין נראה לרבא דתמכור לכתחלה, להכי מוקי לה בלא עבד בה מאמר. אע"ג דלרבה דלעיל מוכרת לכתחלה משום האי טעמא, משום דהויא איהי ודאי — רבא לית ליה האי סברא, בהלכות פסוקות דרב יודאי גאון פסיק כאביי, *דרב פפא בתראה קאי כוותיה. והא דלא חשיב ביע"ל קג"ם — משום דאיירי בה אמוראי*. **אשה** הקנו לו מן השמים. וא"ת: ומה מרויח בכך היבם? כיון דאי לית לה מראשון תקינו לה רבנן משני! וכ"ת: שאם מכר הראשון נכסיו טורפא מלקוחות, אע"פ שיש בני חורין לשני — א"כ תהא קלה בעיניו להוציאה! א) ואר"י: דנפקא מינה שיכול היבם למכור שדותיו, ואפילו אשתדוף אחר כך שדות של מת — לא טרפא ממשעבדי. ואם היתה אשתו — טורפת מהן. ומיהו, למאי דבעי למימר בס"פ "מי שהיה נשוי" (כתובות צה. ושם) דאי אשתדוף בני חרי לא טרפא ממשעבדי — קשה! וי"ל: דנפקא מינה אם גירשה ואח"כ אשתדוף שדותיו של מת, דלא גביא מבני חרי דשני. **ובחרש** ושוטה. מדלא קאמר עד שיתרפא, משמע דאפי' תלה לייבם לאלתר — אין שומעין, לפי שאין חוסמין אותה. וה"ה דה"מ למינקט מוכה שחין. **גבי** אחין לא רצו לא לייבם ולא לחלוץ אמאי חוזרין כו'. אפילו לא רצו לייבם אלא לחלוץ ה"מ למיפרך. אמר

תוספות ישנים

כתובה לגבות מחיים: **וקסבר** אביי ידו כידה. ובהלכות פסוקות דרב יהודאי פסק כאביי ולא נמנו ביע"ל קג"ם משום דאמוראי בתראי סבר כוותיה וא"ל לפסוק כוותיה: **א)** אומר הר"ר דהא דקאמר אשה הקנו לו מן השמים זהו ליתן טעם למה אין לה שתי כתובות אחת מהיבם שהיא אשתו ואין אשה בלא כתובה ואחת מבעלה הראשון שנשתעבדו לה נכסיו. ומשני [אשה] הקנו לו מן השמים בלא כתובה ואין לה כי אם כתובה ראשונה ואי לית לה מראשון אף הכתובה ראשונה תקנו לה וכו' שלא תהא קלה וכו' והרבה יש תירוצים ודחוקים: **ובגדול** עד שיבא ממדינת הים. פי' שיש גדול ממנו במדה"י ואומר לנו להמתין ואין שומעין לו משום דאח שהוא עומד לפנינו מוטלת עליו המצוה וכן משמע בגמ':

מד א מיי' פ"ג מהלכות נחלות הלכה ז טוש"ע אה"ע סימן קס סעיף ה:
מה ב מיי' פ"א מהל' יבום הלכה טו סמג עשין נא טוש"ע שם סימן קסא סע"א:
מו ג מיי' פכ"ב מהל' אישות הלכה יא סמג שם טוש"ע שם סעיף ח וסעיף ט בהגה"ה:
מז ד מיי' פ"ב מהלכו' יבום הלכה ו סמג עשין נא טוש"ע שם סימן קסא סעיף ד:
מח ה מיי' שם הל' ח טוש"ע שם סעיף ה:
[דומה לזה כתבו תוס' מגילה כט: ד"ה והלכתא]
מט ו מיי' שם הל' יג טוש"ע שם סעיף ו:
נ ז מיי' שם הלכה ז טוש"ע שם סעיף ד:
[סוכה לו. וש"נ]

[כתובות פג.]

הגהות הב"ח

(א) במשנה עד שיגדיל ובגדול כצ"ל ותיבת או נמחק: (ב) רש"י ד"ה וקסבר וכו' בנפלו לה כשהיא תחתיו: (ג) ד"ה וקסבר רבא וכו' כודאי ארוסה משוי לה לענין לדחות: (ד) ד"ה ובגדול או שהיה וכו' שמא ייבם אותה והכי מוכח:

לעיל כט. [נ"ב עד.]

הגהות הגר"א

[א] גמ' א"ל רבא אי כו'. נ"ב לדברי רש"י לרבא אף ב"ה מודי דיחלקו. ורי"ף מפרש דהכי לבעל. ורמב"ם מכש לכל האוקימתות הכי לב"ש אבל לב"ה לעולם לאשה ועמש"ש ועי' רמב"ן וכתב דה"ה למכירה ולפירי אבל הרמב"ם פסק דל"ל ליבם פירות ועי' רא"ש פ"ד דכתובות סי' כב וכ"ד הרשב"א (וכמ"ש רבינו באה"ע כ' ק"ס):

לעיל ח: יעי' כתובות פב:

נ"א עברה

לקמן מ. כתובות פב:

ביצה לו. לעיל כד.

דברים כה

[נ"ל ומייבם]

תוס' ל"י אע"ג, דרב פפא בתראה. ע' תוס' ע"ז נט ע"ב ד"ה רב ותוס' ב"ב קמב ע"ב ד"ה ורב

נא א טוש"ע אה"ע סי' קסא סעיף ו:
נב ב מיי' פ"א מהלכות יבום הל' ב ופ"ב הלכה ז סמג עשין נב טוש"ע שם סימן קסה סעיף א:
נג ג שם סעיף א בהג"ה וסימן קסא סעיף ו בהג"ה:
נד ד טוש"ע שם סימן קסה סעיף א בהג"ה:
נה ה ו מיי' פ"ד מהלכו' יבום הלכה ל סמג עשין נב טור אה"ע סימן קסט:
נו ז מיי' שם הל' לא טוש"ע אה"ע סי' קסט ס"א וקנז ס"ב ובפירוש סדר חליצה סעיף לח:
נז ח מיי' פ"א מהלכות יבום הלכה ב סמג עשין נא טוש"ע שם סימן קנו סעיף א:

תורה אור

אִית דְּאָמְרִי: בְּבִיאָה — כּוּלֵּי עָלְמָא לָא פְּלִיגִי דְּבִיאַת קָטָן עֲדִיפָא. כִּי פְּלִיגִי — בַּחֲלִיצַת קָטָן, וְהָכִי אִיתְּמַר: חֲלִיצַת קָטָן וַחֲלִיצַת גָּדוֹל — פְּלִיגִי בָּהּ רַ' יוֹחָנָן וְרַ' יְהוֹשֻׁעַ בֶּן לֵוִי. חַד אָמַר: אחֲלִיצַת גָּדוֹל עֲדִיפָא, וְחַד אָמַר: כִּי הֲדָדֵי נִינְהוּ. מַאן דְּאָמַר חֲלִיצַת גָּדוֹל עֲדִיפָא — דְּהָא מִצְוָה בְּגָדוֹל. וְאִידָךְ: כִּי אָמְרִינַן מִצְוָה בְּגָדוֹל — לְעִנְיַן יִבּוּם, אֲבָל לְעִנְיַן חֲלִיצָה — כַּהֲדָדֵי נִינְהוּ. תְּנַן: לֹא רָצוּ — חוֹזְרִין אֵצֶל גָּדוֹל, מַאי לָאו: לֹא רָצוּ לְיַיבֵּם אֶלָּא לַחֲלוֹץ, וְקָתָנֵי חוֹזְרִין אֵצֶל גָּדוֹל, וְש"מ: חֲלִיצַת גָּדוֹל עֲדִיפָא! לָא, לֹא רָצוּ — לֹא לַחֲלוֹץ וְלֹא לְיַיבֵּם. דִּכְוָותֵיהּ גַּבֵּי גָּדוֹל — לֹא רָצָה לֹא לַחֲלוֹץ וְלֹא לְיַיבֵּם, אֶלָּא אַמַּאי חוֹזְרִין אֵצֶל גָּדוֹל, לְמִכְפְּיֵיהּ? לִכְפַּיְיהוּ לְדִידְהוּ! כֵּיוָן דְּמִצְוָה עֲלֵיהּ דִּידֵיהּ רַמְיָא — לְדִידֵיהּ כָּיְיפִינַן. ת"ש: תָּלָה בְּגָדוֹל עַד שֶׁיָּבֹא מִמְּדִינַת הַיָּם — אֵין שׁוֹמְעִין לוֹ. וְאִי ס"ד חֲלִיצַת גָּדוֹל עֲדִיפָא, אַמַּאי אֵין שׁוֹמְעִין לוֹ? נִינְטַר דִּלְמָא אָתֵי וְחָלֵיץ! וּלְטַעְמִיךְ, בְּקָטָן עַד שֶׁיַּגְדִּיל אֵין שׁוֹמְעִין לוֹ, אַמַּאי? נִינְטַר דִּלְמָא גָּדֵיל וּמְיַיבֵּם, (אִי נַמִי (א) אָתֵי אִיהוּ וּמְיַיבְּמָהּ). [ס"א ל"ג] אֶלָּא כָּל *שֶׁהֲוַיֵי מִצְוָה לָא שָׁהֵינַן. תְּנַן הָתָם: *במִצְוַת יִבּוּם קוֹדֶמֶת לְמִצְוַת חֲלִיצָה — בָּרִאשׁוֹנָה שֶׁהָיוּ מִתְכַּוְּונִין לְשֵׁם מִצְוָה, געַכְשָׁו שֶׁאֵין מִתְכַּוְּונִין לְשֵׁם מִצְוָה — אָמְרוּ: מִצְוַת חֲלִיצָה קוֹדֶמֶת לְמִצְוַת יִבּוּם. אָמַר רַב: דאֵין כּוֹפִין: כִּי אָתוּ לְקַמֵּיהּ דְּרַב אֲמַר לְהוּ: אִי בָּעֵית — חֲלוֹץ, אִי בָּעֵית — יַיבֵּם, בְּדִידָךְ תְּלָא רַחֲמָנָא, °"וְאִם לֹא יַחְפּוֹץ הָאִישׁ", הָא אִם חָפֵץ — אִי [דברים כה] בָּעֵי חָלֵיץ, אִי בָּעֵי יַיבֵּם. וְאַף רַב יְהוּדָה סָבַר אֵין כּוֹפִין. המִדְּאַתְקֵין רַב יְהוּדָה בְּגִיטָּא דַּחֲלִיצָה: אֵיךְ פְּלוֹנִית בַּת פְּלוֹנִי אַקְרְבַת יַת פְּלוֹנִי יְבָמַהּ קַדָּמָנָא לְבֵי דִּינָא, וְאִשְׁתְּמוֹדְעִינְהוּ *דַּאֲחוּהּ דְּמִיתְנָא מֵאַבָּא נִיהוּ, וְאָמְרִי לֵיהּ: אִי צָבֵית לְיַבֵּם — יַבֵּם, *וְאִי לָא — אִיטְּלַע לָהּ רַגְלָיךְ דִּימִינָא. וְאִיטְּלַע לָהּ רַגְלָא דִּימִינָא, וּשְׁרַת סֵינֵיהּ מֵעַל רַגְלוֹהִי, וְיָרְקַת בְּאַנְפּוֹהִי רוּקָא דְּמִתְחַזְיָא לְבֵי דִּינָא עַל אַרְעָא.

ווְרַבִּי חִיָּיא בַּר אָוְיָא מְסַיֵּים בָּהּ מִשְּׁמֵיהּ דְּרַב יְהוּדָה: וְאַקְרִינְהוּ מַה דִּכְתִיב בְּסֵפֶר אוֹרַיְיתָא דְּמֹשֶׁה. אִשְׁתְּמוֹדְעִינְהוּ, פְּלִיגִי בָּהּ רַב אַחָא וְרָבִינָא. חַד אָמַר: בְּעֵדִים, וְחַד אָמַר: אֲפִילּוּ קָרוֹב, אֲפִילּוּ אִשָּׁה. זוְהִלְכְתָא: גִּלּוּיֵי מִילְּתָא בְּעָלְמָא הוּא, וַאֲפִילּוּ קָרוֹב וַאֲפִילּוּ אִשָּׁה. § בָּרִאשׁוֹנָה שֶׁהָיוּ מִתְכַּוְּונִין לְשֵׁם מִצְוָה — מִצְוַת יִבּוּם קוֹדֶמֶת לְמִצְוַת חֲלִיצָה, וְעַכְשָׁיו שֶׁאֵין מִתְכַּוְּונִין לְשֵׁם מִצְוָה — אָמְרוּ: מִצְוַת חֲלִיצָה קוֹדֶמֶת לְמִצְוַת יִבּוּם. אָמַר רָמִי בַּר חָמָא א"ר יִצְחָק: חָזְרוּ לוֹמַר מִצְוַת יִבּוּם קוֹדֶמֶת לְמִצְוַת חֲלִיצָה. א"ל רַב נַחְמָן בַּר יִצְחָק: *אַכְשׁוּר דָּרֵי?! [חולין נג:] מֵעִיקָּרָא סָבְרִי לָהּ כְּאַבָּא שָׁאוּל, וּלְבַסּוֹף סָבְרִי לָהּ כְּרַבָּנַן. דְּתַנְיָא, *אַבָּא [לקמן קט. [לעיל ג.]] שָׁאוּל אוֹמֵר: *הַכּוֹנֵס אֶת יְבִמְתּוֹ לְשֵׁם נוֹי, וּלְשׁוּם אִישׁוּת, וּלְשׁוּם דָּבָר אַחֵר [תוספתא פ"ו ע"ש] — כְּאִילּוּ פּוֹגֵעַ בְּעֶרְוָה, וְקָרוֹב אֲנִי בְּעֵינַי לִהְיוֹת הַוָּלָד מַמְזֵר. וַחֲכָמִים אוֹמְרִים: °"יְבָמָהּ יָבֹא עָלֶיהָ" — מִכׇּל מָקוֹם. מַאן תְּנָא לְהָא דְּתָנוּ רַבָּנַן: *"יְבָמָהּ יָבֹא עָלֶיהָ" מִצְוָה. [דברים כה] [לקמן קט:] שֶׁבַּתְּחִלָּה הָיְתָה עָלָיו בִּכְלַל הֵיתֵר, נֶאֶסְרָה, וְחָזְרָה וְהוּתְּרָה, יָכוֹל תַּחֲזוֹר לְהֶתֵּירָהּ הָרִאשׁוֹן — ת"ל "יְבָמָהּ יָבֹא עָלֶיהָ" מִצְוָה. מַאן תְּנָא? אָמַר רַבִּי יִצְחָק בַּר אַבְדִּימִי: אַבָּא שָׁאוּל הִיא, וְה"ק: "יְבָמָהּ יָבֹא עָלֶיהָ" מִצְוָה, שֶׁבַּתְּחִלָּה הָיְתָה עָלָיו בִּכְלַל הֵיתֵר, רָצָה לְשֵׁם נוֹי — כּוֹנְסָהּ, רָצָה לְשׁוּם אִישׁוּת — כּוֹנְסָהּ. נֶאֶסְרָה, חָזְרָה וְהוּתְּרָה, יָכוֹל תַּחֲזוֹר לְהֶתֵּירָהּ הָרִאשׁוֹן — ת"ל "יְבָמָהּ יָבֹא עָלֶיהָ", לְמִצְוָה. רָבָא אָמַר: אֲפִי' תֵּימָא רַבָּנַן, וְהָכִי קָאָמַר: "יְבָמָהּ יָבֹא עָלֶיהָ" — מִצְוָה. שֶׁבַּתְּחִלָּה הָיְתָה בִּכְלַל הֵיתֵר. רָצָה — כּוֹנְסָהּ, רָצָה — אֵינוֹ כּוֹנְסָהּ. נֶאֶסְרָה, חָזְרָה וְהוּתְּרָה, יָכוֹל תַּחֲזוֹר לְהֶתֵּירָהּ הָרִאשׁוֹן; רָצָה — כּוֹנְסָהּ, רָצָה — אֵינוֹ כּוֹנְסָהּ. רָצָה אֵינוֹ כּוֹנְסָהּ? הָא אֲגִידָה בֵּיהּ, בִּכְדֵי תִּיפּוֹק?! אֶלָּא אֵימָא: רָצָה — כּוֹנְסָהּ, רָצָה — חוֹלֵץ לָהּ. ת"ל: "יְבָמָהּ יָבֹא עָלֶיהָ" — חמִצְוָה. אֵימָא *) רֵישָׁא: °"מַצּוֹת תֵּאָכֵל בְּמָקוֹם קָדוֹשׁ" — מִצְוָה, [ויקרא ו]

*) ס"א סיפא [אבל לע שבת"כ היא רישא ע"ש וכן בילקוט איתא אימא רישא]

רש"י

הָתָם תְּנַן. בְּמַסֶּכֶת בְּכוֹרוֹת. אָמַר רַב אֵין כּוֹפִין. וְאִי נִיחָא לְתַרְוַיְיהוּ לְיַיבּוּמֵי, אֵין כּוֹפִין אוֹתוֹ לַחֲלוֹץ, דְּנֵימָא לָאו לְמִצְוָה מִכַּוְּונֵי וּפָגַע בְּאִיסּוּר אֵשֶׁת אָח. אֶלָּא, אִי בָּעֵי — מְיַיבֵּם. וּמִיהוּ, הֵיכָא דְּהוּא בָּעֵי לְיַיבּוּמֵי וְאִיהִי אָמְרָה לָא בָּעֵינָא לֵיהּ, וְאָמְרָה דְּבָרִים נִיכָּרִים, אִי מָצֵינוּ לְאַטְעוּיֵיהּ וְלוֹמַר לוֹ: חֲלוֹץ לָהּ ע"מ שֶׁתִּתֵּן לְךָ מָאתַיִם זוּז — מַטְעִינַן לֵיהּ, וְאִי לָא — כָּפֵינַן לֵיהּ וְחָלֵיץ. דְּאָמַר רַב שֵׁשֶׁת (לעיל ד.): מִנַּיִן לִיבָמָה שֶׁנָּפְלָה לִפְנֵי מוּכֵּה שְׁחִין שֶׁאֵין חוֹסְמִין אוֹתָהּ, וְלָא תֵּימָא מוּכֵּה שְׁחִין דַּוְקָא, אֶלָּא כׇּל אֲמַתְלָא שֶׁתִּתֵּן לִדְבָרֶיהָ, דְּאָמַר בְּ"הַמַּדִּיר" (כתובות עז.) מַעֲשֶׂה בְּצַיְידָן בְּבוּרְסִי שֶׁמֵּת וְלוֹ אָח בּוּרְסִי, וְאָמְרוּ חֲכָמִים: יְכוֹלָה שֶׁתֹּאמַר: לְאָחִיךָ הָיִיתִי יְכוֹלָה לְקַבֵּל, וּלְךָ אֵינִי יְכוֹלָה לְקַבֵּל. וְעוֹד: פָּסְקִינַן הִלְכְתָא בְּאע"פ (שם סד.): כּוֹתְבִין אִגֶּרֶת מֶרֶד עַל אֲרוּסָה, וְאֵין כּוֹתְבִין אִגֶּרֶת מֶרֶד עַל שׁוֹמֶרֶת יָבָם. וּמִכׇּל הָנֵין טַעֲמֵי כָּפֵינַן לֵיהּ דְּחָלֵיץ, וְשָׁקְלָה כְּתוּבָּה. וְכׇל הָנֵי אֵין כּוֹפִין דְּהָכָא, הֵיכָא דְּתַרְוַיְיהוּ נִיחָא לְהוּ: אִיקְּרְבַת. הִקְרִיבָה. אִטְּלַע. לֵךְ לָהּ רֶגֶל יָמִין. דְּאִיתְחֲזֵי לָנָא. דְּבָעֵינַן רוֹק הַנִּרְאֶה לְעֵינֵי דַּיָּינִין, בְּפֶרֶק "מִצְוַת חֲלִיצָה" (לקמן דף קו:). וְאַקְרִינְהוּ. "לֹא חָפַצְתִּי לְקַחְתָּהּ". בְּעֵדִים. צָרִיךְ לְהָבִיא שְׁנֵי עֵדִים שֶׁהוּא אֲחִי הַמֵּת מֵאָבִיו: אַכְשׁוּר דָּרֵי. בִּתְמִיָּה: וְכִי נִתְכַּשְּׁרוּ הַדּוֹרוֹת?! יְבָמָהּ יָבֹא עָלֶיהָ מִצְוָה. גָּרְסִינַן: וְלָא גָּרַס הָכָא לְמִצְוָה, אֶלָּא לְקַמָּן בְּתֵירוּצָא דְּרַב יִצְחָק בַּר אַבְדִּימִי: שֶׁבַּתְּחִלָּה. עַד שֶׁלֹּא קִידְּשָׁהּ אָחִיו: נֶאֶסְרָה. כְּשֶׁקִּידְּשָׁהּ אָחִיו. וְחָזְרָה וְהוּתְּרָה. כְּשֶׁמֵּת בְּלֹא בָּנִים. יָכוֹל תַּחֲזוֹר לְהֶתֵּירָהּ הָרִאשׁוֹן. מְפָרֵשׁ לְקַמָּן: מַאן תְּנָא. וּמַאי קָאָמַר. אַבָּא שָׁאוּל הִיא. וְה"ק: יְבָמָהּ יָבֹא עָלֶיהָ לְמִצְוָה, מַשְׁמַע: לְשֵׁם מִצְוַת יִבּוּם, דִּכְתַב "וְיִבְּמָהּ". רָבָא אָמַר אֲפִי' תֵּימָא רַבָּנַן. וְלָא תֵּיתְנֵי לְמִצְוָה, אֶלָּא מִצְוָה: יְבָמָהּ יָבֹא עָלֶיהָ מִצְוָה. מִצְוָה עָלָיו לְיַבְּמָהּ, יוֹתֵר מִן הַחֲלִיצָה. יָכוֹל תַּחֲזוֹר לְהֶתֵּירָהּ הָרִאשׁוֹן. וְתוּ לָא. דְּאִי בָּעֵי — לָא כָּנֵיס לָהּ, ת"ל: יְבָמָהּ יָבֹא עָלֶיהָ — מִצְוָה. בִּכְדֵי תִּיפּוֹק. בִּתְמִיָּה. מַצּוֹת תֵּאָכֵל. קְרָא יְתֵירָא הוּא, דִּכְתִיב בְּרֵישָׁא דִּקְרָא "וְהַנּוֹתֶרֶת מִן הַמִּנְחָה יֹאכְלוּ". שֶׁבַּתְּחִלָּה

תוספות

אמר רב אין כופין. פירש בקונטרס: כי ניחא לתרווייהו לייבם — אין כופין (ב) לחלוץ משום מצוה, דנימא דלאו למצוה מכווני. אבל אם לא תרצה לייבם מחמת שתתן אמתלא לדבריה, אם אין יכולין להטעותו — כפינן ליה, וחליץ. וממוכה שחין ובורסי שהביא בקונט' נראה דאין ראיה, שהן מאותם שכופין להוציא מן הבעל. אבל בשאר אמתלא — אין נראה לומר דכופין. דא"כ — למה היו טורחין לקמן בפרק "מצות חליצה" (דף קו.) להטעותו? יכפוהו לחלוץ! ומאגרת מרד אין ראיה, דא"כ — בלא אמתלא נמי, והתם הוי טעמא משום דמצות חליצה קודמת, כדמסיק. (ג) ועוד: דקאמר התם רבי יוחנן תבע לייבם — אין נזקקין לו. השתא לחלוץ כופין — ואין נזקקין לייבם מבעיא? ועוד: מדקאמר בדידך תלה רחמנא — משמע אפי' בזמן הזה, דמצות חליצה קודמת, ור"ת גרים: מצות יבום קודמת למצות חליצה, אמר רב: אין כופין. וקאי אבראשונה שהיו מתכוונין לשם מצוה, וקאמר דאין כופין לייבם. וכי הוו אתו לקמיה דרב, אותן שהיו מתכוונים לשם מצוה. ורב יהודה נמי דאתקין אי צבית לייבומי — באותן שבאין לפנינו לחלוץ איירי, שאותן אם היו מייבמין היו מכוונים לשם מצוה, שהרי לא היו מתכוונים לשם נוי ולשם אישות, שלא היו חוששים לייבם אלא לחלוץ. אבל אחריני — אין מניחין לייבם, אלא אדרבה כופין[א] לחלוץ. ואר"ת: דהלכה כאבא שאול, כשם מתני' דבכורות (דף יג.), ולא כרמי בר חמא דאמר חזרו לומר דמצות ייבום קודמת כרבנן. ועוד: *דבריש מכילתין אוקי מתניתין דפ"ק (דף ג. ושם) כאבא שאול, ובפרק "בית שמאי" (לקמן דף קט. ושם) תני בר קפרא: לעולם ידבק אדם בחליצה, כאבא שאול. וסתמא דגמרא בפרק "אע"פ" (כתובות דף סד. ושם) כאבא שאול. ולעיל בשמעתין דמשמע דביאה עדיפא — במתכוין לשם מצוה איירי. ור"ת פסק כאן דמצות יבום קודמת, וחזר בו בפ' "מצות חליצה", ופסק דמצות חליצה קודמת. דמתחזיא לן בבי דינא על ארעא. נראה דל"ג על ארעא, דלא צריך. כדאמר בפרק "מצות חליצה" (לקמן דף קו: ושם) גבי הוא ארוך והיא גוצא וקלטתו הרוח*).

ולשום אישות. דתיפוק ליה עליה שם אישות. אר"י: כי אין פירושו כההיא דבסמוך רצה לשם נוי — כונסה, רצה לשם אישות — כונסה, דההוא לשם אישות — היינו לשם מצות יבום. וכה"ג איכא בפרק "הבא על יבמתו" (לקמן דף נג: ושם) אפילו שניהם שוגגין או מזידים, דההוא מזיד — *לשם זנות, ולא הוי כההוא דקאמר התם *דרבי רחמנא ביאת שוגג כמזיד, דההוא מזיד במתכוין לשם מצוה, וכן אפילו הוא שוגג והיא מזידה. רלה

*) [ועי' תוס' לקמן קו: ד"ה על דמטי]

צ"ל דבריש מכילתין דף ג. אוקי מתניתין דפ"ק כאבא שאול וכו'.

[תורת כהנים סוף פ"ב]
[דף נד.]

תוספות ישנים

נגמר דלמא אתי וחליץ. וא"ל אפי' לדידיה תקשי דלמא אתי ומייבם דהא כ"ע מודים דביאת גדול עדיפא דאיכא למימר שממעט ממנו שלא היה רוצה לייבם: למה חוזרין אצל גדול למכפייה וכו'. פי' אא"ב דר"ל לא רצה לייבם אלא לחלוץ וכן האחים לא רצו לייבם אלא לחלוץ ניחא שחוזרין אצל גדול לחלוץ כי חליצתו טובה מהם. אא"א שלא רצה לייבם ולא לחלוץ ודכוותה גבי אחין. א"כ אמאי חוזרין אצל גדול היינו ולאי למכפייה וכן נמי נכפייה לדידהו:

תוספות חד מקמאי

כתב הרב אלפס ואשתמודעינן דאחוה [דמיתנא] מאבא הוא אפי' מפי אשה ואפי' מפי קרוב וכיון דמודעי ליה הכי איתחזק גבי [ההוא] סהדא מפומא דהאי קרוב או מפומא דהאי איתתא דהאי ניהו פלניא והא ניהו פלניתא הלכך שרי ליה לסהדא למסמך אפומיה ולמסהד עלוי דההוא [גברא]. או עלוי הך אתתא בין לענין ממונא בין לענין איסורא והוא א) כמ"ש הה"ל ברבי מדבריו שאם היו קרוב או אשה מעידין עכשיו בשעת חליצה דאחוה דמיתנא הוא לא סמכינן עלייהו. וכי סמיכנא עלייהו כגון שכבר קודם מעשה אמרו קמיה דהך סהדי שלא ע"י מעשה דאחוה דהאי הוא ולפיכך כתב הרב שאותו העד יש לסמוך ולהעיד בב"ד על אותו קרוב או אותה אשה שאמרו לו שלא ע"י מעשה דהוא אחוה דהאי גברא ב). ומיהו עיקר הדבר ג) שע"י מעשה קרוב או אשה נאמן דגלויי מלתא בעלמא הוא. והלשון שכתב הרב ז"ל [דלא] שרי לסהדא למסמך אפומייהו ד) משום עובדא דרבה בר חנן דאייתיה מיניה ראיה הוא דכתב עד לפי דברי הרב שכך פירש אמר לה אף אנא. ומיהו אמרי להו דלאו איהי היא ואמרו לי קרובים מקשא הוא דאקשו לה קלא ועתה אני מכיר כי האמת אתך והמניה אביי (לרבא) [לרבה] בר חנן ואילו היו שם עדים כשרים בודאי לא היה נאמן רבה בר חנן. אלמא במקום חשדא אין קרוב [נאמן] אבל לעולם בודאי קרוב או אשה בשעת מעשה נאמן אפי' לדעת הרב אלפס ז"ל: מתניתין

א) נראה דל"ל כמש"כ הרב ז"ל דמדבריו נראה שאם כו'. ב) וכ"כ בריב"ש סימן קפ"ב שדעת הרי"ף דבעת מעשה אין נאמן אשה או קרוב ע"ש. ג) נ"ל נראה שגם בעת מעשה כו'. ד) נ"ל במקום דאיכא חששא דתשלא משום כו' דמייתי מיניה ראיה לפי דברי הרב כך פירושו שאמר לה

[לקמן מז:]
כתובות סד. בכורות יג.

הגהות הב"ח

(א) גמ' אי נמי דלמא אתי איהו ומייבם: (ב) תוס' ד"ה אמר וכו' אין כופין אותו לחלוץ: (ג) בא"ד כדמסיק התם ועוד:

[לקמן קו.]

[גירסת הערוך ערך סלע ואם לאו איטלע לך ריגלא דימינא ואיטלע ליה ריגלא דימינא שלף איש נעלו תרגום שלע גבר ית נרתיק ימיניה וכו']

[לקמן קט:]

הגהות הגר"א

[א] תוס' ד"ה אמר כו' אלא אדרבה כופין. נ"ב ר"ל במילי. תוס' בכתובות (ס"ד א' סד"ה ודינ' ועמ"ש רביעו באה"ע סי' קס"ה ס"ק ט'):

שֶׁבַּתְּחִלָּה הָיְתָה עָלָיו בִּכְלַל הֶיתֵּר, נֶאֶסְרָה, וְחָזְרָה וְהוּתְּרָה, יָכוֹל תַּחֲזוֹר לְהֶיתֵּירָהּ הָרִאשׁוֹן — ת"ל "מַצּוֹת תֵּאָכֵל בְּמָקוֹם קָדוֹשׁ" [א]מִצְוָה. בִּשְׁלָמָא לְרָבָא, דְּאָמַר הָא מַנִּי רַבָּנַן הִיא — הָכָא הָכִי קָאָמַר: "מַצּוֹת תֵּאָכֵל בְּמָקוֹם קָדוֹשׁ" מִצְוָה. שֶׁבַּתְּחִלָּה הָיְתָה עָלָיו בִּכְלַל הֶיתֵּר, רָצָה — אוֹכְלָהּ, רָצָה — אֵינוֹ אוֹכְלָהּ. (נֶאֶסְרָה, חָזְרָה וְהוּתְּרָה, יָכוֹל תַּחֲזוֹר לְהֶיתֵּירָהּ הָרִאשׁוֹן) — רָצָה אוֹכְלָהּ, רָצָה אֵינוֹ אוֹכְלָהּ. רָצָה אֵינוֹ אוֹכְלָהּ?! וְהָכְתִיב °"וְאָכְלוּ אֹתָם אֲשֶׁר כֻּפַּר בָּהֶם" (שמות כט) *[ב]מְלַמֵּד שֶׁהַכֹּהֲנִים אוֹכְלִים וּבְעָלִים מִתְכַּפְּרִין! אֶלָּא: רָצָה — הוּא אוֹכְלָהּ, רָצָה — כֹּהֵן אַחֵר אוֹכְלָהּ, ת"ל "מַצּוֹת תֵּאָכֵל בְּמָקוֹם קָדוֹשׁ" — מִצְוָה. אֶלָּא לְרַב יִצְחָק בַּר אַבְדִּימִי, דְּאָמַר אַבָּא שָׁאוּל הִיא — הָכָא מַאי תְּרֵי גַּוְונֵי אִיכָּא? וְכִי תֵּימָא: רָצָה — לְתֵאָבוֹן אוֹכְלָהּ, רָצָה — אֲכִילָה גַּסָּה אוֹכְלָהּ, אֲכִילָה גַּסָּה מִי שְׁמָהּ אֲכִילָה? וְהָאָמַר ר"ל: *[ג]הָאוֹכֵל אֲכִילָה גַּסָּה בְּיוה"כ — פָּטוּר מִ"לֹּא תְעֻנֶּה"! אֶלָּא: רָצָה — מַצָּה אוֹכְלָהּ, רָצָה — חָמֵץ אוֹכְלָהּ, וְהָכְתִיב °"לֹא תֵאָפֶה חָמֵץ חֶלְקָם" (ויקרא ו), *וְאָמַר רֵישׁ לָקִישׁ: [ד]וַאֲפִילּוּ חֶלְקָם לֹא תֵאָפֶה חָמֵץ! אֶלָּא: רָצָה — מַצָּה אוֹכְלָהּ, רָצָה — חָלוּט אוֹכְלָהּ. הַאי חָלוּט הֵיכִי דָמֵי? אִי מַצָּה הִיא — הָא מַצָּה הִיא, וְאִי לָא מַצָּה הִיא — "מַצּוֹת" אָמַר רַחֲמָנָא! לָא, לְעוֹלָם אֵימָא לָךְ מַצָּה הִיא, וּלְהָכִי *תְּנָא בֵּיהּ קְרָא — לְעַכֵּב. אֶלָּא חָלוּט מַצָּה הִיא דְּקָאָמְרִינַן, לְמַאי הִלְכְתָא? לוֹמַר [ה]שֶׁאָדָם יוֹצֵא בָּהּ יְדֵי חוֹבָתוֹ בְּפֶסַח, אע"פ דְּחָלְטֵיהּ מֵעִיקָּרָא, כֵּיוָן דַּהֲדַר אֲפָיֵיהּ בְּתַנּוּר — "לֶחֶם עוֹנִי" קָרֵינָא בֵּיהּ, וְאָדָם יוֹצֵא בָּהּ יְדֵי חוֹבָתוֹ בְּפֶסַח.§ **מתני'** [ו]הַחוֹלֵץ לִיבִמְתּוֹ — הֲרֵי הוּא כְּאֶחָד מִן הָאַחִין לְנַחֲלָה, וְאִם יֵשׁ שָׁם אָב — נְכָסִים שֶׁל אָב. [ז]הַכּוֹנֵס אֶת יְבִמְתּוֹ זָכָה בַּנְּכָסִים שֶׁל אָחִיו. רַ' יְהוּדָה אוֹמֵר: בֵּין כָּךְ וּבֵין כָּךְ, אִם יֵשׁ שָׁם אָב — נְכָסִים שֶׁל אָב.§ **גמ'** פְּשִׁיטָא! סד"א: חֲלִיצָה בִּמְקוֹם יִבּוּם קַיְימָא, וְנִשְׁקוֹל כּוּלְּהוּ נִכְסֵי, קמ"ל. אִי הָכִי "הֲרֵי הוּא כְּאֶחָד מִן הָאַחִים"? אֵינוֹ אֶלָּא כְּאֶחָד מִן הָאַחִים מִיבְּעֵי לֵיהּ! אֶלָּא, סד"א: הוֹאִיל וְאַפְסְדָהּ מִיבּוּם לִקְנְסֵיהּ, קמ"ל.§ "אִם יֵשׁ שָׁם אָב".§ *דַּאֲמַר מָר: [ח]אָב קוֹדֵם לְכָל יוֹצְאֵי יְרֵכוֹ.§ "הַכּוֹנֵס אֶת יְבִמְתּוֹ וכו'".§ מ"ט? °"יָקוּם עַל שֵׁם אָחִיו" (דברים כה) אָמַר רַחֲמָנָא, וַהֲרֵי קָם.§ "רַ' יְהוּדָה אוֹמֵר וכו'".§ אָמַר עוּלָּא: הֲלָכָה כְּרַ' יְהוּדָה. וְכֵן א"ר יִצְחָק נַפָּחָא: הֲלָכָה כְּרַ' יְהוּדָה. וַאֲמַר עוּלָּא וְאִיתֵּימָא רַ' יִצְחָק נַפָּחָא: מ"ט דְּרַ' יְהוּדָה — דִּכְתִיב °"וְהָיָה הַבְּכוֹר אֲשֶׁר תֵּלֵד" (שם), כִּבְכוֹר: מַה בְּכוֹר אֵין לוֹ בְּחַיֵּי הָאָב — אַף הַאי נַמִי אֵין לוֹ בְּחַיֵּי הָאָב. אִי מַה בְּכוֹר נוֹטֵל פִּי שְׁנַיִם לְאַחַר מִיתַת הָאָב — אַף הַאי נוֹטֵל פִּי שְׁנַיִם לְאַחַר מִיתַת הָאָב! מִידֵי "יָקוּם עַל שֵׁם אָבִיו" כְּתִיב? "יָקוּם עַל שֵׁם אָחִיו" כְּתִיב, וְלֹא "עַל שֵׁם אָבִיו"! אֵימָא: הֵיכָא דְּלֵיכָּא אָב דְּלִשְׁקוֹל נַחֲלָה — תִּתְקַיֵּים מִצְוַת יִבּוּם, הֵיכָא דְּאִיכָּא אָב, [דְּלָא] שָׁקֵיל נַחֲלָה — לֹא תִּתְקַיֵּים מִצְוַת יִבּוּם! מִידֵי *יִבּוּם בְּנַחֲלָה תָּלָה רַחֲמָנָא? יַבּוּמֵי מְיַבְּמֵי, וְאִי אִיכָּא נַחֲלָה — שָׁקוֹלֵי, וְאִי לָא — לָא שָׁקֵיל. יְתֵיב רַ' חֲנִינָא קָרָא קַמֵּיהּ דְּרַ' יַנַּאי, וִיתֵיב וְקָאָמַר: הֲלָכָה כְּרַ' יְהוּדָה. א"ל: *פּוּק קְרֵי קְרָיָיךְ לְבָרָא, אֵין הֲלָכָה כְּרַ' יְהוּדָה. תָּנֵי תַּנָּא קַמֵּיהּ דְּרַב נַחְמָן: אֵין הֲלָכָה כְּרַ' יְהוּדָה. א"ל: אֶלָּא כְּמַאן, כְּרַבָּנַן? פְּשִׁיטָא, *יָחִיד וְרַבִּים הֲלָכָה כְּרַבִּים! א"ל: אַסְמְיֵיהּ?! א"ל: לָא, אַתְּ "הֲלָכָה" אַתְנְיָיךְ, וּמוּקְשֶׁה הוּא דְּאַקְשֵׁי לָךְ, וְאַפֵּכְתְּ, וּלְמַאי דְּאַפֵּכְתְּ — שַׁפִּיר אַפֵּכְתְּ.§ **מתני'** [ט]הַחוֹלֵץ לִיבִמְתּוֹ — הוּא אָסוּר בִּקְרוֹבוֹתֶיהָ, וְהִיא אֲסוּרָה בִּקְרוֹבָיו.

הוא

רש"י

שֶׁבַּתְּחִלָּה. קוֹדֶם שֶׁהוּקְדְּשָׁה מִנְחָה זוֹ, הָיְתָה עָלָיו בִּכְלַל הֶיתֵּר. וְנֶאֶסְרָה. כְּשֶׁהוּקְדְּשָׁה, וְחָזְרָה וְהוּתְּרָה בְּהַקְטָרַת הַקּוֹמֶץ. יָכוֹל תַּחֲזוֹר וכו'. כִּדְמְפָרֵשׁ. בִּשְׁלָמָא לְרָבָא דְּאָמַר רַבָּנַן הִיא. וּמִצְוָה קָתָנֵי, וְלָא קָתָנֵי לְמִצְוָה. ה"ק כו' וְאָכְלוּ אוֹתָם. אֶת הַקֳּדָשִׁים אֲשֶׁר כּוּפַּר בָּהֶם, כִּי הֵיכִי דְּתֶהֱוֵי כַּפָּרָה שְׁלֵימָה. רָצָה הוּא. כֹּהֵן שֶׁעָבַד עֲבוֹדָתָהּ. אֶלָּא לְרַב יִצְחָק. דְּתָנֵי לְמִצְוָה, וְאַבָּא שָׁאוּל הִיא. הָכָא מַאי תְּרֵי גַּוְונֵי אִיכָּא. דְּקָא מְמַעֵט תַּנָּא יָכוֹל תַּחֲזוֹר לְהֶיתֵּירָהּ הָרִאשׁוֹן — ת"ל דְּלָא. וְהָא לֵיכָּא לְמֵימַר תַּחֲזוֹר לְהֶיתֵּירָהּ הָרִאשׁוֹן, רָצָה לְשֵׁם מִצְוָה אוֹכְלָהּ, רָצָה שֶׁלֹּא לְשֵׁם מִצְוָה אוֹכְלָהּ, ת"ל דְּלָא — דְּהָא כָּל כַּמָּה דְּבָעֵי לֵיכְלָהּ, דְּהָתָם הוּא כִּי בָּעֵיל שֶׁלֹּא לְשֵׁם מִצְוָה פָּגַע בְּעֶרְוָה, אֲבָל הָכָא — מַאי קָעָבֵיד? וְע"כ בִּתְרֵי גַּוְונֵי בָּעֵית לְאוֹקְמֵי, דּוּמְיָא דְּרֵישָׁא. אֲכִילָה גַּסָּה מִי מִקַּרְיָא אֲכִילָה וְהָאָמַר ר"ל כו'. וְכֵיוָן דְּלָאו אֲכִילָה הִיא, מִ"וְאָכְלוּ אַהֲרֹן וּבָנָיו" דְּרֵישָׁא נָפְקָא. פָּטוּר. דְּלָא עָבַר עַל "אֲשֶׁר לֹא תְעוּנֶּה", שֶׁאַף זֶה עִינּוּי הוּא, שֶׁמַּזִּיק אֶת עַצְמוֹ. אֶלָּא. תְּרֵי גַּוְונֵי הָכִי תִּיבָּעֵי לְמֵימַר: רָצָה מַצָּה אוֹכְלָהּ רָצָה חָמֵץ אוֹכְלָהּ, ת"ל "מַצּוֹת תֵּאָכֵל" — וְלֹא חָמֵץ. לֹא תֵאָפֶה חָמֵץ חֶלְקָם נָתַתִּי אוֹתָהּ. לְהָכִי סָמֵיךְ "חֶלְקָם" לְ"לֹא תֵאָפֶה חָמֵץ", לוֹמַר: אֲפִי' שְׁיָרֵי מִנְחָה, שֶׁהֵם חֶלְקָם שֶׁל כֹּהֲנִים — לֹא תֵאָפֶה חָמֵץ, וּמֵהָתָם נָפְקָא. חָלוּט. בְּרוֹתְחִים. רָצָה חָלוּט אוֹכְלָהּ. ת"ל: מַצּוֹת, וְלֹא חָלוּט. אִי מַצָּה הִיא* מַצָּה הִיא. וְהֵיכִי מִימְעִיט מִמַּשְׁמָעוּת דְּ"מַצּוֹת תֵּאָכֵל". וְאִי לָאו מַצָּה הִיא מַצּוֹת אָמַר רַחֲמָנָא. בִּשְׁיָרֵי מִנְחַת חוֹבָה, דִּכְתִיב (א) בְּ"צַו אֶת אַהֲרֹן" "וְאִכְלוּהָ מַצּוֹת", וְה"ה לִשְׁאָר מְנָחוֹת, וְלָמָּה לִי "מַצּוֹת תֵּאָכֵל". **מתני'** הֲרֵי הוּא כְּאֶחָד כו'. וְלֹא הִפְסִיד חֶלְקוֹ בְּנִכְסֵי אָחִיו. זָכָה בְּנִכְסֵי הָאָח. וַאֲפִילּוּ גֵּירְשָׁהּ לְמָחָר. **גמ'** פְּשִׁיטָא. דְּלֹא אִיבֵּד זְכוּתוֹ. מַהוּ דְּתֵימָא. כְּלוֹמַר, לָאו לְאַשְׁמוּעִינַן דְּלֹא אִיבֵּד זְכוּתוֹ תְּנָיָא לָהּ, אֶלָּא לְאַשְׁמוּעִינַן דְּלָא שָׁקֵיל כּוּלְּהוּ נִכְסֵי. אִי הָכִי. דְּלְגָרוּעֵי אָתָא, הֲוָה לֵיהּ לְמִיתְנֵי: אֵינוֹ אֶלָּא כְּאֶחָד כו': ה"ג. אֶלָּא סָלְקָא דַּעְתָּךְ אָמִינָא לִיקְנְסֵיהּ הוֹאִיל וְאַפְסְדָהּ מִיִּבּוּם. שֶׁפְּסָלָהּ עַל הָאַחִין. אַף הַאי נַמִי. לְאַחַר מִיתַת הָאָב, אִם מֵת הָאָב לְאַחַר יִבּוּמוֹ שֶׁל זֶה — מוֹדֶה ר"י דְּנוֹטֵל זֶה חֶלְקוֹ וְחֵלֶק אָחִיו. עַל שֵׁם אָחִיו כְּתִיב. וְלֹא עַל שֵׁם אָבִיו כְּתִיב, וְכֵיוָן דִּבְשָׁעָה שֶׁקָּם עַל שֵׁם אָחִיו לֹא שָׁקַל — תּוּ לָא שָׁקֵיל. [דְּאִי שָׁקֵיל הָשְׁתָּא — לָא מִנִּכְסֵי אָחִיו שָׁקֵיל, אֶלָּא מִנִּכְסֵי אָבִיו, דְּהָא יָרְתִינְהוּ]. הֵיכָא דְּאִיכָּא אָב דְּלָא שָׁקֵיל. יָבָם נַחֲלָה — לֹא תִּתְקַיֵּים מִצְוַת יִבּוּם. אִיסְמְיֵיהּ. לְכוּלָּהּ מַתְנִי', דְּמִשְׁנָה שֶׁאֵינָהּ צְרִיכָה הִיא. אֲמַר לֵיהּ לָא. תִּסְמְיֵיהּ, דְּאַתְּ הֲלָכָה כְּרַבִּי יְהוּדָה אַתְנְיָיךְ, וּמִשְׁנָה צְרִיכָה הֲוַאי. וּמִיקְשָׁה הוּא דְּקַשְׁיָא לָךְ. הֵיכִי שָׁבֵיק רַבָּנַן וְעָבֵיד כְּרַבִּי יְהוּדָה, וְאַפֵּכְתְּ לָהּ, וְשַׁפִּיר עֲבַדְתְּ דְּאַפֵּכְתְּ לָהּ. **מתני'** אָסוּר בִּקְרוֹבוֹתֶיהָ. כְּאִילּוּ הִיא אִשְׁתּוֹ, וְכָל קְרוֹבוֹת הַנֶּאֱסָרוֹת מֵחֲמַת אִשָּׁה גְּמוּרָה — אֲסוּרוֹת מִדְּרַבָּנַן בַּחֲלוּצָה.

הוא

תוספות

רצה כהן אחר אוכלה. והא דדרשינן בפ"ב דקדושין (דף נג.) "לכל בני אהרן תהיה איש כאחיו" — היינו של אותו משמר, או של אותו בית אב. א"נ: הכא מרבוי [ילפינן], דכהן המקריב צריך שיאכל ממנה ולא כולה. **מאי** תרי גווני איכא. דליכא למימר רצה לשם סעודה אוכלה רצה לשם מצוה, דאין צריך שיתכוין לשם מצוה, אלא שלא יהא אוכלה אכילה גסה.

אכילה גסה ביוה"כ פטור. וא"ת: דאמר בפרק "מי שאמר הריני נזיר" (נזיר דף כג. ושם): "כי ישרים דרכי ה' צדיקים ילכו בם ופושעים יכשלו בם" (הושע יד) משל לב' בני אדם שצלו פסחיהן, אחד אכלו לשם פסחו ואחד אכלו אכילה גסה, ומשמע התם דתרווייהו נפקי, אלמא הויא אכילה! וי"ל: דתרי עניני אכילה גסה הם א)*.

מצות אמר רחמנא. פי' בקונט': "ואכלוה מצות אצל המזבח" וגו', ובשמיני של מלואים כתיב. ואפילו לשמואל דאמר בריש "הקומץ רבה" (מנחות דף יט:) דלא ילפינן דורות משעה — שמא הכא איכא שום יתור.

שנה בה קרא לעכב. הך דהכא לא הוי כמו "שנה עליו הכתוב לעכב" דעלמא, דמהיכא תיתי לעכב? דדלמא למצוה הוא, דאמר רחמנא דלא ליעבד חלוט. אלא לעכב. כלומר: דבעינן מצה מעלייתא, ולא חלוט*.

כיון דהדר אפייה בתנור. או באילפס, לחם איקרי, ואדם יוצא בה ידי חובתו בפסח. והא דאמר בפ' "כל שעה" (פסחים דף לו:): "לחם עוני" — פרט לחלוט ואשישה — אר"ת: דהתם בלא הדר אפייה בתנור. ועוד אר"ת: דהתם בחלוט גדול, דומיא דאשישה, ולא חשיב לחם עוני לפי שהוא גדול, ולא משום דחלוט. א"נ: התם בבלילתו קשה, והכא בבלילתו רכה, כגון סופגנין או חלת המשרת, דמפרש התם דהיינו חלוט של בעלי בתים, דלא מחייב בחלה, ולא חשיב לחם אלא על ידי אפיה. ולהכי חשיב שפיר לחם עוני, אע"ג דחלטיה. אבל בלילתו עבה — מיפסל לעשות, דחשיב לחם עשירות אפי' לא הדר אפייה. ובפ' "כל שעה" (שם ד"ה פרט) הארכתי.

אבל

עין משפט נר מצוה

נח א מיי' פ"י מהלכות מעשה קרבנות הל' ב סמג עשין קפד קפה:

נט ב מיי' שם הלכה א:

ס ג מיי' פ"ב מהלכות שביתת עשור הלכה ז סמג לאוין סט טוש"ע א"ח סימן תריב סעיף ו:

סא ד מיי' פי"ב מהל' מעשה קרבנות הל' יד סמג לאוין של:

סב ה מיי' פ"ו מהל' חמץ ומצה הלכה ו סמג עשין מ טוש"ע א"ח סימן תנד סעיף ג:

סג ו טוש"ע אה"ע סימן קסג סעיף ב:

[וע"ע תוס' פסחים קז: ד"ה דלמא ותוספות נזיר כג. ד"ה פסח ותוספות ב"ק קי. ד"ה אכילה]

סד ז מיי' פ"ג מהלכות נחלות הלכה ז סמג עשין נא טוש"ע שם סע"א:

סה ח מיי' שם פ"א הל' ב סמג עשין נו טור ש"ע ח"מ סי' רעו סע"א:

סו ט מיי' פ"א מהלכות יבום הלכה יג סמג עשין נב ולאוין קי טור ש"ע אה"ע סמן קסב סעיף ג:

[ועי' היטב תוס' מנחות נג. ד"ה ת"ל תהיה]

תוספות ישנים

א) וי"ל א) דתרי עניני הוו אכילה גסה היכא שאכל כל צרכו והסיח דעתו מלאכול עוד כשאכל יותר לא מקרייא אותה אכילה אכילה גסה אבל היכא דלא הסיח דעתו אכן אוכל הוא יותר מדאי שהיה שבע בפחות מקרי אותה אכילה אכילה גסה עוד י"ל דשאני אכילת פסחים דלא מיעכבא דהא לא ממעטינן מקרא דלפי אוכלו כי אם חולה וזקן שאינו ראוי כלל לאכילה אבל אפילו אכילה גסה גמורה מותרת דפסח מיהא קעביד אבל בכל מקום אכילה גסה לא שמה אכילה ואין חילוק באכילה גסה: מצות אמרה רחמנא פ"ה דכתיב ואכלוה מצות. ולא נהירא דהא בשמיני של מילואים כתיב ודורות משעה לא ילפינן אלא נראה מצות אמר רחמנא דכתיב לא תאפה חמץ חלקם א"נ משום דכתיב מצה תהיה ובזה ניחא דקאמר להכי תנא ביה קרא לעכב וקשה דאין זה לעכב ממש שהרי קרא אחרינא לא כתיב למעוטי חלוט דהא אמרי' לעולם מצה היא ולא חזינן בשום מקום לעכב אם לא כתיבי תרי קראי דמשמע שנה הכתוב לעכב וצ"ל לעכב לאו דוקא אלא ר"ל לעכב שלא יביא חלוט אבל זה אינו לעכב ממש כי אם למצוה ולמאי דפרישית ניחא דודאי לעכב הוי מקרא דמצות תאכל דכבר כתיב קרא אחרינא למעוטי חלוט דכתיב מצה

תנא

הגהות הב"ח

(א) רש"י ד"ה ואי לאו וכו' דכתיב בסדר שמיני ואכלוה מצות.

מסורת הש"ס

לקמן ל. פסחים כו: [יומא סח:]

יומא פ:

שבועות טו. [מנחות נה.]

[מכות יט: וש"נ]

ב"ב קטז.

[עי' לעיל יז: כד.]

[ברכות ל: כתובות נו.]

[שבת ס: וש"נ]

א) נראה דצ"ל וי"ב דתרי ענייני אכילה גסה הוו היכא וכו'. ב) צ"ל ר"ל דהיכי שראוי לנחל [כגון אח מן האב] מייבם אידך לא.

פסים והכי איתא במנחות בריש פ' כל המנחות דף נג ע"א: מידי יבום בנחלה תלה רחמנא והא דאמרינן [דף יז] יבום בנחלה תלה רחמנא ר"ל ב) היכי דמי שראוי לנחלה מייבם אידך לא אבל אם אין נחלה משום הכי לא פקע מצות יבום:

עין משפט נר מצוה

סז א מיי' פ"א מהל' יבום הלכה יג וסמג עשין נ"ב וטוש"ע אה"ע סי' קסב סעיף ד:
סח ב מיי' שם פ"ו הל' כ סמג שם טוש"ע שם סעיף ה:
סט ג מיי' שם פ"א הל' יב סמג שם טוש"ע שם סעיף ג:

הוּא אָסוּר בְּאִמָּהּ, וּבְאֵם אִמָּהּ, וּבְאֵם אָבִיהָ, וּבְבִתָּהּ, וּבְבַת בִּתָּהּ, וּבְבַת בְּנָהּ, וּבַאֲחוֹתָהּ בִּזְמַן שֶׁהִיא קַיֶּימֶת, וְהָאַחִין מוּתָּרִין. וְהִיא אֲסוּרָה בְּאָבִיו, וּבַאֲבִי אָבִיו, וּבִבְנוֹ, וּבְבֶן בְּנוֹ, בְּאָחִיו, וּבְבֶן אָחִיו. *[א]מוּתָּר אָדָם בִּקְרוֹבַת צָרַת חֲלוּצָתוֹ, *[ב]וְאָסוּר בְּצָרַת קְרוֹבַת חֲלוּצָתוֹ.§

גמ' אִיבַּעְיָא לְהוּ: גָּזְרוּ שְׁנִיּוֹת בַּחֲלוּצָה אוֹ לָא? בְּעֶרְוָה דְּאוֹרַיְיתָא גָּזְרוּ בְּהוּ רַבָּנַן שְׁנִיּוֹת, בַּחֲלוּצָה לָא גָּזְרוּ רַבָּנַן שְׁנִיּוֹת, אוֹ דִּלְמָא לָא שְׁנָא? ת"ש: "הוּא אָסוּר בְּאִמָּהּ וּבְאֵם אִמָּהּ", וְאִילּוּ "אֵם אֵם אִמָּהּ" – לָא קָתָנֵי. דִּלְמָא הַיְינוּ טַעְמָא דְּלָא תָּנֵי – מִשּׁוּם דְּקָבָעֵי לְמִיתְנֵי סֵיפָא "וְהָאַחִין מוּתָּרִין", וְאִי תָּנָא "אֵם אֵם אִמָּהּ" ה"א: הָאַחִין מוּתָּרִין דַּוְקָא בְּאֵם אֵם אִמָּהּ, אֲבָל בְּאֵם אִמָּהּ וּבְאִמָּהּ לָא. וְלִיתְנֵי "אֵם אֵם אִמָּהּ" וְלִיתְנֵי "הָאַחִין מוּתָּרִין בְּכוּלָּן"! קַשְׁיָא. ת"ש: הִיא אֲסוּרָה בְּאָבִיו וּבַאֲבִי אָבִיו. קָתָנֵי מִיהָא אֲבִי אָבִיו, מַאי לָאו – מִשּׁוּם חוֹלֵץ, דְּהָוְיָא לָהּ כַּלַּת בְּנוֹ! לָא, מִשּׁוּם מִיתְנָא, דְּהָוְיָא לָהּ כַּלַּת בְּנוֹ. ת"ש: וּבְבֶן בְּנוֹ. מַאי לָאו – מִשּׁוּם חוֹלֵץ, דְּהָוְיָא לָהּ (מִשּׁוּם) אֵשֶׁת אֲבִי אָבִיו! לָא, מִשּׁוּם מִיתְנָא, וְהָוְיָא לָהּ אֵשֶׁת אֲחִי אֲבִי אָבִיו. הָא *אֲמֵימַר מַכְשַׁר בְּאֵשֶׁת אֲחִי אֲבִי אָבִיו! אֲמֵימַר מוֹקֵי לָהּ בְּבַר בְּרָא דְּסָבָא. אִי הָכִי, הַיְינוּ אָחִיו וּבֶן אָחִיו! תָּנָא אָחִיו מִן הָאָב, וְקָתָנֵי אָחִיו מִן הָאֵם. ת"ש, דְּתָנֵי רַ' חִיָּיא: אַרְבַּע מִדִּבְרֵי תוֹרָה, וְאַרְבַּע מִדִּבְרֵי סוֹפְרִים. אָב וּבְנוֹ, אָחִיו וּבֶן אָחִיו – מִדִּבְרֵי תוֹרָה, אֲבִי אָבִיו וַאֲבִי אִמּוֹ, בֶּן בְּנוֹ, וּבֶן בִּתּוֹ – מד"ס. קָתָנֵי מִיהָא אֲבִי אָבִיו, מַאי לָאו מִשּׁוּם חוֹלֵץ, וְהָוְיָא לָהּ כַּלַּת בְּנוֹ! לֹא, מִשּׁוּם מִיתְנָא, דְּהָוְיָא לָהּ כַּלַּת בְּנוֹ. ת"ש: אֲבִי אִמּוֹ – מַאי לָאו מִשּׁוּם חוֹלֵץ, דְּהָוְיָא לָהּ כַּלַּת בִּתּוֹ! לָא, מִשּׁוּם מִיתְנָא, דְּהָוְיָא לָהּ כַּלַּת בִּתּוֹ. ת"ש: וּבֶן בְּנוֹ, מַאי לָאו מִשּׁוּם חוֹלֵץ, דְּהָוְיָא לָהּ אֵשֶׁת אֲבִי אָבִיו! לָא, מִשּׁוּם מִיתְנָא דְּהָוְיָא לָהּ אֵשֶׁת אֲחִי אֲבִי אָבִיו. וְהָא אֲמֵימַר מַכְשִׁיר בְּאֵשֶׁת אֲחִי אֲבִי אָבִיו! אֲמֵימַר מוֹקִים לָהּ מִשּׁוּם חוֹלֵץ, וְקָסָבַר גָּזְרוּ שְׁנִיּוֹת בַּחֲלוּצָה. ת"ש: וּבְבֶן בִּתּוֹ, מַאי לָאו מִשּׁוּם חוֹלֵץ, דְּהָוְיָא לָהּ אֵשֶׁת אֲבִי אִמּוֹ! לָא, מִשּׁוּם מִיתְנָא דְּהָוְיָא לָהּ אֵשֶׁת אֲחִי אֲבִי אִמּוֹ. וְהָא גַּבֵּי שְׁנִיּוֹת דְּעֶרְוָה לָא גָּזְרוּ! אֶלָּא לָאו מִשּׁוּם חוֹלֵץ, [ג]וּשְׁמַע מִינַּהּ: גָּזְרוּ שְׁנִיּוֹת בַּחֲלוּצָה, שְׁמַע מִינַּהּ.§ "מוּתָּר אָדָם וכו'".§ אָמַר רַב טוֹבִי בַּר קִיסְנָא אָמַר שְׁמוּאֵל: הַבָּא עַל צָרַת חֲלוּצָה – הַוָּלָד מַמְזֵר. מַאי טַעְמָא – בְּאִיסּוּרָהּ קַיְימָא. אָמַר רַב יוֹסֵף: אַף אֲנַן נַמִי תְּנֵינָא: מוּתָּר אָדָם בִּקְרוֹבַת צָרַת חֲלוּצָתוֹ. אִי אָמְרַתְּ בִּשְׁלָמָא צָרָה אַבְּרָאֵי – מִשּׁוּם הָכִי מוּתָּר בַּאֲחוֹתָהּ. אֶלָּא אִי אָמְרַתְּ צָרָה כַּחֲלוּצָה דָּמְיָא – אַמַּאי מוּתָּר? לֵימָא תֶּהֱוֵי תְּיוּבְתָּא דְּרַבִּי יוֹחָנָן, דְּאָמַר: *בֵּין הוּא בֵּין אַחִין אֵין חַיָּיבִין לֹא עַל הַחֲלוּצָה כָּרֵת, וְלֹא עַל צָרָתָהּ כָּרֵת! אָמַר לָךְ רַבִּי יוֹחָנָן: וְתִסְבְּרָא אֲחוֹת חֲלוּצָה דְּאוֹרַיְיתָא? וְהָאָמַר ר"ל: *כָּאן שָׁנָה רַבִּי: אֲחוֹת גְּרוּשָׁה – מִדִּבְרֵי תוֹרָה, אֲחוֹת חֲלוּצָה – מִדִּבְרֵי סוֹפְרִים. מַאי שְׁנָא הַאי, וּמַאי שְׁנָא הַאי?
הַךְ

רש"י

הוא אסור כו'. כל הנך עריות דאורייתא נינהו באשתו, וגזרינהו רבנן בחלוצתו. **בזמן שהיא קיימת.** אאחותה קאי, ולא אשאר עריות. **באביו.** משום כלתו. **ובאבי אביו.** משום כלת בנו, אע"ג דבאשתו גמורה אין אסורה לאבי אביו אלא מדברי סופרים, דהא כלת בנו משניות דרבנן היא – ואפילו הכי גזרוה רבנן נמי בחלוצה. **בבנו.** משום אשת אב. **בבן בנו.** משום אשת אבי אביו, שהיא מן השניות. **באחיו.** משום אשת אח. **בבן אחיו.** משום אשת אחי אביו. **מותר אדם בקרובת צרת חלוצתו.** ולא אמרינן צרה כחלוצה, ואסור בקרובותיה. **ואסור בצרת קרובת חלוצתו.** ראובן חלץ ללאה, ורחל נשואה לנכרי ולה צרה, ומת הנכרי – אסורה הצרה לראובן. וטעמא מפרש בגמרא.

גמ' גזרו שניות בחלוצה או לא. כגון אם אם אמה ואם אם אביה, דגבי אשתו מיתסרו עליה משום שניות, כדתני רבי חייא בפרק "כיצד" (לעיל דף כא.): רביעי שבחמיו ושבחמותו. שניה הכא מאי? בערוה דאורייתא. כלומר, באשתו, דאמה ואם אמה הוה ערוה דאורייתא – גזרו רבנן שניות, אבל בחלוצה, דאפילו עריות דידה דרבנן – לא גזרו שניות בהן. או דלמא לא שנא. ומתני' לא דייק. דקתני היא אסורה באבי אביו משום כלת בנו דהוי שניה – הא קמיימינן לה לקמן עלה דהא מילתא, ומדחי ליה, למימר: לאו משום חולץ, אלא בשביל המת שהיתה זו אשתו גמורה, לפיכך אבי אביו אסור בה משום כלת בנו. ה"א **האחין מותרין.** לא קאי אלא אאם אם אמה, דלא גזרו שניות בזיקה. אבל אמה ואם אמה, דהוו להו עריות דאורייתא לגבי אשה גמורה – לא מישתרו אחין, דגזרו עריות בזיקה ואפי' לאחר חליצה. נימא דאיהו שליחותייהו עבד, משום הכי לא תנייה. **ת"ש מבן בנו מאי לאו משום חולץ** דהוי ליה **אשת אבי אביו.** והיא מן השניות. **לא משום מיתנא.** שהיתה זו אשתו גמורה, ואסורה על בן בנו של חולץ, דהויא לה אשת אחי אבי אביו. וקס"ד דהא נמי משניות היא. **והא אמימר מכשר כו'.** בפרק "כיצד" (לעיל דף כא:). **אמימר מוקי לה.** להאי בן בנו דמתני' אסבא, אביהן של מת; וחולץ דתנא ברישא, דקתני: היא אסורה באביו, והדר תני ובבנו של אביו – שהוא אחי המת והחולץ, וקמה עליה בלא יבנה משלך לה האחד, ולבן בנו של אביהם, דהויא ליה אשת אחי אביו. וקתני אחיו מן האם. שהיה זה אחיו מן האם, או בן אחיו מן האם, ולאו משום חולץ – דא"כ הויא לה שניות בחלוצה, דהא ליתא. אלא אשת אחי האב מן האם, והא בשניות תנינן לה. אלא משום מיתנא, דהוי שניה משום ערוה דאורייתא, דאשתו מעלייתא הוה. וכגון שהיו (א) היבם והחולץ אחין מן האב ומן האם, ולשניהם אח מן האם שלא מן האב. דתני רבי חייא. בחלוצה. **ארבע מדברי תורה.** כלומר, דלגבי אשתו הוין דאורייתא. **אב.** של חולץ, אסור בה מן התורה מפני המת, דהויא ליה כלתו של אב. **ובנו.** של חולץ, שהיה המת אחי אביו, וערוה היא לגביה. **ואחיו.** של חולץ, דהוה נמי אחי המת, וקם ליה ב"לא יבנה". **ובן אחיו.** של חולץ, שהיה המת אחי אביו. **ואבי אמו.** משום כלת בתו. **ובן בנו.** קס"ד משום חולץ, דהויא ליה אשת אבי אביו. **ובן בתו.** דהויא ליה אשת אבי אמו, וכל הנך שניות נינהו: ת"ש ובאבי אמו מאי לאו משום חולץ דהויא ליה כלת בתו לא משום מיתנא דהויא ליה כלת בתו וכגון שהיו אחין אף מן האם. **אמימר מוקי לה.** ודאי כדקאמרת משום חולץ, וקסבר גזרו שניות בחלוצה אבל מאן דאסר באשת אחי אבי האב – מצי לאוקמי משום מיתנא, ותיבעי לך אי גזרו שניות בחלוצה או לא. **באיסורה קיימא.** חלוצה היא דקיימא ב"לא יבנה" ותו לא, אבל צרתה קיימא עליה באיסור אשת אח בכרת, והולד ממזר. **אי אמרת בשלמא צרה אבראי קיימא.** באיסורא קמא, ולא אמרינן חלוצה שליחותא דידה עבדא. משום הכי שרי באחותה. דלאו אחות חלוצה היא. ולגבי דידה נמי, כיון דחלוצה לאו שליחות דידה עבדא – לא משוויא ליה ב"לא יבנה", אלא באיסורא קמא קיימא. **אלא אי אמרת צרה כחלוצה דמיא.** דחלוצה שליחותא דידה עבדא, ומשוי לה ב"לא יבנה" – א"כ הויא לה צרה כחלוצה, ואמאי שרי באחותה? **דר' יוחנן.** בפרק קמא (לעיל י:). **ולא על צרתה כרת.** החולץ ליבמתו, וחזר ובא הוא או אחד מן האחין על צרתה. **ותסברא.** דהא ראיה דרב יוסף דאייתי ממתניתין – ראיה היא? וכי *חלוצה גופא דאורייתא (דרבנן היא), דכי אמרינן צרה כחלוצה יאסר באחות הצרה. **והאמר ר"ל.** לקמן אמתניתין דלקמן. **כאן שנה רבי.** במשנה זו למדנו רבי: אחות גרושה מדברי תורה וכו'. ולקמן מפרש לה. וכיון דאחות חלוצה גופה דרבנן, בחלוצה – גזור באחותה, בצרה – לא גזור. **מאי שנא.** רישא קרובת צרת חלוצה דשריא, ומאי שנא סיפא צרת קרובת חלוצתו שאשתהן נכריות, היא וצרתה נשואות לנכרי, וקתני אסור?
הַךְ

תוספות

אבל אמה ואם אמה לא. והא דתנן בפרק ג' (לעיל כג.) אחד חולץ ואחד מייבם, אלמא שרי באחותה! שאני התם משום דלאימור דידיה איתרמי ליה. והא נמי דתנן לקמן בפרקין (דף מא.): החולץ ליבמתו ונשא אחיו את אחותה – היינו דיעבד. **וליתני אחין מותרין בכולן קשיא.** הא דלא קאמר אלא שמע מינה דלא גזרו שניות בחלוצה, היינו משום דלקמן מסיק דגזרו. ולא שייך לשנויי תנא ושייר, כיון דלא תנא שום שניה אלא הני דאורייתא לחוד. **אמימר** מוקי לה כו'. כל סוגיא דשמעתין דלא כאמימר, כדפרשתי לעיל (דף כא: ד"ה "אמימר"). **בבן** בתו לאו משום חולץ. לא בעי לאוקמי בבן בתו דסבא דומיא דבן בנו – דלא מיירי בבן בנו דסבא, דא"כ הויא ליה אשת אחי אביו דאורייתא. **שמע** מינה גזרו שניות בחלוצה. והא דלא תני במתניתין אבי אמו ובן בתו – משום דתנא ושייר. ומיהו רבי חייא, דקתני מנינא, קשה דלא תנא בן אחותו ובן אחיו מן האם! ויש לומר: דלא תנא אלא ארבע, כנגד ארבע של דברי תורה.
הך

תוספות ישנים

תנא אחיו מן האב ותנא אחיו מן האם פי' הא דקאמר ובן אחיו ר"ל אחיו מן האם וא"ת א"כ לפשוט דגזרו שניות בחלוצה דהא אשת אחי האב מן האם היינו שניה וי"ל דזהו משום מיתנא דמיירי שאותו בן אחיו דמיירי בה מתני' שהוא אח מן האם למיתנא ולחולץ אבל החולץ והמיתנא אחין מן האב ומן האם וזה בן אחיו ר"ל שהוא בן אחי האב מן האם לשניהם וא"כ לא תפשוט שניות בחלוצה דהיינו משום מיתנא: **אמימר** מוקים לה בבר ברא דחולץ וקסבר כו' אבל לא קאמר בבר ברא דסבא כדלעיל וא"כ לא תפשוט דגזרו שניה בחלוצה דדוקא לעיל מצינן למימר הכי דהא קאי אהיא אסורה באביו ור"ל בן בנו של אותו אב אבל ר' חייא דהכא לא קתני אביו ועוד נלע"ד דלא מצי מוקי לה בבר ברא דסבא כדלעיל דא"כ בן בנו הוי מן התורה דהיינו לכל הפחות אשת אחי אביו ור' חייא תני ליה בן בנו עם הארבעה שמדברי סופרים: **ותסברא** אחות חלוצה דאורייתא היא. פי' אלא ודאי לאו סיועא היא לעולם מצינן למימר דצרה כחלוצה וליכא להקשות אמאי מותר כי יש טעם גדול בדבר דהא אפי' אי הוי הצרה עצמה חלוצה אחותה אינה אסורה אלא מדרבנן וא"כ לא גזור רבנן באחות הצרה דכי גזור רבנן באחות חלוצה עצמה אבל באחות צרת חלוצה לא גזור:

תוספות חד מקמאי

מתני' (א) אסור בקרובת חלוצתו ומותר בקרובת חלוצתו פירוש אי חליץ לצרת לאה מותר אף ברחל אי חליץ ללאה אסור בצרת רחל ופי' רש"י ז"ל אע"פ שרחל נשואה לנכרי ולה צרה ומת הנכרי אסורה הצרה לראובן החולץ ומפורש טעמא בגמ' הך דאזלא לב"ד גזרו בהו רבנן כלומר כשלאה חולצת מוליכה רחל אחותה עמה לב"ד וכ"ע לא ידעי הי מינייהו יבמתו ואיכא דסברי (ב) דרחל חלץ ואנסיב צרת רחל דהיינו צרת אחות חלוצתו אמרי צרת אחות חלוצתו נסיב ואינהו סברי דרחל וצרת האחין הוו. הך דלא אזלא לב"ד לא גזרו בהו רבנן כשהיבמה חולצת אין צרתה הולכת עמה דמסתפק דלמא חליץ לה הלכך כי נסיב אחות הצרה לא אמרי אחות חלוצתו נסיב כך פירש"י ז"ל ולפי דבריו מצינו חלוצה שהיא מדברי סופרים חמורה מערוה שהיא מד"ת דאילו צרת ערוה שלא במקום מצוה היא שריה וצרת אחות חלוצה שלא במקום מצוה אסורה וי"מ שלא אסרו צרת קרובת חלוצתו אלא במקום יבום כגון שלאה ורחל נשואים לראובן ושמעון ומתו שניהם וכההיא דאמר בפרק ד' אחין התחיל באחיות לא יגמור אפילו בצרות דתנן אסור אדם בצרת קרובת חלוצתו התחיל בצרות יגמור אף באחיות דתנן מותר אדם בקרובת צרת חלוצתו ועל הפירוש הזה איכא לעיוני כיון דרחל אזלא בתרה (דינא) לב"ד וכי חליץ לאה סברי חליץ רחל אלא מעתה תפסול רחל לכהונה ותפסלה רחל לאחי החולץ אלמא תנן החולץ ליבמתו אסור הוא בקרובותיה והאחין מותרים ונפסלת רחל לאחר מיתת לאה אלמה תנן מתה מותר באחותה אלא כיון דאחות חלוצה אינה אסורה אלא מדברי סופרים לא גזרו בה רבנן כולי האי אע"פ שגזרו בצרתה: הא דאמר נפלה לפני יבם קטן לית לה מזוני מבעל מסתברא הני מילי לאחר שלשה חדשים אבל תוך שלשה חדשים אית לה מזוני מבעל:
גרים

א) נ"ל אסור אדם בצרת קרובת חלוצתו ומותר בקרובת צרת חלוצתו. ב) נ"ל ואיכא דסברי דלרחל חלץ ואי נסיב צרת רחל דהיינו צרת אחות חלוצתו אמרי צרת חלוצתו נסיב דאינהו סברי דרחל חלוצת האחין הוה.

מסורת הש"ס

[לעיל כז.]
שם
לעיל כח:
[לעיל י.]
לקמן מא. מד. קדושין מה.
ס"א אחות חלוצה

הגהות הב"ח

(א) רש"י ד"ה וקתני אחיו וכו' וכגון שהיו המת והחולץ אחים מן האב:

גמרא

הַךְ דְּאָזְלָא בַּהֲדַהּ לְבֵי דִינָא — גָּזְרוּ בְּהוּ רַבָּנַן, הַאי דְּלָא אָזְלָא בַּהֲדַהּ לְבֵי דִינָא — לָא גָּזְרוּ בְּהוּ רַבָּנַן.§ **מתני'** [א]הַחוֹלֵץ לִיבִמְתּוֹ, וְנָשָׂא אָחִיו אֶת אֲחוֹתָהּ, וָמֵת — חוֹלֶצֶת וְלֹא מִתְיַבֶּמֶת. [ב]וְכֵן הַמְגָרֵשׁ אֶת אִשְׁתּוֹ, וְנָשָׂא אָחִיו אֶת אֲחוֹתָהּ וָמֵת — הֲרֵי זוֹ פְּטוּרָה. *[ג]שׁוֹמֶרֶת יָבָם שֶׁקִּידֵּשׁ אָחִיו אֶת אֲחוֹתָהּ, מִשּׁוּם רַבִּי יְהוּדָה בֶּן בְּתֵירָא אָמְרוּ: אוֹמְרִים לוֹ: הַמְתֵּן עַד שֶׁיַּעֲשֶׂה אָחִיךָ מַעֲשֶׂה. חָלַץ לָהּ אָחִיו אוֹ כְּנָסָהּ — יִכְנוֹס אֶת אִשְׁתּוֹ. מֵתָה הַיְבָמָה — יִכְנוֹס אֶת אִשְׁתּוֹ. [ד]מֵת יָבָם — יוֹצִיא אֶת אִשְׁתּוֹ בְּגֵט, וְאֵשֶׁת אָחִיו בַּחֲלִיצָה.§ **גמ'** מַאי "וְכֵן"? אֵימָא: אֲבָל הַמְגָרֵשׁ. אָמַר רֵישׁ לָקִישׁ: *כָּאן שָׁנָה רַבִּי: [ה]אֲחוֹת גְּרוּשָׁה — מִדִּבְרֵי תוֹרָה, [ו]אֲחוֹת חֲלוּצָה — מִדִּבְרֵי סוֹפְרִים.§ "שׁוֹמֶרֶת יָבָם שֶׁקִּידֵּשׁ וכו'".§ *אָמַר שְׁמוּאֵל: הֲלָכָה כְּדִבְרֵי רַבִּי יְהוּדָה בֶּן בְּתֵירָא. אִיבַּעְיָא לְהוּ: מֵתָה אִשְׁתּוֹ, מַהוּ בִּיבִמְתּוֹ? רַב וְרַבִּי חֲנִינָא דְּאָמְרִי תַּרְוַיְיהוּ: [ז]מֵתָה אִשְׁתּוֹ מוּתָּר בִּיבִמְתּוֹ, שְׁמוּאֵל וְרַב אַסִּי דְּאָמְרִי תַּרְוַיְיהוּ: מֵתָה אִשְׁתּוֹ אָסוּר בִּיבִמְתּוֹ. אָמַר רָבָא: מַאי טַעְמָא דְּרַב — מִשּׁוּם דַּהֲוַאי יְבָמָה שֶׁהוּתְּרָה, וְנֶאֶסְרָה, וְחָזְרָה וְהוּתְּרָה — תַּחֲזוֹר לְהֶיתֵּירָהּ הָרִאשׁוֹן. מְתִיב רַב הַמְנוּנָא: *ג' אַחִין, ב' נְשׂוּאִין ב' אֲחָיוֹת וְאֶחָד מוּפְנֶה, מֵת אֶחָד מִבַּעֲלֵי אֲחָיוֹת וְעָשָׂה בָּהּ מוּפְנֶה מַאֲמָר, וְאַחַר כָּךְ מֵת אָחִיו הַשֵּׁנִי, וְאַחַר כָּךְ מֵתָה אִשְׁתּוֹ אַחֲרָיו — אוֹתָהּ יְבָמָה חוֹלֶצֶת וְלֹא מִתְיַבֶּמֶת. וְאַמַּאי? תֶּיהֱוֵי כִּיבָמָה שֶׁהוּתְּרָה, וְנֶאֶסְרָה, וְחָזְרָה וְהוּתְּרָה — תַּחֲזוֹר לְהֶיתֵּירָהּ הָרִאשׁוֹן! אִישְׁתִּיק. לְבָתַר דִּנְפַק אֲמַר: אַמַּאי לָא אֲמַרְתְּ לֵיהּ רַבִּי אֶלְעָזָר הִיא, דְּאָמַר: *כֵּיוָן שֶׁעָמְדָה עָלָיו שָׁעָה אַחַת בְּאִסּוּר נֶאֶסְרָה עָלָיו עוֹלָמִית? הֲדַר אֲמַר: אֵימוּר דְּא"ר אֶלְעָזָר — הֵיכָא דְּלָא חַזְיָא בִּשְׁעַת נְפִילָה, אֲבָל הֵיכָא דְּחַזְיָא בִּשְׁעַת נְפִילָה — מִי אֲמַר? הֲדַר אֲמַר: אִין, וְהָתַנְיָא: רַבִּי אֶלְעָזָר אוֹמֵר: מֵתָה יְבִמְתּוֹ — מוּתָּר בְּאִשְׁתּוֹ, מֵתָה אִשְׁתּוֹ אוֹתָהּ יְבָמָה חוֹלֶצֶת וְלֹא מִתְיַבֶּמֶת. לֵימָא שְׁמוּאֵל וְרַב אַסִּי דְּאָמְרִי כְּר' אֶלְעָזָר! אֲפִי' תֵּימָא כְּרַבָּנַן, עַד כָּאן לָא קָמִיפַּלְגִי רַבָּנַן עֲלֵיהּ דְּרַבִּי אֶלְעָזָר — אֶלָּא מִשּׁוּם דְּמִנְּפִילָה וְאֵילָךְ לָא מִיתְּסַר עֲלַיְיהוּ, אֲבָל הָכָא דְּאִיתְּסַר — אֲפִילּוּ רַבָּנַן מוֹדוּ.§ **מתני'** *[ח]הַיְבָמָה לֹא תַּחֲלוֹץ וְלֹא תִּתְיַיבֵּם עַד שֶׁיֵּשׁ לָהּ שְׁלֹשָׁה חֳדָשִׁים. [ט]וְכֵן כָּל שְׁאָר הַנָּשִׁים לֹא יִתְאָרְסוּ וְלֹא יִנָּשְׂאוּ עַד שֶׁיְּהוּ לָהֶן שְׁלֹשָׁה חֳדָשִׁים אֶחָד בְּתוּלוֹת וְאֶחָד בְּעוּלוֹת, אֶחָד גְּרוּשׁוֹת וְאֶחָד אַלְמָנוֹת, אֶחָד נְשׂוּאוֹת וְאֶחָד אֲרוּסוֹת. רַבִּי יְהוּדָה אוֹמֵר: הַנְּשׂוּאוֹת יִתְאָרְסוּ, וְהָאֲרוּסוֹת יִנָּשְׂאוּ, חוּץ מִן הָאֲרוּסוֹת שֶׁבִּיהוּדָה, מִפְּנֵי שֶׁלִּבּוֹ גַּס בָּהּ. *ר' יוֹסֵי אוֹמֵר: כָּל הַנָּשִׁים יִתְאָרְסוּ, חוּץ מִן הָאַלְמָנָה, מִפְּנֵי

רש"י

הַךְ דְּאָזְלָא בַּהֲדַהּ לְבֵי דִינָא. כְּשֶׁלֵּאָה חוֹלֶצֶת מוֹלִיכָה אֲחוֹתָהּ עִמָּהּ לְבֵ"ד, וְכ"ע לָא יָדְעִי הֵי מִינַּיְיהוּ יְבִמְתּוֹ, וְאִיכָּא דְּסָבַר דְּלְרָחֵל חָלַץ. וְכִי נָסֵיב צָרַת רָחֵל, דְּהַיְינוּ צָרַת קְרוֹבַת חֲלוּצָתוֹ, אָמְרִי: צָרַת חֲלוּצָתוֹ נָסֵיב. דְּאִינְהוּ סָבְרִי שֶׁרָחֵל וְצָרָתָהּ נְשֵׁי אָחִיו הֲווּ, שֶׁהֲרֵי חָלַץ לְרָחֵל. הַאי דְּלָא אָזְלָא בַּהֲדַהּ לְבֵי דִינָא. כְּשֶׁהַיְּבָמָה חוֹלֶצֶת אֵין צָרָתָהּ הוֹלֶכֶת עִמָּהּ. הִלְכָּךְ, כִּי נָסֵיב אֲחוֹת צָרָה — לָא אָמְרִינַן אֲחוֹת חֲלוּצָתוֹ נָסֵיב. **מתני'** וְלֹא מִתְיַיבֶּמֶת. דְּהָוְיָא לָהּ אֲחוֹת חֲלוּצָתוֹ. וּמִיהוּ, מֵחֲלִיצָה לָא מִפַּטְרָא, דְּמִדְּאוֹרַיְיתָא רַמְיָא קַמֵּיהּ, וְאע"ג דַּאֲחוֹתָהּ קַיֶּימֶת. דַּאֲחוֹת חֲלוּצָה אֵינָהּ אֶלָּא מִדִּבְרֵי סוֹפְרִים. וְכֵן הַמְגָרֵשׁ. בַּגְּמָרָא בָּעֵי: מַאי "וְכֵן"? פְּטוּרָה. אַף מִן הַחֲלִיצָה, דְּיוֹלְדָהּ מִשּׁוּם אֲחוֹת אִשָּׁה, הוֹאִיל וְאִשְׁתּוֹ קַיֶּימֶת. וַאֲחוֹת גְּרוּשָׁה מִדִּבְרֵי תוֹרָה, דִּכְתִיב (ויקרא יח) "עָלֶיהָ בְּחַיֶּיהָ" — כָּל שֶׁבְּחַיֶּיהָ. שׁוֹמֶרֶת יָבָם שֶׁקִּידֵּשׁ. אֶחָד מִן הָאַחִין אֶת אֲחוֹתָהּ לְאַחַר שֶׁנָּפְלָה זוֹ לִפְנֵיהֶם, וְהוּזְקְקָה לְכוּלָּן. הַמְתֵּן. מִלִּכְנוֹס, דְּקָא פָּגַעְתְּ בַּאֲחוֹת זְקוּקָה. עַד שֶׁיַּעֲשֶׂה מַעֲשֶׂה. שֶׁיִּכְנְסוּ הָאַחִין אֶת הַיְּבָמָה אוֹ יַחְלְצוּ, וְתֵעָקֵר זִיקָתָהּ מִמְּךָ. מֵתָה הַיְבָמָה יִכְנוֹס אֶת אִשְׁתּוֹ. דַּאֲפִילּוּ כְּנָסָהּ וּמֵתָה — מוּתָּר בַּאֲחוֹתָהּ. מֵת הַיָּבָם. וְלֹא נוֹתַר לוֹ אָח אֶלָּא זֶה. וְאֵת אֵשֶׁת אָחִיו בַּחֲלִיצָה. אֲבָל יַבּוּמֵי לָא, דַּאֲחוֹת גְּרוּשָׁתוֹ הִיא. **גמ'** הֲלָכָה כְּרַבִּי יְהוּדָה. דְּיֵשׁ זִיקָה, וְאַלִּימָא לְמֵיסְרָא עָלָיו. מַהוּ בִּיבִמְתּוֹ. מִי אָמְרִינַן: כֵּיוָן דְּמֵתָה — פָּקַע אִיסּוּר אֲחוֹת אִשָּׁה, וְשַׁרְיָא, אוֹ דִּלְמָא, אע"ג דְּפָקַע אִיסּוּר אֲחוֹת אִשָּׁה, קָם עֲלֵיהּ בְּאִיסּוּר אֵשֶׁת אָח, הוֹאִיל וְנֶאֶסְרָה עָלָיו שָׁעָה אַחַת בְּשָׁעָה שֶׁהָיְתָה זְקוּקָה לְיַבֵּם, וְאֵין אֲנִי קוֹרֵא בָּהּ "יְבָמָהּ יָבֹא עָלֶיהָ" — הֲרֵי הִיא כְּאֵשֶׁת אָח שֶׁיֵּשׁ לָהּ בָּנִים, וַאֲסוּרָה עוֹלָמִית עָלָיו. מ"ט דְּרַב. דְּשָׁרֵי, הֲרֵי נֶאֶסְרָה עָלָיו שָׁעָה אַחַת! שֶׁהוּתְּרָה. בִּשְׁעַת נְפִילָתָהּ. נֶאֶסְרָה. כְּשֶׁקִּידֵּשׁ זֶה אֲחוֹתָהּ. וְאח"כ מֵת אָחִיו. הַב', וְנָפְלָה אֲחוֹתָהּ, וַאֲסָרַתָּהּ לָרִאשׁוֹנָה עָלָיו מִשּׁוּם אֲחוֹת זְקוּקָה. וְאע"ג דַּעֲבַד בָּהּ מַאֲמָר, כְּדִתְנַן בְּפֶ' "אַרְבָּעָה אַחִין", ב"ה אוֹמְרִים: אוֹי לוֹ עַל אִשְׁתּוֹ, וְאוֹי לוֹ עַל אֵשֶׁת אָחִיו. וְאח"כ מֵתָה אִשְׁתּוֹ שֶׁל שֵׁנִי אַחֲרָיו. וְנִשְׁאֲרָה בַּעֲלַת מַאֲמָר זוֹ. ר' אֶלְעָזָר הִיא. בְּפֶרֶק ב"ש: הַמְגָרֵשׁ אֶת הָאִשָּׁה וְהֶחֱזִירָהּ — מוּתֶּרֶת לְיַבֵּם, רַבִּי אֶלְעָזָר אוֹסֵר, הוֹאִיל וְעָמְדָה עָלָיו שָׁעָה אַחַת בְּאִיסּוּר גְּרוּשַׁת אָח. דִּבִשְׁעַת נְפִילָה לָא אִיתְחֲזַאי. דְּמִקַּמֵּי נְפִילָה אִיתַּסְרָא עֲלֵיהּ. מֵתָה יְבִמְתּוֹ. אַמְּקַדֵּשׁ אֲחוֹת יְבִמְתּוֹ קָאֵי. חוֹלֶצֶת. כִּשְׁמוּאֵל וְרַב אַסִּי. עַד כָּאן לָא פְּלִיגִי רַבָּנַן עֲלֵיהּ דְּרַבִּי אֶלְעָזָר. בְּפֶרֶק "בֵּית שַׁמַּאי" אֶלָּא גַּבֵּי מְגָרֵשׁ אִשָּׁה וְהֶחֱזִירָהּ, מִשּׁוּם דְּמִנְּפִילָה וְאֵילָךְ לָא אִיתַּסְרָא עֲלֵיהּ, וְאִיסּוּר שֶׁבְּחַיֵּי אָחִיו לָא מְהַנֵּי. הַשְׁתָּא, דְּלֵיכָּא לְמֵימַר אֵין אֲנִי קוֹרֵא בָּהּ בִּשְׁעַת נְפִילָה — דְּלָאו בִּשְׁעַת נְפִילָה הֲוַאי. אֲבָל בְּבָרַיְיתָא דִּמְקַדֵּשׁ אֲחוֹת יְבִמְתּוֹ, דְּמִנְּפִילָה וְאֵילָךְ אִיתַּסְרָא עֲלֵיהּ, וַהֲרֵי אֵין אֲנִי קוֹרֵא בָּהּ בִּשְׁעַת זִיקַּת יִבּוּם "יְבָמָהּ יָבֹא עָלֶיהָ", לָא פְּלִיגִי. **מתני'** לֹא תַחֲלוֹץ. מְפָרֵשׁ טַעְמָא בַּגְּמָרָא. בְּתוּלוֹת וּבְעוּלוֹת אֲרוּסוֹת וּנְשׂוּאוֹת. בַּגְּמָרָא בָּעֵי: מַאי הֶפְרֵשׁ אִיכָּא בֵּין בְּתוּלוֹת לַאֲרוּסוֹת, בֵּין נְשׂוּאוֹת לִבְעוּלוֹת? הַנְּשׂוּאוֹת יִתְאָרְסוּ. דְּטַעְמָא מִשּׁוּם לְהַבְחִין בֵּין זֶרַע רִאשׁוֹן לְזֶרַע שֵׁנִי הוּא. שֶׁלֹּא תֵּלֵד סָפֵק בֶּן ט' לָרִאשׁוֹן סָפֵק בֶּן ז' לָאַחֲרוֹן, וּבְאֵירוּסִין לֵיכָּא לְמֵימַר הָכִי. וְהָאֲרוּסוֹת יִנָּשְׂאוּ. מִיָּד, דְּהָא לָא אִיעַבְּרָא מִן הָרִאשׁוֹן. חוּץ מֵאֲרוּסָה שֶׁבִּיהוּדָה. דִּתְנַן פֶּרֶק קַמָּא דִּכְתוּבּוֹת (דף יב.): בִּיהוּדָה הָיוּ מְיַיחֲדִים הֶחָתָן וְהַכַּלָּה קוֹדֶם כְּנִיסָתָן לַחוּפָּה כְּדֵי שֶׁיְּהֵא לִבּוֹ גַּס בָּהּ — כְּלוֹמַר: רָגִיל וּמְלַחֵק עִמָּהּ — שֶׁלֹּא יְהוּ בּוֹשִׁין זֶה מִזֶּה בִּבְעִילַת מִצְוָה. הִלְכָּךְ, חָיְישִׁינַן דִּלְמָא בָּעֵיל. כָּל הַנָּשִׁים יִתְאָרְסוּ. רַבִּי יוֹסֵי אַנְּשׂוּאוֹת קָאֵי, וְהָכִי *(קא"ל ר' יְהוּדָה): כָּל הַנָּשִׁים נְשׂוּאוֹת יִתְאָרְסוּ, כִּדְקָאָמְרַתְּ, וְלָא גָּזְרִינַן אֵירוּסִין אַטּוּ נִשּׂוּאִין. וּמִיהוּ, בְּהָא פְּלִיגְנָא עָלָךְ, שֶׁלֹּא חִלַּקְתָּ בֵּין אַלְמָנָה לִגְרוּשָׁה, וְהִתַּרְתָּ אַלְמָנָה לֵיאָרֵס בְּתוֹךְ יְמֵי אֶבְלָהּ — וַאֲנָא סְבִירָא לִי: אַלְמָנָה מִן הַנִּשּׂוּאִין לֹא תִּתָּאֵרֵס כָּל שְׁלֹשִׁים יְמֵי אֶבְלָהּ, מִפְּנֵי

תוספות

הך דאזלא בהדה לבי דינא. פי' בקונטרס: כשלאה חולצת מוליכה רחל אחותה עמה לב"ד, ואיכא דסברי שרחל חלצה ולהכי אסורה גם לצרתה, אפילו שתיהן נשואות לנכרי, דאינהו סברי שרחל וצרתה נשי אחיו היו, שהרי חלץ לרחל. ותימה גדולה פירש: דהא תנן במתניתין: ובאחותה בזמן שהיא קיימת, הא מתה – שריא! ותנן נמי לקמן (דף מט.): חלץ לה ומתה מותר באחותה. ואמאי? והא סברי שלאחותה חלץ! ועוד, דתנן: האחין מותרין, אע"ג דאזלי בהדיה לבי דינא! ועוד: דלא מיתסר צרה אלא דוקא במצוה, כדאמרינן בפ' קמא (לעיל ח.), ולעיל בריש "ארבעה אחין" (דף כז. ושם) גבי התחיל באחיות מייתי לה למתני' דהכא, דהיינו ששניהן נשואות לאחיו. ופ"ה יש ליישב קצת בנשואה לאחיו ולא לנכרי. א) ונראה לר"י דגרסי': הא דאזלא בהדיה לבי דינא, פי': שהולכת לחלוץ, וכיון דחלצה – דמיא לגרושה טפי, ואסרו גם צרת קרובתה כנשואה לאחין, דדמיא לצרת ערוה. אבל כשחולצת צרת לאה ולא לאה – לא דמיא לאה לגרושה, ואפילו רחל שהיא קרובת צרת חלוצה שריא. ויש ספרים דלא גרסי לא בהדיה ולא בהדה, אלא: הא דאזלא לבי דינא והא דלא אזלא. **יוציא** את אשתו בגט. בפ' "ארבעה אחין" (לעיל כט.) לא בעי למימר ד"זו היא" למעוטי הך דהכא דפשע, כדפרישית לעיל(א).

מתה אשתו מותר ביבמתו. ומתני' דקתני מתה יבמתו, ולא נקט מתה אשתו, דהוי רבותא טפי – איידי דבעי למיתני מת היבם תנא נמי מתה היבמה. **מאי** טעמא דרב משום דהוי יבמה שהותרה. ואע"פ דבפ' "ארבעה אחין" (שם דף כז:) שרי רב אפילו לא הותרה לכתחלה, דקאמר: מתה הראשונה מותר בשניה – היינו דוקא בזיקה דרבנן, אבל הכא – אחות אשה דאורייתא, דוקא משום דהותרה. **עשה** בה מופנה מאמר. לא אצטריך אלא לאפוקי מב"ש, דאמר (לעיל דף כט.): מאמר קונה קנין גמור. אי נמי: נקט עשה בה מאמר לאשמועינן דאע"ג דאין זיקת השניה גמורה – אפילו הכי אוסרת את זו. **ואמאי** תיהוי יבמה שהותרה כו'. תימה: דלא פריך מהך ברייתא לרב בריש פרק "ארבעה אחין" (לעיל דף כח.), ולישני דרבי אלעזר היא, כדמשני הכא. **הדר** אמר אימור דאמר רבי אלעזר כו'. אכתי הוה מצי למימר דטעמא דר' אלעזר כדמפרש לקמן בפרק "ב"ש" (דף קט. ושם), אבל בהך ברייתא דלמא לא פליגי. אמאי

עין משפט נר מצוה

עט א מיי׳ פ״א מהל׳ יבום הלכה יט:
פ ב מיי׳ פ״ו מהלכות יבום הלכה ז סמג עשין נא טוש״ע אה״ע סימן קעג סעיף טו:
פא ג מיי׳ פי״א מהל׳ גרושין הלכה כ סמג עשין נ טוש״ע אה״ע סימן יג סעיף א:
פב ד מיי׳ פי״ח מהל׳ אישות הלכה טו סמג עשין נא טור ש״ע אה״ע סימן קס סעיף א:
פג ה מיי׳ שם הלכה יז וטוש״ע שם סע״ג:
פד ו מיי׳ פ״א מהלכות יבום הלכה יט סמג עשין נב טוש״ע אה״ע סימן קסד סעיף א:

מִפְּנֵי הָאִיבּוּל.§ **גמ׳** בִּשְׁלָמָא לֹא תִתְיַבֵּם — שֶׁמָּא יִהְיֶה הַוָּלָד בֶּן קַיָּימָא, וְקָא פָּגַע בְּאִיסּוּר אֵשֶׁת אָח דְּאוֹרַיְיתָא. אֶלָּא לֹא תַחֲלוֹץ — אַמַּאי? לֵימָא תֶּיהֱוֵי תְּיוּבְתָּא דְּר״י דְּאָמַר: *חֲלִיצַת מְעוּבֶּרֶת שְׁמָהּ חֲלִיצָה! וְלָאו מִי אוֹתְבִינֵיהּ לְרַ׳ יוֹחָנָן חֲדָא זִימְנָא? לֵימָא מֵהָא נַמִי תֶּיהֱוֵי תְּיוּבְתָּא! לָא, הָכָא הַיְינוּ טַעֲמָא *שֶׁמָּא יְהֵא וָלָד בֶּן קַיָּימָא, וְנִמְצֵאת אַתָּה מַצְרִיכָהּ כָּרוֹז לִכְהוּנָּה. וְנִצְרְכָהּ! דִּלְמָא אִיכָּא דַּהֲוָאי בַּחֲלִיצָה וְלָא הָוֵי בַּהַכְרָזָה, וּמְפַסְלוּהָ מִן הַכְּהוּנָּה. תֵּינַח אַלְמָנָה, גְּרוּשָׁה מַאי אִיכָּא לְמֵימַר? מִשּׁוּם דְּמַפְסִיד לָהּ מְזוֹנוֹת. תֵּינַח נְשׂוּאָה, אֲרוּסָה גְּרוּשָׁה מַאי אִיכָּא לְמֵימַר? אֶלָּא מִשּׁוּם דְּרַבִּי יוֹסֵי. דְּתַנְיָא: *מַעֲשֶׂה בְּאָדָם אֶחָד שֶׁבָּא לִפְנֵי רַבִּי יוֹסֵי, א״ל: מַהוּ לַחֲלוֹץ בְּתוֹךְ ג׳? א״ל: לֹא תַחֲלוֹץ. וְתַחֲלוֹץ וּמַה בְּכָךְ? קְרָא עָלָיו מִקְרָא זֶה: °״וְאִם לֹא יַחְפֹּץ״ הָא אִם חָפֵץ — יַבֵּם, *[א]כָּל הָעוֹלֶה לְיִבּוּם — עוֹלֶה לַחֲלִיצָה כו׳. מְתִיב רַב חִינְּנָא: הַסְּפֵקוֹת חוֹלְצוֹת וְלֹא מִתְיַבְּמוֹת. מַאי סְפֵקוֹת? אִילֵימָא סְפֵק קִדּוּשִׁין אַמַּאי לֹא מִתְיַבְּמוֹת? [ב]תִּתְיַיבֵּם וְאֵין בְּכָךְ כְּלוּם! אֶלָּא לָאו — סְפֵק שֶׁקִּידֵּשׁ אַחַת מִשְּׁתֵּי אֲחָיוֹת וְאֵינוֹ יוֹדֵעַ אֵיזוֹ מֵהֶן קִידֵּשׁ, וְקָתָנֵי: חוֹלֶצֶת! °הָכִי הַשְׁתָּא?! הָתָם, אִם יָבֹא אֵלִיָּהוּ וְיֹאמַר דְּהָא קִידֵּשׁ — בַּת חֲלִיצָה וְיִיבּוּם הִיא, הָכָא אִם יָבֹא אֵלִיָּהוּ וְיֹאמַר דְּהָא לָא אִיעַבְּרָה — מִי מַשְׁגַּח בֵּיהּ וְיַבְּמִינַן לָהּ? [ג]הָא קְטַנָּה דְּלָאו בַּת אִיעַבּוּרֵי הִיא, וְאפ״ה צְרִיכָה לְהַמְתִּין ג׳ חֳדָשִׁים *ת״ר: [ד]יְבָמָה, שְׁלֹשָׁה חֳדָשִׁים הָרִאשׁוֹנִים — נִזּוֹנֶת מִשֶּׁל בַּעַל, מִכָּאן וְאֵילָךְ — אֵינָהּ נִזּוֹנֶת לֹא מִשֶּׁל בַּעַל וְלֹא מִשֶּׁל יָבָם. עָמַד בַּדִּין וּבָרַח — נִזּוֹנֶת מִשֶּׁל יָבָם, נָפְלָה לִפְנֵי יָבָם קָטָן (מַאי)? מִיָּבָם — לֵית לָהּ, מִבַּעַל — מַאי? פְּלִיגִי בָּהּ רַב אַחָא וְרָבִינָא; חַד אָמַר: אִית לָהּ, וְחַד אָמַר: לֵית לָהּ, [ה]וְהִלְכְתָא: לֵית לָהּ, מִשְּׁמַיָּא קְנָסוּהָ. ת״ר: [ו]יְבָמָה שֶׁחָלְצוּ לָהּ אַחִים בְּתוֹךְ שְׁלֹשָׁה — צְרִיכָה לְהַמְתִּין שְׁלֹשָׁה חֳדָשִׁים לְאַחַר

תורה אור: דברים כה

רש״י

מפני האיבול. אבילות. והאי כל הנשים יתארסו — לאו למעוטי ארוסה ליפאה, דהתם כר׳ יהודה סבירא ליה. דגבי הכתנה רבי יוסי מקיל טפי מרבי יהודה, כדאמר בשלהי גמ׳ ד״ארבעה אחים״ (לעיל דף לה.), אלא באבילות אתי לפלוגי עליה. **גמ׳ אלא לא תחלוץ אמאי.** ולאחר ג׳, אם אינה מעוברת — תנשא, או אם הפילה — תנשא, דהא חלוצה. **לימא תיהוי** תיובתיה דר׳ יוחנן. ומשום הכי לא תחלוץ שמא תפיל ותנשא בחליצה זו, וחליצת מעוברת לא שמה חליצה. **ולאו מי אותביניה.** בריש פירקין (דף לה:). **לימא מהא נמי תיהוי תיובתא. ונפקא** מינה דאי מיתרצא קמייתא — תיקום הך. **גרושה מאי איכא למימר.** אמאי לא תחלוץ, אם היתה גרושה מאחר קודם שנשאה אחיו של זה, דהא פסולה היא לכהונה וקיימא, מאי איכא למימר? אמאי לא תחלוץ? **משום מזוני.** דאית לה כל שלשה מנכסי בעלה, כדתניא בברייתא בשמעתין. ואי חלצה — לית לה מזוני. ואיהי לא מצי מינסבא עד לאחר שלשה, ומפסיד לה. **ארוסה וגרושה.** גרושה שנתארסה ומת בעלה, ונפלה ליבום מן האירוסין — תחלוץ בתוך שלשה. דהכא לאו משום מזוני איכא — דארוסה לית לה מזוני מבעל, ולא משום כרוז לכהונה — דהא פסולה היא משום גרושין קמאי. **אלא משום דרבי יוסי. כל העולה ליבום כו׳,** וזו הואיל ואינה עולה ליבום בתוך ג׳, כדאמרן לעיל שמא יפגע באשת אח — אינה עולה השערה לפני הזקנים לחליצה. ולרבי יוחנן לא תיקשי, דאי חלצה — ודאי חליצה, (א) דהאי אינה עולה לחליצה — לאו חליצה פסולה משמע, שהרי כמה נשים שנינו חולצות ולא מתייבמות היכא דלא אפשר, אלמא חליצה היא. ומיהו, היכא דאפשר לאמתוני עד שתראה ליבום משהינן. **אילימא ספק קידושין.** כגון זרק לה אחיו קידושין, ספק קרוב לו ספק קרוב לה. **אמאי לא מתייבמת. תתייבם** ממ״נ: אי היא יבמתו — שפיר מייבם, ואי לאו קידושין הוו — נכרית בעלמא נסיב. **שקידש אחת משתי אחיות ואין יודע** איזה מהן קידש. ומת, שתיהן חולצות ולא מתייבמות, דלא מצי לייבומי, דלמא פגע באחות זקוקה. והא הכא דאינה עולה לייבום ועולה לחליצה, ולא אמרי׳ תמתין עד שיבואו עדים ויבררו את יבמתו. **הכי השתא.** התם עולה לייבום היא, אי הוה ידעינן לה. אבל הכא, אם יבא אליהו ויאמר לא מיעברא — מי משגיחינן ביה ותתייבם. **הרי קטנה דלאו בת איעבורי היא כו׳.** הלכך לא חלצה. וכל הנך דאמרו רבנן חולצות ולא מתייבמות, כגון אחות חלוצתו ואחות זקוקתו וספק ערוה — התם (ב) משום דלא אפשר הוא, דאם כן לעולם תאסר. הלכך, כיון דמדאורייתא בת ייבום היא — חלצה. אבל הכא, דאפשר לשהויי — משהינן, ויצא הדבר בהיתר. **שלשה חדשים הראשונים.** שאינה יכולה להנשא מחמת בעלה. **נזונת משל בעלה.** שכן כתב לה ״את תהא יתבא בביתי ומתזנא מנכסי כל יומי מיגר ארמלותיך״. **מכאן ואילך אינה נזונת לא משל בעל ולא משל יבם.** ואינה דומה לשאר אלמנה. דהתם, כל זמן שלא נשאת לאחר ואומרת מחמת פלוני בעלי שכבודו גדול עלי — יש לה מזונות. אבל הך — אגידא ביבם, לפיכך אין לה על נכסי בעל מזונות. ולא משל יבם — עד שתכנס לחופה. **עמד בדין.** שתבעתו בדין: או כנוס או פטור, וברח. **נזונת משל יבם.** דקנסינן ליה. **צריכה להמתין.** עד שיהיו לה ג׳ חדשים מיום מיתה. הוי

תוספות

אמאי לימא תיהוי תיובתא דרבי יוחנן. וא״ת: דלמא לא תחלוץ משום שמא תסמוך על אותה חליצה לינשא לשוק, וחיישינן שמא תמלא מעוברת ולד של קיימא, וולד אינו פטור עוד שילא לאויר העולם! וי״ל: דלהא ליכא למיחש, דתוך שלשה ודאי לא תנשא, ולאחר ג׳ נמי, אם תמלא מעוברת לא יבא לטעות. ועוד: שלא ישא אדם מעוברת חברו. **משום** דמפסיד לה מזוני. לפי טעם זה לא תחלוץ דמתני׳ — עלה טובה קמ״ל. **אלא** ארוסה גרושה מאי איכא למימר. וא״ת: לר״ל לקיש ארוסה, כיון דלא מיעברה, אמאי לא תחלוץ? וי״ל: דלר״ל גזרו ארוסה אטו נשואה. אבל לר׳ יוחנן, דנשואה גופה משום כרוז בעלמא, ליכא למגזר. ותימה: דאמאי נקט גרושה? דמארוסה גרידא הוה מצי למיפרך. **קרא** עליו המקרא הזה. וא״ת: לר״ל תקשי ליה מרבי יוסי! וי״ל: דלר״ל נמי אינה חולצת תוך ג׳, משום דאינה עולה ליבום. **הספקות** חולצות ולא מתיבמות. מההיא דפ׳ שני (לעיל כג:), [מי] שקידש אחת מב׳ אחיות ואינו יודע איזו קידש, ה״מ למיפרך, אלא שהיה צריך להאריך. אבל מההיא דריש ״ארבעה אחין״ (לעיל דף כו.) דחולצות ולא מתיבמות — לא ה״מ למיפרך, דלעולם אין לה ליבם ולהתעגן, אבל הכא — יכולה להמתין עד שיתברר הספק, כההיא דלעיל שיכולה להמתין עד אחר הג׳. ומיהו, מההיא דספק קידושין דבפ״ד אחין״ (לעיל דף ל:) הוה מצי למפרך. **אילימא** ספק קדושין תתייבם ואין בכך כלום. ולא בעי למימר שנולד ספק קידושין בערוה, דהוי ספק אם היא צרת ערוה או לא — דא״כ הוה ליה למימר הספיקות צרותיהן חולצות ולא מתיבמות. ובספק גירושין ה״מ לאוקמי דלא מתיבמות, שמא היא גרושת אחיו. **הא** קטנה דלאו בת איעבורי. ואפילו למאן דלא גזר לקמן (דף מב:) קטנה אטו גדולה — ה״מ לענין הבחנה בשאר נשים, אבל לענין יבמה — מודה. **עמד** בדין וברח. לאו ברח בשבילה איירי, שרוצה לעגנה ואין רוצה לא לייבם ולא לחלוץ. דהא בפרק בתרא דכתובות (דף קז:) פריך מינה לשמואל דחייש לצררי, ואם בשבילה ברח — אמאי אית לן למיחש לצררי? אלא בברח מחמת מרדין או מחמת ממון איירי. ולאו דוקא ברח, דהוא הדין חלה, דכיון דלא בשבילה ברח, אלא מחמת אונס שאירע לו — מה לי ברח מה לי חלה. ובהדיא אמר בירושלמי בפרק ״אע״פ״ דה״ה חלה. ולא כמו שפירש בקונטרס התם דוקא ברח, אבל חלה לא. והא דבעיא בריש כתובות (דף ב.) חלה מאי — היינו שחלה מיד בהגעת זמן, אבל הכא — שחלה אחר שעמד בדין, דהוה לו לכונסה לאלתר קודם שאירע לו אונס. ונראה לר״י: דוקא בנתרצה ליבום וברח, אבל אם לא נתרצה אלא לחלוץ — אין נראה שיתקנו לה חכמים מזונות מיבם, כיון דאין סופו לייבם אלא לחלוץ. ודוקא ברח תקנו לה מזונות משלו, אבל לא ברח — לא, משום דלא שכיח שיאחר מליבם, כיון דאיתיה קמן ונתרצה, דמשום זמן מועט שרגיל לאחר לא תקנו לה מזונות. ומיהו בפרק ״ד׳ אחין״ (לעיל דף כט: ושם) משמע קצת דכי לא ברח נמי חייב במזונות. דקאמר: כשעמד בדין ופסקו לה מזונות משלו, ואינו מזכיר כלל ברח. אף על גב דהתם איירי בעבד בה מאמר, כדפרישית לעיל — לענין זה אין שום סברא לחלק בין עשה בה מאמר ללא עשה אלא כשיש שני יבמין, דאי לא עשה מאמר לא זה ולא זה לא — מחייב במזונות, לא זה ולא זה, אפילו נתרצה אחד מהם ליבם וברח. ואצטריך התם לאוקמי בעבד בה מאמר, משום דבענין אחר לא הוה מצי מיפר. וקצת נראה דמחמת קנס שקנסוהו חכמים שלא כנסה — תקנו לה מזונות. דהא אין מעשה ידיה שלו. כדאמר בפרק בתרא דכתובות (דף קז: ושם) ״אי משום מעשה ידיה לא משעבדא ליה״. ולמאי דפרישית דבשלא ברח אין לה מזונות — אינו ראיה דמעשה ידיה אינו שלו, דאין לחוש שמא אמר לה נאי מעשה ידיך למזונותיך — דהכתי לא משעבדא ליה עד שיברח ויפסקו לה מזונות. ומיהו, אר״י: דלפירוש זה טפי הוי ליה למימר דלא מיחייב במזונותיה. לאחר

תוספות ישנים

כל שאינה עולה לייבום [אינה] עולה לחליצה. ואין להקשות א״כ איך קאמר ר׳ יוחנן חליצת מעוברת שמה חליצה הא אינה עולה לייבום משום שמא יהא ולד בן קיימא וא״כ לא תהא עולה לחליצה וי״ל דדוקא לכתחלה אין לחלוץ מעוברת משום דלא מצי לייבמה אבל דיעבד מהניא החליצה כי חזינן שהפילה דלא חזיא לייבום:

מסורת הש״ס

[לעיל לה:]
לקמן קיט: [לעיל לו.]
[תוספתא פ״ו]
[לעיל ג. כ. לו. לקמן מד.]
כתובות קז:

הגהות הב״ח

(א) רש״י ד״ה אלא משום וכו׳ חלילה היא דהא אינה: (ב) ד״ה הרי קטנה וכו׳ משום דלא אפשר. נ״ב ע״ל דף ג ע״א:

גליון הש״ס

גמ׳ הכי השתא התם אי יבא אליהו. עיין לקמן דף ס״ז ע״ב תוס׳ ד״ה אי תושבין:

לְאַחַר ג' — אֵין צְרִיכָה לְהַמְתִּין ג' חֳדָשִׁים. הֱוֵי הַג' חֳדָשִׁים שֶׁאָמְרוּ — מִשְּׁעַת מִיתַת הַבַּעַל, וְלֹא מִשְּׁעַת חֲלִיצַת הַיָּבָם. מ"ש מִגֵּט, *דְּרַב אֲמַר מִשְּׁעַת נְתִינָה וּשְׁמוּאֵל אֲמַר ^א^מִשְּׁעַת כְּתִיבָה? אֲמַר רָבָא: ק"ו: *אִיסּוּר כָּרֵת הִתַּרְתָּ, אִיסּוּר לָאו לֹא כ"ש? § "וְכֵן שְׁאָר כָּל הַנָּשִׁים". בִּשְׁלָמָא יְבָמָה — כְּדַאֲמַרַן. אֶלָּא שְׁאָר כָּל הַנָּשִׁים אַמַּאי? אֲמַר *רַב נַחְמָן אֲמַר שְׁמוּאֵל: מִשּׁוּם דְּאָמַר קְרָא °"לִהְיוֹת לְךָ לֵאלֹהִים וּלְזַרְעֲךָ אַחֲרֶיךָ" ^ב^לְהַבְחִין בֵּין זַרְעוֹ שֶׁל רִאשׁוֹן לְזַרְעוֹ שֶׁל שֵׁנִי. מְתִיב רָבָא: לְפִיכָךְ *^ג^גֵּר וְגִיּוֹרֶת צְרִיכִין לְהַמְתִּין ג' חֳדָשִׁים, הָכָא מַאי לְהַבְחִין אִיכָּא? ^ד^ה"נ: אִיכָּא לְהַבְחִין בֵּין זֶרַע שֶׁנִּזְרַע בִּקְדוּשָּׁה לְזֶרַע שֶׁלֹּא נִזְרַע בִּקְדוּשָּׁה. רָבָא אָמַר: גְּזֵירָה שֶׁמָּא יִשָּׂא אֶת אֲחוֹתוֹ מֵאָבִיו, וְיַיבֵּם אֵשֶׁת אָחִיו מֵאִמּוֹ, וְיוֹצִיא אֶת אִמּוֹ לַשּׁוּק, וְיִפְטוֹר אֶת יְבִמְתּוֹ לַשּׁוּק. מְתִיב רַב חֲנַנְיָה: בְּכוּלָּן אֲנִי קוֹרֵא בָּהֶן מִשּׁוּם תַּקָּנַת עֶרְוָה, וְכָאן מִשּׁוּם תַּקָּנַת וָלָד. וְאִם אִיתָא — כּוּלְּהוּ מִשּׁוּם תַּקָּנַת עֶרְוָה! הַאי מִשּׁוּם תַּקָּנַת וָלָד דְּלָא לִפְגַּע בְּהוּ עֶרְוָה. בִּשְׁלָמָא תַּמְתִּין ב' חֳדָשִׁים וְתִנָּשֵׂא, לָא — דְּהַיְינוּ סְפֵיקָא, אִי בַּר תִּשְׁעָה לְקַמָּא אִי בַּר שִׁבְעָה לְבַתְרָא. אֶלָּא, תַּמְתִּין חֹדֶשׁ אֶחָד וְתִנָּשֵׂא: וְאִי לְשִׁבְעָה יָלְדָה — הַאי בַּר שִׁבְעָה לְבַתְרָא הוּא, וְאִי לְתַמַנְיָא יָלְדָה — הַאי בַּר תִּשְׁעָה לְקַמָּא הוּא. אִי נַמִי לְתַמַנְיָא יָלְדָה — אִיכָּא לְמֵימַר דְּבַתְרָא הוּא, דִּלְמָא אִישְׁתַּהוּיֵי אִישְׁתָּהָא חֹדֶשׁ אֶחָד וְאִיעַבַּר. וְתַמְתִּין שְׁנֵי חֳדָשִׁים וּמֶחֱצָה וְתִנָּשֵׂא, דְּאִי לְשִׁבְעָה יָלְדָה — הַאי בַּר שִׁבְעָה לְבַתְרָא הוּא. וְאִי לְשִׁיתָּא וּפַלְגָּא יָלְדָה — הַאי בַּר תִּשְׁעָה לְקַמָּא הוּא, דְּאִי בַּר בַּתְרָא הוּא — בַּר שִׁיתָּא וּפַלְגָּא לָא חַיֵּי! א"נ לְשִׁיתָּא וּפַלְגָּא יָלְדָה — אִיכָּא לְמֵימַר דְּבַתְרָא הוּא, *דְּאָמַר מָר זוּטְרָא: אֲפִילּוּ לְמַאן דְּאָמַר *יוֹלֶדֶת לְט' אֵינָהּ יוֹלֶדֶת לְמִקּוּטָּעִין — יוֹלֶדֶת לְז' יוֹלֶדֶת לְמִקּוּטָּעִין, שֶׁנֶּאֱמַר °"וַיְהִי לִתְקֻפוֹת הַיָּמִים", *מִיעוּט "תְּקוּפוֹת" — ב', מִיעוּט "יָמִים" — ב'. וְתַמְתִּין מֶשֶׁהוּ וְתִנָּשֵׂא, וְכִי מָלוּ שְׁלֹשָׁה חֳדָשִׁים לִבְדְּקָהּ! אָמַר רַב סַפְרָא: אֵין בּוֹדְקִין אֶת הַנְּשׂוּאוֹת, שֶׁלֹּא יִתְגַּנּוּ עַל בַּעֲלֵיהֶן. וְנִבְדְּקָהּ בְּהִלּוּכָהּ? אָמַר רָמִי בַּר חָמָא: אִשָּׁה מְחַפָּה עַצְמָהּ, כְּדֵי שֶׁיִּירַשׁ בְּנָהּ בְּנִכְסֵי בַּעֲלָהּ. הֵיכָא דְּקִים לָן דִּמְעוּבֶּרֶת הִיא תִּנָּשֵׂא, אַלְמָה תַּנְיָא: *^ה^לֹא יִשָּׂא אָדָם מְעוּבֶּרֶת חֲבֵרוֹ וּמֵינֶקֶת חֲבֵרוֹ, וְאִם נָשָׂא יוֹצִיא וְלֹא יַחֲזִיר עוֹלָמִית. גְּזֵרָה שֶׁמָּא תַּעֲשֶׂה עוּבָּרָהּ סַנְדָּל, אִי הָכִי — דִּידֵיהּ נַמִי, אִי לְמ"ד בְּמוֹךְ — וְאִי לְמ"ד מִן הַשָּׁמַיִם יְרַחֲמוּ — מִן הַשָּׁמַיִם יְרַחֲמוּ, הָכָא נַמִי: אִי לְמַאן דְּאָמַר בְּמוֹךְ — בְּמוֹךְ, אִי לְמַאן דְּאָמַר מִן הַשָּׁמַיִם יְרַחֲמוּ — מִן הַשָּׁמַיִם יְרַחֲמוּ! ^ו^אֶלָּא מִשּׁוּם דְּחָסָה. אִי הָכִי דִּידֵיהּ נַמִי! דִּידֵיהּ חָיֵיס עִילָּוֵיהּ. הָכָא נַמִי חָיֵיס עִילָּוֵיהּ! *אֶלָּא: סְתָם מְעוּבֶּרֶת לִמְנִיקָה קַיְימָא, דִּלְמָא

תורה אור: בראשית יז; ש"א א

רש"י

הֲוֵי. כְּגוֹמַר, הֲוֵי לוֹמֵד מִכָּאן שְׁלֹשָׁה חֳדָשִׁים שֶׁאָמְרוּ כו'. וּמ"ש מִגֵּט דְּרַב אָמַר מִשְּׁעַת נְתִינָה. וְאַף עַל גַּב דְּמִשְּׁעַת כְּתִיבָה לֹא נִתְיַיחֵד עִמָּהּ, דְּאִם כֵּן הָוֵה לֵיהּ גֵּט יָשָׁן, וַאֲפִילּוּ הָכִי מִשְּׁעַת נְתִינָה מָנֵינַן, ה"נ נִמְנֵי מִשְּׁעַת חֲלִיצָה. לְאִיסּוּר כָּרֵת. לַיָּבָם, הִתַּרְתָּ לְאַחַר ג' חֳדָשִׁים מִיָּד. לְאִיסּוּר לָאו. לַשּׁוּק לֹא כ"ש דְּמוּתֶּרֶת לְאַחַר חֲלִיצָה מִיָּד, הוֹאִיל וְעָבְרוּ שְׁלֹשָׁה חֳדָשִׁים מִיּוֹם מִיתָה. וּלְזַרְעֲךָ אַחֲרֶיךָ. שֶׁאֵין הַשְּׁכִינָה שׁוֹרָה אֶלָּא עַל הַוַּודָּאִים, שֶׁזַּרְעוֹ מְיוּחָס אַחֲרָיו. וְהָכִי נַמִי קַיְימָא לָן בִּנְדָרִים (דף כ:) "וּבָרוֹתִי מִכֶּם הַמּוֹרְדִים וְהַפּוֹשְׁעִים בִּי" — אֵלּוּ בְּנֵי עִרְבּוּבְיָא. גֵּר וְגִיּוֹרֶת. גֵּר שֶׁנִּתְגַּיֵּיר וְאִשְׁתּוֹ עִמּוֹ — צְרִיכִים לְהַמְתִּין ג' חֳדָשִׁים, לִפְרוֹשׁ זֶה מִזֶּה. וְהָכָא מַאי לְהַבְחִין אִיכָּא, הֲרֵי אֵין כָּאן רִאשׁוֹן וְשֵׁנִי. רָבָא אָמַר שֶׁמָּא יִשָּׂא אֲחוֹתוֹ מֵאָבִיו. אִם נִשֵּׂאת תּוֹךְ שְׁלֹשָׁה וְיָלְדָה, וְהוּא בֶּן ט' לָרִאשׁוֹן וְנוֹלַד בְּבֵיתוֹ שֶׁל שֵׁנִי, וְסָבוּר שֶׁהוּא בְּנוֹ וְיִשָּׂא אֶת בַּת בַּעְלָהּ הָרִאשׁוֹן שֶׁיֵּשׁ לוֹ מֵאִשָּׁה אַחֶרֶת, וְהִיא אֲחוֹתוֹ מִן הָאָב. וּמְיַיבֵּם אֵשֶׁת אָחִיו מֵאִמּוֹ. שֶׁאִם תֵּלֵד לָאַחֲרוֹן בֵּן אַחֵר, וְיִשָּׂא אִשָּׁה וְיָמוּת בְּלֹא בָנִים, וְיִיבְּמֶנָּה זֶה, כְּסָבוּר שֶׁהוּא אָחִיו מֵאָבִיו, וְנִמְצָא מְיַיבֵּם אֵשֶׁת אָחִיו מֵאִמּוֹ שֶׁלֹּא מֵאָבִיו, וְחַיָּיב כָּרֵת. וְיוֹצִיא אֶת אִמּוֹ לַשּׁוּק. אִם לֹא תֵּלֵד אִמּוֹ לַשֵּׁנִי וְלָדוֹת, וְכִסְבוּרִים שֶׁזֶּה בְּנוֹ, וְתִנָּשֵׂא אִמּוֹ לַשּׁוּק בְּלֹא חֲלִיצָה. וְיִפְטוֹר אֶת יְבִמְתּוֹ לַשּׁוּק. אִם יֵשׁ לוֹ אָח מֵאָבִיו הָרִאשׁוֹן, וְלֹא הָיוּ לוֹ בָּנִים וּמֵת, וְאֵין שָׁם אָח אֶלָּא הוּא, וְהוּא סָבוּר שֶׁהוּא בֶּן הָאַחֲרוֹן, וּמַנִּיחַ אֵשֶׁת בְּנוֹ שֶׁל רִאשׁוֹן הַזְּקוּקָה לוֹ נִשֵּׂאת לַשּׁוּק בְּלֹא חֲלִיצָה. וְגַבֵּי גֵּר וְגִיּוֹרֶת לַחֲדָא מֵהָנֵי הוּא דְּאִיכָּא לְמֵיחַשׁ, כְּגוֹן לְשֶׁמָּא יְיַבֵּם אֵשֶׁת אָחִיו מֵאִמּוֹ, שֶׁמָּא מְעוּבֶּרֶת הָיְתָה, וּכְשֶׁתֵּלֵד סְבוּרָה הִיא שֶׁבֶּן ז' הוּא, וּבִקְדוּשָּׁה נִזְרַע, וְתַחֲזוֹר וְתֵלֵד בֵּן אַחֲרָיו וְיִשָּׂא אִשָּׁה וְיָמוּת בְּלֹא בָנִים, וִייַבֵּם זֶה אֶת אִשְׁתּוֹ, דְּסָבוּר שֶׁגַּם הוּא נִזְרַע בִּקְדוּשָּׁה. וְכֵיוָן שֶׁזֶּה נִזְרַע שֶׁלֹּא בִּקְדוּשָּׁה, וּסְתָם גּוֹיָה זוֹנָה הִיא — אִיכָּא לְמֵימַר שֶׁמָּא אֵינוֹ בְּנוֹ שֶׁל זֶה, וְנִמְצָא נוֹשֵׂא אֵשֶׁת אָחִיו מֵאִמּוֹ. בְּכוּלָּן אֲנִי קוֹרֵא בָּהֶן. כָּל נָשִׁים שֶׁאָסְרוּ חֲכָמִים לְהִנָּשֵׂא אוֹ לְהִתְיַיבֵּם, קוֹרֵא אֲנִי בָּהֶן תַּקָּנַת עֶרְוָה, כְּדֵי שֶׁלֹּא יָבֹאוּ לִידֵי עֶרְוָה. וְכָאן. בְּהַמְתָּנָה שֶׁל ג' חֳדָשִׁים שֶׁאָסְרוּ חֲכָמִים לִשְׁאָר נָשִׁים אֵין כָּאן תַּקָּנַת עֶרְוָה, אֶלָּא תַּקָּנַת הַוָּלָד, לְהַבְחִין בֶּן מִי הוּא. וְאִם אִיתָא. דְּחָשׁוּ חֲכָמִים לְשֶׁמָּא יִשָּׂא אֲחוֹתוֹ מִן אָבִיו — הָא נַמִי תַּקָּנַת עֶרְוָה הִיא. דְּלָא לִפְגַּע וָלָד. בְּעֶרְוָה. אֲבָל כָּל שְׁאָר הַנֶּאֱסָרוֹת — אִיכָּא (א) תַּקַּנְתָּא הִיא וּבַעַל עַצְמוֹ דְּלָא לִפְגְּעוּ בְּעֶרְוָה. הָא בַּר ז' לְבַתְרָא הוּא. דְּאִי מִקַּמָּא אִיעַבְּרָא כְּשֶׁמֵּת — אִשְׁתַּכַּח דְּבַר תַּמְנְיָא הוּא, וּבַר תַּמַנְיָא לָא חַיֵּי. א"נ לְתַמְנְיָא יָלְדָה כו'. פֵּירוּשָׁא הוּא. אִישְׁתַּהִי. לְאַחַר שֶׁנִּשֵּׂאת. וְה"ה נַמִי דְּמָצֵי לְתָרוּצֵי אִי נַמִי לְשִׁבְעָה יָלְדָה — אִיכָּא לְמֵימַר בַּר תִּשְׁעָה לְקַמָּא הוּא, מֵעִיקָּרָא חֹדֶשׁ אֶחָד אִיעַבְּרָא קוֹדֶם מִיתָתוֹ. אֶלָּא הוֹאִיל וְתֵירֵץ לְמִילְּתֵיהּ בַּחֲדָא, וְאוֹקֵי דְּאַכַּתִּי אִיכָּא סָפֵק — סַגֵּי לֵיהּ בְּהָכִי. אֲפִילּוּ לְמ"ד. בְּמַסֶּכֶת נִדָּה, בְּפֶרֶק "בְּנוֹת כּוּתִים". וַיְהִי לִתְקוּפוֹת הַיָּמִים. הֲרֵי שִׁשָּׁה חֳדָשִׁים וּב' יָמִים. וְתַמְתִּין מֶשֶׁהוּ. שָׁבוּעַ אוֹ שְׁבוּעַיִם. וְכִי מָלוּ ג' חֳדָשִׁים. לְיוֹם מִיתַת בַּעְלָהּ, שֶׁדֶּרֶךְ עוֹבָּר לִהְיוֹת נִיכָּר — לִיבְדְּקָהּ בְּדַדֶּיהָ, כְּדֶרֶךְ נָשִׁים. וְאִי מִיעַבְּרָא — וַדַּאי בַּר קַמָּא הוּא, דְּאִי בַּר בַּתְרָא הוּא אַכַּתִּי לָא הֲוָה מִינְכַּר, דְּלָא מָלוּ שְׁלֹשָׁה חֳדָשִׁים לְנִישּׂוּאֶיהָ, דְּחָסַר לֵיהּ הַהוּא מֶשֶׁהוּ שֶׁהִמְתִּינָה. וְאִי לָא מִינְכַּר וּלְבָתַר הָכִי מִינְכַּר (ב) — וַדַּאי בַּר בַּתְרָא הוּא. בְּהִילּוּכָהּ. מוֹלִיכִין אוֹתָהּ בֶּעָפָר תִּיחוּחַ, אִי מְעוּבֶּרֶת הִיא — פְּסִיעוֹתֶיהָ נִיכָּרוֹת וּמַעֲמִיקוֹת יוֹתֵר מִשְּׁאָר נָשִׁים, שֶׁהַוָּלָד מַכְבִּידָהּ. כָּךְ מָצָאתִי בִּתְשׁוּבַת הַגְּאוֹנִים. מְחַפָּה עַצְמָהּ. שֶׁלֹּא תֵּרָאֶה מְעוּבֶּרֶת, כְּדֵי שֶׁלֹּא יָדְעוּ שֶׁבֶּן הָרִאשׁוֹן הוּא, וְיִירַשׁ בְּנִכְסֵי בַּעְלָהּ שֵׁנִי. הֵיכָא דְּקִים לָן כו'. הוֹאִיל וְטַעַם הַמְתָּנָה מִשּׁוּם וָלָד הוּא, שֶׁלֹּא יְהֵא סָפֵק, כְּשֶׁהָיוּ יוֹדְעִים וַדַּאי שֶׁהִיא מְעוּבֶּרֶת מֵרִאשׁוֹן — תִּנָּשֵׂא! וּמְשַׁנֵּי: גְּזֵירָה שֶׁמָּא תַּעֲשֶׂה כו'. דִּידֵיהּ נַמִי. לֹא יְשַׁמֵּשׁ עִם אִשְׁתּוֹ מְעוּבֶּרֶת, שֶׁמָּא תַּחֲזוֹר וְתִתְעַבֵּר, וְיִדְחוֹק אָחִיו וְיִמָּעֵךְ צוּרַת פָּנָיו, כְּסַנְדָּל הַזֶּה שֶׁאֵין לוֹ צוּרָה. אִי לְמ"ד בְּמוֹךְ. פְּלוּגְתָּא הִיא בְּפ"ק (לעיל דף יב:). דְּחָסָה. שֶׁמְּמָעֲכוֹ בִּשְׁעַת תַּשְׁמִישׁ. דְּחָסָה — לְשׁוֹן לַחַץ, שֶׁלּוֹחֲצוֹ, כִּדְאָמַר לְקַמָּן (דף קג.) גַּבֵּי חֲלִיצָה: צָרִיךְ לְמִידְחֲסֵיהּ לְכַרְעֵיהּ. ה"נ חַיִּים עִילָּוֵיהּ. שֶׁאֵין אָדָם מִתְכַּוֵּין לַהֲרוֹג הַנֶּפֶשׁ. לִמְנִיקָה קַיְימָא. כְּשֶׁתֵּלֵד מְנִיקָתוֹ. וְאִי

תוספות

לאחר שלשה חדשים אין צריכה להמתין. אמר ר"ת: דוקא חלוץ. שהחליצה מוכחת שלא בא עליה, כדאמר בממאנת דמיאונה מוכיח עליה שהיא קטנה. אבל אם מת היבם לאחר ג' – צריכה להמתין שלשה חדשים, דיותר יבמה קרובה לביאה מארוסה, דגזרינן אטו נשואה. אע"ג דאמר לקמן בפ' "ב"ש" (דף קיב.) ובפסחים פרק "אלו דברים" (דף עג:) יבמתו – בזיז מינה, אשתו – לא בזיז מינה, היינו לענין לאוקמי אנפשיה עד שלשים, אבל לענין גזרה שמא ישא אחותו כו' – איכא למימר יבמתו קרובה לביאה טפי. **מאי** שנא מגט דרב אמר משעת נתינה. אע"ג דודאי לא בא עליה מקמי כתיבה – דאם כן לא היה פוטרה בגט זה, דהוה ליה גט ישן. וטעמא מפרש בפרק שני דגיטין (דף יח. ושם) שלא יאמרו: ב' נשים בחצר אחת זו אסורה וזו מותרת, שהעולם סוברים שכתיבת שניהם היתה סמוך לנתינה, ויבא להתיר תוך שלשה. והכא גבי חליצה נמי יסברו ששתיהן סמוך למיתה חלצו, ויבא להתיר תוך שלשה. ומשני: לאיסור כרת התרת, דאם היה רוצה לייבם אחר שלשה – היה מייבם, לאיסור לאו לא כ"ש? דהיאך אפשר לאסרה להנשא לשוק אחר חליצה, שזה דומה לחוכא ואיטלולא, ולא ישמעו לנו העולם על כך.

לזרעך אחריך. לקמן בפ' "נושאין" (דף ק:) דריש מהאי קרא דאזהר ליה רחמנא לאברהם: לא תינסיב גויה ושפחה, דלא יתייחס זרעך בתרה. **גר** וגיורת. מכאן משמע דגר מותר בגיורת, ודלא כאוסרים כשנשאה מקודם דלא יחזרו לסורם. **בכולן** אני קורא כו'. איבמה לחוד קאי, ונקט לשון כולן – משום דאיירי בכל יבמות, בין ארוסות בין נשואות, בין להתייבם או להנשא לשוק. אם חלצה תוך ג' – כולן צריכות להמתין שלשה חדשים.

ותמתין משהו ותנשא. לאו דוקא משהו, שצריכה להמתין שלשה ימים של קליטת הזרע.

סתם מעוברת למניקה קיימא. רבינו שמשון זקנו של רשב"א היה אומר דגרושה מינקת מותרת לינשא. משום דלא משעבדא להניק, כדאמרי' בפ' "אע"פ" (כתובות נט: ושם) נתגרשה – אינו כופה. ואין נראה לר"ת, דהא למאי דהוה בעי למימר דטעמא משום סנדל, או משום דיתסא – לא היה חילוק בין אלמנה לגרושה. וה"ה להאי טעמא, דאינו חוזר בו אלא מהטעם בלבד. ועוד: אלמנה גופה, אי אמרה איני ניזונית ואיני עושה, או תבעה כתובתה – לא משעבדא, וכן פוסק בשאלתות דרב אחאי* דלא שנא גרושה ולא שנא אלמנה.

תוספות ישנים

אלא שאר כל הנשים מאי טעמא. תימה מאי [לא] קאמר משום דלמא היא מעוברת ואמרי' לא ישא אדם מעוברת. וי"ל דהיינו דוקא בסתם מעוברת אבל כשהיא ספק אם היא מעוברת אם לאו [לא אסרינן לה] משום לא ישא אדם מעוברת חבירו אם לא מקרבה כדמייתי: **ויפטור** את יבמתו לשוק. אבל בגר וגיורת לתנהו לכולהו טעמי דהכא אלא משום דשמא ייבם אשת אחיו מאמו לפי שזה יחשוב כי הוא נזרע בקדושה וא"כ ייבם אשת אחיו הנזרע בקדושה כי הוא יחשוב כי הוא אחיו מן האב ביהדות והוא נזרע בקדושה ושמא הוא אינו אלא אחיו מאמו כי שמא נזרע שלא בקדושה וסתם גויה זונה הוא ואין לו קורבה לאבות אף אם הגר נתגייר עם אשתו: **לפיכך** גר וגיורת צריכות להמתין וכו' מכאן קשה למאי דאיתא בהגדה גר לא ישא גיורת שמא יחזרו לסורן דהכא משמע דשרי: **א"נ** לתמניא ילדה איכא למימר דבתרא הוא. ה"נ מ"מ למימר א"נ לשבעה ילדה איכא למימר אימור בר תשעה לקמא הוא דשמא נתעברה חדש אחד לפני מותו:

הגהות הב"ח

(א) רש"י ד"ה דלא ליפגע וכו' איכא תקנתא היא: (ב) ד"ה וכי מלו ג' וכו' ולבתר הכי מינכר נ"ב ואין להקשות דלמא לא יהא ניכר עובר כלל לשליש כדאיתא לעיל דף ל"ו דאין כולם ניכר רק רובן ובשביל זה [illegible] ספק דיש ספק אם הולכין אחר רוב הנשים שהולדות לט' והוה מן הראשון או אזלינן בתר רוב להנכר לשליש וזו הואיל ולא ניכר הוא מן שני א"כ ע"כ לא תנשא עכשיו [והשאר חסר]:

עין משפט נר מצוה

פה א מיי' פי"א מהל' גירושין הל' יט סמג עשין נ טוש"ע אה"ע סי' יג סעיף א:
פו ב ג ד מיי' שם וטור ש"ע שם סעיף ה:
פז ה מיי' שם הל' כה טוש"ע שם סעיף יא:
פח ו מיי' שם הל' כה:

[פרשת ויקרא ריש סי' יז]
[עי' כ"מ פ' י"א מהל' גירושין דין כה הכרמב"ם לא גרס אלא]

מסורת הש"ס

גיטין יח.
[לקמן לז. קח:]
[בשאלתות פ' וירא סי' ב איתא אר"נ אמר רב]
[עי' תוספות לעיל לה. ד"ה תורן]
ר"ה יא. נדה לח:
[נדה כו.]
[עמ"ש על גליון בנדה לח:]
[לעיל לו:] סוטה כ.

אדלמא איעברה, ומעבר חלבה, וקטלה ליה. אי הכי דידיה נמי! דידיה ממסמסא ליה בביצים וחלב. דידה נמי ממסמסא ליה בבצים וחלב! לא יהב לה בעל. וליתבעיניה ליורשים! אמר אביי: אשה בושה לבא לבית דין, והורגת את בנה. § "אחת בתולות ואחת בעולות". הי ניהו בתולות והי ניהו ארוסות, הי ניהו בעולות והי ניהו נשואות? א"ר יהודה הכי קאמר: אחת בתולות ואחת בעולות שנתארמלו או שנתגרשו, בין מן הארוסין בין מן הנשואין. *ר' אלעזר לא על לבי מדרשא, אשכחיה לר' אסי, אמר ליה: מאי אמור רבנן בבי מדרשא? אמר ליה, הכי א"ר יוחנן: הלכה כר' יוסי. מכלל דיחידאה פליג עליה? אין, והתניא: *בהרי שהיתה רדופה לילך לבית אביה, או שהיה לה כעס בבית בעלה, או שהיה בעלה חבוש בבית האסורין[א], או שהיה בעלה זקן או חולה, או שהיתה היא חולה, או שהפילה אחר מיתת בעלה, או שהיתה עקרה, או זקנה, או קטנה, או אילונית, או שאינה ראויה לילד (א) – צריכה להמתין ג' חדשים, דברי ר' מאיר. *ר' [ב] יהודה מתיר ליארס ולינשא מיד. אמר רבי חייא בר אבא: חזר בו רבי יוחנן. אמר רב יוסף: אי הדר ביה – ממתני' דכרמא הדר ביה. דתניא, *אמר ר' ישמעאל בנו של ר' יוחנן בן ברוקה: שמעתי מפי חכמים בכרם ביבנה: גכולן צריכות להמתין שלשה חדשים. אמר ליה ר' ירמיה לר' זריקא: כי עיילת לקמיה דר' אבהו רמי ליה: מי אמר רבי יוחנן הלכה כרבי יוסי? והאמר ר' יוחנן: *הלכה כסתם משנה, ותנן: כל הנשים לא ינשאו ולא יתארסו עד שיהו להם שלשה חדשים, אחת בתולות ואחת בעולות! אמר ליה: *דרמא לך הא – לא חש לקמחיה; סתם ואח"כ מחלוקת היא, ואין הלכה כסתם. דאמר רב פפא ואיתימא ר' יוחנן: *מחלוקת ואחר כך סתם – הלכה כסתם, סתם ואחר כך מחלוקת – אין הלכה כסתם מסתמיך ואזיל ר' אבהו אכתפיה דרבי נחום שמעיה, מנקיט ואזיל הלכתא מיניה. בעא מיניה: מחלוקת ואחר כך סתם מאי? ⊕א"ל: הלכה כסתם. סתם ואחר כך מחלוקת מאי? אמר ליה: אין הלכה כסתם. סתמא דמתני' ומחלוקת בברייתא מאי? א"ל: הלכה כסתם. מחלוקת במתני' וסתמא בברייתא מאי? א"ל: וכי

ואי מינכבא דלמא מיעברא. לאחר לידתה, ומיעבר עליה חלבה, וקטלה לברה ברעב. **ממסמסא** ליה. מאכילתו. **לא יהב לה בעל.** משום דלאו בריה הוא. **וליתבעיניה ליורשים.** של בעל ראשון. **אשה בושה לבא לב"ד.** ולתבוע יורשים בשביל בנה. **והורגת את בנה.** על כרחה מת בנה ברעב. **הי ניהו בתולות הי ניהו ארוסות.** הא חדא היא, דהיכי משכחת לה בתולה יבמה אם לא ארוסה? **הכי קאמר.** כלומר, לא תתני אחת ואחת, דמשמע תרי מילי, אלא כולה חדא קתני. ופרושי קמפרש: אחת בתולות ואחת בעולות, וכגון שנתארמלו או נתגרשו בין מן האירוסין, דהיינו בתולות, בין מן הנשואין, דהיינו בעולות. **הלכה כר' יוסי.** דשרי ארוסות לינשא, הואיל וליכא למיחש לזרע ראשון, ונשואה ליארס. והאי דנקט ר' יוסי ולא רבי יהודה, דהא רבי יהודה נמי שרי ארוסה לינשא בהדיא, אלא משום דר' יוסי נימוקו עמו. **מכלל דיחידאה פליג עליה.** תנא קמא דאמר לא ינשאו ולא יתארסו אחת ארוסות ואחת בתולות, דאסר אפי' ארוסות ליארס כ"ש לינשא – יחידאה היא, ולאו סתמא דרבים היא. **ה"ג אין והתניא.** בניחותא. **רדופה.** רגילה. וגם סמוך למיתתו עמדה בבית אביה זמן מרובה, דליכא למימר מעוברת היא. **או שהיה לה כעס.** ולא שימשה: **עקרה.** שנעקר רחמה, ונטלה האם שלה. **אילונית.** ממעי אמה לקויה היא, ואין לה סימני שער ודדים. **או שאינה ראויה לילד.** לאיתויי [מעמת] סמא או חולי. **כולן צריכות להמתין.** דגזרו שאינה ראויה אטו ראויה. **ממתני' דכרמא.** שנשנית בכרם ביבנה, מחמת אותה משנה חזר בו. **בכרם ביבנה.** שהיו יושבים שורות שורות כעין (ב) הכרם. **לא חש לקימחיה.** למה שהוא טוחן ומוציא מפיו, כלומר לדיבורו: **סתם ואח"כ מחלוקת היא.** דהא איפלגו עלה ר' יוסי ור' יהודה: **מחלוקת ואחר כך סתם.** בין שסתם אחריה מיד (ג) באחד מהם, בין שסתם אחריה במסכת אחרת באותו הסדר. כגון: נתן למר לצבע, דמחלוקת בב"ק ב"הגוזל" (דף ק:), וסתם בב"מ (ד עו.): כל המשנה ידו על התחתונה, וסתם לן כר"י, דאמר: אם השבח יתר על היציאה כו' – הלכה כסתם. **סתם ואחר כך מחלוקת. כי מתני'.** **מנקיט.** מלקט ממנו הלכות פסוקות, הלכה כפלוני ופלוני.

***רבי** יוסי אומר כל הנשים יתארסו. בעירובין (דף מז.) פי' בקונט' דאפילו ארוסות דוקא יתארסו. אבל ינשאו – לא, דגזר רבי יוסי ארוסה אטו נשואה. ואין נראה. דאי גרס בברייתא דרדופה רבי יוסי מתיר ליארס ולינשא מיד – א"כ קשיא דרבי יוסי אדרבי יוסי, דהכא גזר אפילו ארוסה אטו נשואה, כ"ש דהוה ליה למיגזר נשואה רדופה אטו שאינה רדופה! ואפילו גרס בברייתא דרדופה רבי יהודה – מ"מ קשיא, דהיכי מוכח בפרק "מי שהוציאוהו" (ג"ז שם) ובגמ' דיחידאה פליג עליה מברייתא דרדופה, ותנא קמא דמתניתין הוא ר"מ? דלמא ר"מ דרדופה הוא כר' יוסי דמתניתין, דלא שרי אלא ליארס, אבל לינשא – לא, וצריכות להמתין שלשה חדשים דקאמר ר"מ, היינו: מלינשא, אבל ליארס – מיד שרי, ואף על גב דקתני סתמא צריכות להמתין, הכי נמי קתני בפרק "ד' אחין" (לעיל דף לה. ושם) גבי גיורת ושבויה ואנוסה ומפותה צריכות להמתין סתמא, דברי רבי יהודה. וע"כ היינו דוקא לינשא, דליארס אפי' נשואה שרי הכא ר"י. ועוד: היכי מוכח בגמ' דהדר ביה ר' יוחנן ממתני' דכרמא, דקתני כולן צריכות להמתין. דלמא לינשא קאמר, אבל ליארס שרי? ונראה כמו [שפי' רש"י] כאן, דרבי יוסי שרי נמי ארוסה לינשא, ולא פליג ארבי יהודה אלא באיבול לחודיה ומיהו, מה שהביא ראיה דשמעינן לרבי יוסי דמיקל בהבחנה טפי מרבי יהודה בסוף פרק "ד' אחין" (ג"ז שם) – אינה ראיה, דדלמא בגיורת ואנוסה מיקל, משום דמתהפכת שלא תתעבר, כדאמרינן לעיל (דף לה.). אבל לעולם גזר ארוסה אטו נשואה. ומברייתא דרדופה היה יכול לדקדק אי גרס בה ר' יוסי, דלא גזר אפי' נשואה רדופה – אטו שאין רדופה כ"ש דלא גזר ארוסה אטו נשואה. והא דפסיק רבי יוחנן כר' יוסי, ולא נקט ר' יהודה, כיון דשניהם שוין – משום שבא לפסוק כרבי יוסי גם באיבול. או נקט ר' יוסי כדפי' בקונטרס משום דנימוקו עמו. וא"ת: כשמגיה בגמרא (לקמן מג.) אימא רבי יוסי אומר כל הנשים ינשאו, ופריך: ולית ליה לרבי יוסי להבחין? ומאי קשיא ליה! נימא דכל הנשים לאו דוקא, ואארוסות דוקא קאי, ולא אנשואות, דמעיקרא נמי לא הוי כל דוקא, דלא הוי קאי אלא אנשואות, דארוסות שרי אפילו לינשא! וי"ל: דלא דמי, דהשתא הוי כל דוקא, וקאי שפיר בין אארוסות בין אנשואות, אלא שהדיוק דמשמע יתארסו – אין, ינשאו – לא, לא קאי אכל נשים אלא אנשואות לחוד. אבל פשטא דמתניתין אכל נשים. קאי אבל קשה לר"ת: דקתני לקמן בברייתא: וכולן לא ינשאו עד שיהו להם שלשה חדשים. משמע אפילו ארוסות כמו כל הנשים. ודוחק לחלק בין וכולן לכל הנשים. ואר"ת: דגרס בברייתא דרדופה רבי יוסי מתיר ליארס, ול"ג לינשא. וגזר ר' יוסי ארוסה אטו נשואה. ודוחק הוא למחוק הספרים, דבכולהו גרס לינשא. ועוד, דליארס אפילו נשואה שרי. **הלכה** כרבי יוסי. ול"ג כרבי יהודה, דהא בפ' "מי שהוציאוהו" (עירובין דף מו:) קאמר רבי יעקב בר אידי אמר רבי יוחנן: רבי מאיר ורבי יהודה – הלכה כר"י, ר"י ורבי יוסי – הלכה כרבי יוסי, ואין צ"ל רבי מאיר ורבי יוסי – הלכה כרבי יוסי. ודייק דליתנהו להני כללי מדאיצטריך רבי יוחנן לפסוק כרבי יוסי, אף על גב דיחידאה פליג עליה. ואי גרס הלכה כרבי יהודה – שפיר איצטריך לפסוק הלכה כר' יהודה, לאפוקי מר' יוסי דפליג עליה. **סתם** ואח"כ מחלוקת היא. וא"ת: ⊕והא אמרינן בריש מסכת ביצה (דף ב.) גבי שבת סתם לן תנא כר"ש. דתנן: מחתכין הדלועין כו', אע"ג דפליג ר' יהודה בסיפא, וקאמר אם לא היתה נבילה מערב שבת כו'! ויש לומר: דנהי דלא חשיב סתם גמור – מ"מ חשיב כרבים לגבי יחיד. וא"ת: בפ' "המוציא יין" (שבת פא: ושם) דפריך: ומי סבר רבי יוחנן דבר שאין מתכוין אסור? והאמר ר' יוחנן הלכה כסתם משנה, ותנן: נזיר חופף ומפספס אבל לא סורק! ומאי קושיא? דסתמא בנזיר (דף מב.) ופלוגתא בפ"ב דביצה (דף כג.) גבי קירוד וקרצוף, ובתרי מסכתי אמר בפ"ק דמס' ע"ז (דף ז. ושם) אין סדר למשנה! וליכא למימר דר' יוחנן אית ליה הלכה כסתם, אפי' בסתם ואח"כ מחלוקת – דהא קאמר הכא בהדיא אליבא דר' יוחנן סתם ואח"כ מחלוקת היא! וי"ל: דודאי בסתם ואח"כ מחלוקת מודה ר' יוחנן דאין הלכה כסתם, אבל בתרי מסכתי – אית ליה לר' יוחנן דהלכתא כסתם. וטעמא דר' יוחנן משום דמסתמא אית לן למימר דמחלוקת ואח"כ סתם הוא, ולא סתם ואח"כ מחלוקת, דאין לנו לומר שחזר בו רבי מפסקו עד שנראה בפירוש. ומיהו, שאר אמוראי אית להו דבתרי מסכתי אין סדר למשנה ואין הלכתא כסתם. וא"ת: דבפ' "כל גגות" (עירובין דף צב. ושם) פסק ר' יוחנן כר"ש, בין עירבו בין לא עירבו. ופריך: והא אמר ר' יוחנן הלכה כסתם משנה ומייתי מסתם משנה! דבפרק "חלון" (שם דף עו:) והיינו סתם ואח"כ מחלוקת! ותירץ ה"ר אהרן כהן: דעיקר קושיא לרבי יוחנן אינה אלא דלא גזר בעירבו, ובזה הדבר הוי מחלוקת ואח"כ סתם, מחלוקת בשלש חצירות ב"מי שהוציאוהו" (שם דף מה:) וסתם בפרק "חלון". אבל בפרק "כל גגות" לא פליגי בגזירה. ומיהו קשה, דבסוף פרק קמא דמסכת ע"ז (דף כא.), גבי שכירות בתים, פסק שמואל כרבי יוסי, אע"ג דסתם לן תנא בתר הכי כרבי מאיר!

במקום

עין משפט נר מצוה

[שייך לעיל במשנה מח.]

פט א מיי' פי"א מהל' גירושין הלכה כה:

צ ב ג מיי' שם הל' כ סמג עשין נ טוש"ע אה"ע סימן יג סעיף א:

תוספות ישנים

הלכה כרבי יוסי וה"ה דה"מ למימר כר' יהודה אלא נקט כר' יוסי משום דנימוקו עמו: **ורבי** יוסי מתיר ליארס ולינשא מיד ל"ג ר' יוסי דהא משמע לקמן דמיקל בהבחנה אף בנשואה אלמנה כדמשמע דקאמר (לקמן מג ע"א) אלא אימא כל הנשים ינשאו פי' אף נשואות והכא משמע דלא מתיר לינשא אלא זקנה ואילונית אבל אשה דעלמא לא. א"נ שפיר גרסינן ליה א) דהכי משמע בעירובין (דף מו) דמייתי מהכא ב) דר' יוסי ליתיה להני כללי אלא ודאי גרסי' ליה והאי דנקט מתיר ליארס ולינשא על זקנה ואיילונית וכו' לאו למעוטי שאר נשים אלא משום דלא מיירי ת"ק אלא בהכי לא קאמר מתיר ר' יוסי בכל הנשים משום דת"ק לא איירי בהו אכן ה"נ בשאר נשים ופירש רבינו נתנאל דלעיל גרסי' הלכה כר' יהודה דאי גרסי' ר' יוסי לא הוה ליה למפסק הלכתא כוותיה אלא לקמן על משנת ר' יוסי שרמז הספר לקמן ר' יוסי אומר כל הנשים וכו' א"כ לעיל מיניה הוי ר' יהודה וא"ת אמאי לא בעינן שלשה חדשים וג' ימים להמתין כי שמא לא נקלט הזרע עד לאחר ג' ימים וא"כ אם תנשא מיד לאחר ג' חדשים ותלד לששה חדשים ויום אחד לא נדע אם הוא מן הראשון או מן האחרון דהא יכול להיות אף מן הראשון והוא מט' חדשים ויום א' כי לא נקלט עד יום א' לאחר מיתת הבעל וי"ל דהא דאין אנו מצריכין כולי האי משום דבדקינן אותה בבדיקה אחרת עם ג' חדשים כי בדקינן אותה בהלוכה כדמשמע לקמן פי' מה שהיא מכבדת על עפר תיחוח ופסיעותיה כבדין יותר מאשה אחרת:

א) וכ"כ התוספות עירובין שם. ב) אולי צ"ל דמייתי מהכא דא"ר יוחנן דהלכה כרבי יוסי דלתנייהו להני כללי.

גליון הש"ס

גמ' א"ל הל' כסתם. עיין חידושי הרשב"א בב"ק קב ע"א ד"ה אלא הלכה: **תוס'** ד"ה סתם ואח"כ מחלוקת וכו' ול"ת והא אמרי' וכו'. עיין תשובת הרשב"א סי' קי"ד.

מסורת הש"ס

[עירובין מז.]

שם ע"ש כתובות ס: ע"ש [תוספתא פ"ו]

[בעירובין ובכתובות אי' ר' יוסי וכ"א בשאלתות פ' וירא ס"ס ה' אכן בתוספתא איתא רבי יהודה ועיין תוספות לעיל לו: סד"ה אבל]

[תוספתא שם]

[שבת מו. וש"נ]

[פסחים פד. יומא מו. סוכה נד.]

[ב"ק קב. ע"ז . נדה יא:]

הגהות הב"ח

(א) גמ' שאינה ראויה לילד כולן צריכות להמתין ג': (ב) רש"י ד"ה בכרם וכו' כעין נטיעות הכרם: (ג) ד"ה מחלקת וכו' אחריה מיד באותה מסכת בין שסתם אחריה במסכת אחרת:

הגהות הגר"א

[א] גמ' בבית האסורין. נ"ב בתוספתא ובירושלמי איתא או שהלך בעלה למדינת הים וכ"ה בכתובות ס ע"ב: [ב] שם ר' יהודה. נ"ב בכתובות שם הגירסא רבי יוסי ובזה מתורץ קושית רש"י ד"ה הלכה דנקיט רבי יוסי משום הברייתא

וכי *רבי לא שנאה *ר' חייא מנין לו? אמר ליה: והא תנן: *[א]מסרק של פשתן שניטלו שיניו, ונשתיירו בו שתים – טמאות, ואחת – טהורה. וכולן שניטלו אחת אחת בפני עצמן – טמאות. [ב]של צמר שניטלו שיניו אחת מבינתים – טהור, נשתיירו בו ג' במקום אחד – טמא, היתה החיצונה אחת מהן – טהור. ניטלו ב' ועשאן למלקט – טמאות, אחת והתקינה לנר או למיתוח – טמאה. וקי"ל דאין הלכה כאותה משנה! אמר ליה: בר מינה דההיא, דר' יוחנן ור"ל דאמרי תרוייהו: זו אינה משנה. מ"ט? אמר רב הונא בר מנוח משמיה דרב אידי בריה דרב איקא: משום דקשיא רישא לסיפא. דקתני: של צמר שניטלו שיניו אחת מבינתים – טהור, הא נשתיירו בו שתים במקום אחד – טמא, והדר תני: נשתיירו בו ג' – טמא, ג' – אין, שתים – לא! ומאי קושיא? דלמא הא בגווייתא הא בברייתא! אלא מהכא, דקתני: וכולן שניטלו אחת אחת בפני עצמן טמאות, ואע"ג דלא התקינה. אימא סיפא: אחת והתקינה לנר או למיתוח – טמאה. התקינה – אין, לא התקינה – לא! אמר אביי: ומאי קושיא? דלמא הא בקתייהו, הא בלא קתייהו. א"ר פפא: [ג]ומאי קושיא? ודלמא הא – בקטינתא, הא – באלימתא. אלא: משום דמסיימי בה דווקני: זו דברי ר"ש. שלח ר' חייא בר אבין: מארסין תוך ג', וכן עושים מעשה. וכן היה ר' אלעזר מלמדנו משום רבי חנינא הגדול: רובו של ראשון, ורובו של שלישי, ואמצעי שלם. אמימר שרא ליארס ביום תשעים. אמר ליה רב אשי לאמימר: והא רב ושמואל דאמרי תרוייהו: צריכה להמתין ג' חדשים, חוץ מיום שמת בו וחוץ מיום שנתארסה בו! ההוא לענין מינקת איתמר. דרב ושמואל דאמרי תרוייהו: *צריכה להמתין כ"ד חדש, חוץ מיום שנולד בו וחוץ מיום שנתארסה בו. והא ההוא דעבד סעודת אירוסין ביום תשעים, ואפסדיה רבא לסעודתיה! ההיא סעודת נשואין הואי. [ד]והלכתא: צריכה להמתין כ"ד חודש, חוץ מיום שנולד בו וחוץ מיום שנתארסה בו. וצריכה להמתין ג' חדשים, חוץ מיום שמת בו וחוץ מיום שנתארסה בו.§ "חוץ מן האלמנה וכו'".§ אמר רב חסדא: ק"ו, ומה במקום שאסור לכבס – מותר ליארס, מקום שמותר לכבס – אינו דין שמותר ליארס! מאי היא? דתנן: *[ה]השבת שחל תשעה באב בתוכה – אסור לספר ולכבס, ובחמישי מותר מפני כבוד השבת. ותניא: [ו]קודם הזמן הזה העם ממעטין בעסקיהם מלישא ומליתן, מלבנות ולנטוע, [ז]ומארסין אבל לא כונסין, ואין עושין סעודת אירוסין. כי תניא ההיא – קודם דקודם (תניא). אמר רבא: וקודם דקודם נמי, ק"ו: ומה במקום שאסור לישא וליתן – מותר ליארס, מקום שמותר לישא וליתן – אינו דין שמותר ליארס?! לא תימא דרבי יוסי אומר כל הנשים יתארסו, אלא אימא: כל הנשים ינשאו.

ולית

רש"י

רבי לא שנאה. רבי שסידר את המשנה לא שנאה שתהא משנה, שלא רצה לסותמה. רבי חייא. תלמידו מנין לו שהלכה כמותה, שסתמה בברייתא? שתים טמאות. דחזו למילתיה. אחת טהורה. דלא חזי למידי. אחת בפני עצמה. שאינה תחובה במסרק. טמאה. שראויה לנר, או למיתוח, לפרוש בגדים או חוט זו מזו. אחת מבינתיים. שמכל ג' הסמוכות ניטלה האמצעית – תו לא חזי. היתה החיצונה. אחת מהשלימות הללו, שנשתיירו ג' עם החיצונות. ושן חיצונה רחבה היא, כעין חיצונות שבמסרק של עץ שלנו – הלכך לא מהניא בהדייהו, וטהור. למלקט. מלקטים, שקורין טנל"ש. לנר. לנקר את הנר. ולמיתוח. לפרוש בגד, כעין הסייטים שמותחין עורות במסמרים: טמאה. לקמן פריך: דהא תנא רישא כולן (א) אחת אחת בפני עצמן טמאות, ואע"ג דלא התקינה. הא. דקתני שתים טמא בגווייתא אמצעיות, דחזיין טפי, שהן כנגד בית יד המסרק, וכשהוא אוחז בו מכוונות הן לסרוק. והא. דקתני שלש אין שתים לא – בברייתא. ולא בחיצונות [ממש], דהא אמרינן היתה חיצונה אחת מהן טהור, אלא אותן המשוכות כלפי הראש, דאינן מכוונות כנגד בית יד המסרק, ולא חזו כולי האי – הלכך ג' הוא דחזו במקצת, אבל שתים – לא חזו ולא מידי. ל"א, והוא עיקר: בגווייתא וברייתא – שתי שורות שיניים יש למסרק של צמר, חיצונות ופנימיות. החיצוניות – עיקר המלאכה תלויה בהן, ופנימיות – לקלוט הצמר שלא יפול. והלכך, בחיצונות צריך ג' במקום אחד, והפנימיות – דיין בב': בקתייהו. שנטל עמה חתיכת עץ, והיא נעשית לה בית יד, ואינה צריכה תיקון אחר. אלימתא. עבות, ואינם צריכות בית יד. זו דברי ר"ש. ולאו סתמא הוא. וכן עושין מעשה. כלומר: כך ראיתי מנהג חכמים עושים. רובו. של חדש ראשון, ורובו של אחרון, ואמצעי (ב) שלם. והלכתא. מניקה צריכה להמתין כ"ד חדש חוץ מיום שנולד בו, ואשה שאינה מניקה צריכה להמתין ג' חדשים, חוץ מיום שמת בעלה וחוץ מיום שנתארסה בו (כל הנשים יתארסו – אנשואות קאי, חוץ מן האלמנה – אתא לאשמועינן ולא אארוסות ולמעוטינהו מלינשא. דגבי הבחנה רבי יוסי מיקל טפי מכולהו, כדאמר ב"ארבעה אחין"). ק"ו. רב חסדא מתמיה על דברי רבי יוסי שאוסר ליארס מחמת אבילות כל ל', כדקתני לקמן: כמה איבול שלה – שלשים יום. במקום שאסור לכבס. שבת שחל ט' באב להיות בתוכה. מותר ליארס. דאירוסין לאו שמחה נינהו. מקום שמותר לכבס. תוך ל' יום של אבל, דאבל אין אסור בתכבוסת אלא שבעה ימים, דכל שלשים יום לגיהוץ תנן בפ' "ואלו מגלחין" (מו"ק דף כג.) אבל כיבוס – לא, דהא תספורת גופה, אי לאו דאתיא "פרע" "פרע" מנזיר – לא מיתסרא. קודם הזמן הזה. קא ס"ד: קודם ט' באב, דהיינו כל השבת שחל להיות בתוכה ממעטין כו'. ומארסין. דלאו שמחה היא, ומלוה קעביד. כי תניא ההיא. דמארסין. קודם דקודם. קודם שבת שחל ט"ב בתוכה, דהתם מותר לכבס. אבל תוך השבת, כשם שאסור לכבס – אסור נמי ליארס, וליכא ק"ו.

אלא

תוספות

במקום שמותר לכבס. גרסי', ול"ג לספר. דהא אמרינן [בירושלמי] במועד קטן: לגיהוץ ולתספורת שלשים יום. והר"ר יעקב מאורליינ"ש הביא מהך גרסא דאשה מותרת בנטילת שער, [וכן איתא בה"ג]. ועוד מצינו למימר: דהתם אליבא דר' יוסי קיימי, דשרי תספורת באבל. דהכי כתב בעל ה"ג: כשם שאסור לגלח במועד כך אסור *לגלח בימי אבלו, דברי רבי יהודה. רבי יוסי מתיר, כל ל' יום אסור לתספורת, אחד זקנו, אחד שער ראשו, ואחד כל שער שבו. וכשם שאסור *ליטול לפרניס במועד – כך אסור בימי אבלו, דברי רבי יהודה, ר' יוסי מתיר. והאשה מותרת בנטילת שער לאחר ז'. ומיהו, אין נראה: דשמא אשה, דשריא באבלה – שריא נמי בתשעה באב. וכן ר' יוסי, דשרי לספר באבילות – שרי נמי בתשעה באב. ועוד נראה: דלרבי יוסי נמי אסור לספר, דמסתמא יליף "פרע" "פרע": מנזיר, וכל ראשו הוא דשריא לגלח – דניוול הוא, אבל לספר – אסור. וכן משמע מתוך הלכות גדולות שהבאתי, וא"כ לא גרסינן הכא לספר, דגילוח כל הראש לא מיקרי סיפור*. שמותר לכבס. אחר שבעה ותוך ל'. והא דמשמע בפ' "ואלו מגלחין" (מו"ק דף כג.) דאבל אסור לכבס כסותו במים – היינו תוך ז', דדוקא גיהוץ אסור תוך שלשים יום. ומיהו, גיהוץ דידן שרי, כדאמרינן בפ"ק דכתובות (דף י:) דגיהוץ שלנו ככיבוס שלהם. ואין להאריך*. מאי היא דתנן. למאי דפרישית דבאיבול פליגי רבי יהודה ורבי יוסי קשה, דנוקי הא דשרי לארס בתשעה באב כרבי יהודה, דשרי נמי באבל! וכי תימא: מ"מ תקשה ליה, שסברת רבי יוסי הפוכה מדרבי יהודה, דר' יהודה מחמיר טפי בכיבוס מבאירוסין, ולרבי יוסי איפכא – ע"כ אין הש"ס חושש בכך, דהא לקמן בעי למימר דתנאי היא! וי"ל: דאין נראה להש"ס שום תנא יחלוק אמתני' דשרי לארס בט' באב אם לא ימצא ברייתא בפירוש, דהא לקמן כשמצא ברייתא נמי בהדיא דקתני ממעטין מליארס – דוחק ומוקי לה בסעודת אירוסין כי היכי דלא תפלוג אמתני' [דהתם]. מלישא וליתן מלבנות ולנטוע. בפרק בתרא דתענית [בירושלמי] מוקי בבנין ונטיעה של שמחה, כגון אבורנקי של מלכים. וי"מ דמשא ומתן נמי איירי בשל שמחה, כגון צרכי חופה. ואין נראה: דלא אסר אלא סעודה עצמה. ונראה דריבוי משא ומתן קא אסר, שימעטו יותר מבשאר ימים*). ומה במקום שאסור לישא וליתן. וא"ת: מה לקודם דקודם – שמותר לספר! ועוד תימה: דתספורת יהא אסור בקודם דקודם מק"ו דשלשים יום דאבילות, שמותר לישא וליתן! או משא ומתן ליתסר בשלשים יום דאבילות מק"ו דתספורת בקודם דקודם! או תספורת לישרי בשלשים יום של אבילות! ולפי המסקנא ניחא.

*) [ועיין תוספות מגילה ה: ד"ה ממעטין]

עין משפט נר מצוה

צא א מיי' פי"א מהל' כלים הלכה ז:
צב ב ג מיי' שם הלכה ג ועיין שם בכ"מ:
[ליטול לפרנים במועד רש"ל]
[לגלח בימי אבלו כך אסור ליטול לפרנים בימי אבלו. רש"ל]
צג ד מיי' פי"א מהלכות גירושין הל' כו סמג עשין נ טוש"ע אה"ע סי' יג סעיף א וסעיף יא:
צד ה מיי' פ"ה מהל' תעניות הלכה ו סמג עשין מד"ס ג טוש"ע א"ח סימן תקנא סעיף ג:
[והאריכות בזה מבואר בתוס' מ"ק כג. ד"ה כל]
צה ו מיי' וסמג שם טוש"ע א"ח סימן תקנא סעיף ב [ברמב"ם ליתא גם בריי"ף והרא"ש השמיטו ועי' ב"י סימן תקנ"א טעם להשמטה זו]:
צו ז מיי' פ"י מהלכות אישות הלכה יד טור ש"ע שם:
[ועי' אריכות בתוספות מו"ק כג. ד"ה כל שלשים וכו']

תוספות ישנים

והא בברייתא. פי' הא דאמרי' שלש א) (או שתים) מיירי בברייתא פי' ולא בחיצונות ממש דהא אמרי' (קמייתא) [דהיתה] החיצונה אחת מהן טהורה אלא באותן המשוכות כלפי הראש (כזה). י"מ בברייתא בשורה החיצונה ובגווייתא מיירי בשורה הפנימית דאינם משוכות כלפי בית יד המסרק ולא חזו כולי האי הלכך שלשה ב) (לא) לחזו במקצת אבל שתים לא חזו מידי כי שתי שורות יש למסרק של צמר חיצונה ופנימית והחיצונה עיקר המלאכה תלויה בהם והפנימית לקלוט את הצמר שלא יפול הלכך בחיצונות צריך שלש במקום אחד והפנימית דיין בשתים: מתני' כל הנשים יתארסו אנשואות קאי וחוץ מן האלמנה אתא לאשמעינן ולאו אארוסות ולמעוטינהו מלינשא דגבי הבחנה ר' יוסי מיקל טפי מכלהו כדאמרינן בד' אחין: מה במקום שאסור לכבס ולספר כגון בשבת שחל ט' באב להיות בתוכה מותר לארס נראה דל"ג לספר שהרי איך אמרי' מקום שמותר לספר כגון ג) כל ימי אבלות א"א לומר כן שהרי כן שהרי אסור לספר כל שלשים יום כדילפינן פרע פרע מנזיר ולפי הספרים שגורסים לספר י"ל דמיירי באשה דשריא בנטילת שער כל ל' יום ודוחק הא דמנא לן לאסירא נטילת שער באשה בשבת שחל ט' באב להיות בתוכה הלא אין זה לה אלא ניוול לגלח שערה וי"ת דמוכחינן [מהא] דמותר לספר תוך ל' יום בתכפוהו אבליו אבל בשבת שחל ט' באב להיות בתוכו סברא הוא לאסור משום דלא צריך רק להמתין מעט שיעבור ט' באב אבל באבלות שרי להקל שערו בתכפוהו אבליו. משמע הכא בתוך ל' יום מותר לכבס וא"ת הא אמרינן אבל אסור לכבס כסותו במים וי"ל התם איירי תוך שבעה אבל לאחר שבעה שרי ועתה אף גיהוץ שלנו שרי דגיהוץ שלנו ככיבוס שלהם דהכי אמרינן התם וא"ת הא אמרינן דא"ר שמעון בן אלעזר לא אסרו אלא לכלים חדשים וגם קאמר התם אביי נפק בחומרתא סומקתי ורבא נפק בגלידא דסרבלא משמע דגיהוץ בבבל לא שרי וי"ל דהתם איירי שהיו שם הכלים מגוהצים מארץ ישראל א"נ יכול להיות שיש מקומות בבבל שיש בהם אומנים כמו בארץ ישראל ועתה יש לנו לאסור כל שלשים יום דאמרינן בתוספתא כל שלשים לתכבוסת וא"כ נהי נמי דגיהוץ שלנו ככיבוס שלהם מ"מ אסור דהא אף כיבוס שלהם אסור ועתה יש להזהר בכיבוס שלנו דהוי לבן ביותר והוי כגיהוץ ואסור ככיבוס שלהם ולכן יש להחמיר ולתת חלוק לבן שלו לחברו ללבשו טרם ילבשנו וכן נהגו העולם: לישא וליתן ר"ל משא ומתן של שמחה דומיא דלבנות ולנטוע דמפרש התם כגון אבורנקי של מלכים: וקודם דקודם נמי ק"ו ומה במקום שאסור לישא וליתן דהיינו קודם דקודם מותר ליארס וא"ת וליפרך מה לקודם דקודם שמותר לספר תאמר באבלות שאסור לספר וי"ל דלמסקנא ניחא ד) דאבלות ישנה מתחלה ועד סוף אבל אין להקשות דלשתרי תספורת כל ל' יום מק"ו דקודם דקודם שאסור לישא וליתן ומותר לספר ל' יום של אבלות כו' אינו דין שמותר לספר דזה אינו יכול להיות דהא ילפינן פרע פרע מנזיר לאסור כל ל' יום ואם תאמר ותספורת תיאסר בקודם דקודם בק"ו דאבלות שמותר לישא וליתן ואסור לספר וכן נמי משא ומתן לתסר כל שלשים יום של אבלות מק"ו מקודם דקודם דמותר בתספורת ואסור לישא וליתן וגם בזה יש לומר דלמסקנא ניחא הכל:

א) צ"ל הא דאמרינן שלש אבל לא שתים מיירי בחיצונות. ב) נראה דצ"ל הלכך אם נשתיירו שלש במקום אחד טמא דחזו במקצת וכו'. ג) אולי דצ"ל כגון בל' יום של אבילות א"א לומר כן שהרי אסור לספר כל ל' יום. ד) צ"ל דשאני אבילות חדשה מאבילות ישנה.

מסורת הש"ס

[עירובין לב: נדה סב:]
[עי' תוס' נדה סב: ד"ה ר"ח]
כלים פי"ג מ"ח
כתובות ס:
תענית כו:

תוספות רי"ד מקמאי

גרים הרב אלפס אמר רב נחמן ק"ו ומה במקום שאסור לספר ולכבס מותר לארס מקום שמותר לספר ולכבס אינו דין שמותר לארס ומוכח מהא שהאשה מותרת לספר בשבעת האיבול דהכי איתא באבל רבתי ורש"י ז"ל גרים ומה במקום שאסור לכבס מותר לארס במקום שמותר לכבס אינו דין שמותר לארס ול"ג לספר: ומאי דאיסתפקא לרב אלפס בעובד כוכבים ועבד הבא על בת ישראל אם הולד פגום לכהונה או לא תימה הוא מאי ספיקא איכא דמילתא פסיקא היא ק"ו מאלמנה ועוד דגרים בפ' כיצד לימא קסבר רבינא גוי ועבד הבא על בת ישראל הולד כשר נהי דממזר כיהא לא הוי. ישראל פסול מיהא ליקרי הלכך מילתא פשוטה היא שהולד פגום לכהונה:

הגהות הב"ח

(א) רש"י ד"ה טמאה וכו' רישא כולן שניטלו אחת אחת: (ב) ד"ה רובו של וכו' שלם הס"ד ואח"כ נ"ל ד"ה ביום תשעים. יום השלמת ג' חדשים הס"ד:

גליון הש"ס

רש"י ד"ה מקום שמותר וכו' אבל כבוס לא. עי' מו"ק דף יט ע"א ברש"י ד"ה שמנה ימים וצ"ע:

וְלֵית לֵיהּ לְרַבִּי יוֹסֵי לְהַבְחִין? (א) לֵית לֵיהּ. וְאִיבָּעֵית אֵימָא: לְעוֹלָם אִית לֵיהּ, וְאֵימָא, רַבִּי יוֹסֵי אוֹמֵר: כָּל אֲרוּסוֹת גְּרוּשׁוֹת יִנָּשְׂאוּ. אִי הָכִי הַיְינוּ רַ' יְהוּדָה! אִיכָּא בֵּינַיְיהוּ נְשׂוּאָה לֵיאָרֵס; רַבִּי יְהוּדָה סָבַר: נְשׂוּאָה מוּתֶּרֶת לֵיאָרֵס, וְרַבִּי יוֹסֵי סָבַר: נְשׂוּאָה אֲסוּרָה לֵיאָרֵס. וְסָבַר רַ' יוֹסֵי נְשׂוּאָה אֲסוּרָה לֵיאָרֵס? וְהָתַנְיָא, רַבִּי יוֹסֵי אוֹמֵר: כָּל הַנָּשִׁים יִתְאָרְסוּ, חוּץ מִן הָאַלְמָנָה מִפְּנֵי הָאִיבּוּל, וְכַמָּה אִיבּוּל שֶׁלָּהּ — שְׁלֹשִׁים יוֹם. וְכוּלָּן לֹא יִנָּשְׂאוּ עַד שֶׁיְּהוּ לָהֶן ג' חֳדָשִׁים! הַאי מַאי קוּשְׁיָא? אִילֵימָא דְּקָתָנֵי, רַבִּי יוֹסֵי אוֹמֵר: כָּל הַנָּשִׁים יִתְאָרְסוּ — מִי אַלִּימָא מִמַּתְנִי' דְּאוֹקִימְנָא בַּאֲרוּסוֹת גְּרוּשׁוֹת יִנָּשְׂאוּ — ה"נ כָּל אֲרוּסוֹת גְּרוּשׁוֹת יִנָּשְׂאוּ. אֶלָּא מִסֵּיפָא, דְּקָתָנֵי: וְכוּלָּן לֹא יִנָּשְׂאוּ עַד שֶׁיְּהוּ לָהֶן ג' חֳדָשִׁים. אִינְסוּבֵי הוּא — דְּלָא, הָא אִיתְרוּסֵי — שַׁפִּיר דָּמֵי. אֲמַר רָבָא, תְּרֵיץ וְאֵימָא הָכִי: רַ' יוֹסֵי אוֹמֵר כָּל אֲרוּסוֹת גְּרוּשׁוֹת יִנָּשְׂאוּ, חוּץ מִן הָאַלְמָנָה מִפְּנֵי הָאִיבּוּל, וְכַמָּה אִיבּוּל שֶׁלָּהּ — שְׁלֹשִׁים יוֹם. וּנְשׂוּאוֹת לֹא יִתְאָרְסוּ עַד שֶׁיְּהֵא לָהֶן שְׁלֹשָׁה חֳדָשִׁים. וְאַלְמָנָה מִן הָאֵירוּסִין מִי אִית לָהּ אִיבּוּל? וְהָתָנֵי רַבִּי חִיָּיא בַּר אַמִּי: *אִשְׁתּוֹ אֲרוּסָה — לֹא אוֹנֵן וְלֹא מִיטַּמֵּא לָהּ, וְכֵן הִיא לֹא אוֹנֶנֶת וְלֹא מִיטַּמְּאָה לוֹ. מֵתָה — אֵינוֹ יוֹרְשָׁהּ, מֵת הוּא — גּוֹבָה כְּתוּבָּתָהּ. אֶלָּא תַּנָּאֵי הִיא. דְּתַנְיָא: מֵרֹאשׁ חֹדֶשׁ וְעַד הַתַּעֲנִית הָעָם מְמַעֲטִין מֵעִסְקֵיהֶן, מִלִּישָּׂא וּמִלִּיתֵּן, מִלִּבְנוֹת וְלִנְטוֹעַ, וּמִלֵּיאָרֵס וּמִלִּישָּׂא. *שַׁבָּת שֶׁחָל תִּשְׁעָה בְּאָב בְּתוֹכָהּ — אָסוּר לְסַפֵּר וּלְכַבֵּס (וְאָסוּר לֵיאָרֵס). וי"א: *כָּל הַחֹדֶשׁ אָסוּר. מַתְקִיף לָהּ רַב אַשִׁי: מִמַּאי דְּלֵיאָרֵס — לֵיאָרֵס מַמָּשׁ? [א]דִּלְמָא לְמֵיעֲבַד סְעוּדַת אֵירוּסִין הוּא דְּאָסוּר, הָא לֵיאָרֵס — שַׁפִּיר דָּמֵי. אִי הָכִי, מִלִּישָּׂא? לִינָּשֵׂא נַמִי לְמֵיעֲבַד סְעוּדַת נִשּׂוּאִין הוּא דְּאָסוּר, הָא לִישָּׂא — שַׁפִּיר דָּמֵי! הָכִי הַשְׁתָּא! בִּשְׁלָמָא נִשּׂוּאִין בְּלֹא סְעוּדָה — אִיכָּא שִׂמְחָה, אֶלָּא אֵירוּסִין בְּלֹא סְעוּדָה — מִי אִיכָּא שִׂמְחָה? אֶלָּא אֲמַר רַב אַשִׁי: שָׁאנֵי אֲבֵילוּת חֲדָשָׁה מֵאֲבֵילוּת יְשָׁנָה, וְשָׁאנֵי אֲבֵילוּת דְּרַבִּים מֵאֲבֵילוּת דְּיָחִיד.§

מתני' [ב]אַרְבָּעָה אַחִין נְשׂוּאִין אַרְבַּע נָשִׁים, וָמֵתוּ. אִם רָצָה הַגָּדוֹל שֶׁבָּהֶם לְיַבֵּם אֶת כּוּלָּן — הָרְשׁוּת בְּיָדוֹ. [ג]מִי שֶׁהָיָה נָשׂוּי לִשְׁתֵּי נָשִׁים וָמֵת — בִּיאָתָהּ אוֹ חֲלִיצָתָהּ שֶׁל אַחַת מֵהֶן פּוֹטֶרֶת צָרָתָהּ. הָיְתָה

אלא אימא רבי יוסי אומר כל הנשים ינשאו. חוץ מאלמנה. ורבי יוסי לא איבול אתא לאשמועינן. דבנישואין אפילו רבי יהודה מודה דאסור בימי איבול, דהא שמחה היא. אלא ינשאו אתא לאשמועינן, ופליג אדרבי יהודה, דאמר כל הנשואות יתארסו. ואתא ר' יוסי למימר: אפילו נשואות ינשאו. וג' מחלוקות בדבר: דת"ק אסר אפילו ארוסות ליארס, דגזרו ארוסת ראשון אטו נשואה, וגזרינן ארוסין דאחרון אטו נשואין דאחרון. ור' יהודה סבר: הנשואות יתארסו, ולא גזר אירוסין אטו נשואין, והארוסות ינשאו, ולא גזר ארוסה אטו נשואה. אבל הבחנה מיהא אית ליה, ונשואה לא תנשא. ורבי יוסי – אפילו הבחנה לית ליה. ואי בעית **אימא** אית ליה. ואפ"ה ינשאו קתני. [ולא אנשואות קאי] אלא אארוסות קאי, וה"ק: כל הארוסות שנתגרשו – ינשאו חוץ מן הארוסות אלמנות מחמת האיבול. ולקמן פריך: מי חייל איבול אארוסה? **אי הכי** היינו ר' יהודה. דרבי יהודה נמי שרי ארוסה לינשא. וליכא למימר הכא כדלעיל, דרבי יוסי איבול אתא לאשמועינן, דנשואין אסור כל ל' יום – דהא בנשואין כ"ע מודו דשמחה היא. וינשאו דקאמר רבי יהודה – אגרושה, דליכא איבול, קאמר. **איכא** בינייהו נשואה ליארס. דקאמר רבי יהודה הנשואות יתארסו, דלא גזר אירוסין אטו נשואין. ואתא רבי יוסי למימר: כל ארוסות [גרושות] ינשאו, הואיל וליכא איבול – שרי. ומשום הבחנה – לא מיפסרא, דהא לאו מעוברת היא. וארוסה אטו נשואה לא גזרינן. אבל נשואות לא יתארסו, דאיכא למיחש שמא מעוברת היא, ואי שרית לה להתארס – אתי לאינסובי. **כל הנשים** יתארסו. ואפילו נשואות. **וכולן**. הנשואות, בין גרושה בין אלמנה – לא ינשאו, משום הבחנה עד שלשה חדשים. **הכא** נמי. תני הכי: כל ארוסות גרושות ינשאו, חוץ מן האלמנה אפי' ארוסה, מפני האיבול. **וכולן**. הנשואות לא ינשאו, אפי' גרושה דליכא איבול, דחיישינן להבחנה. **אלא מסיפא** דקתני וכולן לא ינשאו. דעל כרחך אנשואות לא ינשאו קאי, דהא אוקמא רישא אארוסות ינשאו, ולא גזרינן משום הבחנה דנשואות. הלכך, סיפא אנשואות קאי, דקתני לא ינשאו, דבעינן הבחנה. אבל איתרוסי – שפיר דמי, ולא גזרינן אירוסין אטו נשואין. **תריץ ואימא הכי** כו'. דודאי סיפא אנשואין קאי כדקאמרת, ומיהו לא תיתני לא ינשאו, אלא לא יתארסו. **ולא מיטמאה**. (ג) כלומר, אינה מצווה להתעסק בו. **גובה** כתובתה. וכגון דכתב לה מן האירוסין: ה"ג. **אלא תנאי היא**. אלא לעולם כדקתני מתני' כל הנשים יתארסו, וכדפרשינן בריש שמעתין דאנשואות קאי. ואיבול איכא בינייהו, ואשמעינן דאירוסין בימי אבל אסור. ודקשיא לך: קודם הזמן דקתני ומארסין – תנאי היא, דאיכא למאן דאסר. והיא דקתני מארסין – לאו דברי הכל היא, ולא סבירא ליה לרבי יוסי. **אלא אמר רב אשי**. לא תוקמא כתנאי, ורבי יוסי מודה בההיא דמארסין. ודקשיא לך: ק"ו הוא – שאני בין אבילות חדשה, *דתשעה באב דהוי אבילות ישנה ואבלות דרבים, הלכך קילא. **מתני'** היתה

ולית ליה לרבי יוסי להבחין לית ליה. ורדופה וחברותיה דנקט לעיל – משום ר"מ. **אי** הכי היינו רבי יהודה. השתא לא בעי למימר דאיכא בינייהו איבול – דלא מסתברא ליה למימר שלא יחוש רבי יהודה באיבול לענין נישואין, כדפי' בקונטר'. אע"ג דלפי המסקנא ליכא איבול בארוסה, מ"מ, למאי דס"ד השתא דאיכא איבול בארוסה – אין סברא לומר שלא יחוש ר' יהודה לענין נישואין. **שאני** בין אבילות חדשה. פי' בקונט': דאבילות דתשעה באב דהוי ישנה, ודרבים – קילא. וקשיא: דאכתי תקשי ק"ו, כדמעיקרא! ומפרש ר"ת: שאני בין אבילות חדשה שאסרו ליארס, לפי שבחדשה יש להחמיר מבישנה, משא"כ באבילות ישנה ובאבילות דרבים יש להחמיר טפי לענין משא ומתן מאבילות דיחיד. דמשא ומתן שהוא דבר של פרהסיא, אם יעסקו בפרקמטיא כל היום – יבאו ויאמרו שאין חוששין להתאבל על ירושלים. ולא דמי לאירוסין שאין אלא שעה אחת, וכדאוקמי' בקודם דקודם. אבל בשבת שחל תשעה באב להיות בתוכה – אסור ליארס, דאי שרי – אכתי איכא ק"ו דכיבוס. ומיהו, במגילת סתרים מתיר ליארס אפילו בט' באב, שלא יקדמנו אחר ברחמים. והביא ראיה מירושלמי. וצ"ל: דבאבילות דרבים יש להחמיר נמי בכיבוס, דכיבוס נמי דבר של פרהסיא, שלא יהו כולם עוסקים לכבס ולספר וליפות עצמם, ונראים שאין חוששין להתאבל כלל. וא"ת: דהכא אסרי' ליארס תוך שלשים. ובפרק בתרא דמו"ק (דף כג. ושם) תני: כל שלשים יום לנישואין, משמע דליארס שרי! וי"ל: דההיא כרבי יהודה דשרי. אי נמי, נשואין נקט, לאשמועינן דאפילו נשואין שרי מיד לאחר שלשים יום. אע"פ שבאשתו קתני דצריך להמתין ג' רגלים. ונראה לר"ת: דאע"ג דאסרינן באביו ובאמו בית השמחה עד י"ב חדש – מ"מ מותר לישא אחר שלשים, משום מצות פריה ורביה. דכל ל' יום לנשואין סתמא קתני, אפילו באביו ובאמו, דלא מפליג אלא באשתו. ואע"ג דקיים פריה ורביה – שרי, דהלכה כר' יהושע דאמר ב"הבא על יבמתו": *ישא אשה בזקנותו, שנאמר "בבקר זרע את זרעך" (קהלת יא). ואם יש לו בנים קטנים – מותר לכנוס אפילו תוך ז'. או שאין לו בנים כלל, או לכל הפחות אחר שבעה כדמשמע בעובדא *דר' יוסף הכהן (מו"ק דף כג.), דבעוד שהיה בבית הקברות אמר לאחותה לכי וגדלי בני אחותך – ומשמע דכנסה לאלתר, מדקתני: אעפ"כ לא בא עליה אלא לזמן מרובה. ומפרש התם דהיינו ל'. ומשמע דלא בא עליה, אבל נשואין – הוו. ור"ת הביא הירושלמי, דקתני: אע"פ שכנסה – לא הכיר בה עד לאחר שלשים. ומעשה באחת משודכת שמת אחיה לאחר הזמנת קרואים סמוך לחופה, והתיר לכונסה תוך שלשים משום פריה ורביה דבעל, מאחר שאם לא ישא את זו – לא ישא אחרת. ושמא אפי' אם לא היתה משודכת היה מתיר, מאחר שחפץ בה יותר מאחרת, כדאשכחן *ברבי יוסף הכהן דמשום פרנסת בניו אשתראי, אע"פ שהיתה אבילה מאחותה. ומיהו, התם לא אפשר באחרת לפי שמרחמת על בני אחותה יותר משאר נשים. והא דאסר במתני' ליארס תוך שלשים, ולא מפליג אפילו רוצה לינשא למי שיש לו בנים קטנים, או למי שאין לו בנים כלל – לפי שצריכה להמתין עדיין לינשא עד שלשה חדשים משום הבחנה. ועוד אומר ר"ת: דמי שאין לו בנים מותר לישא ולבעול תוך ל', דלא מקיימא מצות פריה ורביה אלא בבעילה. אבל תוך ז' ימי אבילות – אסור לכנוס, כדמוכח בריש כתובות (דף ד. ושם) דלא שרי אלא בטבחו טבוח ויינו מזוג, ובמת אביו של חתן או אמה של כלה דוקא. ובשאין לו בנים מיירי התם, מדקאמרינן התם דאביו של חתן קטרת. *ורבי יוסף הכהן אף על פי שדבר עמה בבית הקברות – לא כנס עד אחר שבעה. או שמא משום פרנסת בנים שרי לכנוס אפילו תוך שבעה. וק"ק לפירוש רבינו תם מדתני במסכת שמחות פרק ז' גבי אשתו דצריך להמתין שלש רגלים כשיש לו בנים, אבל אין לו בנים או שיש לו בנים קטנים – מותר לישא אחרת לאחר שלשים יום, ומותר לישא – צריך לומר דלישא ולבעול קאמר, דלכנוס גרידא אפילו

עין משפט נר מצוה

צז א מיי' פ"י מהלכות אישות הלכה י"ד טור שו"ע א"ח סימן תקנ"א סעיף א:

צח ב מיי' פ"א מהלכות יבום הלכה יא סמג עשין נ טוש"ע אה"ע סימן קסא סעיף ח:

צט ג מיי' שם הלכה ט טור ש"ע שם סעיף א:

הגהות הב"ח

(א) גמ' להבחין איבעית אימא לית ליה ואיבעית אימא: (ב) רש"י ד"ה ולא מיטמאה כלומר אינה מצווה. נ"ב עיין לעיל דף כט ע"ב:

מסורת הש"ס

לעיל כט: ב"מ יח. כתובות נג. ע"ש פט: ע"ש סנהדרין כח: [ב"ש וכ"ע]

תענית כו:

[שם כט:]

צ"ל לתשעה באב. יעב"ץ

[לקמן סב:]

[צ"ל דיוסף הכהן]

[צ"ל ביוסף הכהן]

[צ"ל ויוסף הכהן]

*א הָיְתָה אַחַת כְּשֵׁרָה וְאַחַת פְּסוּלָה, אִם הָיָה חוֹלֵץ — חוֹלֵץ לַפְּסוּלָה, וְאִם הָיָה מְיַיבֵּם — מְיַיבֵּם לַכְּשֵׁרָה.§ **גמ'** אַרְבָּעָה אַחִין ס"ד? אֶלָּא אֵימָא: אַרְבָּעָה מֵאַחִין.§ "הָרְשׁוּת בְּיָדוֹ".§ וְשָׁבְקִי לֵיהּ? וְהַתַּנְיָא: *°"וְקָרְאוּ לוֹ זִקְנֵי עִירוֹ" — ב הֵן וְלֹא שְׁלוּחָן, "וְדִבְּרוּ אֵלָיו" — מְלַמֵּד שֶׁמַּשִּׂיאִין לוֹ עֵצָה הַהוֹגֶנֶת לוֹ, שֶׁאִם הָיָה הוּא יֶלֶד וְהִיא זְקֵנָה, הוּא זָקֵן וְהִיא יַלְדָּה — אוֹמְרִין לוֹ: מַה לְּךָ אֵצֶל יַלְדָּה, מַה לְּךָ אֵצֶל זְקֵנָה? כְּלַךְ אֵצֶל שֶׁכְּמוֹתְךָ, וְאַל (א) תָּשִׂים קְטָטָה בְּבֵיתְךָ. לָא צְרִיכָא, דְּאֶפְשָׁר לֵיהּ. א"ה, אֲפִילּוּ טוּבָא נַמִּי! ג עֵצָה טוֹבָה קמ"ל: ד' — אִין, טְפֵי — לָא, כִּי הֵיכִי דְּנִמְטְיֵיהּ עוֹנָה בְּחֹדֶשׁ.§ "מִי שֶׁהָיָה נָשׂוּי וכו'".§ וְנַיְיבֵּם לְתַרְוַיְיהוּ! א"ר חִיָּיא בַּר אַבָּא א"ר יוֹחָנָן: אָמַר קְרָא °"אֲשֶׁר לֹא יִבְנֶה אֶת בֵּית אָחִיו" — ד בַּיִת אֶחָד הוּא בּוֹנֶה, וְאֵין בּוֹנֶה שְׁנֵי בָתִּים. וְנַחֲלוֹץ לְתַרְוַיְיהוּ! אֲמַר מָר זוּטְרָא בַּר טוֹבִיָּה: אָמַר קְרָא °"בֵּית חֲלוּץ הַנָּעַל" — בַּיִת אֶחָד הוּא חוֹלֵץ, וְאֵין חוֹלֵץ שְׁנֵי בָתִּים. (ג) וְנַיְיבֵּם לַחֲדָא וְנַחֲלוֹץ לַחֲדָא! — אָמַר קְרָא °"אִם לֹא יַחְפּוֹץ" הָא חָפֵץ — יְיַבֵּם, *כָּל הָעוֹלָה לְיִבּוּם — עוֹלָה לַחֲלִיצָה, כָּל שֶׁאֵין עוֹלָה לְיִיבּוּם — אֵין עוֹלָה לַחֲלִיצָה. וְעוֹד: *שֶׁלֹּא יֹאמְרוּ בַּיִת מִקְצָתוֹ בָּנוּי וּמִקְצָתוֹ חָלוּץ. וְיֹאמְרוּ! אִי דִּמְיַיבֵּם וַהֲדַר חָלֵיץ — הָכִי נַמִּי, אֶלָּא [דִּלְמָא] חָלֵיץ וַהֲדַר מְיַיבֵּם, וְקָם לֵיהּ בְּ"לֹא יִבְנֶה". וְאֵימָא: כִּי אִיכָּא חֲדָא — תִּתְקַיֵּים מִצְוַת יִבּוּם, כִּי אִיכָּא תַּרְתֵּי — לֹא תִּתְקַיֵּים מִצְוַת יִבּוּם! א"כ, צָרַת עֶרְוָה דְּאָסַר רַחֲמָנָא לָמָּה לִי? הַשְׁתָּא, ב' בְּעָלְמָא אָמְרַתְּ לָאו בְּנֵי חֲלִיצָה וְיִבּוּם נִינְהוּ, צָרַת עֶרְוָה מִיבַּעְיָא? אַלְמָה לָא? אִצְטְרִיךְ, סד"א עֶרְוָה אַבָּרַאי קַיְּימָא, וְתִתְיַיבֵּם צָרָתָהּ — קמ"ל דַּאֲסִירָא, אֶלָּא: "יְבִמְתּוֹ... יְבִמְתּוֹ" — רִיבָּה.§ "הָיְתָה אַחַת כְּשֵׁרָה".§ אָמַר רַב יוֹסֵף: *כָּאן שָׁנָה רַבִּי: לֹא יִשְׁפּוֹךְ אָדָם מֵי בוֹרוֹ וַאֲחֵרִים צְרִיכִים לָהֶם.§ **מתני'** הַמַּחֲזִיר גְּרוּשָׁתוֹ, וְהַנּוֹשֵׂא חֲלוּצָתוֹ, וְהַנּוֹשֵׂא קְרוֹבַת חֲלוּצָתוֹ — יוֹצִיא, וְהַוָּלָד מַמְזֵר, דִּבְרֵי ר"ע. וחכ"א: אֵין הַוָּלָד מַמְזֵר. וּמוֹדִים בְּנוֹשֵׂא קְרוֹבַת גְּרוּשָׁתוֹ, שֶׁהַוָּלָד מַמְזֵר.§ **גמ'** וְסָבַר ר' עֲקִיבָא הַנּוֹשֵׂא קְרוֹבַת חֲלוּצָתוֹ הַוָּלָד מַמְזֵר? וְהָאָמַר רֵישׁ לָקִישׁ, *כָּאן שָׁנָה רַבִּי: אֲחוֹת גְּרוּשָׁה — מִדִּבְרֵי תוֹרָה, אֲחוֹת חֲלוּצָה — מִדִּבְרֵי סוֹפְרִים! תְּנֵי: קְרוֹבַת גְּרוּשָׁתוֹ. הָכִי נַמִּי מִסְתַּבְּרָא, דְּקָתָנֵי סֵיפָא: וּמוֹדִים בְּנוֹשֵׂא קְרוֹבַת גְּרוּשָׁתוֹ שֶׁהַוָּלָד מַמְזֵר. אִי אָמְרַתְּ בִּשְׁלָמָא אַיְירֵי בָּהּ — הַיְינוּ דְּקָתָנֵי "וּמוֹדִים", אֶלָּא אִי אָמְרַתְּ לָא אַיְירֵי בָּהּ — מַאי "וּמוֹדִים"? וְדִלְמָא הָא קָא מַשְׁמַע לָן: דְּיֵשׁ מַמְזֵר מֵחַיָּיבֵי כָּרֵיתוֹת. הָא קָתָנֵי לָהּ לְקַמָּן: *אֵיזֶהוּ מַמְזֵר — כָּל שְׁאֵר בָּשָׂר שֶׁהוּא בְּ"לֹא יָבֹא" דִּבְרֵי ר"ע, *ר"ש הַתִּימְנִי אוֹמֵר: כָּל שֶׁחַיָּיבִין עָלָיו כָּרֵת בִּידֵי שָׁמַיִם, וַהֲלָכָה כִּדְבָרָיו. וְדִלְמָא קָסָתֵים לָן תַּנָּא *כְּר"ש הַתִּימְנִי. א"כ לִיתְנֵי שְׁאָר חַיָּיבֵי כָּרֵיתוֹת, קְרוֹבַת גְּרוּשָׁתוֹ לָמָּה לִי? אֶלָּא ש"מ אַיְירֵי בָּהּ. [וְדִלְמָא] לְעוֹלָם לָא אַיְירֵי בָּהּ, וְאַיְּידֵי דְּתָנָא מַחֲזִיר גְּרוּשָׁתוֹ וְנוֹשֵׂא חֲלוּצָתוֹ וּקְרוֹבַת חֲלוּצָתוֹ — תָּנֵי נַמִּי קְרוֹבַת גְּרוּשָׁתוֹ. אֶלָּא קְרוֹבַת חֲלוּצָתוֹ לְרַבִּי עֲקִיבָא הָוֵי מַמְזֵר. אָמַר ר' חִיָּיא בַּר אַבָּא א"ר יוֹחָנָן: הַיְינוּ טַעְמָא דר"ע, דְּאָמַר קְרָא "בֵּית חֲלוּץ הַנָּעַל" — הַכָּתוּב קְרָאוֹ בֵּיתוֹ. אָמַר רַב יוֹסֵף אָמַר ר"ש ב"ר: הַכֹּל מוֹדִים בְּמַחֲזִיר גְּרוּשָׁתוֹ שֶׁהַוָּלָד

תורה אור: דברים כה | שם | שם | שם

רש"י

הָיְתָה אַחַת כְּשֵׁרָה. לִכְהוּנָּה, וְאַחַת פְּסוּלָה, כְּגוֹן שֶׁנִּתְגָּרְשָׁה מֵאִישׁ אַחֵר. אִם בָּא יָבָם לַחֲלוֹץ חוֹלֵץ לַפְּסוּלָה. וְלֹא יִפְסוֹל אֶת הַכְּשֵׁרָה לִכְהוּנָּה. דְּלֹא יִשְׁפּוֹךְ אָדָם מֵי בוֹרוֹ וַאֲחֵרִים צְרִיכִים לָהֶם, אע"ג דְּהוּא אֵין צָרִיךְ לָהֶם. גמ' אַרְבָּעָה אַחִין ס"ד. כֵּיוָן דְּלָא הֲווּ אֶלָּא ד' וְכוּלָּן מֵתוּ, כִּדְקָתָנֵי מֵתוּ, מַאן מְיַיבֵּם? וְשָׁבְקִינַן לֵיהּ. בִּתְמִיָּה: וּבַמֶּה יְפַרְנֵס כּוּלָּן? דְּאֶפְשָׁר לֵיהּ. שֶׁעָשִׁיר הוּא, וְיָכוֹל לְזוּנָן. עוֹנָה בְּחֹדֶשׁ. עוֹנָה שֶׁל ת"ח מֵעֶרֶב שַׁבָּת לְעֶרֶב שַׁבָּת, וְזֶהוּ "אֲשֶׁר פִּרְיוֹ יִתֵּן בְּעִתּוֹ" בִּכְתוּבּוֹת (דף סב:), דְּמָטֵי לְכָל חֲדָא עוֹנָה בְּחֹדֶשׁ. וְנַיְיבֵּם לַחֲדָא. בְּרֵישָׁא, וַהֲדַר נַחֲלוֹץ לַאֲחָרָא. כָּל שֶׁאֵינוֹ עוֹלֶה. לְבֵית דִּין לְיִיבּוּם, שֶׁאֵינָהּ זְקוּקָה לְהִתְיַיבֵּם, דְּרַחֲמָנָא פְּטָרָהּ, דִּכְתִיב "אֶת בֵּית אָחִיו" — בַּיִת אֶחָד הוּא בּוֹנֶה, וְלֹא שְׁנֵי בָתִּים — אֵינוֹ עוֹלֶה לַחֲלִיצָה. אַלְמָה לָא. בִּתְמִיָּה, כְּלוֹמַר: וְאִי שְׁתֵּי בָתִּים בְּעָלְמָא פְּטוּרָה — מִי לָא אִיצְטְרִיךְ לְמֵיסַר צָרַת עֶרְוָה? וְהָא אִיצְטְרִיךְ, סד"א עֶרְוָה אַבָּרַאי קַיְּימָא וְלָא רְמִיָא קַמֵּיהּ, וַהֲוָיָא לָהּ צָרַת בַּיִת אֶחָד וְתִתְיַיבֵּם, קמ"ל. כָּאן שָׁנָה רַבִּי. בְּמִשְׁנָה זוֹ לִמְּדָנוּ רַבִּי לֹא יִשְׁפּוֹךְ כו'. מתני' הַמַּחֲזִיר גְּרוּשָׁתוֹ. מִשֶּׁנִּיסֵּאת. וְהַנּוֹשֵׂא אֶת חֲלוּצָתוֹ. דְּקַיְימָא עָלָיו בְּלָאו, דְּשׁוּב לֹא יִבְנֶה. וְהַנּוֹשֵׂא אֶת קְרוֹבַת חֲלוּצָתוֹ. לְקַמָּן בָּעֵי לָן בַּגְּמָרָא: הָא קְרוֹבַת חֲלוּצָתוֹ לָאו דְּאוֹרַיְיתָא הִיא! יוֹצִיא וְהַוָּלָד מַמְזֵר. דְּסָבַר ר"ע: יֵשׁ מַמְזֵר מֵחַיָּיבֵי לָאוִין. קְרוֹבַת גְּרוּשָׁתוֹ. דִּגְרוּשָׁתוֹ כְּאִשְׁתּוֹ, וַאֲחוֹתָהּ אוֹ אִמָּהּ חַיָּיבֵי כָּרֵיתוֹת נִינְהוּ לְגַבֵּיהּ. גמ' אֵימָא קְרוֹבַת גְּרוּשָׁתוֹ. וְרַבָּנַן אַמַּחֲזִיר גְּרוּשָׁתוֹ וְנוֹשֵׂא חֲלוּצָתוֹ פְּלִיגִי. וְדִלְמָא הָא קמ"ל דְּיֵשׁ מַמְזֵר מֵחַיָּיבֵי כָּרֵיתוֹת. וְה"ק: אע"ג דִּפְלִיגִי רַבָּנַן בְּחַיָּיבֵי לָאוִין, מוֹדִים הֵם בְּחַיָּיבֵי כָּרֵיתוֹת שֶׁהַוָּלָד מַמְזֵר. וְדִלְמָא לְעוֹלָם לָא אַיְירֵי בָּהּ. וּדְקָאָמְרַתְּ לְאַשְׁמוּעִינַן שְׁאָר חַיָּיבֵי כָּרֵיתוֹת. אַיְּידֵי דְּתָנָא רֵישָׁא מַחֲזִיר גְּרוּשָׁתוֹ וְנוֹשֵׂא חֲלוּצָתוֹ וּקְרוֹבַת חֲלוּצָתוֹ. וּפְלִיגִי רַבָּנַן עֲלֵיהּ, תָּנָא נַמִּי וּמוֹדִים בִּקְרוֹבַת גְּרוּשָׁתוֹ. (ג) אֲבָל קְרוֹבַת חֲלוּצָתוֹ — ה"נ דִּלְר"ע הָוֵי מַמְזֵר. הַכָּתוּב קְרָאוֹ בֵּיתוֹ. וְלֵית לֵיהּ סְתָמָא דְּמַתְנִי' בְּרֵישׁ פִּרְקִין (מא.) דְּקָתָנֵי: הַחוֹלֵץ לִיבִמְתּוֹ וְנָשָׂא אָחִיו אֶת אֲחוֹתָהּ וּמֵת — חוֹלֶצֶת. דִּלְר"ע פְּטוּרָה לְגַמְרֵי.

תוספות

אפילו תוך שלשים שרי, כדמוכח בעובדא *דר' יוסף, דמשמע אע"פ שאין לו בנים כלל – אין מותר לבעול עד לאחר שלשים. ושמא מילתא דפסיקא לתרוייהו נקט, ולעולם באין לו בנים שרי אפילו תוך שלשים. ולר"י נראה: באין לו בנים כלל – אסור אפילו לכנוס תוך שלשים, כיון דאינו יכול לבעול עד לאחר שלשים. ואתי שפיר דנקט במס' שמחות לישא, משום דאין לו בנים נקטיה, דאפילו לישא אסור, והר"ר יוסף אומר, דהא דאסרינן בית השמחה – היינו דוקא שמחה של רשות, דאמרינן במסכת שמחות (פ"ט): על כל המתים אסור לילך לבית השמחה עד שלשים יום, ועל אביו ועל אמו שנים עשר חדש, אא"כ היתה סעודה של מצוה. דאפשר דלא שרי בסעודה של מצוה אלא אחר שלשים, וקאי אאביו ואמו. אך קלת משמע דשרי אפילו תוך שלשים. **ונייבם** לחדא ונחלוץ לחדא אמר קרא "אם לא יחפוץ כו'". אית ספרים (ד) דגרסי מקמי הכי: ונחלוץ לחדא ונייבם לחדא, אמר קרא "אשר לא יבנה" – כיון שלא בנה שוב לא יבנה. ונראה דל"ג. (ה) דלא צריך קרא להכי, דכיון דחליץ לחדא – א"א לייבם שניה, כיון דאין עולה לחליצה, כדאמר לעיל דאינו חולץ שני בתים. [ועוד, דאינו חולץ שני בתים] משמע דהשניה מותרת לשוק בלא כלום. וקרא ד"לא יבנה" אייתר לכדדרשינן פ"ק (לעיל דף י. ושם) לנתק החלוצה מכרת ללאו. **כל** שאינו עולה כו'. וא"ת: והרי חרש וחרשת, דאינן עולים לחליצה ועולים לייבום כדאמר בפרק "חרש" (לקמן דף קיב:)! ויש לומר: דהתם בני חליצה נינהו, אלא דפומייהו הוא דכאיב להו. **ועוד.** לא גרסינן: ועוד גזרה שמא יאמרו בית מקצתו כו', דאי מדאורייתא מייבם לחדא וחליץ לחדא – משום גזרה לא יניח. **כי איכא תרתי** לא תתקיים מצות ייבום. תימה: דא"כ למה לי קרא דאין חולץ לשני בתים? **אלמה** לא איצטריך סד"א ערוה אבראי קיימא. הקשה הר"ר יו"ט בר' יצחק: אכתי צרת צרה היכי משכחת לה? שהרי צרת ערוה אינה יכולה לינשא לאחיו השני, דאסורה לו מדאורייתא, דגבי דידיה ערוה לאו אבראי קיימא! וי"ל: דמשכחת לה כגון שהערוה היא מחייבי עשה או ל"ת ועשה לכל האחין, דלאו בת יבום היא, וצרתה שריא). **ודלמא** קסתים לן תנא כשמעון התימני. תימה: דסתם ואח"כ מחלוקת היא. דכהאי גוונא פריך בפרק "יש נוחלין" (ב"ב דף קכב:): וכי תאמר סתם לן תנא כרבי יוחנן בן ברוקא – סתם ואח"כ מחלוקת היא! וי"ל: דנהי דאין חשיב סתם, מ"מ חשיב כרבים לגבי יחיד, כדפרישית לעיל*. ובפ' "יש נוחלין" סמיך אקושיא אחריתי, דקאמר: ועוד מאי אלא. **אם** כן לשמעינן שאר חייבי כריתות. אכתי ה"מ למיפרך תנינא, דסתם לן תנא כוותיה בקדושין בפרק "האומר" (דף סו:): כל מקום שאין קדושין כו' ואיזה זה – הבא על אחת מכל העריות. **הכל** מודים במחזיר גרושתו. לרבותא נקט מחזיר גרושתו טפי משאר חייבי לאוין, דאף על גב דכתיב "היא" "תועבה" ואין בניה תועבין – פגום מיהא הוי.

עין משפט נר מצוה

נ"ל דיוסף

ק א מיי' פ"א מהלכות יבום הלכה י סמג עשין נ טור ש"ע אה"ע סי' קסא סעיף ב:

קא ב מיי' פ"ד שם הלכה א סמג עשין נב טוש"ע שם סימן קסו סעיף א:

קב ג מיי' פי"ד מהלכות אישות הלכה א סמג עשין מה ולאוין פא טור ש"ע שם סימן עו סעיף ז:

קג ד מיי' פ"א מהלכות יבום הלכה ט:

תוספות ישנים

כי איכא תרתי לא תתקיים מצות יבום. וא"ת היאך אפשר לומר כן הלא אמרינן בית אחד הוא בונה ואינו בונה שני בתים אם כן הרי מצינו יבום אף בשני בתים שמייבם האחת וי"ל דנימא הכא בית אחד הוא בונה פירוש כי ליכא אלא בית א' אז הוא בונה אבל אינו בונה כלל בשיש שני בתים: **א)** [ועוד י"ל] כגון שגירש הערוה ולמ"ד נשואין הראשונים מפילין לאסורה לשמעון ומותרת ללוי: **אלא** אי אמרת לא איירי בה מאי ומודים. ואע"ג דבפרק האשה שנפלו (דף ע"ח) קאמר ומודים אף על גב דלא איירי בה שאני הכא כיון דלא אשמעינן שום חדוש לא הו"ל למתני ומודים הואיל ולא איירי בה אבל התם אשמעינן חדוש: **בית** חלוץ הנעל הכתוב קראו ביתו. וא"כ לא סבר כמו הסיא דלעיל (דף מ"א) דמגיה המשנה דלאימא אבל המגרש ושפיר גרסינן במתני' וכן וניתני בכלהו באחות חלוצה ובאחות גרושתו (פסולה) דהרי זו פטורה: **הכתוב** קראו ביתו. וא"כ לרבי עקיבא אם בא עליה כהן חייב מן התורה וגם נפקא לן מואשה לרבות חלוצה והא א) דקאמרינן באלו הן הלוקין וקחשיב גרושה וחלוצה לכהן הדיוט הייט כר"ע דלרבנן לא לקי אחלוצה דקרא ב) דהא דכתיב ואשה לא הוי אלא אסמכתא בעלמא אי נמי שפיר אתיא אליבא דרבנן ואגב גרושה נקט חלוצה א"נ בחלוצה נפרש דלוקין ר"ל מדרבנן מכת מרדות: **הכל** מודים במחזיר גרושתו. נ"ע אמאי נקט מחזיר גרושתו טפי מאינך חייבי לאוין נראה משום דס"ד דאין הולד פגום משום דכתיב היא תועבה דמשמע ואין בניה תועבין קמ"ל דהולד פגום ונימא דהיא תועבה אבל אין נרתה

א) והא דקחשיב בר"פ אלו הן הלוקין גרושה וחלוצה כו'. כנ"ל:

ב) נראה דל"ל והא דילפינן מואשה לרבות חלוצה לא הוי אלא כו':

מסורת הש"ס

לעיל ח. | לקמן קח: | [לעיל כ. וש"נ] | לעיל לה: | לעיל יח: יב. לקמן נג. | לעיל מ: וש"נ | לקמן מט. וש"נ | [נ"ל שמעון התימני] | [נ"ל כשמעון התימני]

הגהות הב"ח

(א) גמ' ואל תכניס כטוטה בביתך: (ב) שם ואין חולץ ב' בתים ונחלוץ לחדא ונייבם לחדא אמר קרא אשר לא יבנה כיון שלא בנה שוב לא יבנה נייבם לחדא ונחלוץ לחדא: (ג) רש"י ד"ה אייד דתנא וכו' בקרובת גרושה הס"ד ואח"כ מ"ה אבל קרובת חלוצתו: (ד) תוס' ד"ה ונייבם וכו' אית ספרים. נ"ב ע"ל דף י ע"ב בתוס' ד"ה אינו: (ה) בא"ד דל"ג ליה דלא צריך:

שכן

קד א מיי' פי"א מהל' גירושין הלכה יב סמג לאוין פב:

שֶׁהוּלַד פָּגוּם לִכְהוּנָּה. מַאן "הַכֹּל מוֹדִים" – שִׁמְעוֹן הַתִּימְנִי. דְּאע"ג דְּאָמַר שִׁמְעוֹן הַתִּימְנִי: אֵין מַמְזֵר מֵחַיָּיבֵי לָאוִין – נְהִי דְּמַמְזֵר לָא הָוֵי, פָּגוּם – מִיהָא הָוֵי, מִק"ו מֵאַלְמָנָה. *וּמָה אַלְמָנָה לְכ"ג, שֶׁאֵין אִיסּוּרָהּ שָׁוֶה בַּכֹּל – בְּנָהּ פָּגוּם, זוֹ שֶׁאִיסּוּרָהּ שָׁוֶה בַּכֹּל – אֵינוֹ דִּין שֶׁבְּנָהּ פָּגוּם? אִיכָּא לְמִיפְרַךְ: מַה לְּאַלְמָנָה – שֶׁכֵּן הִיא עַצְמָהּ מִתְחַלֶּלֶת, וְעוֹד: *"הִיא תוֹעֵבָה" כְּתִיב, וְאֵין בָּנֶיהָ תּוֹעֲבִין. וְעוֹד, תַּנְיָא: הַמַּחֲזִיר גְּרוּשָׁתוֹ, וְהַנּוֹשֵׂא חֲלוּצָתוֹ, וְהַנּוֹשֵׂא קְרוֹבַת חֲלוּצָתוֹ. ר"ע אוֹמֵר: אֵין לוֹ בָּהּ קִדּוּשִׁין, וְאֵינָהּ צְרִיכָה הֵימֶנּוּ גֵּט, וְהִיא פְּסוּלָה וּוְלָדָהּ פָּסוּל, אוְכוֹפִין אוֹתוֹ לְהוֹצִיא. וְחכ"א: יֵשׁ לוֹ בָּהּ קִדּוּשִׁין, וּצְרִיכָה הֵימֶנּוּ גֵּט, וְהִיא כְּשֵׁרָה וּוְלָדָהּ כָּשֵׁר. לְמַאן – לָאו לִכְהוּנָּה? לָא, לַקָּהָל. אִי הָכִי, הִיא כְּשֵׁרָה – לְמַאן? אִילֵימָא לַקָּהָל – פְּשִׁיטָא, מִשּׁוּם דְּזַנְיָא אִפַּסְלָה לַקָּהָל? אֶלָּא לָאו – לִכְהוּנָּה, וּמִדְּהִיא לִכְהוּנָּה – וְלָדָהּ נַמִי לִכְהוּנָּה. מִידֵּי אִירְיָא? הָא כִּדְאִיתָא וְהָא כִּדְאִיתָא. הָכִי נַמִי מִסְתַּבְּרָא, דְּקָתָנֵי רֵישָׁא: הִיא פְּסוּלָה וּוְלָדָהּ פָּסוּל. הִיא פְּסוּלָה לְמַאן? אִילֵימָא לַקָּהָל – מִשּׁוּם דְּזַנְיָא אִפַּסְלָה *לֵיהּ לַקָּהָל? אֶלָּא לָאו – לִכְהוּנָּה, וּוְלָדָהּ פָּסוּל, לְמַאן? אִילֵימָא לִכְהוּנָּה – הָא לַקָּהָל כָּשֵׁר? הָאָמַר רַבִּי עֲקִיבָא הַוָּלָד מַמְזֵר! אֶלָּא פְּשִׁיטָא – לַקָּהָל, וּמִדְּרֵישָׁא הָא כִּדְאִיתָא וְהָא כִּדְאִיתָא – סֵיפָא נַמִי הָא כִּדְאִיתָא וְהָא כִּדְאִיתָא. וְ"הִיא תוֹעֵבָה" נַמִי, הִיא תוֹעֵבָה – וְאֵין צָרָתָהּ תּוֹעֵבָה, אֲבָל בָּנֶיהָ – תּוֹעֲבִין. אֶלָּא אַלְמָנָה קַשְׁיָא: מַה לְּאַלְמָנָה שֶׁכֵּן הִיא עַצְמָהּ מִתְחַלֶּלֶת! אֶלָּא אִי אִתְּמַר הָכִי אִתְּמַר: אָמַר רַב יוֹסֵף אָמַר ר' שִׁמְעוֹן בְּרַבִּי: הַכֹּל מוֹדִים בְּבָא עַל חַיָּיבֵי כְּרֵיתוֹת שֶׁהוּלַד פָּגוּם. מַאן "הַכֹּל מוֹדִים" – רַבִּי יְהוֹשֻׁעַ, דְּאע"ג דְּאָמַר ר' יְהוֹשֻׁעַ אֵין מַמְזֵר מֵחַיָּיבֵי כְּרֵיתוֹת, *נְהִי דְּמַמְזֵר לָא הָוֵי – פָּגוּם מִיהָא הָוֵי, מִק"ו מֵאַלְמָנָה. וּמָה אַלְמָנָה לְכ"ג, שֶׁאֵין אִיסּוּרָהּ שָׁוֶה בַּכֹּל – בְּנָהּ פָּגוּם, זוֹ שֶׁאִיסּוּרָהּ שָׁוֶה בַּכֹּל – אֵינוֹ דִּין שֶׁבְּנָהּ פָּגוּם. וְכ"ת: מַה לְּאַלְמָנָה שֶׁכֵּן הִיא עַצְמָהּ מִתְחַלֶּלֶת – הָכָא נַמִי, כֵּיוָן שֶׁבְּעָלָהּ – עֲשָׂאָהּ זוֹנָה. אָמַר רַבָּה בַּר בַּר חָנָה א"ר יוֹחָנָן: הַכֹּל מוֹדִים בְּעֶבֶד וְגוֹי הַבָּא עַל בַּת יִשְׂרָאֵל שֶׁהַוָּלָד מַמְזֵר. מַאן "הַכֹּל מוֹדִים" שִׁמְעוֹן הַתִּימְנִי. דְּאע"ג דְּאָמַר *שִׁמְעוֹן הַתִּימְנִי אֵין מַמְזֵר מֵחַיָּיבֵי לָאוִין – ה"מ מְחַיָּיבֵי

שֶׁהוּלַד פָּגוּם. וְאִם יָלְדָה בַּת – פְּסוּלָה לִכְהוּנָּה כַּחֲלָלָה. שֶׁכֵּן הִיא עַצְמָהּ מִתְחַלֶּלֶת. שֶׁאִם מֵת כֹּהֵן גָּדוֹל – אֲסוּרָה אֲפִילּוּ לְכֹהֵן הֶדְיוֹט, שֶׁפְּסָלָהּ זֶה בְּבִיאָתוֹ וַעֲשָׂאָהּ חֲלָלָה, דִּכְתִיב "לֹא יְחַלֵּל זַרְעוֹ" (ויקרא כא) וְלָא כְּתִיב "וְלֹא יָחֵל". וּמַשְׁמַע: ב' חִילּוּלִים, אֶחָד לָהּ וְאֶחָד לְזַרְעוֹ, וְהָכִי מְפָרֵשׁ בְּקִדּוּשִׁין (דף עז.). אוֹ אִם בַּת כֹּהֵן הִיא פְּסָלָהּ מִן הַתְּרוּמָה, כִּדְאָמַר בִּמְכִילְתִּין לְקַמָּן (דף סח.): תֹּאמַר בְּמַחֲזִיר גְּרוּשָׁתוֹ שֶׁאֵין הִיא עַצְמָהּ מִתְחַלֶּלֶת. דְּאִי לְמִפְסְלָהּ לְכֹהֵן לָא מִפַּסְלָה בְּהַאי חֲזָרָה, דְּהָא פְּסוּלָה וְקַיְימָא מִשְּׁעַת גֵּירוּשִׁין, וְאִי לִתְרוּמָה – לָא מִתַּסְרָא בְּהָכִי, כִּדְאָמַר בְּפֶרֶק "אַלְמָנָה לְכֹהֵן גָּדוֹל" (לקמן דף סט.): הַמַּחֲזִיר גְּרוּשָׁתוֹ. מִשֶּׁנִּשֵּׂאת. אֵין לוֹ בָּהּ קִדּוּשִׁין. דְּקָסָבַר ר"ע אֵין קִדּוּשִׁין תּוֹפְסִין בְּחַיָּיבֵי לָאוִין. וְהִיא פְּסוּלָה. לְכֹהֵן, דְּזוֹנָה הִיא. וּוְלָדָהּ פָּסוּל. מַמְזֵר הוּא. לְמַאן. קָתָנֵי וְלָדָהּ כָּשֵׁר, לָאו לִכְהוּנָּה? הָא כִּדְאִיתָא וְהָא כִּדְאִיתָא. הִיא כְּשֵׁרָה לִכְהוּנָּה, וְלָדָהּ כָּשֵׁר לָבֹא בַּקָּהָל, אֲבָל לִכְהוּנָּה פָּגוּם. ה"נ מִסְתַּבְּרָא. דְּהָא כִּדְאִיתָא וְהָא כִּדְאִיתָא: וְהִיא תוֹעֵבָה. דְּקָא פָּרְכַתְּ הִיא תוֹעֵבָה וְאֵין בָּנֶיהָ תּוֹעֲבִין – לָא תֵּידּוּק הָכִי, אֶלָּא: הִיא תוֹעֵבָה וְאֵין צָרָתָהּ תּוֹעֵבָה, לֵיאָסֵר לְיִיבּוּם, אֶלָּא מִתְיַיבֶּמֶת. ר' יְהוֹשֻׁעַ. דְּאָמַר בְּמַתְנִיתִין (לקמן דף מט.): אֵין מַמְזֵר אֶלָּא מֵחַיָּיבֵי מִיתוֹת. עֲשָׂאָהּ זוֹנָה. וּפְסָלָהּ לִכְהוּנָּה. אֲבָל לְעֵיל, גַּבֵּי מַחֲזִיר גְּרוּשָׁתוֹ, לֵיכָּא לְשַׁנּוּיֵי הָכִי, דְּאָמַר בְּפֶרֶק אַלְמָנָה לְכ"ג לְקַמָּן (דף סט.): וְאֵימָא נִבְעֲלָה לְפָסוּל לָהּ מַחֲזִיר גְּרוּשָׁתוֹ? וּמְשַׁנֵּי: זָר אֶלָּלָה מֵעִיקָּרָא בָּעֵינַן.
חַיָּיבֵי

שכן היא עצמה מתחללת. ליכא למימר דהיא נמי תתחלל מק"ו, דהא אמר בקדושין (דף עז:) דאין חללה אלא מאיסורי כהונה. ולעיל בפ"ק (דף טו: ד"ה "מה") פירשתי. **היא** כשרה. לכהונה איירי, כדמסיק היינו לתרומה, דלכהן אסירא דגרושה היא. וא"ת: לרבי עקיבא, אמאי מיפסלה לתרומה? הא לאו זר אללה מעיקרא הוא! דלקמן בפרק "אלמנה" (דף סט. ושם) פריך: ואימא נבעלה לפסול לה מחזיר גרושתו, ומשני: זר אללה מעיקרא בעינן! וי"ל: דסוגיא דהתם אליבא דרבנן, אבל ר"ע לא בעי זר אללה מעיקרא, כדאמר בפ' "עשרה יוחסין" (קדושין עה:): השתא ממזר הוי, מיפסיל בביאתו מיבעיא? וקצת תימה לר"י: דמאי דריש ר"ע מ"היא תועבה"? דלא דריש ואין בניה תועבין – דהא ממזר הוי, ולא מצי למדרש נמי ואין צרתה תועבה – דלא שייך בה צרתה, דאין קדושין תופסין בחייבי לאוין אליבא דר"ע א). **הכא** נמי כיון דבא עליה עשאה זונה. משמע הכא דזונה פסולה לתרומה, דמתחללת כמו אלמנה. וכן בפ"ק דסוטה (א) (דף ו.) אמתני' דואלו אסורות לאכול בתרומה דקאמר: אילימא מקמי דתסתי – זונה היא, ופשיטא דאסורה בתרומה ב). ותימה לר"י: מנא לן דאסורה בתרומה? ד"אשה זונה לא יקחו" כתיב, אבל לתרומה לא אשכחן! ועוד: לקמן בפ' "אלמנה" (דף סח:) דפריך: ואימא נבעלה לפסול לה – חייבי כריתות, ולמה לי קרא ד"כי תהיה לאיש זר" לחייבי כריתות? כיון דבחייבי כריתות הויא זונה, וזונה אסורה בתרומה! והיה נראה לר"י ד"מכי תהיה לאיש זר" הוא דנפקא לן דזונה אסורה בתרומה. וכל חייבי כריתות, אפילו אותה דע"י קדושין דלא הוי זר אללה מעיקרא, וכן חייבי לאוין לר"ע, ואפי' מחזיר גרושתו, דלא הוי זר אללה מעיקרא, כדמשמע לעיל דמיפסלה לר"ע מתרומה – הוי בכלל "לאיש זר", כדאמרינן ב"עשרה יוחסין" (קדושין עה. ושם): השתא ממזר הוי, מפסיל בביאתו מיבעיא? ואפילו לרבי יהושע דלא הוי ממזר, כיון דחמירי (ג) דזרים אללה חשיבי. והא דבעינן בפרק "אלמנה" (לקמן דף סט. ושם) זר אללה מעיקרא – היינו דוקא בחייבי לאוין, ולרבנן, ולא ממעטו מ"כי תהיה" דמשמע הנך דאית בהו הויה חייבי כריתות דחמירי, אלא דוקא (ג) גוי ועבד. ולהכי איצטריך קרא ד"אלמנה וגרושה" – מי שיש לו אלמנות וגרושין, לאתויי גוי ועבד. ולרבי עקיבא דמגוי ועבד הוי ממזר, ונפיק מ"לאיש זר" – דריש "אלמנה וגרושה" לקמן (דף סט.) לדרשה אחריתי. ומכל הנהו דלא תפסו בהו קדושין הויא זונה, כדאמר בפרק "כל האסורין" (תמורה דף כט: ושם): מה עריות דלא תפסי בהו קדושין והויא זונה כו', דלשון זונה משמע שא"א להיות בה אלא ביאת זנות – לא לאו דמלקות. ואין להקשות: למה לי דכתב רחמנא "זונה לא יקחו" כיון דזונה אסורה בתרומה – ק"ו דאסורה לכהונה, מגרושה דשריא בתרומה ואסורה לכהן? דמהאי ק"ו נפקא לן (לקמן דף סח:) דגר עמוני ומואבי פסלי לכהונה, אע"ג דאין מזהירין מן הדין – קאמר התם דגילוי מילתא בעלמא הוא! דאיצטריך לאו דזונה דלקי תרתי. ועוד איצטריך לזונה מגוי ועבד לרבנן דר"ע, דליכא בה *לאו בתרומה מ"לאיש זר" אלא מ"אלמנה וגרושה", דמאלמנה וגרושה נפקא. אי נמי: משום גיורת ומשוחררת איצטריך לאו דזונה. ואפילו לאביי דאמר בפ' "כל האסורין" (תמורה כט:) דכהן הבא על הזונה גויה אינו לוקה משום זונה, אם נתגיירה – מודה דלקי, דהוי זרעו מיוחס אחריו. ועוד: דמטעם שנעשה זונה ואסרה רחמנא משום זונה – הוא דהוי חייבי כריתות בכלל "לאיש זר", כדמשמע הכא ובכל דוכתי, דשם זונה גורם לה ליפסל. ומיהו מגוי ועבד, אע"ג דהויא זונה, דהא לא תפסי בה קדושין מינייהו – לא הוי בכלל "לאיש זר", אלא דוקא חייבי כריתות דחמירי. וקצת קשה: דבפרק "עשרה יוחסין" (קדושין דף עה: ושם) דפריך: השתא ממזר הוי, מפסיל בביאתו מיבעיא? משמע, היכא דהוי ממזר פשיטא דהוי בכלל "לאיש זר" אפילו לא הויא זונה. ומיהו, לרבי יהושע דלא הוי ממזר מחייבי כריתות, ושם זונה גרם לה דהויא בכלל "לאיש זר". וזהו דוחק, דבכל דוכתין דמשמע דשם זונה גורם לה ליפסל מתרומה אפי' כר' יהושע, ולעיל בסוף פ' "ד' אחין" (דף לה. ד"ה "אע"פ") הביא ר"י דכל הנך דע"י קדושין, כיון דלא הוי זר אללה מעיקרא – לא הוי בכלל "לאיש זר", וזונה דפסולה לתרומה – משום דכללה קרא בהדי חללה, להכי פסולה כחללה. ולפי זה צריך ליישב הא דפריך בפ' "אלמנה" (לקמן דף סח:) ואימא נבעלה לפסול לה – חייבי כריתות. **עשאה** זונה. משמע דלר' יהושע אין קדושין תופסין בחייבי כריתות, דבתפיסת קדושין תלוי שם זנות, כדמשמע בפרק "כל האסורין" (שם), וכן בס"פ "ר"ג" (לקמן נג. ושם) איצטריך לאשמועינן דאין קדושין תופסין בחייבי כריתות, משמע דליכא מאן דפליג. והא דמשמע בסמוך דממזרות תלוי בתפיסות קדושין, וכן לקמן (דף מה:) דקאמר: מה אשת [אב] דלא תפסי קדושין והולד ממזר, משמע דכל היכא דלא תפסי קדושין – הוי ולד ממזר. היינו לשמעון התימני ולר"ע, משום דגלי לן קרא שיש ממזר מחייבי כריתות, כדילפינן בסוף פירקין (דף מט.). וגלי לן נמי דלא תפסי בהו קדושין, כדאמרינן בס"פ "האומר" (קדושין סח. ושם), משום הכי אית לן למימר דהא בהא תליא. אבל לר' יהושע, אע"ג דאין קדושין תופסין בחייבי כריתות – לא הוי ממזר, כדיליף ר' יהושע בסוף פירקין דאין ממזר אלא מחייבי מיתות ב"ד. ולהכי בסמוך, דקאמר: הכל מודים שמעון התימני, לא קאמר: הכל מודים ר' יהושע – אע"ג דאמר ר' יהושע אין ממזר מחייבי כריתות ה"מ כו', דלרבי יהושע אין קדושין תופסין בחייבי כריתות אף על גב דאין הולד ממזר. אבל קצת קשה, דבפ"ק דתמורה (דף ה: ושם) פריך: לרבא דאמר כל היכא דאמר רחמנא לא תעביד אי עביד לא מהני – והרי אלמנה לכהן גדול, דרחמנא אמר "לא יקח" ותנן: כל מקום שיש קדושין ויש עבירה, כגון אלמנה לכהן גדול כו'!
ומשני

תוספות ישנים

תועבה: **היא** פסולה וולדה פסול נראה היא פסולה לתרומה אע"ג דבעינן זר אללה מעיקרא כיון דר' עקיבא אומר אין קדושין תופסין בחייבי לאוין אמרינן כיון שבעלה עשאה זונה אע"ג דבעינן זר אללה מעיקרא כיון שאין קדושין תופסין א"כ הוי כמו חייבי כריתות וחייבי כריתות הוי כמו זר אללה מעיקרא אבל י"מ היא פסולה לכהן ולא נהירא דהא מקודם לכן איפסילא ליה משום גרושה וי"ל דר"ל לכהונה וקאי אקרובי חלוצתו וכן פר"ח: **היא** כשרה. פר"ח ז"ל דלא קאי אמחזיר גרושתו דנהי נמי דולדה כשר משום דכתיב היא תועבה ואין בניה תועבין מ"מ איהי אפסלא מתרומה דבי נשא ובירושלמי מפרש כן ולא עת עתה להאריך: **א)** ושמעתי מתרצים כי רבי עקיבא מפיק מקרא דהיא תועבה למימר ואין צרת סוטה תועבה ובהא שפיר איצטריך דליכא למימר דלא שייך בה צרה דהא מקודם שסטתה היתה זאת צרתה כי קדושי הסוטה היו טובים בתחלה וא"ת ולמה לי קרא דכי תהיה אלמנה וגרושה דגוי ועבד פסלי אשה בביאתן הא ידעת ליה שפיר מלאיש זר אליבא דר"ע דס"ל דאין קדושין תופסין וכיון דאין קדושין תופסין הולד ממזר והשתא ממזר הוי מפסיל בביאתו מבעיא דהא גוי ועבד חייבי לאוין נינהו וזר מעיקרא נינהו וי"ל דס"ד הואיל ולא תפסי בה קדושי כלל דלא פסלי אשה בביאתן להכי אצטריך קרא לובת כהן כי תהיה אלמנה וגרושה: **ב)** גם בפרק כשם משמע כן דקאמר תרומה נמי עשה בה ספק זונה כזונה אלמא דזונה אסורה מלאכול בתרומה וקשה ומנלן דזונה פסולה מלאכול בתרומה אי משום דפסולה לכהונה הלא גרושה פסולה לכהונה ואינה פסולה לתרומה וי"ל דזונה פסולה לתרומה משום דכתיב זונה וחללה אתקש זונה לחללה וחללה פשיטא לן דפסולה לתרומה וקשה דאמרינן לקמן ואימא נבעלה לפסול לה חייבי כריתות ומאי קאמר הא מזונה נפקא דכיון דבעלוה חייבי כריתות עשאוה זונה וזונה פסולה לתרומה לכן נראה דלא ידעינן דזונה פסולה לתרומה אלא מדאמרינן לקמן כיון שנבעלה לפסול לה פסלה מקרא דמייתי לקמן כי תהיה והכי פירושא ואימא נבעלה לפסול לה חייבי כריתות דוקא דלא מצינן למימר הא ידעינן שפיר למ"ד יש ממזר מחייבי כריתות כיון דממזר הוי כ"ש דמפסיל בביאתו א) הא משום הכי לא שמעינן פיסול דתרומה דלא ידעינן פיסול דתרומה מפיסול ביאה כלל ומשני אמר קרא כי תהיה בהנך דאית בהו הויה דהיינו חייבי לאוין דתפסי בהו קדושי מעתה דשמעינן בחייבי לאוין כ"ש בחייבי כריתות דיש מביאתו ממזר וגם לר' יהושע דאמר אין ממזר מחייבי כריתות מ"מ שמעינן דפסלה לתרומה מכ"ש דחייבי לאוין דפסלי לה לקמן: **מאן** הכל מודים שמעון התימני. וא"ת אמאי לא קאמר מאן הכל מודים דר' יהושע דאמר ר' יהושע אין ממזר מחייבי כריתות ה"מ חייבי כריתות דתפסי בהו קדושי אבל גוי ועבד לא וי"ל דפשיטא דר' יהושע סבר דאין קדושין תופסין בחייבי כריתות ואע"ג דסבר דאין ממזר מהם מ"מ לא תפסי בהו קדושי ולא ס"ל הא תליא בהא וכן משמע בריש מכילתין ט"ו נשים פוטרות צרותיהן מחליצה ומיבום וקחשיב חייבי כריתות ואי קדושין תופסין בהן לר' יהושע א"כ בני חליצה נינהו כמו חייבי לאוין לרבנן דאמרי חולצות ולא מתייבמות באיסור קדושה וכאיך חייבי לאוין ואין סברא לומר דפליג רבי יהושע על מתני' דלעיל דהא אמרינן לעיל דבפלוגתא לא קא מיירי ועוד דאמרינן בפרק ארבע מיתות חייבי כריתות מי איכא למ"ד דתפסי בהו קדושי משמע דליכא מאן דפליג וגם משמע כן מהא דאמרינן בכל דוכתא אין קדושין תופסין באחותו והיא חייבי כריתות וליכא מאן דפליג וא"כ משמע דר' יהושע לא סבר הא תליא בהא וקשה דאמרינן פ"ק דתמורה גבי כל מלתא דאמר רחמנא לא תעביד אי עביד לא מהני ופריך מאלמנה לכה"ג ומשני שאני התם דאמר קרא לא יקח [ולא יחלל] חללין הוא עושה ממזרים אינו עושה ולהכי תפסי בהו קדושין משמע דהא תליא בהא וגם הכא קאמר תלמודא לר"ש התימני הא תליא בהא
דקאמר

א) דלאו משום הכי לא שמעינן.

לעיל טו: לקמן מה. נדה סט:

לעיל יז: וש"נ

הגהות הב"ח

(א) תוס' ד"ה הכל וכו' בפ"ק דסוטה. נ"ב דף ו ועי"ש בפרש"י דאיתא זונה היא ופשיטא דאסור בתרומה דהא תני ליה האוכלת טמאה אני: (ב) בא"ד כיון דחמירי כזרים אללה מעיקרא חשיבי וכו' ולא ממעטי מכי תהיה לאיש זר בתרומת הקדשים לא תאכל דמשמע הנך דלאו בכה"ג: (ג) בא"ד אלא דוקא (גוי ועבד) תא"מ ונ"ב ס"ה חייבי לאוין:

נ"ל לה. יעב"ץ

[לעיל טו:]

[וסוטה לקמן מט.]

דלא ילפינן מלאיש זר אלא מאלמנה וגרושה א"כ וכו' כצ"ל רש"ל

מֵחַיְּיבֵי לָאוִין דְּתָפְסֵי בְּהוּ קִדּוּשִׁין, אֲבָל הָכָא — גּוֹי וְעֶבֶד, אכֵּיוָן דְּלָא תָּפְסֵי בְּהוּ קִדּוּשִׁין — כְּחַיָּיבֵי כְּרֵיתוּת דָּמֵי. מֵיתִיבֵי: *גּוֹי וְעֶבֶד הַבָּא עַל בַּת יִשְׂרָאֵל — הַוָּלָד מַמְזֵר, רַבִּי שִׁמְעוֹן בֶּן יְהוּדָה אוֹמֵר: אֵין מַמְזֵר אֶלָּא מִמִּי שֶׁאִיסּוּרוֹ אִיסּוּר עֶרְוָה, וְעָנוּשׁ כָּרֵת. אֶלָּא אֲמַר רַב יוֹסֵף: מַאן "הַכֹּל מוֹדִים" — רַבִּי. אַף עַל גַּב דְּרַבִּי אוֹמֵר: *אֵין הַדְּבָרִים הַלָּלוּ אֲמוּרִים אֶלָּא לְדִבְרֵי ר"ע, שֶׁהָיָה עוֹשֶׂה חֲלוּצָה כְּעֶרְוָה, וְלֵיהּ לָא סְבִירָא לֵיהּ — בְּגוֹי וְעֶבֶד מוֹדֶה. *דְּכִי אֲתָא רַב דִּימִי אֲמַר רַב יִצְחָק בַּר אֲבוּדִימִי מִשּׁוּם רַבֵּינוּ: גּוֹי וְעֶבֶד הַבָּא עַל בַּת יִשְׂרָאֵל — הַוָּלָד מַמְזֵר. רַבִּי אַחָא שַׂר הַבִּירָה וְרַ' תַּנְחוּם בְּרֵיהּ דְּרַבִּי חִיָּיא אִישׁ כְּפַר עַכּוֹ פְּרוּק הָנְהוּ שְׁבוּיָיתָא דְּאָתוּ מֵאַרְמוֹן לְטִבֶרְיָא. הֲוָה חֲדָא דְּאִיעַבְּרָא מִגּוֹי, וַאֲתוּ לְקַמֵּיהּ דְּרַ' אַמִי. אֲמַר לְהוּ: ר' יוֹחָנָן וְרַ' אֶלְעָזָר וְרַ' חֲנִינָא דְּאָמְרִי, גּוֹי וְעֶבֶד הַבָּא עַל בַּת יִשְׂרָאֵל הַוָּלָד מַמְזֵר. אֲמַר רַב יוֹסֵף: *רְבוּתָא לְמִחְשַׁב גַּבְרֵי?! הָא רַב וּשְׁמוּאֵל בְּבָבֶל, וְרַבִּי יְהוֹשֻׁעַ בֶּן לֵוִי וּבַר קַפָּרָא בְּאֶרֶץ יִשְׂרָאֵל, וְאָמְרִי לָהּ: חִלּוּפֵי בַּר קַפָּרָא וְעַיְילֵי זִקְנֵי דָּרוֹם, דְּאָמְרִי: *גּוֹי וְעֶבֶד הַבָּא עַל בַּת יִשְׂרָאֵל — הַוָּלָד כָּשֵׁר. אֶלָּא אֲמַר רַב יוֹסֵף: רַבִּי הִיא. *דְּכִי אֲתָא רַב דִּימִי אֲמַר רַבִּי יִצְחָק בַּר אֲבוּדִימִי מִשּׁוּם רַבֵּינוּ אָמְרוּ: גּוֹי וְעֶבֶד הַבָּא עַל בַּת יִשְׂרָאֵל — הַוָּלָד מַמְזֵר. רַבִּי יְהוֹשֻׁעַ בֶּן לֵוִי אוֹמֵר: הַוָּלָד מְקוּלְקָל. לְמַאן? אִילֵימָא לַקָּהָל — הָא אֲמַר רַבִּי יְהוֹשֻׁעַ הַוָּלָד כָּשֵׁר, אֶלָּא לִכְהוּנָּה — דְּכוּלְּהוּ אֲמוֹרָאֵי דְּמַכְשְׁרֵי מוֹדוּ שֶׁהַוָּלָד בפָּגוּם לִכְהוּנָּה *מִק"ו מֵאַלְמָנָה: מָה אַלְמָנָה לְכֹהֵן גָּדוֹל, שֶׁאֵין אִיסּוּרָהּ שָׁוֶה בַּכֹּל — בְּנָהּ פָּגוּם, זוֹ שֶׁאִיסּוּרָהּ שָׁוֶה בַּכֹּל — אֵינוֹ דִּין שֶׁבְּנָהּ פָּגוּם. מַה לְּאַלְמָנָה לְכֹהֵן גָּדוֹל שֶׁכֵּן הִיא עַצְמָהּ מִתְחַלֶּלֶת! הָכָא נַמִי, כֵּיוָן שֶׁנִּבְעֲלָה פְּסָלָהּ. *דְּאָמַר רַבִּי יוֹחָנָן מִשּׁוּם רַבִּי (א) שִׁמְעוֹן: גמִנַּיִן לְגוֹי וְעֶבֶד הַבָּא עַל הַכֹּהֶנֶת וְעַל הַלְּוִיָּה וְעַל הַיִּשְׂרְאֵלִית שֶׁפְּסָלוּהָ — שֶׁנֶּאֱמַר °"וּבַת כֹּהֵן כִּי תִהְיֶה אַלְמָנָה וּגְרוּשָׁה", מִי שֶׁיֵּשׁ לוֹ אַלְמְנוּת וְגֵירוּשִׁין בָּהּ, יָצְאוּ גּוֹי וְעֶבֶד שֶׁאֵין לָהֶם אַלְמְנוּת וְגֵירוּשִׁין בָּהּ. אֲמַר לֵיהּ אַבַּיֵי: מַאי חֲזֵית דְּסָמְכַתְּ אַדְּרַב דִּימִי? סְמוֹךְ אַדְּרָבִין! דְּכִי אֲתָא רָבִין אֲמַר: רַבִּי נָתָן וְרַבִּי יְהוּדָה הַנָּשִׂיא מוֹרִים בָּהּ לְהֶיתֵּירָא, וּמַאן *רַבִּי יְהוּדָה הַנָּשִׂיא — רַבִּי וְאַף רַב מוֹרֶה בָּהּ הֶיתֵּירָא, דְּהַהוּא דַּאֲתָא לְקַמֵּיהּ דְּרַב, אֲמַר לֵיהּ: גּוֹי וְעֶבֶד הַבָּא עַל בַּת יִשְׂרָאֵל מַהוּ? אֲמַר לוֹ: הַוָּלָד כָּשֵׁר. אֲמַר לֵיהּ: הַב לִי בְּרַתָּךְ! לָא יָהֵיבְנָא לָךְ. אֲמַר שִׁימִי בַּר חִיָּיא לְרַב: אָמְרִי אֱינָשֵׁי: גַּמְלָא בְּמָדַי אַקַּבָּא רַקְדָא, הָא קַבָּא וְהָא גַּמְלָא וְהָא מָדַי — וְלָא רָקְדָא! א"ל: אִי (ג) נֶיהֱוֵי כִּיהוֹשֻׁעַ בִּן נוּן לָא יָהֵיבְנָא לֵיהּ בְּרַתִּי. א"ל: אִי הֲוָה כִּיהוֹשֻׁעַ בִּן נוּן, אִי מָר לָא יָהֵיב לֵיהּ — אַחֲרִינֵי יָהֲבֵי לֵיהּ. הַאי, אִי מָר לָא יָהֵיב לֵיהּ — אַחֲרִינֵי לָא יָהֲבֵי לֵיהּ. לָא הֲוָה קָאָזֵיל מִקַּמֵּיהּ, יָהֵיב בֵּיהּ עֵינֵיהּ וּשְׁכִיב. וְאַף רַב מַתָּנָה מוֹרֶה בָּהּ לְהֶיתֵּירָא, וְאַף רַב יְהוּדָה מוֹרֶה בָּהּ לְהֶיתֵּירָא. דְּכִי אֲתָא לְקַמֵּיהּ דְּרַב יְהוּדָה א"ל: זִיל אִיטְמַר, אוֹ נְסִיב בַּת מִינָּךְ. וְכִי אֲתָא לְקַמֵּיהּ דְּרָבָא א"ל: *אוֹ גְּלֵי, אוֹ נְסִיב בַּת מִינָּךְ. שָׁלְחוּ לֵיהּ בְּנֵי בֵּי מִיכְסֵי לְרַבָּה: מִי שֶׁחֶצְיוֹ עֶבֶד וְחֶצְיוֹ בֶּן חוֹרִין הַבָּא עַל בַּת יִשְׂרָאֵל מַהוּ? א"ל: הָשְׁתָּא עֶבֶד כּוּלּוֹ אָמְרִי' כָּשֵׁר — חֶצְיוֹ מִיבַּעְיָא? אֲמַר רַב יוֹסֵף: מָרָא דִּשְׁמַעְתָּא

מַנּוּ

רש"י

חַיָּיבֵי לָאוִין דְּתָפְסֵי בְּהוּ קִדּוּשִׁין. דְּנָפְקָא לָן בְּפֶרֶק "כֵּילַד" (לעיל דף כג.) מִ"כִּי תִהְיֶין לְאִישׁ שְׁתֵּי נָשִׁים" וגו', וְעֶבֶד וְגוֹי לָאו בְּנֵי קִדּוּשִׁין נִינְהוּ, דִּכְתִיב (בראשית כב) "שְׁבוּ לָכֶם פֹּה עִם הַחֲמוֹר" — עַם הַדּוֹמֶה לַחֲמוֹר. וְגוֹי נַמִי לֵיתֵיהּ בִּכְלַל קִדּוּשִׁין, דִּכְתִיב (דברים ז) בְּז' אוּמּוֹת "לֹא תִתְחַתֵּן בָּם" — לֹא יְהֵא לְךָ בָּהֶן חִיתּוּן. וּבִשְׁאָר אוּמּוֹת כְּתִיב (שם כא) "וְאַחַר כֵּן תָּבֹא" — מִכְּלָל דְּמֵעִיקָּרָא לֵית בָּהּ הֲוָיָה. וּמֵהָנֵי קְרָאֵי נָפְקָא לָן בְּקִדּוּשִׁין (דף סח:) דְּלָא תָּפְסֵי קִדּוּשִׁין בְּגוֹיָה, וְגוֹי נַמִי מָצֵי לְמֵילַף מִינַּיְיהוּ. הִלְכָּךְ, אֵין בִּיאָתוֹ בִּיאָה לְשֵׁם קִדּוּשִׁין, וְדָמְיָא לְחַיָּיבֵי כְרֵיתוּת. וּבִשְׁאִלְתּוֹת דְּרַב אַחַאי* מַפֵּיק מֵהָא "וְהִיא בְּעוּלַת בָּעַל" (בראשית כ) וְדָרְשִׁינַן בְּסַנְהֶדְרִין (דף מז:): בְּעוּלַת בַּעַל יֵשׁ לָהֶם, נִכְנְסָה לַחוּפָּה וְלֹא נִבְעֲלָה — אֵין לָהֶם, וְכָל שֶׁכֵּן דַּאֲרוּסָה לֵית לְהוּ. וּבִיאָה לְשֵׁם קִדּוּשִׁין נַמִי לֵית לְהוּ, דְּאִיתְקוּשׁ הֲוָיוֹת לַהֲדָדֵי*. אֵין מַמְזֵר וכו'. וְהָא הַאי תַּנָּא כְּשִׁמְעוֹן הַתִּימְנִי סְבִירָא לֵיהּ, וְקָתָנֵי בְּגוֹי וְעֶבֶד דְּאֵין מַמְזֵר. אַף עַל גַּב דְּקָאָמַר רַבִּי. בְּפֶרֶק ר"ג אֵין בִּיאָה אַחַר חֲלִיצָה, דְּאִם חָלַץ לָזוֹ וּבָעַל אֶת זוֹ — אֵינָהּ צְרִיכָה הֵימֶנּוּ גֵּט. וְקָאָמַר: אֵין הַדְּבָרִים הַלָּלוּ אֲמוּרִים, דְּבִיאָה אַחַר חֲלִיצָה לֹא תָּפְסָה, אֶלָּא לְדִבְרֵי ר"ע כו', אֲבָל לְדִידֵיהּ לָא סְבִירָא לֵיהּ, אֲפִילּוּ הָכִי, בְּגוֹי וְעֶבֶד — מוֹדִים. דְּכִי אֲתָא רַב דִּימִי כו' מִשּׁוּם רַבֵּינוּ. רַבִּי. שְׁבוּיָיתָא מִן אַרְמוֹן. לְאַנְטוֹכִי. אֶלָּא אֲמַר רַב יוֹסֵף רַבִּי הִיא. לֹא תַּחְשׁוֹב גַּבְרֵי. דְּהַאי מִשּׁוּם רְבוּתָא דְּרַבִּים לָא תַּכְסִיל לֵיהּ, דְּהָא נַמִי רַבִּים אַכְשְׁרֵי, אֶלָּא מִשּׁוּם הַהִיא דְּר' אִיכָּא לְמִיפְסְלֵיהּ, דַּהֲלָכָה כְּמוֹתוֹ. וְהָאָמַר רַבִּי יְהוֹשֻׁעַ בֶּן לֵוִי. לְעֵיל, הַוָּלָד כָּשֵׁר. זוֹ שֶׁאִיסּוּרָהּ שָׁוֶה בַּכֹּל. גּוֹי אָסוּר בֵּין בְּכֹהֶנֶת בֵּין בִּלְוִיָּה בֵּין בְּיִשְׂרְאֵלִית. שֶׁבְּנָהּ פָּגוּם. בְּנָהּ פָּגוּם לָאו דַּוְקָא, דְּהָא פְּשִׁיטָא בֶּן הַגּוֹיָה לָאו כֹּהֵן הוּא. וְאִי מִשּׁוּם דְּלָא יִשָּׂא כֹּהֶנֶת, כֵּיוָן דְּמוּתָּר בְּיִשְׂרְאֵלִית — מוּתָּר נַמִי בְּכֹהֶנֶת, שֶׁאֵין קְדוּשָּׁה בַּנָּשִׁים, דַּאֲפִילּוּ כְּשֵׁרוֹת מוּתָּרוֹת לִפְסוּלִים, דְּקַיְימָא לָן (קדושין דף עג.): לֹא הוּזְהֲרוּ כְּשֵׁרוֹת מִלִּינָּשֵׂא לִפְסוּלִים. אֶלָּא מִשּׁוּם בִּתָּהּ נָקַט, דְּאִם תֵּלֵד בַּת — פְּסוּלָה לִכְהוּנָּה. פְּסָלָהּ. אֲפִי' מִתְּרוּמָה דְּבֵי נָשָׁא, וְכ"ש מִלְּהִנָּשֵׂא לְכֹהֵן. שֶׁפְּסָלוּהָ. כֹּהֶנֶת מִתְּרוּמַת אָבִיהָ, וּלְוִיָּה וְיִשְׂרְאֵלִית כְּגוֹן שֶׁנִּישְּׂאוּ לְכֹהֵן וְיָלְדוּ לוֹ בָּנִים, וּכְשֶׁמֵּתוּ בַּעֲלֵיהֶן הָיוּ אוֹכְלוֹת בִּתְרוּמָה בִּשְׁבִיל בְּנֵיהֶם. וְאִם בָּא עָלֶיהָ גּוֹי וְעֶבֶד — פְּסָלָהּ מִתְּרוּמָה, וְכ"ש מִכְּהוּנָּה. מִי שֶׁיֵּשׁ לוֹ אַלְמְנוּת וְגֵירוּשִׁין בָּהּ. כְּגוֹן א] יִשְׂרְאֵלִית, הוּא דְּכִי מֵת וְזֶרַע אֵין לָהּ — "וְשָׁבָה אֶל בֵּית אָבִיהָ" וגו' (ויקרא כב). יָצְאוּ גּוֹי וְעֶבֶד שֶׁאֵין לוֹ אַלְמְנוּת וְגֵירוּשִׁין בָּהּ. שֶׁאֵין קִדּוּשִׁין תּוֹפְסִין. א"ל אַבַּיֵי. לְרַב יוֹסֵף. מַאי חֲזֵית דְּסָמְכַתְּ אַדְּרַב דִּימִי. דַּאֲמַר מִשְּׁמֵיהּ דְּרַבִּי הַוָּלָד מַמְזֵר, סְמוֹךְ אַדְּרָבִין דְּמַכְשְׁרֵי לֵיהּ מִשְּׁמֵיהּ דְּרַבִּי. דְּהַהוּא דַּאֲתָא. בֶּן גּוֹי מִיִּשְׂרְאֵלִית. אָמְרִי אֱינָשֵׁי גַּמְלָא בְּמָדַי אַקַּבָּא רַקְדָא. גָּמָל גָּדוֹל מְרַקֵּד בְּתוֹךְ קַב קָטָן בְּד' רַגְלָיו בְּמַלְכוּת מָדַי, וְגוּזְמָא. הָא קַבָּא וְהָא גַּמְלָא וְהָא מָדַי. יָבֹא וִירַקֵּד לְפָנֵינוּ. כְּלוֹמַר: אַתָּה שֶׁהִתַּרְתָּ דְּבַר חִידּוּשׁ — הַאֲמֵת דְּבָרֶיךָ וְתֵן לוֹ בִּתְּךָ. לָא הֲוָה אָזֵיל מִקַּמֵּיהּ. אוֹתוֹ בֶּן הַגּוֹי דְּקָא א"ל הַב לִי בְּרַתָּךְ. זִיל אִיטְמַר. לֵךְ בְּמָקוֹם שֶׁלֹּא יַכִּירוּךְ, וְשָׂא בַּת יִשְׂרָאֵל. שֶׁאִילּוּ יַכִּירוּךְ — לֹא יִתְּנוּהָ לָךְ. אַלְמָא לָא מַמְזֵר הוּא, מִדְּאַכְשַׁר לֵיהּ בַּת יִשְׂרָאֵל, שֶׁהֲרֵי מַמְזֵר מוּזְהָר עַל הַכְּשֵׁרָה. בַּת מִינָּךְ. בַּת יִשְׂרָאֵל מִן הַגּוֹי, הַכְּשֵׁרָה כְּמוֹתָךְ. אֲבָל מַמְזֶרֶת וְשִׁפְחָה — לֹא תִּשָּׂא, אַלְמָא כָּשֵׁר הוּא. גְּלֵי. לֵךְ לְגָלוּת בְּמָקוֹם שֶׁלֹּא יַכִּירוּךְ, וְיִתְּנוּ לָךְ בַּת יִשְׂרָאֵל כְּשֵׁרָה. בְּנֵי בֵּי מִיכְסֵי. מָקוֹם. מָרָא דִּשְׁמַעְתָּא. דְּאָמַר: גּוֹי וְעֶבֶד הַבָּא עַל בַּת יִשְׂרָאֵל — בְּנוֹ כָּשֵׁר.

מַנּוּ

תוספות

ומשני: שאני התם דאמר רחמנא: "לא יחלל" — חילולים הוא עושה, ואין עושה ממזרים. פי': וכיון דלא הוי ממזר — תפסו בה קדושין. א"כ לרבי יהושע לא תפסי קדושין באלמנה אליבא דרבא, דלרבי יהושע ליכא לאוקומי מידי דתפסי בה קדושין מדלא הוי ממזרת! ואם תאמר: בקדושין ב"האומר" (דף סח: ושם) אמאי דוחק למצוא שאר עריות דלא תפסי בהו קדושין מנלן, כיון דכבר אשכחן דלא תפסי באשת אב קדושין? דמהשתא תיפוק לן כל עריות דהוי מינייהו ממזר(ג)! וי"ל: דממזרים גופייהו לא שמעינן בכל חייבי כריתות כל כמה דלא מייתי היקישא דרבי יונה. דמ"לא יקח" "ולא יגלה" דמייתי בסוף פירקין (לקמן דף מט.) דכתיבי באשת אב ובשומרת יבם של אביו — לא שמעינן ממזרות בשאר עריות, כגון אשת איש שיש לה היתר בחיי אוסרה, ואחות אשה וכל דכוותייהו. אבל בסוף, דמייתי היקישא — איכא למילף בעלמא, כדפרשי'.

יצאו גוי ועבד שאין לו אלמנות וגירושין בה. וא"ת: והא רבי יוחנן אית ליה לעיל דגוי ועבד הבא על בת ישראל הולד ממזר, אם כן למה לי קרא? דהשתא ממזר הוי, מפסיל בביאתו מיבעיא? וי"ל: הא דידיה והא דרביה. ועוד: דאמוראי נינהו, ואליבא דרבי יוחנן, כדאמרינן ספ"ק (לעיל טז:). ושם פירשתי אמאי הוי ממזר מגוי, כיון דביאת היתר היא מדאורייתא*. **זיל** איטמר. וישיאוך מיוחסת. וא"ת: והא בעי ראיה, כדאמר בפ"ב בכתובות (דף כד: ושם) דמעלין מתרומה ליוחסין! ויש לומר: דהתם להשיא בתו לכהן העובד על גבי המזבח, כמו שמוכיח שם רבינו תם. א"נ: התם כר"מ, אבל חכמים אומרי' כל משפחות בחזקת כשרות הם עומדות, בפרק "עשרה יוחסין" (קדושין דף עג:).

משום

עין משפט נר מצוה

קה א מיי' פ"ד מהלכות איסורי ביאה הל' טו סמג עשין מח טוש"ע אה"ע סימן מד סעיף ח:

קו ב טוש"ע אה"ע סי' ד סעי' ה וסעיף יט:

קז ג מיי' פי"ח מהלכות איסורי ביאה הלכה ב טוש"ע אה"ע סימן ו סעיף ח:

תוספות ישנים

דקאמר אבל גוי ועבד דלא תפסי בהו קדושי הולד ממזר וא"ל דלר"ש התימני וגם לר' עקיבא הא תליא בהא אבל לרבי יהושע לא אמרינן הא תליא בהא וכן מפורש בקדושין: **מיתיבי** גוי ועבד וכו' ר' [שמעון בן] יהודה אומר אין ממזר אלא ממי שאיסורו איסור ערוה וענוש (מיתה) [כרת] א) וכמו האי קאמר ר' שמעון התימני דאין ממזר אלא מחייבי מיתות וכו' וכמו דקך דר"ל דאין ממזר אלא מחייבי כריתות סבר דגוי ועבד הבא וכו' הולד כשר דהכי משמע דפליג את"ק דלעיל מיניה כמו כן יש לנו לומר לרבי שמעון התימני: **זיל** גלי או נסיב בת מינך. וא"ת ומה מועיל לו זה הא אמרינן כשאומר אני כהן אינו נאמן להשיאו אשה וע"ק התם אמאי אינו נאמן להשיאו אשה הא אמרינן כל המשפחות בחזקת כשרות הן עומדות וי"ל דהתם מיירי להשיאו אשה מיוחסת מד' אמהות וזה אינו כן דזה לא מצי להיות בנו כהן דחיישינן ליה משום חללות ובתו פסולה מספק היא דשמא חלל הוא ובת חלל פסולה לכהונה. עי"מ דהתם מיירי בדנפק עליה קלא דבן גרושה ולהכי אמרי' דאינו נאמן להשיאו אשה ולהכי קאמר זיל איטמר דלא ליפוק עליה קלא ודוחק וז"ל מורי דלעולם נימא דהא דקאמר אינו נאמן להשיאו אשה ר"ל אף ישראלית אף להנשא בתו לישראל ומיירי בדנפק עליה קלא דממזרות וא"נ נוכל לומר

א) נראה דל"ל וכמו האי דקאמר שמעון התימני דאין ממזר אלא במי שחייבין עליו כרת בידי שמים וכו'

תוספות חד מקמאי

ואם נשא כהן בת עבד ועובד כוכבים הבא על בת ישראל מוציאין אותה מידו אבל בנו ינשא לכהונה לכתחלה שלא הוזהרו כשרות לינשא לפסולין לכהונה וחציו עבד וחציו בן חורין שבא על בת ישראל הולד פגום לכהונה שהיא עצמה מתחללת ואע"פ שיש אלמנות וגירושין בה מצד החירות אין לה אלמנות וגירושין מצד

גליון הש"ס

גמ' ה"נ כיון שנבעלה פסלה. עיין לקמן עז ע"א תד"ה רבי יוחנן אמר כשרה: **שם** דאמר רבי יוחנן משום ר"ש מנין לגוי וכו'. לקמן סח ע"ב ובסוטה דף כו ע"ב ובקדושין דף עה ע"ב איתא משום רבי ישמעאל:

מסורת הש"ס

[לעיל טז: לקמן נט. קדושין ע.]

[פ' ויטלח סימן כה]

לקמן נב:

[לקמן ע.]

[עי' היטב לקמן סח: ברש"י ד"ה עבד]

[כ"ב לו:]

[לעיל כג. קדושין עח:]

[לקמן ע. ע"ש]

[לעיל טז: מד: נדה סט:]

לקמן סח: סוטה כו: קדושין עה:

[שבת לב: קדושין סג.]

[עי' תוס' לקמן מז. ד"ה במוחזק ותוס' פסחים ג: ד"ה ולא]

הגהות מהר"ב רנשבורג

א] רש"י ד"ה מי שיש לו כו' כגון ישראלית הוא כ' מלת ישראלית נמחק ונ"ב ישראל:

הגהות הב"ח

(א) גמ' דאמר ר' יוחנן משום ר' שמעון. נ"ב עיין בדף סח ע"ב דמשמע מדברי התוספות דגרסי' רבי ישמעאל ע"ש ד"ה כמאן כר"ע: (ב) שם ולא רקדא א"ל אי הוי כיהושע: (ג) תוס' ד"ה עשאה וכו' דהוי מינייהו ממזר לא תפסי בהו קדושין וי"ל דממזרים:

עין משפט נר מצוה

קח א ב מיי' פט"ו מהל' איסורי ביאה הלכה ה סמג לאוין קיז טוש"ע אה"ע סי' ד סעי' יז:

קט ג מיי' שם ה"ג טוש"ע שם סעיף ה וסעיף יט:

קי ד מיי' פ"א מהלכות מלכים הלכה ד:

קיא ה ו מיי' פי"ג מהל' איסורי ביאה הלכה ט סמג לאוין קטז טוש"ע יו"ד סימן רסח סעיף ג:

[וע"ע שבת קנו. ובתוס' שם ובתוס' ב"מ עג: ד"ה רב מרין]

קיב ז מיי' שם הי"א ופ"ח מהל' עבדים הי"ט סמג שם טוש"ע שם סי' רכז סעיף ט:

גמרא

מַנּוּ — רַב יְהוּדָה וְהָא אָמַר רַב יְהוּדָה: [א]מִי שֶׁחֶצְיוֹ עֶבֶד וְחֶצְיוֹ בֶּן חוֹרִין הַבָּא עַל בַּת יִשְׂרָאֵל — אוֹתוֹ וָלָד אֵין לוֹ תַּקָּנָה. כִּי אִיתְּמַר דְּרַב יְהוּדָה כְּגוֹן דְּקַדֵּישׁ בַּת יִשְׂרָאֵל, דְּנִמְצָא צַד עַבְדוּת שֶׁבּוֹ מִשְׁתַּמֵּשׁ בְּאֵשֶׁת אִישׁ. וְהָאָמְרִי נְהַרְדְּעֵי מִשְּׁמֵיהּ דְּרַבִּי יַעֲקֹב: לְדִבְרֵי הַפּוֹסֵל — פּוֹסֵל אֲפִילּוּ בִּפְנוּיָה, לְדִבְרֵי הַמַּכְשִׁיר — מַכְשִׁיר אֲפִי' בְּאֵשֶׁת אִישׁ. וּשְׁנֵיהֶם לֹא לָמְדוּהָ אֶלָּא מֵאֵשֶׁת אָב — מַאן דְּפָסֵיל סָבַר: מָה אֵשֶׁת אָב דְּלָא תָּפְסֵי בָּהּ קִדּוּשִׁין [הַוָּלָד מַמְזֵר] — אַף כָּל דְּלָא תָּפְסֵי בָּהּ קִדּוּשִׁין הַוָּלָד מַמְזֵר. וּמַאן דְּמַכְשַׁר סָבַר: מָה אֵשֶׁת אָב, דִּלְדִידֵיהּ לָא תָּפְסֵי בָּהּ קִדּוּשִׁין לַאֲחֵרִינֵי תָּפְסֵי בָּהּ קִדּוּשִׁין — לְאַפּוּקֵי גּוֹי וְעֶבֶד דְּלָא תָּפְסֵי בְּהוּ קִדּוּשִׁין כְּלָל. אֶלָּא, כִּי אִיתְּמַר דְּרַב יְהוּדָה — [ב]כְּגוֹן שֶׁבָּא עַל אֵשֶׁת, אִישׁ וְנִמְצָא צַד חֵירוּת שֶׁבּוֹ מִשְׁתַּמֵּשׁ בְּאֵשֶׁת אִישׁ. אֲמַר רָבִינָא אֲמַר לִי רַב גַּזָּא: אִיקְלַע רַ' יוֹסֵי בַּר אָבִין לְאַתְרִין, וַהֲוָה עוּבְדָא בִּפְנוּיָה — וְאַכְשַׁר, בְּאֵשֶׁת אִישׁ — וּפְסֵיל. א"ר שֵׁשֶׁת: לְדִידִי אֲמַר לִי רַב גַּזָּא: לָא רַ' יוֹסֵי בַּר אָבִין הֲוָה, אֶלָּא רַבִּי יוֹסֵי בְּרַבִּי זְבִידָא הֲוָה, וְאַכְשַׁר בֵּין בִּפְנוּיָה בֵּין בְּאֵשֶׁת אִישׁ. א"ל רַב אַחָא בְּרֵיהּ *דְּרַבָּה לְרָבִינָא: אִיקְלַע אֲמֵימַר לְאַתְרִין. וְאַכְשַׁר בֵּין בִּפְנוּיָה בֵּין בְּאֵשֶׁת אִישׁ. [ג]וְהִלְכְתָא: גּוֹי וְעֶבֶד הַבָּא עַל בַּת יִשְׂרָאֵל — הַוָּלָד כָּשֵׁר, בֵּין בִּפְנוּיָה בֵּין בְּאֵשֶׁת אִישׁ. *רָבָא אַכְשְׁרֵיהּ לְרַב מָרִי בַּר רָחֵל וּמַנְיֵיהּ בְּפוּרְסֵי דְּבָבֶל. וְאע"ג *דְּאָמַר מָר °"שׂוֹם תָּשִׂים עָלֶיךָ מֶלֶךְ", (א) [ד]כָּל מְשִׂימוֹת שֶׁאַתָּה מֵשִׂים אַל יְהוּ אֶלָּא מִקֶּרֶב אַחֶיךָ, הַאי כֵּיוָן דְּאִמּוֹ מִיִּשְׂרָאֵל — "מִקֶּרֶב אַחֶיךָ" קָרֵינַן בֵּיהּ. עַבְדֵּיהּ דְּרַבִּי חִיָּיא בַּר אַמִּי אַטְבְּלָהּ לְהַהִיא גּוֹיָה לְשֵׁם אִנְתְּתָא. אֲמַר רַב יוֹסֵף: יָכֵילְנָא לְאַכְשׁוּרֵי בָּהּ וּבִבְרַתָּהּ. בָּהּ — כִּדְרַב אַסִי, דַּאֲמַר רַב אַסִי: מִי לֹא טָבְלָה לְנִדּוּתָהּ? בִּבְרַתָּהּ — גּוֹי וְעֶבֶד הַבָּא עַל בַּת יִשְׂרָאֵל הַוָּלָד כָּשֵׁר. הַהוּא דַּהֲווּ קָרוּ לֵיהּ בַּר אֲרַמַּיְיתָא. אֲמַר רַב אַסִי: [ה]מִי לֹא טָבְלָה לְנִדּוּתָהּ? הַהוּא דַּהֲווּ קָרוּ לֵיהּ בַּר אַרְמָאָה, אֲמַר ריב"ל: [ו]מִי לָא טָבַל לְקִרְיוֹ? אֲמַר רַב חָמָא בַּר גּוּרְיָא אָמַר רַב: [ז]הַלּוֹקֵחַ עֶבֶד מִן הַגּוֹי, וְקָדַם וְטָבַל לְשֵׁם בֶּן חוֹרִין — קָנָה עַצְמוֹ בֶּן חוֹרִין. מַאי טַעְמָא? גּוֹי

תורה אור: דברים יז

רש"י

מנו רב יהודה. כדקאמר, ואף רב יהודה מורה בה להיתירא. והאמר רב יהודה. גבי חליו עבד הבא על בת ישראל. הולד אין לו תקנה. בבת ישראל, כלומר: ממזר הוא. כי איתמר. ההיא דאין לו תקנה. כגון דקדיש. מי שחליו עבד וחליו בן חורין את בת ישראל, ואח"כ בא עליה. דכיון דקדושיו הויא מקודשת לצד חירות, אבל לא לצד עבדות, ונמצא צד עבד שבו משמש בא"א, ולפיכך הולד ממזר. דכל הני דמכשרי — בפנויה מכשרי, אבל באשת איש — אפילו בישראל הולד ממזר, וכ"ש גוי ועבד. אבל היכא דבא עליה בלא קידושין — כשר: ה"ג: דנמלא לד עבדות שבו משמש באשת איש. לדברי המכשיר. בעבד הבא על בת ישראל, מכשיר אפי' בא"א. וטעמא מפרש ואזיל. אלא מאשת אב. דממזרות לגבה כתיב, דכתיב "לא יקח איש את אשת אביו" וסמיך ליה "לא יבא ממזר" (דברים כג). כגון שבא על אשת איש. ומשום הכי הולד אין לו תקנה בבת ישראל, דנמלא לד חירות של עבד, כשבא עליה, משמש באשת איש. ואע"ג דאי כולו עבד הולד כשר, כדאמרן לדברי המכשיר מכשיר אפי' בא"א — הכא ממזר משום לד חירות דהוי כשאר ישראל הבא על אשת איש, דהולד ממזר: רב גזא גרסי'. הוה עובדא. בעבד גמור. בין באשת איש. כדאמרן, שאין עושה ממזר אלא מי שיש לו קדושין על אחרים. רב מרי בר רחל. מגוי הבא על ישראלית הוה. בפורסי דבבל. גבאים ממונים על ישראל. ואע"ג דגר בעלמא אסור למנותו פרנס על ישראל, דאמר מר כו', האי, כיון דאמו מישראל — "מקרב אחיך" קרינן ביה. אטבלה לשם אנתתא. לשם טבילת נדה, ולא לשם טבילת גירות. יכילנא לאכשורי בה. להיות גיורת גמורה, ואע"פ שלא טבלה לשם גירות. ואמר לקמן (דף מו:): לעולם אינו גר עד שימול ויטבול. דטבילת נדה סלקא לה לשם גירות, דגויה לא טבלה לנדותה. ובברתה. ואע"ג דבת עבד הבא על בת ישראל היא, דהא נתגיירה זו, וכבת ישראל היא — אפ"ה כשרה בתה. בה כדרב אסי. דאמר בשמעתין: ההוא דהוו קרו ליה בר ארמייתא, שלא טבלה אמו לשם גירות, ואמר רב אסי: מי לא טבלה לנדותה? אלמא: טבילת נדה סלקא לה לשם גירות. ל"א: לשם אנתתא — לשם אישות. וטבילת גירות הוה, אלא שאינה טבילה, דאמר ב"כילד" (לעיל דף כד:) אחד איש שנתגייר לשום אשה ואחד אשה שנתגיירה לשום איש — אינן גרים.

יכילנא לאכשורי בה ע"י טבילות אחרות שטבלה אח"כ לנדותה. כך שמעתי, וקשיא לי: חדא, דקבעינן הלכתא התם הלכה כולן גרים. ואפי' למשנה ראשונה נמי, אי קמייתא לא סלקא לה — בתרא נמי לא סלקא לה, דלאו לשם שמים נתגיירה. ולשון ראשון עיקר, ונראה בעיני. בר ארמייתא. שלא טבלה אמו כשנתגיירה. מי לא טבלה לנדותה. ואותה טבילה עולה לה לטבילת גירות, דדת יהודית היא. וכן מי לא טבל לקריו.

תוספות

משום דאתי צד עבדות ומשתמש באשת איש. והא דמשמע בפ"ק דקדושין (דף ז. ושם) דהתקדשי לחליי לא אמר כלום, אי לאו משום דאי(ב) בעינן למינסב אחריתי נסיבנא קאמר — היינו משום דשייר בקניינו, כדאמר ב"השולח" (גיטין דף מג. ושם) והכא לא שייר. מה אשת אב כו'. וא"ת: מה לאשת אב שכן כרת ומיתה! ויש לומר! דממזרות תלוי בתפיסת קדושין, כדפרישית לעיל. רבא אכשריה לרב מרי בר רחל. רבא גרסי' ולא רב, דרב מרי בריה דאיסור גיורא הוה, שהיה בימי רבא, כדמוכח בפ' "מי שמת" (ג) (ב"ב קמט. ושם*). פורסי דבבל. ממונה, כדאמר בפ"ק דיומא (דף ט.): מאי פרהדרין — פורסי. כיון דאמו מישראל מקרב אחיך קרינן ביה. מכאן קשה לפי' הקונטרס: דפירש "באלו נאמרין" (סוטה דף מא. ושם) גבי אגריפס המלך, שאמרו לו אחינו אתה, וקאמר בגמרא דאותה שעה נתחייבו שונאיהם של ישראל כלייה, שהחניפו לאגריפס, ופי' בקונטרס: שקראוהו אחינו לפי שהיתה אמו מישראל, ולפירושו אמאי נענשו? הא אמרינן הכא כיון דאמו מישראל "מקרב אחיך" קרינן ביה! ואע"ג דתניא בתוספתא (דסנהדרין פ"ד) דאין מעמידין מלך אלא מן המשיאים לכהונה — מ"מ תימה הוא לומר דמשום איסורא דרבנן נתחייבו כלייה! ואומר רבינו שמואל: דהורדוס לא נשא בת ישראל, שעשה תשובה, כדאמרינן בפ"ק דב"ב (דף ד.), ולכך נענשו. ואע"פ שהיה עבד קראוהו אחינו, לפי שהיה אחיהם במצות. ואתי שפיר הא דאמר שמואל בפ' "עשרה יוחסין" (קדושין ע:): כל דאמר מבית חשמונאי קאתינא — עבדא הוא, ושמואל גופיה אית ליה (לעיל עמוד א) דגוי ועבד הבא על בת ישראל הולד כשר. אלא ודאי לא נשא ישראלית. וא"ת: מ"מ אמאי עבדא הוא? והלא מסתמא כשמלך הורדוס נתייאשו בעליו, ושמואל אית ליה (לקמן דף מח.): המפקיר עבדו יצא לחירות, ואין צריך גט שחרור! וי"ל: דשמא היו מצפים שתהא גאותו מושפלת. וא"ת: דהכא משמע דגר שאין אמו מישראל אין כשר לדון, ובפ' "אחד דיני ממונות" (סנהדרין דף לו: ושם) תנן: הכל כשרים לדון, ופריך: תנינא! [ומשני]: חדא לאתויי גר, וחדא לאתויי ממזר. משמע דגר, אע"פ שאין אמו מישראל, אלא שנתגייר בעצמו — דכשר לדון, דקרינן ליה בא מטיפה פסולה דקאמר התם, אבל גר מטיפה פסולה לא! וי"ל: דהתם מיירי לדון גר חברו, כדאמר בפ' "מצות חליצה" (לקמן דף קב. ושם): גר דן את חברו דבר תורה, ואם היתה אמו מישראל — דן אפילו ישראל. וא"ת בפ' "עשרה יוחסין" (קדושין עו:) אמרינן: מי שהוחזקו אבותיו משוטרי הרבים, למימרא דלא מוקמינן פסולים, ורמינהו: הכל כשרים לדון כו', ואמר רב יהודה: לאתויי ממזר. ומאי קושיא? דהתם היינו לדון את חברו! וי"ל: דממזר, כיון דאביו ואמו מישראל — "מקרב אחיך" קרינן ביה. תדע, דהא דרשינן "עליך" הוא דבעינן מקרב אחיך, וחברו ממזר מיקרי שפיר עליך, שבא מזרע ישראל, ואי מיפסל ממזר לדון את ישראל — מיפסל נמי לחברו, ובפרק "אחד דיני ממונות" (סנהדרין דף לו:) דקעביד צריכותא בין גר לממזר, אע"פ שגר וממזר חלוקין, דגר אינו דן אלא חברו — מ"מ נקט צריכותא, לפי שהמשנה שנויה סתם, ואין חילוק זה מפורש בה(א). אטבלה להויא גויה לשום אנתתא. שהיה רוצה לייחדה לו, והיה מטבילה כדרך כל בנות ישראל שטובלות משנתבעות לינשא. וטועה היה, דבעבד לא גזרו נשג"ז, כדאמרינן בנדה[א] (דף כ). מי לא טבלה לנדותה. תימה: דאמר לקמן (דף מו:) דגר צריך שלשה, דמשפט כתיב ביה. ואפילו למאן דאמר בריש סנהדרין (דף ג.) דבר תורה חד נמי כשר — מכל מקום אין דרך נשים להביא איש עמהן בשעת טבילה, ואשה אינה ראויה לדון, כדתנן (נדה דף מט:): כל הכשר לדון כשר להעיד. ובהדיא איתא בירושלמי דיומא: מעתה שאין אשה מעידה אינה דנה. ודבורה לא היתה דנה, אלא מלמדת להן שידונו. אי נמי על פי הדיבור שאני! וי"ל: האי דבעינן שלשה — היינו לקבלת המצות, אבל לא לטבילה. ב) אף על גב דאמרינן לקמן (דף מז:) דשני ת"ח עומדים מבחוץ — היינו לכתחלה, דעדיף טפי. *ויש מפרשים: דכיון דידוע לכל שטבלה — כאילו עומדים שם דמי. ומיהו קשיא: דטבילת נדה בלילה, ולקמן (דף מו:) אמר: אין מטבילין גר בלילה! אבל אי לאו כתיב משפט אלא אקבלת מצוה — אתי שפיר והא דאין מטבילין — היינו לכתחלה, מדרבנן.

הקדש

תוספות ישנים

דפליגא: מקרב אחיך קרינא ביה. קשה לפ"ה דפי' לקמן (ק"ב.) עלה דגר דן את חברו דבר תורה דר"ל דוקא דיני נפשות אבל דיני ממונות דן אפילו ישראל וקשה דהכא משמע דדוקא אמו מישראל מלי לדון אבל אי לאו הכי לא דן ובדיני ממונות איירינן הכא דדיני נפשות ליכא בזמן הזה וצ"ל דאף בדיני ממונות דן חבירו דוקא: א) וקשה לקמן פ' מצות חליצה רב יהודה לאדבריה לר' שמואל בר יהודה והוא היה גר [להיות דיין] בחליצה והדר תניתוה בב"ד של ישראל ולא בב"ד של גרים ולפר"ח דפי' דאף בדיני ממונות לא מלי דיין אפילו ישראל איך היה טועה ר' יהודה להוליכו שם להכשירו לחליצה מי גרע מדיני ממונות ובשלמא לפ"ה ניחא דעלה על דעתו להכשירו לחליצה כמו בשאר דיני ממונות דדן אפי' לישראל ולהכי קאמר תלמודא תניתוה דגלי קרא דפסול בחליצה אבל לפר"ת קשה ונראה לומר דגר פסול לדון ישראל בדיני ממונות בדבר שלריך כפיה וא"כ ניחא דהכא מיירי במילי דכפיה וכן משמע [דמנייה] בפורסי דבבל דמשמע לכפות העולם ובהא בעי' דוקא משום דאמו מישראל אבל בלא כפיה מלי למידן ישראל ומש"ה ניחא ההיא דלקמן דס"ד לעשות מצות חליצה כמו מלתא דלית ביה כפיה ולהכי ס"ד להכשירו עד דמייתי קרא דפסול גם בחליצה ובסנהדרין פי' לפי' ר"ת מאי האי דגביה כל הכשר לדון כשר להעיד ויש כשר להעיד ואינו כשר לדון ואמר ר' יוחנן לאתויי סומא באחת מעיניו ואמאי לא קאמר לאתויי גר כיון דלא מלי לדון ישראל וי"ל דלא פסיקא ליה משום דחבירו מיהו מלי לדון: לשם אנתתא פ"ה לטבילת נדות ולא לשם יהדות ומהניא כדאמרינן לקמן מי לא טבלה לנדותה ולכן רלה להכשיר בה ובברתה וי"מ לשם אנתתא לשם אישות ולא לשם יהדות רק כי היה חפץ בה והיא חפלה בו והכשיר בה ובברתה משום טבילות שעשתה אחרי כן לנדותה דמשום הטבילה שעשתה לשם אישות לא מהניא כדמשמע לעיל ולא נהירא דהא מסקינן הלכה כולם גרים וא"כ הטבילה לשם אישות מהניא ואם לא מהניא משום דלא נתכוונה לשם יהדות כלל א"כ מה אהנו הטבילות של נדות שטבלה אחרי כן אחרי שלא נתכוונה לשם יהדות [ולכן נראה עיקר] כפי' קמא: ב) וצ"ל דהכי מיירי כשקבלה כבר המצות והודיעוה מצות קלות וחמורות דאל"ה לא סגי בטבילת נדותן:

מסורת הש"ס

דרבא. יעב"ץ

[שבת קנו. ע"ש]

קדושין עו:

[וע"ע תוס' קדושין סב: ד"ה גר]

הגהות הב"ח

(א) גמ' תשים עליך מלך מקרב אחיך כל משימות: (ב) תוס' ד"ה משום וכו' דאי בעינן: (ג) ד"ה רבא וכו' בפרק מי שמת נ"ב ע"ש בתוספ' קמט ע"א ובפ' ה"א עג ע"ב ובמה שכתבתי שם ובפרק מי שהתחיל קנה ע"א:

הגהות מהר"ב רנשבורג

א] תוס' ד"ה אטבלה כו'. כדאמרינן בנדה דף כ ע"א ע"ש תוס' ד"ה מסר וכו' כל"ל:

תוספות חד מקמאי

עבודות: עבדיה דר' חייא בר אמי אטבלה להויא גויה לשום אנתתא אמר רב יוסף יכילנא לאכשורי בה ובברתה בה כדרב אסי דאמר רב [אסי] מי לא טבלה לנדותה פירוש עבדיה דר' חייא גיירה להויא גויה וקבלה עליה מקצת מצות קלות ומקצת מצות חמורות ובשעת גירותה לא טבלה לשם גירות אלא שטבלה לאחר ימי נדותה לטהרה לבעלה משום הכי אמר רב אסי מי לא טבלה לנדותה דכיון שטבלה לנדותה או האיש שטבל לקריו ש"מ בקבלת המצות שקבלו עליהם הם עומדים. וכן ההוא דהוו קרו ליה בר ארמאה ואריב"ל מי לא טבל לקריו הכי הוא מעשה שנתגייר ומל וקבל מקצת מצות קלות ומקצת מצות חמורות ולא טבל בשעת גירותו עד לאחר זמן שטבל לקריו ולפיכך אמרינן כיון דטבל לקריו מקצת מצות קלות ומקצת מצות חמורות אע"פ שבשעת הקבלה לא נזדמן להיות שם שלשה ואחר כך טבל לקריו עלתה לו טבילה והא דאמרינן גר צריך שלשה היינו לכתחלה כל שהודיעוהו מקצת מצות קלות ומקצת מצות חמורות בשעת מילה ובשעת טבילה [illegible] (לקמן מז:) נתרפא מטבילין אותו מיד ושני

תלמידי חכמים עומדים על גביו ומודיעין וכו' ופרכינן עלה והא אנן תנן שלשה הא אמר ליה ר"י לתנא תני ג' אבל דיעבד כגון שהודיעוהו מקצת מצות קלות ומקצת מצות חמורות אע"פ שלא נזדמן לו לטבול בשעה שהודיעוהו ואח"כ טבל לקריו או אשה לנדותה גרים גמורים הם ומותרים לבוא בקהל ישראל לכתחלה אבל כשנתגייר בינו לבין עצמו שלא הודיעוהו מקצת מצות קלות וחמורות גוי גמור הוא אפילו נמול ולפיכך אמר גר שנתגייר בינו לבין עצמו אינו גר ומעשה באחד שבא לפני רבי יהודה וכו' ומסקנא לדבריך גוי אתה [illegible] ודר"ל בדיעבד [illegible] טבל לקריו [illegible] דוקא בדאתחזק בגוי אבל לא איתחזק בגוי [illegible] טבל לקריו נאמן במגו:

תניא

גוי גופא לא קני. גוי לא קנאו לגופו של זה מתחלה, כדאמר לקמן: ולא הם קונים זה את זה. הקדש חמץ ושחרור. עשה שורו אפותיקי והקדישו למזבח, דהויא קדושת הגוף – פקע שיעבודא דקמא. אבל קדושת בדק הבית לא מפקעא, כדתנן בערכין (דף כג:): מוסיף עוד דינר ופודה הנכסים כולן. או אם עשה חמצו אפותיקי לגוי, והרי הוא מופקד בידו של ישראל, ובאו שש שעות של ערב הפסח – פקע שיעבוד הגוי, הואיל ולא הוי ממש דידיה, וחייב זה לבערו. ושחרור. עשה עבדו אפותיקי לחבירו ושחררו – משוחרר, ופקע ממונו של מלוה. בבלוריא כו' לפניה אין. לפי שהן גרים, והיא גויה, והגוי – ישראל לא קני לגופיה. לאחריה לא. אלמא גבי ישראל לא אמרינן קנה עבד עצמו בן חורין. בין בסתם. שלא פירש, הרי אנו תולין לשם בני חורין. במפורש. כדרב חמא בר גוריא, דקתני: וקדם וטבל לשם בן חורין. אבל גוי גופיה. גוי שמכר עצמו לישראל – קנהו ישראל לגופיה, ואם קדם וטבל לשם בן חורין – לא קנה עצמו בן חורין. אלא גוי מי לא קני ליה לישראל. למעשה ידיו, והכתיב "או לעקר משפחת גר", ואמר מר: משפחת גר – זה הגוי. אימא בכספא ובטבילה. לשום עבדות הוא דקאמר רחמנא ליקני, אבל אם קדם וטבל לשם בן חורין – ה"נ דבן חורין הוא. לתקפו במים. כשמטבילו לשם יהדות לעבדות, צריך שיתקפנו, לתת עליו עול מלאכה במים, כדי שתהא נראית כטבילת עבדות. שאפילו יאמר הוא לשם בן חורין – לא קנה עצמו בן חורין, ולא יהא ממשות בדבריו. בעי לאטבולי. לשם יהדות לעבד. מינייכו קא בעינא ליה. אם יקדים ויאמר לשם בן חורין. ארויסא. קיסטרי. וצמצמו. דחקוהו לקשור בצוארו, משום לתוקפו במים. ארפו ליה וצמצמו ליה. שהיה לו עניבה, וכשרוצים מושכין ראש החבל והוא דוחק מאליו, וכשאין מושכין – רפוי, והמים נכנסים על בשרו. זולטא דטינא. כלי מלא טיט. דיהבי זוזי לאינשי לכרגייהו. כשאין נותנין כסף גולגלת למלך תופסים אותם גבאי המלך. והני דבי פפא עשירים היו, ופורעים המס לגבאי המלך, וקונין אותם לעבדים מהם. וגוים היו אותן הנקנין, וקא מיבעיא ליה אי הוי קנין, דלכי נפקי מיניה ליבעי גיטא דחירותא, או לא. מוהרקייהו דהני. חותמן של אלו. בטפסא דמלכא. (ב) שהן לו לעבדים. טפסא. ארגז, אשקרי"ן בלע"ז. ומלכא אמר כו'. הילכך מכר הוא, ובעו גיטא דחירותא אי בעו לאיגיורי ולאישתרויי בבת ישראל. לפי שאינם בני תורה. אתורמוסין קאי, דאין בו משום בישולי גוים כדמפרש לקמן, אלא לפי שאינן בני תורה גזה ואסור עליהן, שלא יזלזלו בבשולי גוים. ועל יינם משום יין נסך. דאע"ג דלא נגעי, אלא כאו בעלמא הוא – אסור משום לך לך אמרין לנזירא כו': תורמוס אינו עולה על שלחן מלכים. באבותינו שמלו. בימי משה, כשיצאו ממצרים, ויצאו מכלל בני נח לקבל התורה ולקבל פני השכינה. באמהות. נשותיהם שטבלו כדמפרש לקמן, דאם לא טבלו – במה נכנסו תחת כנפי שכינה? משאי אפשר. אמהות אי אפשר למול. אלא מן החולין. ולא מדמי מעשר שני, דאכתי מעשר שני לא הוה. אין בא אלא מן החולין. למעוטי מדמי מעשר שני: ה"ג במנחות בהתודה (דף פג.). א"ל רבי עקיבא וכי דנין אפשר כו'. ומאן דגרים רבי יהושע קשיא, האמר רבי יהושע דנין מאמהות. משאי אפשר. מפסח מצרים, דהאי דלא בא מן המעשר – דאי אפשר הוא, דאכתי מעשר לא הוה.

גוי גופא לא קני ליה, מאי דקני ליה – הוא דמקני ליה לישראל, וכיון דקדם וטבל לשם בן חורין – אפקעיה לשעבודיה, כדרבא. *דאמר רבא: [א]הקדש, חמץ, [ב]ושחרור – מפקיעין מידי שעבוד. מתיב רב חסדא: *[ג]מעשה בבלוריא הגיורת שקדמו עבדיה וטבלו לפניה. ובא מעשה לפני חכמים ואמרו: קנו עצמן בני חורין. לפניה – אין, לאחריה – לא! אמר רבא: [ד]לפניה – בין בסתם בין במפורש. לאחריה, במפורש – אין, בסתם – לא. אמר רב אויא: לא שנו אלא בלוקח מן הגוי, אבל [ה]גוי גופיה – קני, דכתיב °"וגם מבני התושבים הגרים עמכם מהם תקנו" – *אתם קונים מהם, ולא הם קונים מכם, ולא הם קונים זה מזה. ולא הם קונים מכם, למאי? אילימא למעשה ידיו – אטו גוי לא קני ליה לישראל למעשה ידיו? [ו]והכתיב °"או לעקר משפחת גר" ואמר מר: *"משפחת גר" – זה הגוי! אלא לאו – לגופיה, וקאמר רחמנא "אתם קונין מהם" – אפילו גופיה. *פריך רב אחא: אימא בכספא ובטבילה! קשיא. אמר שמואל: [ז]וצריך לתקפו במים. [ח]כי האי דמניומין, עבדיה דרב אשי, בעא לאטבולי, מסריה ניהלייהו לרבינא ולרב אחא בריה' דרבא, אמר להו: חזו דמינייכו *קבעית ליה. רמו ליה *ארויסא בצואריה, ארפו ליה. וצמצמו ליה. ארפו ליה – כי היכי דלא להוי חציצה, צמצמו ליה – כי היכי דלא לקדים ולימא (א) להו: לשם בן חורין אני טובל. בהדי דדלי רישיה ממיא, אנחו ליה זולטא דטינא ארישיה. ואמרו ליה: זיל אמטי לבי מרך. א"ל רב פפא לרבא: חזי מר הני דבי פפא בר אבא דיהבי זוזי לאינשי לכרגייהו, ומשעבדי בהו. *כי נפקי, צריכי גיטא דחירותא או לא? *א"ל: איכו שכיבי לא אמרי לכו הא מילתא, [ט]הכי א"ר ששת: מוהרקייהו דהני בטפסא דמלכא מנח, ומלכא אמר: מאן דלא יהיב כרגא – משתעבד למאן דיהיב כרגא. *ר' חייא בר אבא איקלע לגבלא. חזא בנות ישראל דמעברן מגרים שמלו ולא טבלו, וחזא חמרא דישראל דמזגי גוים ושתו ישראל, וחזא תורמוסין דשלקי גוים ואכלי ישראל, ולא אמר להו ולא מידי. אתא לקמיה דר' יוחנן. א"ל: צא והכרז על בניהם שהם ממזרים, ועל יינם משום יין נסך, ועל תורמוסן משום בישולי גוים, לפי שאינן בני תורה. על בניהן שהם ממזרים – ר' יוחנן לטעמיה, דאמר ר' חייא בר אבא אמר ר' יוחנן: [י]לעולם אין גר עד שימול ויטבול, וכיון דלא טביל – גוי הוא. ואמר רבה בר בר חנה א"ר יוחנן: גוי ועבד הבא על בת ישראל – הולד ממזר. [כ]ועל יינם משום יין נסך – משום *"לך לך", אמרין נזירא, סחור סחור, לכרמא לא תקרב". ועל תורמוסן משום בשולי גוים – לפי שאינן בני תורה, הא בני תורה שרי? *והאמר רב שמואל בר רב יצחק משמי' דרב: [ל]כל הנאכל כמות שהוא חי – אין בו משום בשולי גוים, והא תורמוס אינו נאכל כמות שהוא חי, ויש בו משום בשולי גוים! ר' יוחנן כאידך לישנא סבירא ליה דאמר רב שמואל בר רב יצחק משמי' דרב: [מ]כל שאין עולה על שולחן מלכים לאכול בו את הפת – אין בו משום בשולי גוים. וטעמא דאינן בני תורה, הא בני תורה – שרי. ת"ר: גר שמל ולא טבל, ר"א אומר הרי זה גר, שכן מצינו באבותינו שמלו ולא טבלו. טבל ולא מל, ר' יהושע אומר: הרי זה גר, שכן מצינו באמהות שטבלו ולא מלו. וחכמים אומרים: טבל ולא מל, מל ולא טבל – [מ] אין גר עד שימול ויטבול. ורבי יהושע נמי – ניליף מאבות, ור"א נמי – ניליף מאמהות! וכי תימא: אין דנין אפשר משאי אפשר – והתניא, *ר"א אומר: [נ]מנין לפסח דורות שאין בא אלא מן החולין – נאמר פסח במצרים ונאמר פסח בדורות, מה פסח האמור במצרים – אין בא אלא מן החולין, אף פסח האמור לדורות – אין בא אלא מן החולין. א"ל ר' עקיבא: *וכי דנין אפשר משאי אפשר? א"ל: אע"פ שאי אפשר – ראיה גדולה היא, ונלמד הימנה. אלא בטבל

הקדש חמץ ושחרור. מפורש ב"השולח" (גיטין דף מ:). **כי נפקי** צריכי גיטא דחירותא או לאו. מספקא ליה אי דינא דמלכותא דינא (ג) או לא. ואע"ג דלא קני גופיה – הכא קני. או דלמא, הכא נמי לא קני אלא למעשה ידיו. ובגויותן מיירי, אם היו באין להתגייר.

רבי יוחנן כאידך לישנא ס"ל. אומר ר"ת: דכולהו מודו דכשנאכל כמות שהוא חי – דאין בו משום בישולי גוים, דאמר ב"אין מעמידין" (ע"ז דף לח.) דאיכא בינייהו דגים קטנים ארזי ודייסא, היינו: דברים שאין עולים על שלחן מלכים ואין נאכלים כמות שהן חיין. ולא נקט כמה דברים הנאכלים כשהן חיין ועולים על שלחן מלכים, כמו פירות וגבינה וכיוצא בהן. והא דאסר רבי יוחנן התם ביצה, אע"ג דראוי לגומעה חיה – אין זו אכילה חשובה, דהכי נמי בשר מליח מותר לטלטלו בשבת (שבת קכח.), דחזי לאכילה. ואפ"ה יש בו משום בישולי גוים. **אמר** ליה ר' עקיבא וכי דנין אפשר משאי

תוספות חד מקמאי
תניא מעשה בבלוריא הגיורת, שקדמו עבדיה וטבלו לפניה ובא מעשה לפני חכמים ואמרו קנו עצמן בן חורין ואסיק רבא בפניה בין בסתם בין במפורש לאחריה במפורש אין בסתם לא ופירוש לפניה הוא קודם שנתגיירה והרב אלפס לא גרים לאחריה אלא שלא בפניה במפרש אין בסתם לא פירוש בפניה כיון שראתה ושתקה בין בסתם בין במפורש. שלא בפניה שלא ראתה כדטבלה במפרש אין בסתם לא וגירסת מכילתא מסייע (א) לרב ז"ל דגרס' התם בפ' בא אל פרעה ר' נתן אמר מה ת"ל המול לו כל זכר ואז יקרב לעשותו להביא את העבד שטבל בפני רבו שיצא בן חורין ומעשה בבלוריא הגיורת שטבלו שפחותיה בפני' ומקצתן לאחריה ובא מעשה לפני חכמים ואמרו את שטבלו בפני' בנות חורין ואת [שטבלו] לאחריה משועבדים ואעפ"כ משמשות אותה עד יום מיתה: **אמר** שמואל וצריך לתקפו במים פירוש שיראה שלשום עבדות טובלין ולא לשום בן חורין והרב ז"ל פירש כדי שתעלה לו טבילה ומסתברא (בפ"ק) כפר"ש ז"ל א"ר יוחנן לעולם אינו גר עד שימול ויטבול דוקא מילה והדר טבילה אבל איפכא לא. וצריך לטבול (עד) אחר המילה וכן נעשה מעשה בלוניל מפי אבא מארי וחבריו ז"ל שהצריכוהו טבילה לאחר המילה. תניא הרי שבא ואמר מלתי ולא טבלתי מטבילין אותו ומה בכך דברי ר"י ור' יוסי אמר אין מטבילין. ומסקנא בהא פליגי דר"י סבר בחד מינייהו סגי או מילה או טבילה ור' יוסי תרתי בעי. והלכתא כר' יוסי דתרתי בעי. ושמעי' מהא הגר שנתגייר כשהוא מהול צריך להטיף ממנו דם ברית וכבר

(א) נראה דל"ל וגירסת מכילתא מסייע לפי' רש"י ז"ל.

עין משפט נר מצוה

קיג א מיי' פ"ז מהל' ערכין הל' יד ופי"ח מהלכות מלוה ולוה הל' ו ז וסמג עשין לד טוש"ע ח"מ סימן קיז סעיף ז:
קיד ב מיי' פ"ח מהל' עבדים הלכה טז סמג עשין פז טוש"ע שם סעיף ו טוש"ע י"ד סימן רסז סעיף סח:
קטו ג מיי' פ"ח מהל' עבדים הל' כא:
מכילת' פרשת בא פ' טו
קטז ד מיי' שם הל' יט ומיי' פי"ג מהל' איסורי ביאה הלכה יא:
קיז ה טוש"ע י"ד סימן רסו סעיף ע:
קיח ו מיי' פ"א מהל' עבדים הלכה ג סמג עשין פג:
קיט ז ח מיי' פי"ג מהל' איסורי ביאה הל' יא טוש"ע י"ד סימן רסז סעיף ע:
קכ ט מיי' פ"ה מהל' גזילה הל' טז ופ"א מהל' עבדים הל' ח סמג עשין עג טוש"ע ח"מ סי' שסט סעי' יא:
קכא י מיי' פי"ג מהל' איסורי ביאה הל' ו סמג לאוין קטז:
קכב כ מיי' פ"א מהל' מאכלות אסורות הל' ג סמג לאוין קמח טוש"ע י"ד סי' קכג סעיף א:
[נ"ל ארוסיה פירוש שלשלת ערוך ערך ארסה]

הגהות הב"ח
(א) גמ' ולימא לשם בן חורין כצ"ל ותיבת להו נמחק: (ב) רש"י ד"ה בטפסא דמלכא וכו' (שהן) תז"מ ונ"ב ס"א שהיו: (ג) תוס' ד"ה כי וכו' דינא ואע"ג כצ"ל ותיבת או לא נמחק:

תוספות ישנים
הקדש חמץ ושחרור מפקיעים וכו'. פירשתי פרק כל שעה בפסחים. וא"ת מאי מדמה הכא לשחרור דמפקע מידי שעבוד הא לא דמי דהתם מיירי כשהרב עצמו משחרר עבדו. אבל הכא מיירי שהוא משחרר עצמו כשטובל לשם בן חורין. וי"ל דמ"מ מדמי שפיר דהכא נמי כיון שטבל אפקע ליה שם עבדות ולא איתא לרב אלא מעשה ידיו דהא גוי גופיה לא קני והעבד יכתוב לו שטר על חצי דמיו ולא יהיה לרב כלום לד עבדות עליו: (לעיל) **מי** לא לא טבלה לנדותה. וא"ת הלא טבילתה בלילה וגר צריך לטבול ביום דמשפט כתיב ביה. וי"ל דאיכא טבילת נדות דהוי שפיר ביום כגון טבילה שלא בזמנה: **ומשתעבד** בהו עבידתא ל"ג יתירתא רק בבבא מליעא גבי רבית ואי גרסינן ליה הכא יש לייטבו משום דאז מוכחא מלת' שגופם קנוי לעבדים:

בְּטָבַל וְלֹא מָל — כּוּלֵּי עָלְמָא לָא פְּלִיגִי דְּמַהֲנֵי. כִּי פְּלִיגִי — בְּמָל וְלֹא טָבַל. רַבִּי אֱלִיעֶזֶר יָלֵיף מֵאָבוֹת, וְרַבִּי יְהוֹשֻׁעַ: בָּאָבוֹת נַמִּי טְבִילָה הֲוָה. מְנָא לֵיהּ? אִילֵימָא מִדִּכְתִיב °"לֵךְ אֶל הָעָם וְקִדַּשְׁתָּם הַיּוֹם וּמָחָר וְכִבְּסוּ שִׂמְלֹתָם", וּמַה בְּמָקוֹם שֶׁאֵין טָעוּן כִּבּוּס — טָעוּן טְבִילָה, מָקוֹם שֶׁטָּעוּן כִּבּוּס — אֵינוֹ דִּין שֶׁטָּעוּן טְבִילָה? וְדִלְמָא נְקִיּוּת בְּעָלְמָא? אֶלָּא מֵהָכָא: °"וַיִּקַּח מֹשֶׁה אֶת הַדָּם וַיִּזְרֹק עַל הָעָם" וּגְמִירִי *דְּאֵין הַזָּאָה בְּלֹא טְבִילָה. וְרַבִּי יְהוֹשֻׁעַ, טְבִילָה בְּאִמָּהוֹת מְנָלַן? סְבָרָא הוּא, דְּאִם כֵּן — בַּמֶּה נִכְנְסוּ תַּחַת כַּנְפֵי הַשְּׁכִינָה? *א"ר חִיָּיא בַּר אַבָּא א"ר יוֹחָנָן: לְעוֹלָם אֵינוֹ גֵּר עַד שֶׁיִּמּוֹל וְיִטְבּוֹל. פְּשִׁיטָא, *יָחִיד וְרַבִּים הֲלָכָה כְּרַבִּים! מַאן חֲכָמִים — *רַבִּי יוֹסֵי. דְּתַנְיָא: הֲרֵי שֶׁבָּא וְאָמַר מַלְתִּי וְלֹא טָבַלְתִּי — מַטְבִּילִין אוֹתוֹ, וּמַה בְּכָךְ, דִּבְרֵי רַ' יְהוּדָה. רַבִּי יוֹסֵי אוֹמֵר: אֵין מַטְבִּילִין. לְפִיכָךְ מַטְבִּילִין גֵּר בְּשַׁבָּת, דִּבְרֵי רַ' יְהוּדָה. וְרַ' יוֹסֵי אוֹמֵר: אאֵין מַטְבִּילִין. אָמַר מָר: לְפִיכָךְ מַטְבִּילִין גֵּר בְּשַׁבָּת, (א) פְּשִׁיטָא, כֵּיוָן דְּא"ר יְהוּדָה בַּחֲדָא סַגְיָא, הֵיכָא דְּמָל לְפָנֵינוּ — מַטְבִּילִין, מַאי לְפִיכָךְ? מַהוּ דְּתֵימָא: לְרַבִּי יְהוּדָה טְבִילָה עִיקָּר, וּטְבִילָה בְּשַׁבָּת — לָא, דְּקָא מְתַקֵּן גַּבְרָא, קמ"ל דְּרַ' יְהוּדָה אוֹ הָא אוֹ הָא בָּעֵי. רַ' יוֹסֵי אוֹמֵר אֵין מַטְבִּילִין. פְּשִׁיטָא, דְּכֵיוָן דְּאָמַר רַבִּי יוֹסֵי תַּרְתֵּי בָּעֵינַן — תַּקּוֹנֵי גַּבְרָא בְּשַׁבָּת לָא מְתַקְּנִינַן! מַהוּ דְּתֵימָא: לְרַ' יוֹסֵי מִילָה עִיקָּר, וְהָתָם הוּא דְּלָא הֲוַאי מִילָה בְּפָנֵינוּ, אֲבָל הֵיכָא דַּהֲוְיָא מִילָה בְּפָנֵינוּ — אֵימָא לִיטְבַּל זֶה בְּשַׁבַּתָּא, קמ"ל דְּרַבִּי יוֹסֵי תַּרְתֵּי בָּעֵי. אֲמַר רַבָּה: עוּבְדָא הֲוָה בֵּי רַבִּי חִיָּיא בַּר רַבִּי, וְרַב יוֹסֵף מַתְנֵי רַבִּי אוֹשַׁעְיָא *בַּר רַבִּי, וְרַב סַפְרָא מַתְנֵי רַ' אוֹשַׁעְיָא בְּרַ' חִיָּיא, דַּאֲתָא לְקַמֵּיהּ גֵּר שֶׁמָּל וְלֹא טָבַל. א"ל שְׁהֵי כָּאן עַד לְמָחָר וְנַטְבְּלִינָךְ. ש"מ תְּלָת: בש"מ גֵּר צָרִיךְ שְׁלֹשָׁה וְשַׁ"מ: אֵינוֹ גֵּר עַד שֶׁיִּמּוֹל וְיִטְבּוֹל, וְשַׁ"מ: גאֵין מַטְבִּילִין גֵּר בַּלַּיְלָה. וְנֵימָא: ש"מ נַמִּי בָּעֵינַן מוּמְחִין! דִּלְמָא דְּאִיקְלַעוּ. אָמַר רַבִּי חִיָּיא בַּר אַבָּא אָמַר רַבִּי יוֹחָנָן: *גֵּר צָרִיךְ ג' "מִשְׁפָּט" כְּתִיב בֵּיהּ. ת"ר: מִי שֶׁבָּא וְאָמַר: "גֵּר אָנִי", יָכוֹל נְקַבְּלֶנּוּ — ת"ל "אִתְּךָ" — בְּמוּחְזָק לְךָ. בָּא וְעֵדָיו עִמּוֹ מִנַּיִן — ת"ל °"וְכִי יָגוּר (ג) אִתְּךָ גֵּר בְּאַרְצְכֶם". אֵין

בְּמָקוֹם שֶׁאֵין טָעוּן כִּיבּוּס. כְּגוֹן בַּעַל קֶרִי בְּעָלְמָא, דִּכְתִיב "וְרָחַץ בַּמַּיִם וְטָמֵא עַד הָעָרֶב" (ויקרא טו) וְלָא כְּתִיב יְכַבֵּס בְּגָדָיו. מָקוֹם שֶׁטָּעוּן כִּיבּוּס. כְּגוֹן בְּקִבּוּל תּוֹרָה, דִּכְתִיב "וְכִבְּסוּ שִׂמְלוֹתָם". דִּלְמָא נְקִיּוּת בְּעָלְמָא. הַהוּא כִּיבּוּס לָאו מִשּׁוּם טוּמְאָה הֲוָה דְּלִטְעוֹן טְבִילָה מִקַּ"ו, אֶלָּא שֶׁיִּהְיוּ בִּגְדֵיהֶם לְבָנִים וַהֲגוּנִים לְקַבֵּל פְּנֵי שְׁכִינָה. וַיִּזְרוֹק עַל הָעָם. הַזָּאָה הוּא. מַטְבִּילִים אוֹתוֹ. וְהָוֵי כְּיִשְׂרָאֵל מְעַלְיָא, וְאֵין צָרִיךְ לִבְדּוֹק בְּעֵדִים אִם מִילָתוֹ לְשֵׁם מִצְוַת מִילָה. וּמַה בְּכָךְ. אִם אֵין מִילָתוֹ לְשֵׁם מִילָה, הוֹאִיל וְטָבַל — בִּטְבִילָה סַגִּי. אֵין מַטְבִּילִים. שֶׁמָּא עַרְבִי מָהוּל* וְגִבְעוֹנִי מָהוּל הוּא, וְצָרִיךְ לְהַטִּיף מִמֶּנּוּ דַּם בְּרִית. דְּרַ' יוֹסֵי תַּרְתֵּי בָּעֵי. לְפִיכָךְ. הוֹאִיל וּלְרַ' יְהוּדָה בַּחֲדָא סַגְיָא — מַטְבִּילִין בְּשַׁבָּת גֵּר שֶׁמָּל אֶתְמוֹל לְפָנֵינוּ, דְּבְמִילָה סַגֵּי לֵיהּ, וְכִי מַטְבְּלֵי לֵיהּ בְּשַׁבַּתָּא — לָא מְתַקְּנֵי גַּבְרָא. הָכִי גָּרְסִינַן: אָמַר מָר לְפִיכָךְ מַטְבִּילִין גֵּר בְּשַׁבָּת דִּבְרֵי רַבִּי יְהוּדָה פְּשִׁיטָא כֵּיוָן דִּלְרַבִּי יְהוּדָה בַּחֲדָא סַגֵּי הֵיכָא דְּמָל לְפָנֵינוּ מַטְבִּילִים. טְבִילָה עִיקָּר. דְּהָא אַמִּילָה שָׁמְעִינַן לֵיהּ דְּקָאָמַר וּמַה בְּכָךְ. ר' יוֹסֵי אוֹמֵר אֵין מַטְבִּילִין. תַּרְתֵּי בָּעֵי, וְאַע"ג דְּמָל בְּפָנֵינוּ — טְבִילָתוֹ תַּקָּנָתוֹ. עוּבְדָא הֲוָה בֵּי ר' חִיָּיא בַּר רַבִּי וְרַב יוֹסֵף מַתְנֵי בְּרַ' אוֹשַׁעְיָא ב"ר. כְּלוֹמַר, ר' אוֹשַׁעְיָא נַמִּי הֲוָה בַּהֲדֵי ר' חִיָּיא. וְרַב סַפְרָא מַתְנֵי. דְּאַף רַבִּי אוֹשַׁעְיָא בְּרַ' חִיָּיא הֲוָה בַּהֲדַיְיהוּ. שְׁהֵי הָאִידָנָא. לַיְלָה הָיָה. ש"מ. מִדְּרַב סַפְרָא, דְּאָמַר תְּלָתָא הֲווּ — גֵּר צָרִיךְ שְׁלֹשָׁה. דְּבָעֵינַן מוּמְחִין. כִּי הָנָךְ תְּלָתָא גַּבְרֵי רַבָּנַן רַבְרְבֵי. דִּלְמָא דְּאִיקְלַעוּ. הָכִי הֲוָה מַעֲשֶׂה דְּאִיתְרַמּוּ רַבָּנַן כִּי הָנֵי. אֲבָל ג' וַדַּאי שָׁמְעִינַן, מִדְּקָפָלֵיג רַב סַפְרָא וּמוֹסִיף עַד דְּהָווּ תְּלָתָא. מִשְׁפָּט כְּתִיב בֵּיהּ. "מִשְׁפָּט אֶחָד יִהְיֶה לָכֶם וְלַגֵּר" (במדבר טו) וְאֵין מִשְׁפָּט פָּחוֹת מִג'. יָכוֹל מְקַבְּלִין אוֹתוֹ. לֹא נִצְרִיכֶנּוּ הַטָּפַת דַּם בְּרִית וּטְבִילָה. בָּא וְעֵדָיו עִמּוֹ מִנַּיִן. שֶׁנֶּאֱמָן. תַּלְמוּד לוֹמַר וְכִי יָגוּר. מִכָּל מָקוֹם. וּלְקַמָּן פָּרֵיךְ: כֵּיוָן דְּעֵדָיו עִמּוֹ — פְּשִׁיטָא, וּמִי בָּעֵי קְרָא? בְּכָל

מִשּׁאי אפשר. תימה: לר' עקיבא, מנלן דאין משלשין במכות? דבפרק קמא דמכות (דף ה.) ילפינן לה ממיתה, והיינו אי אפשר! ואין לומר דהתם דגזירה שוה היא מודה ר"ע דדנין משאי אפשר, משום דאין ג"ש למחצה. אבל הכא, בנין אב הוא. דהא הכא נמי היקישא הוא, כדמסיק בסוף "התודה" (מנחות דף פב: ושם) דדריש רבי אליעזר מ"ועבדת" (שמות יג) – שיהו כל העבודות שוות זה כזה, ולא קיבל ר"ע, אף על גב דאין היקש נמי למחצה* א).

בשטבל ולא מל כולי עלמא לא פליגי. ואם תאמר: ור' יהושע, אדמודי ליה אודויי – לפלוג עליה לפלוגי, דנקט טבל דמודי ר' אליעזר, ולא נקט מילתא דפליג בה! וכי האי גוונא פריך בסוף "שבועת הפקדון" (שבועות דף לח.). וי"ל: דהתם לא דייק אלא משום דהתנא הראשון הזכיר הכל. אבל הכא נקט שפיר ר' יהושע טבל ולא מל, כיון דלא דבר בו ר' אליעזר. **כי** פליגי במל ולא טבל. תימה: דלקמן בריש "הערל" (דף עא.) ממעט ר"ע גר שמל ולא טבל מפסח, מדכתיב "תושב ושכיר", והשתא כמאן סבר ר"ע? אי כר' יהושע – למה לי קרא? פשיטא דלא אכיל בפסח, דגוי גמור הוא! ואי כר' אליעזר, כיון דגר מעליא הוא – אין סברא למעטו מפסח, כדמשמע התם! וי"ל: דלעולם כרבי יהושע סבירא לי', ולאו מטעמיה. דאיהו סבר דבאבות נמי טבילה הוה, ורבי עקיבא סבר מדמעטיה קרא בפסח – שמע מינה דאין גר עד שימול ויטבולב).

דאין הזאה בלא טבילה. מפרש ר"ת: בלא טבילה לפני הזאה, כדי לקבל הזאה. כדאמר בפרק "ארבעה מחוסרי כפרה" (כריתות דף ט.): מה אבותינו לא נכנסו לברית אלא במילה וטבילה והזאת דמים. ואותה טבילה כשרה אף בלילה, כדתנן במסכת פרה (פי"ב מי"א): אבל הוא עצמו טובל בלילה ומַזֶּה ביום. ולענין טומאה יש עוד טבילה אחרת אחר הזאה, שהיא כדי לטהר מטומאה, כדכתיב בקרא "והזה" ברישא והדר "ורחץ במים", ואותה טבילה אינה כשרה אלא ביום, כדתנן בפרק ב' דמגילה (דף כ. ושם): אין טובלין ואין מזין אלא ביום. ויש מפרשים דהתם בטבילת אזוב איירי – אין טובלים אזוב אלא ביום, כדאמרינן בסוף מסכת פרה שאם טבל את האזוב בלילה אפי' הזה ביום הזאתו פסולה. והשתא אתי שפיר הא דתנן טבילה קודם להזאה. והא דקאמר התם בגמ' לא מזין אלא ביום, דכתיב (במדבר יט) "והזה הטהור על הטמא ביום השלישי וגו'" ואיתקש טבילה להזאה – היינו בקרא דלקמיה, דכתיב "ולקח אזוב וטבל במים איש טהור והזה על האהל וגו'". וכן משמע בירושלמי דמגילה דאמר: וטבל והזה, מה הזאה ביום אף טבילה ביום. ואין לתמוה כיון דבעי הזאה היאך מקבלים גרים בזמן הזה? דבפ' ["ארבעה] מחוסרי כפרה" נפקא לן מקרא דלא בעינן*. **ורבי** יהושע טבילה באמהות מנא ליה. אע"ג דאית ליה דאין הזאה בלא טבילה – שמא הנשים לא היו בכלל אותה הזאה. אי נמי, משום רבי אליעזר איצטריך האי טעמא, דמסיק משום דאיהו נמי מודה דבטבילה לחוד סגי, כדאמר לעיל בטבל ולא מל – כולי עלמא לא פליגי דלית ליה, דאין הזאה בלא טבילהג).

כיון דאמר רבי יהודה דבחדא סגי כו'. תימה: דפריך פשיטא, דמנא ליה דסגי במילה לחודה? דלמא כר' יהושע סבר ליה דטבילה בלא מילה – מהניא, אבל מילה בלא טבילה – לא מהני. **תקוני** גברא בשבתא לא מתקנינן. ואע"ג דלענין טומאה שרי לטבול בשבת משום דנראה כמיקר – שאני הכא, דבעי שני ת"ח לעמוד שם בשעת טבילה להודיעו המצות, כדאמרינן לקמן (דף מז:). **דרבי** יוסי תרתי בעי. כתב בה"ג דגר שנתגייר כשהוא מהול צריך להטיף ממנו דם ברית, וקטן שנולד כשהוא מהול אין צריך להטיף. וטעמא: דקטן, שלא היתה לו ערלה מעולם, אין צריך, אבל גר שהיתה לו ערלה ומילתו אינה מילה – צריך להטיף דם ברית. ד) ומיהו, אם נכרת לו כל הגיד ובא להתגייר – אין דומה שמילתו מעכבתו מלהתגייר. ומודי רבי יוסי בההיא דסגי בטבילה לחודה. ור"ת פסק במסכת שבת איפכא מה"ג, וכן משמע בפרק "ר"א דמילה" (שבת דף קלה. ושם) דקאמר: לא נחלקו בית שמאי ובית הלל על נולד כשהוא מהול שצריך להטיף ממנו דם ברית, על מה נחלקו – על גר שנתגייר כשהוא מהול. ונראה שעל זה סמכו ה"ג, דסברי להו כאמוראי דהתם, דאית להו דקטן אין צריך, ובגר סברי כר' יוסי דשמעתין, דמשמע דהלכתא כוותיה. ובפרק "הערל" (לקמן דף עב.) פליגי רבי אלעזר בר"ש ורבנן בגר שנתגייר כשהוא מהול אם נמול ביום או אפי' בלילה, אבל כולהו מודו דצריך הטפת דם ברית. **שמע** מינה דגר צריך שלשה. וא"ת: ודלמא דאיקלעו? וי"ל: דמרב ספרא דייק, שהרי ר' חייא הזכירו לפי שהיה בעל מעשה וראש, ורב יוסף הזכיר רבי אושעיא חברו, אבל רב ספרא – למה הזכיר ר' אושעיא בר' חייא. **אינו** גר עד שימול ויטבול. מהכא לא מצי לדקדק דלא תיסגי בטבילה לחודה, ולא בא לדקדק אלא דמילה בלא טבילה לא מהניא. **אין** מטבילין גר בלילה. דמשפט כתיב ביה, ואע"פ שכבר מל – חשיב ליה כתחילת דין. **משפט** כתיב ביה. "ושפטתם צדק בין איש ובין אחיו ובין גרו" (דברים א). אי נמי – "משפט אחד יהיה לכם ולגר" (במדבר טו). ואפי' למ"ד בסנהדרין (דף ג. ושם) דבר

אין לי אלא בארץ, בחו"ל מנין? תלמוד לומר "אתך" — בכל מקום שאתך. אם כן מה ת"ל "בארץ" — בארץ צריך להביא ראיה, בחו"ל — אין צריך להביא ראיה. דברי ר' יהודה. וחכמים אומרים: בין בארץ בין בחוצה לארץ — צריך להביא ראיה. בא הוא ועדיו עמו — קרא למה לי? אמר רב ששת, דאמרי: שמענו שנתגייר בב"ד של פלוני. סד"א: לא ליהמנייהו, קמ"ל. (א) "בארץ", אין לי אלא בארץ, בח"ל מנין? ת"ל "אתך" — בכל מקום שאתך. והא אפיקתיה! חדא מ"אתך" וחדא[א] מ"עמך". וחכ"א: בין בארץ בין בח"ל צריך להביא ראיה. ואלא, הא כתיב (ב) "בארץ"! ההוא מיבעי ליה דאפילו בארץ מקבלים גרים. דסד"א: משום טיבותא דארץ ישראל קמגיירי, והשתא נמי דליכא טיבותא — איכא לקט שכחה ופאה ומעשר עני, קמ"ל. א"ר חייא בר אבא אמר ר' יוחנן: א הלכה, בין בארץ בין בח"ל — צריך להביא ראיה. פשיטא, *יחיד ורבים הלכה כרבים! מהו דתימא: מסתבר טעמא דרבי יהודה, דקמסייעי ליה קראי, קמ"ל. ת"ר: °"ושפטתם צדק בין איש ובין אחיו ובין גרו" מכאן א"ר יהודה: גר שנתגייר בב"ד — הרי זה גר, בינו לבין עצמו — אינו גר. מעשה באחד שבא לפני רבי יהודה, ואמר לו: נתגיירתי ביני לבין עצמי. א"ל רבי יהודה: יש לך עדים? אמר ליה: לאו. יש לך בנים? א"ל: הן. א"ל: ב נאמן אתה לפסול את עצמך, ואי אתה נאמן לפסול את בניך. — [ומי] א"ר יהודה אבנים לא מהימן? *והתניא: °"יכיר" — יכירנו לאחרים. מכאן א"ר יהודה: ג נאמן אדם לומר: זה בני בכור. ד וכשם שנאמן לומר זה בני בכור כך נאמן לומר: בני זה בן גרושה הוא, או בן חלוצה הוא. וחכ"א: אינו נאמן. א"ר נחמן בר יצחק, ה"ק ליה: לדבריך גוי אתה, ואין עדות לגוי. רבינא אמר: הכי קאמר ליה: יש לך בנים? הן, יש לך בני בנים? הן. א"ל: נאמן אתה לפסול בניך, ואי אתה נאמן לפסול בני בניך. תניא נמי הכי, ר' יהודה אומר: ה נאמן אדם לומר על בנו קטן, ואין נאמן על בנו גדול. ואמר ר' חייא בר אבא א"ר יוחנן: לא קטן קטן ממש, ולא גדול גדול ממש, אלא, קטן ויש לו בנים — זהו גדול, גדול ואין לו בנים — זהו קטן. והלכתא כוותיה דרב נחמן בר יצחק. והתניא כוותיה דרבינא! ו ההוא לענין "יכיר" איתמר. תנו רבנן: ז גר שבא להתגייר בזמן הזה אומרים לו: מה ראית שבאת להתגייר? אי אתה יודע שישראל בזמן הזה דוויים, דחופים, סחופים ומטורפין, ויסורין באין עליהם? אם אומר: יודע אני ואיני כדאי — מקבלין אותו מיד. ומודיעין אותו מקצת מצות קלות, ומקצת מצות חמורות, ומודיעין אותו עון לקט שכחה ופאה ומעשר עני, ומודיעין אותו ענשן של מצות, אומרים לו: הוי יודע שעד שלא באת למדה זו, אכלת חלב — אי אתה ענוש כרת, חללת שבת — אי אתה ענוש סקילה. ועכשיו, אכלת חלב — ענוש כרת, חללת שבת — ענוש סקילה. וכשם שמודיעין אותו ענשן של מצות, כך מודיעין אותו מתן שכרן. אומרים לו: הוי יודע שהעולם הבא אינו עשוי אלא לצדיקים, וישראל בזמן הזה אינם יכולים לקבל

לא

רש"י

בכל מקום שאתך. ולקמן פריך הא אפיקתיה. צריך להביא ראיה. שבב"ד נתגייר, שמא גבעוני מהול הוא, ומשום שבחא דא"י הוא דקאמר הכי, ומשקר: ה"ג: מהו דתימא לא ליהמניהו: [ב] מעמך. "גר ותושב וחי עמך" (ויקרא כה). דליכא טובה. דפסק חלב ודבש. דקמסייעי קראי. דהא עמך — כל מקום שאתך משמע, ואפילו בארץ. "ובארצכם" למה לי? אלא לאו ארחיה קאי. דבארץ צריך להביא ראיה, ולא בחוצה לארץ: מדכתיב (ג) גר אצל "ושפטתם", מכאן אמר ר' יהודה: גר בעי בית דין. יכיר. "את הבכור בן השנואה יכיר". יכירנו לאחרים. שאם אין ב"ד מכירים אותו — נאמן עליו אביו לומר: זה בני בכור ליטול פי שנים. בן גרושה הוא. וכהן חלל הוא. ואין עדות לגוי. ה"אל ובניך מוחזקין בכשרות — אין אתה נאמן להעיד עליהן ולפוסלן. לפסול את בניך. דנפקא לן מ"יכיר", ואי אתה נאמן לפסול את בני בניך. והלכתא כרב נחמן. דאמר לדבריו גוי הוא, ואין עדות לגוי, ואפילו אבניו לא מהימן. והתניא כרבינא. דנאמן הוא על בנו קטן שאין לו בנים. וקס"ד דהא מתני' בגר שבא ואמר גר אני קמיירי. ההיא. דקתני נאמן הוא על בנו קטן. לענין יכיר. תניא, אההיא מתני' דיכיר קאי, דקתני וכשם שנאמן אדם לומר זה בני בכור כך נאמן לומר זה בני בן גרושה. ועלה קתני דנאמן הוא על הקטן, דהא ישראל הוא ויש לו עדות, והתורה האמינתו על בנו, ולא על בן בנו. אבל גבי גר — אפילו אבנו לא מהימן, דאין עדות לגוי. וסחופין. שפלים וכפויין. כמו סחופי כסא (שבת דף סו:) — כפיית הכלי. ואיני כדאי. ואיני ראוי להשתתף בצרתן, ומי יתן ואזכה לכך. ומודיעים אותו. לקמן מפרש טעמא דכולה מתני'.

תוספות

דבר תורה חד נמי כשר — הכא מדמין לגזילות וחבלות, דבעינן שלשה לכ"ע. ור' יוחנן דהכא אית ליה בהדיא (ד) בירושלמי דשנים שדנו אין דיניהם דין. וא"ת: ואנן היכי מקבלין גרים? הא בעינן מומחין! וי"ל: דשליחותייהו עבדינן, כדמשמע נמי בשילהי "המגרש" (גיטין דף פח: ושם). וכמו שחשו לנעילת דלת בפני לווין חשו נמי לנעילת דלת בפני גרים*.

*במוחזק לך. אומר רבינו תם דדוקא בדידעינן דהוה גוי מעיקרא, דאי לא הוה ידעינן — מהימן, מגו דאי בעי אמר, ישראל אני, דמהימן, כדמשמע בריש מסכת פסחים (דף ג: ושם) גבי ההוא גוי דהוה סליק ואכיל פסחים בירושלים. ואין לומר שאני התם דהוו סמכי ארובא דהוו ישראל — דהא בכל מקום נמי איכא רובא, דרוב הבאין לפנינו בתורת יהודות ישראל הם. ועוד ראיה משמעתין, דאמר ליה ר"י: אי אתה נאמן לפסול את בניך. ואיהו גופיה כשר, אלא דשוי נפשיה חתיכה דאיסורא. אבל אם בא על בת כהן לא פסלה, כדפי' לעיל. (ה) ומההיא דלעיל (דף מה.) דא"ל: זיל גלי — אין ראיה, דשמא לא היו בודקים אלא אם הוא ישראל אם לאו, אבל במשפחתו לא היו בודקין.

אין לי אלא בארץ. פי': דמקבלין גרים. ואע"ג דחובת הגוף היא — בעיא ריבויא, כיון דכתיב "בארץ". כדאשכחן בסוף פ"ק דקידושין (דף לח:) גבי שילוח עבדים והשמטת כספים. אי נמי: בארץ לא חיישינן דלמא הדרי בהו, משום דאיכא שבחא דארץ ישראל.

מהו דתימא לא להימניהו. ויש ספרים דגרסי: מהו דתימא ליהמניהו, וה"פ: ליהמניהו כעד מפי עד. **יש** לך עדים. פירוש: שנתגיירת בינך לבין עצמך. ותימה: מיהא, אי הא דבעינן ג' היינו דוקא לכתחלה, אבל דיעבד חד נמי כשר — א"כ אם יש לו עדים לאו בינו לבין עצמו הוא.

נאמן אתה לפסול עצמך כו'. היינו דוקא במילי דמשוי נפשיה חתיכה דאיסורא, אבל אם בא על בת כהן — לא פסלה, כדפרישית לעיל בסוף פ' שני (דף כה: ושם). וא"ת: היכי דמי? אם אשתו גויה — ממה נפשך בניו פסולים, דאין קרוי בנך אלא בנה. ואם היתה אשתו ישראלית — ממה נפשך בניו כשרים, דקי"ל (לעיל דף מה.): גוי ועבד הבא על בת ישראל — הולד כשר. וכי תימא נהי דממזר לא הוי — פגום מיהא הוי, הא השתא נמי דאין נאמן פגומין הם, דר"י אית ליה בפרק "עשרה יוחסין" (קדושין עז.) דבת גר זכר כבת חלל זכר! וי"ל: דקסבר ר"י גוי ועבד הבא על בת ישראל הולד ממזר, דבפרק "ד' מיתות" (סנהדרין דף נג. ושם) אמר דר' יהודה סבר לה כרבי עקיבא דאמר אין קידושין תופסין בחייבי לאוין.

כך נאמן אדם לומר זה בן גרושה. ר' אליהו מפרי"ש מפרש דנפקא לן מדכתיב "בן השנואה יכיר" (דברים כא). וכן משמע בירושלמי בפרק בתרא דקידושין. ולשון הש"ס לא משמע הכי, דקתני: כשם שנאמן אדם לומר זה בני בכור — משמע דמינה גמר. וי"מ דטעמא דר' יהודה, דמשמע ליה קרא דנאמן אדם לומר זה בני בכור אפי' על תינוק בין הבנים. וכשאומר על הקטן שהוא בכור — א"כ הראשון ממזר, אלמא דנאמן לפוסלו. וה"נ דנאמן לומר שהוא בן גרושה.

ואין עדות לגוי. ועל עצמו נאמן, משום דשוי נפשיה חתיכה דאיסורא. **ואין** אתה נאמן לפסול בני בניך. אומר ר"י דה"פ: נאמן אתה לפסול בניך, פי': כשאין לו אלא בנים ואין לו בני בנים, ואי אתה נאמן לפסול בני בניך — כשיש לו בני בנים אין נאמן לפסול אפי' בניו, דאין סברא לומר שיהיו בניו פסולים ובני בניו כשרים. וכן משמע בסמוך, דקאמר: ואין אדם נאמן על בנו גדול, ומפרש כשיש לו בנים, משמע דאבנו נמי לא מהימן. **והלכתא** כוותיה דרב נחמן בר יצחק. משמע דהלכה כר"י, דנאמן אף לפסול בניו, דדוקא משום דאין עדות לגוי דאין יכול לפוסלן. ולא כמו שמפרש רבינו תם דאין הלכה כרבי יהודה אלא כשפוסל אחרים על ידי הכרת בכור, אבל בלא הכרת בכור לא. ובשאלתות בפרשת *"וירא" נמי דקדק מהך דשמעתין דבכל ענין הלכה כרבי יהודה.

מטבילין

עין משפט נר מצוה

קכז א מיי' פי"ג מהל' איסורי ביאה הל' ז סמג לאוין קטז טוש"ע י"ד סי' רסח סעיף י:

[וע"ע תוס' קידושין סב: ד"ה גר]

*שייך לעמוד הקודם

קכח ב מיי' שם הלכה ח טוש"ע שם סי"א:

קכט ג מיי' פ"ב מהל' נחלות הלכה יד סמג עשין צו טוש"ע ח"מ סימן רעז סעי' יב:

קל ד מיי' פט"ו מהל' איסורי ביאה הל' טז סמג לאוין קטז:

קלא ה ו מיי' שם הל' טז וסמג שם טוש"ע אה"ע סימן ד סעיף כט:

קלב ז מיי' פי"ג שם הל' יד ופי"ד הל' א סמג לאוין קטז טוש"ע י"ד סימן רסח סעיף ב:

תוספות חד מקמאי

וכבר כתבתי מזה כל הצורך בפר"א דמילה: א"ר יוחנן בין בארץ בין בחוצה לארץ צריך להביא ראיה כשהוא מוחזק בעובד כוכבים אבל אם אינו מוחזק א"צ להביא ראיה. הפה שאסר הוא הפה שהתיר דאי בעי אמר ישראל אני מאבותי. וראיה לדבר ההוא גוי דהוה אכיל פסחים בירושלים בפרק קמא דפסחים: מעשה באחד שבא לפני ר' יהודה וא"ל נתגיירתי ביני לבין עצמי וכו' פי' לא היו מוחזקים בו שהוא גוי דא"כ היה צריך להביא ראיה עליו ועל בניו אלא היו מוחזקים בו שהיה גר. ושאל לו ר' יהודה יש לך עדים כלו' יש לך עדים שנתגיירת בינך לבין עצמך אפילו בניו פסולים ואם יש עדים שנתגיירת בפני ב"ד או א) בפניהם קבל עליו עול מצות שהודיעוהו [הרי] הוא גר גמור והוא עצמו כשר ומיירי שנתגייר הוא ובניו דאם נתגייר הוא לבדו ובא אח"כ על גיורת או על בת ישראל הרי בניו כשרים. דקי"ל גוי ועבד הבא על בת ישראל הולד כשר ואם לבתה האמר ר' יהודה בת גר זכר כבת חלל זכר. והיכא דאמרי סהדי שמענו שנתגייר בב"ד פלוני מהימנין ליה. תניא א"ר יהודה נאמן הוא על בנו קטן לאמר שהוא בן גרושה או בן חלוצה ואינו נאמן על בנו גדול. א"ר חייא בר אבא א"ר (שמעון) [יוחנן] לא קטן קטן ממש ולא גדול גדול ממש אלא קטן ויש לו בנים זהו גדול גדול ואין לו בנים זהו קטן כלומר נאמן הוא על בנו כשאין לו בנים אבל אם יש לו בנים אינו נאמן אפלו אבנו דאבריה המניה רחמנא ולא אבר בריה:

א) לעתו דבדיעבד אפי' דקבלת עול מצות בלבד הי' בפני ב"ד נמי סגי ועי' בטוש"ע יו"ד סימן רס"ח סעיף ג'.

מסורת הש"ס

[ברכות ע. וש"נ]

קידושין עד עח: ב"ב קכ:

[נ"ל ולאוין ס"ם מ"א]

הגהות הב"ח

(א) גמ' קמ"ל בארצכם אין לי: (ב) שם הא כתיב בארצכם ההוא: (ג) רש"י ד"ה מדכתיב גרו אצל: (ד) תוס' ד"ה משפט (בעמוד הקודם) אית ליה בהדיא. נ"ב עי' סנהדרין ב' ע"ב תוד"ה דברי הכל: (ה) ד"ה במוחזק וכו' כדפי' לעיל. נ"ב בפ' שני דף כה ע"ב בד"ה לימא:

הגהות הגר"א

[א] גמ' מעמך. נ"ל מאתכם (דכתיב כתר וכי יגור כו' הגר אתכם וכ"ה בתורת כהנים ומ"ש הש"י הוא תמוה): [ב] רש"י ד"ה מעמך כו' עד סה"ד. נמחק:

גליון הש"ס

גמ' א"ל נאמן אתה לפסול את עצמך. ע' כתובות כה ע"ב תד"ה הרי נאמר: שם ואי אתה נאמן לפסול את בניך. ע' לעיל כה ע"ב תד"ה לימא רב יוסף: תום' ד"ה במוחזק לך וכו' דרוב הבאין וש' עיין ירושלמי רפ"ב דר"ה וקרבן עדה שם: ד"ה נאמן אתה לפסול וכו' דמשוי נפשיה חתיכה דאיסורא. ע' במרדכי סוף פירקין:

מטבילין אותו מיד. משמע שהמילה קודם טבילה, וכדאמר: אין גר עד שימול ויטבול. ותימה: דאמר ב"הערל" (לקמן דף עח.) מעוברת שנתגיירה בנה אין צריך טבילה! ואר"י: דשאני התם, דאכתי לא חזי למילה. **במקום** שהנדה טובלת. טבילת נדה לא כתב קרא בהדיא, ופי' רב יהודה גאון דנפקא לן בק"ו ממגעה דטעון טבילה – וכ"ש היא עצמה. ור"ת מפרש דנפקא לן מהא דדרשינן בע"ז (דף עה:): "אך במי נדה יתחטא" – מים שהנדה טובלת בהם, וכמה הם – מ' סאה. ורבינו יצחק פירש: דנפקא מהא דדרשינן בפ' "במה אשה" (שבת דף סד:) תהיה בנדתה – תהא בנדתה עד שתבא במים* א). **שם** גר ועבד טובלים. בכולי שמעתין משמע דעבד בעי טבילה כשמשתחרר, ולא סגי ליה בטבילה קמייתא. וקשה: דב"השולח" (גיטין דף מ.) אמרינן: הכותב שטר אירוסין לשפחתו, ואמר לה הרי את מקודשת לי בו והתקדשי בו – משמע דמקודשת, אע"ג דלא טבלה! וי"ל: דאיירי כגון שטבלה מקודם לשם שחרור, שהטבילה של שחרור קודמת לגט, כדמשמע לקמן, דקתני: ומטבילה לשם שחרור ומשחררה, ומותר בה מיד.

וכל דבר שחוצץ בטבילה כו' ובנדה. תימה: דלענין הכשר מקוה פשיטא ליה שאין לחלק בין נדה לבעלה, ובין טהרות, דקאמר: במקום שהנדה טובלת. ולענין חציצה תלי נדה בטבילת טומאה וטהרה! וי"ל: דבחציצה דאיכא מילי טובא דלא הוי אלא מדרבנן, כגון רובו ואינו מקפיד, או מיעוטו ומקפיד, איצטריך לאשמועינן דבחציצה דרבנן נמי אין לחלק בין לבעלה לטהרות, ואיכא מילי דחציצה דאמר בפ' בתרא דנדה (דף סז. ושם): ה"מ – לטהרות, אבל לבעלה – לא, והיינו ספק חציצה, אבל ודאי חציצה, אפילו דרבנן – לא הקילו לבעלה יותר מלטהרות. ובקונטרס לא גרס ליה במסכת נדה משום הא דהכא.

קשים גרים לישראל (ב) כספחת. לפי שאין בקיאין בדקדוקי מצות, וישראל למדין ממעשיהם. ובמס' נדה (דף יג: ושם) פירש בקונטרס עוד לשון אחר: משום דכל ישראל ערבים זה בזה. *וקשה: דבפרק "אלו נאמרים" (סוטה דף לז:) משמע שלא היו ערבין על הגרים, דלא חשיב התם ערבות של ערב רב! ועוד י"ל: דקשים גרים לישראל – לפי שמתערבין בהם, ואין שכינה שורה אלא על משפחות המיוחסות שבישראל. וי"מ: לפי שביותר הוזהרו ישראל על הגרים, ואין יכולין להזהר מאונאתן* ב). אלא

לא רוב טובה ולא רוב פורענות. [א]ואין מרבין עליו, ואין מדקדקין עליו. קיבל – מלין אותו מיד. נשתיירו בו ציצין המעכבין את המילה – חוזרים ומלין אותו שניה. נתרפא – מטבילין אותו מיד. ושני ת"ח עומדים על גביו, ומודיעין אותו מקצת מצות קלות ומקצת מצות חמורות. טבל ועלה – הרי הוא כישראל לכל דבריו. אשה – נשים מושיבות אותה במים עד צוארה, ושני ת"ח עומדים לה מבחוץ, ומודיעין אותה מקצת מצות קלות ומקצת מצות חמורות. [ב]אחד גר ואחד עבד משוחרר. [ג]ובמקום שנדה טובלת – שם גר ועבד משוחרר טובלין. וכל דבר שחוצץ בטבילה – חוצץ בגר ובעבד משוחרר ובנדה. אמר מר: גר שבא להתגייר אומרים לו: מה ראית שבאת להתגייר? ומודיעים אותו מקצת מצות קלות ומקצת מצות חמורות. מ"ט? דאי פריש – נפרוש. *דא"ר חלבו: [ד]קשים גרים לישראל כספחת, דכתיב °"ונלוה הגר עליהם ונספחו על בית יעקב".§ (ישעיה יד) "ומודיעים אותו עון לקט שכחה ופאה ומעשר עני".§ מ"ט? א"ר חייא בר אבא א"ר יוחנן: *[ה]בן נח נהרג על פחות משוה פרוטה, ולא ניתן להשבון. (*ומודיעים אותו עון שכחה ופאה).§ "ואין מרבים עליו ואין מדקדקים עליו".§ אמר רבי אלעזר: מאי קראה – דכתיב °"ותרא כי מתאמצת היא ללכת אתה ותחדל לדבר אליה", (רות א) אמרה לה: אסיר לן תחום שבת – °"באשר תלכי אלך", (שם) אסיר לן יחוד – °"באשר תליני אלין", (שם) מפקדינן שש מאות וי"ג מצות – °"עמך עמי", (שם) אסיר לן עבודה זרה – °"ואלהיך אלהי", (שם) *ארבע מיתות נמסרו לב"ד – °"באשר תמותי אמות", (שם) *ב' קברים נמסרו לב"ד – °"ושם אקבר". (שם) מיד – "ותרא כי מתאמצת היא וגו'".§ "קיבל – מלין אותו מיד".§ מ"ט? *שהויי מצוה לא משהינן.§ "נשתיירו בו ציצין המעכבין המילה וכו'".§ כדתנן: *[ו]אלו הן ציצין המעכבין המילה: בשר החופה את רוב העטרה, ואינו אוכל בתרומה. וא"ר ירמיה בר אבא אמר רב: [ז]בשר החופה רוב גובהה של עטרה.§ "נתרפא מטבילין אותו מיד",§ נתרפא – אין, לא נתרפא – לא. מאי טעמא? משום *דמיא מרזו מכה.§ ו"שני ת"ח עומדים על גביו".§ והא *א"ר חייא א"ר יוחנן: גר צריך שלשה! הא א"ר יוחנן לתנא: תני שלשה.§ "טבל ועלה הרי הוא כישראל לכל דבריו".§ למאי הלכתא? [ח]דאי הדר ביה, ומקדש בת ישראל – ישראל מומר קרינא ביה, וקידושיו קידושין.§ "אחד גר ואחד עבד משוחרר".§ קסלקא דעתך לקבל עליו עול מצות, ורמינהו: במה דברים אמורים – בגר, [ט]אבל בעבד משוחרר – אין צריך לקבל! אמר רב ששת: לא קשיא, הא – ר"ש בן אלעזר, הא – רבנן. דתניא, °"ובכתה את אביה ואת אמה וגו'" (דברים כא) בד"א – שלא קבלה עליה, אבל קבלה עליה – מטבילה, *ומותר בה מיד. ר"ש בן אלעזר אומר: אע"פ שלא קבלה עליה – כופה, ומטבילה לשם שפחות, וחוזר ומטבילה לשם שחרור, ומשחררה, ומותר

לא רוב הטובה. לפי שאין הרע מחזר אחריהן, כדאמרי' במס' סוכה (דף נב:), ושמא תזוח דעתן עלייהו, ויחטאו. ואין מרבין עליו. דברים, לאיים עליו שיפרוש. ציצין. חתיכות בשר, שלא נפרעת המילה כהלכתה. ומודיעין אותו מקצת מצות. דהשתא, ע"י טבילה, הוא נכנס לכלל גירות, הלכך בשעת טבילת מצוה צריך לקבל עליו עול מצות. אחד גר ואחד עבד משוחרר. לקמן מפרש למאי הלכתא אקשינהו. ובמקום שנדה טובלת. בארבעים סאה. שם גר ועבד משוחרר טובלין. ואע"פ שאין טבילתו משום טומאה וטהרה כשאר טבילות. חוצץ בגר ועבד משוחרר ובנדה. לבעלה, ואע"פ שאין טבילתן לענין מגע טהרות כשאר טבילות. דאי פריש. שלא יתגייר. נפרוש. ולא איכפת לן. דאמר מר קשים גרים לישראל כספחת דכתיב ונלוה הגר עליהם ונספחו על בית יעקב. לשון ספחת, שאוחזין מעשיהם הראשונים, ולומדים ישראל מהם, או סומכין עליהם באיסור והיתר. ומודיעין אותו עון לקט שכחה ופאה. שלא יאמרו: עניים הללו המלקטין פאת שדה – גזלנים הם, ועומד עליהם והורגם בדיניהם, שבני נח הוזהרו על הגזל, בסנהדרין (דף נו.), ואזהרתן זו היא מיתתן, דלא בעו התראה. לפיכך בן נח נהרג על פחות משוה פרוטה, דגוי קפיד על דבר מועט, ולגבי ישראל הויא מחילה. ולא ניתן להשבון. אינו בחזרה, אלא נהרג. דגבי ישראל כתיב "והשיב את הגזלה אשר גזל" (ויקרא ה), אבל בני נח אמרינן בסנהדרין (דף נח:): אזהרתן זו היא מיתתן. וכיון שעבר על אחת מז' מצות – נהרג. לישנא אחרינא: מודיעים אותו עון לקט שכחה ופאה. הואיל והן מקפידים על הממון כ"כ, כדאמר דנהרג על פחות משוה פרוטה – מודיעין אותו עון לקט כו' שמא יחזור בו מלהתגייר. ולשון זה עיקר, דאי משום טעמא קמא – מאי לשון עון לקט שכחה ופאה? יודיעוהו (א) שילקטו עניים בשדהו. אסיר לן יחוד. להתייחד עם אשת איש. ב' קברים. אחד לנסקלים ולנשרפים שהרשיעו בעבירות חמורות, ואחד לנהרגים ולנחנקים שאין מיתתן חמורה, ואינם רשעים כל כך. עטרה. שורה גבוהה שסביב הגיד, וממנה הולך ומשפע למעלה ולמטה. רוב גובהה. של אותה שורה, ולא תימא רוב היקיפה. ואין אוכל בתרומה. אם כהן הוא. דכהן ערל אסור בתרומה, כדאמר לקמן בפרק "הערל". מרזו מכה. מכבידין את חולי המכה, כמו מטרא רזיא לאילני במסכת תענית (דף ג:). דאי הדר ביה. לקדמותו, ואח"כ קידש בת ישראל – מקודשת, וצריכה גט. דישראל מומר קידושיו קידושין, דישראל הוא. קס"ד. דהאי דאקיש שיחרור של עבד לגירות הגוי לקבל קאמר, שבשעת טבילת שחרור העבד צריך להודיעו מקצת מצות. אבל עבד אין צריך לקבל. בשעת שחרור, דמשעה שטובל לשם עבדות שייך במצות, דכתיב (דברים ה) "למען ינוח עבדך ואמתך". ועוד: דגמרי' (חגיגה דף ד.) "לה" "לה" מאשה. שלא קבלה עליה. להתגייר. כופה ומטבילה לשם שפחות. דכל טבילות עבדים על כרחן היא. ומשחררה. ומטבילה לשם שחרור בע"כ. ומותר

עין משפט נר מצוה:
קלג א מיי' פי"ד מהל' איסורי ביאה הל' ב סמג לאוין קטז טוש"ע י"ד סימן רסח סעיף ב:
קלד ב מיי' שם הל' ט סמג שם טוש"ע שם סימן רסח סעיף ב:
קלה ג מיי' שם פי"ג הל' יג ד מיי' פ"א מהל' מקואות הל' כב סמג שם טוש"ע שם סימן רסח סעיף ב:
קלו ד מיי' פי"ג מהל' איסורי ביאה הל' יח:
קלז ה מיי' פ"ט מהל' מלכים הלכה ט:
[ע' תוספות חגיגה יח. ד"ה לא נצרכה ותוס' יומא עח. ד"ה מכלל]
קלח ו ז מיי' פי"ד מהל' מילה הל' ג סמג עשין כח טוש"ע י"ד סי' רסד סעיף ד:
קלט ח מיי' פי"ג מהל' איסורי ביאה הל' יז סמג לאוין קטז טוש"ע שם סי' רסח סעי' ב:
קמ ט מיי' שם הל' יב סמג שם טוש"ע שם סי' רסח סעיף ז:
קמא י מיי' פ"ח מהל' מלכים הלכה ה:

גליון הש"ס
גמ' קשים גרים לישראל כספחת. וברמב"ם פי"ג הל' י"ח מהל' א"ב איתא כנגע לרעת:

[צ"ל וקשה]
[וע"ע תוס' קידושין ע: ובנדה יג: ד"ה קשים]

מסורת הש"ס:
קידושין ע: וש"נ נדה יג: לקמן קט:
ע"ז עא: ערובין סב.
רש"ל מ"ז
[סנהדרין מג:]
[שם מו.]
[לעיל לט.]
לקמן שבת קכ.
[לקמן קכ: קכח.]
[לעיל מו:]

הגהות הב"ח
(א) רש"י ד"ה לקמא אחרינא וכו' יודיעוהו שמפיו שילקטו: (ב) תוס' ד"ה קשים גרים לישראל כספחת. כ"ב עיין בתוס' פ' י' יוחסין דף ע ע"ב:

[אין הפירוש שמותר לבא עליה מיד דהא בעיא להמתין ג' חדשים ע' כ"מ פ"ח מהל' מלכים דין ה.]

תוספות ישנים
שתלא נפשו גבי ימול גוי ואל ימול כותי לפי שהוא מל לשם הר גריזים וי"ל דהתם עדיף טפי לפי שהישראל עומד ע"ג של כותי: **א)** עי"מ מק"ו דכתיב יכבס בגדיו כ"ש היא עצמה שצריכה טבילה וי"מ דכתיב ומזה מי הנדה מכאן לנדה שצריכה מים: **ב)** עי"מ לפי שהקב"ה מעניש אותנו על ידם כשמטיבים מעשיהם ואומר כי הוא רואה שאין אנו נזהרים במצות כמותם אע"פ שאינם מזרע כשר כמותו: **ומודיעין** אותו עון לקט שכחה ופאה מפני שאנו חוששין פן ירוא העניים באים בשדותיהם ללקוט לקט שכחה ופאה ויהרגו אותם כמו שהם עושים בדיניהם מפני שבן נח נהרג על פחות משוה פרוטה ולא ניתן להשבון שאזהרה שלהם זו היא מיתתן ולא קרינן בהו והשיב את הגזלה ונהרגין בלא התראה דבן נח א"צ התראה. י"מ מודיעין אותו עון לקט מפני שמקפידים על ממון מועט וחיישינן שמא יחזרו לסורן ומשמע מודיעין אותו לו שינוי ואל יקפיד ואי פריש מהשתא נפרוש לפי שיוסיף עינו לרה. וזה הפי' נראה אבל פירוש קמא לא נהירא דא"כ דלא חיישינן אלא שמא יהרגו עניים בדיניהם העניים. מה לנו להודיעם עון לקט שכחה ופאה נאמר להם הזהרו שלא תהרגו עניים כשיבואו ללקוט בשדותיכם כי דינם בזה אבל השתא ניחא עון לקט וכו':

[גמרא]

וּמוּתָּר בָּהּ מִיָּד. אֲמַר רָבָא: מַאי טַעֲמָא דְּרַבִּי שִׁמְעוֹן בֶּן אֶלְעָזָר – דִּכְתִיב °"כָּל עֶבֶד אִישׁ מִקְנַת כָּסֶף", עֶבֶד אִישׁ •וְלֹא עֶבֶד אִשָּׁה?! אֶלָּא: עֶבֶד אִישׁ אַתָּה מָל בְּעַל כָּרְחוֹ, וְאִי אַתָּה מָל בֶּן אִישׁ בְּעַל כָּרְחוֹ. וְרַבָּנַן? אֲמַר עוּלָּא: כְּשֵׁם שֶׁאִי אַתָּה מָל בֶּן אִישׁ בְּעַל כָּרְחוֹ כָּךְ אִי אַתָּה מָל עֶבֶד אִישׁ בְּעַל כָּרְחוֹ. וְאֶלָּא, הָכְתִיב "כָּל עֶבֶד אִישׁ"! הַהוּא מִיבָּעֵי לֵיהּ לִכְדִשְׁמוּאֵל. *דְּאָמַר שְׁמוּאֵל: [א]הַמַּפְקִיר עַבְדּוֹ יָצָא לְחֵירוּת, וְאֵין צָרִיךְ גֵּט שִׁחְרוּר, שֶׁנֶּאֱמַר "כָּל עֶבֶד אִישׁ מִקְנַת כָּסֶף", עֶבֶד אִישׁ וְלֹא עֶבֶד אִשָּׁה? אֶלָּא: עֶבֶד שֶׁיֵּשׁ לוֹ רְשׁוּת לְרַבּוֹ עָלָיו – קָרוּי עֶבֶד, וְשֶׁאֵין רְשׁוּת לְרַבּוֹ עָלָיו – אֵין קָרוּי עֶבֶד. מַתְקִיף לָהּ רַב פָּפָּא: אֵימוּר דִּשְׁמַעְתְּ לְהוּ לְרַבָּנַן בִּיפַת תּוֹאַר, דְּלָא שַׁיְיכָא בְּמִצְוֹת. אֲבָל עֶבֶד דְּשַׁיֵּיךְ בְּמִצְוֹת – •הָכִי נַמִי דְּאַפִּי' רַבָּנַן מוֹדוּ. דְּתַנְיָא: אֶחָד גֵּר וְאֶחָד לוֹקֵחַ עֶבֶד מִן הַגּוֹי צָרִיךְ לְקַבֵּל. הָא לוֹקֵחַ מִיִּשְׂרָאֵל – אֵין צָרִיךְ לְקַבֵּל, מַנִּי? אִי רַבִּי שִׁמְעוֹן בֶּן אֶלְעָזָר – הָאָמַר לוֹקֵחַ מִן הַגּוֹי נַמִי אֵין צָרִיךְ לְקַבֵּל. אֶלָּא לָאו – רַבָּנַן, וְשׁ"מ: [ב]דְּלוֹקֵחַ מִן הַגּוֹי צָרִיךְ לְקַבֵּל, אֲבָל לוֹקֵחַ מִיִּשְׂרָאֵל – אֵין צָרִיךְ לְקַבֵּל. וְאֶלָּא קַשְׁיָא אֶחָד גֵּר וְאֶחָד עֶבֶד מְשׁוּחְרָר! [ג]כִּי תַּנְיָא הַהִיא – לְעִנְיַן טְבִילָה תַּנְיָא. תָּנוּ רַבָּנַן: °"וְגִלְּחָה אֶת רֹאשָׁהּ וְעָשְׂתָה אֶת צִפָּרְנֶיהָ" רַבִּי אֱלִיעֶזֶר אוֹמֵר: תָּקוֹץ, רַבִּי עֲקִיבָא אוֹמֵר: [ד]תַּגְדִּיל. אָמַר רַבִּי אֱלִיעֶזֶר: נֶאֶמְרָה עֲשִׂיָּה בָּרֹאשׁ וְנֶאֶמְרָה עֲשִׂיָּה בַּצִּפָּרְנַיִם, מָה לְהַלָּן הַעֲבָרָה – אַף כָּאן הַעֲבָרָה. רַבִּי עֲקִיבָא אוֹמֵר: נֶאֱמַר עֲשִׂיָּה בָּרֹאשׁ, וְנֶאֱמַר עֲשִׂיָּה בַּצִּפָּרְנַיִם. מַה לְּהַלָּן נִיוּוּל – אַף כָּאן נִיוּוּל. וּרְאָיָה לְדִבְרֵי רַבִּי אֱלִיעֶזֶר °"וּמְפִבֹשֶׁת בֶּן שָׁאוּל יָרַד לִקְרַאת הַמֶּלֶךְ לֹא עָשָׂה רַגְלָיו וְלֹא עָשָׂה שְׂפָמוֹ". מַאי עֲשִׂיָּה – הַעֲבָרָה. ת"ר: °"וּבָכְתָה אֶת אָבִיהָ וְאֶת אִמָּהּ", רַ'

[גמרא marginal references: שמות יב | דברים כא | שמואל ב יט | דברים כא]

[רש"י]

וּמוּתָּר בָּהּ מִיָּד. אַלְמָא: לְר' שִׁמְעוֹן עֶבֶד אֵין צָרִיךְ לְקַבֵּל בִּשְׁעַת טְבִילַת שִׁחְרוּר. •וּלְרַבָּנַן, דְּלָא הָוֵי תַּקַּנְתָּא כְּהָכִי – סָבְרִי צָרִיךְ לְקַבֵּל. עֶבֶד אִישׁ וְלֹא עֶבֶד אִשָּׁה. בִּתְמִיָּה. וְאִשָּׁה שֶׁקָּנְתָה עֲבָדִים וְלָא מָלוּ, מִי לָא הָווּ כִּשְׁאָר עֲבָדִים? אֶלָּא ע"כ, הַאי אִישׁ – אַגּוֹי שֶׁמְּכָרוֹ קָאֵי, וּלְמַעוּטֵי בֵּן אִישׁ. וְה"ק: עֶבֶד שֶׁלָּקַחְתָּ מִן הַגּוֹי אַתָּה מָל בְּעַל כָּרְחוֹ שֶׁל עֶבֶד, וְאִי אַתָּה מָל בֵּן גּוֹי בְּעָלְמָא, דְּלָאו עֶבֶד, בְּעַל כָּרְחוֹ. •מִדְּכָתַב רַחֲמָנָא "אִישׁ", קְרָא יְתֵירָא, לְמַעוּטֵי בֵּן אִישׁ, ש"מ "וּמַלְתָּה אוֹתוֹ" בְּעַל כָּרְחוֹ מַשְׁמַע, דְּאִי מִדַּעְתּוֹ – הֵיכִי מְמַעֵט לְבֶן אִישׁ? וְאִי לָא כְּתִיב אִישׁ ה"א הַאי עֶבֶד לָאו לְמַעוּטֵי בֵּן אָתָא, אֶלָּא הָא גּוּפָא אִיצְטְרִיךְ לְאַשְׁמוּעִינַן – דְּמִילַת עֲבָדִים מְעַכְּבָא בַּפֶּסַח. לָשׁוֹן אַחֵר, וְעִיקָּר: "עֶבֶד אִישׁ" ה"ק: עֶבֶד שֶׁהוּא אִישׁ, אע"פ שֶׁהוּא גָּדוֹל וּבֶן דַּעַת – "וּמַלְתָּה אוֹתוֹ" בְּעַל כָּרְחוֹ. וְאִי אַתָּה מָל בֵּן [שֶׁהוּא] אִישׁ, גֵּר הַבָּא לְהִתְגַּיֵּיר אֵין לוֹ כֹּחַ לָמוּל בְּנוֹ גָּדוֹל בְּעַל כָּרְחוֹ. דְּגַבֵּי בָּנִים כְּתִיב "הִמּוֹל לוֹ כָּל זָכָר", וְלָא כְּתִיב בְּהוּ "אִישׁ", וְגַבֵּי עֶבֶד כְּתִיב "אִישׁ" לְמַעוּטֵי בֵּן. וְרַבָּנַן. כְּשֵׁם שֶׁאֵין אַתָּה מָל בֶּן אִישׁ [בְּע"כ], דְּהָא לָא כְּתִיב בְּהוּ אִישׁ. כָּךְ אִי אַתָּה מָל כו'. וּמִילְּתָא בְּעָלְמָא הִיא, וְלָא הֶקֵּישָׁא, אֶלָּא ה"ק לֵיהּ: כִּי הֵיכִי דְּמוֹדֵית לָן בְּבֵן – ה"ה לְעֶבֶד נַמִי, דְּאֵין מְגַיְּירִין בֶּן דַּעַת אֶלָּא מֵרְצוֹנוֹ. אֵימוּר דְּקָא שָׁמְעַתְּ לְרַבָּנַן. דִּפְלִיגִי אַדְּרַבִּי שִׁמְעוֹן, דְּלָא הָוְיָא תַּקַּנְתָּא. בִּיפַת תּוֹאַר. דְּלָא שַׁיְיכָא בְּמִצְוֹת. אֲבָל עֶבֶד. שֶׁשָּׁהָא אֶצְלוֹ כַּמָּה יָמִים, וְנִיהֵג עָלָיו מִצְוֹת הַנּוֹהֲגוֹת בְּעֶבֶד – מִי שָׁמְעַתְּ לְהוּ דְּצָרִיךְ לְקַבֵּל? לְעִנְיַן טְבִילָה תַּנְיָא. שֶׁשְּׁנֵיהֶם שָׁוִים בִּטְבִילָה, שֶׁצְּרִיכִים לִטְבּוֹל כְּשֶׁבָּאִין לִכְלַל יִשְׂרָאֵל גָּמוּר. אֲבָל לְעִנְיַן קַבָּלָה לֹא הוּשְׁווּ, דְּעֶבֶד אֵין צָרִיךְ לְקַבֵּל בִּשְׁעַת טְבִילַת שִׁחְרוּר. תָּקוֹץ. לַצִּפָּרְנַיִם קָאֵי, וְאע"ג דְּלָאו נִיוּוּל גְּזֵירַת הַכָּתוּב הִיא. עֲשִׂיָּה בָּרֹאשׁ. כְּלוֹמַר, נֶאֱמַר שָׁם תִּיקּוּן מִצְוָה בָּרֹאשׁ, דִּכְתִיב "וְגִלְּחָה". לֹא עָשָׂה רַגְלָיו. לֹא קִצֵּץ לְפָרְנֵי רַגְלָיו. וְלֹא עָשָׂה שְׂפָמוֹ. לֹא גִּלַּח שְׂעַר שְׂפָמוֹ. אַלְמָא: עֲשִׂיָּה קָרֵי לְהַעֲבָרָה. כִּי

[תוספות]

אלא עבד איש אתה מל בעל כרחו. פי' בקונט' בלשון שני: דעבד איש, אע"ג שהוא גדול ובן דעת – "ומלתה אותו וגו'" בעל כרחו, ואי אתה מל בן איש, גר הבא להתגייר אין לו כח למול בנו גדול בעל כרחו. דגבי בנים כתיב "המול לו כל זכר" ולא כתיב בהו "כל איש" כמו גבי עבד. ודבר תימה פירש; דקרא ד"המול לו כל זכר" מוקמינן למילת זכריו, שמעכבתו מלאכול בפסח, וזה לא שייך אלא בבנים שנולדו בקדושה. אבל מילת בניו שלא נולדו בקדושה – אינה מעכבתו מלאכול בפסח! ונראה דלא צריך קרא למידרש מיניה "ואי אתה מל בן איש בעל כרחו", דממילא ידעינן שלא יגיירוהו בעל כרחו. ועוד: דמיפת תואר שמעינן דאין מלין גר בעל כרחו, דהא יפת תואר אין מטבילין אותה בעל כרחה, מדאיצטריך רחמנא להמתין לה שלשים יום. ובקבלה עליה – אין צריך להמתין. ולא נקטיה אלא לפרושי מילתיה דרשב"א, דקאמר דמתחלה כופין לשם שפחות ולא לשם גירות. אי נמי, משום דנקט לה במילתיה דרבנן "כשם שאי אתה מל בן איש" נקט נמי בדרבי שמעון בן אלעזר, לאשמועינן דאע"פ שאי אתה מל בן איש בעל כרחו – עבד אתה מל בעל כרחו. תימה: דרשב"א קאמר לקמן דאין משהין אותו בא"י מפני הפסד טהרות – עבד שאינו רוצה למול, ומשמע דזקוק למוכרו, •ואמאי? ימהלנו בעל כרחו! וכן קשה, דרבי יהושע בן לוי אית ליה ב"השולח" (גיטין דף לט: ושם): נתיאשתי מפלוני עבדי, אותו העבד אין לו תקנה אלא בשטר. אלמא, לית לי' ההיא דשמואל דבסמוך, וא"כ דריש: עבד איש אתה מל בעל כרחו, ולקמן קאמר: הלוקח עבד מן הגוי ולא רצה למול – מגלגל עמו עד י"ב חודש וימול אותו בעל כרחו! ואומר ר"י: דתקנת חכמים היא שלא יכשיל את רבו באיסור והיתר, כיון דאין מקבל עליו עול מצות. ועוד: דאין טוב לחייבו במצות, מאחר דאין חפץ לקיימם. **המפקיר** עבדו יצא לחירות ואין צריך גט שחרור. תימה: לשמואל תקשי ליה: למה ליה שטרא בעבד כנעני? יפקירנו ולימא ליה באפי בי תרי "זיל", דהכי דייק בפ"ק דקידושין (דף טז. ושם) גבי עבד עברי למה לי שטרא, לימא ליה באפי בי תרי זיל. ומשני: עבד עברי גופו קנוי! ואר"י: דהכי פריך(א): למה לי שטרא, דאותו לשון עצמו הכתוב בשטר "הרי את בן חורין" "הרי את לעצמך" – יאמר לו בעל פה! דס"ד דאין צריך אלא מחילה מחוב שעליו, ומסיק דגופו קנוי ואין הלשון הכתוב בשטר מועיל בעל פה, אבל הפקר, שמסלק רשותו, מועיל אפי' בעל פה לשמואל. וא"ת: אמאי לא חשיב הפקר גבי קניים של עבד בפ"ק דקדושין? (*גז"ש). וי"ל: דלא חשיב אלא קניים שמקנה הרב לעבד עצמו, והפקר אינו אלא סילוק בעלמא, שהרב מסלק עצמו מן העבד. ועוד יש לומר: דמילתא דליתא בכל מילי לא קתני, כדקאמר התם לענין חליפין, ותנא דידן – מילתא דליתא במטלטלין לא קתני. **לא** עשה רגליו. פי' בקונטרס: לפרני רגליו. ולר"י נראה דהיינו שער בית הערוה, דהכי משמע פרק "מצות חליצה" (לקמן קג.) גבי "מן הארכובה ולמעלה חליצתה פסולה", למימרא דלא מיקרי רגל מן הארכובה ולמעלה? תא שמע: ולא עשה את רגליו, ומשני: לישנא מעליא. מכאן אין ראיה דשרי לגלח שער של בית הערוה, דשמא מדרבנן אסור. אבל בריש פרק "ב' נזירים" (נזיר נח:) קאמר רב בהדיא: מיקל אדם כל גופו בתער, אפילו שער בית השחי ובית הערוה, כדמשמע התם דפריך עלה: והתניא המעביר שער בית השחי ובית הערוה הרי זה לוקה! ומשני: כי קאמר רב – במספרים. והא בתער קאמר! כעין תער. וא"ת דבתר הכי קאמר בעי מיניה רב מרבי חייא: מהו לגלח? א"ל: אסור. והא קא גדיל? א"ל: גבול יש לו. משמע דבמספרים בעא מיניה אי שרי, דאי בתער – מאי פריך והא קא גדיל? והלא יכול לגלח במספרים! ושמא רב לא קבלה מרבי חייא. ור"ת מפרש: דבתער בעא מיניה, והא דפריך: והא קא גדיל – ה"פ: והלא אין זה תיקון, ואין דומה כלל לתיקוני אשה, שאין זה משום ייפוי אלא משום נער, שגדל יותר מדאי. ואפילו בתער אית לן למישרי! ולפי זה צריך לומר שלא היה יודע ברייתא דלעיל שאוסרת. ובה"ג גרים הכי, אמר רב: מיקל אדם כל גופו בתער, והתניא המעביר כו' – כי קאמר רב בשאר אברים. ובשאר אברים מי שרי? והתניא העברת שער אינו מדברי תורה אלא מדברי סופרים, ומשמע ליה דאיירי ההיא ברייתא אף *(בשאר אברים, אע"ג דבבית השחי ובבית הערוה נמי איירי, כדמוכח בתר הכי דכי קאמר רב במספרים כי תניא ההיא בתער, ולפי זה בשאר אברים לא שרי אלא במספרים. ובית השחי ובית הערוה – אפי' במספרים אסור, ומדרבנן, דלא תקשי הך דהכא. מיהו, בה"ג של אספמיא כתוב: אלא, הא בתער והא במספרים, והדר ביה משינויא קמא דשני) כי קאמר רב בשאר אבריםא). ולגירסא זו שאר אברים ודאי אסור לגלח בתער, אבל במספרים שרי אף בית השחי ובית הערוה. ובערוך בערך גיוסטרא גורס כגירסת ספרים שלנו. ובתשובת הגאונים שרי לגלח בית השחי ובית הערוה כי מגלח כל גופו מראשו ועד רגליו. ולא משמע דאיירי במצורע, דפשיטא הוא \ אלא במגלח לרפואה, כיון דמגלח כל גופו – אין זה ייפוי אלא ניוול. ותדע, דלא משתמיט בשום דוכתא גבי מצורע שיהא עשה דמצורע דוחה לאו דלא ילבש גבר, אלא לאו דהקפת הראש וזקן גרידא.

רבי

[עין משפט נר מצוה]

קמב א מיי' פ"ח מהל' עבדים הלכה יג טוש"ע י"ד סימן רסז סעיף סד:

קמג ב מיי' פי"ד מהל' איסורי ביאה הל' ט סמג לאוין קיז טוש"ע שם סימן רסח סעיף ג:

קמד ג מיי' שם פי"ג הל' יג סמג שם טוש"ע שם:

קמה ד מיי' פ"ח מהל' מלכים הלכה ה סמג עשין קנב:

[תוספות ישנים]

א) והא דלא מקשי תלמודא התם דבשאר אברים שרי לגמרי בתער והא דקאמר העברת שער אינה אלא מד"ס דמשמע דהא מדברי סופרים מיהא איתא מיירי בבית השחי ובבית הערוה. והא דקאמר המעביר בית השחי ובית הערוה ה"ז לוקה ר"ל מכת מרדות מדרבנן. כדמשני תלמודא התם גבי ר' יוחנן דאמר המעביר בית השחי ובית הערוה ה"ז לוקה. ופריך מהא דהעברת שער אינה אלא מד"ס. ומשני מאי לוקה מכת מרדות מדרבנן. וי"ל משום דס"ל דהעברת שער מיירי בכל אברים מדלא מפרש בית השחי ובית הערוה כמו דמפרש גבי המעביר בית השחי ובית הערוה לוקה:

[מסורת הש"ס]

גיטין לח. נזיר סב: קידושין עב:

[אולי צ"ל דף כב:]

[הגהות הב"ח]

(א) תום' ד"ה המפקיר וכו' ואר"י דהכי פריך. נ"ב כוונתו בתירוץ זה למה שתירצו התוס' בקידושין דף טז בד"ה לימא ליה ע"ש ועיין עוד בפרק השולח דף לח בתוס' ד"ה המפקיר:

[גליון הש"ס]

גמ' ולא עבד אשה. עיין מהרש"א לקמן עא ע"ב ד"ה כגון שהיה אביו: **שם** ה"נ דאפילו רבנן מודו. עיין קידושין דף סב ע"ב תד"ה אלא מעתה: **תום'** ד"ה אלא עבד וכו'. ואמאי ימהלנו בעל כרחו. עיין ע"ז דף נז ע"ב תד"ה עד:

רבי אליעזר אומר אביה כו'. למיסבר קראי פליגי. אי נמי נפקא מינה אם מתו אביה ואמה או נתגיירו. וריב"ן פירש דלר"ע צריכה שתכפור בעבודה זרה קודם שתבעל לו. ולפירושו לא אתי כר"ע הא דקתני לעיל בד"א שלא קיבלה עליה.

כי הני. שלשים, (א) "ואחר כן תבא אליה" – אחר שיעור אחר כזה תבא אליה. הרי הוא אומר וינפש בן אמתך. והאי בעבד ערל כתיב, כדמפרש לקמן. בין השמשות של ע"ש ולא הספיק למולו. ומזהירו הכתוב לרבו על עבדו לנוח ביום המחרת. ולא על שבת הבאה, שהרי צריך למולו בשבת זו. וכיון דמל – מקרא אחר נפקא מ"למען ינוח עבדך", דלקמן מוקי לה בעבד שמל. גר תושב. שקבל עליו שלא לעבוד עבודה זרה, ואוכל נבלות. והזהירו הכתוב על השבת, דמחלל את השבת כעובד עבודה זרה. האמר אין מקיימין. אפילו יום אחד. ה"מ. דאין מקיים. היכא דלא פסקא למילתיה. דלא קיבל מעולם להתגייר, ולא פסק מגיותו. אבל היכא דפסקא למילתיה. בשעת לקיחתו, ונתפייס להתגייר, ואחר כך חזר בו – מגלגלין, שמא יחזור ויתרצה, לשון מורי. לישנא אחרינא: ה"מ – דאין מקיימין, היכא דלא פסק למילתיה, שמקיימין סתם, אבל היכא דפסק דאמר לו הריני מגלגל עמך י"ב חדש, ואם לא תמול אמכור אותך – מותר, דהוי גביה כשכיר בעלמא. לשמעתא. האי מרולא דרב פפא דהיכא דפסק למילתיה – משהינן. לישני ליה הא. כגון דפסק למילתיה, דיכול לקיימו כל י"ב חדש. חד מתרי טעמי. שני ליה. וכל רבותי אמרו לי משמיה. דרבי אלעאי. הפסד טהרות. שמטמא את התרומות. דגוי גזרו עליו שיהא טמא כזב לכל דבריו. לספר. מרק"א בלע"ז, כרך המבדיל בין ארץ ישראל לארץ העמים. שלא קיימו ז' מצות. בעודן גוים. ועד השתא לא איפרעו מינייהו, דפורענות גנוזה להם לעתיד לבא. אבל כשמתגיירין – נפרעין מהם כדי למרק חובתן. כקטן שנולד. ואינו נענש על שעבר. מיראה. מיראת גיהנם והפורענות האמורה עליהם. אשר באת. שמיהרת ולא איחרת.

ר' אליעזר* אומר: "אביה" – אביה ממש, "אמה" – אמה ממש. ר"ע אומר: א"אביה ואמה" – זו עבודה זרה, וכן הוא אומר °"אומרים לעץ אבי אתה וגו'. "ירח ימים" – ב"ירח שלשים יום. ר"ש בן אלעזר אומר: תשעים יום, "ירח" – שלשים, "ימים" – שלשים, "ואחר כן" – שלשים. מתקיף לה רבינא: אימא "ירח" – שלשים, "ימים" – שלשים, "ואחר כן" – כי הני! – קשיא. ת"ר: מקיימין עבדים שאינם מלין, דברי רבי ישמעאל. רבי עקיבא אומר: אין מקיימין. אמר ליה ר' ישמעאל: הרי הוא אומר °"וינפש בן אמתך"! א"ל: בלוקח עבד בין השמשות ולא הספיק למולו הכתוב מדבר. דכ"ע מיהת "וינפש בן אמתך" בעבד ערל כתיב, מאי משמע? דתניא: *"וינפש בן אמתך" – בעבד ערל הכתוב מדבר. אתה אומר בעבד ערל, או אינו אלא בעבד מהול? כשהוא אומר: °"למען ינוח עבדך ואמתך כמוך" – הרי עבד מהול אמור, הא מה אני מקיים "וינפש בן אמתך"! – בעבד ערל. "והגר" – זה גר תושב, אתה אומר זה גר תושב, או אינו אלא גר צדק? כשהוא אומר "וגרך אשר בשעריך" – הרי גר צדק אמור, הא מה אני מקיים "והגר" – זה גר תושב. אמר רבי יהושע בן לוי: גהלוקח עבד מן הגוי ולא רצה למול, מגלגל עמו עד י"ב חדש. לא מל – חוזר ומוכרו לגוים. אמרוה רבנן קמיה דרב פפא: כמאן – דלא כר' עקיבא, דאי ר"ע – האמר אין מקיימין! אמר להו רב פפא: אפילו תימא ר' עקיבא, הני מילי – היכא דלא פסקא למילתיה, אבל היכא דפסקא למילתיה – פסקא. אמר רב כהנא: אמריתא לשמעתא קמיה דרב זביד מנהרדעא, אמר לי: אי הכי, כי אמר ליה ר"ע בלוקח עבד בין השמשות – לישני ליה הא! חדא מתרי טעמי קאמר. שלח רבין משמיה דרבי אילעאי, וכל רבותי אמרו לי משמו: דאיזהו עבד ערל שמותר לקיימו – זה שלקחו רבו על מנת שלא למולו. אמרוה רבנן קמיה דרב פפא: כמאן – דלא כרבי עקיבא, דאי ר"ע – האמר: אין מקיימין! אמר להו רב פפא: אפילו תימא רבי עקיבא, ה"מ – היכא דלא אתני בהדיה, אבל היכא דאתני – אתני. אמר רב כהנא: אמריתא לשמעתא קמיה דרב זביד מנהרדעא, וא"ל: אי הכי, כי קאמר ליה רבי עקיבא בלוקח עבד בין השמשות ולא הספיק למולו – לישני ליה הא! ולטעמיך – לישני ליה הך! אלא: *חד מתרי ותלת טעמי קאמר. יתיב רבי חנינא בר פפי ורבי אמי ור' יצחק נפחא אקילעא דרבי יצחק נפחא, ויתבי וקאמרי: עיר אחת היתה בארץ ישראל ולא רצו עבדיה למול, וגלגלו עמהם עד שנים עשר חדש, וחזרו ומכרום לגוים. כמאן – כי האי תנא. דתניא: הלוקח עבד מן הגוי ולא רצה למול – מגלגל עמו עד שנים עשר חדש, לא מל – חוזר ומוכרו לגוים. ר' שמעון בן אלעזר אומר: אין משהין אותו בארץ ישראל, מפני הפסד טהרות. ובעיר הסמוכה לספר – אין משהין אותו כל עיקר, שמא ישמע דבר, וילך ויאמר לחברו גוי. תניא, רבי חנניא בנו של רבן גמליאל אומר: מפני מה גרים בזמן הזה מעונין, ויסורין באין עליהן – מפני שלא קיימו שבע מצות בני נח. רבי יוסי אומר: *גר שנתגייר כקטן שנולד דמי. אלא מפני מה מעונין – לפי שאין בקיאין בדקדוקי מצות כישראל, אבא חנן אומר משום ר' אלעזר: לפי שאין עושין מאהבה אלא מיראה. אחרים אומרים: מפני ששהו עצמם להכנס תחת כנפי השכינה. אמר ר' אבהו ואיתימא ר' חנינא: מאי קראה – °"ישלם ה' פעלך ותהי משכרתך שלמה מעם ה' אלהי ישראל אשר באת לחסות" וגומר.§

מתני'

שמעון

ירח שלשים יום. וכן בפ"ק דנזיר (דף ה. ושם): ואימא שלשים יום כדכתיב "עד חדש ימים". משמע דסתם חדש שלשים. והא דאמרי' בר"ה (דף יט:) ובסנהדרין (דף יא. ושם) כמה עיבור שנה – שלשים יום, רשב"ג אומר – חודש! היכא דמוכח – שאני* א).

אין מקיימין. פירש ריב"ן: שלא ינסך יינו. וקשיא לר"י: דא"כ, כי אתני בהדיה נמי! ועוד: דמתשובתו של ר' ישמעאל משמע דמדאורייתא פליגי! ונראה לר"י דטעמא דר' עקיבא לפי שצוה הקב"ה לאברהם למול עבדיו, לכך אסור לקיים שאינם מולין.

זה גר תושב. פירש בקונטרס: שקבל עליו שלא לעבוד עבודה זרה, ומחלל שבת כעובד עבודה זרה. וקשה: דאם כן נפישי להו משבע מלות! ובמסכת ע"ז (דף סד:) משמע דבשבע מלות שקבלו בני נח איקרי גר תושב! ועוד, דבפרק "ארבע מיתות" (סנהדרין דף נח:) אמרי' דגוי ששבת חייב מיתה אפילו בחול, כל שכן בשבת. ובפרק "ד' מחוסרי כפרה" (כריתות דף ט. ושם) קאמר ר"ע דגר תושב אין מוזהר על השבת! ונראה דהכא בעושה מלאכה לצורך ישראל, דומיא ד"וינפש בן אמתך".

היכא דלא פסקא וכו'. פר"ת: דהני מילי אדר' יהושע קאי. ולא פסקא למילתיה – היינו שכל שעה דוחה אותו מיום ליום שימול. אבל היכא דפסקא למילתיה שלא ימול כלל – התם אין מקיימין. ולא משמע כן, דה"מ אדר"ע קאי! ונראה לר"י כפירושו, אבל אדר"ע קאי, דהיכא דנתרצה למול ודוחהו – התם אין מקיימין, הואיל ומצוה למול, דשהוי מצוה לא משהינן. אבל היכא דפסק שלא ימול – אינו מחויב למולו בעל כרחו, ומגלגל י"ב חדש עמו, אולי יתרצה. וכן פי' בשערי דרב האי בשער *רביעי.

שאין עושין מאהבה אלא מיראה. בפרק *"נוטל" (בסוטה דף כב: ושם) משמע שניהם רעים, ובפרק "כשם" (שם דף לא. ושם) משמע דשניהם לשבח! ואומר ר"י דמאהבת המקום ומיראת המקום – הוו תרווייהו לשבח, מאהבת אדם ומיראת אדם – תרווייהו לגריעותא. או כמו שפירש שם בקונט': מאהבת שכר, וכגון שאם לא יהיה לו שכר – תוהא על הראשונות ואין עושה אלא על מנת לקבל פרס. ומיראה – היינו מיראת עונש. אבל הכא קשה, דנקט מאהבה לשבח ומיראה לגריעותא, והוי מצי למימר איפכא: או תרווייהו לגריעותא, או תרווייהו לשבח!

אשר באת לחסות. פירוש: שמיהרת. ותימה: דבפ' "מי שאמר הריני נזיר ושמע חבירו ואמר ואני" (נזיר דף כג: ושם) אומר: רות בת בנו של עגלון בנו של בלק מלך מואב היתה, וכשתחשוב שנותיו של אהוד שהרג עגלון עד סוף ימים של אבצן, דהיינו: בועז, תמצא יותר ממאתים שנה, ולעת זקנתו נשאה, דכתיב "לבלתי לכת אחרי הבחורים"! וי"ל: דבת בנו של עגלון לאו דוקא, אלא כלומר דמזרעו היתה, כמו בן בנו של נמרוד הרשע (חגיגה דף יג.), ובקרא קרי לה נערה.

[צ"ל רבינו] [צ"ל מנה מנטל]

עין משפט נר מצוה

קמו א ב מיי' פ"ח מהל' מלכים הלכה ה סמג עשין קנב:
קמז ג מיי' פ"א מהלכות מילה הל' ו ופי"ד מהל' איסורי ביאה הל' ט סמג עשין כח טוש"ע י"ד סימן רסז סעיף ד:
קמח ד מיי' וסמג שם טוש"ע שם בהג"ה:

[ועי' תוס' כתובות נז: ד"ה ואין. ועוד שם עח. ד"ה ר' יהודה]

תוספות ישנים

א) נראה לומר דירח דקרא ר"ל מלא משום שאין חדשה של לבנה פחותה מכ"ט י"ב תשל"ג וכיון שנכנס ביום שלשים מקצת היום ככולו והוי משלשים. אבל חדש לבנה חכמים הוי שפיר מכ"ט יום: זה גר תושב ולא הספיק למולו בין השמשות. פי' ומן שבת ראשון קאמר דאילו מן שבת שני פשיטא דכיון שהיה לו שהות למולו ולא מל לא ישבות. אכן משמע דהשתא ישבות ואם ירצה לחייב עצמו משביתה שבת הרשות בידו. ותימה דאמרינן גוי ששבת חייב וי"ל דזה כיון דלדעתו להתגייר מלי לשבות. וא"נ דאף כי אינו מצווה על שבת מ"מ אנחנו מצווים שלא לחלל שבת על ידינו לצוות לו ישראל לעשות מלאכתו: ה"מ היכא דלא פסקא למלתיה. פ"ה דוקא כי לא אמר מתחלה שימול עצמו אין מקיימין אבל היכא דפסקא למלתיה שאמר מתחלה שהוא רוצה למול ואח"כ חזר בו מגלגלין עמו אולי יתרצה למול כמקודם. וי"מ היכא דלא פסקא למלתיה שלא פי' שום דבר אז מקיימים אבל פסקא פירוש פסק הקונה עמו שאם רוצה למול יגלגל עמו ואם לא ימול ימכרנו לגוי פסקא ומגלגל עמו דהוי גביה כשכיר בעלמא. וקשה [illegible] גר שנתגייר כקטן שנולד דמי. ואינו נענש על אשר עשה בגיותו ובדיני שמים איירי נמי הכא. אבל בדיני אדם אמרינן בן נח שבירך את השם בגיותו ונתגייר היה נהרג. וכמו כן אינו אסור בקרובות מטעם הזה דכקטן שנולד דמי רק היכא דשייך שמא יאמרו באנו מקדושה חמורה לקדושה קלה: שאין עושין מאהבה אלא מיראה. משמע היכא דמיראה אינו טוב ובמגילה (כ"ה) משמע דאף מאהבה אינו טוב דקאמר דלמא אתי למעבד מאהבה ומיראה. וגם (בסמוך) [בסוטה (כ"ב)] נמי משמע דמאהבה נמי אינו טוב (דקאמר חשיב) [דקחשיב ליה] גבי ז' פרושין הם וכולן כגנא. ובסוף כשם משמע דאף מיראה קא חשיב דקאמר תרווייהו לדיקי גמורי נינהו מר מאהבה ומר מיראה משמע מהתם דאף מיראה לדיק הוא. ונראה לפרש דדוקא מאהבת המקום ומיראת המקום הוו לדיקי אבל מיראת העונש ומאהבת השכר לאו לדיקי נינהו והכא ר"ל שאין עושין מאהבת המקום אלא מיראת העונש והמבין יבין: ועוד

א) נראה לנ"ל והתם נמי רב פפא הוא דאמר כן דהיכא דלאתני אתני ולכן נראה דה"ק היכא דלא פסיקא וכו'.
ב) אולי נ"ל א"ע דאמר דאינו רוצה להיות אלא הישראל רק כשכיר יום.

מסורת הש"ס

(סנהדרין נו:) ספרי פרשה כי תצא
ירמיה ב
שמות כג
מכילתא פרשת משפטים פ"ב
דברים ה
[יומא פו: סוטה לא. ב"ק קו: זבחים ל: מנחות פט: כריתות ג.]
[לעיל כב. וש"נ]
רות ב

הגהות הב"ח

(א) רש"י ד"ה כי הני שלשים וכו' ואחר כן:

גליון הש"ס

גמ' גר שנתגייר כקטן. עיין סנהדרין דף עא ע"ב תד"ה בן:

תוספות חד מקמאי

תניא וינפש בן אמתך בעבד ערל הכתוב מדבר למען ינוח עבדך ואמתך כמוך בעבד המל. והגר זה גר תושב. וגרך אשר בשערך זה גר צדק. ודוקא במלאכת ישראל הוא דאסור עבד ערל אבל לעצמו מותר. והכי איתא בכריתות פרק מחוסרי כפרה. דגרים התם גר תושב עושה מלאכה לעצמו כישראל בחולו של מועד ר"ע אומר כישראל בי"ט ר"י אומר גר תושב עושה מלאכה לעצמו כישראל בחולו של מועד. עבד ואמה התושבים עושין מלאכה לעצמן בשבת כישראל בחול ר"ש אומר א' גר תושב וא' עבד ואמה התושבים עושין מלאכה לעצמן בשבת כישראל בחש"מ. אמר רב אידי בר גרשום אמר רב אדא בר אהבה הלכה כר"ש: הא דאר"ש הא גופה ומטבילה לשם עבדות כתב הראב"ד דרבנן פליגי עליה ואמרי אף לשום עבדות צריך לקבל ואינו כופהו והלכתא כרבנן דר"ש ור"ע קיימי כותיה לקמן גבי מקיימין עבדים שאינן מהולים ויש אומרים דלא פליגי רבנן עליה דר"ש אלא בשחרור אבל לשום עבדות כופהו כדי שלא יטבול לשום בן חורין. ור"ש ור"ע פליגי אם אינו רוצה לכופו אם רשאי לקיימן או לא: הכל

מתני' כָּל שְׁאֵר בָּשָׂר שֶׁהוּא בְּלֹא יָבֹא. כָּל קוּרְבָה שֶׁהִיא בְּלָאו, וַאֲפִי' אֵין בָּהּ כָּרֵת, כְּגוֹן אֲנוּסַת אָבִיו, וּכְרַבִּי יְהוּדָה דַּהֲוְיָא בְּלָאו ד"לֹא יְגַלֶּה כְּנַף אָבִיו". וּמֵחֲמַת קוּרְבָה,(א) כְּגוֹן נוֹשֵׂא חֲלוּצָתוֹ, דַּהֲוֵי בְּ"לֹא יִבְנֶה" וַהֲוֵי לָאו דְּקוּרְבָה בְּלֹא כָּרֵת. כָּל שֶׁחַיָּיבִין עָלָיו כָּרֵת. אֲבָל נוֹשֵׂא חֲלוּצָתוֹ לָא הָוֵי מַמְזֵר. לְקַיֵּים דִּבְרֵי רַבִּי יְהוֹשֻׁעַ. לֹא הָיָה כָּתוּב בַּמְּגִלָּה, אֶלָּא אַרֵישָׁא קָאֵי: אָמַר ר"ש בֶּן עַזַּאי לְקַיֵּים דִּבְרֵי ר' יְהוֹשֻׁעַ כו'. מֵאֵשֶׁת אִישׁ. חַיָּיבֵי מִיתוֹת כו'. **גמ'** וּכְתִיב לֹא יָבֹא מַמְזֵר. וְסָמִיךְ לֵיהּ "לֹא יְגַלֶּה". דְּר' יְהוּדָה וְרַבָּנַן. בְּפֶרֶק "נוֹשְׂאִין עַל הָאֲנוּסָה" (לקמן דף צז.). וּלְרַבִּי סִימַאי. בִּכְתוּבּוֹת (דף כט:) וְקִידּוּשִׁין (דף סח.) מִן הַכֹּל הָיָה עוֹשֶׂה ר"ע מַמְזֵרִים, חוּץ מֵאַלְמָנָה לְכ"ג שֶׁעוֹשֶׂה חֲלָלִין וְלֹא מַמְזֵרִי'. מִדְּקָאָמַר חוּץ מֵאַלְמָנָה – אַלְמָא אֲפִי' חַיָּיבֵי לָאוִין שֶׁלֹּא מֵחֲמַת קוּרְבָה מַרְבֶּה, כְּגוֹן מַחֲזִיר גְּרוּשָׁתוֹ מִשֶּׁנִּישֵּׂאת, וּכְגוֹן נְתִינָה לְיִשְׂרָאֵל, דְּקַיְימָא בְּ"לֹא תִתְחַתֵּן בָּם" (דברים ז), וּמִשִּׁבְעָה אוּמּוֹת הוּא, וּכְגוֹן עַמּוֹנִי שֶׁנָּשָׂא בַּת יִשְׂרָאֵל בָּנָיו מַמְזֵרִים. חַיָּיבֵי עֲשֵׂה. מִצְרִי אוֹ אֲדוֹמִי קוֹדֶם ג' דּוֹרוֹת, דִּכְתִיב (דברים כג) "דּוֹר שְׁלִישִׁי יָבֹא לָהֶם" – וְלֹא שֵׁנִי, וְלָאו הַבָּא מִכְּלַל עֲשֵׂה – עֲשֵׂה. וְהָא דְּר' יְשֵׁבָב נַמִי בִּכְתוּבּוֹת (שם): בּוֹאוּ וְנִצְוַח עַל עֲקִיבָא בֶּן יוֹסֵף, שֶׁהָיָה אוֹמֵר: כָּל שֶׁאֵין לוֹ בִּיאָה בְּיִשְׂרָאֵל הַוָּלָד מַמְזֵר. סָבַר לָהּ כְּרַבָּנַן. דִּפְלִיגִי אַדְּרַבִּי יְהוּדָה בְּ"נוֹשְׂאִין עַל הָאֲנוּסָה" (לקמן דף צז.) וְאָמְרֵי: הַאי "לֹא יְגַלֶּה כְּנַף אָבִיו" – בְּשׁוֹמֶרֶת יָבָם שֶׁל אָבִיו הַכָּתוּב מְדַבֵּר, דַּהֲוְיָא לֵיהּ אֵשֶׁת אֲחִי אָבִיו, וּבְכָרֵת. וְהַאי דְּהָדַר כַּתְבָהּ בְּמִשְׁנֵה תוֹרָה – מִשּׁוּם לְמִסְמְכֵיהּ לֵיהּ "לֹא יָבֹא מַמְזֵר", וּלְאַשְׁמְעִינַן דְּיֵשׁ מַמְזֵר מֵחַיָּיבֵי כְּרֵיתוֹת: ה"ג. וְרַבִּי יְהוֹשֻׁעַ לִכְתּוֹב רַחֲמָנָא לֹא יְגַלֶּה. כְּלוֹמַר, אִי בְּשׁוֹמֶרֶת יָבָם שֶׁל אָבִיו מִשְׁתָּעֵי, אוֹ בַּאֲנוּסַת אָבִיו מִשְׁתָּעֵי – לִכְתּוֹב "לֹא יְגַלֶּה כְּנַף אָבִיו" לְחוּדֵיהּ, וּלְאַשְׁמְעִינַן דְּיֵשׁ מַמְזֵר מֵחַיָּיבֵי כְּרֵיתוֹת לְרַבָּנַן, אוֹ מֵחַיָּיבֵי לָאוִין לְרַבִּי יְהוּדָה, וְכָל שֶׁכֵּן מֵאֵשֶׁת אָב דַּהֲוְיָא בְּכָרֵת וּמִיתָה. "לֹא יִקַּח. אִישׁ אֶת אֵשֶׁת אָבִיו" לָמָּה לִי לְמִכְתַּב? אֶלָּא ש"מ מִדִּכְתָבֵיהּ, הָא קמ"ל: דְּ"לֹא יָבֹא מַמְזֵר" עֲלָהּ קָאֵי, דְּמִינָּהּ הוּא דַּהֲוֵי מַמְזֵר, מִשּׁוּם דְּחַיָּיבֵי מִיתוֹת הוּא.(ב) וְאַ"לֹא יְגַלֶּה כְּנַף אָבִיו" לָא קָאֵי. וְאִי קַשְׁיָא: כְּנַף אָבִיו לְמַאי כְּתָבֵיהּ? אִי בְּשׁוֹמֶרֶת יָבָם, לַעֲבוֹר עָלָיו בִּשְׁנֵי לָאוִין – "עֶרְוַת אֲחִי אָבִיךָ לֹא תְגַלֵּה", וְלָאו דְּ"לֹא יְגַלֶּה כְּנַף אָבִיו", וְאִי בַּאֲנוּסַת אָבִיו – אַשְׁמְעִינַן דַּאֲסוּרָה. מִ"לֹּא יִקַּח עַד לֹא יְגַלֶּה". דְּהַיְינוּ אֵשֶׁת אָב הַכְּתוּבָה בֵּין "לֹא יִקַּח" לְ"לֹא יְגַלֶּה". הַכֹּל מוֹדִים. וַאֲפִילוּ שִׁמְעוֹן הַתִּימְנִי. בָּבָא עַל הַנִּדָּה. אע"ג דְּקָאֵי בְּכָרֵת – אֵין הַוָּלָד מַמְזֵר. וְהַבָּא

מתני' אֵיזֶהוּ *מַמְזֵר? כָּל שְׁאֵר בָּשָׂר שֶׁהוּא בְּ"לֹא יָבֹא", דִּבְרֵי ר"ע. *שִׁמְעוֹן הַתִּימְנִי אוֹמֵר: [א]כָּל שֶׁחַיָּיבִים עָלָיו כָּרֵת בִּידֵי שָׁמַיִם. וַהֲלָכָה כִּדְבָרָיו. וְרַבִּי יְהוֹשֻׁעַ אוֹמֵר: כָּל שֶׁחַיָּיבִין עָלָיו מִיתַת בֵּית דִּין. אָמַר *רַבִּי שִׁמְעוֹן בֶּן עַזַּאי: מָצָאתִי מְגִלַּת יוֹחֲסִין בִּירוּשָׁלַיִם וְכָתוּב בָּהּ: אִישׁ פְּלוֹנִי מַמְזֵר מֵאֵשֶׁת אִישׁ, לְקַיֵּים דִּבְרֵי רַבִּי יְהוֹשֻׁעַ. *[ב]אִשְׁתּוֹ שֶׁמֵּתָה – מוּתָּר בַּאֲחוֹתָהּ, גֵּרְשָׁהּ וּמֵתָה – מוּתָּר בַּאֲחוֹתָהּ. נִשֵּׂאת לְאַחֵר וּמֵתָה – מוּתָּר בַּאֲחוֹתָהּ. *יְבִמְתּוֹ שֶׁמֵּתָה – מוּתָּר בַּאֲחוֹתָהּ, חָלַץ לָהּ וּמֵתָה – מוּתָּר בַּאֲחוֹתָהּ, נִשֵּׂאת לְאַחֵר וּמֵתָה – מוּתָּר בַּאֲחוֹתָהּ.§ **גמ'** מ"ט דְּרַבִּי עֲקִיבָא? דִּכְתִיב (דברים כג) °"לֹא יִקַּח אִישׁ אֶת אֵשֶׁת אָבִיו וְלֹא יְגַלֶּה כְּנַף אָבִיו" – *כָּנָף שֶׁרָאָה אָבִיו לֹא יְגַלֶּה, וְסָבַר לָהּ כְּר' יְהוּדָה, דְּאָמַר: בַּאֲנוּסַת אָבִיו הַכָּתוּב מְדַבֵּר, דַּהֲוְיָא לָהּ חַיָּיבֵי לָאוִין. וְסָמִיךְ לֵיהּ (שם) °"לֹא יָבֹא מַמְזֵר בִּקְהַל ה'". אַלְמָא: מֵהָנֵי הָוֵי מַמְזֵר. *וּלְרַבִּי סִימַאי דְּמַרְבֶּה שְׁאָר חַיָּיבֵי לָאוִין דְּלָאו דִּ"שְׁאֵר", וּלְרַבִּי יְשֵׁבָב דְּמַרְבֶּה אֲפִילוּ חַיָּיבֵי עֲשֵׂה – נָפְקָא לְהוּ מִ"וְּלֹא". וְשִׁמְעוֹן הַתִּימְנִי סָבַר לָהּ כְּרַבָּנַן, דְּאָמְרִי: בְּשׁוֹמֶרֶת יָבָם שֶׁל אָבִיו הַכָּתוּב מְדַבֵּר, דַּהֲוְיָא לָהּ חַיָּיבֵי כְּרֵיתוֹת, וְסָמִיךְ לֵיהּ "לֹא יָבֹא מַמְזֵר", אַלְמָא: מֵחַיָּיבֵי כְּרֵיתוֹת הָוֵי מַמְזֵר. וְרַבִּי יְהוֹשֻׁעַ: לִכְתּוֹב רַחֲמָנָא "לֹא יְגַלֶּה", "לֹא יִקַּח" ("וְלֹא יְגַלֶּה") לָמָּה לִי? אֶלָּא לָאו הָכִי קָאָמַר: מִ"לֹּא יִקַּח" עַד "לֹא יְגַלֶּה" – הָוֵי מַמְזֵר, טְפֵי – לָא הָוֵי מַמְזֵר. *)אָמַר אַבָּיֵי: הַכֹּל מוֹדִים בַּבָּא עַל הַנִּדָּה וְעַל

*) [קדושין סח. ע"ש]

שמעון התימני אומר כו' והלכה כדבריו. אע"ג דאין למדין הלכה מפי גמרא(ג) – *הכא הלכתא כוותיה, דסתמא דפרק "האומר" (קדושין דף סו: ושם) נראה עיקר, דכהאי גוונא קרי הלכתא פסיקתא בבבא קמא (ד' קב.) ובמסכת ע"ז (דף ז: ושם) בההיא דכל המשנה ידו על התחתונה, ולעיל בפ' קמא (דף יד. ושם) אמר: פשיטא, בני חייבי לאוין כשרים נינהו. ובפרק שני (לעיל כג.) קאמר רב פפא: מסתברא, חייבי לאוין תפסי בהו קידושין. ולעיל (דף מה.) פסקינן דגוי ועבד הבא על בת ישראל הולד כשר. וכמה אמוראי דאיירי בגרת מחזיר גרושתו. ולר"ע לא משכחת לה גרה דאין קידושין תופסין בחייבי לאוין. וכרבי יהושע נמי יש להוכיח דלא קי"ל כוותיה, דאמר לעיל (שם:): ושניהם לא למדוה אלא מאשת אב, וחייבי כריתות דמו לאשת אב לכולי עלמא. ולעיל בריש פירקין (דף לז.) קאמר ראב"י דהלכתא כוותיה דאין ממזר מספק, משמע דהויא ממזר מאשת אח. ולעיל (ד' מ:) אמר רב טובי בר קיסנא: הבא על גרת חלוצתו הולד ממזר. ואפילו רבי יוחנן לא פליג אלא משום דגרה כחלוצה בלאו). **רבי יהושע** אומר כל שחייבין עליו כו'. יש מגיהים ר' יהודה במקום רבי יהושע, דבפרק "עשרה יוחסין" (קדושין דף עד:) גבי כל האסורין לבא בקהל מותרים לבא זה בזה. ור' יהודה אוסר. ומפרש עלה דר' יהודה סבר דממזר מאחותו לא הוי ממזר, אלא מאשת איש. ופריך עלה: תנינא, מהך דהכא. ואין נראה, דהיאך היה בן עזאי אומר לקיים מילתיה דר' יהודה? והא קשיש מיניה טובא, דהא בן עזאי תלמיד חבר הוה לרבי עקיבא, כדאמר ב"מי שמת" (ב"ב ד' קנח:), ור' יהודה מתלמידי בתראי דר' עקיבא הוה! ועוד: דר' יהודה סבר כרבי עקיבא דיש ממזר מחייבי לאוין, כדפרישית לעיל (ד' מז.) גבי ההוא דאתא לקמיה דרבי יהודה, וכדאמר בפ' "ארבע מיתות" (סנהדרין ד' נג: ושם). אלא ודאי ר' יהושע גרסינן. והתם פריך תנינא – משום דהוה ליה למיתני: וכן היה רבי יהודה אומר כדבריו, אי הוה סבר כר' יהושע. ומיהו, התם דפריך תנינא הוה מצי למיפרך טפי שפיר דלא אפשר לומר דלר' יהודה ממזר מאחותו לא הוי ממזר, כיון דמוקי קרא באנוסת אביו, וסבר כר"ע דיש ממזר מחייבי לאוין. **איש** פלוני ממזר מאשת איש כו'. תימה: דלא נקט חייבי מיתות ב"ד סתם. ואי משום דמעשה שהיה כך היה – א"כ מנ"ל דהוי כר' יהושע? וי"ל: דנקט אשת איש לרבותא, דאע"פ שהוא קל משאר חייבי מיתות, דהוי בחנק ויש לה היתר בחיי אוסרה.

וכתיב לא יבא ממזר. וא"ת: והא מפסיק קרא ד"לא יבא פצוע דכא" בינתים! וי"ל: דכיון דלאו בני בנים נינהו, ולא שייך מינייהו ממזר – לא חשיב הפסק. **לכתוב** רחמנא או לא יקח או לא יגלה. בקונטרס גרס: לכתוב רחמנא "לא יגלה", ופי': דמלא יגלה לחודיה שמעינן דיש ממזר מחייבי כריתות לרבנן, או מחייבי לאוין לר' יהודה לא יקח איש את אשת אביו למה לי למכתב? אלא, ש"מ מדכתביה – דלא יבא ממזר עליה קאי, דמיניה הוא דהוי ממזר, משום דחייבי מיתות ב"ד הוא. אבל א"לא יגלה" לא קאי, ודין לא יקח עד לא יגלה היינו אשת אב הכתובה בין לא יקח ללא יגלה. וקשה: חדא, שמוחק הספרים. ועוד: דבין לא יקח עד לא יגלה לא משמע כפירושו דקאי על אשת אב הכתובה בינתים, ועוד: בחייבי מיתות דקילי, כמו אשת איש, מנ"ל דהוי ממזר? ועוד: דליליף ר' יהושע שאר חייבי כריתות מהיקישא דר' יונה! ונראה לר"י כגירסת הספרים, דגרסי': לכתוב רחמנא או לא יקח או לא יגלה, דמ"לא יקח" נמי שמעינן כריתות, דהא דומיא דאשת אב דלא תפסי בה קידושין, דהא בהא תליא, כדפיר' לעיל (ד' מד: ד"ה "עשאה"), או מהיקישא דרבי יונה אתו דאיתקיש כל העריות, כדאמרי' בריש "הבא על יבמתו" (לקמן ד' נד:). ומדכתב תרוייהו – ש"מ דמ"לא יקח" היינו חייבי סקילה, עד "לא יגלה" דהיינו חייבי כריתות – הוי ממזר. ואתא לרבויי כל חייבי [כריתות] ומיתות קלות. וסבר כרבנן דבשומרת יבם הכתוב מדבר, ולא הוי לא יגלה בכלל, דאי הוי בכלל – לא לכתוב אלא לא יגלה, ושמעון התימני נמי ה"מ למימר דסבר כר' יהודה, דאמר באנוסת אביו הכתוב מדבר, ומלא יקח עד לא יגלה הוי הולד ממזר, ואין לא יגלה בכלל. אלא דניחא ליה למימר דסבר כרבנן. •ולפירוש ר"י נ"ל לתנא דפירקין קמא דסבר כרבי יהודה(ד) דאמר באנוסת אביו הכתוב מדבר, וסבר נמי דאין ממזר מחייבי לאוין, דמלא יקח עד לא יגלה הוי ממזר, ואין לא יגלה בכלל. **הכל** מודים בבא על הנדה ועל הסוטה. פירש בקונטרס: אפי' לר' עקיבא דפליג ארבנן דמתניתין במחזיר גרושתו, וקאמר דהולד ממזר, אע"ג דלאו חייבי לאוין ד"שאר" – הוא הכא בסוטה מודה. וקשה לר"ת: דא"כ ה"ל לאתויי לעיל (ד' מד.) גבי משנה דמחזיר גרושתו! ועוד: אי קאי הכל מודים למ"ד אליבא דר' עקיבא דהוי ממזר אפילו מחייבי לאוין שאין דשאר, הא ע"כ הוי ממזר לרבי עקיבא מיבמה לשוק לשום תנא, כדאמר בפ"ק (לעיל ד' יג.) דאמר ר' אלעזר: אע"פ שנחלקו ב"ש וב"ה בצרות – מודים שאין ממזר כו', וקאמר: לאפוקי מדרבי עקיבא, דאמר אין קידושין תופסין בחייבי לאוין. משמע בהדיא דלר' עקיבא הוי ממזר משומרת יבם! ועוד אמר בפרק "עשרה יוחסין" (קדושין דף עה.), גבי כותים שהיו מייבמים את הארוסות ופוטרים את הנשואות, ורבי עקיבא לטעמיה דאמר אין קידושין תופסין בחייבי לאוין. ובפרק "האשה רבה" (לקמן ד' צב. ושם), גבי אשה שהלך בעלה וכנה למדינת הים קאמר: זו דברי רבי עקיבא, דאמר אין קידושין תופסין בחייבי לאוין. אבל חכמים אומרים דאין ממזר מיבמה. ולימא אין ממזר מחייבי לאוין! האי תנא הך תנא דר"ע הוא, דמחייבי לאוין דשאר הוא דהוי ממזר, מחייבי לאוין גרידא – לא הוי ממזר. משמע בהדיא דלמאן דלא בעי אליבא דרבי עקיבא שיהא לאו דשאר הוי ממזר מיבמה לשוק. ושם נפרש בעזרת השם מנא ליה דאתיא כרבי עקיבא, דלמא תאמר אפילו כרבנן והוי ממזר מדרבנן? ונראה לר"ת דמחזיר גרושתו וסוטה הוו חייבי לאוין דשאר, שהיא אסורים אלא משום אישות, ואליבא דתנא דמתני'

מסורת הש"ס

קידושין עה: [לעיל מד. לקמן פח.]

[ע' בכ' הרב מברטנורה ריש פ"ד דאבות]

[לעיל יז: יח.]

לעיל ד:

לעיל ד. [לקמן לג.]

[כתובות כט: קידושין סח. כה.]

גליון הש"ס

רש"י ד"ה לכתוב רחמנא וכו' ולפירש"י נ"ל כו'. וכפירש"י נ"ל כצ"ל.

תוספות חד מקמאי

הכל מודים בבא על הנדה ועל הסוטה ועל שומרת יבם שאין הולד ממזר [illegible]

עין משפט נר מצוה

[כדאיתא ב"ב קב: נדה ז:]

קמט א מיי' פט"ו מהל' איסורי ביאה הל' א סמג לאוין קיז טוש"ע אה"ע סימן ד סעיף יג:

[לעיל מד.]

קנ ב מיי' שם פ"ב הל' ט סמג לאוין שם טוש"ע שם סי' טו סעיף כז:

תוספות ישנים

א) ועוד ראיה דאמר רב נחמן (בקדושין ע"ו) גבי כותי ממזר מאחותו וממזר מאשת איש נתערבו בהם משמע שיש ממזר מאחותו דהוי חייבי כריתות ויש לדחות דהתם קאי אליבא דר' אלעזר ולר' אלעזר אין ראיה דהא ודאי איהו סבר דיש ממזר מחייבי כריתות כדאמרי' לעיל א"ר אלעזר אע"פ שנחלקו ב"ש וב"ה בצרות מודים שאין ממזר אלא ממי שאיסורו איסור ערוה וענוש כרת.

הגהות הב"ח

(א) רש"י ד"ה כל שאר וכו' ומחמת קורבה דלאו וכגון נושא: (ב) ד"ה לא יקח וכו' דמחייבי מיתות הוא אבל לא יגלה: (ג) תוס' ד"ה שמעון וכו' מפי גמרא. נ"ב בפרק יש נוחלין דף קל ע"ב: (ד) ד"ה לכתוב וכו' דפירקין קמא דסבר כרבי יהודה. נ"ב ע"ל דף ק' בתוספות ד"ה ורבי יהודה.

תוספות חד מקמאי

[illegible]

[illegible]

ועל הסוטה שאין הולד ממזר. [א]נדה – דהא תפסי בה קידושין, שנאמר "ותהי נדתה עליו" – אפי' בשעת נדתה – תפסי בה קידושין. סוטה נמי – דהא תפסי בה קידושין. תניא נמי הכי: *[ב]הכל מודים בבא על הנדה, ועל הסוטה, ועל שומרת יבם – שאין הולד ממזר. ואביי: שומרת יבם מספקא ליה, אי *כרב אי כשמואל. § "א"ר שמעון בן עזאי כו'". § תני, שמעון בן עזאי אומר: מצאתי מגלת יוחסין בירושלים, וכתוב בה: איש פלוני ממזר מאשת איש. וכתוב בה: *משנת ר' אליעזר בן יעקב קב ונקי. וכתוב בה: מנשה הרג את ישעיה. אמר רבא: מידן דייניה וקטליה. אמר ליה: משה רבך אמר °"כי לא יראני האדם וחי" ואת אמרת °"ואראה את ה' יושב על כסא רם ונשא", משה רבך אמר °"מי כה' אלהינו בכל קראנו אליו" ואת אמרת °"דרשו ה' בהמצאו". משה רבך אמר °"את מספר ימיך אמלא" ואת אמרת °"והוספתי על ימיך חמש עשרה שנה"! אמר ישעיה: ידענא ביה דלא מקבל מה דאימא ליה, ואי אימא ליה – אישוייה מזיד. אמר שם, איבלע בארזא. אתיוה לארזא ונסרוה. כי מטא להדי פומא – נח נפשיה, משום דאמר °"ובתוך עם טמא שפתים אנכי יושב". מכל מקום קשו קראי אהדדי! "ואראה את ה'" – כדתניא: [ג]כל הנביאים נסתכלו *באספקלריא שאינה מאירה, משה רבינו נסתכל באספקלריא המאירה. "דרשו ה' בהמצאו" – *[ד]הא ביחיד הא בצבור. ויחיד אימת? אמר רב נחמן אמר רבה בר אבוה: [ה]אלו עשרה ימים שבין ראש השנה ליום הכפורים, "את מספר ימיך אמלא" – תנאי היא. דתניא: "את מספר ימיך אמלא" אלו

תורה אור: ויקרא טו | שמות לג | ישעיה ו | דברים ד | ישעיה נה | שמות כג | מ"ב כ | ישעיה ו

רש"י

והבא על הסוטה. אשת איש שזינתה, וקיימא לן דאסורה לבעלה, בפ"ק (לעיל דף יא:) מה אני מקיים "אחרי אשר הוטמאה" (דברים כד) – לרבות סוטה שנסתרה. ואע"ג דחייבי לאוין היא – מודה בה רבי עקיבא, דפליג אדרבנן במתני' (לעיל מד.) במחזיר גרושתו, וקאמר דהולד ממזר אע"ג דלאו חייבי לאוין ד"שאר" הוא – הכא מודי דאין ולד ממזר. וכל שכן לאידך רבי עקיבא בר פלוגתא דשמעון התימני לא הוי ממזר, משום דסוט' לאו מחייבי לאוין דשאר היא. **דהא תפסי בה קידושין.** לאשה, דאף לאחר שזינתה לא פקעו מינה קידושיה הראשונים. **נדה** דכתיב ותהי נדתה עליו. "תהי" – לשון הויה דקידושין עליו. **שומרת יבם.**(א) לאחד מן השוק בלא חליצה, שאין הולד ממזר. ואפילו לרבי עקיבא דפליג אדרבנן במתני'. וטעמא – משום דקידושין תופסין בה, מדאפקיה רחמנא ללאו דידה בלשון הויה, דכתיב (דברים כה) "לא תהיה" – בת הויה היא. והכי קאמר: לא תהיה אשת המת – לא תתקדש אשת המת בקידושין לאיש זר, אלמא: קידושין תפסי בה. **ואביי מספקא ליה.** האי לא תהיה לאיש זר. **אי כרב.** דאמר בפרק "האשה רבה" (לקמן דף צב:) מנין שאין קידושין תופסין ביבמה – דכתיב "לא תהיה אשת המת לאיש זר" – לא תהיה בה הויה לזר, והולד ממזר. **אי כשמואל.** דאמר (שם): בעניותינו, בעניות דעתינו, צריכה גט. דמספקא לן אי להכי הוא דאתא כדקאמר רב, או דלמא לאוקמה בלאו אתא, וקידושין תפסי בה, מדאפיק לאו דידיה בלשון הויה. **משנת רבי אליעזר ב"י קב ונקי.** קב מדה קטנה, כלומר: במקומות מועטים הוא נזכרא במשנה [או בברייתא]. **ונקי.** בכל מקום שנזכר – הלכה כמותו. **בהמצאו.** משמע: פעמים שאינו מצוי. **אמלא.** לאו לשון תוספת, אלא משלים ולא יותר. **ידענא ביה.** במנשה דלא מקבל פירושא דטעמא דקראי, אלא קטיל לי. ואי אימא ליה ולא מקבל – אישויי' ליה מזיד בהריגתי, דעכשיו הוא סבור להורגני בדין – מיטב שאברח מפניו. **כי מטא.** נרגא. **להדי פומא.** דישעיה. נסרוה לפומיה ונח נפשיה. ומשום הכי איענש לנסורי פומיה, משום דקרינהו לישראל "עם טמא שפתים" מדעתו, שלא צוה לו הקב"ה, ולא מחמת תוכחה, דכתיב "ואומר אוי לי כי נדמיתי". **נסתכלו באספקלריא שאין מאירה.** וכסבורים לראות ולא ראו. ומשה נסתכל באספקלריא המאירה, וידע שלא ראהו בפניו.

שני

תוספות

דמתני' קאי, דלא אסר אלא חייבי לאוין ד"שאר". וא"ת: א"כ, אמאי איצטריך למנקט הכל מודים בשומרת יבם? אמאי תיסק אדעתא למימר דהוי ממזר טפי מבשאר חייבי לאוין דלאו דשאר? וי"ל: דאליבא דרב, דאמר אין קידושין תופסין ביבמה, איצטריך לאשמועינן שפיר דלא הוי ממזר. וטעמא, אר"ת: דהוי כגוי ועבד, שאין בה קידושין לשום אדם. וליבם נמי לאו בת קידושין היא, אלא ביאה הוא דאית בה. ואפי' למ"ד דהוי ממזר מגוי ועבד – מ"מ אין ממזר מיבמה, דכיון דיבמה עומדת לחלוץ כמו ליבם – חשיבא בת תפיסת קידושין. וא"ת: לשמואל תפשוט מהך ברייתא דאין קידושין תופסין ביבמה, דאי תופסין – לא הוה צריך לאשמועינן דאין הולד ממזר! וי"ל: דשמואל מספקא ליה, דלמא ברייתא היא גופה אתא לאשמעינן דקידושין תופסין ביבמה. וא"ת: היכי קמ"ל דתפסי, הא אפי' לא תפסי לא הוי ממזר, דשמואל אית ליה לעיל (דף מה.) דגוי ועבד הבא על בת ישראל הולד כשר! וי"ל: דשפיר משמע דתפסי בה קידושין, מדכייל לה בהדי סוטה ונדה – משמע דכולהו לא הוי הולד ממזר, משום דתפסי בהו קידושין. והא דקאמר ואביי מספקא ליה אי כרב אי כשמואל – לא כפירוש הקונטרס דאפי' לרב אין הולד ממזר, כדפי', אלא להכי לא נקט שומרת יבם – משום דשמא תפסי בה קידושין כדשמואל, ופשיטא דלא הוי ממזר, ואין שום חידוש להשמיענו. וא"ת: ואמאי הוי ממזר משומרת יבם לשום תנא (ג)כיון דהוי כגוי ועבד דלא תפסי קדושין לא לדידיה ולא לאחריני? וברייתא ד"האשה רבה" (לקמן דף צב. ושם) נמי, דקתני זו דברי ר' עקיבא דאמר אין קידושין תופסין בחייבי לאוין אבל חכמים אומרים כו' – משמע דלרבנן לא הוי ממזר משום דקידושין תופסין, ולפי' ר"ת אפי' אין קידושין תופסין לא הוי ממזר? ואר"י: דלמ"ד דהוי ממזר לר' עקיבא מחייבי לאוין דלאו דשאר – נמי הוי ממזר מיבמה לשוק ומגוי ועבד, אע"ג דלא דמו לאשת אב, דהא מוי"ו ד"ולא יגלה" נפקי כולהו, וסמיך ליה לא יבא ממזר. ולא ילפינן מידי מאשת אב, אלא בהדיא כתיב בכולהו ממזרות. אבל לתנא דמתניתין, דאין ממזר לר' עקיבא אלא מחייבי לאוין דשאר, ולא דריש וי"ו ד"ולא יגלה" – לא נפקי שום חייבי לאוין אלא מאשת אב, בעינן דליהוי דומיא דאשת אב דלא תפסי בה קידושין לדידיה ותפסי בה לאחריני. וה"פ דברייתא ד"האשה רבה" (ג"ז שם): זו דברי ר' עקיבא דאמר אין קדושין נמי תפסי בכל חייבי לאוין דלאו דשאר. פי': מוי"ו ד"ולא יגלה" שמעינן בכולהו דהוה ממזר, ולהכי אין קידושין תופסין נמי בכולן, ולהכי אין לחלק בין לאו יבמה לשוק לשאר לאוין, כדפירשתי. אבל חכמים אומרים אין ממזר מיבמה, דכיון דקידושין תופסין בחייבי לאוין דלאו דשאר, ולא הוי ממזר מינייהו – לא הוי ממזר נמי מיבמה לשוק, אע"ג דאין קידושין תופסין בה, כיון דלא דמיא לאשת אב. **סוטה** נמי דהא תפסי בה קדושין. פי' בקונט': דאף לאחר שזינתה לא פקעי מינה קידושיה הראשונים. וק' לר"י: דנדה נמי לא פקעי קידושיה ואפילו הכי איצטריך קרא לאתויי דתפסי בה קידושין! ואר"י: דגרס, וכן ברוב ספרים, סוטה נמי הא כתיב בה הויה ותפסי בה קידושין. פי': שגרשה ומחזירה, והויה דכתיב בה היינו קרא "להיות לו לאשה" דמוקמינן בפ"ק (לעיל יא: ושם) לרבות סוטה. וכן משמע בפרק "יש מותרות" (לקמן ד' פה:) דבסוטה ודאי תפסי קידושין. ולא פליגי אלא אי אית לה כתובה אי לאו, דקאמר: סוטה ודאי איכא בינייהו, דמ"ד דאורייתא – הא נמי דאורייתא, ואית לה כתובה כו'. והיינו על כרחך במחזיר סוטה אחר שגירשה, דאי לא גירשה, כיון דזנתה – הפסידה כתובתה. ובפרק "עשרה יוחסין" (קדושין ד' עח.) נמי משמע ד"להיות לו" משמע לשון הויה, דקאמר: ושניהם מודים במחזיר גרושתו, שאם בעל ולא קידש – שאין לוקה, דרך הויה אסרה תורה. וא"ת: בסוף "האומר" בקידושין (ד' סח. ושם) ור' עקיבא "כי תהיין" במאי מוקי לה? לוקמה במחזיר סוטה! וכ"ת דכי תהיין מיותר, וסוטה נפקא לן מקרא ד"להיות לו לאשה" – א"כ היכי מוקי לה באלמנה לכ"ג וכדר' סימאי, הא כתיב "לא יחלל" – חילולין הוא עושה, ואין עושה ממזרים! וי"ל: דלא בעי לאוקמא בסוטה, משום דשנואה משמע שהיא שנואה בתחלת נישואין. וא"ת: ולוקמה בסוטה ולבועל! וי"ל: דמי כתיב כי תהיין לבועל, כדקאמר התם מי כתיב כי תהיין לכהן? א"נ: בבועל לא כתיב הויה, ולא תפסי בה קידושין. פר"ת: דמסוטה, נהי דלא הוי ממזר מדאורייתא – מדרבנן מיהא הוי ממזר, מידי דהוי (לקמן פז:) אאשה שהלך בעלה למדינת הים, ואמרו לה מת בעליך ונישאת, ואח"כ בא בעלה, דהולד ממזר ותלא מזה ומזה. ואין ראיה, דהתם קנסוה כי היכי דתידוק, אבל הכא – אין צריך לקונסה כדי שלא תזנה תחת בעלה. ועוד דבריש "יש מותרות" (לקמן ד' פה: ושם) קאמר גבי סוטה למ"ד דמרגלא ליה – הא איהי מרגליתו, ואי הוי ממזר – אפילו מדרבנן לא מרגלא ליה, כדאמר התם גבי חלוצה(א). **אי כרב אי כשמואל.** מתוך פי' הקונט' משמע דלרב ליכא לאו ביבמה. דפי': אי כרב, דאמר ב"האשה רבה" (לקמן ד' צב:) מנין שאין קידושין תופסין ביבמה, שנאמר "לא תהיה וגו'" – לא תהא בה הויה לזר, והולד ממזר, ואי כשמואל דמספקא ליה אי להכי הוא דאתא כדקאמר רב, או לאוקומי ללאו הוא דאתא, וקידושין תפסי בה, מדאפיק לאו דידה בלשון הויה. ואין נראה, דאמרינן ב"האומר" בקידושין (ד' סח. ושם) מאי יבמה שהיא בלאו *לא תפסי בה קידושין. אלמא איכא לאו אפילו למ"ד דלא תפסי בה קידושין – ובכל מקום חשיב יבמה לשוק חייבי לאוין! ואותם ששאלו לר' יהושע בני נרות דבית הלל לב"ש (לעיל ד' טו:) דקבעי למילף יבמה לשוק בקל וחומר מאלמנה, משמע דאיכא לאו! ואומר רבינו תם: דלכולי עלמא אית בה לאו, וה"ק לקמן: ושמואל מספקא ליה אי ללאו הוא דאתא, ותהיה אורחיה *דקרא(ג), או לאשמועינן דלקי אקידושין, או לקידושין דלא תפסי נמי הוא דאתא. **אשוייה** מזיד. פר"ח: שרצה להשיבו דמשה *)כתיב "ויראו את אלהי ישראל" (שמות כד).

*) נ"ל דבמשה נמי כתיב. יעב"ץ

מוסיפין

עין משפט נר מצוה

קנא א מיי' פ"ד מהל' איסורי ביאה הל' יב סמג עשין מח טוש"ע אה"ע סימן מד סעיף ו:

קנב ב מיי' פט"ו מהל' איסורי ביאה הלכה א סמג לאוין קטז טוש"ע שם סימן ד סעיף יג:

קנג ג מיי' פ"ז מהלכות יסודי התורה הל' ו:

קנד ד מיי' פ"ב מהל' תשובה הל' ו:

מסורת הש"ס

קדושין סח.

[לעיל יג. לקמן לב: נב.]

[[לעיל לו.] לקמן ב עירובין סב: גיטין ס. בכורות כג:]

[שני פרקים אמלה זו חמלה בתו"כ פ' לב כלים מ"ב]

לקמן קה. ר"ה יח.

[נ"ל ולא תפסי כו']

הגהות הב"ח

(א) רש"י ד"ה שומרת יבם שנשאה אחד מן וכו' במתניתין למחזיר גרושתו וטעמא: (ב) תום' ד"ה (בעמוד הקודם) הכל מודים וכו' מידי דהוי אגוי ועבד כו': (ג) ד"ה אי כרב וכו' אורחיה דקרא ולאשמעינן דלקי אקידושין או אתי נמי לאשמעינן דלא תפסי קידושין הס"ד:

תוספות חד מקמאי

שלא ב"ל. וס"ל לרב דלא מתוקמה התם מתניתא כר"מ דהא לר"מ אדם מקנה דשלב"ל כדתניא קונם שאיני עושה לפיך א"צ להפר ר"מ אומר יפר שמא תעדיף עליו יותר מן הראוי לו ולא ס"ל לרב התם אוקימתא דאוקמ' רבה בר רב הונא בריה דר"י באומר יקדשו ידים לעושיהם. ושמואל מספקא ליה וס"ל אין ממזר מיבמה ממזר ודאי אבל ספק ממזר הוי וכיון דקי"ל כשמואל יש ממזר ספק מיבמה והא דתניא הכל מודים בבא על הנדה ועל הסוטה ועל שומרת יבם שאין הולד ממזר. (בנדרים) [לצדדין] קתני בנדה אינו ממזר כלל אפי' בספק בשומרת יבם אינו ממזר ודאי אבל ממזר ספק הוי. ואסור בממזרת ואסור בישראלית. ואית דבעי מימר דאע"ג דס"ל לרב דאין קדושין תופסין מודה הוא דאין הולד ממזר ולא פליג אמתניתא. ושמואל נמי אע"ג דמספקא ליה אם קדושין תופסין בה אי לא מודה הוא דאין הולד ממזר [ואמנם] ממאי דאמר הכא דלאביי מספקא בשומרת יבם או כרב או כשמואל לא משמע הכי אלא משמע דהא בהא תליא אם אין קדושין תופסין בה הולד ממזר ואם קדושין תופסין בה הולד כשר:

גירסת רש"ל ולאשמועינן דלקי אקדושין או אתי למה דלא תפסי קדושין הס"ד

תוספות ישנים

א) והקשה הר' נתנאל כיון דנפקא לן מחזיר סוטתו מלא יוכל בעלה הראשון וכו' ואמרינן הכא דהולד כשר א"כ מאי טעמא דרבי עקיבא דאמר במחזיר גרושתו הולד ממזר. בשלמא לפ"ה ניחא דנימא דקרא דלא יוכל לא איירי כלל במחזיר סוטתו [אלא] במקיים סוטתו איירינן הכא דאית בה ראיה דאין הולד ממזר מטעם דלא פקעי קדושי ואפי' החזירה אין הולד ממזר לר"ע נמי כיון דאנתק לאו דלא יוכל לגבי מקיים סוטתו דהא אית בה הויה משום דלא פקעי קדושי מעתה נאמר הואיל ואשתראי הלאו איפשרי ואפילו החזירה לא יהיה הולד ממזר אבל במחזיר גרושתו יהא הולד ממזר אבל לפי הר"י דמקרא דלא יוכל שמעי' דאית הויה במחזיר סוטתו ואין הולד ממזר מאי שנא מחזיר גרושתו ממחזיר סוטתו. הא כולהו נפקי מחד קרא מלא יוכל וכו' וכתיב בתר כן הויה להיות לו לאשה. וי"ל דר"ע יתרץ שאני מחזיר גרושתו דכתיב בגופה תועבה אבל בסוטה לא. ואומר רא"ש כי מזה נוכל לתרץ קושיא דלעיל דפריך לעיל לר' עקיבא למאי איצטריך היא תועבה וכו' וצ"ע לעיל. והשתא נוכל לומר דשפיר איצטריך היא תועבה להיא גופה למימר דלא תפסי בה קדושי. דאי לא כתיב בגופה תועבה ה"א דתפסי בה קדושי ולא הוי הולד ממזר כמו בסוטה דכולהו מחד קרא נפקי דכתיב להיות וכו' א"כ תפסי בהו קדושי דקרא דלהיות קאי נמי אמחזיר גרושה עם סוטה וכו' [קמ"ל קרא דתועבה] כ"נ לרא"ש:

הגהות מהר"ב רנשבורג

א] רש"י ד"ה משנת ראב"י קב ונקי וכו'. במשנה או בברייתא עכ"ל. ובד"ה ונקי בכל מקום שנזכר הלכה כמותו עכ"ל. מבואר מזה שדעתו כדעת האומרים בזה דקיי"ל משנת ראב"י קב ונקי דהלכה כמותו היינו אף בברייתא וכן מוכיחין דברי רש"י בקידושין (דף סב ע"ב) בד"ה כמאן וכו'. וכן מוכיחין דברי הש"ס ביבמות דף לז ע"א ומוקי לה ראב"י אליבא דהלכתא דלא תקשי הלכתא אהלכתא ויעוי"ש דף לז ע"ב ברש"י ד"ה הלכתא אהלכתא דקיי"ל משנת ראב"י קב ונקי וכו' עכ"ל. והתם בברייתא הוא וש"מ דאף בברייתא איתא לכללא הדין. ולהאומרים דוקא במשנה קשה מסוגיא זו דאיך ובמה יפרשוה אם לא שידחקו לומר דידע הש"ס דבמקום הזה הלכה כראב"י אף שהוא בברייתא וצ"ע. אחרי העיון למתני לייתב בזה. די"ל בהכרח יעקב סוגיות מחולקות בזה. דלקמן דף ס ע"א פריך ומי סבר לה כוותיה והא קיי"ל משנת ראב"י קב ונקי ואילו בהא אמר ר"ע אמר רב אין הלכה כר"א ומסיק קשיא ולפי הכלל הידוע דכל דלא אמר הש"ס תיובתא אלא אמר קשיא יש תירוץ להקושיא צריך שהבין מה תירוץ יש בזה ובהכרח לומר דרב ס"ל דבברייתא אין הלכה כראב"י וא"כ תו לא ק"מ להני בעלי כללים ודו"ק ועי' מחנה לראובן בחדושי יבמות לקף ס ע"א מ"ש בזה:

(א) רש"י ד"ה נתן גט וכו' לאפקועי. נ"ב ע"ל דף נב ע"ב דיש לאו בגט ג"כ רק דהוא אסמכתא: (ב) ד"ה וחליצה וכו' לא מפטרא כשאר יבם שכונס את יבמתו:

אֵלּוּ שְׁנֵי דוֹרוֹת, זָכָה — מַשְׁלִימִין לוֹ, לֹא זָכָה — פּוֹחֲתִין לוֹ. דִּבְרֵי רַ' עֲקִיבָא. וַחֲכָמִים אוֹמְרִים: זָכָה — מוֹסִיפִים לוֹ, לֹא זָכָה — פּוֹחֲתִין לוֹ. אָמְרוּ לוֹ לְרַבִּי עֲקִיבָא: הֲרֵי הוּא אוֹמֵר "וְהוֹסַפְתִּי עַל יָמֶיךָ חֲמֵשׁ עֶשְׂרֵה שָׁנָה"! אָמַר לָהֶם: מִשֶּׁלּוֹ הוֹסִיפוּ לוֹ. תֵּדַע, שֶׁהֲרֵי נָבִיא עוֹמֵד וּמִתְנַבֵּא (מ"א יג) "הִנֵּה בֵן נוֹלָד לְבֵית דָּוִד יֹאשִׁיָּהוּ שְׁמוֹ" וַעֲדַיִין לֹא נוֹלַד מְנַשֶּׁה. וְרַבָּנַן: מִי כְּתִיב מֵחִזְקִיָּה? "לְבֵית דָּוִד" כְּתִיב, אִי מֵחִזְקִיָּה נוֹלַד, אִי מֵאֱינָשׁ אַחֲרִינָא.§ "אִשְׁתּוֹ שֶׁמֵּתָה וכו' יְבִמְתּוֹ שֶׁמֵּתָה וכו'".§ אָמַר רַב יוֹסֵף: כָּאן שָׁנָה רַבִּי מִשְׁנָה שֶׁאֵינָהּ צְרִיכָה.§

הדרן עלך החולץ

רַבָּן גַּמְלִיאֵל אוֹמֵר: אֵין גֵּט אַחַר גֵּט, וְלֹא מַאֲמָר אַחַר מַאֲמָר, וְלֹא בְּעִילָה אַחַר בְּעִילָה, וְלֹא חֲלִיצָה אַחַר חֲלִיצָה. וַחֲכָמִים אוֹמְרִים: [א]יֵשׁ גֵּט אַחַר גֵּט, [ב]וְיֵשׁ מַאֲמָר אַחַר מַאֲמָר, [ג]אֲבָל לֹא אַחַר בְּעִילָה וְלֹא אַחַר חֲלִיצָה כְּלוּם. [ד]כֵּיצַד? עָשָׂה מַאֲמָר בִּיבִמְתּוֹ, וְנָתַן לָהּ גֵּט — צְרִיכָה הֵימֶנּוּ חֲלִיצָה. עָשָׂה מַאֲמָר וַחֲלִיצָה — צְרִיכָה הֵימֶנּוּ גֵּט. עָשָׂה מַאֲמָר וּבָעַל — הֲרֵי זוֹ כְּמִצְוָתָהּ. [ה]נָתַן גֵּט וְעָשָׂה מַאֲמָר — צְרִיכָה גֵּט וַחֲלִיצָה. נָתַן גֵּט וּבָעַל — צְרִיכָה גֵּט וַחֲלִיצָה. נָתַן גֵּט וְחָלַץ — [ו]אֵין אַחַר חֲלִיצָה כְּלוּם. חָלַץ וְעָשָׂה מַאֲמָר, נָתַן גֵּט וּבָעַל, אוֹ בָּעַל וְעָשָׂה מַאֲמָר, נָתַן גֵּט וְחָלַץ — אֵין אַחַר חֲלִיצָה כְּלוּם.

אַחַת

רש"י

שְׁנֵי דוֹרוֹת. שָׁנִים שֶׁפּוֹסְקִין לְאָדָם בִּשְׁעַת לֵידָתוֹ. זָכָה מוֹסִיפִין לוֹ. וְהַאי "מַשְׁלִימִין" – לְשׁוֹן תּוֹסֶפֶת הוּא. מִשֶּׁלּוֹ הוֹסִיפוּ לוֹ. אֶלָּא שֶׁמִּתְּחִלָּה הָיוּ רוֹצִים לִפְחוֹת מִשָּׁנָיו. תֵּדַע. שֶׁמִּתְּחִלָּה כְּשֶׁנּוֹלַד נִפְסְקוּ לוֹ כָּל אוֹתוֹ תּוֹסֶפֶת. שֶׁהֲרֵי נָבִיא נִתְנַבֵּא. בִּימֵי יָרָבְעָם שָׁנִים הַרְבֵּה קוֹדֶם "הִנֵּה בֵן נוֹלָד לְבֵית דָּוִד יֹאשִׁיָּהוּ שְׁמוֹ", וּבִשְׁעַת חָלְיוֹ שֶׁל חִזְקִיָּה עֲדַיִין לֹא נוֹלַד מְנַשֶּׁה שֶׁמִּמֶּנּוּ יָצָא יֹאשִׁיָּהוּ, הֲוֵי אוֹמֵר: בִּשְׁעַת חָלְיוֹ גָּזְרוּ לִפְחוֹת מִשָּׁנָיו, וּכְשֶׁזָּכָה – הִשְׁלִימוּ לוֹ. מִשְׁנָה שֶׁאֵינָהּ צְרִיכָה. דְּזִיל קְרִי בֵּי רַב הוּא "עָלֶיהָ בְּחַיֶּיהָ", שֶׁלֹּא נֶאֶסְרָה אֲחוֹתָהּ אֶלָּא בְּחַיֶּיהָ.

הדרן עלך החולץ

רַבָּן גַּמְלִיאֵל אוֹמֵר. סֵדֶר מִשְׁנָה זוֹ – שֶׁלֹּא תִּטְעֶה לְשַׁבֵּשׁ הַגִּירְסָא שֶׁבַּסְּפָרִים – סֵדֶר יָבָם אֶחָד וִיבָמָה אַחַת: תְּחִלָּה מְפָרֵשׁ דִּין גֵּט וַחֲלִיצָה וּבִיאָה שֶׁאַחַר מַאֲמָר, וְאַחַר כָּךְ מְפָרֵשׁ דִּין מַאֲמָר וּבִיאָה וַחֲלִיצָה שֶׁאַחַר הַגֵּט, וְאַחַר כָּךְ דִּין מַאֲמָר וְגֵט וּבִיאָה שֶׁאַחַר הַחֲלִיצָה, וְאַחַר כָּךְ דִּין מַאֲמָר וְגֵט וַחֲלִיצָה שֶׁאַחַר הַבִּיאָה. וְכֵן סֵדֶר יָבָם א' וּשְׁתֵּי יְבָמוֹת. אֵין גֵּט אַחַר גֵּט. שְׁתֵּי יְבָמוֹת לְאָדָם אֶחָד מֵאָח אֶחָד, וְנָתַן גֵּט לָזוֹ וְגֵט לָזוֹ – אֵינוֹ אָסוּר בִּקְרוֹבוֹת שְׁנִיָּה, דְּאִי קַמָּא אַהֲנֵי – הָא פָּקְעָה זִיקָה דְּתַרְוַיְיהוּ, וַהֲוֵי כִּמְגָרֵשׁ נָכְרִית. וְאִי קַמָּא לָא אַהֲנֵי לְמִידְחֵי – בַּתְרָא נָמֵי לָא אַהֲנֵי, וְהִלְכָּךְ לָאו גְּרוּשָׁתוֹ הִיא. וְכֵן שְׁנֵי יְבָמִין לִיבָמָה אַחַת, וְנָתַן זֶה גֵּט וְזֶה גֵּט – הָאַחֲרוֹן אֵינוֹ כְּלוּם, וּמוּתָּר בִּקְרוֹבוֹתֶיהָ. וְטַעְמָא כִּדְפָרֵישִׁית. וְלֹא מַאֲמָר אַחַר מַאֲמָר. בֵּין בְּיָבָם אֶחָד לִשְׁתֵּי יְבָמוֹת, בֵּין שְׁנֵי יְבָמִים לִיבָמָה אַחַת – הָאַחֲרוֹן אֵין כְּלוּם לִפְסוֹל אֶת הָרִאשׁוֹנָה עָלָיו, וְאֵינָהּ צְרִיכָה הֵימֶנּוּ גֵּט, וְלֹא לֵיאָסֵר בִּקְרוֹבוֹת הַשְּׁנִיָּה. וְלֹא בְּעִילָה אַחַר בְּעִילָה. בָּא עַל זוֹ וְחָזַר וּבָא הוּא אוֹ אָחִיו עַל צָרָתָהּ – בִּיאַת זְנוּת בְּעָלְמָא הוּא, וְאֵין אָסוּר בִּקְרוֹבוֹתֶיהָ. יֵשׁ גֵּט אַחַר גֵּט. דְּקַמָּא לָא דָּחָה לְגַמְרֵי, הִלְכָּךְ אַכַּתִּי אִיכָּא פַּלְגָּא זִיקָה, דְּהָא בָּעְיָא חֲלִיצָה. הִלְכָּךְ, אַהֲנֵי בַּתְרָא וַהֲוָיָא גְּרוּשָׁתוֹ, וְאָסוּר בִּקְרוֹבוֹתֶיהָ. כֵּיצַד. לָאו אַפְּלוּגְתָּא קָאֵי, אֶלָּא מִלְּתָא בְּאַנְפֵּי נַפְשָׁהּ הִיא, וְאַיָּבָם אֶחָד וְאַיְּבָמָה אַחַת קָאֵי. וְהָכִי קָאָמַר: כֵּיצַד דִּין יָבָם וִיבָמָה, וְהָכִי מְפָרֵשׁ בַּגְּמָ'. צְרִיכָה הֵימֶנּוּ חֲלִיצָה. וְאִם רָצָה לִכְנוֹס – לֹא יִכְנוֹס, דְּכֵיוָן דְּהִתְחִיל בְּגֵירוּשִׁין – קַיְימָא עֲלֵיהּ בְּ"לֹא יִבְנֶה". צְרִיכָה הֵימֶנּוּ גֵּט. דַּחֲלִיצָה אַפְקַעְתָּהּ לְזִיקָתָהּ, וּבָעֵי גֵּט לְאַפְקוּעֵי קִדּוּשִׁין דִּילֵיהּ, דַּחֲלִיצָה לֹא מַפְקַעַת קִידּוּשִׁין. הֲרֵי זוֹ כְּמִצְוָתָהּ. מְפָרֵשׁ בַּגְּמָרָא: אַף זוֹ כְּמִצְוָתָהּ. נָתַן גֵּט וְעָשָׂה מַאֲמָר. בְּאוֹתָהּ יְבָמָה עַצְמָהּ, אֲפִי' ר"ג מוֹדֶה דְּיֵשׁ מַאֲמָר אַחַר הַגֵּט. דְּמִסְפְּקָא לֵיהּ אִי גֵּט דָּחֵי אִי לָא, וְדִלְמָא גֵּט לָא דָּחֵי, וְאַהֲנֵי מַאֲמָר יְבָמִין בָּהּ. וְכ"ש לְרַבָּנַן דְּאָמְרִי גֵּט דּוֹחֶה קְצָת וּמְשַׁיֵּיר קְצָת – אַהֲנֵי מַאֲמָר לְמִיקְנֵי שִׁיּוּרָא דְּגֵט, וְצָרִיךְ גֵּט לְמַאֲמָרוֹ וַחֲלִיצָה לְזִיקָתוֹ. וְיַבּוּמֵי – לָא, דְּמִגֵּט קַמָּא קַיְימָא עֲלֵיהּ בְּ"לֹא יִבְנֶה". נָתַן גֵּט וּבָעַל. אָסוּר לְקַיְּימָהּ, דְּקָמָה עֲלֵיהּ בְּ"לֹא יִבְנֶה", וּצְרִיכָה גֵּט לְבִיאָתוֹ וַחֲלִיצָה לְזִיקָתוֹ. גֵּט לְבִיאָתוֹ, וַאֲפִילּוּ לְר' עֲקִיבָא דְּאָמַר אֵין קִידּוּשִׁין תּוֹפְסִין בְּחַיָּיבֵי לָאוִין, דְּהָא הָךְ מַתְנִי' כּוּלָּהּ ר' עֲקִיבָא הִיא, כִּדְמְפָרֵשׁ בַּגְּמָ', הָכָא מוֹדֵי דְּתָפְסֵי קִידּוּשֵׁי בִּיאָה. דְּגֵט לָאו כַּחֲלִיצָה דָּמֵי (א) לְאַפְקוּעֵי כּוּלָּהּ זִיקָה, הִלְכָּךְ לֹא עָמְדָה עָלָיו בְּלָאו גָּמוּר. וַחֲלִיצָה. לְזִיקָתוֹ. וּבְגֵט לְחוּדֵיהּ לָא מִפַּטְרָא (ב), [כְּמוֹ] שֶׁאַחֵר כּוֹנֵס אֶת יְבִמְתּוֹ שֶׁיָּכוֹל לְפוֹטְרָהּ בְּגֵט. מִשּׁוּם דַּהֲוֵי בִּיאָה פְּסוּלָה מִשּׁוּם גֵּט קַמָּא, וְלָא קַנְיָא לְגַמְרֵי. אֵין לְאַחַר חֲלִיצָה כְּלוּם. וְאַע"ג דַּחֲלִיצָה פְּסוּלָה הִיא. דְּאִי הֲוָה בָּעֵי לְיַיבּוּמֵי – לָא מָצֵי, וְאַפ"ה דָּחְיָא לְגַמְרֵי, וְאֵין אַחֲרֶיהָ כְּלוּם. דְּאִי הָדַר וּמְקַדֵּשׁ לָהּ בְּמַאֲמָר אוֹ בְּבִיאָה – לָא בָּעֵינַן גֵּט, וְכִדְרַבִּי עֲקִיבָא דְּאָמַר אֵין קִידּוּשִׁין תּוֹפְסִין בְּחַיָּיבֵי לָאוִין. וְהָכִי מְפָרֵשׁ בַּגְּמָ', דְּמַתְנִי' ר"ע הִיא. חָלַץ וְעָשָׂה בָּהּ מַאֲמָר. אוֹ נָתַן גֵּט אַחַר חֲלִיצָה, אוֹ בָּעַל אַחַר חֲלִיצָה – אֵינוֹ כְּלוּם, כִּדְתָנֵי בְּסֵיפָא: אֵין אַחַר חֲלִיצָה כְּלוּם. שֶׁאֵין מַאֲמָר וּבִיאָה תּוֹפְסִין בָּהּ אַחַר חֲלִיצָה כְּר' עֲקִיבָא, וְגֵט דְּאַחַר חֲלִיצָה לָא הֲוָה צָרִיךְ לְמִיתְנֵי לְאַשְׁמוּעִינַן דְּאֵין כְּלוּם, דִּלְמַאי לִיהֲנֵי? לִיתְסוּרֵי בִּקְרוֹבוֹתֶיהָ – הָא מִיתְּסַר וְקָאֵי מֵחֲמַת חֲלִיצָה. אֶלָּא אַיְּדֵי דְּבָעֵי לְמִיתְנֵי גֵּט דְּאַחַר בְּעִילָה, כִּדְקָתָנֵי אוֹ בָּעַל וְעָשָׂה מַאֲמָר וְנָתַן גֵּט, לְאַשְׁמוּעִינַן דְּאֵין לְאַחַר בִּיאָה כְּלוּם זִיקַת יִבּוּמִים, וּבְהַאי גֵּט סַגִּי לֵיהּ בְּלֹא חֲלִיצָה – תָּנָא נָמֵי גֵּט דְּאַחַר חֲלִיצָה, וְהָכִי מְפָרֵשׁ בַּגְּמָ'. אוֹ בָּעַל וְעָשָׂה מַאֲמָר. אוֹ נָתַן גֵּט אַחַר בִּיאָה, אוֹ חָלַץ אַחַר בִּיאָה – אֵין לְאַחַר בִּיאָה כְּלוּם. זִיקַת יְבָמִים דְּגֵט שֶׁנָּתַן אַחַר בִּיאָה מְגָרֵשׁ לָהּ כְּאִשְׁתּוֹ גְּמוּרָה, וְלָא בָּעְיָא חֲלִיצָה. וְאִם רָצָה לְהַחֲזִיר – מַחֲזִירָהּ. וַחֲלִיצָה שֶׁעָשָׂה אַחַר בִּיאָה – אֵינָהּ מוֹעֶלֶת כְּלוּם, דְּאֵין עָלֶיהָ זִיקַת יְבָמִין. וּמַאֲמָר דְּאַחַר בִּיאָה לָא הֲוָה צָרִיךְ לְמִיתְנֵי, דִּפְשִׁיטָא לָן דְּלָא מְהַנֵּי. דִּלְמַאי לִיהֲנֵי? הָא אֲפִילּוּ מַאֲמָר אַחַר מַאֲמָר בְּיָבָם אֶחָד וִיבָמָה אַחַת – בַּתְרָא כְּמַאן דְּלֵיתֵיהּ דָּמֵי, דְּמַאי קָעָבֵיד? הָא מִיתְּסַר וְקָאֵי בִּקְרוֹבוֹתֶיהָ. אֶלָּא אַיְּדֵי דְּתָנָא רֵישָׁא חָלַץ וְעָשָׂה מַאֲמָר, דְּאִיצְטְרִיךְ לְאַשְׁמוּעִינַן כְּר' עֲקִיבָא דְּאֵין קִידּוּשִׁין תּוֹפְסִין בַּחֲלוּצָתוֹ – תָּנָא נָמֵי בָּעַל וְעָשָׂה מַאֲמָר, וְהָכִי מְפָרֵשׁ בַּגְּמָ'. אֵין אַחַר חֲלִיצָה כְּלוּם. אַרֵישָׁא קָאֵי, וּכְדְפָרֵישִׁית לְעֵיל. וְאַלִּישָּׁנָא דְּסֵיפָא, דְּקָתָנֵי אוֹ בָּעַל וְעָשָׂה מַאֲמָר אוֹ נָתַן גֵּט וְחָלַץ, הֲוָה שַׁיָּיךְ לְמִיתְנֵי אֵין אַחַר בִּיאָה כְּלוּם, וּבַגְּמָרָא קָא בָּעֵי לֵיהּ.

אַחַת

תוספות

מוסיפין לו. והא דאמר במועד קטן (דף כח. ושם): בני חיי ומזוני לאו בזכותא תליא מילתא אלא במזלא תליא מילתא – פשיטא דזכות גדול מועיל, כדאמר בשבת (דף קנו: ושם): אין מזל לישראל. ומיהו, לא שכיח שישתנה המזל, כדמוכח בתענית (דף כה.) גבי עובדא דר"א בן פדת.

משלו הוסיפו לו. וקרי ליה תוספת – לפי מה שנגזר לפחות ע"י עון. והא דאמר בפ"ק דחגיגה (דף ד: ושם) גבי איתתא מגדלא נשיא כי חזינן צורבא מרבנן דמעבר אמיליה מוסיפין ליה – אר"י דניחא אפילו לר"ע, דאין זה תוספת, כיון שנגזרו לשום אדם.

תדע שהרי נביא עומד. וא"ת: והלא אם לא התפלל חזקיהו על עצמו היה מת, והיתה נבואה בטלה! אלא ע"כ אין הנביא מתנבא אלא מה שראוי להיות אם לא היה חוטא. א"כ, היכי מוכח מכאן דמשלו הוסיפו לו? אפי' לא הוסיפו לו משלו, והיה כבר כל שנותיו שנגזרו לו – מה שלא נתקיימה הנבואה לפי שחטא, ואילו לא חטא ונשא אשה בשנים הראשונים – היה מוליד! ואר"י: דשמא הדורות נגזרו להוולד באותו הזמן ובאותו הפרק שהם נולדים. ובשני התוספת נגזר לו להוליד מנשה.

שנה רבי משנה שאינה צריכה. פ"ה: דזיל קרי בי רב הוא. וקשה: דבכמה מקומות שונה התנא מה שבפסוק בפירוש! ועוד: דגרשה ומתה מותר באחותה איצטריך למידק, הא לא מתה – אסירא, דלא כתיב בהדיא, ודרשינן לה בפ"ק (דף ח:) מ"עליה בחייה" – כל שבחייה, אפילו נתגרשה! אלא נראה לר"י דיבמתו היא משנה שאין צריכה, דכיון דתנא אשתו – כ"ש יבמתו(א).

הדרן עלך החולץ

רבן גמליאל. אין מאמר אחר מאמר. אתי אפי' כרבנן דרבי עקיבא, אע"ג דקידושין לדידהו תופסין בחייבי לאוין. ותפסי קידושין אחר ביאה – התם הוא משום דהוו קדושין דאורייתא, דע"י ביאה פקעה זיקה. אבל הכא, שהיא זקוקה לו – אין לו לתפוס אלא מדרבנן, ולא תקון רבנן שיהא מאמר אחר מאמר. ולהכי לא קאמר בגמרא עלה זו דברי ר' עקיבא. ולא כמו שפי' ריב"ן דר"ג כר"ע.

ולא בעילה אחר בעילה. היינו אחר בעילה כשרה, אבל אחר בעילה פסולה, כגון ביאה שאחר הגט – יש אחריה ביאה, כי היכי דיש אחריה מאמר, כמו שמפרש בגמ'.

ולא חליצה אחר חליצה. היינו אפילו אחר חליצה פסולה.

עשה מאמר ביבמתו ונתן לה גט צריכה חליצה. היינו בנתן גט סתם, אף לזיקתו. אבל אם נתן גט למאמרו – שריא אף ליבם, דאמר בפ' "ד' אחין" (לעיל דף לב.) דהותרה אפי' היא, דמאי דעבד – שקליה.

עשה מאמר וחליץ צריכה הימנו גט. הכא לא תני אין אחר חליצה כלום – משום דאכתי צריכה גט למאמר שכבר ולא תני ליה אלא היכא דאחר חליצה אין צריך לעשות כלום.

חליץ ועשה מאמר כו'. אומר ריב"ן: לא הוה צריך למיתני כלל, דכיון דתנא נתן גט וחלץ אין אחר חליצה כלום, אע"פ שהיא חליצה פסולה – כ"ש דאחר חליצה כשירה אין אחריה כלום, אלא כל העניינים שונה.

עשה

תוספות ישנים

א) ואע"ג דגבי יבמה איכא למידק באחותה אין באמה לא כדדייקי' בפ"ב. ר' יוסף לית ליה ההוא דיוקא דקסבר אין זיקה אבל בבא דאשתו צריכה שלא תדרוש כל שבחייה לדרשא אחריתא כדבעיא למדרשיה בפ"ק [דף ח ע"ב] ונשאת לאחר נמי אצטריך דלא תימא כי לא מתה נמי כיון שנשאת לאחר כמתה דמיא. מאחר דאסור להחזיר גרושתו משנשאת והוה אמינא דשרי באחותה:

עין משפט נר מצוה

א א מיי' פ"ה מהלכות יבום הלכה יד טוש"ע אה"ע סימן קע סעיף ג:
ב ב מיי' שם טוש"ע שם סעיף ו:
ג ג מיי' שם טוש"ע שם סעיף יב:
ד ד מיי' שם הלכה ד טוש"ע שם סעי' ב:
ה ה מיי' שם הלכה ז טוש"ע שם סעיף ט וסעיף י:
ו ו מיי' שם טוש"ע שם סעיף יד:

ז א מיי' פ"ה מהלכות יבום הלכה יז טוש"ע אה"ע סימן קע סעיף ו:
ח ב מיי' שם הלכה ו טוש"ע שם סעיף ז:
ט ג מיי' שם טוש"ע שם סעיף ח:
י ד מיי' שם טוש"ע שם סעיף ז:
יא ה מיי' שם הלכה טו טוש"ע שם סעיף א וסעיף ה:
יב ו טוש"ע שם סעיף יד:
יג ז שם סעיף יא:
יד ח שם סעיף יד:
טו ט שם סעיף יג:
טז י מיי' שם הלכה ט טוש"ע שם סעיף יד:
יז כ מיי' שם הלכה ז טוש"ע שם סעי' א:
יח ל מיי' שם הלכה ב טוש"ע שם סעי' ב:
יט מ מיי' שם הלכה ט טוש"ע שם סעיף יד:

עשה מאמר בזו ומאמר בזו צריכות ב' גיטין וחליצה. הכא שייך להקשות: דיתן גט לאחת מהן למאמרו ותשתרי אידך. ולעיל פי' (דף לב. ד"ה "גט"). **צריכות** ב' גיטין וחליצה. למ"ד חליצה פסולה צריכה לחזור – הכא בעו ב' חליצות, וקאי נמי צריכות אחליצה.

ובסמוך דקתני עשה מאמר ונתן גט צריכה גט וחליצה, הא דלא קתני וצריכות חליצה לשון רבים – איידי דקתני צריכה גט, לשון יחיד, נקט נמי גבי חליצה לשון יחיד. **מדגט** לא מהני חליצה נמי לא מהניא. בקשה דעלמא ליכא למיחש שמא יאמרו: מדחליצה לא מהני – גט נמי לא מהני, דבאשה לא שייך חליצה וקריאה. ואין לומר דתיבעי יבמה גט וחליצה משום דלא יאמרו מדחליצה לחודה מהניא גט נמי מהני – דבהא לא יטעו שיפטרוה בלא חליצה, דבהדיא הצריך הכתוב חליצה. אבל הכא, חיישינן שיאמרו מה שהצריך הכתוב חליצה, היינו מלבד הגט שהוא בכל הנשים, ויאמרו: מדגט לחודיה לא מהני – חליצה נמי לא מהניא, ואתי למיבעל אחר חליצה. **ואתי** למיבעל אחר ביאה. אבל השתא דמהני לא חיישינן שמא יאמרו: כי היכי דמהני ביאה אחר גט ומאמר – מהני נמי אחר ביאה וחליצה, ואתי למיבעל אחר ביאה כמו אחר מאמר. דאחר מאמר נמי אסור למיבעל.

דמספקא

אַחַת יְבָמָה אַחַת לְיָבָם אֶחָד, וְאַחַת שְׁתֵּי יְבָמוֹת לְיָבָם אֶחָד. ^א כֵּיצַד? עָשָׂה מַאֲמָר בָּזוֹ וּמַאֲמָר בָּזוֹ — צְרִיכוֹת שְׁנֵי גִּיטִּין וַחֲלִיצָה. ^ב מַאֲמָר בָּזוֹ וְגֵט לָזוֹ — צְרִיכָה גֵּט וַחֲלִיצָה. ^ג מַאֲמָר בָּזוֹ וּבָעַל אֶת זוֹ — צְרִיכוֹת ב' גִּיטִּין וַחֲלִיצָה. ^ד מַאֲמָר בָּזוֹ וְחָלַץ לָזוֹ — הָרִאשׁוֹנָה צְרִיכָה גֵּט. ^ה גֵּט לָזוֹ וְגֵט לָזוֹ — צְרִיכוֹת הֵימֶנּוּ חֲלִיצָה. ^ו גֵּט לָזוֹ וּבָעַל אֶת זוֹ — צְרִיכָה גֵּט וַחֲלִיצָה. ^ז גֵּט לָזוֹ וּמַאֲמָר בָּזוֹ — צְרִיכָה גֵּט וַחֲלִיצָה. ^ח גֵּט לָזוֹ וְחָלַץ לָזוֹ — אֵין אַחַר חֲלִיצָה כְּלוּם. ^ט חָלַץ וְחָלַץ, אוֹ חָלַץ וְעָשָׂה מַאֲמָר, נָתַן גֵּט וּבָעַל, אוֹ בָּעַל וּבָעַל, אוֹ בָּעַל וְעָשָׂה מַאֲמָר, נָתַן גֵּט וְחָלַץ — אֵין אַחַר חֲלִיצָה כְּלוּם, בֵּין יָבָם אֶחָד לִשְׁתֵּי יְבָמוֹת. בֵּין שְׁנֵי יְבָמִין לִיבָמָה אַחַת. חָלַץ וְעָשָׂה מַאֲמָר, נָתַן גֵּט וּבָעַל, אוֹ בָּעַל וְעָשָׂה מַאֲמָר, וְנָתַן גֵּט וְחָלַץ — אֵין אַחַר חֲלִיצָה כְּלוּם, בֵּין בַּתְּחִלָּה בֵּין בָּאֶמְצַע בֵּין בַּסּוֹף. ^י וְהַבְּעִילָה, בִּזְמַן שֶׁהִיא בַּתְּחִלָּה — אֵין אַחֲרֶיהָ כְּלוּם. בָּאֶמְצַע וּבַסּוֹף — יֵשׁ אַחֲרֶיהָ כְּלוּם. *רַבִּי נְחֶמְיָה אוֹמֵר: אַחַת בְּעִילָה וְאַחַת חֲלִיצָה, בֵּין בַּתְּחִלָּה בֵּין בָּאֶמְצַע בֵּין בַּסּוֹף — אֵין אַחֲרֶיהָ כְּלוּם.§ **גמ'** עַד כָּאן לָא פְּלִיגִי אֶלָּא בְּגֵט אַחַר גֵּט וּמַאֲמָר אַחַר מַאֲמָר, ^כ אֲבָל גֵּט אֶחָד בִּיבָמָה [וּמַאֲמָר אֶחָד בִּיבָמָה] — מְהַנֵּי, מ"ט אָמוּר רַבָּנַן גֵּט בִּיבָמָה מְהַנֵּי — מִשּׁוּם דִּמְהַנֵּי בְּעָלְמָא. דְּאִי אָמְרַתְּ לָא מְהַנֵּי, אָמְרִי: גֵּט לְהוֹצִיאָהּ וַחֲלִיצָה לְהוֹצִיאָהּ וּמִדְּגֵט לָא מְהַנֵּי — חֲלִיצָה נַמִּי לָא מְהַנֵּי, וְאָתֵי לְמִיבְעַל אַחַר חֲלִיצָה. וּמַאי טַעְמָא ^ל אָמוּר רַבָּנַן מַאֲמָר בִּיבָמָה מְהַנֵּי — מִשּׁוּם דִּמְהַנֵּי בְּעָלְמָא. דְּאִי אָמְרַתְּ לָא מְהַנֵּי, אָמְרִי: מַאֲמָר לִקְנוֹת וּבִיאָה לִקְנוֹת, וּמִדְּמַאֲמָר לָא מְהַנֵּי — בִּיאָה נַמִּי לָא מְהַנְיָא וְאָתֵי לְמִבְעַל אַחַר בִּיאָה. וּמ"ט אָמוּר רַבָּנַן ^מ בִּיאָה פְּסוּלָה יֵשׁ אַחֲרֶיהָ כְּלוּם — אָמְרִי: אִי בִּיאָה אַחַר הַגֵּט הִיא — גְּזֵירָה בִּיאָה אַחַר הַגֵּט מִשּׁוּם בִּיאָה אַחַר חֲלִיצָה, וְאִי בִּיאָה אַחַר מַאֲמָר הִיא — גְּזֵירָה בִּיאָה אַחַר מַאֲמָר מִשּׁוּם בִּיאָה אַחַר בִּיאָה. וּמ"ט אָמוּר רַבָּנַן ^נ הַאי חֲלִיצָה פְּסוּלָה אֵין אַחֲרֶיהָ כְּלוּם — אָמְרִי: מַאי לִגְזוֹר? נִגְזוֹר חֲלִיצָה אַחַר הַגֵּט מִשּׁוּם חֲלִיצָה אַחַר חֲלִיצָה — כָּל כִּי הָנֵי תַּחְלוֹץ וְתֵיזִיל?! לִיגְזוֹר חֲלִיצָה אַחַר מַאֲמָר מִשּׁוּם חֲלִיצָה אַחַר בִּיאָה — אַטּוּ חֲלִיצָה אַחַר מַאֲמָר מִי לָא בָּעֲיָא גֵּט לְמַאֲמָרוֹ? חֲלִיצָה אַחַר בִּיאָה נַמִּי — בָּעֲיָא גֵּט לְבִיאָתוֹ. אָמַר רָבָא:

מ"ט

אַחַת יְבָמָה אַחַת לְיָבָם אֶחָד וְאַחַת שְׁתֵּי יְבָמוֹת לְיָבָם אֶחָד. שָׁוִין, כְּמוֹ שֶׁאָמַרְנוּ, שֶׁיֵּשׁ אַחַר גֵּט רִאשׁוֹן אוֹ אַחַר מַאֲמָר רִאשׁוֹן כְּלוּם, וְאֵין אַחַר בִּיאָה שֶׁבַּתְּחִלָּה, אוֹ אַחַר חֲלִיצָה, כְּלוּם. כֵּיצַד. בִּשְׁתֵּי יְבָמוֹת לְיָבָם אֶחָד. צְרִיכוֹת שְׁנֵי גִיטִּין. כְּרַבָּנַן, דְּיֵשׁ מַאֲמָר אַחַר מַאֲמָר. וְיַיבּוּמֵי לָא, דְּהֵיכִי לִיעֲבִיד? אִי לְיַיבּוּמֵי לְתַרְוַיְיהוּ – הָווּ לְהוּ שְׁנֵי בָּתִּים. וְאִי לַחֲדָא, הוֹאִיל וַחֲבֶרְתָּהּ בֵּיהּ אֲגִידָא – הָוֵה לֵיהּ בּוֹנֶה שְׁנֵי בָּתִּים. וַחֲלִיצָה. לְאַחַת מֵהֶן, וּפוֹטֶרֶת צָרָתָהּ. מַאֲמָר לָזוֹ וְגֵט לָזוֹ. פָּסַל גֵּט שֶׁל אַחֲרוֹנָה אֶת הָרִאשׁוֹנָה, דְּקָם לֵיהּ בְּ"לֹא יִבְנֶה", וּצְרִיכָה גֵּט לְמַאֲמָרוֹ וַחֲלִיצָה לְזִיקָתוֹ. דַּחֲלִיצָה לָא מַפְקְעָא קִידּוּשִׁין, וְגֵט לָא מַפְקַע זִיקָה. מַאֲמָר לָזוֹ וּבָעַל אֶת זוֹ. אָסוּר לְקַיְּימָהּ, דְּהוֹאִיל וְקַמַּיְיתָא אֲגִידָא בֵּיהּ – הָווּ לְהוּ שְׁנֵי בָּתִּים. וּצְרִיכוֹת שְׁנֵי גִיטִּין: זוֹ גֵּט לְמַאֲמָרוֹ, וְזוֹ גֵּט לְבִיאָתוֹ, וַחֲלִיצָה לְאַחַת מֵהֶן, וּפוֹטֶרֶת צָרָתָהּ. אֲבָל בְּגֵט לְחוּדֵיהּ לָא נָפְקָא בַּעֲלַת בִּיאָה, הוֹאִיל דְּבִיאָה פְּסוּלָה הִיא. מַאֲמָר בָּזוֹ וְחָלַץ לָזוֹ. בַּעֲלַת מַאֲמָר הָרִאשׁוֹנָה צְרִיכָה גֵּט לְמַאֲמָר, דַּחֲלִיצָה דְּאִידָךְ לָא מַפְקְעָה לְמַאֲמָרוֹ. צְרִיכוֹת הֵימֶנּוּ חֲלִיצָה. אַחַת, וְאָסוּר בִּקְרוֹבוֹת שְׁנִיָּה. דְּרַבָּנַן הוּא דְּאָמְרִי: יֵשׁ גֵּט אַחַר גֵּט. גֵּט לָזוֹ וּבָעַל אֶת זוֹ צְרִיכָה גֵּט וַחֲלִיצָה. וְאָסוּר לְקַיְּימָהּ, דְּקָמָה עֲלֵיהּ בְּ"לֹא יִבְנֶה", מִשּׁוּם גֵּט דְּרִאשׁוֹנָה. וּבְגֵט לְחוּדֵיהּ לָא נָפְקָא, מִשּׁוּם דְּבִיאָה פְּסוּלָה הִיא. אֵין לְאַחַר חֲלִיצָה כְּלוּם. דְּאִי הֲדַר מְקַדֵּשׁ לָהּ לְצָרָתָהּ לָא תָּפְסִי בָּהּ קִידּוּשִׁין, כְּרַבִּי עֲקִיבָא. חָלַץ וְחָלַץ אוֹ חָלַץ וְעָשָׂה מַאֲמָר וְנָתַן גֵּט וּבָעַל וְקָתָנֵי סֵיפָא אֵין לְאַחַר חֲלִיצָה כְּלוּם. וְהָכִי פֵּירוּשׁוֹ: חָלַץ לָזוֹ וְחָלַץ לָזוֹ – מוּתָּר בִּקְרוֹבוֹת שְׁנִיָּה, שֶׁאֵין אַחַר חֲלִיצָה רִאשׁוֹנָה שׁוּם זִיקַת יְבָמִין, וַחֲלִיצָה בַּתְרַיְיתָא לָאו כְּלוּם הִיא. וְכֵן חָלַץ לָזוֹ וּמַאֲמָר לָזוֹ, וְכֵן נָתַן גֵּט לָזוֹ אַחַר חֲלִיצַת זוֹ, וְכֵן בָּעַל לָזוֹ אַחַר חֲלִיצָה שֶׁל זוֹ – אֵין מַעֲשֶׂה הָאַחֲרוֹן כְּלוּם. אוֹ בָּעַל. תְּחִלָּה, וְחָזַר וּבָעַל לַשְּׁנִיָּה. אוֹ בָּעַל וְעָשָׂה מַאֲמָר. בַּשְּׁנִיָּה, אוֹ נָתַן גֵּט לַשְּׁנִיָּה, אוֹ חָלַץ לַשְּׁנִיָּה – אֵין אַחַר בִּיאָה רִאשׁוֹנָה כְּלוּם, וּמַעֲשֶׂה אַחֲרוֹן לָא חָשִׁיב, וּמוּתָּר בִּקְרוֹבוֹת שְׁנִיָּה. אֵין אַחַר חֲלִיצָה כְּלוּם. אַרֵישָׁא קָאֵי. וְאַסֵּיפָא שַׁיָּיךְ לְמֵימַר אֵין אַחַר בִּיאָה כְּלוּם, וּבִגְמָרָא קָמִיבַּעְיָא לֵיהּ. בֵּין שְׁנֵי יְבָמִין לִיבָמָה אַחַת. בְּכָל הַדִּין הָאָמוּר לְמַעְלָה, כְּנָס א' וּבְב' יְבָמוֹת. חָלַץ וְעָשָׂה מַאֲמָר וְנָתַן גֵּט וּבָעַל כו'. אַיְּיבָם א' וְאַיְּבָמָה אַחַת קָמַהֲדַר. וְאע"ג דְּתַנְיָא לְעֵיל – הֲדַר תַּנְיָא הָכָא מִשּׁוּם סֵיפָא, דְּבָעֵי לְפַלּוּגֵי בֵּין בִּיאָה לַחֲלִיצָה, כִּדְקָתָנֵי: חֲלִיצָה, בֵּין בַּתְּחִלָּה בֵּין בָּאֶמְצַע בֵּין בַּסּוֹף אֵין אַחֲרֶיהָ כְּלוּם, וְהַבְּעִילָה בִּזְמַן שֶׁהִיא בַּתְּחִלָּה כו'. וּלְאַשְׁמוּעִינַן פְּלוּגְתָּא דְּרַבִּי נְחֶמְיָה וְרַבָּנַן. בֵּין בַּתְּחִלָּה בֵּין **בָּאֶמְצַע**. בֵּין מַאֲמָר לְגֵט, כְּגוֹן גֵּט לָזוֹ וְחָלַץ לָזוֹ, וְחָזַר וְעָשָׂה בָּהּ מַאֲמָר, אוֹ בְּבַעֲלַת הַגֵּט – לָא מְהַנֵּי מַאֲמָר, וְלָא בָּעֲיָא גֵּט לְמַאֲמָרוֹ. בַּסּוֹף. אַחַר מַאֲמָר וְגֵט חָלַץ – אֵין אַחֲרֶיהָ כְּלוּם, וַחֲלִיצָה גְּמוּרָה הִיא. וְאִי הֲדַר עָבֵיד מַאֲמָר – לָא בָּעֲיָא גֵּט, דַּחֲלִיצָה גֵּירוּשִׁין גְּמוּרִים הִיא, וְקָמָה בְּלָאו גָּמוּר עֲלֵיהּ, וְאע"ג דַּחֲלִיצָה פְּסוּלָה הָוַאי. הַבִּיאָה **בָּאֶמְצַע**. כְּגוֹן גֵּט לָזוֹ וּבָעַל לָזוֹ, וְחָזַר וְעָשָׂה מַאֲמָר בַּשְּׁלִישִׁית – אָסוּר בִּקְרוֹבוֹתֶיהָ. וּבַסּוֹף. גֵּט לָזוֹ וּמַאֲמָר לָזוֹ, וְחָזַר וּבָא עַל הָאַחַת – יֵשׁ אַחַר בִּיאָה זוֹ זִיקַת יְבָמִין, וְכִי מַפִּיק לָהּ – בָּעֲיָא חֲלִיצָה, וְלָא סַגִּי לָהּ בְּגֵט. אֵין **אַחֲרֶיהָ** כְּלוּם. וְנַפְקָא בְּגֵט וּבְלָא חֲלִיצָה. וְאִי הֲדַר קָדֵישׁ לְאִידָךְ אַחַר בִּיאָה – לָא מְהַנֵּי. **גמ'** אֲבָל גֵּט אֶחָד בִּיבָמָה. אוֹ מַאֲמָר אֶחָד בִּיבָמָה – מְהַנֵּי גֵּט בִּיבָמָה לְמֵיקַם עֲלֵיהּ בְּ"לֹא יִבְנֶה", וְשׁוּב לֹא יְיַבֵּם. וּמַאֲמָר בִּיבָמָה מְהַנֵּי לָהּ לְהַצְרִיכָהּ גֵּט לְמַאֲמָרוֹ, אִי בָּעֵי לְאַפּוּקַהּ. מ"ט **אָמוּר** רַבָּנַן גֵּט בִּיבָמָה מְהַנֵּי. הָא מִדְּאוֹרַיְיתָא חֲלִיצָה הוּא דִּמְהַנֵּי בָּהּ, וּמִשּׁוּם גֵּט לָא קָרֵינָא בָּהּ שֶׁלֹּא בָּנָה. מִשּׁוּם **דִּבְעָלְמָא** מְהַנֵּי. בְּכָל הַנָּשִׁים לְהִתְגָּרֵשׁ, וְאִי אָמְרַתְּ הָכָא לָא מְהַנֵּי, וְאִם רָצָה לְכוֹנְסָהּ אַחַר הַגֵּט יִכְנוֹס. **אָמְרִי**. אֱינָשֵׁי: גֵּט לְהוֹצִיא, וַחֲלִיצָה נַמִּי לְהוֹצִיא, מִדְּגֵט לָא מְהַנֵּי לֵיהּ כו'. וּמ"ט **אָמוּר** רַבָּנַן מַאֲמָר בִּיבָמָה מְהַנֵּי. לֶאֱסוֹר חֲבֶרְתָּהּ עָלָיו? הָא מִן הַתּוֹרָה קִנְיָן לָא הָוֵי בִּיבָמָה אֶלָּא בְּבִיאָה. מִשּׁוּם דִּמְהַנֵּי **בְּעָלְמָא**. קִידּוּשֵׁי אִשָּׁה קוֹנִים אוֹתָהּ, וְאָתֵי לְמִבְעַל אַחַר בִּיאָה, וְהָוֵה לֵיהּ בּוֹנֶה שְׁתֵּי בָּתִּים, דְּאִיסּוּרָא דְּאוֹרַיְיתָא. וּמ"ט **אָמוּר** רַבָּנַן **בִּיאָה פְּסוּלָה** יֵשׁ **אַחֲרֶיהָ**. זִיקַת יְבָמִין, כְּדִתְנַן לְעֵיל: מַאֲמָר בָּזוֹ וּבָעַל לָזוֹ צְרִיכוֹת שְׁנֵי גִיטִּין וַחֲלִיצָה, וְלָא אָמְרִינַן תִּיסְגֵּי לְבַעֲלַת בִּיאָה בְּגֵט בְּלָא חֲלִיצָה, וְתִיפָּטֵר אַף חֲבֶרְתָּהּ בְּבִיאָתָהּ מִן הַחֲלִיצָה. **אִי בִּיאָה אַחַר הַגֵּט הִיא**. כְּגוֹן גֵּט לָזוֹ וּבָעַל לָזוֹ, דְּאָמְרִינַן צְרִיכָה גֵּט וַחֲלִיצָה, וְלָא סַגִּי בְּגֵט לְחוּדֵיהּ כִּשְׁאָר יְבָמָה שֶׁכּוֹנְסָהּ. גְּזֵירָה בִּיאָה אַחַר הַגֵּט מִשּׁוּם בִּיאָה אַחַר חֲלִיצָה. דְּאִי אָמְרַתְּ תִּיסְגֵּי לָהּ בְּגֵט – אָתֵי לְמֵימַר: מִדְּקָנְיָא בִּיאָה אַחַר הַגֵּט בְּבִיאָה גְּרֵידְתָּא, אַלְמָא מְעַלְּיוּתָא הִיא, וְאָתֵי לְמִיבְעַל לְכַתְּחִלָּה אַחַר חֲלִיצָה. וְאִי **בִּיאָה אַחַר מַאֲמָר הִיא**. כְּגוֹן מַאֲמָר לָזוֹ וּבָעַל לָזוֹ, לְהָכִי תְּנַן צְרִיכוֹת (א) שְׁנֵיִם גֵּט וַחֲלִיצָה. דְּאִי אָמְרַתְּ בְּגֵט סַגִּי לָהּ – אָמְרִי: בִּיאָה שֶׁל זוֹ אַחַר קִנְיָן שֶׁל זוֹ מְעַלְּיוּתָא הִיא, וְאָתֵי לְמֶעֱבַד בִּיאָה אַחַר בִּיאָה, וְקָא פָּגַע בְּאִיסּוּר אֵשֶׁת אָח. **חֲלִיצָה פְּסוּלָה**. שֶׁאַחַר גֵּט אוֹ אַחַר מַאֲמָר. אֵין **אַחֲרֶיהָ** כְּלוּם. דְּאִי הֲדַר עָבֵד מַאֲמָר אוֹ גֵּט לַשְּׁלִישִׁית – לָא מְהַנֵּי. מִשּׁוּם חֲלִיצָה **אַחַר** חֲלִיצָה. דְּלָא לֵיתֵי לְמֵיחְלַץ לִשְׁתֵּי יְבָמוֹת זוֹ אַחַר זוֹ, אוֹ שְׁנֵי יְבָמִין לִיבָמָה אַחַת זֶה אַחַר זֶה. כָּל כִּי הָנֵי תַּחֲלוֹץ וְתֵיזִיל. כְּלוֹמַר, מַאי אִיכְפַּת לָן? כָּל יָמֶיהָ תַּחֲלוֹץ. מִשּׁוּם חֲלִיצָה **אַחַר** בִּיאָה. דְּלָא לֵיתֵי לְמֵימַר: יְבָמָה כְּנוּסָה יוֹצְאָת בַּחֲלִיצָה בְּלֹא גֵט – לָא אָתוּ לְמֵימַר הָכִי, דְּאַטּוּ חֲלִיצָה אַחַר מַאֲמָר מִי לָא בָּעֲיָא גֵּט לְמַאֲמָרוֹ? וְהָא דְּאָמְרִינַן אֵין אַחֲרֶיהָ כְּלוּם – בְּדָבָר הֶעָשׂוּי אַחֲרֶיהָ קָאָמַר, דְּאִי הֲדַר עָבֵיד גֵּט אוֹ מַאֲמָר אוֹ חֲלִיצָה בַּחֲבֶרְתָּהּ, לָא מִיתְּסַר בִּקְרוֹבוֹתֶיהָ.

מַאי

[לקמן נג: קיח.]

תוספות ישנים

ומדגט לא מהני חליצה נמי לא מהניא. ואם תאמר והלא כתיבה בקרא בהדיא חליצה וי"ל שיאמרו לצריך חליצה עם גט דשאר נשים ויצטרך ביבמה גט וחליצה אבל אין לומר דבקשה בעלמא נמי תועיל חליצה דאי חליצה לא מהניא יאמרו דגט נמי לא מהניא והא דכתב בהדיא גט נאמר דהיינו עם חליצה כמו דאמרינן בחליצה שביבמה. וי"ל דדוקא ביבמה שייך שפיר גט וחליצה אבל בשאר נשים לא שייך קריאה כמו ביבמה ולא שייך בהו חליצה כלל ולא אתי למטעי שלא יועיל גט בשאר נשים:

הגהות הב"ח

(א) רש"י ד"ה ואי ביאה וכו' להכי תנן צריכות שני גיטין וחליצה:

מ"ט דְּר"ג – דִּמְסַפְּקָא לֵיהּ: גֵּט, אִי דָּחֵי אִי לָא דָּחֵי, מַאֲמָר, אִי קָנֵי אִי לָא קָנֵי. גֵּט אִי דָּחֵי אִי לָא דָּחֵי, אִי קַמָּא דָּחֵי – בַּתְרָא מַאי קָעָבֵיד? אִי קַמָּא לָא דָּחֵי – בַּתְרָא נַמִי לָא דָּחֵי. מַאֲמָר אִי קָנֵי אִי לָא קָנֵי, אִי קַמָּא קָנֵי – בַּתְרָא מַאי קָעָבֵיד? וְאִי קַמָּא לָא קָנֵי – בַּתְרָא נַמִי לָא קָנֵי. אֵיתִיבֵיהּ אַבַּיֵי: *וּמוֹדֶה ר"ג שֶׁיֵּשׁ גֵּט אַחַר מַאֲמָר, וּמַאֲמָר אַחַר הַגֵּט, וְגֵט אַחַר בִּיאָה וּמַאֲמָר, וּמַאֲמָר אַחַר בִּיאָה וְגֵט. וְאִי מְסַפְּקָא לֵיהּ לְר"ג – תֶּהֱוֵי כְּבִיאָה דִּלְכַתְּחִלָּה, וְתִקְנֵי! דְּהָא תְּנַן: הַבְּעִילָה, בִּזְמַן שֶׁהִיא בַּתְּחִלָּה – אֵין אַחֲרֶיהָ כְּלוּם. אֶלָּא אֲמַר אַבַּיֵי: לְעוֹלָם פְּשִׁיטָא לֵיהּ לְר"ג בְּגֵט דְּדָחֵי, וּמַאֲמָר דְּקָנֵי. מִיהוּ, אֲמוּר רַבָּנַן: הָא יְבָמָה, בְּחַד צַד מְהַנֵּי בָּהּ גֵּט, וּבְחַד צַד מְהַנֵּי בָּהּ מַאֲמָר. גֵּט אַחַר גֵּט – לָא דָּחֵי, דְּהָא דָּחָה לֵיהּ קַמָּא, וּמַאֲמָר אַחַר מַאֲמָר – לָא קָנֵי, דְּהָא קָנֵי לֵיהּ קַמָּא. גֵּט אַחַר מַאֲמָר, וּמַאֲמָר אַחַר הַגֵּט – הַאי מִילְּתָא קָא דָּחֵי, וְהַאי מִילְּתָא קָא קָנֵי. וְרַבָּנַן: כָּל חַד וְחַד תַּקִּינוּ לֵיהּ רַבָּנַן גֵּט וּמַאֲמָר בִּיבָמָה. וְהַאי בִּיאָה פְּסוּלָה עֲדִיפָא מִמַּאֲמָר, וּגְרִיעָא מִמַּאֲמָר. עֲדִיפָא מִמַּאֲמָר, דְּאִילּוּ מַאֲמָר אַחַר מַאֲמָר לָא מְהַנֵּי, וְאִילּוּ בִּיאָה אַחַר מַאֲמָר – מְהַנֵּי. וּגְרִיעָא מִמַּאֲמָר, דְּאִילּוּ מַאֲמָר אַחַר הַגֵּט קָנֵי לְכוּלֵּיהּ שִׁיּוּרָא דְּגֵט, וְאִילּוּ בִּיאָה אַחַר הַגֵּט – לָא קָנְיָא לֵיהּ לְכוּלֵּיהּ שִׁיּוּרָא דְּגֵט. ת"ר: כֵּיצַד אר"ג אֵין גֵּט אַחַר גֵּט? שְׁתֵּי יְבָמוֹת שֶׁנָּפְלוּ לִפְנֵי יָבָם אֶחָד, וְנָתַן גֵּט לָזוֹ וְגֵט לָזוֹ – ר"ג אוֹמֵר: חוֹלֵץ לָרִאשׁוֹנָה וְאָסוּר בִּקְרוֹבוֹתֶיהָ, וּמוּתָּר בִּקְרוֹבוֹת שְׁנִיָּה. וַחֲכָמִים אוֹמְרִים: [א]נָתַן גֵּט לָזוֹ וְגֵט לָזוֹ – אָסוּר בִּקְרוֹבוֹת שְׁתֵּיהֶן, וַחֲלִיצָה לְאַחַת מֵהֶן. וְכֵן אַתָּה אוֹמֵר בִּשְׁנֵי יְבָמִים וִיבָמָה אַחַת, כֵּיצַד אָמַר ר"ג אֵין מַאֲמָר אַחַר מַאֲמָר? שְׁתֵּי יְבָמוֹת שֶׁנָּפְלוּ לִפְנֵי יָבָם אֶחָד וְעָשָׂה מַאֲמָר בָּזוֹ וּמַאֲמָר בָּזוֹ, רַבָּן גַּמְלִיאֵל אוֹמֵר: נוֹתֵן גֵּט לָרִאשׁוֹנָה, וְחוֹלֵץ לָהּ, וְאָסוּר בִּקְרוֹבוֹתֶיהָ, וּמוּתָּר בִּקְרוֹבוֹת שְׁנִיָּה. וַחֲכָמִים אוֹמְרִים: [ב]נוֹתֵן גֵּט לִשְׁתֵּיהֶן, וְאָסוּר בִּקְרוֹבוֹת שְׁתֵּיהֶן, וַחֲלִיצָה לְאַחַת מֵהֶן. וְכֵן אַתָּה אוֹמֵר בִּשְׁנֵי יְבָמִים וִיבָמָה אַחַת. אָמַר מָר: נוֹתֵן גֵּט לָזוֹ וְגֵט לָזוֹ, ר"ג אוֹמֵר: חוֹלֵץ לָרִאשׁוֹנָה וְאָסוּר בִּקְרוֹבוֹתֶיהָ, וּמוּתָּר בִּקְרוֹבוֹת שְׁנִיָּה. לֵימָא תֶּהֱוֵי תְּיוּבְתָּא דִּשְׁמוּאֵל, דְּאָמַר שְׁמוּאֵל: *חָלַץ לְבַעֲלַת הַגֵּט – לֹא נִפְטְרָה צָרָה! אָמַר לָךְ שְׁמוּאֵל: כִּי אָמְרִי אֲנָא – אַלִּיבָּא דְּמַאן דְּאָמַר יֵשׁ זִיקָה, וְר"ג סָבַר *אֵין זִיקָה. וּמִדְּר"ג סָבַר אֵין זִיקָה – רַבָּנַן

רש"י

מַאי טַעְמָא דְּר"ג. דְּקָאָמַר אֵין גֵּט אַחַר גֵּט בִּשְׁתֵּי יְבָמוֹת אוֹ בִּשְׁנֵי יְבָמִין, דְּלָא מִיתְּסַר בַּתְרָא בִּקְרוֹבוֹתֶיהָ. שֶׁיֵּשׁ גֵּט אַחַר מַאֲמָר. מַאֲמָר לָזוֹ וְגֵט לָזוֹ, פָּסַל אֶת הָרִאשׁוֹנָה וְאָסוּר בִּקְרוֹבוֹת שְׁתֵּיהֶן. וּמַאֲמָר אַחַר גֵּט. גֵּט לָזוֹ וּמַאֲמָר לָזוֹ, בַּעֲלַת מַאֲמָר צְרִיכָה גֵּט. (א) וְגֵט אַחַר בִּיאָה וּמַאֲמָר. אַחַר בִּיאָה שֶׁאַחַר מַאֲמָר, כְּגוֹן מַאֲמָר לָזוֹ וּבָעַל לָזוֹ וְגֵט לַשְּׁלִישִׁית – מְהַנֵּי גֵּט וְאָסוּר בִּקְרוֹבוֹתֶיהָ: (דְּבִיאָה פְּסוּלָה הִיא בַּשְּׁנִיָּה, דְּמֵאַחַר שֶׁעָשָׂה מַאֲמָר בָּרִאשׁוֹנָה – פְּסוּלוֹת בַּשְּׁנִיָּה). וּמַאֲמָר אַחַר בִּיאָה וְגֵט. גֵּט לָזוֹ וּבָעַל לָזוֹ וּמַאֲמָר לַשְּׁלִישִׁית – קוֹנֶה מַאֲמָר, וּצְרִיכָה גֵּט וְאָסוּר בִּקְרוֹבוֹתֶיהָ. וְאִי אָמְרַתְּ מְסַפְּקָא לֵיהּ. בִּדְחִיַּית הַגֵּט וּקְנִיַּית מַאֲמָר. תֶּיהֱוֵי. הָךְ בִּיאָה הָאֶמְצָעִית כְּבִיאָה בַּתְּחִלָּה, וְתִיקְנֵי, וְלָא תֶּהֱנֵי מַעֲשֶׂה שְׁלִישִׁית, בֵּין בְּגֵט אַחַר בִּיאָה וּמַאֲמָר, בֵּין בְּמַאֲמָר אַחַר בִּיאָה וְגֵט – מִמָּה נַפְשָׁךְ: גֵּט אַחַר בִּיאָה וּמַאֲמָר לָא לִיהֲנֵי, דְּאִי מַאֲמָר קַמָּא קָנֵי לְגַמְרֵי – תּוּ לָא מְהַנֵּי בִּיאָה וְגֵט אַבַּתְרֵיהּ, וְאִי מַאֲמָר לָא קָנֵי מִידֵּי – נִמְצֵאת בִּיאָה שֶׁל אַחֲרָיו בִּיאָה בַּתְּחִלָּה וּכְשֵׁרָה, וְתוּ לָא מְהַנֵּי גֵּט בַּשְּׁלִישִׁית. דְּהָא תְּנַן: הַבְּעִילָה בִּזְמַן שֶׁהִיא בַּתְּחִלָּה – אֵין אַחֲרֶיהָ כְּלוּם. וְכֵן בְּמַאֲמָר אַחַר בִּיאָה וְגֵט, דְּאִי גֵּט קַמָּא דָּחֵי – תּוּ לָא מְהַנֵּי בִּיאָה וּמַאֲמָר אַבַּתְרֵיהּ, וְאִי גֵּט לָא דָּחֵי מִידֵּי – נִמְצָא בִּיאָה שֶׁלְּאַחֲרֵיהֶן בַּתְּחִלָּה, וּכְשֵׁרָה הִיא, וְקוֹנָה, וּמַאֲמָר דְּבַתְרֵיהּ לָאו כְּלוּם הִיא. אֶלָּא. פְּשִׁיטָא לֵיהּ דְּגֵט דָּחֵי קְצָת וּמַאֲמָר קָנֵי קְצָת. הִלְכָּךְ, בִּיאָה שֶׁל אַחֲרֵיהֶן אֵינָהּ תְּחִלָּה. וּמִיהוּ, מ"ט יֵשׁ מַאֲמָר אַחַר גֵּט וְגֵט אַחַר מַאֲמָר, וְאֵין מַאֲמָר אַחַר מַאֲמָר וְלָא גֵּט אַחַר גֵּט – דַּאֲמוּר רַבָּנַן: בְּחַד צַד מְהַנֵּי בָּהּ גֵּט לִדְחוֹת חֶלְיָהּ, וְחַד צַד מְהַנֵּי בָּהּ מַאֲמָר לִקְנוֹת חֶלְיָהּ. גֵּט אַחַר גֵּט לָא דָּחֵי דְּהָא דָּחָה לֵיהּ קַמָּא. כָּל כֹּחַ גֵּט. הִלְכָּךְ לָאו כְּלוּם הוּא, וּמוּתָּר בִּקְרוֹבוֹתֶיהָ. וְכֵן מַאֲמָר אַחַר מַאֲמָר, דְּהָא קָנָה קַמָּא כָּל כֹּחַ מַאֲמָר. הַאי מִילְּתָא כו'. גֵּט אַחַר מַאֲמָר, מַאי דְּשַׁיֵּיר מַאֲמָר מִן קַמַּיְיתָא – דָּחֵי גֵּט בְּבַתְרַיְיתָא. וְכֵן בִּשְׁנֵי יְבָמִין, מַאי דְּשַׁיֵּיר מַאֲמָר דְּקַמָּא – דָּחֵי גֵּט דְּבַתְרָא. מַאֲמָר אַחַר הַגֵּט. מַאי דְּשַׁיֵּיר גֵּט דְּקַמָּא מִן הַזִּיקָה, דְּלָא דַּחְיֵיהּ – קָנֵי מַאֲמָר דְּבַתְרָא. וְרַבָּנַן. דִּפְלִיגִי עֲלֵיהּ דְּר"ג, דְּאָמְרִי: יֵשׁ גֵּט אַחַר גֵּט, אָמְרִי לָךְ: כָּל חַד וְחַד. מִן הַיְבָמִין תִּיקְנוּ לֵיהּ רַבָּנַן גֵּט וּמַאֲמָר בְּכָל הַיְבָמוֹת. הִלְכָּךְ, לֵיכָּא לְמֵימַר קַמָּא דָּחָה כָּל כֹּחַ הַגֵּט, דְּקַמָּא, כָּל כֹּחַ הַגֵּט דִּידֵיהּ דְּאִית לֵיהּ בְּהָךְ יְבָמָה הוּא דְּדָחָה, אֲבָל כֹּחַ גֵּט דְּאָחוּהּ בְּהַךְ יְבָמָה, וְכֹחַ גִּיטָּא דִּידֵיהּ בְּצָרָתָהּ – לָא דָּחָה, וְכֵן לְעִנְיַן מַאֲמָר. וְהַאי בִּיאָה פְּסוּלָה כו'. כְּלוֹמַר, לְהָכִי קָאָמַר ר"ג יֵשׁ גֵּט אַחַר בִּיאָה שֶׁאַחַר מַאֲמָר וְיֵשׁ מַאֲמָר אַחַר בִּיאָה וְגֵט, דְּהָא בִּיאָה אֶמְצָעִית, שֶׁהִיא פְּסוּלָה, עֲדִיפָא מִמַּאֲמָר וּגְרִיעָא מִמַּאֲמָר. עֲדִיפָא מִמַּאֲמָר כו'. דְּאִילּוּ בִּיאָה אַחַר מַאֲמָר מְהַנְּיָא, כִּדְקָתָנֵי: גֵּט אַחַר בִּיאָה וּמַאֲמָר, אַלְמָא יֵשׁ בִּיאָה אַחַר מַאֲמָר. וּגְרִיעָא מִמַּאֲמָר דְּאִילּוּ מַאֲמָר אַחַר הַגֵּט קָנֵי לֵיהּ לְכוּלֵּיהּ שִׁיּוּרָא דְּגֵט. כָּל מַה שֶּׁשַּׁיֵּיר גֵּט לַמַּאֲמָר, וְאֵין מַאֲמָר אַחַר מוֹעִיל כְּלוּם אַחֲרָיו, אִם חָזַר וְעָשָׂה מַאֲמָר בַּשְּׁלִישִׁית, כִּדְקָאָמַר רַבָּן גַּמְלִיאֵל: אֵין מַאֲמָר אַחַר מַאֲמָר, וְלָא שְׁנָא אִי הָוֵה מַאֲמָר רִאשׁוֹן אַחַר גֵּט אִי לָא – אֵין מַאֲמָר אַחֲרָיו, וְלָא פְּלוּג בֵּין שֶׁהָיָה מַאֲמָר רִאשׁוֹן בַּתְּחִלָּה, בֵּין שֶׁהָיָה אַחַר הַגֵּט, מִדְּלָא קָתָנֵי: מוֹדֶה רַבָּן גַּמְלִיאֵל שֶׁיֵּשׁ מַאֲמָר אַחַר מַאֲמָר וְגֵט. וְאִילּוּ בִּיאָה אַחַר הַגֵּט לָא קָנְיָא לֵיהּ לְכוּלֵּיהּ שִׁיּוּרָא דְּגֵט. כָּל מַה שֶּׁשַּׁיֵּיר גֵּט לְבִיאָה, דְּיֵשׁ מַאֲמָר אַחַר בִּיאָה וְגֵט, כִּדְתְנַן: הַבְּעִילָה בִּזְמַן שֶׁהִיא בַּתְּחִלָּה אֵין אַחֲרֶיהָ כְּלוּם, אֲבָל בָּאֶמְצַע יֵשׁ אַחֲרֶיהָ כְּלוּם, וּכְדַאֲמַר טַעְמָא לְעֵיל: מ"ט אֲמוּר רַבָּנַן בִּיאָה פְּסוּלָה יֵשׁ אַחֲרֶיהָ כְּלוּם כו': ה"ג: וְנָתַן גֵּט לָזוֹ וְגֵט לָזוֹ ר"ג כו'. חוֹלֵץ לָרִאשׁוֹנָה. וְכ"ש דְּאִי חָלַץ לַשְּׁנִיָּה הָוֵי חֲלִיצָה מַעַלְיְיתָא לְאִיפְטוּרֵי קַמַּיְיתָא, דְּכֵיוָן דְּגֵט דִּשְׁנִיָּה (ב) אֵין גֵּט – חֲלִיצָה דִּידָהּ מַעַלְיְיתָא הִיא. אֶלָּא עֵצָה טוֹבָה קָא מַשְׁמַע לַן, שֶׁלֹּא יֵאָסֵר עַצְמוֹ בִּקְרוֹבוֹת שְׁנִיָּה, שֶׁאִם יַחֲלוֹץ לָהּ – נִמְצְאוּ זוֹ גְּרוּשָׁתוֹ וְזוֹ חֲלוּצָתוֹ, וְאָסוּר בִּקְרוֹבוֹת שְׁתֵּיהֶן. וְכֵן אַתָּה אוֹמֵר בִּשְׁנֵי יְבָמִין וִיבָמָה אַחַת. נָתַן זֶה גֵּט וְזֶה גֵּט, ר"ג אוֹמֵר חוֹלֵץ לָהּ הָרִאשׁוֹן וְהַשֵּׁנִי מוּתָּר בִּקְרוֹבוֹתֶיהָ, וּלְדִבְרֵי חֲכָמִים שְׁנֵיהֶם אֲסוּרִין בִּקְרוֹבוֹת. מַאֲמָר בָּזוֹ וּמַאֲמָר בָּזוֹ ר"ג אוֹמֵר נוֹתֵן גֵּט לָרִאשׁוֹנָה כו'. לְקַמָּן פָּרֵיךְ: כֵּיוָן דְּאֵין מַאֲמָר אַחַר מַאֲמָר, יִיבּוּמֵי נַמִי תִּתְיַיבֵּם קַמַּיְיתָא, דְּהָא לָא אִיפַּסְלָה עֲלֵיהּ! לֵימָא תֶּהֱוֵי תְּיוּבְתָּא דִּשְׁמוּאֵל דְּאָמַר שְׁמוּאֵל חָלַץ לְבַעֲלַת הַגֵּט. נָפְלוּ לְפָנָיו שְׁתֵּי יְבָמוֹת, וְנָתַן גֵּט לְאַחַת מֵהֶן, וְאַחַ"כ חָלַץ לָהּ – לֹא נִפְטְרָה צָרָתָהּ, מִשּׁוּם דְּקְלִישָׁא זִיקָתָהּ, וְלָאו חֲלִיצָה לְאַפְקוּעֵי זִיקָה מְעַלְיְיתָא דְּצָרָתָהּ. וְהָא הָכָא, כֵּיוָן דְּאָמַר ר"ג אֵין גֵּט אַחַר גֵּט – נִמְצֵאת זִיקָה שְׁנִיָּה שְׁלֵימָה, וְקָתָנֵי: חוֹלֵץ לָרִאשׁוֹנָה, וְקַשְׁיָא לִשְׁמוּאֵל. וּמִדְּרַבָּנַן לֵיכָּא לְאוֹתוּבֵי לִשְׁמוּאֵל, אע"ג דְּאָמְרִי רַבָּנַן וַחֲלִיצָה לְאַחַת מֵהֶן, אַלְמָא חֲלִיצַת בַּעֲלַת גֵּט פּוֹטֶרֶת צָרָתָהּ – לָא קַשְׁיָא לִשְׁמוּאֵל, דְּהָכָא הַיְינוּ טַעְמָא דְּתַרְוַיְיהוּ זִיקָתָא קְלִישָׁא, דְּהָא אָמְרִי רַבָּנַן: יֵשׁ גֵּט אַחַר גֵּט. יֵשׁ זִיקָה. שְׁלֵימָה זִיקָתָהּ, וְלָא פָּקְעָה זִיקָה שְׁלֵימָה אֶלָּא בַּחֲלִיצָה מַעַלְיְיתָא. ר"ג סָבַר אֵין זִיקָה. כִּדְאָמַר בְּפֶרֶק ב"ש (לְקַמָּן דף קט.): אִם מֵיאֲנָה – מֵיאֲנָה כו'. הִלְכָּךְ, כֵּיוָן דְּלָאו שְׁלֵימָא זִיקָה – פָּקְעָה בַּחֲלִיצָה כָּל דְּהוּ.

רבנן

תוספות

דמספקא ליה גט אי דחי אי לא דחי. לא מצי למימר דפשיטא ליה דגט ודאי דחי ומאמר ודאי קונה – דא"כ אמאי מהני מאמר אחר הגט וגט אחר מאמר? ואע"ג דאכתי לא ידע ברייתא דבסמוך דמודה ר"ג דיש גט אחר מאמר כו' – מתניתין משמע ליה דיש גט אחר מאמר לר"ג, דדוקא נקט גט אחר גט ומאמר אחר מאמר דלא מהני, אבל מאמר אחר הגט או איפכא – מהני.

עדיפא ממאמר דאילו מאמר כו'. דמאמר האחרון אין יכול לתפוס במקום שתפס הראשון, וביאה פסולה תופסת אחר מאמר אותו צד עצמו שתפס המאמר, דסברא הוא שאין תופס אלא אותו צד שתופס המאמר, דתרווייהו לקנות. והיינו משום דעדיף ממאמר, לפי שהיא דאורייתא וגריעא ממאמר – דאילו מאמר אחר הגט קני לכוליה שיורא דגט. שהרי אין מאמר מועיל אחריו, אבל ביאה לא קני לכוליה שיורא דגט, שהרי מאמר מועיל אחריה, ואם היתה קונה כל השיור – לא היה מאמר מועיל אחריה לתפוס מה שתפסה הביאה. דביאה עדיפא ואלימא לפי שהיא דאורייתא, כדפרישית. ואתי לפרושי טעמא דלא תקשה הא דביאה עדיפא ממאמר, אע"ג דגריעא נמי ממאמר. ובקונטרס פירש: דאילו ביאה אחר גט לא קניא לכוליה שיורא דגט, דיש ביאה אחר ביאה פסולה. ותימה: דלא אשכחן בהדיא להאי מילתא שתהא לר"ג ביאה אחר ביאה פסולה! מיהו, יש לדקדק דיש ביאה אחר ביאה פסולה לר"ג. דאי אין ביאה אחרי ביאה פסולה, משום שכל קנין הראוי לביאה עשתה ביאה הראשונה ואין האחרונה יכולה לתפוס אחריה אע"ג דראשונה לא קניא כוליה שיורא דגט, א"כ – מנא ליה שמאמר קונה כוליה שיורא דגט? שמא גט ומאמר משייר אלא שאין במאמר אחר כח לחול אחריו במה ששייר, כמו שאין ביאה אחר ביאה פסולה אף על פי ששייר לקונה מאמר אחריה.

כולהו

תוספות ישנים

עדיפא ממאמר. אין להקשות ומאי עדיפותא הוא הלא כמו כן יש גט אחר מאמר אע"ג דלא עדיף ממאמר אלא דכוותיה די"ל שאני גט ומאמר דזה דוחה וזה קונה אבל הכא הכי פירושא עדיפא ממאמר דמאמר אחר מאמר לא מהני דלא עדיף מאמר בתרא ממאמר קמא ואינו יכול לתפוס במה שתפס מאמר ראשון. וביאה פסולה אע"פ שאינה יכולה לתפוס מסברא רק בצד שתפס המאמר שלפניה שהרי כיון דתרווייהו לקנות סברא הוא דהוא צד דחזי למאמר חזי לביאה ואפ"ה מהניא אחר מאמר ותופסת באותו צד עצמו א"כ אלימא היא ממאמר וגריעא ממאמר דאילו מאמר אחר הגט קני לכולא שיורא דגט שאין מאמר מועיל אחריו דכי אמרי' במתני' אין מאמר אחר מאמר ר"ל בין לאחר מאמר כשר בין לאחר מאמר פסול מדלא מפליג בין כשר לפסול כמו גבי ביאה וחליצה. ואילו ביאה לא קניא ליה לכולא שיורא דגט שהרי מאמר מועיל אחריה ואם הוה קני לכולא שיורא דגט כמו מאמר לא היה מועיל מאמר אחריה שאין מאמר יכול לתפוס הצד שהביאה תפסה: הא אמר שמואל חלץ לבעלת הגט לא נפטרה צרה. פ"ה דדוקא לר"ג קא פריך דאמר חולץ לראשונה ומפטרא אידך אבל לרבנן לא פריך אע"ג וכו' ותימה דלעיל משמע דאף בפסולות קאמר שמואל דבחלה לא מפטרא אידך גבי התחיל בחיות לא יגמרו בגרות ונ"ל דה"ה דהוי מצי למפרך לרבנן אלא פריך בהדיא לר"ג דפטר שניה דמגלה לחלוץ חליצה כשרה בחליצה לראשונה שהיא פסולה:

תוספות חד מקמאי

פרק ר"ג ת"ר (כיוצא בו) [כיצד] אמר ר"ג אין גט אחר גט ב' יבמות שנפלו לפני יבם א' ונתן גט לזו וגט לזו ר"ג אומר חולץ ראשונה ואסור בקרובותיה ומותר בקרובות שניה. וחכ"א אסור בקרובות שתיהן וחולץ לאחת וכן אתה מוצא בב' יבמין ויבמה אחת פי' כשתחלוץ לאחת מהן ופרכינן מיניה לרב דאמר חליצה פסולה צריכה לחזור על כל האחין. ופריק דבין לר"ג בין לרבנן אין זיקה ס"ל ובגט אחר גט ובמאמר אחר מאמר נמי פליגי וכיון דקי"ל יש זיקה לפום מאי דפסיקנא בפ' ד' אחין כרב דאמר חליצה פסולה צריכה לחזור על כל האחין לית הלכתא כי הא שתני' דקתני וכן אתה מוצא בב' יבמין ויבמה אחת ומדאקשינן לרב מסיפא דשני יבמין ולא מקשינן מרישא דשתי יבמות דקתני חליצה לא' מהן אלמא לרב לא פליג בהדי שמואל דאמר חלץ לבעלת הגט לא נפטרת צרה. לצרה נפטרת בעלת הגט ולא מילתא דתליין אהדדי נינהו והא דאמר נמי חולץ לראשונה לית הלכתא כותיה דאיהו ס"ל אין זיקה. וקי"ל דיש זיקה וקי"ל כשמואל חלץ לבעלת הגט לא נפטרת צרה:

בעא

עין משפט נר מצוה

כ א מיי' פ"ה מהלכות יבום הלכה טו טוש"ע אה"ע סימן קע סעי' ג ז:

כא ב מיי' שם וטוש"ע שם סעיף ו:

מסורת הש"ס

ס"א כל זה אינו

לעיל כז:

לעיל כז.

[לעיל יז: וש"נ]

הגהות הב"ח

(א) רש"י ד"ה וגט אחר וכו' הד"א עם ד"ה ביאה וכו' פסול בשניה: הס"ד: (ב) ד"ה חולץ וכו' דשניה אינו וכו':

רַבָּנַן סָבְרִי יֵשׁ זִיקָה. וְקָתָנֵי סֵיפָא: וְכֵן אַתָּה אוֹמֵר בִּשְׁנֵי יְבָמִין וִיבָמָה אַחַת. לֵימָא תֶּיהֱוֵי תְּיוּבְתָא דְּרַבָּה בַּר רַב הוּנָא אָמַר רַב. דְּאָמַר רַבָּה בַּר רַב הוּנָא אָמַר רַב: *חֲלִיצָה פְּסוּלָה — צְרִיכָה לַחֲזוֹר עַל כָּל הָאַחִין! אָמַר לָךְ רַבָּה בַּר רַב הוּנָא: בֵּין לְר"ג בֵּין לְרַבָּנַן סָבְרִי אֵין זִיקָה, וְהָכָא בְּגֵט אַחַר גֵּט וּמַאֲמָר אַחַר מַאֲמָר קָמִיפַּלְגִי. אָמַר מָר: עָשָׂה מַאֲמָר בָּזוֹ וּמַאֲמָר בָּזוֹ, רַבָּן גַּמְלִיאֵל אוֹמֵר: נוֹתֵן גֵּט לָרִאשׁוֹנָה וְחוֹלֵץ לָהּ, וְאָסוּר בִּקְרוֹבוֹתֶיהָ, וּמוּתָּר בִּקְרוֹבוֹת שְׁנִיָּה. מִכְּדִי קָסָבַר רַבָּן גַּמְלִיאֵל אֵין מַאֲמָר אַחַר מַאֲמָר — רִאשׁוֹנָה נַמִי תִּתְיַיבֵּם! גְּזֵירָה דִּלְמָא אָתֵי לְיַיבּוּמֵי לִשְׁנִיָּה. אָמַר רַבִּי יוֹחָנָן: רַבָּן גַּמְלִיאֵל, וּב"ש, *וְר"ש, וּבֶן עַזַּאי וְרַבִּי נְחֶמְיָה — כּוּלְּהוּ סְבִירָא לְהוּ: מַאֲמָר קוֹנֶה קִנְיָן גָּמוּר. רַבָּן גַּמְלִיאֵל — הָא דַּאֲמָרַן. ב"ש — דִּתְנַן(א): *שְׁלֹשָׁה אַחִין, שְׁנַיִם מֵהֶם נְשׂוּאִין לִשְׁתֵּי אֲחָיוֹת וְאֶחָד מוּפְנֶה, מֵת אֶחָד מִבַּעֲלֵי אֲחָיוֹת וְעָשָׂה בָּהּ מוּפְנֶה מַאֲמָר, וְאח"כ מֵת אָחִיו הַשֵּׁנִי, ב"ש אוֹמְרִים: אִשְׁתּוֹ עִמּוֹ, וְהַלָּזוּ תֵּצֵא מִשּׁוּם אֲחוֹת אִשָּׁה. ר"ש — דְּתַנְיָא, *אָמַר(ב) לְהוּ ר"ש לַחֲכָמִים: אִם בִּיאַת רִאשׁוֹן בִּיאָה — בִּיאַת שֵׁנִי אֵינָהּ בִּיאָה, אִם בִּיאַת רִאשׁוֹן אֵינָהּ בִּיאָה — בִּיאַת שֵׁנִי נַמִי אֵינָהּ בִּיאָה. וְהָא בִּיאַת בֶּן תֵּשַׁע, דִּכְמַאֲמָר שַׁוְיוּהָ רַבָּנַן, וְקָאָמַר רַ' שִׁמְעוֹן אֵינָהּ בִּיאָה. בֶּן עַזַּאי — דְּתַנְיָא, *בֶּן עַזַּאי אוֹמֵר: יֵשׁ מַאֲמָר אַחַר מַאֲמָר בִּשְׁנֵי יְבָמִין וִיבָמָה אַחַת, וְאֵין מַאֲמָר אַחַר מַאֲמָר בִּשְׁתֵּי יְבָמוֹת וְיָבָם אֶחָד. רַ' נְחֶמְיָה — דִּתְנַן, *רַ' נְחֶמְיָה אוֹמֵר: אַחַת בְּעִילָה וְאַחַת חֲלִיצָה, בֵּין בַּתְּחִלָּה בֵּין בָּאֶמְצַע בֵּין בַּסּוֹף — אֵין אַחֲרֶיהָ כְּלוּם. וְהָא בִּיאָה פְּסוּלָה, דִּכְמַאֲמָר שַׁוְיוּהָ רַבָּנַן וְקָתָנֵי: אֵין אַחֲרֶיהָ כְּלוּם.§ "כֵּיצַד עָשָׂה מַאֲמָר כו'".§ הַאי

רש"י

רַבָּנַן סָבְרִי יֵשׁ זִיקָה. לְאַקְשׁוּיֵי אָתֵי, כְּלוֹמַר: קס"ד דְּכִי הֵיכִי דִּפְלִיגִי רַבָּנַן אַדְּרַבָּן גַּמְלִיאֵל בְּגֵט אַחַר גֵּט, הָכִי פְּלִיגִי בְּזִיקָה. וְאע"ג דְּמִמִּילְּתַיְיהוּ לָא שָׁמְעִינַן לֵיהּ. וְקָתָנֵי סֵיפָא וְכֵן אַתָּה אוֹמֵר בִּשְׁנֵי יְבָמִין. דְּאִם נָתְנוּ שְׁנֵיהֶם גֵּט – חוֹלֵץ לָהּ אֶחָד מֵהֶם. וַאֲפִילּוּ לְרַבָּנַן דְּאָמְרִי יֵשׁ זִיקָה – סַגִּי לָהּ בְּהַךְ חֲלִיצָה רְעוּעָה דְּחַד מִינַּיְיהוּ. לֵימָא תֶּיהֱוֵי תְּיוּבְתָא כו'. דְּהָא נַמִי חֲלִיצָה פְּסוּלָה הִיא, שֶׁאַחַר הַגֵּט בָּאָה: הָכִי גָּרְסִינַן. בֵּין לְרַבָּן גַּמְלִיאֵל בֵּין לְרַבָּנַן אֵין זִיקָה וְהָכָא כו'. וְהָנָא דְּאָמְרִי – אַלִּיבָּא דְּמַאן דְּאָמַר יֵשׁ זִיקָה. קִנְיָן גָּמוּר. לָא גָּמוּר מַמָּשׁ, אֶלָּא קִנְיָן חָשׁוּב. הָא דַּאֲמַרַן. אֵין מַאֲמָר אַחַר מַאֲמָר – אַלְמָא חָשִׁיב קַמָּא לְמִיקְנֵי כָּל כֹּחַ מַאֲמָר. אִשְׁתּוֹ עִמּוֹ. דְּקָנְיֵיהּ בְּמַאֲמָר, וְכִי נָפְלָה אֲחוֹתָהּ – לָא רַמְיָא קַמֵּיהּ, דַּאֲחוֹת אִשָּׁה הִיא, וְלָא מִיתַּסְרָא קַמַּיְיתָא עֲלֵיהּ מִשּׁוּם אֲחוֹת זְקוּקָה. וְהַלָּזוּ תֵּצֵא. אַף מִן הַחֲלִיצָה. הַלָּזוּ. כְּמוֹ "הָאָרֶץ הַלֵּזוּ הַנְּשַׁמָּה" (יחזקאל לו). אָמַר לָהֶם ר"ש כו'. לְקַמָּן בְּפֶרֶק "הָאִשָּׁה רַבָּה": בֶּן תֵּשַׁע שָׁנִים וְיוֹם אֶחָד הַבָּא עַל יְבִמְתּוֹ, וְחָזַר וּבָא אָחִיו בֶּן תֵּשַׁע שָׁנִים וְיוֹם אֶחָד עָלֶיהָ – פְּסוּלָה עַל יָדוֹ, דְּבִיאַת בֶּן תֵּשַׁע שָׁנִים כְּמַאֲמָר שַׁוְיוּהָ רַבָּנַן, וְהָוֵה לֵיהּ מַאֲמָר אַחַר מַאֲמָר, וּמְקוּדֶּשֶׁת אַף לַשֵּׁנִי, וּפְסָלָהּ אַף עַל רִאשׁוֹן, כְּרַבָּנַן דְּאָמְרִי יֵשׁ מַאֲמָר אַחַר מַאֲמָר. ר"ש אוֹמֵר: לֹא פְּסָלָהּ. אָמַר לָהֶם ר' שִׁמְעוֹן אִם בִּיאַת רִאשׁוֹן בִּיאָה. קָנְיָהּ לְגַמְרֵי. בִּיאַת שֵׁנִי אֵינָהּ בִּיאָה. דְּהַבִּיאָה בִּזְמַן שֶׁהִיא בַּתְּחִלָּה – אֵין אַחֲרֶיהָ כְּלוּם, וְאֵינָהּ מְקוּדֶּשֶׁת לַשֵּׁנִי, וְלֹא פְּסָלָהּ עַל הָרִאשׁוֹן. וְאִי מִשּׁוּם דִּזְנוּתָהּ, דְּקי"ל בִּיאָתוֹ בִּיאָה, דִּתְנַן (נדה דף מה.): בָּא עַל אַחַת מִכָּל הָעֲרָיוֹת שֶׁבַּתּוֹרָה – מֵתוֹת עַל יָדוֹ, אֲפִילּוּ הָכִי לָא מִיתַּסְרָא עַל בַּעְלָהּ, דְּקַיְימָא לַן (כתובות דף ט.) אֵין הָאִשָּׁה נֶאֱסֶרֶת עַל בַּעְלָהּ אֶלָּא עַל עִיסְקֵי קִינּוּי וּסְתִירָה. כְּמַאֲמָר שַׁוְיוּהָ רַבָּנַן. דְּהָכִי תַּנְיָא בְּפֶרֶק "הָאִשָּׁה": עָשׂוּ בִּיאַת בֶּן תֵּשַׁע כְּמַאֲמָר בְּגָדוֹל. וְקָאָמַר רַבִּי שִׁמְעוֹן: בִּיאַת שֵׁנִי אֵינָהּ בִּיאָה, אַלְמָא: מַאֲמָר רִאשׁוֹן חָשׁוּב לִקְנוֹת כָּל כֹּחַ מַאֲמָר: ה"ג. יֵשׁ מַאֲמָר אַחַר מַאֲמָר בִּשְׁנֵי יְבָמִין וִיבָמָה אַחַת. דְּכָל חַד וְחַד תַּקִּינוּ לֵיהּ רַבָּנַן מַאֲמָר בָּהּ. וְאֵין מַאֲמָר אַחַר מַאֲמָר בִּשְׁתֵּי יְבָמוֹת וְיָבָם אֶחָד. דְּכָל כֹּחַ שֶׁתִּקְּנוּ חֲכָמִים בַּמַּאֲמָר – קָנָה בְּמַאֲמָר רִאשׁוֹן, לְשׁוֹן מוֹרִי. ל"א ה"ג: אֵין מַאֲמָר אַחַר מַאֲמָר בִּשְׁנֵי יְבָמִין וִיבָמָה אַחַת דְּדוּמְיָא דְּקִידּוּשִׁין בְּעָלְמָא תַּקִּינוּ רַבָּנַן לְמַאֲמָר, וְאֵין קִידּוּשִׁין אַחַר קִידּוּשִׁין בְּאִשָּׁה אַחַת. וְיֵשׁ מַאֲמָר אַחַר מַאֲמָר בִּשְׁתֵּי יְבָמוֹת וְיָבָם אֶחָד – דְּהָא תַּרְוַייהוּ קַמֵּיהּ רַמְיָין, וְכָל חֲדָא אִית לָהּ כֹּחַ יְבָמִין, דְּלָא כֹּחַ בִּיאָה יָהֲבִי רַבָּנַן לְמַאֲמָר לְמִיקְנֵי לְגַמְרֵי. *וְלָא פָּקַע זִיקָה דַּחֲבֶרְתָּהּ, דְּבִיאָה הוּא דְּפָטְרָה. וְלָשׁוֹן רִאשׁוֹן עִיקָּר, דִּלְקַמָּן מוּכְחָא מִילְּתָא בְּפִירְקִין. וְהָא בִּיאָה פְּסוּלָה כְּמַאֲמָר שַׁוְיוּהָ רַבָּנַן. דְּלָא נָפְקָא מִינֵּיהּ בְּגֵט, דְּקָא בָּעְיָא נַמִי חֲלִיצָה לְזִיקָתוֹ. הַאי

תוספות

כולהו סבירא להו. אין התנאים כולן שוין, דלבית שמאי קונה מדאורייתא, כדמשמע בפ' "ד' אחין" (לעיל דף כט. ושם) ולכולהו תנאי לא קני אלא מדרבנן, ולר"ג לא קני אלא בהא דלא מהני מאמר בתריה, ובן עזאי מפליג בין שני יבמין ויבמה אחת ובין יבם אחד ושתי יבמות, ולר"ש מספקא ליה אי קני אי לא קני. וכה"ג איכא בפ"ק(ג) דסוטה (דף ז: ושם)*. **אי** ביאת ראשון ביאה כו'. משנה היא לקמן ב"האשה רבה" (דף נו:) וקאמר תנא קמא דשני פוסל על ידו לראשון. ואם תאמר: לרבי שמעון נמי תיאסר לראשון, משום דזינתה תחתיו, ובקונטרס פירש דאין נאסרת על בעלה אלא על ידי קינוי וסתירה! ואר"י: שהוא טעות סופר, ולא פירשו רש"י מעולם. דבעד אחד ודאי אינה נאסרת אלא בקינוי וסתירה, אבל בעדי טומאה – נאסרת בלא קינוי. ואין לומר משום דהני נשואין דרבנן נינהו לא חשו לאוסרה – דכל דתיקון רבנן כעין דאורייתא תיקון. ועוד, דתיתסר משום דרב המנונא, דאמר: *שומרת יבם שזינתה אסורה ליבמה! ואר"י: דמיירי בבא עליה בשוגג, שאינה נאסרת. אי נמי בקטנה, דפיתוי קטנה אונס הוא. אי נמי בבא עליה בעל כרחה. ונאמר אע"ג דביאת בן תשע כמאמר, ומאמר בעל כרחה לא מהני. כדאמר בפ"ב (לעיל יט:) – עשו חכמים ביאת בן תשע בעל כרחה כמאמר מדעת, דלא שני לן בביאה דיבמה בין מדעת לבע"כ. **בן** עזאי אומר כו'. בקונט' נראה לו עיקר דגרסינן אין מאמר אחר מאמר בשתי יבמות ויבם אחד, משום דלקמן (דף נג.) אמתני' בעשה מאמר בזו ומאמר בזו כו' קאמר: מתני' דלא כבן עזאי. ור"י אומר דשפיר גרים איפכא, ולקמן סמיך אסיפא, דקתני בין שני יבמין ויבמה אחת, ולהכי נקטיה אמתניתין דעשה מאמר בזו ומאמר בזו, לפרושי דעלה קאי מתניתין, דלא כבן עזאי, וכה"ג איכא לקמן, דקתני גט לזו וגט לזו צריכות הימנו חליצה, ומסיק: לימא מסייע ליה לרבה בר רב הונא דאמר חליצה פסולה צריכה לחזור על כל האחין. ומההיא ליכא סייעתא, שיש לחלק בין מיפטר נפשה למיפטר צרה, כדאמר בריש פ' "ד' אחין" (לעיל דף כח.) אלא אסיפא סמיך, דקתני בין שני יבמין ויבמה אחת. ויש ספרים שכתוב בהם: כילד עשה מאמר ביבמתו כו' עד בין שני יבמין ליבמה אחת, ועלה מסיק מתניתין דלא כבן עזאי. **ביאה** פסולה כמאמר שויוה רבנן וקתני דאין אחריה כלום. פי': וה"ה אחר מאמר. תימה: דבסוף פירקין מפרש טעמא דרבי נחמיה דליכא למיגזר ביאה שאחר הגט ומאמר אטו ביאה שאחר חליצה וביאה, כיון דחליצה וביאה מדאורייתא – מידע ידיע. ואם כן, מנלן דלא יהא כלום אחר מאמר? ואומר ה"ר יצחק ב"ר ברוך דע"כ לרבי נחמיה גט ומאמר דאורייתא, דילפינן מק"ו משאר נשים. ולית ליה הני מיעוטי דבפ"ק דקידושין (דף יד.). דאי אפשר לומר שיהא מדרבנן לרבי נחמיה, דכיון דאית ליה דביאה וחליצה דאורייתא מידע ידיע, דאם כן לא שייך למיגזר הני גזירות דאמר לעיל: גט להוציא וחליצה להוציא, וביאה לקנות ומאמר לקנות. ותימה גדולה הוא לומר כן(ד), ולא מישתמיט שום תנא ולימא דגט פוטר ביבמה. ועוד: דא"כ הוה ליה למימר נמי דאין אחר הגט כלום! ועוד: דלישנא דהש"ס לא משמע שבא לדקדק מכח זה. א)ונראה לר"י, דה"פ: והא ביאה(ה) כמאמר שויוה רבנן, שיהא אחריה כלום משום גזירות דלעיל, ואל אחריה מאמר. [ומשום הכי תקינו נמי] רבנן שיהא מאמר אחר מאמר, אע"ג דמסברא הוה לן למימר כר"ג דאין מאמר אחר מאמר, לפי שקנה המאמר הראשון כל מה שיש למאמר לקנות. אלא טעמא דרבנן, דאי אמרינן דאין מאמר אחר מאמר – אתי למימר נמי דאין מאמר אחר ביאה פסולה, דלא גרעא ביאה ממאמר, לכך תיקנו שיהא מאמר אחר מאמר וגט אחר גט. דגט ומאמר ענין אחד, דשניהן דרבנן. ואי אמרת דאין גט אחר גט – אתי למימר נמי דאין מאמר אחר מאמר, ולא מאמר אחר ביאה פסולה. אם כן לרבי נחמיה אין מאמר אחר מאמר, דלדידיה ליכא למגזר מידי, דהא לית ליה נמי מאמר אחר ביאה פסולה, דקתני: (ביאה פסולה) אין אחריה כלום. ואם תאמר: אמאי תקינו רבנן לר' נחמיה גט ומאמר כלל ביבמה? כיון דביאה וחליצה מידע ידיע – ליכא למיגזר דגט להוציא וחליצה להוציא כו'! ויש לומר: דהעולם סוברים דגט ומאמר מהני מן התורה מקל וחומר דבפרק קמא דקידושין (ג"ז שם). ואע"ג דאימעוט – מכל מקום אהני קצת, כמו מאמר לבית שמאי. ולהכי, אי שרית למיבעל אחר גט ומאמר – אתי למיבעל אחר חליצה וביאה. אבל בהא לא טעו שיאמרו אחר הגט ומאמר בשביל שתקנה ביאה קנין גמור תקנה כמו כן קנין גמור אחר ביאה וחליצה, ויבא לבעול אחריה, דהא ודאי ידעי דחליצה וביאה עדיפא מגט ומאמר, שכתובין בהדיא, וגט ומאמר נתמעטו.ב) ר"י. אם

תוספות ישנים

לימא תהוי תיובתא דרבה בר רב הונא דאמר חליצה פסולה צריכה לחזור על כל האחין. וא"ת ואמאי לא פריך מיבם א' ושתי יבמות דאמרו חכמים (חלצה) [דחולץ] לאחת מהם ואמאי הלא יש לנו לומר צריכה לחזור על כל הבית כמו על כל האחין. וי"ל דניחא ליה לאותוביה שפיר בהדיא מחיזור דאחין לחיזור דאחין: **א)** ונראה א) דקאמר והא ביאה פסולה וכו' דפריך מכח שאין לנו לומר שמועיל ביאה יותר ממאמר לשום תנא שהרי ר"ג סבר אין מאמר אחר מאמר ואפ"ה מהני מאמר וביאה אחר ביאה פסולה כדפרישית בריש פרקין וכן לרבנן לא גרע מאמר מביאה פסולה ושוין הם דיש מאמר אחר מאמר וכן יש ביאה אחר ביאה פסולה וא"כ אין לנו לומר לר' נחמיה שמועיל ביאה פסולה יותר ממאמר וקאמר דאין מאמר אחר ביאה פסולה וא"כ כמו כן אין מאמר אחר מאמר. ולא נהירא שהרי סברא גדולה יש לחלק דהא ביאה פסולה דיש ב) אומרים לר"ג ולרבנן היינו משום דאיכא למגזר כדמפרש תלמודא בריש פרקין ור' נחמיה לא ס"ל משום דביאה וחליצה הוו מדאורייתא ומידע ידיע: **ב)** גם נ"ל דטעמא רבא איכא דאין לטעות למבעל אחר ביאה דאדרבה סברי כ"ע דחשיבות דביאה היא ואפילו פסולה אין אחריה כלום וכ"ש דביאה כשרה ואין לה שיור דאין אחריה כלום ולא אתי למבעל אחר ביאה. ורבנן לית להו האי טעמא דקסברי דכיון שתקנו חכמים גט ומאמר להודייהו ביבמה דלא ליתי למיבעל אחר ביאה. כמו כן תקנו דביאה פסולה יש אחריה דלא ליתו למטעי בביאה אחר ביאה והמוסיף יוסיף:

לעיל כו: לקמן נג.

[עי' תוספות לעיל יט. ד"ה דתניא]

עדיות פ"ד מ"ח

לקמן נו:

[לקמן נג. נו:]

[לעיל כ: לקמן קיח.]

ס"א ולמסקנא

רש"ל מ"ז

[ועי' תוס' ב"ב פח:]

[לקמן נב:]

הגהות הב"ח

(א) גמ' ב"ש דתנן. נ"ב קנ' כט ע"ב: (ב) שם אמר להם ר' שמעון: (ג) תוס' ד"ה כולהו וכו' בפ"ק דסוטה דף ז הס"ד: (ד) ד"ה ביאה וכו' לא משתמיט וכו': (ה) בא"ד והא ביאה פסולה כמאמר

תורה אור

הַאי גֵּט אַחַר גֵּט הוּא! אֲמַר רַב יְהוּדָה, הָכִי קָאָמַר: גֵּט אַחַר הַגֵּט וּמַאֲמָר אַחַר מַאֲמָר כְּדַאֲמַרַן, יָבָם אֶחָד וִיבָמָה אַחַת כֵּיצַד (א) הַתָּרָתָן? עָשָׂה מַאֲמָר בִּיבִמְתּוֹ וְנָתַן לָהּ גֵּט — צְרִיכָה הֵימֶנּוּ חֲלִיצָה.§ "עָשָׂה מַאֲמָר וּבָעַל הֲרֵי זוֹ כְּמִצְוָתָהּ".§ לֵימָא מְסַיֵּיע לֵיהּ לְרַב הוּנָא, דְּאָמַר רַב הוּנָא: [א]מִצְוַת יְבָמָה — מְקַדֵּשׁ וְאַחַר כָּךְ בּוֹעֵל. אֵימָא: אַף זֶה כְּמִצְוָתָהּ. פְּשִׁיטָא! סד"א: (ב) כֵּיוָן דְּאָמַר מָר: *הָעוֹשֶׂה מַאֲמָר בִּיבִמְתּוֹ — פָּרְחָה הֵימֶנּוּ זִיקַת יְבָמִין, וְחָלָה עָלָיו זִיקַת אֵרוּסִין וְנִשּׂוּאִין, אֵימָא לָאו מִצְוָה קָעָבֵיד — קמ"ל. גּוּפָא, אָמַר רַב הוּנָא: מִצְוַת יְבָמִין מְקַדֵּשׁ וְאַחַר כָּךְ בּוֹעֵל, וְאִם בָּעַל וְעָשָׂה מַאֲמָר — קָנָה. אִם בָּעַל וְעָשָׂה מַאֲמָר — פְּשִׁיטָא, דְּהָא קָנְיָהּ בְּבִיאָה! אֶלָּא אֵימָא: [ב]אִם בָּעַל בְּלֹא מַאֲמָר — קָנָה. וְהָתַנְיָא: לוֹקֶה! *מַכַּת מַרְדּוּת [ג]מִדְּרַבָּנַן. *דְּרַב מְנַגֵּיד [ד]מַאן דִּמְקַדֵּשׁ בְּבִיאָה, [ה]וּמַאן דִּמְקַדֵּשׁ בְּשׁוּקָא, [ו]וּמַאן דִּמְקַדֵּשׁ בְּלֹא שִׁדּוּכֵי, [ז]וּמַאן דִּמְבַטֵּל גִּיטָּא, [ח]וּמַאן דְּמָסַר מוֹדָעָא אַגִּיטָּא, [ט]וּמַאן דְּפָקַר שְׁלִיחָא דְּרַבָּנַן, [י]וּמַאן דְּשָׁהֵי שַׁמְתָּא דְּרַבָּנַן עֲלֵיהּ תְּלָתִין יוֹמִין וְלָא אָתֵי לְבֵי דִּינָא וְתָבַע לְשַׁמְתֵיהּ, [כ]וְעַל חַתְנָא דְּדָאֵיר בְּבֵי חֲמוּהִי. דְּדָאֵיר — אִין, דְּחָלֵיף — לָא. וְהָא הַהוּא דְּחָלֵיף אַבָּבָא דְּבֵי חֲמוּהִי, וְנַגְדֵיהּ רַב שֵׁשֶׁת! [ל]הַהוּא — מֵידַם הֲוָה דַּיֵּים מֵחֲמָתֵיהּ. נְהַרְדְּעֵי אָמְרִי: בְּכוּלְּהוּ לָא מְנַגֵּיד רַב אֶלָּא לִמְקַדֵּשׁ בְּבִיאָה וּבְלֹא שִׁדּוּכֵי. וְאִיכָּא דְּאָמְרִי: אֲפִילּוּ בְּשִׁדּוּכֵי נַמִי, מִשּׁוּם פְּרִיצוּתָא. ת"ר: [מ]כֵּיצַד מַאֲמָר — נָתַן לָהּ כֶּסֶף אוֹ שָׁוֶה כֶּסֶף, וּבִשְׁטָר כֵּיצַד? בִּשְׁטָר כֵּיצַד?! כְּדַאֲמַרַן: *[נ]כָּתַב לָהּ עַל הַנְּיָיר אוֹ עַל הַחֶרֶס, אע"פ שֶׁאֵין בּוֹ שָׁוֶה פְּרוּטָה, "הֲרֵי אַתְּ מְקוּדֶּשֶׁת לִי"! אֲמַר אַבָּיֵי, ה"ק: [ס]שְׁטַר כְּתוּבַּת יְבָמִין כֵּיצַד — כָּתַב לָהּ: אֲנָא פְּלוֹנִי בַּר פְּלוֹנִי קַבֵּילִית יַת פְּלוֹנִית יְבִמְתִּי עֲלַי לָזוּן וּלְפַרְנָסָה כָּרָאוּי, *וּבִלְבַד שֶׁתְּהֵא כְּתוּבָּתָהּ עַל נִכְסֵי בַּעְלָהּ הָרִאשׁוֹן. *וְאִי לֵית לָהּ מֵרִאשׁוֹן — תַּקִּינוּ לָהּ רַבָּנַן מִשֵּׁנִי, כְּדֵי שֶׁלֹּא תְּהֵא קַלָּה בְּעֵינָיו לְהוֹצִיאָהּ. בְּעָא מִינֵּיהּ אַבָּיֵי מֵרַבָּה: נָתַן לָהּ גֵּט, וְאָמַר: הֲרֵי אַתְּ מְגוֹרֶשֶׁת הֵימֶנִּי, וְאִי אַתְּ מוּתֶּרֶת לְכָל אָדָם, מַהוּ? גֵּט יְבָמָה דְּרַבָּנַן הוּא, גֵּט דְּמַהֲנֵי בְּאֵשֶׁת אִישׁ מַהֲנֵי בִּיבָמָה. גֵּט דְּלָא מַהֲנֵי בְּאֵשֶׁת אִישׁ — לָא מַהֲנֵי בִּיבָמָה. אוֹ דִּלְמָא אָתֵי לְאַחְלוּפֵי בְּגִיטָּא? [א"ל: חָיְישִׁינַן דִּלְמָא אָתֵי לְאַחְלוּפֵי בְּגִיטָּא]. מַתְקִיף לָהּ רַבָּה בַּר חָנָן: אֶלָּא מֵעַתָּה, יָהֵיב לָהּ נְיָירָא בְּעָלְמָא ה"נ דְּפָסְלָהּ? א"ל: הָתָם לָא פָּסֵיל בִּכְהוּנָּה, [ע]הָכָא — קָפָסֵיל בִּכְהוּנָּה. דְּתַנְיָא: "°וְאִשָּׁה גְּרוּשָׁה *מֵאִישָׁהּ לֹא יִקָּחוּ" [פ]אֲפִילּוּ לֹא נִתְגָּרְשָׁה אֶלָּא מֵאִישָׁהּ — לֹא יִקָּחוּ, וְהַיְינוּ רֵיחַ הַגֵּט שֶׁפּוֹסֵל בִּכְהוּנָּה. אָמַר רָמֵי בַּר חָמָא: *הֲרֵי אָמְרוּ, [צ]אָמַר אֶחָד לַלַּבְלָר "כְּתוֹב גֵּט לַאֲרוּסָתִי, לִכְשֶׁאֶכְנָסֶנָּה אֲגָרְשֶׁנָּה" הֲרֵי זֶה גֵּט, מִפְּנֵי שֶׁבְּיָדוֹ לְגָרְשָׁהּ. וּלְאִשָּׁה

רש"י

הַאי גֵּט אַחַר גֵּט הוּא. בִּתְמִיָּה: וְכִי זֶהוּ גֵּט אַחַר גֵּט? דְּקָתָנֵי רֵישָׁא וַחֲכָמִים אוֹמְרִים יֵשׁ גֵּט אַחַר כו'? וּמְפָרֵשׁ כֵּיצַד עָשָׂה מַאֲמָר כו' — דְּהַיְינוּ גֵּט אַחַר מַאֲמָר. כְּדַאֲמָרַן. בְּבָרַיְיתָא דִּלְעֵיל, כֵּיצַד אָמַר ר"ג כו' וּבְמַתְנִי' לֹא פֵּירֵשׁ. הוֹאִיל דְּאָמַר מַר. בְּפֶרֶק "ד' אַחִין" (לעיל דף כט:). וְהָתַנְיָא לוֹקֶה. וְאֵין מַלְקוֹת אַרְבָּעִים אֶלָּא עַל דִּבְרֵי תוֹרָה. אַלְמָא דְּאוֹרַיְיתָא הִיא, וְהֵיכִי אָמְרַתְּ קָנָה? וְקָמְשַׁנֵּי: הַאי לוֹקֶה לָאו מַלְקוֹת אַרְבָּעִים הוּא, אֶלָּא מַכַּת מַרְדּוּת, מַכַּת רִידּוּי מִדְּרַבָּנַן, שֶׁנָּהַג קַלּוּת רֹאשׁ בְּעַצְמוֹ, וּלְעוֹלָם קָנָה. דְּרַב מְנַגֵּיד. מַכַּת מַרְדּוּת. אַמַּאן דִּמְקַדֵּשׁ בְּבִיאָה. מִשּׁוּם פְּרִיצוּתָא. וְאַמַּאן דִּמְקַדֵּשׁ בְּשׁוּקָא. אֲפִילּוּ בְּכַסְפָּא, דְּמִנְהַג זִילוּת וּפְרִיצוּת הִיא. דְּמִתְפַּקֵּר. לְשׁוֹן חוּצְפָּא, שֶׁמֵּעִיז פָּנָיו לְהִתְרִיס עִם שְׁלִיחַ ב"ד. מֵידַם הֲוָה דַּיְימָא חֲמָתֵיהּ מִינֵּיהּ. חֲשׁוּדָה הָיְתָה חֲמוֹתוֹ מִמֶּנּוּ. נָתַן לָהּ כֶּסֶף אוֹ שָׁוֶה כֶּסֶף. וְאָמַר לָהּ: הִתְקַדְּשִׁי לִי בְּמַאֲמַר יְבָמִין. וְאַע"ג דְּיָהֵב לָהּ מִידֵּי — לָאו קִידּוּשִׁין גְּמוּרִים הֵן כְּקִידּוּשֵׁי תוֹרָה, שֶׁהֲרֵי אֵין קִידּוּשִׁין תּוֹפְסִין בְּאֵשֶׁת אָח, וְהַתּוֹרָה לֹא הִתִּירָהּ לוֹ לַעֲשׂוֹת כְּאִשָּׁה נָכְרִית אֶלָּא כְּסֵדֶר הַמִּצְוָה, וּבִיאָה הוּא דִּכְתָבָהּ בָּהּ רַחֲמָנָא. וּבִשְׁטָר כֵּיצַד. וְאִם קִידֵּשׁ בִּשְׁטָר כֵּיצַד כָּתַב בּוֹ? וְהָוֵינַן: כֵּיצַד?! בִּתְמִיָּה. וְהָא כֵּיוָן דְּקִידּוּשֵׁי כֶּסֶף אָמְרַתְּ נָתַן לָהּ כֶּסֶף כִּשְׁאָר נָשִׁים, מִמֵּילָא שָׁמְעִינַן שְׁטָר נַמִי כִּשְׁאָר כָּל שְׁטַר אֵירוּסִין בְּעָלְמָא, כִּדְאָמַר בְּקִידּוּשִׁין: כָּתַב עַל הַנְּיָיר אוֹ עַל הַחֶרֶס, אע"פ שֶׁאֵין בּוֹ שָׁוֶה פְּרוּטָה, הֲרֵי אַתְּ מְקוּדֶּשֶׁת כו'. אָמַר אַבָּיֵי. הַאי תַּנָּא לָאו אִשְׁטַר מַאֲמָר קָאֵי, אֶלָּא אִשְׁטַר כְּתוּבָּה קָאֵי. עַל נִכְסֵי בַּעְלָהּ הָרִאשׁוֹן. וְלֹא עַל שֶׁל יָבָם. מַאי טַעְמָא — כִּדְאָמַר בְּ"הַחוֹלֵץ" (לעיל דף לט.) אִשָּׁה הִקְנוּ לוֹ מִן הַשָּׁמַיִם. נָתַן לָהּ גֵּט. יָבָם לִיבִמְתּוֹ. מַהוּ. לְפוֹסְלָהּ עַל אָחִיו וְעָלָיו בְּהַאי גִּיטָּא, דְּקָיְימָא עֲלֵיהּ בְּ"לֹא יִבְנֶה". הַאי גֵּט לָא מְהַנֵּי בְּאֵשֶׁת אִישׁ לְהַתִּירָהּ לִינָּשֵׂא, וְהָכָא נַמִי — לָאו גֵּירוּשִׁין לְמֵיקַם בְּלֹא יִבְנֶה. לְאִיחְלוּפֵי בְּגִיטָּא. וְלִכְנוֹס יְבָמָה אַחַר הַגֵּט. הָכָא פָּסֵיל בִּכְהוּנָּה. כֹּהֵן שֶׁנָּתַן גֵּט כָּזֶה לְאִשְׁתּוֹ אֲסָרָהּ עָלָיו, וְהִלְכָּךְ תִּיבָּעֵי לָן (ג) אִי מְהַנֵּי מִדְּרַבָּנַן. אֶלָּא מֵאִישָׁהּ. וְלֹא הִתִּירָהּ לְכָל אָדָם. הֲרֵי זֶה גֵּט. וְאִם נְתָנוֹ (ד) מִשֶּׁכְּנָסָהּ — הֲרֵי זוֹ מְגוֹרֶשֶׁת, הוֹאִיל וּבְיָדוֹ לְגָרְשָׁהּ מִשֶּׁנִּכְתַּב. וְאִי מִשּׁוּם גֵּט יָשָׁן, דְּקי"ל (גיטין דף עט:) בֵּית הִלֵּל פּוֹסְלִין, וּתְנַן: אֵיזֶהוּ גֵּט יָשָׁן — כָּל שֶׁנִּתְיַיחֵד עִמָּהּ אַחַר כְּתִיבָה, הָא אִיתְּמַר בְּפֶרֶק "הַזּוֹרֵק" (שם): אִם נִתְגָּרְשָׁה — תִּנָּשֵׂא לְכַתְּחִלָּה. וּלְאִשָּׁה

תוספות

אם בעל ועשה מאמר פשיטא דהא קניה בביאה. הא לא פריך פשיטא דקניה בביאה לחודה — דמהא לא הוה משני מידי. אלא הכי פריך: פשיטא שמאמר אחר ביאה אינו מגרע, ואם בביאה לחוד קנה — בשביל מאמר שאחריו לא גרע! ומשני: אימא אם בעל בלא מאמר קנה, דס"ד לא קני אלא אם כן עושה כמלותה: מקדש ואחר כך בועלה. ומתניתין דתנן בריש קידושין (דף ב.): היבמה נקנית בביאה — לא שמעינן ליה, דדלמא היינו מדאורייתא, וכן הא דתנן הכא במתני' (לעיל נ:) הבעילה, בזמן שהיא בתחילה אין אחריה כלום — דלמא נמי היינו משום דמדאורייתא קני ופריך: והתניא לוקה! וידע שפיר דמדרבנן לוקה, אלא דס"ד דלוקה מדרבנן משום דעשאוהו חכמים כפוגע באשת אח שלא במקום מצוה, וא"כ מדרבנן לא קני לה בלא מאמר. ומשני: מכת מרדות מדרבנן, ומשום פריצותא בעלמא, כדרב.

דמבטל גיטא. אע"ג דרב משמע דסבירא ליה בריש "השולח" (גיטין דף לג:) דביטלו אינו מבוטל *כר"ג, גבי הא דאמר רב יוסף ניחזי אנן, מ"מ קאמר הכא דלקי — משום דמוליא לעז על הגט.

דמסר מודעא אגיטא. אפילו היה מבטל כל מודעי, מ"מ היה מלקה אותו, משום דמוליא לעז על הגט, דאיכא דשמע במודעא ולא שמע בביטול.

דמתפקר בשליח דבי דינא. כך גירס' הקונטרס. ויש ספרים שכתוב בהן: מאן דמלעיר שליחא דרבנן. וכן כתוב בכל הספרים בפ"ק דקידושין (דף יב:). ומיהו, גם שם פי' בקונטרס: שליחא דרבנן — שליח ב"ד. ונראה דבכל שליחא דרבנן יש ללקות, אע"ג דלא הוי שליח ב"ד. כדאשכחן בפ' "עשרה יוחסין" (קדושין ע.) דשמתיה רב יהודה לההוא *טבחא דליער שלוחו. ואע"ג דשמתא חמור מנגדא, כדמוכח ב"מקום שנהגו" (פסחים דף נב.) — שמא החמיר עליו משום שביזה את רב יהודה עצמו.

דמקדש בביאה. אר"ת דאפי' ביבמה דצריך ביאה — דפריצותא הוא שעושה תחלת קנינו בביאה.

הדר בבית חמיו. אנן סמכינן אנהרדעי, דאמרי: בכולהו לא מנגיד רב אלא אמאן דמקדש בביאה, דבשל סופרים הלך אחר המיקל.

על הנייר או על החרס. אר"ת: כר' אליעזר אתיא, דלרבי מאיר, דאמר עדי חתימה כרתי — לא מהני, דדבר שיכול להזדייף הוא, דבשטר קידושין נמי בעי ר' מאיר עדי חתימה, כדמוכח בפ"ב דקידושין (דף מח.). ובפ"ק דקידושין (דף ט. ד"ה "כתב") פירשתי.

שאין בו שוה פרוטה. פירוש: ואינה מתקדשת משום כסף — מקודשת מטעם שטר, גבי שדי מכורה לך בפרק קמא דקידושין (דף כו. ושם) שהמוכר נותן שטר. תימה: אמאי נקט אע"פ שאין בו שוה פרוטה דאין בו שום רבותא! דכך לי שוה פרוטה כמו אין שוה פרוטה! ויש לומר: דמשום דכתב ביה נתינה אחרי תיבת את ספר המקנה, ס"ד דליבעי שוה פרוטה*.

לכשאכנסנה אגרשנה הרי זה גט. תימה דבפרק "כל הגט" (גיטין דף כו:) אמרינן דאינו גט, שלא יאמרו גטה קודם לבנה ובקונטרס פי': דהכא נמי לא קאמר דהוי גט אלא בדיעבד, שכבר נתגרשה בו. ואין נראה: דהתם דקאמר אין גט משמע דלא הוי גט כלל! ואר"ת דהכא כשכתב בו זמן שאחר נשואין, שהוא זמן נתינה — דאפילו גט ישן לא הוי, שלא נתייחד עמה אחר זמן הכתוב בגטה. והרי

עין משפט נר מצוה

כב א ב ג מיי' פ"א מהל' יבום ה"א ופ"ב הלכה א ב סמג עשין נא טוש"ע אה"ע סימן קסו סעיף ב:

כג ד ה ו מיי' פ"ג מהל' אישות הלכה כא כב ופכ"א מהלכו' איסורי ביאה הלכה יד סמג עשין מח טוש"ע שם סימן כו סעיף ד:

כד ז ח מיי' פ"ו מהל' גירושין הלכה כו סמג שם טוש"ע שם סי' קמא סעיף סז:

כה ט מיי' פכ"ה מהל' סנהדרין הלכה ה סמג לאוין רח טוש"ע ח"מ סי' ח סעיף ה:

כו י מיי' פ"א מהלכו' טוען ונטען הלכה ה טוש"ע שם סי' פז ס"ט:

כז כ מיי' פכ"א מהל' איסורי ביאה הלכה טו סמג לאוין קפו:

כח ל מיי' פ"ב מהל' איסורי ביאה הל' יב:

כט מ מיי' פ"ב מהלכות יבום הלכה א סמג עשין נא טוש"ע אה"ע סי' קסו סעי' ב:

[נ"ל כרשב"ג]

ל נ מיי' פ"ג מהלכות אישות הלכה ג סמג עשין מח טוש"ע שם סימן לב סעיף א ב:

לא ס מיי' פ"ד מהלכות יבום הלכה לב:

לב ע מיי' פ"ה שם הלכה א סמג עשין נא נב טוש"ע שם סי' קע סעיף א:

לג פ מיי' פ"י מהל' גרושין הלכה א סמג לאוין קסג טוש"ע שם סימן ו סעיף א:

לד צ מיי' פ"ג שם הל' ו סמג עשין נ טוש"ע שם סי' קלב סעיף א:

נ"ל גברא

תוספות ישנים

ועל דמלעיר שליחא דרבנן. לאו שליחא ממש אלא צורבא מרבנן ולאו מלעיר לוקא אלא מחרף כדאמרי' בעשרה יוחסין גבי רבי יהודה דקריא ליה ההוא גברא [יהודה בר] שויסקאל:

תוספות חד מקמאי

בעא מניה אביי מרב' נתן לה גט ואמר לה הרי את מגורשת ממני ואי את מותרת לכל אדם מהו גט יבמ' מדרבנן הוא [גט] דמהני בא"א מהני ביבמה גט דלא מהני בא"א לא מהני ביבמה או דלמא אתי לאחלופי בגיטא מעליא ולא איפשיטא: תניא ואשה גרושה מאישה אפילו לא נתגרשה אלא מאישה פסולה לכהונה וזהו ריח הגט שפוסל בכהונה אמר רמי בר חמא הרי שאמר ללבלר כתוב גט לארוסתי לכשאכנסנה אגרשנה ה"ז גט מפני שבידו לגרשה. לאשה דעלמא אינו גט. ובפ' כל הגט אמרינן אמר ללבלר כתוב גט לארוסתי לכשאכנסנה אגרשנה אינו גט מפני תקנת ולד שמא יאמרו גיטה קודם יבנה התם כגון דכתב בו זמן מהשתא דאיכא משום תקנת ולד הכא דכתב זמן דשעת גירושין דליכא תקנת ולד. א"נ הכא מדאורייתא קא' ה"ז גט א"נ כגון שנתגרשה הקי"ל אין מגרשין בגט ישן גזרה שמא

מסורת הש"ס

[לעיל כט:]

[שבת מ: וש"נ]

קידושין יב:

קידושין כ. ע"ש ב"כ נח.

לעיל לח. וש"נ

שם לב.

ויקרא כא

[גיטין פב:] לקמן לב.

גיטין כו:

וע"ע תוס' קידושין ט. ד"ה אע"פ

הגהות הב"ח

(א) גמ' כיצד התרתן: (ב) שם סד"ה הואיל דאמר מר: (ג) רש"י ד"ה הכא וכו' תיבעי לן הכא אי מהני: (ד) ד"ה הרי וכו' נתנו לה משנכנסה:

וְלָאִשָּׁה בְּעָלְמָא — אֵין גֵּט, מִפְּנֵי שֶׁאֵין בְּיָדוֹ לְגָרְשָׁהּ. בָּעֵי רָמִי בַּר חָמָא: לִיבִמְתּוֹ מַהוּ? כֵּיוָן דַּאֲגִידָא בֵּיהּ — כַּאֲרוּסָתוֹ דָּמְיָא, אוֹ דִלְמָא: כֵּיוָן דְּלָא עֲבַד בָּהּ מַאֲמָר — לָא? תֵּיקוּ. בָּעֵי רַב חֲנַנְיָה: כָּתַב גֵּט לְזִיקָתוֹ וְלֹא לְמַאֲמָרוֹ, לְמַאֲמָרוֹ וְלֹא לְזִיקָתוֹ, מַהוּ? מַאֲמָר עִילָּוֵי זִיקָה קָא רָמֵי, וַהֲוָה לֵיהּ כִּמְגָרֵשׁ חֲצִי אִשָּׁה, וְהַמְגָרֵשׁ חֲצִי אִשָּׁה לֹא עָשָׂה וְלֹא כְּלוּם, אוֹ דִלְמָא: הַאי לְחוּדֵיהּ קָאֵי וְהַאי לְחוּדֵיהּ קָאֵי? וְתִפְשׁוֹט לֵיהּ מִדְּרָבָא, דְּאָמַר רָבָא: נָתַן גֵּט לְמַאֲמָרוֹ — הוּתְּרָה צָרָתָהּ! לְרָבָא — פְּשִׁיטָא לֵיהּ, לְרַב חֲנַנְיָה — מִיבַּעְיָא לֵיהּ, מַאי? תֵּיקוּ. § "חָלַץ וְעָשָׂה מַאֲמָר". § אָמַר רַב יְהוּדָה אָמַר רַב: זוֹ דִּבְרֵי רַ' עֲקִיבָא, דְּאָמַר: אֵין קִדּוּשִׁין תּוֹפְסִין בְּחַיָּיבֵי לָאוִין. אֲבָל חכ"א: יֵשׁ אַחַר חֲלִיצָה כְּלוּם. וּמִי מָצֵית מוֹקְמַתְּ לָהּ כְּרַבִּי עֲקִיבָא? וְהָא קָתָנֵי רֵישָׁא: נָתַן גֵּט וְעָשָׂה מַאֲמָר — צְרִיכָה גֵּט וַחֲלִיצָה, וְאִי רַבִּי עֲקִיבָא — כֵּיוָן דִּיהַב לָהּ גֵּט מִי מְהַנֵּי בָּהּ מַאֲמָר? וְהָתַנְיָא, רַבִּי עֲקִיבָא אוֹמֵר: מִנַּיִן לְנוֹתֵן גֵּט לִיבִמְתּוֹ שֶׁנֶּאֶסְרָה עָלָיו עוֹלָמִית — שֶׁנֶּאֱמַר "לֹא יוּכַל בַּעְלָהּ הָרִאשׁוֹן אֲשֶׁר שִׁלְּחָהּ" אַחַר שִׁילּוּחַ. (דברים כד) אָמַר רַב אַשִׁי: גֵּט יְבָמִין מִדְּרַבָּנַן. וּקְרָא — אַסְמַכְתָּא בְּעָלְמָא. תַּנְיָא נַמִי הָכִי, אָמַר רַבִּי: אֵין הַדְּבָרִים הַלָּלוּ אֲמוּרִים אֶלָּא לְדִבְרֵי רַ' עֲקִיבָא, שֶׁהָיָה עוֹשֶׂה חֲלוּצָה כְּעֶרְוָה. אֲבָל חֲכָמִים אוֹמְרִים: יֵשׁ אַחַר חֲלִיצָה כְּלוּם. וַאֲנִי אוֹמֵר: אֵימָתַי — בִּזְמַן שֶׁקִּדְּשָׁהּ לְשׁוּם אִישׁוּת, אֲבָל קִדְּשָׁהּ לְשׁוּם יַבְמוּת — אֵין אַחַר חֲלִיצָה כְּלוּם. תַּנְיָא אִידָךְ: הַחוֹלֵץ לִיבִמְתּוֹ, וְחָזַר וְקִדְּשָׁהּ. רַבִּי אוֹמֵר: אִם קִדְּשָׁהּ לְשׁוּם אִישׁוּת — צְרִיכָה הֵימֶנּוּ גֵּט, לְשׁוּם יַבְמוּת — אֵין צְרִיכָה הֵימֶנּוּ גֵּט וַחֲכָמִים אוֹמְרִים: בֵּין שֶׁקִּדְּשָׁהּ לְשׁוּם אִישׁוּת, בֵּין שֶׁקִּדְּשָׁהּ לְשׁוּם יַבְמוּת — צְרִיכָה הֵימֶנּוּ גֵּט. אָמַר רַב יוֹסֵף: מ"ט דְּרַבִּי — עֲשָׂאוּהָ כְּעוֹדֵר בְּנִכְסֵי הַגֵּר וּכְסָבוּר שֶׁלּוֹ הֵן דְּלָא קָנֵי. א"ל אַבַּיֵי: מִי דָּמֵי? הָתָם — לָא קָא מְכַוֵּין לְמִיקְנֵי, הָכָא — קָא מְכַוֵּין לְמִיקְנֵי. הָא לָא דָּמְיָא אֶלָּא לְעוֹדֵר בְּנִכְסֵי גֵּר זֶה, וּכְסָבוּר שֶׁל גֵּר אַחֵר הוּא, דְּקָנֵי. אֶלָּא אָמַר אַבַּיֵי: הָכָא בְּמַאי עָסְקִינַן — כְּגוֹן דְּאָמַר לָהּ "הִתְקַדְּשִׁי לִי בְּמַאֲמַר יְבָמִין". רַבִּי סָבַר: מַאֲמָר עִילָּוֵי זִיקָה קָא רָמֵי, וַאֲתַאי חֲלִיצָה אַפְקַעְתָּהּ לְזִיקָה. וְרַבָּנַן סָבְרִי: הַאי לְחוּדֵיהּ קָאֵי וְהַאי לְחוּדֵיהּ קָאֵי. מֵעִיקָּרָא, אִילּוּ אֲמַר לָהּ "הִתְקַדְּשִׁי לִי בְּמַאֲמַר יְבָמִין" מִי לָא מְהַנֵּי? הַשְׁתָּא נַמִי מְהַנֵּי. רָבָא אֲמַר: אִי דְּאָמַר לָהּ "בְּמַאֲמַר יְבָמִין" כּוּלֵּי עָלְמָא לָא פְּלִיגִי דִּמְהַנְּיָא, וְהָכָא בְּמַאי עָסְקִינַן — כְּגוֹן דְּאָמַר לָהּ "הִתְקַדְּשִׁי לִי בְּזִיקַּת יְבָמִין". רַבִּי סָבַר: יֵשׁ

רש"י

וּלְאִשָּׁה בְּעָלְמָא. וּכְנָסָהּ וְגֵירְשָׁהּ בּוֹ — אֵינוֹ גֵּט, הוֹאִיל כְּשֶׁנִּכְתַּב לֹא הָיָה רָאוּי לְגֵירוּשִׁין. לִיבִמְתּוֹ מַהוּ. כְּתָבוֹ קוֹדֶם שֶׁכְּנָסָהּ, וּכְשֶׁכְּנָסָהּ נְתָנוֹ לָהּ, מַהוּ שֶׁתִּתְגָּרֵשׁ בּוֹ? כָּתַב גֵּט לְזִיקָתוֹ וְלֹא לְמַאֲמָרוֹ אוֹ לְמַאֲמָרוֹ וְלֹא לְזִיקָתוֹ. וְהוּא עָשָׂה בָּהּ מַאֲמָר תְּחִלָּה, מַהוּ שֶׁתִּיפָּסֵל עָלָיו בְּכָךְ? מַאֲמָר עִילָּוֵי זִיקָה רָמֵי. כְּשֶׁעָשָׂה מַאֲמָר נִדְבַּק עִם הַזִּיקָה, וְנִיתּוֹסֵף עָלֶיהָ — וְאֵין גֵּט מוֹעִיל לָזֶה בְּלֹא זֶה. וְכֵיוָן שֶׁנִּכְתַּב בְּתוֹךְ הַגֵּט שֶׁלֹּא עֲשָׂאוֹ אֶלָּא לְאֶחָד מֵהֶן — הָוֵה לֵיהּ מְגָרֵשׁ חֲצִי אִשָּׁה, וְלֹא כְלוּם הִיא, וּמוּתֶּרֶת לוֹ. אוֹ דִלְמָא הַאי לְחוּדֵיהּ קָאֵי וְהַאי לְחוּדֵיהּ קָאֵי. וּמְהַנֵּי. וְהֵיכָא דְּכָתַב לְזִיקָתוֹ וְלֹא לְמַאֲמָרוֹ — אֲסוּרָה עָלָיו וְעַל אָחִיו, דְּפָקַע זִיקָה, וְקָמָה בְּ"לֹא יִבְנֶה", וְאִי כָּתַב לְמַאֲמָרוֹ וְלֹא לְזִיקָתוֹ — אֲסוּרָה לוֹ וּמוּתֶּרֶת לְאָחִיו, דְּמַאֲמָר דַּעֲבַד שַׁקְלֵיהּ, וּפָשָׁה לֵיהּ זִיקָה כְּמֵעִיקָּרָא. נָתַן גֵּט לְמַאֲמָרוֹ. וְלֹא לְזִיקָתוֹ, בְּ"אַרְבָּעָה אַחִין" (לעיל לב.) גַּבֵּי זִיקַת [ב'] יְבָמִין — ג' אַחִין נְשׂוּאִין ג' נָכְרִיּוֹת, וּמֵת אֶחָד מֵהֶן, וְעָשָׂה בָּהּ הַשֵּׁנִי מַאֲמָר וּמֵת — הֲרֵי אֵלּוּ חוֹלְצוֹת כו', וְקָאָמַר (א) רָבָא עֲלָהּ: נָתַן גֵּט לְמַאֲמָרוֹ וְאַחַ"כ מֵת — הוּתְּרָה אִשְׁתּוֹ הָרִאשׁוֹנָה שֶׁהִיא צָרָתָהּ לְאָחִיו הַשֵּׁנִי, דְּאִי לָאו גֵּט הֲוָה אֲסוּרָה עָלָיו מִשּׁוּם זִיקַת שְׁנֵי יְבָמִין. אַלְמָא, הַאי לְחוּדֵיהּ קָאֵי, מִדְּאַהֲנֵי גֵּט לְאִישְׁתַּרוּיֵי צָרָתָהּ לְאָחִיו הַשֵּׁנִי. וְהוּא הַדִּין דְּהִיא גּוּפָהּ נַמִי שַׁרְיָא לְאָחִיו, אֶלָּא דְּמִחַלְּפָא בְּבַעֲלַת גֵּט גָּמוּר לְזִיקָה דִּמְקַמֵּי מַאֲמָר, אוֹ לְזִיקָה וּמַאֲמָר. וְהָכִי אָמְרִינַן בְּ"אַרְבָּעָה אַחִין". זוֹ דִּבְרֵי רַבִּי עֲקִיבָא. אַחֲלַץ וְעָשָׂה בָּהּ מַאֲמָר קָאֵי, דְּקָתָנֵי: לֹא תָּפִיס מַאֲמָר. אַחַר שִׁילּוּחַ. כְּלוֹמַר, מִדִּכְתִיב "אֲשֶׁר שִׁלְּחָהּ" קְרָא יְתֵירָא דְּלָא צְרִיךְ, הָכִי קָאָמַר: יֵשׁ לְךָ מְשַׁלֵּחַ שֶׁאָסוּר לְהַחֲזִיר אַחַר שִׁילּוּחַ אֲפִילּוּ לֹא נִישֵּׂאת, וְאֵיזוֹ — זוֹ יְבָמָה. וְכֵיוָן דִּבְלָאו קָאֵי — הֵיכִי מְהַנֵּי בָּהּ תּוּ מַאֲמָר? אֵימָתַי. יֵשׁ אַחַר חֲלִיצָה תְּפִיסַת קִידּוּשִׁין. בִּזְמַן שֶׁקִּדְּשָׁהּ לְשׁוּם אִישׁוּת. בְּקִידּוּשִׁין גְּמוּרִים, וְלֹא בְּמַאֲמַר יְבָמִין. דְּוַדַּאי קִידּוּשִׁין תּוֹפְסִין בְּחַיָּיבֵי לָאוִין. אֲבָל קִדְּשָׁהּ לְשׁוּם יַבְמוּת. אֵינָן קִידּוּשִׁין, שֶׁהֲרֵי אֵין כָּאן לַד יִיבּוּם, וְהָווּ לְהוּ קִידּוּשֵׁי טָעוּת. כְּעוֹדֵר. סוֹפֵר וּכְסָבוּר שֶׁלּוֹ הֵן. שֶׁהָיָה קַרְקַע הַגֵּר סָמוּךְ לְקַרְקָעוֹ, וּמֵת הַגֵּר וְאֵין לוֹ יוֹרְשִׁין, וְהַמַּחֲזִיק בִּנְכָסָיו קָנָה. וְזֶה סִיפֵּר בְּקַרְקַע הַגֵּר, וּכְסָבוּר שֶׁזֶּה קַרְקַע שֶׁלּוֹ, וְלֹא נִתְכַּוֵּין לְהַחֲזִיק — דְּלָא קָנֵי. וְהַאי נַמִי סָבוּר שֶׁקִּידּוּשֵׁי יְבָמָה תּוֹפְסִין בָּהּ, וְלֹא נִתְכַּוֵּין לִקְנוֹת אֶלָּא מִכֹּחַ יִיבּוּמֵי אָחִיו — וְהָא פָּקְעוּ לְהוּ. הָתָם לָא קָמִיכַּוֵּין לְמִיקְנֵי. דְּהָא סָבוּר שֶׁלּוֹ הֵן. הָכָא מְכַוֵּין לְמִיקְנֵי. מ"מ. הָא לָא דָּמְיָא כו'. אַבַּיֵי הוּא דְּאַקְשֵׁי וְאָזֵיל. וּכְסָבוּר שֶׁל גֵּר אַחֵר הוּא. וּמִתְכַּוֵּין לִקְנוֹת מִכָּל מָקוֹם. וְהַאי נַמִי קָסָבַר לִקְנוֹת מִכֹּחַ אָחִיו, וְאֵינוֹ קוֹנֶה אֶלָּא מִכֹּחוֹ — וּמ"מ קִנְיָן הוּא. מַאֲמָר עִילָּוֵי זִיקָה רָמֵי. מַאֲמָר דְּתַקִּינוּ רַבָּנַן לְכָל הַיְבָמִין, לֹא תִּקּוּן אֶלָּא הֵיכָא דְּקַיְימָא זִיקָה, וְאָתָא מַאֲמָר וְאִיתּוֹסַף עֲלָהּ. וְהָכָא לֵיכָּא לְמֵימַר הָכִי, דְּאָתְיָא חֲלִיצָה מַפְקְעָה לְזִיקָה. הַאי לְחוּדֵיהּ קָאֵי כו'. וְלָא מְהַנֵּי זִיקָה לְמַאֲמָר. הִילְכָּךְ, הַשְׁתָּא כְּמֵעִיקָּרָא: מֵעִיקָּרָא, אִילּוּ אֲמַר לָהּ הִתְקַדְּשִׁי לִי בְּמַאֲמַר יְבָמִין, מִי לָא קָנֵי? וְאַף עַל גַּב דְּלָא מְהַנְּיָא לֵיהּ זִיקָה, דְּהַאי לְחוּדֵיהּ קָיְימָא — הַשְׁתָּא נַמִי מְהַנֵּי.

תוספות

והרי זה גט* [דקאמר, היינו:] לגרש בו לכתחלה. והיא ד"כל הגט" — שכתב זמן דקודם נישואין, וגרע טפי מגט ישן. דבגט ישן ליכא אלא ייחוד בעלמא, לכך אם נתגרשה בו תנשא לכתחלה. אבל התם דכנסה, ואיכא ודאי ביאה — אינו גט כלל* א). ולאשה בעלמא אין גט. ואפילו כתוב בו זמן דאחר נשואים. כיון דאין בידו לגרשה בשעה שעשאו שליח. ונראה לר"י דהיינו דוקא למ"ד אין אדם מקנה דבר שלא בא לעולם, אבל למאן דאמר אדם מקנה — הוי גט, דבידו לגרשה, כמו בשחרור דמהני לוקח עבד על מנת לשחררו וכתב לו לכשאקחך הרי עצמך קנוי לך מעכשיו, כדאמר ב"האשה רבה" (לקמן דף צג:) ובקידושין בפרק "האומר" (דף סג.). וגט שחרור וגט אשה שוים לכל דבר, דהא ילפינן "לה" "לה" מאשה. ליבמתו מהו. אין לפרש דמיבעיא ליה אם גירשה בגט זה לאחר שיבמה יבומין גמורין אי הוי גט אי לא — דפשיטא דאין ניתרת בגט זה לשוק. דהא בההיא שעתא לא היה בידו לגרשה ולהתירה לשוק על ידי גט זה. ומאי קאמר נמי או דלמא כיון דלא עבד בה מאמר לא, אי בלא מאמר לא מהני — עבד בה מאמר נמי לא מהני להתגרש אחר שתתייבם, דמאמר לא הוי אלא מדרבנן. ואמר ר"י: דלפוסלה מכהונה מיבעיא ליה, אי חשיב ריח הגט דפסיל לכהונה אי לא. ב) וריב"ם הגיה בפירושיו דמיבעיא ליה אי כְּתָבוֹ קודם מאמר, ועשה מאמר וגירש בו, מהו שיפקיע את מאמר. או דלמא האי לחודיה קאי כו'. פירש בקונטרס: ואי כתב גט למאמרו ולא לזיקתו — אסורה לו ומותרת לאחיו, דמאמר דעבד ליה שקליה, ופשה ליה זיקה כמעיקרא. ולר"י נראה דללישנא דאמר רבא — הותרה אפילו היא. ואם כן, הכא נמי שריא לדידיה. וללישנא דהיא אסורה, דמיחלפא בבעלת הגט, הכא נמי אסורה אפי' לאחיו, דהא בעלת הגט אסורה על כל האחין. והא דשרי רבא צרתה בנתן גט למאמרו — משום דבאות משני בתים הן, ואפילו היה נותן גט גם לזיקתו היתה צרתה מותרת. כעודר בנכסי הגר. אר"י: דמיירי לרב יוסף כגון דאמר לה התקדשי לי סתם, ולשם יבמות היינו — דגלי אדעתיה שבתורת יבמין מקדשה. דאי באמר לה בהדיא במאמר יבמין — לא הוי פריך ליה אביי מי דמי, דהא אביי קאמר בסמוך דהיכא דאמר לה במאמר יבמין — דלא קני לרבי, אלא בסתם איירי. א"נ: באמר לה התקדשי לי לשם יבמות, ולא משמע בתורת מאמר יבמין. דבמאמר יבמין משמע — בתורת מאמר ולא בתורת קידושין. אבל לשם יבמות — לא משמע בתורת יבמות, אלא שסבור שעדיין היא זקוקתו. אי אמר לה התקדשי לי בזיקת (ג) מאמר יבמין מי לא מהני. דאפילו למ"ד אין זיקה — היינו לענין אחות זקוקתו וכיוצא בה, אבל פשיטא דמהני לשון זיקה, שהרי היא זקוקתו ועומדת בפניו.

תוספות ישנים (סוף)

...נאסרה אלא מטעם האחרת שעשה בה בעלה מאמר וכשנתן גט פקע ליה למאמרו וזו שלא עשה בה מידי מותרת לאחין אבל היא אסורה על כולן דמחלפא בבעלת הגט. אבל הכא דליכא אלא חדא שקידש תחלה במאמרו ואח"כ נתן גט אי שרית לה באחיו משום דמאי דעבד שקליה כ"ש לדידיה ואי אסרי' לה עליה משום דמחלפא כ"ש על האחין. וא"כ נ"ל דכי אמרינן האי לחודיה קאי והאי לחודיה קאי כשכתב גט למאמרו ולא לזיקתו אסורה בין לו בין לאחיו ומייתי ראיה מסוף דברי [רבא] דאמר נתן גט למאמרו הותרה צרתה אבל היא אסורה משום דמחלפא בבעלת הגט ור"ל לאסרה על האחין: מנין לנותן גט ליבמתו שנאסרה עליו עולמית שנאמר לא יוכל בעלה הראשון לשוב לקחתה לו לאשה. ומוכח מדקאמר לא יוכל בעלה לשוב לקחתה אחרי אשר הוטמאה ויש לך אחרת אע"ג דלא הוטמאה אסורה ואיזו זו מגרש יבמתו דכיון ששלחה שוב אינה חוזרת: וכסבור שלו הן דלא קני. וקשה למשמע הכא דלקניה בעינן כוונה ובב"ק [כ"ט ע"ב] אמרינן טוקמה בלמעלה משלשה ובשלא מתכוין וי"ל דהתם בקנין מטלטלין א"נ כוונה דלא אליס חזקת הבעלים עליהם דהם נכסים שאין להם אחריות ונקנים בקל. אבל בקרקע [אליס] חזקת הבעלים וצריך כוונה לקנותה קודם שתצא מרשות הבעלים: אלא אמר אביי הב"ע כגון דאמר לה התקדשי במאמר יבמין. והא דאביי קא מתמה לעיל שמן הדין היתה קנויה לו והשתא פשיטא ליה דאינה נקנית הכא דלעיל הייתי טעמא משום דלא אמר לה לשום מאמר יבמין בהדיא ודין הוא שיקנה להיות אשתו:

תוספות חד מקמאי (סוף)

...שני אביי כגון שאמר במאמר יבמין א"נ מעיקרא קס"ד שקדשה סתם ומסתמה לשום יבמות קדשה. והראב"ד פירש דמעיקר' דהוה מדמי לה לעודר בנכסי הגר הוא קס"ד כגון דאמר פלונית יבמתי התקדשי לי ולא תלי הקידושין במאמר יבמין וזיקת יבמין ודלמא הכי קאמר פלונית שהיתה יבמתי תתקדשי לי והשתא שני אביי כגון דא"ל התקדשי במאמר יבמין וס"ל לרבנן האי לחודיה קאי והאי לחודיה קאי מעיקרא אי א"ל התקדשי לי במאמר מי לא מהני השתא נמי מהני וכיון דקי"ל כרבא דאמר נתן לה גט למאמרו הותרה צרתה אלמא הלכתא כרבנן והיינו דאמר רבא אי דא"ל במאמר יבמין דכ"ע לא פליגי דרבא לטעמיה דאמר הותרה צרתה אלא הכא במ"ע כגון דא"ל התקדשי לי בזיקת יבמין. ר' סבר יש זיקה אתאי חליצה ואפקעיה לזיקה

א) נ"ל והאי לחודיה קאי ומהני. ופי' הקונטרס דהיכא דכתב גט לזיקתו ולא למאמרו אסורה עליו ועל אחיו דפקעה זיקה וכו'.

*יש זיקה, ואתאי חליצה אפקעתיה לזיקה. ורבנן סברי, *אין זיקה. מעיקרא אילו אמר לה "התקדשי לי בזיקת יבמין" מי לא מהני? השתא נמי מהני. רב שרביא אמר: בחליצה כשירה, אי דאמר לה "התקדשי לי בזיקת יבמין" כ"ע לא פליגי דלא מהני. והכא בחליצה פסולה קמיפלגי. מר סבר: חליצה פסולה פוטרת, ומר סבר: חליצה פסולה אינה פוטרת. רב אשי אמר: דכ"ע חליצה פסולה אינה פוטרת. והכא ביש תנאי בחליצה קמיפלגי. מר סבר: יש תנאי בחליצה, ומר סבר: [א]אין תנאי בחליצה. רבינא אמר: דכ"ע יש תנאי בחליצה. והכא *בתנאי כפול קמיפלגי; מר סבר: [ב]בעינן תנאי כפול, ומר סבר: לא בעינן תנאי כפול.§ "חלץ ועשה מאמר ונתן גט ובעל וכו'".§ וניתני נמי אין אחר ביאה כלום (א)אביי ורבא דאמרי תרוייהו, תני: [ג]אין אחר ביאה כלום. ותנא דידן — התרת יבמה לשוק עדיפא ליה.§ "אחד יבמה אחת אחד שתי יבמות".§ מתני' דלא כבן עזאי. דתניא, *בן עזאי אומר: יש מאמר אחר מאמר בשני יבמין ויבמה אחת, ואין מאמר אחר מאמר בשתי יבמות ויבם אחד.§ "כיצד מאמר לזו וכו'".§ לימא מסייע ליה לשמואל, דאמר שמואל: *חלץ לבעלת מאמר לא נפטרה צרתה, ותיובתא *דרב יוסף! מי קתני "חולץ"? "חלץ" קתני, דיעבד.§ "גט לזו וגט לזו כו'".§ לימא מסייע ליה לרבה בר רב הונא, דאמר *רבה בר רב הונא: [ד]חליצה פסולה — צריכה לחזר על כל האחין. מאי "צריכות" צריכות דעלמא.§ "גט לזו וחלץ לזו".§ לימא מסייע ליה לשמואל ותהוי תיובתא דרב יוסף! מי קתני "חולץ"? "חלץ" קתני, דיעבד.§ "חלץ וחלץ או חלץ וכו'".§ וליתני נמי אין אחר ביאה כלום(א)! אביי ורבא דאמרי תרוייהו, תני: אין אחר ביאה כלום. ותנא דידן — התרת יבמה לשוק עדיפא ליה.§ "בין יבם אחד לשתי יבמות כו'".§ בשלמא *לרבי יוחנן, דאמר: כולה ביתא בלאו קאי, איצטריך לאשמועינן דאין קידושין תופסין בחייבי לאוין. אלא לר"ל, דאמר: כולה ביתא בכרת קאי — איצטריך לאשמועינן [ה]דאין קידושין תופסין בחייבי כריתות?! אמר לך ר"ל: ולטעמיך, סיפא דקתני: בעל ועשה מאמר, איצטריך לאשמועינן דאין קידושין תופסין באשת איש? אלא: איידי דתנא התרת יבם אחד ויבמה אחת — תנא נמי שתי יבמות ויבם אחד, *ואיידי דתנא שתי יבמות ויבם אחד — תנא נמי שתי יבמין ויבמה אחת.§

הדרן עלך רבן גמליאל

חלץ

רש"י

יש זיקה. האי דתפיס מאמר בעלמא בכי האי לישנא — משום דיש זיקה, והשתא אתאי חליצתה פקעתה, וליכא למימר הכי. **אין זיקה.** אין כאן זיקה. ואפי' הכי מעיקרא הוי מאמר. **רב שרביא אמר.** אי דאמר לה בזיקת יבמין — כ"ע לא פליגי דלא מהני, דיש זיקה, ואתיא חליצה אפקעתה. **והכא בחליצה פסולה.** כגון שחלץ אחר הגט קמיפלגי, רבנן [לעיל יח: וש"נ] סברי: לא אפקעתה שפיר, ויש אחריה [שם] כלום, הלכך קני מאמר. **יש תנאי בחליצה.** שחלץ לה על מנת שתתן לו מאתים זוז. רבי סבר: אין תנאי מועיל בחליצה, ואפילו לא נתנה לו אין תנאי מועיל, והוי חליצה. הלכך לא תפיס מאמר שעשה בלשון זיקת יבמין אבתרה, דהא אפקעתה לזיקתו. ולרבנן יש תנאי, וכל כמה דלא קיימא לא פקע זיקה. וכי אמר לה התקדשי לי ע"י כסף זה בזיקת יבמין — קני: ה"ג. **רבינא אמר דכ"ע יש תנאי בחליצה.** אע"ג דקי"ל (לקמן דף קו.) [קידושין סב.] חליצה מוטעת כשירה — הני תנאי לא סבירא להו. **והכא בתנאי כפול קמיפלגי.** וכגון דלא כפליה לתנאי. לרבי בעינן תנאי כפול כתנאי בני גד ובני ראובן, והאי דלא כפליה: אם תתני תהא חליצה, ואם לא תתני לא תהא חליצה — לא הוי תנאי לבטולי לחליצה. **וניתני נמי אין לאחר ביאה** [לעיל נא: לקמן נו:] **כלום.** דהא ביאה שייכא למימר בסיפא, דקתני: או בעל ועשה מאמר ונתן גט וחלץ, דהא או או קתני. ובבעל ועשה מאמר, או בבעל ונתן גט, מאי חליצה איכא? תני אין לאחר ביאה [לעיל כז.] **כלום.** ולא צריך למיתני נמי אין [לעיל יח: יט: מד.] לאחר חליצה כלום, דכיון דתנא אין אחר ביאה כלום — ה"ה נמי דאין אחר חליצה כלום. ולישנא קלילא הוא למיתני [לעיל כו: נח.] חדא, או ביאה או חליצה. **ותנא דידן.** דלא נקט ביאה, ואע"ג דאיירי בה בסיפא — משום דהיתר יבמה לשוק חביבא ליה לאורויי, ומינה שמעינן דאין אחר ביאה כלום. וטריחא לתנא למיתני תרתי: אין אחר ביאה, ואין אחר חליצה כלום. **מתניתין.** דקתני אחת שתי יבמות עשה מאמר בזו ומאמר בזו צריכות שני גיטין. **דלא כבן עזאי.** דאמר: אין מאמר אחר מאמר בשתי יבמות ויבם אחד. ומתני' בשתי יבמות [לעיל י:] ויבם אחד קא מיירי. וללישנא בתרא דגרסינן למילתיה דבן עזאי איפכא, קיימא הך אתקפתא אסיפא דמתני', דקתני: בין יבם אחד לשתי יבמות בין שני יבמין ויבמה אחת. ומיסתברא כלישנא קמא, דא"כ לא הוה לן לאיתויי הך אתקפתא הכא, אלא [לעיל ג. וש"נ] בגמרא דסיפא דלקמן. **לימא מסייע ליה לשמואל.** אמאמר לזו וחלץ לזו קאי, מדלא נקט חליצה אבעלת מאמר — מסייע לשמואל, דאמר: חלץ לבעלת מאמר לא נפטרה צרתה, דכיון דבעי גט למאמרו — לא הויא חליצה מעלייתא לאפוקי זיקה דחברתה. **ותיובתא דרב יוסף.** דאמר ב"החולץ" (לעיל דף מד.) לא ישפוך אדם מי בורו ואחרים צריכים להם. דהא הכא דחלץ לחברתה, וקמייתא בעיא גט, ונמצא פוסל את שתיהן מן הכהונה, ולא אמרינן ליחלוץ לקמייתא ותהא חברתה כשירה. **צריכות.** משמע חליצה לכל אחת, דכיון דחליצת שתיהן רעועה — אין אחת מהן פוטרת חברתה, וקתני סיפא: וכן שני יבמין ליבמה אחת. דאם נתן זה גט וזה גט צריכה חליצה משניהן: לימא מסייע ליה לרבה כו': ה"ג. **גט לזו וחלץ לזו לימא מסייע ליה לשמואל.** מדלא נקט חליצה לבעלת הגט אלא לחברתה — מסייע ליה לשמואל דאמר בפ' "ד' אחין": חלץ לבעלת הגט — לא נפטרה צרה. **וליתני נמי אין אחר ביאה כלום.** בסיפא, דקתני או בעל ובעל או בעל ועשה מאמר כו', דהא משום הכי נקט לה, דהתם לא שייך למיתני אין אחר חליצה כלום — דהא ליכא חליצה. **כולה ביתא.** כל האחין על הבתולה ועל צרתה בלאו בעלמא, כחולץ עצמו, דשליחות דידהו עבד. **איצטריך לאשמועינן.** מתני' חלץ לזו ועשה מאמר בזו אינו כלום, דאע"ג דלאו בעלמא היא גביה לא תפסי קידושין. וקסים לן בכולן כר' עקיבא, וכן בשני יבמין ויבמה אחת. **אלא לר"ש בן לקיש דאמר.** בפ"ק (דף י:): כולה ביתא בכרת קאי, לבד מחולץ בחלוצה. אבל חולץ לגבי צרה, וכל האחין, בין בחלוצה בין בצרה, בכרת, מאי איצטריך למיתני גבי ב' יבמות ויבם אחד, וב' יבמין ויבמה אחת דאין מאמר השני תופס אחר חליצה? **ולטעמיך סיפא.** בב' יבמין ויבמה אחת, דקתני: בעל הראשון ועשה השני מאמר — אין אחר ביאה כלום, מי איצטריך לאשמועינן דאין קידושין תופסין בא"א? הרי כנסה, וכאשתו היא לכל דבר. **אלא איידי דתני התרת יבם ויבמה אחת.** דאיצטריך לאשמועינן אפילו לר"ל דאין מאמר אחר חליצה, דהא ליתא גביה אלא בלאו ד"לא יבנה", ואיצטריך לאשמועינן כרבי עקיבא, תנא נמי כו'.

חלץ

תוספות

רבינא אמר דכ"ע יש תנאי בחליצה. תימה לר"י: דהני אמוראי אתו דלא כהלכתא, דקי"ל בפרק "מצות חליצה" (לקמן דף קו.) וב"המדיר" (כתובות דף עד. ושם) דחליצה מוטעת כשירה, דאין תנאי בחליצה, משום דגמרינן מתנאי בני גד ובני ראובן, דבעינן דאיפשר לקיימו ע"י שליח. דאי סבירא להו דאין תנאי — לא הוה להו לאוקמי פלוגתא דרבי ורבנן בהכי! ועוד: אדמיפלגי ביש תנאי בחליצה לענין מאמר שאחריה — ליפלגו לענין התרה לשוק! ואר"י דלענין התרה לשוק לכ"ע הויא חליצה, כדקי"ל דאין תנאי בחליצה. אלא לענין דהויא חליצה פסולה דלא מפקע לה זיקה לגמרי, שלא יועיל אחריה מאמר בלשון זיקת יבמין קאמר דיש תנאי. ושוב מצא ר"י כשם ר"ת א). **לימא** מסייע ליה לשמואל ותיובתא לרב יוסף. אמאמר לזו וחלץ לזו קאי. ואם תאמר: אמאי הוי תיובתא לרב יוסף? דהא דאין חולץ לבעלת מאמר — משום דשמואל, דחלץ לבעלת מאמר לא נפטרה צרה! וי"ל דה"ק: לימא מסייע ליה לשמואל, או תיהוי תיובתא דרב יוסף. דאי לא תסייע לשמואל ומיפטרה צרה בחליצת בעלת מאמר — א"כ, האי דנקט מאמר לזו וחלץ לזו לאשמועינן דחולץ לאיזו שירצה, לאפוקי מדרב יוסף, דקאמר לא ישפוך מי בורו ואחרים צריכים לו. **איצטריך** לאשמועינן דאין קידושין תופסין בחייבי לאוין. אע"ג דכבר אשמועינן לעיל — קתני לה נמי הכא אגב שאר גווני. כיון דלאו מילתא דפשיטא היא. **איצטריך** לאשמועינן דאין קידושין תופסין באשת איש. פירוש: דקתני סיפא: וכן בשני יבמין ויבמה אחת. ותימה: דלמא הא דנקט בעל ועשה מאמר — משום שתי יבמות ויבם אחד נקטיה. *[ע"ש בגליון] **סלקא** דעתך אמינא ליגזור מאמר דבתר חליצה כו'. תימה: מה צריך לטעם זה? דלעיל הוה ניחא לר' יוחנן דאיצטריך לאשמועי' דאין קידושין תופסין בחייבי לאוין, אע"ג דכבר אשמועינן ליה מרישא. והכי נמי תינח ליה הכא, מהאי טעמא גופיה.

עין משפט נר מצוה

מב א מיי' פ"ד מהלכות יבום הלכה כד סמג עשין נב טוש"ע אה"ע סימן קסט סעיף כ:
מג ב מיי' פ"ו מהל' אישות הלכה ג סמג עשין מח טוש"ע שם סימן לח סעי' ב:
מד ג מיי' פ"ה מהלכות יבום הלכה יד טוש"ע שם סימן קע סעיף יב:
מה ד מיי' שם הלכה יא טוש"ע שם סעיף ה:
מו ה מיי' פ"ד מהל' אישות הלכה יב סמג עשין מח טוש"ע שם סימן מד סעי' ו:

תוספות ישנים

א) **ועוד** דקאמר לעיל דכ"ע חליצה פסולה אינה פוטרת ובכולהי מתני' אמרינן אין אחר חליצה כלום וכן הא דקאמר רב אשי דכו"ע חליצה פסולה אינה פוטרת היינו לענין דחייל מאמר אבתרה: **לימא** מסייעא ליה לרבה בר רב הונא פי' לעיל בהאי פרקא: **אביי** ורבא דאמרי תרוייהו תני אין אחר ביאה כלום ותנא דידן התרת יבמה לשוק עדיפא ליה והקשה הר' נתנאל למאי קאמר ותנא דידן הא אמר תני במתני' וא"כ אינו כ"א מגיה המשנה ואין זה תנא אחר ותירץ דה"ג תנא אין אחר ביאה כלום דברייתא היא בתוספתא א) והשתא ניחא דקאמר ותנא דידן דלא תני במתני' הכי ומשני התרת יבמה לשוק עדיפא ליה וכו':

א) כ"ה באמת בתוספתא פ"ז חלץ את זו וכו' אין אחר בעילה כלום אך דיש שם ט"ס דבבבא קמייתא גבי בעל את זו נצריך לסיים אין אחר בעילה כלום ע"ש.

תוספות חד מקמאי

לזיקה ורבנן סברי אין זיקה מעיקרא כו' (וקי"ל יש זיקה): רב שרביא אמר בחליצה פסולה קא מיפלגי רבי סבר חליצה פסולה פוטרת ורבנן סברי חליצה פסולה אינה פוטרת [פי' רבי סבר דפוטרת] ושריא לעלמא ודחי' לה מהאי ביתה ואין (כלל) [כאן] יבמות כלל. ולפיכך אינה צריכה הימנו גט ורבנן סברי אינה פוטרת ולא אידחיא מהאי ביתא ויש כאן יבמות. והרב אלפס פי' דבחליצה פסולה צריכה לחזור על כל האחין קמיפלגי וס"ל לרבנן צריכה לחזור על כל האחין וכל זה סיוע למפסק הלכתא כרב דאמר חליצה פסולה צריכה לחזור אחר כל האחין דהא רבנן קיימי כותיה אעפ"י שפסק הרב אלפס דכל הני טעמי דאתמר (בהו) [גבי] פלוגתא דרבי ורבנן לא סמכינן עלייהו איכא מינייהו דסמכינן כגון האי טעמי דאיתמר לעיל מתוקמי' כרבי דלא סמכינן אדרבנן דקי"ל דיש זיקה כדפרישנא. רב [אשי] אמר ביש תנאי בחליצה קא מיפלגי רבי סבר אין תנאי בחליצה ורבנן סברי יש תנאי בחליצה וכיון דלא נתקיים התנאי אין כאן חליצה ויש כאן יבמות רבינא אמר דכ"ע דיש תנאי בחליצה והכא בתנאי כפול קמיפלגי דרבנן סברי דלא בעי תנאי כפול ואע"ג דלא כפילנא לתנאיה התנאי תנאי וצריך לקיימו וכיון שלא קיימו אין כאן חליצה ויש כאן יבמות. א) הכי אוקימנא דרב אסי ורבינא הוו להו לרבנן דלא כהלכתא דקי"ל אין תנאי בחליצה דתניא חליצה מוטעת כשרה ואוקימנא בפרק המדיר דאין תנאי בחליצה. דמכדי כל תנאי מהיכא גמרינן ליה מתנאי בני גד ובני ראובן תנאה דאפשר לקיומי ע"י שליח כי התם הוי תנאיה תנאה דלא אפשר לקיומי ע"י שליח לא הוי תנאיה תנאה. ומיהו מעיקרא קס"ד בפ' המדיר דהיינו טעמא דחליצה מוטעת כשירה דכיון דעבד מעשה אחולי אחליה לתנאיה ולהאי טעמא אי אדכר תנאיה בשעת חליצה הוי תנאיה תנאה ואפ"ה הלכתא כטעמא בת"אה כהאי מסקנא ואפי' אידכר התנאי בשעת חליצה לא הוי תנאיה תנאה דלא אפשר לקיומי ע"י שליח: הא דתנן מאמר לזו וחלץ לזו צריכה גט ואמר עלה בגמ' לימא (תהוי תיובתא) [מסייע ליה] לשמואל דאמר חלץ לבעלת מאמר לא נפטרת צרתה ותיובתא דרב יוסף דאמר לא ישפוך אדם מי בורו ואחרים צריכים לו מי קתני חולץ חלץ קאמר דיעבד וכיון דקי"ל כשמואל לכתחלה נמי אית ליה למעבד אם עשה מעשה לזו חולץ לאחרת ונפטרת בעלת מאמר לא נפטרת צרה ג) וכי חליץ לאחרת לא הוי תיובתא דרב יוסף כלומר לית ליה לשמואל דאם חלץ לבעלת מאמר נפטרת צרתה וה"ל למחלץ לבעלת מאמר שאחרים פסולין לה בלא חליצה ולא לצרתה שאחרים כשירים לה בלא חליצה והשתא נפסלה לאחרים בחליצה זו ג):

א) נראה דל"ל ולהך אוקימתא דרב אשי ורבינא. ב) אינו מובן ונראה דל"ל ולכן חולץ לאחרת ורב יוסף לית ליה לשמואל וס"ל דאם חלץ וכו'. ג) הדבר צ"ע דמנ"ל דרב יוסף פליג אדשמואל הא רב יוסף לא אמר זה רק אמתניתין דלעיל דף מד

הגהות הב"ח

(א) גמ' (אביי ורבא דאמרי תרוייהו תני) תא"מ ונ"ב ס"א אביי ורבא תנו:

"חָלַץ וְעָשָׂה מַאֲמָר וְנָתַן וכו'".§ בִּשְׁלָמָא חָלַץ וְעָשָׂה מַאֲמָר אִיצְטְרִיךְ, סד"א: נִגְזוֹר מַאֲמָר דְּבָתַר חֲלִיצָה אַטּוּ מַאֲמָר דְּקַמֵּי חֲלִיצָה — קמ"ל דְּלָא גָּזְרִינַן. אֶלָּא חָלַץ וְנָתַן גֵּט לָמָּה לִי? וּלְטַעְמִיךְ אֵימָא סֵיפָא: בָּעַל וְעָשָׂה מַאֲמָר, בָּעַל וְנָתַן גֵּט — בִּשְׁלָמָא בָּעַל וְנָתַן גֵּט אִיצְטְרִיךְ, סד"א: נִגְזוֹר גֵּט דְּבָתַר בְּעִילָה אַטּוּ גֵּט דְּקַמֵּי בְּעִילָה, קמ"ל דְּלָא גָּזְרִינַן. אֲבָל בָּעַל וְעָשָׂה מַאֲמָר לָמָּה לִי? אֶלָּא: אַיְּדֵי דְּתָנָא חָלַץ וְעָשָׂה מַאֲמָר — תָּנָא נַמִי בָּעַל וְעָשָׂה מַאֲמָר, וְאַיְּדֵי דְּבָעֵי לְמִיתְנֵי בָּעַל וְנָתַן גֵּט — תָּנָא נַמִי חָלַץ וְנָתַן גֵּט.§ "בִּזְמַן שֶׁהִיא וכו'".§ מַתְנִיתִין דְּלָא כִּי הַאי תַּנָּא. דְּתַנְיָא, אַבָּא יוֹסֵי בֶּן יוֹחָנָן אִישׁ יְרוּשָׁלַיִם אוֹמֵר מִשּׁוּם רַבִּי מֵאִיר: אַחַת בְּעִילָה וְאַחַת חֲלִיצָה, בַּתְּחִלָּה — אֵין אַחֲרֶיהָ כְּלוּם, בָּאֶמְצַע וּבַסּוֹף — יֵשׁ אַחֲרֶיהָ כְּלוּם. *וְשָׁלֹשׁ מַחֲלוֹקוֹת בַּדָּבָר, תַּנָּא קַמָּא סָבַר: בִּיאָה דְּאִיכָּא לְמִיגְזַר — גָּזְרִינַן, חֲלִיצָה דְּלֵיכָּא לְמִיגְזַר — לָא גָּזְרִינַן. וְרַ' נְחֶמְיָה סָבַר: בִּיאָה נַמִי לֵיכָּא לְמִיגְזַר. וּדְקָאָמְרַתְּ: לִיגְזוֹר בִּיאָה אַחַר הַגֵּט מִשּׁוּם בִּיאָה אַחַר חֲלִיצָה — כֵּיוָן דַּחֲלִיצָה דְּאוֹרַיְיתָא, מֵידַע יָדְעִי. וּדְקָאָמְרַתְּ לִיגְזוֹר בִּיאָה אַחַר מַאֲמָר מִשּׁוּם בִּיאָה אַחַר בִּיאָה — כֵּיוָן דְּבִיאָה דְּאוֹרַיְיתָא, הָא מֵידַע יָדְעִי. וְאַבָּא יוֹסֵי בֶּן חָנָן סָבַר לָהּ כְּרַבָּנַן דְּגָזְרִי בְּבִיאָה, וְגָזַר חֲלִיצָה מִשּׁוּם בִּיאָה.§

הדרן עלך רבן גמליאל

חָלַץ וְעָשָׂה מַאֲמָר. אַיְּבָם אֶחָד וִיבָמָה אַחַת קָאֵי. דְּאוֹקְמֵיהּ דְּצָרִיךְ לְמִתְנְיֵיהּ. בִּשְׁלָמָא חָלַץ וְעָשָׂה מַאֲמָר אִיצְטְרִיךְ. לְמִיתְנֵי דְּאֵינוֹ כְּלוּם. סד"א. אַפִּי' לְר' עֲקִיבָא. לִיגְזוֹר מַאֲמָר דְּבָתַר חֲלִיצָה. דְּלִיבָּעֵי גֵּט אַטּוּ מַאֲמָר דְּמִקַּמֵּי חֲלִיצָה, קמ"ל דְּלָא גָּזְרִינַן. אֶלָּא חָלַץ וְנָתַן גֵּט. בְּיָבָם אֶחָד וִיבָמָה אַחַת, לָמָּה לִי כו'? לְמַאי לִיהֲנֵי הַאי גֵּט? אִי לְמֵיסְרָהּ — הָא אִיתַּסְרָא הִיא וְקְרוֹבוֹתֶיהָ עָלָיו. וּלְטַעְמִיךְ בָּעַל וְעָשָׂה מַאֲמָר. בְּיָבָם וִיבָמָה אַחַת לָמָּה לִי? בִּשְׁלָמָא בָּעַל וְנָתַן גֵּט — אִיצְטְרִיךְ לְמִתְנֵי אֵין אַחַר בִּיאָה כְּלוּם, דְּנָפְקָא בְּהַאי גִּיטָּא וְלָא בָּעְיָא חֲלִיצָה, דְּבִיאָה קַמַּיְיתָא אַפְקַעְתָּהּ לְזִיקָה. סד"א לִגְזוֹר גֵּט דְּבָתַר בִּיאָה. דְּלָא תִּסְגֵּי לֵיהּ בְּגֵט בְּלָא חֲלִיצָה — אַטּוּ גֵּט דְּמִקַּמֵּי בִּיאָה, דְּלָא לֵימְרוּ גֵּט סַגִּי בִּיבָמָה בִּמְקוֹם חֲלִיצָה. אֶלָּא בָּעַל וְעָשָׂה מַאֲמָר. לְמַאי קָבָעֵי אִיתְנוּיֵי? הֲלֹא אִשְׁתּוֹ הִיא. אֶלָּא. אַיְּדֵי דְּתָנָא חָלַץ וְעָשָׂה מַאֲמָר דְּאִיצְטְרִיךְ לֵיהּ, כִּדְאָמְרַן, תָּנָא נַמִי כו'. וְשָׁלֹשׁ מַחֲלוֹקוֹת בַּדָּבָר תַּנָּא קַמָּא. דְּמַתְנִיתִין, דְּאָמַר חֲלִיצָה פְּסוּלָה אֵין אַחֲרֶיהָ כְּלוּם, אֲבָל בִּיאָה פְּסוּלָה יֵשׁ אַחֲרֶיהָ כְּלוּם. וְרַבִּי נְחֶמְיָה. דְּאָמַר: אַחַת זוֹ וְאַחַת זוֹ אֵין אַחֲרֶיהָ כְּלוּם. וְאַבָּא יוֹסֵי בַּר חָנָן. דְּאָמַר: אַחַת זוֹ וְאַחַת זוֹ יֵשׁ אַחֲרֶיהָ כְּלוּם בָּאֶמְצַע וּבַסּוֹף. כִּדְפָרֵישְׁנָא לֵיהּ בְּמַתְנִיתִין. בִּיאָה — דְּאִיכָּא לְמִיגְזַר כִּדְאָמְרַן בְּרֵישׁ פִּירְקִין (לעיל נ:), אִי בִּיאָה אַחַר הַגֵּט הִיא — גְּזֵירָה בִּיאָה אַחַר הַגֵּט מִשּׁוּם בִּיאָה אַחַר חֲלִיצָה, דְּלָא לֵיתֵי לְמִיבְעַל אַחַר חֲלִיצָה. וְאִי בִּיאָה אַחַר מַאֲמָר כו' חֲלִיצָה לֵיכָּא לְמִיגְזַר, כִּדְאָמַר בְּרֵישׁ פִּירְקִין (שם).

הדרן עלך רבן גמליאל

[עירובין עה. וש"נ]

הגהות הב"ח

(א) גמ' ואפילו הוא שוגג והיא מזידה הוא מזיד והיא שוגגת דתרווייהו לא: (ב) רש"י ד"ה פסלה. מיפסלא בהך ביאה מתרומה:

הַבָּא עַל יְבִמְתּוֹ, בֵּין בְּשׁוֹגֵג בֵּין בְּמֵזִיד בֵּין בְּאוֹנֶס בֵּין בְּרָצוֹן, אֲפִי' הוּא שׁוֹגֵג וְהִיא מְזִידָה, הוּא מֵזִיד וְהִיא שׁוֹגֶגֶת, הוּא אָנוּס וְהִיא לֹא אֲנוּסָה, הִיא אֲנוּסָה וְהוּא לֹא אָנוּס. אֶחָד הַמְעָרֶה וְאֶחָד הַגּוֹמֵר — קָנָה, וְלֹא חִילֵּק בֵּין בִּיאָה לְבִיאָה. וְכֵן הַבָּא עַל אַחַת מִכׇּל הָעֲרָיוֹת שֶׁבַּתּוֹרָה, אוֹ פְּסוּלוֹת, כְּגוֹן: אַלְמָנָה לְכ"ג, גְּרוּשָׁה וַחֲלוּצָה לְכֹהֵן הֶדְיוֹט, מַמְזֶרֶת וּנְתִינָה לְיִשְׂרָאֵל, בַּת יִשְׂרָאֵל לְמַמְזֵר וּלְנָתִין — פְּסָלָהּ, וְלֹא חִילֵּק בֵּין בִּיאָה לְבִיאָה.§

גמ' מַאי אֲפִי'? לָא מִיבַּעְיָא קָאָמַר: לָא מִיבַּעְיָא הוּא שׁוֹגֵג וְהִיא קָמְכַוְּונָה לְמִצְוָה, אִי נַמִי הוּא מֵזִיד וְהִיא קָמְכַוְּונָה לְמִצְוָה, אֶלָּא אֲפִי' הוּא שׁוֹגֵג וְהִיא מְזִידָה(א), דְּתַרְוַיְיהוּ לָא קָמְכַוְּונִי לְשֵׁם מִצְוָה — אֲפִילּוּ הָכִי קָנָה. תָּנֵי ר' חִיָּיא: אֲפִי' *שְׁנֵיהֶם שׁוֹגְגִים, שְׁנֵיהֶם מְזִידִים, שְׁנֵיהֶם אֲנוּסִים. אָנוּס דְּמַתְנִיתִין הֵיכִי דָּמֵי? אִילֵימָא כְּשֶׁאֲנָסוּהוּ גּוֹיִם וּבָא עָלֶיהָ — וְהָאָמַר רָבָא: אֵין אוֹנֶס לְעֶרְוָה, לְפִי שֶׁאֵין קִישּׁוּי אֶלָּא לְדַעַת. אֶלָּא בְּיָשֵׁן — וְהָאָמַר רַב יְהוּדָה: יָשֵׁן